An Introduction to the Aquatic Insects of North America

Second Edition

An Introduction to the Aquatic Insects of North America

Second Edition

Edited by

Richard W. Merritt

Department of Entomology
Michigan State University

and

Kenneth W. Cummins

Department of Fisheries & Wildlife
Oregon State University

*To Ethan,
With best
regards,
Rich Merritt*

KENDALL/HUNT PUBLISHING COMPANY
2460 Kerper Boulevard P.O. Box 539 Dubuque, Iowa 52004-0539

C 403180 01

Dedication

This book is dedicated to the memory of Dr.'s Justin W. Leonard and Herbert H. Ross, who contributed immensely to the field of aquatic entomology through their teachings and writings.

Contents

Preface

As in the first edition, this revised edition is intended as a standard guide to the aquatic insects of North America. The revision includes generic keys for each order, the completeness of which varies with order, life stage, and the present state of knowledge. We hope this new edition will be of even greater use to both professional and lay groups. In response to critiques by users of the first edition, the coverage of general biology and morphology has been expanded for each group. Chapters dealing with respiration and life history have been added, and the coverage of ecology, phylogeny, and sampling has been expanded. In addition, the ecological tables appearing in each order (or family) chapter have been updated. As with any compendium, coverage of the literature is only partial and is a continuing problem as the literature treating aquatic insects grows exponentially. The ever-increasing number of papers appearing in additional journals is overwhelming. Our coverage has expanded from over 1700 (through 1977) to over 2800 references (1983). As before, we strongly encourage all users of the book to continually update material in their own areas of interest.

Preface to the First Edition

This treatment is intended to provide a standard guide to North American families of aquatic insects: their taxonomy, phylogeny, morphology, ecology, and distribution, as well as collection and rearing techniques. The coverage should allow a variety of groups, both lay and professional, to identify and categorize the immatures or adults they collect and, having done so, to associate pertinent ecological and distributional information with the group in question. The book is directed at students and professionals in entomology, fisheries and wildlife, limnology, freshwater biology, invertebrate zoology, water resources, conservation and natural resources, water quality, and public health. It should also be of use to lay groups such as fishermen and amateur naturalists.

In order to meet the publication schedule, the literature review was terminated in April 1977. Interested students and professionals are encouraged to continually update the literature sections of this book related to their areas of interest. We have not included a glossary at the end of the book since most of the terms have been defined in the text. For a further explanation of terms, the student should consult Torre-Bueno (1937).

Acknowledgments

Many people have helped in the preparation of the second edition in many different ways. As in the first edition, we especially acknowledge Dr. Jim Bath, Chairman of the Department of Entomology, Michigan State University, for providing his continual support and optimism during the entire project. We gratefully acknowledge the assistance of the following individuals for either manuscript review, table preparation, reference verification and/or editorial suggestions: Tom Burton, Mike and Sue Kaufman, Dave Cornelius, Dave and Terry Grant, Jim Keller, Dan Lawson, Bill Taft, Kevin Webb, and Peggy Wilzbach. We thank R. Mattingly for assistance in editing. A special thanks goes to Gail Motyka for the extra hours devoted to the book in lieu of finishing her thesis. We are grateful to Lana Tackett for scientific illustration, Josephine Maybee, Susan Battenfield, Patti Vuich, and Carol Asbahr for various aspects of manuscript preparation. Our special thanks goes to Ken Dimoff, computer coordinator for the MSU Department of Entomology, for designing the data management program to merge the old and new reference lists. Finally, we would like to again thank Pam, Brett, and Scott Merritt for their patience and understanding, as well as their permission to convert the entire home living room into "book central" for a two-year period.

Acknowledgments and credits by contributors and the editors for specific chapters are as follows: *General Morphology*—Roger Akre (Washington State Univ.) and H. V. Daly (Univ. of California) for review; Ken Manuel (Duke Power Co.) for critical comments; *Aquatic Insect Respiration*—Doug Craig (Univ. of Alberta) and Mike Wiley (Illinois Nat. Hist. Surv.) for review; *Habitat, Life History and Behavioral Adaptations*—Chuck Hawkins (Oregon State Univ.) for review; *Ecology and Distribution of Aquatic Insects*—Doug Ross (Biochem Products), Jean Stout, Dan Lawson (Michigan State Univ.) and Peggy Wilzbach (Oregon State Univ.) for review; Al Grigarick (Univ. of California) for critical comments; *Phylogenetic Relationships and Evolutionary Adaptations*—R. Garrison and M. Westfall, Jr. (Odonata), G. Edmunds (Ephemeroptera), P. Harper, and K. Stewart (Plecoptera), J. Polhemus (Hemiptera), G. Wiggins and J. Wood (Trichoptera), and E. Schlinger (Diptera) for their comments on the genealogical trees prepared for the second edition; *Plecoptera*—the Plecoptera nymph key was developed, in part, from a study by K. W. Stewart, supported by the National Science Foundation; *Aquatic and Semiaquatic Hemiptera*—Drs. R. F. Denno (Univ. of Maryland) and J. P. Kramer (USDA, USNM) for their suggestions and comments on the semiaquatic Homoptera; Dan A. Polhemus for preparing many original figures; the Entomological Society of Canada for permission to use figures from Brooks and Kelton (1967); the University of California Press for permission to use figures from Usinger (1956a) and Menke et al. (1979); R. Aiken (Erindale College) for critical comments; *Megaloptera and Aquatic Neuroptera*—D. C. Tarter (Marshall Univ.) for providing larval material for study and O. S. Flint (Smithsonian Institution) for suggestions relative to revising the chapter; *Trichoptera*—Zile Zichmanis for illustrations of adults and pupae; Anker Odum for illustrations of larvae and cases; Toshio Yamamoto for assistance in reviewing characters for the keys; John Morse (Clemson Univ.) for critical comments; *Trichoptera (Genera)*—O. S. Flint, Jr., S. W. Hamilton, R. W. Kelley, J. S. Weaver, III, and G. B. Wiggins for their cooperation in providing specimens, inforamtion, and comments; J. P. Norton for selected illustrations; S. W. Hamilton and W. R. English for editorial tasks; N. H. Brewer for typing the final manuscript; *Aquatic and Semiaquatic Lepidoptera*—Fred Stehr (Michigan State Univ.) and Dale Habeck (Univ. of Florida) for comments and review; *Aquatic Coleoptera*—H. B. Leech who reviewed the chapter for the original edition and to F. N. Young, Jr., who has offered many suggestions for this edition; Kathleen Sweeney (Univ. of Michigan), Aleta Holt (INHS), and Celeste Green (Univ. of California) for their artistic abilities in producing most of the more than 300 illustrations; C. Millenbach, M. L. Giovannini, and E. Rogers for their assistance in producing the manuscript; "We gratefully acknowledge G. Ulrich (Univ. of California) for his significant contributions to the original edition." *Aquatic Hymenoptera*—F. E. Skinner and Natalie Vandenberg for several drawings; *Aquatic Diptera*—R. Foote, R. Gagné, C. Thompson, D. D. Wilder, W. Wirth (Systematic Entomology Laboratory, USDA, Washington, D.C.), Lloyd Knutson (IIBIII, USDA/ARS), Wayne Mathis (Smithsonian Institution), Ben Foote (Kent State Univ.), Robert Lane (Univ. of California), W. Turner (Washington State Univ.), J. B. Wallace (Univ. of Georgia), J. Burger (Univ. of New Hampshire) assisted with revisions of the Diptera table; *Chironomidae*—S. Roback (Philadelphia Acad. Sciences) and Don Oliver (Biosystematics Research Instit., Ottawa) for review. Additional credits for figure use are given in specific chapters.

Original research supported, in part, by the Michigan State and Oregon State University Agricultural Experiment Stations, Ecosystem Studies of the National Science Foundation (grants DEB–80–22634; DEB–81–12455), and the Department of Energy, Ecological Sciences Division (Contract DE–AT06–79E1004).

Acknowledgments to the First Edition

We gratefully acknowledge the continual encouragement and support on this project by James E. Bath, Chairman, Department of Entomology, Michigan State University. Original research reported by R. W. Merritt was supported, in part, by the Michigan State University Agricultural Experiment Station, Ecosystem Studies of the National Science Foundation (grant DEB76–20122) and the Office of Water Research and Technology (grant A–085–MICH). Original research reported by K. W. Cummins was supported by the U.S. Energy Research and Development Administration (contract EY–76–S–2002. A001) and Ecosystem Studies of the National Science Foundation (grant GB–36069X).

We would like to acknowledge Drs. Herbert H. Ross (Department of Entomology, University of Georgia) and Carl W. Richards (Rockford, Michigan) for evaluating the prepublication copy of the manuscript. We are also grateful to Lana Tackett for art work, Paul Mescher and Vivian Napoli for graphics, John E. Stuurwold (Graphics Department, Pest Management Curriculum, Michigan State University) for cover design, Josephine Maybee and Charlotte Seeley for manuscript and table preparation, and Doug Ross, Neil Kagan, and Edward F. Gersabeck, Jr., for proofing. We would also like to thank Jane Cummins for bibliographic work and Pam, Brett, and Scott Merritt for their patience and understanding. Others have been acknowledged in specific chapters.

List of Contributors

N. H. ANDERSON, Department of Entomology, Oregon State University, Corvallis, Oregon 97331.

S. S. BALLING, Department of Entomological Sciences, University of California, Berkeley, California 94720.

W. U. BRIGHAM, Illinois Natural History Survey, 607 East Peabody Drive, Champaign, Illinois 61820.

G. W. BYERS, Department of Entomology, University of Kansas, Lawrence, Kansas 66044.

I. J. CANTRALL, Museum of Zoology, University of Michigan, Ann Arbor, Michigan 48104.

K. CHRISTIANSEN, Department of Biology, Grinnell College, Grinnell, Iowa 50112.

W. P. COFFMAN, Department of Biological Sciences, University of Pittsburgh, Pittsburgh, Pennsylvania 15213.

K. W. CUMMINS, Department of Fisheries and Wildlife, Oregon State University, Corvallis, Oregon 97331.

H. V. DALY, Department of Entomological Sciences, University of California, Berkeley, California 94720.

J. T. DOYEN, Department of Entomological Sciences, University of California, Berkeley, California 94720.

G. F. EDMUNDS, JR., Department of Biology, University of Utah, Salt Lake City, Utah 84112.

C. H. ERIKSEN, Joint Sciences Department, The Claremont Colleges, Claremont, California 91711.

E. D. EVANS, Michigan Department of Natural Resources, P.O. Box 30028, Lansing, Michigan 48909.

L. C. FERRINGTON, JR., State Biological Survey of Kansas, University of Kansas, Lawrence, Kansas 66044.

K. S. HAGEN, Department of Entomological Sciences, University of California, Berkeley, California 94720.

P. P. HARPER, Department of Biology, Université de Montréal, Montreal, Quebec, Canada.

R. W. HOLZENTHAL, Department of Entomology, Fisheries and Wildlife, Clemson University, Clemson, South Carolina, 29631.

G. A. LAMBERTI, Department of Entomological Sciences, University of California, Berkeley, California 94720.

W. H. LANGE, Department of Entomology, University of California, Davis, California 95616.

R. W. MERRITT, Department of Entomology, Michigan State University, East Lansing, Michigan 48824.

J. C. MORSE, Department of Entomology, Fisheries and Wildlife, Clemson University, Clemson, South Carolina 29631.

H. D. NEWSON, Department of Entomology, Michigan State University, East Lansing, Michigan 48824.

H. H. NEUNZIG, Department of Entomology, North Carolina State University, Raleigh, North Carolina 27650.

B. V. PETERSON, Biosystematics Research Institute, Canada Agriculture, Ottawa, Ontario, Canada KIA OC6.

J. T. POLHEMUS, 3115 S. York, Englewood, Colorado 80110.

V. H. RESH, Department of Entomological Sciences, University of California, Berkeley, California 94720.

E. I. SCHLINGER, Department of Entomological Sciences, University of California, Berkeley, California 94720.

R. J. SNIDER, Department of Zoology, Michigan State University, East Lansing, Michigan 48824.

J. O. SOLEM, The Museum, University of Trondheim, Royal Norwegien Society of Sciences and Letters, Trondheim, Norway.

K. W. STEWART, Department of Biological Sciences, North Texas State University, Denton, Texas 76203.

H. J. TESKEY, Biosystematics Research Institute, Canada Agriculture, Ottawa, Ontario, Canada KIA OC6.

J. B. WALLACE, Department of Entomology, University of Georgia, Athens, Georgia 30602.

M. J. WESTFALL, JR., Department of Zoology, University of Florida, Gainesville, Florida 32611.

D. S. WHITE, Benthos Laboratory, 1081 N. University Bldg., University of Michigan, Ann Arbor, Michigan 48109.

G. B. WIGGINS, Department of Entomology, Royal Ontario Museum, Toronto, Ontario, Canada M5S2C6.

Introduction

Richard W. Merritt
Michigan State University, East Lansing

Kenneth W. Cummins
Oregon State University, Corvallis

Interest in North American aquatic ecosystems has grown since the early work of limnologists and fisheries biologists (e.g., Forbes 1887; Needham 1934). This interest has intensified recently, due to concerns for environmental quality (Kuehne 1962; Bartsch and Ingram 1966; Wilhm and Dorris 1968; Warren 1971; Hart and Fuller 1974) and the ever-increasing sophistication of anglers (e.g., Swisher and Richards 1971; Schweibert 1973; Caucci and Nastasi 1975; McCafferty 1981; Whitlock 1982). Aquatic insects are also of concern to those involved in teaching (Resh and Rosenberg 1979; ref. 2840) and in outdoor recreation activities, since certain groups (e.g., mosquitoes, black flies, horse flies) are frequently pests of humans and animals in water-based environments (Merritt and Newson 1978). Identification is the first step toward a basic understanding of the biology and ecology of aquatic insects; this will eventually allow for the development of proper management strategies. The amateur naturalist and primary or secondary school educator also require basic identifications as an important initial step in familiarization. Thus, for all concerned, identification is important to biologically categorize the organisms collected.

Interest groups, both lay and professional, have continually suffered from our incomplete knowledge of aquatic insects, particularly the immature forms, which are most frequently encountered in the water. Several well-known general works (Usinger 1956a; Edmondson 1959; Klots 1966) and specific studies (Ross 1944; Burks 1953) are taxonomically at least partially out-of-date. Recent comprehensive treatments of Ephemeroptera (Edmunds *et al.* 1976) and Trichoptera (larvae; Wiggins 1977) are currently available; however, no new general treatments of other major aquatic orders are now in print. Therefore, except for the revision of Pennak (1978), which includes many genera of freshwater invertebrates, no comprehensive, updated, generic treatment of immature and adult stages of aquatic insects of North America exists. The first edition of our book (Merritt and Cummins 1978) was intended to serve as a standard reference on the biology and ecology of aquatic insects with keys to separate life stages of major taxonomic groupings—orders and families (or subfamilies). This was coupled with summaries of related information on phylogeny, methods, and techniques. The revised edition has been significantly updated and expanded to include *generic* keys to all major groups of aquatic and semiaquatic insects of North America and additional related information on respiration, sampling, life history, behavior, and ecology. In most orders, generic keys are provided to both immatures and adults; however, in the Diptera, generic keys to all families having aquatic representatives would have made the text prohibitive in size. Therefore, larval generic treatment is limited to those dipteran families that are: (1) of significant interest to aquatic workers, (2) dominant and abundant in fresh or marine waters, (3) economically important, and (4) in need of treatment because of the present lack of available information.

The distinction between aquatic or semiaquatic and terrestrial insects is arbitrary. We have attempted to include those orders and families with one or more life stages associated with aquatic habitats and frequently encountered in collections made from aquatic environments. The orders treated in Usinger (1956a) have been included, although some (Collembola, Orthoptera, and Hymenoptera) are marginally associated with aquatic habitats. Since terrestrial insects frequently become trapped in the surface film of aquatic systems (e.g., Collembola), a wide range of species are encountered with varying frequency. A specimen not fitting the keys included in this book probably belongs to a terrestrial taxon. Terrestrial forms generally can be identified using Borror *et al.* (1981).

An annotated list of general references to works dealing with aquatic insect taxonomy is given in table 1A. As indicated above, many of these works are taxonomically outdated; however, they include a great deal of useful, particularly biological, information. More specific references are given in the appropriate order (or family) chapter.

Various combinations of taxa can be categorized so that we may address ecological questions at the functional level. For example, some groups are based on morpho-behavioral adaptations for food gathering, habitat selection, or habits of attachment, concealment, and movement (see chap. 6 and ecological tables in chaps. 9–25). Different levels of taxonomic identification are required to classify aquatic insects according to general functional groups. The ordinal level may be sufficient to define functional trophic relations of the Odonata (chap. 11), but even the generic level may be insufficient in some of the Chironomidae (chap. 25). Ecologists have also resorted to "habitat taxonomy" (e.g., Coffman et al. 1971), where the fauna of a given aquatic system is studied for an extended period in sufficient detail to permit system-specific keys to be written. This allows for significant simplification in such keys, but changes in species composition can be masked by the restricted nature of this approach and such keys must be used cautiously and verified continually.

Table 1A. North American literature dealing with general aquatic insect identification.

Source	Coverage				General Comments
	Immatures	Adults	Keys	Biology	
Ward and Whipple (1918)	x	x	Generic	x	Contains much information on biology
Chu (1949)	x		Family	x†	Generalized treatment of immatures
Peterson (1951)	x		Family	x†	Limited to holometabolous groups; descriptive in nature
Usinger (1956a)	x*	x	Primarily generic level, with keys to Calif. species	x	Considerable information on West Coast species
Edmondson (1959)	x	x*	Generic		A standard reference on freshwater invertebrates; some keys outdated
Eddy and Hodson (1961)	x		Order		Keys to common animals, including water mites, of the North Central states
Needham and Needham (1962)	x	x*	Generic		Keys to many genera; field manual
Klots (1966)	x	x*	Primarily family level, with keys to some genera	x†	Field manual; some keys based on ecology and behavior of group
Borror and White (1970)	x§	x	Key to orders, some keys to families	x	Comprehensive field manual on insects; primarily based on examination of insects in the hand; color plates
Swisher and Richards (1971)	x	x	Generic (mayflies only)	x	Anglers' guide, primarily to mayflies; color photographs; seasonal data
Schweibert (1973)	x		None	x	Extensive treatment of immature aquatic insects for anglers; color plates; seasonal and distributional data
Caucci and Nastasi (1975)	x	x	None	x	Anglers' guide to mayflies and stoneflies; color photographs; seasonal and distributional data
Parrish (1975)	x		Generic		Keys only to Southeastern United States; limited to water quality indicator organisms
Smith and Carlton (1975)		x	Primarily family level, with keys to some species	x†	Keys only to intertidal insects of the central California coast
Tarter (1976)	x	x‡	Generic	x†	Keys only to West Virginia genera and occasionally species
Merritt and Cummins (1978)	x	x	Keys to orders, families, and some genera of North American aquatic insects	x	Chapters on morphology, ecology, phylogeny, and sampling; summary tables on ecology and distribution
Pennak (1978)	x	x*	Generic	x	Extensive treatment on biology of some groups
Lehmkuhl (1979a)	x	x*	Families	x†	Field guide to aquatic insects
Borror *et al.* (1981)		x	Families	x†	Generalized treatment of adults
Hilsenhoff (1981)	x		Generic	x†	Keys only to Wisconsin genera, but generally applicable to Great Lakes region
McCafferty (1981)	x	x	Pictorial keys to aquatic insect families	x	A thorough scientific introduction to aquatic insects for the fly fisherman; excellent illustrations
Brigham *et al.* (1982)	x	x*	Families and genera for eastern North America; species for the Carolinas'	x	A thorough treatment of the aquatic insects and oligochaetes of the Carolinas'
Whitlock (1982)	x		None	x†	A new practical book on fly-fishing entomology

* Only adult keys to Hemiptera and Coleoptera.
† Contains notes on biology or ecology.
‡ Covers adults of some groups.
§ Primarily adult coverage, brief treatment of immatures of some groups.

As noted in the first edition, the emphasis on ecology and field techniques in this book reflects our conviction that a critical task in the near future will be the integration of taxonomic and ecological approaches in a manner that will permit important questions concerning environmental quality and management to be addressed. It is hoped that the first edition provided some of the tools and initial direction for such analyses of aquatic ecosystems. Our hope is that this second, expanded edition will work further toward this goal.

General Morphology of Aquatic Insects

2

Kenneth W. Cummins
Oregon State University, Corvallis

Richard W. Merritt
Michigan State University, East Lansing

OVERVIEW

A stonefly (order Plecoptera, family Pteronarcyidae) serves to illustrate the general external morphological features of aquatic insects used in taxonomic determinations. This primitive insect exhibits basic morphological features in a relatively unmodified or nonspecialized form. However, modifications of the general morphological plan are found in each insect order having aquatic representatives. These modifications and associated terminology are presented with the introductory material for each group and should be carefully studied before attempting to use the keys in the following chapters.

The insect body represents the fusion and modification of the basic segmentation plan characteristic of the Annelida–Arthropoda evolutionary line (e.g., Snodgrass 1935; Manton and Anderson 1979). Each segment of the body can be compared to a box, with the dorsal (top) portion, the *tergum* or *notum,* joined to the ventral (bottom) portion, the *sternum,* and to the sides or lateral portions, the *pleura,* by membranes. The legs and wings are hinged (articulated) on the pleura of the mid body region, the *thorax.* The body regions, head, thorax, and abdomen, and associated appendages of a stonefly nymph or naiad are shown in figures 2.1 and 2.2. The life cycle of stoneflies is representative of those orders characterized by *simple* (*incomplete* by some authors) metamorphosis, consisting of egg, naiad or nymph (immature), and adult stages; more advanced orders exhibit *complete* metamorphosis, consisting of egg, larva (immature), pupa, and adult stages.

Head

The generalized insect head represents the evolutionary fusion of six or seven anterior segments in the ancestral Annelida–Arthropoda line (e.g., Snodgrass 1935; Rempel 1975). Two or three preoral (procephalic) segments, or *somites,* were fused and now bear important sensory structures used by present-day insects to monitor their environment—the compound eyes, light-sensitive ocelli (simple eyes), and the antennae (figs. 2.1–2.2). The *labrum,* which forms the upper lip, is joined at its base to the *clypeus,* which in turn is fused to the *frons,* or face. The margins of the clypeus and frons

are bounded by the anterior portion of the Y-shaped *epicranial suture* (in fig. 2.1, the line of joining between the clypeus and frons, termed a *suture* [sulcus], is not externally visible so the structure is referred to as the *frontoclypeus* [Nelson and Hanson 1971]).

Three postoral (gnathocephalic) segments are fused in modern insects to form the posterior portion of the head and bear the remaining structures of the feeding apparatus (Snodgrass 1935). As described above, the labrum forms the upper lip and the paired *mandibles* and *maxillae* form the mouth region laterally (figs. 2.2–2.3). The bottom of the mouth is set by the *labium* or lower lip (figs. 2.2–2.3). The maxillae and the labium bear *palps* (palpi), which are sensory in function (figs. 2.2–2.3). The mandibles are used for chewing or crushing the food or may be modified for piercing (piercing herbivores or predators) or scraping (scraping herbivores that graze on attached algae). The maxillae and labium are variously used for tearing and manipulating food, or they may be highly modified as in the Hemiptera, adult Lepidoptera, Hymenoptera, and Diptera. The *hypopharynx* or insect "tongue," located just anterior to the labium, is a small inconspicuous lobe in some nymphal forms, but is subject to extreme modification in some orders (e.g., Diptera).

The sides of the head are referred to as *genae* (singular, gena; fig. 2.2) and the top of the head as the *vertex.* Immediately behind the vertex is a large area called the *occiput* (fig. 2.1). The head is joined to the thorax by a membranous neck region or *cervix* (fig. 2.1). If the head is joined to the thorax so that the mouthparts are directed downward (ventrally), the condition is termed *hypognathous* (e.g., many caddisfly larvae). Mouthparts directed forward (anteriorly) are *prognathous* (e.g., beetle larvae) and those directed backward (posteriorly) are *opisthognathous* (e.g., some true bugs).

In aquatic insects that are dorsoventrally flattened, as are some stoneflies and mayflies, the sensory structures (eyes, ocelli, and antennae) are dorsal and the food-gathering apparatus is ventral. These modifications allow certain groups to move through the interstices of coarse sediments and cling to exposed surfaces in rapidly flowing streams.

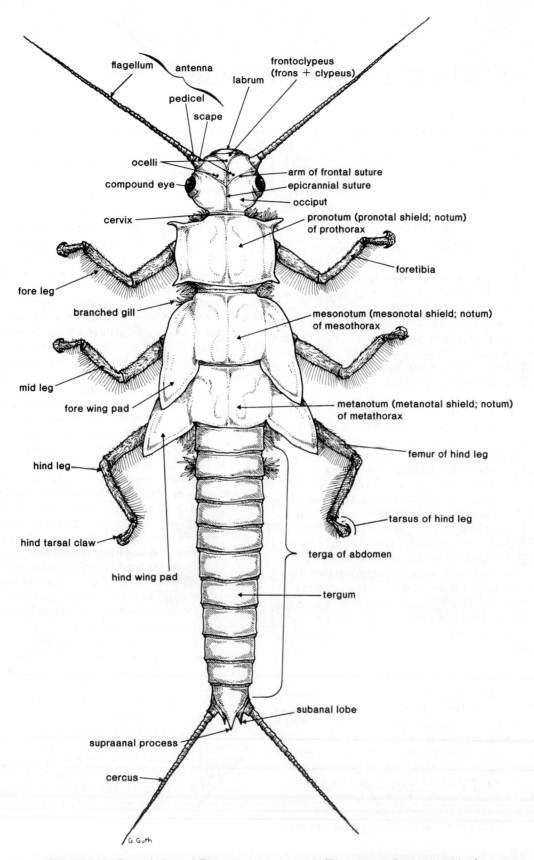

Figure 2.1. Dorsal view of *Pteronarcys* sp. nymph (Plecoptera: Pteronarcyidae).

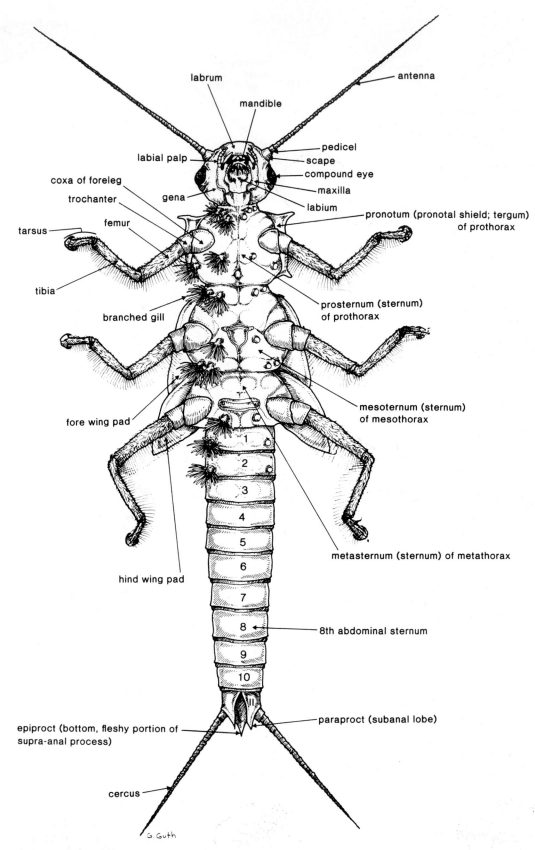

Figure 2.2. Ventral view of *Pteronarcys* sp. nymph (Plecoptera: Pteronarcyidae). Gills of left side of thorax and first two abdominal segments removed to show underlying structures.

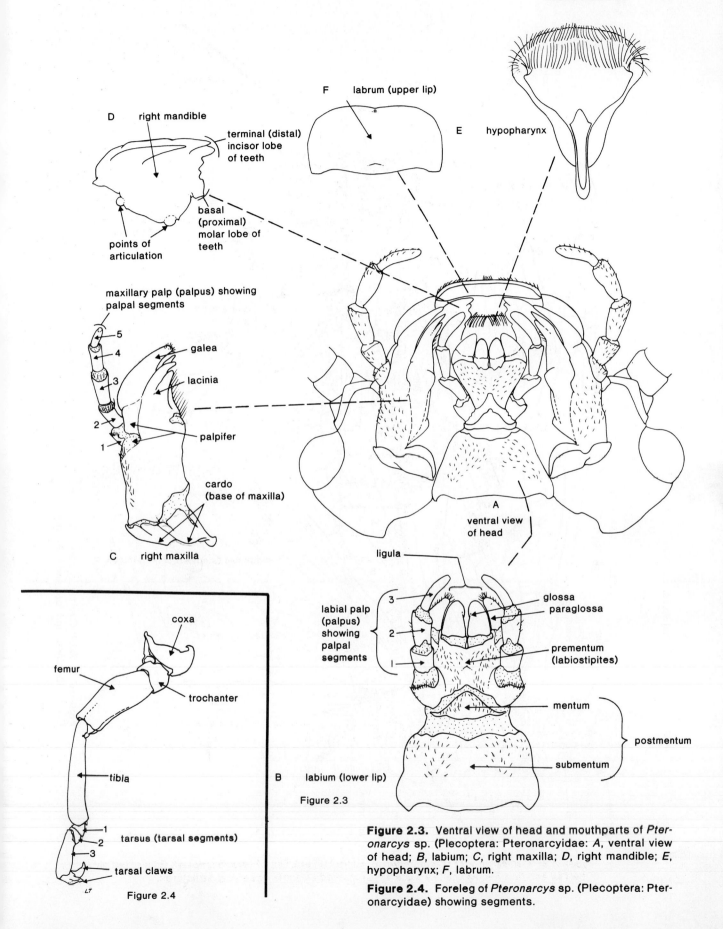

Figure 2.3. Ventral view of head and mouthparts of *Pteronarcys* sp. (Plecoptera: Pteronarcyidae: *A*, ventral view of head; *B*, labium; *C*, right maxilla; *D*, right mandible; *E*, hypopharynx; *F*, labrum.

Figure 2.4. Foreleg of *Pteronarcys* sp. (Plecoptera: Pteronarcyidae) showing segments.

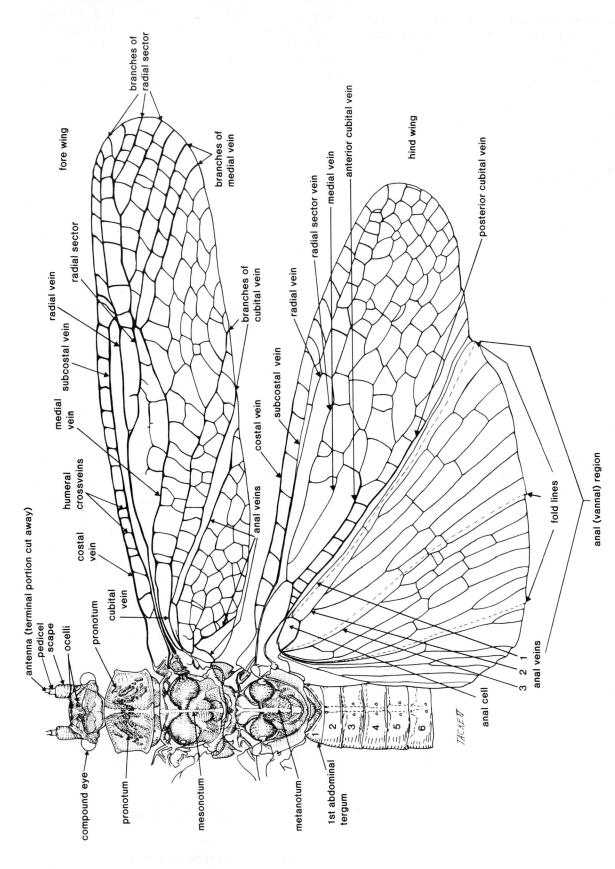

Figure 2.5. Adult *Pteronarcys* sp. (Plecoptera: Pteronarcyidae) showing head, thorax, basal portion of abdomen, and fore and hind wings.

Thorax

The mid region of the body, or *thorax,* bears the jointed *legs* (fig. 2.4) and the *wings,* and is divided into three segments (figs. 2.1–2.2, 2.5–2.6). The *prothorax* bears the forelegs, the *mesothorax* the mid legs and fore wings, and the *metathorax* the hind legs and hind wings (if wings are present).

The jointed legs are five-segmented: the *coxa, trochanter, femur, tibia,* and the three- to five-segmented *tarsus,* which terminates in one or two *tarsal claws* (fig. 2.4). In aquatic insects, modifications of the hind legs for swimming (e.g., a fringe of tibial hairs) are common in certain adult Coleoptera, some nymphal and adult Hemiptera, and a few larval Trichoptera. The forelegs are modified for burrowing in Ephemeridae (Ephemeroptera), Gomphidae (Odonata), and some semiaquatic Orthoptera.

Most adult forms of aquatic insects bear two pairs of wings; some mayflies and all Diptera have only one pair. The second pair of wings in Diptera is modified into balancing organs (*halteres;* fig. 2.6) that function somewhat as gyroscopes. Collembola are wingles (apterous), as are females of certain species of Trichoptera and Diptera.

The structures that extend into the wings are termed *veins.* The form and location of these veins are used extensively in insect taxonomy. Two extreme types of wing venation are shown in figures 2.5–2.6. The primitive stonefly wings have many branches of the major veins with many crossveins between them. The highly evolved wing of a dipteran Tipulidae (*Tipula* sp.) is characterized by the fusion of veins and the loss of branches and crossveins.

The general venation pattern (figs. 2.5–2.6) consists of: a *costal vein* (C), the anterior marginal vein; a *subcostal vein* (Sc) just behind the costal vein and often with two branches near the wing tip; a *radial vein* (R), often the heaviest vein of the wing, which forks near the middle of the wing, with the main part forming the *radial sector vein* (Rs), which typically divides into two branches, each of which may divide into two or more branches near the wing margin; a *medial vein* (M) (the fourth major vein), which has a maximum of four major branches (typically two or three); a *cubital vein* (Cu), which has two major branches, the anterior of which usually forks into two branches; and an *anal* (vannal) *vein* (A), which has a maximum of three major branches with considerable secondary branching, particularly in the more primitive forms. Although crossveins are highly variable, certain ones are usually present. There are generally at least one *humeral crossvein* (h) between the base of the wing and the apex (tip) of the subcosta; a *radial crossvein* (r) between the radius and the first branch of the radial sector; a *radial-medial crossvein* (r-m) between the lower first fork of the radial sector and the upper first fork of the medial vein; and a *medial-cubital crossvein* (m-cu) between the lower first fork of the medial and the upper first fork of the cubital (see Snodgrass 1935; Daly *et al.* 1978; Borror *et al.* 1981; and discussion of taxonomically significant wing veins given in the order and family chapters below).

Abdomen

There are primitively eleven abdominal segments, although in most adults fusion of the last two makes them difficult to distinguish. In some immature forms (notably Ephemeroptera and Megaloptera), gills arise from the pleural regions—being extensions of the tracheal system borne in variously shaped plates or filaments (fingerlike gills). In the stonefly shown in figure 2.2, the branched filamentous gills are attached to the sterna of the thorax and the first two abdominal segments.

The end of the abdomen of paurometabolous and hemimetabolous insects (i.e., Hemiptera, Orthoptera, Ephemeroptera, Odonata, and Plecoptera) bears the reproductive structures (figs. 2.1–2.2, 2.7–2.9). The eleventh segment bears the *anus* at its apex and the *cerci* laterally. The dorsal surface is covered by a triangular or shield-shaped tergal plate, the *epiproct,* and the ventral surface bears two lobes, the *paraprocts.* In males, the ninth sternum often bears two lateral *styli* or *claspers (harpagones).* These accessory structures bound the *phallobase* and *aedeagus* that comprise the main reproductive organ, the *penis* or *phallus.*

The terminal segments of adult females, in addition to the dorsal epiproct and lateral paraprocts below the cerci, generally consist of three pairs of lobes or *valvae* (valves), which form the visible portion of the ovipositor and arise from the eighth and ninth sterna. The bases of the valvae are usually covered by the projecting eighth sternum (fig. 2.9).

Specific morphological modifications in each of the orders (or families receiving special treatment) are detailed in the introductory material covering the respective groups. The modifications usually represent fusion or specialization of the basic structures discussed above. However, some of the terms used in naming the various segments of the genitalia have restricted meanings, and homology with primitive forms is not always possible (Tuxen 1970; Scudder 1971a). For a more complete treatment of insect morphology the student should consult Snodgrass (1935), DuPorte (1959), Matsuda (1965, 1970, 1976), and Chapman (1982). Consult Torre-Bueno (1937) for further explanation of terms.

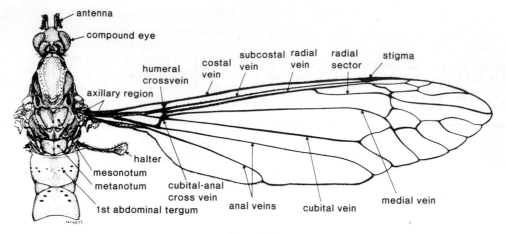

Figure 2.6

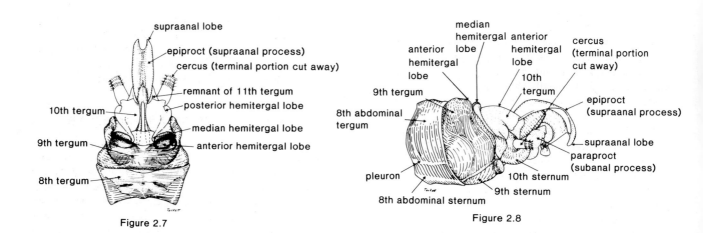

Figure 2.7

Figure 2.8

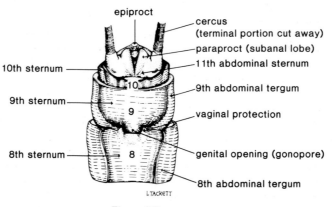

Figure 2.9

Figure 2.6. Dorsal view of adult *Tipula* sp. (Diptera: Tipulidae) showing head, thorax, basal portion of abdomen, fore wing and halter.

Figure 2.7. Dorsal view of terminal male abdominal segments of *Pteronarcys* sp. (Plecoptera: Pteronarcyidae); terminology after Snodgrass (1935) and Nelson and Hanson (1971).

Figure 2.8. Lateral view of terminal male abdominal segments of *Pteronarcys* sp. (Plecoptera: Pteronarcyidae).

Figure 2.9. Ventral view of terminal female abdominal segments of *Pteronarcys* sp. (Plecoptera: Pteronarcyidae).

3

Collecting, Sampling, and Rearing Methods for Aquatic Insects

Richard W. Merritt
Michigan State University, East Lansing

Kenneth W. Cummins
Oregon State University, Corvallis

Vincent H. Resh
University of California, Berkeley

COLLECTING AND SAMPLING METHODS

The following outline and table 3A on collecting and sampling methods for aquatic macroinvertebrates are intended to serve as a guide for those interested in aquatic entomology and ecology. The table is not a complete listing of the references on sampling methods, and students and researchers should continually check the current literature for methods more suited to specific objectives. As noted by Cummins (1962), the number of different samplers used for benthic macroinvertebrates is nearly proportional to the number of benthic investigations! Nevertheless, the table should provide the student with a knowledge of the major qualitative and quantitative sampling techniques used to collect different stages of aquatic macroinvertebrates in a variety of freshwater habitats.

For the beginning student we have placed an asterisk in table 3A after some of the more commonly used samplers for aquatic insects; however, the decision to use a specific sampler or collecting device should depend on the objectives of the study (e.g., Andre *et al*. 1981) and a thorough characterization of the habitat to be sampled. The references cited are generally those that have used or described a particular sampling technique, or compared a technique with other standard methods. In many cases, a supplier of the equipment is also listed.

Since the classification system used here is based primarily on the habitat and community being sampled, the physical nature of the substrate has not been outlined in detail. However, substrate composition may be an important consideration when sampling the benthos (e.g., Minshall and Minshall 1977; Rabeni and Minshall 1977; Lamberti and Resh 1978; Reice 1980), and the equipment and techniques listed below may require modification depending on the substrate type. For a comprehensive review and discussion of different collecting and sampling methods for macroinvertebrates, the reader is referred to Welch (1948), Macan (1958), Albrecht (1959), Cummins (1962), Hrbáček (1962), Hynes (1970a), Edmondson and Winberg (1971), Hellawell (1978), and Southwood (1978). Factors that affect benthic sampling devices and may result in sampling bias are discussed by Resh (1979a, tables 1–3), and Rosenberg (1978)

and Elliott and Tullett (1978) provide extensive bibliographies on samplers for benthic invertebrates. The North American Benthological Society and the Freshwater Biological Association (Great Britain) publish annual bibliographies that include a section on methods and techniques. Rosenberg and Resh (1982) reviewed the use of artificial substrates for studying freshwater macroinvertebrates.

SAMPLING DESIGN AND ANALYSIS

As mentioned previously, sampling can be qualitative (a general assessment of the taxa of aquatic insects present, possibly with some observations of their relative abundance) or quantitative (an estimate of the numbers [total or by taxa] present made so that a statistical confidence of the estimate can be obtained) (e.g., Elliott 1977; Sokal and Rohlf 1981). All representative subhabitats (categories in table 3A) of a given system should be thoroughly sampled. A widely used semiquantitative method for stream benthos is kick sampling (table 3A; Hynes 1970a), whereby a standard number of kicks dislodge organisms from comparable areas into a collection net. Qualitative sampling is also suitable for determining ratios of various functional feeding groups of aquatic insects, for example, the ratio of the number of forms that skeletonize leaf litter (shredders) to the number that graze on attached algae (scrapers) (see chap. 6).

Quantitative sampling requires not only the selection of the most appropriate collection device given the habitat type and composition of the macroinvertebrate community (table 3A), but also consideration of sample site location, sampling frequency, and adequate numbers of samples for each collection date. Sampling frequency should be related to the type of study. For example, production estimates (chap. 6) of one to several species require a sampling regime keyed to specific life cycle patterns, whereas complete faunal studies require at least seasonal frequency. A useful approach is to sample every 100–300 degree-days (chap. 6; i.e., cumulated mean daily temperature [e.g., 10 days at a mean temp. of $10°C = 100$ deg.-days]; Southwood 1978) because most aquatic insect life cycles are under general thermal control.

Table 3A. Collecting and sampling methods for aquatic macroinvertebrates based on the habitat and community being sampled.

Major Sampling Habitat	Subhabitat and Ecological Community	Quantitative Sampler	Figure	Reference(s)	Supplier†	Qualitative or Semi-quantitative Sampler	Figure	Reference(s)	Supplier
LOTIC HABITATS									
I. Shallow Streams, Rivers, and Springs	A. Riffles (erosional zones)								
	1. Benthos								
	a. Sediments	Surber sampler*	3.7	401, 1134, 1490, 1681, 1785, 2375	A, C, H	Aquatic net	3.2	2495	C, E
		Hess or modified Hess sampler*	3.6	1039, 1122, 1207, 2593	B	Hand screen collector	3.3	2495	E
		T-sampler	3.8	1517		Artificial substrate samplers	3.23	1134, 1490, 1562, 1681, 1785, 2078, 2375	A, B, C, E
		Wilding or stovepipe sampler; box-type sampler	3.5	34, 2324, 2613, 2687		Kick sampling		815, 1168, 1939	
						Recolonization		2702	
						Hand collection		1490, 2495	
						Leaf packs	3.25	1638, 1905, 2207	
		Portable invertebrate box sampler	3.9		D	Photographic methods		477, 478	
		Riffle sampler		421		Graded sieves	3.33	100, 1735, 2495	C, I, J
	b. Hyporheic area (subterranean)	Implants*		199, 426, 864, 1173, 1710, 1940		Frozen corer		646, 2343, 2543	
		Standpipe corer		695, 2700, 2701, 2703					
	c. Plants	Bag sampler		1172, 2613		Needham apron net		2495	C
		Surber sampler	3.7		A, C, H	Aquatic net	3.2	2495	C, E
		Stovepipe sampler	3.5	34, 2602					
		Lambourn sampler		1050					
	d. Drift and Neuston (surface)	Drift net*	3.10	70, 653, 2587, 2702	A, C	Aquatic net	3.2	2495	C, E
		Plankton net	3.11	653, 1172	A, B, C, H, I, K, L				
		Cushing-Mundie drift sampler		493, 1733					
		Hardy plankton indicator type sampler		651, 1172					
		Surface film sampler		420					

*Commonly used samplers for aquatic insects.
†See Section III of this chapter for sources and addresses.

le 3A. — *Continued*

Major Sampling Habitat	Subhabitat and Ecological Community	Quantitative Sampler	Figure	Refer- ence(s)	Supplier†	Qualitative or Semi- quantitative Sampler	Figure	Refer- ence(s)	Supplier†
	2. Emerging Adults	Surface film sampler		420		Hand screen col- lector	3.3	2495	E
		Mundie pyra- mid trap*	3.26	1731		Pan traps		922, 1372	
		Stationary screen trap		949, 1179, 1568		Window traps		386, 2379	
		Enclosed channels		2580		Light traps*		2283	
		Floating emergence traps*		1457, 1492, 1705					
	B. Pools (depositional zones) 1. Benthos a. Sediments	Ekman grab with pole*	3.16	1172	A	Aquatic net	3.2	2495	C, E
		Wilding or stovepipe sampler	3.5			Graded sieves	3.33	2495	I, J
		Single corer with pole	3.12	428, 823, 2534					
	b. Plants	Bag sampler		1172		Needham apron net		2495	C
	c. Drift and Neuston	See Section I.A.I.C.				See Section I.A.I.C.			
	2. Emerging Adults	See Section I.A.Z.				See Section I.A.Z.			
Large Rivers	A. Riffles 1. Benthos a. Sediments	Suction samplers		660, 827, 928, 2520		Basket or cylin- drical-type artifi- cial substrate samplers*	3.24	43, 63, 124, 467, 734, 825, 948, 1050, 1054, 1565, 1567, 1848, 2093, 2603	F
		SCUBA diving		825, 826, 1050, 1976		Single or multi- ple-plate sam- plers	3.23	562, 734, 988, 1040, 2093	A, B, C
		Grab samplers*		26, 658, 660		Drag-type sam- plers		659, 660, 2497	A, B
	b. Drift and Neuston	Floating drift trap (with floats)		653, 1734					
		Hardy plank- ton indicator- type sampler		651, 1172					
	2. Emerging Adults	Insect emer- gence traps		1392, 1705					
		Floating drift trap (with floats)		1734					

ommonly used samplers for aquatic insects.
ee Section III of this chapter for sources and addresses.

Table 3A. — *Continued*

Major Sampling Habitat	Subhabitat and Ecological Community	Quantitative Sampler	Figure	Reference(s)	Supplier†	Qualitative or Semi-quantitative Sampler	Figure	Reference(s)	Supplier
	B. Pools								
	1. Benthos								
	a. Sediments	Ponar grab*	3.17	658, 660, 1462, 1951	A, B, C	Basket-type artificial substrate samplers*	3.24	734, 825, 1565, 2093	F
		Peterson-type grabs*	3.19	658, 1462, 1914		SCUBA diving		660, 1172	
		Ekman grab*	3.16	650, 658, 660, 1172, 1462	A, B, C				
		Core sampler	3.12, 3.13	660, 733, 823	A, B, C				
		Allan hand-operated grab	3.18	26					
		Also, see **LENTIC HABITATS**							
	b. Plants	See **Lentic Habitats,** Section III.A.1.b.				See **Lentic Habitats,** Section III.A.1.b			
	c. Drift and Neuston	See Section II.A.1.b.							
	2. Emerging Adults	See Section II.A.Z.							
LENTIC HABITATS **III. Shallow Standing-Water Habitats** (ponds, oxidation lakes, marshes, bogs, rice fields, etc.) 1. Benthos	A. Vegetated								
	a. Sediments	Core sampler with pole	3.12	122, 428, 823, 2534		Aquatic net	3.2	2495	C, E
		Wilding or Hess-type sampler	3.5, 3.6	1039, 1050, 2687	B	Graded sieves	3.33	1389, 2413, 2495	C, I, J
		Kellen grab	3.15	1284, 2583					
		Water column sampler*		1438, 2381					
	b. Rooted Plants, Periphyton	Macan sampler	3.20	1127, 1267, 1488		Glass slides, plastic squares, and other artificial substrates		1498, 2242, 2243	
		Lambourn sampler		1050					
		Gerking sampler*	3.21	853		Modified sweep net		1276, 2527	
		Modified Gerking sampler	3.22	1276, 1680		Needham apron net		2495	C
		Removal of natural substrates		2243					
		Plexiglass or metal tubes		1386, 2243					
		Douglas method		581					

*Commonly used samplers for aquatic insects.
†See Section III of this chapter for sources and addresses.

ble 3A.—*Continued*

Major Sampling Habitat	Subhabitat and Ecological Community	Quantitative Sampler	Figure	Reference(s)	Supplier†	Qualitative or Semi-quantitative Sampler	Figure	Reference(s)	Supplier†
	c. Neuston	Water column sampler		1438		Subaquatic light traps*	3.28	2, 352, 353, 1153, 1155, 2583, 2826	
		D-Vac vacuum sampler		832		Telescope method		915	
		Funnel-trap sampler		1029		Plankton tow net	3.11		A, B, C, I, K, L
						Hand dipper*	3.4	2209, 2283	C, E, F
						Aquatic net	3.2	2495, 2527	C, E
	2. Emerging Adults	Emergence traps (primarily surface traps which float*	3.27	443, 687, 934, 1254, 1304, 1384, 1457, 1464, 1600, 1705, 1706, 1731, 1736, 1960, 2094		Subaquatic light traps*	3.28	2, 66, 352, 353, 683, 1153, 1155, 2583, 2826	
	B. Nonvegetated 1. Benthos a. Sediments	Ekman with or without pole*	3.16	650, 1127, 1267	A, B, C	Dredges		1267	A, B, C, G, I, K, L
		Kellen grab	3.15	1284		Aquatic net	3.2	2495	C, E
		Petite Ponar grab			A				
		Core sampler with pole	3.12	122, 428, 823, 1267, 2534					
		Water column sampler		2381					
	b. Neuston	See Section III.A.1.c.				See Section III.A.1.c.			
	2. Emerging Adults	See Section III.A.2.				See Section III.A.1.c.			
. Lakes	A. Littoral 1. Benthos a. Nonvegetated (wave swept)	Wilding or stovepipe sampler	3.5	1267, 2613, 2687		Basket-type artificial substrate samplers*	3.21	64, 71, 124, 734, 1691, 2093, 2530, 2603	
		Suction samplers		723, 928					
		Core sampler with or without pole*	3.12, 3.13	122, 428, 733, 823, 2534	A, B, C	Graded sieves	3.33	2495	C, I, J
		Ekman or similar type grab with pole*	3.16	538, 658, 1125, 1833, 2749	A				
		Ponar grab*	3.17	64, 658, 733, 1125, 1267, 1951	A, B, C				
		SCUBA diving with sampling gear		696, 824					
		Also, see Section III.B.1.a.							

ommonly used samplers for aquatic insects.
ee Section III of this chapter for sources and addresses.

Table 3A. — *Continued*

Major Sampling Habitat	Subhabitat and Ecological Community	Quantitative Sampler	Figure	Reference(s)	Supplier†	Qualitative or Semi-quantitative Sampler	Figure	Reference(s)	Supplier
	b. Vegetated (plant zone)	Wilding or stovepipe sampler	3.5	2602, 2687		Dredges and grabs			A, B, C, I, K, L
		Gillespie and Brown sampler		859		Photographic methods		2602	
		Macan sampler with attachment rod	3.20	1267, 1833					
		Removal of natural substrate by SCUBA		2633					
	2. Emerging Adults	See Section III.A.2.							
	B. Profundal 1. Benthos a. Sediments	Single core sampler*	3.13	253, 733, 1110, 1267, 1270, 1279, 1654, 2613, 2651	A, B, C, G	Dredges			A, B, C, G, I, K,
		Multiple core sampler	3.14	733, 950, 1267, 1654	A				
						Photographic methods		1267	
		Ekman or modified Ekman grab*	3.16	650, 733, 1267, 1747	A, B, C				
		Ponar grab*	3.17	733, 1267, 1951	A, B, C				
		Peterson-type grab*	3.19	1267, 1914, 2268, 2613	A, B, C, F, G, K				
		SCUBA diving with sampling gear		696, 1267, 2530					
	2. Emerging Adults	Emergence traps (mainly funnel and submerged traps)	3.27	292, 706, 934, 1254, 1705, 1706,* 1731, 1736, 2094, 2651					
TERRESTRIAL HABITATS **V. Stream and Lake Margins** (floodplains and beach zones)									
	A. Adult Aquatic or Semiaquatic Insects	Light traps	3.30, 3.31	1122, 1726, 2209, 2283, 2372	C, E	Aerial insect net		2495	C, E, K
						Aspirator		2495	
		Malaise traps and other emergence traps*	3.29	1530, 2209, 2254, 2461, 2463	E, L	Graded sieves	3.33		C, I, J
	B. Immatures and Adults	Berlaise or Tullgren funnels	3.32	2283, 2495					
		Modified Ladell apparatus		1423					

*Commonly used samplers for aquatic insects.
†See Section III of this chapter for sources and addresses.

Table 3B. Symbols and formulas for calculating numbers of requisite samples for a desired level of precision (from Elliott 1977 and other sources).

Symbol	Formula	Description
n		Total number of sampling units in sample.
$\bar{x}$	$\dfrac{\Sigma x}{n}$	Mean number of individuals ($\bar{x}$) in n sample units in which each x is the number in a given sample unit (Σ = summation).
s^2	$s^2 = \dfrac{\Sigma(x - \bar{x})^2}{n - 1}$ or $s^2 = \dfrac{\Sigma(x^2) - \bar{x}\Sigma x}{n - 1}$	Variance (s^2) is the sum of the deviations of $\bar{x}$ from each x divided by the degrees of freedom (one less than the number of sampling units). It is also equal to the standard deviation (s) squared.
SE	$SE = \sqrt{\dfrac{s^2}{n}}$	Standard error
D	$D = \dfrac{SE}{\bar{x}}$	Precision (D) is the standard error expressed as a proportion (or, if multiplied by 100, as %) of the mean. The usual range of D in benthic studies is 0.10–0.40, but choice of D should be a function of sampling objectives.
t^2		$t \approx 2$ ($t^2 \approx 4$) if $n > 30$ for 95% probability level of D in Student's t-distribution.
$n_{est.}$	$n_{est.} = \dfrac{t^2 s^2}{D^2 \bar{x}^2}$	General formula for sample size; if 95% confidence limits of $\pm$ 40% of $\bar{x}$, $n_{est.} = \dfrac{25\, s^2}{\bar{x}^2}$

Stratified random or randomly placed transects are useful methods of selecting sites for individual sample collection (Cummins 1975; Elliott 1977; Southwood 1978; Resh 1979a; Sokal and Rohlf 1981). These are likely to ensure that all general habitats and their biotic associations are adequately represented.

As indicated by Elliott (1977) in his excellent treatment of benthic sampling and analysis, the number of samples (i.e., sample units or n) to take is a difficult and critical decision. The number of sampling units required is a function of: (1) the size of the mean, (2) the degree of aggregation exhibited by the population, and (3) the desired precision of the mean estimate (Resh 1979a). If (2) and (3) are the same, a population with higher density will require fewer samples than one that is less dense. In terms of (2), most ecological studies of aquatic insects have indicated that the majority of species are distributed in a patchy fashion (clumped, nonrandom, and aggregated distributions are all synonyms for this phenomenon), but interpretations of aggregation may be a function of the size of the sampling unit and the number of samples collected (Elliott 1977). Assuming (1) and (3) are equal, populations with nonrandom distributions require greater numbers of samples than those that are randomly distributed. The higher the desired precision of the mean estimate, the greater the number of samples required. If the tolerable 95% confidence limits are cut by half (e.g., from $\pm$ 40% to $\pm$ 20%), four times as many samples will be required. The formula for sample size determination is given in table 3B and an example using a caddisfly population is presented in table 3C. Detailed treatment of sampling design in aquatic insect studies is provided by Cummins (1975), Elliott (1977, especially chap. 8), Green (1979), Resh (1979a), and Waters and Resh (1979).

A graphic (i.e., mean stabilization) technique can also be used to approximate the number of sample units required to adequately sample aquatic insect populations. With this approach, a cumulative plot of mean and total numbers of individuals from a pilot study is made, and the number of samples after which the change in the mean becomes less than 10% with increased number of individuals is chosen as the sample size. Confidence limits of the mean can then be established based on mean and variance estimates.

If a sample unit contains a very large number of individuals in a given taxon, e.g., midge (Chironomidae) larvae, it may be necessary to subsample to obtain an estimate because the time required for a total count is prohibitive (Waters 1969; Elliott 1977; Wrona *et al.* 1982; fig. 3.1). If the subsample counts fulfill the criteria of randomness, then a single subsample count can be used to estimate the number in the original sample unit. To satisfy randomness, the mean of at least five subsample counts should be within the 95% confidence interval, that is, have a chi-square (χ^2) value between the 5% significance levels for n-1 degrees of freedom found in a standard statistical table $\left(\dfrac{\Sigma(x - \bar{x})^2}{\bar{x}^2}\right)$. The count should be of the category of interest, e.g., all taxa or a particular taxon such as a species, age class, or life stage of a species or functional group. For a further discussion of subsampling, see Elliott (1977).

Once the sample has been collected, it must be treated according to the nature of the substrate materials and the types of analyses to be made. We have presented a generalized flow diagram summarizing some general procedures that might be used in analyzing stream bottom samples (fig. 3.1). For a more thorough treatment and discussion of methods of

Table 3C. Determination of the number of sample units required to estimate age-specific and total population size of the caddisfly *Glossosoma nigrior* Banks (Trichoptera: Glossosomatidae) in two first-order Michigan streams. See Table 3B for sample size formula.

Stream	n	*Glossosoma nigrior* Age Class	$\bar{x}$/0.016 m²	s²	Sample Sizes (to nearest integer) for 95% Confidence Limits where D = ± 40%	± 20%	± 10%
Augusta Creek (August)	62	Instar 1	2.6	16.8	63	249	994
		2	13.4	292.4	41	165	652
		3	7.8	44.9	19	74	296
		4	1.8	4.0	31	124	494
		5	5.6	19.4	16	62	248
		Prepupae	2.2	5.8	30	120	480
		Pupae	4.5	51.8	64	256	1024
		Total	32.8	681.2	16	64	254
Spring Brook (July)	44	Instar 1	0.5	1.0	100	400	1600
		2	4.3	21.2	29	115	459
		3	6.7	37.2	21	83	332
		4	5.3	22.1	20	79	315
		5	1.7	4.0	35	139	554
		Prepupae and pupae	2.1	6.3	36	143	571
		Total	20.6	201.6	12	49	196

sorting and sample analysis, the reader is referred to Cummins (1962, 1975), Kajak (1963), Edmondson and Winberg (1971), Weber (1973), Elliott (1977), Hellawell (1978), Southwood (1978), Resh (1979a; table 2), Sokal and Rohlf (1981), and appropriate references in Rosenberg (1978).

OUTLINE OF CLASSIFICATION SYSTEM USED IN TABLE 3A BASED ON THE HABITAT AND COMMUNITY BEING SAMPLED

Lotic Habitats

I. Shallow Streams, Rivers, and Springs
- A. Riffles (erosional zones)
  - 1. Benthos
    - a. Sediments
    - b. Hyporheic area (subterranean)
    - c. Plants
    - d. Drift and Neuston (surface)
  - 2. Emerging Adults
- B. Pools (depositional zones)
  - 1. Benthos
    - a. Sediments
    - b. Plants
    - c. Drift and Neuston
  - 2. Emerging Adults

II. Large Rivers
- A. Riffles
  - 1. Benthos
    - a. Sediments
    - b. Drift and Neuston
  - 2. Emerging Adults
- B. Pools
  - 1. Benthos
    - a. Sediments
    - b. Plants
    - c. Drift and Neuston
  - 2. Emerging Adults

Lentic Habitats

III. Shallow Standing-Water Habitats (ponds, oxidation lakes, marshes, bogs, rice fields, etc.)
- A. Vegetated
  - 1. Benthos
    - a. Sediments
    - b. Rooted Plants
    - c. Neuston
  - 2. Emerging Adults
- B. Nonvegetated
  - 1. Benthos
    - a. Sediments
    - b. Neuston
  - 2. Emerging Adults

IV. Lakes
- A. Littoral
  - 1. Benthos
    - a. Nonvegetated (wave-swept)
    - b. Vegetated (plant zone)
  - 2. Emerging Adults
- B. Profundal
  - 1. Benthos
    - a. Sediments
  - 2. Emerging Adults

Terrestrial Habitats

V. Stream and Lake Margins (floodplains and beach zones)
- A. Adult Aquatic and Semiaquatic Insects
- B. Immatures and Adults

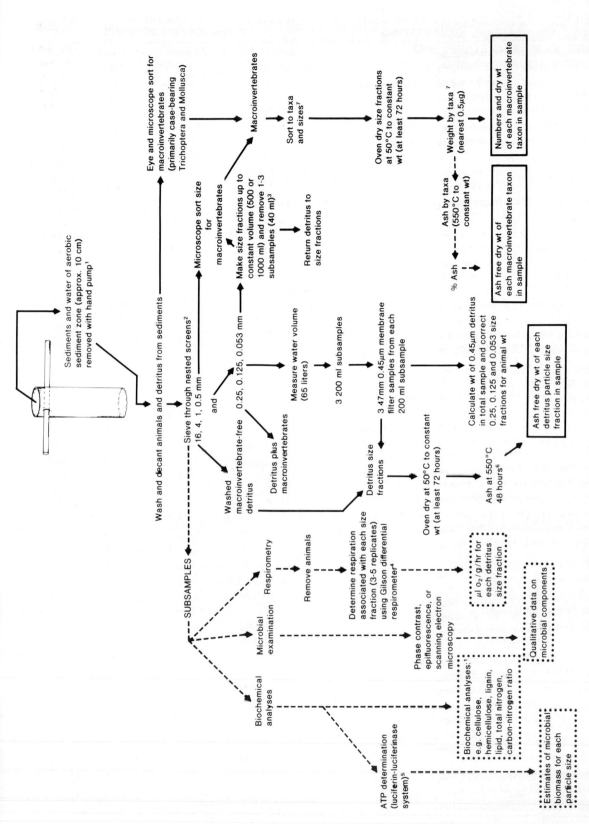

Figure 3.1. A flow diagram summarizing general procedures for analyzing stream bottom samples. *Solid arrows* indicate procedures used on all samples, *dashed arrows* are procedures used only on selected samples or subsamples. Notations: *1*, bilge-type hand pump or dipped out with a scoop; *2*, size classes are based on the Wentworth (1922) scale (modified by Cummins *et al.* [1973]); *3*, size fraction and subsample volumes should be based on the nature of the sample, especially the density of macroinvertebrates. (Waters [1969b] has devised an efficient subsampler and subsampling is discussed by Elliott [1977]); *4*, Gilson (1963); *5*, Asmus (1973); *6*, long ashing times are required to achieve constant weight, particularly with large detritus samples. If sample contains significant clay content, peroxide digestion may be preferable to combustion; *7*, animals can be classed into length or weight groups by sieve size (Reger *et al.* 1982).

19

SOURCES OF GENERAL COLLECTING AND SAMPLING EQUIPMENT FOR AQUATIC INSECTS

In addition to the sources listed below, the investigator should also consult: (1) "Sources of Limnological and Oceanographic Apparatus and Supplies" (Special Publ. No. 1, 3rd revision) available from the American Society of Limnology and Oceanography; (2) "Guide to Scientific Instruments," a special issue of *Science* published each year by the American Association for the Advancement of Science; and (3) "Directory of Entomological Services," published by Ent. Res. Publishers, P.O. Box 3686, Santa Fe Springs, Calif. 90670.

    A. Wildlife Supply Co.
        301 Cass St.
        Saginaw, Mich. 48602

    B. Kahl Scientific Instrument Corp.
        P.O. Box 1166
        El Cajon, Calif. 92022

    C. Ward's Natural Science Establishment, Inc.
        P.O. Box 1712
        Rochester, N.Y. 14603 (Eastern Office)

        Ward's of California
        P.O. Box 1749
        Monterey, Calif. 93942 (Western Office)

    D. Ellis-Rutter Associates
        P.O. Box 401
        Punta Gorda, Fla. 33950

    E. BioQuip Products
        P.O. Box 61
        Santa Monica, Calif. 90406

    F. Entomological Supplies, Inc.
        5655 Oregon Ave.
        Baltimore, Md. 21227

    G. GM Mfg. and Instrument Co.
        Box 947
        El Cajon, Calif. 92022

    H. Van Waters and Rogers
        P.O. Box 182
        Buffalo, N.Y. 14240 (Eastern Office)

        Van Waters and Rogers
        P.O. Box 3200, Rincon Annex
        San Francisco, Calif. 94119 (Western Office)

        (Regional Offices in 17 states)

    I. Cole-Parmer
        7425 North Oak Park Ave.
        Chicago, Ill. 60648

    J. Carolina Biological Supply Co.
        Burlington, N.C. 27215

    K. Hydro-Bios Apparatebau Gnblt.
        Wismarerstrasse 14
        23 Kiel, Germany

    L. D. A. Focks and Associates
        P.O. Box 12852
        University Station
        Gainesville, Fla. 32604

REARING METHODS

Most ecological studies of aquatic insects have dealt with their immature stages. This is largely because nymphs and larvae occur in aquatic habitats and represent the major portion of insect life cycles, whereas adults are mainly terrestrial and short-lived. For this reason, aquatic sampling techniques are primarily designed to collect many immatures but few adults.

The identification of most aquatic immatures is difficult because: (1) taxonomic names are generally based on characteristics present in the adult stage, (2) larvae have been associated with their corresponding adult stages for relatively few species, and (3) the comparative analysis of congeneric (i.e., in the same genus) larvae necessary to produce species-level keys is lacking since the immature stages of relatively few species are known in some groups.

Species-level identifications are important in ecological studies since congeneric species do not necessarily have identical ecological requirements or water quality tolerances. Also, the inability to distinguish between coexisting species may mask population dynamics or trends, and, without species identification, comparisons with results obtained from other studies (possibly even with related species) are difficult (see individual order chapters for exceptions). The calculation of diversity indices, a technique widely used in aquatic insect community studies, may result in significant underestimates when generic- or family-level identifications, rather than those made at the species level, are used (Resh 1979b).

The taxonomic problems of identifying the immature stages of aquatic insects can be solved either by rearing the larva or nymph to the adult stage, or in some groups by collecting associated adult and immature stages. For example, associations can be made by examining mature pupae (Milne 1938) and cast larval skins (e.g., Trichoptera), or by collecting exuviae in organic foam accumulations, drift (streams), or windrows (lakes) (e.g., Chironomidae). Rearing techniques range from very simple to highly complex, and no single technique is suitable for all aquatic insects or even all species of a given family. In table 3D, general references to techniques for obtaining adult stages of immature insects from lotic and lentic habitats are given, as are rearing (i.e., a single generation) and culturing (i.e., rearing through subsequent generations) methods appropriate for the different orders of aquatic insects. In the future, the use of innovative rearing methods should greatly increase the number of species that have associated immature and adult stages.

Published reports of rearing techniques generally fall into three categories: (1) descriptions of various running-water systems (artificial streams; see discussion in Vogel and LaBarbera 1978), (2) methods of maintaining larvae and pupae until emergence occurs, and (3) methods of obtaining eggs from adult females and then rearing the newly hatched larvae as in (2). Because lotic insects are often more difficult to rear than lentic ones, a greater number of techniques has been published on the former. In recent years, culturing methods (i.e., for continuous generations) have been improved, largely in response to the need for maintaining organisms for bioassay tests (e.g., Anderson 1980). The methods outlined by Lawrence (1981) and references in table 3D

Table 3D. Selected references on aquatic insect rearing methods.

Order	Immature to Adult Rearing Methods				Laboratory Culture Methods References
	Field		Laboratory		
	References	Figures	References	Figures	
Lentic insects in most orders†			71*	3.37	
Rheophilic (current-loving) insects in all orders		3.35	201, 453*, 455, 1414, 1566, 2184	3.38–3.39	
Collembola					2293
Ephemeroptera	535, 637*, 1782, 1963	3.34	535, 801, 1489, 1887	3.37–3.39	141, 801, 802, 1745, 2295
Odonata	1764	3.35	119*, 330, 1518*, 1884, 2636	3.38	918, 1366, 1518, 2163, 2636
Plecoptera	805, 1166	3.34	247, 804, 805, 846, 1166*, 1278, 1887, 2780	3.37–3.39	201, 1278
Hemiptera			119*, 1620	3.37	665, 1099, 1228
Trichoptera	1454	3.34–3.35	50–52*, 55, 1049, 1917, 2014*, 2663*	3.37–3.39	54, 201, 2014
Neuroptera			275*, 1836		
Megaloptera			1959*, 2253*		
Lepidoptera		3.35	1390		
Hymenoptera	See methods for rearing specific hosts				
Coleoptera					
Lentic species			45, 119*, 2794		281, 2643
Lotic species			281, 2643*		
Diptera					
Ceratopogonidae			1298, 2429		943, 1470
Chironomidae		3.36	119*, 237, 640	3.36	196, 461, 584, 1628, 2806
Culicidae			852*		852, 2252
Sciomyzidae			1788		
Simuliidae	1409		354, 946, 997, 2394, 2395*, 2426*		242*, 716, 793, 1724, 1725, 1986, 2229, 2230, 2753, 2754, 2774
Tabanidae			1388, 1543, 2073, 2074, 2191*, 2414		
Tipulidae	1953		1022, 2086		
Parasitic mites on aquatic insects			468, 469, 2022		

*Recommended techniques.
†Hemimetabolous or with aquatic pupal stage.

should be consulted for more detailed information on the approaches used. The subject of invertebrate bioassays has recently been covered by Buikema and Cairns (1980).

The types of decisions necessary for choosing an appropriate rearing technique are outlined in figure 3.40. Field rearings are generally more successful but are often impractical because of the time or frequency required to be on-site. The choice of mass (many species per container) versus individual rearings is based on the degree of similarity among larvae being reared. Collection of adults in the vicinity of the larval aquatic habitat with sweep nets or light traps can give some idea of the presence of systematically related species whose immature stages may not be distinguished easily from those under examination. This information may help avoid the situation in which two or more species of adults emerge from a presumed single-species rearing. An alternative approach is to obtain eggs from known females and rear these to maturity (Solem and Resh 1981).

One of the most common problems encountered in rearing aquatic insects involves mortality during transport from the field to the laboratory, due to inadequate oxygen supply and/or temperature control. Agitation during transport will maintain oxygen levels, but may damage delicate specimens. Alternative methods include transporting the animals in damp moss, burlap, or paper towels; using small "bait bucket" aerators; or attaching tubing to an exterior funnel that can pick up a "wind stream" while a vehicle is moving. To maintain cool temperatures, thermos containers or ice coolers should be used.

Laboratory rearings can be maintained at field temperatures using an immersible refrigeration unit or by recirculating water through a cooling reservoir. If laboratory temperatures do not match those in the field, mortality can be reduced by allowing temperatures to equilibrate slowly. To maintain water quality in the laboratory, tap water should be dechlorinated and distilled water added to replace evaporation loss.

Algal and detrital food supplies are often best maintained by periodic replenishment from the field. Detritivores that eat leaf litter (shredders) require conditioned material, that is, leaves colonized by aquatic hyphomycete fungi and bacteria. Wheat and other grains can be used to supplement the diets of detritivores; herbivores and scrapers can frequently be fed spinach leaves. The addition of enchytraeid worms to a detritus-based diet not only reduced development time but also increased the weight of individuals in a limnephilid caddisfly culture (Anderson 1976). Larvae of *Drosophila,* house flies, mosquitoes, and tubificid or enchytraeid worms can serve as food for predators. The most critical problem in rearing aquatic insects that require a highly specific food (e.g., freshwater sponges, bryozoans) may be in the culture of the food source itself.

Mortality can be reduced in rearings by choosing only nymphs close to emergence or larvae about to pupate. Because adult males are normally required for specific identification, a special effort should be made to select more males for rearing (as can be done with many hemimetabolous species) or collect sufficiently large numbers for rearing to ensure at least some male emergence. Adjustments of photoperiod (using a light/dark regime similar to that in the field during emergence) or temperature may be required to break the arrested development of species that undergo diapause.

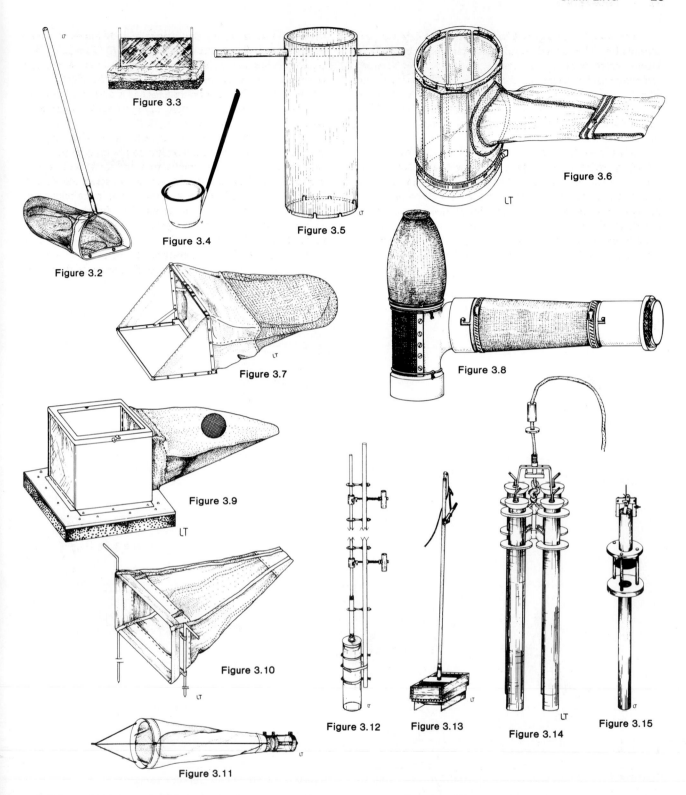

Figure 3.3

Figure 3.4

Figure 3.5

Figure 3.6

Figure 3.2

Figure 3.7

Figure 3.8

Figure 3.9

Figure 3.10

Figure 3.11

Figure 3.12

Figure 3.13

Figure 3.14

Figure 3.15

Figure 3.2. D-frame aquatic net.

Figure 3.3. Hand screen collector.

Figure 3.4. Hand dipper.

Figure 3.5. Wilding or stovepipe sampler.

Figure 3.6. Modified Hess sampler.

Figure 3.7. Surber sampler.

Figure 3.8. Stream bottom T-sampler.

Figure 3.9. Portable invertebrate box sampler.

Figure 3.10. Drift net.

Figure 3.11. Plankton tow net.

Figure 3.12. Core sampler with pole.

Figure 3.13. Kellen grab.

Figure 3.14. Multiple core sampler.

Figure 3.15. Single core sampler.

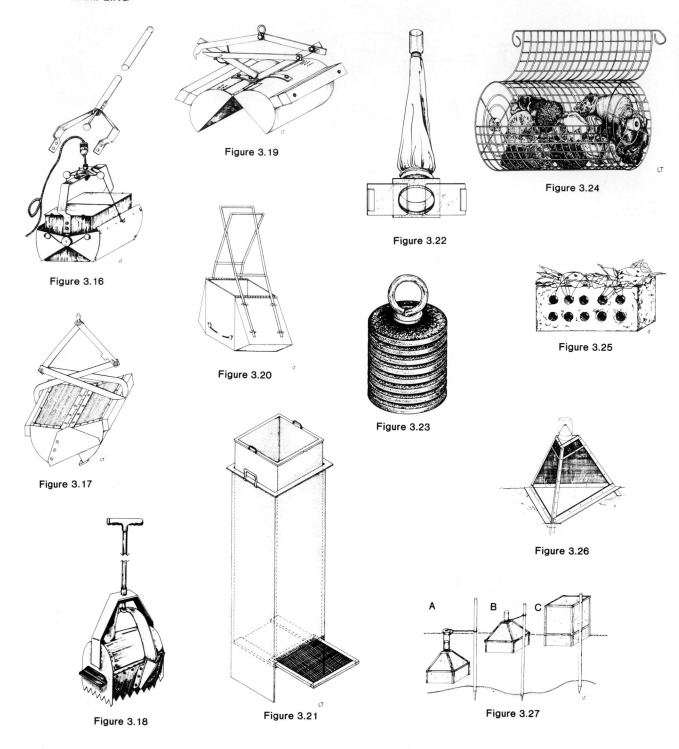

Figure 3.16. Ekman grab (with and without pole attachment).

Figure 3.17. Ponar grab.

Figure 3.18. Allan grab.

Figure 3.19. Petersen grab.

Figure 3.20. Macan sampler.

Figure 3.21. Gerking sampler.

Figure 3.22. Modified Gerking sampler.

Figure 3.23. Multiple-plate artificial substrate sampler.

Figure 3.24. Basket-type artificial substrate sampler.

Figure 3.25. Leaf pack sampler.

Figure 3.26. Mundie pyramid trap.

Figure 3.27. Emergence traps: *A*, submerged; *B*, floating pyramid; *C*, staked box.

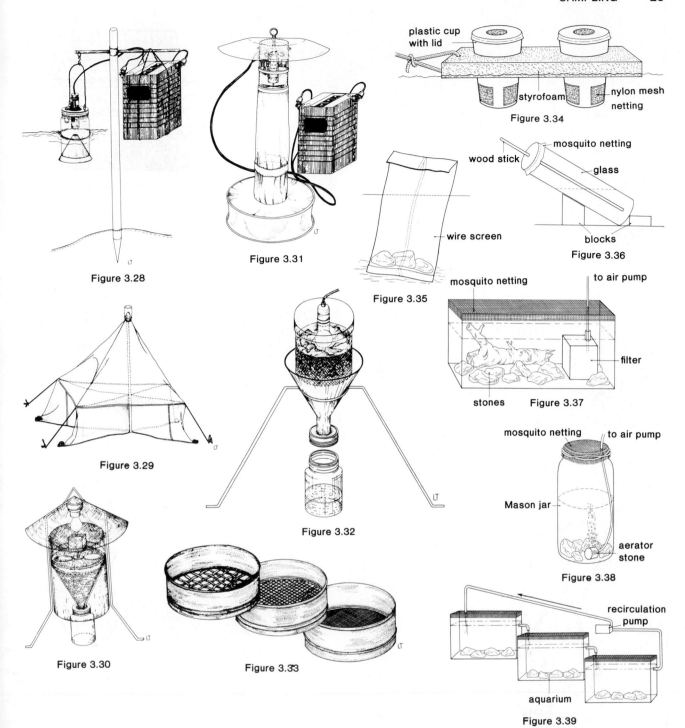

plastic cup
with lid

Figure 3.34

styrofoam

nylon mesh
netting

mosquito netting

wood stick

glass

wire screen

blocks

Figure 3.36

Figure 3.35

mosquito netting

to air pump

filter

stones   Figure 3.37

mosquito netting

to air pump

Mason jar

aerator
stone

Figure 3.38

recirculation
pump

aquarium

Figure 3.39

Figure 3.28

Figure 3.31

Figure 3.29

Figure 3.32

Figure 3.30

Figure 3.33

Figure 3.28. Subaquatic light trap.

Figure 3.29. Malaise trap.

Figure 3.30. New Jersey light trap.

Figure 3.31. CDC light trap.

Figure 3.32 Berlese-Tullgren funnel.

Figure 3.33. Graded sieves.

Figure 3.34. Floating cages (drawn after Edmunds *et al.* [1976]). A mesh lining attached along the inside wall of the cups will allow the subimagos to cling to the side and not slip back into the water.

Figure 3.35. Pillow cage (drawn after Peterson [1934]). The inclusion of larger stones to serve as ballast may prevent the pillow cage from being washed away. The top portion of the cage must be above the water surface.

Figure 3.36. Vial rearings (drawn after Peterson [1934]). Fungal growth will be retarded if distilled water is used and the temperature is kept 16°C or lower.

Figure 3.37. Aquarium rearing method.

Figure 3.38. Quart jar rearing method.

Figure 3.39. Artificial stream rearing design.

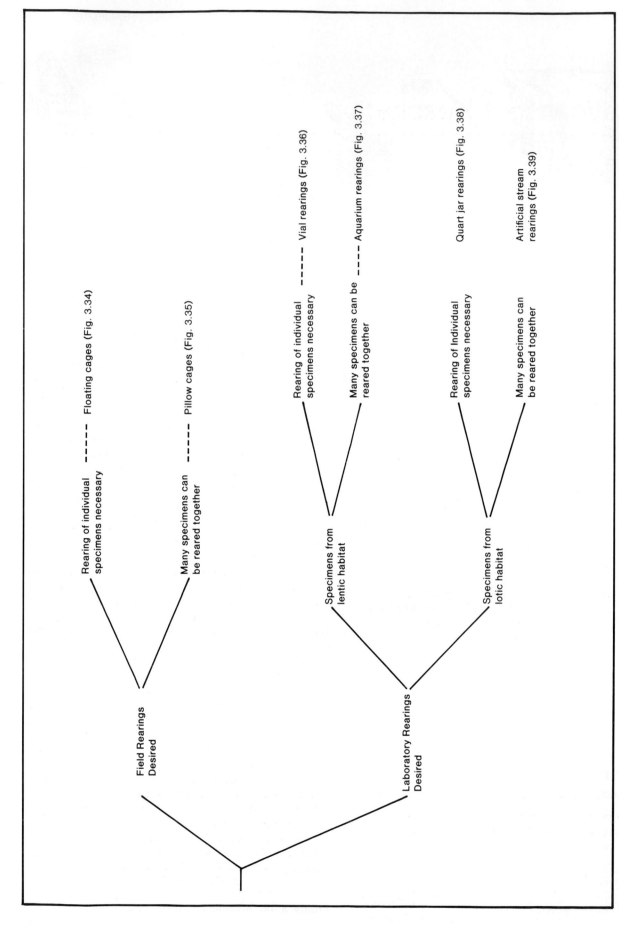

Figure 3.40. Schematic presentation of rearing decisions.

Aquatic Insect Respiration

4

Clyde H. Eriksen
The Claremont Colleges, Claremont, California

Vincent H. Resh
Steven S. Balling
Gary A. Lamberti
University of California, Berkeley

INTRODUCTION

A major challenge for any aquatic insect is to obtain sufficient oxygen (O_2). Aquatic habitats contain much less O_2 than terrestrial environments, even under the most favorable conditions. In addition, the aquatic O_2 supply is often highly variable and in some habitats may be totally lacking (anaerobic). This difference between terrestrial and aquatic environments must have created a considerable challenge for insects that evolved under terrestrial selective pressures. On land, insects developed a gas-filled (tracheal) respiratory system and thus were committed to take that structural plan with them as they invaded water.

Several options exist for obtaining O_2 with a tracheal system and, as might be expected, insects have been extremely successful in exploiting such options. Whatever the aquatic habitat and the O_2 supply, insects are normally present. The general structural and behavioral adaptations they demonstrate are conspicuous, as are the variations of the basic adaptive themes.

Regardless of the feeding mechanism used by an aquatic insect (chap. 6), the main requirement for food is to provide fuel for cellular processes that collectively produce bodily work. As ingested, food is not a satisfactory fuel. It must be digested and transported to cells, where it is used in cellular respiration. Oxygen is an important commodity in the latter process. Its use as the final electron acceptor in a series of mitochondrial reactions that allow energy release from organic molecules makes available about nineteen times more energy than is produced by anaerobic metabolism. Because energy demands of most multicellular and all highly active organisms exceed energy made available by anaerobic metabolism, obtaining O_2 is absolutely essential.

OXYGEN: FROM SOURCE TO CELL

Oxygen in the Environment

Since the insect respiratory system evolved to obtain and transport the abundant O_2 from the atmosphere, aquatic insects that use air directly do not encounter O_2 limitations. However, insects that use O_2 dissolved in water face a far different situation.

When water and air are in contact, an equilibrium is established between the gaseous components of each. Because gases that make up "air" have different solubilities in water, their proportions and absolute amounts in water and air are quite different. For example, O_2 comprises approximately 21% of air, but over 33% of the total dissolved gases in water. Carbon dioxide (CO_2) is only 0.03% of air, but almost 3% of water. Nitrogen (N_2) is 78% of air, but comprises less than 67% of the dissolved gases in water. However, even though O_2 is more soluble in water than some other gases (e.g., N_2), its absolute amount in water is miniscule compared with that in an equal amount of air (i.e., over 200 thousand ppm in air compared with a maximum of approximately 15 ppm in saturated water!).

Environmental conditions affect gas solubility in water; the amount of gas dissolved in water is inversely proportional to temperature and salinity, but directly proportional to pressure (e.g., solubility decreases with increasing altitude and increases with greater water depth). The water surface serves as a diffusion boundary through which gases exchange. Turbulence increases the speed of exchange by increasing the water surface area, by forcing aeration, and by moving less-oxygenated water to the surface. Once dissolved, if O_2 were distributed in an anoxic system by diffusion alone, it would take years for even traces of the gas to reach several meters of depth. Thus wind-generated currents and turbulence are vital to the mixing of gases within the water column. In fact, gas exchange and mixing are significantly reduced by anything that inhibits the effect of wind on water, such as limited water surface area, protective vegetation, and ice cover.

Typically, dissolved O_2 levels are higher in lotic than in lentic environments. However, since O_2 may occur in excess of equilibrium (supersaturation) as a result of photosynthesis by phytoplankton, periphyton, and macrophytes, a warm, algae-rich pond may be higher in O_2 during the day than is a cold, cascading stream. Oxygen supersaturation persists when photosynthesis adds O_2 to the system in excess of that lost to community respiration, mixing, and diffusion into the atmosphere. At night, as during the day, dissolved O_2 is consumed, but because O_2 is not produced, dissolved O_2 levels decline. Thus, the normally higher daytime and lower nighttime dissolved O_2 levels clearly reflect the diel cycle in photosynthesis and its relation to respiration of the aquatic community. The ratio of daily gross photosynthesis to daily respiration (P/R) is often used as an index of aquatic community metabolism (Cummins 1974).

Groundwater is often nearly devoid of O_2 because of the bacterial respiration that occurs during its slow movement through the soil. Once groundwater surfaces, O_2 is replaced at a rate determined by local conditions, especially substrate, gradient, current, and turbulence. More-detailed treatments of O_2 in aquatic environments are given in Welch (1948), Ruttner (1953), Hutchinson (1957), Reid (1965), Hynes (1970a), Wetzel (1975), and Cole (1983).

Obtaining Oxygen from the Environment

Whatever the environmental conditions, diffusion ultimately moves gases the final distance to and through the respiratory surface. The speed of that movement depends on the molecular weight of the gas, the permeability of the medium through which it must pass, the concentration gradient over the distance to be moved, and the distance itself. The interrelationship among these parameters determines the diffusion rate for any particular gas and is described by Fick's law: diffusion rate equals permeability constant times gradient/distance.

Oxygen diffuses rapidly through air, but in water the permeability of O_2 is a staggering 324 thousand times slower. If that is not problem enough, insect cuticle is even less permeable, slowing O_2 diffusion through its structure almost 850 thousand times (Miller 1964a). The difference in gas concentration between the respiratory system of the animal and the surrounding medium determines the diffusion gradient. The distance over which that gradient exists includes not only the cuticle-tissue thickness, but also the adjacent layer of water (fig. 4.1). As water moves over a respiratory surface (or any surface), frictional resistance increasingly slows adjacent molecules until flow ceases at the surface. When very slow, water movement changes from turbulent to laminar. This region of laminar flow is termed the *boundary layer* and, because this layer lacks turbulence and mixing, gases must move through it by diffusion alone (Ambühl 1959; Feldmeth 1968). The thickness of the boundary layer is inversely proportional to the rate of flow in the adjacent water, which is a function of the stream's velocity or, in still water, the organism's self-generated ventilation currents. Nevertheless, even in the most rapid flow, a thin boundary layer remains.

Because of their flattened shape or small size, a number of aquatic insects can dwell within the boundary layer created as stream water flows over rock surfaces. Here, removed from significant water movement,[1] the insects nonetheless remain close enough to turbulent water flow to obtain adequate O_2 supplies.

Tracheal System and Respiratory Surfaces

In most insects, gas distribution takes place through a network of internal, air-filled tubes known as the *tracheal system*. The blood, or *hemolymph*, plays little or no role in this process. The larger tubes, or *tracheae*, exchange respiratory gases with the atmosphere through segmentally arranged pores called *spiracles*. Tracheae, which are cuticular invaginations, branch internally from the spiracles and become progressively smaller (to 2–5 µm in diameter). Further branching forms capillaries called *tracheoles*, which are generally less than 1 µm across and end blindly where they contact or indent individual cells. Diffusional gas exchange with the cells occurs here.

This respiratory system evolved terrestrially and was probably the basic design that insects carried into the water. Thus, most terrestrial and some aquatic insects have multiple pairs of spiracles (usually 8–10) that open on the body surface (*polypneustic* systems; fig. 4.2A–B). Developing secondarily from this ancestral design were the *oligopneustic* systems, which have only one or two pairs of open spiracles, often located terminally (fig. 4.2C). Both designs are frequently referred to as *open* tracheal systems because of the presence of functional spiracles. In contrast, tracheal systems with no functional spiracles are *closed* (*apneustic;* fig. 4.2D–F), and, although otherwise complete, lack direct communication with the outside and rely on gaseous diffusion through the cuticle for respiratory exchange.

The amount of exchange is partially determined by the amount of surface through which gas molecules can pass. In air, where O_2 concentration is high, open spiracles suffice as the respiratory surface; in water, where dissolved O_2 is sparse, larger respiratory surfaces are necessary. The body surface of a small, elongate organism (e.g., an early instar chironomid larva) may be large enough to allow sufficient O_2 diffusion to meet the organism's metabolic needs (fig. 4.2D). However, as that animal increases in size, its volume will increase more rapidly than its surface area and, unless there is some means of relatively increasing the latter, O_2 intake will become surface limited. Additional gas exchange surfaces or *gills*, which are either large, thin, tracheated body evaginations (fig. 4.2E–F) or air bubbles (fig. 4.3), serve to counter this. As an insect grows, these surfaces often become disproportionately larger to maintain a permeable surface-to-volume ratio sufficient to meet the insect's respiratory needs.

RESPIRATORY OPTIONS WITH AN OPEN TRACHEAL SYSTEM

Open tracheal systems are characteristic of insects that breathe air. Aquatic insects with open tracheal systems must therefore establish spiracle-air contact, either by connecting directly with a stationary air source, or by using a transportable air store (see table 4A).

Stationary Air Sources

Aquatic insects that connect with a stationary air source have an oligopneustic tracheal system with the functional spiracles located at the end of the abdomen (larvae) or on the thorax (pupae). The insect gains access to the O_2 supply either by bringing its spiracles into contact with the air-water interface (*atmospheric breathers*) or by forcing them into plant air stores (*plant breathers*).

---

1. Some recently published preliminary data (Statzner and Holm 1982) suggest that velocities and pressures affecting small, flattened, benthic organisms are greater and more complicated than the boundary layer concept indicates.

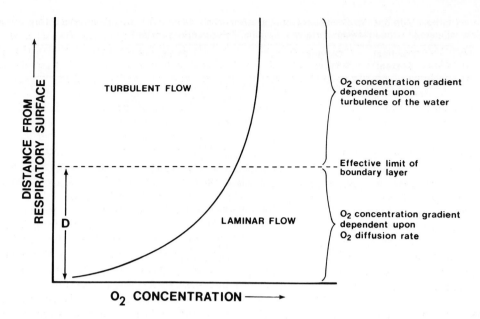

Figure 4.1

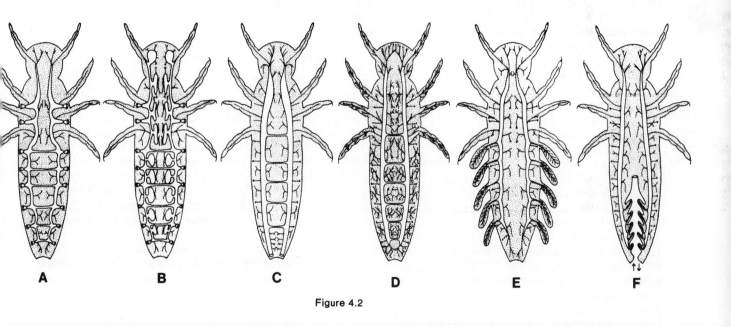

Figure 4.2

Figure 4.1. The boundary layer and its effect upon O_2 reaching an organism's respiratory surface. The *dashed line* demarcates the boundary layer's outer limit. An O_2 concentration gradient *(solid line)* is established because O_2 is consumed at the organism's surface and is replaced within the boundary layer only by diffusion. The diffusion rate is dependent on the thickness *(D)* of the boundary layer and the steepness of the O_2 gradient (modified from Feldmeth 1968).

Figure 4.2. *A.* Open polypneustic tracheal system; *B.* Polypneustic tracheal system with air-sacs for ventilation; *C.* Oligopneustic tracheal system, terminal spiracles alone functional; *D.* Closed tracheal system, cutaneous respiration only; *E.* Closed tracheal system with abdominal tracheal gills; *F.* Closed tracheal system with rectal tracheal gills (modified from Wigglesworth 1972).

Table 4A. Respiratory options with open and closed tracheal systems. (The life stages known or inferred to use a particular respiratory option are indicated by the following: L=larvae/nymphs; P=pupae; A=adults.)

Respiratory Option	Tracheal System	Oxygen Source	Examples	Selected References
Atmospheric Breathers	open	atmosphere	Diptera: Culicidae (L, P), Dolichopodidae (L), Ephydridae (L, P), Psychodidae (L), Stratiomyidae (L, P), Syrphidae (L, P), Tabanidae (L, P), Tipulidae (L, P), Ptychopteridae (L, P) Coleoptera: Amphizoidae (L), Dytiscidae (L, A), Hydrophilidae (L, A) Hemiptera: Nepidae (L, A)	1283, 1361
Plant Breathers	open	plants	Coleoptera: Chrysomelidae (L, P, A), Curculionidae (L) Diptera: Culicidae (L, P), Ephydridae (L, P), Syrphidae (L)	1119, 1120, 1121, 2513
Temporary Air Store	open	atmosphere and dissolved	Coleoptera: Dytiscidae (A), Gyrinidae (A), Haliplidae (A), Helodidae (A), Hydraenidae (A), Hydrophilidae (A) Hemiptera: Belostomatidae (L, A), Corixidae (L, A), Naucoridae (L, A), Notonectidae (L, A), Pleidae (L, A)	647, 1861, 1862, 1942, 1980
Permanent Air Store 　Plastrons	open	dissolved	Coleoptera: Curculionidae (A), Dryopidae (A), Elmidae (A), Hydraenidae (A), Hydrophilidae (A) Hemiptera: Naucoridae (L, A) Lepidoptera: Pyralidae (L, P)	981, 982, 1080, 2431, 2432, 2433, 2434, 2435
Spiracular Gills	open	dissolved	Coleoptera: Psephenidae (L) Diptera: Blephariceridae (L, P), Canaceidae (L, P), Deuterophlebiidae (L, P), Dolichopodidae (L, P), Empididae (L, P), Simuliidae (L, P), Tipulidae (L, P)	1076
Tracheal Gills	closed	dissolved	Ephemeroptera (L), Odonata (L), Plecoptera (L), Megaloptera (L), Neuroptera (Sisyridae) (L), Coleoptera (several families), Diptera (several families), Trichoptera (L), Lepidoptera (Pyralidae) (L)	675, 676, 677, 1703, 2727
Cutaneous	closed	dissolved	Diptera: Chaoboridae (L, P), Chironomidae (L, P), Simuliidae (L, P)	785
Hemoglobin	open or closed	atmosphere or dissolved	Hemiptera: Notonectidae (L, A) Diptera: Chironomidae (L, P)	1667, 2564, 2565, 2566

Atmospheric breathers seldom maintain continuous connection with an air source. Therefore, spiracles must be adapted to prevent flooding both when the insect submerges and when it reestablishes contact with the air. Spiracles are commonly surrounded with a water-repellent *(hydrofuge)* cuticle or hairs (figs. 21.47, 21.50). On submergence, flooding is prevented by hydrofuge hairs, by retractile fleshy lobes that seal the spiracular opening, or by the maintenance of an air bubble that covers the opening.

Atmospheric breathers include larvae of dytiscid and hydrophilid beetles and most dipteran larvae and pupae. Most Diptera larvae have posterior functional spiracles at the end of a tube called the *respiratory siphon* (e.g., figs. 21.20, 21.22, 21.58, 21.63, 21.76, 21.86). In *Eristalis* sp. (Syrphidae) this siphon, which can extend to six times the body length (fig. 21.76), gave rise to the common name, rat-tailed maggot. Larvae of species with shorter siphons often are restricted to shallow seeps (e.g., ephydrids, ptychopterids), to moving up and down in the water column (e.g., culicids, ephydrids), or to living near the surface in algal mats (e.g., dolichopodids, ptychopterids) or along pond and stream margins (e.g., tabanids).

Plant breathers have spiracles modified to pierce submerged portions of aquatic plants and tap aerenchymal air stores. Larvae of the syrphid *Chrysogaster* sp., the brine fly *Notiphila* sp., and the weevil *Lissorhaptrus* sp. all live in anoxic mud at the base of aquatic plants and obtain their O_2 in this manner. Larvae, pupae, and, less frequently, adults of the chrysomelid beetle *Donacia* sp. use the air source in the roots of such aquatic macrophytes as *Typha* sp. (cattails), *Juncus* sp. (rushes), and *Nymphaea* sp. (water lilies). During winter when these plants die back and are often completely submerged, O_2 concentrations in the root air spaces decline and *Donacia* sp. goes into metabolic diapause, greatly reducing its O_2 requirements (Houlihan 1969b, 1970). The sharp, barbed respiratory siphons of larval *Mansonia* sp., *Coquillettidia* sp., and *Taeniorhynchus* sp. (Culicidae; fig. 4.4) can pierce the roots and stems of plants in open water; this allows larvae to remain submerged until adult emergence (Keilin 1944). Because these larvae have a thin cuticle and inhabit the open water, plant-derived O_2 intake can be supplemented with cutaneous respiration. Nonetheless, such larvae appear unable to gain sufficient O_2 for an active life; they move and feed slowly and have an extended life cycle (Gillett 1972).

Transportable Air Stores

Aquatic insects that rely on fixed O_2 sources either venture away from those sources only briefly or remain relatively inactive, whereas aquatic insects carrying their own supply can stay submerged longer and are more active. When a transportable air supply is exposed to the water, it can serve not only as an air reserve, but also as a *physical gill*. As such, the gas bubble is able to supply more O_2 than it contained originally and diving time is extended, sometimes permanently.

Temporary Air Stores: When an insect initiates a dive with its temporary air store (bubble; fig. 4.3), gases in the atmosphere, the bubble, and the water are in equilibrium. As the insect consumes O_2, this gas is replaced by CO_2. However, CO_2 diffuses so rapidly into the surrounding water that it has essentially no effect on the bubble's size or gas composition. As O_2 pressure in the bubble decreases, O_2 from the water diffuses inward, but replacement is not immediate; this results in a net increase in the bubble's N_2 concentration causing N_2 diffusion outward and ultimately decreasing the volume. Because O_2 diffuses into the bubble 2–3 times faster than N_2 diffuses out, this temporary physical gill (sometimes called a *compressible gill;* Mill 1973) continues to extract O_2 from the water, supplying about eight times more O_2 than the original air store.

The length of time a bubble can act as a gill depends upon the ratio of O_2 consumption to gill surface—the larger the ratio, the shorter the lifetime of the gill (Rahn and Paganelli 1968). Large insects that have high O_2 demands must replenish their air stores often because they carry bubbles with relatively less surface exposed. For example, so little of the air stores of *Belostoma* sp. (Belostomatidae), *Hydrous* sp. (Naucoridae), and *Dytiscus* sp. (Dytiscidae) are exposed that the bubbles serve as effective physical gills only during winter. At that time lower temperatures allow increased dissolved O_2 concentrations and decrease the insect's metabolic rate and therefore its O_2 consumption (Ege 1915; de Ruiter *et al.* 1952; Popham 1962). The water scorpion *Ranatra* sp. (Nepidae) does not achieve the physical gill effect because its air store is held completely beneath the hemelytra. Smaller diving insects with relatively more bubble area exposed, such as notonectid, pleid, and corixid bugs, use a physical gill year round (Ege 1915; Gittelman 1975). Consequently, such small insects seem less tied to the surface, and corixids, which are generally the smallest diving Hemiptera, have essentially become bottom dwellers, thereby avoiding competition at the surface (Popham 1960).

Several factors decrease the effectiveness of the physical gill, and therefore, increase the surfacing frequency of the insect. Deeper dives increase hydrostatic pressure causing N_2 to diffuse out of the bubble faster. Lower O_2 concentrations in surrounding water decrease the diffusion gradient and therefore the inward diffusion rate of O_2. Finally, increased water temperature causes both lower O_2 concentrations and higher O_2 consumption by the insect. Hutchinson (1981) has suggested that this relationship between gill efficiency and water temperature may explain the predominance, within the Corixidae and many other aquatic taxa using temporary air stores, of smaller species in warmer climates.

Permanent Air Stores (Plastrons): A number of aquatic insects have hydrofuge hairs or cuticular meshworks that hold water away from the body surface and form a permanent gas film (mainly N_2). The gas film is permanent because N_2 will not diffuse out, and since it is in contact with open spiracles and at the same time presents a considerable surface to the water, it serves as a physical gill, allowing continuous diffusion of O_2 inward. This system is known as a *plastron* (sometimes called an *incompressible gill;* Mill 1973).

Many aquatic insects with plastrons need never surface to replenish air stores. Their oxygen consumption and, thus, metabolic rate are determined by the rate of O_2 diffusion through the fixed and limited surface area of the plastron. As a consequence, most insects with plastrons are slow moving and limited to habitats with high O_2. Those insects using plastrons in still water must be good swimmers (hydrophilid beetles) or capable of crawling out of the water (curculionid beetles) to avoid low O_2 conditions (Hinton 1976a). The ability of these still-water insects to detect and avoid low O_2 conditions is absolutely necessary because a plastron gives up O_2 to the water if the diffusion gradient is reversed.

Plastrons are quite variable in structure. Hydrofuge hair systems have evolved in a wide variety of taxa, including the lepidopteran *Acentropus* sp., the weevil *Phytobius* sp., and the elmid beetles. A European naucorid bug (*Aphelocheirus* sp.) has one of the most efficient plastrons, consisting of a dense pile of hydrofuge hairs (4.3×10^6 hairs/mm^2) that are bent at the tips (fig. 4.5). This pile covers most of the ventral surface and, since *Aphelocheirus* sp. is apterous, most of the dorsal surface as well (Hinton 1976a). The elmids have a plastron formed by short, dense hairs located on the lateral and lateroventral body surfaces and on the dorsum of the thorax. It is overlain by a second, temporary air store, sometimes referred to as a *macroplastron,* which is formed by longer, less dense hairs. The temporary air store is used when the elmid's O_2 demands are high (Thorpe 1950).

Hydrofuge cuticular networks are always associated with outgrowths of the area around the spiracles. They often rise as columns from the body surface and divide at the top to form an open canopy (fig. 4.6). An air film held beneath the canopy serves as a physical gill. These *spiracular gills* are found in pupae of many beetles and flies, and in larvae of sphaeriid and hydroscaphid beetles (Hinton 1968). Such insects often inhabit the margins of highly fluctuating streams where spiracular gills serve the two functions of O_2 acquisition when submerged and water retention when exposed.

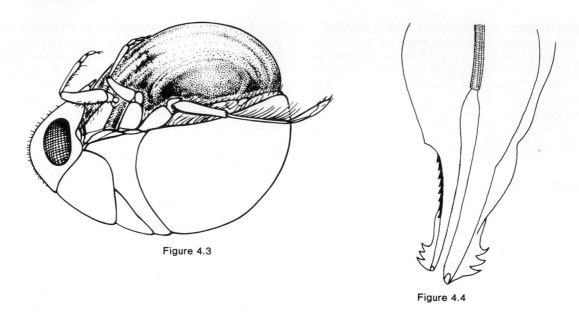

Figure 4.3

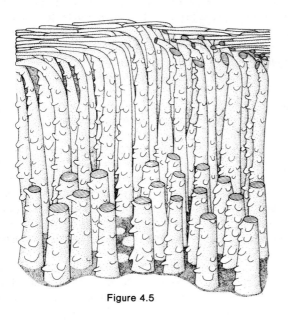

Figure 4.5

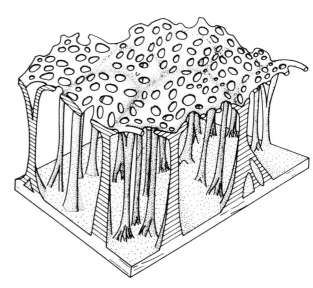

Figure 4.4

Figure 4.6

Figure 4.3. Ventral air bubble, which also serves as a temporary physical gill, of the pleid backswimmer *Neoplea* sp. (after Gittelman 1975).

Figure 4.4. Longitudinal section of postabdominal respiratory siphon of a *Taeniorhynchus* sp. (Culicidae) larva. Barbed hooks allow the larva to maintain contact between the spiracle and the plant air stores (modified from Keilin 1944).

Figure 4.5. Hydrofuge hairs comprising the plastron of the naucorid bug *Aphelocheirus* sp. (after Hinton 1976a).

Figure 4.6. Hydrofuge cuticular network found in the spiracular gill of the tipulid *Dicranomyia* sp. (after Hinton 1968).

RESPIRATORY OPTIONS WITH A CLOSED TRACHEAL SYSTEM

Closed tracheal systems have no functional spiracles so gas exchange occurs by diffusion through the cuticle. Such cuticle is thin and permeable and is closely underlain by a dense network of tracheoles that provides a large area for exchange between the respiratory surface and the tracheal system. Because of either surface-to-volume considerations or the presence of impermeable cuticular surfaces, most insects with closed tracheal systems cannot meet their O_2 requirements solely through the general body surface (cutaneous respiration). Therefore, cutaneous respiration has commonly been supplemented with highly tracheated, minimum bulk, body wall evaginations called tracheal gills (see table 4A).

Cutaneous Respiration

Since the amount of gas exchanged is proportional to surface area, only aquatic insects having a high surface-to-volume ratio rely on cutaneous respiration alone. Such a situation is demonstrated by the smallest of the aquatic Hemiptera (non-North American Idiocoris sp. and Paskia sp., the only known free-living adult apneustic insects; Esaki and China 1927, cited by Hutchinson 1981). However, most of the strictly cutaneously respiring species are small, worm-shaped larvae, such as chironomids (Fox 1920), some tipulids (Pritchard and Stewart 1982), simuliids, and gill-less trichopterans. Cutaneous respiration may account for all gas exchange in the early life stages of a large number of other aquatic insects as well. For example, young Trichoptera larvae respire exclusively through the cuticle; gill filaments are added only in later instars (Wiggins 1977), presumably to maintain the needed surface-to-volume ratio. Even with the presence of tracheal gills, cutaneous respiration probably accounts for a significant but variable portion of total O_2 intake in most insects. The zygopteran Lestes, whose gills are ". . . so large that one may suppose it would be an embarrassment to them if they grew any bigger . . ." (MacNeill 1960), normally uses cutaneous respiration to meet 70 to 80% of its needs (Eriksen, unpubl. data).

Tracheal Gills

Tracheal gills are present in the immature stages of at least some species of every truly aquatic insect order, except the Hemiptera. Whether or not tracheal gills are used in respiration has been the subject of considerable debate. For example, removal of such gills from larvae of the caddisfly Macronema sp. resulted in no difference in O_2 intake between normal and gill-less individuals (Morgan and O'Neil 1931). In fact, gill-less larvae generally behaved normally and eventually pupated. However, such experiments were typically conducted under the favorable conditions of high dissolved O_2 and low temperature. Respiratory studies of the mayfly Cloeon under varying O_2 and temperature conditions demonstrated that nymphs maintained a high metabolic rate down to 1 ppm O_2 when gills were intact, but gill-less individuals experienced O_2 stress below 3 ppm (Wingfield 1939). Eriksen

(unpubl. data) showed that gills of the damselfly Lestes disjunctus performed no respiratory role at 7°C and 5.5 ppm O_2, but became more important with increasing temperature and decreasing O_2, ultimately accounting for up to 80% of total O_2 intake. In general, tracheal gills apparently are not very important as O_2 intake sites under high environmental O_2 conditions, but become progressively more important as O_2 concentration decreases and temperature increases.

Besides their principal role as O_2 intake sites, tracheal gills may also serve in ventilation, protection, streamlining, and salt exchange. Because they are permeable to gases and are active uptake sites, gills are probably highly susceptible to damage by environmental contaminants. For example, chlorine and crude oil may stunt and deform gills of net-spinning hydropsychid caddisflies (Simpson 1980).

Segmental pairs of lateral abdominal gills are found on some species in a number of groups (e.g., Megaloptera, Coleoptera, Zygoptera, Neuroptera), but show the greatest structural diversity in the Ephemeroptera. Mayfly gills vary from leaflike protrusions (e.g., Ameletus sp.; fig. 10.34) to biramous (two-branched) arrangements with single (e.g., Paraleptophlebia sp.; fig. 10.5) or multiple (e.g., Habrophlebia sp.; fig. 10.26) filaments. Combinations of leaflike and filamentous gills occur in a number of genera including Ephoron (fig. 10.4) and Caenis (fig. 10.15). In Tricorythodes sp. the first gill pair is enlarged to cover the posterior pairs (fig. 10.14), presumably to shield them from fouling by fine sediments. In a number of fast-water insects (e.g., Iron sp.) gills overlap and are held against the substrate to provide a flattened shape.

The abdominal gills of trichopteran larvae appear as scattered single (fig. 16.77) or clustered (fig. 16.39) filaments, which may or may not be branched. Their number and size tend to increase with increasing body size. Wichard (1977) reported that gill number in Molanna angustata was inversely related to the average environmental O_2 concentration, a phenomenon also suggested by Dodds and Hisaw (1924b).

The terminal abdominal placement of tracheal gills is typical of damselfly nymphs (Odonata: Zygoptera). These caudal gills are usually leaflike structures, two placed laterally and one medially (fig. 11.12). MacNeill (1960) describes two gill types among Zygoptera: (1) the simplex type, which increases in size uniformly as the damselfly grows and is typical of the Lestidae; and (2) the duplex gill, which consists of a thick proximal and thin distal zone, the latter becoming disproportionately larger at each molt. Duplex gills are typical of the Coenagrionidae.

Internal placement of tracheal gills is found in dragonflies (Odonata: Anisoptera). Six longitudinal rows of gills are located in an enlarged, anterior portion of the rectum, the branchial chamber. Dragonfly nymphs pump water through the anus and over the gills; thus, in nymphs that burrow in mud, the anus is protruded above the surface to prevent fouling (Corbet et al. 1960).

Tracheal gills located on the head and thorax are not common but do occur in several orders including Plecoptera, Diptera, and Lepidoptera. Many species of Plecoptera, for example, have tufts of filamentous gills on the cervical region of the head (fig. 13.20), the thorax (fig. 13.14), or even the coxae (fig. 13.5). Some stoneflies retain gills in the adult stage, and Tozer (1979) has suggested that cervical gills of adult *Zapada cinctipes* (Nemouridae) function in respiration when individuals enter the water to avoid subzero air temperatures.

RESPIRATORY PIGMENTS

One of the most vivid images in aquatic entomology is the discovery of bright red "bloodworms" in dark, reduced sediment. The red color of these chironomids is caused by the respiratory pigment, hemoglobin. Although hemoglobin is most characteristic of vertebrate blood, it occurs in some species of most phyla (Terwilliger 1980). Among insects, hemoglobin is restricted to species of Chironomidae, Notonectidae (see table 4A), and the terrestrial dipteran family Gasterophilidae.

The many types of hemoglobin differ mainly in peptide composition and higher order structure. These differences produce somewhat different O_2-combining and -releasing characteristics. Insect hemoglobin differs from that of vertebrates in containing two instead of four heme groups. *Chironomus* sp. has a high affinity pigment (i.e., it unloads O_2 at low external O_2 pressures. By contrast, vertebrate and other insect hemoglobins tend to be low affinity pigments. Low affinity hemoglobin is adapted to the high O_2 concentrations found in air, whereas high affinity hemoglobin is adapted to the low concentrations found in water and mud.

The Bohr effect (inverse relationship between CO_2 concentration and O_2 loading by hemoglobin) is a major adaptation for organisms that obtain O_2 from a high O_2 environment (lungs) and release it in a high CO_2 environment (tissues). However, in environments where O_2 concentration is always low and the pH varies considerably (e.g., lake muds), low affinity hemoglobin would be maladaptive.

When chironomid larvae undulate in their mud burrows to bring in oxygenated water, their hemoglobin becomes O_2-saturated and apparently performs no function. However, when O_2 is depleted between periods of undulation, hemoglobin gives up O_2 to the tissues. The hemoglobin's nine-minute supply of O_2 (as determined by Walshe [1950] for a species of chironomid) may be less than is needed in the interval between undulations, so anaerobic respiration becomes necessary. When undulation resumes, hemoglobin facilitates rapid recovery from these periods because it takes up O_2 and passes it to the tissues more quickly than is possible by diffusion alone (Walshe 1950).

Two genera of Notonectidae *(Anisops* and *Buenoa)* have a low affinity hemoglobin that performs a very different function. Miller (1964b, 1966) has observed that O_2 released from the hemoglobin contained in certain richly tracheated abdominal cells markedly reduced the rate of depletion of the external air store during diving. The resultant ability to remain submerged longer has allowed exploitation of the sparsely colonized midwater habitat.

VENTILATION AND REGULATION

Oxygen ultimately reaches an organism's tissues by diffusion, but the amount obtained can be influenced by the organism's structural and behavioral adaptations that control the diffusion rate. For example, if thickness of the boundary layer around respiratory surfaces is reduced, the distance over which diffusion must occur is shortened. This may be accomplished by ventilation, which is defined as air or water flow by active or passive means over respiratory surfaces or through part of the tracheal system. Ventilation currents may result from stationary structural-muscle activity (e.g., gill beating), swimming through the water, movement to a more favorable microhabitat (see chap. 5), or a combination of these mechanisms (table 4B).

Because the air-filled tracheal system is noncollapsing and ends blindly among the cells, diffusion is the only manner by which O_2 can be delivered directly to the cells. However, some large or highly active insects can advantageously ventilate at least an outer portion of the system. In those species, abdominal contractions compress nonrigid air-sacs located along the longitudinal tracheal trunks (fig. 4.2B), thus flushing the trunks via the spiracles. Such ventilations can occur continuously in terrestrial insects because spiracles are always in contact with the atmosphere; but in diving aquatic insects, ventilation probably occurs only during atmospheric contact. At that time, apparently, the large air-sacs are deeply ventilated. For example, although air-sacs in most terrestrial insects seldom compresss more than 10 to 20% (Miller 1964a), *Dytiscus* sp. (Dytiscidae) and *Eristalis* sp. (Syrphidae) can ventilate two-thirds of their entire system per stroke (Krogh 1920, 1943), and *Hydrocyrius* sp. (Belostomatidae) may completely collapse some parts of its air-sac system (Miller 1961). High-volume ventilation conveys a substantial advantage to divers that only briefly contact the atmosphere.

The problems in obtaining sufficient O_2 from a dissolved source are considerably more difficult. Because O_2 diffuses slowly through the boundary layer, ventilation may be necessary to enable O_2 to reach respiratory surfaces. Such ventilation generally moves water posteriorly over the gills and dorsal body surface. Eastham (1934, 1936, 1937, 1939) demonstrated that mayflies beat their gills to create respiratory currents. The frequency of gill beat, at least in burrowing mayflies, is inversely related to O_2 concentration (Eriksen 1963a). Trichopterans, chironomids, and aquatic lepidopterans use body undulations to pump water through their cases or tubes (Welch and Sehon 1928; Walshe 1950; Feldmeth 1970). For some Trichoptera, efficient ventilation may depend on the presence of a case that restricts and directs flow, as some larvae removed from their cases ultimately die even though they continue to undulate.

Dragonfly nymphs possess an especially effective ventilatory mechanism for their internal gills. Contraction, mainly of dorsoventral abdominal muscles, increases pressure in the branchial chamber and forces water out the anus. When muscular relaxation occurs, negative pressure in the chamber allows water to return. Ventilations increase in frequency with decreasing O_2 and increasing temperature (Mantula 1911; Mill and Hughes 1966).

Table 4B. Ventilation methods for insects utilizing dissolved oxygen.

System Ventilated	Ventilation Method	Taxon	References
Cutaneous	Undulation	Chironomidae	1283, 2566
		Trichoptera (gills lacking)	
		Lepidoptera (gills lacking)	1390
	Swimming	Chaoboridae	*
		Chironomidae	*
	Natural water flow	Trichoptera (caseless, gills lacking)	567
		Plecoptera (gills lacking)	567
		Simuliidae	2781
Tracheal Gills	Beating gills	Ephemeroptera	618, 619, 620, 621, 675, 2727
		Psephenidae	2255
		Corydalidae	1529
		Gyrinidae	1436
	Undulation	Trichoptera	710, 1427, 1918, 1919, 1920, 1921
		Lepidoptera	2615
		Chironomidae	2566
	Leg contractions which move body (push-ups)	Plecoptera	142, 846, 1277, 1321, 1322, 1605, 1759, 1760
		Lestidae	*
	Rectal pump	Anisoptera	1656, 1657
	Natural water flow	Heptageniidae	33
		Plecoptera	567
		Zygoptera	2809
		Trichoptera (caseless)	33
		Trichoptera (with case)	710, 1920, 1921
		Blephariceridae	*
Temporary and Permanent Air Stores	Leg movements	Notonectidae	560
		Naucoridae	560
		Corixidae	560, 1942
	Swimming	All taxa that swim with exposed air bubble	560
	Natural water flow	Simuliidae (pupae)	1076
		Dryopidae (adult)	*
		Lepidoptera (larvae and pupae)	158, 159

*Eriksen, C. H. Personal observation or unpublished data.

Some organisms, such as stoneflies and lestid damselflies (Knight and Gaufin 1963; Eriksen, unpubl. data), perform "push-up" ventilatory movements that, though helpful, are inefficient because the surrounding water is merely stirred up; freshly oxygenated water is not passed over the gills.

Whether or not an insect uses ventilation to compensate for a changing environmental O_2 supply determines whether it is considered a *respiratory regulator* or a *respiratory conformer*. Since aquatic insects that utilize atmospheric air do not encounter variable O_2 concentration, they are undoubtedly respiratory regulators, controlling the supply of O_2 to cells by the length of time the spiracles are open, the number of ventilation movements, or the frequency of surfacing.

Regulators that use dissolved O_2 often face a decreasing supply. Under such conditions they maintain fairly constant intake, and thus activity, by increasing the ventilation rate. However, upon reaching some minimum threshold, metabolism is significantly disrupted and the animal dies if more highly oxygenated water is not soon forthcoming.

In contrast to regulators, respiratory conformers are unable to create significant respiratory currents, and as a result, their O_2 intake is proportional to O_2 availability in the microhabitat.

Studies of aquatic insect respiration have shown an array of abilities ranging from absolute conformance to strict regulation. Yet Eriksen (1963a) and Nagell (1973) have demonstrated that some mayfly and stonefly species can perform either as respiratory regulators or as conformers depending on experimental conditions. In contrast, experimental conditions apparently did not affect the response curve of a lestid damselfly, which was intermediate between regulation and conformity (Eriksen, unpubl. data). Whether or not the array of abilities described to date is real, or due to conditions of the experiments, has yet to be clearly determined.

RESPIRATORY MECHANISMS AND OXYGEN ENVIRONMENTS

The switch to an aquatic existence has resulted in a broad range of adaptations of the original terrestrial insect respiratory system. Aquatic insects have refined their major structural and behavioral adaptations to their various habitats via seemingly endless variations. The lotic-depositional and lentic-littoral habitats (chap. 6) contain such a variety of microenvironments that most respiratory adaptations are found

Table 4C. Demonstrations of respiratory processes (*superscripts* refer to Section C. *Useful Equipment*). Table 4B contains relevant literature.

A. *Closed Respiratory System* (larvae only)
  1. Ventilation Methods and Behavior
      a. Beating gills[1,2,6]   (e.g., burrowing, climbing, sprawling Ephemeroptera; Corydalidae)
      b. Push-ups[1,6]   (e.g., Plecoptera, Lestidae)
      c. Undulation[1,2,3]   (e.g., Trichoptera, Lepidoptera, Chironomidae)
      d. Muscular rectal pump[1,6]   (Anisoptera)
      e. Swimming[1]   (e.g., Chaoboridae, Chironomidae)
      f. None (other than possible position (e.g., Blephariceridae, Simuliidae, fast-water Ephemeroptera, Plecop-
         change)   tera)
  2. Respiratory Currents Produced by Insect (Section A.1.a–d)[8]
  3. Micro-areas from which Respiratory Water Obtained (Section A.1.a–d)[8]
  4. Environmental Effects on Ventilation Frequency and Volume of Respiratory Flow (Section A.1.a–d)
      Vary: O_2 concentration[10]
             water current[7]
             temperature[11]
B. *Open Respiratory System* (larvae and adults)
  1. Ventilation Methods and Behavior
      a. Leg movements[4]   (e.g., Corixidae, Naucoridae, Notonectidae)
      b. Swimming[5]   (any species with exposed air store)
  2. Environmental Effects on Diving Time (any species with temporary air store)
      Vary: dissolved O_2 concentration[5,10]
             dissolved CO_2 concentration[5,10]
             temperature[5,11]
  3. Diving Stimulus (any species with temporary air store)
      Provide: air atmosphere[5,10]
               O_2 atmosphere[5,10]
               CO_2 atmosphere[5,10]
               N_2 atmosphere[5,10]
  4. Need for Surface Tension to Establish Atmospheric Connection[5,9] (e.g., Culicidae, Tipulidae, Syrphidae, Notonectidae, Dytiscidae)
  5. Plastron (any species using plastron respiration only)
      Vary: dissolved O_2 concentration[1,10]
             current velocity[1,7]
             temperature[1,11]
C. *Useful Equipment*
  1. Narrow (e.g., < 3 cm) plexiglass observation aquarium.
  2. U-shaped glass burrows simulating natural dimensions. Portion restricted with coarse mesh screen for containing animal but allowing current flow.
  3. Artificial Trichoptera case: glass or plastic tubing approximating case interior diameter and length with one end restricted to a 1 mm central pore (Feldmeth 1970).
  4. Vertical, clear "diving tube," 2–3 cm by about 30 cm. Vertical strip of plastic screening near surface simulating vegetation. Horizontal screening just below water level. No bottom substrate.
  5. Vertical, clear "diving tube," 2–3 cm by 100–200 cm. Horizontal screening on bottom as substrate.
  6. Plastic window screen cut to appropriate shapes.
  7. Water current generation:
     —gravitational, from reservoir via appropriate tubing with flow control valves
     —air hose pump
     —magnetic stirrers. Note: these create centrifugal currents; however an organism can be restricted to one area and experience essentially longitudinal current flows (e.g., Philipson 1954; Morris 1963)
     —water current respirometer (e.g., Eriksen and Feldmeth 1967)
  8. Carmine or carbon-black suspension introduced where desired with narrow aperture eyedropper. Observe particle movement.
  9. Detergent or thin oil added to water surface with eyedropper.
  10. Gas concentrations: control concentration of dissolved gases in reservoir with gas mixing valves or a combination of compressed air, O_2, N_2, or CO_2. Monitor with O_2 electrode if available.
  11. Temperature: many heating/cooling devices may be used to adjust reservoir temperature, or use temperature controlled environmental rooms.

---

there. The lentic-profundal zone lacks those insects that use atmospheric O_2 because of the dual problem of renewing O_2 supplies and the diffusional loss of O_2 from those supplies to the surrounding oxygen-poor water. Those that do occur commonly possess hemoglobin and strong ventilatory or migratory abilities. The few species that inhabit the lentic-limnetic zones have a high surface-to-volume ratio and therefore use cutaneous respiration. The constantly high-O_2 lotic-erosional habitat is suitable for species using plastrons, cutaneous respiration, or tracheal gills. No doubt those insects requiring air contact are eliminated because surface connection is often impossible in this turbulent habitat. More specific generalizations cannot be made because the major habitat categories encompass so many different O_2 microhabitats.

APPENDIX 1: DEMONSTRATIONS OF RESPIRATORY PROCESSES

The respiratory structures and processes that have been described are best appreciated when seen in action. As a means to that end, simple experiments are summarized in table 4C that help demonstrate the structural and behavioral abilities and limitations of aquatic insects subjected to varying environmental conditions. When conducting these experiments, avoid stressing the organisms unless it is part of the design. Always provide suitable substrate (pebbles, plastic mesh, glass burrows, etc.) and other appropriate environmental conditions (e.g., oxygen, current; see Rearing Methods, chap. 3) when holding and using the insects in experiments and as controls. Detailed explanations of additional experiments can be found in Kalmus (1963) and Cummins *et al.* (1965).

Habitat, Life History, and Behavioral Adaptations of Aquatic Insects

5

N. H. Anderson
Oregon State University, Corvallis

J. Bruce Wallace,
University of Georgia, Athens

INTRODUCTION

The observed patterns of distribution and abundance of aquatic insects indicate successful adaptations to a wide variety of habitats. To demonstrate how organisms adapt to particular niches of the freshwater community, examples of species using certain environments are presented in this chapter and the life cycle is used as a framework for describing diverse modes of coping with environmental characteristics.

Factors that influence utilization of a particular habitat can be grouped into four broad categories: (1) physiological constraints (e.g., oxygen acquisition, temperature effects, osmoregulation; (2) trophic considerations (e.g., food acquisition); (3) physical constraints (e.g., coping with habitat); and (4) biotic interactions (e.g., predation, competition). However, these categories are so interrelated that detailed analysis of each factor is not appropriate. Aquatic insect respiration is covered in detail in chapter 4, but it is considered here because activities related to oxygen acquisition are central to behavioral and morphological features associated with most other activities.

The traditional division of freshwater systems into standing (lentic) and running (lotic) waters is useful for indicating physical and biological differences. Most insects are adapted to either a lentic or a lotic habitat, but overlaps are common. For example, insects inhabiting pools in streams have "lentic" respiratory adaptations, whereas those on wave-washed shores of lakes are similar to stream riffle inhabitants in both oxygen requirements and clinging adaptations.

Despite their success in exploiting most types of aquatic environments, insects are only incompletely or secondarily adapted for aquatic life. With very few exceptions, aquatic insects are directly dependent on the terrestrial environment for part of the life cycle. Even Hemiptera and Coleoptera with aquatic adults may require access to surface air for respiration. This dependence on the terrestrial environment probably contributes to the prevalence of insects in shallow ponds and streams as compared with deep rivers or lakes and to their virtual absence from the open sea.

ADAPTATION TO HABITAT

Osmoregulation

Aquatic insects need to maintain a proper internal salt and water balance. Body fluids usually contain a much higher salt concentration than does the surrounding water and water tends to pass into the hypertonic (higher osmotic pressure) hemolymph. The insect integument, especially the wax layer of the epicuticle, appears to be especially important in preventing flooding of the tissues (Chapman 1982). Some freshwater insects take in large quantities of water during feeding. Their feces contain more water than the frass of terrestrial counterparts since many aquatic insects excrete nitrogenous wastes as ammonia, which is generally toxic unless diluted with large quantities of water (Chapman 1982). The production of a hypotonic urine (lower osmotic pressure, or more dilute than the body fluids) is an important osmoregulatory mechanism in aquatic insects. Specialized areas of the hindgut reabsorb ions before wastes are eliminated.

In contrast, saltwater and terrestrial insects produce a rectal fluid that is hypertonic to the hemolymph (Stobbart and Shaw 1974). For example, the dipteran *Ephydra cinerea,* which occurs in Great Salt Lake (salinity > 20% NaCl), maintains water and salt balance by drinking the saline medium and excreting rectal fluid that is more than 20% salt.

Concentrations of freshwater ions vary tremendously. Many insects absorb salts directly from the surrounding water by active transport across specialized regions of the body. Such regions include the rectal gills of the mosquito, *Culex pipiens;* the rectal gills are larger in larvae reared in water with low ionic concentrations, which increases the surface area available for absorption of chloride ions (Wigglesworth 1938). Specialized areas of the integument, including the gills and anal papillae in larvae[1] of Ephemeroptera, Plecoptera, and Trichoptera, facilitate uptake of ions from the hypotonic external media (Wichard and Komnick 1973, 1974; Wichard et al. 1975; Wichard 1976, 1978). In the mayfly *Callibaetis* sp. the number of cells involved with chloride uptake decreases as the salinity of the environment increases, an adaptation to the increasing salinity of drying temporary ponds (Wichard and Hauss 1975; Wichard et al. 1975).

---

1. Throughout this chapter we use the term "larva" for the immature stages of all orders of insects.

Temperature

Virtually all facets of life history and distribution of aquatic insects are influenced by temperature. Aquatic insects occur at temperatures ranging from zero to about 50°C. Metabolism, growth, emergence, and reproduction are directly related to temperature, whereas food availability, both quantity and quality, may be indirectly related (Anderson and Cummins 1979). The thermal death point of most freshwater invertebrates is between 30 and 40°C (Pennak 1978), so species such as the ephydrid fly, *Scatella thermarum,* found at 47.7°C in Icelandic hot springs (Tuxen 1944), have developed considerable thermal acclimation.

In contrast to the limited number of species found at high temperatures, a diverse fauna exists at the freezing point and many lotic species can grow at winter temperatures. Hynes (1963) and Ross (1963) suggest that this is an adaptation to exploit the seasonal pulse of leaf input in the autumn. The ancestral aquatic habitat of many insects is postulated to be cool streams; Hynes (1970a, 1970b) comments that the extant taxa of Plecoptera, Ephemeroptera, Trichoptera, Corydalidae, and nematocerous Diptera occur in cool streams and these are survivors of primitive groups.

Shallow lentic waters will generally reach higher summer temperatures than streams of the same area, resulting in a greater algal food supply and faster insect growth rates. However, oxygen may become a limiting factor because O_2 concentration is inversely proportional to temperature and high algal respiration during darkness may deplete the available O_2. Thus, a greater proportion of lentic than lotic species utilizes atmospheric O_2 or has developed other more efficient respiratory devices.

Life cycle adaptations have evolved that enable species to utilize favorable periods for growth, coupled with appropriate timing for aerial existence. This may involve diapause or quiescent periods in a resistant life stage for avoiding inclement periods of excessively high or low temperatures. Asynchronous larval cohorts and extended emergence periods occur in springs, where temperature is uniform year around. Cold springs can also be refugia for species normally found in colder climates, e.g., arctic insects in temperate region springs.

Sweeney and Vannote (1978) and Vannote and Sweeney (1980) suggest that an optimal thermal regime exists for a given species and that deviations into warmer (southern) or cooler (northern) waters adversely affect fitness by decreasing body size and fecundity. Alteration of thermal regimes, for example by removal of riparian vegetation or by hypolimnionic release from dams, will obviously affect insect life cycles or species composition (Lehmkuhl 1972a; Ward 1976).

Lotic Habitats

The velocity of moving water influences substrate particle size. Substrates may range from large boulders to fine sediments in a relatively short reach, resulting in a wide range of microhabitats. Flowing water continuously replenishes water surrounding the body and turbulence provides reaeration; thus, dissolved oxygen is rarely limiting to stream inhabitants. The transport of inorganic and organic materials by the current may be either detrimental (e.g., scouring action) or beneficial (as a food source).

The range of current velocities associated with a rubble or cobble substrate also increases habitat diversity, and various taxa are adapted for maintaining position at different velocities. Filter-feeding collectors exploit the current for gathering food with minimal energy expenditure. Other fast-water forms feed by predation, scraping the periphyton-detrital film, or gathering fine particles that collect in crevices.

An important microhabitat for the stream biota is the "boundary layer" on stones (Ambühl 1959; Hynes 1970a). Current velocity is greatly reduced due to frictional drag and, as the layer extends for 1–4 mm above the surface, many insects are small or flat enough to live within it. Bournaud (1963) provides a discussion of problems and methods of measuring velocity in microsites actually occupied by stream-dwelling organisms. Recent studies by Statzner and Holm (1982) using laser doppler anemometry indicate that velocity patterns around the body of benthic invertebrates are much more complicated than is suggested by the currently accepted boundary layer concept.

Morphological and Behavioral Adaptations to Current: A general flattening of the body and smooth, streamlined dorsum are typical of many rheophilic (current-loving) insects: e.g., heptageniid mayflies, perlid stoneflies, and psephenid beetles. Many mayflies and stoneflies have legs that project laterally from the body, thereby reducing drag and simultaneously increasing friction with the substrate. In some caddisflies (e.g., Glossosomatidae), the shape of the case rather than the insect modifies turbulent flow to a laminar sublayer.

True hydraulic suckers are apparently found only in the larvae of the dipteran family Blephariceridae (fig. 21.11). A V-shaped notch at the anterior edge of each of the six ventral suckers works as a valve out of which water is forced when the sucker is pressed to the substrate. The sucker operates as a piston with the aid of specialized muscles. In addition, a series of small hooks and glands that secrete a sticky substance aid sucker attachment (Brodsky 1980). Blepharicerids move in a "zigzag" fashion, releasing the anterior three suckers, lifting the front portion of the body to a new position, and reattaching the anterior suckers before releasing and moving the posterior ones to a new position. The larvae are commonly found on smooth stones, and Hora (1930) attributes their absence from certain Indian streams to the presence of moss or roughened stones that would interfere with normal sucker function.

Several aquatic insects have structures that simulate the action of suckers. The enlarged gills of some mayflies (e.g., *Epeorus* sp. and *Rhithrogena* sp.) function as a friction pad, and *Drunella doddsi* has a specialized abdominal structure for the same purpose. Brodsky (1980) describes a "pushing-proleg" in some chironomids; it has a circlet of small spines that function as a false sucker when pressed to the substrate. Mountain midge larvae (Deuterophlebiidae) possibly use a similar mechanism to attach their suckerlike prolegs.

Larval black flies (Simuliidae) use a combination of hooks and silk for attachment. The thoracic proleg resembles that of chironomids and deuterophlebiids, described above, and the last abdominal segment bears a circlet of hooks. The larva spreads a web of silk on the substrate to which it attaches either the proleg or posterior hooks. The larva moves forward in an inchwormlike manner, spins silk over the substrate, and attaches the proleg and then the posterior circlet of hooks to the silken web.

Silk is used for attachment by a number of caddisflies (e.g., Hydropsychidae, Philopotamidae, and Psychomyiidae), which build fixed nets and retreats. Some case-making caddisflies (e.g., *Brachycentrus* sp.) also use silk for attaching their cases to the substrate in regions of fairly rapid flow, and free-living caddisflies may use "security threads" as they move over the substrate in fast currents. The line is used in combination with their large anal prolegs, which are employed as grapples. Many chironomid larvae construct fixed silken retreats for attachment, and black fly pupae are housed in silken cases that are attached to the substrate. Other morphological adaptations to running water are given in table 7A.

Despite the fact that unidirectional current is the basic feature of streams, the majority of lotic insects have not adapted to strong currents but instead have developed behavior patterns to *avoid* current. Very few lotic insects are strong swimmers, probably because of the energy expenditure required to swim against a current; downstream transport requires only a movement off the substrate to enter the current. Streamlined forms, such as the mayflies *Baetis* sp., *Isonychia* sp., and *Ameletus* sp., are capable of short rapid bursts of swimming, but most lotic insects move by crawling or passive displacement. The benthic fauna chiefly occurs in cracks and crevices, between or under rocks and gravel, within the boundary layer on surfaces, or in other slack-water regions. Presumably, much of the benthic population seeks refuge deeper in the substrates during floods; insects are difficult to find at such times, but normal population levels are found soon after the flows subside.

The *hyporheic* region is the area below the bed of a stream where interstitial water moves by percolation. In gravelly soils or glacial outwash areas it may also extend laterally from the banks. An extensive fauna occurs down to one meter in such substrates (Williams and Hynes 1974; Williams 1981b). Most orders are represented, especially those taxa with slender flexible bodies or small organisms with hard protective exoskeletons. Stanford and Gaufin (1974) report that some stoneflies spend most of their larval period in this subterranean region of a Montana River. They collected larvae in wells over 4 m deep, located 30–50 m from the river.

Drift. Downstream drift is a characteristic phenomenon of invertebrates in running waters. Despite the adaptations for maintaining their position in the current or avoiding it, occasional individuals could be expected to lose attachment or orientation and be transported downstream. However, the large numbers of some taxa that drift indicate that this is more than a passive activity. Waters (1965) divided drift into three categories: (1) *catastrophic*, resulting from physical disturbance of the bottom fauna, e.g., by floods, high temperatures, and pollutants; (2) *behavioral*, indicated by characteristic behavior patterns resulting in a consistent diel periodicity (usually at night); and (3) *constant*, the continual occurrence of low numbers of most species. Mayflies of the genus, *Baetis* consistently exhibit high behavioral drift rates with a night-active periodicity. Other mayflies, stoneflies, caddisflies, black flies, and the amphipod *Gammarus* sp. are frequently abundant in drift. Drift is important to stream systems in the recolonization of denuded areas, as a dispersal mechanism, and particularly as a food source for visual predators. Many fish, especially salmonids, select and defend territories best suited for the interception of drift (Waters 1972).

Irrespective of its causes, drift results in a net downstream displacement of some portion of the benthic population. Whether drift losses from upstream areas represent excess production or whether compensatory upstream movements are required is not known. Müller (1954) proposed that upstream flight of adults could be the mechanism to complete the "colonization cycle," and upstream migrations of some mayflies and amphipods in the slow water near shore have been recorded (e.g., Neave 1930; Minckley 1964; Hayden and Clifford 1974). However, the relative importance of upstream movement, or even its necessity for most taxa, remains an open question. Several workers (Bishop and Hynes 1969; Waters 1972; Müller 1974, Williams 1981a) have reviewed the extensive literature on the significance of drift to production biology, population dynamics, and life histories.

Unstable Substrates. Sandy substrates of rivers and streams are poor habitats because the shifting nature of the bed affords unsuitable attachment sites and poor food conditions. An extreme example of this instability is the Amazon River, where strong currents move bedload downstream as dunes of coarse sand reaching 8 m in height and up to 180 m in length, largely preventing the establishment of a riverbed fauna (Sioli 1975). Despite substrate instability, some sandy streams are quite productive. Blackwater streams of the Southeast have extensive areas of sand with an average standing stock, primarily small Chironomidae less than 3 mm in length, exceeding $18000/m^2$. Though their biomass is small, rapid growth rates result in a significant annual production and an important food source for predaceous invertebrates and fish (Benke *et al.* 1979).

The inhabitants of sandy or silty areas are mostly sprawlers or burrowers (table 6B), with morphological adaptations to maintain position and to keep respiratory surfaces in contact with oxygenated water. The predaceous mayflies *Pseudiron* sp. and *Analetris* sp. have long, posterior-projecting legs and claws that aid in anchoring the larvae as they face upstream. Some mayflies (e.g., Caenidae and Baetiscidae) have various structures for covering and protecting gills, and others (e.g., Ephemeridae, Behningiidae) have legs and mouthparts adapted for digging. The predaceous mayfly *Dolania* sp. burrows rapidly in sandy substrates of Southeastern streams. The larva utilizes its hairy body and legs to form a cavity underneath the body where the ventral abdominal gills are in contact with oxygenated water.

Many dragonflies (e.g., *Cordulegaster* sp., *Hagenius* sp., Macromiidae, and many Libellulidae) have flattened bodies and long legs for sprawling on sandy and silty substrates. They are camouflaged by dull color patterns and hairy integuments that accumulate a coating of silt. The eyes, which cap the anteriolateral corners of the head, are elevated over the surrounding debris. Many gomphid larvae actually burrow into the sediments using the flattened, wedge-shaped head, and fossorial tibiae. The genus *Aphylla* (Gomphidae) is somewhat unusual in that the last abdominal segment is upturned and elongate, allowing the larvae to respire through rectal gills while buried fairly deep in mucky substrate.

Wood-Associated Insects. Wood debris provides a significant portion of the stable habitat for insects in small streams where water power is insufficient to transport it out of the channel. In addition to the insect component using wood primarily as a substrate, a characteristic xylophilous fauna is associated with particular stages of degradation. These include: chironomid midges and scraping mayflies (*Cinygma* sp. and *Ironodes* sp.) as early colonizers; the elmid beetle, *Lara* sp., and the caddisfly, *Heteroplectron* sp., as gougers of firm waterlogged wood; and the tipulids, *Lipsothrix* spp., in wood in the latest stages of decomposition (Anderson *et al.* 1978; Dudley and Anderson 1982). Wood debris is most abundant in small forested watersheds, but it is also an important habitat in larger streams with unstable beds. Cudney and Wallace (1980) found that submerged wood in the Coastal Plain region of the Savannah River was the only substrate suitable for net-spinning caddisflies, but that high standing crops and production could be supported in a relatively small space because the caddisflies were exploiting the food resource transported to them by the current. Benke *et al.* (1979) reported that snags in a small Southeastern blackwater river were highly productive, not only for net-spinning caddisflies, but also for filter-feeding Diptera and other typical "benthic" insects. Even in the Amazon situation mentioned above, large logs in the lee of dunes are heavily colonized by chironomid midges (Sioli 1975).

Lentic Habitats

Standing-water habitats range from temporary pools to large, deep lakes. They tend to be more closed than are lotic environments, with recycling occurring within the lake basin. The physical environment is governed by the climate and geology of the area and the shape of the basin. The habitats for insects are illustrated in a typical cross section from the surface film, through open waters, to the shallow and deep benthos (fig. 5.1). Similar habitats occur in lotic situations so many of the insects discussed below can also be found in lotic environments.

Surface Film. The unique properties of the water surface constitute the environment for the *neuston* community. Water striders (Gerridae), whirligig beetles (Gyrinidae), mosquito larvae (Culicidae), and springtails (Collembola) are common examples. The surface film results from the attractive forces among water molecules. Within the body of water the forces are equal on all sides, but at the surface the attraction is less between air and water than on the other three sides. This results in a slight pull toward the center of the water mass and the surface acts as if it were a stretched elastic membrane. "To an organism of small size, this air-water interface can be an impenetrable barrier, a surface on which to rest, or a ceiling from which to hang suspended" (Usinger 1956a).

Water striders and bugs of the related family Veliidae have preapical claws that enable them to move about without breaking the surface film and a velvety hydrofuge hair pile on the venter that is nonwettable. The skating motion of gerrids is more accurately described as rowing. The weight causes a slight dimpling of the surface film (easily seen in the shadow cast on the bottom of clear shallow waters). The long tarsi of the middle legs are pressed against the depression in the film for propulsion while the hind legs are held outstretched behind as rudders for steering.

The gerrids also exploit the surface film by detecting vibrations from surface ripples with sensors located between the tarsal segments on the meso- and metathoracic legs. The

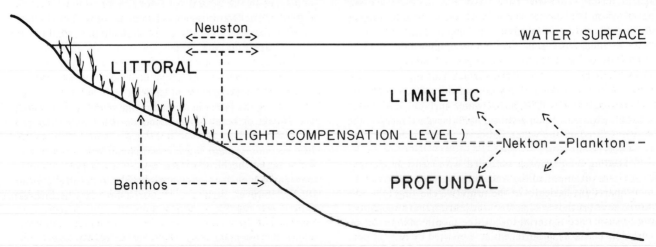

Figure 5.1. Diagram of lentic zones *(capital letters)* and aquatic communities *(lower case letters)*.

sequence in which these sensors perceive an oncoming ripple tells the insect how much to turn to face the disturbance caused, for example, by a potential prey. The strider turns by moving its rowing legs in opposite directions much as an oarsman would turn a boat. At this juncture, a combination of visual and vibratory information allows the strider to choose between approaching the disturbance or fleeing from it. If the former, it rows forward, pausing between each stroke to evaluate further ripple signals (Milne and Milne 1978). Some gerrids also use vibrations of the surface film for communication in courtship and mating (Wilcox 1979).

Some semiaquatic insects have developed chemical propulsion mechanisms for a quick return to shore. The beetles *Dianus* sp. and *Stenus* sp. (Staphylinidae) can skim across the surface at a rate of 60–70 cm/sec. Glands at the tip of their abdomens discharge a secretion that lowers the surface tension behind the abdomen so that the insect is being drawn forward by the normal surface tension of the water in front (Jenkins 1960).

Whirligig beetles have divided eyes; the lower part detects events under the water and the upper part detects events on or above the water surface. Glands keep the upper portion of the body greased to repel water, whereas the lower surface and lower eyes are wettable. Whirligig gyrations on the surface are effected by rapid propulsion with paddle-shaped swimming legs. The hind legs are unique in that the segments can be folded up during the forward stroke and spread apart like a fan for the powerful backward stroke. In addition to propulsion, the swimming activity causes a series of ripples or bow waves that, when reflected back by obstacles, are detected by the antennae touching the surface film, allowing quick course correction even in the dark (Milne and Milne 1978).

Neuston insects are potentially vulnerable to predation by visual aquatic predators because they are silhouetted against the sky; however, both gerrids and gyrinids seem to be avoided by fish, apparently because secretions produced by repugnatorial glands make them distasteful.

Hydrofuge structures are important adaptations for obtaining atmospheric air through the surface film. The openings of terminal spiracles have glands that discharge a waxy secretion on the cuticle; contact with the surface film repels the water exposing the spiracles to the air. The waxy lining of the tracheae prevents water from running into them by capillarity. Some insects (e.g., *Culex* sp., *Limonia* sp., *Stratiomys* sp.) can hang from the surface film supported by a crown of semihydrofuge hairs around the spiracles. The semihydrofuge hair will lie in the water surface, half wetted and half exposed. When a stratiomyiid larva submerges, the crown is lifted off the water and envelops an air bubble that is used as an air store.

Feeding adaptations associated with neuston specialization are exemplified by mosquito larvae. Though the mouthparts are basically of the primitive chewing type, the larvae have brushes arising from the labrum that sweep floating or suspended material toward the mouth. *Anopheles* sp. larvae lie beneath the surface film supported by tufts of float hairs on each segment. The larva rotates its head so that the mouth brushes are uppermost and sets up a current that draws the microbial-rich layer of water along the underside of the surface film and into the mouth.

Limnetic Zone. In open waters, to the depth of effective light penetration, a broad distinction is made between *nektonic* and *planktonic* organisms: nekton are swimmers able to navigate at will (e.g., Coleoptera, Hemiptera, some Ephemeroptera), whereas plankton are floating organisms whose horizontal movements are largely dependent on water currents.

The phantom midge *Chaoborus* sp. is the most common insect plankter; it is abundant in many eutrophic (nutrient-rich) ponds, lakes, and some large rivers. *Chaoborus* sp. exhibits vertical migrations, occurring in benthic regions during the day but migrating vertically into the water column at night. These migrations are dependent on light and oxygen concentrations of the water (LaRow 1970). Larvae avoid predation by being almost transparent except for two crescent-shaped air-sacs or buoyancy organs (fig. 21.30); they lie horizontally in the water, slowly descending or rising by adjusting the volume of the air-sacs. Their prehensile antennae are used as accessory mouthparts to impale zooplankton and deliver them to the mouth.

Many lentic insects are strong swimmers but relatively few are nektonic. They pass through the limnetic zone when surfacing for emergence, but the vast majority of lentic insects occurs in shallow water with emergent plants. As mentioned previously, the scarcity of insects in limnetic areas may be a consequence of the secondary adaptations for aquatic life. There are no resting supports in the limnetic zone so maintaining position requires continuous swimming or neutral buoyancy.

Littoral Zone: The littoral zone, the shallow region with light penetration to the bottom, is typically occupied by macrophytes (macroalgae and rooted vascular plants). It contains a diverse assemblage of insects with representatives of most aquatic orders. Habitats include benthic and plant surfaces, the water column, and the surface film (table 6A); occupants include burrowers, climbers, sprawlers, clingers, swimmers, and divers (table 6B). Morphological and behavioral types in the littoral zone are similar to those in slow-moving or backwater regions of lotic habitats. The diversity and abundance of littoral species results in biological factors (e.g., competition and predation) assuming importance in shaping community structure.

The biomass and diversity of invertebrates associated with aquatic macrophytes in lentic or lotic habitats may exceed that of the fauna in the sediments at the same location. The impact of herbivorous insects on many living plants is low, and it has been suggested that aquatic macrophytes produce secondary plant substances that serve as chemical defenses against herbivores (Otto and Svensson 1981b), or that they may be deficient in some essential amino acids (Smirnov 1962). However, herbivore–chewers (shredders-herbivores), miners, and stem borers (see chap. 6) feed on macrophytes, and these include pests of economic importance such as the weevil *Lissorhoptrus simplex* (Curculionidae) on rice (Leech and Chandler 1956), and the caddisfly *Limnephilus lunatus* (Limnephilidae) on watercress (Gower 1967). Berg (1949) and McGaha (1952) recorded a diverse fauna feeding on *Potomogeton* sp. and other aquatic plants. Such feeding adaptations may be recent because only the more advanced orders (Lepidoptera, Trichoptera, Coleoptera, and Diptera) are represented.

Insects may also use macrophytes as a substrate rather than as food. For example, macrophytes in both lentic and lotic habitats may harbor a number of filter-feeding Ephemeroptera, Trichoptera, and Diptera. Many species found in weed beds are green in color and blend in with their surroundings. Dragonflies of the family Aeshnidae often have contrasting bands of pale and dark green or light brown that adds to the effectiveness of the camouflage. Some species in most orders utilize macrophytes as oviposition sites. Larvae of some Coleoptera and Diptera rely on the intracellular air spaces for respiration and are thus limited in their distribution by that of their macrophyte "host."

Profundal Zone: The number of taxa of aquatic insects occurring below about 10 m is limited, but the few species that do occur there may be very abundant. This area includes the sublittoral and profundal regions. The latter is the zone below which light penetration is inadequate for plant growth. The deep water is a stable region because water movement is minimal and temperature varies only slightly between summer and winter. Periodic depletion or absence of dissolved oxygen may occur, especially in eutrophic situations. Substrates are usually soft or flocculent and offer little in the way of habitat diversity or cover. The inhabitants are mostly burrowers that feed on suspended or sedimented materials and are capable of tolerating low dissolved oxygen or even anaerobic conditions. Typical deep-water insects are ephemerid mayflies (e.g., *Hexagenia* sp., *Ephemera* sp.) and many genera of Chironomidae (e.g., *Chironomus, Tanytarsus*). Predaceous deep-water insects include *Sialis* sp. (Megaloptera) and *Chaoborus* sp. (Diptera).

Dense populations of the midge *Chironomus* are characteristic of profundal sediments. The larvae build U-shaped tubes with both openings at the mud-water interface. Body undulations cause a current of water, providing oxygen, and particulate food in the form of phytoplankton and fine detritus with its accompanying microbes to be drawn through the tube. Hemoglobin serves as an oxygen store during periods of low dissolved oxygen, but the larvae become quiescent under anaerobic conditions. The life cycle of profundal *Chironomus* typically requires two years, compared with a year or less for the same species in shallow waters. This is due to the slow growth at cold temperatures, low food quality, and to extended periods of quiescence when the water is anoxic (Jonasson and Kristiansen 1967; Danks and Oliver 1972).

The profundal chironomid community has been used extensively as an indicator of the nutrient conditions or productivity status of lakes. Saether (1980b) lists about twenty genera of chironomids that are characteristic of particular oxygen-nutrient-substrate combinations, which, in conjunction with other noninsect assemblages, can be used in lake typology classifications. Warwick (1980) documented over 2500 years of land-use practices around Lake Ontario using the subfossil chironomid head capsules in a sediment core; changes in species composition of midges were associated with various periods of eutrophication, deforestation, sedimentation, and contamination.

LIFE CYCLE ADAPTATIONS

Diverse life history patterns have evolved to enable species to exploit foods that are seasonably available, to time emergence for appropriate environmental conditions, to evade unfavorable physical conditions (e.g., droughts, spates, and lethal temperature), and to minimize repressive biotic interactions such as competition and predation. Typically, a seasonal succession of species can be cataloged at a given location by determining the emergence and flight periods of adults or by studying the larval growth periods. However, comparison of a given species at different sites may indicate considerable flexibility in life histories. Some important adaptations include: (1) responses to temperature and oxygen levels; (2) use of daylength or temperature as environmental cues to synchronize life stages; (3) resting stages to avoid unfavorable conditions; and (4) extended flight, oviposition, or hatching periods to spread the risk in coping with environmental conditions that cannot be avoided entirely.

The duration of aquatic insect life cycles ranges from less than two weeks (e.g., some Culicidae and Chironomidae) to 4–5 years (e.g., some Megaloptera and Odonata), but in the north temperate zone an annual cycle is most common. Hynes (1970a) distinguished three main types of life cycles for insects in a temperate stream: slow seasonal, fast seasonal, and nonseasonal cycles. In seasonal cycles a distinct change of larval size occurs with time, i.e., the progression of growth by cohorts can be discerned by periodic sampling of field populations. In nonseasonal taxa, individuals of several ages are present at all times. The three types are illustrated by three species of glossosomatid caddisflies, all collected from one emergence trap (fig. 5.2).

Slow-seasonal cycles are common in cool streams and typified by some Plecoptera, Ephemeroptera, and Trichoptera. Eggs hatch soon after deposition, and larvae grow slowly, reaching maturity nearly a year later. In many species, an extended hatching period results in recruitment over several months. Larvae grow during winter and most species have a flight period early in the year.

Fast-seasonal cycles are those in which growth is rapid after a long egg or larval diapause or after one or more intermediate generations. The caddisfly *Agapetus bifidus* has an egg diapause of 8–9 months and a larval growth period of only 2–3 months (fig. 5.2). Various fast-seasonal cycles reach full term in spring, early and late summer, and fall. Two or more fast cycles may be exhibited by the same species when rapid generations succeed one another, as in the mayfly *Baetis* sp. and the black fly *Simulium* sp. Individuals that grow rapidly at warm temperatures tend to be much smaller than those of the earlier, slow-growing generation (Hynes 1970b; Ross and Merritt 1978; Sweeney 1978; Cudney and Wallace 1980; Georgian and Wallace 1983).

In nonseasonal cycles, individuals of several stages or size classes are present in all seasons. This may be because the life cycle spans more than a year as in some large Plecoptera and Megaloptera, or because a series of overlapping generations occurs, or for other unexplained reasons. Chironomidae often exhibit nonseasonal patterns probably because two or more species have not been distinguished or because short life cycles result in overlapping cohorts.

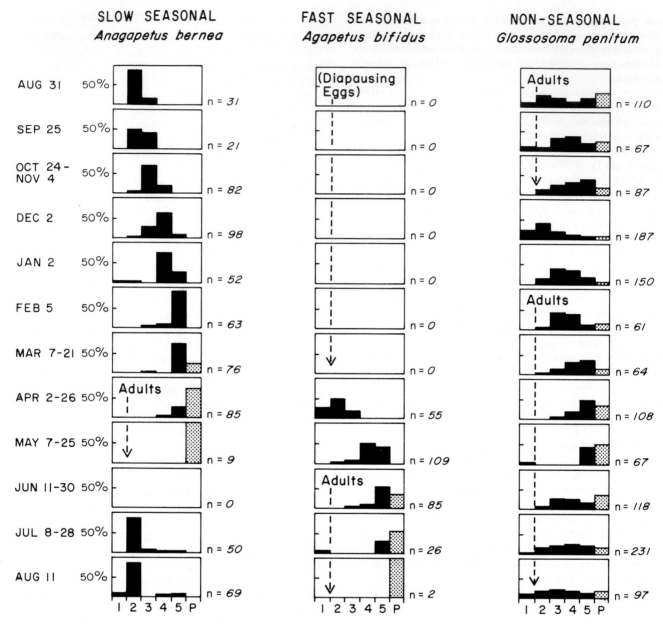

Figure 5.2. Age distribution of three glossosomatid caddisflies, illustrating life cycles. Field data are expressed as percentage composition per month for each instar. There are five larval instars; P = prepupa + pupa; n = number per sample. Flight period of adults is also indicated. (Data from Anderson and Bourne [1974].)

Poorly synchronized life cycles would be expected to occur in situations where limiting factors for growth or reproduction (e.g., temperature, food, and moisture) are not seasonally dependent. Thus in the tropics the unvarying temperature and light conditions could result in continuous periods of growth and reproduction. It is somewhat surprising that aquatic insects in the southern hemisphere are predominantly of the nonseasonal type in contrast to the situation in the north temperate zone (Winterbourn 1974, 1978; Hynes and Hynes 1975; Corbet 1978; Towns 1981).

Habitat Selection

On a gross level, habitat selection is primarily the province of the mated females as deposition of eggs determines where the larvae will initially occur. The chain of behavioral cues leading to oviposition has rarely been elucidated but habitat selection may involve visual, tactile, and chemosensory cues. Coleoptera and Hemiptera detect water while in daytime flight apparently from the reflective surface so they are attracted to ponds, swimming pools, and other shiny surfaces. For most aquatic insects, oviposition occurs near the location from which the adult emerged, but dispersal flights are common especially in species from temporary habitats.

Species that overwinter as adults (e.g., Coleoptera, Hemiptera) may have a fall dispersal flight to overwintering sites, and also a spring flight for oviposition.

The widespread tropical dragonfly, *Pantala flavescens* (Libellulidae), an obligate migrant that breeds in temporary ponds, exhibits long-distance dispersal in search of oviposition sites. The adults fly upward at emergence and are then transported by the wind to places where rain will later fall. Wind may transport the adults over 1400 km across the Indian Ocean toward the cold front produced by monsoons (Corbet 1963).

Caddisflies from temporary streams (*Hesperophylax* sp., *Grammotaulius* sp.) and ponds *(Limnephilus indivisus)* (table 5A) deposit eggs in damp channels or depressions before the habitat fills with autumnal rains or snow. A similar selection of habitat before it is suitable for the larva occurs with snow-pool mosquitos *(Aedes),* which deposit diapausing eggs in depressions, and hatching occurs the following spring when eggs are wetted by the melting snow.

Males are responsible for habitat selection in many odonates; they establish territories, over ponds or streams depending on the species, and actively court females to oviposit within that locale. A male in tandem flight may even remain coupled while the female is ovipositing below the surface. Belostomatid bugs, which incubate eggs on the back of the male (table 5A), are another instance of male influence on habitat selection. Movement by the male through swimming or overland crawling to nearby pools will determine the site in which the larvae develop.

In general, taxa with specialized habitat requirements might be expected to exhibit the greatest degree of habitat selection by the ovipositing female. Insect parasitism (which is rare in aquatic insects) requires habitat specialization. The Palaearctic wasp, *Agriotypus* sp., crawls into the water enveloped by a film of air and seeks out a mature larva or pupa of the caddisflies *Silo* sp. or *Goera* sp. (Goeridae). An egg is then deposited within the caddisfly case so that the *Agriotypus* sp. larva can develop as a parasite of the pupal stage of the caddisfly (Clausen 1931).

Oviposition and Eggs

The diversity of oviposition strategies is illustrated in table 5A. Hinton (1981) provides a comprehensive treatment of insect eggs. Much of the life cycle can be deduced from the timing and habits of oviposition and the location of the eggs, but this aspect of natural history frequently receives less attention than it deserves. Elliott and Humpesch (1980) point out that information on fecundity, oviposition behavior, and hatching is essential for: (1) interpretation of life cycles; (2) identification of larval cohorts; (3) study of spatial patterns and movements; (4) construction of life tables; and (5) estimation of growth rates, mortality, and production.

The number of eggs varies greatly among taxa and among individuals of a species. Within the Ephemeroptera, *Dolania* sp. deposits about 100 eggs (Peters and Peters 1977), whereas the fecundity of *Ecdyonurus* sp. is 5000–8000 eggs per female (Elliott and Humpesch 1980). The number of eggs

produced by *Baetis rhodani* ranges from 600 to 2400 per female (Elliott and Humpesch 1980). The within-species variation in fecundity is related to size of the female, which in turn is associated with growth conditions of the larvae. In taxa in which feeding by adults is required for egg maturation, fecundity will depend not only on food availability but also on appropriate oviposition conditions, because eggs may be resorbed if conditions are unsuitable for oviposition.

The eggs of some insects mature in the pupa or last larval stage (e.g., Megaloptera, Ephemeroptera, some Plecoptera) and are ready to be laid soon after emergence and mating. At the other extreme (e.g., Odonata, Hemiptera, some Plecoptera, and Coleoptera), adults emerge with undeveloped ovaries, require a feeding period before oviposition (or overwintering), and deposit eggs over an extended period or in discontinuous clutches. Potential fecundity can be estimated by dissection of newly emerged females if eggs mature all at one time. However, when egg maturation is a continuing process or when successive clutches are produced, total egg production depends on the length of life of individual adults.

The egg is potentially a vulnerable stage because it lacks mobility. However, in many instances the egg is the most resistant stage of the life cycle and spans periods of cold, heat, drought, or food shortages. The hatching period may extend for several months, which spreads the risk over a range of environmental conditions. Extended hatching may be due to irregular rates of development of individual embryos, to irregular breaking of diapause, or to extended oviposition periods.

Larval Growth and Feeding

Differences in duration of the larval stage and in growth patterns provide for much of the variation in life histories. The examples presented below illustrate food acquisition strategies and larval growth patterns that adapt species to particular environments.

Though the fauna of temporary habitats is quite limited, most orders of aquatic insects are represented and these exhibit extreme seasonal regulation of life cycles. Wiggins *et al.* (1980) describe several life-cycle patterns for temporary ponds, depending on the timing of adult colonization and kind of resistant stage. The prime requisite for all species is rapid larval development during the wet phase. Many mosquitoes are temporary-habitat breeders; under optimum conditions some species can complete their growth in five days. Rapid growth implies adaptation to warm waters as even the species that emerge early in snow-melt pools (e.g., limnephilid caddisflies) will be exposed to high temperatures when water volume diminishes. The timing of recruitment in temporary pools is correlated with feeding behavior. The earliest larvae are detritivores, either shredders (e.g., limnephilid caddisflies) or fine-particle feeders (e.g., siphlonurid mayflies, *Aedes* sp. mosquitoes, Chironomidae); then algal feeders (e.g., *Callibaetis* sp. mayflies, haliplid beetles) and finally predators (e.g., Odonata, Hemiptera, dytiscid and gyrinid beetles) are recruited coinciding with abundant prey resources.

Table 5A. Summary of data for oviposition and egg stage of selected aquatic insects.

Taxon	Preoviposition Period	Oviposition Season	Oviposition Site	Oviposition Behavior
EPHEMEROPTERA				
Baetidae				
Baetis spp.	1 day (including subimago)	extended (spring–fall)	Shallow riffles, underside of stones	♀ folds wings along abdomen walks into water and selects site
Callibaetis floridanus	5–7 days (including subimago)	entire year	Lentic, often temporary habitats	♀ lands on water and extrudes milky mass; dies on site
Ephemeridae				
Hexagenia spp.	2–4 days (including subimago)	May–Sept	Lakes, large rivers	♀♀ plummet to water and extrude egg packets; on contact with water eggs separate and sink. Some ♀♀ can take off and repeat
Leptophlebiidae				
Leptophlebia cupida	2 days (including subimago)	mid May–early July	Mainstream of slow-moving rivers	♀ dips abdomen in water, release few eggs at a time; completed in min; flies up or down stream, daytime only
Ephemerellidae				
Ephemerella ignita	2 days (including subimago)	late June–Sept	Turbulent streams, in moss	♀ flies upstream with extruded egg ball; contact with water releases ball, and eggs then separate
Heptageniidae				
Epeorus pleurialis	3 days (including subimago)	Mar–May	Streams, fast water	♀ touches water several times, washes eggs off in batches
ODONATA				
Lestidae				
Lestes congener	3 wk	Aug	Temporary ponds; only in dry stems of *Scirpus* sp., 5–30 cm above water	♂ + ♀ in tandem; eggs inserted singly in incisions 2 cm apart
Archilestes grandis	—	mid June–late July	Lentic; in branches or petioles up to 13 m above water	♂ + ♀ in tandem; oviposition during daytime. Endophytic oviposition; 2 eggs per incision in petiole but about 10 in pithy stems
Aeshnidae				
Anax imperator	11–14 days	early June–early Aug	Ponds; warmest area	♀ alights on floating plants and deposits eggs endophytically; egg may penetrate leaf; 1 egg per incision
Corduliidae				
Tetragoneuria spp.	1 wk	mid May–July (ca. 1 mo at a site) (individuals live 2 wks)	Lotic, ca. 10 or more feet from shore	♀ makes 2 passes to select a site; on 3rd pass she drags abdomen through water trailing egg string until it adheres to solid object. Several ♀♀ add to egg-string aggregations on same day

scription of Egg or Egg Mass	Number of Eggs*	Incubation and Hatching Period	Comments	Geographic Area	Reference
tiguous rows of yel-, spherical eggs, form at semicircular plate	*B. rhodani,* winter generation up to 2500; summer generation up to 1200	*B. rhodani,* start of hatching 17 wks @ 3°C, 1 wk @ 22°C. Hatching interval 34 days @ 3°C, 3 days @ 22°C	Hatching period is variable for species and site. Delayed hatch of some eggs for 40 wk	Europe North America	655, 1181 415
cous, reddish brown mass on venter of domen; mass is re-sed and eggs separate en abdomen touches ter	450–500	Hatch in 5–10 sec (ovoviviparous)	Adapted for temporary habitats. ♀♀ mate, and embryonic development complete before oviposition	Florida	170, 2474
s ellipsoid, –.19 × .28–.32 mm; ky surface results in s adhering in clumps	2260–7684; x̄ = 4000 for average-size ♀♀ (24–25 mm)	11–26 days; 2 wk @ summer temp	Both low temp. and low D.O. will delay incubation (Fremling 1967)	Midwest	800, 801, 1154
id, .23 × .12 mm; s anchored by peg-structures that ing out after wetting	x̄ (mean-sized ♀), 2959; *Fecundity, F = 2.02 L³·⁰⁴	Hatching started in 10–14 days @ 20°C; 50% emerge on day 1, hatching continues for 43 days	Latitude effect on oviposition period and fecundity. 1072–2065 eggs per ♀ in Penn.	Alberta Pennsylvania	416, 2385
enish egg ball; eggs ve polar anchoring chanism to attach to strate	eggs per mass, 156–603; x̄ = 322	112–392 days @ 8.2°C; 56–294 days @ 15.8°C. In stream, 10% hatch by 100 days, 90% by 300 days	Extended hatching period. Temp. > 14.5°C delays hatching; egg diapause in some populations	England, Lake District	657
am colored; ellipsoid, –.09 × .13–.15 mm; here firmly to sub-ate	2000–6000, x̄ = 4260 (dissected ♀♀)	Estimated 7 mo in field @ 11–14°C	Extended hatching period, with peak of small larvae in Feb	Kentucky	1678
ngate, 1.2 mm long; t and greyish when osited; cuticle then rdens and darkens	87–297 (x̄=205) mature oocytes; no. of egg clutches per ♀ not determined	Prediapause development for 1 wk; 3 mo diapause; 6–7 wk postdiapause; synchronous hatching (1 wk, in May)	Diapause occurs under snow cover; postdiapause embryogenesis triggered by snowmelt. Hatching threshold is 5°C	Saskatchewan	2165
ite with dark anterior d; 1.9 × .3 mm	up to 149/♀; 70–180 (Smith and Pritchard 1956)	15 days; eggs hatch without wetting	At emergence, prolarva "jumps" to water; use of deciduous petioles for egg site possible because eggs do not overwinter	Oklahoma	191
ngate cylinder, × .4 mm, with ante-r bladelike projection anchor egg in leaf	no data; can mature successive batches of eggs	Direct development; at field temp., 22–26 days; in lab, range of 28–51 days @ 15–20°C	Long oviposition period results in many larval size classes overwintering; thus, synchrony required in final instar	Southern England	436, 439, 441
al, brown eggs, × .4 mm, within a ring of gelatinous ma-x that swells to 3.5 n wide × 11 cm long	up to 1000 per string. Egg-string aggregation averages 250 thousand eggs; exceptionally large mass contained over 1 million	Individual strings in lab, hatching began @ 2 wk, 50% complete by 3 wk, continues for 7 wk	Hatching of eggs within large aggregations is retarded and thousands fail to hatch	Michigan	1344

ecundity of many mayflies conforms to power law: F = aLᵇ, where *L* = body length, and *a* and *b* are constants (Elliott 1972; Clifford and Boerger 1974).

Table 5A.—*Continued*

Taxon	Preoviposition Period	Oviposition Season	Oviposition Site	Oviposition Behavior
PLECOPTERA				
Nemouridae				
Nemoura trispinosa	2–3 wk (feeding required)	mid June–early July	Lotic, midstream	Extruded as mass; flying ♀ dips abdomen into water; mass "explodes" when jelly expands
Amphinemura nigritta	as above	June	As above	As above (?)
Perlodidae				
Hydroperla crosbyi	2–5 days	Feb–Mar	Lotic, head of riffle	♀ alights on water, extrudes egg mass. Mass separates and eggs sink
Perlidae				
Paragnetina media	< 1 day	June (synchronous emergence)	Lotic	Extruded as mass
HEMIPTERA				
Gerridae				
Gerris spp.	several mo (adults overwinter)	spring and summer	Pools and running water	♀ glues eggs to floating objects or at water's edge, at or below water line; deposited in parallel rows
Corixidae				
Ramphocorixa acuminata	—	early spring–fall; some eggs overwinter	Ponds, stock watering holes	Preferentially on crayfish (*Cambarus* sp.); also on other smooth surfaces. Several ♀♀ oviposit on one crayfish
Notonectidae				
Notonecta undulata	(*Buenoa* sp. = 16 days; Bare 1926)	early spring through summer	Lentic, widespread (clear pools to slimy ponds)	Eggs glued to submerged plants and other objects; irregular spacing
Belostomatidae				
Abedus herberti	—	nonseasonal	Warm streams and ponds	Starting at apex of wings and moving forward, ♀ deposits a solid mass of eggs on dorsum of ♂
MEGALOPTERA				
Corydalidae				
Orohermes crepusculus	few days	July–early Sept	Above lotic waters; bridges, trees, rocks	♀ deposits rows of eggs; she may add 3–4 smaller tiers on top of the base layer
Sialidae				
Sialis rotunda	1 day	late Apr–June	On vegetation or other objects overhanging lentic waters	♀ secretes adhesive, then deposits upright rows of eggs forming a tight mass

escription of Egg or Egg Mass	Number of Eggs	Incubation and Hatching Period	Comments	Geographic Area	Reference
cky coating attaches gs to substratum	114–833/batch; $\bar{x} = 514$	Immediate development @ 10°C. Incubation minimum of 3 wk, 80% by 6 wk; continues to 12 wk	In field, hatching from mid July to mid Sept	Ontario	972
	90–188/batch; $\bar{x} = 121$	4-mo embryonic diapause (germ disk stage)	In lab, hatching began @ 12°C in Sept; continued to Nov with temp. decrease from 12 to 8°C	Ontario	972
own, oval, triangular oss section. Gelatinous ating glues eggs to bstratum	172–330 eggs/mass; up to 3 masses/♀; 442–1418, $\bar{x} = 787$ (dissected ♀♀)	7 mo egg diapause to Sept–Oct	Synchronous hatching with decreasing temp. from 25 to 19°C	Texas	1831
	3–7 batches; 1207–2929 egg/♀ (dissected ♀♀)	At 20°C, 32 days; continues for 58 days	Partial hatch in fall, remainder in spring. Some parthenogenesis	Ontario	971
ongate, cylindrical, × 1 mm; white, turning amber brown before atching	—	2 wk incubation	♂ of *Rhagadotarsus* calls ♀ with wave patterns; defends oviposition territory (Wilcox 1979)	Kansas	1140
ongate, oval, .9 × .4 m, with apical nipple. gg attached by elastic destal and disk with rong glue	up to 22 mature eggs in abdomen at one time; successive batches are matured	5–10 day incubation	Continuous reproduction and asynchronous incubation. Synchrony of oviposition induced by freezing or recolonization. Oviposition on crayfish gives protection, aeration, and solid, nonsilted, attachment surface	Kansas	920
ongate, oval, 1.7 × .6 m; with small tubular icropyle; rough surce with hexagonal ulpturing	—	5–14 day incubation	Continuous oviposition in summer and overlapping broods. Some notonectids insert eggs into plants	Kansas, and New York	1140
al with rounded top; llow, darkening to tan. gg swells during development from 3.1 × 1.7 m to 5.0 × 2.0 mm	one ♀ produced 4 masses in 13 mo, total = 344 eggs	Incubation in lab @ 18°C = 21–23 days	♂ aerates eggs by raising and lowering wings. Encumbered ♂♂ occur throughout the year	Arizona	2262
long mass, 30 × 25 m. Eggs, 1.0 × .5 m, with micropylar ojection; greyish yelw, becoming reddish hatching	1000–1700 eggs/mass $\bar{x} = 1500$	In field, 26–63 days, $\bar{x} = 43$ days; in lab (20°C), 25 days	Synchronous hatching within a mass	Oregon	688
ylindrical, rounded at p with micropylar tuercle; .7 × .3 mm; hite when laid, turning ark brown before atching	300–500 eggs/mass; ♀ may deposit a second, smaller mass	8–12 days	Synchronous hatching within a mass, usually at night. Larvae drop from egg mass into the water	Oregon	77, 78

Table 5A.—*Continued*

Taxon	Preoviposition Period	Oviposition Season	Oviposition Site	Oviposition Behavior
TRICHOPTERA				
Glossosomatidae				
Agapetus fuscipes	few days	Apr–Oct	Chalk streams, slow flow over clean gravel	♀ swims underwater and oviposits on rock, then places "capstone" of small gravel on egg mass before cement is dry; submerged for 15–20 min
Agapetus bifidus	—	July–early Aug	Streams, in crevices on cobble	♀ probably swims to substrate
Hydropsychidae				
Hydropsyche sp. *Cheumatopsyche* sp.	few days	May–Sept	Large rivers, on submerged objects	♀ swims underwater, deposits egg mass on firm surface. Masses concentrated 3–5 ft below surface
Limnephilidae				
Limnephilus indivisus	several wk (ovarial diapause over summer)	early fall	Dry basin of temporary pool	♀ attaches gelatinous egg mass under log or to other protected site
Limnephilus lunatus	variable: 2–3 wk in fall; > 3 mo in spring	fall	Chalk streams, attached to watercress	♀ deposits egg mass on plants above water. Mass absorbs water and swells to 10 mm in diameter
Clistoronia magnifica	2 wk (in lab)	July–Aug	Lentic, attached to submerged logs or plants, or loose in littoral benthos	In lab, ♀ observed to enter water for 5 min and attach egg mass. May also oviposit on surface and egg mass sinks to substrate
Calamoceratidae				
Heteroplectron spp.	few days? (pupae contain mature eggs)	early summer	Small streams; loosely attached masses near waterline; also in drop zones not attached	Some ♀♀ may oviposit underwater, but site of eggs suggests that most oviposit at the waterline
Leptoceridae				
Ceraclea spp.	< 1 day	spring, or spring and mid-late summer	Lentic and lotic	♀ oviposits on surface. Mass floats until it absorbs water, then sinks and adheres to submerged objects
Chathamiidae				
Philanisus plebeius	few wk	summer–fall	Marine; in starfish *(Patiriella)* in tidepools	♀ probably inserts ovipositor through pores on aboral surface of starfish to deposit eggs in coelom

escription of Egg or Egg Mass	Number of Eggs	Incubation and Hatching Period	Comments	Geographic Area	Reference
ınd, .2–.25 mm in di-ıeter, creamy white; posited in single-lay-d, compact mass	eggs/mass = 12–94, $\bar{x}$ = 27. In lab, 12 ♀♀ deposited 70 masses	Direct development. At 12°C, hatching starts @ 1 mo, and continues for 3 wk	In cold springbrook, eggs hatched from early May—Oct	Southern England	51
ıss, firm matrix, $\times$ 1.6 mm. Eggs ınd, .2–.3 mm in di-ıeter	30–100 eggs/mass	7 mo to hatching	Eggs overwinter in obligatory diapause	Oregon	56
ıcentric rows of sely packed eggs ıdcock 1953)	*Hydropsyche,* dissected ♀♀ = 331–465 eggs (Fremling 1960a). 820 deposited in 50 min by a ♀ (Badcock 1953)	In lab, 8–11 days	—	England, Iowa	82, 799
	—	Larvae hatch in few wk, but remain in matrix until flooded	Emergence from egg mass dependent on time of flooding; may be in fall or the following spring	Ontario	2670, 2678
ıne-shaped mass, ıque yellow when de-ısited. When swollen, ıy is colorless with ıs in rows. Eggs ıntly elliptical, $\times$ .3 mm	270–636/mass	Duration of egg stage (room temp.) averages 17 days	Fall oviposition synchro-nized by decreasing duration of ovarial dia-pause as summer pro-gresses	Southern England	905
ıerical colorless mass, to 3 cm in diameter, ıes 8 hr to achieve l size. Eggs greenish, ıanged in lines	200–300 eggs per mass; ♀ may deposit a second smaller mass	2–2½ wk @ 16°C; lar-vae continue to emerge from a mass for 1 wk	Field oviposition period extended by long flight period. May be 2–3 mo ovarial diapause in spring	Oregon, British Columbia	54, 2728
ı mass spherical, 15 mm, coated with ı, jelly very fluid; eggs lowish, arranged in ıvs	132–348 eggs per mass, $\bar{x}$ = 209. Dissected ♀♀ contain 300–400 eggs	At 20°C, hatching @ 12 days; 15 days @ 15°C; larvae remain in matrix 2–9 days	Short, synchronous ovi-position period. Eggs above waterline require 100% humidity; larvae remain in mass until in-undated, then all emerge in ca. 1 min	Pennsylvania Oregon	1868 R. Wisseman (unpublished)
ıss, dark green, ca. 1 ı sphere when depos-d. Eggs, spherical, ıen yolk, transparent ırion; eggs swell from ımm to .2 mm in ımeter by time of ıtching	100–300 eggs per mass	In lab, 1–3 wk	Direct embryonic development	Kentucky	2017
ıgs spherical, .4 mm, low-yellowish gray; ıgle or in small ımps in coelomic ıvity of host	dissected ♀♀ contain up to 400 mature eggs, $\bar{x}$ = ca. 160. Variable numbers in starfish: mostly < 10, but up to 112	At least 5 wk incubation @ 16–18°C	Extended incubation and hatching periods as eggs were found in star-fish throughout the year	New Zealand	2732

Table 5A.—*Continued*

Taxon	Preoviposition Period	Oviposition Season	Oviposition Site	Oviposition Behavior
COLEOPTERA Gyrinidae *Dineutus* spp.	—	May–Aug	Ponds, on underside of *Potamogeton* sp. leaves	Deposited in clusters; each egg glued separately to leaf
Haliplidae *Peltodytes* sp., *Haliplus* sp.	—	May–early July	Lentic, in beds of *Chara* sp. and *Nitella* sp.	*Peltodytes*, eggs glued to macrophytes or algae. *Haliplus*, ♀ chews hole in hollow stems and deposits several eggs within
Dytiscidae *Agabus erichsoni*	—	May–June	Temporary woodland pools	Eggs deposited in clumps of 2–3 among root fibers or moss on bottom of pond
Colymbetes sculptilis	—	late Mar–April	Temporary woodland pools	Eggs firmly attached to submerged vegetation or to edge of rearing container
Hydrophilidae *Hydrophilus triangularis*	—	early–mid summer	Eutrophic ponds, with some vegetation	♀ spins a silken egg case; ellipsoidal shape with elongate "mast." Construction takes > 1 hr
Psephenidae *Psephenus falli*	1 day? (mature ovaries at emergence)	early May–mid Aug	In riffles, under rocks	♀ crawls down a rock and remains submerged for life (1–3 days)
Elmidae *Stenelmis sexlineata*	—	May–Aug	Lotic, in riffles, on sides and bottom of rocks	Submerged ♀ selects depressions cracks on rocks; deposits group of eggs usually touching each other, each egg pressed against surface for 10–20 sec to glue it down
LEPIDOPTERA Pyralidae *Nymphula* sp.	1 day	July–Aug	Lentic, underside of floating *Potamogeton* sp. leaves	♀ generally does not enter water but extends tip of abdomen to attach egg mass on underside near margin of leaf. Oviposition occurs at night
HYMENOPTERA Agriotypidae *Agriotypus* sp.	few days	May–July	Lentic or lotic; in cases of goerid or odontocerid caddisflies	♀ crawls down a support into water and searches for a host. Eggs only deposited on prepupa or pupa. ♀ may stay underwater for several hr, enveloped in air bubble

scription of Egg or Egg Mass	Number of Eggs	Incubation and Hatching Period	Comments	Geographic Area	Reference
te, elongated ellips- 1.9 × .6 mm; clus- arranged diagonally 45° angle from mid-	7–40 eggs per cluster (Wilson 1923b); 12–17 eggs per ♀ per day (Istock 1966)	5–6 days	Synchronous hatching of clusters; extended oviposition period of the population	Iowa, Michigan	1188, 2722
odytes, oval, with ecting plug, .5 × .3 , yellowish brown; *iplus*, oval, .4 × .2 , whitish	30–40 eggs within a wk	8–10 days @ 21°C	♀♀ live over 1 yr, so several batches of eggs are matured	Michigan	1045, 1570
rt oval; pale cream oming light brown age; 1.7 × 1.1 mm	♀♀ contain 14–31 eggs at one time; ovaries continue to develop eggs	8–9 mo; some embryonic development before pond dries up, then diapause; hatching occurs the following spring	Eggs from dry pond bottom were chilled for 3 mo @ 0°C, then flooded and larvae emerged within a few hr	Ontario	1215
gate oval, somewhat ney-shaped; pale yel- with smooth cho- ; 1.8 × .7 mm	—	6 days @ 19°C; longer in field as oviposition occurs at < 14°C	Apparently a short incubation and hatching period, as 1st-instar larvae only found for 3 wk in April	Ontario	1215
case is yellow, turns wn; eggs, elongate el- oid, 4.4 × 1 mm; ght yellow	10–130 eggs per case; ♀ probably matures more than 1 batch	—	Egg case floats and eggs do not hatch if case turns over; mast assumed to aid in stabilizing the case	Iowa	2721
erical, lemon yellow s, deposited in com- t, single-layered ss	ca. 500 eggs per ♀; several may oviposit together, forming masses of over 2000 eggs	16–17 days @ 23°C	Apparently synchronous hatching within a mass, but extended oviposition period	Southern California	1750
ong; whitish-yellow; –.62 mm long	—	6–10 days @ 22–25°C	Protracted oviposition period; adults live underwater for > 1 yr	Kentucky	2639
ptical eggs, .45 × .6 n; light grey or whi- ; about 20 eggs/ ss	♀ of *N. badiusalis* laid 441 eggs in one night	6–11 days	Direct development of eggs; synchronous hatching within a mass	Michigan	159
gate, .9 × .2 mm; ered to a stalk which nserted into the t's integument	—	In lab, 5–8 days	Several eggs may be deposited on one host but only one larva can develop per host	Japan, France	407, 917

Table 5A.—*Continued*

Taxon	Preoviposition Period	Oviposition Season	Oviposition Site	Oviposition Behavior
DIPTERA				
Tipulidae				
Tipula sacra	< 1 day	June–July	Lentic, in soil or algae mats near shore	♀♀ emerge during the day; mate and begin ovipositing immediate
Lipsothrix nigrilinea	< 12 hr	Mar–Aug; peak in May–June	In saturated wood in streams	♀ searches for suitable site on w near waterline with ovipositor. [posits egg ca. 1 mm deep in soft wood or crack; then moves to m another insertion
Ptychopteridae				
Ptychoptera lenis	< 1 day	late May–June	Lentic, stagnant water	Mating and oviposition occur shortly after emergence. Eggs occur loose on substrate, so prob bly scattered at pond surface an sink to substrate
Simuliidae				
Simulium spp.	variable; blood meal may be required for egg maturation	spring and summer; multivoltine	Lotic; various sites (wet-ted vegetation, dam faces, debris, etc.)	Variable even within a species; may oviposit in flight, but more commonly on solid surface in masses or strings, at or below waterline
Culicidae				
Aedes aegypti	variable; blood meal re-quired for egg development	nonseasonal	artificial containers: cis-terns, cans, old tires	Eggs deposited singly, at or near waterline
Culex pipiens	variable; blood meal re-quired, except in autogen-ous strains; some overwinter as nulliparous ♀♀	spring–late autumn	Lentic; small catch-ments and pools with high organic content	♀ lands on water and deposits eg in raftlike masses. Oviposition u ally at night
Chironomidae				
Chironomus plumosus	2–5 days	mid May, July–Sept	Lentic; on water or on flotsam	♀ flies over water (sometimes sev eral mi); extrudes egg mass be-tween hind tibiae and deposits it on first surface that she touches
Tabanidae				
Tabanus atratus	1 wk	June–Oct	On plants, near or over water	♀ faces head downward while de positing egg mass on vertical por tion of plant
Ephydridae				
Dichaeta sp. (=*Notiphila*) (Mathis 1979a)	5–15 days	throughout summer	Marshy areas with ac-cumulation of decaying vegetation	♀ scatters eggs along shore or on floating detritus. Eggs not glued substrate but many in crevices
Sciomyzidae				
Sepedon spp.	4–24 days	—	Lentic; on emergent vegetation, from 5 cm to > 1 m above water	♀ in head downward position, de posits eggs in vertical row

scription of Egg or Egg Mass	Number of Eggs	Incubation and Hatching Period	Comments	Geographic Area	Reference
ning black, elongate, vex on one side; 1.0 .4 mm; posterior fila-nt uncoils when wet-as anchoring device	dissected ♀♀, $\bar{x}$ = 925, range, 500–1600 eggs	In lab, few days; in field, < 1 mo	Direct development of eggs; hatching period from early July–mid Aug	Alberta	1953, 1958
am colored, elongate, ooth; no anchoring ice	dissected ♀♀, $\bar{x}$ = 185, range, 106–380 eggs	About 3 wk @ 16°C	Direct development, but extended hatching period because of long flight period	Oregon	605
ngate oval; whitish low; longitudinal re-lations on chorion; .9 mm long	dissected ♀♀ contain 530–806 eggs	In field, 14–20 days	Egg maturation occurs during pharate adult stage	Alberta	1094
l to triangular .25 × × .13 mm; whitish, ning brown as they ture.	300–600 eggs per ♀. Eggs may occur in large aggregations (72 000/ft²)	5 days @ 23°C	Successive generations in summer; overwinter often as diapausing eggs	Ontario	517
ngate oval	average about 140 eggs when fed on humans; may be 2 or more egg cycles	Highly variable; embry-onic development com-pleted in 2–4 days after flooding	Direct development in water but eggs with-stand desiccation for at least 1 yr	Southeastern states	1001
indrical, tapered	100–400 eggs per mass; ♀ lays 2–4 masses	1–3 days	First batch of eggs may mature without a blood meal. Size of later masses depends on blood meals. Several genera-tions per yr.	Holarctic	1001
g mass is dark brown, ar-shaped; swells to 25 5 mm. Eggs, cream lored, oval, .5 × .2 m	eggs per mass: $\bar{x}$ = 1676, range, 1154–2014	3 days @ 24°C; 14 days @ 9°C	Egg mass floats and lar-vae remain in it for 1 day after hatching. 2 generations per yr	Wisconsin	1053
g mass is subconical, al at base, with 4–5 ers of eggs, 5–25 mm 2–10 mm. Eggs hite when laid, then rken	500–800 eggs per mass	4–12 days	—	Florida	1256
g ellipsoidal, convex venter; longitudinally dged; white; .9 × .3 m	—	1–2 days @ 21–25°C	Eggs float when marsh floods and have plastron for underwater respira-tion	Ohio, Montana	617
ggs lie horizontal uching preceding one. gg elongate with arse, longitudinal riations; white, becom-g colored during de-lopment	Up to 25 eggs per row; ♀ probably deposits sev-eral rows	3–5 days		USA	1788

Fast development is characteristic of temporary inhabitants of water, but larval diapause or quiescence may extend the life cycle to several years. Corydalidae (Megaloptera) larvae in intermittent streams burrow into the streambed when surface water dries up; growth only occurs during the wet cycle so larval duration may be 3–4 years, depending on the annual duration of stream flow. The extreme example of tolerance of drought is the chironomid, *Polypedilum vanderplanki,* from ephemeral pools in Africa. The larvae can withstand complete dehydration and exist in a state of suspended metabolism, or cryptobiosis. The dehydrated larvae can survive immersion in liquid helium and heating to over 100°C (Hinton 1960). In their natural habitat, they can survive several years in sun-baked mud and rehydrate when wetted (McLachlan and Cantrell 1980). They are normally the first invaders of small pools and can inhabit the shallowest and most ephemeral pools with virtually no competitors.

Many stream insects are adapted to a narrow range of cool temperatures (cold stenothermy). Hynes (1970b) attributes winter growth not only to use of leaf detritus as a food base, but also suggests that this growth pattern may have been selected for because predation by fish would be less at low temperatures. Larval diapause to avoid high summer temperatures occurs in some early-instar Plecoptera (e.g., Capniidae, Taeniopterigidae) and in mature larvae or prepupae of some limnephilid caddisflies (e.g., *Dicosmoecus* sp., *Neophylax* sp., *Pycnopsyche* sp.).

Habitat partitioning may be effected by segregation by functional feeding groups. Thus, in addition to shredders, the winter-growing stream species include scrapers (e.g., heptageniid mayflies, glossosomatid caddisflies), filter-feeders (e.g., Simuliidae), and deposit feeders (e.g., several mayflies, some Chironomidae). Within a group, coexistence may be based on differential responses to food and temperature. For example, three coexisting species of the caddisfly genus *Pycnopsyche* are all shredders and winter growers, but the food resource is partitioned by the species having different timing of rapid growth intervals and also some differences in microhabitat preferences (Mackay 1972).

Elaborate and specialized feeding adaptations occur in the filter-feeding Ephemeroptera, Trichoptera, and Diptera (Wallace and Merritt 1980). The adaptations include specialized anatomical structures (e.g., leg setae in *Isonychia* spp. mayflies and *Brachycentrus* spp. caddisflies, mouth brushes in mosquitoes, head fans in *Simulium* spp.), and silk nets in many caddisflies and some chironomid midges. Habitat partitioning within the filter-feeding guild occurs along the water velocity gradient. Also, there is some selectivity in feeding habits. Georgian and Wallace (1981) demonstrated that the hydropsychid caddisflies that build large-meshed nets filter larger volumes of water than do those species with small nets and mesh size; the former will select for animal or algal foods rather than detritus.

Black fly larvae select areas where the current is fast and the boundary layer is thin so that the cephalic fans reach into the current. They show no selectivity with respect to food quality and will readily ingest inorganic as well as organic materials. Their food includes detritus, bacteria, diatoms, and animal fragments. The particle size of ingested material ranges from colloidal to 350 μm; a mucuslike secretion on the fans aids in trapping the minute particles (Ross and Craig 1980). Though they do not select for food quality, the type of food available will affect growth rates. Carlsson *et al.* (1977) found that black fly larvae at lake outfalls occurred in very dense aggregations and had exceptionally high growth rates associated with the availability of colloidal-sized organic material washed into the river at ice melt.

The above examples are primarily winter-growing lotic taxa. Most stream species respond to increasing temperatures in the spring by increasing their rate of growth. Multivoltine stream taxa include *Baetis* sp., *Glossosoma* sp., some hydropsychid caddisflies, and several black fly species. Though typical life cycles are univoltine, the duration and timing are more indeterminate than is usually suggested. Pritchard (1978) cites examples of cohort splitting in which individuals of the same cohort may have 1-, 2-, or even 3-year life cycles, depending on food availability and environmental conditions.

Aquatic insect predators include large conspicuous species with relatively long life cycles compared with those of their prey and have a range of morphological specializations and behavior patterns. Some are ambush or "sit-and-wait" predators, whereas others actively pursue their prey. The Hemiptera and some Coleoptera (e.g., Dytiscidae, Gyrinidae) are aquatic predators both as larvae and adults, whereas all others (e.g., Odonata, Megaloptera, some Diptera) are aquatic only as larvae.

Some of the most specialized predators are larval Odonata; the hinged prehensile labium, or mask, is unique to this order. The mask is projected forward by elevated blood pressure induced by abdominal muscles. Prey are impaled by hooks or setae on the labial palpi. The food is then returned to the mouth when the labium is folded back by adductor muscles. Prey perception involves receptor organs on the antennae and tarsi as well as use of the eyes. Sight is more important in later instars and in climbing species that live on vegetation than in bottom-sprawling or burrowing forms (Corbet 1963). In mature larvae of visual hunters, such as *Anax* sp., prey capture involves a highly integrated binocular vision, resulting from stimulation of certain ommatidia in each eye that enables the distance of the prey to be accurately judged. Feeding behavior of odonates is influenced by factors such as degree of hunger, time since the last molt, and the density, size, and movement of potential prey. As larvae grow, individual prey items become larger and more varied because larger larvae can also consume small prey (Corbet 1980).

Preoral digestion is a feature of hemipteran and some beetle predators. Salivary secretions are injected to immobilize prey and to liquefy tissues with hydrolytic enzymes. In Hemiptera the mouthparts are modified into a 3- or 4-segmented beak that is used to pierce the prey and suck the fluids. Dytiscid beetle larvae have chewing mouthparts, but their long sickle-shaped mandibles are grooved for fluid feeding. Larvae of some hydrophilid beetles (e.g., *Tropisternus* sp. and *Hydrophilus* sp.) are unusual in that the prey is held out of the water. In this position, the prey juices flow down the mandibles and into the oral opening rather than being lost into the surrounding water.

Territoriality and intraspecific competition were shown by Macan (1977) to be important factors affecting growth rate and life cycle of the damselfly *Pyrrhosoma* sp. In years when the larvae were abundant and prey populations were low, two size classes existed at the end of the summer. Macan attributed this to cohort splitting; larvae in superior feeding territories grew rapidly whereas those occupying poorer feeding sites grew slowly and would either require an extra year or die of starvation. Furthermore, Macan suggests that fish predation was selective for the larger specimens, which led to vacancies in the superior feeding sites, and that these were then readily filled by smaller larvae. Thus, predation by fish did not greatly reduce the numbers of damselflies reaching maturity because elimination of large larvae allowed smaller ones to exploit the food resource.

The prevalence of insect predators suggests that predation may be a dominant biotic factor influencing aquatic insects. Selective pressures due to predation have produced behavioral responses by prey species. For example, mayfly prey may react to predators by drifting or displaying scorpionlike threat postures (Peckarsky 1980; Peckarsky and Dodson 1980). The mayflies can apparently detect predators by noncontact chemical cues, and they may be able to distinguish between predaceous and detritivorous stoneflies that have a similar body form.

Metamorphosis and Eclosion

Molting during the larval stages results in a larger insect of essentially the same body form, whereas the final molt produces a more complete change associated with the development of wings and other adult structures. These are considered two distinct types of physiological differentiation, and Chapman (1982) suggests that the term *metamorphosis* be restricted to the latter. Molting and metamorphosis are mediated by hormones. There is no fundamental physiological difference between the metamorphosis of hemimetabolous and holometabolous insects; the difference is a matter of degree rather than kind. The pupal instar may be regarded as the equivalent of the last larval instar of hemimetabolous insects (Gillott 1980).

Control of molting involves the interaction of a molting hormone (ecdysone) and a juvenile hormone. The latter exerts an influence on development only in the presence of the former. When the concentration of juvenile hormone in the blood is high, the next molt will be larval-larval. At intermediate concentrations, a larval-pupal molt occurs, and when there is little or no circulating juvenile hormone (due to inactivity of the corpora alata) an adult insect will emerge at the next molt (Gillott 1980).

The primary morphological difference between hemimetabolous (Exopterygota) and holometabolous (Endopterygota) insects is the external development of the wings in the former and the delayed eversion of wings in the latter (Hinton 1963). The gradual development of adult structures is apparent in hemimetabolous insects by the progressive development of external wing pads and rudiments of the genitalia. Changes also occur in the last larval instar of the Holometabola, but these are internal and major differentiation is constrained by lack of space. During the pupal instar, the wings are evaginated to outside of the body; this makes room for development of the indirect flight muscles and the reproductive system. The pupal instar is usually of short duration. In the strict sense, the insect becomes an adult immediately after the apolysis (separation) of the pupal cuticle and the formation of the adult epicuticle to which the musculature is now attached (Hinton 1971a). Thus, in most instances, locomotion and mandibular chewing are activities, not of the pupa, but of the *pharate* adult that is enclosed within the pupal exuviae.

The final event in metamorphosis is *eclosion,* or emergence, which is the escape of the adult from the cuticle of the pupa or last larval instar. See chapter 8 for a further discussion of aquatic insect metamorphosis.

The development of a pupal stage has permitted the great divergence of larval and adult forms in the Holometabola. Larvae exploit environments and food resources that result in growth, whereas the activities of the adult center on dispersal and reproduction. If the number of species is considered to be a measure of biological success, complete (holometabolous) metamorphosis is a prime contributor to the success of insects. Hinton (1977) states that this is a focal point of insect evolution because about 88% of the extant insect species belong to the Endopterygota.

Metamorphosis in hemimetabolous aquatic insects differs in detail among the various taxa but the behaviors involved are mostly associated with switching from an aquatic to a terrestrial mode of life (especially respiration and flight) and overcoming the abiotic and biotic hazards during an especially vulnerable stage. Data from Corbet (1963) for Odonata illustrate both morphological and behavioral changes occurring during metamorphosis and eclosion.

The onset of metamorphosis in some dragonflies can be detected several weeks before emergence when the facets of the adult compound eye begin to migrate to the top of the head. Respiration rate also increases prior to metamorphosis associated with increased metabolic requirements. Behavioral changes characteristically involve movement to shallow water or up the stems of plants towards the surface. In *Anax imperator,* histolysis of the labium occurs and feeding stops several days before emergence.

Nearly all Odonata have a diurnal rhythm of emergence. The timing is presumably to restrict emergence to an interval when weather conditions are favorable and when predation is least likely to occur. The major predators are birds or mature adult dragonflies that hunt by sight, so night is the safest time to leave the water. In the tropics, most of the large dragonflies emerge after dusk; they eclose, expand their wings, and are then ready to fly before sunrise. In the temperate regions or at high altitudes where nocturnal temperatures are low, odonates tend to emerge in early morning or during the daytime. Mortality during emergence of *Anax imperator* may amount to 16% of the annual population (Corbet 1963). The individuals are immobile and defenseless for several hours during eclosion and while the wings expand and harden. Cold and wind increase mortality by prolonging ecdysis or by postponing emergence and thereby exposing more individuals to predation. Overcrowding is common in species that have mass emergences; competition for emergence supports is so intense that the first larva to climb a support may be used as a platform by others that follow. Although overcrowding is an ecological disadvantage of mass emergence, this type of synchronization is apparently adaptive, perhaps because it satiates predators and affords the appropriate synchronization of males and females.

Adaptations of pupae pertain to respiration, protection, and emergence from the water. These factors also operate on the pharate adult, so it is convenient to discuss the two stages together. This is usually a quiescent stage, but mosquito pupae (tumblers) are relatively active swimmers, and Hinton (1958a) demonstrated that some black fly pupae both feed and spin a cocoon. Pupation occurs out of water in Megaloptera, Neuroptera, most Coleoptera, and many Diptera. Larvae construct a chamber in the soil (e.g., Megaloptera, Coleoptera) for metamorphosis, and eclosion may occur within the chamber (Coleoptera) or after the pharate adult has worked its way to the soil surface (Megaloptera).

Many nematocerous Diptera have aquatic pupae, some of which are active swimmers (e.g., Culicidae, Dixidae, Chaoboridae) throughout the pupal stage, whereas others (e.g., Chironomidae, some Tipulidae) only swim to the surface for emergence. In taxa in which the pupa is glued to a substrate (e.g., Blephariceridae, Deuterophlebiidae, Simuliidae), the adult emerges underwater and rises to the surface enveloped in a gas bubble. These adults expand their wings and are capable of flying immediately after reaching the surface. Species with swimming pupae will emerge using the exuviae as a platform at the water surface. All Chironomidae emerge in this manner, and the cast skins remain trapped in the surface film for some time. Collections of exuviae are useful for taxonomic purposes and also as a rapid method of sampling the entire chironomid fauna of a water body (Wartinbee and Coffman 1976; also see chap. 25).

Respiration in most aquatic Diptera pupae differs from that of the larvae in which the terminal abdominal spiracles are generally the most important. The pupae have respiratory horns or other extensions of the prothoracic spiracles. Depending on the species, these may be used for breathing at the surface, in the water column, or even to pierce the tissues of submerged plants.

The case-making caddisflies illustrate several morphological and behavioral adaptations in the pupal stage. The mature larva selects a protected site, such as under a stone or in a crevice in wood, and attaches the case with silk. Then the case is shortened, and the ends are closed with mineral or detrital particles and a silk mesh that allows for water flow.

Metamorphosis occurs within the case. The pupa (pharate adult) is active within the case, maintaining a flow of water for respiratory purposes by undulating the body. The pupa has elongate bristles on the labrum and on anal processes that are used for removing debris from the silk grating at either end of the case. The back-and-forth movement within the case is effected by the dorsal hook-plates on the abdomen. The pharate adult has large mandibles used for cutting an exit hole at emergence. It then swims to the surface or crawls to shore where eclosion occurs.

CONCLUDING COMMENTS

The critical importance of systematics to basic life-history studies has been emphasized on numerous occasions (e.g., Wiggins 1966; Ross 1967a; Waters 1979a, 1979b). Excellent progress has been made for several aquatic insect groups in North America (e.g., Edmunds et al. 1976; Wiggins 1977); however, eggs and all instars of immatures cannot always be identified. Studies of aquatic insect life histories require that individual investigators develop reliable methodologies for separating early instars of closely related species (e.g., Mackay 1978). It is unfortunate that life histories of so many aquatic insect species remain unknown. In some quarters, the mistaken impression still persists that such efforts are unfashionable and of little value. Ecosystem-level studies are often directed to studies of the processing of organic matter by various groups of animals, and insects are frequently the most abundant group considered. The integration of production, feeding habit, and bioenergetic data can yield a much better understanding of the role of individual species in ecosystems. Benke (1979), Benke et al. (1979), and Waters (1979a, 1979b) have emphasized that a knowledge of basic life histories is mandatory for reasonable estimates of production. Waters has pointed out that voltinism and length of aquatic life (=CPI, or Cohort Production Interval [Benke 1979]) are two of the most important life history features influencing secondary production estimates. The "once-per-month" sampling program of most studies is not adequate for many estimates of aquatic insect secondary production, and sampling schedules need to be tailored to the life histories of the organisms being studied (Cummins 1975; Waters 1979a).

Both temperature and food may influence life-history patterns; however, data on the potential combined effects of temperature and food quality on life histories of various groups of aquatic insects are too meager for any broad generalizations as yet. All students are encouraged to develop an appreciation for the importance of systematics, life histories, secondary production, and bioenergetics as interconnecting links toward the basic understanding of the structure and function of aquatic communities.

Ecology and Distribution of Aquatic Insects

6

Kenneth W. Cummins
Oregon State University, Corvallis

Richard W. Merritt
Michigan State University, East Lansing

INTRODUCTION

The emphasis on aquatic insect studies, which has expanded exponentially in recent decades, has been largely ecological. From its roots in sport fishery-related investigations of the '30s and '40s, through growing interest in indicators for water quality studies of the '50s and '60s, the work on aquatic insects has embraced most major areas of ecological inquiry (e.g., population dynamics, predator-prey interactions, physiological and trophic ecology, competition; Resh and Rosenberg 1984). In addition, fly fishermen have enthusiastically sought knowledge about aquatic insects, both as fish foods to be imitated and as interesting coinhabitants of their quarry. A major justification for this book is that systematics of aquatic insects has lagged behind the needs of aquatic ecologists.

The imperfect state of our present knowledge of aquatic insect species, together with pressing environmental and intriguing theoretical problems, provide incentives for understanding aquatic systems by utilizing different levels of taxonomic resolution. Although the species may be the appropriate basic unit for many types of ecological questions (e.g., Mayr 1969), such resolution may not always be required for significant insights, particularly in process-oriented studies. Separations ranging from orders to genera, and species in cases requiring a detailed level of taxonomic resolution, hopefully can be matched with the requirements of a given study. Stated in this fashion, the goal should be to maximize ecological information and insight per unit of taxonomic effort.

Several ecological topics are covered in separate chapters (chap. 3, Sampling; chap. 4, Physiology; chap. 5, Life History and Behavior; chap. 7, Evolution; and in the general material given in each order chapter). Thus, the major topics covered in this chapter are: (1) organization and functional relationships of aquatic insects with respect to habitat and nutritional resources, and (2) various aspects of the distribution, abundance, and production of aquatic insects. To summarize a large amount of information on the ecology and geographical distribution of aquatic insects, and to better indicate the numerous gaps in our knowledge, a generalized scheme has been presented in tabular form (tables 6A–6C, and the ecological tables in each order chapter). Ecological data have been organized in three categories: (1) habitats in which the aquatic nymphs and larvae occur (table 6A); (2) habits or modes of maintaining habitat location (table 6B);

and (3) modes of food acquisition (functional feeding groups; table 6C). Tables 6A–6C are definitions of terms to be used in conjunction with the ecological-distributional tables that appear in each order chapter (chaps. 9–25). The habitat, habit, and food acquisition classifications are based on our own research (e.g., Cummins 1962, 1964, 1972, 1973, 1974, 1975, 1980a, 1980b; Merritt *et al.* 1978, 1982, 1984; Cummins and Klug 1979; Merritt and Lawson 1979; Wallace and Merritt 1980; Merritt and Wallace 1981), a combination of systems proposed by others (e.g., Usinger 1956a; Edmondson 1959; Klots 1966; Pennak 1978), and two decades of teaching aquatic insect-related courses.

HABITAT ORGANIZATION

Aquatic insect adaptations to habitat types are treated in chapters 5 and 7. As above, the summary classification used here (table 6A) also stresses the basic distinction between lotic (running waters, streams-rivers) and lentic (standing waters, ponds-lakes) habitats. This separation is generally useful in partitioning aquatic insect genera (as well as families, and species in some cases). The key features of habitat organization appear to be the physical-chemical differences among erosional, depositional, and semiaquatic conditions (Moon 1939). Thus, often the same genera (or even species) occur in both stream riffles and along rocky, wave-swept (erosional) lakeshores or in stream-river pools and the soft sediments of pond or lake bottoms (depositional). Similar overlap is found in semiaquatic habitats along either running or standing waters or in intermittent ponds and streams. An example of lotic and lentic cooccurrence is the Eastern snail-case caddisfly *Helicopsyche borealis* (Trichoptera; Helicopsychidae), which inhabits cobble substrates in erosional habitats of both lakes and streams.

Within a given habitat, the modes by which individuals maintain their location (e.g., clingers to surfaces in fast-flowing water or burrowers in soft sediments) or move (e.g., swimmers or surface skaters) have been categorized in table 6B. The distribution pattern resulting from habitat selection by a given aquatic insect species reflects the optimal overlap between habit and physical environmental conditions that comprise the habitat: substrate, flow, turbulence, etc. Because food is almost always distributed in a patchy fashion,

Table 6A. Aquatic habitat classification system.

General Category	Specific Category	Description
Lotic—erosional (running-water riffles)	Sediments	Coarse sediments (cobbles, pebbles, gravel) typical of stream riffles.
	Vascular hydrophytes	Vascular plants growing on (e.g., moss *Fontinalis*) or among (e.g., pondweed *Potamogeton pectinatus*) coarse sediments in riffles.
	Detritus	Leaf packs (accumulations of leaf litter and other coarse particulate detritus at leading edge or behind obstructions such as logs or large cobbles and boulders) and debris (e.g., logs, branches) in riffles.
Lotic—depositional (running-water pools and margins)	Sediments	Fine sediments (sand and silt) typical of stream pools and margins.
	Vascular hydrophytes	Vascular plants growing in fine sediments (e.g., *Elodea*, broad-leaved species of *Potamogeton, Ranunculus*).
	Detritus	Leaf litter and other particulate detritus in pools and alcoves (backwaters).
Lentic—limnetic (standing water)	Open water	On the surface or in the water column of lakes, bogs, ponds.
Lentic—littoral (standing water, shallow shore area)	Erosional	Wave-swept shore area of coarse (cobbles, pebbles, gravel) sediments.
	Vascular hydrophytes	Rooted or floating (e.g., duckweek *Lemna*) aquatic vascular plants (usually with associated macroscopic filamentous algae).
	Emergent zone	Plants of the immediate shore area, e.g., *Typha* (cattail), with most of the leaves above water.
	Floating zone	Rooted plants with large floating leaves, e.g., *Nymphaea* (pond lily), and non-rooted plants (e.g., *Lemna*).
	Submerged zone	Rooted plants with most leaves beneath the surface.
	Sediments	Fine sediments (sand and silt) of the vascular plant beds.
Lentic—profundal (standing water, basin)	Sediments	Fine sediments (fine sand, silt and clay) mixed with organic matter of the deeper basins of lakes.
Beach zone	Freshwater lakes	Moist sand beach areas of large lakes.
	Marine interitidal	Rocks, sand, and mud flats of the intertidal zone.

Table 6B. Categorization of aquatic insect habits, that is, mode of existence.

Category	Description
Skaters	Adapted for "skating" on the surface where they feed as scavengers on organisms trapped in the surface film (example: Hemiptera, Gerridae—water striders).
Planktonic	Inhabiting the open water limnetic zone of standing waters (lentic: lakes, bogs, ponds). Representatives may float and swim about in the open water, but usually exhibit a diurnal vertical migration pattern (example: Diptera, Chaoboridae—phantom midges) or float at the surface to obtain oxygen and food, diving when alarmed (example: Diptera: Culicidae—mosquitoes).
Divers	Adapted for swimming by "rowing" with the hind legs in lentic habitats and lotic pools. Representatives come to the surface to obtain oxygen, dive and swim when feeding or alarmed; may cling to or crawl on submerged objects such as vascular plants (examples: Hemiptera, Corixidae—water boatmen; Coleoptera, adult Dytiscidae—predaceous diving beetles).
Swimmers	Adapted for "fishlike" swimming in lotic or lentic habitats. Individuals usually cling to submerged objects, such as rocks (lotic riffles) or vascular plants (lentic), between short bursts of swimming (examples: Ephemeroptera in the families Siphlonuridae, Leptophlebiidae).
Clingers	Representatives have behavioral (e.g., fixed retreat construction) and morphological (e.g., long, curved tarsal claws, dorsoventral flattening, and ventral gills arranged as a sucker) adaptations for attachment to surfaces in stream riffles and wave-swept rocky littoral zones of lakes (examples: Ephemeroptera, Heptageniidae; Trichoptera, Hydropsychidae; Diptera, Blephariceridae).
Sprawlers	Inhabiting the surface of floating leaves of vascular hydrophytes or fine sediments, usually with modifications for staying on top of the substrate and maintaining the respiratory surfaces free of silt (examples: Ephemeroptera, Caenidae; Odonata, Libellulidae).
Climbers	Adapted for living on vascular hydrophytes or detrital debris (e.g., overhanging branches, roots and vegetation along streams, and submerged brush in lakes) with modifications for moving vertically on stem-type surfaces (examples: Odonata, Aeshnidae).
Burrowers	Inhabiting the fine sediments of streams (pools) and lakes. Some construct discrete burrows which may have sand grain tubes extending above the surface of the substrate or the individuals may ingest their way through the sediments (examples: Ephemeroptera, Ephemeridae—burrowing mayflies; Diptera, most Chironominae, Chironomini—"blood worm" midges). Some burrow (tunnel) into plant stems, leaves, or roots (miners).

Table 6C. General classification system for aquatic insect trophic relations. (Applicable only to immature and adult stages that occur in the water.)

Functional Group (General category based on feeding mechanism)	Subdivision of Functional Group — Dominant Food	Subdivision of Functional Group — Feeding Mechanism	General Particle Size Range of Food (microns)	Collembola	Plecoptera	Odonata	Ephemeroptera	Hemiptera	Megaloptera	Neuroptera	Trichoptera	Lepidoptera	Coleoptera	Hymenoptera	Diptera
Shredders	Living vascular hydrophyte plant tissue	Herbivores—chewers and miners of live Macrophytes									+	+	+		+
	Decomposing vascular plant tissue—coarse particulate organic matter (CPOM)	Detritivores—chewers of CPOM	$>10^3$		+						+		+		+
	Wood	Gougers—excavate and gallery, wood					(+)				+		+		+
Collectors	Decomposing fine particulate organic matter (FPOM)	Detritivores—filterers or suspension feeders	$<10^3$												
		Detritivores—gatherers or deposit (sediment) feeders (includes feeders on loose surface films)		+			+	+			+		+		+
Scrapers	Periphyton—attached algae and associated material	Herbivores—grazing scrapers of mineral and organic surfaces	$<10^3$				+	+			+	+	+		+
Macrophyte Piercers	Living vascular hydrophyte cell and tissue fluids or filamentous (macroscopic) algal cell fluids	Herbivores—pierce tissues or cells and suck fluids	$>10^2-10^3$						+	+					
Predators	Living animal tissue	Engulfers—carnivores, attack prey and ingest whole animals or parts	$>10^3$		+	+	(+)		+		+		+		+
		Piercers—carnivores, attack prey, pierce tissues and cells, and suck fluids						+		+			+		
Parasites	Living animal tissue	Internal parasites of eggs, larvae and pupae. External parasites of larvae, prepupae and pupae in cocoons, pupal cases or mines. Also, external parasites of adult spiders.	$>10^3$											+	+

Orders Having Dominant Representatives

certain locations within a species habitat-habit match will constitute areas with the highest probability of occurrence. Thus, the discontinuous (= patchy, contagious, negative binomial) distribution pattern of an aquatic insect population is the result of interplay among habitat (e.g., sediment particle size, large wood debris), habit (i.e., mode of existence), and food availability (Cummins 1964; Lauff and Cummins 1964, Anderson *et al.* 1978, Reice 1980, Williams 1981a).

TROPHIC ORGANIZATION AND FUNCTION

A major observation stemming from insect feeding studies (e.g., Cummins and Klug 1979) is that based on food ingested, essentially all aquatic insects are omnivorous. Insects that chew leaf litter in a stream (shredders), for instance, particularly large species in their later instars, ingest not only the leaf tissue (and associated microbiota: fungi, bacteria, protozoans, and microarthropods), but diatoms and other algae that may be attached to the leaf surface in addition to

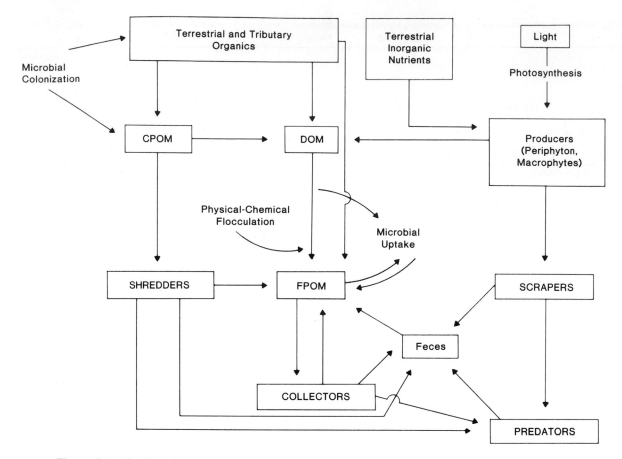

Figure 6.1. Nutritional resource categories and invertebrate functional feeding group categories in lotic ecosystems.

very small macroinvertebrates (e.g., first-instar midge larvae). For this reason, the trophic level analysis pioneered by Lindeman (1942) and used extensively in investigations of trophic relationships in marine and terrestrial communities, does not yield much information regarding linkages between insects and their food resources or the manner in which food resources might be partitioned among aquatic insect assemblages (figs. 6.1, 6.2).

A more promising approach is a classification that is based on morpho-behavioral mechanisms of food acquisition. The same morpho-behavioral mechanisms can result in the ingestion of a wide range of food items, the intake of which constitutes herbivory (living plants), detritivory (dead organic matter), or carnivory (live animal prey) (table 6D). Although food type intake would be expected to change from season to season, habitat to habitat, and with growth stage, limitations in food acquisition mechanisms have been shaped over evolutionary time and these are relatively more fixed. An example of similar morphological apparati enabling insects to scrape attached periphyton is shown in figure 6.3. The similarity in structure of the scraping mandibles in four families representing two orders is striking.

Since the mouthparts and associated feeding behavior probably change as part of the nymphal or larval developmental process, many species may initiate growth as members of the most generalized food acquisition group, i.e., gathering collectors. This would be a logical consequence of eggs generally hatching in protected locations where fine particulate detritus should be an omnipresent, abundant food resource. The early developmental food acquisition process would then consist of moving the tiny particles, in which the animals are immersed, into the mouth. As individuals grow, feeding morphology would be expected to become more restrictive. In many instances, the morphology obviously limits the food type that can be acquired, although the corresponding behavior that manipulates the structures may not be apparent.

Food resource categories (table 6A; Cummins 1973, 1974; Merritt and Cummins 1978; Cummins and Klug 1979) relating to food acquisition mechanisms have been chosen on the basis of: (1) size range (e.g., coarse and fine) of the material and (2) general location (e.g., attached to surfaces [periphyton], suspended in the water column, deposited in the sediments, in litter accumulations, in the form of live invertebrates). This categorization also reflects biochemical differences in the nutritional resources, such as presence of living chlorophyll or microbial-substrate interactions, and the major

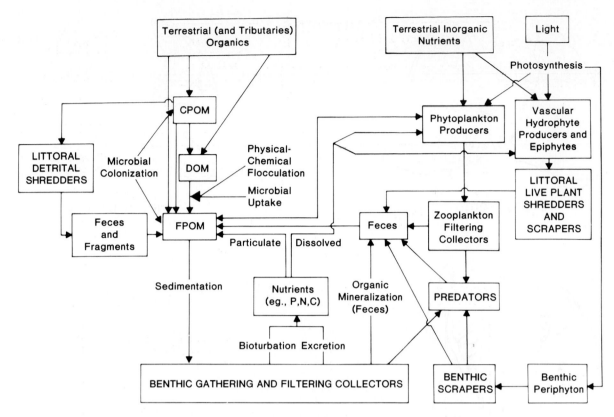

Figure 6.2. Nutritional resource categories and invertebrate functional feeding group categories in lentic ecosystems.

Table 6D. Comparison of functional feeding groups and trophic levels.

Functional Feeding Group	Trophic Level Based on Ingestion*
Shredders (live plant or dead plant)	Detritivores Herbivores (Carnivores)
Collectors Filtering (suspension feeders)	Detritivores Herbivores (Carnivores)
Gathering (deposit feeders)	Detritivores Herbivores (Carnivores)
Scrapers (grazers)	Herbivores Detritivores
Predators (engulfers)	Carnivores (Detritivores)
Piercers (plant or animal)	Unrecognizable fluids

*The occasional or minor component (on a biomass basis) of a trophic classification is shown in parentheses.

source of the resource, either from within the aquatic system (autochthonous) or from the stream-side (riparian) terrestrial areas (allochthonous).

This classification of feeding adaptations is a "functional group" classification in that it distinguishes insect taxa that perform different functions within aquatic ecosystems with respect to processing of nutritional resource categories. The functional approach reflects both convergent (i.e., interordinal, -familial, or -generic) and parallel evolution leading to functionally similar organisms (e.g., MacMahon *et al.*

1981). As an example, Wiggins and Mackay (1979) have presented an analysis of Trichoptera functional feeding groups that indicates a reasonable functional consistency at the generic level. The functional groups described in the classification are analogous to "guilds" or sets of organisms using a particular resource class (Root 1973; MacMahon *et al.* 1981; Georgian and Wallace 1983), inasmuch as function is defined as use of similar resource classes.

SCRAPERS

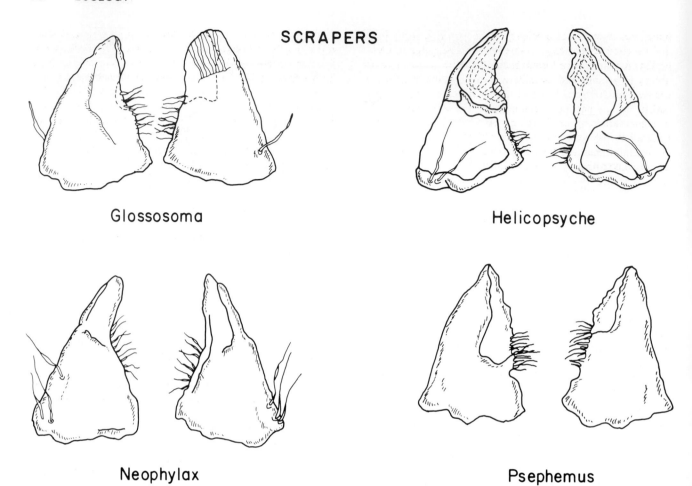

Glossosoma   Helicopsyche

Neophylax   Psephemus

Figure 6.3. Mandible structure in scraper species representing four families and two orders (Trichoptera: Glossosomatidae, Helicopsychidae, Linnephilidae; Coleoptera: Psephenidae).

Use of the functional feeding group approach is advantageous in that it enables an assessment, numerically or by standing crop biomass and more significantly by production, of the degree to which the invertebrate biota of a given aquatic system is dependent upon a particular food (nutritional) resource. It also makes more apparent the linkages that exist between food sources and insect morpho-behavioral adaptations (Cummins 1973, 1974; figs. 6.1–6.2). In an increasing number of cases, freshwater invertebrate assemblages have been analyzed according to relative functional feeding group assemblages (e.g., Cummins *et al.* 1981; Hawkins and Sedell 1981; Vannote *et al.* 1981; Minshall *et al.* 1983). These analyses support the notion that linkages exist in riparian-dominant headwater streams between coarse particulate organic matter (CPOM) and shredders, and fine particle organic matter (FPOM) and collectors, and between primary production (e.g., periphyton in mid-sized rivers) and scrapers.

The efficiency with which ingested food is converted to growth of aquatic insects (ECI, Waldbauer 1968) is dependent on the assimilation system. In general, aquatic insects would be expected to ingest foods that are most efficiently assimilated. Within a food resource category, such as CPOM

or FPOM, there may be selection for quality of food, as by shredders which select the most densely microbially colonized leaf tissue (e.g., Cummins and Klug 1979), or selection by many collectors for particle size, somewhat independent of quality (e.g., Chance 1970; Cummins and Klug 1979; Wallace and Merritt 1980; Mattingly *et al.* 1981). One of the most intriguing features of food assimilation by aquatic insects involves the roles played by microorganisms associated with food and as gut symbionts, which may produce enzymes and/or metabolites that can be used by the insects (e.g., Martin *et al.* 1980, 1981a,b). Although insect metabolism and growth are generally under thermal control (Sweeney and Vannote 1978; Vannote and Sweeney 1980; Ward 1982), there is some temperature compensation as evidenced by growth of many fall-winter species at temperatures below 5°C (Anderson and Cummins 1979) and a strong effect on food quality. The growth rate of detrital-associated microbes increases with temperature, increasing food quality by virtue of their increased biomass and activity (Cummins and Klug 1979).

Efficiency of food conversion to growth should reflect the degree of correspondence between the acquisition and assimilation systems operating together, and the food being consumed. Obligate specialists within a functional group should have maximum loss of efficiency if the match between food and function is poor (e.g., a shredder scraping algae). Generalists (or facultative forms) should be more plastic in their ability to acquire and assimilate a wider range of food resources, but presumably not with the same efficiency as a specialist, for any particular resource (e.g., a collector capable of some shredding or scraping). A survival advantage for generalists may accrue during unpredictable changes in environmental conditions when particular resources are unavailable. Predictably, such generalists should perform better than specialists in disturbed aquatic habitats.

DISTRIBUTION, ABUNDANCE, AND PRODUCTION

Distribution of an aquatic insect population is ultimately set by physical-chemical tolerance to an array of environmental factors. Within its range of occurrence, population abundance is determined by interaction of habitat and food suitability and availability. Recent experimental studies suggest that, at least under certain circumstances, competitors and/or predators may significantly influence or modify habitat or food associations and local distribution patterns of a population (e.g., Hart and Resh 1980; Peckarsky 1980; Peckarsky and Dodson 1980; Allan 1982).

Inventory methods for qualitative and quantitative sampling are reviewed in chapter 3. In lotic waters and fluctuating lentic systems such as reservoirs (Ward and Stanford 1979), the expansion and contraction of overall habitat with changing flow regimes alter aquatic insect distribution seasonally. This may give the appearance of differences in abundance, expressed as number of organisms per unit area, if care is not taken when analyzing distribution patterns (Elliott 1977; chap. 3).

Quite often, one objective of an aquatic insect study is to estimate production of one or more key species. Production is defined as the elaboration of new biomass per unit area per unit time, regardless of its fate, e.g., death by predation or adult emergence. Techniques for estimating production have been reviewed and discussed in a number of publications (e.g., Cummins 1975; Benke 1977, 1979; Waters 1977, 1979a). Most techniques require the same basic field and laboratory data. Several size-specific (usually instar or length-class) estimates of a species' density (e.g., number/m²) are made over a period of time (usually one year). These densities are converted to size-specific standing stock biomass (e.g., g/m²). Biomass can be determined by directly weighing specimens on a microbalance or by using size-mass (or volume-mass) regressions. If fresh specimens are not available for weighing, a correction for any change in biomass caused by the preservative may be necessary. Size-specific biomasses are then used to estimate production.

In a typical study, the investigator will estimate production of a single species or a few individual species. Several techniques are applicable for such estimates (Waters 1977,

1979a). Sometimes it may be desirable to estimate production of a group of related species (e.g., a taxonomic family or functional group) or the entire benthic insect community (e.g., Benke et al. 1984). The size-frequency method can be used to estimate both "group" and single species production (Waters 1977; Waters and Hokenstrom 1980). When using this method for a group of species, the researcher must be aware of complications caused by differences in the life cycles, growth rates, and maximum weights of the species in the group. Several papers discuss these problems and methods for dealing with them (Waters 1977, 1979a; Benke et al. 1984).

Size-frequency production estimates are greatly influenced by a species' life cycle. If the insect has any prolonged nongrowing stages, such as eggs, adults, or diapausing larvae or nymphs, the size-frequency calculations will produce an underestimate of annual production (Benke 1979). Therefore, size-frequency estimates must be corrected using the cohort production interval of the insect (CPI, Benke 1979). CPI is the time in days from hatching to largest larval or nymphal size. The production estimate is multiplied by 365/CPI to correct for nongrowing stages. Another advance in the use of the size-frequency method has recently been made. Krueger and Martin (1980) developed a formula to calculate confidence intervals for size-frequency production estimates. This allows critical comparisons of production between species from the same habitat and different locations.

Aquatic insect growth approaches a logarithmic function in most cases, so instantaneous growth can be approximated as $G = (\ln \bar{x}$ final or maximum mass $- \ln \bar{x}$ initial or minimum mass$) \times (1/$time interval$)$ (Waters 1977). If the initial mass is at hatching and the final at the last nymphal stadium, or at larval pupation, the estimate is for life cycle instantaneous growth rate. The growth rate of an average individual in the population can also be expressed as relative growth rate (Waldbauer 1968): $RGR = (\bar{x}$ final mass $- \bar{x}$ initial mass$) \times (1/$median mass$) \times (1/$time interval$)$, where median mass is (initial mass + final mass)/2. The resulting expression multiplied by 100 is growth as % body weight/day and is essentially equal to instantaneous growth rate for short time intervals, especially during periods of rapid growth (Cummins et al. 1973).

Another concept involved in production estimation is the expression $P/\bar{B}$, where P = annual (or cohort) production and $\bar{B}$ = mean annual (or cohort) standing stock biomass (Waters 1969a). This expression describes the rate at which biomass of a species is turning over (replacing itself), i.e., how many units of new biomass are produced per unit standing stock biomass per unit area. For most univoltine aquatic insects, this turnover ratio ranges from 3 to 6, with a mean of about five (Waters 1969a, 1979a). Bivoltine and multivoltine species have turnover ratios ≥ 6 (Waters 1969a, 1979; Benke et al. 1983). Interestingly, the $P/\bar{B}$ ratio of a species approximates the instantaneous growth rate G (see above) calculated over the entire life cycle.

Phylogenetic Relationships and Evolutionary Adaptations of Aquatic Insects

7

Vincent H. Resh
University of California, Berkeley

John O. Solem
*The Royal Norwegian Society of Sciences and Letters
Trondheim, Norway*

Evolutionary biologists generally accept the hypothesis that life originated in the sea and from there all species of plants and animals evolved. Of the animals, the insects have perhaps undergone the most remarkable adaptive radiation, and today representatives of this arthropod class can be found in almost every conceivable terrestrial and aquatic habitat.

The origin of the insects has been the subject of numerous discussions in the entomological literature and some controversy still exists as to whether or not insects are primarily or secondarily adapted to aquatic environments. That is, did insects originally evolve in freshwaters, or did they first evolve in terrestrial habitats and then secondarily occupy habitats in freshwater environments?

Ross (1965a) assumes that the preterrestrial progenitor of the myriapod-insect group (millipedes, centipedes, insects) lived in leaf litter areas along margins of pondlike environments. In this moist terrestrial environment many present-day myriapods (centipedes and millipedes) are found along with many primitive species of insects. However, Riek (1971) postulates that the original insects were aquatic and spent their whole lives in water. These primitive insects lacked the tracheal respiratory system that is typical of the modern-day terrestrial forms, and their descendents developed a tracheal system when they left the water for part of their life cycle. After tracheae developed in the terrestrial adult stage, they eventually became incorporated in the immature stages. Currently, the majority of the evidence seems to favor the terrestrial origin of both aquatic and terrestrial insects (Wooten 1972).

The Odonata and the Ephemeroptera are the only Paleoptera (primitive orders of insects whose adults cannot fold their wings) that are known to have had aquatic juveniles. The Plecoptera originated from a complex of Paleozoic protorthopteroid groups (precursors of the grasshoppers, cockroaches, crickets, etc.), many of which are known to have been terrestrial. However, even though the aquatic insects may have originated from terrestrial species, their survival and success through geologic time probably resulted from the exploitation of freshwater environments by their immature stages (fig. 7.1).

The understanding of aquatic insect evolution and phylogeny has been hampered by the relatively poor fossil record of freshwater animals. Marine animals with calcareous ($CaCO_3$) exoskeletons tend to be preserved as fossils in fairly good condition, and, as a result, our knowledge of the evolution of marine organisms is far more complete than our knowledge of the evolution of freshwater groups. One reason that few freshwater fossils exist is that the deposition of sediment occurs at a slower rate in freshwater than in marine environments. Since the chitin in the exoskeleton of aquatic insects slowly dissolves in water, insects usually decompose too rapidly for preservation as fossils (Corbet 1960).

The fossil record can be valuable in reconstructing evolutionary patterns by indicating: (1) intermediates between two higher taxonomic categories (such as families); (2) the direction of the evolutionary trend within a group; (3) the time of occurrence of evolutionary grades within phylogenetic lines; and (4) distributions of phylogenetic lines in geographical regions from which they are now extinct (Edmunds 1972). Interpretations of the fossil record must be made with great caution. For example, fossils used in evaluating the terrestrial/aquatic origin of insects were recently found to be not primitive insects at all, but merely fossilized segments of crustaceans! With so few insect fossils available and fossils absent from critical geologic periods, it is difficult to base evolutionary trends in any of the insect orders solely on the fossil record.

The lack of a complete fossil record does not preclude systematic studies of aquatic insects or the construction of phylogenetic trees. Systematists use a wide variety of evidence, including the determination of ancestral and derived character states (often referred to as *plesiomorphic* and *apomorphic* characters, respectively). The interpretation and use of these characteristics vary depending on the approach of the systematist. There are many sound arguments in favor of each of the three main approaches to systematic research: the classical phylogenetic method (in which taxonomic groupings are deduced by similarity of characteristics; e.g., fig. 7.2), the numerical taxonomic methods (in which the arrangement is based on overall similarity of all available characters), and the cladistic approach (in which the emphasis is on recency

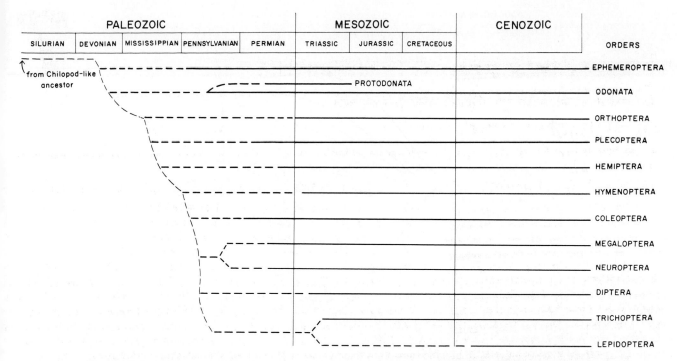

Figure 7.1. Phylogeny of the insect orders containing aquatic representatives plotted against geologic time (after Ross 1965).

of common ancestry; e.g., fig. 7.3). Many systematists use combinations of these techniques, and, for further discussions on systematic methods, the texts of Hennig (1966), Mayr (1969), Sneath and Sokal (1973), and Ross (1974) should be consulted.

The Protodonata are presumed to have been carnivores as are their immediate successors, the Odonata. The largest Protodonata, with a wingspan of 75 cm, probably had nymphs that required a number of years to reach maturity and that in their late instars may well have eaten fish (Hutchinson 1981).

The fossil record of damselflies and dragonflies is more complete than the records of other aquatic insect orders and is mainly composed of wing fragment impressions. From examining a genealogical tree of odonate phylogeny (fig. 7.4), the Anisozygoptera (a suborder of the Odonata whose members possess characteristics of each of the other suborders Anisoptera and Zygoptera; represented in fig. 7.4 by the family Epiophlebiidae) is not placed at the point of divergence of the damselflies from the dragonflies, but rather is interpreted as representing an advanced and specialized stage of zygopteran evolution that finally led to the Anisoptera (Corbet 1960). In addition, Fraser (1957) concluded that the suborder Zygoptera (in particular the family Coenagrionidae) represented the most primitive origins of all the present-day odonates. From this relationship, the evolutionary role of the Carboniferous dragonflies of the Meganeuridae, whose large size initially gave the false impression that the Anisoptera were the most primitive, is now placed in a new perspective.

The order Odonata has retained a recognizable individuality for at least 200 million years. How has this order survived for such a vast period of time without appreciable change? Corbet (1960) suggests that part of the explanation lies in the ecological niche that the adults occupy, which places a premium on aerial agility and visual acuity, but not the specialization of feeding. By retaining generalized feeding habits and living in an environment where overcrowding and competition for food are virtually absent, the adult odonates have avoided two of the most severe selective forces with which other animals must contend. Odonate nymphs may have a limited food supply or live in a habitat with severe environmental restrictions, but it is the immature stage that exhibits the greatest diversity of form and habit.

Edmunds (1972, 1975) has reviewed evolutionary trends within the Ephemeroptera, an aquatic order with a poor fossil record. Mayflies may be regarded as "flying Thysanura," since they are almost certainly derived from lepismatoid (bristletails) origins and are similar in having three caudal filaments (Edmunds and Traver 1954). Studies of mayfly evolution have had a unique orientation when compared with those of the other insect orders in that both immature and adult stages have been considered in the development of phylogenetic relationships (fig. 7.5). The reviews of Edmunds (1972, 1975) are recommended, not only as evolutionary studies of mayflies, but also for their thought-provoking comments on systematic methodology.

AQUATIC HEMIPTERA

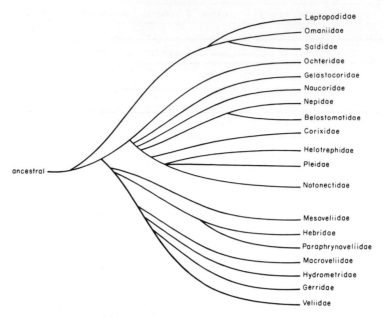

Figure 7.2. Phylogeny of aquatic Hemiptera (modified from China [1955] and Usinger [1956b] by J. T. Polhemus).

AQUATIC DIPTERA

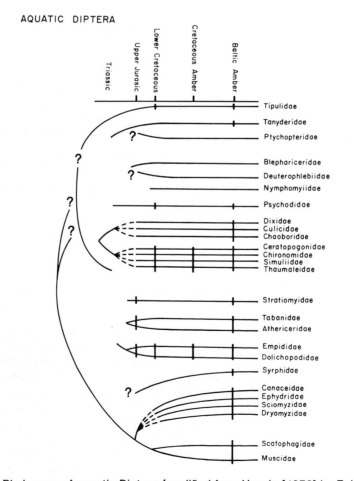

Figure 7.3. Phylogeny of aquatic Diptera (modified from Hennig [1973] by E. I. Schlinger).

ODONATA

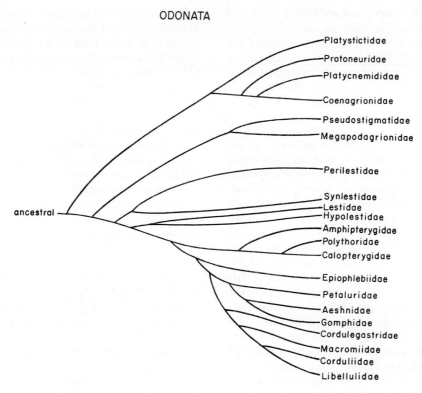

Figure 7.4. Genealogical tree of Odonata (after Fraser 1957), including extant North American and European families and Epiophlebiidae in Japan and India.

EPHEMEROPTERA

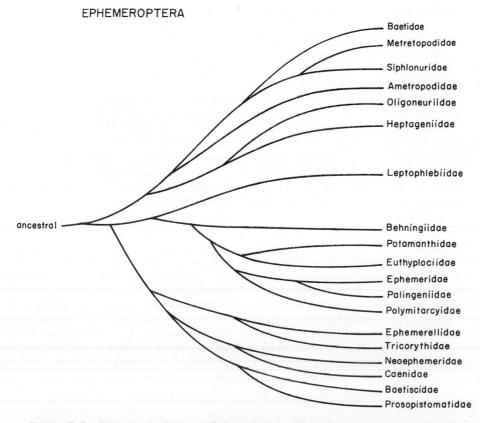

Figure 7.5. Genealogical tree of Ephemeroptera (after Edmunds, unpubl. data).

Illies (1965) reviews the evolutionary history of the Plecoptera (fig. 7.6), and discusses their ancestral relationship to the Orthoptera and the Blattoidea (which includes the cockroaches). The stonefly fossil record includes over thirty species that have been described from the different strata of the Permian to the middle Tertiary periods (Wooten 1972). Extant stonefly families are restricted to either the northern or southern hemispheres, and there is a pattern indicating that the more primitive families occur in the southern hemisphere (Illies 1965). The present distribution of stoneflies can be explained by continental drift patterns. Whereas Illies' study concentrates on worldwide distribution patterns, the study of Ross and Ricker (1971) on the winter stonefly genus *Allocapnia* provides interesting information on the distribution and dispersal routes used during the Pleistocene glaciation.

The order Trichoptera appears to have arisen from a megalopteranlike ancestor with a larval stage much like that of the present-day caddisfly family Philopotamidae (Ross 1956). The evolution of the approximately thirty families of Trichoptera is more apparent in the structure and habits of the immature stages (fig. 7.7), whereas adult structures are valuable in elucidating the evolution of genera within these families (Ross 1956). Both the Trichoptera and Lepidoptera are closely related to a third group, the Zeugloptera (considered a suborder by some authors to include those Lepidoptera with functional mandibles). In fact, certain authors have suggested that these three groups should be considered as distinct suborders within one single order (Hinton 1958b). Kristensen (1975, 1981) recently concluded that the monophyly of the Trichoptera is generally accepted and substantiated, although the Zeugloptera is cladistically a member of the Lepidoptera.

During their evolution and adaptation to aquatic environments, insects have solved the problems of respiration in many different ways. These include the use of air-tubes to obtain atmospheric oxygen, cutaneous and gill respiration, the extraction of air from plants, hemoglobin pigments, air bubbles, and plastrons. Air-tubes, which tend to restrict activity to the water surface, have evolved in the Hemiptera (Nepidae, Belostomatidae) and the Diptera (*Aedes, Culex,* and *Eristalis*). Cutaneous and gill respiration is widespread in the immature stages of most of the aquatic insect orders and these mechanisms enable the submerged species to occupy habitats below the water surface and within the substrate. Most of the species that rely on this type of respiration require well-oxygenated water, although certain species of the Chironominae that are found in the profundal regions of eutrophic lakes and may normally rely on cutaneous respiratory mechanisms survive periods of oxygen depletion through the use of hemoglobin pigments that aid in oxygen transfer. Respiration by adult aquatic insects such as the beetles and true bugs is often facilitated by the use of an air bubble, although certain species have evolved a more advanced respiratory mechanism, the plastron (a system of microhairs or papillae that hold an air film), which enables the adult to stay submerged for far longer periods than would be possible if an air bubble mechanism were used (Thorpe 1950). (For a detailed description of aquatic insect respiration, see chap. 4.)

The distribution of aquatic insects in the wide variety of habitats present in freshwater environments has led to the evolution of many types of adaptation. These occur in all stages of the insect life cycle and are characterized by their great flexibility in terms of the evolution of several different mechanisms in response to a specific selective pressure. Many unique adaptations in the egg stage are found in species that occupy temporary pool habitats. The adult females of these species may deposit egg masses close to the ground on the underside of pieces of wood or bark, thereby gaining the advantage of increased humidity and protection from the sun and wind. Certain caddisfly species that are primarily adapted for life in temporary pools have evolved mechanisms that delay or suspend development of the immature stages until soil moisture or the surface water in the basin is sufficient to sustain the newly hatched larvae (Wiggins 1973a). In addition, modifications of the gelatinous egg mass matrix protect the eggs and larvae from desiccation and freezing for periods up to seven months (Wiggins 1973a). Other mechanisms used by species inhabiting temporary pools include delaying oviposition until the pools contain water, followed by the prompt hatching and development of the eggs (Corbet 1964; Wiggins *et al.* 1980).

The time spent in the egg stage varies considerably from species to species, but the time may also vary within a single species population. Whereas all eggs of *Lestes sponsa* (Odonata) will diapause through the late summer, autumn, and winter (Macan 1973), both diapausing and nondiapausing eggs will be found in the same batch of *Diura bicaudata* (Plecoptera) eggs (Hynes 1970a). These two egg types of this latter species imply that not all nymphs hatch at the same time. Similarly, eggs of *Baetis rhodani* (Ephemeroptera) hatch at different intervals (Macan 1973). The diapause during the egg stage may enable insects to survive unfavorable periods. A staggered hatching pattern may also prevent overcrowding of newly hatched nymphs in an area that may have limited food resources. The exploding egg masses in the stonefly family Nemouridae, which disperse eggs over a wide area, and the swimming ability of newly hatched caddisfly larvae in genera such as *Phryganea, Agrypnia,* and *Triaenodes* may also aid in enhancing dispersal and preventing overcrowding.

Morphological adaptations of larvae and nymphs of freshwater insects (table 7A, based on the discussion of Hynes 1970a, 1970b; also see Hora 1930; Nielsen 1951b) are closely followed by behavioral adaptations. In running-water environments, many of the adaptations can be directly related to the current velocity and the continuous struggle of the organisms to cling tightly to the substrate. There are, however, species that actively exhibit what Waters (1972) has termed *behavioral drift,* in which individuals enter into the water column and move downstream from their original points of attachment during certain well-defined periods of their daily cycle. In standing water, current does not force animals into the open water, but insects such as *Chaoborus* sp. (Diptera) and many Coleoptera and Hemiptera actively move through the water column in these environments. (For a detailed description of aquatic insect behavior, see chap. 5.)

PLECOPTERA

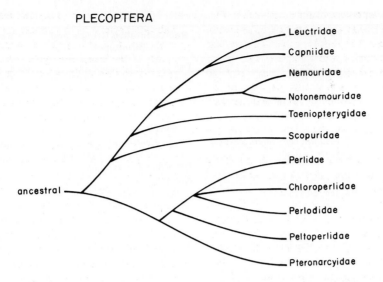

Figure 7.6. Genealogical tree of Plecoptera (after Illies 1965).

TRICHOPTERA

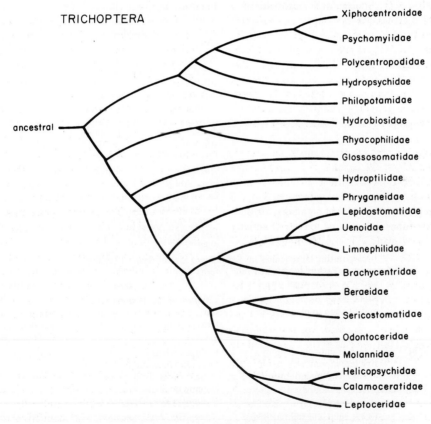

Figure 7.7. Genealogical tree of Trichoptera (after Ross 1967b).

Table 7A. Morphological adaptations of aquatic insects to running-water environments.

Adaptation	Significance	Representative Groups and Structures	Exceptions or Comments
Flattening of body surface	Allows species to live on top of flattened stones in the slow-current boundary layer; allows them to crawl through closely compacted substrate	Psephenidae (Coleoptera); *Epeorus, Rhithrogena* (Ephemeroptera); Gomphidae, Libellulidae (Odonata); *Molanna, Glossosoma, Ceraclea ancylus* (Trichoptera)	Many stream inhabitants that do not live on exposed surfaces are also flattened
Streamlining	A fusiform body offers least resistance to fluids	*Baetis, Centroptilum* (Ephemeroptera); *Simulium* (Diptera); Dytiscidae (Coleoptera)	Except in the Coleoptera, this body shape is relatively rare
Reduction of projecting structures	Projecting structures increase water resistance	Gills of *Baetis* and loss of central cerci in many mayflies (Ephemeroptera)	*Atherix* (Diptera), Corydalidae (Megaloptera), and Gyrinidae have large lateral projections; gills of *Baetis* may reflect respiratory physiology
Suckers	Provide attachment to smooth surfaces	Blephariceridae (Diptera); some Dytiscidae (Coleoptera)	Rare in stream animals; if surfaces are irregular due to moss, algae, etc., suckers are inefficient
Friction pads and marginal contact with substrate	Close contact with substrate increases frictional resistance and reduces chances of being dislodged by current	*Psephenus* (Coleoptera); *Dicercomyzon, Ephemerella doddsi, Rhithrogena* (Ephemeroptera)	Marginal contact devices are not confined to insects living in the torrential parts of streams
Hooks and grapples	Attachment to rough areas of substrate	Elmidae, Dryopidae (Coleoptera); Rhyacophilidae (Trichoptera); Corydalidae (Megaloptera)	Modified structures include tarsal claws, clawlike legs, and posterior prolegs
Small size	Small sizes permit utilization of the slow-current boundary layer on top of stones	Water mites (Hydracarina) in streams are never as large as still-water Hydracarina and lack the swimming hairs that are found in these latter water mites; large hydrophilids and dytiscids (Coleoptera) inhabit still water; nearly all beetles in fast water are small	Stream animals in other groups are not noticeably smaller than still-water relatives
Silk and sticky secretions	Allows attachment to stones in swift current	*Rheotanytarsus*, Orthocladiinae, *Simulium* (Diptera); Psychomyiidae, Hydropsychidae, Leptoceridae (Trichoptera); *Paragyractis* (Lepidoptera); Plecoptera and Ephemeroptera eggs	Even free-living caddisflies use silk attachments as do the cased species when they molt and pupate
Ballast	Incorporating large stones in cases makes the insects heavier and less easily swept away	*Goera, Stenophylax* (Trichoptera)	This is at least partially due to these sized particles being the only ones available for case building
Attachment claws and dorsal processes	Stout claws aid in attachment and fixation to plants	Calopterygidae (Odonata); some *Taeniopteryx* (Plecoptera); *Ephemerella* (Ephemeroptera)	Most animals which live in vegetation show no particular adaptations that distinguish them from still-water species in vegetation
Reduction in powers of flight	A loss of individuals from a restricted habitat may result in smaller populations in following generations	Reduced wings of stoneflies *Allocapnia* (Plecoptera); loss of hind wings in Elmidae (Coleoptera); wingless females of *Dolophiloides* (Trichoptera)	Reduced flight powers may be a disadvantage because it reduces dispersal ability
Hairy bodies	Keeps sand and soil particles away while burrowing in substrate	*Hexagenia, Potamanthus* (Ephemeroptera)	Permits open spaces for water to flow over body

Of the holometabolous insects, aquatic pupae are found in nearly all species of Trichoptera (cf. Anderson 1967), aquatic Lepidoptera, and Diptera. Terrestrial pupae are found in all Megaloptera and aquatic Neuroptera, while the aquatic Coleoptera have species of both types. A terrestrial pupa is by far the most common condition among the aquatic beetles, and aquatic pupae are found only in *Donacia, Neohaemonia,* and *Macroplea* of the Chrysomelidae, *Lissorhoptrus* of the Curculionidae, *Psephenoides* of the Psephenidae, and *Noterus* of the Noteridae. As far as is known, of all aquatic beetles, only the pupae of species in the European genus *Psephenoides* are surrounded with water and could be described as truly aquatic since the other taxa mentioned pupate in air-filled cocoons (Leech and Chandler 1956).

The different climatic zones in which aquatic insects exist expose these species to a variety of abiotic factors, the most pronounced being temperature, which varies considerably on a yearly basis (although generally less than terrestrial temperatures) within the different geographical regions of the world. Temperature fluctuations greatly affect the poikilothermous (cold-blooded) insects. Possibly due to the relatively constant temperature, more types of emergence patterns are seen in the tropical regions of the world than in either the arctic or temperate zones. In permanent water bodies of the tropics, many insects have continuous emergence throughout the year (Corbet 1964; McElravy *et al.* 1982). This occurs primarily in areas that are located near the equator and undergo small fluctuations in temperature. However, continuous emergence has recently been demonstrated also in constant low-temperature mountain brooks where two species of caddisflies, *Philopotamus ludificatus* and *Wormaldia copiosa* (Philopotamidae), have acyclic development and show continuous emergence (Malicky 1980).

Several species also show a rhythmic emergence pattern, and lunar emergence rhythms have been recognized in several species of aquatic insects that live in tropical climates (Tjonneland 1960; Corbet 1964). The peak of emergence pattern coincides with different lunar phases depending on the species. The chironomid *Tanytarsus balteatus* has an emergence pattern that follows the phases of the new moon (Corbet 1964), whereas other species may have two emergence peaks where the minimum activity occurs during the new and full moon phases (Tjonneland 1960).

In temperate regions, the lunar periodicity in emergence patterns is exemplified by the chironomid *Clunio marinus* (Neumann 1976). This midge larva lives in the intertidal zone of sandy seashores and emergence is restricted to a few days at the time of the new and full moon (Caspers 1951). The sporadic pattern, in which emergence appears to occur at irregular intervals and seemingly without any environmental cues, seems to be present in only a few aquatic insects (Corbet 1964).

Distinct seasonal emergence is typical of insects living at high latitudes where regular changes in temperature occur. However, wet and dry season climatic patterns may also lead to seasonal emergence patterns as has been demonstrated in the tropics (Corbet 1964). As one moves from the tropics to higher latitudes, emergence periods become increasingly shorter, with the extreme condition occurring in the arctic regions where many species have adapted to cycles in which emergence is limited to a few days out of the entire year.

The most widespread rhythm exhibited by aquatic insects is the diel pattern (Remmert 1962), which may influence initial hatching from the egg, feeding behavior of the immature stages, emergence, flight activity, oviposition, and other life history features. The significance of diel emergence patterns is that in a short-lived adult insect, such as a mayfly or caddisfly, simultaneous emergence and swarming of males and females help to ensure the continuity of the population through the next generation.

There are several excellent reviews of the biology of aquatic insects in the above orders (Odonata: Corbet 1980; Ephemeroptera: Brittain 1982; Plecoptera: Hynes 1976; Trichoptera: Mackay and Wiggins 1979).

The Hemiptera (fig. 7.2), Diptera (fig. 7.3), and Coleoptera are large orders that contain representative aquatic species in several different families. In all these groups the invasion into aquatic habitats probably occurred independently several different times. This polyphyletic pattern is especially true in the Coleoptera, the largest order of insects.

The phylogenetic studies of the aquatic insect orders mentioned above (Fraser 1957; Edmunds 1972, 1975; etc.), along with studies of more specialized groups such as Brundin's (1966) study of the Chironomidae, have greatly increased our knowledge of animal dispersal patterns. In discussing the present-day distribution of all these groups, the question of dispersal mechanisms is logically raised. Active dispersal is accomplished by adult females, although species can also be dispersed passively as windblown eggs or by birds. The short adult life span of mayflies, stoneflies, and caddisflies would prevent long dispersal flights, but a windblown egg mass that could withstand desiccation for long periods would certainly aid in widespread distribution. Examination of the present-day distribution of aquatic insect species suggests that the question of how the species initially arrived in the habitat is less interesting than what are the ecological conditions that have enabled it to survive there.

LIFE CYCLE ADAPTATIONS

Of the major groups of freshwater insects, almost all are regularly represented throughout the world. However, several groups only occur in running-water habitats and many others reach their maximum development and diversity there. Hynes (1970a) suggests that this may be a consequence of the permanence of streams and rivers when compared with the longevity of most lake and pond habitats. Many river systems have been in continuous existence for long periods of geologic time, whereas lakes persist for relatively short periods and have had little opportunity to develop a *purely* lacustrine fauna. Lakes are certainly capable of producing evolutionary change as shown in the endemic species that occupy such ancient lakes as Lake Baikal in Russia. In time, however, all lakes fill in and disappear; their faunas perish (Wetzel 1975). River faunas have a much greater chance for continuity and development, and although rivers and river systems may change, they rarely disappear entirely. They are not "evolutionary traps" and, because of this, many of the most primitive species of freshwater organisms are primarily found in lotic environments (Hynes 1970a).

In addition, most primitive species of aquatic insects are found in lotic habitats because the groups probably first entered aquatic habitats under lotic conditions where respiration for larvae and resistance to desiccation for adults were most propitious. These factors seem to apply for the Plecoptera, Ephemeroptera, Odonata, Trichoptera, and Chironomidae. Thus, the absence of primitive members of these groups from lentic habitats could be explained by the hypothesis that they never lived there (G. B. Wiggins, pers. comm.). Wiggins *et al.* (1980) give support to this speculation in that insects that occur in temporary pools are primarily derivative groups because the specialized features required to sustain dry periods arose from permanent lentic-dwelling species and these, in turn, arose from lotic species.

Aquatic insects exhibit the same versatility as terrestrial insects in their ability to use a wide variety of food sources (see chap. 6). In pre-Tertiary times, the main food items available to the primitive aquatic insects probably were floating and encrusting algae, plant debris (with its associated decomposing microorganisms), and animals, including smaller insects, other invertebrates, and fish fry (Wooten 1972). As small predators feeding on primary consumers, these early aquatic insects probably had few competitors. In time, they developed morphological and behavioral adaptations in response to increased competition and other selective pressures. Eventually, these adaptations were such that the aquatic insects were able to exploit a wider range of food sources and develop into the variety of macro- and micro-feeders that operate from deep within the substrate to the top of the surface film (Wooten 1972).

Very few aquatic insects have adapted to a completely submerged life cycle (see Plecoptera exception, Jewett 1963). At one time or another, nearly all species spend a period in the terrestrial habitat. A major problem in being submerged for even part of the life cycle is respiration, since, to respire while submerged, the insect must receive oxygen from the surrounding aquatic environment (see chap. 4). Many species have evolved respiratory systems that function in well-aerated water but have not adapted survival mechanisms for low oxygen concentrations. In regard to the latter, there is a major difference between running- and standing-water environments. Normally, streams have higher oxygen concentrations due to turbulence than do either ponds or lakes. This is certainly a factor in the distribution of Plecoptera and most species of Ephemeroptera and Trichoptera, groups that have their maximum development in running water. Oxygen saturation and temperature are integrally related, and the cooler temperatures that often prevail in running water aid in survival. In high-altitude (or latitude) lakes where the water is cold and highly oxygenated at all times, the distinction between standing- and running-water faunas becomes less clear.

In addition to the adaptations in the immature and adult stages of aquatic insects, the life cycles often exhibit unique phenological patterns. Aquatic insect populations may produce single or multiple generations during a year or, in some species, greater than a year. In addition, life cycle completion time may vary greatly throughout the range of a species and even between populations of the same species in the upper and lower reaches of the same stream (e.g., Mackay 1979).

The presence of a diapause in the egg stage, or the formation of a quiescent prepupa, is an important modification that enables the insect to conserve energy or survive unfavorable conditions. Certain life history patterns in aquatic insects may have a definite selective advantage, particularly in maximizing the efficient use of food sources that have only seasonal availability. An example of this can be seen in the leptocerid caddisflies of the genus *Ceraclea* that feed on freshwater sponge. Since the sponge is available only certain times of the year (only the nonedible gemmules are present during the winter months), life cycles have been modified and alternative food sources are used (Resh 1976a). The significance of life cycle flexibility in the presence of coexisting, systematically related species has yet to be fully understood, but the ability of these species to share available resources presents interesting implications for habitat partitioning and community evolution. This and many other fascinating aspects of aquatic insect evolution provide fertile areas for future research.

PROSPECTS FOR FUTURE RESEARCH

As Ross (1974) points out, the future of systematic research can best be predicted by examining the future of biology. This is especially true in considering evolutionary studies of aquatic insects. Thousands of species of aquatic insects have been described. However, in all groups, and particularly in the holometabolous orders, the immature stages are poorly known. Since it is the larval stages that are usually collected by aquatic entomologists, the lack of association of the immature and the taxonomically named adult stage has limited the precision of many studies in aquatic ecology. Associations between immature and adult stages are needed, and they can be made by a variety of rearing techniques (see chap. 3, especially table 3D for rearing method references). Association of the egg and pupal stages with the adult is also important in elucidating phylogenetic relationships (Wiggins 1966; Koss 1970). This is an area of research in which all students of aquatic entomology can make valuable contributions since these rearing techniques do not require elaborate equipment and they provide definitive associations that eventually can be used in constructing taxonomic keys.

Studies of systematically related, coexisting species often reveal both obvious and subtle mechanisms of resource partitioning and ecological segregation (e.g., Cummins 1964; Grant and Mackay 1969; Mackay 1972). Similarly, studies of water quality tolerances of congeneric species have been useful in developing the important concept of biological indicators of environmental quality (e.g., Resh and Unzicker 1975).

In almost all cases, evolutionary relationships of aquatic insects have been based on studies of morphological structures and this has proven to be a useful way of analyzing systematically related groups. However, species are often assigned to different higher taxa because of conflicting opinions on the validity of the various morphological characteristics. In these cases, behavioral studies may be valuable. For instance, behavior patterns of nymphs of two European species of the mayfly genus *Leptophlebia* (Solem 1973) agree with that reported for a North American *Leptophlebia* (Hayden and Clifford 1974). If the diversity of rhythms is comparable at the generic level, behavioral studies could provide valuable information on the higher classification of the aquatic insects. By combining behavior and other alternative approaches to descriptive systematics, classification and taxonomy may soon be used extensively in predicting ecological aspects of systematically related species.

General Classification and Key to the Orders of Aquatic and Semiaquatic Insects

8

Howell V. Daly
University of California, Berkeley

GENERAL CLASSIFICATION

Although only three percent of the insect species are aquatic or semiaquatic, that is, with one or more life stages living in or closely associated with aquatic habitats, representatives may be found in about half (13) of all the insect orders. Since many species are aquatic only during their immature stages, the study of aquatic insects involves both terrestrial and aquatic or semiaquatic life forms.

Insects are named according to strict international rules of nomenclature that apply to all animals. The hierarchical system is exemplified by the classification of a species of burrowing mayfly below:

Taxon	Name
Kingdom	Animalia
Phylum	Arthropoda
Class	Insecta
Subclass	Pterygota
Infraclass	Paleoptera
Order	Ephemeroptera
Superfamily	Ephemeroidea
Family	Ephemeridae
Subfamily	Ephemerinae
Genus	*Hexagenia*
Subgenus	*(Hexagenia)*
Species	*limbata*
Author	(Jean G. A. Serville)

Each species is assigned a specific name and placed in a genus with related species. The combination of Latin or Latinized generic and specific names is unique for each species of insect and is printed in italics with the generic name capitalized, e.g., *Hexagenia limbata* (Serville). The name of the first person to publish a description of and assign a specific name to the insect is cited after the name. If, as in this case, the author initially placed the species in another genus, the author's name is enclosed in parentheses. A more detailed coverage of the principles of classification is given in Mayr (1969).

A named group of insects at any level is referred to as a *taxon* (plural, taxa)—a species or group of species, a genus or group of genera, etc. One or more genera that share certain common characteristics are placed in a *tribe* designated by the ending -ini. Tribes are grouped in subfamilies (-inae), subfamilies in *families* (-idae) and phylogenetically related families are grouped in superfamilies (-oidea). Related superfamilies and their families are included in an *order*. The names of most insect orders have the ending "-ptera," from the Greek word meaning wing, but a few such as Collembola (springtails) and Odonata (dragonflies and damselflies) simply end with "-a". Finally, all insect orders are included in the class Insecta, sometimes referred to as Hexapoda (six legs).

Although scientific names of taxa may be hard to remember and difficult to pronounce, they eliminate the confusion that often surrounds common names. The mayfly, *Hexagenia limbata,* is also commonly known as the Michigan caddis, fishfly, sandfly, and Great Olive-Winged Drake. Entomologists and knowledgable anglers use caddis or caddisflies to refer to the order Trichoptera, fishflies for certain Megaloptera, and sandflies for certain Diptera. Even the angler's "Drake" applies to mayflies belonging to at least six genera and three families.

Below is a list of orders that have at least some aquatic or semiaquatic species. Orders with almost all species having one or more aquatic stages are marked by an asterisk (*), followed by the common names where appropriate.

Class Insecta (Insects)
  Subclass Apterygota
      Order Collembola (Springtails)
  Subclass Pterygota
    Infraclass Paleoptera
      Order Ephemeroptera* (Mayflies)
      Order Odonata* (Dragonflies and damselflies)
    Infraclass Neoptera
      Division Exopterygota
        Order Orthoptera (Grasshoppers and their allies)
        Order Plecoptera* (Stoneflies)
        Order Hemiptera (True bugs, leaf hoppers, etc.)

Division Endopterygota
    Order Neuroptera (Spongillaflies)
    Order Megaloptera* (Dobsonflies, fishflies, and al-
       derflies)
    Order Trichoptera* (Caddisflies)
    Order Lepidoptera (Moths)
    Order Coleoptera (Beetles)
    Order Diptera (Flies)
    Order Hymenoptera (Wasps)

INSECT LIFE HISTORIES

Identification of insects is complicated by the existence of several distinctive forms during the life cycle. The change in structure and form during the life of an insect is called *metamorphosis.*

To increase in size or change form, an insect periodically sheds (or casts) its rigid exoskeleton, a process called *molting.* A portion of the old cuticle is digested and absorbed, while a new cuticle is deposited beneath. The outer part of the old cuticle is loosened and finally split, beginning at the top of the head and thorax. The brief act of casting or shedding the old skin is termed *ecdysis.* The discarded skin, termed the *exuviae,* is known as the "shuck" by anglers.

The act of ecdysis provides a useful means for subdividing an insect's life history. The form of an insect between ecdyses is called an *instar,* and the period of time between ecdyses is termed the *stadium.* After hatching from the egg, the insect is a first instar in the first stadium; after the initial ecdysis, the second instar is in the second stadium, etc. Most insects have four to six instars, but there may be fifteen to thirty or more in some mayflies, dragonflies, and stoneflies. The adult insect or *imago* is the imaginal instar, is distinguished by functional external reproductive organs, and is usually winged.

The Collembola, an order of tiny, primitive insects that never evolved wings, has some semiaquatic species. They change little in form after hatching except to become larger as they pass through the immature instars. After the reproductive organs become functional, the adults may continue to molt. This type of life history, with no change in body form, is termed *ametabolous* metamorphosis (meaning without change).

Among the winged insects, two major types can be recognized: (1) the Exopterygota, with wings developing externally as wing pads in the immatures, and (2) the Endopterygota, with wings developing internally. In the Exopterygota the rudimentary wings are recognizable as stiff, immovable pads on the thorax, and well-developed legs, antennae, and compound eyes are visible. Wing development of the immatures culminates when the wings become functional after the last ecdysis.

Two distinct groups may be distinguished within the Exopterygota, the *paurometabolous* and *hemimetabolous* insects. The paurometabolous insects may be distinguished by the striking similarity between the adult form and the immature, known as a nymph. Subtle changes in general shape and body proportions occur gradually with each instar; hence, this type of metamorphosis is often termed gradual. Adults and nymphs live in the same habitat and feed similarly.

Two paurometabolous orders are aquatic or semiaquatic. In the order Orthoptera, species of the family Tridactylidae (pygmy mole crickets) are associated with wet habitats throughout their lives. Many families of the order Hemiptera are found near or in water as both nymphs and adults.

The *hemimetabolous* insects, or those undergoing simple or incomplete metamorphosis, include all species of the orders Odonata, Ephemeroptera, and Plecoptera. The aquatic immatures of these orders, termed *naiads* by some workers, have respiratory gills and are otherwise modified for life under water, whereas the adults are terrestrial (one plecopteran species has aquatic adults). The immatures of the hemimetabolous insects resemble the adult in general appearance less than in paurometabolous forms, and usually have different feeding habits and occupy different habitats than the adults (fig. 8.1B). The change in appearance from naiad to adult is generally much greater than in the other exopterygotes.

The Ephemeroptera are unique among all winged insects in having two winged instars. The first winged instar, called the *subimago,* or dun by the angler, emerges from the water. Usually within 24 hours, the insect molts again to the *imago,* or spinner in angler terminology. Reproduction is usually restricted to the imaginal or last instar.

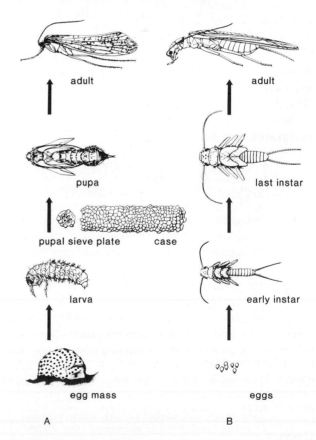

Figure 8.1. Examples of life stages in aquatic insects: *A.* holometabolous metamorphosis of a caddisfly (Trichoptera); *B.* hemimetabolous metamorphosis of a stonefly (Plecoptera). (Figure by Bonnie Hall.)

The second major group of winged insects, the endopterygotes (largely holometabolous), contain the largest number of aquatic or semiaquatic species. After hatching, the early instars are totally unlike the adult. There is no external evidence of the wings, which develop internally as tissue buds. The legs and antennae may be reduced or missing entirely, and the eyes are simple ocelli as opposed to the compound eyes of adults. The insect is wormlike and called a *larva* (caterpillar [Lepidoptera]; maggot [Diptera]; or wiggler [mosquito]). Once fully grown, the larva transforms to a nonfeeding, usually less active instar, the *pupa*. The wings, legs, antennae, and compound eyes of the adult are formed during the pupal stage, but are not functional since further development is necessary before the pupa transforms into the winged adult. This type of life cycle is termed *holometabolous* metamorphosis (meaning complete change; fig. 8.1A).

Seven orders of endopterygotes have at least some aquatic or semiaquatic species, primarily during the immature stages: Megaloptera, Neuroptera (only the family Sisyridae or spongillaflies are aquatic), Trichoptera, Lepidoptera (certain moth families), Hymenoptera (some parasitic wasps have aquatic hosts), Coleoptera (many families), and Diptera (many families). Terminal instar aquatic larvae of Megaloptera, Neuroptera, and most Coleoptera pupate in terrestrial sites whereas the other orders remain in the water. The pupae of Trichoptera, Megaloptera, Neuroptera (Sisyridae), and the dipterans, Culicidae (mosquitoes) and Chironomidae (midges), are fairly active. Adults of all orders return near to, or actually reenter, the water to lay their eggs. However, only species of aquatic Coleoptera regularly spend their adult life in water.

Taxonomic Keys

A key is simply an aid for identifying different kinds of organisms. Once you are familiar with the higher taxa, most can be recognized at a glance. A dichotomous key consists of numbered, paired statements of contrasting characteristics. In using a key, one reads the first couplet and decides which statement best describes the specimen at hand. Each statement indicates the number of the next couplet to be read. Couplet by couplet, the number of possible choices is reduced until the search terminates with the name of a taxon.

If the specimen does not exactly match either statement, try both possible routes to an identification. It usually becomes evident that a wrong choice was made when the specimen clearly lacks the features mentioned in both statements of subsequent couplets. To confirm a tentative identification, consult texts describing or illustrating the taxon. Of course, if possible, specimens already identified should be examined. (Locations of good reference collections of aquatic specimens are listed at the end of the chapter.)

KEY TO THE ORDERS OF AQUATIC INSECTS

The following key is designed to identify the orders of all stages of insects treated in this text. The key is a modification of several previous keys, especially that of Bentinck (1956). In the great majority of cases, insects normally found living on the water surface or submerged are included in the key. Insects found at the water's edge, flying near water, or trapped in the surface film may be mainly terrestrial in habit. If the characters of such insects do not correspond with the choices in the key, then a key to all orders of insects should be consulted (e.g., Daly *et al.* 1978; Borror *et al.* 1981).

Immatures and Adults

1.	Wings or wing pads present, fore wings sometimes hard and shell-like, concealing hind wings; legs present (figs. 2.5, 10.1, 10.81, 11.1, 14.4, 19.97, 21.98)	2
1'.	Wings or wing pads entirely absent; legs present or absent (figs. 15.5, 16.23, 18.4, 21.1)	27
2(1).	Wings fully developed, usually conspicuous and movable (figs. 10.81, 14.1, 15.8–15.9, 21.98). Adults	3
2'.	Wings developing in fixed wing pads (figs. 10.1, 11.12, 13.1, 14.4). Nymphs and pupae	15
3(2).	Fore wings leathery or hard, at least in the basal (nearest the body) half (figs. 12.3, 14.1, 19.97)	4
3'.	Wings entirely membranous (figs. 10.81, 15.8, 16.34, 18.36)	6
4(3).	Chewing mouthparts, mandibles visible (fig. 19.229)	5
4'.	Sucking mouthparts united in a jointed beak, mandibles concealed (figs. 14.1–14.3)	*Hemiptera*
5(4).	Fore wings leathery, veins distinct; femora of hind legs greatly enlarged, suited for jumping (fig. 12.3)	*Orthoptera*
5'.	Fore wings hard (called elytra), veins indistinct (figs. 19.97–19.98); hind legs suited for walking or swimming (figs. 19.99–19.101)	*Coleoptera*
6(3').	One pair of wings (figs. 21.98–21.122)	7
6'.	Two pairs of wings (figs. 10.81, 15.8, 16.34, 18.38)	8

7(6).   Abdomen ending in 2 or 3 long filaments; mouthparts inconspicuous; thorax
           without halteres (fig. 10.81) .... ***Ephemeroptera*** (in part)

7'.   Abdomen without conspicuous filaments (figs. 21.98–21.122); mouthparts well
           developed, forming a proboscis (figs. 21.107–21.108); thorax with halteres (fig.
           21.99) .... ***Diptera***

8(6').   Wings covered with scales or hairs, obscuring venation (figs. 8.1A, 16.112,
           18.38–18.43) 9

8'.   Wings bare or with minute hairs, venation clearly visible (figs. 10.81, 11.1–11.2,
           15.8–15.9) 10

9(8).   Wings with scales (figs. 18.38–18.43); mouthparts usually fitted with a coiled
           sucking tube (fig. 18.28) .... ***Lepidoptera***

9'.   Wings with hairs (figs. 8.1A, 16.112); mouthparts without a coiled sucking tube
           (fig. 16.32) .... ***Trichoptera***

10(8').   Antennae short, bristlelike, and inconspicuous (figs. 10.81, 11.3–11.4) 11

10'.   Antennae of various shapes, conspicuous, not bristlelike (figs. 13.1, 15.8, 15.52,
           20.20) 12

11(10).   Abdomen ending in 2 or 3 long filaments; hind wings much smaller than fore wings
           (fig. 10.81) .... ***Ephemeroptera*** (in part)

11'.   Abdomen without long filaments; wings about equal in size (figs. 11.1–11.2) .... ***Odonata***

12(10').   Tarsi 2- or 3-segmented; abdomen ending with 2 conspicuous cerci (reduced in
           some adult Nemouridae) (fig. 13.1) .... ***Plecoptera***

12'.   Tarsi 5-segmented (except in a few Hymenoptera, with 3 [fig. 20.11]); abdomen
           without conspicuous appendages (figs. 15.8–15.9, 20.13) 13

13(12').   Abdomen broadly joined to thorax (figs. 15.8–15.9); front margin of fore wing in
           basal half with many small veins perpendicular to edge; wings with more than
           20 closed cells (figs. 15.32–15.35, 15.48–15.49) 14

13'.   Abdomen with narrow constriction at junction with the thorax (fig. 20.13);
           marginal veins in basal half of fore wing parallel to leading edge; wings with
           fewer than 20 closed cells (figs. 20.19–20.20); aquatic forms are very small,
           usually less than 3 mm long (figs. 20.13, 20.16) .... ***Hymenoptera***

14(13).   Hind wings folded or pleated lengthwise (figs. 15.8–15.9) .... ***Megaloptera***

14'.   Hind wings not folded (fig. 15.52) .... ***Neuroptera***

15(2').   Active insects with legs freely movable; not in cocoons or capsulelike cases (figs.
           10.1, 11.12, 11.21, 13.1, 14.4). Nymphs or naiads 16

15'.   Usually inactive insects, "mummylike" with appendages drawn up and free or
           fused to body (figs. 15.6–15.7, 16.30, 20.10); sometimes in cocoons or sealed in
           capsulelike cases or puparia (figs. 18.7, 24.27). Pupae 20

16(15).   Chewing mouthparts with mandibles distinct (figs. 10.2, 11.3) 17

16'.   Sucking mouthparts united in a jointed beak with mandibles concealed (fig. 14.3) .... ***Hemiptera***

17(16).   Hind legs suited for jumping, hind femora greatly enlarged; abdomen without long
           cerci; found in moist places and only temporarily in water (fig. 12.2) .... ***Orthoptera***

17'.   Hind legs suited for crawling, hind femora not greatly enlarged, approximately the
           same size as front and middle femora (figs. 10.1, 11.12); abdomen with or
           without conspicuous terminal appendages; usually submerged, truly aquatic 18

18(17').   Labium (lower lip) masklike, extendable into a scooplike structure longer than
           head (figs. 11.34, 11.12, 11.21) .... ***Odonata***

18'.   Labium normal, smaller than head, not large and masklike (figs. 2.3, 10.2, 13.8) 19

19(18').   Tarsi with one claw (fig. 10.1); abdomen ending in 3 long filaments, less commonly
           with 2 filaments; gills located on sides of abdomen, may be platelike,
           filamentous, or feathery (figs. 10.1, 10.26–10.30) .... ***Ephemeroptera***

19'.   Tarsi with 2 claws (fig. 13.1); abdomen ending in only 2 filaments; gills present,
           fingerlike and located at base of mouthparts (inconspicuous), head, or legs, or on
           thorax or abdomen (figs. 2.1, 13.1, 13.4a–13.4d) .... ***Plecoptera***

20(15'). Appendages free, distinct, not fused to body (termed *exarate* pupae) (figs. 15.6, 16.30, 20.10, 23.2, 24.27) 21

20'.   Appendages fused to body or concealed in hardened capsule (termed *obtect* and *coarctate* pupae, respectively) (fig. 18.7) 26

21(20). Abdomen broadly joined to thorax (figs. 15.6–15.7, 16.30) 22

21'.   Abdomen with constriction where joined to thorax (fig. 20.10) .... *Hymenoptera*

22(21). One pair of wing pads (figs. 23.2, 24.27–24.28) .... *Diptera*

22'.   Two pairs of wing pads (figs. 15.6–15.7, 16.30) 23

23(22'). Pads of fore wings thickened; antennae usually 11-segmented or less .... *Coleoptera*

23'.   Pads of fore wings not thickened; antennae of 12 or more segments (figs. 15.6–15.7, 16.30) 24

24(23'). Mandibles stout, not crossing each other; pupae terrestrial (near water's edge), not normally submerged (figs. 15.6–15.7, 15.47) 25

24'.   Mandibles curved, projecting forward and usually crossing each other (figs. 16.89, 16.91); pupae usually submerged in water (may be in damp areas of overhanging stream banks); always in cases (figs. 8.1A, 16.30) .... *Trichoptera*

25(24). Smaller, 10 mm or less in length; pupae in double-walled, meshlike cocoons in sheltered places (fig. 15.47) .... *Neuroptera*

25'.   Larger, 12 mm or more; pupae in chambers in soil or rotten wood, without cocoons (figs. 15.6–15.7) .... *Megaloptera*

26(20'). Appendages visible on surface of pupa; without obvious breathing tubes or gills; two pairs of wing pads present (hind wings mostly concealed beneath fore wings) (figs. 18.1d, 18.7) .... *Lepidoptera*

26'.   Appendages visible or entirely concealed in barrel-shaped capsule; if appendages visible, then usually with projecting respiratory organs (figs. 24.27–24.28) or paired, dorsal, prothoracic breathing tubes (fig. 23.2); sometimes with gills at the abdominal tip; one pair of wing pads .... *Diptera*

27(1'). Abdomen with 6 or fewer segments and with a ventral tube; minute, 5 mm or less (fig. 9.1) .... *Collembola*

27'.   Abdomen with more than 6 segments and without a ventral tube; usually larger than 5 mm (figs. 15.5, 18.4, 21.1, 19.71) 28

28(27'). Three pairs of jointed legs present on thorax (figs. 15.5, 18.4, 19.74) 29

28'.   True legs absent; fleshy, leglike protuberances or prolegs may be present on thorax, but fewer than three pairs and not jointed (figs. 21.1–21.3, 21.38–21.46) 34

29(28). Middle and hind legs long and slender, extending considerably beyond the abdomen; compound eyes present (wingless Gerridae) .... *Hemiptera*

29'.   Legs not longer than the abdomen; compound eyes absent (figs. 15.5, 18.4, 19.195) 30

30(29'). Abdomen with at least two pairs of ventral, fleshy, leglike protuberances tipped with tiny hooks (prolegs with crochets) (figs. 18.4–18.6) .... *Lepidoptera*

30'.   Abdomen without leglike protuberances, or, if present, not tipped with tiny hooks (figs. 15.5, 16.23, 16.39, 19.231) 31

31(30'). Last abdominal segment with lateral appendages bearing hooks (anal hooks) (figs. 16.39, 16.42), antennae 1-segmented, inconspicuous; gills, if present, seldom confined to lateral margins of body; larvae free-living or in cases made of sand grains and/or bits of plant matter (figs. 16.1–16.22) .... *Trichoptera*

31'.   Last abdominal segment without anal hooks; or, if anal hooks present, antennae of more than 1 segment, and gill insertions lateral (figs. 15.22–15.23, 19.71, 19.131) 32

32(31'). Mandibles and maxillae united at each side to form long, straight or slightly recurved, threadlike suctorial tubes; laterally inserted, segmented gills folded beneath abdomen; small, 10 mm or less, and found in or on freshwater sponges (fig. 15.43) .... *Neuroptera*

32′.   Mandibles not united with maxillae (figs. 15.17, 19.133); if mandibles suctorial, then strongly curved; gills seldom segmented and not folded beneath abdomen (figs. 15.22–15.23, 19.52, 19.46); not associated with sponges 33

33(32′).   Abdomen with 7 or 8 pairs of lateral filaments or gills, arranged 1 pair on each segment (figs. 15.5, 15.17, 15.22–15.23); segment 9 with hooked lateral appendages (anal hooks) (figs. 15.22–15.23) or a single, medial, caudal filament (fig. 15.5) .... *Megaloptera*

33′.   Abdomen usually without lateral gills; if segmental gills present, than (a) anal hooks absent, or (b) segment 10 with 4 gills, or (c) caudal appendage paired or absent, never single (figs. 19.46, 19.52, 19.71, 19.183, 19.195–19.196) .... *Coleoptera*

34(28′).   Head capsule distinct, partly or entirely hardened, and usually pigmented (figs. 19.15, 21.10–21.37), but may be deeply withdrawn in prothorax (figs. 21.1–21.3) 35

34′.   Head capsule absent, not distinct, hardened, or pigmented, often consisting of a few pale rods (figs. 21.66–21.88) 36

35(34).   Posterior end of body with at least one or a combination of gills, hair brushes, a sucker, or breathing tube (figs. 21.1–21.37) .... *Diptera* (in part)

35′.   Posterior end of body simple or with small processes or isolated hairs, but without gills, brushes, suckers, or breathing tubes (fig. 19.15) .... (Curculionidae) *Coleoptera*

36(34′).   Body usually 5 mm or larger, elongate, somewhat cylindrical, spindle-shaped or maggotlike; mouthparts may be reduced to a pair of retractile mouth hooks that move vertically (figs. 21.66–21.88) .... *Diptera* (in part)

36′.   Body usually 5 mm or less; mouthparts may be reduced to a pair of opposable, acute mandibles that move horizontally; parasitoids on or inside insect hosts (fig. 20.9) .... *Hymenoptera*

Collections of identified aquatic immatures are maintained at several North American universities and museums, such as: Illinois Natural History Survey, Urbana; Philadelphia Academy of Natural Sciences, Pennsylvania; American Museum of Natural History, New York; California Academy of Sciences, San Francisco; United States National Museum of Natural History and Smithsonian Institute, Washington, D.C.; Ohio State University, Columbus; University of Wisconsin, Madison; Cornell University, Ithaca, New York; Oregon State University, Corvallis; Canadian National Collection of Insects, Ottawa; and the Royal Ontario Museum, Toronto.

Aquatic Collembola

9

Kenneth A. Christiansen
Grinnell College, Iowa

Richard J. Snider
Michigan State University, East Lansing

INTRODUCTION

Collembola are primarily inhabitants of soil, litter, and moist vegetation. Their ubiquitous distribution and small size suggest that almost any species may accidentally be found on the water surface. Their size and hydrophobic (water-repelling) integument keep them afloat on the surface film. However, a number of specialized aquatic species form part of the freshwater neuston and others are regularly found in the intertidal zone (Christiansen 1964). A variety of individual species from different genera are inhabitants of one or another of these habitats.

Rapoport and Sanchez (1963) recognized two types of neustonic conditions occupied by Collembola: *transitory*, formed by rain into temporary pools, and *permanent*, typically lakes, lagoons, or ponds. They also concluded that rivers, streams, and floods act as dispersal mechanisms. Waltz and McCafferty (1979) ranked the Collembola into categories based on the relative degree of association and adaptation to the aquatic environment. First, the *primary aquatic associates* are those found exclusively in aquatic habitats; the *secondary aquatic associates* may be found in and around aquatic habitats, but may also inhabit other areas where high humidity exists; and the *tertiary aquatic associates* are those typical (in part) of the *transitory* neuston of Rapoport and Sanchez (1963) and having the least apparent adaptation to aquatic habitats. Waltz and McCafferty (1979) were able to classify some 50 species representing 29 genera most commonly associated with freshwater habitats. The great majority of Nearctic neustonic Collembola are either *Podura aquatica* (fig. 9.4) or members of the genus *Sminthurides* (fig. 9.43).

Among intertidal species the most common is *Anurida maritima* (fig. 9.7), which is frequently found in tidal marshes, rocky coasts, and sometimes sandy beaches (Joosse 1966). Commonly, it clusters together among shells during low tide before inundation occurs. Short body setae hold an air bubble that functions as a physical gill. When currents are not too strong, clustering individuals form "nests" in rock cracks or under shells where the animals seek refuge and deposit eggs. In late fall the population dies out, leaving diapausing eggs until spring (Joosse 1966). *Anurida maritima* is widespread, but *Entomobrya (Mesentoma) laguna* (fig. 9.23) and *Archisotoma besselsi* (fig. 9.39) are locally more common in southern California.

Collembolans have also been reported from two specialized aquatic habitats, interstitial (water-filled spaces between sand grains) littoral habitats (Delamare-Deboutteville 1960) and the surface film in cave habitats (Vandel 1964). No Nearctic species are presently known to be limited to such habitats, although some members of the genus *Arrhopalites* appear to be largely inhabitants of the latter. Because the interstitial habitat intergrades with the true littoral zone, some Nearctic species are found in both environments.

The Collembola are generally detritus feeders capable of consuming a wide variety of dead plant material and microflora; however, most species show a strong preference for particular foods (Christiansen 1964). Neustonic forms often feed primarily on diatoms, unicellular algae, and plankton trapped in the surface film. In a number of species, the highly modified mouthparts (fig. 9.9) suggest fluid or bacterial diets. This postulate agrees with the work of Rapoport and Sanchez (1963) who reported fluid intestinal contents and the observation of biting the surface film by some species. They concluded that the springtails fed on a lipoprotein layer of the film or bacterial populations beneath it.

Collembola display a number of unusual features including a great divergence in total instar number (2–50+) and the absence of a definitive adult form in many species (Christiansen and Bellinger 1980–81). Although the great majority of Collembola show little sexual differentiation, the aquatic genera *Sminthurides* and *Bourletiella* have a strong dimorphism associated with an elaborate behavior pattern during reproduction. The neustonic *Isotomurus (Hydroisotoma) schaefferi* shows sexual dimorphism only in certain localities.

EXTERNAL MORPHOLOGY

The Collembola are apterygote (wingless) insects characterized by the presence of a *collophore* or ventral tube (respiratory, adhesive, osmoregulatory organ) on the venter of the first abdominal segment (fig. 9.1). Primitive forms are equipped on the venter of the fourth abdominal segment with a peculiar bifurcate jumping organ or *furcula* (fig. 9.1), which is held in place by the *tenaculum* (fig. 9.1) when the animal is at rest. Also eight eyes on two generally trapezoidal, pigmented eye patches are located on each side of the head (fig.

9.1). Both features are often reduced or absent in specialized forms. Mouthparts vary from primitive chewing forms to complex filtering types, or have specialized piercing and sucking structures (fig. 9.9). Primitive forms have three thoracic and six abdominal segments, which may be fused in various ways. Each tarsus is typically equipped with a single *unguis* and a small opposable *unguiculus* (fig. 9.1).

The body is clothed with various types of setae and sometimes with complex scales. The antennae are always present and generally four-segmented. Cerci are absent, although anal horns or anal appendages of various sorts may be present (fig. 9.1). There is no metamorphosis (ametabolous) and molting continues after the adult stage is reached. All aquatic species are small, being rarely larger than 3 mm.

KEY TO FAMILIES AND GENERA OF COLLEMBOLA

1.	Body linear (fig. 9.1) (Suborder Arthropleona)	2
1′.	Body subglobular (figs. 9.42–9.43) (Suborder Symphypleona)	73
2(1).	First thoracic segment dorsally visible, with dorsal setae (fig. 9.2) (Poduromorpha)	3
2′.	First thoracic segment without dorsal setae and frequently not visible dorsally (fig. 9.3) (Entomobryomorpha)	29
3(2).	Dentes more than 3 times as long as manubrium (fig. 9.4) .... *PODURIDAE—Podura*
3′.	Dentes absent or less than 2.5 times as long as manubrium	4
4(3′).	Pseudocelli present (figs 9.5–9.6); eyes always absent .... *ONYCHIURIDAE* 5
4′.	Pseudocelli absent; eyes present or rarely absent (fig. 9.7) .... *HYPOGASTRURIDAE* 8
5(4).	Furcula with dens and mucro present; tenaculum present (fig. 9.1) .... *Lophognathella*
5′.	Furcula of paired knobs, single fold, or absent; mucro and tenaculum absent 6
6(5′)	Last 2 antennal segments completely fused .... *Sensiphorura*
6′.	Last 2 antennal segments distinctly separated 7
7(6′).	Apical sense organ of 3rd antennal segment with 2 sense clubs behind 4–6 integumentary papillae (fig. 9.8A) .... *Onychiurus**
7′.	Apical sense organ of 3rd antennal segment with 1–3 exposed sense clubs (fig. 9.8B) .... *Tullbergia**
8(4′).	Mandible with a basal molar plate (fig. 9.9A) .... (HYPOGASTRURINAE) 9
8′.	Mandible absent or without a molar plate (figs. 9.9B–C) .... (NEANURINAE) 20
9(8).	PAO absent (fig. 9.2) 10
9′.	PAO present (fig. 9.1) 11
10(9).	Four or 5 eyes per side .... *Xenylla**
10′.	Eyes absent .... *Acherontiella*
11(9′).	Anal spines 3; 9 or more dorsal dental setae .... *Triacanthella*
11′.	Anal spines 0 or 2 (fig. 9.1); 7 or fewer dorsal dental setae 12
12(11′).	Eyes 8 + 8 13
12′.	Eyes 6 + 6 or fewer 15
13(12).	Furcula absent .... *Knowltonella*
13′.	Furcula present 14
14(13′)	Mandible with apical teeth (fig. 9.10A); PAO lobed .... *Hypogastrura**
14′.	Mandible without apical teeth (fig. 9.10B); PAO simple .... *Stenogastrura*
15(12′).	Furcula absent 16
15′.	Furcula present 18
16(15).	PAO elongate with 2 rows of oblong tubercles (fig. 9.11A) .... *ONYCHIURIDAE—Sensiphorura*
16′.	PAO circular with triangular tubercles (fig. 9.11B) 17
17(16′).	Unguis strongly toothed; 3 clavate tenent hairs (fig. 9.1) .... *Tafallia*
17′.	Unguis without tooth; at most 1 clavate tenent hair .... *Willemia*
18(15′).	More than 1 clavate (clubbed) tenent hair per foot (fig. 9.1) .... *Mesachorutes*
18′.	One acuminate (tapering) or clavate tenent hair per foot 19

*These genera are often found on water surface. Those marked † have truly aquatic species. The remainder are terrestrial or rarely associated with water but are included to ensure reliable determination of the primarily aquatic or semiaquatic genera.

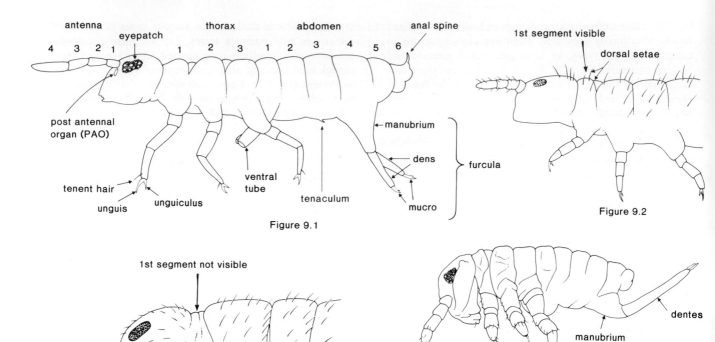

Figure 9.1

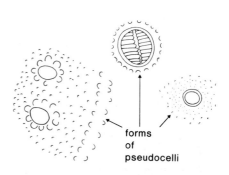

Figure 9.2

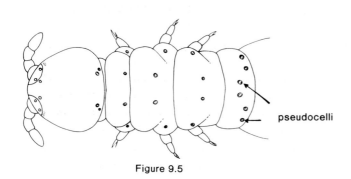

Figure 9.5

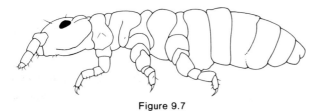

Figure 9.7

Figure 9.8

Figure 9.1. Generalized diagram of collembolan anatomy.

Figure 9.2. Lateral view of podurimorph thorax and head.

Figure 9.3. Lateral view of entomobryomorph thorax and head.

Figure 9.4. *Podura aquatica* (Poduridae).

Figure 9.5. Onychiurid thorax and first abdominal segment showing pseudocelli.

Figure 9.6. Various forms of pseudocelli.

Figure 9.7. *Anurida maritima* (Hypogastruridae).

Figure 9.8. Typical apical organs of third antennal segment: *A, Onychiurus* sp. and *B, Tullbergia* sp. (Onychiuridae).

19(18′).	Mandible with strong molar plate and several apical teeth (fig. 9.10A)	*Schaefferia**
19′.	Mandible with weak molar plate and at most 1 apical tooth (fig. 9.12)	*Microgastrura*
20(18′)	Mucro trilamellate (fig. 9.13)	*Odontella* (Odontella)
20′.	Mucro not trilamellate; frequently reduced or absent	21
21(20′).	Unguiculus present (fig. 9.1); PAO triradiate	*Odontella* (Xenyllodes)
21′.	Unguiculus absent; PAO when present, lobed	22
22(21′).	Maxilla sickle-shaped (fig. 9.14A); 3 or more anal spines or spinelike setae, or 2 such setae and mucro fused to dens	*Friesa**
22′.	Maxilla quadrate (fig. 9.14B), narrow and lamellate (fig. 9.16C), or needlelike (fig. 9.14D); anal spines absent, or 2 anal spines and mucro separate from dens	23
23(22′).	Furcula present with all segments distinct	24
23′.	Furcula reduced or absent; mucro always absent	26
24(23).	Head of maxilla quadrate (fig. 9.14B)	*Brachystomella*
24′.	Maxilla otherwise (figs. 9.14C–D)	25
25(24′).	PAO present; anal spines absent	*Pseudachorutes**
25′.	PAO absent; 2 anal spines	*Oudemansia†*
26(23′)	Last abdominal segment bilobed; body usually with conspicuous tubercles (fig. 9.15A)	27
26′.	Last abdominal segment rounded; body without conspicuous tubercles (fig. 9.15B)	28
27(26).	PAO present	*Morulina*
27′.	PAO absent	*Neanura**
28(26′).	PAO present (fig. 9.1)	*Anurida†*
28′.	PAO absent	*Paranura*
29(2′).	Dentes with spines (fig. 9.17)	30
29′.	Dentes without spines	33
30(29).	Mucro bidentate (with 2 teeth) and short (fig. 9.17C)	*ISOTOMIDAE—Semicerura**
30′.	Mucro elongate, 3 or more teeth (figs. 9.17 A–C) (ENTOMOBRYIDAE)	31
31(30′).	Dental spines relatively small, on basal portion of dens only (fig. 9.17A) ..... (TOMOCERINAE) .... *Tomocerus**
31′.	Dental spines relatively large, most conspicuous toward apex of dens (fig. 9.17B) (Oncopodurinae)	32
32(31′).	Eyes and pigment present	*Harlomillsia**
32′.	Eyes and pigment absent	*Oncopodura**
33(29′).	Body with scales	*ENTOMOBRYIDAE* 34
33′.	Body without scales	40
34(33).	Mucro elongate (fig. 9.17A)	(CYPHODERINAE) *Cyphoderus*
34′.	Mucro short (fig. 9.18)	(ENTOMOBRYINAE) 35
35(34′).	Mucro falcate (sickle-shaped) (fig. 9.18A)	*Seira*
35′.	Mucro bidentate (fig. 9.18B)	36
36(35′).	Dentes with scales on ventral surface (fig. 9.19)	37
36′.	Dentes without scales	39
37(36).	Fourth abdominal segment at midline more than twice as long as 3rd	38
37′.	Fourth abdominal segment at midline less than twice as long as 3rd	*Heteromurus*
38(37).	Eyes 8 + 8 (fig. 9.20)	*Lepidocyrtus**
38′.	Eyes 6 + 6 or less	*Pseudosinella**
39(36′).	Scales narrow, without clear markings (fig. 9.21A)	*Janetschekbrya*
39′.	Scales broad, and clearly striate (fig. 9.21B)	*Willowsia**
40(33′).	PAO present (fig. 9.16A) or (2 species) absent; setae at most unilaterally ciliate	*ISOTOMIDAE* 45

*These genera are often found on water surface. Those marked † have truly aquatic species. The remainder are terrestrial or rarely associated with water but are included to ensure reliable determination of the primarily aquatic or semiaquatic genera.

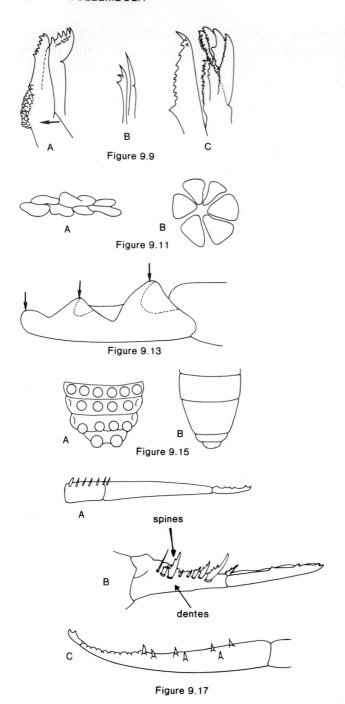

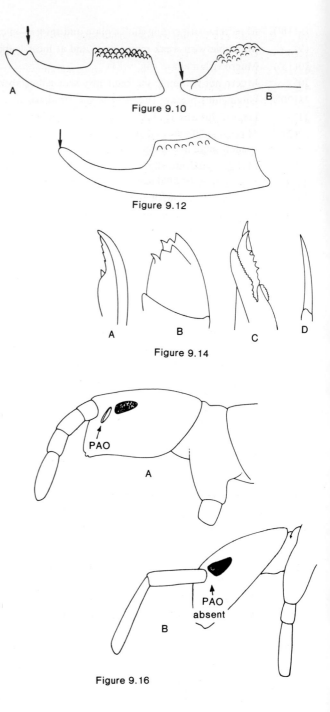

Figure 9.9. Mouthparts: *A*, chewing grinding sort typical of Hypogasturinae; *B* and *C*, piercing and sucking sorts typical of Neanurinae.

Figure 9.10. Mandible typical of *A*, *Hypogastrura* sp. and *B*, *Stenogastura* sp. (Hypogastruridae).

Figure 9.11. Postantennal organ typical of *A*, *Sensiphorura* sp. (Onychiuridae) and *B*, *Tafallia* sp. (Hypogastruridae) and *Willemia* sp. (Hypogastruridae).

Figure 9.12. Mandible of *Microgastrura* sp. (Hypogastruridae).

Figure 9.13. Mucro typical of *Odontella* sp. (Hypogastruridae).

Figure 9.14. Maxillae typical of *A*, *Friesea* sp.; *B*, *Brachystomella* sp.; *C*, *Anurida* sp.; and *D*, *Neanura* sp. (Hypogastruridae).

Figure 9.15. Diagram of dorsal view of the end of the abdomen: *A*, *Morulina* sp. and *Neanura* sp. (Hypogastruridae), and *B*, other genera of Neanurinae (Hypogastruridae).

Figure 9.16. Diagrammatic lateral view of entomobryomorph heads: *A*, with postantennal organs and *B*, without postantennal organs.

Figure 9.17. Mucro and dens showing spines: *A*, *Tomocerus* sp.; *B*, *Oncopodura* sp. (Entomobryidae); and *C*, *Semicerura* sp. (Isotomidae).

40'.   PAO absent (fig. 9.16B); some setae multilaterally ciliate .... *ENTOMOBRYIDAE* 41

41(40'). Eyes 6 + 6 or fewer .... *Sinella**

41'.   Eyes 8 + 8 42

42(41'). Fourth abdominal segment at midline less than 3 times as long as 3rd 44

42'.   Fourth abdominal segment at midline more than 3 times as long as 3rd 43

43(42') Dens dorsally crenulate (with small scallops) and curving upward, basally in line
         with manubrium (figs. 9.22A–9.23) .... (ENTOMOBRYINAE) *Entomobrya*†

43'.   Dens not crenulate, straight and usually forming a basal angle with manubrium
         (fig. 9.22B) .... (PARONELLINAE) *Salina*

44(42). Unguis with 2 unpaired and 2 paired inner teeth (fig. 9.24A); 1st and 2nd antennal
         segments subsegmented .... *Orchesella*

44'.   Unguis with 3 unpaired inner teeth (fig. 9.24B); antennal segments not
         subsegmented .... *Corynothrix**

45(40). Anal spines 2–4, terminal at end of abdomen on projecting papillae (fig. 9.25A);
         furcula never reaching end of abdomen; eyes 8 + 8 46

45'.   Abdominal spines absent, or subterminal (fig. 9.25B), or not on papillae (fig.
         9.25C); furcula extending beyond end of abdomen; eyes 8 + 8 or fewer 47

46(45). Four anal spines .... *Tetracanthella**

46'.   Two anal spines .... *Uzelia*

47(45'). Abdominal segments 4–6 fused (no clear nonsetaceous bands separating these
         segments) (fig. 9.26) .... *Folsomia*

47'.   At least 4th and 5th abdominal segments separated by a clear nonsetaceous band
         or suture 48

48(47'). Furcula well developed; mucro with 2 (fig. 9.27A) or more teeth, or lamellate (fig.
         9.27B) 54

48'.   Furcula reduced or absent; mucro absent or unidentate and hooklike (fig. 9.27C) 49

49(48'). Furcula bifurcate (fig. 9.28A); tenaculum present 50

49'.   Furcula without paired distal projections (fig. 9.28B) or absent; tenaculum absent 51

50(49). Integument coarsely granulate (fig. 9.29) .... *Coloburella (Coloburella)*

50'.   Coarse integumentary granulations absent .... *Stachanorema*

51(49). Eyes 2 + 2 or more; antenna with apical retractile papilla .... *Anurophorus (Anurophorus)*

51'.   Eyes 1 + 1 or absent; no apical retractile antennal papilla 52

52(51'). Rudimentary furcula present (fig. 9.27B); integument coarsely granulate (fig.
         9.29) .... *Coloburella (Paranurophorus)*

52'.   Furcula completely absent; integument finely granulate 53

53(52'). Fifth and 6th abdominal segments fused .... *Micranurophorus*

53'.   Fifth and 6th abdominal segments separate .... *Anurophorus (Pseudanurophorus)**

54(48). Abdomen with 2–6 subterminal spines set in strongly rugose (wrinkled)
         surface .... *Isotoma* ("Spinisotoma" ecomorphs)

54'.   Abdominal spines absent or not set on rugose surface 55

55(54). Head wider than 2nd thoracic segment; antennae shorter than head (fig. 9.30A) .... *Metisotoma*

55'.   Head subequal to or narrower than 2nd thoracic segment; antennae longer than
         head (fig. 9.30B) 56

56(55'). PAO absent; eyes and pigment absent .... *Isotomiella**

56'   PAO present; eyes and pigment present or not 57

57(56). Ventral manubrial setae 10 or more (usually 14 or more) 58

57'.   Ventral manubrial setae 9 or fewer (usually 6 or fewer) 63

58(57). Sense organ of 3rd antennal segment with more than 10 blunt setae (figs. 9.31A,
         9.32) .... *Axelsonia*†

---

*These genera are often found on water surface. Those marked † have truly aquatic species. The remainder are terrestrial or rarely
associated with water but are included to ensure reliable determination of the primarily aquatic or semiaquatic genera.

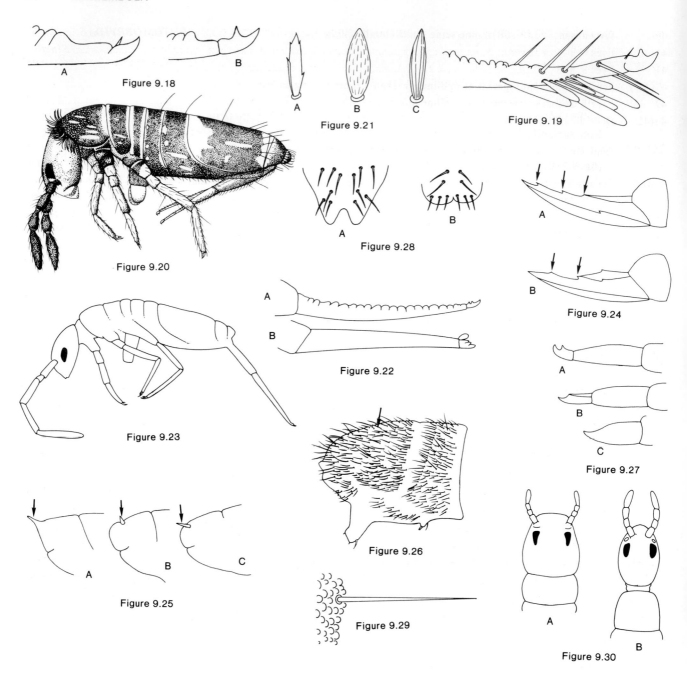

Figure 9.18. Apex of dens and mucro showing: *A*, falcate and *B*, bidentate conditions.

Figure 9.19. Apex of dens and mucro of *Lepidocyrtus* sp. (Entomobryidae) showing ventral scales.

Figure 9.20. *Lepidocyrtus* sp. (Entomobryidae) (after Christiansen and Bellinger 1980–81).

Figure 9.21. Scales typical of *A, Janetschekbrya* sp.; *B* and *C, Willowsia* sp. (Entomobryidae).

Figure 9.22. Dens and mucro typical of *A*, Entomobryinae and *B*, Paronellinae (Entomobryidae).

Figure 9.23. *Entomobrya laguna* (Entomobryidae).

Figure 9.24. Ungues, characteristic of *A, Orchesella* sp. and *B, Corynothrix* sp. (Entomobryidae).

Figure 9.25. Lateral view of abdomen showing: *A*, terminal anal spines; and *B* and *C*, subterminal anal spines.

Figure 9.26. Posterior 4 abdominal segments of typical *Folsomia* sp. (Isotomidae). The *arrow* shows the location of the unsetaceous band in other genera.

Figure 9.27. Dentes and mucrones showing: *A*, bidentate; *B*, lamellate; and *C*, fused conditions.

Figure 9.28. Reduced furculae showing *A*, presence and *B*, absence of distal projections.

Figure 9.29. Coarsely granulate integument.

Figure 9.30. Dorsal views of anterior thorax and head of: *A, Metisotoma* sp. and *B*, a characteristic Isotomidae.

58′.	Sense organ of 3rd antennal segment with 2 (usually) to 4 or 5 blunt setae (fig. 9.31B)	59
59(58′).	Dentes dorsally smooth (fig. 9.33) .... ***Isotomurus (Hydroisotoma)***†	
59′.	Dentes dorsally crenulate or tuberculate (fig. 9.36)	60
60(59′).	Abdominal macrochaetae coarsely, multilaterally ciliate (fig. 9.34A); 2nd to 4th abdominal segments with bothriotrichia (long, fringed hairs) (fig. 9.35) .... ***Isotomurus (Isotomurus)***†	
60′.	All setae smooth or unilaterally ciliate (fig. 9.34B); bothriotrichia absent	61
61(60′)	Dentes dorsally tuberculate (tubercle-shaped) (fig. 9.36A)	62
61′.	Dentes dorsally crenulate (scallop-shaped) (fig. 9.36B) .... ***Isotoma****	
62(61)	Subapical dental seta greatly exceeding apex of mucro (fig. 9.36A) .... ***Agrenia***†	
62′.	No dental setae exceed apex of mucro (fig. 9.36B) .... ***Isotoma (Panchaetoma)***	
63(57′).	Cephalic integument reticulate (fig. 9.38A); 8 anal spines present on papillae .... ***Weberacantha***	
63′.	Cephalic integument granulate (fig. 9.38C), tuberculate (fig. 9.38B), or smooth; anal spines present or absent, *rarely* on papillae	64
64(63′).	Manubrium ventrally without setae	65
64′.	Manubrium ventrally with setae	69
65(63).	Mucro with 2 basal flaps (fig. 9.39) .... ***Archisotoma***†	
65.	Mucro without basal flaps	66
66(65′).	Dorsal dental setae 7 or more	67
66′.	Dorsal dental setae 3 or fewer	68
67(66).	Dentes without ventrolateral setae (fig. 9.40A) .... ***Bonetrura***	
67′.	Dentes with 1 or more ventrolateral setae (fig. 9.40B) .... ***Proisotoma*** (in part)	
68(66′).	Abdomen with spinelike setae on 6th segment; dens with 2 setae in ventral half .... ***Isotomodes****	
68′.	Abdomen without posterior spinelike setae; dens with 1 or no setae in ventral half .... ***Folsomides****	
69(64′)	PAO with margin divided into 4 quadrants (fig. 9.41A); some macrochaetae conspicuously ciliate .... ***Micrisotoma***	
69′.	PAO margin not divided into quadrants (fig. 9.41B); no clearly ciliate setae	70
70(69′).	Mucro with 3 or more teeth .... ***Proisotoma*** (in part)*	
70′.	Mucro bidentate	71
71(70′)	Fifth and 6th abdominal segments separated by clear nonsetaceous band or suture .... ***Proisotoma*** (in part)*	
71′	Fifth and 6th abdominal segments fused	72
72(71′).	Dens with 6 or fewer setae in ventral half .... ***Dagamaea****	
72′.	Dens with 7 or more setae in ventral half .... ***Cryptopygus****	
73(2′).	Antennae shorter than head; eyes absent (fig. 9.42) .... NEELIDAE—*Neelus*	
73′.	Antennae longer than head, or at least 1 + 1 eyes (sometimes unpigmented) (fig. 9.43) .... SMINTHURIDAE	74
74(73).	Fourth antennal segment less than half as long as 3rd .... ***Dicyrtoma****	
74′.	Fourth antennal segment more than half as long as 3rd	75
75(74′).	Antennae shorter than head .... ***Sminthurides (Denisiella)***†	
75′.	Antennae longer than head	76
76(75′).	With 2 or more clavate tenent hairs (fig. 9.45)	77
76′.	Without clavate tenent hairs	80
77(76).	Body with heavy, outstanding serrate setae on greater abdomen (fig. 9.44) .... ***Vesicephalus***	
77′.	Body without such setae	78
78(77′).	Tenent hairs 2–3, parallel to long axis of tibiotarsus, very strongly clavate (fig. 9.45A) .... ***Bourletiella***†	
78′.	Tenent hairs often more than 3, outstanding, less strongly clavate (fig. 9.45B)	79

*These genera are often found on water surface. Those marked † have truly aquatic species. The remainder are terrestrial or rarely associated with water but are included to ensure reliable determination of the primarily aquatic or semiaquatic genera.

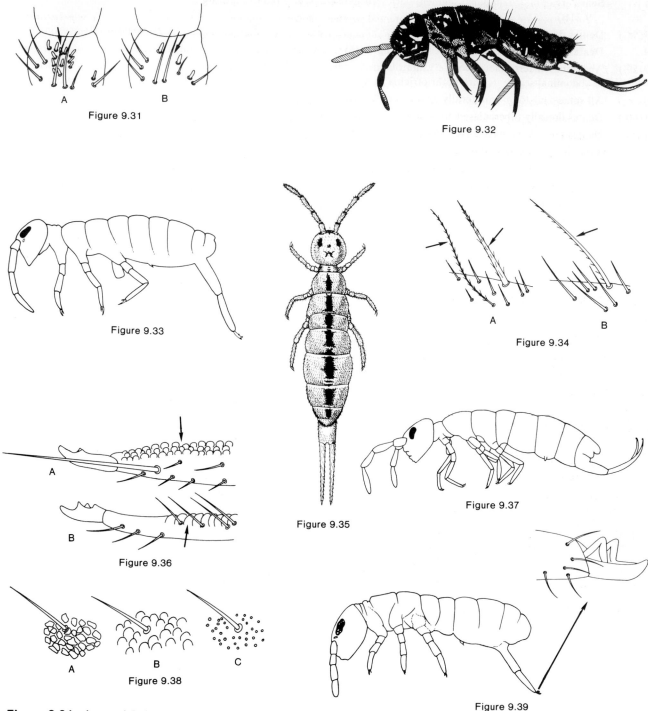

Figure 9.31

Figure 9.32

Figure 9.33

Figure 9.34

Figure 9.35

Figure 9.36

Figure 9.37

Figure 9.38

Figure 9.39

Figure 9.31. Apex of 3rd antennal segment of *A, Axelsonia* sp. and *B*, a typical isotomid.

Figure 9.32. *Axelsonia* sp. (Isotomidae) (after Christiansen and Bellinger 1980–81).

Figure 9.33. *Isotoma schaefferi* (Isotomidae).

Figure 9.34. Abdominal setae of *A, Isotomurus* sp. showing large ciliate setae and slender bothriotrichium and *B, Isotoma* sp.

Figure 9.35. *Isotomurus tricolor* (Isotomidae) seen from above (after Folsom 1937).

Figure 9.36. Apex of dens and mucro typical of *A, Agrenia* sp. and *B, Isotoma* sp. (Isotomidae).

Figure 9.37. *Agrenia bidenticulata* (Isotomidae).

Figure 9.38. Integumentary types of the family Isotomidae: *A*, reticulate; *B*, coarsely granulate; and *C*, finely granulate.

Figure 9.39. *Archisotoma besselsi* (Isotomidae) with enlargement of mucro.

79(78′)   Trochanteral organ (posterior distal seta in pit) on hind trochanter (fig. 9.46A); 4 or more clavate tenent hairs, or 4th antennal segment simple .... *Sminthurinus**

79′.   Trochanteral organ absent (hind trochanter without modified external seta) (fig. 9.46B); 3 clavate tenent hairs; 4th antennal segment subsegmented .... *Sminthurus**

80(76′).   Eyes 2 + 2 or less .... *Arrhopalites**

80′.   Eyes 4 + 4 or more 81

81(80′).   Fourth antennal segment with 8 or more subsegments or annulations 82

81′.   Fourth antennal segment with 7 or fewer subsegments 84

82(81).   Metathoracic trochanter with inner spine (fig. 9.47A) 83

82′.   Metathoracic trochanter without inner spine (fig. 9.47B) .... *Sminthurus* sens. str.*

83(82).   Female subanal appendage palmate (fig. 9.48) .... *Sminthurus (Allacma)*

83′.   Female subanal appendage truncate or acuminate .... *Sphyrotheca*

84(81′).   Body with heavy, denticulate setae (fig. 9.49) .... *Neosminthurus*

84′.   Body without such setae 85

85(84′).   Eyes at least 6 + 6 (fig. 9.43) .... *Sminthurides*†

85′.   Eyes 4 + 4 .... *Collophora*

ADDITIONAL TAXONOMIC REFERENCES

General
Heymons and Heymons (1909); Rimski-Korsakov (1940); Phillips (1955); Gisin (1960); Salmon (1964); Pedigo (1970); Martynova (1972); Joosse (1976); Pennak (1978); Waltz and McCafferty (1979); Betsch (1980).

Regional Faunas
California: Wilkey (1959).
Canada: James (1933).
Indiana: Hart (1970, 1971, 1973, 1974).
Louisiana: Hepburn and Woodring (1963).
Michigan: Snider (1967).
Pacific Coast: Scott and Yosii (1972).
West Virginia: Lippert and Butler (1976).

Taxonomic treatments at the family and generic levels
General: Guthrie (1903); Mills (1934); Maynard (1951); Hammer (1953); Uchida (1971, 1972a, 1972b); Ellis and Bellinger (1973); Christiansen and Bellinger (1980–81).
Entomobryidae: Stach (1960, 1963); Pedigo (1968).
Hypogastruridae: Folsom (1916); Stach (1949a, 1949b, 1951); Yosii (1960).
Isotomidae: Folsom (1937); Stach (1947).
Onychiuridae: Folsom (1917); Stach (1954).
Sminthuridae: Folsom and Mills (1938); Stach (1956, 1957).

---

*These genera are often found on water surface. Those marked † have truly aquatic species. The remainder are terrestrial or rarely associated with water but are included to ensure reliable determination of the primarily aquatic or semiaquatic genera.

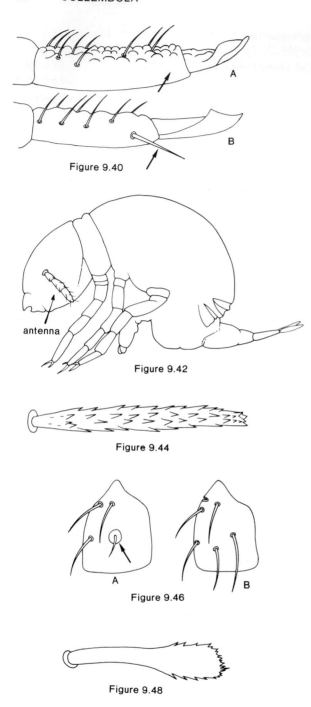

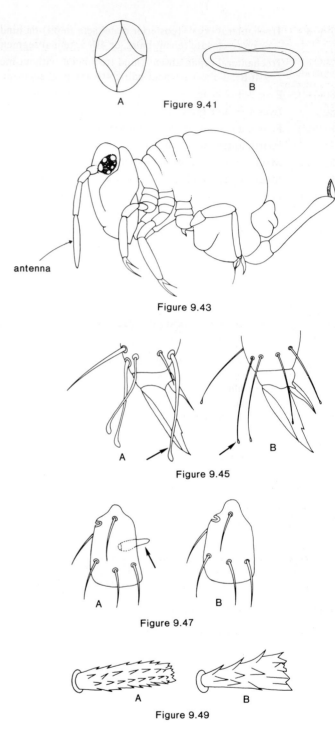

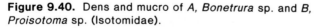

Figure 9.40. Dens and mucro of A, *Bonetrura* sp. and B, *Proisotoma* sp. (Isotomidae).

Figure 9.41. Postantennal organ typical of A, *Microisotoma* sp. and B, other isotomid Collembola.

Figure 9.42. Typical Neelidae form.

Figure 9.43. *Sminthurides aquaticus* (Sminthuridae).

Figure 9.44. Large body seta characteristic of *Vesicephalus* sp. (Sminthuridae).

Figure 9.45. Foot complex typical of A, *Bourletiella* sp. and B, *Sminthurinus* sp. (Sminthuridae).

Figure 9.46. Trochanter typical of A, *Sminthurinus* sp. and B, some species of *Sminthurus* (Sminthuridae).

Figure 9.47. Trochanter characteristic of A, *Sminthurus* sp. *(Allacma)* and *Sphyrotheca* sp., and B, most species of *Sminthurus* (Sminthuridae).

Figure 9.48. Female subanal appendage of *Allacma* sp. (Sminthuridae).

Figure 9.49. Heavy body setae *(A and B)* characteristic of *Neosminthurus* sp. (Sminthuridae).

ble 9A. Summary of ecological and distributional data for *Semiaquatic Collembola (springtails)*. (For definition of terms see Tables 6A–6C; table pared by K. Christiansen, R. J. Snider, and K. W. Cummins; only genera with normally aquatic or semiaquatic species are included.)

Taxa (number of species in parentheses)	Habitat	Habit	Trophic Relationships	North American Distribution	Ecological References
ᵈuridae(1) Podura(1)	Lotic—margins (on surface film)	"Skaters" (on water surface, "sprawlers" (at margins)	Collectors—gatherers (scavengers)	Widespread	514, 759, 2170, 2177, 2197
pogastruridae(3)					118, 289, 539, 540, 1847, 1886, 1983, 2170, 2190, 2197, 2360, 2504
Oudemansia(1)	Beach zone—marine (intertidal)	"Sprawlers" (active at low tide, hide in protected microhabitats when submerged)	Collectors—gatherers (scavengers?)	Washington coast	2197
Anurida(2)	Beach zone—marine (intertidal), estaurine marshes	"Sprawlers" (active at low tide, aggregate at high tide in protected microhabitats)	Collectors—gatherers (scavengers on dead invertebrates, especially Molluska)		
Anurida*(1)				East and West Coasts	
Anuridella*(1)				New York coast	
tomidae(4)	Generally marine—intertidal: lotic—margins	Generally "skaters"	Generally collectors—gatherers (scavengers)		118, 289, 380, 1847, 1886, 1983, 2170, 2190, 2197
Axelsonia(1)	Beach zone—marine intertidal (on surface film)	"Skaters"	Collectors—gatherers (scavengers)	Florida coast	
Archistoma(1)	Beach zone—marine intertidal (on surface film)	"Skaters"	Collectors—gatherers (scavengers)	Widespread	
Agrenia(1)	Lotic—margins (on surface film)	"Skaters"	Collectors—gatherers (scavengers)	Widespread	
Isotomurus(1) Hydroistoma*(1)	Lotic—margins (on surface film)	"Skaters"	Collectors—gatherers (scavengers)	Widespread	2190
tomobryidae(2)					1847, 1886, 1983, 2170, 2197
Entomobrya Mesentotoma*(1)	Beach zone—marine	"Sprawlers" (active at low tide, hide in protected microhabitats when submerged)	Collectors—gatherers (scavengers)	Southern California coast	
Salina(1)	Lotic—margins	"Sprawlers"	Collectors—gatherers	Eastern United States	1882
ᵐinthuridae(17)	Generally lotic—margins (on surface film)	Generally "skaters"	Generally collectors—gatherers (scavengers), shredders—herbivores (chewers)		397, 1847, 1886, 1983, 2170, 2197
Sminthurides(14)	Lotic—margins (on surface film)	"Skaters," "clingers–sprawlers" (on *Lemna*)	Collectors—gatherers (scavengers), shredders—herbivores (chewers of *Lemna*)	Widespread	699, 759, 1886, 1983, 2195, 2197
Bourletiella Pseudobourletiella*(2)	Lotic—margins (on surface film)	"Skaters"	Collectors—gatherers (scavengers)	Eastern United States	
Sminthurus(1)	Lotic—margins (on surface film)	"Skaters" (on submerged vegetation)	Collectors—gatherers	Florida	2273

ubgenera.

Ephemeroptera

10

G. F. Edmunds, Jr.
University of Utah, Salt Lake City

INTRODUCTION

Mayflies occur in an extremely wide variety of standing- and running-water habitats, the greatest diversity being found in rocky-bottomed, second- and third-order, headwater streams. Most of the taxonomic and biological studies on mayflies have been centered on the nymphs. This is primarily a result of the abbreviated adult life and the limited range of adult activities, viz., mating and egg laying. Adult mayflies can be so elusive that adults of some genera remain unknown and others are rarely seen except by specialists. Unless adults come to lights or form conspicuous swarms during daylight hours they are rarely encountered.

The eggs are usually deposited at the water surface, a few at a time or all in one or two clusters. In at least some species of *Baetis,* the female crawls beneath the water and lays rows of eggs on the substrate. A few adults drop clusters of eggs from the air. Eggs of most mayflies have sticky coverings, frequently with specialized anchoring devices (Koss and Edmunds 1974). Egg structure is useful in taxonomic and phylogenetic analyses. Embryonic development usually takes a few weeks. Although diapause has been confirmed experimentally in only a few species, it is almost certainly common in many temperate zone mayflies. In most species, egg hatching may be delayed three to nine months and eggs of *Parameletus* may remain dormant for over 11 months. In others, e.g., some Western *Ephemerella,* development proceeds directly. A number of species are known to depend on specific hatching temperatures. The combination of specific cool periods to break diapause and specific warm temperatures for hatching appears to play a significant role in the distribution of certain species.

The nymphs undergo numerous molts; examples of reported numbers are 12 for *Baetisca rogersi* Berner, 27 for *Baetis vagans* McDunnough, and 40–45 for *Stenacron interpunctatum canadense* (Walker). Because more mortality tends to occur at than between molts, reduced numbers of instars should be adaptive. Measures of the number of molts are difficult to obtain and the totals reported may be overestimated. Length of nymphal life varies with temperature and is usually 3–6 months. The period can be as short as 16–22 days, in *Parameletus columbiae* McDunnough, or as long as two years, in *Hexagenia limbata* Serville. Development of *Hexagenia limbata* varies from one to two years in Lake Winnipeg in northern Canada but the same species may develop in less than 17 weeks in warm canals in Utah and can

be laboratory reared in 13 weeks. Some of the Baetidae, Caenidae, and Tricorythidae may produce several broods a year. Various species of *Baetis* develop much faster in summer than do their overwintering broods.

Adults of some species of *Baetis* emerge throughout the year even in strongly seasonal climates. Long emergence periods for mayflies are characteristically found where winters are relatively mild, such as along the Pacific Coast area and in the Southeast. Subimagos (winged, but sexually immature adults) may be an extremely brief part of the life cycle. Some may remain in this stage for as little as minutes, but most species are subimagos from 24 to 48 hours. Subimagos usually perch on shoreline vegetation, but many short-lived ones alight for only 1 to 2 minutes or shed the subimaginal exoskeleton from all but wings without alighting. Imagos of most species live 2 hours to 3 days, but many live less than 90 minutes and the females of some genera with species that hold the eggs until they are ready to hatch *(Callibaetis, Cloeon)* may live for weeks.

Most mayfly nymphs are collectors or scrapers (chap. 6) and feed on a variety of detritus and algae, and some macrophyte and animal material. A few species are true carnivores (table 10A). Frequently food habits vary during the growth period. Newly hatched nymphs tend to feed largely on fine particle detritus. Many shift to ingestion of algae, and some eventually increase the amount of animal material eaten as they increase in size.

EXTERNAL MORPHOLOGY

The following account of the external morphology of mayflies will facilitate use of the keys.

Mature Nymphs

Head (fig. 10.1): The shape of the nymphal head is variable and the head may possess a variety of processes, projections, and armature. The eyes are usually moderately large and are situated laterally or dorsally near the posterolateral margin. The antennae usually arise anterior or ventral to the eyes and vary in length from less than the width of the head to more than twice the width of the head. The mouthparts are illustrated in figure 10.2.

Thorax (fig. 10.1): The three thoracic segments each bear a pair of legs and the developing wing pads are found on the meso- and metathorax. The legs of some genera are modified for such special functions as burrowing, filtering food, grooming, and gill protection.

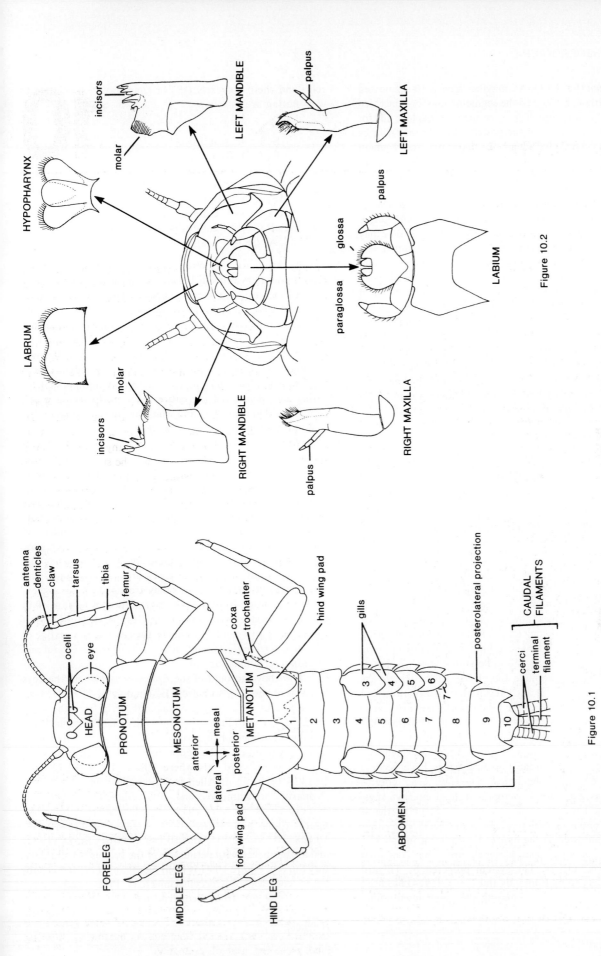

Figure 10.1. Dorsal view of *Ephemerella* sp. nymph (Ephemerellidae).

Figure 10.2. Ventral view of mouthparts of *Ephemerella* sp. nymph (Ephemerellidae).

Figure 10.1

Figure 10.2

Figure 10.1 labels: antenna, denticles, claw, tarsus, tibia, femur, ocelli, eye, HEAD, PRONOTUM, MESONOTUM, anterior, mesal, lateral, posterior, METANOTUM, coxa, trochanter, hind wing pad, fore wing pad, FORELEG, MIDDLE LEG, HIND LEG, gills, ABDOMEN, posterolateral projection, cerci, terminal filament, CAUDAL FILAMENTS

Figure 10.2 labels: incisors, molar, LEFT MANDIBLE, HYPOPHARYNX, LABRUM, palpus, LEFT MAXILLA, palpus, paraglossa, glossa, LABIUM, molar, incisors, RIGHT MANDIBLE, palpus, RIGHT MAXILLA

95

Abdomen (fig. 10.1): All mayflies have a 10-segmented abdomen, although some of the segments may be concealed beneath the mesonotum. The terga may have spines and/or tubercles and the shape of the posterolateral corners can be used as taxonomic characters. To determine the segment number *always count forward from segment 10*. The gills, which are the most variable nymphal structures, are usually located entirely on the abdomen, although in some species they also occur at the bases of the coxae *(Isonychia, Dactylobaetis)*, or at the bases of the maxillae *(Isonychia, Oligoneuriinae)*. Gill position on the abdomen is variable: they may be ventral, lateral, or dorsal, and occur on abdominal segments 1 through 7, or they may be absent from one or more segments in various combinations. In referring to gill position, gill 4, for example, refers to the gills on segment 4 whether or not there are gills on the first three segments.

Most species have three caudal filaments, comprising a terminal filament and two cerci (fig. 10.5). In others, only the cerci are well developed, the terminal filament being represented by a short rudiment or entirely absent. When present, the terminal filament may vary in length and thickness relative to the cerci. Length of the caudal filaments varies from shorter than the body to two or three times its length.

Adults

Head (fig. 10.81): The eyes are usually sexually dimorphic, those of the male being larger than those of the female. In males, the eye facets may be uniform in size or the upper facets may be larger and in the Baetidae the upper facets are turbinate, i.e., raised on a stalklike portion (fig. 10.112). The mouthparts are vestigial and nonfunctional in the adult.

Thorax (figs. 10.81–10.82): The thorax consists of three regions, each with one or two pairs of appendages; the prothorax with the fore legs, the mesothorax with the middle pair of legs and the fore wings, and metathorax with the hind legs and hind wings (which may be absent in some forms). The fore legs of most mayflies show sexual dimorphism, with those of the male having very long tibiae and tarsi and usually being much longer than the middle and hind legs and often as long as or longer than the body. In the Polymitarcyidae, the middle and hind legs of the male and all legs of the female are vestigial (much reduced) and presumably nonfunctional. In *Dolania* (Behningiidae), all the legs of both sexes are vestigial but apparently are somewhat functional. Most mayflies have two pairs of wings; the somewhat triangular fore wings and the much smaller hind wings. In the families Caenidae, Tricorythidae, and Baetidae the hind wings have become greatly reduced or completely lost. The three wing margins are known as the costal, outer, and hind margin (figs. 10.81–10.82). The surface of the wing has a regular series of corrugations or fluting with the longitudinal veins lying either on a ridge (indicated in the figures by +) or a furrow (indicated by −). Venational nomenclature is not consistent among various authors. The system proposed by Tillyard (1932) as discussed by Edmunds and Traver (1954) has been followed. Abbreviations designating the major longitudinal veins and their convexity ($+$) or concavity ($-$) relative to wing fluting are as follows:

$$C \, (+) = \text{costa}$$
$$Sc \, (-) = \text{subcosta}$$
$$R_1 \, (+), R_2 \, (-), R_3 \, (-), R_{4+5} \, (-) = \text{radius}_1,$$
$$\text{radius}_2, \text{etc.}$$
$$MA_1 \, (+), MA_2 \, (+) = \text{medius anterior}_1, \text{etc.}$$
$$MP_1 \, (-), MP_2 \, (-) = \text{medius posterior}_1, \text{etc.}$$
$$CuA \, (+) = \text{cubitus anterior}$$
$$CuP \, (-) = \text{cubitus posterior}$$
$$A_1 \, (+) = \text{anal}_1$$

R_2 through R_5 are often referred to as the radial sector (Rs). Intercalary veins lie between the principal veins. When intercalaries are long, they lie opposite the principal veins on either side; for example, IMA (intercalary medius anterior) is a furrow ($-$) vein lying between the two ridge ($+$) branches of MA (MA_1 and MA_2). Conversely, IMP is a ridge vein ($+$) in between the furrow veins of MP. The longer veins alternate as ridges and furrows at the wing margin. Two ridge veins of the fore wing, MA and CuA, are important landmarks in locating and identifying the entire venation. Learning which veins are ridge veins ($+$) and which are furrow veins ($-$) is important for efficient use of the keys.

Abdomen (figs. 10.81, 10.83–10.84): The abdomen is composed of 10 segments. Each segment is ring shaped and consists of a dorsal tergum and a ventral sternum. The posterior portion of sternum 9 of the female is referred to as the *subanal plate* and in males (fig. 10.83) as the *subgenital plate* or *styliger plate*. The posterior margin of the subgenital plate, which is variable in shape, gives rise to a pair of slender and usually segmented appendages called the *forceps* (or claspers). Dorsal to the subgenital plate are the paired *penes* (fig. 10.83). In most mayflies the penes are well developed and sclerotized, but in the Baetidae they are membranous and extrudable. Arising from the posterior portion of tergum 10 in both sexes are the *caudal filaments* (figs. 10.81, 10.84). Most species have two caudal filaments, the *cerci,* and a vestige of a median *terminal filament;* others have three, the cerci and a median terminal filament.

The above account of the *Ephemeroptera* and the keys below have been rewritten from Edmunds *et al.* (1976). Many of the figures are modified or taken directly from the same source. I am grateful to the University of Minnesota Press and the coauthors for permission to use this material and the figures. A number of the figures have been taken from work that I coauthored elsewhere (figs. 10.71–10.72 and 10.142–10.148 from Allen and Edmunds; fig. 10.63 from Bednarik and Edmunds; and 10.67 from Traver and Edmunds). Dr. R. K. Allen has kindly allowed me to republish figure 10.68 and 10.78–10.80. Figures 10.116–10.118, 10.128–10.131, 10.135, and 10.149 are from Burks (1953) and are published with permission of the Illinois Natural History Survey. Figure 10.41 is from Needham *et al.* and is published courtesy of Cornell University Press, and figures 10.57–10.59 are from Bednarik and McCafferty (1979), courtesy of the Canadian Bulletin of Fisheries and Aquatic Science.

KEYS TO THE FAMILIES AND GENERA OF EPHEMEROPTERA

Considerable disagreement exists concerning the classification of mayflies above the family level, and some disagreement exists concerning family classification. We follow the classification proposed by McCafferty and Edmunds (1979); this differs from that used by Edmunds *et al.* (1976) in placing the genus *Pentagenia* in the family Palingeniidae rather than Ephemeridae, and in placing *Isonychia* in the Oligoneuriidae rather than Siphlonuridae.

The most recent changes in generic-level classification are the splitting of *Heptagenia* into four genera *(Heptagenia, Macdunnoa, Leucrocuta,* and *Nixe)* and the elevation of the subgenera of Ephemerellidae to genera.

The family Leptophlebiidae has been divided into two subfamilies (Leptophlebiinae and Atalophlebiinae) on the basis of characters that are in some cases difficult for nonspecialists. In the keys I ignore this division only because of its difficulty for students. The genus *Farrodes* (Texas) is not keyed.

The genus *Spinadis* is unknown as an adult and the genus *Anepeorus* is so rare as an adult that I have not keyed it. In other cases I have lumped genera of adults together because some of them are rarely encountered *and* they are difficult to separate. The most severe case concerns adults of the genera *Pseudocloeon, Paracloeodes, Baetodes,* and *Apobaetis. Pseudocloen* is geographically widespread and occurs in a wide variety of streams. *Paracloeodes* is a genus of Neotropical origin that occurs in warm rivers as far north as Minnesota and as far east as Indiana. *Baetodes* occurs in Oklahoma, Texas, New Mexico, and Arizona, and *Apobaetis* is known only from California. Persons wishing to distinguish these adults should use the keys and drawings in Edmunds *et al.* (1976). The genus *Acanthametropus* is unknown as an adult, but probably keys with *Analetris*.

Generic determinations of adults can be difficult for certain Heptageniidae (e.g., distinguishing *Stenonema* from *Heptagenia*) and for some Ephemerellidae (e.g., distinguishing some species as being *Ephemerella* or *Serratella*). In some cases, I have keyed two genera of nymphs out in the same couplet because the genera are rarely encountered (e.g., *Spinadis* and *Anepeorus, Acanthametropus* and *Analetris*); generally, however, the larval keys are more complete than are the adult keys.

All known distributions are tentative and should be regarded as incomplete. Such terms as abundant, common, uncommon, or rare are all relative to place, time, and collector. Rare can be interpreted as hard to collect, active at the wrong time of day, or perhaps, in some cases, truly at low population levels. In any case, a collector using the best technique at the right places at an appropriate time may collect large numbers of a "rare" genus or species.

The family Palingeniidae is now represented in North America because of the recent transfer of the genus *Pentagenia* from Ephemeridae to Palingeniidae (McCafferty and Edmunds 1976). For a list of valid species and references to keys see Edmunds *et al.* (1976). Major changes have been made concerning the valid species and taxonomy in *Stenonema* and *Baetis.* The same book provides a relatively complete bibliography for 1935 to 1974.

Nymphs

1. Thoracic notum enlarged to form a shield extended to abdominal segment 6, gills enclosed beneath shield (fig. 10.3) .... *BAETISCIDAE—Baetisca*

1′. Thoracic notum not enlarged as above; abdominal gills exposed 2

2(1′). Gills on abdominal segments 2–7 forked, with margins fringed (fig. 10.4); mandibles usually with large tusks projected forward and visible from above head (figs. 10.6–10.7); if tusks absent, head and thorax with pads of long spines (fig. 10.8) 3

2′. Gills on abdominal segments 2–7 variable; if gills forked, margins not fringed (fig. 10.5); tusks rarely present on mandibles 7

3(2). Head and prothorax with dorsal pad of long spines on each side (fig. 10.8); without mandibular tusks; gills ventral .... *BEHNINGIIDAE—Dolania*

3′. Head and prothorax without pads of spines; mandibular tusks present (figs. 10.6–10.7); gills lateral or dorsal 4

4(3′). Fore tibiae more or less modified, either flattened or with tubercles, adapted for burrowing (fig. 10.6); abdominal gills held dorsally 5

4′. Fore tibiae cylindrical, unmodified (fig. 10.7); abdominal gills held laterally .... *POTAMANTHIDAE—Potamanthus*

5(4). Mandibular tusks curved upward apically as viewed laterally (fig. 10.9); ventral apex of hind tibiae projected into distinct acute point (fig. 10.11) 6

5′. Mandibular tusks curved downward apically as viewed laterally (fig. 10.10); ventral apex of hind tibiae rounded (fig. 10.12) .... *POLYMITARCYIDAE* 67

6(5). Mandibular tusks with a distinct dorsolateral keel that is more or less toothed and with a line of spurs along the toothed edge; teeth extend to apical half of tusks; common; infrequently collected, large rivers (fig. 10.6) .... *PALINGENIIDAE—Pentagenia*

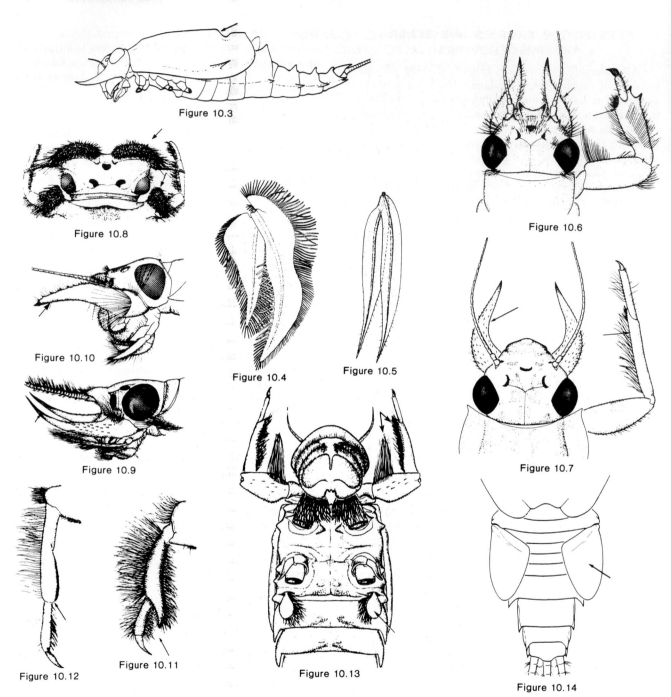

Figure 10.3.

Figure 10.8.

Figure 10.10.

Figure 10.9.

Figure 10.4.

Figure 10.5.

Figure 10.6.

Figure 10.7.

Figure 10.12.

Figure 10.11.

Figure 10.13.

Figure 10.14.

Figure 10.3. Lateral view of *Baetisca* sp. nymph (Baetiscidae).

Figure 10.4. Gill 4 of *Ephoron* sp. nymph (Polymitarcyidae).

Figure 10.5. Gill 4 of *Paraleptophlebia* sp. nymph (Leptophlebiidae).

Figure 10.6. Dorsal view of head and foreleg of *Pentagenia* sp. nymph (Palingeniidae).

Figure 10.7. Dorsal view of head and foreleg of *Potamanthus* sp. nymph (Potamanthidae).

Figure 10.8. Dorsal view of head and prothorax of *Dolania* sp. nymph (Behningiidae).

Figure 10.9. Lateral view of head of *Ephemera* sp. nymph (Ephemeridae).

Figure 10.10. Lateral view of head of *Ephoron* sp. nymph (Polymitarcyidae).

Figure 10.11. Hind leg of *Hexagenia* sp. nymph (Ephemeridae).

Figure 10.12. Hind leg of *Ephoron* sp. nymph (Polymitarcyidae).

Figure 10.13. Ventral view of anterior portion of *Lachlania* sp. nymph (Oligoneuriidae).

Figure 10.14. Dorsal view of abdomen of *Tricorythodes* sp. nymph (Tricorythidae).

6'.   Mandibular tusks more or less circular in cross section, without a distinct toothed
       keel (fig. 10.9) .... *EPHEMERIDAE* 65

7(2'). A double row of long setae on inner margins of femora and tibiae of fore legs (fig.
       10.13) .... *OLIGONEURIIDAE* 33

7'.   Long setae absent on fore legs, or not arranged as above 8

8(7'). Gills on abdominal segment 2 operculate or semioperculate, covering succeeding
       pairs (fig. 10.14) 9

8'.   Gills on abdominal segment 2 neither operculate nor semioperculate, either similar
       to those on succeeding segments or absent 11

9(8).   Gills on abdominal segment 2 triangular, subtriangular, or oval, not meeting
       medially (fig. 10.14); gill lamellae on segments 3–6 simple or bilobed, without
       fringed margins .... *TRICORYTHIDAE* 63

9'.   Gills on abdominal segment 2 quadrate, meeting or almost meeting medially (fig.
       10.15a); gill lamellae on segments 3–6 with fringed margins (fig. 10.15b) 10

10(9'). Mesonotum with distinct rounded lobe on anterolateral corners (fig. 10.16);
        operculate gills fused medially; developing hind wing pads present; East, mostly
        Southeast .... *NEOEPHEMERIDAE—Neoephemera*

10'.   Mesonotum without anterolateral lobes (fig. 10.17); operculate gills not fused
        medially; without developing hind wing pads; widespread .... *CAENIDAE* 64

11(8'). Gills *absent* on abdominal segment 2, rudimentary or absent on segment 1, and
        present or absent on segment 3 (figs. 10.18, 10.41); gills on segments 3–7 or 4–7
        consist of anterior (dorsal) oval lamella and posterior (ventral) lamella with
        numerous lobes (fig. 10.19); paired tubercles often present on abdominal
        terga .... *EPHEMERELLIDAE* 56

11'.   Gills present on abdominal segments 1–5, 1–7, or 2–7; paired tubercles rarely
        present on abdominal terga 12

12(11'). Nymph distinctly flattened; head flattened; eyes and antennae dorsal; mandibles
         not visible in dorsal view (fig. 10.20) .... *HEPTAGENIIDAE* 35

12'.   Nymph not flattened (figs. 10.21–10.22) or, if flattened, mandibles visible and
        forming part of the flattened dorsal surface of head (fig. 10.23) 13

13(12') Claws of forelegs differ in structure from those on middle and hind legs (figs.
        10.24–10.25); claws of middle and hind legs long and slender, about as long as
        tibiae (figs. 10.24–10.25) 14

13'.   Claws of all legs similar in structure, usually sharply pointed, rarely spatulate;
        claws variable in length, if those of middle and hind legs long and slender, then
        usually shorter than tibiae (longer than tibiae in 3 rare genera) 15

14(13). Claws on fore legs simple, with long slender denticles; spinous pad present on fore
        coxae; from Michigan west (fig. 10.24a) .... *AMETROPODIDAE—Ametropus*

14'.   Claws on fore legs bifid (fig. 10.25a); without spinous pad on fore coxae; Canada,
        Midwest, and East .... *METRETOPODIDAE* 48

15(13'). Abdominal gills on segments 2–7 either forked (fig. 10.5), in tufts (fig. 10.26),
         with all margins fringed (fig. 10.27), or with double lamellae terminated in
         filaments or points (figs. 10.28–10.30); apicolateral margin of maxillae with a
         dense brush of hairs (fig. 10.31) .... *LEPTOPHLEBIIDAE* 49

15'.   Abdominal gills not as above; gills either more or less oval or heart-shaped;
        lamellae either single, double, or triple (figs. 10.33–10.36); fringed on inner
        margin in 1 rare genus (fig. 10.37); never terminating in filaments or points;
        apicolateral margin of maxillae variable, never with dense brush of hairs (figs.
        10.32, 10.40) 16

16(15'). Median terminal filament shorter than tergum 10, or, if well developed, then
         antennae long, 2 to 3 times width of head (fig. 10.39) .... *BAETIDAE* 22

16'.   Median terminal filament subequal to cerci; antennae shorter than twice width of
        head (fig. 10.38) .... *SIPHLONURIDAE* 17

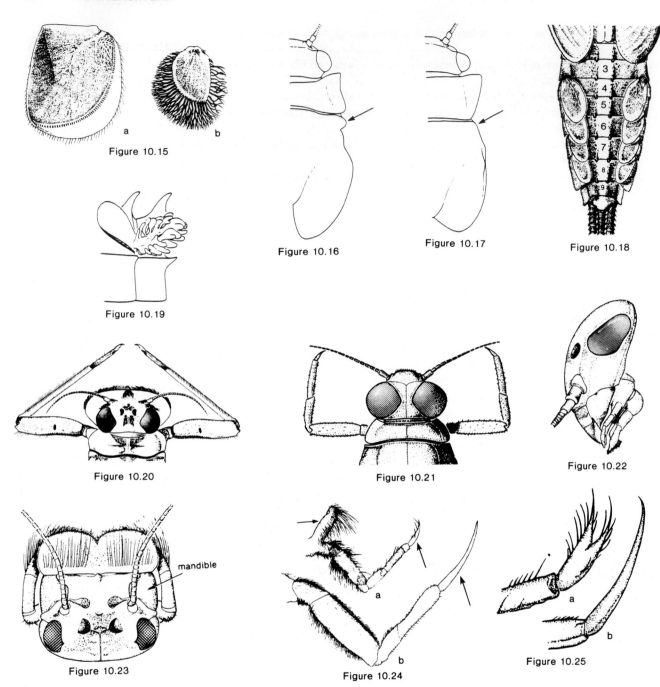

Figure 10.15

Figure 10.16

Figure 10.17

Figure 10.18

Figure 10.19

Figure 10.20

Figure 10.21

Figure 10.22

mandible

Figure 10.23

Figure 10.24

Figure 10.25

Figure 10.15. Gills 2 *(a)* and 4 *(b)* of *Caenis* sp. nymph (Caenidae).

Figure 10.16. Dorsal view of head and thorax of *Neoephemera* sp. nymph (Neoephemeridae).

Figure 10.17. Dorsal view of head and thorax of *Caenis* sp. nymph (Caenidae).

Figure 10.18. Dorsal view of abdomen of *Serratella* sp. nymph (Ephemerellidae).

Figure 10.19. Gill of segment 3 (lamella raised) of *Drunella* sp. nymph (Ephemerellidae).

Figure 10.20. Dorsal view of head and prothorax of *Epeorus* sp. nymph (Heptageniidae).

Figure 10.21. Dorsal view of head and prothorax of *Parameletus* sp. nymph (Siphlonuridae).

Figure 10.22. Lateral view of head of *Baetis* sp. nymph (Baetidae).

Figure 10.23. Dorsal view of head of *Traverella* sp. nymph (Leptophlebiidae).

Figure 10.24. Foreleg *(a)* and hind leg *(b)* of *Ametropus* sp. (Ametropodidae).

Figure 10.25. Claws of foreleg *(a)* and hind leg *(b)* of *Siphloplecton* sp. nymph (Metretopodidae).

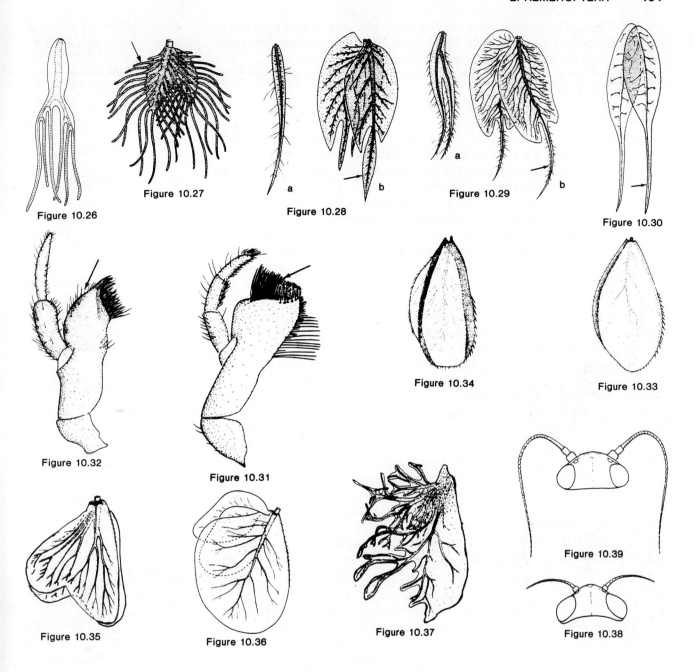

Figure 10.26. Gill 5 of *Habrophlebia* sp. nymph (Leptophlebiidae).

Figure 10.27. Gill 4 of *Traverella* nymph (Leptophlebiidae).

Figure 10.28. Gills 1 *(a)* and 4 *(b)* of *Choroterpes* sp. nymph (Leptophlebiidae).

Figure 10.29. Gills 1 *(a)* and 4 *(b)* of *Leptophlebia* sp. nymph (Leptophlebiidae).

Figure 10.30. Gill 4 of *Leptophlebia* nymph (Leptophlebiidae).

Figure 10.31. Right maxilla of *Leptophlebia* sp. nymph (Leptophlebiidae).

Figure 10.32. Right maxilla of *Callibaetis* sp. nymph (Baetidae).

Figure 10.33. Gill 4 of *Ameletus* sp. nymph (Siphlonuridae).

Figure 10.34. Gill 4 of *Ameletus* sp. nymph (Siphlonuridae).

Figure 10.35. Gill 2 of *Siphlonurus* sp. nymph (Siphlonuridae).

Figure 10.36. Gill 4 of *Analetris* sp. nymph (Siphlonuridae).

Figure 10.37. Gill 4 of *Acanthametropus* sp. nymph (Siphlonuridae).

Figure 10.38. Dorsal view of head of *Siphlonurus* sp. nymph (Siphlonuridae).

Figure 10.39. Dorsal view of head of *Baetis* sp. nymph (Baetidae).

17(16'). Tibia and tarsi bowed; claws very long and slender, claws of hind legs about as long as tarsi (similar to fig. 10.24b); rare; large rivers; scattered distribution .... ***Acanthametropus, Analetris***

17'. Tibiae and tarsi not bowed; claws usually not long and slender 18

18(17'). Abdominal gills with double lamellae on segments 1–2 (in some, double also on segments 3–7) (fig. 10.35) 19

18'. Gills on all abdominal segments with single lamellae, more or less oval (figs. 10.33–10.34) or heart-shaped 20

19(18). Gills on abdominal segments 1–2 subtriangular, broadest near apex (fig. 10.35); claws of middle and hind legs slightly longer than those of forelegs .... ***Siphlonurus***

19'. Gills on abdominal segments 1–2 oval; claws of middle and hind legs distinctly longer than those of fore legs; rare, California .... ***Edmundsius***

20(18'). Maxillae with crown of pectinate spines (fig. 10.40); gills more or less oval with a sclerotized band along lateral margin and usually with a similar sclerotized band on (fig. 10.33) or near mesal margin (fig. 10.34) .... ***Ameletus***

20'. Maxillae without pectinate spines; gills more or less heart-shaped 21

21(20'). Sterna of mesothorax and metathorax each with a median tubercle; abdominal segments 5–9 greatly expanded laterally; rare, New York to Labrador .... ***Siphlonisca***

21'. Sterna of thorax without tubercles; abdominal segments 5–9 not greatly expanded; uncommon; Canada or West, mountains .... ***Parameletus***

22(16). Claws distinctly spatulate with large apical denticles, tarsi distinctly bowed (Fig. 10.42); Southwest .... ***Dactylobaetis***

22'. Claws sharply pointed; denticles, if present, smaller and ventral (Figs. 10.43–10.45) 23

23(22'). Abdominal gills present on segments 1–5 only, extended ventrally from the pleura; median tubercle present on anterior abdominal terga; Southwest .... ***Baetodes***

23'. Abdominal gills present on segments 1–7 or 2–7, held laterally or dorsally; no tubercles on abdomen 24

24(23'). Middle caudal filament as long as lateral cerci 25

24'. Middle caudal filament shorter than cerci, or apparently absent 30

25(24). Apex of labial palpi simple and truncate (fig. 10.46); trachea of gills palmate (fig. 10.47) or asymmetrical with most branches on median side (fig. 10.48); tails with distinct dark band every 3rd to 5th segment (fig. 10.49a,b) 26

25' Apex of labial palpi variable, not as above; trachea variable, not as above; tails rarely banded as above 27

26(25). Hind wing pads present .... ***Centroptilum***

26'. Hind wing pads absent .... ***Cloeon***

27(25). Gills on one or more segments with recurved flap, (fig. 10.50); when flap large, gills may appear double or triple .... ***Callibaetis***

27'. Gills of simple, flat plates (fig. 10.51) 28

28(27'). Claws clearly less than half as long as respective tarsi (fig. 10.43) .... ***Baetis*** (in part)

28'. Claws one-half or more as long as respective tarsi (figs. 10.44–10.45) 29

29(28). Claws almost as long as respective tarsi (fig. 10.45); rare; California .... ***Apobaetis***

29'. Claws about one-half as long as respective tarsi (fig. 10.44) .... ***Paracloeodes***

30(24'). Middle caudal filament at least one-eighth as long as cerci .... ***Baetis*** (in part)

30'. Middle caudal filament shorter than one-eighth as long as cerci, may appear absent 31

31(30'). Fore coxae each with a single filamentous gill .... ***Heterocloeon***

31' Fore coxae without gills 32

32(31'). Hind wing pads present, but may be very small .... ***Baetis*** (in part)

32'. Hind wing pads absent .... ***Pseudocloeon***

33(7). Gills on segment 1 dorsolateral, similar in position and structure to other gills; fibrils shorter than gill plates; widespread and common .... ***Isonychia***

33'. Gills on segment 1 ventral (fig. 10.13); fibrils longer than plate or gill plate absent 34

34(33').   Gill plates oval on segments 2–7 (similar to abdominal gill 1 (fig. 10.13); claws present on forelegs .... *Lachlania*

34'.   Gill plates slender and elongate on segments 2–7; claws absent on fore legs .... *Homoeoneuria*

35(12).   Claws as long as or longer than tarsi; tibiae and tarsi bowed; rare; large rivers .... *Pseudiron*

35'.   Claws much shorter than tarsi; tibiae and tarsi straight 36

36(35).   Gills ventral on segments 1–2, lamellae slender and curved; rare; large rivers .... *Anepeorus, Spinadis*

36'.   Gills dorsal or lateral; if gills extend ventrally they are at least 1/3 as broad as long 37

37(36').   Second segment of maxillary palpi longer than head is broad, conspicuous at side or behind head (fig. 10.52); in pools and swamps .... *Arthroplea*

37'.   Second segment of maxillary palpi not greatly elongated, inconspicuous; in lotic waters 38

38(37').   Two well-developed caudal filaments, terminal filament rudimentary or absent 39

38'   Three well-developed caudal filaments 40

39(38).   Well-developed paired tubercles present on hind margin of abdominal terga 1–9 .... *Ironodes*

39'.   Abdominal terga without paired tubercles .... *Epeorus*

40(38').   Gills on abdominal segments 1 and 7 enlarged and meet or almost meet beneath abdomen to form ventral disk (fig. 10.53) .... *Rhithrogena*

40'.   Gills on abdominal segments 1 and 7 do not meet beneath abdomen and usually smaller than intermediate pairs 41

41(40').   Maxillary palpi protrude at sides of head (fig. 10.54); fibrilliform portion of gills 2–6 absent or with only a few filaments (fig. 10.55) .... *Cinygmula*

41'.   Maxillary palpi rarely protrude at sides of head; fibrilliform portion of gills 2–6 of many fibrils 42

42(41).   Gills on segment 7 minute, no longer than the posterolateral projections of that segment (fig. 10.56) .... *Macdunnoa*

42'.   Gills on segment 7 much larger than above 43

43(42').   Gills on segment 7 reduced to slender filaments; trachea absent or with few or no lateral branches (figs. 10.57b–10.59b) 44

43'.   Gills on segment 7 similar to preceding pairs but smaller; trachea of gill 7 with lateral branches 45

44(43).   Gills on abdominal segments 1–6 with apex pointed (fig. 10.57a) .... *Stenacron*

44'.   Gills on abdominal segments 1–6 with apex rounded (fig. 10.58a) or truncate (fig. 10.59a) .... *Stenonema*

45(43').   Gill lamellae on segment 1 less than 1/2 as long as those on segment 2, with fibrilliform portion of gill 1 much longer than lamella (fig. 10.60); Northwest .... *Cinygma*

45'.   Gill lamellae on segment 1 two-thirds as long as those on segment 2; fibrilliform portion of gill 1 usually subequal to or shorter than lamella 46

46(45').   Gills on segment 7 with fibrilliform portion present and with numerous fibrils; claws without denticles but with one basal tooth (fig. 10.61) .... *Heptagenia*

46'.   Gills on segments 7 without fibrilliform portion; claws with denticles (fig. 10.62) 47

47(46').   Head large, wider than pronotum, many dark spots near anterior margin (fig. 10.63) .... *Leucrocuta*

47'.   Head not as wide as pronotum, without numerous dark spots .... *Nixe*

48(14').   Margins of claws of fore legs densely covered with spines (more than 30) that are only slightly smaller than the short terminal spines (fig. 10.64); outer margin of gill 4 with 2–7 stout spines in addition to small setae; rare; Canada, Michigan to Maine .... *Metretopus*

48'.   Margins of claws of fore legs sparsely covered with spines (less than 20) that are more slender than the long terminal spines (fig. 10.25); Midwest and East .... *Siphloplecton*

49(15).   Labrum as wide as or wider than head capsule; (fig. 10.23); abdominal gills oval with fringed margins (fig. 10.27) .... *Traverella*

49'.   Labrum much narrower than head capsule (fig. 10.67) 50

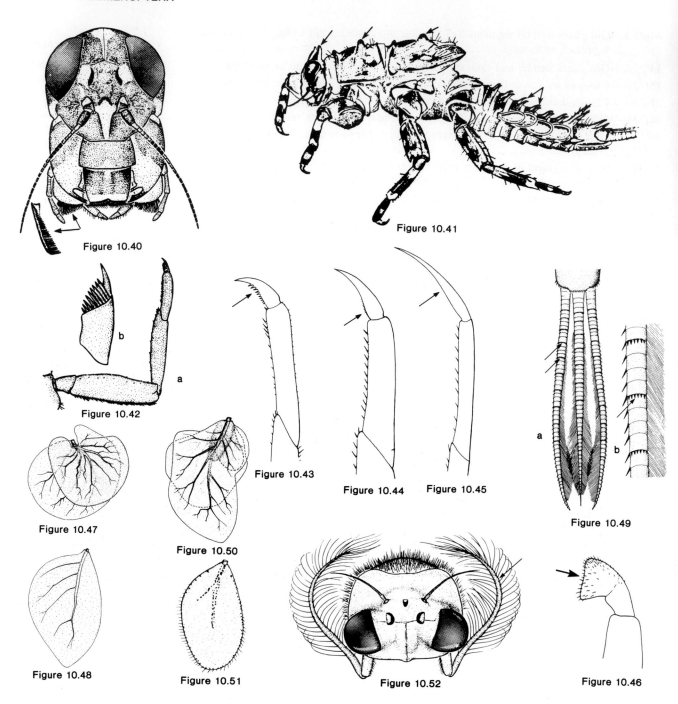

Figure 10.40. Anterior view of head and enlarged pectinate spine of *Ameletus* sp. (Siphlonuridae).

Figure 10.41. Lateral view of *Drunella grandis* nymph (Ephemerellidae).

Figure 10.42. Leg *(a)* and claw *(b)* of *Dactylobaetis* sp. nymph (Baetidae).

Figure 10.43. Tarsus and claw of *Baetis* sp. nymph (Baetidae).

Figure 10.44. Tarsus and claw of *Paracloeodes* sp. nymph (Baetidae).

Figure 10.45. Tarsus and claw of *Apobaetis* sp. nymph (Baetidae).

Figure 10.46. Labial palpus of *Centroptilum* sp. nymph (Baetidae).

Figure 10.47. Gill 1 of *Cloeon* sp. nymph (Baetidae).

Figure 10.48. Gill 4 of *Centroptilum* sp. nymph (Baetidae).

Figure 10.49. Caudal filaments *(a)* and detail of cercus *(b)* of *Centroptilum* sp. nymph (Baetidae).

Figure 10.50. Gill 2 of *Callibaetis* sp. nymph (Baetidae).

Figure 10.51. Gill 4 of *Baetis* sp. nymph (Baetidae).

Figure 10.52. Dorsal view of head of *Arthroplea* sp. (Heptageniidae).

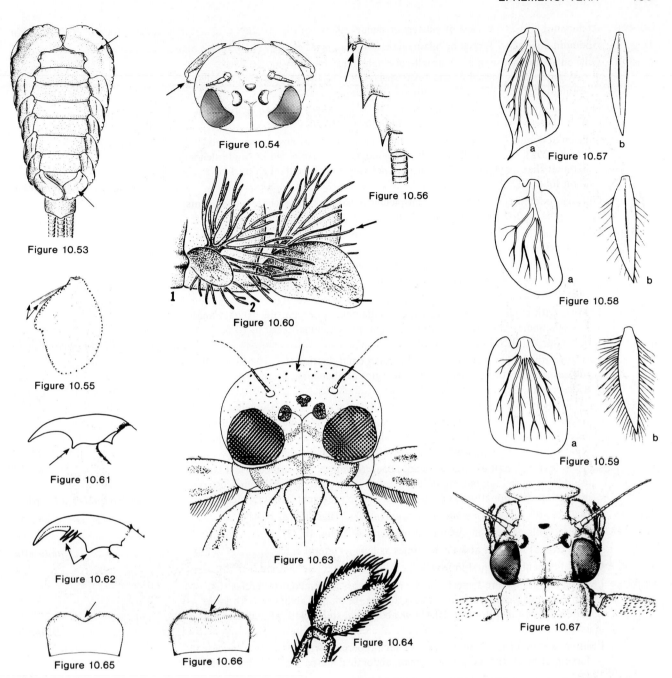

Figure 10.54

Figure 10.56

Figure 10.53

Figure 10.57

Figure 10.55

Figure 10.58

Figure 10.60

Figure 10.59

Figure 10.61

Figure 10.62

Figure 10.63

Figure 10.67

Figure 10.64

Figure 10.65

Figure 10.66

Figure 10.53. Ventral view of abdomen of *Rhithrogena* sp. nymph (Heptageniidae).

Figure 10.54. Dorsal view of head of *Cinygmula* sp. nymph (Heptageniidae).

Figure 10.55. Gill 4 of *Cinygmula* sp. nymph (Heptageniidae).

Figure 10.56. Abdominal segments 7–10 of *Macdunnoa* sp. nymph (Heptageniidae).

Figue 10.57. Gills 4 *(a)* and 7 *(b)* of *Stenacron* sp. nymph (Heptageniidae).

Figure 10.58. Gills 4 *(a)* and 7 *(b)* of *Stenonema* sp. nymph (Heptageniidae).

Figure 10.59. Gills 4 *(a)* and 7 *(b)* of *Stenonema* sp. nymph (Heptageniidae).

Figure 10.60. Gills of segments 1 and 2 of *Cinygma* sp. nymph (Heptageniidae).

Figure 10.61. Claw of *Heptagenia* sp. nymph (Heptageniidae).

Figure 10.62. Claw of *Nixe* sp. nymph (Heptageniidae).

Figure 10.63. Head and part of thorax of *Leucrocuta* sp. nymph (Heptageniidae).

Figure 10.64. Claw of foreleg of *Metretopus* sp. (Metretopodidae).

Figure 10.65. Labrum of *Habrophlebiodes* sp. nymph (Leptophlebiidae).

Figure 10.66. Labrum of *Paraleptophlebia* sp. nymph (Leptophlebiidae).

Figure 10.67. Head of *Thraulodes* sp. nymph (Leptophlebiidae).

50(49).   Abdominal gills 2–7 consist of clusters of slender filaments (fig. 10.26) .... *Habrophlebia*

50′.   Abdominal gills 2–7 forked or bilamellate, not as above (figs. 10.28–10.30) 51

51(50′).   Gills on abdominal segment 1 usually of single linear lamella (fig. 10.28a) (asymmetrically forked in one Texas species, fig. 10.68a,b), those on succeeding segments broadly bilamellate with apex 3-lobed (fig. 10.28b) .... *Choroterpes*

51′.   Gills on abdominal segment 1 forked (fig. 10.29a), either similar to or different from those on succeeding segments (figs. 10.29b, 10.30) 52

52(51′).   Gills on abdominal segment 1 forked, much narrower than those on segments 2–7 (fig. 10.29a); each lamella of gills on segments 2–7 terminated in single slender filament that may (fig. 10.29b) or may not (fig. 10.30) be flanked by 1 or 2 blunt lobes .... *Leptophlebia*

52′.   Gills on abdominal segment 1 not conspicuously narrower than those on segments 2–7; gills on 2–7 forked or bilamellate 53

53(52′).   Gills on middle abdominal segments shaped as in figure 10.69; lateral tracheal branches conspicuous 54

53′.   Gills on middle abdominal segments forked or bilamellate, but either broader, narrower, more deeply forked, or with lateral tracheal branches less conspicuous than above 55

54(53).   Labrum with moderately deep V-shaped median emargination (fig. 10.65); small row of spinules present on posterior margins of abdominal terga 6–10 or 7–10 only (fig. 10.70); Midwest or East .... *Habrophlebiodes*

54′.   Labrum with shallow, variably shaped median emargination (fig. 10.66); small rows of spinules present on posterior margins of abdominal terga 1–10; widespread .... *Paraleptophlebia* (in part)

55(53′).   Labrum about two-thirds as wide as head in front of eyes distinctly wider than clypeus (fig. 10.67); gills variable, but each lamella up to one-fourth as broad as long; posterolateral spines present on abdominal segments 2–9, usually small on segments 2–3 or 2–4; Utah, Texas, New Mexico, and Arizona .... *Thraulodes*

55′.   Labrum less than half as wide as head, about as wide as clypeus; each gill lamella usually no more than one-eighth as broad as long; posterolateral spines usually present on abdominal segments 6–9 or 8–9 or on segment 9 only; widespread .... *Paraleptophlebia* (in part)

56(11).   Lamellate gills present on abdominal segments 3–7 (figs. 10.18, 10.41) 57

56′.   Lamellate gills present on abdominal segments 4–7 (fig. 10.72) 60

57(56).   Middle caudal filament at least 1⅓ times as long as lateral cerci .... *Caudatella*

57′.   Caudal filaments subequal in length 58

58(57′).   Leading margin of fore femora usually armed with conspicuous tubercles (fig. 10.71); if not (some western species), thorax, head, *and* abdomen with large paired dorsal tubercles (fig. 10.41) *or* abdominal sterna with attachment disk of long hair .... *Drunella*

58′.   Leading margin of fore femora without such tubercles, without large tubercles on dorsum of head, thorax, *and* abdomen, abdominal sterna without disk of long hair 59

59(58′).   Caudal filaments with whorls of spines at apex of each segment, otherwise with only sparse setae or none (fig. 10.76); maxillary palpi reduced in size (figs. 10.73, 10.74) or absent .... *Serratella*

59′.   Caudal filaments with or without whorls of spines at apex of each segment, apical half of caudal filaments with long intersegmental setae extending laterally (fig. 10.77); maxillary palpi well developed (fig. 10.75) .... *Ephemerella*

60(56′).   Gills on tergum 4 operculate, largely covering those on segments 5–7, only about one-third of any following gill visible (fig. 10.72) 61

60′.   Gills on tergum 4 not operculate, apical half of gills 5 and 6 visible .... *Attenella*

61(60).   Apex of each femur developed into an acute point; head broadest near anterior margin, West .... *Timpanoga*

61′.   Apex of each femur rounded or angulate, but not acutely pointed; head variable 62

62(61′).   Abdominal terga without paired tubercles on or near posterior margin; Midwest,
           East .... *Dannella*

62′.   Abdominal terga with paired tubercles on or near posterior margin of at least
           segments 3–7 (fig. 10.72); Midwest, East, Pacific Coast .... *Eurylophella*

63(9).   Femora with transverse row of long setae (fig. 10.79); operculate abdominal gill 2
           triangular or subtriangular in shape, over two-thirds as wide as long (fig. 10.14) .... *Tricorythodes*

63′.   Femora with transverse row of spines (fig. 10.78); operculate abdominal gill 2 oval
           in shape, less than two-thirds as wide as long (fig. 10.80) .... *Leptohyphes*

64(10′).   Head with 3 prominent ocellar tubercles; maxillary and labial palpi 2-segmented .... *Brachycercus*

64′.   Head without ocellar tubercles; maxillary and labial palpi 3-segmented .... *Caenis*

65(6′).   Antennae with whorls of long setae on each segment (fig. 10.9); the small
           unfringed gills on segment 1 forked 66

65′.   Antennae with only short setae; the small gills on segment 1 single .... *Litobrancha*

66(65).   Frontal process of head forked (similar to fig. 10.6) .... *Ephemera*

66′.   Frontal process of head rounded, not forked .... *Hexagenia*

67(5′).   Mandibular tusks with numerous tubercles on upper surface (fig. 10.10); fore tarsi
           rounded and clearly separated from fore tibiae .... *Ephoron*

67′.   Mandibular tusks with 1–3 tubercles on *inner margin;* fore tarsi flattened and
           largely fused with tibiae 68

68(67′).   Tubercles present almost at apex of inner margin of tusks (Midwest, Southeast) .... *Tortopus*

68′.   Tubercles present in basal half of tusks only (Texas only) .... *Campsurus*

Adults

1.   Fore wing venation greatly reduced, apparently only 3–4 longitudinal veins behind
           R$_1$ (fig. 10.85); body black .... *OLIGONEURIIDAE* (in part) 30

1′.   Fore wing venation complete or only moderately reduced, numerous longitudinal
           veins present behind R$_1$ (figs. 10.86–10.87, 10.107); body variable in color 2

2(1′).   Penes of male longer than forceps (fig. 10.92); antennae of female inserted on
           prominent anterolateral projections (fig. 10.93); 4 or more long cubital
           intercalaries connected by crossveins usually present in fore wing (fig. 10.86) .... *BEHNINGIIDAE—Dolania*

2′.   Penes of male shorter than forceps (fig. 10.94); antennae of female not inserted as
           above; cubital intercalaries in fore wing variable, 3 or less, or crossveins few or
           absent (figs. 10.87–10.91, 10.97–10.102) 3

3(2′).   In fore wings, base of veins MP$_2$ and CuA strongly divergent from base of vein
           MP$_1$; MP$_2$ strongly bent towards CuA basally (figs. 10.87–10.90) and
           sometimes fused at base with CuA; hind wings with numerous veins and
           crossveins; vein MA of hind wings unforked (figs. 10.87–10.90) 4

3′.   In fore wings, base of veins MP$_2$ and CuA little divergent from vein MP$_1$ (vein
           MP$_2$ only may diverge from MP$_1$), fork of MP usually more symmetrical (figs.
           10.91, 10.97–10.107); hind wings variable, may be reduced or absent; if hind
           wings present, vein MA variable 8

4(3).   Costal angulation of hind wings acute or at a right angle (fig. 10.87b); vein A$_1$ of
           fore wing unforked; costal crossveins basal of bullae of fore wings weak or
           atrophied (fig. 10.87a); East, mostly Southeast .... *NEOEPHEMERIDAE—Neoephemera*

4′.   Costal angulation of hind wings usually rounded (figs. 10.88–10.90); if nearly
           acute or at right angles (fig. 10.89), fore wing vein A$_1$ forked near margin (fig.
           10.89); costal crossveins basal of bullae of fore wings well developed (fig. 10.89) 5

5(4′).   Middle and hind legs of male and all legs of female feeble and nonfunctional; color
           usually pale; wings often somewhat translucent and colorless or with gray or
           purplish gray shading .... *POLYMITARCYIDAE* 60

5′.   All legs of both sexes well developed and functional; color variable 6

6(5′).   Fore wing vein A$_1$ forked near wing margin (fig. 10.89); abdomen usually
           yellowish, in some species with reddish lateral stripes or spots on terga ...... *POTAMANTHIDAE—Potamanthus*

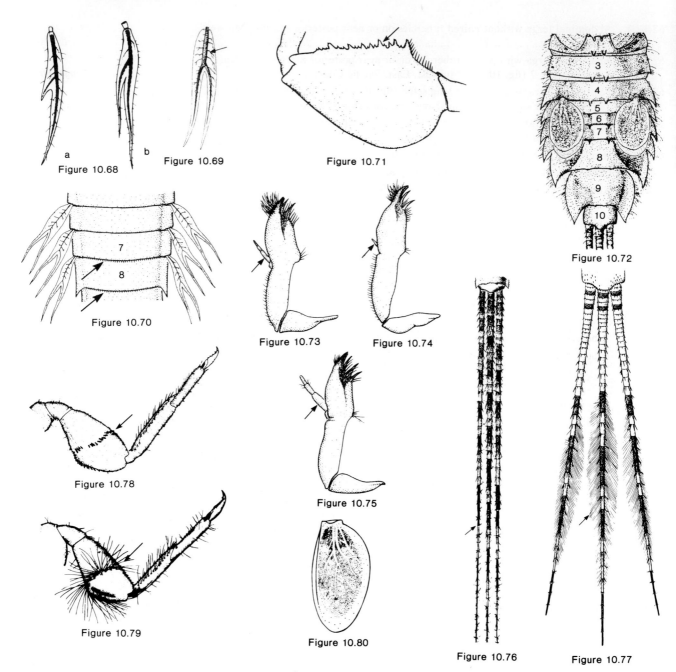

Figure 10.68. Variations (a and b) of gill 1 of Choro-terpes (Neochoroterpes) sp. nymph (Leptophlebiidae).

Figure 10.69. Gill 4 of Habrophlebiodes sp. nymph (Leptophlebiidae).

Figure 10.70. Abdominal segments 5–8 of Habrophlebiodes sp. nymph (Leptophlebiidae).

Figure 10.71. Forefemur of Drunella sp. nymph (Ephemerellidae).

Figure 10.72. Abdominal terga of Eurylophella sp. nymph (Ephemerellidae).

Figure 10.73. Maxilla of Serratella sp. nymph (Ephemerellidae).

Figure 10.74. Maxilla of Serratella sp. nymph (Ephemerellidae).

Figure 10.75. Maxilla of Ephemerella sp. nymph (Ephemerellidae).

Figure 10.76. Caudal filaments of Serratella sp. nymph (Ephemerellidae).

Figure 10.77. Caudal filaments of Ephemerella sp. nymph (Ephemerellidae).

Figure 10.78. Foreleg of Leptohyphes sp. nymph (Tricorythidae).

Figure 10.79. Foreleg of Tricorythodes sp. nymph (Tricorythidae).

Figure 10.80. Gill 2 of Leptohyphes sp. nymph (Tricorythidae).

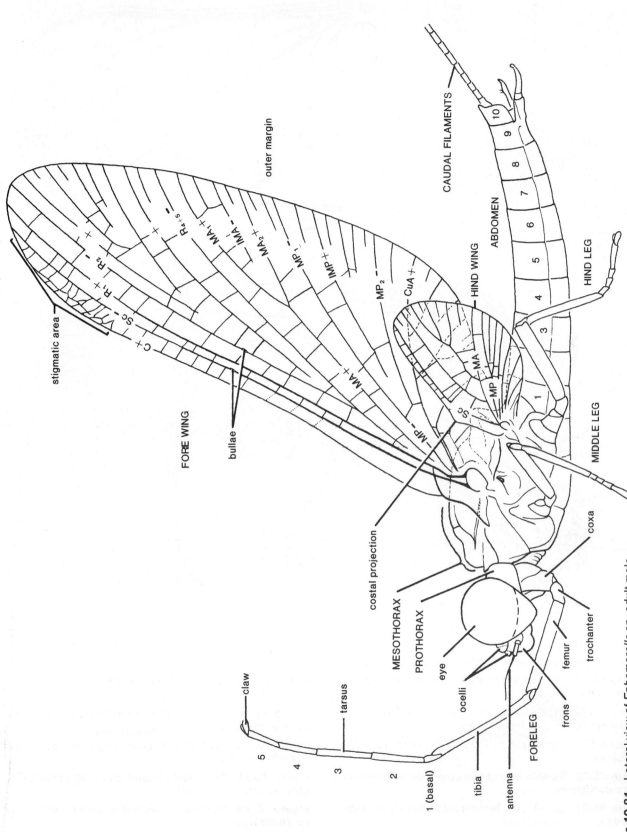

Figure 10.81. Lateral view of *Ephemerella* sp. adult male (Ephemerellidae).

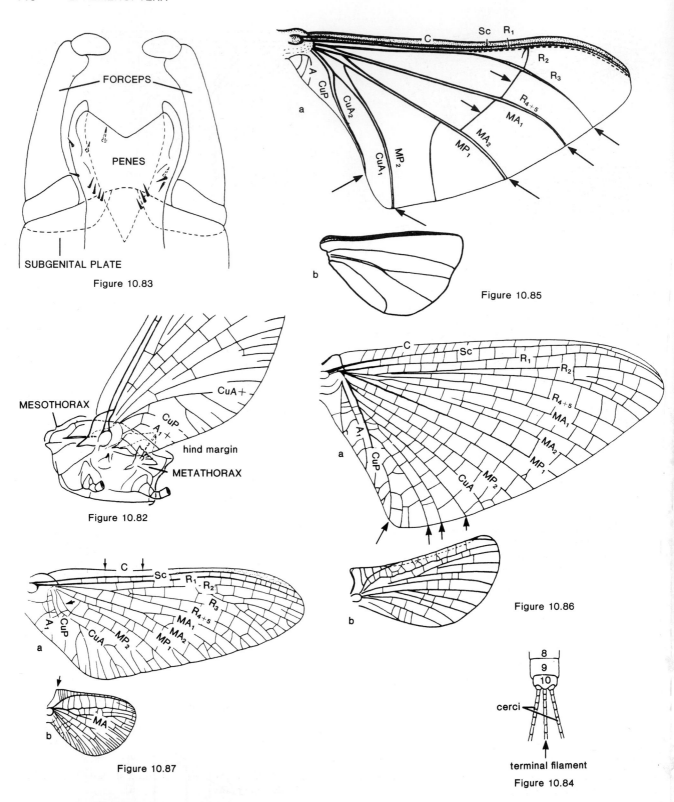

Figure 10.83

Figure 10.85

Figure 10.82

Figure 10.86

Figure 10.87

Figure 10.84

Figure 10.82. Lateral view of thorax and wing of *Ephemerella* sp. (Ephemerellidae).

Figure 10.83. Ventral view of genitalia of *Ephemerella* sp. adult male (Ephemerellidae).

Figure 10.84. Dorsal view of apex of abdomen of *Ephemerella* sp. adult female (Ephemerellidae).

Figure 10.85. Fore wing *(a)* and hind wing *(b)* of *Lachlania* sp. (Oligoneuriidae).

Figure 10.86. Fore wing *(a)* and hind wing *(b)* of *Dolania* sp. (Behningiidae).

Figure 10.87. Fore wing *(a)* and hind wing *(b)* of *Neoephemera* sp. (Neoephemeridae).

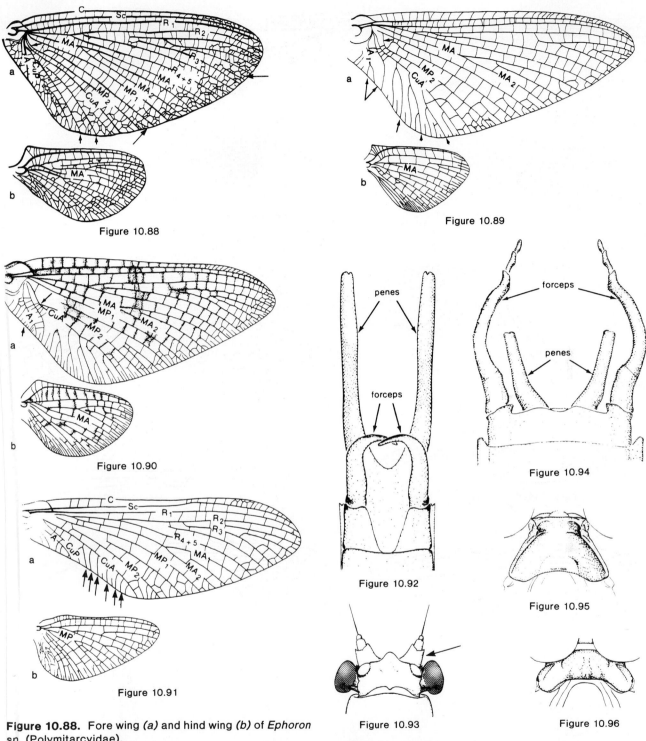

Figure 10.88.

Figure 10.89.

Figure 10.90.

Figure 10.91.

Figure 10.92.

Figure 10.93.

Figure 10.94.

Figure 10.95.

Figure 10.96.

Figure 10.88. Fore wing *(a)* and hind wing *(b)* of *Ephoron* sp. (Polymitarcyidae).

Figure 10.89. Fore wing *(a)* and hind wing *(b)* of *Potamanthus* sp. (Potamanthidae).

Figure 10.90. Fore wing *(a)* and hind wing *(b)* of *Ephemera* sp. (Ephemeridae).

Figure 10.91. Fore wing *(a)* and hind wing *(b)* of *Siphlonurus* sp. (Siphlonuridae).

Figure 10.92. Ventral view of male genitalia of *Dolania* sp. (Behningiidae).

Figure 10.93. Dorsal view of head of *Dolania* sp. adult female (Behningiidae).

Figure 10.94. Ventral view of genitalia of *Pentagenia* sp. adult male (Palingeniidae).

Figure 10.95. Dorsal view of pronotum of *Ephemera* sp. adult male (Ephemeridae).

Figure 10.96. Dorsal view of pronotum of *Pentagenia* sp. adult male (Palingeniidae).

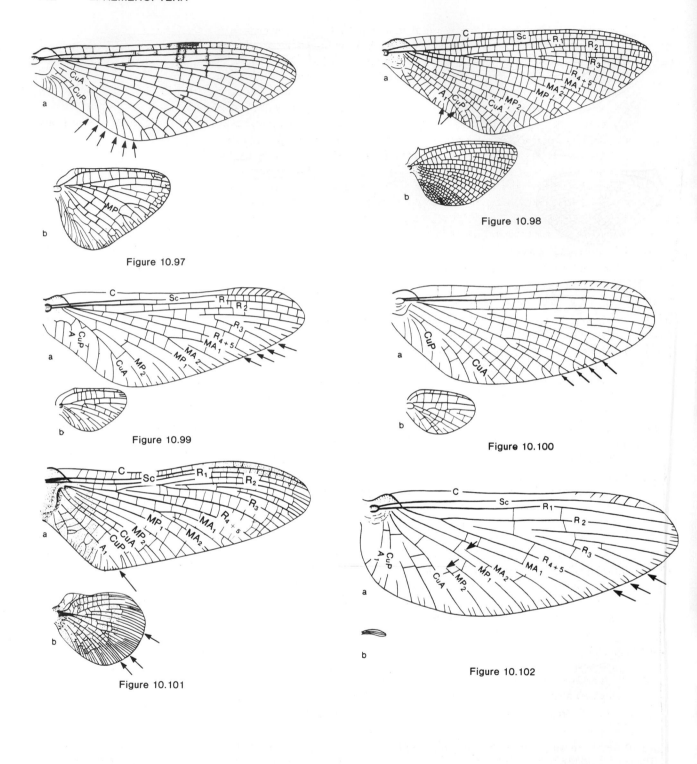

Figure 10.97

Figure 10.98

Figure 10.99

Figure 10.100

Figure 10.101

Figure 10.102

Figure 10.97. Fore wing *(a)* and hind wing *(b)* of *Isonychia* sp. (Oligoneuriidae).

Figure 10.98. Fore wing *(a)* and hind wing *(b)* of *Ametropus* sp. (Ametropodidae).

Figure 10.99. Fore wing *(a)* and hind wing *(b)* of *Ephemerella* sp. (Ephemerellidae).

Figure 10.100. Fore wing *(a)* and hind wing *(b)* of *Paraleptophlebia* sp. (Leptophlebiidae).

Figure 10.101. Fore wing *(a)* and hind wing *(b)* of *Baetisca rogersi* (Baetiscidae).

Figure 10.102. Fore wing *(a)* and hind wing *(b)* of *Baetis* sp. (Baetidae).

6'. Fore wing vein A₁ unforked, attached to hind margin by 3 or more veinlets (fig. 10.90); abdomen of most species with striking dark pattern on terga and sterna 7

7(6'). Pronotum of male well developed, no more than twice as wide as long (fig. 10.95); penes variable, not long and tubular (figs. 10.152, 10.155); caudal filaments of female longer than body .... *EPHEMERIDAE* 58

7'. Pronutum of male shortened, about 3 times as wide as long (fig. 10.96); penes long and tubular (fig. 10.94); caudal filaments of female shorter than body .... *PALINGENIIDAE—Pentagenia*

8(3'). Cubital intercalaries of fore wing consist of a series of veinlets, often forking or sinuate, attaching vein CuA to hind margin (figs. 10.91, 10.97); hind tarsi 4-segmented 9

8'. Cubital intercalaries of fore wing variable but not as above (figs. 10.98–10.100, 10.103–10.104); sometimes absent (fig. 10.101); hind tarsi 4- or 5-segmented 10

9(8). Fore legs largely or entirely dark and middle and hind legs pale; vein MP of hind wing forked near margin (fig. 10.97b) .... *OLIGONEURIIDAE* (in part)—*Isonychia*

9'. Leg color not as above; vein MP of hind wing forked near base to mid-length ...... *SIPHLONURIDAE* 19

10(8'). Three well-developed caudal filaments present 11

10'. Two well-developed caudal filaments (the cerci) present, terminal filament rudimentary or absent 14

11(10). Hind wings present and usually relatively large with 1 or more veins forked; costal projection shorter than wing width (figs. 10.98–10.100) 12

11'. Hind wings absent (figs. 10.106–10.107) or small and with 2 or 3 simple veins only; costal projection long (1½ to 3 times width of wing) and straight or recurved (fig. 10.105) 18

12(11). Vein A₁ of fore wings attached to hind margin by a series of veinlets (fig. 10.98), and with 2 pairs of cubital intercalaries present, anterior pair long, posterior pair very short .... *AMETROPODIDAE—Ametropus*

12'. Vein A₁ not attached to hind margin as above (figs. 10.99–10.100); cubital intercalaries not as above 13

13(12'). Short, basally detached marginal intercalaries present between veins along entire outer margin of wings (fig. 10.99); genital forceps of male with 1 short terminal segment (figs. 10.142–10.148) .... *EPHEMERELLIDAE* 49

13'. No true basally detached marginal intercalaries in positions indicated above, usually absent along entire outer margin of wings (fig. 10.100); genital forceps of male with 2 or 3 short terminal segments (fig. 10.141) .... *LEPTOPHLEBIIDAE* 43

14(10'). Hind wings with numerous, long, free marginal intercalaries (fig. 10.101); cubital intercalaries absent in fore wings with vein A₁ terminating in outer margin of wings (fig. 10.101) .... *BAETISCIDAE—Baetisca*

14'. Hind wings not as above, sometimes absent; cubital intercalaries present in fore wings with vein A₁ terminating in hind margin of wings (figs. 10.102–10.104) 15

15(14'). Short, basally detached, single or double marginal intercalaries present in each interspace of fore wings; and veins MA₂ and MP₂ detached basally from their respective stems (Fig. 10.102); hind wings small or absent; penes of male membranous; upper portion of eyes of male turbinate (raised on a stalklike portion; fig. 10.112) .... *BAETIDAE* 24

15'. Marginal intercalaries attached basally to other veins; MA₂ and MP₂ attached basally (figs. 10.104–10.105); hind wings relatively large; penes of male well developed; eyes of male not turbinate 16

16(15'). Hind tarsi apparently 4-segmented, the basal segment of the 5 fused or partially fused to tibiae (figs. 10.109–10.110), the fusion line being in basal half of tibiae plus tarsi; cubital intercalaries consist of 1 or 2 pair (figs. 10.104–10.105) 17

16'. Hind tarsi distinctly 5-segmented (fig. 10.111); tarsi shorter than tibiae; cubital intercalaries consist of 2 pairs similar to fig. 10.103 .... *HEPTAGENIIDAE* (in part) 31

17(16). Eyes of male contiguous (touching) or nearly contiguous dorsally (similar to fig. 10.125); fore tarsi 3 times length of fore tibiae; abdomen of female with apical and basal segments subequal to middle segments in length and width; subanal plate evenly convex .... *METRETOPODIDAE* 42

17'. Eyes of male separated dorsally by twice width of median ocellus; fore tarsi 2 times length of fore tibiae; abdomen of female long and slender, apical segments distinctly more elongate and slender than basal segments; subanal plate with medial emargination (fig. 10.108); rare .... *HEPTAGENIIDAE—Pseudiron*

18(11'). Vein MA of fore wings forming a more or less symmetrical fork, and veins MP_2 and IMP extend less than three-fourths of distance to base of vein MP (figs. 10.105–10.106); genital forceps of male 2- or 3-segmented; thorax usually black or gray .... *TRICORYTHIDAE* 56

18'. Vein MA of fore wing not as above, MA_2 attached basally by a crossvein; wing veins MP_2 and IMP almost as long as vein MP, and extend nearly to base (fig. 10.107); genital forceps of male 1-segmented; thorax usually brown .... *CAENIDAE* 57

19(9'). Three caudal filaments; middle filament distinctly longer than tergum 10; rare; scattered distribution .... *Acanthametropus*(?), *Analetris*

19'. Two apparent caudal filaments; middle filament vestigial 20

20(19'). Claws of each pair dissimilar (1 sharp, 1 blunt) (fig. 10.114); costal projection of hind wings acute (fig. 10.113) .... *Ameletus*

20'. Claws of each pair similar, sharp (fig. 10.115); costal projection of hind wings obtuse or weak (fig. 10.91b) 21

21(20'). Abdominal segments 5–9 of male greatly expanded laterally; tubercles present on sterna of mesothorax and metathorax; rare; New York to Labrador .... *Siphlonisca*

21'. Abdominal segments 5–9 not expanded laterally; without tubercles on sterna of thorax 22

22(21'). Vein MP of hind wings simple, unforked; uncommon; northern or montane .... *Parameletus*

22'. Vein MP of hind wings forked (fig. 10.91b) 23

23(22'). Abdominal sterna 3–6 pale with a brown transverse bar; rare; California .... *Edmundsius*

23'. Ventral markings not as above, usually with dark spots, longitudinal stripes, oblique stripes, U-shaped marks, or mostly dark; abundant; widespread .... *Siphlonurus*

24(15). Hind wings present, although may be minute (as in fig. 10.102b) 25

24'. Hind wings absent 29

25(24). Hind wings with blunt costal projection and 10 or more crossveins; abdomen with distinct dark speckles .... *Callibaetis*

25'. Hind wings usually with less than 6 crossveins; costal projection of hind wings never blunt, either sharply pointed (fig. 10.116), hooked (fig. 10.117), or absent (fig. 10.118); abdomen variable, rarely with speckles 26

26(25'). Marginal intercalaries of fore wings occur singly; costal projection of hind wings hooked or recurved (similar to fig. 10.117) .... *Centroptilum*

26'. Marginal intercalaries of fore wings occur in pairs as in figure 10.102a; costal projection of hind wings variable, rarely hooked 27

27(28'). Costal projection of hind wings broadly based, acute at apex, giving hind wings characteristic shape (fig. 10.119a,b); uncommon; medium to large rivers .... *Dactylobaetis*

27'. Costal projection of hind wings present or absent (if present, variable in shape); if similar to above, costal projection not broadly based so that hind wings are not shaped as above (fig. 10.120a,b) 28

28(27'). Hind wings minute in male and female; hind wings without veins (similar to fig. 10.102b, but without veins); Midwest or East .... *Heterocloeon*

28'. Hind wings variable (figs. 10.116–10.118, 10.120), may be minute in female, if so 1 or 2 longitudinal veins present (fig. 10.102b) .... *Baetis*

29(24'). Marginal intercalaries of wings occur singly .... *Cloeon*

29'. Marginal intercalaries of wings occur in pairs (similar to fig. 10.102a) (see discussion before keys) .... *Pseudocloeon, Paracloeodes, Baetodes, Apobaetis*

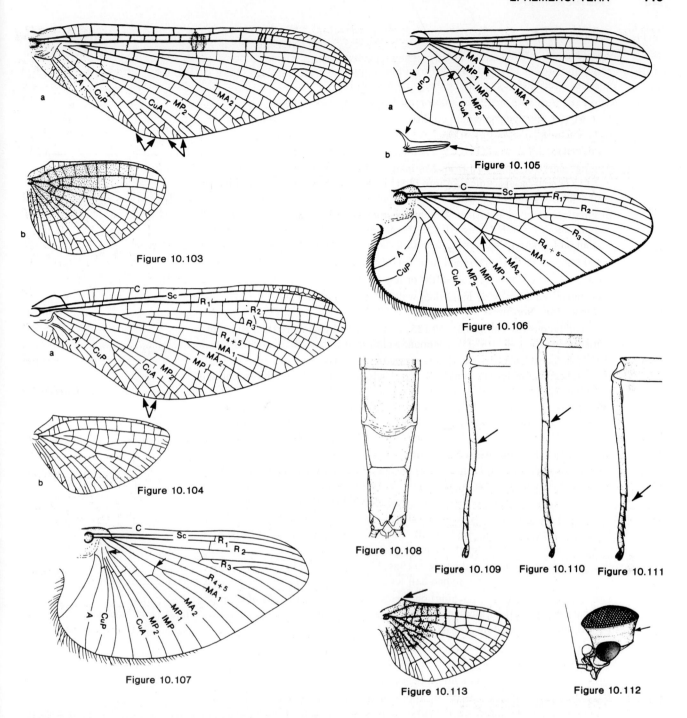

Figure 10.103. Fore wing *(a)* and hind wing *(b)* of *Siphloplecton* sp. (Metretopodidae).

Figure 10.104. Fore wing *(a)* and hind wing *(b)* of *Metretopus* sp. (Metretopodidae).

Figure 10.105. Fore wing *(a)* and hind wing *(b)* of *Leptohyphes* sp. (Tricorythidae).

Figure 10.106. Wing of *Tricorythodes* sp male (Tricorythidae).

Figure 10.107. Wing of *Caenis* sp. (Caenidae).

Figure 10.108. Ventral view of apex of abdomen of *Pseudiron* sp. female (Heptageniidae).

Figure 10.109. Hind tibia and tarsi of *Pseudiron* sp. (Heptageniidae).

Figure 10.110. Hind tibia and tarsi of *Siphloplecton* sp. (Metretopodidae).

Figure 10.111. Hind tibia and tarsi of *Heptagenia* sp. (Heptageniidae).

Figure 10.112. Lateral view of head of *Baetis* sp. male (Baetidae).

Figure 10.113. Hind wing of *Ameletus* sp. (Siphlonuridae).

30(1). Three caudal filaments present .... *Homoeoneuria*

30' Two caudal filaments present .... *Lachlania*

31(16'). Stigmatic area of fore wing divided by a fine, more or less straight vein into 2
series of cellules (fig. 10.121); uncommon; Northwest .... *Cinygma*

31'. Stigmatic area with simple or anastomosed crossveins, not as above 32

32(31'). Vein MA of hind wing simple, unforked; uncommon; Midwest or Northeast .... *Arthroplea*

32'. Vein MA of hind wing forked (fig. 10.126) (females not keyed beyond this
couplet) 33

33(32'). Stigmatic area of wing with from 2 to many anastomoses of crossveins (fig.
10.122), and basal segment of fore tarsi one-third or less than one-third length
of segment 2; femora usually with dark longitudinal streak near middle .... *Rhithrogena*

33'. Stigmatic area of wing with or without anastomosed crossveins; if crossveins
anastomosed (similar to fig. 10.122) basal segment of fore tarsi half or more
than half length of segment 2; femora usually without dark longitudinal streak 34

34(33'). Basal segment of fore tarsi equal to or slightly longer than segment 2 35

34'. Basal segment of fore tarsi four-fifths or less than four-fifths length of segment 2 36

35(34). Eyes separated dorsally by more than width of median ocellus (fig. 10.124);
uncommon; Northwest .... *Ironodes*

35'. Eyes contiguous (touching) (fig. 10.125) or separated by no more than width of
median ocellus (fig. 10.123); common; widespread .... *Epeorus*

36(35'). Penis lobes separated or appearing separated to near base medially (fig. 10.127);
basal segment of fore tarsi usually two-thirds or more than two-thirds length of
segment 2 .... *Cinygmula*

36'. Penis lobes fused medially at least in basal half (figs. 10.128–10.131); basal
segment of fore tarsi two-thirds or less than two-thirds length of segment 2,
usually less than half length of segment 2 37

37(36'). Wings with 2 or 3 crossveins below bullae between veins R_1 and R_2 connected or
nearly connected by dark pigmentation (fig. 10.132), rarely only a dark spot;
basal crossveins between R_1 and R_2 dark margined .... *Stenacron*

37'. Wings may have crossveins below bullae clouded but never as above; crossveins
between R_1 and R_2 rarely dark margined 38

38(37). Penes distinctly L-shaped (figs. 10.130–10.131); basal segment of fore tarsi usually
one-third to two-thirds length of segment 2 .... *Stenonema*

38'. Penes not distinctly L-shaped as above (figs. 10.128–10.129); basal segment of
fore tarsi usually one-fifth to one-half length of segment 2 39

39(38'). Eyes of male contiguous (touching) on vertex (similar to fig. 10.125) of head or
separated by width of median ocellus (similar to fig. 10.123) 40

39'. Eyes of male separated by at least width of a *lateral* ocellus 41

40(39). Eyes of male separated by width of median ocellus (similar to fig. 10.123); male
penes without spines or ridges; rare (fig. 10.128) .... *Macdunnoa*

40'. Eyes of male contiguous (touching); penes with spines or ridges (i.e., fig. 10.129) .... *Nixe*

41(39'). Eyes of male separated at vertex by approximately the width of one compound
eye; crossveins behind costa and subcosta usually margined in brown .... *Leucrocuta*

41'. Eyes of male separated at vertex by a little more than diameter of a lateral ocellus
(see fig. 10.124) .... *Heptagenia*

42(17). One pair of cubital intercalaries present (fig. 10.104) .... *Metretopus*

42'. Two pairs of cubital intercalaries present (fig. 10.103) .... *Siphloplecton*

43(13'). Hind wings without costal projection (fig. 10.100b) 44

43'. Hind wings with distinct costal projection (figs. 10.136–10.140) 45

44(43). Penes of male with long, decurrent, median appendages (figs. 10.134–10.135);
median terminal filament often shorter and thinner than lateral cerci .... *Leptophlebia*

44'. Penes of male variable (e.g., fig. 141), not as in figures 10.134–10.135; 3 subequal
caudal filaments .... *Paraleptophlebia*

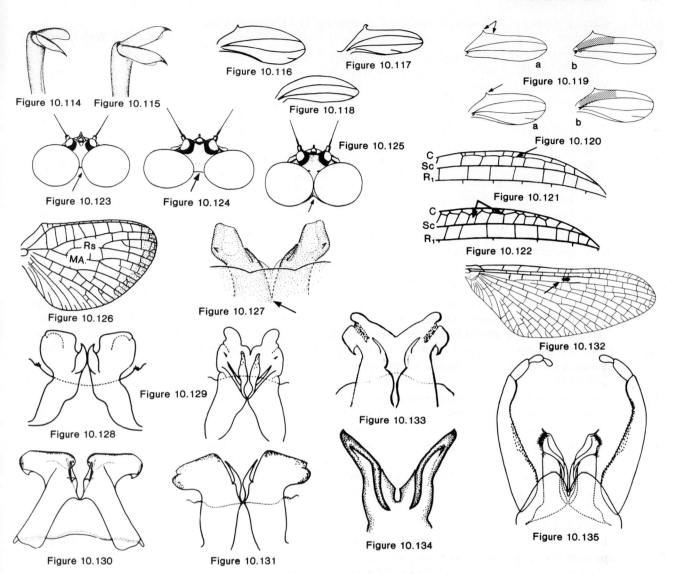

Figure 10.125. Dorsal view of head of *Epeorus* sp. adult male (Heptageniidae).

Figure 10.126. Hind wing of *Stenonema* sp. adult (Heptageniidae).

Figure 10.127. Penes of *Cinygmula* sp. adult male (Heptageniidae).

Figure 10.128. Penes of *Macdunnoa* sp. adult male (Heptageniidae).

Figure 10.129. Penes of *Nixe* sp. adult male (Heptageniidae).

Figure 10.130. Penes of *Stenonema* sp. adult male (Heptageniidae).

Figure 10.131. Penes of *Stenonema* sp. adult male (Heptageniidae).

Figure 10.132. Fore wing of *Stenacron* sp. adult male (Heptageniidae).

Figure 10.133. Penes of *Epeorus* sp. adult male (Heptageniidae).

Figure 10.134. Penes of *Leptophlebia* sp. adult male (Leptophlebiidae).

Figure 10.135. Penes of *Leptophlebia* sp. adult male (Leptophlebiidae).

Figure 10.114. Claws of adult *Ameletus* sp. (Siphlonuridae).

Figure 10.115. Claws of adult *Siphlonurus* sp. (Siphlonuridae).

Figure 10.116. Hind wing of *Baetis* sp. adult (Baetidae).

Figure 10.117. Hind wing of *Baetis* sp. adult (Baetidae).

Figure 10.118. Hind wing of *Baetis* sp. adult (Baetidae).

Figure 10.119. Hind wing *(a,b)* of *Dactylobaetis* sp. adult (Baetidae).

Figure 10.120. Hind wing *(a,b)* of *Baetis* sp. adult (Baetidae). Shaded arc on Figures 10.119b and 10.120b to emphasize shape of costal projection.

Figure 10.121. Stigmatic area at apex of *Cinygma* sp. adult fore wing (Heptageniidae).

Figure 10.122. Stigmatic area at apex of *Rhithrogena* sp. adult fore wing (Heptageniidae).

Figure 10.123. Dorsal view of head of *Epeorus* sp. adult male (Heptageniidae).

Figure 10.124. Dorsal view of head of *Ironodes* sp. adult male (Heptageniidae).

45(43'). Costal projection of hind wings in apical half of wing (fig. 10.137); uncommon;
Eastern .... *Habrophlebiodes*

45'. Costal projection of hind wing near midpoint of length of wings (figs. 10.136,
10.138–10.140) 46

46(45). Vein Sc of hind wings extends well beyond costal projection (fig. 10.136);
uncommon; Eastern .... *Habrophlebia*

46'. Vein Sc of hind wings ends at or slightly beyond costal projection (figs. 10.138,
10.139b, 10.140) 47

47(46'). Vein MP of hind wing forked (fig. 10.140); uncommon; Utah, Texas, New Mexico,
Arizona .... *Thraulodes*

47'. Vein MP of hind wing simple, unforked (figs. 10.138–10.139) 48

48(47'). Costal projection of hind wings rounded (fig. 10.138); widespread .... *Choroterpes*

48'. Costal projection of hind wings acute (fig. 10.139); large rivers, mostly West ...... *Traverella*

49(13). Cerci one-fourth to three-fourths as long as terminal filament; Northwest .... *Caudatella*

49'. Cerci and terminal filament subequal in length (females not keyed beyond this
couplet) 50

50(49'). Terminal segment of genital forceps 6 times as long as broad .... *Attenella*

50'. Terminal segment of genital forceps less than 4 times as long as broad (figs.
10.142–10.148) 51

51(50'). Terminal segment of genital forceps more than twice as long as broad; inner
margin of long 2nd segment distinctly incurved (fig. 10.142) or strongly bowed .... *Drunella*

51'. Terminal segment of genital forceps less than twice as long as broad (fig. 10.148);
inner margin of long 2nd segment variable but not strongly bowed 52

52(51'). Abdomen with well-developed posterolateral projections on segment 9; smaller
projections on segment 8 and vestiges of gills on segments 4–7; fore wings 12
mm or longer; West .... *Timpanoga*

52'. Abdomen without the above appendages; fore wing size variable, rarely as large as
12 mm 53

53(52). Penes with dorsal and/or ventral spines and shaped similar to figure 10.83, *or* with
long anterolateral lobes (figs. 10.143–10.144), *or* (one western species) as in
figure 10.145 .... *Ephemerella*

53'. Penes different than above 54

54(53'). Penes with lateral subapical projections as in figures 100.146–10.147 .... *Serratella*

54'. Penes lacking lateral subapical projections 55

55(54'). Segment 3 of fore tarsi shorter than segment 2; penes relatively narrow apically,
expanded basally (fig. 10.148) .... *Eurylophella*

55'. Segment 3 of fore tarsi longer than segment 2; penes expanded apically, relatively
narrow basally (fig. 10.149) .... *Dannella*

56(18). Wings of male greatly expanded in cubitoanal areas; vein CuP evenly recurved in
male and female (fig. 10.106); hind wings absent, abundant, widespread .... *Tricorythodes*

56'. Wings not expanded in cubitoanal area, broadest near midpoint of length; vein
CuP abruptly recurved (fig. 10.105a); hind wings of male with long costal
projection (fig. 10.105b); hind wings absent in female; uncommon; Southwest .... *Leptohyphes*

57(18'). Prosternum half as long as broad, rectangular in shape; fore coxae widely
separated on venter (fig. 10.151); uncommon .... *Brachycercus*

57'. Prosternum 2–3 times as long as broad, triangular in shape; fore coxae close
together on venter (fig. 10.150); abundant .... *Caenis*

58(7). Crossveins of wings crowded together near bullae; wings with distinct pattern of
dark markings (fig. 10.90); terminal filament as long as cerci .... *Ephemera*

58'. Crossveins of wings not crowded near bullae; wings without pattern of dark
markings although crossveins may be darkened; terminal filament vestigial or
distinctly shorter than cerci 59

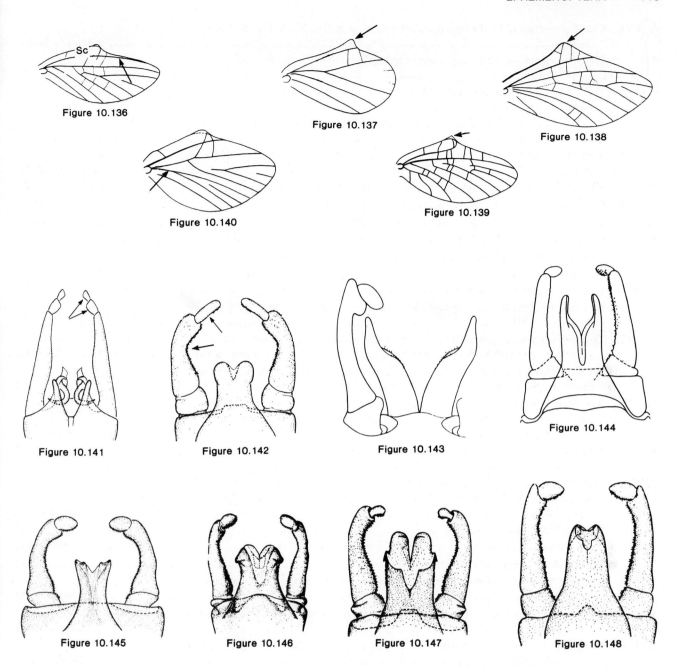

Figure 10.136.
Figure 10.137.
Figure 10.138.
Figure 10.139.
Figure 10.140.
Figure 10.141.
Figure 10.142.
Figure 10.143.
Figure 10.144.
Figure 10.145.
Figure 10.146.
Figure 10.147.
Figure 10.148.

Figure 10.136. Hind wing of *Habrophlebia* sp. adult (Leptophlebiidae).

Figure 10.137. Hind wing of *Habrophlebiodes* sp. adult (Leptophlebiidae).

Figure 10.138. Hind wing of *Choroterpes* sp. adult (Leptophlebiidae).

Figure 10.139. Hind wing of *Traverella* sp. adult (Leptophlebiidae).

Figure 10.140. Hind wing of *Thraulodes* sp. adult (Leptophlebiidae).

Figure 10.141. Genitalia of *Paraleptophlebia* sp. adult male (Leptophlebiidae).

Figure 10.142. Genitalia of *Drunella* sp. adult male (Ephemerellidae).

Figure 10.143. Genitalia of *Ephemerella* sp. adult male (Ephemerellidae).

Figure 10.144. Genitalia of *Ephemerella* sp. adult male (Ephemerellidae).

Figure 10.145. Genitalia of *Ephemerella* sp. adult male (Ephemerellidae).

Figure 10.146. Genitalia of *Seratella* sp. adult male (Ephemerellidae).

Figure 10.147. Genitalia of *Serratella* sp. adult male (Ephemerellidae).

Figure 10.148. Genitalia of *Eurylophella* sp. adult male (Ephemerellidae).

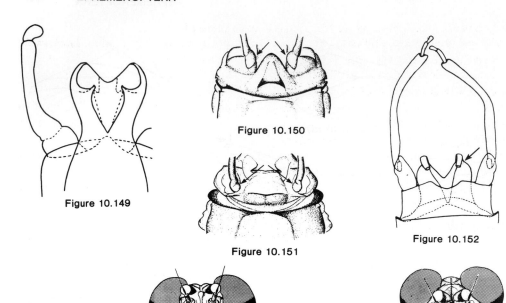

Figure 10.149

Figure 10.150

Figure 10.151

Figure 10.152

Figure 10.155

Figure 10.154

Figure 10.153

Figure 10.149. Genitalia of *Dannella* sp. adult male (Ephemerellidae).

Figure 10.150. Ventral view of pronotum of *Caenis* sp. adult (Caenidae).

Figure 10.151. Ventral view of pronotum of *Brachycercus* sp. adult (Caenidae).

Figure 10.152. Genitalia of *Litobrancha* sp. adult male (Ephemeridae).

Figure 10.153. Anterior view of head of *Litobrancha* sp. adult male (Ephemeridae).

Figure 10.154. Anterior view of head of *Hexagenia* sp. adult male (Ephemeridae).

Figure 10.155. Genitalia of *Hexagenia* sp. adult male (Ephemeridae).

59(58′). Head with frons greatly expanded below eyes (fig. 10.153); penes of male recurved
 ventrally (fig. 10.152); uncommon; East, Midwest .... *Litobrancha*

59′. Head with frons not extending below eyes (fig. 10.154); penes of male not recurved
 (e.g., fig. 10.155); abundant; widespread .... *Hexagenia*

60(5). Outer margin of fore wings with dense network of reticulate veinlets (fig. 10.88);
 abundant, widespread .... *Ephoron*

60′. Outer margin of fore wings with few or no veinlets 61

61(60′). Middle and hind legs with all segments present, but reduced and shriveled;
 abundant; Midwest, Southeast .... *Tortopus*

61′. Middle and hind legs greatly reduced, terminating in a bladelike femur;
 uncommon; Texas .... *Campsurus*

ADDITIONAL TAXONOMIC REFERENCES

General

Tillyard (1932); Needham *et al.* (1935); Edmunds and Traver (1954); Day (1956); Edmunds (1959); Koss (1968); Koss and Edmunds (1974); Edmunds *et al.* (1976); Pennak (1978); McCafferty and Edmunds (1979); McCafferty (1981).

Regional faunas

Illinois and region: Burks (1953).
Florida: Berner (1950).
Michigan: Leonard and Leonard (1962).
Saskatchewan: Lemkuhl (1976a).
Wisconsin: Hilsenhoff (1981).

Taxonomic treatments at the family and generic levels *

Ametropodidae: Allen and Edmunds (1976).
Baetidae: Morihara and McCafferty (1979).
Baetiscidae: Berner (1955); Berner and Pescador (1980); Pescador and Berner (1981).

Behningiidae: Edmunds and Traver (1959); McCafferty (1975).
Ephemerellidae: Allen and Emunds (1965; obtain citations for Parts I–VII from this reference); Allen (1980).
Ephemeridae: Spieth (1941); McCafferty (1975).
Heptageniidae: Edmunds and Allen (1964); Lewis (1974); Flowers and Hilsenhoff (1975); Bednarik and McCafferty (1979); Lehmkuhl (1979b); Bednarik and Edmunds (1980); Flowers (1980).
Leptophlebiidae: Traver and Edmunds (1967); Berner (1975); Peters (1980).
Metretopodidae: Berner (1978).
Neoephemeridae: Berner (1956).
Oligoneuriidae: Edmunds *et. al.* (1958); Edmunds (1961).
Palingeniidae: McCafferty and Edmunds (1976).
Polymitarcyidae: McCafferty (1975).
Potamanthidae: McCafferty (1975).
Tricorythidae: Allen (1967).

---

*Other regional treatments and lists can be found in Edmunds *et. al.* (1976).

Table 10A. Summary of ecological and distributional data for *Ephemeroptera (mayflies).* (For definition of terms see Tables 6A–6C; table prepared by K. W. Cummins, G. F. Edmunds, and R. W. Merritt.)

Taxa (number of species in parentheses)	Habitat	Habit	Trophic Relationships	North American Distribution	Ecological References[*]
Siphlonuridae(56)	Generally lotic—erosional and depositional	Generally swimmers, clingers	Generally collectors		535, 628, 629, 632, 63 1316, 1453, 1782, 188
Acanthametropus(1)	Lotic—depositional (large rivers)	Swimmers, clingers	Predators (engulfers)	Illinois (Rock River), South Carolina, Georgia (Savannah River)	305
Analetris(1)	Lotic—depositional (large rivers)	Swimmers, clingers	Predators (engulfers)	Wyoming, Utah, Saskatchewan	637, 1445
Ameletus(31)	Lotic—erosional and depositional	Swimmers, clingers	Collectors—gatherers (detritus, diatoms)	Northeast, West and Southeast mountains, Illinois	535, 863, 1756, 1782, 1811
Edmundsius(1)	Lotic—erosional			California mountains	637
Parameletus(4)	Lentic—vascular hydrophytes	Swimmers, climbers		West, Ontario, Quebec	637
Siphlonisca(1)	Lentic—littoral		Predators (engulfers)	Northeast	856
Siphlonurus(17)	Lentic—littoral (vascular hydrophytes or sediments), lotic—depositional	Swimmers, climbers	Collectors—gatherers, scrapers, predators (engulfers; especially *Tanytarsus* in pools), shredders—herbivores?	Widespread	258, 630, 637, 863, 1259, 1701, 1782, 184 2210, 2529
Metretopodidae(6)	Generally lotic—erosional	Generally swimmers, clingers	Generally predators (engulfers), collectors—gatherers		535, 629, 632, 637, 1453, 1782, 1886
Metretopus(1)	Lotic—erosional	Swimmers, clingers		Canada, upper Midwest, Northeast	637
Siphloplecton(5)	Lotic—erosional and depositional, lentic—margins	Swimmers, clingers	Collectors—gatherers	Canada, upper Midwest, Southeast	413
Baetidae(130)	Generally lotic—erosional and depositional	Generally swimmers, clingers	Generally collectors—gatherers, scrapers		535, 629, 632, 637, 1316, 1453, 1782, 188
Apobaetis(1)	Lotic—depositional (sand)	Swimmers, clingers		California	637, 1527
Baetis(41)	Lotic—erosional and depositional, lentic—littoral, vascular hydrophytes	Swimmers, climbers, clingers	Collectors—gatherers (detritus, diatoms), scrapers	Widespread	83, 258, 382, 413, 449, 606, 863, 1136, 1259, 1346, 1525, 1671, 167 1698, 1701, 1756, 218 2222, 2591
Baetodes(2)	Lotic—erosional	Clingers	Scrapers	Texas, Arizona, Oklahoma	637
Callibaetis(23)	Lentic—vascular hydrophytes	Swimmers, climbers	Collectors—gatherers	Widespread	494, 637, 1782
Centroptilum(24)	Lotic—erosional and depositional	Swimmers, clingers	Collectors—gatherers (detritus, diatoms), scrapers	Widespread	421, 632, 863, 1674‡
Cloeon(12) (includes *Neocloeon*)	Lotic—erosional	Swimmers, clingers	Collectors—gatherers, scrapers	West, Texas, Midwest, East	272, 273
Dactylobaetis(2)	Lotic—erosional and depositional	Swimmers, clingers		West, Northwest, Oklahoma	637
Heterocloeon(4)	Lotic—erosional	Clingers	Scrapers	Midwest, Southeast, Ontario	637, 1340
Paracloeodes(2)	Lotic—depositional (sand)	Swimmers, clingers		West, South	637
Pseudocloeon(19)	Lotic—erosional	Swimmers, clingers	Scrapers, collectors—gatherers	Widespread	421, 2210

[*]Emphasis on trophic relationships.
‡Unpublished data, K. W. Cummins, Kellogg Biological Station; Oregon State University.

ble 10A.—*Continued*

Taxa (number of species in parentheses)	Habitat	Habit	Trophic Relationships	North American Distribution	Ecological References[*]
netropodidae(3)					
Ametropus(3)	Lotic—erosional (gravel-sand) and depositional (sand) (large rivers)	Burrowers (shallow, with eyes and gills exposed)	Collectors—gatherers (fine particles)	West, Northwest	414, 535, 629, 632, 637, 1782, 1886
goneuriidae(32)	Generally lotic	Clingers and Burrowers			414
Lachlania(3)	Lotic—erosional and depositional	Clingers	Collectors—filterers	West	535, 629, 632, 637, 1170, 1782, 1886
Homoeoneuria(4) (=Oligoneuria of Spieth and Burks)	Lotic—depositional (large rivers)	Burrowers	Collectors—filterers	Southwest, lower Midwest (north to Indiana, Nebraska), Southeast	637, 1896
sonychia(25)	Lotic—erosional	Swimmers, clingers	Collectors—filterers (very fine particles), predators (engulfers)	Widespread	305, 411, 421, 910, 2210‡, 2383, 2550
ptageniidae(105†)	Generally lotic and lentic—erosional	Generally clingers	Generally scrapers, collectors—gatherers		173, 535, 566, 629, 632, 637, 1316, 1453, 1527, 1782, 1886
Anepeorus(2)	Lotic—erosional and depositional (large rivers)	Swimmers, clingers	Predators (engulfers, primarily midges)	West, Midwest, Southeast	305, 628
Arthroplea(1)	Lentic—littoral, lotic—depositional	Swimmers, clingers	Collectors—filterers	Northeast (to Wisconsin and Ohio)	637
Cinygma(3)	Lotic—erosional	Clingers	Scrapers, collectors—gatherers	West	637
Cinygmula(11)	Lotic—erosional	Clingers	Scrapers (diatoms), collectors—gatherers (detritus, diatoms)	West, Northeast, Southeast	382, 637, 863, 1698
Epeorus(19) (=Iron = Ironopsis)	Lotic—erosional	Clingers	Collectors—gatherers, scrapers	Widespread	382, 863, 1678, 1679, 2210
Heptagenia(13)	Lotic—erosional	Clingers (swimmers)	Scrapers, collectors—gatherers	Widespread	1259, 1702, 1755, 1756, 2210
Leurocuta(10) (formerly in Heptagenia)	Lotic—erosional and depositional (slow-flowing warm waters)	Clingers	Scrapers, collectors—gatherers	Widespread	750, 1701
Macdunnoa(2) (formerly in Heptagenia)	Lotic-erosional and depositional	Clingers	Scrapers, collectors	Midwest, Southeast	1447
Nixe(12) (formerly in Heptagenia)	Lotic—erosional and depositional	Clingers	Scrapers, collectors—gatherers	Widespread	750, 863, 1756
Ironodes(6)	Lotic—erosional	Clingers	Scrapers, collectors—gatherers	West	637, 1782, 1889
Pseudiron(2)	Lotic—depositional (large rivers on sand)	Sprawlers	Predators (engulfers)	West, Manitoba, Midwest, Southwest	628, 637, 2478
Rhithrogena(21)	Lotic—erosional	Clingers	Collectors—gatherers (detritus, diatoms), scrapers	Widespread	637, 863, 1259, 2210
Stenacron(7)	Lotic and lentic—erosional	Clingers	Scrapers, collectors—gatherers	East and Central (to Arkansas, Minnesota)	421, 637, 1385, 2748‡
Stenonema(17)	Lotic and lentic—erosional (depositional)	Clingers (under loose cobbles and boulders)	Scrapers, collectors—gatherers	Widespread	421, 637, 1339, 1385, 1671, 1701, 1702, 1709, 2030, 2210, 2297‡, 2467
Spinadis(1)	Lotic—erosional and depositional		Predators (engulfers, primarily midges)	Midwest, Southeast	636, 637

nphasis on trophic relationships.
bgenera.
npublished data, K. W. Cummins, Kellogg Biological Station; Oregon State University.

Table 10A.—*Continued*

Taxa (number of species in parentheses)	Habitat	Habit	Trophic Relationships	North American Distribution	Ecological References*
Ephemerellidae(85)	Lotic—erosional, some depositional and in macrophytes, a few lentic—vascular hydrophytes	Generally clingers, some sprawlers and swimmers	Generally collectors—gatherers (detritus, algae), some scrapers, few shredders (detritivores and herbivores), 1 predator (engulfer)	Widespread	59, 173, 382, 421, 62* 632, 637, 1453, 1671, 1782, 1886, 2210, 27:
Attenella (= *Attenuatella*)(4)	Lotic—erosional and depositional	Clingers	Collectors—gatherers (detritus, algae)	West, East	637
Caudatella(5)	Lotic—erosional and depositional	Clingers	Collectors—gatherers (detritus, algae), scrapers?	West	413, 637
Dannella(2)		Clingers	Collectors—gatherers	Widespread	637
Drunella(15)		Clingers, sprawlers	Scrapers, (*D. spinifera* and possibly *D. doddsi* and *D. coloradensis,* predators [engulfers])	Widespread	637, 863
Ephemerella(28)	Lotic—erosional and depositional	Clingers, some swimmers	Collectors—gatherers, scrapers (*E. infrequens,* a shredder)	Widespread	637, 1009, 1259, 175* 1888, 2386
Eurylophella(12)	Lotic—erosional and depositional; Lentic—vascular hydrophytes	Clingers, sprawlers	Collectors—gatherers, (*E. funeralis,* a shredder)	West, East	637, 952
Serratella(14)	Lotic—erosional and depositional	Clingers	Collectors—gatherers (detritus)	Widespread	637, 1701
Timpanoga(1)	Lotic—erosional and depositional	Sprawlers	Collectors—gatherers	West	637
Tricorythidae(21)	Generally lotic—depositional and lentic—littoral	Generally clingers, sprawlers	Generally collectors—gatherers		535, 629, 632, 637, 1453, 1782, 1886
Tricorythodes(13)	Lotic—depositional, lentic—littoral (sediments)	Sprawlers, clingers	Collectors—gatherers	Widespread	637, 863, 947, 1346, 1525, 1604, 1805, 2210, ‡
Leptohyphes(8)	Lotic-depositional	Clingers		Southwest, Utah, Texas, Maryland	637
Neoephemeridae(4)					535, 629, 632, 637, 1782, 1886
Neoephemera(4)	Lotic—depositional	Sprawlers, clingers	Collectors—gatherers?	East	637
Caenidae(18)					535, 629, 632, 637, 1316, 1453, 1782, 188
Brachycercus(5)	Lotic—depositional (large rivers)	Sprawlers	Collectors—gatherers	East, Central, Southwest, Idaho, and Wyoming	637
Caenis(13)	Lotic—depositional, lentic—littoral (sediments)	Sprawlers	Collectors—gatherers, scrapers	Widespread	421, 1525, 1692, 2185, ‡
Baetiscidae(12)					535, 629, 632, 637, 1316, 1453, 1782, 188
Baetisca(12)	Lotic—depositional (sand, with detritus)	Sprawlers, clingers	Collectors—gatherers, scrapers	Widespread	171, 372, 637, 1443, 1894, 1895, 2210
Leptophlebiidae(70)	Generally lotic—erosional	Generally swimmers, clingers	Generally collectors—gatherers, scrapers		173, 535, 629, 632, 63 1177, 1316, 1453, 178 1886
Choroterpes(12)	Lotic—erosional and depositional, lentic—littoral (sediments)	Clingers, sprawlers	Collectors—gatherers, scrapers	Widespread	421, 1527, 1601, 1782

*Emphasis on trophic relationships.

‡Unpublished data, K. W. Cummins, Kellogg Biological Station; Oregon State University.

able 10A.— *Continued*

Taxa (number of species in parentheses)	Habitat	Habit	Trophic Relationships	North American Distribution	Ecological References[*]
Habrophlebia(1)	Lotic—depositional and erosional			East	637
Habrophlebiodes(4)	Lotic—erosional and depositional	Swimmers, clingers, sprawlers	Scrapers, collectors— gatherers	East, Midwest	170
Farrodes (=*Homothraulus*)(1)	Lotic			Texas	637
Leptophlebia(10)	Lotic—erosional (sediments and detritus)	Swimmers, clingers, sprawlers	Collectors—gatherers (fine particles)	Northwest, Midwest, East	174, 257, 258, 415, 416, 448, 1011, 1178, 1692, 1698, 1761, 2210‡
Paraleptophlebia (33)	Lotic—erosional (sediments and detritus)	Swimmers, clingers, sprawlers	Collectors—gatherers (coarse detritus, diatoms), shredders— detritivores	Widespread	382, 448, 637, 863, 1176, 2210‡
Thraulodes(5)	Lotic—erosional	Clingers, sprawlers		Southwest	637, 2468
Traverella(4)	Lotic—erosional and depositional	Clingers	Collectors—filterers	West, Southwest, Indiana, and North Dakota	637
hningiidae(1)					535, 629, 632, 637, 639, 1782, 1886, 1900
Dolania(1)	Lotic—depositional (sand)	Burrowers	Predators (engulfers, Chironomidae)	Southeast	637, 999, 2478, ‡
tamanthidae(8)					535, 629, 632, 637, 1316, 1782, 1886
Potamanthus(8)	Lotic—depositional	Sprawlers, clingers	Collectors—gatherers	East, Midwest	637, 1178, 1627, 2210, ‡
hemeridae(13)					173, 535, 629, 632, 637, 1316, 1453, 1469, 1782, 1886
Ephemera(7)	Lotic and lentic—depositional (sand-gravel)	Burrowers	Collectors—gatherers, predators (engulfers)	Widespread	254, 421, 1648, 1745, 2210, 1845 ‡
Hexagenia(5)	Lentic and lotic—depositional (sand-silt)	Burrowers	Collectors—gatherers (fine particles, possibly also filter at mouth of burrow)	Widespread	259, 800, 801, 802, 1116, 1117, 1154, 1701, 1782, 2210, 2822, 2823, 2824
Litobrancha(1)	Lotic—depositional (small streams and rivers)	Burrowers		East	369, 637
lingeniidae(2)					637
Pentagenia(2)	Lotic—depositional (hard clay banks, large rivers)	Burrowers	Collectors—gatherers?	Central, Southeast	637, 414
lymitarcyidae(6)					629, 632, 634, 1648, 1782, 1886
Ephoron(2)	Lotic—erosional and depositional, lentic— littoral (sediments)	Burrowers	Collectors—gatherers	Widespread	254, 637, 1178, 2210
Campsurus(1)		Burrowers		Texas	637
Tortopus(3)	Lotic—depositional (hard clay banks, large rivers)	Burrowers		Midwest (north to Manitoba), Southeast	414, 2199

mphasis on trophic relationships.
npublished data, K. W. Cummins, Kellogg Biological Station; Oregon State University.

Odonata

11

Minter J. Westfall, Jr.
University of Florida, Gainesville

INTRODUCTION

Adults of Odonata, or dragonflies (Anisoptera) and damselflies (Zygoptera) are found flying on sunny, warm days near almost any body of fresh water where their nymphs live. A few species tolerate water with a considerable saline content in the nymphal stage, especially *Erythrodiplax berenice* (Drury) and *Ischnura ramburii* (Selys). Because these graceful, long-bodied insects are conspicuous in flight, they have been noticed by the casual observer and given a variety of common names, such as "mosquito hawks," "devil's darning needles," and "snake doctors." Mosquitoes do comprise a significant part of the diet of both adults and nymphs of Odonata; the adult catches the flying mosquito with its spiny fore legs, and the nymph thrusts out the labium to grasp the mosquito larva in the water. Other insect pests are also captured and eaten, giving the adult dragonfly its reputation as an agile and beneficial predator. The nymphs, on the other hand, form an important link in food chains for fish and other aquatic vertebrates. Dragonflies have been used in scientific research on the effects of stream pollution and in certain medical fields. The worldwide population of described species of Odonata numbers about 5,500, with approximately 650 species occurring within the North American range.

The scientific name, Odonata, is derived from the Greek "odon," meaning tooth, and was suggested by the presence of sharp teeth on the jaws. Originally, dragonflies were included in the order Neuroptera. The wings are unique in the development of their rich venation. Wing structure is an important odonate feature, as much of their time is spent in the aerial pursuit of food or mates. Odonates grasp their prey on the wing, and some species oviposit while flying. Flight speeds have been calculated at between 25 and 35 km per hour, possibly as much as 56 km per hour. Sight is the most highly developed sense; hence, the importance of the two large compound eyes in the detection of prey and in the selection of habitat.

Flight habits vary with the species. Some rarely alight during hours of flight, but others occupy favorite perches from which they go forth to capture food. Some males (e.g., *Tetragoneuria* sp., *Epicordulia* sp.) defend a territory over a stretch of water where eggs will be laid, and often patrol back and forth across this area. Most species fly only in bright sunlight and instantly alight when the sun is darkened by clouds. A preponderance of cloudy days can discourage flights for food to the extent that a local population can be dangerously decimated before sunny weather returns. A few, such as *Neu-*

rocordulia sp., which feed upon mayflies, *Enallagma vesperum* Calvert, and *Gynacantha nervosa* Rambur, fly only briefly at dawn or dusk. *Tauriphila argo* (Hagen) sometimes flies tree-top high, defying capture. The complete flight period of most individuals lasts only a few weeks. Some temperate species have an explosive annual emergence and soon disappear, whereas others continue to emerge throughout the summer, or all year long in the tropics. Migrations of dragonflies have been recorded. Longfield (1948) describes the appearance on the south coast of Ireland of thousands of individuals of *Sympetrum* sp. over a period of six weeks, probably traveling 500 miles from the coast of Spain, and Federley (1908) reports migrations of *Libellula quadrimaculata* Linnaeus in Finland.

Mating may take place over the water, near the water, or, in several species, some distance from the water, and at various times of the day. Most Corduliidae appear to oviposit at dawn or twilight. As an initial step in mating, the male transfers sperm from the opening of the sperm duct near the end of the abdomen to the penis on the second abdominal segment. In Anisoptera, the male clasps the female by the back of the head, whereas in Zygoptera, the caudal appendages of the male fit precisely into grooves of the pro- and mesothorax of the female. If the male is of the same species, the female will respond by bringing the tip of her abdomen forward to the male's second segment where fertilization occurs, and the two form an interesting heart-shaped configuration. In some species, the two fly in tandem during egg laying, but in others the female oviposits alone, repeatedly dipping the end of the abdomen in the water and washing off some eggs each time.

The total number of eggs laid by a female in one batch varies from a few hundred to a few thousand, the maximum recorded being 5,200. Because a few corduliid species will lay eggs in closely associated gelatinous strings, masses of hundreds of thousands of eggs have been erroneously credited to one female. The damselflies (Zygoptera) and some dragonflies (Anisoptera), notably the Aeshnidae, have sharp ovipositors and insert the eggs into plant tissues above or below the water (fig. 11.8), presumably an adaptation to avoid predation and mediate temperature extremes. On occasion, this endophytic trait has resulted in excessive damage to plant tissue during oviposition by great numbers of females, especially of the family Lestidae. Needham (1900) reports considerable damage to the stems of the aquatic plant "blue flag" (*Iris versicolor* Linnaeus) from the oviposition of numerous *Lestes* sp. females. A few species, such as *Calopteryx aequabilis* Say, submerge entirely, sometimes descending to a depth of 30 cm or more to oviposit in the plant stem, remaining submerged for as long as 30 minutes before finally floating to the surface. The male may descend and remain with the female or rise to the surface soon after submerging. They are able to derive oxygen from the air adhering to the hairs of the body surface and that which is trapped by the wings.

In the Cordulegastridae, the females have a blunt ovipositor used to insert eggs into the sand or silt in shallow areas of streams. Most Libellulidae tap the surface of the water periodically with the end of the abdomen in flight, each time releasing a cluster of eggs that scatter and settle to the bottom. Some species (especially of the genus *Sympetrum*) have been observed to release eggs in mid air several feet above the water. Most odonate eggs hatch within 12–30 days, depending upon weather conditions. In the temperate zone, some species go through a winter diapause in the egg stage. Eggs laid in plant tissue above a drying temporary pond may not hatch until rains fill the pond again.

Dragonflies and damselflies have an incomplete metamorphosis with the immature stage (nymph, naiad) going through 10–15 instars. Most species in the last few days of the final instar eat little food and are sluggish while great internal changes are taking place in preparation for emergence. Snodgrass (1954) likens this period to the pupa of holometabolous insects.

Upon hatching, the unique *pronymph* (sometimes termed *instar one*) almost immediately molts to produce the nymph, usually considered as the *first instar*. The newly hatched nymphs are nourished for a few days by yolk retained in the body, but very soon begin to feed on protozoa or other minute animals. Dragonfly nymphs are generalized carnivores, feeding on any aquatic animal of an appropriate size that they can capture. Feeding behavior has been described as following three phases: detecting prey and adjusting position in relation to it; next, ejecting the labium to grasp the prey; and, finally, employing the mandibles to devour the prey. The labium, when extended, is approximately as long as the fore leg, and, when back in place, may mask the face up to the eyes. It is uniquely outfitted for grasping and holding the prey. When an organism is sighted close by, the immense labium, resembling a large prehensile arm, shoots out with lightning speed to grasp the prey and draws back again so swiftly that the observer cannot follow it. The sharp hooks and spines of the palpal lobes, which are situated at the front of the labium, clutch the prey and the jaws cut it into pieces for ingestion. Any fragments remaining are caught in the prementum and also consumed. This efficient mechanism requires enough room to reach out for prey and is occasionally subject to entanglement in threads of filamentous algae and other slender, multicellular plants, probably explaining the scarcity of nymphs in dense mats of such plants.

Nymphs are typically concealed in habitats by burrowing, sprawling amongst fine sediment and detritus, or climbing on vascular plants. With a few exceptions, the Petaluridae and Gomphidae nymphs burrow in mud, coarse sand, or light silt, and characteristically have a flat, wedge-shaped head and short antennae, which are probably helpful in prey detection.

The fore and middle legs are much shorter than the hind legs and are modified, e.g., with burrowing hooks in some species, for shallow burrowing. The end of the abdomen is generally upturned slightly, allowing it to protrude above the mud or silt into the water for respiration. The genus *Aphylla* (fig. 11.96), which burrows more deeply, bears a cylindrical abdomen with an elongated tenth segment forming a siphon. In rare instances some Libellulidae have been found buried beneath the surface of the sand, possibly to escape predators.

Sprawlers are typically more active foragers (with some exceptions, e.g., the sluggish *Hagenius* sp. and *Macromia* sp.), having longer—often spiderlike—legs. Numerous setae give them a rather hairy appearance, and particles of mud and silt adhering to the setae camouflage the nymphs. The setae are probably also tactile organs that assist in prey detection. Color is advantageously protective in patterns of mottled greens and browns. The body is generally flatter than that of the burrowers. The Cordulegastridae includes species intermediate between the sprawlers and burrowers. They are found in clean sand or silt, buried by sand swept over the subcylindrical bodies by the lateral kicking movements of the legs, which are slender and without burrowing hooks. When deep enough, sand covers them except for the tips of the eyes and the tip of the abdomen.

Most Zygoptera and Aeshnidae are classified as *climbers,* lurking in vegetation or resting on stems of aquatic plants. These nymphs stalk their prey, halting their pursuit when the movements of the prey stop. Some weed dwellers have developed specialized forms of protective coloration that may match their immediate background. *Aeshna* sp. nymphs are apparently able to distinguish different colors (Koehler 1924). Nymphs of *A. grandis* Linnaeus are said to become green in summer and brown in winter, and *Anax* sp. is reported to possess a highly characteristic type of juvenile coloration. A few species of Protoneuridae, Coenagrionidae, Aeshnidae, and Corduliidae (especially *Neurocordulia*), are *clingers,* holding tenaciously to rocks, sticks, and roots submerged in streams.

Most Odonata nymphs are found in permanent lakes, ponds, or streams. However, some with short life cycles have adapted to temporary aquatic habitats, and a few are semiaquatic, living in bog moss or under damp leaves in seepage areas. In tropical regions, several species are adapted for life in the water that collects in bromeliads or in tree holes. Other species are able to withstand long periods of desiccation. The 10–15 instar nymphal stage lasts from a few weeks in some species to about five years in the Petaluridae. Wing pads appear after the third or fourth molt and become swollen, indicating imminent emergence, in the final instar. Some univoltine (one generation per year) species have a synchronized emergence, and all adults disappear after a few weeks, whereas some with southern distributions continue to emerge throughout the year. The most favorable condition for emergence is a dry, sunny period following wet, cold weather.

Respiration in the Odonata adult takes place through the thoracic spiracles. In Anisoptera, nymphal respiration is chiefly rectal, occurring through the regular expansion and contraction of the rectal walls. This movement brings about an inflow and outflow of water through the anus. A sudden expulsion of water also serves in nymphal jet-propulsion locomotion. The caudal lamellae or gills of the Zygoptera nymphs are supplementary respiratory structures. In later instars, oxygen may also be absorbed through the surface of the wing pads.

Predators of the nymphs of Odonata include aquatic birds, fish (e.g., Percidae, Centrarchidae, Salmonidae), and large predaceous insects. A list of the predators of adult Odonata would include many species of birds (e.g., falcons, kingbirds, kingfishers, herons, terns, gulls, sandpipers, blackbirds, swallows, swifts, grackles, and red-winged blackbirds), amphibians, bats, spiders, wasps, and other dragonflies. Nymphs of *Aeshna cyanea* Müller have been observed climbing up plant stems to grasp and devour teneral adults of their own species. Because of the predation activity during daylight hours, emergence most often occurs at night. Weather is also responsible for considerable mortality. For example, cloudy, rainy days may shorten feeding hours, and severe windstorms may drive adults out to sea or onto large lakes, where they drown and are washed ashore in large numbers.

Immature stages of water mites (*Hydracarina* spp.) may parasitize lentic odonate nymphs. Several species of Hymenoptera parasitize eggs, especially those of species that oviposit endophytically (Aeshnidae and Coenagrionidae). The adults of Ceratopogonidae (biting midges) and some internal parasites are also causes of mortality. Comprehensive accounts of the biology and ecology of the Odonata are given by Walker (1953) and Corbet (1963).

EXTERNAL MORPHOLOGY

Nymphs

The nymphs of the Odonata are quite different in structure from the adults. They are cryptically colored with body structures adapted for different aquatic microhabitats.

The nymphal body plan is the same as the adult's, and body parts bear the same names. Compared with the adult, the head is smaller and not so freely movable. The three segments of the nymphal thorax are more aligned and equal in size than in the adults. The legs are farther apart and adapted for walking. The nymphs of the Zygoptera are more slender than those of the Anisoptera; the head is wider than the thorax or abdomen, and the antennae are relatively longer than in the Anisoptera.

Head: The most unique structure of the nymphal head is the *labium* or lower lip. It is folded upon itself at midlength and turned backward (caudally) beneath the front legs (figs. 11.33–11.34). At the front are a pair of strong, hinged *palpal lobes* or labial palpi (formerly called *lateral lobes*) armed with hooks, spines, teeth, and raptorial setae that vary with family and genus (figs. 11.22, 11.26). Each palpal lobe is two-segmented, the larger first segment (articulated with the prementum) is prolonged apically to meet almost the one on the opposite side. The palpal lobe usually bears strong, raptorial *palpal setae* (formerly called *lateral setae*) on its dorsal surface (fig. 11.27). The lobe often terminates in an apical projection, the *end hook* (fig. 11.66). The second segment is a

slender, curved or sharp-pointed *movable hook,* which may bear strong, raptorial setae and is articulated at a movable joint with the first segment on its outer margin; it usually overlaps the hook of the opposite side (figs. 11.13, 11.16, 11.28–11.29). The central portion of the front margin of the prementum may have a projection known as the *ligula* (figs. 11.22, 11.26). On each side of the midline are usually some prominent *premental setae* (formerly called *mental setae*), and their number and placement are used taxonomically (figs. 11.13, 11.26, 11.30). The antennae are usually composed of six or seven segments, but in the Gomphidae the number is reduced to three or four, the fourth usually being vestigial (figs. 11.90–11.94).

Thorax: The prothorax is freely movable as in the adult, although relatively larger and less contracted. The propleura may be useful taxonomically when they are raised into a pair of prothoracic *supracoxal processes.* The mesothorax and metathorax are solidly fused to form the *synthorax.* The wing cases are moved more caudad and the metepisterna meet in front of them. The legs are still in a position to permit walking, not forced so far forward as in the adult. The legs are usually shorter and more robust than in the adult, although in some groups, such as Macromiidae, they are quite long. The setae and spines so characteristic of the adult are missing. The first two pairs of legs of some Anisoptera (especially Gomphidae) may have burrowing hooks. In late instars the two inner cases enclose the front wings and the two outer cases enclose the hind wings; the ventral side of the hind wings is exposed. The longitudinal veins are clearly seen in the swollen wing cases prior to emergence, and in some species, before the wings are crumpled and swollen, triangles, crossveins, and other features may also be seen clearly. If the wing cases are removed from fresh, mature nymphs, slit open, and placed into a weak potassium hydroxide solution, the wings will expand to their full size and allow adult venational characters to be observed.

Abdomen: The nymphal abdomen of Anisoptera is always much shorter and stouter than the adult's. In the Anisoptera and very few Zygoptera, the lateral abdominal carina often ends in a sharp projection, the *lateral spine,* usually longest on segment 9 (fig. 11.23). There may be variously shaped, middorsal projections *(dorsal hooks)* on the posterior margin of the segments (figs. 11.23, 11.25). The abdomen may be long, slender, and tapering to the end, as in Aeshnidae and the Zygoptera, or blunt-tipped, even broad and subcircular, as in some Gomphidae (*Hagenius* sp.) (fig. 11.101) and in the Macromiidae. On the sternum of segment 2 of the male (even in exuviae), the rudiments of the adult genitalia often may be seen as swellings, and the developing ovipositor of the female is in the sternal region of segment 9. The terminal anal pyramid of Anisoptera is composed of a *dorsal epiproct* (formerly called *superior appendage*) and two ventral *paraprocts* (formerly called *inferior appendages*), which surround the anal opening from the rectal chamber (fig. 11.23). Two *cerci* (formerly called *lateral appendages*) develop later. In the Zygoptera, the epiproct and paraprocts are specialized to form the three *gills* (caudal lamellae), one median and two lateral (fig. 11.12), the shape, tracheation, and markings of which are important taxonomic characters. In the Coenagrionidae, the gills usually have a nodus or point on the edge of the gill where there is a change in the marginal setae, often marked by a notch. The antenodal setae are short and stiff, whereas the postnodal setae may be only fine hairs. The setae are more numerous and stronger on the dorsal margin of the median gill and on the ventral margins of the lateral gills. The cerci are quite small, but in some Zygoptera the shape may be used to separate two species that otherwise appear almost identical. All North American species have easily-shed gills that regenerate when broken off. Because these regenerated gills may be much smaller and quite different from the original ones, gills must be used with caution in making taxonomic identifications.

Adults

Detailed accounts of adult odonate structure are given in Walker (1953) and Needham and Westfall (1955), but structures used in the keys are discussed below.

Head: The huge compound eyes with many facets, which occupy a large portion of the head, are more widely separated in the Zygoptera (fig. 11.3) than in the Anisoptera (fig. 11.4). The labium or lower lip has a median cleft in some families (fig. 11.42), but not in others (fig. 11.43). The short and bristlelike antennae are of little use in taxonomy (fig. 11.4). The top of the head between the compound eyes, the *vertex*, bears three *ocelli*. Behind the vertex and fused with it is the *occiput*, forming the rear of the head. In some Anisoptera, as the Aeshnidae (fig. 11.4), the compound eyes meet and separate the vertex from the occiput. Many Zygoptera have conspicuous, pale *postocular spots* behind the ocelli.

Thorax: The head is freely movable, attached to the small prothorax by a very slender neck. The dorsal sclerite, or *pronotum*, is divided into three lobes. In most Zygoptera, during mating the posterior lobe of the female is grasped by the inferior appendages of the male, and it consequently bears structural modifications matching the specific form of the male appendages. The meso- and metathorax of Odonata are fused into a pterothorax (or synthorax). The dorsal sclerites or plates *(nota)* and the ventral ones *(sterna)* are much reduced. The side sclerites *(pleura)* slope backward and upward, with the legs displaced forward and the wings backward. Immediately anterior to the first abdominal sternum is the *intersternum,* which is sometimes raised into a distinct tubercle. The mesopleural suture is termed the *humeral suture.* The intersegmental or interpleural suture (between meso- and metathorax) is called the *first lateral,* and the metapleural suture, the *second lateral.* The middorsal thoracic carina runs the length of the dorsum and between it and the humeral suture there is often an *antehumeral stripe.*

Legs: Each of the six legs is composed of a basal *coxa* (fig. 11.118), followed by a thinner *trochanter.* The *femur* and *tibia* (fig. 11.118) are long and armed with various spines and hairs. The *tarsus* is composed of three segments, increasing in size from first to third. The last segment ends in a pair of *tarsal claws* that may have hooks on the ventral margin. Some species of Corduliidae possess conspicuous *tibial keels.*

Wings: The two pairs of wings of Odonata are well developed. In Anisoptera the wings are held horizontally when at rest, whereas in most Zygoptera they are held folded vertically above the body. In some Zygoptera genera, such as *Lestes* and *Chromagrion,* the wings are held partly spread, although some Libellulidae may bend the wings down below the horizontal. In the Zygoptera, the front and hind wings are about equal in length and similar in form (fig. 11.1). Both wings are narrowed toward the base and usually stalked or petiolate, i.e., each is paddlelike with a proximally narrowed portion and an expanded distal portion on the posterior side (fig. 11.68). In the Anisoptera (fig. 11.2) the hind wing is much broader at the base than the front wing and has a more or less distinct *anal margin,* which may meet the hind margin of the wing at a distinct angle, the *anal angle,* as in males of most families. The anal margin may meet the hind margin of the wing in a broad curve, as in the females of all families and males of the Libellulidae (fig. 11.135). Bordering the anal margin of the hind wing of Anisoptera, there is an opaque *membranule* (fig. 11.83). Most Odonata have an enlarged cell, the *pterostigma* (fig. 11.2), bordered by the *costa* and near the apex of each wing. It is often wider than the neighboring cells and pigmented so as to be opaque.

Wing venation: The most stable and reliable characters for identifying the major groups of Odonata to genus are found in the wing venation (Needham 1903, 1951; Tillyard 1917; Munz 1919). The veins are either longitudinal or crossveins. The longitudinal veins appear early in the wing pads of the nymphs, generally along the path of the tracheae. The crossveins, which appear later, are more variable than the longitudinal veins.

The following account is chiefly for the Anisoptera, but many structures are common to both suborders. The *costa* (fig. 11.2) marks the front border of the wing. The notch near the middle of that border indicates the position of the thickened crossvein called the *nodus.* The *subcosta,* immediately behind the costa, ends at the nodus. The *radius* (R) is a strong vein parallel to the costa. At its base it is fused with the *media* (M) as far as the *arculus,* and at the nodus it gives off a strong branch posteriorly, the *radial sector* (Rs). Rs descends by way of the subnodus and the *oblique vein* (fig. 11.83) to its position behind the first two branches of media (M_1 and M_2). The media is composed of four branches, and as noted, at the base it is fused with the radius. At the arculus the media descends to meet a crossvein and then bends sharply outward toward the wing tip. At the arculus it gives off a branch rearward (M_4), another (M_3) farther distad, and still another at the subnodus (M_2). From the terminal branch, M_1 runs parallel to the main radial stem (R_1), whereas M_2 parallels the radial sector. The two branches at the first forking are called the *sectors of the arculus.* The *cubitus* (Cu) is a two-branched vein (fig. 11.83). It is straight to the arculus, but soon turns sharply rearward, forming the inner (proximal) side of the *triangle* (fig. 11.83). At the hind angle of the triangle, the cubitus is forked and its branches (Cu_1 and Cu_2) run more or less parallel to the hind margin. The *anal vein* (A), when present, lies posterior to cubitus, and has three branches,

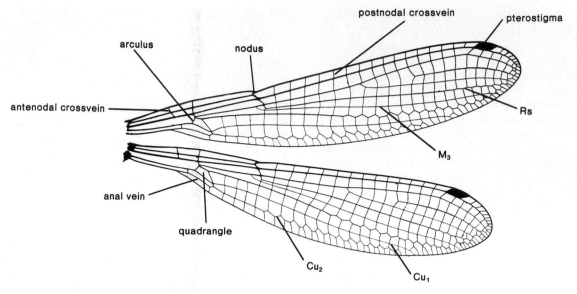

Figure 11.1

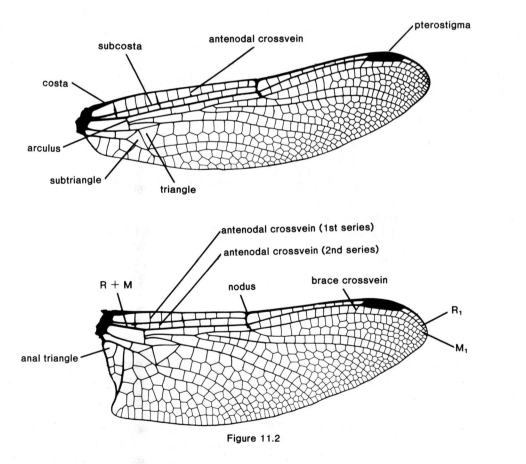

Figure 11.2

Figure 11.1. Wings of male *Argia moesta* (Hagen) (Coenagrionidae).

Figure 11.2. Wings of male *Ophiogomphus carolus* Needham (Gomphidae).

A_1–A_3. The path of these veins and their degree of development varies in different groups. At the pterostigma may be a crossvein, the *brace vein,* at its proximal end (figs. 11.82–11.83). Two crossveins between M and Cu complete the triangle and form the front (appears to be a part of Cu) and outer sides. A *cubito-anal crossvein* forms the front side of the *subtriangle* and added cubito-anal crossveins are present in some genera (fig. 11.82). Behind the costa, as far as the nodus, are two series of *antenodal crossveins.* The first and sixth hind wing crossveins of the first series (fig. 11.83) are thickened and usually only they are continuous from the costa to R + M. This is true only for some families and genera; in others antenodals are not thickened and the first and second series are aligned. The single series of *postnodal crossveins* extends from the nodus to the pterostigma between the costa and R_1. Bordering the triangle on its front side is the *supertriangle* (or supratriangle; fig. 11.82). All triangles may or may not contain crossveins. A stout, perpendicular *anal crossing* (Ac) connects Cu and A near the wing base; this is especially important in Zygoptera (figs. 11.52, 11.72). In both wings the cells behind the anal vein, between the hind angle of the triangle and the wing base, are the *paranal cells* (fig. 11.82). In the male hind wing of some genera, the basal one or two paranals may lie in a strongly bordered *male anal triangle* (figs. 11.82, 11.86–11.87). Below the radial sector may be a *radial planate* (figs. 11.82–11.83), formed by a number of cells lined up evenly and subtending one or more rows of cells. Below M_4 may be a *median planate,* and below M_1 toward the apex of the wing, an *apical planate* (fig. 11.138). In some genera (e.g., *Hagenius*), a *trigonal planate* runs from the triangle toward the wing tip (fig. 11.113). Between M_1 and M_2 near the nodus, the Libellulidae have a *reverse vein,* which may be strongly slanted as compared with the adjacent crossveins (fig. 11.136). An *anal loop,* which is markedly foot-shaped in the Libellulidae may be formed between A_1 and A_2 of the hind wing. It has a thick midrib between A_1 and A_2, which may be strongly angulated at the heel (fig. 11.137) or more nearly straight (fig. 11.136). Proximal to the arculus is a clear space (with or without crossveins), the *midbasal space* (median space), bounded by R + M in front and Cu behind.

Figures of the wings of Zygoptera show readily apparent differences from the Anisoptera. For example, a *quadrangle* replaces the triangle of the Anisoptera, and there is no subtriangle, supertriangle, or anal loop (fig. 11.1).

Abdomen: The abdomen consists of ten segments, which are usually subcylindrical, and a portion of an eleventh segment bearing terminal appendages (fig. 11.5). Segments 1 and 10 are shorter than the intervening ones. In Anisoptera, segments 2 and 3 are swollen, and in the male these bear on the ventral side the unique copulatory organs in the *genital pocket* (genital fossa). The anterior margin of the genital pocket, the *anterior lamina,* may be flat, as in *Stylurus* sp., or project above the rim of the genital pocket. It also may be bilobed and armed with spines or denticles. In the pocket is located the penis and accessory genitalia, including two pairs of *hamules* (anterior and posterior) that assist in copulation and often constitute good diagnostic characters. In some families of Anisoptera the males possess earlike projections on the sides of segment 2, which may be armed with a series of spines. Anisoptera males have one inferior and two superior appendages at the end of the abdomen (figs. 11.5, 11.9), whereas males of Zygoptera have two of each (fig. 11.7). The genital aperture of the male is on the sternum of segment 9. In Aeshnidae and the Zygoptera, the ovipositor of the female is composed of two pairs of sharp, pointed stylets and a pair of covering genital valves, tipped with a slender stylus on each side (fig. 11.8).

KEY TO THE SUBORDERS OF ODONATA

Nymphs

1.   Nymphs slender, head wider than thorax and abdomen; 3 long, caudal tracheal gills at tip of abdomen (fig. 11.12) .... *Zygoptera* (p. 133)

1'.   Nymphs stout, head usually narrower than thorax and abdomen; 3 short, stiff, pointed valves at tip of abdomen (figs. 11.21, 11.24) .... *Anisoptera* (p. 133)

Adults

1.   Front and hind wings similar in size and shape, the triangle and subtriangle represented by a quadrangle (fig. 11.1); eyes separated by more than their own width (fig. 11.3); males with 2 inferior appendages (fig. 11.7); females with a fully developed ovipositor, bearing styli (fig. 11.8); wings in repose (at rest) meeting above the body or only partly expanded .... *Zygoptera* (p. 133)

1'.   Front and hind wings dissimilar in size and shape, the hind wing considerably wider at base than the front wing, each having a triangle and subtriangle (fig. 11.2); eyes meeting middorsally or not separated by a space greater than their own width (fig. 11.4); males with a single inferior appendage (fig. 11.9); females with or without an ovipositor; wings held horizontally in repose .... *Anisoptera* (p. 136)

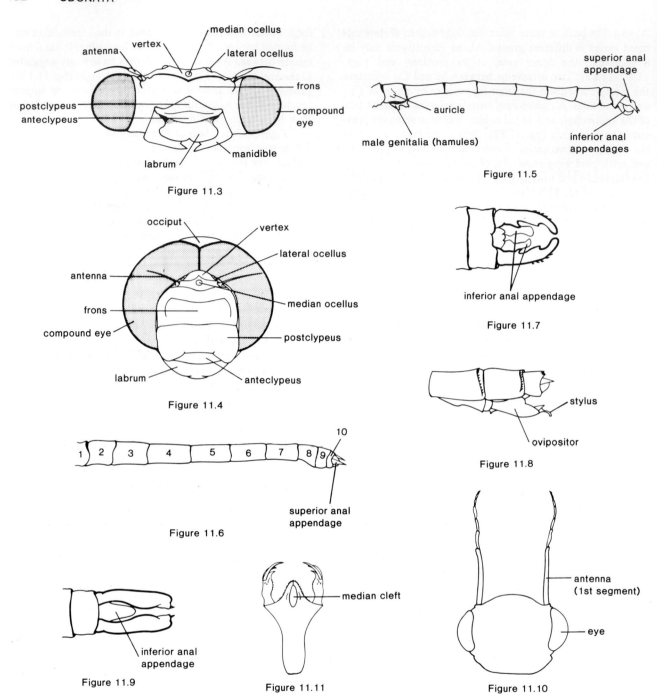

Figure 11.3. Anterior view of head of adult *Calopteryx* sp. (Calopterygidae).

Figure 11.4. Anterior view of head of adult *Aeshna* sp. (Aeshnidae).

Figure 11.5. Lateral view of male abdomen of adult *Erpetogomphus* sp. (Gomphidae).

Figure 11.6. Lateral view of female abdomen of adult *Erpetogomphus* sp. (Gomphidae).

Figure 11.7. Dorsal view of anal appendages of adult male *Lestes* sp. (Lestidae).

Figure 11.8. Lateral view of abdominal segments 8–10 of adult female *Lestes* sp. (Lestidae).

Figure 11.9. Dorsal view of anal appendages of adult male *Aeshna* sp. (Aeshnidae).

Figure 11.10. Dorsal view of head of nymph *Calopteryx* sp. (Calopterygidae).

Figure 11.11. Prementum of labium of nymph *Hetaerina* sp. (Calopterygidae).

KEY TO THE FAMILIES OF ZYGOPTERA

Nymphs

1.   First antennal segment greatly elongate, as long as the combined length of the remaining segments (fig. 11.10); prementum with deep median cleft (fig. 11.11); lateral caudal gills triangular in cross section .... *CALOPTERYGIDAE* (p. 138)

1'.   First antennal segment not so elongate, distinctly less than the combined length of the remaining segments (fig. 11.12); prementum with small closed cleft or none (fig. 11.13); lateral caudal gills flat or somewhat inflated 2

2(1').   Prementum distinctly petiolate (stalked) and spoon-shaped, the narrow proximal part (nearest the body) as long as or longer than the expanded distal part (farthest from the body) (fig. 11.16); movable hook of each palpal lobe with 2 or 3 setae; usually 5–8 dorsal premental setae on each side of median line (when only 4 or 5 prementals present, then with only 3 palpal setae) (fig. 11.16) .... *LESTIDAE* (p. 141)

2'.   Prementum not distinctly petiolate, more or less triangular or subquadrate in shape (fig. 11.13); movable hook of each palpal lobe without setae; dorsal premental setae 0–3 on each side of median line (some Coenagrionidae with 4 or 5 have 5–6 palpal setae (fig. 11.13) 3

3(2').   One dorsal premental seta on each side of median line; palpal setae 3–5; proximal portion of gills thickened and darkened, apical portion thinner and more lightly pigmented, thus nodus very distinctly delineated across entire width of gill (fig. 11.17) .... *PROTONEURIDAE* (p. 148)

3'.   Dorsal premental setae usually 3–5 on each side of median line or absent (if only 1 present, gills not as above and usually 6 palpal setae present) (fig. 11.13); palpal setae 0–6; proximal portion of gills usually not differing markedly from distal portion, thus nodus not delineated across entire width of gill (*Nehalennia* and *Argiallagma,* with gills in exception to this, have 3–4 dorsal premental setae on each side of median line) (fig. 11.15) .... *COENAGRIONIDAE* (p. 141)

Adults

1.   Antenodal crossveins numerous (fig. 11.18); postnodal crossveins not in line with the veins below them; anal vein at its base separate from posterior border of wing; quadrangle with several crossveins (fig. 11.18) .... *CALOPTERYGIDAE* (p. 138)

1'.   Only 2 antenodals present (fig. 11.19); postnodals in line with the veins below them; anal vein joined with wing margin for a distance from the wing base; quadrangle never with crossveins (fig. 11.19) 2

2(1').   Veins M_3 and Rs arising nearer the arculus than the nodus (fig. 11.19) .... *LESTIDAE* (p. 141)

2'.   Veins M_3 and Rs arising nearer the nodus than the arculus (fig. 11.20) 3

3(2').   Anal vein absent or greatly reduced; Cu_2 absent or at most only as long as 1 cell; quadrangle somewhat rectangular (fig. 11.20) .... *PROTONEURIDAE* (p. 148)

3'.   Anal vein and Cu_2 of normal length (fig. 11.1); quadrangle distinctly trapezoidal (fig. 11.1) .... *COENAGRIONIDAE* (p. 145)

KEY TO THE FAMILIES OF ANISOPTERA

Nymphs

1.   Prementum and palpal lobes of labium flat or nearly so, without dorsal premental and usually without palpal setae (fig. 11.22) 2

1'.   Prementum and palpal lobes of labium forming a spoon-shaped structure, usually with dorsal premental and always with palpal setae (figs. 11.26–11.27) 4

2(1).   Antennae 4-segmented; fore- and middle tarsi 2-segmented; ligula without a median cleft (figs. 11.21–11.22) .... *GOMPHIDAE* (p. 153)

2'.   Antennae 6- and 7-segmented; fore and middle tarsi 3-segmented; ligula with a median cleft 3

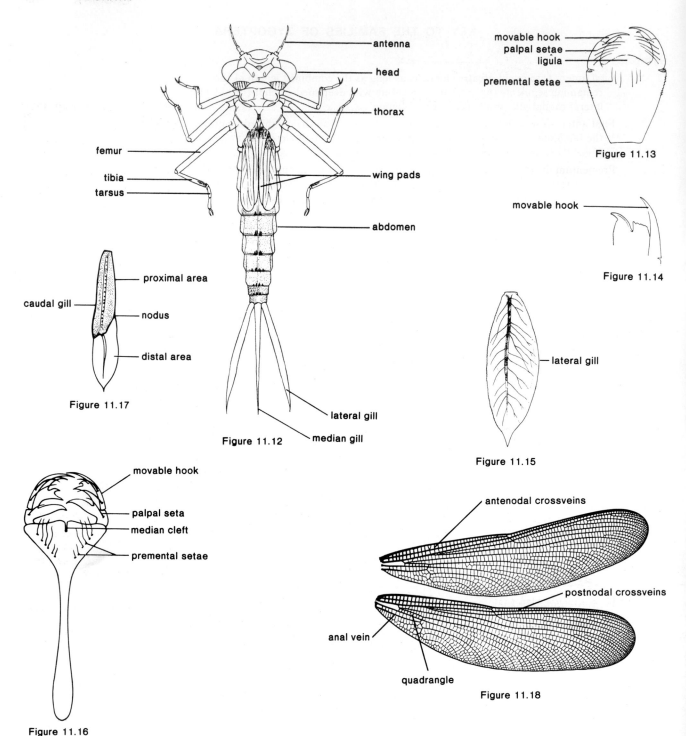

Figure 11.17

Figure 11.12

Figure 11.16

Figure 11.13

Figure 11.14

Figure 11.15

Figure 11.18

Figure 11.12. Dorsal view of nymph *Protallagma titicacae* (Calvert) (Coenagrionidae) (South American genus and species).

Figure 11.13. Prementum of labium of nymph *Protallagma titicacae* (Calvert) (Coenagrionidae).

Figure 11.14. Tip of palpal lobe of prementum of nymph *Protallagma titicacae* (Calvert) (Coenagrionidae).

Figure 11.15. Left lateral caudal gill of nymph *Protallagma titicacae* (Calvert) (Coenagrionidae).

Figure 11.16. Prementum of labium of nymph *Lestes* sp. (Lestidae).

Figure 11.17. Left lateral caudal gill of nymph *Protoneura viridis* Westfall (Protoneuridae).

Figure 11.18. Wings of male *Calopteryx angustipennis* (Selys) (Calopterygidae).

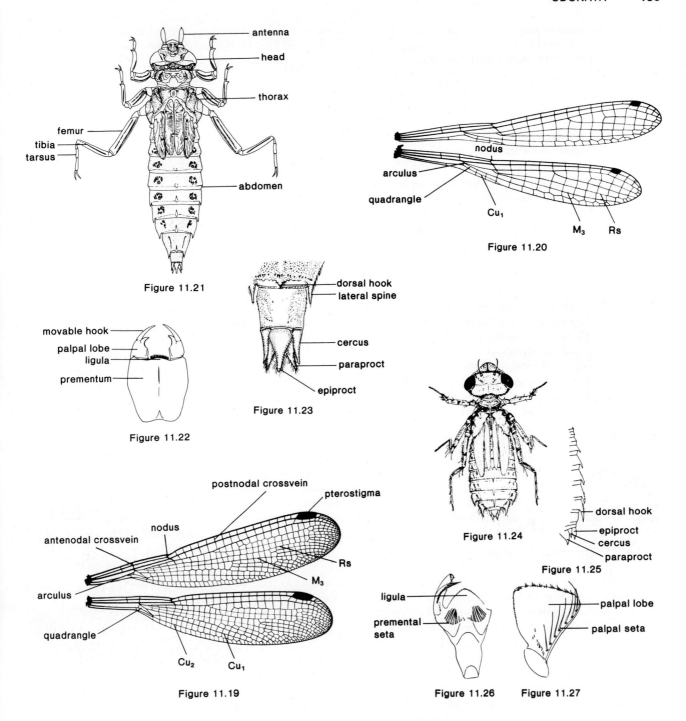

Figure 11.21

Figure 11.20

Figure 11.23

Figure 11.22

Figure 11.24

Figure 11.25

Figure 11.19

Figure 11.26   Figure 11.27

Figure 11.19. Wings of *Lestes vigilax* Hagen (Lestidae).

Figure 11.20. Wings of *Protoneura capillaris* (Rambur) (Protoneuridae).

Figure 11.21. Dorsal view of nymph *Gomphus hodgesi* Needham (Gomphidae).

Figure 11.22. Prementum of labium of nymph *Gomphus hodgesi* Needham (Gomphidae).

Figure 11.23. Tip of abdomen of nymph *Gomphus hodgesi* Needham (Gomphidae).

Figure 11.24. Dorsal view of nymph *Miathyria marcella* Selys (Libellulidae).

Figure 11.25. Lateral view of abdomen of nymph *Miathyria marcella* Selys (Libellulidae).

Figure 11.26. Prementum of labium of nymph with one palpal lobe attached, *Miathyria marcella* Selys (Libellulidae).

Figure 11.27. Palpal lobe of prementum of nymph *Miathyria marcella* Selys (Libellulidae).

3(2').   Segments of antennae short, thick, hairy (fig. 11.91); prementum with sides subparallel in distal three-fifths, abruptly narrowed near base (fig. 11.28); each palpal lobe bearing a strong dorsolateral spur at base of movable hook (fig. 11.28) .... *PETALURIDAE* (p. 153)

3'.   Segments of antennae usually slender, bristlelike (fig. 11.90); prementum widest in distal half, much narrower in basal half or more (fig. 11.29); no spur at base of movable hook (fig. 11.29) .... *AESHNIDAE* (p. 148)

4(1').   Distal margin of each palpal lobe cut into large and irregular dentations (toothed projections) without associated setae (fig. 11.30); ligula represented by a toothlike process cleft in the middle (fig. 11.30) .... *CORDULEGASTRIDAE—Cordulegaster*

4'.   Distal margin of each palpal lobe smooth or with smaller and more regular dentations (figs. 11.27, 11.31–11.32), each crenation (rounded projection) bearing 1 or more setae (fig. 11.27); ligula not as above 5

5(4').   Head with a prominent, almost erect, frontal horn between bases of antennae (fig. 11.33); metasternum with a broad mesal tubercle near posterior margin; legs very long, the hind femur extending to or beyond the hind margin of abdominal segment 8; abdomen strongly depressed, almost circular in outline when viewed from above .... *MACROMIIDAE* (p. 160)

5'.   Head without a prominent, almost erect, frontal horn (*Neurocordulia molesta* has a triangular almost flat frontal shelf—fig. 11.34); legs shorter, the hind femur usually not extending to the hind margin of abdominal segment 8 (fig. 11.24); metasternum without a tubercle near posterior margin; abdomen less depressed, more cylindrical in outline (figs. 11.24, 11.35–11.36) 6

6(5').   Crenations (rounded projections) on distal margins of palpal lobes of labium separated by deep notches, crenations usually one-fourth to one-half as high as they are broad (as in fig. 11.133); cerci generally more than one-half as long as paraprocts; lateral spines of abdominal segment 9 usually longer than its middorsal length; middorsal hooks on abdomen often cultriform (sicklelike) .... *CORDULIIDAE* * (p. 161)

6'.   Crenations on distal margins of palpal lobes of labium generally separated by shallow notches, crenations usually one-tenth to one-sixth as high as they are broad (fig. 11.134); cerci generally not more than one-half as long as paraprocts; lateral spines of abdominal segment 9 usually shorter than its middorsal length but, if longer, then middorsal hooks on abdomen are not cultriform, but more spinelike, stubby, or absent .... *LIBELLULIDAE* * (p. 162)

Adults

1.   Triangles of fore wings less than twice as far from the arculus as those of hind wings (fig. 11.37); triangles of both wings similar in shape, generally elongated in long axis of wings; 2 antenodal crossveins thickened, most of the other antenodals of the 1st series not aligned with those of the 2nd series (fig. 11.37) 2

1'.   Triangles of fore wings at least twice as far from the arculus as those of hind wings (fig. 11.38); triangles of the fore wings generally elongated transversely, those of hind wings longitudinally; no thickened antenodal crossveins, those of the 1st series aligned with those of the 2nd series (fig. 11.38) 5

2(1).   Eyes meeting for a considerable distance (fig. 11.4); pterostigma supported by an oblique brace crossvein at or very near its inner end (fig. 11.2); inferior appendage of male generally triangular, rarely bifurcate (forked) or truncate (cut off squarely at tip) (fig. 11.9); ovipositor well developed, both genital valves with a stylus (as in fig. 11.8) .... *AESHNIDAE* (p. 150)

2'.   Eyes wide apart or barely meeting (fig. 11.41); pterostigma with or without a brace crossvein; inferior appendage of male usually bifurcate or truncate, never triangular; ovipositor small or vestigial (fig. 11.44), rarely long as in figure 11.45; genital valves, if present, without stylus (fig. 11.45) 3

*No single character will reliably separate all nymphs of Corduliidae from those of Libellulidae. For this reason, some specialists have recognized only one family, Libellulidae, and two subfamilies, Libellulinae and Corduliinae. Specimens difficult to place in couplet 6 may need to be studied through keys to genera of both families and compared with available figures.

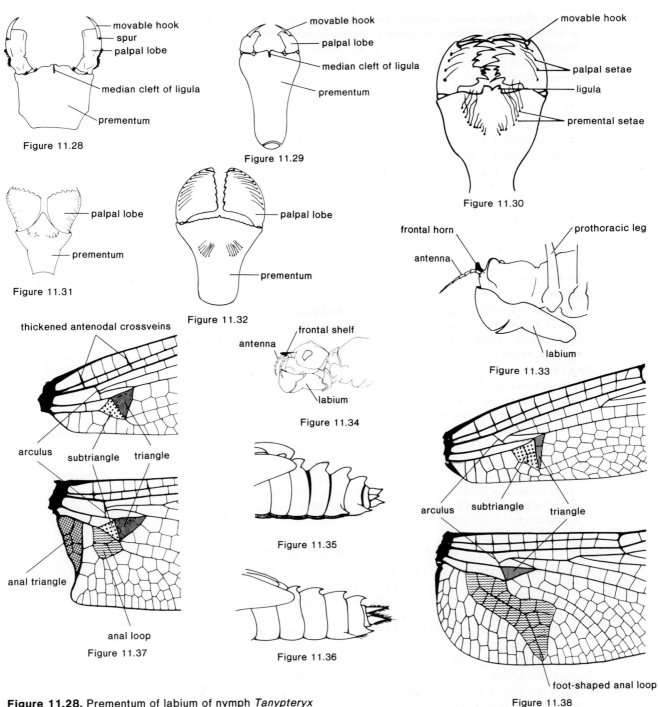

Figure 11.28

Figure 11.29

Figure 11.30

Figure 11.31

Figure 11.32

Figure 11.33

Figure 11.34

Figure 11.35

Figure 11.36

Figure 11.37

Figure 11.38

Figure 11.28. Prementum of labium of nymph *Tanypteryx* sp. (Petaluridae).

Figure 11.29. Prementum of labium of nymph *Aeshna* sp. (Aeshnidae).

Figure 11.30. Prementum of labium of nymph *Cordulegaster* sp. (Cordulegastridae).

Figure 11.31. Prementum of labium of nymph *Paltothemis* sp. (Libellulidae).

Figure 11.32. Prementum of labium of nymph *Plathemis* sp. (Libellulidae).

Figure 11.33. Lateral view of head of nymph *Macromia* sp. (Macromiidae).

Figure 11.34. Lateral view of head of nymph *Neurocordulia molesta* (Walsh) (Corduliidae).

Figure 11.35. Lateral view of abdomen of nymph *Neurocordulia alabamensis* Hodges (Corduliidae).

Figure 11.36. Lateral view of abdomen of nymph *Perithemis* sp. (Libellulidae).

Figure 11.37. Bases of wings of male *Ophiogomphus carolus* Needham (Gomphidae).

Figure 11.38. Bases of wings of male *Erythemis simplicicollis* (Say) (Libellulidae).

3(2').   Eyes close together or barely meeting; labium with a median cleft (fig. 11.42);
           pterostigma without a brace crossvein; ovipositor extending beyond tip of
           abdomen .... *CORDULEGASTRIDAE—Cordulegaster*

3'.   Eyes wide apart (fig. 11.41); labium with or without a median cleft (fig. 11.43);
           pterostigma with a brace crossvein (fig. 11.2); ovipositor never reaching tip of
           abdomen 4

4(3').   Front margin of labium with a median cleft (fig. 11.42); pterostigma longer than
           one-fourth the distance from nodus to distal end of R_1; subtriangle of fore wing
           generally divided into 2 or more cells; last segments of abdomen not enlarged;
           ovipositor small but complete, both genital valves with a stylus .... *PETALURIDAE* (p. 153)

4'.   Front margin of labium entire (fig. 11.43); pterostigma shorter than one-fourth the
           distance from nodus to distal end of R_1 (fig. 11.2); subtriangle of fore wing
           generally single-celled (fig. 11.37); last segments of abdomen usually enlarged;
           ovipositor represented by a bifid vulvar lamina (fig. 11.44) .... *GOMPHIDAE* (p. 158)

5(1').   Anal loop about as broad as long, without a midrib (fig. 11.39); triangle of hind
           wing remote from arculus (fig. 11.39); hooks of tarsal claws nearly equal in size,
           the ventral one usually longer; no ventrolateral carinae (ridges) on abdomen;
           anterior hamules relatively well developed (fig. 11.5) .... *MACROMIIDAE* (p. 160)

5'.   Anal loop, if present, long and narrow, with 2 rows of cells divided by a midrib,
           somewhat foot-shaped (fig. 11.38); triangle of hind wing opposite the arculus
           (fig. 11.38); hooks of tarsal claws unequal, the ventral one much shorter;
           ventrolateral carinae on abdominal segments 3 or 4 to 8 or 9; anterior hamules
           hardly, if at all, discernible 6

6(5').   Anal loop generally foot-shaped, with well-developed toe (fig. 11.38); males
           without anal triangle, and anal margin of hind wings rounded as in females (fig.
           11.38); no tubercle on rear margin of eye; coloration varied, but not metallic (in
           North American species); males without anterior hamules or auricles on
           segment 2; legs without tibial keels (elevated ridges) .... *LIBELLULIDAE* (p. 167)

6'.   Anal loop somewhat foot-shaped, but with little development of the toe (fig.
           11.40); hind wing of males with an anal triangle and anal margin angulate (fig.
           11.37); usually with a low tubercle on rear margin of each compound eye;
           coloration usually metallic; males with small anterior hamules, and an auricle on
           each side of abdominal segment 2 (fig. 11.5); tibial keels on some legs .... *CORDULIIDAE* (p. 161)

KEYS TO THE GENERA OF ZYGOPTERA

Calopterygidae

Nymphs

1.   Prementum cleft nearly halfway to its base (fig. 11.46); posterolateral margins of
           abdominal segments 9 and 10 without spines; lateral caudal gills flat or not
           strongly triquetral in cross section .... *Calopteryx*

1'.   Prementum cleft only to base of palpal lobes (fig. 11.47); posterolateral margins of
           segments 9 and 10 with small, distinct spines; lateral caudal gills strongly
           triquetral in cross section .... *Hetaerina*

Adults

1.   Space proximal to arculus (midbasal or median space) without crossveins; arculus
           bent where its sectors (M_3 and M_4) arise, the sectors not proximally curved;
           anterior margin of quadrangle straight; anal branch of Cu_2 forming somewhat of
           a loop (fig. 11.50) .... *Calopteryx*

1'.   Space proximal to arculus with several crossveins; arculus not bent where its
           sectors arise, the sectors proximally curved; anterior margin of quadrangle
           convex; anal branch of Cu_2 not evident (fig. 11.51) .... *Hetaerina*

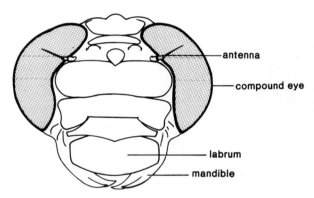

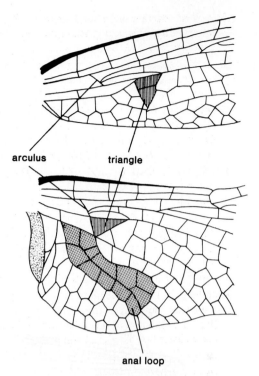

Figure 11.39

Figure 11.40

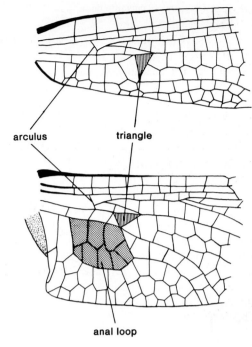

Figure 11.41

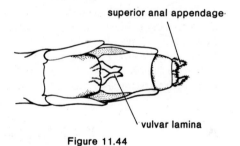

Figure 11.44

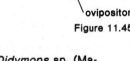

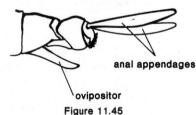

Figure 11.42

ovipositor
Figure 11.45

Figure 11.43

Figure 11.39. Base of wings of male *Didymops* sp. (Macromiidae).

Figure 11.40. Base of wings of male *Tetragoneuria* sp. (Corduliidae).

Figure 11.41. Anterior view of head of adult *Gomphus* sp. (Gomphidae).

Figure 11.42. Ventral view of head of adult *Cordulegaster maculata* Selys (Cordulegastridae).

Figure 11.43. Ventral view of head of adult *Gomphus dilatatus* Rambur (Gomphidae).

Figure 11.44. Ventral view of abdominal segments 8–10 of adult female *Gomphus* sp. (Gomphidae).

Figure 11.45. Lateral view of abdominal segments 9–10 of adult female *Somatochlora* sp. (Corduliidae).

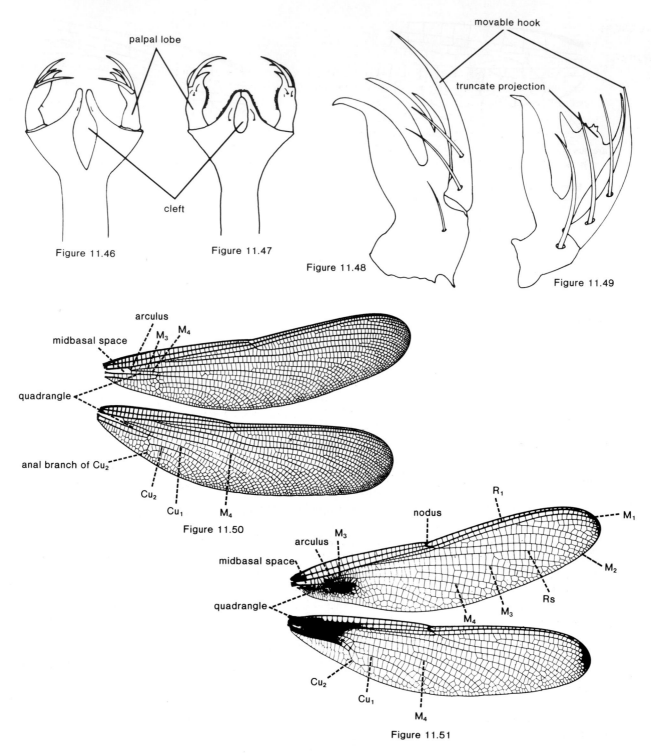

Figure 11.46. Prementum of labium of nymph, dorsal view, *Calopteryx maculata* (Beauvois) (Calopterygidae) (drawn by M. S. Westfall).

Figure 11.47. Prementum of labium of nymph, dorsal view, *Hetaerina titia* (Drury) (Calopterygidae) (drawn by M. S. Westfall).

Figure 11.48. Right palpal lobe of prementum of nymph, dorsal view, *Archilestes grandis* (Rambur) (Lestidae) (drawn by M. S. Westfall).

Figure 11.49. Right palpal lobe of prementum of nymph, dorsal view, *Lestes inaequalis* Walsh (Lestidae) (drawn by M. S. Westfall).

Figure 11.50. Wings of *Calopteryx angustipennis* (Selys) (Calopterygidae). (From *Manual of the Damselflies of North America,* M. J. Westfall, in prep.)

Figure 11.51. Wings of *Hetaerina titia* (Drury) (Calopterygidae) (Westfall manuscript).

Lestidae

Nymphs

1.   Distal margin of each palpal lobe divided into 3 sharp processes, the outermost one
        much shorter than the movable hook (fig. 11.48); caudal gills with 2 well-
        defined, dark crossbands .... *Archilestes*

1'.   Distal margin of each palpal lobe divided into 4 processes—3 sharp hooks and a
        short, serrate, truncate projection between the 2 outer hooks, the outermost hook
        reaching almost as far distad as the tip of the movable hook (fig. 11.49); caudal
        gills never with 2 distinct and complete dark crossbands .... *Lestes*

Adults

1.   The proximal side (inner end) of the quadrangle of the fore wing almost one-half
        the length of the inferior side; in species in the United States, vein M_2 arises
        about one cell beyond the nodus (fig. 11.52) .... *Archilestes*

1'.   The proximal side (inner end) of the quadrangle of the fore wing one-third or less
        of the length of the inferior side; in species in the United States, vein M_2 arises
        several cells beyond the nodus (fig. 11.53) .... *Lestes*

Coenagrionidae

Nymphs

1.   Dorsal premental setae absent; palpal lobes with 2 distal, pointed hooks (fig.
        11.54); palpal setae 0–3 (rarely 4–5); body form usually short and stout; caudal
        gills of some species, in dorsal view, quite thick or triquetral (fig. 11.55) .... *Argia*

1'.   Dorsal premental setae present; palpal lobes with 1 distal, pointed hook and a
        truncate, denticulate lobe (fig. 11.56); palpal setae 3–7; body form usually
        longer and more slender; caudal gills in dorsal view never thick or triquetral (fig.
        11.12) 2

2(1').   Apices of caudal gills rounded, without a trace of a pointed tip (fig.
        11.57) .... *Hesperagrion*

2'.   Apices of caudal gills acute, with a sharply pointed tip of variable length (fig.
        11.58) 3

3(2').   Posterolateral margins of head greatly produced and sharply angulate (fig.
        11.59) 4

3'.   Posterolateral margins of head not so greatly produced, broadly rounded (fig.
        11.60) 5

4(3).   Apices of caudal gills with acute tip long and sharply pointed; gills about one-sixth
        as broad as long, margins with widely separated setae; antennae 7-segmented .... *Chromagrion*

4'.   Apices of caudal gills with tip not so long and acute; gills about one-third as broad
        as long, margins thickly and closely beset with setae (fig. 11.58); antennae 5- or
        6-segmented .... *Amphiagrion*

5(3').   Apices of lateral caudal gills with long, tapering, almost filamentouslike tips, thus
        apical 6th with a terminal angle of less than 20° (fig. 11.61) 6

5'.   Apices of lateral caudal gills with short, tapering tips, apical 6th with a terminal
        angle of 25° or more (fig. 11.64 a, b) 7

6(5).   Proximal portion of caudal gills conspicuously thicker and darker than apical
        portion, thus nodus conspicuous; caudal gills with extratracheal dark pigment in
        form of marginal spots (fig. 11.61); eyes unpatterned; dorsum of abdomen with
        a row of small, dark, paired spots (Florida) .... *Argiallagma*

6'.   Proximal portion of caudal gills not conspicuously thicker or darker than apical
        portion, nodus not so conspicuous; caudal gills without extratracheal dark
        pigment (tracheae in widely separated clusters) (fig. 11.62); eyes with a checker
        pattern; abdomen without such a row of spots (California) .... *Zoniagrion*

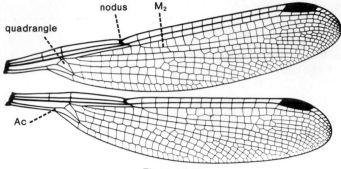

Figure 11.52

Figure 11.58

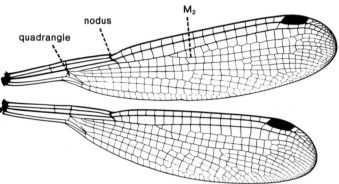

Figure 11.53

Figure 11.57

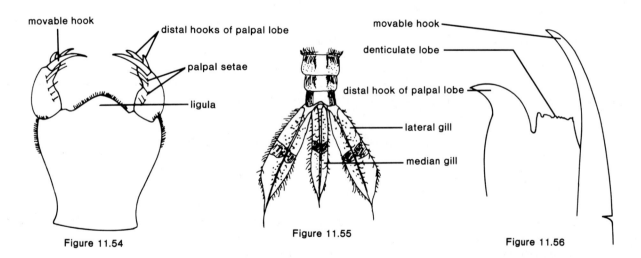

Figure 11.54

Figure 11.55

Figure 11.56

Figure 11.52. Wings of *Archilestes grandis* (Rambur) (Lestidae) (Westfall manuscript).

Figure 11.53. Wings of *Lestes vigilax* Hagen (Lestidae) (Westfall manuscript).

Figure 11.54. Prementum of labium of nymph, dorsal view, *Argia extranea* (Hagen) (Coenagrionidae) (Westfall manuscript).

Figure 11.55. Dorsal view, apex of nymphal abdomen with caudal gills, *Argia extranea* (Hagen) (Coenagrionidae) (Westfall manuscript).

Figure 11.56. Tip of palpal lobe of prementum of nymph, *Protallagma titicacae* (Calvert) (Coenagrionidae) (Westfall manuscript).

Figure 11.57. Right lateral caudal gill of nymph, *Hesperagrion heterodoxum* (Selys) (Coenagrionidae) (Westfall manuscript).

Figure 11.58. Right lateral caudal gill of nymph, *Amphiagrion saucium* (Burmeister) (Coenagrionidae) (Westfall manuscript).

7(5′). Lateral caudal gills one-third as broad as long, apical 6th of each with a terminal angle of 70° or more 8

7′. Lateral caudal gills one-fourth (or less) as broad as long, apical 6th of each with a terminal angle of about 60° or less 9

8(7). Dorsal premental setae 5 each side of median line; apical half of lateral caudal gills, in dorsal view, with outer margin convex, and with tips incurved (forcepslike) (fig. 11.63) (Arizona) .... *Apanisagrion*

8′. Dorsal premental setae 1–3 each side of median line; apical half of lateral caudal gills, in dorsal view, not conspicuously convex, and with tips straight (as in fig. 11.12); gills in lateral view broad and often with marginal dark spots (fig. 11.64) .... *Telebasis*

9(7′). Lateral caudal gills four-fifths the length of the body from anterior margin of head to posterior tip of abdomen; caudal gills with algalike patches of pigmented tracheae (fig. 11.65); dorsal premental setae 3 each side of median line; palpal setae 4 (southern Texas) .... *Acanthagrion*

9′. Lateral caudal gills not more than two-thirds length of body; caudal gills usually without such algalike patches of tracheae; almost always a different combination of premental and palpal setae than above 10

10(9′). One dorsal premental seta of normal length present on each side of median line, although 1–3 small setae may be present on mesal side of principal seta 11

10′. At least 2 dorsal premental setae of normal length present on each side of median line 12

11(10). Palpal setae 3–4; numerous long, stiff setae on lateral carinae of all abdominal segments beyond 1st; length of final-instar nymph 17 mm or more .... *Enallagma* (in part)

11′. Palpal setae 5–6; no long, stiff setae present on lateral carinae of anterior abdominal segments, although often present on posterior segments; length of final-instar nymph 15 mm or less .... *Nehalennia*

12(10′). Lateral carinae of abdominal segments 2–8, in dorsal view, slightly concave, with apices prominent and bearing 2 or more stout, curved setae; usually 3 dorsal premental setae each side of median line; eyes with dark pattern of spots, or lines, forming hexagonal-shaped cells (fig. 11.66) 13

12′. Lateral carinae of abdominal segments 2–8 with margins straight or only slightly convex, apices not prominent, and with apical setae, if present, not noticeably larger than the preceding setae; 2–5 dorsal premental setae each side of median line; eyes, if patterned, usually not as above 14

13(12). Venter of abdominal segments 2–4 (often 2–6) with a more or less transverse, apical group of stiff, conspicuous setae, or nearly all segments devoid of conspicuous ventral setae, at most with tiny brown specks; lateral carinae of abdominal segment 9 less prominent than those of preceding segments and with no stout setae; usually 4 palpal setae .... *Enallagma* (in part)

13′. Venter of all abdominal segments without such a conspicuous, transverse, apical group of setae; instead, setae of equal size and evenly scattered; lateral carinae of abdominal segment 9 nearly as prominent as those of segment 8; segments 8 and 9 bearing 1 stout apical seta; usually 5 palpal setae (southern Florida) .... *Neoerythromma*

14(12′). Eyes usually with a pattern of lateral, alternating pale and dark bands (fig. 11.67); antennae usually with 7 distinct segments; lateral carinae of abdominal segments 2–7 with numerous small setae not arranged in a single row .... *Ischnura, Anomalagrion*

14′. Eyes with no such pattern of lateral pale and dark bands, although dark spots may be apparent; antennae usually 6-segmented, although apical 6th segment often with a scarcely discernible median transverse line that is not similar to joints dividing preceding segments; lateral carinae of abdominal segments 2–8 usually with a single row of setae of variable stoutness .... *Coenagrion, Enallagma* (in part)

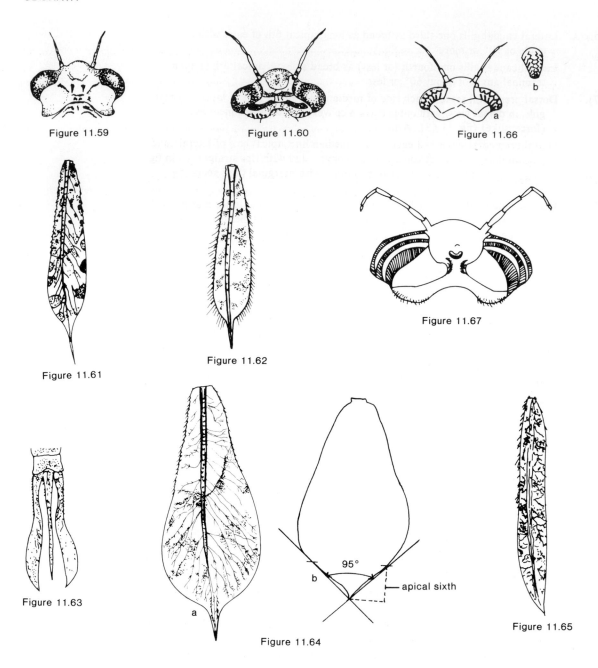

Figure 11.59

Figure 11.60

Figure 11.66

Figure 11.61

Figure 11.62

Figure 11.67

Figure 11.63

Figure 11.64

95°

apical sixth

Figure 11.65

Figure 11.59. Dorsal view of head of nymph, *Amphiagrion saucium* (Burmeister) (Coenagrionidae) (Westfall manuscript).

Figure 11.60. Dorsal view of head of nymph, *Argiallagma minutum* (Selys) (Coenagrionidae) (Cuba) (Westfall manuscript).

Figure 11.61. Left lateral caudal gill of nymph, *Argiallagma minutum* (Selys) (Coenagrionidae) (Cuba) (Westfall manuscript).

Figure 11.62. Left lateral caudal gill of nymph, *Zoniagrion exclamationis* (Selys) (Coenagrionidae) (Westfall manuscript).

Figure 11.63. Apex of abdomen of nymph, with caudal gills, dorsal view, *Apanisagrion lais* (Selys) (Coenagrionidae) (Westfall manuscript).

Figure 11.64. *a,* Left lateral caudal gill of nymph, *Telebasis salva* (Hagen) (Coenagrionidae); *b,* outline of lateral caudal gill, *Telebasis byersi* Westfall (Coenagrionidae) illustrating measurement of angle of apical sixth (drawn by M. S. Westfall).

Figure 11.65. Left lateral caudal gill of nymph, *Acanthagrion quadratum* Selys (Coenagrionidae) (Westfall manuscript).

Figure 11.66. *a,* Dorsal view of head of nymph, *Enallagma divagans* Selys (Coenagrionidae); *b,* anterolateral view of eye showing pattern (Westfall manuscript).

Figure 11.67. Dorsal view of head of nymph, *Ischnura posita* (Hagen) (Coenagrionidae) (drawn by M. S. Westfall).

Adults

1. Tibial spines twice the length of intervening spaces, at least proximally 2

1'. Tibial spines at most barely longer than the intervening spaces 4

2(1). Vein M_{1a} extending at least the length of 8 cells; M_2 arising near 6th or 7th postnodal crossvein in fore wing, near 5th or 6th in hind wing; wings stalked (narrowed) only to level of 1st antenodal crossvein (fig. 11.68) .... ***Argia***

2'. Vein M_{1a} extending at most the length of 6 cells; M_2 arising near 4th or 5th postnodal crossvein in fore wing, near 4th in hind wing; wings stalked to level beyond 1st antenodal crossvein (fig. 11.69) 3

3(2'). Pale postocular spots present; 2 crossveins present between M_4 and Cu_1 proximal to origin of M_3; a pale (often blue) antehumeral (or humeral) stripe present (Florida) .... ***Argiallagma***

3'. Pale postocular spots absent, although crest of occiput may be pale; usually only one crossvein between M_4 and Cu_1 proximal to origin of M_3; no pale, antehumeral or humeral stripe present, these areas solid metallic green .... ***Nehalennia*** (in part)

4(1'). Intersternum with a prominent, moundlike tubercle bearing numerous long, stiff setae; wings nearly equal in length to abdomen; stocky, red or reddish brown and black species .... ***Amphiagrion***

4'. No prominent intersternal tubercle present; wings at most three-fourths the length of the abdomen; usually not stocky, red and black species 5

5(4'). Dorsum of thorax and abdomen mostly metallic green; length of abdomen 19–25 mm; prothoracic femora with 2 distinct external black stripes, 1 at base of spines .... ***Nehalennia*** (in part)

5'. Dorsum of thorax and abdomen usually not metallic green; length of abdomen variable; prothoracic femora without black or with one black stripe which may cover entire external surface 6

6(5'). Postocular area entirely pale or with pale spots ranging from narrow linear areas to large round spots, sometimes confluent with each other or with pale crest of occiput 7

6'. Postocular area dark, without pale spots, although crest of occiput may be pale 22

7(6). Vein M_2 arising proximal to or near 4th postnodal crossvein in fore wing, and proximal to or near 3rd postnodal in hind wing 8

7'. Vein M_2 arising near 5th postnodal crossvein or beyond in fore wing, near 4th or beyond in hind wing (figs. 11.70–11.71) 11

8(7). Black humeral stripe divided along its entire length by a narrow, pale stripe; prothorax with a pale dorsomedial spot .... ***Enallagma*** (in part)

8'. Black humeral stripe entire along its length or lacking; prothorax without a pale, dorsomedial spot or entirely pale 9

9(8'). Anterior margin of fore wing quadrangle less than one-half as long as distal margin; femora with a black apical band; costal margin of pterostigma usually twice as long as proximal margin .... ***Neoerythromma*** (in part)

9'. Anterior margin of fore wing quadrangle nearly as long as distal margin; femora without a dark apical band; costal margin of pterostigma at most slightly longer than proximal margin 10

10(9'). Pterostigma of fore wing of male removed from costa; segment 10 of male with a posterodorsally projecting process nearly equal in length to segment 9; female without an external black stripe on meso- and metatibiae, without a black humeral stripe (suture may be black) and with a pale triangular spot at base of median ocellus .... ***Anomalagrion***

10'. Pterostigma of fore wing of male bordered anteriorly by costa; segment 10 of male with posterodorsal process, if present, not nearly equal in length to segment 9; female usually with a black stripe on meso- and metatibiae, usually with a black humeral stripe, and usually without a pale spot at base of median ocellus .... ***Ischnura*** (in part)

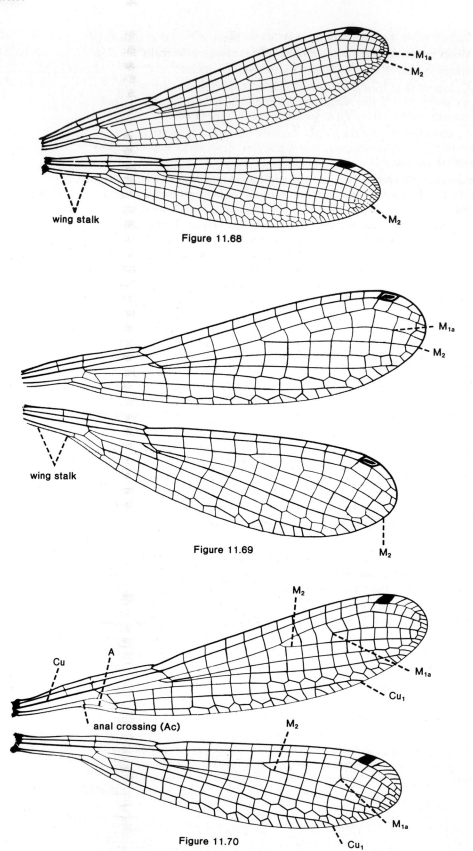

Figure 11.68

Figure 11.69

Figure 11.70

Figure 11.69. Wings of *Nehalennia irene* (Hagen) (Coenagrionidae) (Westfall manuscript).

Figure 11.68. Wings of *Argia moesta* (Hagen) (Coenagrionidae) (Westfall manuscript).

Figure 11.70. Wings of *Hesperagrion heterodoxum* (Selys) (Coenagrionidae) (Westfall manuscript).

11(7'). Vein Cu$_1$ of fore wing extends well beyond level of origin of M$_{1a}$, whereas Cu$_1$ of hind wing usually extends only to level of origin of M$_{1a}$; costal margin of fore wing pterostigma (and often hind wing pterostigma) may be shorter than proximal margin (fig. 11.70) 12

11'. Vein Cu$_1$ similar in fore and hind wings, either extending well beyond level of origin of M$_{1a}$ (usually), or nearly to this level; costal margin of pterostigma as long as or longer than proximal margin in both pairs of wings 13

12(11). Hind wings of male with dense, dark venation at apex (fig 11.71); abdominal segment 8 of female without a ventroapical spine (Arizona) .... *Apanisagrion*

12'. Hind wings of male with normal venation at apex (fig. 11.70); segment 8 of female with a distinct, ventroapical spine .... *Hesperagrion* (in part)

13(11'). Anal crossing linking Cu to posterior border in fore and hind wings 14

13'. Anal crossing linking Cu to A in fore and usually hind wings, not reaching posterior border (as in fig. 11.70) 16

14(13). Abdominal color of male predominantly red, sometimes with black; segment 8 of female without a ventroapical spine .... *Telebasis* (in part)

14'. Abdominal colors of male blue and black; segment 8 of female with a ventroapical spine 15

15(14'). Segment 10 of male in lateral view two and one-half times higher than long, the dorsum projecting dorsoposteriorly; female with a pit on each side of the synthoracic middorsal carina, and apical abdominal appendages approximated at base (southern Texas) .... *Acanthagrion*

15'. Segment 10 of male in lateral view less than twice as high as long, the dorsum flat, directed straight rearward; female without pits near middorsal carina, and abdominal appendages separated at base, usually by width of one appendage .... *Enallagma* (in part)

16(13'). Males 17

16'. Females 19

17(16). Pterostigma of fore wing different in shape, color, or size from pterostigma of hind wing; segment 10 with a posterodorsally projecting bifid process at least one-half as long as the segment .... *Ischnura* (in part)

17'. Pterostigma of fore and hind wings similar in color, shape, and size; segment 10 with at most a very low, widely bifid prominence one-fourth as long as the segment 18

18(17'). Segment 10 with a low, bifid prominence raised slightly above the dorsum of the segment; penis with a transverse row of short spines at base of spatulate lobe; pale antehumeral stripe interrupted posteriorly by black cross-stripe (California) .... *Zoniagrion*

18'. Segment 10 without bifid prominence, although posterior margin may be notched; penis without a transverse row of spines at base of spatulate lobe; pale antehumeral stripe usually entire (except *Coenagrion interrogatum*) .... *Coenagrion, Enallagma* (in part)

19(16'). Humeral suture usually pale, but, if black stripe present, then no apical spine on venter of abdominal segment 8 .... *Ischnura* (in part)

19'. Humeral suture usually with a black stripe, but, if pale, an apical spine is present on venter of segment 8 20

20(19'). Abdominal segment 8 without a ventroapical spine .... *Coenagrion*

20'. Abdominal segment 8 with a ventroapical spine 21

21(20'). Pale antehumeral stripe constricted by black at three-fourths its length; metapleural suture black along entire length; outer surface of all femora wholly black (California) .... *Zoniagrion*

21'. Pale antehumeral stripe usually not constricted posteriorly; metapleural suture pale anteriorly; outer surface of all femora not wholly black .... *Enallagma* (in part)

22(6'). Costal margin of pterostigma of fore wing (and usually hind wing) shorter than proximal margin (fig. 11.70); female with ventroapical spine on segment 8; thoracic middorsal black marking reaching humeral suture, thus pale antehumeral stripe appearing only as anterior and posterior spots (young specimens with thorax entirely pale orange to yellow) (Arizona) .... *Hesperagrion* (in part)

22'.   Costal margin of pterostigma much longer than length of proximal margin (as in
         fig. 11.68); female without a ventroapical spine on segment 8; thoracic markings
         not as above 23

23(22').   M₂ of hind wing arising near 3rd postnodal crossvein; humeral stripe black and of
         even width along entire length (southern Florida) .... *Neoerythromma* (in part)

23'.   M₂ of hind wing nearly always arising near 4th postnodal crossvein; humeral stripe
         pale and of various widths (extremely narrow in some *Telebasis*) 24

24(23').   M₁ₐ extending for the length of 7–8 cells; metepimeron largely bright yellow; male
         predominantly blue and green .... *Chromagrion*

24'.   M₁ₐ extending for the length of 4–5 cells; metepimeron pale, but not bright yellow;
         males of species in United States predominantly red or reddish brown .... *Telebasis* (in part)

Protoneuridae

Nymphs

1.   Before wing pads become crumpled just prior to emergence, they are transparent,
         so that underlying abdominal segments are visible; pterostigma of developing
         wings conspicuous; ventral margin of apical portion of lateral caudal gills evenly
         and slightly convex (Texas) .... *Protoneura*

1'.   Wing pads opaque, so that underlying abdominal segments are not visible;
         pterostigma of developing wings not conspicuous; dorsal or ventral margin (or
         both) of apical portion of lateral caudal gills undulate and not smoothly convex
         (Texas) .... *Neoneura*

Adults

1.   Anal vein (A) present in both pairs of wings for length of one cell (fig. 11.72); M₂
         arising near 4th postnodal crossvein in fore wing, near 3rd in hind wing (fig.
         11.72); M₁ₐ of fore wing usually arising only 1–2 cells beyond origin of M₂ (fig.
         11.72) (Texas) .... *Neoneura*

1'.   Anal vein (A) absent in both pairs of wings (fig. 11.73); M₂ arising near 5th
         postnodal crossvein or beyond in fore wing, near 4th or beyond in hind wing (fig.
         11.73); M₁ₐ of fore wing arising 3–4 cells beyond origin of M₂ (fig. 11.73)
         (Texas) .... *Protoneura*

KEYS TO THE GENERA OF ANISOPTERA

Aeshnidae

Nymphs

1.   Palpal lobes of labium with stout raptorial setae on dorsal surface (fig. 11.74) 2
1'.   Palpal lobes of labium without stout raptorial setae on dorsal surface (fig. 11.75) 3
2(1).   Palpal setae about 9, nearly uniform in length, palpal lobe without end hook (fig.
         11.76); total length of last instar nymph less than 40 mm .... *Triacanthagyna*
2'.   Palpal setae about 12–14, less robust, very unequal in length, diminishing to very
         small ones at proximal end of row, papal lobe with pronounced end hook (fig.
         11.74); total length of last instar nymph more than 40 mm .... *Gynacantha*
3(1').   Posterolateral margins of head decidedly angulate (fig. 11.79) 4
3'.   Posterolateral margins of head rounded (sometimes bluntly angular in *Aeshna*)
         (fig. 11.80) 8
4(3).   Head flattened and elongate, rectangular in dorsal view; low, broadly rounded eyes
         directed laterally (fig. 11.79); ligula usually with a long marginal spine each
         side of the median cleft and adjacent to it (fig. 11.75) .... *Coryphaeschna*
4'.   Head roughly trapezoidal, strongly narrowed posteriorly; ligula without a long
         marginal spine each side of median cleft, at most a small tubercle present 5

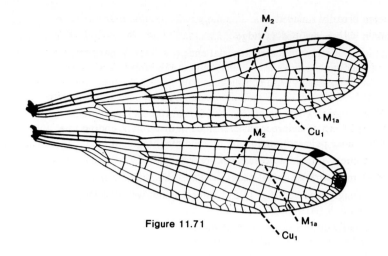

Figure 11.71

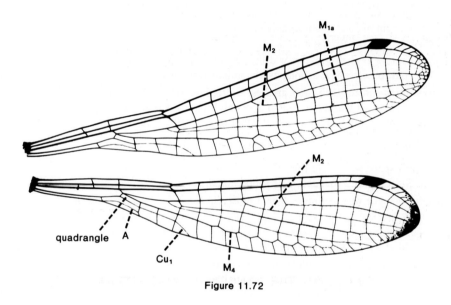

Figure 11.72

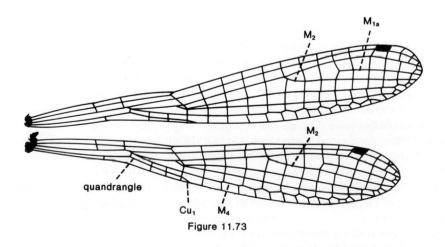

Figure 11.73

Figure 11.72. Wings of *Neoneura aaroni* Calvert (Proto-neuridae) (Westfall manuscript).

Figure 11.71. Wings of *Apanisagrion lais* (Selys) (Coen-agrionidae) (Westfall manuscript).

Figure 11.73. Wings of *Protoneura capillaris* (Rambur) (Protoneuridae) (Westfall manuscript).

5(4′).   Dorsum of abdomen broadly rounded 6

5′.   Dorsum of abdomen with a low median ridge 7

6(5).   Palpal lobes of labium squarely truncated at distal ends (fig. 11.77); paraprocts
about as long as abdominal segments 9 + 10; epiproct tapering to apex that
may be pointed or cleft; usually with conspicuous pale spot on dorsum of
abdominal segment 8 .... *Boyeria*

6′.   Palpal lobes of labium tapering to a point (fig. 11.78); paraprocts longer than
abdominal segments 9 + 10; epiproct parallel-sided in distal half, ending in a
cleft tip; no conspicuous pale spot on dorsum of abdominal segment 8 .... *Basiaeschna*

7(5′).   Median ridge of abdomen with blunt dorsal hooks on segments 7–9 .... *Nasiaeschna*

7′.   Median ridge of abdomen without dorsal hooks .... *Epiaeschna*

8(3′).   Tips of paraprocts strongly incurved (fig. 11.81); lateral spines well developed on
abdominal segments 5–9 (Arizona) .... *Oplonaeschna*

8′.   Tips of paraprocts usually quite straight; lateral spines usually on abdominal
segments 6 or 7–9 (rarely on 5–9); widely distributed 9

9(8′).   Antennae longer than distance from their base to rear of head (fig. 11.80); distal
margin of ligula deeply bilobed, with a V-shaped notch .... *Gomphaeschna*

9′.   Antennae about half as long as distance from their base to rear of head (as in fig.
11.79); distal margin of ligula obtusangulate, at most very slightly bilobed, with
the notch closed 10

10(9′).   Compound eyes as long as their greatest width; lateral spines only on abdominal
segments 7–9; paraprocts about as long as abdominal segments 8 + 9 .... *Anax*

10′.   Compound eyes much shorter than their greatest width; lateral spines usually on
abdominal segments 6–9 (rarely on 5–9 or 7–9 only); paraprocts shorter than
abdominal segments 8 and 9 (usually about equal to 9 + 10) .... *Aeshna*

Adults

1.   Midbasal (median) space with more than one crossvein; sides of thorax in species
in the United States with 2 rounded, pale spots .... *Boyeria*

1′.   Midbasal (median) space with not more than 1 crossvein (as in fig. 11.82); sides of
thorax variously marked but never with only 2 rounded pale spots 2

2(1′).   Sectors of arculus arising from its upper end (fig. 11.83); thorax uniform green;
anal border of hind wing rounded in both sexes; auricles absent .... *Anax*

2′.   Sectors of arculus arising near its middle (fig. 11.82); thorax usually brown,
marked with blue, green, or yellow; male with anal border of hind wing angulate
and with auricles on abdominal segment 2 (as in fig. 11.5) 3

3(2′).   Vein Rs forked (fig. 11.82) 4

3′.   Vein Rs not forked (fig. 11.83) 9

4(3).   Stalk of Rs straight and fork symmetrical (fig. 11.82) 5

4′.   Stalk of Rs bending forward to an asymmetrical fork (fig. 11.84) 6

5(4).   Radial planate subtending one row of cells (fig. 11.82); viewed from the side, frons
prominent and face flat; superior appendages of male about as long as
abdominal segment 9, anal appendages of female much shorter; anterior lamina
of male without a spine .... *Nasiaeschna*

5′.   Radial planate subtending more than one row of cells (as in fig. 11.83); viewed
from the side, frons not noticeably prominent and face slightly convex; superior
appendages of male about as long as abdominal segments 9 + 10, anal
appendages of female somewhat longer; anterior lamina of male bearing a
curved spine on each side .... *Epiaeschna*

6(4′).   Vein Rs forked under the pterostigma (fig. 11.84); two rows of cells in fork of Rs
(fig. 11.84) .... *Coryphaeschna*

6′.   Vein Rs forked proximal to the pterostigma (as in fig. 11.82); usually more than
two rows of cells in fork of Rs (as in fig. 11.82) 7

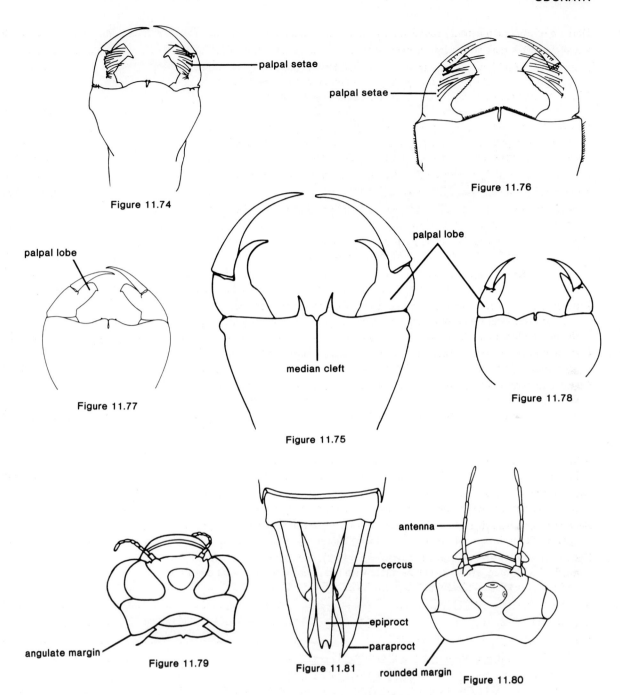

Figure 11.74

Figure 11.76

palpal setae

palpal setae

palpal lobe

palpal lobe

median cleft

Figure 11.77

Figure 11.78

Figure 11.75

antenna

cercus

epiproct

paraproct

angulate margin

Figure 11.79

Figure 11.81

rounded margin

Figure 11.80

Figure 11.74. Prementum of labium of nymph, dorsal view, *Gynacantha nervosa* Rambur (Aeshnidae) (drawn by M. S. Westfall).

Figure 11.75. Prementum of labium of nymph, dorsal view, *Coryphaeschna ingens* (Rambur) (Aeshnidae) (drawn by M. S. Westfall).

Figure 11.76. Prementum of labium of nymph, dorsal view, *Triacanthagyna trifida* (Rambur) (Aeshnidae) (drawn by M. S. Westfall).

Figure 11.77. Prementum of labium of nymph, dorsal view, *Boyeria vinosa* (Say) (Aeshnidae) (drawn by M. S. Westfall).

Figure 11.78. Prementum of labium of nymph, dorsal view, *Basiaeschna janata* (Say) (Aeshnidae) (drawn by M. S. Westfall).

Figure 11.79. Dorsal view of head of nymph, *Coryphaeschna ingens* (Rambur) (Aeshnidae) (drawn by M. S. Westfall).

Figure 11.80. Dorsal view of head of nymph, *Gomphaeschna furcillata* (Say) (Aeshnidae) (drawn by M. S. Westfall).

Figure 11.81. Dorsal view, tip of abdomen of nymph, *Oplonaeschna armata* (Hagen) (Aeshnidae) (drawn by M. S. Westfall).

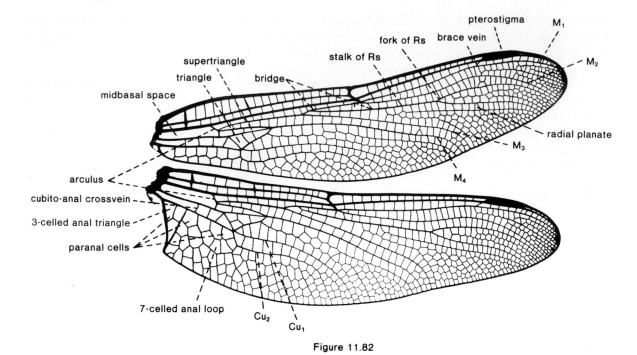

Figure 11.82

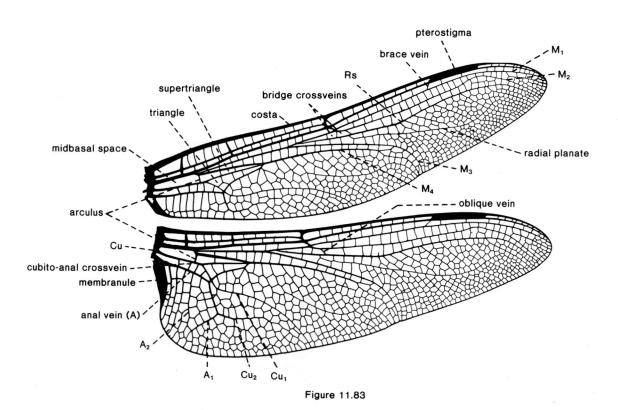

Figure 11.83

Figure 11.82. Wings of *Nasiaeschna pentacantha* (Rambur) (Aeshnidae) (Needham and Westfall 1955).

Figure 11.83. Wings of *Anax junius* (Drury) (Aeshnidae) (Needham and Westfall 1955).

7(6').   Supertriangle as long as, or shorter than, midbasal space (as in fig. 11.82) .... *Aeshna*

7'.   Supertriangle distinctly longer than midbasal space (as in fig. 11.83) 8

8(7').   Hind wing with two rows of cells between M₁ and M₂ beginning distad to base of
pterostigma; female with 3-pronged process on venter of abdominal segment 10
(fig. 11.88) .... *Triacanthagyna*

8'.   Hind wing with 2 rows of cells between M₁ and M₂ beginning at base of
pterostigma or proximal to it; female with 2-pronged process on venter of
abdominal segment 10 (fig. 11.89) .... *Gynacantha*

9(3').   Two cubito-anal crossveins on both fore and hind wings (fig. 11.85); pterostigma
surmounting 1 crossvein, not counting brace vein (fig. 11.85); supertriangle
without crossveins (fig. 11.85); inferior appendage of male deeply forked .... *Gomphaeschna*

9'.   Three or more cubito-anal crossveins (fig. 11.86); pterostigma surmounting 2 or
more crossveins (figs. 11.86–11.87); supertriangle with crossveins (fig. 11.87);
inferior appendage of male triangular (as in fig. 11.9) 10

10(9').   Anal triangle of male 2-celled (fig. 11.87); base of wings with large brown spot;
one row of cells between Cu₁ and Cu₂ beginning at the triangle (fig. 11.87) .... *Basiaeschna*

10'.   Anal triangle of male 3-celled (fig. 11.86); base of wings hyaline; hind wing with
two rows of cells between Cu₁ and Cu₂ beginning at the triangle (fig. 11.86) .... *Oplonaeschna*

Petaluridae

Nymphs

1.   Antennae 6-jointed; abdomen more slender, lateral margins of segments not
expanded and with spines inconspicuous .... *Tanypteryx*

1'.   Antennae 7-jointed (fig. 11.91); abdomen broader, lateral margins of segments
expanded and with conspicuous spines on segments 3–9 (fig. 11.98) .... *Tachopteryx*

Adults

1.   Thorax black, spotted on front and sides with yellow; metathorax bearing a round
hairy tubercle beneath; 1st and 4th or 5th antenodals thickened; anal loop poorly
developed and very variable; subtriangle of fore wing 1- or 2-celled; anal angle
of hind wing produced and rather sharply angulated in male (West Coast states) .... *Tanypteryx*

1'.   Thorax grayish in front, with carina narrowly black; sides lighter gray, with 2
oblique black stripes; metathorax without a round, hairy tubercle beneath; 1st
and 6th or 7th antenodals thickened; subtriangle of fore wing usually 3-celled;
anal angle of hind wing very obtusely angulated in male (eastern United States) .... *Tachopteryx*

Gomphidae

Nymphs

1.   Abdominal segment 10 cylindrical, more than half as long as all the other
abdominal segments combined (fig. 11.96) .... *Aphylla*

1'.   Abdominal segment 10 shorter than abdominal segments 8 and 9 combined (fig.
11.97) 2

2(1').   Middle (mesothoracic) legs closer together at base than fore (prothoracic) legs
(fig. 11.99); 4th antennal segment in species in the United States elongate,
about one-fourth as long as the hairy 3rd antennal segment (fig. 11.94) .... *Progomphus*

2'.   Middle (mesothoracic) legs not closer together at base than (prothoracic) forelegs
(fig. 11.100); 4th antennal segment vestigial or merely a small, rounded knob
(figs. 11.92–11.93) 3

3(2').   Abdomen subcircular, very flat (fig. 11.101); head behind the eyes bearing 2 large
and 2 smaller spines (fig. 11.101); fore and middle legs without tibial burrowing
hooks .... *Hagenius*

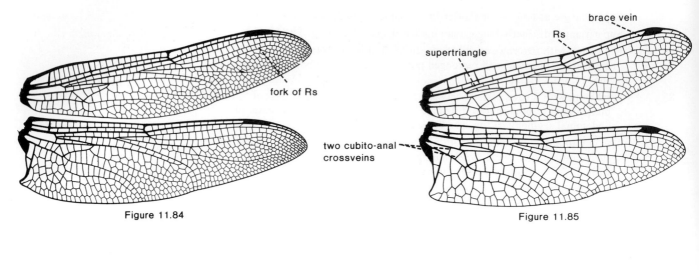

Figure 11.84

Figure 11.85

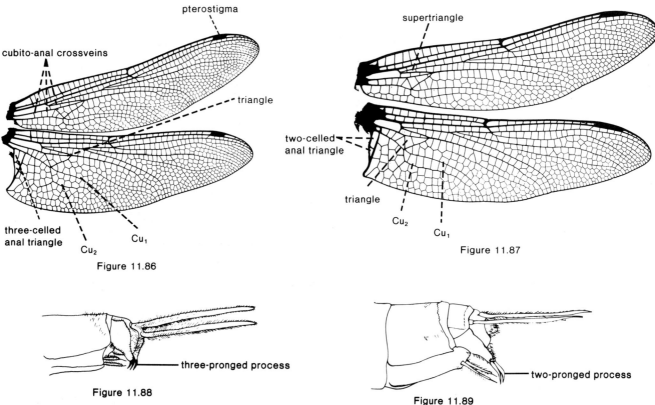

Figure 11.86

Figure 11.87

Figure 11.88

Figure 11.89

Figure 11.84. Wings of male *Coryphaeschna ingens* (Rambur) (Aeshnidae) (Needham and Westfall 1955).

Figure 11.85. Wings of male *Gomphaeschna furcillata* (Say) (Aeshnidae) (Needham and Westfall 1955).

Figure 11.86. Wings of male *Oplonaeschna armata* (Hagen) (Aeshnidae) (Needham and Westfall 1955).

Figure 11.87. Wings of male *Basiaeschna janata* (Say) (Aeshnidae) (Needham and Westfall 1955).

Figure 11.88. Lateral view, tip of abdomen of adult female, *Triacanthagyna trifida* (Rambur) (Aeshnidae) (drawn by M. S. Westfall).

Figure 11.89. Lateral view, tip of abdomen of adult female, *Gynacantha nervosa* Rambur (Aeshnidae) (drawn by M. S. Westfall).

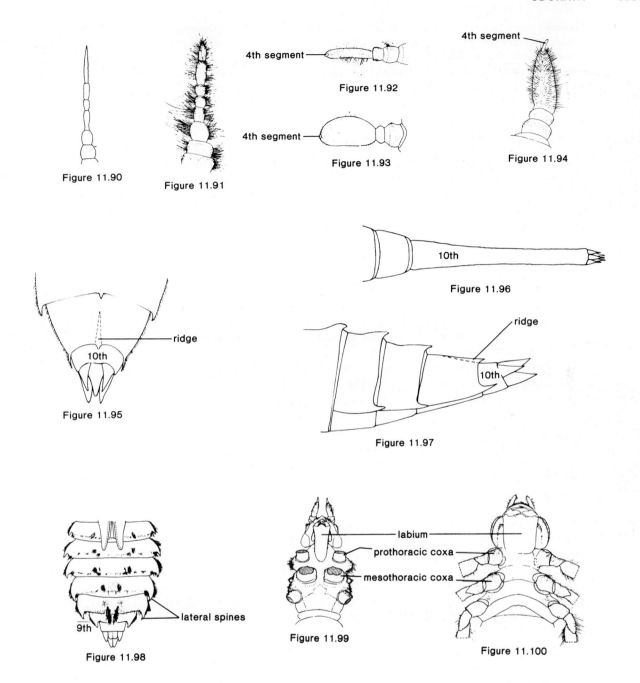

Figure 11.90

Figure 11.91

4th segment

Figure 11.92

4th segment

Figure 11.93

4th segment

Figure 11.94

10th

Figure 11.96

ridge

10th

Figure 11.95

ridge

10th

Figure 11.97

lateral spines

9th

Figure 11.98

labium

prothoracic coxa

mesothoracic coxa

Figure 11.99

Figure 11.100

Figure 11.90. Antenna of nymph, *Aeshna* sp. (Aeshnidae) (Wright and Peterson 1944).

Figure 11.91. Antenna of nymph, *Tachopteryx thoreyi* (Hagen) (Petaluridae) (Wright and Peterson 1944).

Figure 11.92. Antenna of nymph, *Dromogomphus* (Gomphidae) (Wright and Peterson 1944).

Figure 11.93. Antenna of nymph, *Octogomphus specularis* (Hagen) (Gomphidae) (Wright and Peterson 1944).

Figure 11.94. Antenna of nymph, *Progomphus* sp. (Gomphidae) (Wright and Peterson 1944).

Figure 11.95. Dorsal view, tip of abdomen of nymph, *Dromogomphus* sp. (Gomphidae) (drawn by M. S. Westfall).

Figure 11.96. Dorsal view, tip of abdomen of nymph, *Aphylla williamsoni* (Gloyd) (Gomphidae) (Wright and Peterson 1944).

Figure 11.97. Lateral view, tip of abdomen of nymph, *Dromogomphus spinosus* Selys (Gomphidae) (drawn by M. S. Westfall).

Figure 11.98. Dorsal view, abdomen of nymph, *Tachopteryx thoreyi* (Hagen) (Petaluridae) (Wright and Peterson 1944).

Figure 11.99. Ventral view, head and thorax of nymph, *Progomphus obscurus* (Rambur) (Gomphidae) (Wright and Peterson 1944).

Figure 11.100 Ventral view, head and thorax of nymph, *Gomphus* sp. (Gomphidae) (Wright and Peterson 1944).

3'.   Abdomen much longer than broad, not so flat (fig. 11.102); head behind the eyes without spines (fig. 11.102); fore- and middle legs usually with at least vestigial burrowing hooks on tibiae. 4

4(3'). Palpal lobes of labium rounded, without an end hook, and usually bearing only microscopic teeth on the inner margin (fig. 11.104); wing cases may be divergent 5

4'.   Palpal lobes of labium usually with recurved end hook at apex (fig. 11.105), but, if without, then either a sharp dorsal ridge on abdominal segment 9 that ends in a long, sharp spine (figs. 11.95, 11.97), or the inner margins of the palpal lobes bear coarse teeth that may be irregular and obliquely truncated (fig. 11.106); wing cases not divergent (fig. 11.21) 9

5(4'). Wing cases divergent (fig. 11.102); some abdominal segments with middorsal hooks or knobs (fig. 11.102) 6

5'.   Wing cases parallel along midline (fig. 11.21); no abdominal segment with a middorsal hook or knob 7

6(5).   Cerci in full-grown nymphs usually about three-fourths or less as long as paraprocts; dorsal hooks always well developed on abdominal segments 2 or 3–9 (fig. 11.102); lateral spines usually absent on segment 6, but, if present, then species is far Western .... *Ophiogomphus*

6'.   Cerci in full-grown nymphs about as long as paraprocts; dorsal hooks usually wanting or rudimentary on some posterior segments, but, if well developed, then dorsal surface of abdomen very granular .... *Erpetogomphus*

7(5'). Short lateral spines on abdominal segments 7–9; 3rd segment of antennae about half as wide as long, widest in distal half (fig. 11.93); far Western .... *Octogomphus*

7'.   Very short lateral spines only on abdominal segments 8 and 9; third segment of antennae about three-fourths as wide as long, widest in proximal half (fig. 11.103); Eastern 8

8(7'). Wide 3rd antennal segment 3 inequilateral, straight on its inner margin (fig. 11.103); denticles on front border of prementum usually 3; sides of prementum somewhat convergent toward base; lateral spines of abdominal segment 9 wide, short, and stout .... *Stylogomphus*

8'.   Wide 3rd antennal segment 3 nearly oval, its inner margin convex; denticles on front border of prementum usually 4; sides of prementum parallel toward base; lateral spines of abdominal segment 9 more slender, longer, and more clawlike .... *Lanthus*

9(4'). Abdominal segment 9 with an acute middorsal ridge usually bearing a long, sharp dorsal hook at its apex (seen best in lateral view; figs. 11.95, 11.97); segment 9 never as long as wide at its base 10

9'.   Abdominal segment 9 quite rounded dorsally and without such a long, sharp dorsal hook at its apex (figs. 11.108–11.109); segment 9 may be longer than wide at its base 11

10(9). Prementum moderately produced in a low, rounded spinulose border; abdominal segment 10 a little longer than segment 9; dorsal hook of abdominal segment 9 elevated at apex, seen in lateral view (Western) .... *Phyllogomphoides*

10'.   Prementum with straight front border; abdominal segment 10 shorter than segment 9 (fig. 11.95); dorsal hook of abdominal segment 9 straight to apex and not elevated when seen in lateral view (fig. 11.97) .... *Dromogomphus*

11(9'). Tibial burrowing hooks absent or vestigial; abdomen elongate, regularly tapering all the way rearward; lateral spines of abdominal segment 9 not noticeably flattened dorsoventrally and with only hairs on the outer margin; each palpal lobe of labium ending in a strong, recurved end hook, followed by 1–4 usually shallow teeth (fig. 11.105) .... *Stylurus*

11'.   Tibial burrowing hooks well developed; abdomen usually not so elongate, and not tapering regularly all the way rearward; lateral spines of abdominal segment 9 may be noticeably flattened dorsoventrally and with the outer margins spinulose-serrate; palpal lobe of labium usually ending in less of a recurved end hook, followed by more than 4 (sometimes deeply cut) teeth (figs. 11.106–11.107) 12

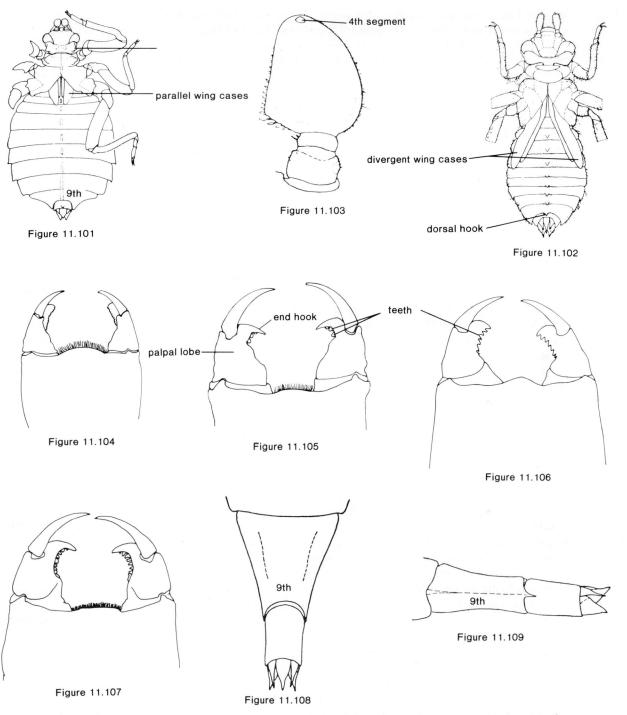

Figure 11.101

Figure 11.103

4th segment

parallel wing cases

9th

divergent wing cases

dorsal hook

Figure 11.102

Figure 11.104

Figure 11.105

end hook

teeth

palpal lobe

Figure 11.106

Figure 11.107

9th

Figure 11.108

9th

Figure 11.109

Figure 11.105. Prementum of labium of nymph, dorsal view, *Stylurus laurae* Williamson (Gomphidae) (drawn by M. S. Westfall).

Figure 11.106. Prementum of labium of nymph, dorsal view, *Arigomphus pallidus* (Rambur) (Gomphidae) (drawn by M. S. Westfall).

Figure 11.107. Prementum of labium of nymph, dorsal view, *Gomphus lividus* Selys (Gomphidae) (drawn by M. S. Westfall).

Figure 11.108. Dorsal view, tip of abdomen of nymph, *Gomphus* sp. (Gomphidae) (Wright and Peterson 1944).

Figure 11.109. Lateral view, tip of abdomen of nymph, *Gomphus* sp. (Gomphidae) (Wright and Peterson 1944).

Figure 11.101. Dorsal view, nymph of *Hagenius brevistylus* Selys (Gomphidae) (Wright and Peterson 1944).

Figure 11.102. Dorsal view, nymph of *Ophiogomphus* (Gomphidae) (Wright and Peterson 1944).

Figure 11.103. Antenna of *Stylogomphus albistylus* (Hagen) (Gomphidae) (Wright and Peterson 1944).

Figure 11.104. Prementum of labium of nymph, dorsal view, *Erpetogomphus designatus* Hagen (Gomphidae) (drawn by M. S. Westfall).

12(11′). Abdomen acuminate, rapidly narrowing on segment 8; segment 10 is longer than wide; lateral spines of abdominal segment 9 laterally flattened and closely appressed to the sides of 10; palpal lobes of labium without a well-developed end hook, but with inner margins bearing 5–8 coarse teeth that are irregular and obliquely truncate (fig. 11.106) .... *Arigomphus*

12′. Abdomen not or scarcely acuminate; segment 10 is usually wider than long; lateral spines of abdominal segment 9 usually neither laterally flattened nor closely appressed to the sides of 10; palpal lobes of labium usually with a well-developed end hook and the inner margins with a series of 4–10 rather regular teeth (fig. 11.107) .... *Gomphus*
(including subgenera *Gomphus, Gomphurus,* and *Hylogomphus*)

Adults

1. Basal subcostal crossvein present (fig. 11.112); at least 1 crossvein in fore wing subtriangle (fig. 11.112) 2

1′. Basal subcostal crossvein absent (fig. 11.113); no crossvein in fore wing subtriangle (fig. 11.113) 4

2(1). Supertriangles with 1 or more crossveins (fig. 11.112) 3

2′. Supertriangles without crossveins .... *Progomphus*

3(2). Hind wing subtriangle of 2 or more cells (fig. 11.112); anal loop of 3–5 cells formed by convergence of veins A_1 and A_2 (fig. 11.112) .... *Phyllogomphoides*

3′. Hind wing subtriangle usually 1-celled; veins A_1 and A_2 run directly to hind wing margin and form no anal loop .... *Aphylla*

4(1′). Triangles with a crossvein (fig. 11.113); each triangle with a supplementary longitudinal vein (trigonal planate) arising from its distal side (fig. 11.113); hind femora reaching a little beyond the base of abdominal segment 3; very large insects, generally more than 70 mm in length .... *Hagenius*

4′. Triangles without crossveins, and without a supplementary longitudinal vein arising from distal side; hind femora usually not reaching beyond middle of segment 2; smaller insects, rarely 69 mm in length 5

5(4′). Hind wing with semicircular anal loop typically of 3 cells; inferior appendage of male with the 2 branches separated either by a mere slit with the apices contiguous or by a U-shaped or V-shaped notch (figs. 11.114–11.115); vulvar lamina nearly as long as sternum of segment 9 .... *Ophiogomphus*

5′. Hind wing with anal loop absent or of 1–2 weakly bordered cells; inferior appendage of male usually with more or less widely separated divergent branches (except in *Erpetogomphus*); vulvar lamina usually less than half as long as sternum of segment 9 6

6(5′). Hind femur long, reaching the base of abdominal segment 3 and bearing 4–7 long ventral spines in addition to the usual short ones (fig. 11.118) .... *Dromogomphus*

6′. Hind femur not extending beyond the middle of abdominal segment 2 and usually bearing only the usual numerous, short, ventral spines 7

7(6′). Pterostigma of fore wing short and thick, at its widest about twice as long as wide; hind wing with 5 paranal cells (see fig. 11.82); branches of inferior caudal appendage of male long, parallel full length, and strongly hooked upward (figs. 11.116–11.117) .... *Erpetogomphus*

7′. Pterostigma of fore wing usually more elongate, about 3 times as long as wide; hind wing with 4–5 paranal cells; branches of inferior caudal appendage of male shorter and divergent 8

8(7′). Dorsum of thorax pale between broad dorsolateral dark stripes; pterostigma of fore wing scarcely 3 times as long as wide and more than twice as wide as the space immediately behind its middle; inferior appendage of male 4-branched; far Western .... *Octogomphus*

8′. Dorsum of thorax usually mesally dark between pale dorsolateral stripes; pterostigma more than 3 times as long as wide and usually less than twice as wide as the space behind its middle; inferior appendage of male 2-branched 9

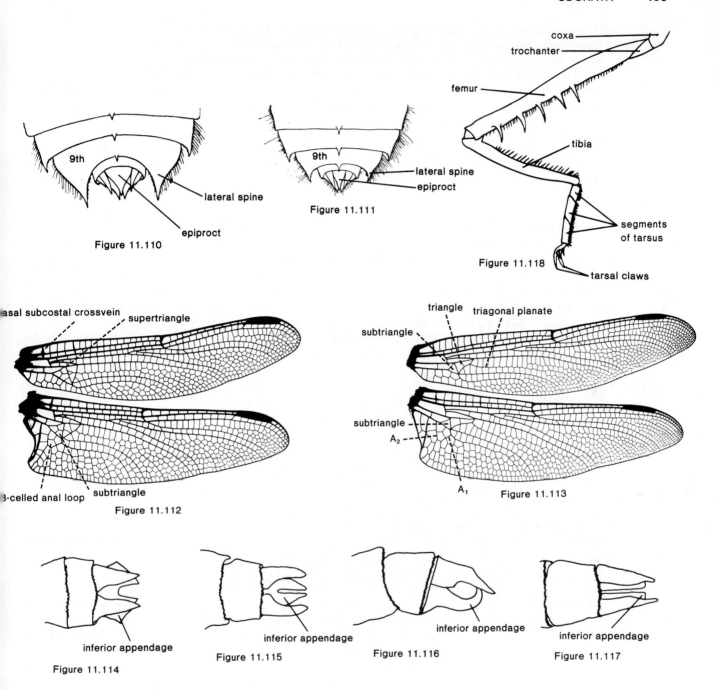

Figure 11.110

Figure 11.111

Figure 11.118

Figure 11.112

Figure 11.113

Figure 11.114

Figure 11.115

Figure 11.116

Figure 11.117

Figure 11.110. Dorsal view, tip of abdomen of nymph, *Didymops* sp. (Macromiidae) (Wright and Peterson 1944).

Figure 11.111. Dorsal view, tip of abdomen of nymph, *Macromia* sp. (Macromiidae) (Wright and Peterson 1944).

Figure 11.112. Wings of *Phyllogomphoides stigmatus* (Say) (Gomphidae) (Needham and Westfall 1955).

Figure 11.113. Wings of *Hagenius brevistylus* Selys (Gomphidae) (Needham and Westfall 1955).

Figure 11.114. Dorsal view, tip of abdomen, adult male, *Ophiogomphus carolus* Needham (Gomphidae) (Needham and Westfall 1955).

Figure 11.115. Dorsal view, tip of abdomen, adult male, *Ophiogomphus colubrinus* Selys (Gomphidae) (Needham and Westfall 1955).

Figure 11.116. Lateral view, tip of abdomen, adult male, *Erpetogomphus designatus* Hagen (Gomphidae) (Needham and Westfall 1955).

Figure 11.117. Dorsal view, tip of abdomen, adult male, *Erpetogomphus designatus* Hagen (Gomphidae) (Needham and Westfall 1955).

Figure 11.118. Hind (metathoracic) leg of adult, *Dromogomphus spinosus* Selys (Gomphidae) (drawn by M. S. Westfall).

9(8').   Pterostigma less than 4 times as long as wide, more than twice as wide as the space behind its middle; inferior appendage of the males with its lateral edges subparallel, its 2 branches shorter than the median length of the appendage; size small, less than 40 mm 10

9'.   Pterostigma rarely less than 4 times as long as wide, less than twice as wide as the space behind its middle; inferior appendage of male with lateral edges widely divergent, its 2 branches longer than the median length of the appendage; size larger, usually more than 40 mm 11

10(9).   Outer side of fore wing triangle slightly angulated near middle; anteclypeus pale; superior appendages of the male pale yellow or white, laterally angulate with apices very slender and curved upward .... *Stylogomphus*

10'.   Outer side of fore wing triangle straight or nearly so; anteclypeus blackish; superior appendages of male black, sides not angulate, and apices straight and not very slender .... *Lanthus*

11(9').   Usually pale species with darker stripe each side of pale middorsal carina of thorax faint or absent; thoracic side stripes much reduced; male with end hook of posterior hamules long and falciform (fig. 11.119); the abdomen usually constricted at segment 9 and the apices of superior appendages usually convergent and very slender .... *Arigomphus*

11'.   Usually darker species, with conspicuous dark stripes on the thorax; male posterior hamule often with a sharp shoulder, but the end hook is not so long or falciform (fig. 11.120); the abdomen usually not constricted at segment 9, and apices of superior appendages variable, but usually not convergent or very slender 12

12(11').   Top of frons 4 times as wide as long; typically long, slender species in which the male superior appendages are simple, horizontal, without angular processes and only rarely with lateral margins angular; branches of male inferior appendage diverging at about same angle as superiors, so they are usually not seen from above; anterior hamules vestigial, slender, unarmed, and difficult to see, whereas posterior hamules are usually upright or leaning forward (fig. 11.120); anterior lamina of male flat, not projecting above rim of genital pocket; vulvar lamina of female very short, sometimes vestigial .... *Stylurus*

12'.   Top of frons about 3 times as wide as long; form varied, with male superior appendages usually with sharply angular processes; branches of male inferior appendage often diverge more strongly than superiors so that their apices are conspicuous when seen from above; anterior hamules not vestigial and always bearing at least 1 hook or spine; posterior hamules upright or leaning backward; anterior lamina of male variable, but usually projecting above rim of genital pocket; vulvar lamina of female usually not vestigial, often half as long as segment 9 (fig. 11.44) .... *Gomphus*
           (including the subgenera *Gomphus, Gomphurus,* and *Hylogomphus*)

Macromiidae

Nymphs

1.   Lateral spines of abdominal segment 9 reaching posteriorly to tip of epiproct or beyond (fig. 11.110); width of head across the eyes about equal to the greatest width behind the eyes; abdominal segment 10 without a middorsal hook .... *Didymops*

1'.   Lateral spines of abdominal segment 9 not reaching posteriorly to tip of epiproct (fig. 11.111); width of head greater across the eyes than behind the eyes; abdominal segment 10 with a small middorsal hook .... *Macromia*

Adults

1.   Nodus of fore wing about midway between base and apex of wing; vertex simple, rounded, smaller than occiput, which has a bulbous swelling behind; coloration light brown and yellow, nonmetallic .... *Didymops*

1'.   Nodus of fore wing distinctly beyond middle of wing; vertex bilobed, larger than occiput, which lacks a bulbous swelling behind; coloration dark, with a metallic lustre and bright yellow markings .... *Macromia*

Corduliidae

Nymphs

1.	Middorsal hooks present and well developed on some of the abdominal segments	2
1'.	Middorsal hooks absent or reduced to low knobs	7
2(1).	Without lateral spines on abdominal segment 8, but present on segment 9 (as far as known)	*Williamsonia*
2'.	With lateral spines on abdominal segments 8 and 9	3
3(2').	Crenations on distal margin of palpal lobes nearly semicircular or even more deeply cut; lateral spines of abdominal segments 8 and 9 about equal in length, those on 8 divergent (figs. 11.121–11.122)	*Neurocordulia*
3'.	Crenations on distal margin of palpal lobes much shallower than a semicircle; lateral spines on abdominal segment 9 about equal in length to those on segment 8 or much longer	4
4(3').	Lateral spines on abdominal segment 9 more than 3 times as long as those on segment 8, being at least as long as the middorsal length of segment 9 or longer	5
4'.	Lateral spines on abdominal segments 8 and 9 short and about equal in length, those of segment 9 never as much as twice as long as those of segment 8	6
5(4).	Distal half of dorsal surface of prementum heavily setose (fig. 11.123); palpal setae usually 4, rarely 5	*Epicordulia*
5'.	Distal half of dorsal surface of prementum with few or generally no setae; palpal setae usually 6–7	*Tetragoneuria*
6(4').	Middorsal hooks on abdominal segments 6–9 only, minute on segment 6, on the other segments as long as the segment or longer	*Helocordulia*
6'.	Middorsal hooks on abdominal segments 3 or 4–9 spinelike and usually curved	*Somatochlora* (in part)
7(1').	Sides of thorax uniformly colored	*Somatochlora* (in part)
7'.	Sides of thorax with a broad, dark, longitudinal stripe	8
8(7').	Middorsal hooks absent or vestigial, but, if present, then highest on segment 8; lateral spines of abdominal segment 9 about one-fifth the length of lateral margin of that segment	*Cordulia*
8'.	Middorsal hooks distinct, stubby, and the highest on segment 5; lateral spines of abdominal segment 9 about two-fifths the length of lateral margin of that segment	*Dorocordulia*

Adults

1.	Veins M_4 and Cu_1 in fore wing diverging towards wing margin	2
1'.	Veins M_4 and Cu_1 converging towards wing margin, often being parallel for most of the distance	3
2(1).	Small dragonflies (abdomen and hind wing each less than 25 mm); top of head metallic green; triangles and subtriangles of fore wing and usually of hind wing, of a single cell; hind wing without a basal spot	*Williamsonia*
2'.	Medium-sized dragonflies (abdomen and hind wing each more than 30 mm) without metallic lustre; fore wing triangle divided into 2–3 cells; hind wing may have a basal amber spot	*Neurocordulia*
3(1').	Wings usually with large brown spots at nodus and wing tip, especially in Southern specimens, and always with large basal spot in hind wing; length of hind wing 38 mm or more	*Epicordulia*
3'.	Wings never with spots at nodus or wing tip, and usually with no more than a trace of color at base of hind wing; length of hind wing much less than 38 mm	4
4(3').	Body without or almost without metallic lustre; tibiae of males with well developed keels on all 3 pairs of legs; vulvar lamina elongate, deeply bilobed and generally flexible, usually longer than sternum of abdominal segment 9	5

4'. Body usually with a metallic green or blue lustre; mesotibiae of males without a keel or with only a vestige at the distal end; vulvar lamina bilobed or entire, sometimes shorter than sternum of abdominal segment 9, and, when as long, more or less rigid, forming an ovipositor (fig. 11.45) 6

5(4). Abdomen of male widest at segments 6–7; superior appendages of male separated at base by a space often no wider than one of the appendages; vulvar lamina bilobed at the base, the lobes longer than sternum of segment 9; wings with one crossvein behind the stigma .... *Tetragoneuria*

5'. Abdomen of male widest at segment 8; superior appendages of male separated at base by a space at least twice the width of one of the appendages; vulvar lamina bilobed but not to base, the lobes usually shorter than sternum of segment 9; wings usually with 2 crossveins behind the stigma .... *Helocordulia*

6(4'). Hind wing with 2nd cubito-anal crossvein forming a subtriangle; mesotibiae of males without a keel; inferior appendage of male normally triangular, rarely divided once .... *Somatochlora*

6'. Hind wing with only 1 cubito-anal crossvein; mesotibiae of males with a vestigial keel at the distal end; inferior appendage of male triangular or strongly bifurcate 7

7(6'). Fore wing triangle without a crossvein; each superior appendage of male tapering to an upturned point; inferior appendage of male triangular .... *Dorocordulia*

7'. Fore wing triangle with a crossvein; each superior appendage of male cylindrical without apex upturned or pointed; inferior appendage of male strongly bifurcate, each ramus being bifid .... *Cordulia*

Libellulidae

Nymphs

1. Eyes capping frontolateral part of head and sometimes high, extending from one-fourth to less than one-half the length of head, so that a line joining their tips will not touch another part of head (figs. 11.124–11.125); abdomen usually long and tapering 2

1'. Eyes lower, more broadly rounded and more lateral in position, usually occupying more than one-half the length of head; abdomen usually ending more bluntly 6

2(1). Anterior margin of prementum quite smooth (fig. 11.31) 3

2'. Anterior margin of prementum noticeably crenate (figs. 11.32, 11.125) 4

3(2). Lateral spines of abdominal segments 8 and 9 absent or very small, not more than one-tenth of their lateral margins; abdomen shorter, less tapering (western United States) .... *Belonia*

3'. Lateral spines of abdominal segments 8 and 9 much more than one-tenth of their lateral margins; abdomen longer, more tapering .... *Libellula*

4(2'). Middorsal hooks absent on middle abdominal segments; eyes very high so that a line joining their tips will not touch another part of the head (fig. 11.125) .... *Orthemis*

4'. Middorsal hooks present on middle abdominal segments; eyes variable 5

5(4'). Middorsal hook absent on abdominal segment 8; segments 7–9 each bearing a dark, shining, middorsal ridge; dorsal premental setae 8–11 each side of median line .... *Plathemis*

5'. Middorsal hook present on abdominal segment 8, segments 7–9 not bearing a dark, shining, middorsal ridge; dorsal premental setae 0–3 each side of median line, short and inconspicuous when present .... *Ladona*

6(1'). Paraprocts strongly decurved at tip (fig. 11.126) 7

6'. Paraprocts straight or nearly so 8

7(6). Lateral spines absent on abdomen; palpal setae 7–9 .... *Erythemis*

7'. Minute lateral spine present on segment 9; palpal setae 11–12 .... *Lepthemis vesiculosa*

8(6'). Middorsal hooks, spines, or knobs present on some of abdominal segments 5–9, the low knobs each bearing a conspicuous tuft of hair 9

8'. Middorsal hooks, spines, or knobs absent on abdominal segments 5–9 22

9(8). Middorsal hook, spine, or knob present on adominal segment 9 10

9'. Middorsal hook, spine, or knob absent on abdominal segment 9 16

10(9). Epiproct less than half as long as paraprocts; lateral spine of abdominal segment 9 at least half as long as the lateral margin of which it is a part; middorsal hook of abdominal segment 8 twice as long as that segment .... ***Tauriphila***

10'. Epiproct about as long as paraprocts; lateral spine of abdominal segment 9 much less than half as long as the lateral margin of which it is a part; middorsal hook of abdominal segment 8 less than twice as long as that segment 11

11(10'). Middorsal hooks of abdomen cultriform, the series in lateral view like teeth of a circular saw (fig. 11.36); crenations of distal margin of each palpal lobe deep; palpal setae 5–6 .... ***Perithemis***

11'. Middorsal hooks of abdomen more upright, spinelike, or low and blunt 12

12(11'). Epiproct about twice as long as its basal width, and longer than middorsal length of abdominal segments 8 + 9 (fig. 11.127); small middorsal hook present on abdominal segment 10 13

12'. Epiproct as long as, or only slightly longer than, its basal width, and much shorter than middorsal length of abdominal segments 8 + 9; no middorsal hook on abdominal segment 10 14

13(12). Cerci about one-third to one-half as long as epiproct in final instar; lateral spine of abdominal segment 9 about one-third as long as lateral margin of which it is a part; palpal setae 6–10 .... ***Brachymesia***

13'. Cerci about one-fifth as long as epiproct in final instar; lateral spine of abdominal segment 9 about one-half as long as lateral margin of which it is a part; palpal setae 6 .... ***Idiataphe***

14(12'). Crenations of distal margin of each palpal lobe obsolete (as in fig. 11.27); surface of nymph smooth; palpal setae 7–10 .... ***Dythemis***

14'. Crenations of distal margin of each palpal lobe evident (fig. 11.31); surface of nymph smooth or granulose; palpal setae 6–9 15

15(14'). Palpal setae 6; dorsal premental setae in North American species almost in even, smoothly curved line (fig. 11.128); surface of nymph smooth .... ***Macrothemis***

15'. Palpal setae 7–9; 2 outermost premental setae set apart from the others and almost at a right angle to them (fig. 11.129); surface of nymph granulose or rough .... ***Brechmorhoga***

16(9'). Middorsal hook on abdominal segment 8 17

16'. No middorsal hook on abdominal segment 8 18

17(16). Palpal setae 7; dorsal premental setae 9–11 each side of median line (figs. 11.26–11.27); epiproct about two-thirds as long as paraprocts .... ***Miathyria***

17'. Palpal setae 10; dorsal premental setae 16–21 each side of median line; epiproct equal in length to paraprocts .... ***Macrodiplax***

18(16'). Lateral spines of abdominal segment 9 long and straight, longer than its middorsal length and extending about to tips of paraprocts .... ***Celithemis***

18'. Lateral spines of abdominal segment 9 much shorter than its middorsal length and not extending to tips of paraprocts 19

19(18'). Crenations of distal margin of each palpal lobe very conspicuous; median lobe of prementum markedly angulate (fig. 11.31) .... ***Paltothemis***

19'. Crenations of distal margin of each palpal lobe much smaller; median lobe of prementum more rounded (fig. 11.27) 20

20(19'). Abdomen with low, blunt middorsal prominences on segments 4–9, each bearing a conspicuous tuft of hairs .... ***Erythrodiplax*** (in part)

20'. Abdomen with definite middorsal hooks on some segments, with no conspicuous tufts of hairs on low prominences 21

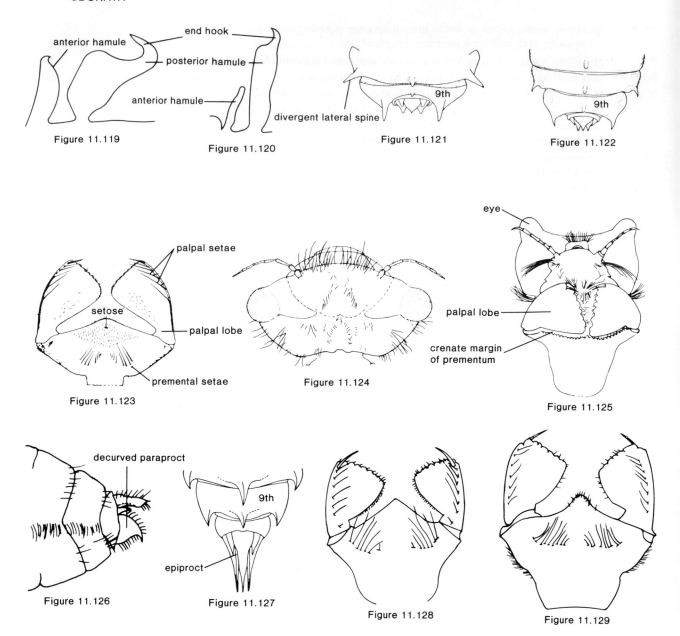

Figure 11.119

Figure 11.120

Figure 11.121

Figure 11.122

Figure 11.123

Figure 11.124

Figure 11.125

Figure 11.126

Figure 11.127

Figure 11.128

Figure 11.129

Figure 11.119. Lateral view, hamules of adult male, *Arigomphus villosipes* (Selys) (Gomphidae) (drawn from Needham and Westfall 1955).

Figure 11.120. Lateral view, hamules of adult male, *Stylurus ivae* Williamson (Gomphidae) (drawn from Needham and Westfall 1955).

Figure 11.121. Dorsal view, tip of abdomen of nymph, *Neurocordulia obsoleta* (Say) (Corduliidae) (Wright and Peterson 1944).

Figure 11.122. Dorsal view, tip of abdomen of nymph, *Neurocordulia yamaskanensis* (Provancher) (Corduliidae) (Wright and Peterson 1944).

Figure 11.123. Dorsal view, labium of nymph, *Epicordulia princeps* (Hagen) (Corduliidae) (Wright and Peterson 1944).

Figure 11.124. Dorsal view, head of nymph, *Libellula* sp. (Libellulidae) (Wright and Peterson 1944).

Figure 11.125. Anterior view, head of nymph, *Orthemis ferruginea* (Fabricius) (Libellulidae) (drawn by M. S. Westfall).

Figure 11.126. Lateral view, tip of abdomen of nymph, *Erythemis simplicicollis* (Say) (Libellulidae) (after Wright and Peterson 1944).

Figure 11.127. Dorsal view, tip of abdomen of nymph, *Brachymesia gravida* (Calvert) (Libellulidae) (Wright and Peterson 1944).

Figure 11.128. Dorsal view, labium of nymph, *Macrothemis celeno* (Selys) (Libellulidae) (Cuba) (drawn by M. S. Westfall).

Figure 11.129. Dorsal view, labium of nymph, *Brechmorhoga mendax)* (Hagen) (Libellulidae) (drawn by M. S. Westfall).

21(20′). Middorsal hook on abdominal segment 3; epiproct and paraprocts about equal in length .... *Leucorrhinia* (in part)

21′. No middorsal hook on abdominal segment 3; epiproct distinctly shorter than paraprocts .... *Sympetrum* (in part)

22(8′). Lateral spines of abdominal segment 9 not longer than its middorsal length; no dark ridge running mesad from mesoposterior part of eye; antennae not light with dark bands 23

22′. Lateral spines of abdominal segment 9 much longer than its middorsal length, or, if equal, with a dark ridge running mesad from mesoposterior part of eye, and antennae light with dark bands 29

23(22). Small species: length of final instar nymph 10 mm; palpal setae 6; end of abdomen truncated and very hairy .... *Nannothemis*

23′. Larger species: length of final instar nymph 12–20 mm; palpal setae more than 6 24

24(23′). Dorsum of abdominal segments 1–5 conspicuously pale, segments 6–10 much darker 25

24′. Dorsum of abdominal segments 1–5 not conspicuously paler than segments 6–10 26

25(24). Lateral margins of abdominal segments 8 and 9 somewhat concave, each bearing 15–16 stout spinules; legs faintly banded; maximum width of abdomen of final instar nymph about 6.3 mm (southern Florida) .... *Crocothemis servilia*

25′. Lateral margins of abdominal segments 8 and 9 straight, each bearing 5–6 stout spinules, interspersed with long, thin hairs; legs strongly banded; maximum width of abdomen of final instar nymph about 5 mm (southwestern United States) .... *Micrathyria hageni*

26(24′). Three wide longitudinal dark bands on underside of abdomen .... *Leucorrhinia* (in part)

26′. No distinct band on underside of abdomen 27

27(26′). Abdomen rather abruptly rounded to tip; abdominal segment 6 is about one-fifth as long as wide measured ventrally; epiproct as long as paraprocts; lateral spines of abdominal segments 8 and 9 very small, that of 9 no more than one-fifth of the middorsal length of that segment .... *Pseudoleon*

27′. Abdomen not so abruptly rounded to tip; abdominal segment 6 is about one-fourth as long as wide measured ventrally; epiproct no more than nine-tenths as long as paraprocts; lateral spines of abdominal segments 8 and 9 larger, that of 9 at least two-fifths the middorsal length of that segment 28

28(27′). Epiproct about nine-tenths as long as the paraprocts; cerci usually no more than one-half as long as paraprocts in full-grown nymphs; lateral spine of abdominal segment 8 at least three-tenths the length of the lateral margin of which it is a part .... *Erythrodiplax* (in part)

28′. Epiproct ususally no more than four-fifths as long as paraprocts; cerci at least three-fifths as long as paraprocts in full-grown nymphs, if only one-half, then lateral spines of abdominal segment 8 are minute or absent .... *Sympetrum* (in part)

29(22′). Epiproct no more than two-thirds length of paraprocts, nearly equal to middorsal length of segment 9 (fig. 11.130); a dark ridge running mesad from mesoposterior part of eye; antennae light with dark bands .... *Pachydiplax*

29′. Epiproct four-fifths or more the length of paraprocts, longer than middorsal length of segment 9 (figs. 11.131–11.132); no dark ridge running mesad from mesoposterior part of eye; antennae not light with dark bands 30

30(29′). Epiproct shorter than paraprocts; lateral spines on abdominal segment 8 only slightly shorter than those on segment 9; lateral spines on abdominal segment 9 extending posteriorly beyond tips of cerci (fig. 11.131); crenations of distal margin of each palpal lobe almost obsolete (fig. 11.134); movable hook of labial palpus long and slender (fig. 11.134) .... *Tramea*

30′. Epiproct as long as or longer than paraprocts; lateral spines on abdominal segment 8 only about one-third as long as those on segment 9; lateral spines on abdominal segment 9 not extending posteriorly as far as tips of cerci (fig. 11.132); crenations of distal margin of each palpal lobe large (fig. 11.133); movable hook of labial palpus short and robust (fig. 11.133) .... *Pantala*

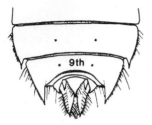

Figure 11.130

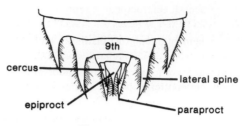

Figure 11.131

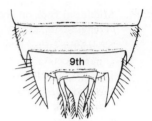

Figure 11.132

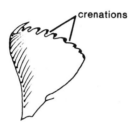

Figure 11.133

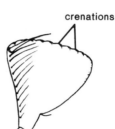

Figure 11.134

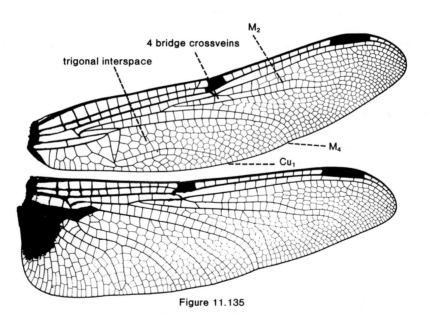

Figure 11.135

Figure 11.130. Dorsal view, tip of abdomen of nymph *Pachydiplax longipennis* (Burmeister) (Libellulidae) (Wright and Peterson 1944).

Figure 11.131. Dorsal view, tip of abdomen of nymph, *Tramea* sp. (Libellulidae) (Wright and Peterson 1944).

Figure 11.132. Dorsal view, tip of abdomen of nymph, *Pantala flavescens* (Fabricius) (Libellulidae) (Wright and Peterson 1944).

Figure 11.133. Dorsal view, left palpal lobe of nymph, *Pantala falvescens* (Fabricius) (Libellulidae) (Wright and Peterson 1944).

Figure 11.134. Dorsal view, left palpal lobe of nymph, *Tramea* sp. (Libellulidae) (Wright and Peterson 1944).

Figure 11.135. Wings of male, *Libellula quadrimaculata* Linnaeus (Libellulidae) (Needham and Westfall 1955).

Adults

1.   Fore wing triangle with anterior (costal) side broken, thus making the space it
        encloses a quadrangle; anal loop of hind wing incomplete, open rearward .... *Nannothemis*

1'.   Fore wing triangle usually normal, 3-sided; anal loop usually complete, and more
        or less foot-shaped 2

2(1').   Antenodal crossveins of both wings with row of roundish brown to black spots and
        distinctive pattern .... *Pseudoleon*

2'.   Crossveins with no such coloration 3

3(2').   Mature males brilliant red; front surface of frons with 2 conspicuous flat areas
        which are roughly triangular; golden basal wing spots; fore wing triangle 2-
        celled; radial planate subtending one row of cells; single bridge crossvein; Cu_1 in
        hind wing separated from anal angle of triangle (southern Florida) .... *Crocothemis*

3'.   No such combination of characters 4

4(3').   Vein M_2 waved (undulation slight in *Brechmorhoga* and *Macrothemis* (fig.
        11.135) 5

4'.   Vein M_2 smoothly curved (fig. 11.136) 14

5(4).   Wings with several bridge crossveins (except in many *Libellula semifasciata*,
        which have large spots at nodus and pterostigma; wing tips clear) (fig. 11.135) 6

5'.   Wings with a single bridge crossvein 9

6(5).   Fore wing triangle of 2 cells .... *Ladona*

6'.   Fore wing triangle of 3 or more cells 7

7(6').   First abdominal sternum of male bearing a pair of large, conspicuous processes;
        abdomen of female with side margins of middle abdominal segments parallel;
        wings of male and female very differently marked .... *Plathemis*

7'.   First abdominal sternum of male bare; abdomen of female slowly tapered rearward
        on side margins of middle segments; wing markings of male and female alike 8

8(7').   Reddish species usually with reddish color at base of wings that may extend to
        nodus; body form quite stout; (2 far Western species) .... *Belonia*

8'.   Usually not reddish species, and wing markings, if present, are usually black,
        white, or brown; body form more slender; (widespread) .... *Libellula*

9(5').   Pterostigma very long, surmounting 5–6 crossveins .... *Orthemis*

9'.   Pterostigma moderately long, surmounting 1–4 crossveins 10

10(9').   Hind wing with 2 cubito-anal crossveins .... *Pantala*

10'.   Hind wing with a single cutito-anal crossvein 11

11(10').   Fore wing with 2 rows of cells beyond triangle 12

11'.   Fore wing with 3 rows of cells beyond triangle 13

12(11).   Fore wing subtriangle with 1–2 cells in species in the United States; median
        planate absent in fore wing; inner tooth of tarsal claw elongated in species in the
        United States .... *Macrothemis*

12'.   Fore wing subtriangle with 3 cells; median planate present in fore wing; inner tooth
        of tarsal claw not elongated, not reaching tip of claw .... *Brechmorhoga*

13(11').   Two–4 parallel rows of cells between vein A_2 and marginal row at hind angle of
        hind wing .... *Dythemis*

13'.   Four–5 very irregular rows in this space .... *Paltothemis*

14(4').   Midrib of anal loop nearly straight or very slightly bent at ankle (fig. 11.136);
        reverse vein, postnodal crossveins of 2nd series, and 1st crossvein under
        pterostigma usually strongly aslant 15

14'.   Midrib of anal loop more angulated (fig. 11.137); reverse vein and crossveins much
        less, if at all, aslant 18

15(14).   Fore wing triangle of 2–4 cells, and usually with 3–4 rows of cells beyond in
        trigonal interspace; radial planate often subtends 2 rows of cells .... *Celithemis*

15'.   Fore wing triangle of 1 cell (except in some *Perithemis*) and with 2 rows of cells
        beyond in trigonal interspace; radial planate subtends a single row of cells 16

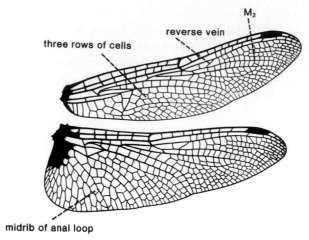

Figure 11.136

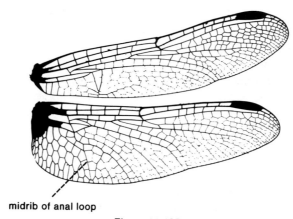

Figure 11.137

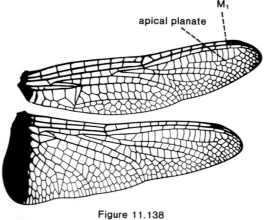

Figure 11.138

Figure 11.137. Wings of male, *Pachydiplax longipennis* (Burmeister) (Libellulidae) (Needham and Westfall 1955).

Figure 11.136. Wings of male, *Celithemis verna* Pritchard (Libellulidae) (Needham and Westfall 1955).

Figure 11.138. Wings of male, *Miathyria marcella* (Selys) (Libellulidae) (Needham and Westfall 1955).

16(15′). Fore wing triangle with inner side about as long as front side; more than a single bridge crossvein .... *Perithemis*

16′. Fore wing triangle with inner side much longer than front side; usually with a single bridge crossvein 17

17(16′). Fore wing subtriangle of 1 cell; 2 paranal cells before anal loop .... *Idiataphe*

17′. Fore wing subtriangle of 2 cells; 3 paranal cells before anal loop .... *Macrodiplax*

18(14′). Wings with more than a single bridge crossvein .... *Micrathyria*

18′. Wings with 1 bridge crossvein only 19

19(18′). Wings with triple-length vacant space before single crossvein that is either under distal end of pterostigma or just beyond it (fig. 11.137) .... *Pachydiplax*

19′. Wings with one or more crossveins under pterostigma, with no triple-length space adjacent to them 20

20(19′). Wings with a single crossvein under the pterostigma; without a dark band across entire base of hind wing .... *Sympetrum*

20′. Wings usually with 2 or more crossveins under pterostigma; there may be a dark band across entire base of hind wing 21

21(20′). Fore wing triangle with inner side less than twice as long as front side; pterostigma short and thick, about twice as long as wide, at least in male; face white .... *Leucorrhinia*

21′. Fore wing triangle with inner side more than twice as long as front side; pterostigma about 3 times as long as wide; face not white 22

22(21′). Hind wing with 2 paranal cells before anal loop .... *Brachymesia*

22′. Hind wing with 3 paranal cells before anal loop 23

23(22′). Wings with pterostigma trapezoidal, front side distinctly longer than rear; some double-length cells above apical planate, reaching from planate to M_1 (fig. 11.138) 24

23′. Wings with front and rear sides of pterostigma about equal in length; apical planate poorly developed and with no double-length cells above it 26

24(23). All cells above apical planate double-length and in a single row (fig. 11.138); one crossvein under pterostigma (fig. 11.138) .... *Miathyria*

24′. About half of these cells in a single row, then a double row; 2 crossveins under pterostigma 25

25(24′). Fore wing with 3 rows of cells in trigonal interspace (distal to triangle, between veins M_4 and Cu_1) (as in fig. 11.136) .... *Tauriphila*

25′. Fore wing with 4 rows of cells in trigonal interspace .... *Tramea*

26(23′). Spines on outer angle of hind femur gradually increasing in length distally; fore wing with 5 paranal cells before subtriangle .... *Erythrodiplax*

26′. Spines on basal half or two-thirds of outer angle of hind femur short and of about equal length, with 2–4 large spines on distal half or third 27

27(26′). Radial planate subtends 2 rows of cells; base of midrib of anal loop 4 times as far from triangle as from vein A_2 .... *Lepthemis vesiculosa*

27′. Radial planate subtends a single row of cells; base of midrib of anal loop 3 times as far from triangle as from vein A_2 .... *Erythemis*

ADDITIONAL TAXONOMIC REFERENCES

General
Muttkowski (1910); Munz (1919); Needham and Heywood (1929); Wright and Peterson (1944); Snodgrass (1954); Needham and Westfall (1955); Gloyd and Wright (1959); Smith and Pritchard (1971); Pennak (1978); Corbet (1980).

Regional faunas
Alaska: Walker (1953, 1958); Walker and Corbet (1975).
British Columbia: Whitehouse (1941); Scudder *et al.* (1976); Cannings and Stuart (1977).
California: Kennedy (1917); Smith and Pritchard (1971).
Canada: Walker (1953, 1958); Walker and Corbet (1975).
Connecticut: Garman (1927).
Florida: Byers (1930); Paulson (1966); Johnson and Westfall (1970).
Illinois: Needham and Hart (1901); Garman (1917).
Indiana: Williamson (1900).
Nevada: Kennedy (1917).
New England: Howe (1917–1923).
New York: Needham (1901, 1903).
North Carolina: Huggins and Brigham (1982).
Oregon: Kennedy (1915).
Philadelphia and Vicinity: Calvert (1893).
Quebec: Robert (1963).
South Carolina: Huggins and Brigham (1982).
Southeastern United States: Louton (1982).
Texas: Johnson (1972).
Utah: Musser (1962).
Washington: Kennedy (1915).
Wisconsin: Muttkowski (1908).
Wyoming: Molnar and Lavigne (1979).

Regional species lists
Arkansas: Bick (1959); Harp and Rickett (1977).
British Columbia: Whitehouse (1941); Scudder *et al.* (1976); Cannings (1981, 1982a).
Canada: Corbet (1979).
Colorado: Bick and Hornuff (1974).
Florida: Pearse (1932); Westfall (1953); Dunkle and Westfall (1982).
Indiana: Williamson (1917); Montgomery (1941, 1947, 1948).
Iowa: Miller (1906); Hummel and Haman (1975).
Kansas: Huggins *et al.* (1976).
Kentucky: Garman (1924).
Louisiana: Bick (1957a).
Maine: Borror (1944).
Manitoba: Conroy and Kuhn (1977).
Maryland: Fisher (1940).
Massachusetts: Gibbs and Gibbs (1954).
Michigan: Byers (1927); Kormondy (1958); Hamrum *et al.* (1971).

Minnesota: Whedon (1914).
Mississippi: Bick (1950); Westfall (1952); Lago *et al.* (1979).
Missouri: Williamson (1932).
Montana: Bick and Hornuff (1974).
Nebraska: Pruess (1968); Bick and Hornuff (1972).
Nevada: LaRivers (1940).
New Hampshire: White and Morse (1973).
New Jersey: Gillespie (1941).
New York: Needham (1901, 1928).
North Carolina: Brimley (1938); Westfall (1942); Wray (1967); Paulson and Jenner (1971).
Northcentral United States: Montgomery (1967).
North Dakota: Bick *et al.* (1977).
Ohio: Borror (1937).
Oklahoma: Bird (1932); Bick (1957b); Bick and Bick (1958).
Pacific Coast States: Paulson and Garrison (1977).
Pennsylvania: Beatty and Beatty (1968); Beatty *et al.* (1969).
Quebec: Hutchinson and Larochell (1977).
South Carolina: Montgomery (1940); Cross (1955); White *et al.* (1980).
South Dakota: Bick and Hornuff (1972); Bick *et al.* (1977).
Southeastern United States: Cuyler (1968).
Tennessee: Williamson (1903); Wright (1938).
Texas: Ferguson (1940); Gloyd (1958); Donnelly (1978); Young and Bayer (1979); Williams (1982).
Utah: Brown (1934).
Virginia: Byers (1951); Gloyd (1951); Matta (1978); Voshell and Simmons (1978); Carle (1979b).
Washington: Paulson (1970).
Washington, D.C. and vicinity: Donnelly (1961a).
West Virginia: Cruden (1962); Harwood (1971).
Western United States: Montgomery (1968).
Wisconsin: Ries (1967, 1969).
Wyoming: Bick and Hornuff (1972).

Taxonomic treatments at the suborder, family, and generic levels (N = nymphs; A = adults)
Aeshnidae: Martin (1908, 1909)–A; Walker (1912)–N, A; Calvert (1934)–N; Dunkle (1977)–N.
Calopterygidae: Johnson (1974)–A.
Cordulegastridae: Fraser (1929)–A.
Corduliidae: Martin (1906)–A; Walker (1925)–N, A; Davis (1933)–A; Byers (1937)–N, A; Kormondy (1959)–N, A.
Gomphidae: Walker (1928)–N, A; Walker (1933)–N; Byers (1939)–A; Needham (1941)–N; Belle (1973)–A; Carle (1979a, 1980)–N, A; Westfall and Tennessen (1979)–N, A.
Libellulidae: Ris (1909–1916)–A; Ris (1930)–A; Davis (1933)–A; Kormondy (1959)–N, A; Bennefield (1965)–A.
Petaluridae: Fraser (1933)–A.
Zygoptera: Munz (1919)–A.

le 11A. Summary of ecological and distributional data for *Odonata (dragonflies and damselflies).* (For definition of terms see Tables 6A–6C;
le prepared by K. W. Cummins, R. W. Merritt, and M. J. Westfall, Jr.)

Taxa (number of species in parentheses)	Habitat	Habit	Trophic Relationships	North American Distribution	Ecological References†
soptera (dragonflies)	Wide variety of lentic and lotic habitats	Sprawlers, climbers, burrowers	Predators (engulfers)		316, 335, 441, 446, 516, 837, 1250, 1783, 1886, 2066, 2440, 2531, 2540, 2541, 2648
etaluridae(2)	Lotic-depositional, lentic—littoral	Primarily burrowers	Predators (engulfers)		1783, 2259
Tachopteryx(1)	Lotic—depositional (margins and moss of spring streams; upper edges of hillside seepages in deciduous forests), lentic—littoral (bogs)	Sprawlers	Predators (engulfers)	East (particularly mountains)	611, 1290, 1783, 2259
Tanypteryx(1)	Bogs	Burrowers	Predators (engulfers)	West (mountains)	334, 1783, 2259, 2380, 2540
Cordulegastridae(8) (biddies, flying adders)	Lotic—depositional	Burrowers	Predators (engulfers)		888, 1316, 1783, 1886, 2259
Cordulegaster(8) (= *Thecaphora, Zoraena, Taeniogaster*)	Lotic—depositional (headwater streams, sand, silt, detritus)	Burrowers	Predators (engulfers, await prey)	East, West	1290, 1783, 2259, 2540
Gomphidae(93)	Generally lotic—depositional, lentic—littoral (sediments)	Primarily burrowers	Predators (engulfers, generally await prey)		888, 1316, 1783, 1886, 2259
Aphylla(3)	Lotic—depositional, lentic—littoral	Burrowers	Predators (engulfers)	Widespread (primarily South)	189, 888, 1783
Arigomphus(7) (= *Orcus*)	Lentic—littoral, some lotic—depositional (sediments, primarily silt)	Burrowers	Predators (engulfers)	East, Southwest	888, 1783, 2546
Dromogomphus (3)	Lotic—erosional and depositional (detritus, larger rivers)	Burrowers	Predators (engulfers)	East	888, 1783, 2540, 2631
Erpetogomphus(5)	Lotic—depositional	Burrowers	Predators (engulfers)	Widespread (except North)	1783, 2259
Gomphurus(14)	Lotic—depositional, some lentic—littoral (sediments, primarily silt)	Burrowers	Predators (engulfers)	East, Central, South	1767, 1783, 2540, 2625, 2628, 2629, 2632
Gomphus(16)	Lotic—depositional, lentic—littoral (sediments, primarily silt)	Burrowers	Predators (engulfers)	Widespread	1766, 1780, 2259, 2540, 2627
Hagenius(1)	Lotic—erosional and depositional (detritus, at margins), lentic—littoral (at margins)	Sprawlers	Predators (engulfers)	East, Southwest	888, 1783, 2540
Hylogomphus(7)	Lotic—depositional, some lentic—littoral (sediments, primarily silt)	Burrowers	Predators (engulfers)	East	347, 575, 1783, 2540
Lanthus(2)	Lotic—erosional and depositional (sand and detritus in spring streams)	Burrowers (active)	Predators (engulfers)	East, Southeast	349, 888, 1767, 2540
Octogomphus(1)	Lotic—depositional (detritus)	Burrowers	Predators (engulfers)	West Coast	349, 1783, 2259, 2540

metimes considered subgenera of *Gomphus*.
nphasis on trophic relationships.

Table 11A.—*Continued*

Taxa (number of species in parentheses)	Habitat	Habit	Trophic Relationships	North American Distribution	Ecological References[†]
Ophiogomphus (15)	Lotic—erosional and depositional (sand) of small cold streams	Burrowers	Predators (engulfers)	Widespread (particularly mountains and high latitudes)	350, 351, 607, 888, 1294, 1346, 1767, 178 2538, 2540
Phyllogomphoides (2)	Lotic—depositional	Burrowers	Predators (engulfers)	Texas	887, 888
Progomphus(4)	Lotic—erosional and depositional (sand including intermittent streams), lentic—littoral (sand)	Burrowers	Predators (engulfers)	Widespread (except North)	887, 1327, 1771, 178C 2259, 2478
Stylogomphus(1) *(albistylus)*	Lotic—erosional and depositional (sand and detritus in spring streams)	Burrowers (active)	Predators (engulfers)	East, Southeast	888
Stylurus(12)	Lotic—depositional, lentic—littoral (sediments, primarily silt)	Burrowers	Predators (engulfers)	Widespread	881, 888, 1778, 1783, 2540
Aeshnidae(38) (darners) (=Aeschnidae)	Primarily lentic—littoral (especially vascular hydrophytes)	Generally climbers	Predators (engulfers, usually stalk prey)		888, 1316, 1783, 1886
Aeshna(20)	Lentic—vascular hydrophytes (lakes, ponds, marshes, and bogs)	Climbers	Predators (engulfers, stalk prey; Diptera, Coleoptera, Trichoptera, Ephemeroptera)	Widespread	335, 336, 572, 1783, 1952, 2259, 2540
Anax(4)	Lentic—vascular hydrophytes	Climbers	Predators (engulfers, stalk prey)	Widespread (especially South and except far North)	329, 439, 760, 1519, 1768, 1830, 2259, 254
Basiaeschna(1)	Lotic—depositional (detritus and sediments, under rocks)	Climbers—sprawlers, clingers	Predators (engulfers)	East, Southwest	1780, 2540
Boyeria (2) (=Fonscolombia)	Lotic—erosional and depositional (detritus, vascular hydrophytes)	Climbers—sprawlers (clingers under rocks)	Predators (engulfers)	East	1780, 2540
Coryphaeschna(4)	Lentic—vascular hydrophytes	Climbers	Predators (engulfers)	Southeast, Arizona	888, 1783
Epiaeschna(1)	Lentic—littoral (detritus—woodland ponds) and vascular hydrophytes (marshes)	Climbers—sprawlers	Predators (engulfers)	East, Southwest	888, 1783, 2540, 2716
Gomphaeschna(2)	Lentic—vascular hydrophytes (bogs)	Climbers—clingers	Predators (engulfers)	East, Central	609, 888, 1783, 2540
Gynacantha(1)	Lentic—vascular hydrophytes (temporary ponds)	Climbers—sprawlers	Predators (engulfers)	Florida, Georgia, California, and Oklahoma	1783, 2259
Nasiaeschna(1)	Lotic—erosional (detritus and debris jams) and depositional (detritus)	Climbers—clingers	Predators (engulfers)	East, Southwest	888, 1783, 2540
Oplonaeschna(1)	Lotic—erosional (detritus and sediments under rocks)	Clingers—climbers	Predators (engulfers)	Arizona, New Mexico	884, 1244, 1783
Triacanthagyna(1)	Lentic—vascular hydrophytes (temporary ponds)	Climbers—sprawlers	Predators (engulfers)	Southeast, California	888, 1783

*Sometimes considered subgenus of *Gomphus*.
†Emphasis on trophic relationships.

le 11A.— *Continued*

Taxa (number of species in parentheses)	Habitat	Habit	Trophic Relationships	North American Distribution	Ecological References†
Macromiidae(10)	Generally lentic—littoral (sediments—sand and silt), lotic—depositional (larger rivers)	Sprawlers	Predators (engulfers)		884, 1783, 2259
Didymops(2)	Lentic—littoral (sand and silt), lotic—depositional	Sprawlers	Predators (engulfers, await prey)	East, Central, Southeast	1783, 2259
Macromia(8)	Same as *Didymops*	Sprawlers	Predators (engulfers, await prey)	East, West Coast	1289
Corduliidae(50)	Primarily lotic—depositional (small streams) and lentic—littoral (bogs)	Both sprawlers and climbers	Predators (engulfers)		1783, 2259
Cordulia(1)	Lentic—littoral (detritus at margins of bogs and ponds)	Sprawlers	Predators (engulfers; Diptera, amphipods)	North	1783, 1952, 2259, 2541
Dorocordulia(2)	Lentic—littoral (bogs)	Sprawlers—climbers?	Predators (engulfers)	North	888, 1783
‡*Epicordulia*(1)	Lotic—depositional, lentic—littoral	Climbers	Predators (engulfers)	East	888, 1783
Helocordulia (2)	Lotic—depositional	Sprawlers	Predators (engulfers)	East	888, 1783
Neurocordulia(6)	Lotic—depositional, lentic—littoral	Climbers, clingers (on rocks, roots, and sticks)	Predators (engulfers)	Widespread (particularly Southeast)	888, 1783, 2694, 2696, 2698
Somatochlora(26)	Lentic—littoral (bogs), lotic—depositional (springs)	Sprawlers	Predators (engulfers)	North	574, 608, 1783, 2259, 2410, 2541, 2693
‡*Tetragoneuria*(10)	Lentic—littoral (pond margins in detritus), lotic—depositional (detritus)	Climbers—sprawlers	Predators (engulfers)	Widespread	147, 1344, 1345, 1483, 1485, 1783, 2259, 2541
Williamsonia(2)	Lentic—littoral (bogs)	Sprawlers	Predators (engulfers)	Northeast	1783, 2645
Libellulidae(93)	Generally lentic—vascular hydrophytes	Primarily sprawlers	Predators (engulfers)		229, 888, 1776, 1783, 2259
Belonia(2)	Lentic—littoral (silt of ponds)	Sprawlers	Predators (engulfers)	West	2259, 2695
Brachymesia (3) (=*Cannacria*)	Lentic—littoral (brackish)	Sprawlers	Predators (engulfers)	South	888, 1783
Brechmorhoga(1)	Lotic—depositional (sediments in pools of torrential streams)	Sprawlers	Predators (engulfers)	Southwest	1783, 2259
Cannaphila(1)			Predators (engulfers)	Texas	888, 1783
Celithemis(8)	Lentic—vascular hydrophytes	Climbers	Predators (engulfers)	East	148, 149, 151, 888, 1783
Dythemis(3)	Lotic—erosional and depositional (sand)	Sprawlers (active)	Predators (engulfers, stalk prey)	Far South (particularly Southwest)	1783, 2259
Erythemis(3) (=*Mesothemis*)	Lentic—littoral (silt in ponds)	Sprawlers	Predators (engulfers)	Widespread (except far North)	183, 1783, 2259
Erythrodiplax(4)	Lentic—vascular hydrophytes	Climbers	Predators (engulfers)	South, East	614, 1783, 2259
Idiataphe(1) (=*Ephidatia*)	Lentic—vascular hydrophytes (emergent zone—brackish) water	Sprawlers	Predators (engulfers)	Florida	888, 1783

phasis on trophic relationships.
metimes considered subgenera or synonyms of *Epitheca*.

Table 11A.— *Continued*

Taxa (number of species in parentheses)	Habitat	Habit	Trophic Relationships	North American Distribution	Ecological References†
Ladona (3)	Lentic—littoral (sediments in ponds)	Sprawlers	Predators (engulfers)	Widespread	147, 148, 149, 151, 88 1783
Lepthemis (1)	Lentic—littoral (silt in ponds)	Sprawlers	Predators (engulfers)	South, Southwest	888, 1783
Leucorrhinia (7)	Lentic—vascular hydrophytes (including bogs)	Climbers	Predators (engulfers, await prey; Diptera, Coleoptera, Trichoptera, Ephemeroptera)	Widespread in North	1783, 1830, 1952, 196 2259, 2541
Libellula (16)	Lentic—littoral (silt and detritus, vascular hydrophytes), lotic—depositional (sediments)	Sprawlers	Predators (engulfers)	Widespread	147, 1690, 1783, 1962 2259
Macrodiplax (1)	Lentic—littoral (brackish water)	Sprawlers	Predators (engulfers)	South (particularly Southeast)	888, 1783
Macrothemis (2)	Lentic—littoral	Sprawlers	Predators (engulfers)	Arizona, Texas	888, 1783
Miathyria (1) (=*Nothifixis*)	Lentic—littoral (in water hyacinth roots)	Climbers	Predators (engulfers)	Extreme South	888, 1783
Micarathyria (2)	Lentic—littoral (vascular hydrophytes	Sprawlers	Predators (engulfers)	Texas, Arkansas	888, 1783
Nannothemis (1) (=*Aino*)	Lentic—vascular hydrophytes (emergent zone in small puddles away from water's edge)	Sprawlers—climbers	Predators (engulfers)	East	888, 1783
Orthemis (1) (=*Neocysta*)	Lentic—littoral	Sprawlers	Predators (engulfers)	South	1783, 2259
Pachydiplax (1)	Lentic—littoral (detritus and silt), lotic—depositional (detritus)	Sprawlers	Predators (engulfers)	Widespread (except far North)	1783, 2259
Paltothemis (1)	Lotic—erosional (among rocks)	Sprawlers	Predators (engulfers)	Southwest	610, 1783, 2259
Pantala (2)	Lentic—littoral (sediments and macroalgae in temporary ponds)	Sprawlers (active foragers)	Predators (engulfers; Chironomidae)	Widespread	121, 319, 1783, 2259
Perithemis (3)	Lotic—depositional (margins)	Sprawlers (active)	Predators (engulfers)	Widespread (except North)	888, 1783
Plathemis (2)	Lentic—littoral	Sprawlers	Predators (engulfers)	Widespread	1783, 2259
Pseudoleon (1)	Lotic—depositional	Sprawlers	Predators (engulfers)	Southwest	2259
Sympetrum (13) (=*Diplax*, =*Tarnetrum*)	Lentic—littoral (detritus and vascular hydrophytes in ponds)	Sprawlers—climbers	Predators (engulfers)	Widespread	437, 1783, 1803, 1952 2259, 2776
Tauriphila (2)	Lentic—littoral	Sprawlers	Predators (engulfers)	Florida, Texas	1783
Tramea (7) (=*Trapezostigma*)	Lentic—littoral (silt and detritus, vascular hydrophytes, and macroalgae)	Sprawlers	Predators (engulfers)	Widespread	185, 541, 1430, 1783, 2259
Zygoptera (damselflies)	Both lentic and lotic habitats	Generally climbers	Predators (engulfers)		5, 229, 470, 516, 888, 1250, 1316, 1425, 142 1874, 1886, 2066, 225 2531, 2539, 2648
Calopterygidae (8) (=*Agrionidae* =*Agriidae*)	Generally lotic—erosional (margins and detritus) and depositional (detritus)	Generally climbers	Predators (engulfers)		888, 1316, 1886, 2259 2539

†Emphasis on trophic relationships.

ble 11A.—*Continued*

Taxa (number of species in parentheses)	Habitat	Habit	Trophic Relationships	North American Distribution	Ecological References†
Calopteryx(5) (= *Agrion*)	Lotic—erosional and depositional (margins and detritus)	Climbers	Predators (engulfers)	Widespread	332, 1554, 1953, 2259, 2539
Hetaerina(3)	Lotic—erosional and depositional (margins and detritus)	Climbers—clingers	Predators (engulfers)	Widespread	2259, 2539
Lestidae(18)	Lotic—depositional and lentic—littoral	Climbers	Predators (engulfers)		888, 1316, 1886, 2259, 2539
Archilestes(2)	Lotic—depositional (detritus and vascular hydrophytes), lentic—vascular hydrophytes	Climbers	Predators (engulfers)	West	1186, 2259
Lestes(16)	Lentic—vascular hydrophytes, lotic—depositional (vascular hydrophytes)	Climbers—swimmers	Predators (engulfers)	Widespread	337, 437, 726, 834, 1186, 1484, 1767, 2164, 2259, 2539, 2630
Protoneuridae(2)	Lotic—erosional and depositional	Generally climbers—clingers	Predators (engulfers)		888, 1316, 1886, 2259, 2539
Neoneura(1)	Lotic—erosional (on rocks)	Climbers—clingers	Predators (engulfers)	Texas	888
Protoneura(1)	Lotic—depositional (vascular hydrophytes)	Climbers—clingers (on floating leaves)	Predators (engulfers)	Texas	
Coenagrionidae(93) (= *Agrionidae*)	Wide range of lentic and lotic habitats	Generally climbers	Predators (engulfers)		888, 1316, 1886, 2259, 2539
Acanthagrion(1)	Lentic—vascular hydrophytes	Climbers	Predators (engulfers)	Texas	848
Amphiagrion(2)	Lotic—depositional (vascular hydrophytes), lentic—vascular hydrophytes (emergent zone) including bogs	Climbers	Predators (engulfers)	Widespread (particularly North)	2259, 2539, 2650
Anomalagrion(1)	Lentic—vascular hydrophytes (emergent zone), small spring seeps	Climbers	Predators (engulfers)	East, Southwest	888, 1249, 1767, 2539
Apanisagrion(1)	Lotic—depositional (spring fed regions)	Sprawlers?	Predators (engulfers)	Arizona	
Argia(27) (= *Hyponeura*)	Lotic—erosional (sediments and detritus) and depositional, lentic—erosional and littoral (sediments)	Clingers, climbers—sprawlers	Predators (engulfers)	Widespread	225, 885, 886, 1289, 1346, 1956, 2259, 2539
Argiallagma(1)	Lentic—littoral (vascular hydrophytes)	Climbers	Predators (engulfers)	Florida	833, 848
Chromagrion(1)	Lotic—erosional (detritus) and depositional (detritus and vascular hydrophytes in small spring streams)	Climbers	Predators (engulfers)	East	836, 888, 1778, 2539
Coenagrion(3) (= *Agrion*)	Lotic—erosional and depositional (emergent vascular hydrophytes at margin), lentic—vascular hydrophytes (marshes and bogs)	Climbers	Predators (engulfers)	North, West	89, 90, 341, 1857, 2259, 2539

Emphasis on trophic relationships.

Table 11A.—*Continued*

Taxa (number of species in parentheses)	Habitat	Habit	Trophic Relationships	North American Distribution	Ecological References[†]
Enallagma(35) (= *Teleallagma*)	Lentic—vascular hydrophytes (including brackish and alkaline waters), lotic—depositional (vascular hydrophytes)	Climbers	Predators (engulfers; Cladocera)	Widespread	836, 1129, 1130, 118 1290, 1346, 1768, 17 1962, 2259, 2411, 25
Hesperagrion(1)	Lentic—vascular hydrophytes	Climbers	Predators (engulfers)	Southwest	888
Ischnura(13) (including *Ischnuridia, Celaenura,* and *Anomalura*)	Lentic—vascular hydrophytes, lotic—depositional (vascular hydrophytes)	Climbers	Predators (engulfers; Cladocera, Chironomidae)	Widespread	338, 575, 838, 839, 9 1248, 1249, 1289, 18 1857, 2259, 2427, 24
Nehalennia(3)	Lentic—vascular hydrophytes (including edges of bog mats)	Climbers	Predators (engulfers)	East, North	888, 2539
Neoerythromma(1)	Lentic—vascular hydrophytes	Climbers	Predators (engulfers)	Florida	833
Telebasis(2)	Lentic—vascular hydrophytes	Climbers	Predators (engulfers)	Widespread in South, Southwest	2259, 2626
Zoniagrion(1)	Lotic—depositional (vascular hydrophytes—*Sparganium*)	Climbers (bases of *Sparganium*)	Predators (engulfers)	California	1290, 2259

[†]Emphasis on trophic relationships.

12

Semiaquatic Orthoptera

Irving J. Cantrall
University of Michigan, Ann Arbor

INTRODUCTION

Orthopterans are generally terrestrial, yet numerous forms are hydrophilous to some extent, and a few are adapted to live on emergent aquatic vegetation. Most species have one-year life cycles, although some may require up to three years. Nymphs undergo gradual metamorphosis and adults lay their eggs in loose soil, plant tissue, or in burrows. Most Orthoptera shred live plant tissue; however, some tettigoniids are predators and some gryllids are collectors adapted to feed on detrital particles. Many of the semiaquatic forms have distinctive morphological and behavioral adaptations.

Numerous species of Tetrigidae (grouse or pygmy locusts; fig. 12.1) live in moist areas along edges of aquatic habitats, and several species of Tettigoniidae (katydids; figs. 12.7, 12.8) in the genera *Conocephalus* and *Orchelimum* commonly inhabit marshes and the marginal vegetation of freshwater environments. The Tetrigidae have no special adaptations for swimming, but can move readily through or on water. The semiaquatic tetrigids and the tettigoniid *Orchelimum bradleyi* have been observed to dive and swim to submerged objects.

Two species of Tridactylidae (pygmy mole crickets; fig. 12.2) inhabit wet shores of streams and back bays (minimal wave action) of small lakes where they dig shallow burrows in moist sand. Pairs of long slender plates on the hind tibiae aid in swimming. Of the Acrididae (grasshoppers; fig. 12.3) known from North America, only three species in two genera commonly occur on emergent aquatic plants and sometimes dive and cling to submerged vegetation. The hind tibiae aid in swimming; they are widened distally and have a flattened upper surface with laminate edges bearing fine hairs between the spines.

Approximately 10% if the nearly 100 North American species of Gryllidae (crickets; fig. 12.5) occur on the ground or in foliage along margins of aquatic habitats. They belong to the subfamilies Nemobiinae, Eneopterinae, Mogoplistinae, and especially Trigonidiinae.

Two species in the genus *Neocurtilla* of the Gryllotalpidae (mole crickets; fig. 12.6) are semiaquatic. They burrow with flattened front tibiae in moist or muddy sand along margins of freshwater habitats. A body covering of short, fine hairs traps air and increases buoyancy.

EXTERNAL MORPHOLOGY

Orthoptera (grasshoppers, pygmy locusts, katydids, crickets) are distinctive insects having generally four wings, chewing mouthparts, and enlarged hind femurs for jumping. The front wings, when present, vary from being fully developed to being reduced to small scalelike structures (Tetrigidae). The fore wings (tegmina) are thickened, leathery, or parchmentlike in texture. The hind wings, when present, are membranous, broad, and folded fanlike beneath the front wings. Many orthopterans produce sound with a stridulating apparatus at the base of the tegmina (figs. 12.7, 12.8).

KEY TO FAMILIES OF ORTHOPTERA CONTAINING ONE OR MORE SEMIAQUATIC SPECIES

1. Front and middle tarsi 2-segmented 2
1'. Front and middle tarsi 3- or 4-segmented 3
2(1). Pronotum prolonged posteriorly to or surpassing apex of abdomen (fig. 12.1) (pygmy or grouse locusts) .... *TETRIGIDAE*
2'. Pronotum not prolonged posteriorly (fig. 12.2) (pygmy mole crickets) .... *TRIDACTYLIDAE* (p. 179)
3(1'). All tarsi 3-segmented; antennae longer or shorter than body 4
3'. All tarsi 4-segmented; antennae longer than body (figs. 12.7, 12.8) (katydids) .... *TETTIGONIIDAE*
4(3). Front legs similar to middle legs; body not velvety in appearance 5
4'. Front legs strongly flattened, front tibiae enlarged and fitted for digging; body covered with very short hairs, giving a velvety appearance; antennae shorter than body length (fig. 12.6) (mole crickets) .... *GRYLLOTALPIDAE* (p. 179)

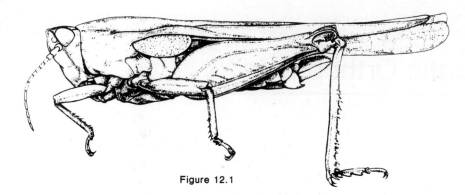

Figure 12.1

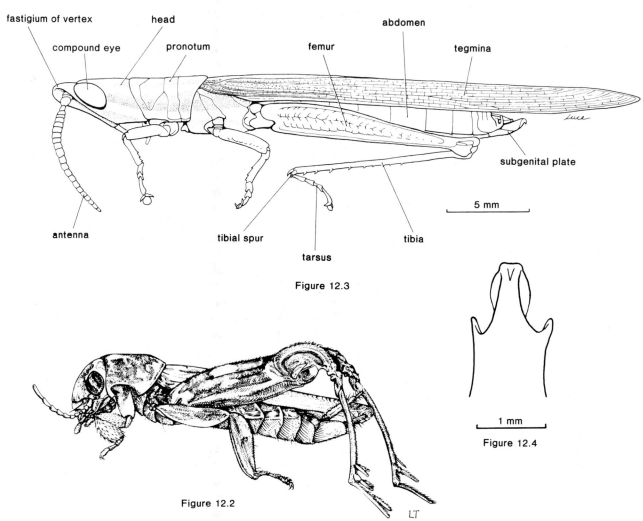

fastigium of vertex

head

compound eye

pronotum

abdomen

femur

tegmina

subgenital plate

antenna

tibial spur

tibia

tarsus

Figure 12.3

5 mm

1 mm

Figure 12.4

Figure 12.2

Figure 12.1. Adult female grouse locust, *Textrix subulata* (Linnaeus) (Tetrigidae).

Figure 12.2. Adult male pygmy mole cricket, *Ellipes minuta* (Scudder) (Tridactylidae).

Figure 12.3. Adult male *Leptysma marginicollis* (Serville) (Acrididae).

Figure 12.4. Subgenital plate of adult male *Stenacris vitreipennis* (Marschall) showing well-developed lateral processes.

5(4). Antennae longer than body; tegmina flat above, bent rather abruptly downward at sides; male with stridulatory apparatus at the base of the tegmina; female with an elongate and cylindrical ovipositor (Fig. 12.5) (crickets) .... *GRYLLIDAE*

5'. Antennae shorter than body; tegmina flattened above and reflexed downward, but not so strongly in either case; tegmina without a stridulatory mechanism at the base; female with ovipositor consisting of 4 short, horny pieces projecting from the tip of the abdomen (fig. 12.3) (grasshoppers) .... *ACRIDIDAE* (p. 179)

KEYS TO SELECTED GENERA BY FAMILY

Tridactylidae

1. Tarsus of hind leg almost as long as large tibial spur; hind tibiae with 4 pairs of slender plates used in swimming; body more than 5.5 mm in length (one species only, *apicialis* [Say]) .... *Neotridactylus*

1'. Tarsus of hind leg absent; hind tibiae with one pair of long slender plates used in swimming (fig. 12.2); body less than 5.5 mm in length (one species only, *minuta* [Scudder]) .... *Ellipes*

Acrididae

1. Head as long or longer than pronotum; fastigium of vertex as long as eyes and with an obvious median groove; male subgenital plate without a lateral process on each side (fig. 12.3) .... *Leptysma*

1'. Head shorter than pronotum; fastigium of vertex shorter than eyes and without a median groove; male subgenital plate with well-developed lateral process on each side (fig. 12.4) (Coastal area from North Carolina into Texas) (only one species, *vitreipennis* [Marschall]) .... *Stenacris*

Gryllotalpidae

1. Front tibiae with 2 dactyls (fingerlike structures); hind femora usually longer than pronotum .... *Scapteriscus*

1'. Front tibiae with 4 dactyls; hind femora shorter than pronotum 2

2. Apical half of hind tibiae armed above with 3–4 long spines on inner margins .... *Gryllotalpa*

2'. Apical half of hind tibiae spined only at apices (fig. 12.6) .... *Neocurtilla*

ADDITIONAL TAXONOMIC REFERENCES

General
Blatchley (1920); Rehn and Grant (1961); Borror *et al.* (1981).

Taxonomic treatments at the family and generic levels
Acrididae: Rehn and Eades (1961).
Gryllidae: Blatchley (1920); Vickery and Johnstone (1970).
Gryllotalpidae: Blatchley (1920).
Tetrigidae: Rehn and Grant (1961).
Tettigoniidae: Rehn and Hebard (1915a, 1915b); Thomas and Alexander (1962); Walker (1971).
Tridactylidae: Günther (1975).

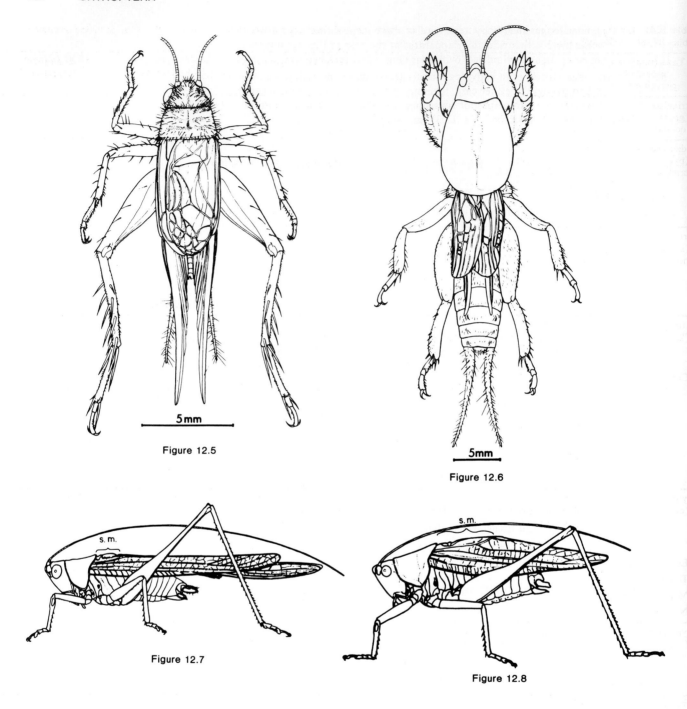

Figure 12.5

5mm

Figure 12.6

5mm

Figure 12.7

Figure 12.8

Figure 12.5. Adult male of a small field cricket, *Allonemobius allardi* (Alexander and Thomas) (Gryllidae).

Figure 12.6. Adult male mole cricket, *Neocurtilla hexadactyla* (Perty) (Gryllotalpidae).

Figure 12.7. Adult male *Conocephalus fasciatus* (De Geer) (Tettigoniidae) (Courtesy Michigan Entomological Society), *s.m.*, stridulating mechanism.

Figure 12.8. Adult male *Orchelium vulgare* Harris (Tettigoniidae) (Courtesy Michigan Entomological Society), *s.m.*, stridulating mechanism.

ble 12A. Summary of ecological and distributional data for *Semiaquatic Orthoptera (grasshoppers, crickets, etc.)* (For definition of terms see bles 6A–6C; table prepared by I. J. Cantrall and K. W. Cummins.)

Taxa (number of species in parentheses)	Habitat	Habit	Trophic Relationships	North American Distribution	Ecological References*
rigidae(?) (grouse or pygmy ocusts)	Lentic—vascular hydrophytes (emergent zone, margins)	Sprawlers (semiaquatic)	Generally shredders— herbivores (chewers), collectors—gatherers	Widespread	205, 1993
dactylidae(2) (pygmy mole crickets)	Lentic and lotic margins (near quiet water away from wave or splash effects)	Burrowers; skaters, "swimmers" (semiaquatic)	Shredders—herbivores (chewers)		205, 931
Neotridactylus(1)				Widespread	931
Ellipes(1)				Widespread	931
rididae(3) (short-horned grasshoppers)	Lentic—vascular hydrophytes (emergent zone, margins)	Skaters, "swimmers," climbers (semiaquatic)	Shredders—herbivores (chewers)		205, 1992
Stenacris(1)				East Coast, Gulf	
Leptysma(2)				East to edge of Great Plains, Southwest	
tigoniidae(12) (katydids)			Generally shredders— herbivores (chewers), some predators (engulfers)		
Conocephalinae(12)					
Orchelimum(2)	Lentic (and lotic)— vascular hydrophytes (emergent zone, margins)	Climbers, "swimmers" (semiaquatic)	Shredders—herbivores (chewers), predators (engulfers)	Northern Midwest to edge of Great Plains, East Coast	205, 1994, 2425, 2542
Conocephalus(10)	Lentic and lotic—margins (and vascular hydrophytes, emergent zone)	Climbers (semiaquatic)	Shredders—herbivores	Widespread	1995
yllidae(?) (crickets)	Generally lentic— vascular hydrophytes (emergent zone, margins)	Sprawlers (semiaquatic)	Generally shredders— herbivores (chewers), collectors—gatherers, some predators (engulfers)	Widespread	205, 2521
Eneopterinae					
Trigonidiinae					
Mogoplistinae					
Nemobiinae					
yllotalpidae(2) (mole crickets)	Lentic and lotic—margins (near quiet water away from wave or splash effects)	Burrowers (semiaquatic)	Collectors—gatherers, predators (engulfers)	East, Midwest	205
Neocurtilla(2)					

mphasis on general ecology, life history.

13

Plecoptera

P. P. Harper
Université de Montréal, Canada

K. W. Stewart[1]
North Texas State University, Denton

INTRODUCTION

Plecoptera (stoneflies) are primarily associated with clean, cool running waters, although a number of species are adapted to life in large oligotrophic, alpine, and boreal lakes. Several species inhabit streams that warm or dry up in summer or that are organically enriched. Eggs and nymphs of all North American species are aquatic, and, with the exception of an *Utacapnia* species living in the depths of Lake Tahoe, adults are terrestrial. The following account of the biology and ecology of stoneflies can be supplemented with the comprehensive works of Hitchcock (1974) and Hynes (1976).

Stonefly nymphs tend to have specific water temperature, substrate type, and stream size requirements reflected in their distribution and succession along the course of streams and rivers. In addition, a distinct microdistribution of species and of size classes of individual species is frequently observed within a particular stream reach. Microhabitats include boulder surfaces, cobble and gravel interstices, debris accumulations and leaf packs, as well as the hyporheal (*Isocapnia* sp., *Paraperla* sp., some European *Leuctra* spp., and early instars of many other species). Stonefly adults live on riparian vegetation or among rocks or debris.

Food ingested by nymphs may vary depending on species, developmental stage, or time of day. Some species are, for example, shredders or predators throughout development;

1. The Plecoptera nymph key was developed, in part, from a study by K. W. Stewart, supported by the National Science Foundation.

however, others may change their feeding habit as development proceeds. Gut content analyses indicate that shifts from herbivory-detritivory in the earliest instars to omnivory-carnivory in later periods are common. Predators usually ingest their prey whole. Stoneflies may either be opportunistic or select for particular food items in low abundance. Details on individual families are given in table 13B. Adults of Taeniopterygidae, Nemouridae, Leuctridae, Capniidae, Chloroperlidae, and some Perlodidae feed on epiphytic algae or young leaves and buds of riparian vegetation.

Plecoptera species emerge in clear succession throughout the year, except at latitudes or altitudes experiencing seasons of drought or frost. In general, species with predaceous nymphs have an emergence period restricted to the spring and summer months (table 13A). Adults live about 1–4 weeks, although winter species often have greater longevity.

In many stonefly species, male and female adults are attracted by drumming (Rupprecht 1967; Zeigler and Stewart 1977), which is a tapping upon the substrate with the tip of the abdomen. Male drummers continue this activity throughout their adult life, but only virgin females respond to males. Males initiate the communication, and females answer either during or immediately after the male drumming roll. Male and female signals are species specific, and dialects have been detected in European *Diura* spp. (Rupprecht 1972) and North American *Pteronarcella* spp. (K. W. Stewart, unpubl. data).

Little courtship has been observed in stoneflies prior to mating, although some Peltoperlidae do a dance involving

Table 13A. Life history data for North American stonefly families. (Only about 15% of the species have been studied in this respect.)

Family	Emergence	Life Cycle	Diapause
Pteronarcyidae	Early summer	1–3 years	none
Peltoperlidae	Early summer	1–2 years	none
Taeniopterygidae	Winter and spring	Univoltine	nymph (egg?) in summer
Nemouridae	Succession of spp. throughout the year	1–2 years	egg in summer or in winter in some spp.
Leuctridae	Succession of spp. throughout the year	1–2 years	egg diapause in a few spp.
Capniidae	Winter and spring	Univoltine	nymph in summer
Perlidae	Summer	1–3 years	eggs in summer, some eggs in winter
Perlodidae	Spring—fall	Univoltine	egg (1 species)
Chloroperlidae	Spring—fall	1–2 years	none

considerable wing lifting during drumming. Males mount females, curve the abdomen to the left or right side, and, using structures such as the hooks of the subanal lobes or the epiproct, gain apposition with the subgenital plate (chap. 2). The aedeagus is everted from beneath the ninth sternum and curves upward between the male cerci into the female genital opening. Sperm are either conveyed internally directly from the aedeagus or through a specially grooved epiproct (Brinck 1956), or introduced externally into a pocket just outside the genital opening, after which the female aspirates the sperm into the bursa (Stewart and Stark 1977). The gravid female releases eggs over the stream surface or deposits them in the water. Eggs are attached to the substrate by either a sticky gelatinous covering or specialized anchoring devices.

In most species, embryonic development proceeds directly and is complete within 3–4 weeks; hatchlings then undergo gradual development requiring some 12–24 months, depending on the species, sex, and environmental conditions. In most cases, growth requires 10–11 months (annual life cycle, univoltine), although growth rates are often low during winter months. Semivoltine (2–3 year) cycles are known or suspected in many Pteronarcyidae and Perlidae, as well as in a few species of Nemouridae, Leuctridae, and Perlodidae (table 13A). Such cycles are termed *slow seasonal* in Hynes' (1961) classification.

In other species, particularly those inhabiting intermittent aquatic habitats or streams subjected to extremes in temperature, embryonic development may be arrested for 3–6 months and hatching delayed until environmental conditions are more favorable (table 13A). Hatchlings must then develop rapidly in order to complete a univoltine cycle in the remaining 6–8 months. A variation of this strategy is found in some Taeniopterygidae, Capniidae, and Leuctridae in which diapause occurs in the early nymphal instars (Harper and Hynes 1970). This type of cycle is called *fast seasonal*. Under drought conditions, species of *Zealeuctra* are able to extend the embryonic diapause for an extra year (Snellen and Stewart 1979). These observations and Hynes and Hynes' (1975) studies on Australian stoneflies suggest considerable flexibility in stonefly life cycles.

EXTERNAL MORPHOLOGY

Nymphs and Adults

Nymphs and adult stoneflies fit the general morphological pattern of a primitive insect (see chap. 2). Metamorphosis is hemimetabolous, and the main characters used for identifying adults are the wings and the external genitalia. The more difficult key characters are explained below:

Mouthparts: The mouthparts are of the primitive mandibular type, and the maxillae (figs. 13.39–13.40, 13.72, 13.76–13.77) and labium (figs. 13.7–13.8, 13.46–13.47, 13.80) are of considerable taxonomic importance. The relative positions of the glossae and paraglossae (figs. 13.7–13.8) are used extensively both in nymphal and adult determinations. The mouthparts of nonfeeding adults remain typical, even though they are membranous and somewhat degenerate.

Gills: Nymphs of many species possess gills at various body locations: the submentum (figs. 13.8, 13.24, 13.80, 13.89), neck (figs. 13.18–13.20), thorax (figs. 13.5–13.6, 13.14, 13.79), abdomen (figs. 13.5, 13.78), anal region (figs. 13.56–13.57), and bases of legs (fig. 13.9). These gills are of two main types: simple flat or cylindrical gills set individually (figs. 13.6, 13.9, 13.19, 13.78–13.79, 13.89) and tufts of gills set on a common stock ("branched gills"; figs. 13.5, 13.14, 13.18, 13.20, 13.24, 13.56–13.57). Gills may persist in adult stages, but tend to shrivel and sometimes leave scars (fig. 13.121) or stubs (figs. 13.111, 13.118, 13.134).

Cerci: As a rule, cerci of both adults and nymphs are long whiplike appendages divided into numerous segments (figs. 13.1–13.2); however, in a few families, cerci of the adults of one or both sexes are reduced to the basal segment (figs. 13.135–13.136, 13.144–147, 13.172–13.173), and, in some cases, are modified as accessory male copulatory organs (figs. 13.142, 13.170–13.171).

Wings: The wings appear in half-grown nymphs as tiny buds on the thorax. They grow with each successive instar and wing pads reach their full development in the terminal instar (figs. 13.1, 13.36, 13.38). Most species are winged; however, some may be apterous or brachypterous (shortened wings; fig. 13.37), often depending on sex. Venation is simple and veins are easily recognized (fig. 13.2).

External genitalia: Adult males possess various types of external genitalia. Accessory copulatory structures are formed from one or more of the following: epiproct (figs. 13.114, 13.124, 13.126, 13.139, 13.146), paraprocts (figs. 13.136, 13.139, 13.184), cerci (figs. 13.142, 13.170–13.171, 13.202), abdominal sternites (figs. 13.126–13.127), and abdominal tergites (figs. 13.144, 13.170, 13.182, 13.195, 13.207). Adult females lack extensive external genitalia. In most instances, sternum 8 is modified into a subgenital plate covering the gonopore (fig. 13.4).

KEY TO FAMILIES AND GENERA OF NORTH AMERICAN PLECOPTERA NYMPHS

The gill system of Ricker (1959b) is used in the following key. Mature nymphs can usually be sexed by the developing genitalia. In addition, males are smaller than females and the latter have a subgenital plate, usually manifested by the absence of mesal hairs of the Ab8 posterior sternal fringe. Determination of mouthpart characters may require extraction, mounting, and observation at a magnification of 100–400×. Selected references used in key construction include: (a) general (Ricker 1959b; B. P. Stark, unpubl. key to Utah Plecoptera nymphs); (b) Peltoperlidae (Stark and Stewart 1981); (c) Nemouridae (Baumann 1975); and (d) Perlidae (Stark and Gaufin 1976). Geographic range of the genera is indicated in table 13B.

Nymphs of *Hansonoperla* sp. Nelson (Perlidae), *Calliperla* sp. Banks (Perlodidae), and *Chernokrilus* sp. Ricker (Perlodidae) are unknown. Definitive separation of the genera *Capnia, Mesocapnia,* and *Utacapnia* (Capniidae), and *Suwallia, Sweltza,* and *Triznaka* (Chloroperlidae) is not possible at present (see Surdick 1981, ref. #2854). Mature nymphs of these and other homogeneous groups often can be distinguished by the underlying adult genitalia.

Nymphs

1. Ventral tufts of gills present on Th and Ab$_{1-2}$ or Ab$_{1-3}$ (fig. 13.5) ....
    .... *PTERONARCYIDAE* (figs. 2.1, 2.2, 13.4a) 9

1'. Without ventral gill tufts on Ab$_{1-2}$ or Ab$_{1-3}$ 2

2(1'). Single, double, or forked conical gills at least behind coxae$_{2-3}$ (fig. 13.6); Th sterna
    posteriorly produced, overlapping succeeding segment; some genera roachlike
    .... *PELTOPERLIDAE* (fig. 13.4b) 10

2'. Gills, if present, not conical; Th sterna not overlapping 3

3(2'). Paraglossae and glossae produced forward about the same distance (fig. 13.7) 4

3'. Paraglossae much longer than glossae (fig. 13.8) 7

4(3). First and 2nd tarsal segments ca. equal in length (fig. 13.9); midline of wing pads
    strongly divergent from body axis .... *TAENIOPTERYGIDAE* (fig. 13.4c) 15

4'. Second tarsal segment much shorter than first (fig. 13.10); midline of wing pads
    parallel or divergent 5

5(4'). Small, robust, hairy nymphs, less than 12 mm in body length; extended hind legs
    reach about tip of Ab; midline of metathoracic wing pads strongly divergent
    from body axis; cervical gills present (figs. 13.18–13.20) or absent
    .... *NEMOURIDAE* (fig. 13.4d) 20

5'. Elongate nymphs, extended hind legs reach far short of Ab tip; midline of
    metathoracic wing pads if present about parallel with body axis; no cervical gills 6

6(5'). Terga and sterna of Ab$_{1-9}$ separated by membranous pleural fold (fig. 13.11); Ab
    terga with posterior setal fringe (fig. 13.12); Ab segments widest posteriorly;
    hind wing pads about as broad as long, reduced, or absent .... *CAPNIIDAE* (fig. 13.4e) ... 31

6'. At most Ab$_{1-7}$ separated by membranous pleural fold (fig. 13.13); Ab terga of
    some genera without posterior setal fringe (*Despaxia, Perlomyia, Paraleuctra,
    Zealeuctra*) (figs. 13.49, 13.51); Ab segments cylindrical; hind wing pads
    usually longer than wide .... *LEUCTRIDAE* (fig. 13.4f)   37

7(3'). Highly branched filamentous gills on sides and venter of Th (fig. 13.14) .... *PERLIDAE* (fig. 13.4g) 43

7'. Branched, filamentous gills absent from Th 8

8(7'). Cerci 3/4 or less length of Ab; head, Th terga usually without distinct pigment
    pattern; midline of metathoracic wing pads ca. parallel to body
    axis .... *CHLOROPERLIDAE** (fig. 13.4h) 56

8'. Cerci as long or longer than Ab; head, Th terga usually with distinct pigment
    pattern; midline of metathoracic wing pads strongly divergent from body
    axis .... *PERLODIDAE* (fig. 13.1) 63

9(1). Ab$_3$ with gills similar to those on Ab$_{1-2}$ .... *Pteronarcella* Banks (fig. 13.4a)

9'. Ab$_3$ without gills (Eastern species, previously in *Allonarcys*, with lateral spinelike
    processes on Ab) .... *Pteronarcys* Newman (figs. 2.1, 2.2)

10(2). Posterior supracoxal gills on Th$_1$ (PSC$_1$) present (fig. 13.6) 14

10'. Gill PSC$_1$ absent 11

11(10'). Gill posterior supracoxal$_{2-3}$ single; gill posterior Th$_3$ present or absent 12

11'. Gill PSC$_{2-3}$ double; gill PT$_3$ present 13

12(11). Gill posterior Th$_3$ absent: .... *Soliperla* Ricker

12'. Gill PT$_3$ present, single; .... *Viehoperla* Ricker

13(11). Four paired, light-colored round spots on pronotum .... *Peltoperla* Needham

13'. Pronotum without paired, light round spots .... *Tallaperla* Stark and Stewart

14(10). Apex Ab rounded; dorsal femora with transverse rows of long setae; close-set,
    median transverse row of spinules and a double posterior row of stout setae on
    all Th nota .... *Yoraperla* Ricker (fig. 13.4b)

14'. Apex Ab with prominent spinelike process (fig. 13.15); no transverse rows of
    spinules on femora or Th nota; Western .... *Sierraperla* Jewett

*See Surdick (1981; ref. #2854) for upgraded key and descriptions (includes genera *Bisancora* Surdick, *Plumiperla* Surdick and *Chloroperla* Newman not treated here.

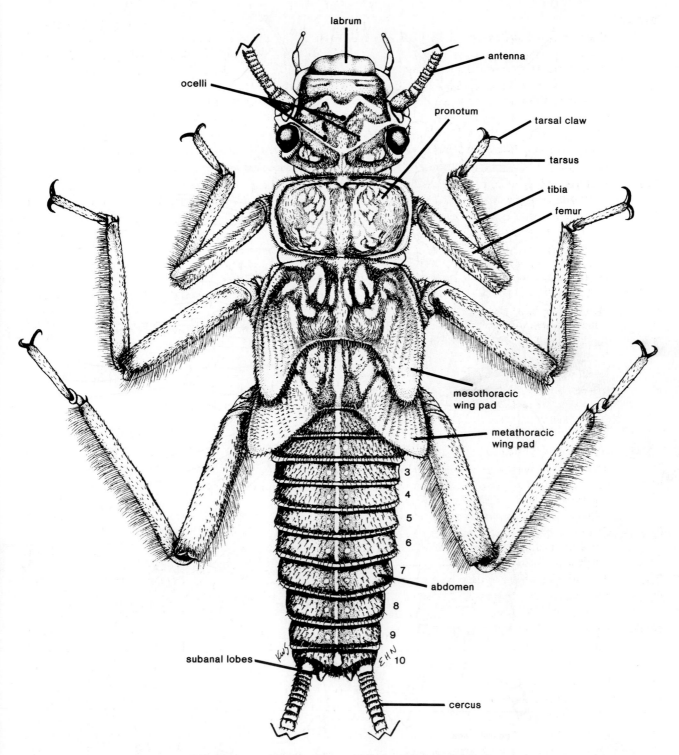

Figure 13.1. Dorsal view of *Skwala parallela* (Perlodidae).

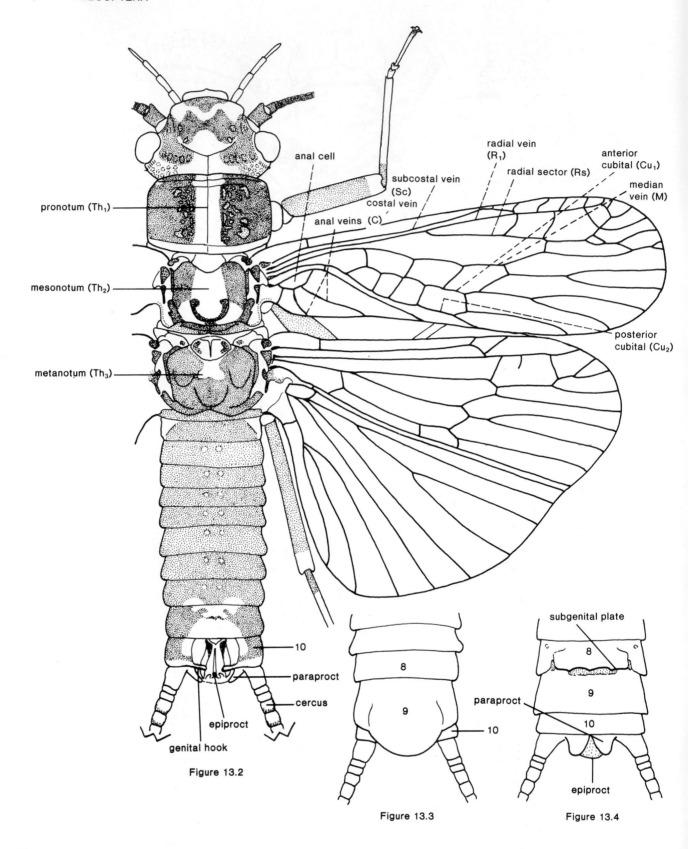

pronotum (Th₁)

mesonotum (Th₂)

metanotum (Th₃)

anal cell

subcostal vein (Sc)

costal vein

anal veins (C)

radial vein (R₁)

radial sector (Rs)

anterior cubital (Cu₁)

median vein (M)

posterior cubital (Cu₂)

10

paraproct

cercus

epiproct

genital hook

Figure 13.2

subgenital plate

8

9

10

paraproct

8

9

10

epiproct

Figure 13.3

Figure 13.4

Figure 13.2. Adult male of *Skwala parallela* (Perlodidae).

Figure 13.3. Ventral view of terminal abdominal segments of male *Skwala parallela* (Perlodidae).

Figure 13.4. Ventral view of terminal abdominal segments of female *Skwala parallela* (Perlodidae).

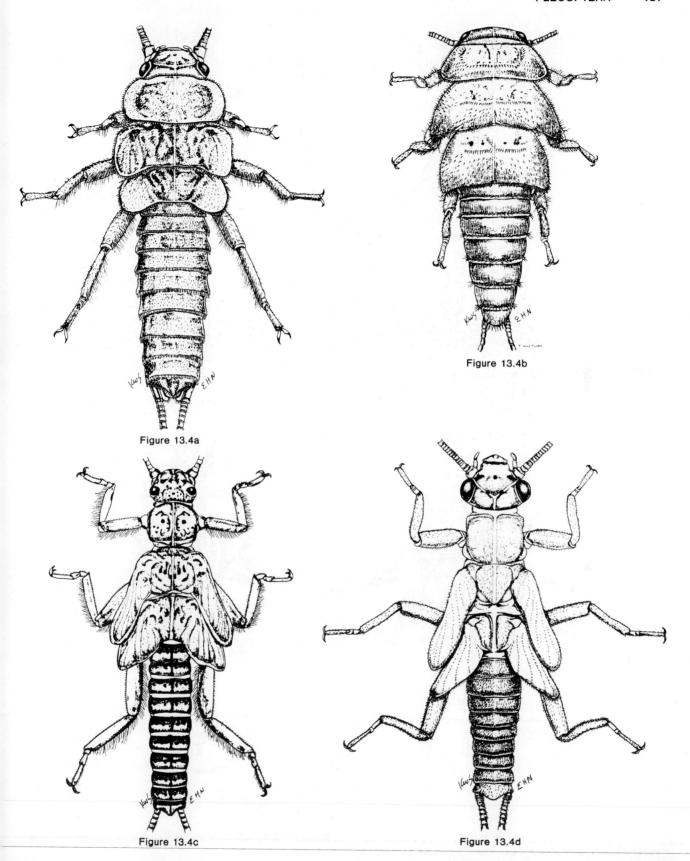

Figure 13.4a

Figure 13.4b

Figure 13.4c

Figure 13.4d

Figure 13.4a. *Pteronarcella badia* (Pteronarcyidae) nymphal habitus.

Figure 13.4b. *Yoraperla* sp. (Peltoperlidae) nymphal habitus.

Figure 13.4c. *Strophopteryx fasciata* (Taeniopterygidae) nymphal habitus.

Figure 13.4d. *Shipsa rotunda* (Nemouridae) nymphal habitus.

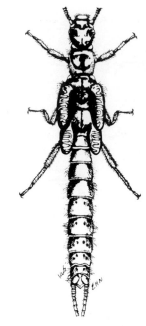

Figure 13.4e

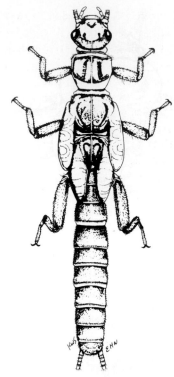

Figure 13.4f

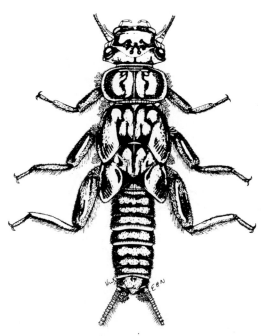

Figure 13.4g

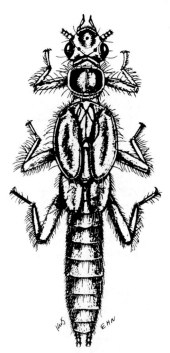

Figure 13.4h

Figure 13.4e. *Eucapnopsis brevicauda* (Capniidae) nymphal habitus.

Figure 13.4f. *Leuctra* sp. (Leuctridae) nymphal habitus.

Figure 13.4g. *Eccoptura xanthenes* (Perlidae) nymphal habitus.

Figure 13.4h. *Haploperla brevis* (Chloroperlidae) nymphal habitus.

15(4). Single, fingerlike, segmented gill on each coxa (fig. 13.9): .... *Taeniopteryx* Pictet

15'. Coxae without gills 16

16(15'). At least basal 8 cercal segments with dorsal hair fringe (fig. 13.16) 17

16'. Basal cercal segments without dorsal hair fringe, or a single long hair present on
each segment (fig. 13.17) 18

17(16). Twenty-five or more cercal segments with distinct dorsal hair fringe (fig. 13.16);
cercal and antennal segments uniformly light brown; Western .... *Doddsia* Needham and Claassen

17'. Basal 8–10 cercal segments with short, fine dorsal hair fringe; cercal and antennal
segments distinctly ringed with narrow brown pigment bands at joints; Eastern .... *Bolotoperla* Ricker

18(16'). Basal cercal segments each with a single, dorsal fine hair (fig. 13.17) .... *Oemopteryx* Klapálek

18'. Basal cercal segments without long dorsal hairs 19

19(18'). Body brown, pattern indistinct, legs uniformly brown (Western except *Atlanticum*) .... *Taenionema* Banks

19'. Body light or yellow, with distinct darker mottled pattern on head and thorax; Ab
distinctly banded, darker basally; legs light, femur darker apically (Eastern) .. *Strophopteryx* Frison (fig. 13.4c)

20(5). A pair of cervical gills present each with 5 or more branches, arising from the
cervical sclerites on each side (fig. 13.18); submental gills absent; no dorsal
transverse row or whorl of femoral spines on forelegs 21

20'. Cervical gills usually absent; if present each of the 4 gills is simple or 2–4
branched and submental gills are absent (fig. 13.19), *or* there are 2 short
cervical knobs and branched submental gills are present (fig. 13.24) 22

21(20). Gill filaments of different length, arranged palmately from base (fig. 13.18) .... *Malenka* Ricker

21'. Gill filaments approximately equal in length emerging equally from base (fig.
13.20) .... *Amphinemura* Ris

22(20'). Distinct, single lateral fringe of spines on pronotum, sometimes longer on posterior
corners (fig. 13.21); lateral spine fringes on wing pads 23

22'. No lateral fringe of pronotal spines, or, if present, not arrranged in single row, or
of unequal lengths; meso- and metanotum without lateral fringes of spines or
with sparse fringes near posterolateral corners 25

23(22). Pair of simple or 2–4 branched cervical gills present on each side of midline (fig.
13.19); transverse row of spines on all femora .... *Zapada* Ricker

23. Cervical gills absent; no transverse femoral spine whorls 24

24(23). Pronotum with round corners, without a definite lateral notch (fig. 13.22) .... *Nemoura* Latrielle

24'. Pronotum angular at corners, with a definite lateral notch (fig. 13.23) .... *Soyedina* Ricker

25(22'). Submental gills absent; fore tibia with outer row of spines and 2 to many fine
hairs, or fine hairs only 26

25'. Branched submental gills present (fig. 13.24) and fore tibia with outer row of
spines and fringe of fine hairs *or* submental gills absent and fore tibia without
fine hair fringe 29

26(25). Pronotum with irregular fringe of moderate to large spines (fig. 13.25) .... *Ostrocerca* Ricker

26'. Pronotum without distinct fringe of heavy spines (fig. 13.26) 27

27(26'). Fore tibia with outer fringe of long hairs, with or without stout outer spines 28

27'. Fore tibia without outer fringe of long hairs, but with occasional single hairs (fig.
13.27) .... *Podmosta* Ricker

28(27). Fore tibia with outer row of stout spines, in addition to hairs (fig. 13.28) .... *Prostoia* Ricker

28'. Fore tibia with outer hair fringe only; no stout spines (fig. 13.29) .... *Shipsa* Ricker (fig. 13.4d)

29(25'). Branched submental gills present (fig. 13.24); fore tibia with outer row of long
stout black spines and fringe of long hairs .... *Visoka* Ricker

29'. Submental and cervical gills absent; fore tibia with only occasional or no longer
outer hairs (fig. 13.30) 30

30(29'). Female nymphs with distinct posterior vesiclelike lobe on Ab$_7$ sternum (fig. 13.31);
Glacier N. P., Montana .... *Lednia* Ricker

30'. Female nymphs without a distinct posterior vesiclelike lobe on Ab$_7$ sternum;
Eastern .... *Paranemoura* Needham and Claassen

(Recurved epiprocts of mature male *Lednia* and *Paranemoura* nymphs visible under Ab$_{10}$ cuticle)

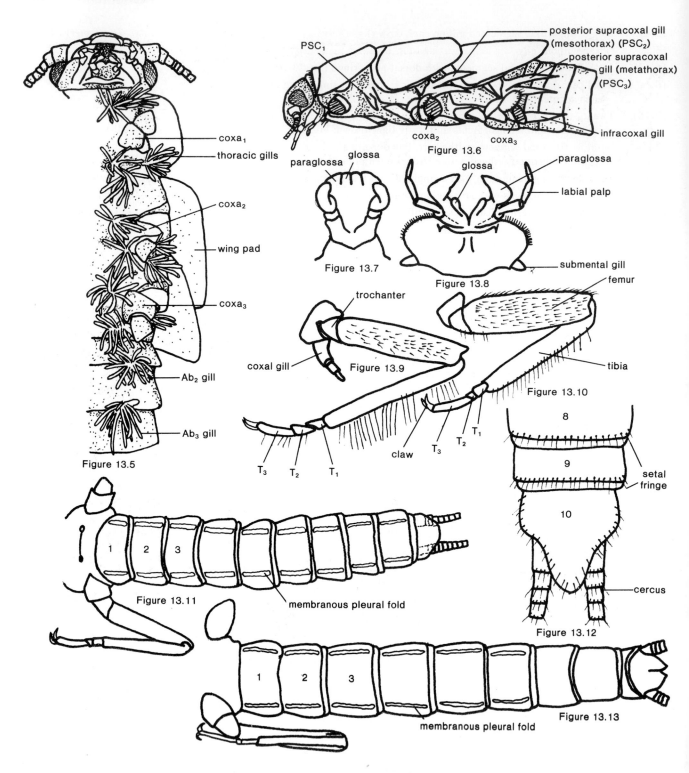

Figure 13.5

Figure 13.6

Figure 13.7

Figure 13.8

Figure 13.9

Figure 13.10

Figure 13.11

Figure 13.12

Figure 13.13

Figure 13.9. *Taeniopteryx maura* (Taeniopterygidae) left rear leg with gill.

Figure 13.5. *Pteronarcella badia* (Pteronarcyidae) ventrum with gills.

Figure 13.6. *Peltoperla arcuata* (Peltoperlidae) left side with gills.

Figure 13.7. *Taeniopteryx maura* (Taeniopterygidae) labium (ventral).

Figure 13.8. *Setvena bradleyi* (Perlodidae) labium (ventral).

Figure 13.10. *Utacapnia lemoniana* (Capniidae) left rear leg.

Figure 13.11. *Allocapnia granulata* (Capniidae) abdominal ventrum.

Figure 13.12. *Allocapnia granulata* (Capniidae) terminal abdomen (dorsal).

Figure 13.13. *Zealeuctra claasseni* (Leuctridae) abdominal ventrum.

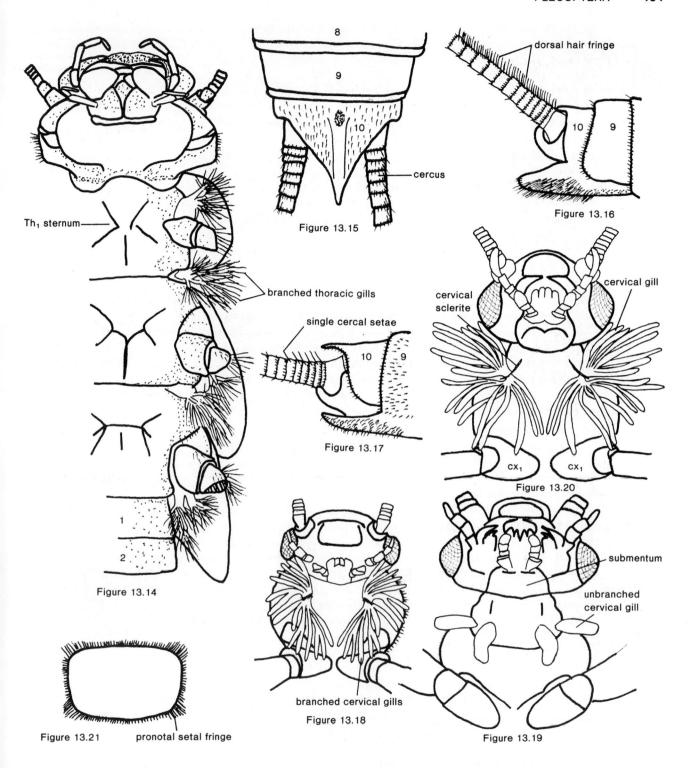

Figure 13.14. *Eccoptura xanthenes* (Perlidae) thorax ventrum with gills.

Figure 13.15. *Sierraperla cora* (Peltoperlidae) terminal abdomen (dorsal).

Figure 13.16. *Doddsia occidentalis* (Taeniopterygidae) right cercus (lateral).

Figure 13.17. *Oemopteryx glacialis* (Taeniopterygidae) right cercus (lateral).

Figure 13.18. *Malenka californica* (Nemouridae) cervical gills (ventral).

Figure 13.19. *Zapada haysi* (Nemouridae) cervical gills (ventral).

Figure 13.20. *Amphinemura banksi* (Nemouridae) cervical gills (ventral).

Figure 13.21. *Zapada haysi* (Nemouridae) pronotum.

31(6). Basal and/or apical cercal segments with multiple long, fine hairs forming a prominent vertical fringe (figs. 13.32–13.33) 32

31′. Long cercal hairs restricted to apical segmental whorls; no prominent vertical fringe 33

32(31). Cerci with about 20 segments (fig. 13.32), cercal length about equal to length of Ab; Western .... *Isocapnia* Banks

32′. Cerci with about 15 segments (fig. 13.33), length equal to last 7 Ab segments together; Eastern .... *Nemocapnia* Banks

33(31). Body and appendages densely clothed with stout hairs; Ab terga with posterior fringe of long bristles (fig. 13.34) .... *Paracapnia* Hanson

33′. Bristles on body and appendages few and inconspicuous, or absent; Ab terga with posterior fringe of short setae and scattered intercalary setae (fig. 13.35) 34

34(33′). Inner margin of hind wing pad unnotched or notched close to the tip (fig. 13.36) (hind wing pad sometimes much reduced fig. 13.37) .... *Allocapnia* Claassen

34′. Inner margin of hind wing pad notched at about mid length (fig. 13.38) (notch weak in *Bolshecapnia*) 35

35(34′). Lacinia with single, weakly sclerotized, emarginate cusp; galea longer than lacinia (fig. 13.39); cercal segments about 17 .... *Eucapnopsis* Okamoto (fig. 13.4e)

35′. Lacinia with 2 sharp cusps; galea shorter than lacinia (fig. 13.40); cercal segments 25 or more 36

36(35′). Mature male nymphs with developing vesicle (dark lobe) visible through nymphal skin at base of Ab₉ sternum (fig. 13.41); body length 8–10 mm .... *Bolshecapnia* Ricker

36′. No developing vesicle evident at base of Ab₉ sternum of male nymphs; body length variable, 5–10 mm .... *Capnia* Pictet, *Mesocapnia* Raušer, *Utacapnia* Nebeker and Gaufin

37(6′). Ab₁₋₇ divided ventrolaterally by membranous pleural fold (fig. 13.42) 38

37′. Fewer than 7 Ab segments divided by membrane (fig. 13.43) 39

38(37). Body robust, length less than 8 times width; body conspicuously clothed with hairs about one fifth the length of middle Ab segment; subanal lobes of mature male a fused strongly keeled plate, much produced with no posterior notch (fig. 13.44) .... *Megaleuctra* Neave

38′. Body more elongate, fine hair pile inconspicuous, appearing naked; subanal lobes of mature male nymph fused 1/2–2/3 length, leaving a notch at tip .... *Perlomyia* Banks

39(37′). Surface of Ab and Th nearly naked of hairs; Ab₁₋₅ divided by membrane (fig. 13.45); .... *Despaxia* Ricker

39′. Ab and Th clothed with sparse or numerous hairs; Ab with 1–4 or 1–6 segments ventrolaterally divided by pleural membrane 40

40(39′). Ab₁₋₄ divided ventrolaterally by membrane (fig. 13.43); labial palps long, apical segment fully reaching beyond tips of paraglossae when palp is appressed (fig. 13.46); clothing of stout hairs on apical Ab segments and subanal lobes; subanal lobes with 2 long innerapical hairs .... *Leuctra* Stephens (fig. 13.4f)

40′. Ab₁₋₆ divided ventrolaterally; labial palps shorter, tips barely reaching near or beyond tips of paraglossae at most, when appressed (fig. 13.47) 41

41(40′). Body nearly naked; subanal lobes of male nymphs half fused (fig. 13.48); developing V- or U-shaped cleft sometimes evident in Ab₉ tergum of mature male (fig. 13.49) .... *Zealeuctra* Ricker

41′. Body clothed with distinct short hairs and/or bristles; subanal lobes of male nymphs separate (fig. 13.50) 42

42(41′). Body covered with long bristles, many whose length is subequal to greatest width of femora .... *Moselia* Ricker

42′. Pronotum with a few long bristles only on corners; wing pads and Ab with sparse, scattered bristles (fig. 13.51), but covered with tiny clothing hairs .... *Paraleuctra* Hanson

43(7). Occiput with transverse row of regularly spaced spinules (fig. 13.52), or distinctly elevated ridge 44

43′. Occiput without spinules, except possibly laterally near the eyes (figs. 13.53, 13.62), *or* with a sinuate, irregularly spaced spinule row (fig. 13.54) 47

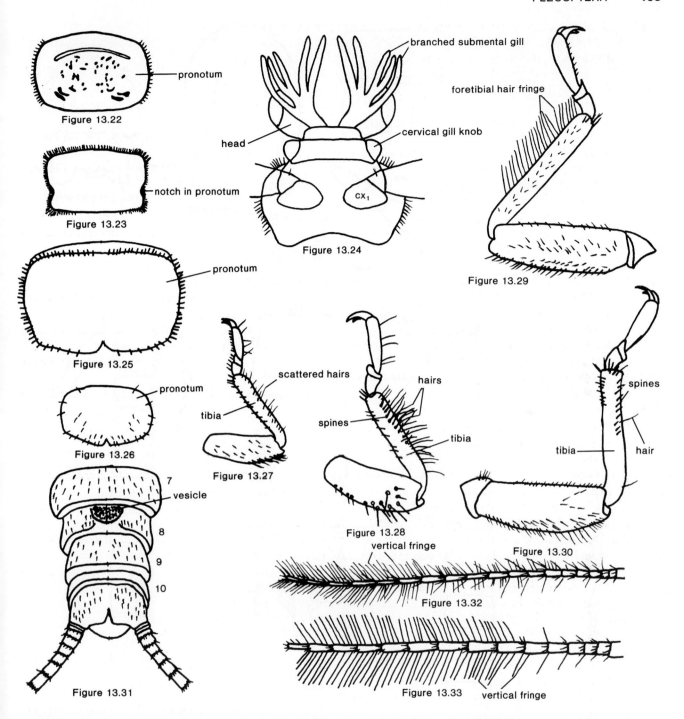

Figure 13.22. *Nemoura arctica* (Nemouridae) pronotum.

Figure 13.23. *Soyedina vallicularia* (Nemouridae) pronotum.

Figure 13.24. *Visoka cataractae* (Nemouridae) submental gills.

Figure 13.25. *Ostrocerca truncata* (Nemouridae) pronotum.

Figure 13.26. *Podmosta decepta* (Nemouridae) pronotum.

Figure 13.27. *Podmosta decepta* (Nemouridae) right front leg.

Figure 13.28. *Prostoia* sp. right front leg.

Figure 13.29. *Shipsa rotunda* (Nemouridae) left front leg.

Figure 13.30. *Paranemoura perfecta* (Nemouridae) right front leg.

Figure 13.31. *Lednia tumana* (Nemouridae) abdominal ventrum.

Figure 13.32. *Isocapnia integra* (Capniidae) left cercus (inside view).

Figure 13.33. *Nemocapnia carolina* (Capniidae) right cercus (outer view).

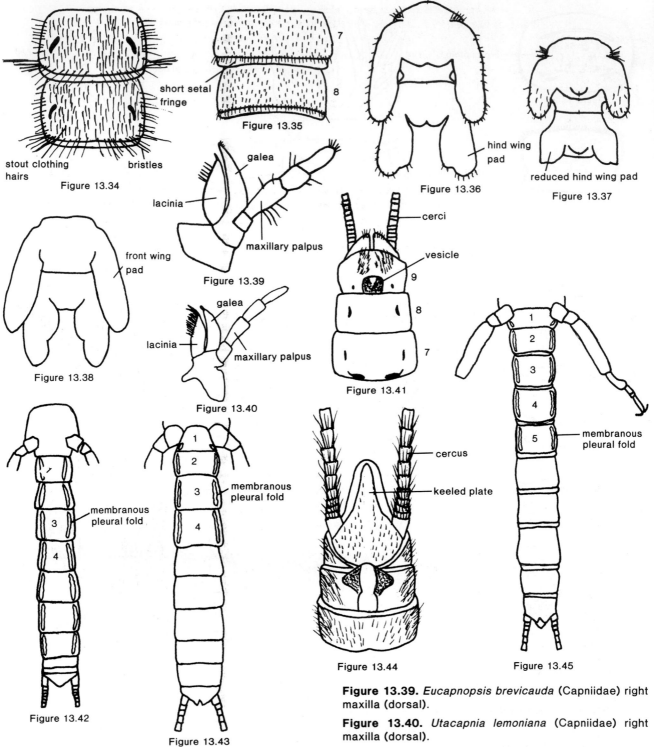

short setal fringe

Figure 13.35

hind wing pad

Figure 13.36

reduced hind wing pad

Figure 13.37

stout clothing hairs   bristles

Figure 13.34

galea

lacinia

maxillary palpus

Figure 13.39

front wing pad

Figure 13.38

galea

lacinia

maxillary palpus

Figure 13.40

cerci

vesicle

9

8

7

Figure 13.41

membranous pleural fold

membranous pleural fold

cercus

keeled plate

membranous pleural fold

Figure 13.42

Figure 13.43

Figure 13.44

Figure 13.45

Figure 13.34. *Paracapnia angulata* (Capniidae) abdominal terga.

Figure 13.35. *Capnia vernalis* (Capniidae) abdominal terga.

Figure 13.36. *Allocapnia* sp. (Capniidae) wing pads.

Figure 13.37. *Allocapnia granulata* (Capniidae) male nymph wing pads.

Figure 13.38. *Capnia vernalis* (Capniidae) wing pads.

Figure 13.39. *Eucapnopsis brevicauda* (Capniidae) right maxilla (dorsal).

Figure 13.40. *Utacapnia lemoniana* (Capniidae) right maxilla (dorsal).

Figure 13.41. *Bolshecapnia spenceri* (Capniidae) male nymph abdominal ventrum.

Figure 13.42. *Perlomyia utahensis* (Leuctridae) abdominal ventrum.

Figure 13.43. *Leuctra sibleyi* (Leuctridae) abdominal ventrum.

Figure 13.44. *Megaleuctra kinkaidi* (Leuctridae) abdominal ventrum.

Figure 13.45. *Despaxia augusta* (Leuctridae) abdominal ventrum.

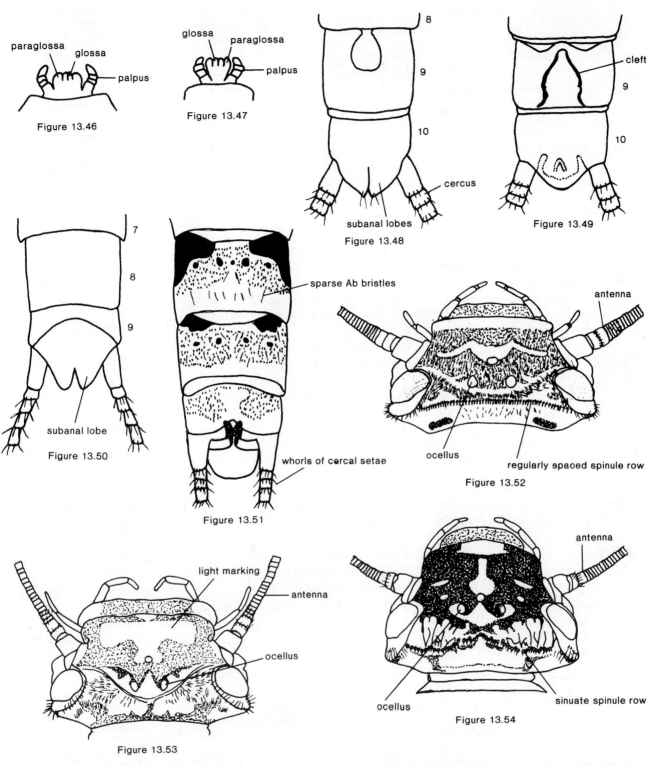

Figure 13.46.

Figure 13.47.

Figure 13.48.

Figure 13.49.

Figure 13.50.

Figure 13.51.

Figure 13.52.

Figure 13.53.

Figure 13.54.

Figure 13.46. *Leuctra sibelyi* (Leuctridae) labium.

Figure 13.47. *Paraleuctra vershina* (Leuotridae) labium.

Figure 13.48. *Zealeuctra claasseni* (Leuctridae) abdominal ventrum.

Figure 13.49. *Zealeuctra claasseni* (Leuctridae) male nymph, abdominal dorsum.

Figure 13.50. *Paraleuctra vershina* (Leuctridae) abdominal dorsum.

Figure 13.51. *Paraleuctra vershina* (Leuctridae) abdominal dorsum.

Figure 13.52. *Claassenia sabulosa* (Perlidae) head.

Figure 13.53. *Eccoptura xanthenes* (Perlidae) head.

Figure 13.54. *Hesperoperla pacifica* (Perlidae) head.

44(43). Two ocelli .... *Neoperla* Needham

44'. Three ocelli 45

45(44') Ab terga with more than 5 intercalary spinules (fig. 13.55) .... *Claassenia* Wu

45'. Ab terga with no more than 4 intercalary spinules 46

46(45'). Posterior spinule fringe of Ab₇ sternum complete (fig. 13.56); cerci without a long
      setal fringe .... *Phasganophora* Klapálek

46'. Posterior spinule fringe of Ab sternum incomplete (fig. 13.57); cerci with at least a
      few long silky setae .... *Paragnetina* Klapálek

47(43'). Occipital spinules in a sinuate, irregularly spaced row, more or less complete
      behind ocelli (fig. 13.54) 48

47'. No distinct occipital spinule row; a few scattered spinules may be present near the
      postocular setal fringe (fig. 13.53) 52

48(47). Ab terga with fewer than 5 or no intercalary spinules .... *Hesperoperla* Banks

48'. Ab terga with more than 5 intercalary spinules 49

49(48'). Pronotum laterally fringed with a complete, close-set row of long setae (fig. 13.58);
      posterior fringe of Ab terga with numerous long setae whose length is three-
      fourths or more the length of Ab segments .... *Attaneuria* Ricker

49'. Pronotum fringed laterally with short setae, not so closely set (fig. 13.59); posterior
      fringe of Ab terga mostly of short setae whose length is about one-fourth the
      length of Ab segments 50

50(49'). Cerci without a dorsal fringe of long silky hairs; Ab of most species speckled with
      dark pigment at bases of intercalary setae .... *Perlesta* Banks

50'. Cerci with prominent dorsal fringe of long silky hairs (fig. 13.60); Ab not speckled 51

51(50'). Dorsum of Th and Ab with a mesal, longitudinal row of long, fine, silky hairs (fig.
      13.61) (best seen in lateral view); Ab₇ sternum usually with incomplete posterior
      fringe .... *Doroneuria* Needham and Claassen

51'. No mesal longitudinal row of silky hairs on Th-Ab dorsum; Ab₇ sternum usually
      with a complete posterior fringe .... *Calineuria* Ricker

52(47'). Postocular fringe reduced to 1–3 long setae (fig. 13.62); eyes set forward on head;
      pronotal fringe of 2–3 setae at corners .... *Perlinella* Banks

52'. Postocular fringe with a close-set row of several thick spinules (fig. 13.53);
      pronotal fringe well developed, consisting of a close-set row of spinules or setae,
      occasionally incomplete laterally 53

53(52'). Two ocelli (fig. 13.63); lateral pronotal fringe complete .... *Anacroneuria* Klapálek

53'. Three ocelli (fig. 13.52–54); lateral pronotal fringe incomplete 54

54(53'). Head with large areas of yellow in front of median ocellus (fig. 13.53) .... *Eccoptura* Klapálek (fig. 13.4g)

54'. Head mostly brown (fig. 13.64), often with yellow, flat, M-shaped mark in front of
      median ocellus 55

55(54'). Cerci with fringe of long, silky setae, at least on basal segments .... *Acroneuria* Pictet

55'. Cerci without basal fringe of silky setae .... *Beloneuria* Needham and Claassen

56(8). Eyes set far forward, head margin behind eye forms a right angle (fig. 13.65);
      body elongate (except *Utaperla* which has ecdysial suture truncate, fig. 13.67,
      and dark colored body) 57

56'. Eyes normally placed, posterolateral angles of head convex (fig. 13.66); ecdysial
      suture Y-shaped; body less elongate 59

57(56). Ecdysial suture truncate (fig. 13.67) .... *Utaperla* Ricker

57'. Ecdysial suture normal, Y-shaped (fig. 13.66) 58

58(57'). Head longer than wide (fig. 13.65); cerci about 0.7 length of Ab .... *Kathroperla* Banks

58'. Head ca. as wide as long; cerci about 0.5 length of Ab .... *Paraperla* Banks

59(56'). Inner margin of hind wing pads nearly parallel to body axis (fig. 13.68); body
      length 5–7 mm .... *Haploperla* Navás (fig. 13.4h)

59'. Inner margins of hind wing pads distinctly divergent from body axis (fig. 13.69) 60

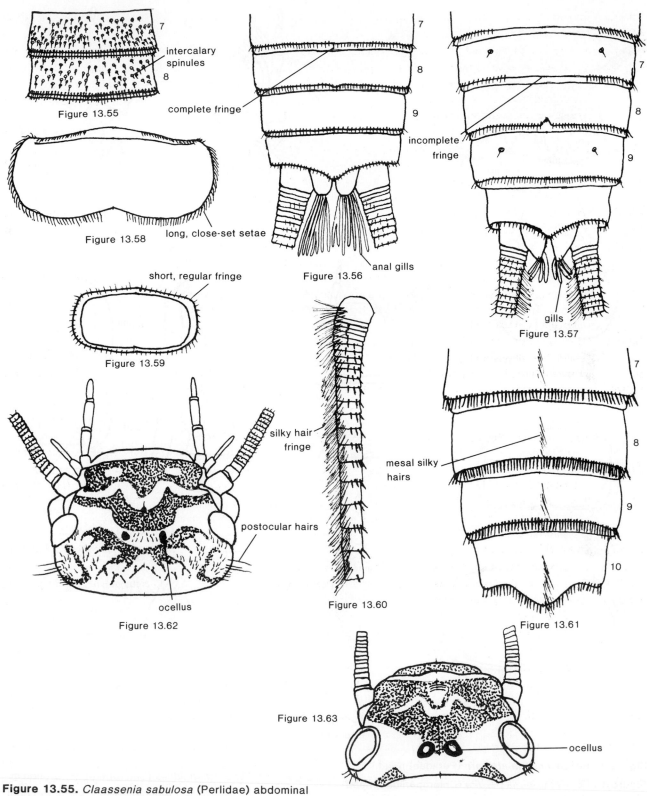

intercalary spinules

complete fringe

Figure 13.55

long, close-set setae

Figure 13.58

short, regular fringe

Figure 13.59

silky hair fringe

postocular hairs

ocellus

Figure 13.62

7
8
9

incomplete fringe

anal gills

Figure 13.56

gills

Figure 13.57

mesal silky hairs

Figure 13.60

Figure 13.61

Figure 13.63

ocellus

Figure 13.55. *Claassenia sabulosa* (Perlidae) abdominal terga.

Figure 13.56. *Phasganophora capitata* (Perlidae) abdominal ventrum.

Figure 13.57. *Paragnetina fumosa* (Perlidae) abdominal ventrum.

Figure 13.58. *Attaneuria ruralis* (Perlidae) pronotum.

Figure 13.59. *Perlesta placida* (Perlidae) pronotum.

Figure 13.60. *Doroneuria baumanni* (Perlidae) basal right cercus (dorsal).

Figure 13.61. *Doroneuria baumanni* (Perlidae) abdominal dorsum.

Figure 13.62. *Perlinella drymo* (Perlidae) head.

Figure 13.63. *Anacroneuria* sp. (Perlidae) head.

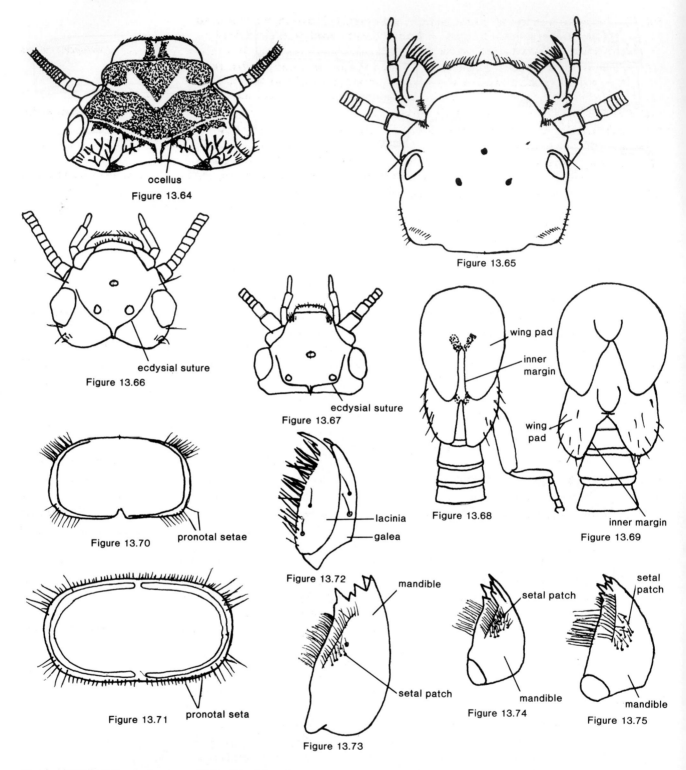

ocellus

Figure 13.64

Figure 13.65

ecdysial suture

Figure 13.66

ecdysial suture

Figure 13.67

wing pad

inner margin

wing pad

Figure 13.68

inner margin

Figure 13.69

pronotal setae

Figure 13.70

lacinia

galea

Figure 13.72

mandible

setal patch

Figure 13.73

setal patch

mandible

Figure 13.74

setal patch

mandible

Figure 13.75

pronotal seta

Figure 13.71

Figure 13.64. *Beloneuria stewarti* (Perlidae) head.

Figure 13.65. *Kathroperla perdita* (Chloroperlidae) head.

Figure 13.66. *Alloperla imbecilla* (Chloroperlidae) head.

Figure 13.67. *Utaperla sopladora* (Chloroperlidae) head.

Figure 13.68. *Haploperla brevis* (Chloroperlidae) wing pads.

Figure 13.69. *Suwallia pallidula* (Chloroperlidae) wing pads.

Figure 13.70. *Alloperla* sp. (Chloroperlidae) pronotum.

Figure 13.71. *Sweltsa fidelis* (Chloroperlidae) pronotum.

Figure 13.72. *Neaviperla forcipata* (Chloroperlidae) right maxilla (dorsal).

Figure 13.73. *Suwallia* sp. (Chloroperlidae) right mandible (dorsal).

Figure 13.74. *Sweltsa fidelis* (Chloroperlidae) right mandible (dorsal).

Figure 13.75. *Triznaka diversa* (Chloroperlidae) right mandible (dorsal).

60(59'). Pronotum with few or no setae on front, and especially hind margins; setae mostly on corners (fig. 13.70); apical 7–10 cercal segments with vertical, feathery fringe of hairs; mature nymphs often green .... ***Alloperla*** Banks

60'. Pronotum with variable setation, but always with some setae along hind margin (fig. 13.71) extending to near midline; no vertical fringe of hairs on apical cercal segments 61

61(60'). Dorsum of Ab with 4 longitudinal stripes .... ***Rasvena*** Ricker

61'. Dorsum of Ab unicolorous except when adult coloration is evident, appearing as median longitudinal band 62

62(61'). Inner, dorsal surface of galea with 2 stout setae (fig. 13.72); modified basal cercal segments of developing adult sometimes distinguishable in mature male nymphs .... ***Neaviperla*** Ricker

62'. Galea without pair of stout setae; mature male nymph with normal basal cercal segments .... ***Suwallia*** Ricker, ***Sweltsa*** Ricker, ***Triznaka*** Ricker (Separations of couplet 62 require mounting of mouth parts. Some Western species of 62' have the following arrangements of setal numbers on right mandible: *Suwallia*, 8 (fig. 13.73); *Sweltsa*, 20–22 (fig. 13.74); *Triznaka*, 15 (fig. 13.75). Eastern and Western *Sweltsa* nymphs and some *Triznaka* are unique with lateral dark depressed clothing hairs near coxae on all thoracic sternae).

63 (8'). Gills absent; Ab usually with dark longitudinal stripes or transverse bands (See also *Cascadoperla* and *Osobenus*, couplets 65 and 71) .... ***Isoperla*** Banks

63'. Submental gills and sometimes other gills present (figs. 13.78–13.80, 13.82) or absent; Ab without longitudinal stripes (except *Cascadoperla* and *Osobenus*) 64

64(63'). Lacinia broad apically, almost quadrate (fig. 13.76) 65

64'. Lacinia narrowed apically (figs. 13.77, 13.90) 66

65(64). Lacinia with apical and subapical teeth, and brush of long, stout hairs and 3 stout spines on the elevated ridge or "shoulder" below subapical teeth (inner margin) (fig. 13.76); Western .... ***Cascadoperla*** Szczytko and Stewart

65'. Lacinia with 12–14 long stout spines on the elevated ridge; median pairs of small light spots on Ab_{1-8}; Eastern .... ***Clioperla*** Needham and Claassen

66(64'). Some combination of gills present on Th 67

66. Gills absent from Th 70

67(66). Lateral, single gills on Ab_{1-7}; double gills on Th_{1-3}; (fig. 13.78) .... ***Oroperla*** Needham

67'. Gills absent from Ab_{1-7} 68

68(67'). Gill combination = submental, cervical, and Th_{1-3} (fig. 13.79); gill-like lateral knobs on Ab_{1-4} pleura; mandibles with strongly serrated cusps .... ***Perlinodes*** Needham and Claassen

68'. Cervical gills absent; submental gills and some simple thoracic gills present 69

69(68'). Single, fingerlike anterolateral gills on Th_{1-3}; submental gills about twice as long as their basal width (fig. 13.80); arms of mesosternal Y-ridge join anterior corners of furcal pits (fig. 13.81) .... ***Megarcys*** Klapálek

69'. Gills present only on Th_{2-3}; submental gills short, about 1.0–1.5 times as long as basal width (fig. 13.8); arms of mesosternal Y-ridge join posterior corners of furcal pits (fig. 13.82) .... ***Setvena*** Illies

70(66'). Arms of mesosternal Y-ridge meet or approach anterior corners of furcal pits (fig. 13.81) 71

70'. Arms of mesosternal Y-ridge meet posterior corners of furcal pits (fig. 13.82), or arms absent (no fork) (fig. 13.83) 74

71(70). Transverse ridge *and* arms of the mesosternal Y-ridge meet anterior corners of the furcal pits; Ab with 2 broad, dark longitudinal bands .... ***Osobenus*** Ricker

71'. Transverse ridge absent from mesosternum 72

72(71'). Terminal tooth of lacinia short, ca. one-fourth as long as whole lacinia, fore femoral hair fringe as wide as width of femur .... ***Frisonia*** Ricker

72'. Terminal tooth of lacinia almost one-half as long as lacinia; fore femoral hair fringe one-half to three-fourths as wide as width of femur (fig. 13.84) 73

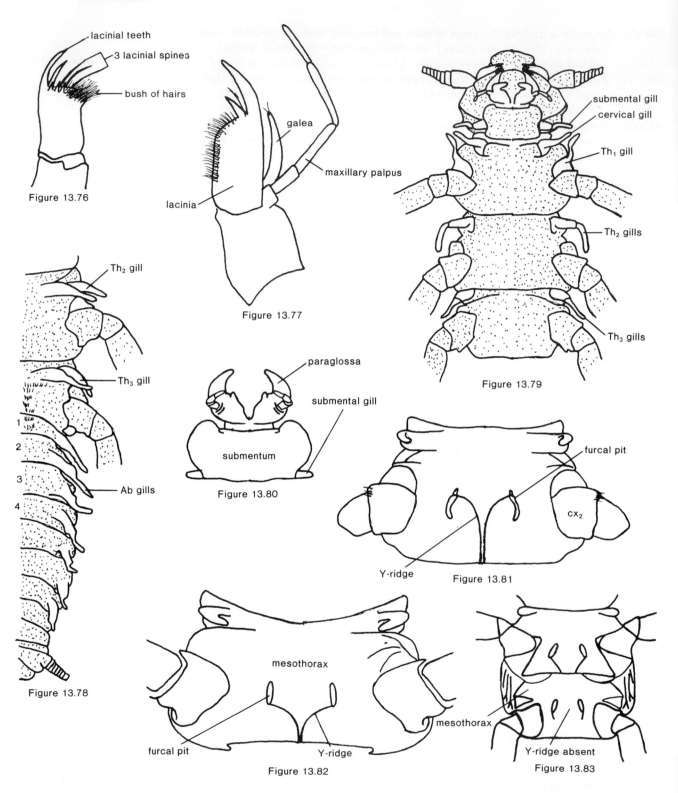

Figure 13.76. *Cascadoperla trictura* (Perlodidae) left maxilla (dorsal).

Figure 13.77. *Isoperla sobria* (Perlodidae) right maxilla (dorsal).

Figure 13.78. *Oroperla barbara* (Perlodidae) left abdomen (ventral).

Figure 13.79. *Perlinodes aurea* (Perlodidae) ventral head, thorax.

Figure 13.80. *Megarcys watertoni* (Perlodidae) labium.

Figure 13.81. *Megarcys watertoni* (Perlodidae) mesoternum.

Figure 13.82. *Setvena bradleyi* (Perlodidae) mesosternum.

Figure 13.83. *Diploperla morgani* (Perlodidae) meso-, metasternum.

73(72'). Arms of mesosternal Y-ridge approach but do not meet anterior corners of furcal pits; only the major outer cusp of left mandible slightly serrated if at all; serrations or denticles usually absent from cusps of right mandible (fig. 13.85) .... *Arcynopteryx* Klapálek

73'. Arms of mesosternal Y-ridge meet anterior corners of furcal pits; serrations (denticles) numerous along inside of the outer cusps of both mandibles (fig. 13.86) .... *Skwala* Ricker (fig. 13.1)

74(70'). Lacinia terminating in a single, major spine (figs. 13.87–13.88); submental gills absent 75

74'. Lacinia with 2 prominent terminal spines (figs. 13.84, 13.90–13.91); submental gills present or absent 77

75(74). Transverse ridge connecting anterior corners of mesosternal furcal pits .... *Rickera* Jewett

75'. Transverse ridge absent from mesosternum 76

76(75'). Maxilla broad at base, abruptly narrowed into a long, terminal spine (fig. 13.87) .... *Remenus* Ricker

76'. Maxilla gradually narrowed from base to terminal spine (fig. 13.88) .... *Kogotus* Ricker

77(74'). Submental gills absent; posterolateral swelling of submentum sometimes fleshy, resembling a short gill (fig. 13.89) 78

77'. Submental gills present, about twice as long as greatest width (fig. 13.80) 81

78(77). Arms of mesosternal ridge pattern separate; no forked Y pattern (fig. 13.83); terminal lacinial spine long, one-half as long as lacinia .... *Diploperla* Needham and Claassen

78'. Arms of mesosternal ridge pattern present, meeting posterior corners of furcal pits (fig. 13.82) 79

79(78'). Stout hairs distributed in a continuous row along inner margin of lacinia (fig. 13.91) .... *Yugus* Ricker*

79'. Stout hairs sparse or absent along the middle one-half of inner margin of lacinia (fig. 13.90) 80

80(79'). Apical lacinial tooth one-half length of lacinia, only 1 or 2 stout hairs near base of subapical tooth; segments of Ab with anterior, transverse dark bands .... *Cultus* Ricker

80'. Apical lacinial tooth one-third length of lacinia, tuft of stout hairs on small knob near base of subapical tooth; Ab with broad lateral longitudinal bands .... *Diura* Billberg

81(77'). Mesosternal ridge pattern with a median, longitudinal ridge connecting fork of Y with transverse ridge (fig. 13.93) .... *Isogenoides* Klapálek

81'. Mesosternum without median longitudinal ridge 82

82(81'). Apical lacinial tooth about one-half length of lacinia; stout hairs sparse or absent along middle one-half of inner margin of lacinia, restricted to near base of subapical tooth and posterior inner margin; apical half of cerci dark brown to black; western United States .... *Pictetiella* Illies

82'. Apical lacinial tooth about one-third length of lacinia; stout hairs distributed continuously along inner lacinial margin; eastern United States 83

83(82'). Abdominal terga uniform brown; distinct single, sinuate row of occipital spinules; slight transverse furrow sometimes evident on mesosternum (fig. 13.92) .... *Malirekus* Ricker

83'. Ab terga with anterior dark transverse bands; occipital spinule row scattered, or an irregular band, 1–3 spinules wide 84

84(83'). Broad, dark transverse band of pigment across head between eyes (fig. 13.94); ventral cusps (1st tooth) of mandible serrate; occipital spinules an irregular band, 1–3 spinules wide .... *Helopicus* Ricker

84'. M-shaped band of dark pigment across head between eyes, with light M-band anterior to it (fig. 13.95); ventral cusps of mandibles unserrated; sparse, scattered occipital spinules .... *Hydroperla* Frison

---

Oconoperla Stark and Stewart (1982) will key here; unlike *Yugus*, nymphs have no prominent femoral hair fringe or complete ventral transverse setal band on the lacinia (Proc. Ent. Soc. Wash. 84:746–752).

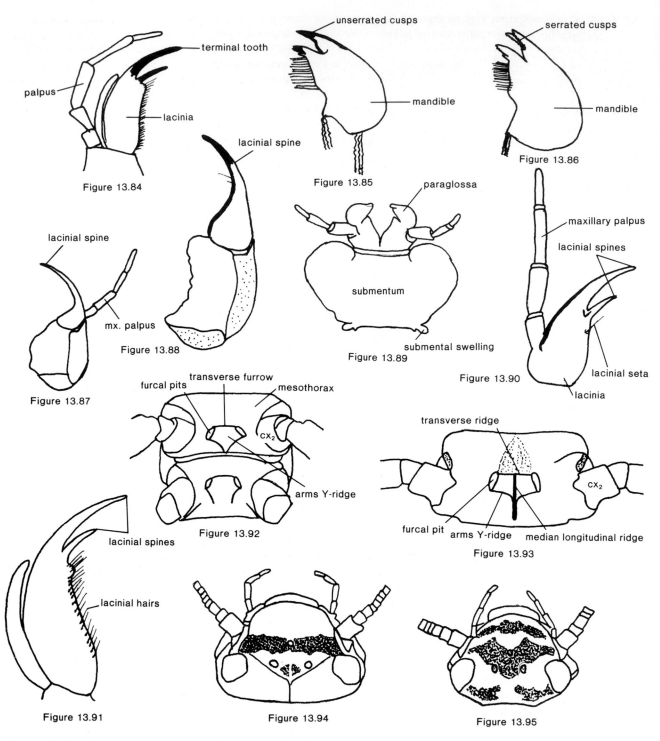

Figure 13.84. *Arcynopteryx compacta* (Perlodidae) left maxilla (dorsal).

Figure 13.85. *Arcynopteryx compacta* (Perlodidae) right mandible (dorsal).

Figure 13.86. *Skwala parallela* (Perlodidae) right mandible (dorsal).

Figure 13.87. *Remenus bilobatus* (Perlodidae) left maxilla (ventral).

Figure 13.88. *Kogotus nonus* (Perlodidae) left maxilla (dorsal).

Figure 13.89. *Diploperla morgani* (Perlodidae) labium.

Figure 13.90. *Cultus aestivalis* (Perlodidae) left maxilla (dorsal).

Figure 13.91. *Yugus bulbosus* (Perlodidae) left maxilla (dorsal).

Figure 13.92. *Malirekus hastatus* (Perlodidae) meso-, metasternum.

Figure 13.93. *Isogenoides zionensis* (Perlodidae) mesosternum.

Figure 13.94. *Helopicus nalatus* (Perlodidae) head.

Figure 13.95. *Hydroperla crosbyi* (Perlodidae) head.

KEY TO FAMILIES AND GENERA OF NORTH AMERICAN PLECOPTERA ADULTS

The following key is tentative and artificial in many respects; nonetheless, it reflects the current state of knowledge about the classification of North American Plecoptera adults. Keys by Jewett (1956) and Hitchcock (1974) are based on a conservative definition of genus. The nomenclature of Illies (1966), followed here, gives generic status to most categories previously considered as subgenera by North American authors. In addition to the classic works of Ricker (1944, 1952), Hitchcock (1974), and Baumann *et al.* (1977), revisions of Baumann (1975), Ricker and Ross (1975), Stark and Gaufin (1976), Stark and Stewart (1981), and others have been used in preparation of this key.

Characters are given to identify genera irrespective of the sex of the specimen whenever possible; however, in many instances males and females must be considered separately. Males are characterized by an elongate abdominal segment 9 (fig. 13.3) and various modifications of the paraprocts, epiproct, cerci, and/or terga into genital hooks and accessory copulatory organs (fig. 13.2). Females have no such structures, their only diagnostic feature being the transformation of sternum 8 into a subgenital plate covering the gonopore (fig. 13.4). The key is based almost exclusively on external characters, but identifications of some females requires an examination of the vagina or eggs.

Adults

1.	Labium with glossae and paraglossae of approximately same length and size and set at same level (figs. 13.7, 13.106–13.107, 13.132)	2
1'.	Labium with glossae much reduced and set below paraglossae (figs. 13.8, 13.181)	7
2(1).	First segment of each tarsus short (fig. 13.96); gill remnants present on the sides of thorax (figs. 13.6, 13.111, 13.118)	3
2'.	First segment of each tarsus longer (figs. 13.97–13.98); no gill remnants on sides of thorax	4
3(2).	Three ocelli; gill remnants on the sides of Ab_{1-2}, or AB_{1-3} (figs. 13.99–13.100); 2 rows of anal crossveins in fore wing (fig. 13.101) ... *PTERONARCYIDAE*	9
3'.	Two ocelli; no gill remnants on sides of abdomen; no rows of anal crossveins (fig. 13.102) ... *PELTOPERLIDAE*	10
4(2').	Second segment of tarsus of approximately same length as first (fig. 13.97) ... *TAENIOPTERYGIDAE*	15
4'.	Second segment of tarsus much shorter than 1st (fig. 13.98)	5
5(4').	Cerci with many segments; in fore wing, 2A simple and unforked; intercubital crossveins few, usually 1–2 (fig. 13.103) ... *CAPNIIDAE*	45
5'.	Cerci 1-segmented; in fore wing, 2A forked; intercubital crossveins numerous, usually 5 or more (figs. 13.104–13.105)	6
6(5').	At rest, wings folded flat over back; terminal segment of labial palpus circular and larger than preceding segment (fig. 13.106); a crossvein in costal space just beyond cord, forming with adjoining veins a X-pattern (fig. 13.104) ... *NEMOURIDAE*	27
6'.	At rest, wings rolled, covering both back and sides of abdomen, giving insect a sticklike appearance; terminal segment of labial palpus more elongate, not much larger than preceding segment (fig. 13.107); no crossvein in costal space beyond cord (fig. 13.105) ... *LEUCTRIDAE*	56
7(1').	Remnants of branched gills on sides of thorax (fig. 13.14); cubito-anal crossvein of fore wing usually reaching anal cell or not distant from it by more than its own length (fig. 13.108) ... *PERLIDAE*	112
7'.	Remnants of branched gills absent; in a few Perlodidae, remnants of single unbranched gills occur on the thorax or elsewhere (figs. 13.176, 13.181); cubito-anal crossvein of fore wing, if present, usually removed from anal cell by at least its own length (figs. 13.109–13.110)	8
8(7').	Fork of 2A of fore wing set in anal cell; hind wing with 5–10 anal veins (fig. 13.109) ... *PERLODIDAE*	62
8'.	Fork of 2A of fore wing set beyond anal cell or absent; hind wing usually with 1–4 anal veins (fig. 13.110) (if 5 or more, either 2A of fore wing forked or hind corners of head angulate; fig. 13.199) ... *CHLOROPERLIDAE**	100

*See Surdick (1981; ref. #2856) for revised key and diagnoses of genera *Bisancora* Surdick, *Plumiperla* Surdick, and *Chloroperla* Newman.

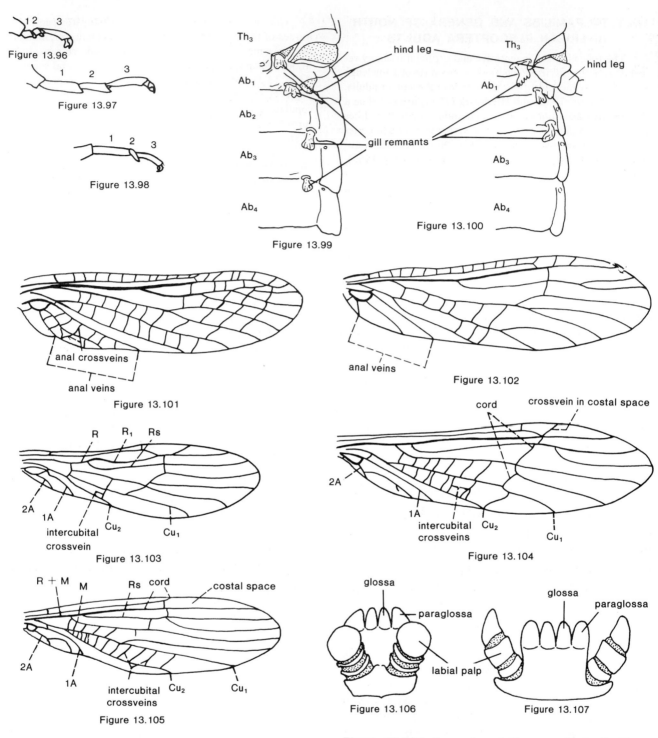

Figure 13.96. Tarsus of *Peltoperla* sp. (Peltoperlidae).

Figure 13.97. Tarsus of *Taeniopteryx* sp. (Taeniopterygidae).

Figure 13.98. Tarsus of *Paracapnia* sp. (Capniidae).

Figure 13.99. Ventral view of metasternum (Th₃) and abdominal sterna 1-4 of *Pteronarcella regularis* (Pteronarcyidae).

Figure 13.100. Ventral view of metasternum (Th₃) and abdominal sterna 1-4 of *Pteronarcys biloba* (Pteronarcyidae).

Figure 13.101. Fore wing of *Pteronarcella badia* (Pteronarcyidae).

Figure 13.102. Fore wing of *Tallaperla maria* (Peltoperlidae).

Figure 13.103. Fore wing of *Capnia* sp. (Capniidae).

Figure 13.104. Fore wing of *Nemoura trispinosa* (Nemouridae).

Figure 13.105. Fore wing of *Leuctra tenuis* (Leuctridae).

Figure 13.106. Labium of *Nemoura trispinosa* (Nemouridae).

Figure 13.107. Labium of *Leuctra tenuis* (Leuctridae).

9(3).   Gill remnants on Ab$_{1-3}$ (fig. 13.99); body length 12–20 mm .... ***Pteronarcella*** Banks

9'.   Gill remnants on Ab$_{1-2}$ (fig. 13.100); body length 23–40 mm. .... ***Pteronarcys*** Newman (including ***Allonarcys*** Needham and Claassen)

10(3').   Gill remnants present on cervix and prothorax (fig. 13.111); male epiproct reduced (fig. 13.112) or absent, and vesicle on sternum 9 wide and oval and set at middle of sternum (fig. 13.113); female with eggs flat or hemispherical 11

10'.   No gill remnants on cervix and prothorax; male epiproct developed into a rod or plate (figs. 13.114, 13.120); if undeveloped, vesicle round or quadrate and set at base of sternum (figs. 13.115–13.116); female with eggs spherical 12

11(10).   Male cerci with 7 segments; female sternum 9 with distinct diagonal sclerotized bars (fig. 13.117) .... ***Yoraperla*** Ricker

11'.   Male cerci with 10 segments; female sternum 9 without such bars .... ***Sierraperla*** Jewett

12(10').   Remnants of supracoxal gills on meso- and metathorax simple; male sternum 9 with vesicle 2 or 3 times as wide as long (fig. 13.113); vagina of female without large central sclerite, though a pair of weak sclerites are present near vaginal opening, and sometimes another near junction of spermathecal duct 13

12'.   Remnants of supracoxal gills on meso- and metathorax double (fig. 13.118); male sternum 9 with vesicle about as wide as long (figs. 13.115–13.116); vagina of female with a well-developed central sclerite (fig. 13.119) 14

13(12).   Eastern species; male epiproct long and pointed; subgenital plate of female reaching about middle of sternum 9; remnants of an infracoxal gill on metathorax (fig. 13.118) .... ***Viehoperla*** Ricker

13'.   Western species; epiproct of male a large crenulate plate (fig. 13.120); subgenital plate of female large, reaching tip of sternum 9; no infracoxal gill .... ***Soliperla*** Ricker

14(12').   Male epiproct developed into a slender rod (fig. 13.114); subgenital plate of female long and notched .... ***Peltoperla*** Needham

14'.   Male epiproct undeveloped (as in fig. 13.112); female subgenital plate short and entire .... ***Tallaperla*** Stark and Stewart

15(4).   Gill scar on inner surface of each coxa (fig. 13.121) .... ***Taeniopteryx*** Pictet

15'.   No such scar 16

16(15').   Males (epiproct and paraprocts complex) 17

16'.   Females (epiproct and paraprocts unmodified) 21

17(16).   Hind margin of sternum 9 asymmetrical (fig. 13.122) .... ***Bolotoperla*** Ricker and Ross

17'.   Sternum 9 symmetrical 18

18(17').   Costal crossveins absent (fig. 13.123); epiproct with 2 prongs (fig. 13.124) .... ***Oemopteryx*** Klapálek

18'.   One–5 costal crossveins (figs. 13.125, 13.128); epiproct with one prong (figs. 13.126–13.127) 19

19(18').   Rs with 3 branches, Cu$_1$ with 4–5 branches (fig. 13.128); tip of epiproct asymmetrical .... ***Doddsia*** Needham and Claassen

19'.   Rs with 2 branches, Cu$_1$ with 2–3 branches (fig. 13.125); tip of epiproct symmetrical (fig. 13.126) 20

20(19').   Hind corners of sternum 9 elevated (fig. 13.126) .... ***Taenionema*** Banks

20'.   Middle of hind margin of sternum 9 elevated, corners low (fig. 13.127) .... ***Strophopteryx*** Frison

21(16').   Costal crossveins absent (figs. 13.123, 13.129) 22

21'.   Costal crossveins present (figs. 13.125, 13.128) 24

22(21).   Crossvein c–r present (fig. 13.129) 23

22'.   Crossvein c–r absent (fig. 13.123) .... ***Oemopteryx*** Klapálek (in part)

23(22).   Western species (California) .... ***Oemopteryx*** Klapálek (in part)

23'.   Eastern species .... ***Bolotoperla*** Ricker and Ross

24(21').   Rs with 3 branches, Cu$_1$ with 4–5 branches (fig. 13.128) .... ***Doddsia*** Needham and Claassen

24'.   Rs with 2 branches, Cu$_1$ with 2–3 branches (fig. 13.125) 25

25(24').   Western species .... ***Taenionema*** Banks (in part)

25'.   Eastern species 26

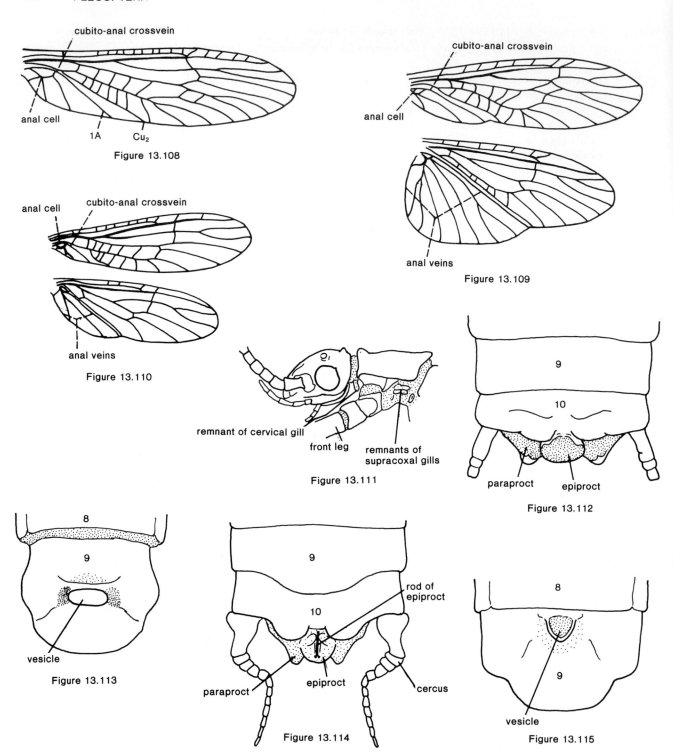

Figure 13.108

Figure 13.109

Figure 13.110

Figure 13.111

Figure 13.112

Figure 13.113

Figure 13.114

Figure 13.115

Figure 13.108. Fore wing of *Paragnetina media* (Perlidae).

Figure 13.109. Wings of *Isoperla frisoni* (Perlodidae).

Figure 13.110. Wings of *Sweltsa onkos* (Chloroperlidae).

Figure 13.111. Side view of head and prothorax of *Yoraperla brevis* (Peltoperlidae).

Figure 13.112. Dorsal view of terminal abdominal segments of male *Yoraperla brevis* (Peltoperlidae).

Figure 13.113. Ventral view of abdominal sternum 9 of male *Yoraperla brevis* (Peltoperlidae).

Figure 13.114. Dorsal view of terminal abdominal segments of *Peltoperla arcuata* (Peltoperlidae).

Figure 13.115. Abdominal sternum 9 of male *Peltoperla arcuata* (Peltoperlidae).

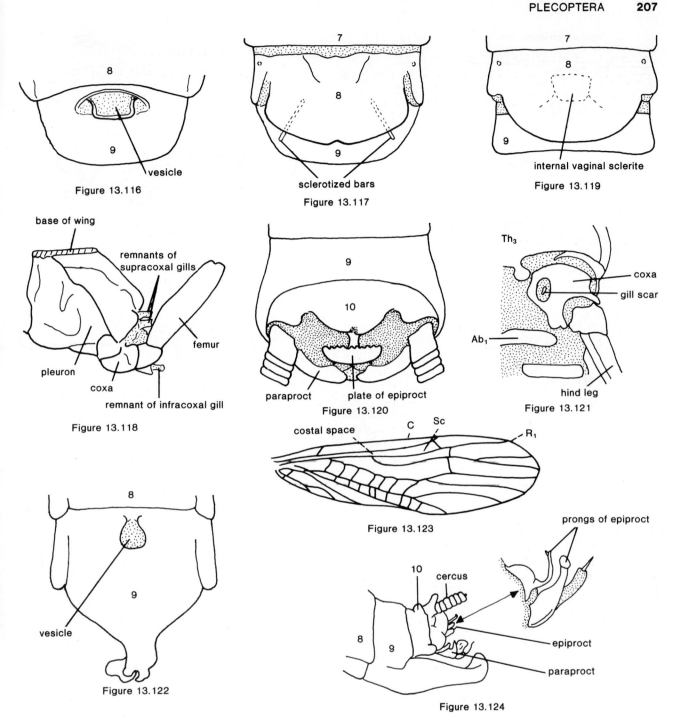

Figure 13.116

Figure 13.117

Figure 13.119

Figure 13.118

Figure 13.120

Figure 13.121

Figure 13.123

Figure 13.122

Figure 13.124

Figure 13.116. Abdominal sternum 9 of male *Tallaperla maria* (Peltoperlidae).

Figure 13.117. Abdominal sterna 8 and 9 of female *Yoraperla brevis* (Peltoperlidae).

Figure 13.118. Side view of Th$_3$ of *Tallaperla maria* (Peltoperlidae).

Figure 13.119. Subgenital plate of female *Peltoperla arcuata* (Peltoperlidae).

Figure 13.120. Dorsal view of terminal abdominal segments of *Soliperla* sp. (Peltoperlidae).

Figure 13.121. Ventral view of Th$_3$ of *Taeniopteryx* sp. (Taeniopterygidae).

Figure 13.122. Abdominal sternum 9 of male *Bolotoperla rossi* (Taeniopterygidae)

Figure 13.123. Fore wing of *Oemopteryx glacialis* (Taeniopterygidae).

Figure 13.124. Side view of terminal abdominal segments of *Oemopteryx glacialis* (Taeniopterygidae). Details of the epiproct.

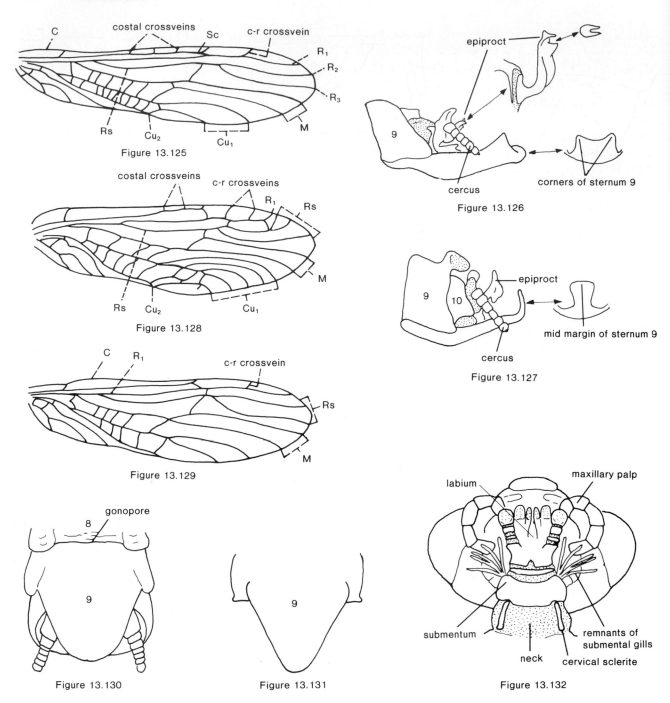

Figure 13.125

Figure 13.126

Figure 13.128

Figure 13.127

Figure 13.129

Figure 13.130

Figure 13.131

Figure 13.132

Figure 13.125. Fore wing of *Taenionema oregonense* (Taeniopterygidae).

Figure 13.126. Side view of terminal abdominal segments of *Taenionema oregonense* (Taeniopterygidae). Details of epiproct; hind view of sternum 9.

Figure 13.127. Side view of terminal abdominal segments of *Strophopteryx fasciata* (Taeniopterygidae). Details of epiproct; hind view of sternum 9.

Figure 13.128. Fore wing of *Doddsia occidentalis* (Taeniopterygidae).

Figure 13.129. Fore wing of *Bolotoperla rossi* (Taeniopterygidae).

Figure 13.130. Sternum 9 of female *Taenionema pacificum* (Taeniopterygidae).

Figure 13.131. Sternum 9 of female *Strophopteryx* sp. (Taeniopterygidae).

Figure 13.132. Ventral view of the head of *Visoka cataractae* (Nemouridae).

26(25').	Sternum 9 subtriangular or narrower (fig. 13.131). .... *Strophopteryx* Frison
26'.	Sternum 9 wider, more rounded (fig. 13.130) .... *Taenionema* Banks (in part)
27(6).	Gill remnants on submentum or cervix (figs. 13.18–13.20, 13.24, 13.132–13.134) 28
27'.	No gill remnants 32
28(27).	Gill remnants on cervix (figs. 13.18–13.20, 13.133–13.134) 29
28'.	Gill remnants on submentum (figs. 13.24, 13.132) .... *Visoka* Ricker
29(28).	Each gill unbranched (figs. 13.19, 13.133) .... *Zapada* Ricker (in part)
29'.	Each gill divided into 3 or more branches (figs. 13.18, 13.20, 13.134) 30
30(29').	Each gill composed of 3–4 branches; male paraprocts with 2 lobes (fig. 13.135); female sternum 7 covering most of sternum 8 (fig. 13.147) .... *Zapada* Ricker (in part)
30'.	Each gill composed of 5–18 branches (figs. 13.18, 13.20, 13.134); male paraprocts with 3 lobes (fig. 13.136); female sternum 7 shorter (figs. 13.137–13.138) 31
31(30').	All gills divided down to gill base (fig. 13.20); male cerci unmodified; female sternum 7 broadly rounded (fig. 13.137) .... *Amphinemura* Ris
31'.	Gill branches arising at different levels (fig. 13.18); male cerci with dorsal lobe at base (fig. 13.139); female sternum 7 forming a nipplelike projection (fig. 13.138) .... *Malenka* Ricker
32(27')	Veins A1 and A2 joined near margin in fore wing (fig. 13.140) .... *Soyedina* Ricker
32'.	Veins A1 and A2 separate (figs. 13.104, 13.141) 33
33(32')	Terminal costal crossvein joining Sc (fig. 13.141) .... *Paranemoura* Needham and Claassen
33'	Terminal crossvein joining R (fig. 13.104) 34
34(33')	Males (epiproct and paraprocts modified) 35
34'.	Females (epiproct and paraprocts not modified) 40
35(34)	Cerci sclerotized or enlarged (figs. 13.142–13.143) 36
35'.	Cerci membranous, unmodified (figs. 13.144, 13.145, 13.146) 37
36(35).	Cerci with spines (fig. 13.142) .... *Nemoura* Latreille
36'.	Cerci without spines, but elongated and curved (fig. 13.143) .... *Ostrocerca* Ricker
37(35').	Sternum 9 without vesicle .... *Lednia* Ricker
37'.	Sternum 9 with vesicle (figs. 13.135–13.136, 13.144–13.146) 38
38(37').	Tergum 10 produced into 2 large lobes covering cerci (figs. 13.144) .... *Shipsa* Ricker
38'.	Lobes of tergum 10, if produced, not so large (fig. 13.145) 39
39(38').	Epiproct long and simple (fig. 13.146) .... *Prostoia* Ricker
39'.	Epiproct short and complex (fig. 13.145) .... *Podmosta* Ricker
40(34').	Sternum 7 large and extending over sternum 8 (fig. 13.147) .... *Nemoura* Latreille
40'.	Sternum 7 short or unmodified 41
41(40')	Sternum 8 extending over sternum 9 as a distinct subgenital plate (figs. 13.148–13.149) 42
41'.	Sternum 8 not extending over sternum 9, though its margin may be sclerotized (figs. 13.150–13.152) 43
42(41).	Sternum 8 small (fig. 13.148) .... *Shipsa* Ricker
42'.	Sternum 8 large; sternum 7 often with a small nipplelike projection (fig. 13.149) .... *Ostrocerca* Ricker
43(41').	Sternum 8 with a distinct median sclerotized patch (figs. 13.151–13.152); wings unmarked 44
43'.	Sternum 8 unsclerotized except at margin (fig. 13.150); wings distinctly banded .... *Prostoia* Ricker
44(43).	Sternum 8 with lateral sclerotized patches in addition to the median sclerotization (fig. 13.151) .... *Lednia* Ricker
44'.	Sternum 8 with only median sclerotization (fig. 13.152) .... *Podmosta* Ricker
45(5).	Wings present 48
45'.	Wings absent 46
46(45').	Eastern species .... *Allocapnia* Claassen
46'.	Western species 47

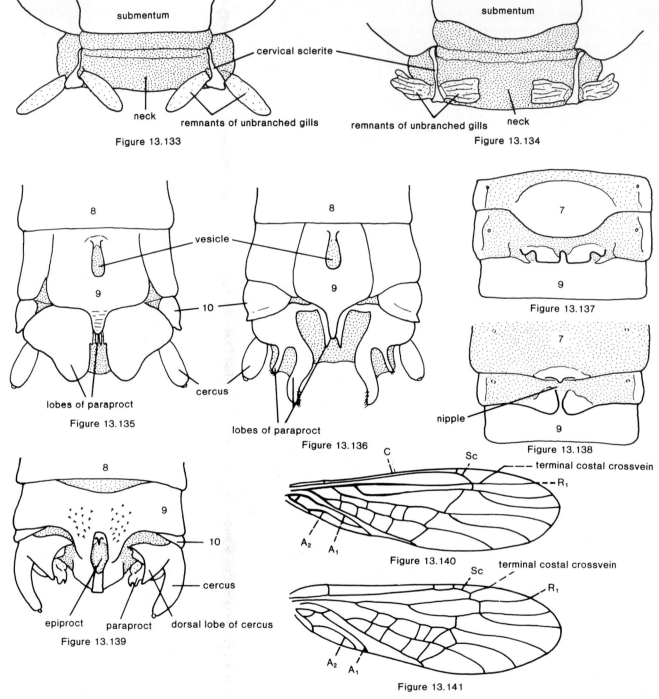

Figure 13.133

Figure 13.134

Figure 13.135

Figure 13.136

Figure 13.137

Figure 13.138

Figure 13.139

Figure 13.140

Figure 13.141

Figure 13.133. Ventral view of neck region of *Zapada* sp. (Nemouridae).

Figure 13.134. Ventral view of neck region of *Amphinemura delosa* (Nemouridae).

Figure 13.135. Ventral view of terminal abdominal segments of male *Zapada* sp. (Nemouridae).

Figure 13.136. Ventral view of terminal abdominal segments of male *Amphinemura delosa* (Nemouridae).

Figure 13.137. Subgenital plate of female *Amphinemura delosa* (Nemouridae).

Figure 13.138. Subgenital plate of female *Malenka* sp. (Nemouridae).

Figure 13.139. Dorsal view of terminal abdominal segments of male *Malenka* sp. (Nemouridae).

Figure 13.140. Fore wing of *Soyedina producta* (Nemouridae).

Figure 13.141. Fore wing of *Paranemoura perfecta* (Nemouridae).

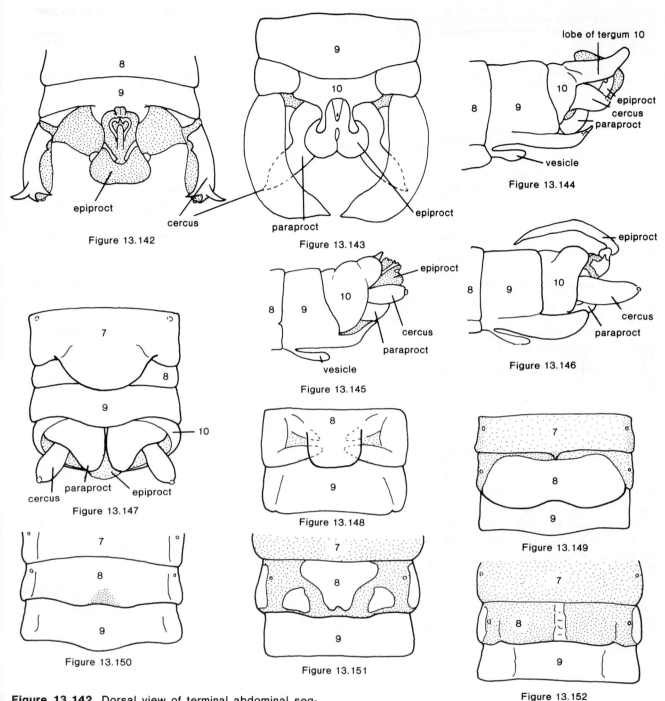

Figure 13.142. Dorsal view of terminal abdominal segments of male *Nemoura trispinosa* (Nemouridae).

Figure 13.143. Dorsal view of terminal abdominal segments of male *Ostrocerca dimicki* (Nemouridae).

Figure 13.144. Side view of terminal abdominal segments of *Shipsa rotunda* (Nemouridae).

Figure 13.145. Side view of terminal abdominal segments of male *Podmosta macdunnoughi* (Nemouridae).

Figure 13.146. Side view of terminal abdominal segments of male *Prostoia besametsa* (Nemouridae).

Figure 13.147. Ventral view of terminal abdominal segments of female *Nemoura trispinosa* (Nemouridae).

Figure 13.148. Subgenital plate of female *Shipsa rotunda* (Nemouridae).

Figure 13.149. Subgenital plate of female *Ostrocerca albidipennis* (Nemouridae).

Figure 13.150. Subgenital plate of female *Prostoia besametsa* (Nemouridae).

Figure 13.151. Subgenital plate of female *Lednia tumana* (Nemouridae).

Figure 13.152. Subgenital plate of female *Podmosta macdunnoughi* (Nemouridae).

47(46') Postfurcasternal plates of mesosternum fused to furcasternum (fig. 13.153) .... *Isocapnia* Banks

47'. Postfurcasternal plates free (fig. 13.154) 50

48(45). R₁ of fore wing curved cephalad just beyond origin of Rs (fig. 13.103) 49

48'. R₁ of fore wing straight at this point (fig. 13.155) 52

49(48). Sternum 9 of male with vesicle (fig. 13.156); male epiproct with lateral hooks (fig. 13.156); sternum 8 of female often produced into a subgenital plate which extends over sternum 9 (fig. 13.157); body length of female 9 mm or more .... *Bolshecapnia* Ricker

49'. Sternum 9 of male without vesicle; if vesicle present, male epiproct without lateral hooks; sternum 8 of female usually not produced over sternum 9; if produced, marked with a distinct dark pattern (fig. 13.158); size of female smaller 50

50(47',49'). Epiproct of male divided into 2 slender processes, upper process forked at tip (fig. 13.159); female sternum 8 with a striking color pattern, its margin usually notched (fig. 13.158) .... *Utacapnia* Nebeker and Gaufin

50'. Epiproct of male usually simple (fig. 13.160); if not, processes are short, or tip of upper process not forked; female sternum 8 not as above 51

51(50'). Epiproct of male simple, terminated by a slender spine, abdominal terga unmodified (fig. 13.160); female sternum 8 little produced or produced into a short point (fig. 13.161) .... *Mesocapnia* Rauser

51'. Epiproct of male variable; if simple, either not ending in a slender spine, or 1 or more abdominal terga with knobs or humps; female sternum 8 variable (Note: females not satisfactorily separable from *Mesocapnia*). .... *Capnia* Pictet

52(48'). Cerci with fewer than 11 segments 53

52'. Cerci with more than 11 segments 54

53(52). Eastern species; A₁ of fore wing sharply bent just beyond anal cell (fig. 13.162) .... *Nemocapnia* Banks

53'. Western species; A₁ of fore wing straight (fig. 13.155) .... *Eucapnopsis* Okamoto

54(52'). Anal lobe of hind wing nearly as large as rest of wing (fig. 13.168) .... *Allocapnia* Claassen

54'. Anal lobe much smaller 55

55(54'). Zero–3 costal crossveins in fore wing (fig. 13.163) .... *Paracapnia* Hanson

55'. Five–6 costal crossveins in fore wing (fig. 13.164) .... *Isocapnia* Banks

56(6'). Hind wing with 6 anal veins (fig. 13.165) .... *Megaleuctra* Neave

56'. Hind wing with 3 anal veins (fig. 13.166–13.167) 57

57(56'). Rs and M arising at same point or close together on R in fore wing (fig. 13.169) .... *Perlomyia* Banks

57'. Rs and M arising separately from R in fore wing (fig. 13.105) 58

58(56'). m-cu joining Cu beyond fork of Cu in hind wing (fig. 13.166) 59

58'. m-cu joining Cu before fork in hind wing (fig. 13.167) 60

59(58). Male tergum 9 entire (fig. 13.171); female abdomen sclerotized dorsally .... *Paraleuctra* Hanson

59'. Male tergum 9 deeply cleft (fig. 13.170); female abdomen membranous dorsally .... *Zealeuctra* Ricker

60(58'). Cerci of male long; 2 hooklike processes arising from sides of epiproct (fig. 13.172); female abdomen with sclerotized mid-dorsal stripe .... *Moselia* Ricker

60'. Cerci of male short, no hooklike processes on epiproct (fig. 13.173); female abdomen membranous dorsally 61

61(60'). Eastern species; sternum 9 of male with vesicle; female sternum 8 produced into a bilobed plate reaching over sternum 9 (fig. 13.174) .... *Leuctra* Stephens

61'. Western species; sternum 9 of male without vesicle (fig. 13.173); female sternum 8 not produced posteriorly, shallowly excavated (fig. 13.175) .... *Despaxia* Ricker

62(8). Male tergum 10 usually deeply cleft (figs. 13.182–13.183, 13.185–13.188); when entire, paraprocts extended as long, erect half cylinders (fig. 13.184); often with gill remnants on submentum, cervix, thorax, or abdomen (figs. 13.176, 13.181); arms of mesoscutal ridge leading to front end (fig. 13.177) or hind end of furcal pits (figs. 13.178–13.179), or absent (fig. 13.180); sometimes with supplementary crossveins in R₁–Rs space (fig. 13.2); pronotum with narrow, median, light stripe, margins of disk usually dark (fig. 13.2) .... Perlodinae 63

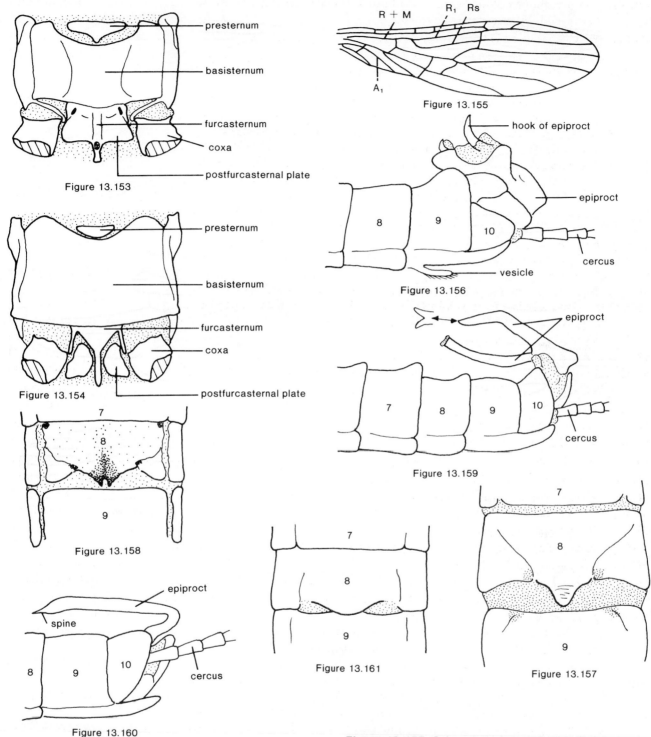

Figure 13.153

Figure 13.154

Figure 13.155

Figure 13.156

Figure 13.158

Figure 13.159

Figure 13.161

Figure 13.157

Figure 13.160

Figure 13.153. Ventral view of mesosternum of *Isocapnia agassizi* (Capniidae).

Figure 13.154. Ventral view of mesosternum of *Capnia* sp. (Capniidae).

Figure 13.155. Fore wing of *Eucapnopsis brevicauda* (Capniidae).

Figure 13.156. Side view of terminal abdominal segments of male *Bolshecapnia spenceri* (Capniidae).

Figure 13.157. Subgenital plate of female *Bolshecapnia spenceri* (Capniidae).

Figure 13.158. Subgenital plate of female *Utacapnia labradora* (Capniidae).

Figure 13.159. Side view of terminal abdominal segments of male *Utacapnia labradora* (Capniidae).

Figure 13.160. Side view of terminal abdominal segments of male *Mesocapnia frisoni* (Capniidae).

Figure 13.161. Subgenital plate of female *Mesocapnia frisoni* (Capniidae).

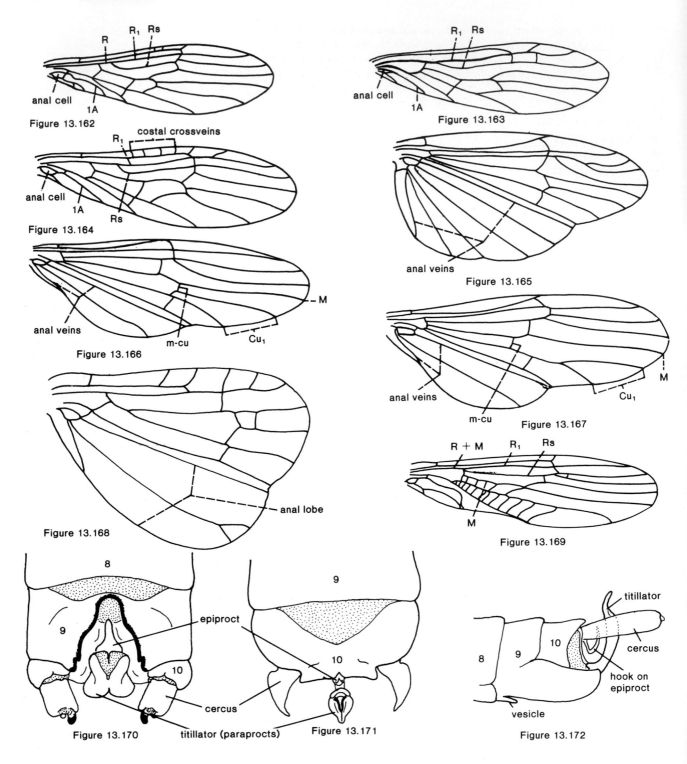

Figure 13.162

Figure 13.163

Figure 13.164

Figure 13.165

Figure 13.166

Figure 13.167

Figure 13.168

Figure 13.169

Figure 13.170

Figure 13.171

Figure 13.172

Figure 13.162. Fore wing of *Nemocapnia carolina* (Capniidae).

Figure 13.163. Fore wing of *Paracapnia opis* (Capniidae).

Figure 13.164. Fore wing of *Isocapnia agassizi* (Capniidae).

Figure 13.165. Hind wing of *Megaleuctra* sp. (Leuctridae).

Figure 13.166. Hind wing of *Paraleuctra* sp. (Leuctridae).

Figure 13.167. Hind wing of *Leuctra* sp. (Leuctridae).

Figure 13.168. Hind wing of *Allocapnia granulata* (Capniidae).

Figure 13.169. Fore wing of *Perlomyia collaris* (Leuctridae).

Figure 13.170. Dorsal view of terminal abdominal segments of male *Zealeuctra hitei* (Leuctridae).

Figure 13.171. Dorsal view of terminal abdominal segments of male *Paraleuctra occidentalis* (Leuctridae).

Figure 13.172. Side view of terminal abdominal segments of male *Moselia infuscata* (Leuctridae).

62'.   Male tergum 10 entire, paraprocts unmodified or transformed into recurved hooks or knobs (fig. 13.196); cleft, if present, shallow or narrow (fig. 13.195); no gill remnants; arms of mesoscutal ridge leading to hind end of furcal pits (fig. 13.178); no supplementary veins in R_1–Rs space (fig. 13.109), though rarely in Rs–M space; pronotal light stripe wider, margins of disk usually light .... Isoperlinae 93

63(62).   Gill remnants on abdominal segments 1–7 (fig. 13.78) .... ***Oroperla*** Needham

63'.   No such gill remnants 64

64(63').   Gill remnants on the thorax (fig. 13.176) 65

64'.   No gill remnants on the thorax 67

65(64).   Gill remnants on all 3 thoracic segments (fig. 13. 176) 66

65'.   Gill remnants only on meso- and metathorax .... ***Setvena*** Illies

66(65).   Gill remnants on the cervix (fig. 13.176) .... ***Perlinodes*** Needham and Claassen

66'.   No gill remnants on the cervix .... ***Megarcys*** Klapálek

67(64').   Arms of mesosternal ridge lead to front end of furcal pits (fig. 13.177) 68

67'.   Arms of mesosternal ridge lead to hind end of furcal pits (figs. 13.178–13.179), or arms absent (fig. 13.180) 72

68(67).   An irregular network of supplementary crossveins in apical area of wings (fig. 13.2) 69

68'.   This network absent (fig. 13.109) 71

69(68).   Transverse ridge present on mesosternum (figs. 13.178–13.179) .... ***Frisonia*** Ricker

69'.   Transverse ridge absent (fig. 13.177) 70

70(69').   Male epiproct blunt (fig. 13.2); lateral stylets present; inhabits temperate zone .... ***Skwala*** Ricker

70'.   Male epiproct a long needlelike structure; inhabits arctic and alpine zones .... ***Arcynopteryx*** Klapálek

71(68').   Wings dark .... ***Chernokrilus*** Ricker (in part)

71'.   Wings pale .... ***Osobenus*** Ricker

72(67').   Median ridge present between arms of mesosternal ridge (fig. 13.179) .... ***Isogenoides*** Klapálek

72'.   Median ridge absent (figs. 13.178, 13.180) 73

73(72').   Submental gills long, at least twice as long as wide (fig. 13.181) 74

73'.   Submental gills shorter (figs. 13.80, 13.89) or absent 75

74(73).   Male epiproct with lateral stylets (fig. 13.182); no lobes (vesicles) on sternum 7 and sternum 8; female subgenital plate reaching at most middle of sternum 9 .... ***Hydroperla*** Frison

74'.   Male epiproct without lateral stylets (fig. 13.183); lobes on sternum 7 and sternum 8 marked at least with light pigment; female subgenital plate reaching beyond the middle of sternum 9 .... ***Helopicus*** Ricker

75(73').   Lateral arms of mesosternal ridge absent (fig. 13.180) .... ***Diploperla*** Needham and Claassen

75'.   Lateral arms of mesosternal ridge present (fig. 13.178) 76

76(75').   Males 77

76'.   Females 84

77(76).   Tergum 10 cleft; epiproct prominent (figs. 13.185–13.188) 78

77'.   Tergum 10 entire; epiproct undeveloped (fig. 13.184) .... ***Diura*** Billberg

78(77).   Lateral stylets present on epiproct (figs. 13.186–13.187) 79

78'.   No lateral stylets on epiproct (figs. 13.185, 13.188) 81

79(78).   Lateral stylets of epiproct slender and acute (fig. 13.186) .... ***Cultus*** Ricker

79'.   Lateral stylets hooked (fig. 13.187) or with a rounded tip 80*

80(79').   Lateral stylets hooked at tip (fig. 13.187) .... ***Malirekus*** Ricker

80'.   Lateral stylets with rounded tips .... ***Chernokrilus*** Ricker

81(78')   Tip of epiproct with coiled inner band (fig. 13.185) .... ***Kogotus*** Ricker

81'.   Epiproct without coiled inner band 82

*****Oconoperla** Stark and Stewart (1982) will key here; lateral stylets truncate (Proc. Ent. Soc. Wash. 84:746–752).

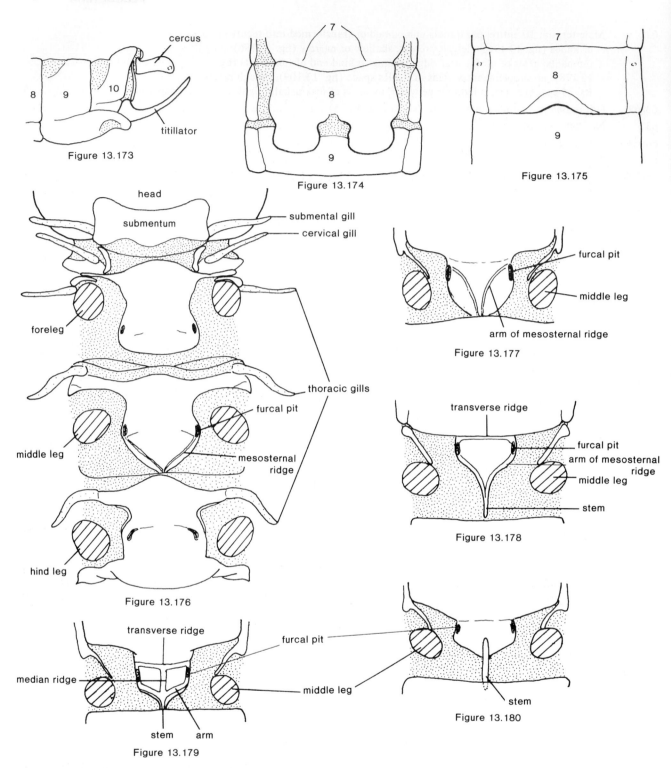

Figure 13.173. Side view of terminal abdominal segments of male *Despaxia augusta* (Leuctridae).

Figure 13.174. Subgenital plate of female *Leuctra tenuis* (Leuctridae).

Figure 13.175. Subgenital plate of female *Despaxia augusta* (Leuctridae).

Figure 13.176. Ventral view of neck and thorax of *Perlinodes aurea* (Perlodidae).

Figure 13.177. Mesosternum of *Skwala curvata* (Perlodidae).

Figure 13.178. Mesosternum of *Clioperla clio* (Perlodidae).

Figure 13.179. Mesosternum of *Isogenoides doratus* (Perlodidae).

Figure 13.180. Mesosternum of *Diploperla duplicata* (Perlodidae).

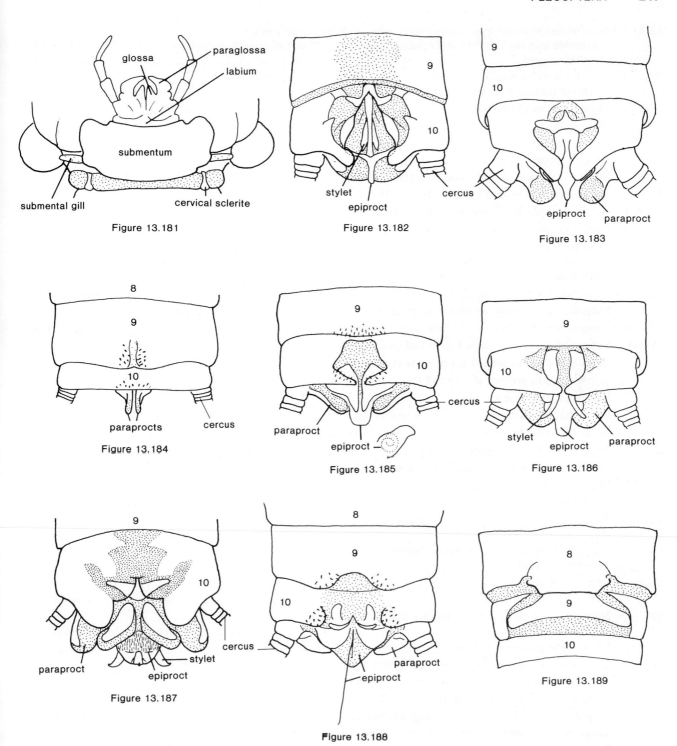

Figure 13.181

Figure 13.182

Figure 13.183

Figure 13.184

Figure 13.185

Figure 13.186

Figure 13.187

Figure 13.188

Figure 13.189

Figure 13.181. Submentum and labium of *Helopicus subvarians* (Perlodidae).

Figure 13.182. Dorsal view of terminal abdominal segments of male *Hydroperla crosbyi* (Perlodidae).

Figure 13.183. Dorsal view of terminal abdominal segments of male *Helopicus subvarians* (Perlodidae).

Figure 13.184. Dorsal view of terminal abdominal segments of male *Diura knowltoni* (Perlodidae).

Figure 13.185. Dorsal view of terminal abdominal segments of male *Kogotus modestus* (Perlodidae).

Figure 13.186. Dorsal view of terminal abdominal segments of male *Cultus decisus* (Perlodidae).

Figure 13.187. Dorsal view of terminal abdominal segments of male *Malirekus hastatus* (Perlodidae).

Figure 13.188. Dorsal view of terminal abdominal segments of male *Remenus bilobatus* (Perlodidae).

Figure 13.189. Subgenital plate of female *Diura knowltoni* (Perlodidae).

82(81'). No crossvein in costal space beyond cord; epiproct of male ending in a long
eversible lash (fig. 13.188); lobes (vesicles) on sternum 7 and sternum 8 equally
well developed .... ***Remenus*** Ricker

82'. One–3 crossveins in costal space beyond cord (fig. 13.190); epiproct without lash;
lobe on sternum 8 much smaller than on sternum 7 or absent 83

83(82'). Eastern species (Appalachian) .... ***Yugus*** Ricker

83'. Western species .... ***Pictetiella*** Illies

84(76'). Eastern species 89

84'. Western species 85

85(84'). Sternum 8 forming a short subgenital plate (fig. 13.189) .... ***Diura*** Billberg

85'. Subgenital plate larger (figs. 13.191–13.193) 86

86(85'). Subgenital plate large covering most of sternum 9 (fig. 13.191) .... ***Pictetiella*** Illies

86'. Subgenital plate smaller (figs. 13.192–13.193) 87

87(86'). Color pale, yellowish or brownish; no crossveins in costal space beyond cord (fig.
13.109); wings pale; submental gills absent 88

87'. Color dark; a few crossveins in costal space beyond cord (fig. 13.190); wings dark;
submental gills present, albeit small .... ***Chernokrilus*** Ricker (in part)

88(87). Subgenital plate nearly as wide as segment at base (fig. 13.192) .... ***Kogotus*** Ricker

88'. Subgenital plate only about 3/4 the width of sternum 8 at base (fig. 13.193) .... ***Cultus*** Ricker

89(84). Subgenital plate on sternum 8 short and truncate (fig. 13.189) .... ***Diura*** Billberg

89'. Subgenital plate larger and not truncate (fig. 13.194) 90

90(89'). Submental gills present, albeit small (figs. 13.80, 13.89) 91

90'. Submental gills absent 92

91(70). Subgenital plate evenly rounded, small species, less than 15 mm .... ***Remenus*** Ricker

91'. Subgenital plate broadly excavated (fig. 13.194), larger species, more than 20 mm .... ***Malirekus*** Ricker

92(90'). No crossvein in costal space beyond cord (fig. 13.109) .... ***Cultus*** Ricker

92'. One–3 crossveins in costal space beyond cord (fig. 13.190) .... ***Yugus*** Ricker

93(62'). Males 94

93'. Females 98

94(93). Tergum 10 partially cleft or slightly excavated with small hooks on each side of
the cleft (fig. 13.195) 95

94'. Tergum 10 usually entire, no hooks developed from hind margin of tergum (figs.
13.196, 13.197) 96

95(94). Ventral lobe present on sternum 8 (fig. 13.200); epiproct present but largely
membranous .... ***Calliperla*** Banks

95'. No ventral lobe on abdominal sternites; epiproct undeveloped (fig.
13.195) .... ***Cascadoperla*** Szczytko and Stewart

96(94'). Ventral lobe on sternum 7 only .... ***Rickera*** Jewett

96'. Ventral lobe present usually only on sternum 8 (fig. 13.200); in some species, there
is no lobe, and in one, therre is an extra lobe on sternum 7 97

97(96'). Tergum 10 with elevated ridges on its hind margin (figs. 13.197) .... ***Clioperla*** Needham and Claassen

97'. Tergum 10 without elevated ridges (fig. 13.196) .... ***Isoperla*** Banks

98(93'). Subgenital plate produced only as a small nipple on hind margin of sternum
8 .... ***Cascadoperla*** Szczytko and Stewart

98'. Subgenital plate larger 99

99(98'). Subgenital plate large covering most of sternum 9 .... ***Rickera*** Jewett

99'. Subgenital plate otherwise, smaller .... ***Isoperla*** Banks, ***Calliperla*** Banks, ***Clioperla*** Needham and Claassen

100(8'). Eyes set far forward on the sides of the head; hind corners of head rather angulate
(figs. 13.65, 13.201) 101

100'. Eyes set in normal position, hind corners of head rounded (fig. 13.2) 102

101(100). Head longer than wide (fig. 13.201) .... ***Kathroperla*** Banks

101'. Head as long as wide .... ***Paraperla*** Banks

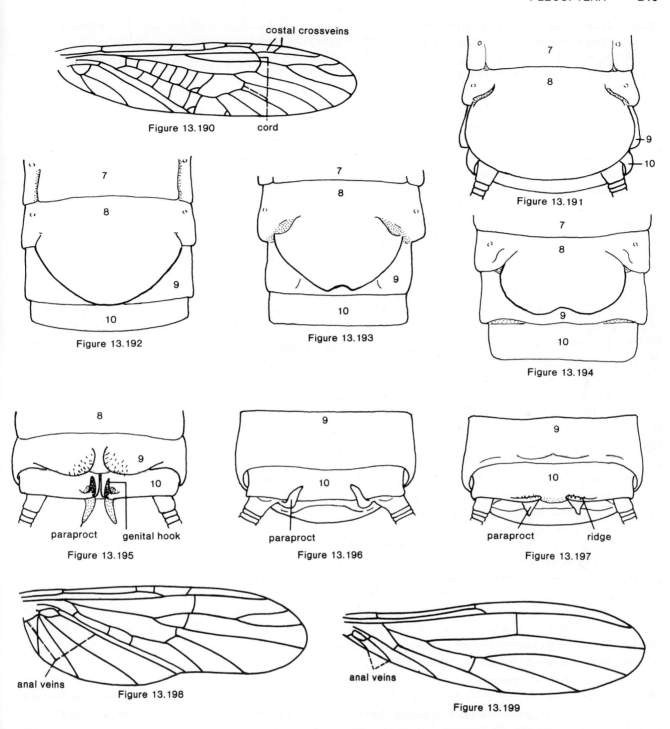

Figure 13.190

costal crossveins

cord

Figure 13.191

Figure 13.192

Figure 13.193

Figure 13.194

Figure 13.195

paraproct   genital hook

Figure 13.196

paraproct

Figure 13.197

paraproct   ridge

Figure 13.198

anal veins

Figure 13.199

anal veins

Figure 13.190. Fore wing of *Helopicus subvarians* (Perlodidae).

Figure 13.191. Subgenital plate of female *Pictetiella expansa* (Perlodidae).

Figure 13.192. Subgenital plate of female *Kogotus modestus* (Perlodidae).

Figure 13.193. Subgenital plate of female *Cultus decisus* (Perlodidae).

Figure 13.194. Subgenital plate of female *Malirekus hastatus* (Perlodidae).

Figure 13.195. Dorsal view of terminal abdominal segments of male *Cascadoperla trictura* (Perlodidae).

Figure 13.196. Dorsal view of terminal abdominal segments of male *Isoperla* sp. (Perlodidae).

Figure 13.197. Dorsal view of terminal abdominal segments of male *Clioperla clio* (Perlodidae).

Figure 13.198. Hind wing of *Utaperla sopladora* (Chloroperlidae).

Figure 13.199. Hind wing of *Haploperla brevis* (Chloroperlidae).

102(100′) Hind wing with 5 or more anal veins (fig. 13.198) .... ***Utaperla*** Ricker

102′.   Hind wing with 4 or fewer anal veins (figs. 13.110, 13.199) 103

103(102′) Folded anal area of hind wing absent (fig. 13.199) .... ***Haploperla*** Naʹvas

103′.   Folded anal area of hind wing present (fig. 13.110) 104

104(103′) Basal segment of cercus more than 3 times as long as wide, and curved (in male, it
          bears knobs and a basal spine) (fig. 13.202) .... ***Neaviperla*** Ricker

104′.   Basal segment of cercus shorter, straight 105

105(104′) Body concolorous (uniform in color) without dark markings, generally green in life
          (yellow in alcohol) .... ***Alloperla*** Banks

105′.   Body with dark markings on head, thoracic nota, or abdomen 106

106(105′) Anal lobe of hindwing small (1/2 as large as in fig. 13.110) .... ***Rasvena*** Ricker

106′.   Anal lob of hind wing larger as in Fig. 13.110 107

107(106′) Males 108

107′.   Females (following key tentative) 110

108(107) Fingerlike process at base of cercus (fig. 13.203) .... ***Suwallia*** Ricker

108′.   No process at base of cercus 109

109(108′) Epiproct large, set in a deep groove in tergum 10 (fig. 13.204) .... ***Sweltsa*** Ricker*

109′.   Epiproct small, about as wide as long, tergum 10 entire or just slightly depressed .... ***Triznaka*** Ricker†

110(107′) Meso- and metanota marked as in figure 13.205 .... ***Triznaka*** Ricker†

110′.   Nota marked differently, median bar absent or faint (fig. 13.206) 111

111(110′) Sternum 8 forming a large subgenital plate covering most of sternum 9; if plate is
          shorter, pronotum pale with only narrow dark lateral margins .... ***Suwallia*** Ricker

111′.   Subgenital plate variable, shorter; disk of pronotum with a dark median line, wide
          dark borders or with a dark reticulate pattern .... ***Sweltsa*** Ricker*

112(7).   Two ocelli 113

112′.   Three ocelli 115

113(112). Male tergum 10 cleft and forming genital hooks (fig. 13.207); subgenital plate
          scarcely developed on female sternum 8 (fig. 13.208) .... ***Neoperla*** Needham

113′.   Male tergum 10 entire, genital hooks developed from paraprocts (fig. 13.214);
          subgenital plate of female either very large or notched (figs. 13.209–13.210) 114

114(113′) Male sternum 9 with small hammer; female sternum 8 forming a large subgenital
          plate; sternum 9 with spicule patch (fig. 13.209) .... ***Anacroneuria*** Klapálek

114′.   Male sternum 9 with a large hammer (fig. 13.211); female sternum 8 forming a
          short subgenital plate bearing a large quadrate notch (fig. 13.210) .... ***Perlinella*** Banks (in part)

115(112′) Males 116

115′.   Females 128

116(115) Genital hooks arising from tergum 10 (figs. 13.212–13.213) 117

116′.   Genital hooks arising from paraprocts (figs. 13.214–13.215) 119

117(116). Hammer (vesicle) present on sternum 9 .... ***Claassenia*** Wu

117′.   No hammer on sternum 9 118

118(117′) Genital hooks long, reaching forward to midline of tergum 8 (fig. 13.212) .... ***Phasganophora*** Klapálek

118′.   Genital hooks shorter, not reaching beyond the midline of tergum 9 (fig. 13.213) .... ***Paragnetina*** Klapálek

119(116′) Mesal tergite differentiated on tergum 10 (fig. 13.215) 120

119′.   Tergum 10 without differentiated mesal tergite (fig. 13.214) 121

120(119). Hammer on sternum 9 twice as wide as long (fig. 13.216) .... ***Hesperoperla*** Banks

120′.   Hammer on sternum 9 twice as long as wide (fig. 13.217) .... ***Calineuria*** Ricker

121(119′) No hammer on sternum 9 .... ***Perlesta*** Banks

121′.   Hammer present on sternum 9 122

---

*Bisancora Surdick will key kere
†*Plumiperla* Surdick and *Chloroperla* Newman will key here

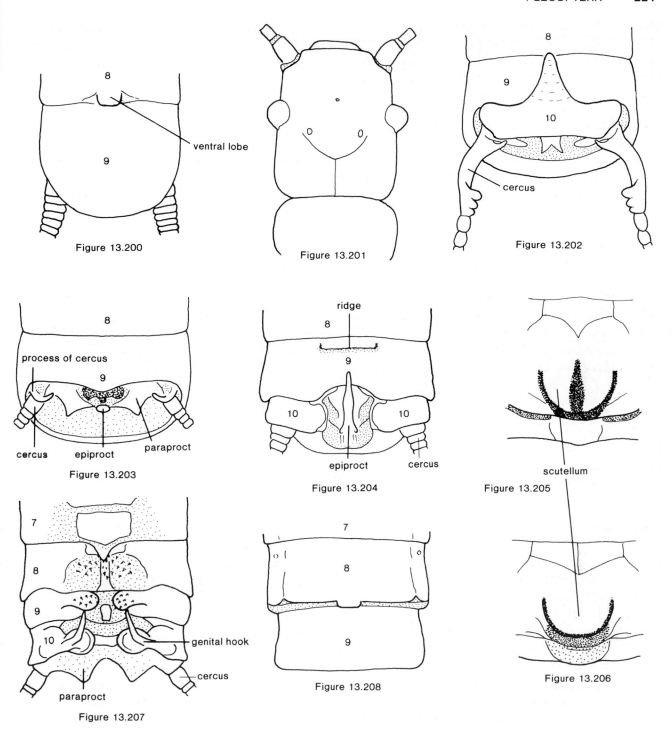

Figure 13.200

Figure 13.201

Figure 13.202

Figure 13.203

Figure 13.204

Figure 13.205

Figure 13.207

Figure 13.208

Figure 13.206

Figure 13.200. Ventral view of terminal abdominal segments of male *Isoperla* sp. (Perlodidae).

Figure 13.201. Outline of head and pronotum of *Kathroperla perdita* (Chloroperlidae).

Figure 13.202. Dorsal view of terminal abdominal segments of male *Neaviperla forcipata* (Chloroperlidae).

Figure 13.203. Dorsal view of terminal abdominal segments of male *Suwallia marginata* (Chloroperlidae).

Figure 13.204. Dorsal view of terminal abdominal segments of male *Sweltsa* sp. (Chloroperlidae).

Figure 13.205. Meso- and metanota of *Triznaka* sp. (Chloroperlidae).

Figure 13.206. Meso- and metanota of *Suwallia* sp. (Chloroperlidae).

Figure 13.207. Dorsal view of terminal abdominal segments of male *Neoperla* sp. (Perlidae).

Figure 13.208. Subgenital plate of female *Neoperla* sp. (Perlidae).

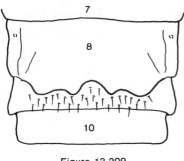

Figure 13.209

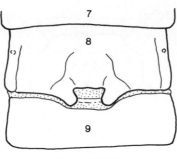

Figure 13.210

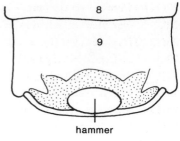

hammer

Figure 13.211

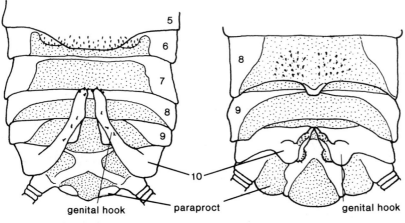

genital hook   paraproct

Figure 13.212

genital hook

Figure 13.213

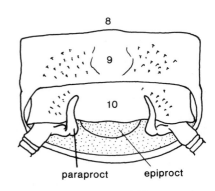

paraproct   epiproct

Figure 13.214

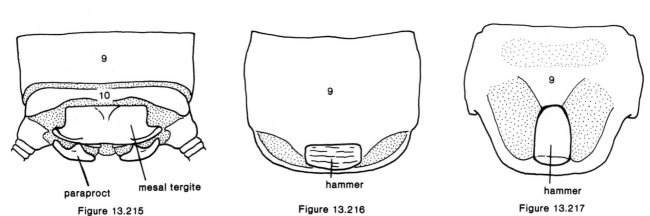

paraproct   mesal tergite

Figure 13.215

hammer

Figure 13.216

hammer

Figure 13.217

Figure 13.213. Dorsal view of terminal abdominal segments of male *Paragnetina immarginata* (Perlidae).

Figure 13.214. Dorsal view of terminal abdominal segments of male *Hesperoperla pacifica* (Perlidae).

Figure 13.215. Dorsal view of terminal abdominal segments of male *Acroneuria* sp. (Perlidae).

Figure 13.216. Sternum 9 of male *Hesperoperla pacifica* (Perlidae).

Figure 13.217. Sternum 9 of male *Calineuria californica* (Perlidae).

Figure 13.209. Subgenital plate of female *Anacroneuria* sp. (Perlidae).

Figure 13.210. Subgenital plate of female *Perlinella* sp. (Perlidae).

Figure 13.211. Sternum 9 of male *Perlinella* sp. (Perlidae).

Figure 13.212. Dorsal view of terminal abdominal segments of male *Phasganophora capitata* (Perlidae).

122(121') Hammer on sternum 9 a small raised knob .... *Eccoptura* Klapálek

122'.   Hammer not raised in side view 123

123(122') Hammer oval (fig. 13.211) 124

123'.   Hammer rectangular on triangular (figs. 13.216, 13.218) 126

124(123). Small species (fore wing less than 13 mm); aedeagus with large lateral sclerites .... *Perlinella* Banks (in part)

124'.   Larger species (fore wing over 15 mm); aedeagus without such sclerites 125

125(124') Spinule patches on both tergum 9 and tergum 10 (fig. 13.214) .... *Acroneuria* Pictet

125'.   Spinule patches absent, a few spinules on tergum 10 .... *Attaneuria* Ricker

126(123') Hammer rectangular (fig. 13.216) .... *Doroneuria* Needham and Claassen

126'.   Hammer triangular (fig. 13.218) 127

127(126') Crossveins present between 1A and 2A, and 2A and 3A (as in fig. 13.223, but with
         additional crossveins between 2A and 3A) .... *Hansonoperla* Nelson

127'.   No such crossveins .... *Beloneuria* Needham and Claassen

128(115') Subgenital plate of sternum 8 not produced over sternum 9 129

128'.   Subgenital plate extending over sternum 9 133

129(128). Subgenital plate notched (fig. 13.219) 130

129'.   Subgenital plate entire 131

130(129). Notch of subgenital plate bordered by a membranous area (fig. 13.219) .... *Calineuria* Ricker

130'.   Notch bordered by a dark, sclerotized area .... *Hansonoperla* Nelson

131(129') Vagina with accessory glands; spermatheca with few or no glands 132

131'.   Vagina without accessory glands; spermatheca with numerous glands (fig. 13.220) .... *Acroneuria* Pictet (in part)

132(131). Vagina covered internally with golden brown spinules .... *Doroneuria* Needham and Claassen

132'.   Vagina without such spinules .... *Claassenia* Wu

133(128') Egg collar stalked (fig. 13.221) 134

133'.   Egg collar not stalked (fig. 13.222) or absent 137

134(133). A squarish dark area on margin of subgenital plate; apex of egg flanged around
         collar (fig. 13.221) .... *Hesperoperla* Banks

134'.   No such dark area; egg without apical flange 135

135(134') Fore wing 15 mm or more in length .... *Paragnetina* Klapálek

135'.   Fore wing 14 mm or less in length 136

136(135') Crossveins present in fore wing between 1A and 2A (fig. 13.223) .... *Perlinella* Banks (in part)

136'.   Crossveins absent between 1A and 2A .... *Perlesta* Banks (in part)

137(133') Egg collar developed as a small button (fig. 13.222) 138

137'.   Egg collar absent 141

138(137). Vagina with sclerites (fig. 13.224) .... *Phasganophora* Klapálek

138'.   Vagina without sclerites 139

139(138') Vagina covered with spinules .... *Acroneuria* Pictet (in part)

139'.   Vagina membranous, without spinules 140

140(139') Subgenital plate large, reaching middle of sternum 9 (fig. 13.225) .... *Eccoptura* Klapálek

140'.   Subgenital plate shorter, reaching about one-third of length of sternum 9, notched
         (fig. 13.226) .... *Perlesta* Banks (in part)

141(137') Subgenital plate with submarginal tubercle (fig. 13.227) .... *Attaneuria* Ricker

141'.   Subgenital plate without such a tubercle 142

142(141') Subgenital plate triangular and notched .... *Beloneuria* Needham and Claassen

142'.   Subgenital plate large, expanding distally, margin entire or shallowly notched (fig.
         13.228) .... *Acroneuria* Pictet (in part)

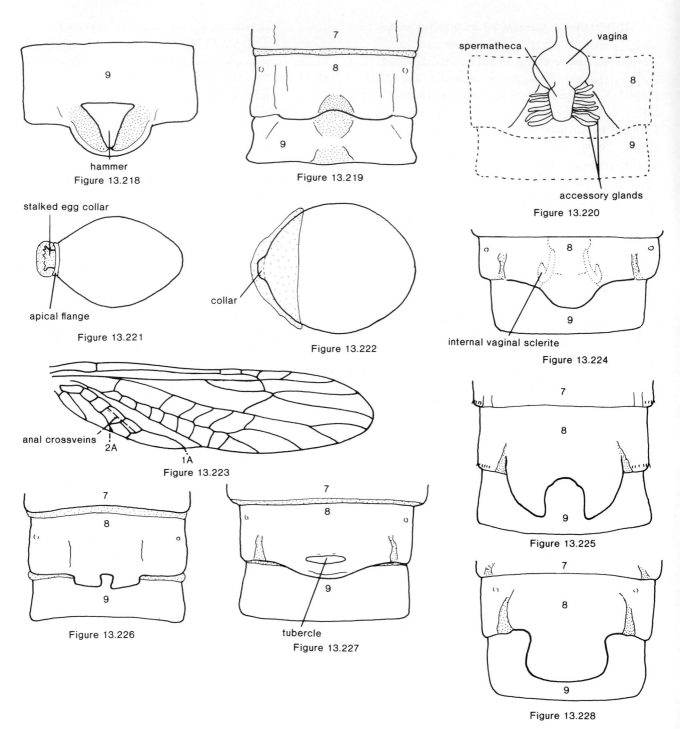

hammer
Figure 13.218

spermatheca   vagina

accessory glands
Figure 13.220

stalked egg collar

apical flange

Figure 13.221

collar

Figure 13.222

internal vaginal sclerite

Figure 13.224

anal crossveins

2A

1A

Figure 13.223

Figure 13.225

tubercle
Figure 13.227

Figure 13.226

Figure 13.228

Figure 13.218. Sternum 9 of male *Beloneuria georgiana* (Perlidae).

Figure 13.219. Subgenital plate of female *Calineuria californica* (Perlidae).

Figure 13.220. Vagina and spermatheca of female *Acroneuria abnormis* (Perlidae).

Figure 13.221. Egg of *Hesperoperla pacifica* (Perlidae).

Figure 13.222. Egg of *Phasganophora capitata* (Perlidae).

Figure 13.223. Fore wing of *Perlinella* sp. (Perlidae).

Figure 13.224. Subgenital plate of female *Phasganophora capitata* (Perlidae).

Figure 13.225. Subgenital plate of female *Eccoptura xanthenes* (Perlidae).

Figure 13.226. Subgenital plate of female *Perlesta placida* (Perlidae).

Figure 13.227. Subgenital plate of female *Attaneuria ruralis* (Perlidae).

Figure 13.228. Subgenital plate of female *Acroneuria evoluta* (Perlidae).

ADDITIONAL TAXONOMIC REFERENCES

General
Needham and Claassen (1925); Claassen (1931); Ricker (1952).

Regional faunas
British Columbia: Ricker (1943); Ricker and Scudder (1975).
California: Jewett (1956, 1960).
Connecticut: Hitchcock (1974).
Florida: Stark and Gaufin (1979).
Illinois: Frison (1935).
Louisiana: Stewart *et al.* (1976).
Minnesota: Harden and Mickel (1952).
Montana: Gaufin *et al.* (1972); Gaufin and Ricker (1974).
Pacific Northwest: Jewett (1959).
Pennsylvania: Surdick and Kim (1976).
Rocky Mountains: Baumann *et al.* (1977).
Saskatchewan: Dosdall and Lehmkuhl (1979).
Texas: Szczytko and Stewart (1977).
Utah: Gaufin *et al.* (1966); Baumann *et al.* (1977).
Wisconsin: Hilsenhoff (1981).

Regional species lists
Alaska: Jewett (1971; ref. #2835); Ellis (1975).
Canadian Far North: Ricker (1944).
Canadian Maritime Provinces: Ricker (1947); Brinck (1958).
Canadian Prairie Provinces: Ricker (1946).
Colorado: Stark *et al.* (1973).
Delaware: Lake (1980).
Idaho: Newell and Minshall (1976).
Indiana: Ricker (1945); Bednarik and McCafferty (1977).
Kansas: Stewart and Huggins (1977).
Minnesota: Lager *et al.* (1979).
Mississippi: Stark (1979).
Nevada: Cather *et al.* (1975).
New Mexico: Stark *et al.* (1975).

Ohio: Gaufin (1956); Tkac and Foote (1978).
Oklahoma: Stark and Stewart (1973).
Quebec: Ricker *et al.* (1968).
South Carolina: McCaskill and Prins (1968).
Southwestern United States: Stewart *et al.* (1974).
Virginia: Kondratieff and Voshell (1979).
Western Intermountain Area: Gaufin (1964; ref. #2833); Logan and Smith (1966)).
West Virginia: Farmer and Tarter (1976); Hissom and Tarter (1976); Steele and Tarter (1977); Tarter and Kirchner (1980).

Taxonomic treatments at the family and generic levels
(N = nymphs; A = adults)
Capniidae: Ricker (1959a)–A; Nebeker and Gaufin (1965)–A; Baumann and Gaufin (1970)–A; Harper and Hynes (1971b)–N; Ross and Ricker (1971)–A.
Chloroperlidae: Gaufin (1964)–A; Hitchcock (1968)–A; Fiance (1977)–N.
Leuctridae: Ricker (1943)–A; Ricker and Ross (1969)–A; Harper and Hynes (1971a)–N; Nelson and Hanson (1973)–A.
Nemouridae: Ricker (1952)–A; Harper and Hynes (1971d)–N; Bauman (1975)–N, A.
Peltoperlidae: Stark and Stewart (1981)–N, A.
Perlidae: Stark and Gaufin (1974a, 1976a, 1976b; ref. #2853)–N, A; Stark and Szczytko (1976)–A; Stark and Baumann (1978)–A.
Perlodidae: Ricker (1952)–N, A; Hilsenhoff and Billmyer (1973)–N; Stark and Gaufin (1974b)–A; Szczytko and Stewart (1979)–N, A.
Pteronarcyidae: Nelson and Hanson (1971)–A; Nelson *et al.* (1977)–N, A.
Taeniopterigidae: Ricker and Ross (1968, 1975)–A; Harper and Hynes (1971c)–N; Fullington and Stewart (1980)–N.

Table 13B. Summary of ecological and distributional data for *Plecoptera (stoneflies).* (For definition of terms see Tables 6A-6C; table prepared K. W. Cummins, P. P. Harper, K. W. Stewart, and R. W. Merritt.)

Taxa (number of species in parentheses)	Habitat	Habit	Trophic Relationships	North American Distribution	Ecological References[*]
Pteronarcyidae(10)	Generally lotic—erosional and depositional (debris jams, leaf packs)	Generally clingers—sprawlers	Generally shredders—detritivores, some scrapers		480, 488, 805, 906, 9 1087, 1166, 1174, 11 1234, 1756, 1886, 20 2041, 2210
Pteronarcella(2)	Lotic—erosional and depositional (logs, leaf litter)	Clingers—sprawlers	Shredders—detritivores and herbivores (macroalgae), predators (engulfers)	West, Southwest	238, 819, 820, 1881
Pteronarcys(8)	Lotic—erosional and depositional (logs, leaf litter)	Clingers—sprawlers	Shredders—detritivores and herbivores (macroalgae), predators (engulfers), scrapers	Widespread	107, 238, 488, 819, 8 965, 1108, 1109, 155 1605, 1658, 1762, 17 2029, 2210
Peltoperlidae(16)	Generally lotic—erosional and depositional (leaf litter)	Generally clingers—sprawlers	Generally shredders—detritivores		965, 1087, 1174, 123 1316, 1886, 2041
Peltoperla(1)	Lotic—erosional and depositional (leaf litter)	Clingers—sprawlers	Shredders—detritivores (leaf litter)	East	1087, 1661
Sierraperla(1)				West (Nevada, California)	
Soliperla(5)				Pacific Northwest	
Tallaperla(6)	Lotic—erosional and depositional (leaf litter)	Clingers—sprawlers	Shredders—detritivores (leaf litter)	East	672, 1087, 2557, 275
Viehoperla(1)				Appalachians	
Yoroperla(2)			Shredders—detritivores, scrapers	West (mountain, intermountain)	382
Taeniopterygidae(31)	Generally lotic—erosional (coarse sediments, debris jams, leaf packs) and depositional at margins	Generally sprawlers, clingers	Generally shredders—detritivores, collectors—gatherers, scrapers		804, 965, 1087, 1174, 1234, 1756, 1886, 20 2210
Taeniopteryginae(10)					
Taeniopteryx(10)	Lotic—erosional (coarse sediments, wood, leaf packs) and depositional at margins	Sprawlers—clingers	Shredders—detritivores, collectors—gatherers (scrapers)	East (1 in Northwest; Texas, Colorado, New Mexico)	107, 145, 421, 427, 7 804, 821, 979, 1325, 2029, 2569, 2647
Brachypterinae(21)			Generally scrapers (some shredders)		1166, 1523, 2029
Bolotoperla(1)				East	
Doddsia(1)				West	
Oemopteryx(4)				East, Central, California	
Strophopteryx(7)				East	979
Taenionema(8)				West, Northwest	
Nemouridae(61)	Generally lotic—erosional (coarse sediments, wood, leaf packs) and depositional (leaf litter), lentic—erosional	Generally sprawlers, clingers	Shredders—detritivores, collectors—gatherers	Widespread	255, 382, 972, 1524, 1674, 1775, 2780

[*]Emphasis on trophic relationships.

le 13.B— *Continued*

Taxa (number of species in parentheses)	Habitat	Habit	Trophic Relationships	North American Distribution	Ecological References[*]
mphinemurinae 4)					
Amphinemura(13)	Lotic—erosional and depositional (in detritus)	Sprawlers—clingers	Shredders—detritivores, collectors—gatherers	Widespread	427, 972, 1508, 1523, 1524, 2210, 2780
Malenka(11)				West	571
emourinae(37)					
Lednia(1)				Montana	116
Nemoura(4)	Lotic—erosional (detritus)	Sprawlers—clingers	Shredders—detritivores (herbivores [macroalgae])	West, North, Northeast	143, 146, 972, 2210, 2647
Ostrocerca(6)				East, Northwest	1508
Paranemoura(1)				Northeast	
Podmosta(5)				West, Northeast	1441
Prostoia(3)	Lotic—erosional and depositional	Shredders—detritivores (scrapers)		Northwest, Northeast	427, 972, 1178, 2210
Shipsa(1)	Lotic—erosional and depositional	Shredders—detritivores, (scrapers)		North, Northeast	107, 972, 2210
Soyedina(7)	Spring outflows			Widespread	1296, 1508, 2780
Visoka(1)				West	
Zapada(8)	Lotic—erosional (detritus)	Sprawlers—clingers	Shredders—detritivores (leaf litter)	West, East	367, 996, 1296, 1978, 2222, 2224
ctridae(45)	Generally lotic—erosional (coarse sediments, debris jams, leaf packs) and depositional	Generally sprawlers—clingers	Generally shredders—detritivores		972, 1259, 2133
egaleuctrinae(5)					
Megaleuctra(5)	Springs, seeps			Northwest, Appalachians	
euctrinae(40)					
Despaxia(1)	Spring outflows			West	
Leuctra(20)	Lotic-erosional and depositional		Shredders—detritivores	East, North Central	143, 972, 2210, 2649
Moselia(1)				Pacific Northwest	
Paraleuctra(8)				Widespread	
Perlomyia(2)				West	
Zealeuctra(8)	Small streams (some intermittent)			East, Central, Texas	2270
niidae(130)	Generally lotic—erosional (coarse sediments, wood, leaf packs) and depositional	Generally sprawlers—clingers	Generally shredders—detritivores		804, 979
Allocapnia(39)		Clingers	Shredders—detritivores	East	145, 427, 718, 719, 720, 721, 979, 1508
Bolshecapnia(4)	Small streams, alpine lakes			West	
Capnia(50)			Shredders—detritivores	West, North, Northeast	83, 571, 979, 1296, 1302, 1441, 2040, 2222, 2224, 2424
Eucapnopsis(1)				West	571, 1296

phasis on trophic relationships.

Table 13.B—*Continued*

Taxa (number of species in parentheses)	Habitat	Habit	Trophic Relationships	North American Distribution	Ecological References[*]
Isocapnia(11)	Hyporheal			West	2311
Mesocapnia(11)				West	
Nemocapnia(1)				East	
Paracapnia(3)				West, East	979, 980
Utacapnia(10)	Lotic (1 sp. in Lake Tahoe)			West, East	
Perlidae(43)	Generally lotic and lentic—erosional	Clingers	Predators (engulfers)		247, 480, 805, 906, 9● 1087, 1166, 1174, 11● 1234, 1316, 1756, 18● 2041
Perlinae(15)					
Claassenia(1)		Clingers	Predators (engulfers; Trichoptera, Ephemeroptera, Chironomidae, Simuliidae)	West, North	27, 107, 819, 820, 82●
Neoperla(8)	Lotic—erosional	Clingers	Predators (engulfers)	East, Southwest	2331, 2515
Paragnetina(5)	Lotic—erosional	Clingers	Predators (engulfers; Diptera, Ephemeroptera, Trichoptera)	East	421, 971, 1016, 1253, 2210, 2400†
Phasganophora(1)	Lotic—erosional	Clingers	Predators (engulfers; Diptera, Ephemeroptera, Trichoptera)	East	421, 971, 1253, 1352, 2210†
Acroneuriinae(28)					
Acroneuria(11)	Lotic and lentic—erosional	Clingers	Predators (engulfers; Diptera, Trichoptera, Ephemeroptera, Plecoptera)	Widespread	421, 1017, 1253, 187● 1881, 1253, 2569, 25●
Anacroneuria(1?)				Texas, Arizona	2331
Attaneuria(1)				East, Central	1879
Beloneuria(3)				Southern Appalachian	
Calineuria(1)	Lotic—erosional	Clingers	Predators (engulfers; Chironomidae, Trichoptera, Ephemeroptera)	West	382, 1296, 1756, 221● 2213, 2225
Doroneuria(2)				West	
Eccoptura (1)				East, Central	1879
Hansonoperla(1)				Appalachian	
Hesperoperla(1)			Predators (engulfers; Chironomidae, Trichoptera, Ephemeroptera)	West	820, 821
Perlesta(2)	Lotic—erosional and depositional (in detritus)	Clingers	Predators (engulfers; Chironomidae, Simuliidae, Ephemeroptera, Trichoptera), collectors—gatherers (first instars)	East, Central	2210, 2271†
Perlinella(3)				East	
Perlodidae (103+)	Generally lotic and lentic—erosional	Generally clingers	Generally predators (engulfers) (some scrapers, collectors—gatherers)		1234, 1886, 2041, 219●
Perlodinae					
Arcynopteryx(1)			Predators (engulfers) (collectors—gatherers?)	Arctic, alpine	1418, 1698, 2212
Chernokrilus(3)				West	

*Emphasis on trophic relationships.
†Unpublished data, K. W. Cummins, Oregon State University.

ble 13.B—*Continued*

Taxa (number of species in parentheses)	Habitat	Habit	Trophic Relationships	North American Distribution	Ecological References[*]
Cultus(4)	Lotic—erosional	Clingers	Predators (engulfers; Chironomidae, Simuliidae)	West, East	819, 1674, 1675
Diploperla(3)			Predators (engulfers)	East	74
Diura(3)			Scrapers, predators (engulfers)	West, North, East	2132, 2193, 2212, 2489
Frisonia(1)				West	2834
Helopicus(2)			Predators (engulfers)	East	1671
Hydroperla(2)	Lotic—depositional and erosional	Clingers	Predators (engulfers; Simuliidae, Chironomidae, Emphemeroptera)	East	1831
Isogenoides(9)	Lotic—erosional and depositional		Predators, (engulfers; Diptera, especially Chironomidae)	East, North, West	107, 2210
Kogotus(3)	Lotic—erosional	Clingers	Predators (engulfers; Ephemeroptera, Trichoptera, Diptera—Simuliidae, Chironomidae) (some scrapers)	West	27, 2439, 2852
Malirekus(1)				East	
Megarcys(5)	Lotic—erosional	Clingers	Predators (engulfers; Ephemeroptera, Trichoptera, Diptera—Simuliidae, Chironomidae)	West	27, 366, 1881
Oroperla(1)				West (California)	
Osobenus(1)				West	1978
Perlinodes(1)				West	1978, 2852
Pictetiella(1)				West (intermountain)	
Remenus(1)				East	
Setvena(2)			Predators (engulfers) (scrapers?)	West	2439
Skwala(2)			Predators (engulfers)	West	2223, 2852
Yugus(3)				East (Appalachian)	2758
Isoperlinae(54+)	Lotic—erosional and depositional	Generally clingers, sprawlers	Predators, (engulfers) (collectors—gatherers)		
Calliperla(1)				West	
Cascadoperla(1)		Clingers, sprawlers		West	
Clioperla(1)				East	971
Isoperla(50+)	Lotic—erosional and depositional, large cold lake	Clingers—sprawlers	Predators (engulfers; Chironomidae, Simuliidae, Ephemeroptera, Plecoptera), collectors—gatherers (early instars)	Widespread	107, 698, 805, 819, 912, 971, 1508, 1674, 1675, 2193, 2210
Rickera(1)	Lotic—erosional	Clingers	Predators (engulfers)	West	2439, 2852
loroperlidae(62)	Generally lotic—erosional	Generally clingers	Generally predators (engulfers), scrapers, collectors—gatherers		421, 668, 698, 805, 819, 820, 971, 1808
Paraperlinae(5)					
Kathroperla(1)			Collectors—gatherers, scrapers	West	Blank
Paraperla(2)	Hyporheal			West	2311
Utaperla(2)				East, West	Blank

mphasis on trophic relationships.

Table 13B—*Continued*

Taxa (number of species in parentheses)	Habitat	Habit	Trophic Relationships	North American Distribution	Ecological References*
Chloroperlinae(57)			Generally collectors— gatherers, engulfers (predators)		
Alloperla(21)				East, West	
Haploperla(4)			Scrapers, predators (engulfers; Chironomidae)	East, West	107, 980, 2210
Neaviperla(1)				West	
Rasvena(1)				East	
Suwallia(4)			Predators (engulfers; Chironomidae, Simuliidae)	East, West	820
Sweltsa(23)			Predators, (engulfers; Chironomidae, Simuliidae)	East, West	495, 571, 820, 971, 15
Triznaka(3)			Predators (engulfers; Chironomidae, Simuliidae)	West	820

*Emphasis on tropic relationships.

Aquatic and Semiaquatic Hemiptera

14

John T. Polhemus
Englewood, Colorado

Heteroptera

INTRODUCTION

Fifteen of the 16 major families of Heteroptera associated with the aquatic habitat are represented in the North American insect fauna, with only the pantropical Helotrephidae missing. Six families are totally aquatic; they leave the water only to migrate. Three families of the water striders live on the surface film and adjacent banks, and the remaining six groups live at aquatic margins although some are often found on the water surface. All of these families belong to three infraorders of the suborder Heteroptera: Leptopodomorpha, Gerromorpha, and Nepomorpha.

Two other families occur in North America whose members are essentially terrestrial, but they have species that are occasionally found near water. They are the introduced Leptopodidae (related to Saldidae) and Dipsocoridae (infraorder Dipsocoromorpha). These are not treated in this work except to list ecological and taxonomic references for the Dipsocoridae that provide an entry to the literature.

About 3,200 species of aquatic and semiaquatic Heteroptera occur worldwide; Jaczewski and Kostrowicki (1969) give an underestimate of 2,900, excluding approximately 230 species of Saldidae and some recently described species. Presently 69 genera and 404 species are recognized from North America. The Nearctic fauna has been enriched by the addition of tropical forms, whereas transverse mountain ranges have blocked such invasions into the Palaearctic, which has a comparatively poor fauna. Holarctic species are known only in the cold-adapted Corixidae and Saldidae, the latter being the most numerous with 15 species. A discussion of the world distribution of water bugs is given by Hungerford (1958) and of Gerromorpha by Andersen (1982). The zoogeography of North American water bugs has been discussed by Menke (1979; California) and Slater (1974; Connecticut). Dispersal of most aquatic Hemiptera occurs by flight, but there is also evidence for hurricane transport (Herring 1958). A habitat key and other significant data on biology are furnished by Hungerford (1920) in his classic work on water bugs; this has been updated by Usinger (1956b) and further by Menke *et al.* (1979). The characterization of a habitat for each group is only a rough generalization due to the many exceptions (table 14A).

The aquatic and semiaquatic Heteroptera are remarkable for their diversity of form, reflecting adaptions to a wide variety of niches. They occupy many varied habitats, including saline ponds, high mountain lakes, hot springs, and large rivers. Basically they are predators; many species seem to be relatively resistant to predation, which is often attributed to the possession of characteristic heteropteran scent glands. Only the Corixidae differ significantly: many genera are primarily collectors, feeding on detritus, and are heavily preyed upon (table 14A).

Some aquatic Heteroptera are of recognized economic importance, and the role of additional forms is presently being investigated. Biting genera such as *Notonecta, Belostoma,* and *Lethocerus* are attracted to lights and may be a nuisance to swimming pools. *Lethocerus,* a large belostomatid, can also be a nuisance at fish hatcheries (Wilson 1958). Corixidae have long been a relished food item in Mexico under the name "Ahuautle" and are also used extensively as food for pet fish and turtles; Belostomatidae are considered a delicacy in Asia. Corixidae have been shown to be good indicators of lentic water quality (Jansson 1977). Both surface and aquatic bugs can be important predators of mosquito larvae and adults (Jenkins 1964; table 14A). *Notonecta undulata* Say prefers mosquito larvae over other food (Ellis and Borden 1970; Toth and Chew 1972b), and these authors and Laird (1956) urge further study of aquatic Hemiptera as biological control agents.

Although there are exceptions, most aquatic Heteroptera lay their eggs in the spring, develop during the warmer months, overwinter as adults, and repeat the cycle. Some saldids overwinter as eggs, many gerrids are bivoltine, and in southern regions a number of species breed throughout the year. Eggs are of various forms and are laid in a wide variety of places, either glued to a substrate or inserted in the earth or plants. They have a wide variety of shapes: spindle-shaped, oval, or occasionally stalked. The chorion is tough, often hexagonally reticulate and successful hatching usually takes place submerged or in damp habitats (see chap. 5, table 5A). A splendid review of heteropteran eggs and embryology is given by Cobben (1968). All but a few species have five nymphal instars; the exceptions have four and include some *Mesovelia* sp., *Microvelia* sp., and *Nepa* sp.

Some true water bugs (Pleidae, Notonectidae, Naucoridae, Corixidae) swim with synchronous oarlike strokes of the hind legs, and other families (i.e., Nepidae, Belostomatidae), by synchronous strokes of the middle and hind pair of legs, those on each side working alternately. When swimming vigorously the latter families stroke both pairs in unison. The belostomatids are the strongest, the nepids the weakest, and the corixids the most agile swimmers.

The water striders (Gerromorpha) are supported by surface tension of the water and the unwettable hydrofuge pile of their tarsi and sometimes their tibiae. The wettable claws can be retracted in the most specialized families (Gerridae and Veliidae). These bugs are able to easily glide over the water because of the low resistance and use their wettable claws or other pretarsal structures to penetrate the surface for "traction." Forward thrust in the gerrid and veliid species by rowing is caused by the surface film "packing up" behind the tarsi during the thrust. These animals usually steer with the hind legs and unequal strokes of the middle legs (Menke 1979; Andersen 1982).

Most other surface-dwelling Gerromorpha walk over the surface film with tripodal locomotion, each leg alternating movement with its opposite. Some veliids are also able to move very rapidly when alarmed by "expansion skating," being carried forward on a contracting surface film caused by lowering of the surface tension by saliva discharged from the beak (review in Andersen 1982).

Most of the true water bugs (Nepomorpha) breathe by means of an air store usually carried dorsally between the wings and abdomen plus an exposed thin bubble (physical gill) on the ventral surface held in place by hydrofuge hairs (chap. 4). Means of air store replenishment are often distinctive for each family, e.g., through tubes (Nepidae), air straps (Belostomatidae), the pronotum (Corixidae), or the tip of the abdomen (Notonectidae, most Naucoridae). A few naucorid bugs can remain submerged indefinitely utilizing plastron respiration (chap. 4; Menke 1979).

Sound production in the Gerromorpha has been reported only for the Veliidae (Leston and Pringle 1963); however, a few Gerridae may also stridulate. Many Saldidae (Leptopodomorpha) possess evident stridulatory mechanisms, as do some, if not most, of the families of Nepomorpha. Stridulatory mechanisms have been described in the Nepidae, Notonectidae, and Corixidae, and the "songs" of the latter family have been studied in detail (Jansson 1976).

EXTERNAL MORPHOLOGY

Nymphs and Adults

The nymphs of aquatic and semiaquatic Heteroptera have one-segmented tarsi, a useful characteristic in separating them from adults, especially the apterous gerromorphans (water striders), which always have two tarsal segments, at least on some legs. Nymphs of Hemiptera resemble the adults but the body parts have different proportions and developing wings are present as wing pads (fig. 14.4) in the ultimate and penultimate instars. Keys to the nymphs of North American families and subfamilies of Heteroptera based in a large part on the *trichobothria* (hair-bearing spots on abdomen) and dorsal abdominal scent gland openings (fig. 14.4) have been published (DeCoursey 1971; Herring and Ashlock 1971). A key and synopsis of the families and genera of adult North American Heteroptera has been published by Slater and Baranowski (1978), but differs somewhat in arrangement from this work (e.g., genus *Limnoporus* included in *Gerris*, family Macroveliidae included in Mesoveliidae).

With the exception of a few families with head and thorax joined (e.g., Pleidae, Naucoridae), the head, thorax, and abdomen are generally well defined in aquatic and semiaquatic Hemiptera.

Head: The eyes are usually prominent and well developed. Ocelli may be present but are lacking in many aquatic families and ocelli are present only in winged forms of some semiaquatic species. Antennae are three-, four-, or five-segmented and are ordinarily quite conspicuous in semiaquatic bugs, but hidden in the true aquatics. Two semiaquatic families (Ochteridae, Gelastocoridae), which inhabit the margins of fresh waters and are closely allied to the true aquatics, have short antennae that are largely or entirely hidden. The *rostrum* or beak is segmented, varies in length, and has either three or four visible segments (except for Corixidae; fig. 14.17). It attaches to the apex of the head and is directed posteriorly underneath (Cobben 1978). The ventral region between the base of the beak and the collar, called the *gula* (fig. 14.100), is one of the primary characters used in separating the Hemiptera-Heteroptera from the Homoptera (leaf hoppers; see Homoptera section).

Thorax: The three-segmented thorax bears the legs and wings and, due to fusions or extra sutures, the segments are difficult to identify except in the wingless forms (fig. 14.145). The metasternum usually bears one or more scent glands (fig. 14.81) and sometimes lateral scent channels (fig. 14.145). The legs often represent striking adaptations of aquatic Heteroptera to their environment (figs. 14.80, 14.143, 14.146). Leg segments are variable in length; however, each leg always consists of a coxa articulating with the body followed by a trochanter joining the coxa and femur. The femur and tibia are usually the longest segments, and the tarsi are one-, two-, or three-jointed and bear the claws.

Alary (wing) polymorphism in water bugs is a common phenomenon, but a few groups, such as the marine water strider *Halobates* sp. and the macroveliid *Oravelia* sp., are known only in the wingless state. The hind wings of Heteroptera are membranous, whereas the fore wings or *hemelytra* have a leathery *clavus* and *corium* plus a thin membrane portion (fig. 14.2), which may appear to be lacking in some aquatic species (e.g., Pleidae). Winged forms are more common in southern regions and wingless or short winged forms are more common in the groups of surface bugs. The most extensive studies of alary polymorphism and its mechanisms have concerned the Gerridae (Brinkhurst 1959, 1960; Vepsalainen 1971a, 1971b, 1974; Andersen 1973).

Abdomen: The abdomen bears the spiracles and genitalia. The first visible segment ventrally is actually the second, and the first seven segments are similar. The eighth through tenth segments form the genitalia and may or may not be distinguishable. In some families of Nepomorpha (e.g., Ochteridae, Gelastocoridae, and Corixidae) the last few abdominal segments are asymmetrical in males but symmetrical or nearly so in females.

Homoptera

INTRODUCTION

The Homoptera have not adapted to truly aquatic life as have some Heteroptera. However, some species of Homoptera can be considered marginally semiaquatic as they have a more or less permanent association with the margins of both the intertidal zone and fresh water, where they feed on aquatic plants.

Homopteran species commonly found in semiaquatic habitats belong to a half dozen or more families. *Draeculacephala* spp. (Cicadellidae) are found along stream margins, and the transcontinental *Helochara communis* Fitch (Cicadellidae) is apparently always associated with low marshy grasses. Adults and nymphs of *Megamelus* sp. (Delphacidae) frequent the upper leaf surfaces of water lilies (*Nuphar* sp.) and pickerelweed (*Pontaderia* sp.).

Although few, if any, of the homopterans are subjected to significant aquatic inundation, the eggs of *Prokelisia marginata* (Van Duzee) (Delphacidae) are deposited in *Spartina* sp., an intertidal grass, which is sometimes completely submerged. Many intertidal Homoptera (Delphacidae, Cicadellidae, Issidae) inhabit salt marsh vegetation (Denno 1976) that is occasionally inundated, but the adults of these species move up the culms of vegetation to escape rising tides (Davis and Gray 1966). Conversely, Cameron (1976) has suggested that certain Homoptera can withstand long periods of submergence in California marshes, which typically have a steeper littoral gradient than those studied by Davis and Gray

(1966) in North Carolina. Certain of the Auchenhorrhyncha may locate in an air bubble trapped in leaf or blade axils during inundation; the bubble could function as a physical gill.

EXTERNAL MORPHOLOGY

Although the inclusion of Homoptera in a work on aquatic insects is problematic, collectors of semiaquatic insects will find them and have the need for identifications. Homoptera differ morphologically from Heteroptera primarily in having the posteriorly directed beak apparently arise from the underside of the thorax rather than the head (fig. 14.1), and sometimes in having a uniformly leathery, hyaline, or membranous corium rather than the differentiated heteropteran wing described above (see figs. 14.2, 14.100, and 14.116).

Within the Sternorrhyncha, *Haliaspis spartinae* (Comstock) (Diaspididae), *Eriococcus* sp. (Eriococcidae), and various pseudococcids inhabit intertidal vegetation and are at least occasionally inundated by tides. In Britain the aphid *Pemphigus trehernei* Foster occurs on the roots of an intertidal aster (Foster 1975).

For the most part, the Homoptera have not evolved the sophisticated respiratory mechanisms found in aquatic Heteroptera. They can be considered no more than semiaquatic, although some scale insects and mealybugs approach an aquatic existence. The respiratory adaptations of salt marsh homopterans have been reviewed by Foster and Treherne (1976; see chap. 4 also).

KEY TO THE FAMILIES OF AQUATIC AND SEMIAQUATIC HEMIPTERA

1. Head without a gula (fig. 14.1) .... (Suborder Homoptera)

1'. Head with a gula (fig. 14.100) (Suborder Heteroptera) 2

2(1'). Antennae shorter than head, inserted beneath eyes, not plainly visible from above (fig. 14.100) except in Ochteridae (fig. 14.5); aquatic or semiaquatic bugs (at margins of standing- or running-water habitats) 3

2'. Antennae longer than head, inserted forward of eyes, plainly visible from above (figs. 14.2–14.3); bugs on surface or at aquatic margins 10

3(2). Beak triangular, very short, unsegmented (sometimes transversely striated), appearing as apex of head (fig. 14.15); front tarsus with a single segment, scooplike, fringed with stiff setae forming a rake (fig. 14.22) .... *CORIXIDAE* (p. 236)

3'. Beak cylindrical, short to long, 3- or 4-segmented (fig. 14.100); front tarsus not scooplike or fringed with stiff setae 4

4(3'). Apex of abdomen with respiratory appendages (figs. 14.12–14.111) 5

4'. Apex of abdomen without respiratory appendages 6

5(4). Apex of abdomen with a pair of flat, retractile air straps (fig. 14.12) .... *BELOSTOMATIDAE* (p. 235)

5'. Apex of abdomen with cylindrical breathing tube (siphon) composed of 2 slender, nonretractile filaments (fig. 14.111) .... *NEPIDAE* (p. 246)

6(4'). Middle and hind legs without fringelike swimming hairs; ocelli present (fig. 14.64) except in *Nerthra rugosa* Desjardins. Bugs at margins of aquatic habitats 7

6'. Middle and hind legs with fringelike swimming hairs (fig. 14.115); ocelli absent. Aquatic bugs 8

7(6). Front legs raptorial (grasping), femora broad (figs. 14.60–14.61); rostrum short, not reaching hind coxae; antennae not visible from above (fig. 14.64) .... *GELASTOCORIDAE* (p. 239)

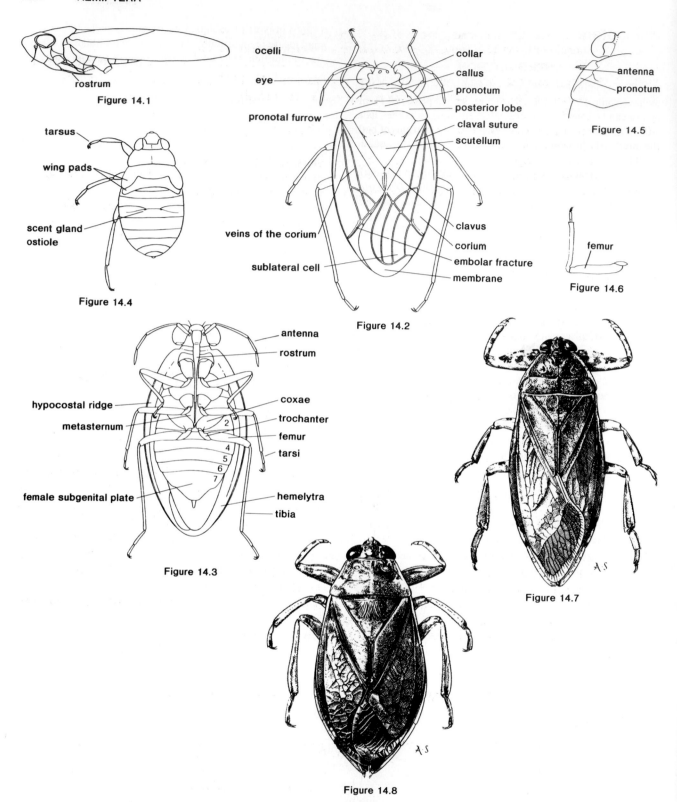

rostrum

Figure 14.1

tarsus

wing pads

scent gland
ostiole

Figure 14.4

ocelli

eye

pronotal furrow

collar

callus

pronotum

posterior lobe

claval suture

scutellum

veins of the corium

sublateral cell

clavus

corium

embolar fracture

membrane

Figure 14.2

antenna

pronotum

Figure 14.5

femur

Figure 14.6

antenna

rostrum

hypocostal ridge

metasternum

coxae

trochanter

femur

tarsi

female subgenital plate

hemelytra

tibia

Figure 14.3

Figure 14.7

Figure 14.8

Figure 14.5. Dorsal view of head and pronotum of Ochteridae.

Figure 14.6. Leg of Ochteridae.

Figure 14.7. *Lethocerus americanus* (Leidy), dorsal view (Belostomatidae; from Usinger 1956).

Figure 14.8. *Belostoma bakeri* Montandon, dorsal view (Belostomatidae; from Usinger 1956).

Figure 14.1. Lateral view of adult Cicadellidae (Homoptera).

Figure 14.2 Dorsal view of adult *Saldula* sp. (Saldidae).

Figure 14.3. Ventral view of adult *Saldula* sp. (Saldidae).

Figure 14.4. Dorsal view of Saldidae nymph.

7'. Front legs not raptorial, femora not broad (fig. 14.6); rostrum long, reaching, or extending beyond hind coxae; tips of antennae usually visible from above (fig. 14.5, 14.69) .... ***OCHTERIDAE—Ochterus***

8(6'). Front legs raptorial, femora broad; body dorsoventrally flattened (fig. 14.100) .... ***NAUCORIDAE*** (p. 246)

8'. Front legs slender, femora not broad; body strongly convex dorsally (figs. 14.95–14.116) 9

9(8'). Body form ovoid; 3 mm or less in length (fig. 14.95); all legs similar; hind tarsus with 2 well-developed claws (fig. 14.97) .... ***PLEIDAE*** (p. 246)

9'. Body form elongate, 5 mm or more in length (fig. 14.116); hind legs long, oarlike; claws of hind tarsus inconspicuous (fig. 14.115) .... ***NOTONECTIDAE*** (p. 246)

10(2'). Membrane of wing with 4 or 5 distinct similar cells (fig. 14.2); hind coxae large, transverse, with broad coxal cavity (fig. 14.3) .... ***SALDIDAE*** (p. 249)

10'. Membrane of wing without distinct similar cells (fig. 14.139); hind coxae small, cylindrical, or conical; coxal cavity socketlike (fig. 14.145) 11

11(10'). Claws of at least front tarsus inserted before apex (fig. 14.144) 12

11'. Claws of all legs inserted at tips of tarsi (fig. 14.92) 13

12(11). Hind femur short, distally either scarcely or not surpassing apex of abdomen; metasternum with a pair of lateral scent grooves terminating on pleura in front of hind coxae (fig. 14.145); dorsum of head usually with median longitudinal sulcus or glabrous (smooth) stripe; mid legs inserted about midway between front and hind legs, except *Trochopus* and *Rhagovelia,* which have featherlike structures on the middle tarsus (fig. 14.146), and *Husseyella,* which has bladelike structures instead of claws on middle tarsus (fig. 14.143) .... ***VELIIDAE*** (p. 252)

12'. Hind femur long, distally greatly exceeding apex of abdomen; metasternal region with single median scent gland opening (omphalium; fig. 14.81), lateral scent grooves absent; dorsum of head without median groove or line except in *Rheumatobates;* mid legs inserted closer to hind legs than forelegs .... ***GERRIDAE*** (p. 242)

13(11'). Body long, slender; head as long or longer than combined length of pronotum and scutellum (fig. 14.94) .... ***HYDROMETRIDAE—Hydrometra***

13'. Body stout; head length not greater than combined length of pronotum and scutellum, or pronotum alone in wingless forms (fig. 14.90) 14

14(13'). Tarsi two-segmented; head ventrally with deep longitudinal channel for reception of rostrum (fig. 14.86) .... ***HEBRIDAE*** (p. 242)

14'. Tarsi 3-segmented; head ventrally without longitudinal channel (fig. 14.91) 15

15(14'). Inner margins of eyes converging anteriorly; femora with at least 1 or 2 black spines on dorsum distally; winged forms with exposed bilobed scutellum (fig. 14.90) .... ***MESOVELIIDAE—Mesovelia***

15'. Inner margins of eyes arcuate, not converging anteriorly (fig. 14.88); femora without black spines; winged forms with scutellum concealed by pronotum (fig. 14.88) .... ***MACROVELIIDAE*** (p. 242)

KEYS TO THE GENERA OF AQUATIC AND SEMIAQUATIC HEMIPTERA

Belostomatidae

1. Tibia and tarsus of hind leg strongly compressed, thin, much broader than middle tibia and tarsus (figs. 14.7, 14.11); basal segment of beak about half length of 2nd; length 40 mm or more .... (Lethocerinae) .... ***Lethocerus*** Mayr

1'. Tibia and tarsus of middle and hind leg similar (figs. 14.8–14.10); basal segment of beak subequal to 2nd; length 37 mm or less .... (Belostomatinae) 2

2(1'). Membrane of hemelytron reduced (figs. 14.9, 14.12) .... ***Abedus*** Stål

2'. Membrane of hemelytron not reduced (figs. 14.8, 14.13); length 26 mm or less .... ***Belostoma*** Latreille

Corixidae

1.   Scutellum exposed, covered by pronotum only at anterior angles (fig. 14.21) .... (Micronectinae) .... *Tenagobia* Bergroth

1'.   Scutellum concealed (fig. 14.28) 2

2(1'). Rostrum (beak) without transverse striations; nodal furrow absent (fig. 14.16) .... (Cymatinae) ..... *Cymatia* Flor

2'.   Rostrum with transverse striations (figs. 14.15, 14.17); nodal furrow present (fig. 14.19) .... (Corixinae) 3

3(2'). Fore tarsus with rather thick, well-developed apical claw; pala of both sexes narrowly digitiform (fingerlike) (figs. 14.24, 14.28) .... (Graptocorixini) 4

3'.   Fore tarsus with spinelike apical claw usually resembling spines along lower margin of palm; pala not digitiform (figs. 14.22, 14.35) 5

4(3).   Tergal lobes on left side of male abdomen produced posteriorly (i.e., abdomen sinistral) (fig. 14.23); strigil absent. Female abdomen slightly asymmetrical; female face slightly concave, densely pilose (hairy) .... *Neocorixa* Hungerford

4'.   Tergal lobes on right side of male abdomen produced posteriorly (i.e., abdomen dextral) (fig. 14.27); strigil present on right side. Female abdomen asymmetrical; female face not concave, not densely pilose .... *Graptocorixa* Hungerford

5(3'). Eyes protuberant (produced above surface) with inner anterior angles broadly rounded. Face depressed in both sexes, with dense hair covering; postocular space broad, head transversely depressed behind eyes (fig. 14.14) .... (Glaenocorisini) 6

5'.   Eyes not protuberant, inner anterior angles acute (fig. 14.15). Face of females usually not densely hairy or depressed; if postocular space is broad, then head is not transversely depressed behind eyes .... (Corixini) 7

6(5).   Pronotum and clavus strongly rastrate (with longitudinal scratches). Metaxyphus (fig. 14.17) broadly triangular (fig. 14.26) .... *Glaenocorisa* Thomson

6'.   Pronotum and clavus not strongly rastrate. Metaxyphus (fig. 14.17) narrowly triangular (fig. 14.25) .... *Dasycorixa* Hungerford

7(5'). Apices of hemelytral clavi not or scarcely surpassing a line drawn through the costal margins at the nodal furrows; abdominal asymmetry of males sinistral, strigil on left; foretibia of male produced over base of pala (figs. 14.29, 14.34); species smaller than 5.6 mm in length .... *Trichocorixa* Kirkaldy

7'.   Apices of hemelytral clavi clearly surpassing a line drawn through the costal margins at the nodal furrows (figs. 14.19, 14.33); abdominal asymmetry of males dextral, strigil on right (fig. 14.27); foretibia of male not produced over base of pala (greatly expanded distally in *Centrocorisa* sp. but not over base of pala; fig. 14.37); spp. longer than 5.9 mm 8

8(7'). Pruinose (frosted) area at base of claval suture (clavopruina) short and broadly rounded, usually about one-half to two-thirds as long as postnodal pruinose area (postnodal pruina) (figs. 14.30, 14.32) .... *Hesperocorixa* Kirkaldy

8'.   Pruinose area at base of claval suture (clavopruina) either broadly rounded, narrowly rounded or pointed distally, subequal to or longer than postnodal pruinose area (postnodal pruina) (fig. 14.33) 9

9(8'). Body short, broad, more than one-third as broad as long (width measured across pronotum) 10

9'.   Body elongate, distinctly less than one-third as broad as long 12

10(9). Pronotum and clavus only faintly rugulose (wrinkled). Male foretarsi expanded distally (fig. 14.37); male without strigil or pedicel (fig. 14.38) .... *Centrocorisa* Lundblad

10'.   Pronotum and clavus distinctly rastrate. Male foretarsi not expanded distally in United States species (fig. 14.35); male with strigil or at least pedicel 11

11(10'). Middle femora of both sexes with a longitudinal groove on the ventral surface (fig. 14.31); males with a strigil .... *Pseudocorixa* Jaczewski

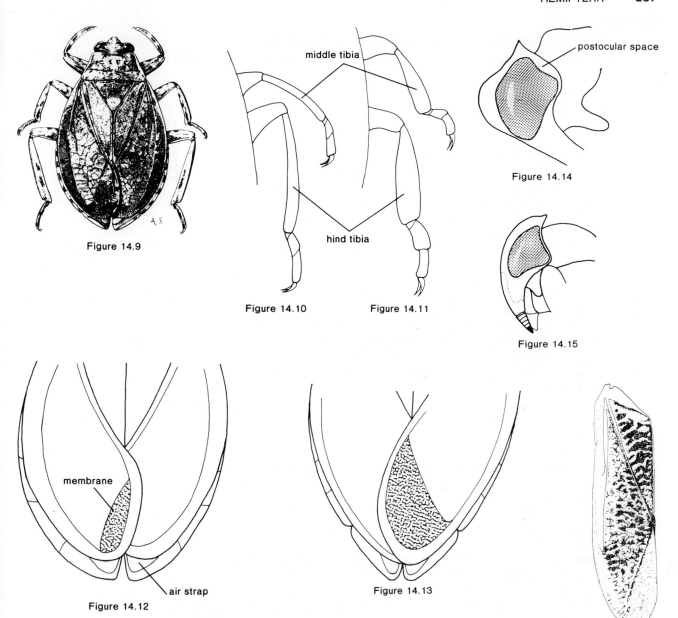

Figure 14.9

middle tibia

hind tibia

Figure 14.10   Figure 14.11

postocular space

Figure 14.14

Figure 14.15

membrane

air strap

Figure 14.12

Figure 14.13

Figure 14.16

Figure 14.9. *Abedus indentatus* (Haldeman), dorsal view (Belostomatidae; from Usinger 1956).

Figure 14.10. Middle and hind legs of *Belostoma* sp. (Belostomatidae).

Figure 14.11. Middle and hind legs of *Lethocerus* sp. (Belostomatidae).

Figure 14.12. Hemelytra of *Abedus* sp. (Belostomatidae).

Figure 14.13. Hemelytra of *Belostoma* sp. (Belostomatidae).

Figure 14.14. Side view of head of *Glaenocorisa* sp. (Corixidae).

Figure 14.15. Side view of head of *Hesperocorixa* sp. (Corixidae).

Figure 14.16. Left hemelytron of *Cymatia* sp. (Corixidae; from Brooks and Kelton 1967).

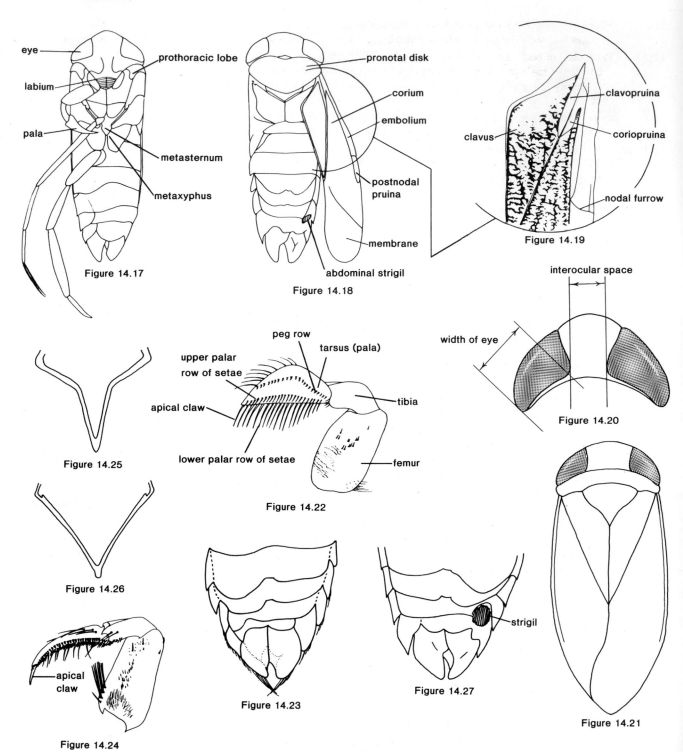

Figure 14.17

Figure 14.18

Figure 14.19

Figure 14.20

Figure 14.25

Figure 14.22

Figure 14.26

Figure 14.23

Figure 14.27

Figure 14.24

Figure 14.21

Figure 14.17. Ventral view of *Corisella* sp. (Corixidae; from Menke *et al.* 1979).

Figure 14.18. Dorsal view of *Corisella* sp. (Corixidae; from Menke *et al.* 1979).

Figure 14.19. Enlarged portion of hemelytron of *Corisella* sp. (Corixidae) showing pruinose areas (from Menke *et al.* 1979).

Figure 14.20. Dorsal view of head of *Palmacorixa* sp. (Corixidae).

Figure 14.21. Dorsal view of *Tenagobia* sp. (Corixidae).

Figure 14.22. Male foreleg of *Cenocorixa* sp. (Corixidae; from Menke *et al.* 1979).

Figure 14.23. Abdominal tergites of *Neocorixa* sp. (Corixidae).

Figure 14.24. Male foreleg of *Graptocorixa* sp. (Corixidae; from Menke *et al.* 1979).

Figure 14.25. Metaxyphus of *Dasycorixa* sp. (Corixidae).

Figure 14.26. Metaxyphus of *Glaenocorisa* sp. (Corixidae).

Figure 14.27. Abdominal tergites of *Graptocorixa* sp. (Corixidae; from Menke *et al.* 1979).

11′. Middle femora of both sexes without a longitudinal groove on the ventral surface; males without a strigil, but with a pedicel (fig. 14.36) .... *Morphocorixa* Jaczewski

12(9′). Palar claw of both sexes minutely serrate (sawlike) at base (fig. 14.46); upper surface of male pala deeply incised (fig. 14.45); vertex of male acuminate (tapering to a point) (fig. 14.42); usually with hemelytral pattern indistinct or obscure .... *Ramphocorixa* Abbott

12′. Palar claw not serrate; upper surface of male pala not deeply incised; vertex of male not acuminate (fig. 14.43); hemelytral pattern usually distinct 13

13(12′). Posterior margin of head sharply curved, embracing very short pronotum (fig. 14.43); interocular space much narrower than width of an eye (fig. 14.20); median lobe of male abdominal tergite VII with a hooklike projection (fig. 14.44) .... *Palmacorixa* Abbott

13′. Posterior margin of head not sharply curved, pronotum longer (fig. 14.40); interocular space at least subequal to width of an eye; median lobe of male abdominal tergite VII without a hooklike projection 14

14(13′). Pronotum and clavus smooth and shining, at most faintly rugulose (wrinkled) (fig. 14.39) .... *Corisella* Lundblad

14′. Part or all of pronotum and clavus rough, either rastrate (with longitudinal scratches) or rugulose, or both (fig. 14.40) 15

15(14′). Markings on clavus and corium narrow and broken, usually open reticulate (covered with network of fine lines) with much anastomosing (merging) (fig. 14.55); pronotal carina (ridge) distinct on at least anterior one-third (fig. 14.41) 16

15′. Markings on clavus transverse, those of corium transverse, longitudinal or reticulate (figs. 14.56–14.59); pronotal carina absent or faintly expressed on anterior border at most (figs. 14.40, 14.54) 17

16(15). Median carina of pronotum well defined on anterior two-thirds or more. Male fore pala usually digitiform with rather evenly curved row of pegs (fig. 14.47); peg row interrupted and pala broadened basally only in *A. chancea* Hungerford (fig. 14.48) .... *Arctocorisa* Wallengren

16′. Median carina of pronotum well defined only on anterior one-third (fig. 14.41). Male fore pala broadened medially, peg row sharply curved (fig. 14.22) or disjunct medially (fig. 14.51) .... *Cenocorixa* Hungerford

17(15′). Male strigil present; palar pegs usually in 1 row (fig. 14.50) with notable exceptions (fig. 14.49); ground color usually yellowish, dark pattern on hemelytra strongly contrasting (fig. 14.54, 14.56–14.58) .... *Sigara* Fabricius

17′. Male strigil absent; palar pegs in 2 rows (fig. 14.52); ground color greenish yellow, dark pattern on hemelytra weakly contrasting (figs. 14.40, 14.59). In all except *C. audeni,* posterior first tarsal segment with black spot (fig. 14.53) .... *Callicorixa* White

Gelastocoridae

1. Fore tarsus articulating with tibia, 1-segmented with 2 claws in nymphs and adults; fore femur only moderately enlarged at base, twice as long as basal width, not subtriangular (fig. 14.61); closing face of fore femur flat and bordered by 2 rows of short spines; beak clearly arising at front of head, directed posteriorly; dorsal aspect of body as in figure 14.62 .... (Gelastocorinae) ....*Gelastocoris* Kirkaldy

1′. Fore tarsus fused with tibia and terminated by a single claw (adults) or 2 claws (nymphs); fore femur very broad at base, about as long as broad, subtriangular (fig. 14.60); closing face of fore femur with a dorsal flangelike extension that projects over tibia when it is closed against femur: beak appearing to arise from the back of the head, L-shaped; dorsal aspect of body as in figure 14.63 .... (Nerthrinae) .... *Nerthra* Say

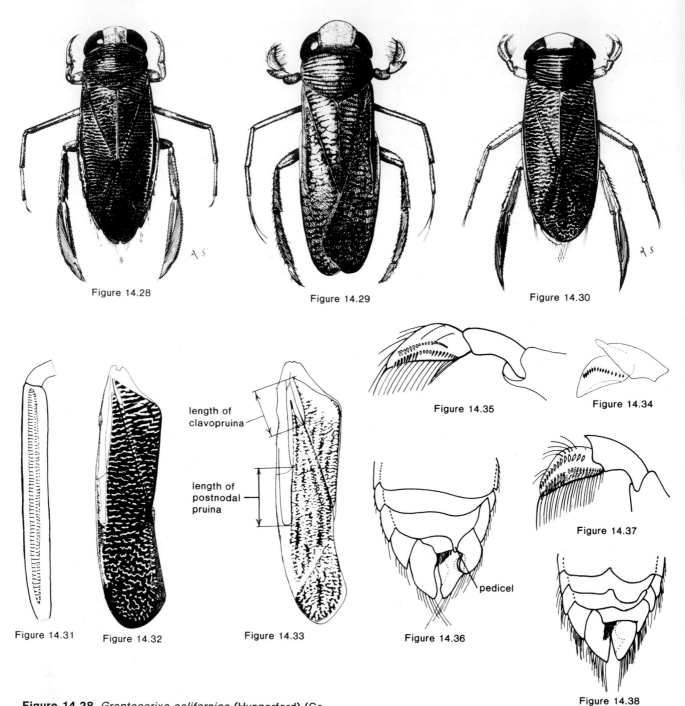

Figure 14.28

Figure 14.29

Figure 14.30

Figure 14.35

Figure 14.34

Figure 14.31   Figure 14.32

length of clavopruina

length of postnodal pruina

Figure 14.33

Figure 14.37

pedicel

Figure 14.36

Figure 14.38

Figure 14.28. *Graptocorixa californica* (Hungerford) (Corixidae; from Usinger 1956).

Figure 14.29. *Trichocorixa reticulata* (Guerin-Meneville) (Corixidae; from Usinger 1956).

Figure 14.30. *Hesperocorixa vulgaris* (Hungerford) (Corixidae; from Usinger 1956).

Figure 14.31. Dorsal view of middle femur of *Pseudocorixa* sp. (Corixidae).

Figure 14.32. Left hemelytron of *Hesperocorixa* sp. (Corixidae; from Brooks and Kelton 1967).

Figure 14.33. Left hemelytron of *Corisella* sp. (Corixidae; from Menke *et al.* 1979).

Figure 14.34. Male foreleg of *Trichocorixa* sp. (Corixidae; from Brooks and Kelton 1967).

Figure 14.35. Male foreleg of *Morphocorixa* sp. (Corixidae).

Figure 14.36. Abdominal tergites of *Morphocorixa* sp. (Corixidae).

Figure 14.37. Male foreleg of *Centrocorisa* sp. (Corixidae).

Figure 14.38. Abdominal tergites of *Centrocorisa* sp. (Corixidae).

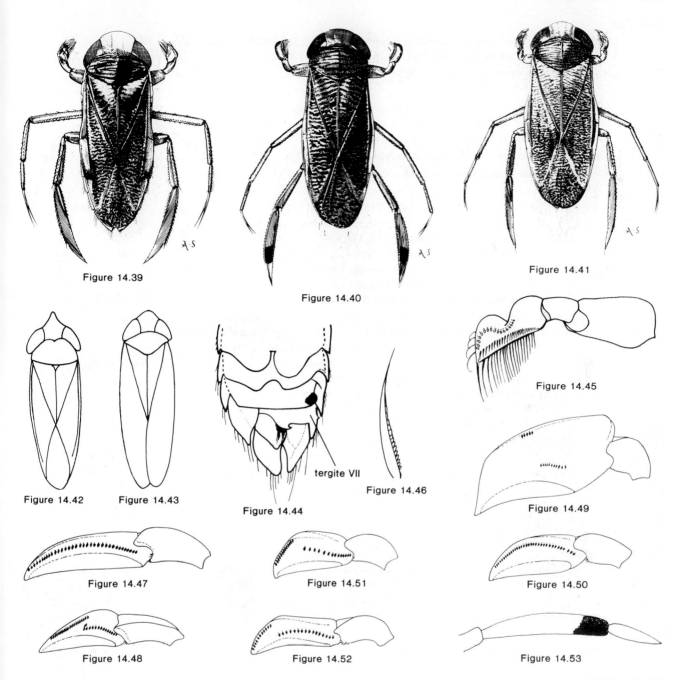

Figure 14.39

Figure 14.40

Figure 14.41

Figure 14.45

Figure 14.42 Figure 14.43

Figure 14.44

tergite VII

Figure 14.46

Figure 14.49

Figure 14.47

Figure 14.51

Figure 14.50

Figure 14.48

Figure 14.52

Figure 14.53

Figure 14.39. *Corisella decolor* (Uhler) (Corixidae; from Usinger 1956b).

Figure 14.40. *Callicorixa vulnerata* (Uhler) (Corixidae; from Usinger 1956b).

Figure 14.41. *Cenocorixa kuiterti* Hungerford (Corixidae; from Usinger 1956b).

Figure 14.42. Dorsal view of *Ramphocorixa* sp. (Corixidae).

Figure 14.43. Dorsal view of *Palmacorixa* sp. (Corixidae).

Figure 14.44. Abdominal tergites of *Palmacorixa* sp. (Corixidae).

Figure 14.45. Male foreleg of *Ramphocorixa* sp. (Corixidae).

Figure 14.46. Palar claw of *Ramphocorixa* sp. (Corixidae).

Figure 14.47. Male foreleg of *Arctocorisa sutilis* (Uhler), semidiagrammatic view (from Brooks and Kelton 1967).

Figure 14.48. Male foreleg of *Arctocorisa chanceae* (Hungerford), semidiagrammatic view (from Brooks and Kelton 1967).

Figure 14.49. Male foreleg of *Sigara fallenoidea* (Hungerford), semidiagrammatic view (from Brooks and Kelton 1967).

Figure 14.50. Male foreleg of *Sigara mathesoni* (Hungerford), semidiagrammatic view (from Brooks and Kelton 1967).

Figure 14.51. Male foreleg of *Cenocorixa* sp. (Corixidae), semidiagrammatic view (from Brooks and Kelton 1967).

Figure 14.52. Male foreleg of *Callicorixa* sp. (Corixidae), semidiagrammatic view (from Brooks and Kelton 1967).

Figure 14.53. Posterior tarsus of *Callicorixa* sp. (Corixidae).

Gerridae

1.   Inner margins of eyes sinuate or concave behind the middle (figs. 14.75–14.77); body comparatively long and narrow (fig. 14.79) .... (Gerrinae) 2

1'.   Inner margins of eyes convex (fig. 14.78), body comparatively short and broad (figs. 14.66–14.68) 5

2(1). Pronotum shining 3

2'.   Pronotum dull 4

3(2). Fore lobe of pronotum with pair of long, pale lines (fig. 14.76) .... *Limnogonus* Stål

3'.   Fore lobe of pronotum with single, median, pale spot (fig. 14.77) .... *Neogerris* Matsumura

4(2'). Antennal segment I equal to or longer than combined lengths of II and III (fig. 14.71) .... *Gerris* Fabricius

4'.   Antennal segment I less than combined lengths of II and III (fig. 14.70) .... *Limnoporus* Stål

5(1'). Tibia and first tarsal segment of middle leg with fringe of long hairs (fig. 14.80); always apterous (without trace of wing pads); the meso- and metanotum fused, without trace of a dividing suture; marine forms .... (Halobatinae) .... *Halobates* Eschscholtz

5'.   Tibia and first tarsal segment of middle leg without a fringe of long hairs; dimorphic (have both apterous and long-winged forms), the meso- and metanotum of apterous forms with a distinct dividing suture 6

6(5'). Third antennal segment with several stiff bristles that are at least as long as diameter of segment (fig. 14.74); length of 1st antennal segment much shorter than remaining 3 taken together; abdomen as long as remainder of body (fig. 14.67) .... *Rheumatobates* Bergroth

6'.   Third antennal segment with fine pubescence or tuft of short, stiff bristles, but these not as long as diameter of segment; abdomen shorter than remainder of body (fig. 14.68), or if subequal then length of 1st antennal segment about equal to remaining 3 taken together (fig. 14.73) .... (Trepobatinae) 7

7(6'). Length of 1st antennal segment subequal to remaining 3 taken together (fig. 14.73) .... *Metrobates* Uhler

7'.   Length of 1st antennal segment much shorter than remaining 3 taken together (fig. 14.72) .... *Trepobates* Uhler

Hebridae

1.   Antennae distinctly shorter than greatest width of pronotum. Antennal segments stout, 4th segment subequal in length to 1st segment (fig. 14.83) .... *Merragata* White

1'.   Antennae distinctly longer than greatest width of pronotum. Antennal segments slender, 4th segment much longer than 1st segment (figs. 14.84–14.85) 2

2(1'). Fourth antennal segment without a constriction (false joint structure) in the middle (fig. 14.84) .... *Lipogomphus* Berg

2'.   Fourth antennal segment with a constriction (false joint structure) in the middle, appearing 5-segmented (figs. 14.82, 14.85) .... *Hebrus* Curtis

Macroveliidae

1.   Ocelli absent; apterous; posterior margin of pronotum arcuate (arched), scutellum exposed (fig. 14.89); antennal segments I–III each longer than head width across eyes .... *Oravelia* Drake and Chapman

1'.   Ocelli present, well developed (fig. 14.88); macropterous or brachypterous; posterior margin of pronotum angular, concealing scutellum (fig. 14.88); antennal segments I–III each shorter than head width across eyes (fig. 14.87) .... *Macrovelia* Uhler

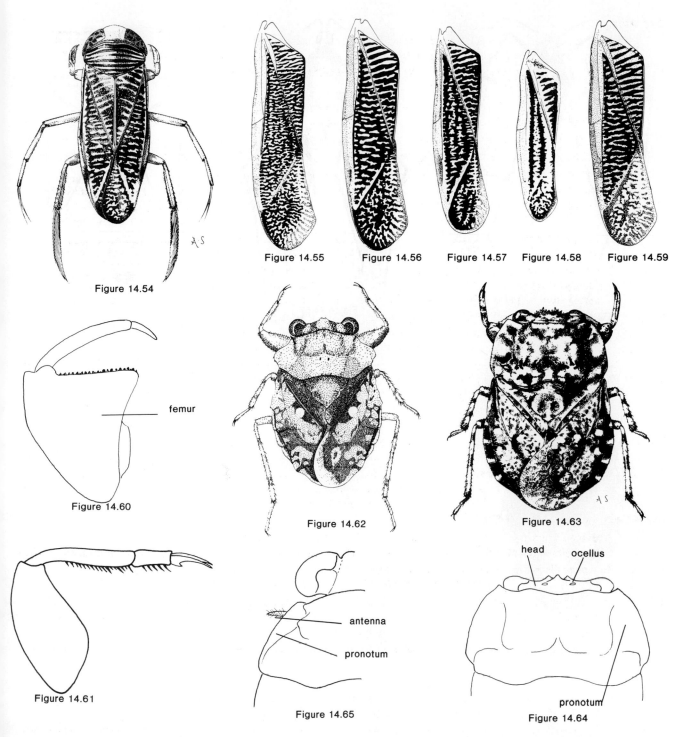

Figure 14.55   Figure 14.56   Figure 14.57   Figure 14.58   Figure 14.59

Figure 14.54

femur

Figure 14.60

Figure 14.62

Figure 14.63

Figure 14.61

antenna

pronotum

Figure 14.65

head   ocellus

pronotum

Figure 14.64

Figure 14.54. Dorsal view of *Sigara mckinstryi* Hungerford (Corixidae; from Usinger 1956b).

Figure 14.55. Left hemelytron of *Arctocorisa* sp. (Corixidae; from Brooks and Kelton 1967).

Figure 14.56. Left hemelytron of *Sigara decoratella* (Hungerford) (Corixidae; from Brooks and Kelton 1967).

Figure 14.57. Left hemelytron of *Sigara mullettensis* (Hungerford) (Corixidae; from Brooks and Kelton 1967).

Figure 14.58. Left hemelytron of *Sigara lineata* (Forster) (Corixidae; from Brooks and Kelton 1967).

Figure 14.59. Left hemelytron of *Callicorixa audeni* Hungerford (Corixidae; from Brooks and Kelton 1967).

Figure 14.60. Foreleg of *Nerthra* sp. (Gelastocoridae).

Figure 14.61. Foreleg of *Gelastocoris* sp. (Gelastocoridae).

Figure 14.62. Dorsal view of *Gelastocoris oculatus* (Fabricius) (Gelastocoridae; from Brooks and Kelton 1967).

Figure 14.63. Dorsal view of *Nerthra martini* Todd (Gelastocoridae; from Usinger 1956).

Figure 14.64. Dorsal view of head and pronotum of *Nerthra* sp. (Gelastocoridae).

Figure 14.65. Dorsal view of head and pronotum of *Ochterus* sp. (Ochteridae).

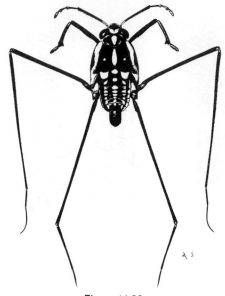

Figure 14.66

Figure 14.67

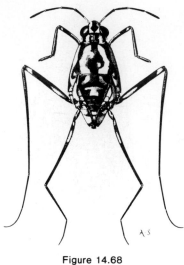

Figure 14.68

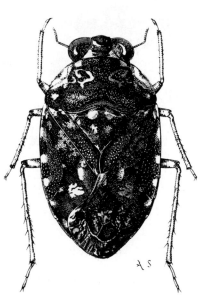

Figure 14:69

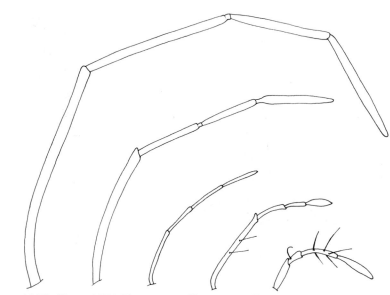

Figure 14.70   Figure 14.71 Figure 14.72   Figure 14.73   Figure 14.74

Figure 14.66. Dorsal view of *Metrobates trux infuscatus* Usinger (Gerridae; from Usinger 1956b).

Figure 14.67. Dorsal view of *Rheumatobates rileyi* Bergroth (Gerridae; from Brooks and Kelton 1967).

Figure 14.68. Dorsal view of *Trepobates becki* Drake and Harris (Gerridae; from Usinger 1956b).

Figure 14.69. Dorsal view of *Ochterus barberi* Schell (Ochteridae; from Usinger 1956b).

Figure 14.70. Antenna of *Limnoporus* sp. (Gerridae).

Figure 14.71. Antenna of *Gerris* sp. (Gerridae).

Figure 14.72. Antenna of *Trepobates* sp. (Gerridae).

Figure 14.73. Antenna of *Metrobates* sp. (Gerridae).

Figure 14.74. Antenna of *Rheumatobates* sp. (Gerridae).

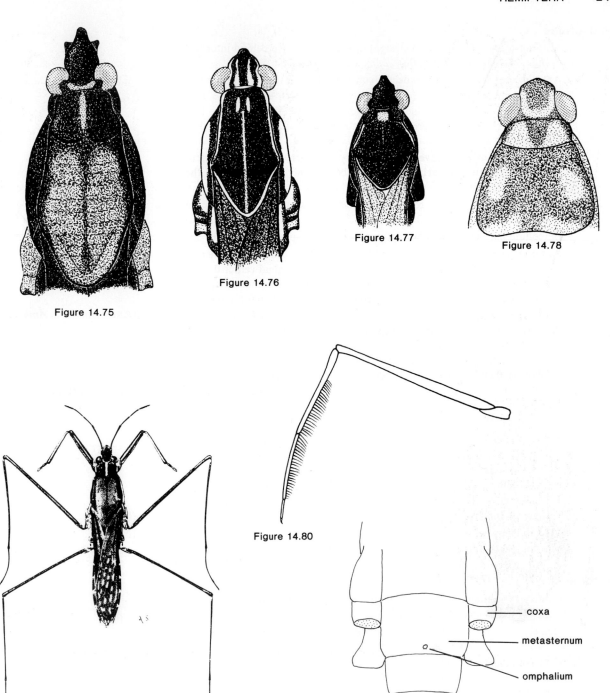

Figure 14.75

Figure 14.76

Figure 14.77

Figure 14.78

Figure 14.79

Figure 14.80

Figure 14.81

coxa

metasternum

omphalium

Figure 14.75. Dorsum of head and thorax of *Gerris* sp. (Gerridae).

Figure 14.76. Dorsum of head and thorax of *Limnogonus* sp. (Gerridae).

Figure 14.77. Dorsum of head and thorax of *Neogerris* sp. (Gerridae).

Figure 14.78. Dorsum of head and thorax of *Trepobates* sp. (Gerridae).

Figure 14.79. Dorsal view of *Gerris remigis* Say (Gerridae; from Usinger 1956b).

Figure 14.80. Hind leg of *Halobates* sp. (Gerridae).

Figure 14.81. Ventral view of thorax of Gerridae.

Naucoridae

1.   Anterior margin of pronotum straight or slightly concave behind interocular space
        (figs. 14.103, 14.105–14.106) 2

1′.   Anterior margin of pronotum deeply concave behind interocular space (fig. 14.104) 4

2(1).   Inner margins of eyes diverging anteriorly (figs. 14.103, 14.106); meso- and
        metasterna bearing prominent longitudinal carinae (keels) that are broad and
        foveate (with a deep impression) along middle; body broadly oval, sub-
        flattened .... (Limnocorinae) 3

2′.   Inner margins of eyes converging anteriorly (fig. 14.105); meso- and metasterna
        without longitudinal carinae at middle; body strongly convex above, the
        embolium rounded .... (Naucorinae) .... *Pelocoris* Stål

3(2).   Embolium produced outward and backward as an arcuate (arched), acute spine
        (fig. 14.106) .... *Usingerina* LaRivers

3′.   Embolium may be dilated, but not produced into a spine (fig. 14.103) .... *Limnocoris* Stål

4(1′). Posterior part of prosternum covered by platelike extensions of propleura which
        are nearly contiguous at midline (fig. 14.102); abdominal venter densely
        pubescent (hairy), except glabrous (shining) around spiracles, each spiracle also
        with a transverse row of small glabrous areas behind; macropterous (fig.
        14.104) .... (Ambrysinae) .. *Ambrysus* Stål

4′.   Prosternum completely exposed, separated from flattened pleura by simple sutures
        (fig. 14.101); abdominal venter bare and with a perforated disklike area near
        each spiracle; dimorphic, the brachypterous forms with hemelytra truncate
        (shortened and squared-off) at apices, about half as long as
        abdomen .... (Cryphocricinae) *Cryphocricos* Signoret

Nepidae

1.   Anterior lobe of pronotum not wider than head; body long, slender, cylindrical (fig.
        14.107); abdominal sterna of adult undivided; adult female subgenital plate
        laterally compressed, keel-like .... (Ranatrinae) .... *Ranatra* Fabricius

1′.   Anterior lobe of pronotum wider than head (fig. 14.110); body flattened;
        abdominal sterna of adult divided longitudinally into median and parasternites
        (figs. 14.108-14.109); adult female subgenital plate broad, flattened .... (Nepinae) 2

2(1′). Median length of 6th sternite twice median length of 5th (fig. 14.109) .... (Nepini) .... *Nepa* Linnaeus

2′.   Median length of 6th sternite about equal to length of 5th (fig. 14.109) .... (Curictini) .... *Curicta* Stål

Notonectidae

1.   Hemelytral commissure with a definite hair-lined pit at anterior end (figs. 14.113,
        14.117); antennae 3-segmented .... *Buenoa* Kirkaldy

1′.   Hemelytral commissure without a definite hair-lined pit at anterior end (figs.
        14.112, 14.114); antennae 4-segmented 2

2(1′). Eyes not holoptic (touching), separated dorsally (fig. 14.114); intermediate femur
        with anteapical (before apex) pointed protuberance; anterolateral margins of
        prothorax not foveate (with a deep impression) .... *Notonecta* Linnaeus

2′.   Eyes holoptic, contiguous dorsally (fig. 14.112); intermediate femur without
        anteapical pointed protuberance; anterolateral margins of prothorax foveate .... *Martarega* White

Pleidae

1.   Anterior tarsi each with 2 segments (fig. 14.98); abdominal carinae (keels) on
        ventrites 2–6 .... *Paraplea* Esaki and China

1′.   Anterior tarsi each with 3 segments (fig. 14.99); abdominal carinae on ventrites
        2–5 .... *Neoplea* Esaki and China

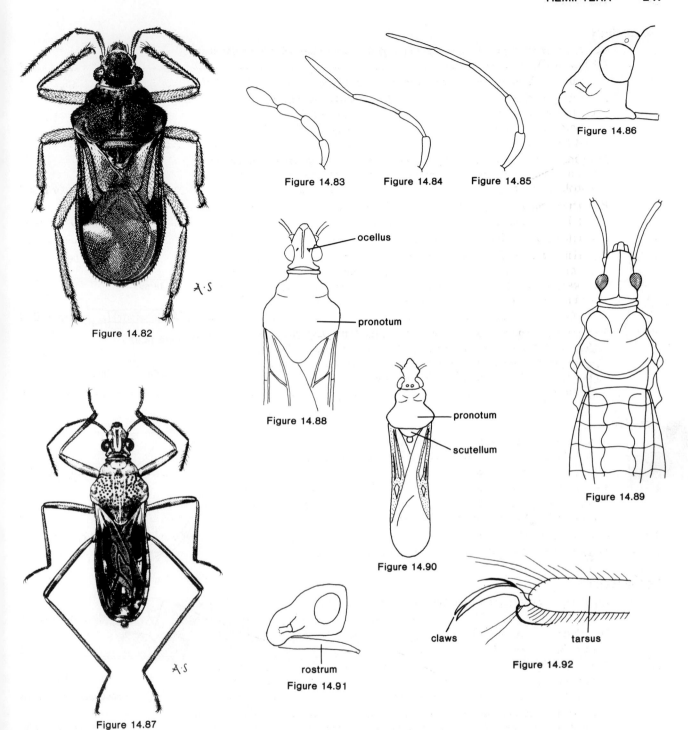

Figure 14.82. Dorsal view of *Hebrus sobrinus* Uhler (Hebridae; from Usinger 1956b).

Figure 14.83. Antenna of *Merragata* sp. (Hebridae).

Figure 14.84. Antenna of *Lipogomphus* sp. (Hebridae).

Figure 14.85. Antenna of *Hebrus* sp. (Hebridae).

Figure 14.86. Lateral view of head of Hebridae.

Figure 14.87. Dorsal view of *Macrovelia hornii* Uhler (Macroveliidae; from Usinger 1956b).

Figure 14.88. Dorsum of head and pronotum of *Macrovelia* sp. (Macroveliidae).

Figure 14.89. Dorsal view of *Oravelia pege* Drake and Chapman (Macroveliidae).

Figure 14.90. Dorsal view of *Mesovelia* sp. (Mesoveliidae).

Figure 14.91. Lateral view of head of *Mesovelia* sp. (Mesoveliidae).

Figure 14.92. Tarsus and claws of Macroveliidae.

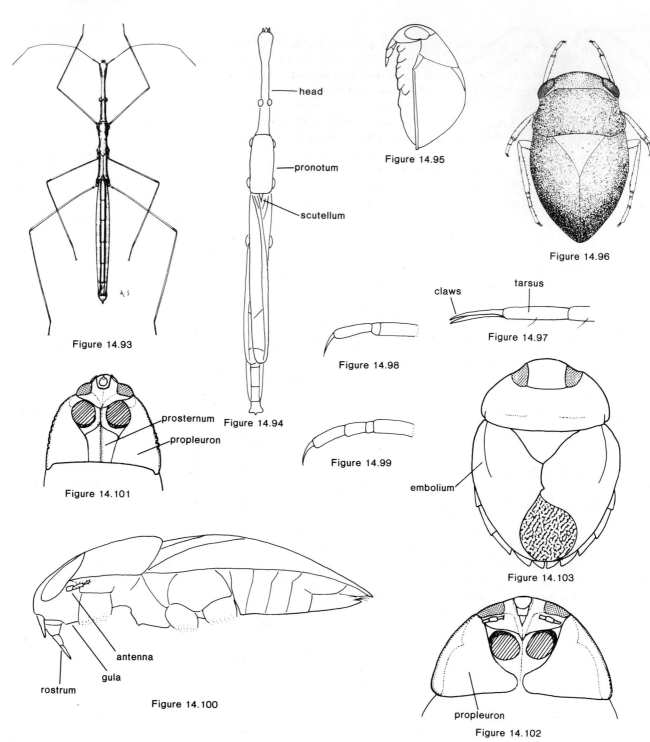

Figure 14.93.

Figure 14.94

head

pronotum

scutellum

Figure 14.95

Figure 14.96

claws   tarsus

Figure 14.97

Figure 14.98

Figure 14.99

embolium

Figure 14.103

prosternum

propleuron

Figure 14.101

antenna

gula

rostrum

Figure 14.100

propleuron

Figure 14.102

Figure 14.93. Dorsal view of *Hydrometra australis* Say (Hydrometridae; from Usinger 1956b).

Figure 14.94. Dorsal view of *Hydrometra* (Hydrometridae).

Figure 14.95. Lateral view of adult Pleidae.

Figure 14.96. Dorsal view of *Plea striola* Fieber (Pleidae; from Brooks and Kelton 1967).

Figure 14.97. Hind tarsus of Pleidae.

Figure 14.98. Foretarsus of *Paraplea* sp. (Pleidae).

Figure 14.99. Foretarsus of *Neoplea* sp. (Pleidae).

Figure 14.100. Lateral view of adult Naucoridae.

Figure 14.101. Ventral view of head and thorax of *Cryphocricos* sp. (Naucoridae).

Figure 14.102. Ventral view of head and thorax of *Ambrysus* sp. (Naucoridae).

Figure 14.103. Dorsal view of *Limnocoris* sp. (Naucoridae).

Saldidae

1.   Hemelytra with long embolar fracture reaching forward at least to level of posterior end of claval suture (fig. 14.121) .... (Chiloxanthinae) 2

1′.   Hemelytra with short embolar fracture, not reaching forward more than half-way from beginning of fracture on costal margin to level of posterior end of claval suture (figs. 14.2, 14.128) .... (Saldinae) 3

2(1).   Sublateral cell of membrane short, only half as long as lateral cell (fig. 14.127) .... ***Chiloxanthus*** Reuter

2′.   Sublateral cell of membrane subequal in length to lateral cell (figs. 14.121, 14.133) .... ***Pentacora*** Reuter

3(1′).   Pronotum with 2 prominent conical tubercles on anterior lobe (fig. 14.126) .... ***Saldoida*** Osborn

3′.   Pronotum without prominent tubercles on anterior lobe (fig. 14.2) 4

4(3′).   Lateral margins of pronotum concave, humeral (posterolateral) angles produced. (fig. 14.132) .... ***Lampracanthia*** Reuter

4′.   Lateral margins of pronotum straight or convex, humeral angles rounded (fig. 14.131) 5

5(4′).   Hypocostal ridge simple, secondary hypocostal ridge absent (fig. 14.137) 6

5′.   Hypocostal ridge complex, secondary hypocostal ridge present (figs. 14.134–14.136) 7

6(5).   Innermost cell of membrane produced anteriorly one-half its length beyond base of 2nd cell (fig. 14.120). First and 2nd antennal segments of male flattened, oval in cross section, the flattened sides glabrous (shining) .... ***Calacanthia*** Reuter

6′.   Innermost cell of membrane produced anteriorly only slightly, not more than one-third its length beyond base of 2nd cell (fig. 14.118). First and 2nd antennal segments of male not flattened, round in cross section, evenly pubescent (hairy) or pilose over entire surface. .... ***Rupisalda*** Polhemus

7(5′).   Second segment of tarsi usually nearly half again as long as 3rd (fig. 14.129). Innermost cell of membrane short, usually reaching only four-fifths the distance to apex of adjacent cell. Outer corium with large, pale spots. Clavus with yellow spot on each side in velvety black area (fig. 14.131). Secondary hypocostal ridge present, oblique, meets or projects to costal margin .... ***Teloleuca*** Reuter

7′.   Second segment of tarsi subequal or slightly longer than 3rd segment (fig. 14.130). Innermost cell of membrane long, usually reaching almost to apex of adjacent cell (figs. 14.119, 14.128). Outer corium with or without pale spots. Clavus with or without yellow spot on each side in velvety black area. Secondary hypocostal ridge present, may or may not meet or project to costal margin 8

8(7′).   Males longer than 5.5 mm, females longer than 6 mm or, *if* shorter, then innermost cell of membrane produced two-fifths to one-half its length anteriorly beyond base of 2nd (fig. 14.119), and dorsal surface unicolorous or with a few small, pale spots on corium and membrane (fig. 14.125). Secondary hypocostal ridge does not meet or project to costal margin (fig. 14.134) .... ***Salda*** Fabricius

8′.   Males shorter than 5.5 mm, females shorter than 6 mm; innermost cell of membrane produced anteriorly only slightly beyond base of 2nd (fig. 14.128) *or, if* inner cell is produced more strongly anteriorly, then dorsum has more or less extensive pale markings. Secondary hypocostal ridge meets or projects to costal margin (figs. 14.35–14.36) 9

9(8′).   Antennae relatively thick, the 3rd and 4th segments thicker than the distal end of the 2nd segment (fig. 14.123). Secondary hypocostal ridge (hrs) meets or projects to costal margin at approximately three-fourths distance from base to embolar fracture. Strigil (file) present on hrs (fig. 14.136), plectrum (rasp) on distal portion of hind femur .... ***Ioscytus*** Reuter

9′.   Antennae relatively slender, the third and fourth segments not thicker than the distal end of the second segment (figs. 14.122, 14.124). Secondary hypocostal ridge meets or projects to costal margin at three-fifths or less distance from base to embolar fracture (fig. 14.135). Strigil and plectrum absent 10

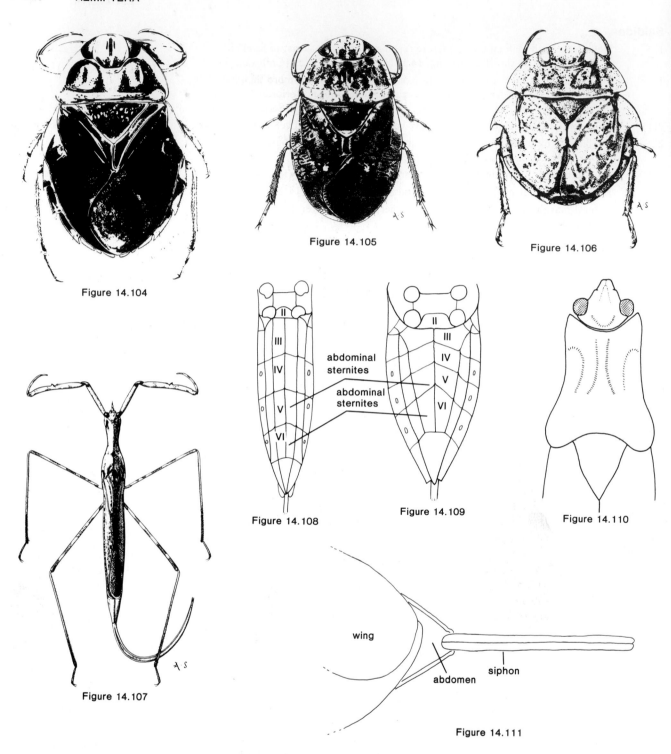

Figure 14.104.

Figure 14.105.

Figure 14.106.

Figure 14.107.

Figure 14.108.

Figure 14.109.

Figure 14.110.

Figure 14.111.

Figure 14.104. Dorsal view of *Ambrysus mormon* Montandon (Naucoridae; from Menke *et al.* 1979).

Figure 14.105. Dorsal view of *Pelocoris shoshone* LaRivers (Naucoridae; from Usinger 1956).

Figure 14.106. Dorsal view of *Usingerina moapensis* LaRivers (Naucoridae; from Usinger 1956b).

Figure 14.107. Dorsal view of *Ranatra brevicollis* Montandon (Nepidae; from Usinger 1956b).

Figure 14.108. Ventral view of abdomen of *Curicta* sp. (Nepidae).

Figure 14.109. Ventral view of abdomen of *Nepa* sp. (Nepidae).

Figure 14.110. Dorsal view of head and pronotum of *Curicta* sp. (Nepidae).

Figure 14.111. Dorsal view of breathing tube of *Nepa* sp. (Nepidae).

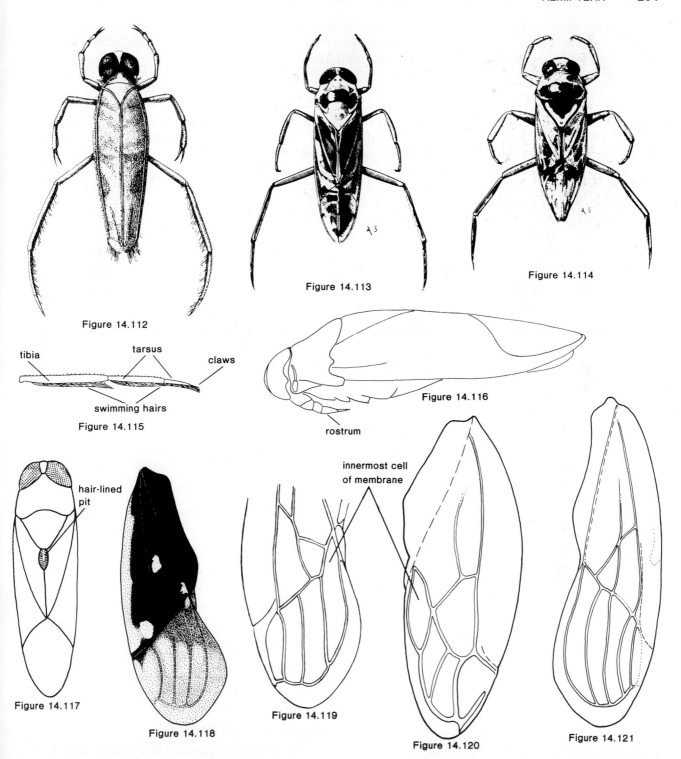

Figure 14.112

Figure 14.113

Figure 14.114

tibia   tarsus   claws

swimming hairs

Figure 14.115

rostrum

Figure 14.116

hair-lined pit

innermost cell of membrane

Figure 14.117

Figure 14.118

Figure 14.119

Figure 14.120

Figure 14.121

Figure 14.112. Dorsal view of *Martarega mexicana* Truxal (Notonectidae; from Menke *et al.* 1979).

Figure 14.113. Dorsal view of *Buenoa scimitra* Bare (Notonectidae; from Usinger 1956b).

Figure 14.114. Dorsal view of *Notonecta unifasciata* Guerin-Meneville (Notonectidae; from Usinger 1956b).

Figure 14.115. Hind leg of Notonectidae.

Figure 14.116. Lateral view of adult Notonectidae.

Figure 14.117. Dorsal view of *Buenoa* sp. (Notonectidae).

Figure 14.118. Left hemelytron of *Rupisalda* sp. (Saldidae).

Figure 14.119. Left hemelytron of *Salda* sp. (Saldidae).

Figure 14.120. Right hemelytron of *Calacanthia* sp. (Saldidae).

Figure 14.121. Right hemelytron of *Pentacora* sp. (Saldidae).

10(9′).   Veins of corium more or less distinct (fig. 14.122). Body usually more than 3.5 mm
long; *if* less, then anterior margin of pronotum wider than collar .... ***Saldula*** Van Duzee

10′.   Veins of corium obsolete (fig. 14.124). Body usually less than 3.5 mm long.
Anterior margin of pronotum usually narrower than collar .... ***Micracanthia*** Reuter

Veliidae

1.   Middle tarsi deeply cleft, with leaflike claws and plumose (plumelike) hairs arising
from base of cleft (fig. 14.146). .... (Rhagoveliinae) 2

1′.   Middle tarsi not deeply cleft and without plumose hairs arising from base of cleft 3

2(1).   Hind tarsi 2-segmented, the basal segment very short (fig. 14.141). Apterous.
Marine .... ***Trochopus*** Carpenter

2′.   Hind tarsi 3-segmented, the basal segment very short (fig. 14.144). Apterous or
macropterous. Riffles of streams and rivers or (rarely) lakes .... ***Rhagovelia*** Mayr

3(1′).   Tarsal formula 1:2:2. (fig. 14.142) .... (Microveliinae) 4

3′.   Tarsal formula 3:3:3. .... (Veliinae) ... ***Paravelia*** Breddin

4(3).   Middle tarsi with 4 leaflike blades arising from cleft (fig. 14.143) .... ***Husseyella*** Herring

4′.   Middle tarsi with narrow claws arising from cleft (fig. 14.142) .... ***Microvelia*** Westwood

ADDITIONAL TAXONOMIC REFERENCES

General

VanDuzee (1917); Hungerford (1920, 1958, 1959); Parshley (1925); Blatchley (1926); China (1955); Usinger (1956a); China and Miller (1959); Lawson (1959); Polhemus (1966, 1973); Brooks and Kelton (1967); Ruhoff (1968); Cobben (1968); Jaczewski and Kostrowicki (1969); DeCoursey (1971); Herring and Ashlock (1971); Miller (1971); Bobb (1974); Cheng (1976); Slater and Baranowski (1978); Andersen (1981a, 1982).

Regional faunas

Arizona: Polhemus and Polhemus (1976).
Arkansas: Kittle (1980).
California: Usinger (1956a); Menke *et al.* (1979).
Central Canada: Strickland (1953); Brooks and Kelton (1967).
Connecticut: Britton (1923).
Florida: Herring (1950, 1951a); Chapman (1958).
Illinois: Lauck (1959).
Kansas: Slater (1981).
Louisiana: Ellis (1952); Gonsoulin (1973a,b,c, 1974, 1975).
Minnesota: Bennett and Cook (1981).
Mississippi: Wilson (1958).
Missouri: Froeschner (1949, 1962).
New Jersey: Chapman (1959).
North Carolina: Sanderson (1982a).
Oklahoma: Schaefer (1966).
Quebec: Chagnon and Fournier (1948).
Rhode Island: Reichart (1976, 1977, 1978).
South Carolina: Sanderson (1982a).
Virginia: Bobb (1974).
Wisconsin: Hilsenhoff (1981).

Taxonomic treatments at the family and generic levels

Belostomatidae: Menke (1958, 1960, 1963); Lauck and Menke (1961); Lauck (1963, 1964).
Corixidae: Hungerford (1948); Sailer (1948); Lansbury (1960); Hilsenhoff (1970); Applegate (1973); Scudder (1976); Nieser (1977); Jansson (1978, 1981); Dunn (1979).
Dipsocoridae: McAtee and Malloch (1925); Štys (1970).
Gelastocoridae: Martin (1928); Todd (1955, 1961).
Gerridae: Anderson (1932); Drake and Harris (1932, 1934); Deay and Gould (1936); Kuitert (1942); Hussey and Herring (1949); Hungerford (1954); Hungerford and Matsuda (1960); Matsuda (1960); Herring (1961); Cheng and Fernando (1970); Scudder (1971b); Calabrese (1974); Kittle (1977b,c, 1982); Stonedahl and Lattin (1982).
Hebridae: Porter (1950); Drake and Chapman (1954, 1958a); Polhemus and Chapman (1966); Andersen (1981b); Polhemus and McKinnon (1983).
Hydrometridae: Torre-Bueno (1926); Hungerford and Evans (1934); Drake and Lauck (1959).
Macroveliidae: McKinstry (1942).
Mesoveliidae: Jaczewski (1930); Andersen and Polhemus (1980).
Naucoridae: Usinger (1941); LaRivers (1949, 1951, 1971, 1974, 1976).
Nepidae: Hungerford (1922c); Polhemus (1976b).
Notonectidae: Hungerford (1933); Hutchinson (1945); Truxal (1949, 1953); Scudder (1965); Reichart (1971); Voigt and Garcia (1976); Zalom (1977).
Ochteridae: Schell (1943); Polhemus and Polhemus (1976).
Pleidae: Drake and Chapman (1953); Drake and Maldonado (1956).
Saldidae: Hodgden (1949a,b); Drake (1950, 1952); Drake and Hoberland (1950); Drake and Hottes (1950); Drake and Chapman (1958b); Chapman (1962); Polhemus (1967, 1976c, 1977); Schuh (1967).
Schizopteridae: Emsley (1969).
Veliidae: Drake and Hussey (1955); Bacon (1956); Polhemus (1974, 1976a); Smith and Polhemus (1978); Smith (1980).

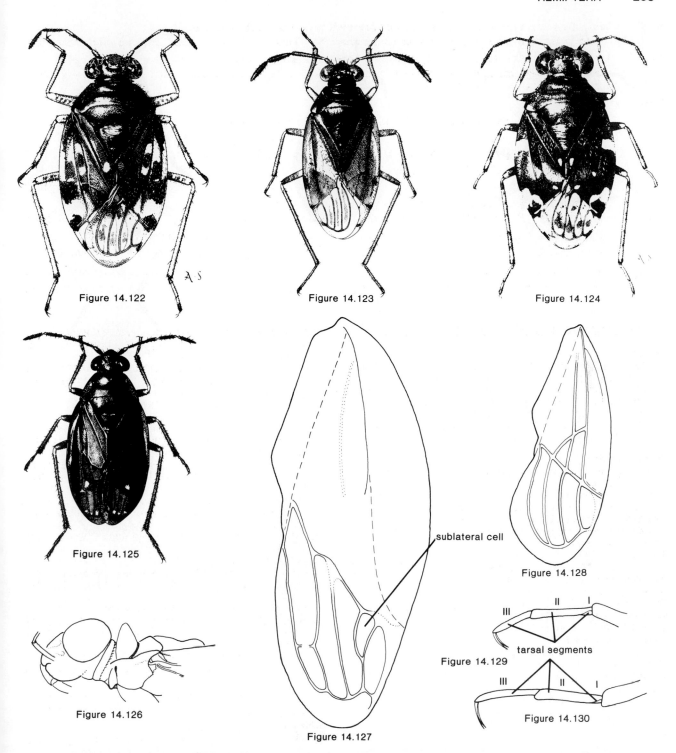

Figure 14.122

Figure 14.123

Figure 14.124

Figure 14.125

Figure 14.126

Figure 14.127

sublateral cell

Figure 14.128

III   II   I

tarsal segments

Figure 14.129

III   II   I

Figure 14.130

Figure 14.122. Dorsal view of *Saldula pexa* Drake (Saldidae; from Usinger 1956b).

Figure 14.123. Dorsal view of *Ioscytus politus* (Uhler) (Saldidae; from Usinger 1956b).

Figure 14.124. Dorsal view of *Micracanthia quadrimaculata* (Champion) (Saldidae; from Usinger 1956b).

Figure 14.125. Dorsal view of *Salda buenoi* (McDunnough) (Saldidae; from Usinger 1956b).

Figure 14.126. Lateral view of head and thorax of *Saldoida* sp. (Saldidae).

Figure 14.127. Right hemelytron of *Chiloxanthus* sp. (Saldidae).

Figure 14.128. Right hemelytron of *Saldula* sp. (Saldidae).

Figure 14.129. Tarsus of *Teloleuca* sp. (Saldidae).

Figure 14.130. Tarsus of *Salda* sp. (Saldidae).

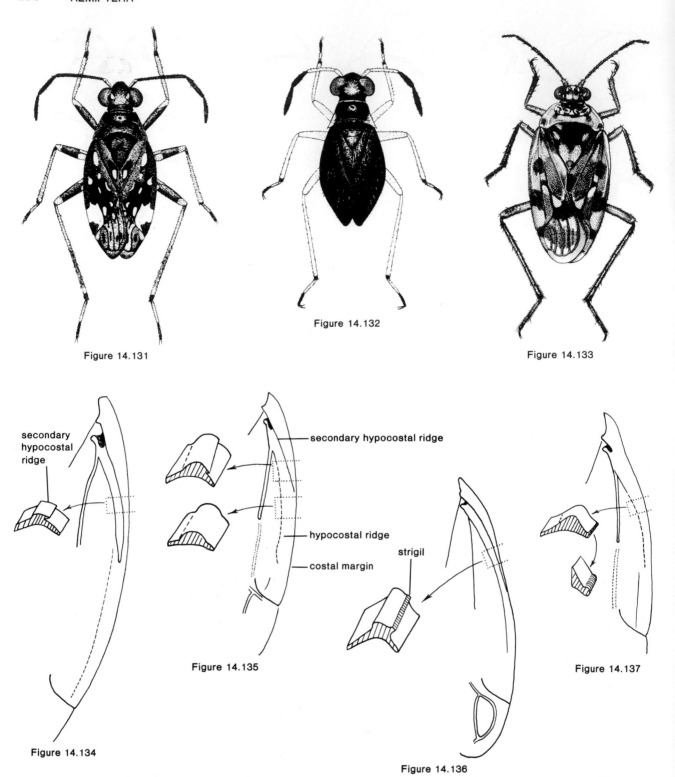

Figure 14.132

Figure 14.131

Figure 14.133

Figure 14.135

Figure 14.134

Figure 14.137

Figure 14.136

Figure 14.131. Dorsal view of *Teloleuca bifasciata* Thomson (Saldidae; from Brooks and Kelton 1967).

Figure 14.132. Dorsal view of *Lampracanthia crassicornis* (Uhler) (Saldidae; from Brooks and Kelton 1967).

Figure 14.133. Dorsal view of *Pentacora signoreti* (Guerin-Meneville) (Saldidae; from Usinger 1956b).

Figure 14.134. Ventral view of hemelytron of *Salda* sp. (Saldidae).

Figure 14.135. Ventral view of hemelytron of *Saldula* sp. (Saldidae).

Figure 14.136. Ventral view of hemelytron of *Ioscytus* sp. (Saldidae).

Figure 14.137. Ventral view of hemelytron of *Rupisalda* sp. (Saldidae).

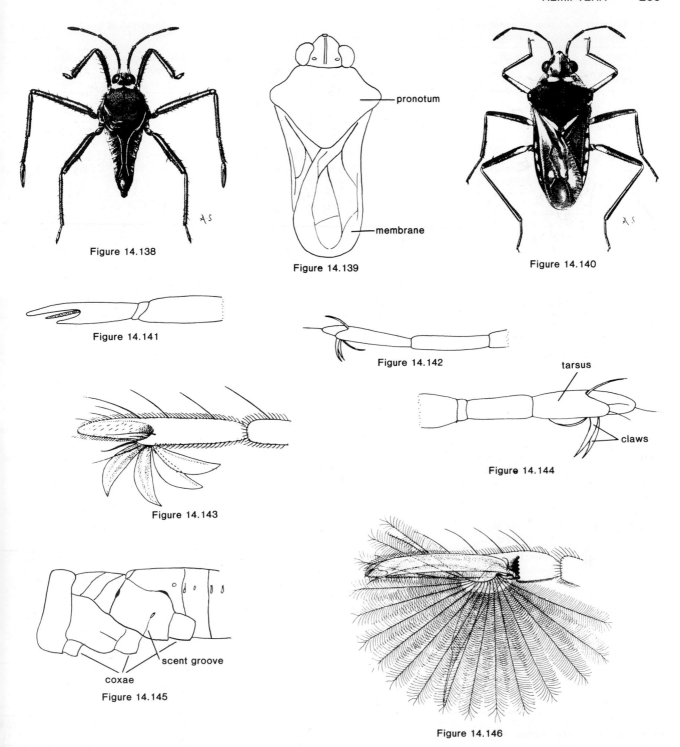

Figure 14.138

Figure 14.139

pronotum

membrane

Figure 14.140

Figure 14.141

Figure 14.142

tarsus

claws

Figure 14.144

Figure 14.143

scent groove

coxae

Figure 14.145

Figure 14.146

Figure 14.138. Dorsal view of *Rhagovelia distincta* Champion (Veliidae; from Usinger 1956b).

Figure 14.139. Dorsal view of *Microvella* sp. (Veliidae).

Figure 14.140. Dorsal view of *Microvella beameri* Mc-Kinstry (Veliidae; from Usinger 1956b).

Figure 14.141. Dorsal view of hind tarsus of *Trochopus* sp. (Veliidae).

Figure 14.142. Lateral view of middle tarsus of *Microvelia* sp. (Veliidae).

Figure 14.143. Lateral view of middle tarsus of *Husseyella* sp. (Veliidae).

Figure 14.144. Lateral view of hind tarsus of *Rhagovelia* sp. (Veliidae).

Figure 14.145. Lateral view of thorax of *Microvelia* sp. (Veliidae).

Figure 14.146. Middle tarsus of *Trochopus* sp. (Veliidae) showing swimming plume.

Table 14A. Summary of ecological and distributional data for *Hemiptera (aquatic and semiaquatic bugs).* (For definition of terms see Tables 6A–6C; table prepared by K. W. Cummins, R. W. Merritt, and J. T. Polhemus.)

Taxa (number of species in parentheses)	Habitat	Habit	Trophic Relationships	North American Distribution	Ecological References[*]
Hemiptera					
Hydrometridae(9) (water measurers)					40, 206, 217, 1150, 1167, 1316, 1381, 13 1886, 2155, 2496, 26
Hydrometra(9)	Lentic—limnetic, surface (in littoral zone), lotic—margins	"Skaters" (slow walkers on surface film)	Predators (piercers) (adult arthropods, dead or live, especially mosquito larvae and pupae, and ostracods)	Widespread	563, 1063, 1140, 131 1526, 1633, 1715, 18 2013, 2300
Macroveliidae(2)	Lotic—margins (semiaquatic)	Climbers—sprawlers (rarely in or on the water)	Predators (piercers)		40, 206, 1150, 1316, 1614, 1886, 2496
Macrovelia(1)	Lotic—erosional and depositional margins (in protected areas)	Climbers—sprawlers	Predators (piercers)	West	1614, 1633, 2496
Oravelia(1)	Lotic—margins	Climbers—sprawlers	Predators (piercers)	West	1633
Veliidae(33) (broad-shouldered water striders)	Generally lentic—limnetic surface, lotic surface	Skaters	Generally predators (piercers) (live and dead arthropods)		40, 41, 206, 217, 103 1063, 1140, 1150, 11 1316, 1381, 1395, 16 1886, 2013, 2155, 24 2620
Husseyella(1)	Lotic and lentic—surface (brackish water)	Skaters	Predators (piercers)	Southern Florida	41, 1633
Microvelia(18)	Lentic—limnetic and lotic—depositional surface	Skaters	Predators (piercers)	Widespread	563, 570, 803, 1633, 1715, 2003, 2005, 24 2453, 2496
Paravelia(4)	Lentic—limnetic and lotic—depositional surface	Skaters	Predators (piercers)	South, Southwest, East, Midwest	563, 1102, 1633, 249
Rhagovelia(9)	Lotic—erosional surface	Skaters	Predators (piercers) (scavengers)	Widespread	393, 561, 563, 1633, 1715, 1867, 2005, 20
Trochopus(1)	Lentic—limnetic (saltwater bays)	Skaters	Predators (piercers)	Southern Florida coast	41, 1633
Dipsocoridae(4) (=Cryptostemmatidae)	Generally lotic—erosional margins	Generally burrowers		West, South, East	2155, 2496
Cryptostemma(3)	Lotic—erosional margins (under stones at stream edge)	Burrowers (active)		California, Georgia	2493, 2496
Ceratocombus(1)	Lentic			Southeast, Maryland, Louisiana	673
Schizopteridae(2)					673
Corixoidea(1)				Tennessee, Louisiana,	673
Nannocoris(1)				Florida	
Gerridae(46) (water striders)	Generally lentic—limnetic surface, lotic surface	Skaters	Generally predators (piercers) (scavengers)		40, 41, 206, 217, 103 1063, 1140, 1150, 11 1316, 1381, 1395, 16 1886, 1997, 2051, 20 2155, 2291, 2292, 24 2620
Gerrinae(21)					
Gerris(15)	Lotic—depositional surface, lentic—limnetic and littoral surface	Skaters	Predators (piercers) (scavengers)	Widespread	290, 324, 325, 327, 5 822, 1219, 1220, 135 1633, 1715, 1743, 18 2005, 2013, 2290, 24 2514, 2683

[*]Emphasis on trophic relationships.

ble 14.A—*Continued*

Taxa (number of species in parentheses)	Habitat	Habit	Trophic Relationships	North American Distribution	Ecological References[*]
Limnogonus(1)	Lentic—limnetic	Skaters	Predators (piercers)	South (primarily tropical)	390, 1167, 1633
Limnoporus(4)	Lentic—limnetic	Skaters	Predators (piercers)	Widespread	215, 325, 1633
Neogerris(1)	Lentic—limnetic	Skaters	Predators (piercers)	South, East	
Halobatinae(2)					
Halobates(2)	Marine (open ocean and protected reefs)	Skaters	Predators (piercers) (scavengers)	East and West Coasts	41, 1037, 1633, 2496
Rhagadotarsinae(8)					
Rheumatobates(8)	Lotic and lentic—surfaces	Skaters	Predators (piercers)	East, Central, South	41, 1633, 1867, 2228
Trepobatinae(15)					
Metrobates(6)	Lotic—erosional surface (usually large rivers)	Skaters	Predators (piercers)	Widespread (especially East)	1633, 1715, 1867, 2496
Trepobates(9)	Lentic—limnetic surface, lotic—depositional surface	Skaters	Predators (piercers)	East, West, South	1633, 1867, 2496
Belostomatidae(19) (giant water bugs)	Generally lotic—depositional—vascular hydrophytes and detritus, lentic—littoral	Climbers—swimmers	Predators (piercers)		206, 217, 476, 1035, 1063, 1140, 1150, 1167, 1316, 1381, 1633, 1634, 1715, 1886, 1997, 2155, 2370, 2496, 2620
Abedus(6)	Lotic—depositional	Climbers—swimmers	Predators (piercers)	Southwest, Southeast	1157, 1633, 2262, 2264, 2496, 2582
Belostoma(8)	Lotic—depositional, lentic—littoral	Climbers—swimmers	Predators (piercers)	Widespread	475, 569, 894, 1342, 1633, 1867, 2263, 2328, 2496, 2582
Lethocerus(5)	Lotic—depositional, lentic—littoral	Climbers—swimmers	Predators (piercers)	Widespread	475, 563, 1167, 1633, 1982, 2065, 2496
Nepidae(13) (water scorpions)	Generally lotic—depositional—vascular hydrophytes and detritus, lentic—littoral	Climbers (poor swimmers)	Predators (piercers)		206, 217, 1035, 1140, 1143, 1150, 1167, 1886, 1316, 1381, 1395, 1633, 1997, 2155, 2496
Curicta(2)	Lentic—littoral	Climbers (poor swimmers)	Predators (piercers)	Southwest, South	1633, 1886, 2689
Nepa(1)	Lentic—vascular hydrophytes	Climbers (poor swimmers)	Predators (piercers)	Central, East	1633, 2496
Ranatra(10)	Lotic—depositional vascular hydrophytes, lentic—littoral	Climbers (poor swimmers)	Predators (piercers)	Widespread	212, 524, 527, 563, 1063, 1633, 1715, 1840, 1867, 1979, 2065, 2450, 2620
Pleidae(5) (pigmy back swimmers)					1381, 1395, 2155
Neoplea(3)	Lentic—vascular hydrophytes (especially dense stands)	Swimmers—climbers	Predators (piercers) (especially microcrustacea)	Widespread	102, 206, 217, 563, 664, 870, 872, 969, 1140, 1150, 1316, 1368, 1886, 2005, 2027, 2496
Paraplea(2)	Lentic—vascular hydrophytes (especially dense stands)	Swimmers—climbers	Predators (piercers) (especially microcrustacea)	Southeast	592
Naucoridae(19) (creeping water bugs)	Generally lotic—erosional, lentic—littoral	Generally clingers, swimmers	Predators (piercers)		206, 314, 1035, 1140, 1150, 1171, 1316, 1395, 1633, 1886, 1985, 2155, 2496, 2620

mphasis on trophic relationships.

Table 14.A— *Continued*

Taxa (number of species in parentheses)	Habitat	Habit	Trophic Relationships	North American Distribution	Ecological References[*]
Ambrysus(13)	Lotic and lentic—erosional (sediments and vascular hydrophytes)	Clingers—swimmers	Predators (piercers)	West, Southwest	99, 290, 1633, 2494, 2496
Cryphocricos(1)	Lotic—erosional (sediments)	Clingers	Predators (piercers)	Texas	1863, 1864, 2357, 24•
Limnocoris(1)	Lotic—erosional (in sediments)	Clingers	Predators (piercers)	Texas	1633, 1863, 2357, 24•
Pelocoris(3)	Lentic—vascular hydrophytes	Climbers—swimmers	Predators (piercers) (Diptera, Belostomatidae)	East, Central, Southwest	217, 563, 969, 1145, 1398, 1545, 1633, 17 1867, 2065, 2449, 24•
Usingerina(1)	Lotic—erosional (warm springs)	Clingers	Predators (piercers)	Nevada	1633, 2496
Corixidae(123) (water boatmen)	Generally lentic—vascular hydrophytes, lotic—depositional (vascular hydrophytes)	Generally swimmers	Generally piercers—herbivores and some predators (engulfers and piercers) or scrapers		206, 217, 290, 314, 4• 869, 920, 1035, 1063, 1137, 1140, 1147, 11: 1167, 1189, 1224, 12: 1316, 1381, 1393, 13• 1487, 1491, 1493, 16. 1715, 1850, 1886, 19• 1967, 1997, 2051, 20• 2155, 2204, 2334, 23: 2378, 2452, 2496, 26: 2790
Arctocorisa(4)	Lentic			North	1849, 1850, 1851, 18: 2328
Callicorixa(6)	Lentic		Predators (piercers)	North	1633, 1849, 1850, 18: 2149
Cenocorixa(8)	Lentic			Northwest	1229
Centrocorisa(1)			Predators (piercers)	Southwest	
Corisella(4)	Lentic—littoral (including brackish water and saline lakes)		Predators (piercers)	West, North	1633, 1715, 2496, 25•
Cymatia(1)				North	1394
Dasycorixa(3)				North	
Glaenocorisa(1)				North	
Graptocorixa(6)			Predators (piercers)	Southwest, West	787, 1633
Hesperocorixa(18)	Lotic—depositional	Swimmers, climbers	Piercers—herbivores	Widespread	216, 563, 1633, 1715
Krizousacorixa (=*Ahautlea*)(3)				Extreme South	1633, 1901
Morphocorixa(2)				Southwest	
Neocorixa(1)				Southwest	
Palmacorixa(4)				Widespread (except extreme North)	1715
Pseudocorixa(1)			Predators (piercers)—herbivores	Southwest	
Ramphocorixa(2)	Lentic—littoral		Predators (engulfers)	Widespread (except West)	920, 1633, 1715
Sigara(46)	Lotic—depositional	Swimmers, climbers	Piercers—herbivores, collectors—gatherers	Widespread	563, 1138, 1140, 114: 1346, 1633, 1715, 20• 2384
Tenagobia(1)	Lotic—depositional			Southwest (primarily tropical)	
Trichocorixa(11)	Lentic—littoral (freshwater, some brackish or saltwater including intertidal pools and offshore sea)	Swimmers, climbers	Predators (piercers) (especially chironomid larvae, Oligochaeta; some collectors—gatherers as early instars)	Widespread	333, 529, 530, 930, 1167, 1633, 1715, 18• 2155, 2496

*Emphasis on trophic relationships.

ole 14.A—*Continued*

Taxa (number of species in parentheses)	Habitat	Habit	Trophic Relationships	North American Distribution	Ecological References[*]
Notonectidae(32) (back swimmers)					121, 206, 217, 1035, 1064, 1140, 1141, 1146, 1167, 1316, 1381, 1395, 1430, 1493, 1886, 1997, 2027, 2155, 2370, 2496, 2620
Buenoa(14)	Lentic—littoral, lotic—depositional	Swimmers (rest submerged in hydrostatic balance)	Predators (piercers)	Widespread	563, 873, 1167, 1633, 1715, 2334, 2457, 2496, 2582, 2811
Martarega(1)	Lotic—depositional	Swimmers (rest at surface in open water)	Predators (piercers)	Southwest	1633
Notonecta(17)	Lentic—littoral, lotic—depositional	Swimmers—climbers (rest submerged or at surface)	Predators (piercers) (including cannibalism)	Widespread	102, 290, 527, 563, 666, 684, 787, 788, 858, 869, 872, 1063, 1355, 1368, 1619, 1633, 1867, 2027, 2065, 2226, 2328, 2358, 2359, 2409, 2456, 2496, 2582, 2811
Mesoveliidae(3) (water treaders)					
Mesovelia(3)	Lentic—vascular hydrophytes (emergent and floating zone including salt marshes)	Skaters—climbers (or sprawlers at water's edge, semiaquatic)	Predators (piercers) (scavengers)	Widespread	40, 206, 217, 563, 1098, 1139, 1140, 1144, 1150, 1167, 1288, 1316, 1381, 1633, 1715, 1867, 1886, 2065, 2245, 2328, 2496, 2620
Hebridae(15) (velvet water bugs)	Generally lentic—littoral vascular hydrophytes (emergent zone and detritus)	Generally climbers (at shore, semiaquatic)	Generally predators (piercers)		40, 206, 217, 1140, 1150, 1316, 1633, 1634, 1886, 1946, 2155, 2496, 2620
Hebrus(12)	Lentic—littoral vascular hydrophytes (emergent zone and sediments at water's edge)	Climbers—"burrowers" (under stones at water's edge)	Predators (piercers)	Widespread	1140, 1633, 2496
Merragata(2)	Lentic—littoral (on mats of floating algae)	Skaters—climbers	Predators (piercers)	Widespread	589, 969, 1633, 1886
Lipogomphus(1)	Lentic—littoral vascular hydrophytes (emergent zone and sediments at water's edge)	Climbers—"burrowers" (under stones at water's edge)	Predators (piercers)	South	
Saldidae(72) (shore bugs)	Generally lentic—vascular hydrophytes (emergent zone), lotic—depositional, beach zone—freshwater	Generally climbers (at shore, semiaquatic)	Predators (piercers) (scavengers, especially Diptera larvae)		84, 206, 217, 1140, 1150, 1633, 1886, 1934, 1935, 2155, 2496
Calacanthia(1)	Lentic—vascular hydrophytes (emergent zone)	Climbers (at shore, semiaquatic)	Predators (piercers)	Alaska, northern Canada	1935
Chiloxanthus(2)	Lentic and lotic—margins (tundra zone)	Climbers (at shore, semiaquatic)	Predators (piercers)	Alaska, northern Canada	1934, 1935
Isocytus(7)	Lentic (including alkaline marshes) and lotic—margins	Climbers (at shore, semiaquatic)	Predators (piercers) (scavengers)	California, Southwest	1633, 1934, 1935
Lampracanthia(1)	Lentic (marshy meadows)	Climbers (semiaquatic)	Predators (piercers)	Arctic (widespread in boreal zone)	1633, 1935

phasis on trophic relationships.

Table 14.A—*Continued*

Taxa (number of species in parentheses)	Habitat	Habit	Trophic Relationships	North American Distribution	Ecological References[*]
Micracanthia(10)	Lentic (marshy meadows)	Climbers (at shore, semiaquatic)	Predators (piercers)	Widespread	1633, 1935
Pentacora(5)	Beaches—marine and freshwater, lotic—depositional	Climbers (semiaquatic)	Predators (piercers) (scavengers)	Widespread	1633, 1934, 1935
Rupisalda(3)	Lentic and lotic—margins	Clingers (on wet or dry vertical rock surfaces)	Piercers—carnivores	Arizona, Idaho	1935
Salda(8)	Beach zone—freshwater, lentic (marshy meadows)	Climbers (semiaquatic)	Predators (piercers) (scavengers)	Widespread	1633, 1934, 1935, 26
Saldoida(3)	Lentic (marshy meadows)	Climbers (semiaquatic)	Predators (piercers) (scavengers)	East, South, Texas, Michigan, Kansas	1934
Saldula(30)	Lentic—littoral and lotic—shorelines (also salt marshes)	Climbers (at shore, semiaquatic)	Predators (piercers) (scavengers)	Widespread	1140, 1468, 1633, 19 1935, 2065, 2334, 23 2496, 2688
Teloleuca(2)	Lotic—margins	Climbers (at shore, semiaquatic)	Predators (piercers) (scavengers)	Arctic, midlatitude mountains	1633, 1935
Gelastocoridae(7) (toad bugs)	Generally lentic—vascular hydrophytes (emergent zone), lotic—depositional, beaches—freshwater	Generally sprawlers (at shore, semiaquatic)	Generally predators (piercers)		206, 1140, 1150, 131 1633, 1886, 2155, 24 2620
Gelastocoris(2)	Lentic—littoral (water's edge) and beaches—freshwater	Sprawlers (jumpers)	Predators (piercers)	Widespread	217, 557, 1142, 1516 1633, 1867, 2003, 20 2496
Nerthra (=*Mononyx*)(5)	Lentic—littoral (water's edge) and beaches—freshwater and marine	"Burrowers" (in mud at water's edge and terrestrial under logs, etc.)	Predators (piercers)	Southwest, Southeast	1633, 1934, 2496
Ochteridae(6)					
Ochterus(6)	Lentic—vascular hydrophytes, lotic—margins and seeps on rock surfaces	Climbers (at shore, semiaquatic), clingers (on seeping vertical rock faces)	Predators (piercers)	Widespread, particularly South and Southwest, North to Nebraska and Great Lakes	214, 217, 1633, 1934 1938, 2155, 2174, 24

[*]Emphasis on trophic relationships.

15

Megaloptera and Aquatic Neuroptera

Elwin D. Evans
Michigan Department of Natural Resources, Lansing

H. H. Neunzig
North Carolina State University, Raleigh

INTRODUCTION

The Megaloptera (alderflies, dobsonflies, fishflies, hellgrammites) and aquatic Neuroptera (spongillaflies) constitute a small worldwide fauna of probably less than 300 species, representing three families (Sialidae, Corydalidae, and Sisyridae). This group of holometabolous aquatic insects contains some of the largest and most spectacular species. The aquatic larvae are predaceous and inhabit both lotic and lentic environments in tropical and temperate climates; however, all eggs, pupae, and adults are terrestrial. Large numbers of adults are seldom seen in nature because they are short-lived, secretive, and many species are nocturnal.

Larval sialids are usually abundant in streams, rivers, or lakes where the substrate is soft and detritus is abundant. Larvae usually burrow into the substrate and feed nonselectively on small animals, such as insect larvae, annelids, crustaceans, and mollusks, in the habitat. Sialids pass through as many as 10 instars during a one- to two-year life cycle. Prior to pupation, larvae leave the stream, river, or lake and pupate in an unlined chamber dug 1–10 cm deep in shoreline soil and litter. Adults (alderflies) usually emerge from late spring to early summer and are active during warm midday hours. Flight is brief and infrequent, and most individuals stay in the same general area where the larvae occur. Apparently, the adults do not feed. Eggs are laid in masses primarily on leaves or branches overhanging the aquatic habitat, on large rocks overhanging or projecting from the water, or on bridge abutments.

Larval corydalids (sometimes called hellgrammites) occur in a wide variety of habitats including spring seeps, streams, rivers, lakes, ponds, swamps, and even temporarily dry streambeds. The life cycle is 2–5 years long with the larvae passing through 10–12 instars. As with sialids, corydalid larvae feed on a wide variety of small aquatic invertebrates. Pupation occurs mostly in chambers in the soil adjacent to the larval habitat. However, some species pupate in dry streambeds, and others prefer soft, rotting shoreline logs or stumps. Adults (dobsonflies, fishflies) emerge from late spring to midsummer. Most species of adult corydalids are nocturnal and may fly considerable distances; some are attracted to lights. Diurnal species are usually found resting or flying near the larval habitats. Oviposition habits are similar to those of adult sialids.

Larvae of the sisyrids are usually found associated with freshwater sponges. They occur on the surface or in the cavities of the host, and pierce the sponge cells and suck the fluids with their elongated mouthparts. Larvae pass through three instars, and some species have several generations each year. Just before pupation, the larvae leave the water, climb onto shoreline plants or other objects, and spin a silk cocoon in which to pupate. Sites chosen for pupation are frequently somewhat secluded, and usually near shore, but larvae may migrate inland up to 20 m before pupating. The cocoon is usually double walled, i.e., composed of an inner, close-meshed enclosure and an additional, more loosely constructed outer envelope. No feces are voided by the larvae prior to pupation; this is typical of many neuropterans but unique among aquatic insects. Adults (spongillaflies) appear to be primarily nocturnal.

EXTERNAL MORPHOLOGY

Megalopteran eggs are quite distinct and can be separated by the size and appearance of the egg mass, and the size, color, sculpturing, and shape of the micropylar process of individual eggs. The egg-burster, left with the hatched egg by a newly emerged larva, is also diagnostic. Identification of larval Megaloptera is based primarily on the number of abdominal filaments, the presence or absence of ventral abdominal gill tufts, and the appearance and location of the eighth abdominal spiracles. Setae and color patterns are also used, particularly for separating species. Pupal identifications of sialids and corydalids can be made based on size and color patterns. Familial and generic identification of adult Megaloptera relies mainly on wing venation; species identification is based primarily on male and female genitalic characters.

Eggs of the two genera of aquatic Neuroptera have not been studied adequately to provide diagnostic characters. Larval sisyrids are best separated at the generic level by the presence or absence and the location of certain setae, and by the presence or absence of spines associated with setae. The labium is useful in separating pupal sisyrids, and there are possibly some differences in the appearance of the cocoons of the two genera. Adult aquatic Neuroptera are identified mainly by wing venation and genitalia.

Megaloptera (Sialidae, Corydalidae)

Eggs: Sialid eggs are laid in even rows of about 200–900 eggs, in compact, more or less quadrangular masses with the eggs vertical (fig. 15.1) or horizontal (fig. 15.2) to the substrate. Each egg is cylindrical, about 0.2 by 0.6 mm in size, with rounded ends; the outer surface is partially or completely covered with small, very short, shield-shaped projections. The micropylar process is cylindrical or slightly fusiform (fig. 15.13). The egg-burster is V-shaped and sharply toothed (fig. 15.3).

Corydalid egg masses of 300–3,000 eggs are compact, rounded to quadrangular in shape, and have 1–5 layers (figs. 15.12, 15.15–15.16); sometimes the eggs have a white or brown protective covering (fig. 15.12). Individual eggs, in general, appear similar to sialid eggs; sometimes the eggs are covered with shield-shaped processes (fig. 15.14), but usually they are relatively smooth. The size of each egg is about 0.5 by 1.5 mm. The position of the eggs relative to the substrate is as in the Sialidae, and the micropylar process is apically enlarged. Egg-bursters are elongate, rounded, or ridged apically, and toothed (fig. 15.4).

Larvae: Terminal instar sialids (fig. 15.5) reach a maximum length of approximately 25 mm, including the unsegmented, median caudal filament. Mouthparts consist of a labrum, two well-developed mandibles (for grasping and engulfing the prey), two maxillae, and a labium. Antennae are four-segmented. The quadrate head is patterned, as is the 10-segmented abdomen, which ranges in color from purplish or reddish brown to yellow. Thoracic legs have two claws. Abdominal segments 1–7 bear four- or five-segmented lateral filaments (fig. 15.5).

Corydalid larvae (figs. 15.17, 15.22–15.23) are larger than sialids, reaching 30–65 mm or more in length when full grown. Mouthparts are similar to those of sialid larvae but the mandibles are usually more robust. Antennae are four- or five-segmented. Thoracic legs have two claws. The head and thorax may be of a uniform color or patterned. Abdominal segments 1–8 bear two-segmented (a short, basal segment and a long, distal segment) lateral filaments (figs. 15.17, 15.22–15.23) and the abdomen terminates in a pair of anal prolegs. Each proleg bears paired claws and a dorsal filament (figs. 15.17–15.23). The last pair of spiracles on the abdomen (segment 8) sometimes is modified with regard to size and location.

Pupae: Both sialid (fig. 15.6) and corydalid (fig. 15.7) pupae are exarate (appendages free, not fastened to body), and range in length from 10 to 12 mm and from 30 to 60 mm, respectively.

Adults: Adults of Sialidae are approximately 10–15 mm in length. Their bodies are black, brown, or yellowish orange with similarly colored wings (fig. 15.8). The head lacks ocelli, and the fourth tarsal segment is dilated (fig. 15.11).

Corydalid adults are 40–75 mm long, with black, brown, or gray bodies; many species have pale smoky wings mottled with brown (fig. 15.9). Some species (*Nigronia* spp.) have darker, almost black, wings with white markings (fig. 15.36). The head has three ocelli and males of some species (*Corydalus* sp.) have very long mandibles (figs. 15.39–15.40). All tarsal segments are simple (fig. 15.10).

Aquatic Neuroptera (Sisyridae)

Eggs: Masses are of 2–5, or occasionally as many as 20, oval, whitish to yellowish eggs covered with a web of white silk. Each egg is about 0.1 by 0.3 mm in size with a short micropylar process (fig. 15.42). The egg-burster is elongate (fig. 15.41).

Larvae: Terminal instars (fig. 15.43) are small (4–8 mm in length), stout, and with conspicuous setae. Body color varies from yellowish brown to dark green. Mouthparts are modified into elongate, unsegmented stylets (usually separated in preserved specimens). Antennae are relatively long and legs are slender and bear a single claw. Second and third instars bear two- or three-segmented, transparent ventral gills, which are folded medially and posteriorly on abdominal segments 1–7.

Pupae: All species are exarate (exposed) and housed in hemispherical, usually double-walled, silken cocoons (fig. 15.47).

Adults: Spongillaflies lack ocelli, have brown bodies with brown wings (fig. 15.52), and are 6–8 mm in length.

KEYS TO THE FAMILIES AND GENERA OF MEGALOPTERA

1.   *Eggs* in masses of approximately 15 mm diameter (figs. 15.1–15.2); egg-burster V-shaped (fig. 15.3).

    Larvae with 7 pairs of 4–5-segmented lateral filaments on abdominal segments 1–7 and a single long caudal filament (fig. 15.5); 25 mm or less when full grown.

    Pupae 10–12+ mm (fig. 15.6).

    Adults less than 25 mm in length (many 10–15 mm) (fig. 15.8); ocelli absent; 4th tarsal segment dilated (fig. 15.11) .... *SIALIDAE*—Sialis Latreille

2.   *Eggs* in masses of 20+ mm diameter (figs. 15.12, 15.15–15.16); egg-bursters
         elongate, apically rounded, or ridgelike and toothed (fig. 15.4).

         Larvae with 8 pairs of 2-segmented lateral filaments on abdominal segments 1–8,
         and a pair of 1-segmented filaments on abdominal segment 10 (fig. 15.17); apex
         of abdomen with 2 anal prolegs, each bearing a pair of claws; 30–65 mm when
         full grown.

         Pupae greater than 30 mm in length (fig. 15.7).

         Adults over 25 mm in length (fig. 15.9); ocelli present; 4th tarsal segment simple
         (fig. 15.10) .... *CORYDALIDAE*

Corydalidae

Eggs

1.   Egg mass 3-layered with a thick, white chalky covering (fig. 15.12) .... *Corydalus* Latreille
1′.   Egg mass not as above 2
2(1′).   Egg mass single layered, may have a thin coating 3
2′.   Egg mass with more than one layer 4
3(2).   Egg chorion with peltate (shield-shaped) processes on dorsum (fig. 15.14) .... *Chauliodes* Latreille
3′.   Egg chorion smooth; a thin coating may cover egg mass .... *Neohermes* Banks, *Protochauliodes* Weele
4(2′).   Egg mass 3–5 layered; western United States and Canada (fig. 15.16) 5
4′.   Egg mass with up to 50 eggs in a second layer; eastern and central United States .... *Nigronia* Banks
5(4).   Egg approximately 2.0 mm long .... *Dysmicohermes* Munroe
5′.   Egg approximately 1.0 mm long .... *Orohermes* Evans

Larvae

1.   Abdominal segments 1–7 with ventral gill tufts at base of lateral filaments (fig.
         15.17) .... *Corydalus* Latreille
1′.   Abdominal ventral gill tufts absent 2
2(1′).   Last pair of abdominal spiracles (segment 8) at the apex of 2 long dorsal
         respiratory tubes extending beyond prolegs (fig. 15.18) .... *Chauliodes* Latreille
2′.   Last pair of abdominal spiracles not at apex of long respiratory tubes 3
3(2′).   Larval head not conspicuously patterned 4
3′.   Larval head with a conspicuous pattern (figs. 15.22–15.23) 6
4(3).   West coast of United States and Canada; last pair of abdominal spiracles either
         dorsal, large, and raised on short tubes (figs. 15.19, 15.30–15.31), or lateral and
         about same size as elsewhere on abdomen (figs. 15.20, 15.29) 5
4′.   East and central United States and Canada; last pair of abdominal spiracles
         dorsal, similar in size to other abdominal spiracles, and borne at apex of short
         respiratory tubes (figs. 15.21, 15.27–15.28) .... *Nigronia* Banks
5(4).   Last pair of spiracles dorsal, large, and raised on short tubes (figs. 15.19,
         15.30–15.31) .... *Dysmicohermes* Munroe
5′.   Last pair of spiracles lateral, similar in size to other abdominal spiracles and
         sessile (figs. 15.20, 15.29) .... *Orohermes* Evans
6(3′).   Spiracles on abdominal segment 8 distinct, associated with raised areas of the
         integument (figs. 15.25–15.26); eastern and western United States and Canada .... *Neohermes* Banks
6′.   Spiracles of abdominal segment 8 less conspicuous, integument not raised around
         spiracle (fig. 15.24); west coast of United States and Canada .... *Protochauliodes* Weele

Adults

1.   Fore wing with white spots in many cells; 20 veins or more reaching wing margin
         posteriad of R_1; M vein with 3 branches reaching wing margin (fig. 15.32) .... *Corydalus* Latreille
1′.   Fore wing lacking white spots (fig. 15.9), or white spots less widely distributed (fig.
         15.36); less than 20 veins reaching wing margin posteriad of R_1; M vein with 2
         branches reaching wing margin (figs. 15.33–15.36) 2

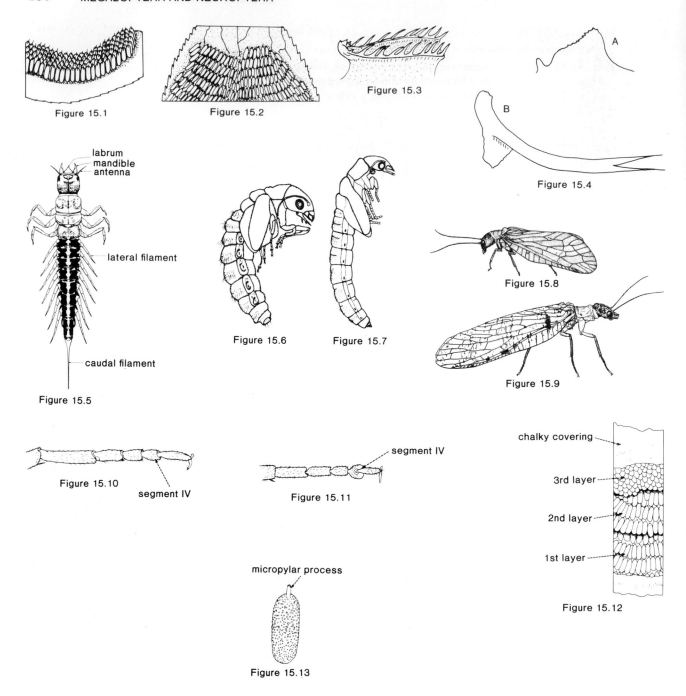

Figure 15.1.

Figure 15.2.

Figure 15.3.

Figure 15.4.

Figure 15.5.

Figure 15.6.

Figure 15.7.

Figure 15.8.

Figure 15.9.

Figure 15.10.

Figure 15.11.

Figure 15.12.

Figure 15.13.

Figure 15.1. Eggs of *Sialis rotunda* Ross (Sialidae).

Figure 15.2. Eggs of *Sialis hamata* Ross (Sialidae).

Figure 15.3. Lateral view of V-shaped egg-burster of *Sialis* sp. (Sialidae) (length 90 μm).

Figure 15.4. Lateral view of corydalid egg-bursters (Corydalidae): *a, Orohermes crepusculus* (Chandler) (length, 115 μm); *b, Corydalus* sp. (length, 160 μm).

Figure 15.5. Dorsal view of larva of *Sialis rotunda* Ross (Sialidae).

Figure 15.6. Lateral view of pupa of *Sialis cornuta* Ross (Sialidae) (after Leischner and Pritchard 1973).

Figure 15.7. Lateral view of *Neohermes* sp. pupa (Corydalidae); length 30+mm.

Figure 15.8. Adult of *Sialis californica* Ross (Sialidae).

Figure 15.9. Adult of *Orohermes crepusculus* (Chandler) (Corydalidae).

Figure 15.10. Distal part of tibia and the tarsus of *Orohermes crepusculus* (Chandler) with a simple 4th tarsal segment (Corydalidae).

Figure 15.11. Distal part of tibia and the tarsus of *Sialis* sp. with a dilated 4th tarsal segment (Sialidae).

Figure 15.12. Section of *Corydalus* egg mass (Corydalidae); covering partially removed.

Figure 15.13. Egg of *Sialis hasta* Ross (Sialidae) (length, 0.6 mm).

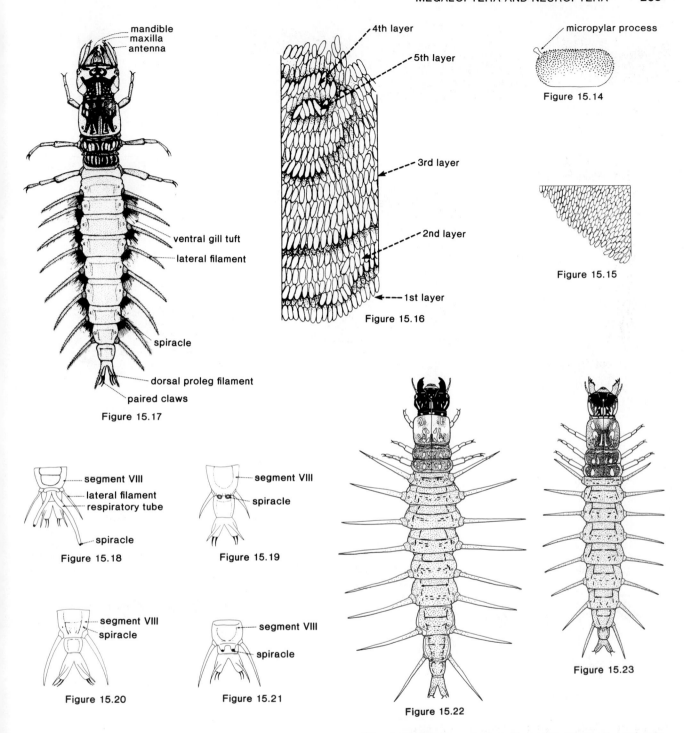

Figure 15.14. Egg of *Chauliodes pectinicornis* (L.) (Corydalidae) (length, 1.0 mm).

Figure 15.15. Section of a *Neohermes* sp. egg mass (Corydalidae).

Figure 15.16. Section of a multilayered egg mass of *Orohermes orepusculus* (Chandler) (Corydalidae).

Figure 15.17. Dorsal view of larva of *Corydalus* sp. (Corydalidae).

Figure 15.18. Dorsal view of caudal segments, respiratory tubes and spiracles of segment VIII of *Chauliodes* sp. larva (Corydalidae).

Figure 15.19. Dorsal view of caudal segments and spiracles of segment VIII of *Dysmicohermes ingens* Chandler larva (Corydalidae).

Figure 15.20. Dorsal view of caudal segments and spiracles of segment VIII of *Orohermes crepusculus* (Chandler) larva (Corydalidae).

Figure 15.21. Dorsal view of caudal segments and spiracles of segment VIII of *Nigronia serricornis* (Say) larva (Corydalidae).

Figure 15.22. Dorsal view of larva of *Neohermes filicornis* (Banks) (Corydalidae).

Figure 15.23. Dorsal view of larva of *Protochauliodes spenceri* Munroe (Corydalidae).

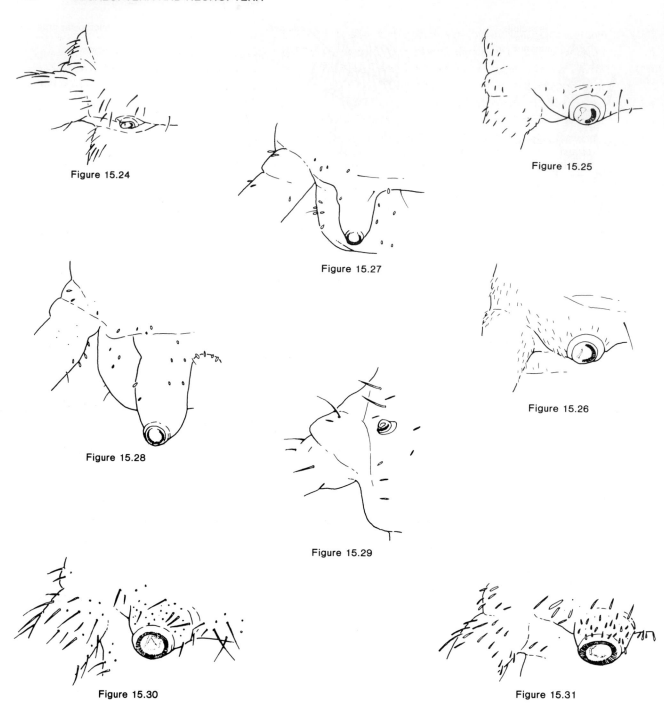

Figure 15.24

Figure 15.25

Figure 15.27

Figure 15.26

Figure 15.28

Figure 15.29

Figure 15.30

Figure 15.31

Figure 15.24. Dorsal view of left spiracle on segment VIII of *Protochauliodes spenceri* Munroe larva (Corydalidae).

Figure 15.25. Dorsal view of left spiracle on segment VIII of *Neohermes concolor* (Davis) larva (Corydalidae).

Figure 15.26. Dorsal view of left spiracle on segment VIII of *Neohermes filicornis* (Banks) larva (Corydalidae).

Figure 15.27. Dorsal view of left spiracle on segment VIII of *Nigronia serricornis* (Say) larva (Corydalidae).

Figure 15.28. Dorsal view of left spiracle on segment VIII of *Nigronia fasciatus* (Walker) larva (Corydalidae).

Figure 15.29. Dorsal view of left spiracle on segment VIII of *Orohermes crepusculus* (Chandler) larva (Corydalidae).

Figure 15.30. Dorsal view of left spiracle on segment VIII of *Dysmicohermes ingens* Chandler larva (Corydalidae).

Figure 15.31. Dorsal view of left spiracle on segment VIII of *Dysmicohermes disjunctus* (Walker) larva (Corydalidae).

2(1').   Posterior branch of Rs forked in both pair of wings (fig. 15.33) 3

2'.   Posterior branch of Rs simple in both pair of wings (fig. 15.34) 4

3(2).   Hind wing with posterior branch of M forked (fig. 15.33) .... *Dysmicohermes* Munroe

3'.   Hind wing with posterior branch of M simple .... *Orohermes* Evans

4(2').   M vein of hind wing with 3 branches reaching wing margin (fig. 15.34) 5

4'.   M vein of hind wing with 2 branches reaching wing margin (fig. 15.35) 6

5(4).   Crossvein present between R_3 and R_4 in fore wing (fig. 15.34); antennae of male
    elongate, moniliform (beadlike), setigerous (bearing setae) (fig. 15.37); apical
    papilla of gonapophysis lateralis absent in female (compare with fig. 15.38) .... *Neohermes* Banks

5'.   Crossvein absent between R_3 and R_4 in fore wing; antennae filiform (threadlike):
    apical papilla of gonapophysis lateralis present in female (fig. 15.38) .... *Protochauliodes* Weele

6(4').   Wings dark with white spots and patches (fig. 15.36) .... *Nigronia* Banks

6'.   Wings pale gray-brown, mottled (fig. 15.35) .... *Chauliodes* Latrielle

KEYS TO THE GENERA OF AQUATIC NEUROPTERA

Sisyridae

Larvae (after Poirrier and Arceneaux 1972)

1.   Pair of dorsal setae present on abdominal segment 8 (fig. 15.43); ventral pair of
    medial setae on abdominal segment 8 raised on tubercles and only slightly closer
    together than those on segment 9 (fig. 15.46); small acute spines at bases of
    thoracic setae (fig. 15.44) (not present in *Climacia californica*) .... *Climacia* McLachlan

1'.   Pair of dorsal setae absent on abdominal segment 8; pair of ventral medial setae on
    abdominal segment 8 sessile and distinctly closer together than those on segment
    9 (fig. 15.45); small acute spines at bases of thoracic setae absent .... *Sisyra* Burmeister

Pupae

1.   Segments of labial palp similar (fig. 15.51) .... *Climacia* McLachlan

1'.   Last palpal segment of labium greatly enlarged and triangular (fig. 15.50) .... *Sisyra* Burmeister

Adults

1.   Rs of fore wing with one fork before pterostigmata (fig. 15.48), fore wing with
    brown markings; last segment of labial palp similar in size and shape to other
    segments (fig. 15.51) .... *Climacia* McLachlan

1'.   Rs of fore wing with more than one fork before pterostigmata (fig. 15.49), fore
    wing uniformly brown; last segment of labial palp greatly enlarged and
    triangular in shape (fig. 15.50) .... *Sisyra* Burmeister

ADDITIONAL TAXONOMIC REFERENCES

General
Pennak (1978); Chandler (1956a,b); Gurney and Parfin (1959); McCafferty (1981).

Regional faunas
California: Chandler (1954, 1956a,b).
Canada: Kevan (1979).
Kansas: Huggins (1980).
Minnesota: Parfin (1952).
Mississippi: Stark and Lago (1980); Poirrier and Holzenthal (1980).
New York: Needham and Betten (1901a).

North Carolina: Cuyler (1956); Brigham et. al. (1982).
Pacific Coastal Region: Evans (1972).
South Carolina: Brigham et al. (1982).
West Virginia: Watkins *et al.* (1975); Tarter (1976).

Taxonomic treatments at the family and generic levels
Corydalidae: Munroe (1951b, 1953); Cuyler (1958); Hazard (1960); Flint (1965); Neunzig (1966); Baker and Neunzig (1968); Glorioso (1981); Evans (1984).
Sialidae: Davis (1903); Ross (1937); Cuyler (1956); Canterbury (1978); Canterbury and Neff (1980).
Sisyridae: Parfin and Gurney (1956); Poirrier and Arceneaux (1972).

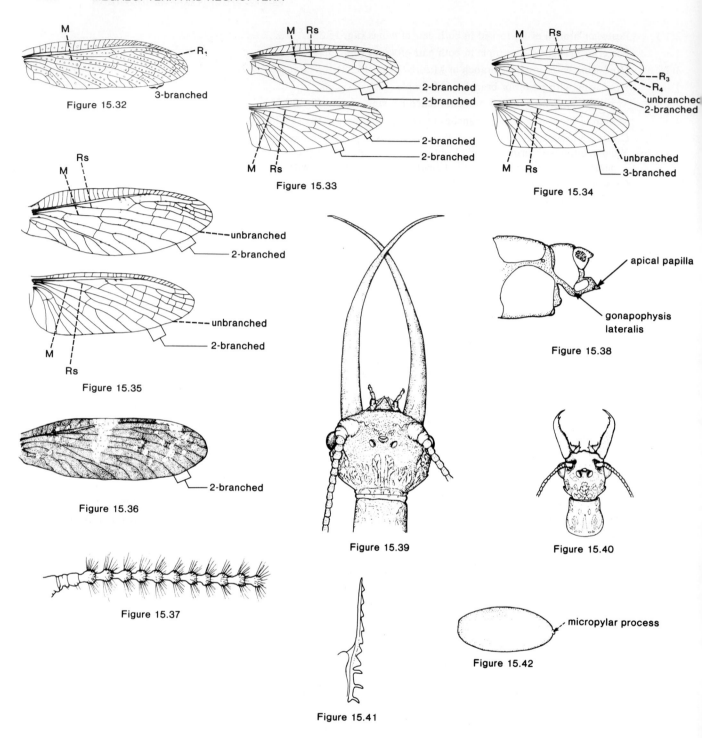

Figure 15.32. Fore wing of *Corydalus* sp. (Corydalidae).

Figure 15.33. Wings of *Dysmicohermes disjunctus* (Walker) (Corydalidae).

Figure 15.34. Wings of *Neohermes* sp. (Corydalidae).

Figure 15.35. Wings of *Chauliodes* sp. (Corydalidae).

Figure 15.36. Fore wing of *Nigronia* sp. (Corydalidae).

Figure 15.37. Basal part of antenna of male *Neohermes* sp. (Corydalidae).

Figure 15.38. Lateral view of female genitalia of *Protochauliodes spenceri* Munroe (Corydalidae).

Figure 15.39. Dorsal view of head and part of prothorax of male *Corydalus* sp. (eastern North America) (Corydalidae).

Figure 15.40. Dorsal view of head and prothorax of male *Corydalus* sp. (western North America) (Corydalidae).

Figure 15.41. Lateral view of egg-burster of *Climacia* sp. (Sisyridae) (after Brown 1952).

Figure 15.42. Egg of *Climacia* sp. (Sisyridae) (after Brown 1952).

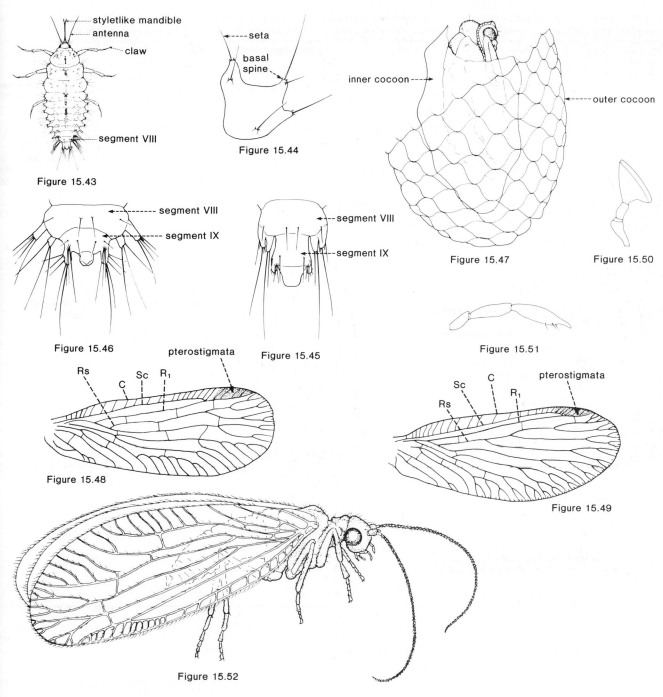

Figure 15.43

Figure 15.44

Figure 15.47

Figure 15.50

Figure 15.46

Figure 15.45

Figure 15.51

Figure 15.48

Figure 15.49

Figure 15.52

Figure 15.43 Dorsal view of larva of *Climacia* sp. (Sisyridae) (after Brown 1952).

Figure 15.44. Right dorsal plate of pronotum of *Climacia* sp. (Sisyridae) (after Parfin and Gurney 1956).

Figure 15.45. Ventral view of caudal abdominal segments of *Sisyra vicaria* (Walker) (after Parfin and Gurney 1956).

Figure 15.46. Ventral view of caudal abdominal segments of *Climacia areolaris* (Hagen) (after Parfin and Gurney 1956).

Figure 15.47. Lateral view of pupa and cocoons of *Sisyra* sp. (Sisyridae).

Figure 15.48. Fore wing of *Climacia* sp. (Sisyridae) (after Parfin and Gurney 1956).

Figure 15.49. Fore wing of *Sisyra* sp. (Sisyridae) (after Parfin and Gurney 1956).

Figure 15.50. Labial palp of *Sisyra* sp. (Sisyridae) (after Chandler 1956a).

Figure 15.51. Labial palp of *Climacia* sp. (Sisyridae) (after Chandler 1956a).

Figure 15.52. Female *Climacia* sp. (Sisyridae) (after Brown 1952).

Table 15A. Summary of ecological and distributional data for the *Megaloptera (alderflies, dobsonflies, hellgrammites)* and the *Aquatic Neuropte.. (spongillaflies).* (For definition of terms see Tables 6A–6C; table prepared by K. W. Cummins, R. W. Merritt, E. D. Evans, and H. H. Neunzig.)

Taxa (number of species in parentheses)	Habitat	Habit	Trophic Relationships	North American Distribution	Ecological References*
Megaloptera Sialidae (alder-flies)(23)					379, 932, 1886
Sialis(23)	Lotic—erosional and depositional (detritus, sediments), lentic—erosional (sediments)	Burrowers—climbers—clingers	Predators—(engulfers) (one species reported to be a collector-gatherer)	Widespread	77, 78, 267, 342, 379, 688, 847, 855, 932, 1048, 1265, 1448, 146. 1773, 1853, 1886, 195' 2098, 2388, 2402, 246. 2562, 2759
Corydalidae(20) Corydalinae (dobson-flies, hellgrammites) (2)	Generally lotic—erosional (lentic—littoral)	Generally clingers—climbers	Predators—(engulfers)		88, 379, 688, 932, 185. 1886
Corydalus(2)	Lotic—erosional and depositional (sediments, detritus)	Clingers—climbers (swimmers)	Predators—(engulfers)	Widespread	88, 270, 379, 688, 932 1323, 1853, 2053, 2332,†
Chauliodinae (fish-flies)(18)					
Chauliodes(2)	Lentic—littoral (sediments, detritus, logs)	Clingers—climbers—burrowers	Predators—(engulfers)	East, Central	88, 498, 531, 1012, 1853, 2053, 2401
Dysmicohermes(2)	Lotic—erosional and depositional (sediments, detritus)	Clingers—climbers	Predators—(engulfers)	West	377, 688, 1739, 1740
Neohermes(5)	Lotic—erosional and spring seeps (sediments, vascular hydro-phytes, leaf detritus)	Clingers—climbers	Predators—(engulfers)	West, East	688, 742, 1885, 2253, 2403
Nigronia(2)	Lotic—erosional and depositional (coarse sediments, detritus, especially under bark and in crevices of woody debris)	Clingers—climbers—burrowers (in crevices and under bark)	Predators—(engulfers)	East, Central	88, 326, 419, 421, 499 1324, 1674, 1796, 190. 2401, 2404,†
Orohermes(1)	Lotic—erosional	Clingers—climbers	Predators—(engulfers)	West	377, 688, 689
Protochauliodes(6)	Lotic—erosional (sediments, detritus), lotic—depositional (detritus) (including intermittent habitats)	Clingers—climbers	Predators—(engulfers)	West	377, 688, 1522, 1739, 1740
Neuroptera Sisyridae(6) (spongillaflies)	Generally lotic—erosional (on sponges), lentic—littoral (on alpine sponges)	Generally climbers—clingers, burrowers (live in or on freshwater sponges)	Predators—(piercers of *Spongilla, Ephydatia,* etc.)		378, 932, 1836, 1853, 1854, 1886, 1925, 192. 2016
Climacia(3)				Widespread (2 Central and Eastern, 1 Western)	378, 932, 2016, 2638
Sisyra(3)				Widespread	378, 924, 1853, 2016

*Emphasis on trophic relationships.
†Unpublished data, K. W. Cummins, Kellogg Biological Station.

Trichoptera

16

Glenn B. Wiggins
Department of Entomology, Royal Ontario Museum and
Department of Zoology, University of Toronto

INTRODUCTION

The Trichoptera, or caddisflies, one of the largest groups of aquatic insects, are closely related to the Lepidoptera. They are holometabolous and, except for a few land-dwelling species (Flint 1958; Anderson 1967) that are secondarily adapted to life out of water, are aquatic in the immature stages in which respiration is independent of the surface and atmospheric oxygen. Adults of almost all species are active, winged insects, although females of at least one North American species are wingless (see Ross 1944, fig. 171). More than 1,200 species are now known in North America north of the Rio Grande, and these are currently assigned to approximately 145 genera in 21 families. This taxonomic richness is a consequence of the broad ecological diversity of the order (Wiggins and Mackay 1978). Caddisflies occur in most types of freshwater habitats: spring streams and seepage areas, rivers, lakes, marshes, and temporary pools. They have been particularly successful in subdividing resources within these habitats. General summaries of information on the biology of Trichoptera are available in several references: Betten (1934), Balduf (1939), Lepneva (1964), Malicky (1973), Wiggins (1977) Mackay and Wiggins (1979), and table 16A.

All North American families are represented in cool, lotic waters, and they have also been successful, to varying degrees, in exploiting freshwater habitats that are larger, warmer, and more lentic. Most larvae eat plant materials in one form or another—algae, especially diatoms on rocks, decaying vascular plant tissue, and the associated microorganisms—but living vascular plant tissue evidently is seldom ingested; some larvae are mainly predaceous. Generally, larval Trichoptera show little selectivity of food, but they are highly and diversely specialized for food acquisition (table 16A).

Caddisfly larvae are perhaps best known for the remarkable nets, retreats, and portable cases they construct. Silk, emitted through an opening at the tip of the labium (fig. 16.26), is used either by itself (e.g., figs. 16.1–16.2, 16.6) or to fasten together rock fragments and pieces of plant materials (e.g., figs. 16.7–16.22). Retreats and cases differ widely in design, materials, and function, but on the whole are consistent at the generic level. Case-making behavior coincides so closely with the diverse ecological roles the larvae fill, that

North American families are usefully categorized into five groups on this basis:

1. *Free-living forms.* Rhyacophilidae, Hydrobiosidae (superfamily Rhyacophiloidea, in part). Larvae move actively about and do not construct a retreat or case of any kind until just before pupation when a crude cell of rock fragments is fastened to some substrate, usually a large rock. Within the cell the larva spins a characteristic tough, brown, ovoid cocoon of silk and undergoes metamorphosis inside the cocoon. Larvae are predators for the most part, although some species feed on algae and vascular plant tissue. Most inhabit cool running waters, some occur in transient streams. The Rhyacophilidae (figs. 16.48–16.49) are generally regarded as the most primitive living family in the Trichoptera. The genus *Rhyacophila,* alone comprising more than 500 species in the northern hemisphere and the largest genus in the order, is abundant and highly diverse in streams especially in western North America. The Hydrobiosidae (fig. 16.50), a family mainly of the southern hemisphere, extend into North America only in the Southwest.

2. *Saddle-case makers.* Glossosomatidae (superfamily Rhyacophiloidea, in part; figs. 16.21, 16.40, 16.47). Using rock fragments, larvae construct portable cases resembling the shell of a tortoise. They live in running waters and occasionally along the wave-swept shores of lakes, grazing on diatoms and fine particulate organic matter on the upper exposed surfaces of rocks and entirely covered by dome-shaped cases. Freshly aerated water for respiration enters the case through spaces between rock pieces. In preparation for pupation, the larva removes the ventral strap and fastens the dome firmly to large rocks or logs with silk; a brown, silken cocoon is spun within the case as in the Rhyacophilidae.

3. *Purse-case makers.* Hydroptilidae (superfamily Rhyacophiloidea, in part; figs. 16.22, 16.37, 16.42). Larvae are extremely small, and are free living until the final instar when they construct purse-shaped or barrel-shaped cases, which are portable in most genera. The first four larval instars, completed within three weeks in some species, differ considerably in morphology from the fifth instar, and represent the only example of larval heteromorphosis known in the Trichoptera. Larvae live in all types of permanent habitats, including springs, streams, rivers, and lakes. Their primary food is algae, mainly the cellular contents of filamentous forms, but diatoms are ingested by species in some genera. One of the few examples known in the Trichoptera of specific

association with a plant occurs in the genus *Dibusa* where larvae have been collected only on the freshwater red alga *Lemanea sp.* Although fifth instar larvae in most genera construct portable cases, those in the tribe Leucotrichiini are sedentary, fixing flattened silken cases resembling the egg cases of leeches to rocks in running waters; the head and thorax are extended through a small opening at either end to graze periphyton and particulate matter from the area surrounding the case. Food reserves of fifth instars cause the abdomen to grow disproportionately large—depressed in the Leucotrichiini and Ptilocolepinae genera but compressed in most others.

4. *Net-spinners or retreat-makers.* Philopotamidae, Psychomyiidae, Xiphocentronidae, Polycentropodidae, Hydropsychidae (superfamily Hydropsychoidea). Most of these families are sedentary and construct fixed retreats, often with capture nets, to strain food particles from the current. Most are dependent on currents of running water to carry food to their retreats, although some also live along wave-washed shorelines of lakes. Larvae of the Philopotamidae (figs. 16.52–16.53) live in elongate, fine-meshed nets (fig. 16.6) in reduced currents on the underside of rocks, where they filter particles smaller than those filtered by other Trichoptera (Wallace and Malas 1976a); the specialized membranous labrum (fig. 16.52) serves to clear accumulated particles from the net.

Larval Hydropsychidae (figs. 16.38–16.39) construct retreats of organic and mineral fragments (fig. 16.4), with a silken sieve net placed adjacent to the anterior entrance to filter particles from the current. Mesh size of the filter net differs: larvae in the Arctopsychinae, living in cold upstream sites with strong currents, spin the largest meshes and feed mainly on other insects; larvae in the Macronematinae, living in downstream sites with slow currents, spin the smallest mesh size and filter small particles; and those in the Hydropsychinae, occupying sites intermediate between these two, spin sieve nets with meshes in a range of intermediate sizes (Wallace 1975a,b; Hauer and Stanford, 1981). By rubbing the femur across ridges on the underside of the head, *Hydropsyche* sp. larvae produce sound (Jansson and Vuoristo 1979). Evidently the sound is a defensive behavior of larvae in protecting their retreat against other hydropsychids, but whether this protective role extends to predators generally is not known.

Larvae in the Polycentropodidae (figs. 16.54, 16.56) construct shelters of several types. Predaceous genera such as *Nyctiophylax* make a flattened tube of silk (fig. 16.1) in depressions in rocks or logs; from concealment within the tube, the larva darts out to capture prey that strike the silk threads emanating from each opening. Larvae in other genera such as *Neureclipsis* construct a funnel-shaped filter net of silk (fig. 16.2) in slow currents and rest in the narrowed base; a single net may be 12 cm long. Larvae of the genus *Phylocentropus* (subfamily Dipseudopsinae, treated as a family by some authors) fashion branching tubes of silk and sand in loose sediments (fig. 16.3), with the ends of the tubes protruding above the sediment; water with food particles in suspension enters the upstream tube, passes through a filter of silk threads that retains the particles, and out of the downstream tube (Wallace *et al.* 1976).

Although larvae of the Psychomyiidae (fig. 16.55) live mainly in running waters, they do not filter food from the current, but graze on the periphyton and fine particulate matter around the entrances to their tubelike retreats. Constructed of fine sand and organic material over a silken lining (fig. 16.5), the retreats are fastened to rocks and logs. Larvae of the Xiphocentronidae (fig. 16.57) construct similar tubes (Edwards 1961).

5. *Tube-case makers.* Phryganeidae, Brachycentridae, Limnephilidae, Uenoidae, Lepidostomatidae, Beraeidae, Sericostomatidae, Odontoceridae, Molannidae, Helicopsychidae, Calamoceratidae, Leptoceridae (superfamily Limnephiloidea). Larvae of these families construct portable cases, essentially tubular in form, of various shapes and materials. Although serving as shelters, portable cases enable larvae to move from place to place seeking food. Moreover, respiratory dependence on natural currents is moderated because undulating movements by the larva cause a current of water to move through the tubular case, bathing the tracheal gills. Experimental work has shown that larvae remove more oxygen from water and thereby survive longer at low oxygen levels when in their cases than when deprived of them (Jaag and Ambuhl 1964); the rate of ventilation increases at lower oxygen levels (Van Dam 1938; Fox and Sidney 1953). Portable cases seem, therefore, to have released some groups from respiratory dependence on stream currents and to have been an asset in the exploitation of the resources of lentic habitats particularly by the Limnephilidae, Phryganeidae, Leptoceridae, and Molannidae. Most larvae of the tube-case families are detritivorous shredders; some are scrapers, and a few are collector-gatherers or predators (table 16A).

The dominant family is the Limnephilidae (figs. 16.41, 16.59, 16.63, 16.69–16.70, 16.77, 16.79) with over 300 species, representing more than 50 genera, in North America alone; the genera are highly diverse in case-making behavior (e.g., figs. 16.7–16.11), habitat, and food (table 16A). Most larvae in subfamilies Dicosmoecinae, Limnephilinae, and Pseudostenophylacinae are detritivorous or omnivorous and have toothed mandibles (as in fig. 16.26); larvae in the Apataniinae, Neophylacinae, and Goerinae have specialized mandibles without teeth (fig. 16.27) and feed mainly by scraping exposed rock surfaces for diatoms and fine organic particles. The Goerinae (fig. 16.79) are often treated as a separate family. Larval Phryganeidae (figs. 16.15–16.16, 16.45–16.46) are large, up to 40 mm in length, and often have conspicuous yellow and black markings on the head and pronotum. Pupae in several genera are unusual in having pupal mandibles reduced to membranous lobes, a specialized feature correlated with the fact that they do not close the anterior end of the pupal case with a silken sieve membrane prior to metamorphosis as do other larvae (Wiggins 1960b). Leptoceridae (figs. 16.43–16.44) are biologically diverse and some are able to swim with their cases; larvae in several genera are predaceous, some in *Ceraclea* feeding on sponges (Resh *et al.* 1976). Larvae of the Odontoceridae (figs. 16.73, 16.75) and Sericostomatidae (figs. 16.71–16.72, 16.74) are primarily burrowers in loose sediments; some odontocerids

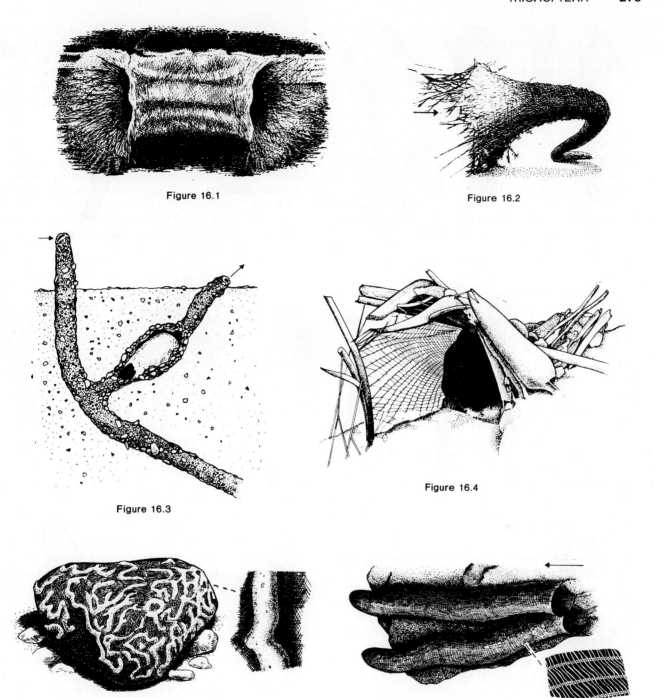

Figure 16.1

Figure 16.2

Figure 16.3

Figure 16.4

Figure 16.5

Figure 16.6

Figure 16.1. *Nyctiophylax* sp. (Polycentropodidae) retreat.

Figure 16.2. *Neureclipsis* sp. (Polycentropodidae) net.

Figure 16.3. *Phylocentropus* sp. (Polycentropodidae) buried branching tube.

Figure 16.4. *Hydropsyche* sp. (Hydropsychidae) net and retreat.

Figure 16.5. *Psychomyia* sp. (Psychomyiidae) tubular retreats on rock, detail of tube.

Figure 16.6. *Dolophilodes* sp. (Philopotamidae) nets, detail of mesh.

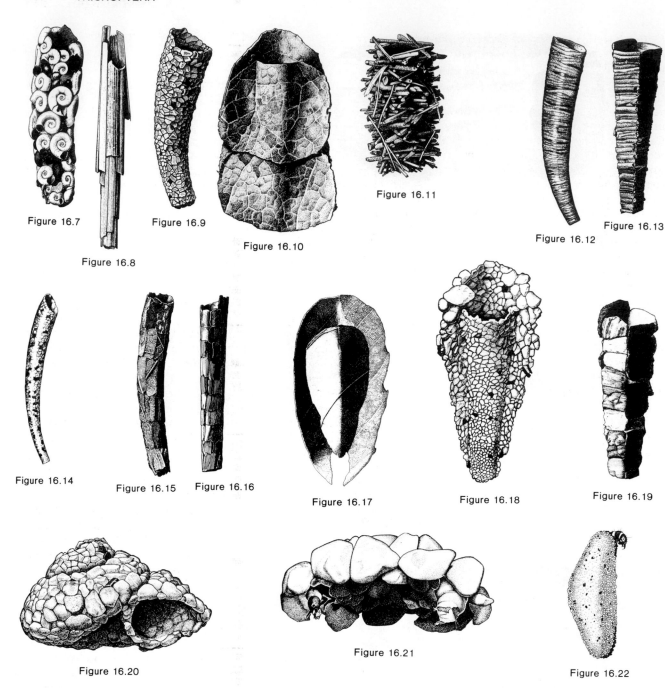

Figure 16.7

Figure 16.8

Figure 16.9

Figure 16.10

Figure 16.11

Figure 16.12

Figure 16.13

Figure 16.14

Figure 16.15

Figure 16.16

Figure 16.17

Figure 16.18

Figure 16.19

Figure 16.20

Figure 16.21

Figure 16.22

Figure 16.7. *Philarctus* sp. (Limnephilidae) portable case.

Figure 16.8. *Arctopora* sp. (Limnephilidae) portable case.

Figure 16.9. *Pseudostenophylax* sp. (Limnephilidae) portable case.

Figure 16.10. *Clostoeca* sp. (Limnephilidae) portable case.

Figure 16.11. *Platycentropus* sp. (Limnephilidae) portable case.

Figure 16.12 *Micrasema* sp. (Brachycentridae) portable case.

Figure 16.13. *Brachycentrus* sp. (Brachycentridae) portable case.

Figure 16.14. *Neothremma* sp. (Uenoidae) portable case.

Figure 16.15. *Oligostomis* sp. (Phryganeidae) portable case.

Figure 16.16. *Agrypnia* sp. (Phryganeidae) portable case.

Figure 16.17. *Anisocentropus* sp. (Calamoceratidae) portable case.

Figure 16.18. *Molanna* sp. (Molannidae) portable case.

Figure 16.19. *Lepidostoma* sp. (Lepidostomatidae) portable case.

Figure 16.20. *Helicopsyche* sp. (Helicopsychidae) portable case.

Figure 16.21. *Glossosoma* sp. (Glossosomatidae) portable case.

Figure 16.22. *Hydroptila* sp. (Hydroptilidae) portable case.

(*Psilotreta* sp.) pupate in dense clusters on rocks. Larval Brachycentridae (figs. 16.12–16.13, 16.58, 16.60) are confined to running waters, those of *Brachycentrus* sp. unusual among the tube-case groups in filtering food from the current with their outstretched legs. The flattened and dorsally cowled larval cases of Molannidae (figs. 16.18, 16.61–16.62) are unusually cryptic; even more so are those of some Calamoceratidae (figs. 16.17, 16.65), particularly *Heteroplectron* species using hollow twigs or pieces of bark as cases. Many larvae of the Lepidostomatidae (fig. 16.76), important components of the shredder community in cool streams, construct cases of sand grains or silk in early instars, later changing to four-sided cases of leaf and bark pieces (fig. 16.19). Uenoidae larvae (figs. 16.14, 16.78) in western montane streams often occur in aggregations on rocks. Beraeidae (figs. 16.51, 16.67–16.68) are extremely local in North America and have been recorded only from the water-saturated muck of spring seepage areas in the East. Perhaps the most unusual larvae of all belong to the Helicopsychidae (figs. 16.20, 16.35), which construct cases coiled like the shell of a snail; these larvae graze diatoms and fine particulate matter from exposed surfaces of rocks in rivers and along wave-swept shorelines of lakes.

Although most species of North American caddisflies are univoltine, some require two years for development, and others less than a year. Larvae of most species have five instars (a few, up to seven), after which they fasten the case with silk to a solid substrate, sealing off the ends. The actual pupal stage lasts from two to three weeks, although in some groups it is preceded by a prepupal phase of up to several weeks' duration when the larva is in diapause (Wiggins 1977). When metamorphosis is complete, the active adult within the pupal cuticle (figs. 16.29–16.30) leaves the pupal case and swims to the surface. Eclosion occurs either on the water surface (e.g., in large lakes) or on some emergent object.

Adults of most species are quiescent during the day, but fly actively during evening and night hours. Some are known to feed on plant nectar (Crichton 1957). Although most adult caddisflies probably live less than one month, adults of the Limnephilidae whose larvae inhabit temporary pools live for at least three months; their reproductive maturity is delayed by diapause until late summer and early autumn when drought conditions are waning (Novak and Sehnal 1963; Wiggins 1973a). Diapause intervenes to suspend development at various points in the life cycles of other species. Eggs are deposited in water in most families, but above water in some groups of the Limnephilidae, and entirely in the absence of surface water by some species inhabiting temporary vernal pools. A further specialization for drought occurs in some Polycentropodidae whose eggs remain in the dry basin of temporary pools and do not hatch until water is replenished the following spring (Wiggins *et al.* 1980). Eggs are enclosed in a matrix of spumaline (a polysaccharide complex; Hinton 1981), which, in the Limnephiloidea, becomes greatly enlarged as water is absorbed.

EXTERNAL MORPHOLOGY

Larvae

Viewed dorsally (fig. 16.28), the head capsule is subdivided into three parts by Y-shaped dorsal ecdysial lines (sutures); the frontoclypeal apotome is separated on each side by frontoclypeal sutures from the rounded parietals. Posteromesally, the parietals meet along the coronal suture. Ventrally, they come together along the ventral ecdysial line, but frequently the parietals are partially or completely separated mesally by the ventral apotome. Peglike antennae (fig. 16.28) are visible on larvae in families constructing portable cases, but are not apparent in other groups. The eyes are groups of ocelli. Cutting edges of the mandibles are of two basic types correlated with the method of feeding—a series of separate points or teeth (fig. 16.26) or an entire scraping edge (fig. 16.27); silk is emitted from an opening at the tip of the labium (fig. 16.26).

The pronotum is covered by a heavily sclerotized plate subdivided by a mid-dorsal ecdysial line (fig. 16.28); the prosternum sometimes bears small sclerites and, in certain families, a membranous prosternal horn (fig. 16.23). The trochantin is a derivative of the prothoracic pleuron. The mesonotum may bear sclerotized plates (fig. 16.28), small sclerites (fig. 16.46), or be entirely membranous (fig. 16.52); the metanotum (fig. 16.28) in most families is largely membranous. Notal setae on the last two thoracic segments may be single or grouped on sclerites, but their basic arrangement into three setal areas—sa1, sa2 and sa3—is usually apparent (figs. 16.25, 16.28). In families with ambulatory larvae, the middle and hind pairs of legs are substantially longer than the first (fig. 16.23).

The abdomen (fig. 16.23) consists of nine segments, usually entirely membranous except for a dorsomedian sclerite on segment IX in some families. This sclerite is not always pigmented and may be difficult to distinguish in certain groups. Segment I of the abdomen in families constructing portable tube-cases usually bears prominent humps—one on each side and one dorsally; these humps, which serve as "spacers" facilitating the movement of the respiratory current through the case, are retractile and may not be prominent in preserved specimens. Tracheal gills are filamentous extensions of the body wall that contain fine tracheoles in the epithelium. Some larvae lack gills entirely. Gills may be single (fig. 16.23) or branched (e.g., fig. 16.39) and are generally arranged in dorsal, lateral, and ventral pairs of gills on each side of a segment. Lightly sclerotized ovoid rings are discernible ventrally on most abdominal segments in larvae of the Limnephilidae (fig. 16.23) and dorsally and laterally in certain limnephilid subgroups; these rings enclose chloride epithelia that are areas of the hypodermis specialized for ionic absorption in osmoregulation (Wichard and Komnick 1973). Anal prolegs terminating the abdomen bear a pointed anal claw that sometimes has a small accessory hook. The prolegs are short and laterally directed (fig. 16.23) in larvae with portable cases, enabling them to hold fast to the silken lining of the case, but are longer in net-spinning larvae (fig. 16.24).

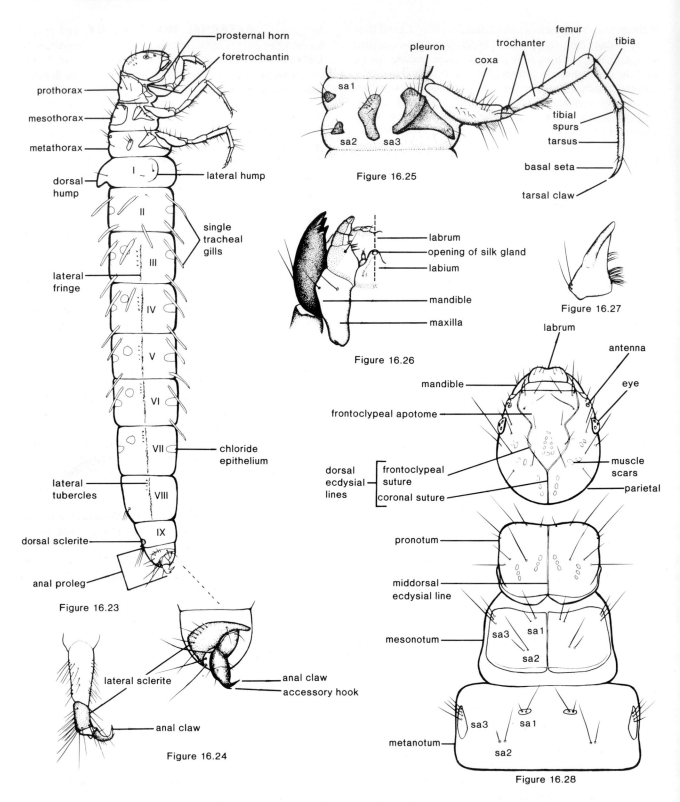

Figure 16.23

Figure 16.24

Figure 16.25

Figure 16.26

Figure 16.27

Figure 16.28

Figure 16.23. Lateral view of larva (Limnephilidae), abdominal segments numbered, detail of anal proleg.

Figure 16.24. Lateral view of anal proleg of larva (Polycentropodidae).

Figure 16.25. Lateral view of metathorax and leg of larva (Limnephilidae).

Figure 16.26. Ventral view of larval mouthparts (Leptoceridae: *Mystacides* sp.), mandible with pointed teeth.

Figure 16.27. Ventral view of larval mandible (Limnephilidae: *Neophylax* sp.) with uniform scraping edge.

Figure 16.28. Dorsal view of larval head and thorax (Limnephilidae).

Pupae

Heavily sclerotized pupal mandibles (fig. 16.29) serve to cut an opening in the pupal case through which the insect escapes to swim to the surface for emergence (Wiggins 1960b). Stout single setae occur on various parts of the head, those on the labrum are hooked apically in some groups; dorsal and ventrolateral tufts of setae often occur near the bases of the antennae (fig. 16.29).

The compacted wings conform tightly to the body, and the legs are folded ventrolaterally. The middle tarsi bear a dense fringe of hairs (fig. 16.30), rendering the leg more effective for swimming from the pupal case to the surface.

Several of the abdominal segments bear paired dorsal sclerites—the hookplates (fig. 16.30); hookplates are designated as anterior (a) or posterior (p) in accordance with their position on a particular segment, with at least segment V usually having both pairs. Hooks on anterior plates are directed posteriorly, and those on posterior plates directed anteriorly. In several families, segment I bears a rough spined ridge. These abdominal sclerites engage with the silken lining of the pupal case, enabling the insect to move within—especially important when it is ready to vacate the case for emergence. Pupal gills generally coincide with larval gills. A lateral fringe of setae is variously developed in a number of families, absent in others; when present, the lateral fringe extends along the side of several segments (fig. 16.30), turning ventrad on segment VIII (fig. 16.31). At the apex of the abdomen in many families is a pair of anal processes (fig. 16.31); these are often elongate, but may also be short and lobate (e.g., fig. 16.106).

Adults

Structural characters of adult Trichoptera are identified in figures 16.32 to 16.34. Setal warts are widely used in the key as diagnostic characters for families; usually clearly delineated by color and texture, the warts are somewhat dome-shaped in profile and bear setae, only the basal pits of which are illustrated in the figures. Setal warts of the head in most families are reduced in various ways from the generalized condition of figure 16.33. The three ocelli occurring on the head in some families can be distinguished by their rounded, beadlike appearance (fig. 16.33). The number and relative length of segments in the maxillary palp is an important diagnostic character; segments are numbered 1–5 from base to apex (fig. 16.32). The terminal segment (no. 5) of the maxillary palp in some families is flexible, and numerous transverse striations can often be seen in the cuticle (fig. 16.133). Sexual dimorphism occurs in the maxillary palpi of some families of the Trichoptera: palpi of all females are five-segmented and largely unmodified, but those of males are reduced in the number of segments—Phryganeidae, 4; Limnephilidae, Brachycentridae, and Helicopsychidae, 3. Maxillary palpi and basal segments of the antennae may be markedly enlarged and distorted in males of the Lepidostomatidae and Sericostomatidae.

Tibial spurs of the legs are large, modified setae occurring in pairs at the apex of the tibia, and singly or paired in a preapical position (fig. 16.32). The full complement of spurs is expressed in an abbreviated form, e.g., 3, 4, 4 for figure 16.32, giving the respective number of spurs on the fore, middle, and hind legs. Wings of caddisflies (figs. 16.34, 16.128) provide a wealth of taxonomic characters involving shape, venation, and other aspects.

Segment I of the abdomen is reduced ventrally, a point to be remembered when locating a particular segment (fig. 16.32). A pair of glands, probably pheromonal, open on the sternum of segment V, often in a raised ovoid sclerotized area (fig. 16.150) or in a slender filament. These are present in at least some representatives of the Rhyacophilidae, Glossosomatidae, Hydroptilidae, Hydropsychidae, Psychomyiidae, Polycentropodidae, Phryganeidae, Brachycentridae, Limnephilidae, Beraeidae, and Molannidae (Schmid 1980). Males are readily distinguished from females (Nielsen 1980) by the paired forcepslike claspers or inferior appendages, and generally more complex genitalic structures terminating the abdomen (fig. 16.32). (See Ross [1944] for examples of genitalic structures in all families.)

An illustration of the head and first two thoracic segments is provided for each family as a means of confirming identifications based on other characters.

KEYS TO THE FAMILIES OF TRICHOPTERA

Generic keys to the Nearctic fauna are given in Wiggins (1977) and in chapter 17 of this volume. Diagnostic characters to pupae of some genera are given by Ross (1944) but are not yet available for most genera. Keys to adults of many genera are given by Ross (1944) and Schmid (1980).

Larvae

1.   Anal claw comb-shaped (fig. 16.35); larva constructing portable case of sand
         grains or small rock fragments, coiled to resemble a snail shell (fig. 16.20).
         Widespread in rivers, streams, and wave-swept shorelines of lakes .... *HELICOPSYCHIDAE—Helicopsyche*

1'.   Anal claw hook-shaped (figs. 16.36, 16.39); larval case straight or nearly so, not
         resembling a snail shell, or larva not constructing a portable case 2

2(1').   Dorsum of each thoracic segment covered by sclerites, usually closely appressed
         along the mid-dorsal line (fig. 16.37), sometimes subdivided with thin transverse
         sutures (fig. 16.38), or some sclerites undivided 3

2'.   Metanotum and sometimes mesonotum entirely membranous, or largely so and
         bearing several pairs of smaller sclerites (figs. 16.40–16.41) 4

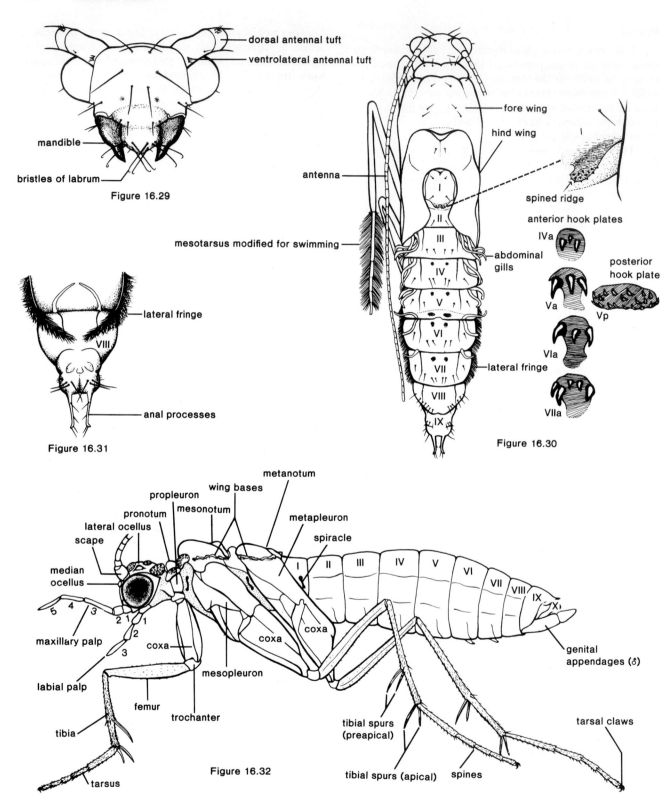

— dorsal antennal tuft

— ventrolateral antennal tuft

mandible —

bristles of labrum —

Figure 16.29

fore wing

hind wing

antenna —

mesotarsus modified for swimming —

spined ridge

anterior hook plates

IVa

abdominal gills

posterior hook plate

Va

Vp

lateral fringe

VIa

VIIa

Figure 16.30

lateral fringe —

VIII

anal processes —

Figure 16.31

metanotum

wing bases

propleuron

metapleuron

pronotum   mesonotum

spiracle

lateral ocellus

scape

median ocellus

coxa

coxa

coxa

maxillary palp

labial palp

mesopleuron

coxa

trochanter

femur

tibia

tibial spurs (preapical)

tarsus

Figure 16.32

tibial spurs (apical)   spines

genital appendages (♂)

tarsal claws

Figure 16.29. Frontal view of pupal head (Limnephilidae).

Figure 16.30. Dorsal view of pupa (Limnephilidae), abdominal segments numbered, detail of hook plates.

Figure 16.31. Ventral view of pupal abdominal segments VIII and IX with anal processes (Limnephilidae).

Figure 16.32. Lateral view of adult (Rhyacophilidae), wings not shown.

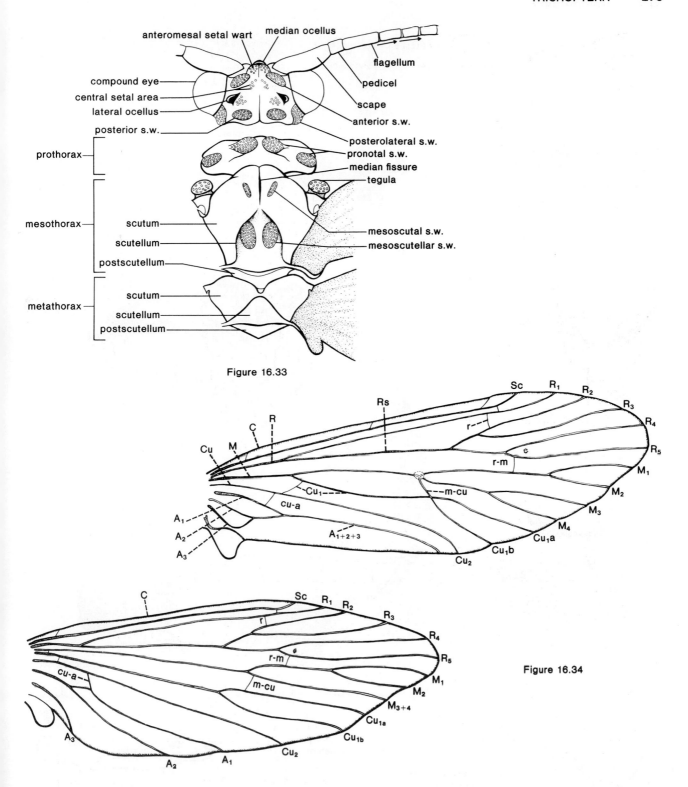

Figure 16.33

Figure 16.34

Figure 16.33. Dorsal view of head and thorax of adult trichopteran, generalized; *s.w.,* setal wart.

Figure 16.34. Wing venation of adult (Rhyacophilidae). Major longitudinal veins R$_1$, M, etc.; crossveins connecting major veins r-m, m-cu, etc.

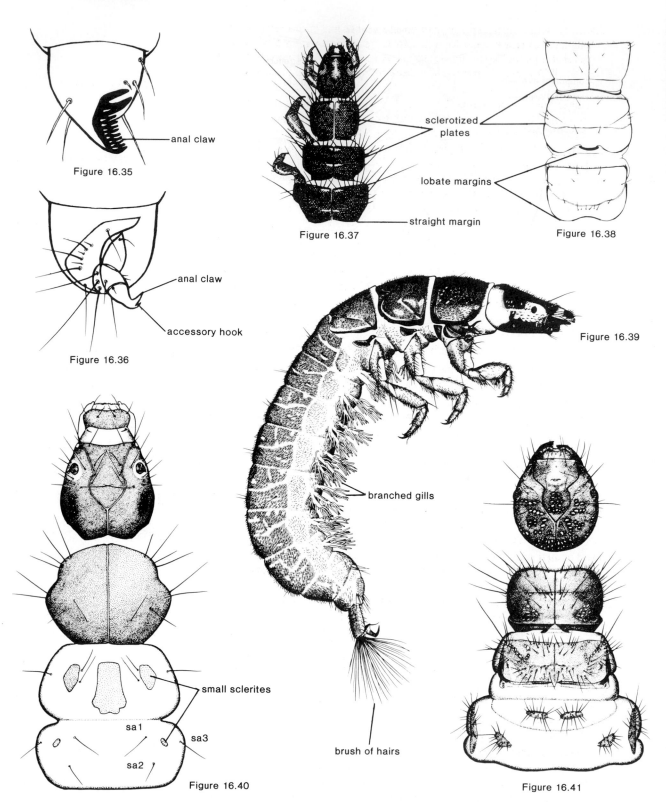

Figure 16.35

anal claw

Figure 16.36

anal claw

accessory hook

sclerotized plates

lobate margins

straight margin

Figure 16.37

Figure 16.38

Figure 16.39

branched gills

brush of hairs

small sclerites

sa1

sa3

sa2

Figure 16.40

Figure 16.41

Figure 16.35. Lateral view of anal proleg of *Helicopsyche* sp. (Helicopsychidae) larva.

Figure 16.36. Lateral view of larval anal proleg (Limnephilidae).

Figure 16.37. Dorsal view of head and thorax of *Ochrotrichia* sp. (Hydroptilidae) larva.

Figure 16.38. Dorsal view of thorax of *Homoplectra* sp. (Hydropsychidae) larva.

Figure 16.39. Lateral view of *Hydropsyche* sp. (Hydropsychidae) larva.

Figure 16.40. Dorsal view of head and thorax of *Matrioptila* sp. (Glossosomatidae) larva.

Figure 16.41. Dorsal view of head and thorax of *Homophylax* sp. (Limnephilidae) larva.

3(2). Abdomen with ventrolateral rows of branched gills, and with prominent brush of long hairs at base of anal claw (fig. 16.39); posterior margin of meso- and metanotal plates lobate (fig. 16.38); larvae construct fixed retreats (e.g., fig. 16.4). Widespread in rivers and streams, occasionally along rocky shores of lakes .... *HYDROPSYCHIDAE* (p. 318)

3′. Abdomen lacking ventrolateral gills, and with only 2 or 3 hairs at base of anal claw (fig. 16.42); posterior margin of meso- and metanotal plates usually straight (fig. 16.37); minute larvae usually less than 6 mm long, constructing portable cases of sand (e.g., fig. 16.22), algae, or fixed cases of silk. Widespread in rivers, streams, and lakes .... *HYDROPTILIDAE** (p. 321)

4(2′). Antennae very long and prominent, at least 6 times as long as wide (fig. 16.43); and/or sclerites on mesonotum lightly pigmented except for a pair of dark curved lines on posterior half (fig. 16.44); larvae construct portable cases of various materials. Widespread in lakes and rivers .... *LEPTOCERIDAE* (p. 324)

4′. Antennae of normal length, no more than 3 times as long as wide (fig. 16.45); or not apparent; mesonotum never with a pair of dark curved lines as above 5

5(4′). Mesonotum largely or entirely membranous (fig. 16.45), or with small sclerites covering not more than half of notum (fig. 16.46); pronotum never with an anterolateral lobe (fig. 16.46) 6

5′. Mesonotum largely covered by sclerotized plates, variously subdivided and usually pigmented (fig. 16.41), although sometimes lightly; pronotum sometimes with a transverse carina terminating in prominent anterolateral lobes (fig. 16.51) 13

6(5). Abdominal segment IX with sclerite on dorsum (fig. 16.48) 7

6′. Abdominal segment IX with dorsum entirely membranous (fig. 16.53) 10

7(6). Metanotal sa3 usually consisting of a cluster of setae arising from a small rounded sclerite (figs. 16.45–16.46); prosternal horn present (fig. 16.45); larvae construct tubular portable cases, mainly of plant materials (e.g., figs. 16.15–16.16). Widespread in lakes, ponds, and slow streams .... *PHRYGANEIDAE* (p. 340)

7′. Metanotal sa3 consisting of a single seta not arising from a sclerite (fig. 16.40); prosternal horn absent; larvae either constructing a tortoiselike case of stones or free-living 8

8(7′). Basal half of anal proleg broadly joined with segment IX, anal claw with at least one dorsal accessory hook (fig. 16.47); larvae construct tortoiselike portable cases of small stones (fig. 16.21). Widespread in rivers and streams .... *GLOSSOSOMATIDAE* (p. 313)

8′. Most of anal proleg free from segment IX, anal claw without dorsal accessory hooks (fig. 16.48); larvae free living without cases or fixed retreats until pupation 9

9(8′). Tibia, tarsus, and claw of fore leg articulating against ventral lobe of femur to form a chelate leg (fig. 16.50). Southwest, running waters .... *HYDROBIOSIDAE—Atopsyche*

9′. Fore leg normal, not chelate as above (fig. 16.49). Widespread in running waters ... *RHYACOPHILIDAE* (p. 345)

10(6′). Labrum membranous and T-shaped (fig. 16.52), often withdrawn from view in preserved specimens; larvae construct fixed sac-shaped nets of silk (fig. 16.6). Widespread in rivers and streams .... *PHILOPOTAMIDAE* (p. 340)

10′. Labrum sclerotized, rounded and articulated in normal way (fig. 16.54) 11

11(10′). Mesopleuron extended anteriorly as a lobate process, tibiae and tarsi fused together on all legs (fig. 16.57); larvae construct fixed tubes of sand in small streams. Southern Texas .... *XIPHOCENTRONIDAE—Xiphocentron*

11′. Mesopleuron not extended anteriorly, tibiae and tarsi separate on all legs (fig. 16.55) 12

12(11′). Trochantin of prothoracic leg with apex acute, fused completely with episternum without separating suture (fig. 16.56); larvae construct exposed funnel-shaped capture nets (fig. 16.2), flattened retreats (fig. 16.1), or tubes buried in loose sediments (fig. 16.3). Widespread in most types of aquatic habitats .... *POLYCENTROPODIDAE* (p. 343)

*The larva of Ecnomidae, recently described from Texas (Waltz and McCafferty 1983), keys to Hydroptilidae, but it is 5–7 mm long when mature, its abdominal tergum 9 is entirely membranous, and it never lives in a portable case.

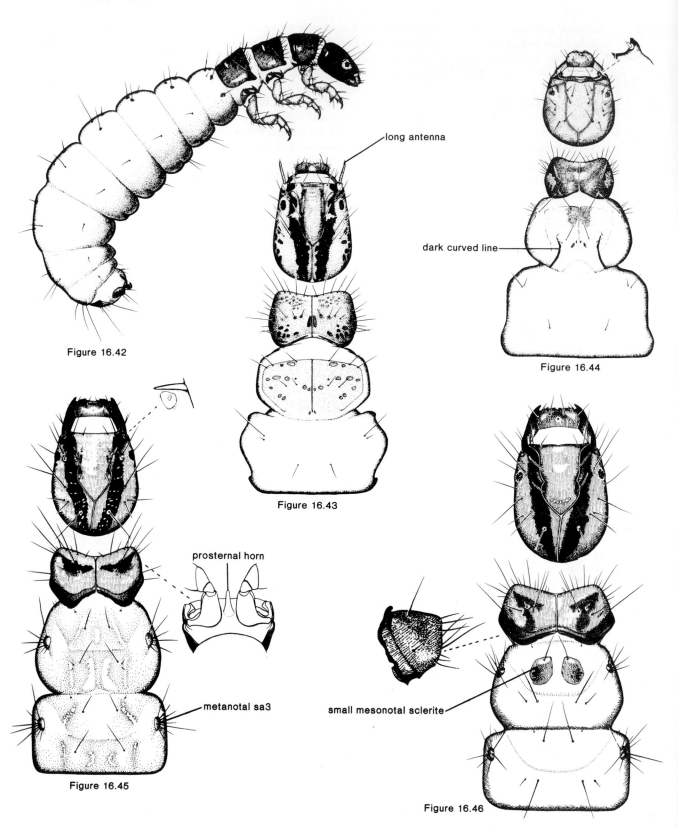

long antenna

dark curved line

Figure 16.42

Figure 16.44

Figure 16.43

prosternal horn

metanotal sa3

small mesonotal sclerite

Figure 16.45

Figure 16.46

Figure 16.42. Lateral view of *Ochrotrichia* sp. (Hydroptilidae) larva.

Figure 16.43. Dorsal view of head and thorax of *Triaenodes* sp. (Leptoceridae) larva.

Figure 16.44. Dorsal view of head and thorax of *Ceraclea* sp. (Leptoceridae) larva, detail of antenna.

Figure 16.45. Dorsal view of head and thorax of *Ptilostomis* sp. (Phryganeidae) larva, details of antenna and prosternum.

Figure 16.46. Dorsal view of head and thorax of *Oligostomis* sp. (Phryganeidae) larva, detail of pronotum (lateral).

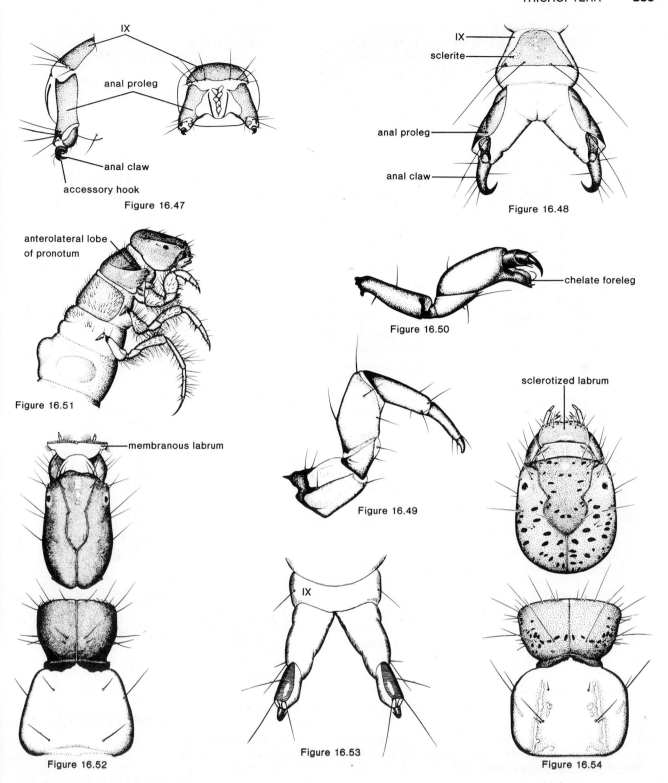

IX

anal proleg

anal claw

accessory hook

Figure 16.47

IX

sclerite

anal proleg

anal claw

Figure 16.48

anterolateral lobe
of pronotum

Figure 16.51

chelate foreleg

Figure 16.50

sclerotized labrum

Figure 16.49

membranous labrum

IX

Figure 16.52

Figure 16.53

Figure 16.54

Figure 16.47. Lateral and caudal view of segment IX and anal prolegs of *Glossosoma* sp. (Glossosomatidae) larva.

Figure 16.48. Dorsal view of segment IX and anal prolegs of *Rhyacophila* sp. (Rhyacophilidae) larva.

Figure 16.49. Lateral view of foreleg of *Rhyacophila* sp. (Rhyacophilidae) larva.

Figure 16.50. Lateral view of foreleg of *Atopsyche* sp. (Hydrobiosidae) larva.

Figure 16.51. Lateral view of head, thorax, and abdominal segment I of *Beraea* sp. (Beraeidae) larva.

Figure 16.52. Dorsal view of head and thorax of *Dolophilodes* sp. (Philopotamidae) larva.

Figure 16.53. Dorsal view of segment IX and anal prolegs of *Chimarra* sp. (Philopotamidae) larva.

Figure 16.54. Dorsal view of head and thorax of *Polycentropus* sp. (Polycentropodidae) larva.

12'.   Trochantin of prothoracic leg broad and hatchet-shaped, separated from episternum by dark suture line (fig. 16.55); larvae construct tubular retreats on rocks and logs (e.g., fig. 16.5). Widespread in running waters .... *PSYCHOMYIIDAE* (p. 345)

13 (5'). Abdominal segment I lacking both dorsal and lateral humps (fig. 16.60); each metanotal sa1 usually lacking entirely (fig. 16.58), or, if represented only by a single seta without a sclerite, mesonotal sclerites subdivided similarly to figure 16.58; larvae construct portable cases of various materials and arrangements (e.g., figures 16.12–16.13). Widepsread in running waters .... *BRACHYCENTRIDAE* (p. 312)

13'.   Abdominal segment I always with a lateral hump on each side although not always prominent, and with (fig. 16.63) or without (fig. 16.76) a median dorsal hump; metanotal sa1 always present, usually represented by a sclerite bearing several setae (fig. 16.59) but with at least a single seta; larvae construct portable cases of various materials and arrangements 14

14(13'). Tarsal claw of hind leg modified to form a short setose stub (fig. 16.61), or a slender filament (fig. 16.62); larval case of sand grains with a dorsal cowl and lateral flanges (fig. 16.18). Transcontinental through Canada to Alaska, and eastern, in lakes and large rivers, less commonly in spring streams .... *MOLANNIDAE* (p. 338)

14'.   Tarsal claws of hind legs no different in structure from those of other legs (fig. 16.64) 15

15(14'). Labrum with transverse row of approximately 16 long setae across central part (fig. 16.65); larval case a hollowed twig, or of leaves (fig. 16.17) and bark variously arranged. Eastern and western streams .... *CALAMOCERATIDAE* (p. 313)

15'.   Labrum with no more than 6 long setae across central part (fig. 16.66) 16

16(15'). Anal proleg with lateral sclerite much reduced in size and produced posteriorly as a lobe from which a stout apical seta arises (fig. 16.67); base of anal claw with ventromesal membranous surface bearing a prominent brush of 25–30 fine setae (fig. 16.68); larval case of sand grains. Eastern, exceedingly local, in wet muck of spring seepage areas .... *BERAEIDAE—Beraea*

16'.   Anal proleg with lateral sclerite not produced posteriorly as a lobe around base of apical seta (fig. 16.69); base of anal claw with ventromesal surface lacking prominent brush of fine setae (fig. 16.70) although setae may be present dorsally (fig. 16.72) 17

17(16'). Antenna situated at or very close to the anterior margin of the head capsule (fig. 16.71); prosternal horn lacking (fig. 16.74); larval cases mainly of rock fragments 18

17'.   Antenna removed from the anterior margin of the head capsule and approaching the eye (figs. 16.76–16.77); prosternal horn present although sometimes short (fig. 16.77); larval cases of rock fragments or of plant materials 19

18(17).   Anal proleg with dorsal cluster of approximately 30 or more setae posteromesad of lateral sclerite (fig. 16.72); foretrochantin relatively large, the apex hook-shaped (fig. 16.74); larval case mainly of sand. Widespread in running waters and along lake shorelines .... *SERICOSTOMATIDAE* (p. 345)

18'.   Anal proleg with no more than 3–5 dorsal setae posteromesad of lateral sclerite, sometimes short spines (fig. 16.73); foretrochantin small, the apex not hook-shaped (fig. 16.75); larval case mainly of small rock fragments. Widespread in running waters .... *ODONTOCERIDAE* (p. 338)

19(17'). Antenna situated close to the anterior margin of the eye, median dorsal hump of segment I lacking (fig. 16.76); larval cases of various materials and arrangements, frequently 4-sided (e.g., fig. 16.19). Widespread, mainly in lotic habitats .... *LEPIDOSTOMATIDAE* (p. 324)

19'.   Antenna situated approximately halfway between the anterior margin of the head capsule and the eye; median dorsal hump of segment I almost always present (fig. 16.77) 20

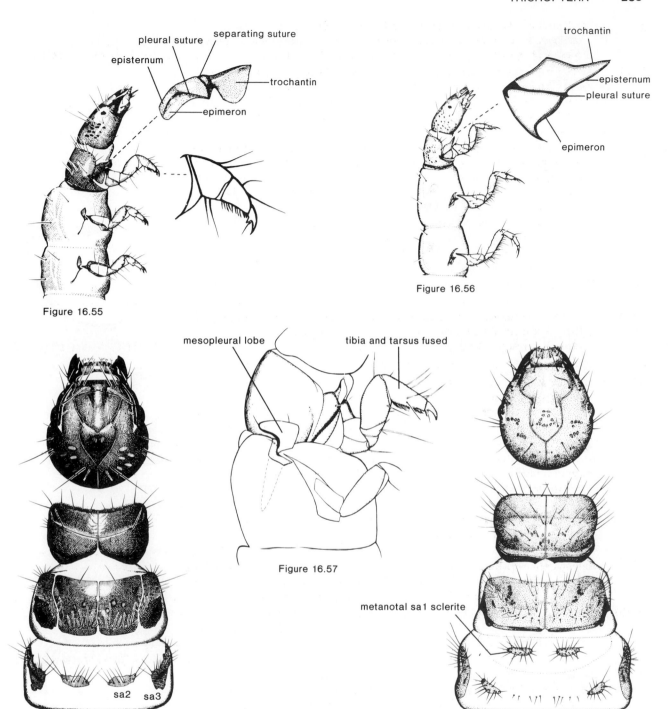

Figure 16.55

Figure 16.56

Figure 16.57

Figure 16.58

Figure 16.59

Figure 16.55. Lateral view of head and thorax of *Tinodes* sp. (Psychomyiidae) larva, details of trochantin and foreleg.

Figure 16.56. Lateral view of head and thorax of *Neureclipsis* sp. (Polycentropodidae) larvae, detail of trochantin.

Figure 16.57. Lateral view of prothorax and mesothorax of *Xiphocentron* sp. (Xiphocentronidae) larva.

Figure 16.58. Dorsal view of head and thorax of *Brachycentrus* sp. (Brachycentridae) larva.

Figure 16.59. Dorsal view of head and thorax of *Pseudostenophylax* sp. (Limnephilidae) larva.

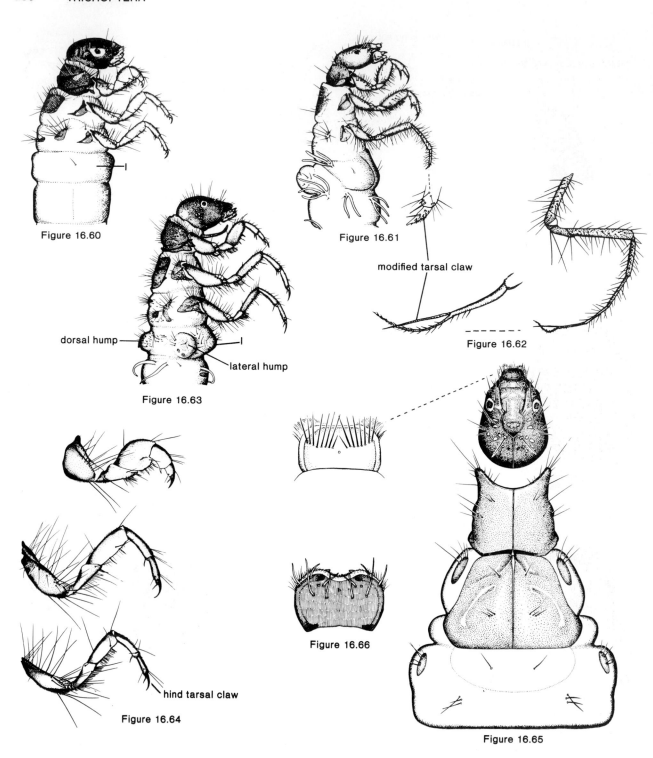

Figure 16.60

dorsal hump

lateral hump

Figure 16.63

Figure 16.61

modified tarsal claw

Figure 16.62

hind tarsal claw

Figure 16.64

Figure 16.66

Figure 16.65

Figure 16.60. Lateral view of *Micrasema* sp. (Brachycentridae) larva.

Figure 16.61. Lateral view of *Molanna* sp. (Molannidae) larva, detail of hind tarsal claw.

Figure 16.62. Lateral view of hind leg of *Molannodes* sp. (Molannidae) larva, detail of tarsal claw.

Figure 16.63. Lateral view of *Desmona* sp. (Limnephilidae) larva.

Figure 16.64. Lateral view of legs of *Eobrachycentrus* sp. (Brachycentridae) larva.

Figure 16.65. Dorsal view of head and thorax of *Anisocentropus* sp. (Calamoceratidae) larva, detail of labrum.

Figure 16.66. Dorsal view of labrum of *Homophylax* sp. (Limnephilidae) larva.

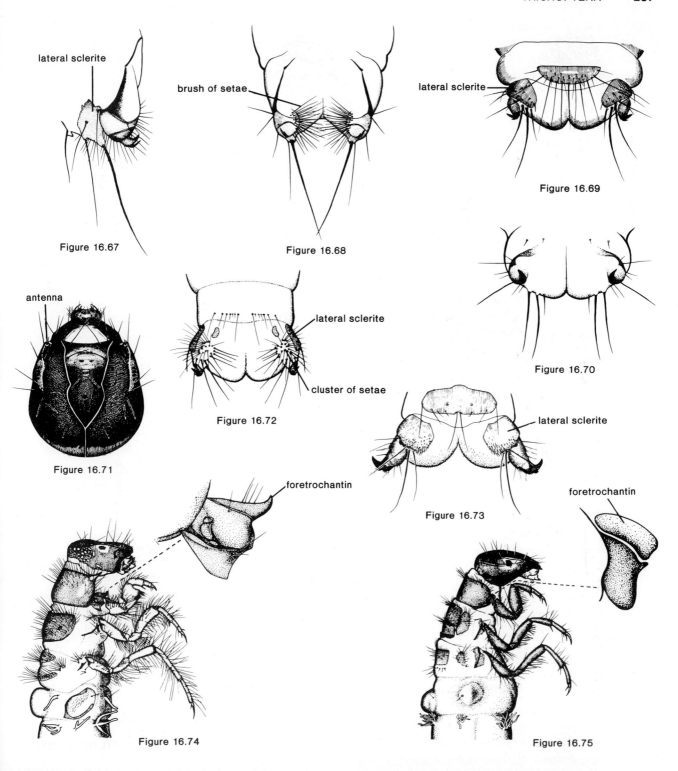

Figure 16.67

Figure 16.68

Figure 16.69

Figure 16.70

Figure 16.71

Figure 16.72

Figure 16.73

Figure 16.74

Figure 16.75

Figure 16.67. Lateral view of anal proleg of *Beraea* sp. (Beraeidae) larva.

Figure 16.68. Ventral view of anal prolegs of *Beraea* sp. (Beraeidae) larva.

Figure 16.69. Dorsal view of segment IX and anal prolegs of *Homophylax* sp. (Limnephilidae) larva.

Figure 16.70. Ventral view of anal prolegs of *Homophylax* sp. (Limnephilidae) larva.

Figure 16.71. Dorsal view of head of *Agarodes* sp. (Sericostomatidae) larva.

Figure 16.72. Dorsal view of segment IX and anal prolegs of *Agarodes* sp. (Sericostomatidae) larva.

Figure 16.73. Dorsal view of segment IX and anal prolegs of *Pseudogoera* sp. (Odontoceridae) larva.

Figure 16.74. Lateral view of *Fattigia* sp. (Sericostomatidae) larva, detail of trochantin.

Figure 16.75. Lateral view of *Marilia* sp. (Odontoceridae) larva, detail of trochantin.

20(19′)   Larvae very slender, pronotum longer than wide, metanotal sa1 a single seta (fig. 16.78); larval cases smooth and very slender, of fine mineral materials (fig. 16.14), sometimes of silk alone. Western montane streams .... *UENOIDAE* (p. 345)

20′.   Larvae not as slender as above, pronotum usually wider than long, metanotal sa1 almost always with more than one seta (fig. 16.59); larval cases of many types, constructed of plant materials or rock fragments, usually of rough, irregular texture (e.g., figs. 16.7–16.11). Widespread in all types of aquatic habitats .... *LIMNEPHILIDAE* (sens.lat.) (p. 327) 21

21(20′).   Mesopleuron modified, usually extended anteriorly as a prominent process (fig. 16.79) .... *LIMNEPHILIDAE* (Goerinae) (p. 327)

21′.   Mesopleuron unmodified (fig. 16.77) .... *LIMNEPHILIDAE* (excl. Goerinae) (p. 327)

Pupae

1.   Two pairs of hook plates present on each of segments III, IV, and V (figs. 16.80, 16.95) 2

1′.   Two pairs of hook plates never present together on each of segments III, IV, and V 3

2(1).   Insects very small, less than 5–6 mm long .... *HYDROPTILIDAE*

2′.   Insects larger, more than 6 mm long 12

3(1′).   Abdomen lacking lateral fringe of setae (figs. 16.81, 16.84), although isolated setal tufts sometimes present (figs. 16.85, 16.100) 4

3′.   Abdomen with lateral fringe, the fringe continuous where present (figs. 16.30–16.31) 16

4(3).   Mandibles with only a single apical point (fig. 16.99), although this is sometimes extended as a slender filament (fig. 16.83) 5

4′.   Mandibles with at least one subapical toothlike point more prominent than the others in addition to an apical point (figs. 16.89, 16.94) 12

5(4).   Hook plates on segment VII, frequently also on segment VIII (fig. 16.84) 6

5′.   Hook plates not extending posteriorly beyond segment VI (fig. 16.87) 10

6(5).   Hook plate Vp with 6 or more hooks (fig. 16.81) 7

6′.   Hook plate Vp with only 2 or 3 hooks (fig. 16.100) 20

7(6).   Hook plates present on segment II (fig. 16.81) 8

7′.   Hook plates absent from segment II (fig. 16.84) 9

8(7).   Hooks of plates on segments II, III, and IV arranged in an arc curved concavely anteriorly (fig. 16.81) .... *PSYCHOMYIIDAE**

8′.   Hooks of plates on segments II, III, and IV arranged in an arc curved concavely posteriorly (fig. 16.82) .... *XIPHOCENTRONIDAE*

9(7′).   Anal processes rounded lobes, pair of hook plates usually present on segment VIII (fig. 16.84) .... *POLYCENTROPODIDAE*

9′.   Anal processes very slender and pointed, frequently hooked apically, segment VIII lacking hook plates (fig. 16.86) .... *UENOIDAE*

10(5′).   Antennae little if any longer than body, not coiled around anal processes (fig. 16.30) 11

10′.   Antennae much longer than body, coiled around anal processes (fig. 16.109) 25

11(10).   Anal processes simple lobes closely appressed along midline, with stout apical bristles longer than processes themselves (fig. 16.87) .... *HELICOPSYCHIDAE*

11′.   Anal processes divergent in dorsal aspect, each one forked apically in lateral aspect, and lacking apical bristles (figs. 16.102–16.103) .... *BERAEIDAE*

12(2′,4′).   Abdominal gills present, 2 pairs of hook plates present on segment III (fig. 16.104) .... *HYDROPSYCHIDAE*

12′.   Abdominal gills absent, 1 or 2 pairs of hook plates on segment III (figs. 16.88, 16.95) 13

*The pupa of Ecnomidae, recently described from Texas (Waltz and McCafferty 1983), keys to Psychomyiidae, but its mandibles are elongate, curved without mesal serrations, and without a long, thin, filiform apical process.

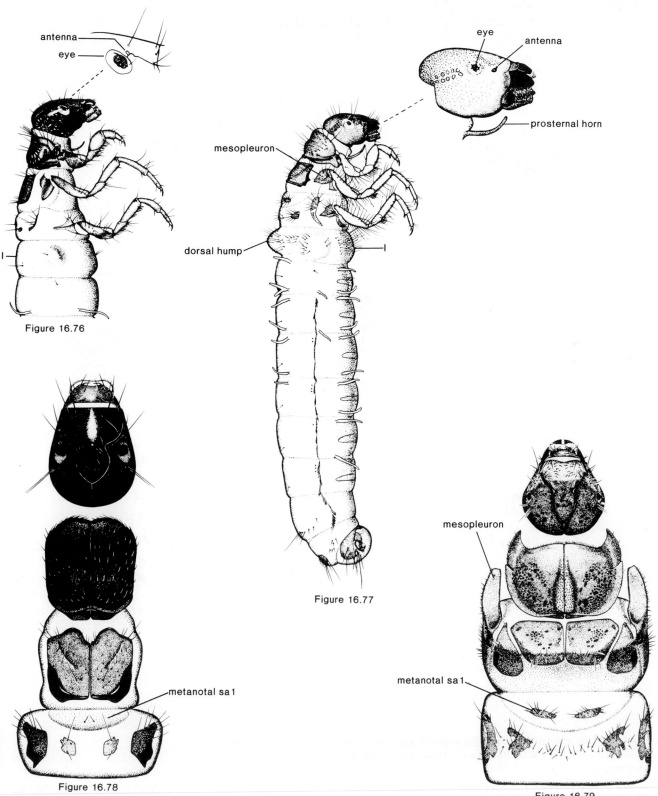

Figure 16.76

Figure 16.77

Figure 16.78

Figure 16.79

Figure 16.76. Lateral view of *Lepidostoma* sp. (Lepidostomatidae) larva, detail of antenna.

Figure 16.77. Lateral view of *Pseudostenophylax* sp. (Limnephilidae) larva, detail of head.

Figure 16.78. Dorsal view of head and thorax of *Neothremma* sp. (Uenoidae) larva.

Figure 16.79. Dorsal view of head and thorax of *Goera* sp. (Limnephilidae: Goerinae) larva.

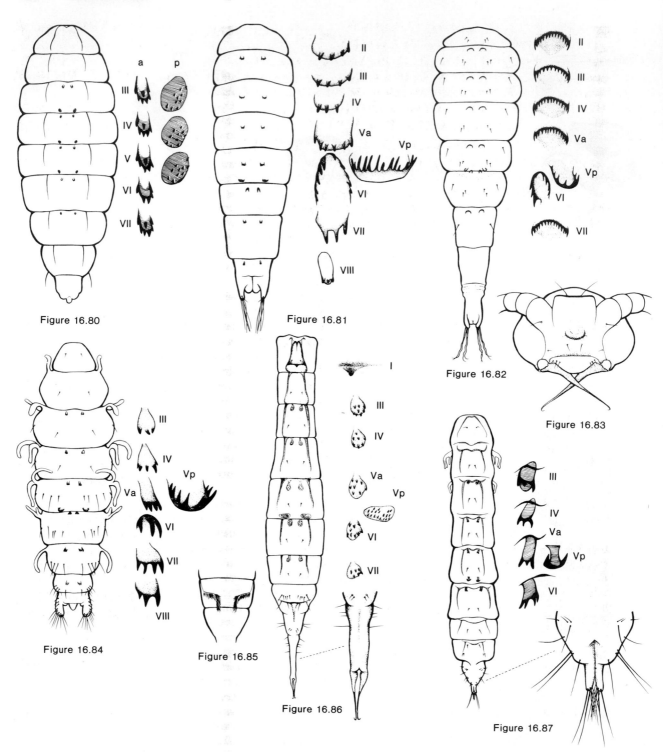

Figure 16.80. Dorsal view of abdomen of *Agraylea* sp. (Hydroptilidae) pupa, detail of hook plates: *a*, anterior; *p*, posterior.

Figure 16.81. Dorsal view of abdomen of *Psychomyia* sp. (Psychomyiidae) pupa, detail of hook plates.

Figure 16.82. Dorsal view of abdomen of *Xiphocentron* sp. (Xiphocentronidae) pupa, detail of hook plates.

Figure 16.83. Frontal view of head of *Xiphocentron* sp. (Xiphocentronidae) pupa.

Figure 16.84. Dorsal view of abdomen of *Polycentropus* sp. (Polycentropodidae) pupa, detail of hook plates.

Figure 16.85. Ventral view of abdominal segments VIII and IX of *Neothremma* sp. (Uenoidae) pupa.

Figure 16.86. Dorsal view of abdomen of *Neothremma* sp. (Uenoidae) pupa, detail of hook plates and anal processes.

Figure 16.87. Dorsal view of abdomen of *Helicopsyche* sp. (Helicopsychidae) pupa, detail of hook plates and anal processes.

13(12').   One pair of hook plates on segment IV (fig. 16.88) .... *PHILOPOTAMIDAE*

13'.   Two pairs of hook plates on segment IV (fig. 16.95) 14

14(13').   Segments VIII and/or IX with a pair of small hook plates, and/or 2 patches of
    long setae at apex of abdomen (fig. 16.93) .... *GLOSSOSOMATIDAE*

14'.   Segments VIII and IX lacking hook plates (fig. 16.90) 15

15(14').   Apex of abdomen bearing 2 patches of setae (fig. 16.90) .... *HYDROBIOSIDAE*

15'.   Apex of abdomen lacking patches of setae (fig. 16.95) .... *RHYACOPHILIDAE*

16(3').   Lateral fringe of abdomen extending anteriorly from segments VII or VIII to V or
    VI (fig. 16.96) 17

16'.   Lateral fringe of abdomen extending anteriorly from segments VII or VIII to III
    or IV (fig. 16.106) 22

17(16).   Anal processes short or lobate, less than 5 times longer than wide (figs.
    16.105–16.106) 18

17'.   Anal processes long and slender, more than 5 times longer than wide (fig. 16.100) 19

18(17).   Anterior hook plates longer than wide or both dimensions approximately the same,
    and most plates with 2–4 hooks (fig. 16.30) 20

18'.   Anterior hook plates wider than long (fig. 16.106) and usually each with 5 or more
    hooks (fig. 16.96) 23

19(17').   Anterior hook plates wider than long (fig. 16.96) .... *BRACHYCENTRIDAE*

19'.   Anterior hook plates longer than wide, or the two dimensions approximately equal
    (fig. 16.30) 20

20(6',18   Bristles of labrum usually hooked apically, antennae usually with dorsal tuft (fig.
    19').   16.29); hook plate Vp usually with more than 3 hooks (fig. 16.30) .... *LIMNEPHILIDAE*

20'.   Bristles of labrum never hooked apically, antennae usually with ventrolateral tuft
    (fig. 16.99); hook plate Vp with 2–3 hooks (fig. 16.97) 21

21(20').   Mesal margin of mandible concave in outline, apex pointed (fig. 16.99); anterior
    hook plates with 2 or 3 hooks (fig. 16.97) .... *SERICOSTOMATIDAE*

21'.   Mesal margin of mandible straight in outline, apex usually attenuate (fig. 16.101);
    most anterior hook plates with 1 hook (fig. 16.100) .... *ODONTOCERIDAE*

22(16').   Anal processes short and quadrate (fig. 16.106) or triangular (fig. 16.105) in
    dorsal aspect 23

22'.   Anal processes long and slender (fig. 16.108) 24

23(18',22)   Segment I with dorsomesal spined lobe, anal processes in dorsal aspect short and
    roughly quadrate (fig. 16.106) .... *PHRYGANEIDAE*

23'.   Segment I lacking dorsomesal spined lobe, anal processes more elongate than
    above in dorsal aspect and roughly triangular (fig. 16.105) .... *LEPIDOSTOMATIDAE*

24(22').   Dorsal abdominal setae arising in clusters (fig. 16.107) .... *CALAMOCERATIDAE*

24'.   Dorsal abdominal setae arising singly (fig. 16.108) 25

25(10',24')   Anal processes with apical bristles approximately one-half as long as processes
    themselves, antennae little longer than body and not coiled apically (fig. 16.108) .... *MOLANNIDAE*

25'.   Anal processes with much shorter apical bristles (fig. 16.110) or with none,
    antennae much longer than body and coiled around base of anal processes (fig.
    16.109) .... *LEPTOCERIDAE*

Adults

1.   Small insects, usually 5 mm or less in length; mesoscutum lacking setal warts,
    mesoscutellar setal warts transverse and meeting mesally to form an angulate
    ridge (fig. 16.111); hind wings narrow and apically acute (fig. 16.112), often
    with a posterior fringe of long hairs, the longest approximating the width of the
    hind wing .... *HYDROPTILIDAE*

1'.   Insects usually more than 5 mm long; mesoscutum frequently with setal warts (fig.
    16.117), mesoscutellar setal warts usually rounded or elongate (figs. 16.115,
    16.120); hind wings usually broader and rounded apically (fig. 16.34), posterior
    fringe, when present, of relatively shorter hairs 2

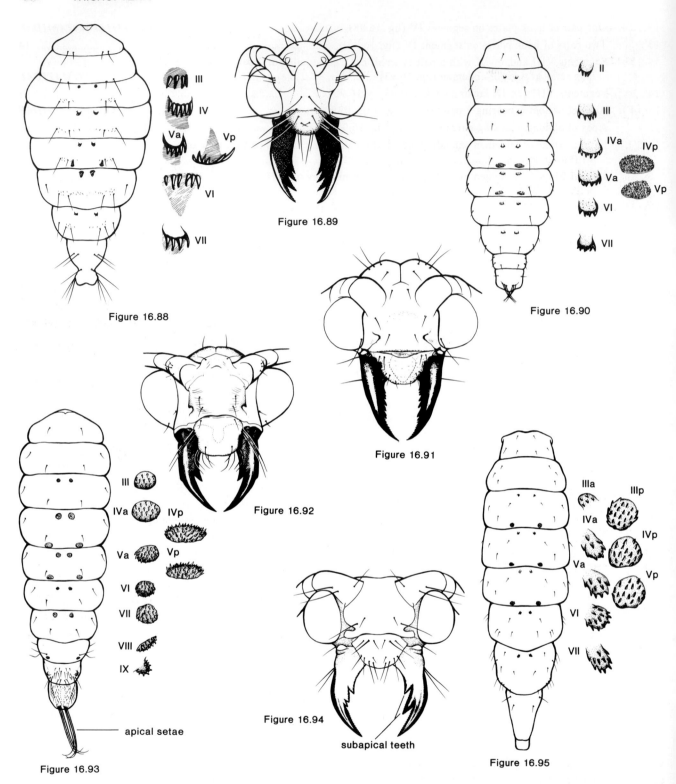

Figure 16.88

Figure 16.89

Figure 16.90

Figure 16.91

Figure 16.92

apical setae

Figure 16.93

subapical teeth

Figure 16.94

Figure 16.95

Figure 16.88. Dorsal view of abdomen of *Dolophilodes* sp. (Philopotamidae) pupa, detail of hook plates.

Figure 16.89. Frontal view of head of *Dolophilodes* sp. (Philopotamidae) pupa.

Figure 16.90. Dorsal view of abdomen of *Atopsyche* sp. (Hydrobiosidae) pupa, detail of hook plates.

Figure 16.91. Frontal view of head of *Atopsyche* sp. (Hydrobiosidae) pupa.

Figure 16.92. Frontal view of head of *Glossosoma* sp. (Glossosomatidae) pupa.

Figure 16.93. Dorsal view of abdomen of *Glossosoma* sp. (Glossosomatidae) pupa, detail of hook plates.

Figure 16.94. Frontal view of head of *Rhyacophila* sp. (Rhyacophilidae) pupa.

Figure 16.95. Dorsal view of abdomen of *Rhyacophila* sp. (Rhyacophilidae) pupa, detail of hook plates.

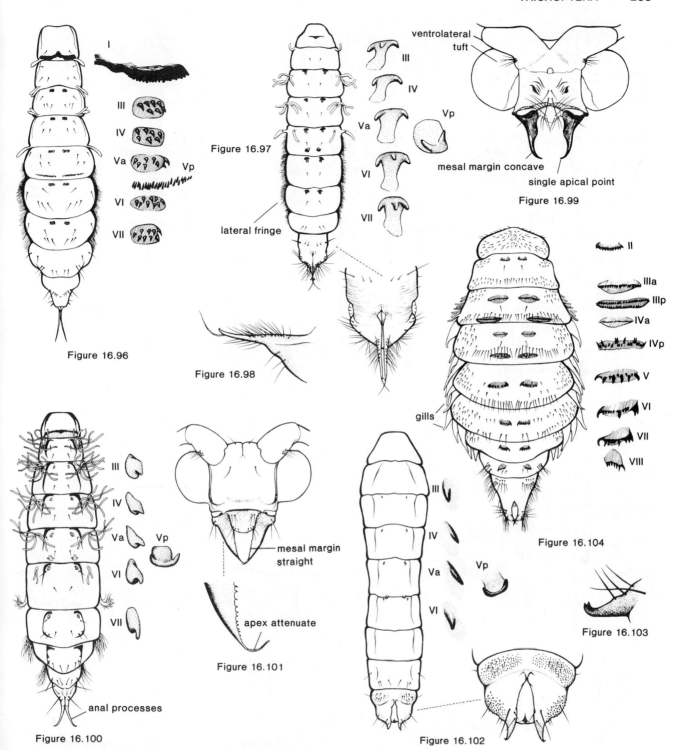

ventrolateral tuft

mesal margin concave

single apical point

lateral fringe

mesal margin straight

apex attenuate

anal processes

gills

Vp

Figure 16.96. Dorsal view of abdomen of *Brachycentrus* sp. (Brachycentridae) pupa, detail of hook plates.

Figure 16.97. Dorsal view of abdomen of *Fattigia* sp. (Sericostomatidae) pupa, detail of hook plates and anal processes.

Figure 16.98. Lateral view of anal process of *Fattigia* sp. (Sericostomatidae) pupa.

Figure 16.99. Frontal view of head of *Fattigia* sp. (Sericostomatidae) pupa.

Figure 16.100. Dorsal view of abdomen of *Psilotreta* sp. (Odontoceridae) pupa, detail of hook plates.

Figure 16.101. Frontal view of head of *Psilotreta* sp. (Odontoceridae) pupa, detail of mandible.

Figure 16.102. Dorsal view of abdomen of *Beraea* sp. (Beraeidae) pupa, detail of hook plates and anal processes.

Figure 16.103. Lateral view of anal process of *Beraea* sp. (Beraeidae) pupa.

Figure 16.104. Dorsal view of abdomen of *Hydropsyche* sp. (Hydropsychidae) pupa, detail of hook plates.

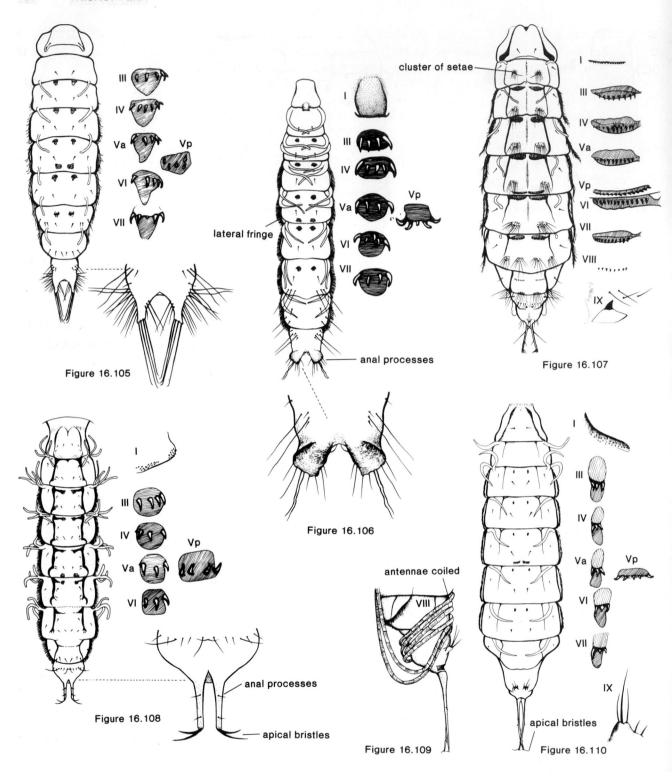

Figure 16.105

Figure 16.106

Figure 16.107

Figure 16.108

Figure 16.109

Figure 16.110

Figure 16.105. Dorsal view of abdomen of *Lepidostoma* sp. (Lepidostomatidae) pupa, detail of hook plates and anal processes.

Figure 16.106. Dorsal view of abdomen of *Banksiola* sp. (Phryganeidae) pupa, detail of hook plates and anal processes.

Figure 16.107. Dorsal view of abdomen of *Heteroplectron* sp. (Calamoceratidae) pupa, detail of hook plates.

Figure 16.108. Dorsal view of abdomen of *Molanna* sp. (Molannidae) pupa, detail of hook plates and anal processes.

Figure 16.109. Lateral view of terminal abdominal segments and antennae of *Oecetis* sp. (Leptoceridae) pupa.

Figure 16.110. Dorsal view of abdomen of *Oecetis* sp. (Leptoceridae) pupa, detail of hook plates.

2(1′). Dorsum of head with 3 ocelli (fig. 16.120) 3

2′. Dorsum of head lacking ocelli (fig. 16.129) 10

3(2). Maxillary palp of 5 segments, terminal segment 5 flexible, usually at least twice as long as preceding segment 4 (fig. 16.114) .... ***PHILOPOTAMIDAE***

3′. Maxillary palp of 3, 4, or 5 segments, terminal segment similar to others in structure, usually approximately same length as preceding segment (figs. 16.118, 16.123) 4

4(3′). Maxillary palp of 5 segments, segment 2 short, often rounded, and approximately same length as segment 1 (fig. 16.118) 5

4′. Maxillary palp of 3, 4, or 5 segments, segment 2 slender and longer than segment 1 (figs. 16.123, 16.125) 8

5(4). Maxillary palp with 2nd segment rounded and globose (fig. 16.118) 6

5′. Maxillary palp with 2nd segment not globose, but of same general cylindrical shape as 1st (fig. 16.121) .... ***HYDROBIOSIDAE***

6(5). Fore tibia with a preapical spur (fig. 16.116) .... ***RHYACOPHILIDAE***

6′. Fore tibia lacking a preapical spur (fig. 16.119) 7

7(6′). Mesal setal warts of pronotum widely spaced (fig. 16.117) .... ***GLOSSOSOMATIDAE***

7′. Mesal setal warts of pronotum close together (as in fig. 16.111, although not in contact .... ***HYDROPTILIDAE (Ptilocolepinae)***

8(4′). Middle tibia with 2 preapical spurs (fig. 16.136); spurs usually 2,4,4 .... ***PHRYGANEIDAE***

8′. Middle tibia with 1 or no preapical spurs; spurs usually 1,2–3,4 9

9(8′). Antenna with scape longer than head, mesoscutum with a pair of discrete setal warts, mesoscutellum long and narrow, the anterior apex acute, extending anterad beyond the midpoint of the mesonotum and bearing a narrow setal wart approximately 3–4 times longer than wide (fig. 16.127); hind wings little wider than fore wings because of reduced anal area (fig. 16.128); slender insects not exceeding 7 mm in length excluding antennae .... ***UENOIDAE***

9′. Antenna with scape shorter than head, mesoscutum with setae diffuse or concentrated in discrete warts, mesoscutellum usually shorter than above with the anterior apex usually neither acute nor reaching the midpoint of the mesonotum and bearing a broad setal wart usually less than 3 times longer than wide (fig. 16.122); hind wings usually much wider than fore wings because of a broad anal area (fig. 16.126); insects ranging in length from 5 to 30 mm .... ***LIMNEPHILIDAE*** (major part)

10(2′). Maxillary palp with 5 or more segments (fig. 16.133) 11

10′. Maxillary palp with fewer than 5 segments 15

11(10). Terminal segment of maxillary palp flexible, with numerous cross-striae and different in structure from preceding segments; usually at least twice as long as preceding segment (fig. 16.131) 12

11′. Terminal segment of maxillary palp similar to others in structure and usually of approximately the same length as preceding segment (fig. 16.121), or some segments with long hair brushes (fig. 16.147) 15

12(11). Mesoscutum lacking setal warts or setae (fig. 16.152) .... ***HYDROPSYCHIDAE***

12′. Mesoscutum with setal warts (fig. 16.129) 13

13(12′). Mesoscutal setal warts quadrate and appressed along the median line over a large area approximately the size of the entire mesoscutellum (fig. 16.137) .... ***XIPHOCENTRONIDAE***

13′. Mesoscutal setal warts circular, sometimes touching at the median line, but much smaller than the mesoscutellum (fig. 16.129) 14

14(13′). Fore tibia with a preapical spur, or if spur absent *(Cernotina)*, length of basal segment of tarsus less than twice the length of the longer apical spur (fig. 16.130) .... ***POLYCENTROPODIDAE†***

14′. Fore tibia lacking a preapical spur, and length of basal segment of tarsus at least twice the length of the longer apical spur (fig. 16.134) .... ***PSYCHOMYIIDAE***

†The adult of Ecnomidae, recently described from Texas (Waltz and McCafferty 1983), keys to Polycentropodidae, but its fore wing has vein R_1 branched.

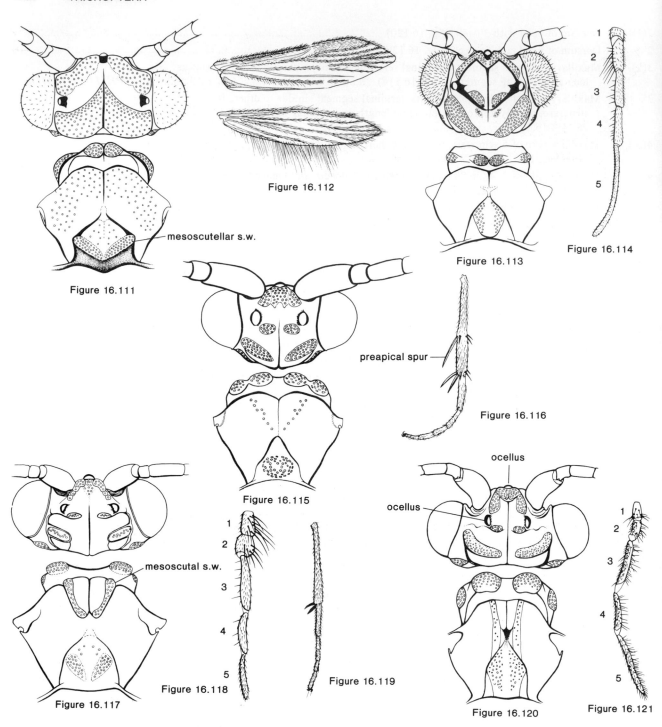

Figure 16.111. Dorsal view of head, pro-, and mesonotum of *Agraylea* sp. (Hydroptilidae) adult.

Figure 16.112. Dorsal view of wings of *Agraylea* sp. (Hydroptilidae).

Figure 16.113. Dorsal view of head, pro-, and mesonotum of *Dolophilodes* sp. (Philopotamidae) adult.

Figure 16.114. Maxillary palp of *Dolophilodes* sp. (Philopotamidae) adult.

Figure 16.115. Dorsal view of head, pro-, and mesonotum of *Rhyacophila* sp. (Rhyacophilidae) adult.

Figure 16.116. Tibia and tarsus of foreleg of *Rhyacophila* sp. (Rhyacophilidae) adult.

Figure 16.117. Dorsal view of head, pro-, and mesonotum of *Glossosoma* sp. (Glossosomatidae) adult.

Figure 16.118. Maxillary palp of *Glossosoma* sp. (Glossosomatidae) adult.

Figure 16.119. Tibia and tarsus of foreleg of *Glossosoma* sp. (Glossosomatidae) adult.

Figure 16.120. Dorsal view of head, pro-, and mesonotum of *Atopsyche* sp. (Hydrobiosidae) adult.

Figure 16.121. Maxillary palp of *Atopsyche* sp. (Hydrobiosidae) adult.

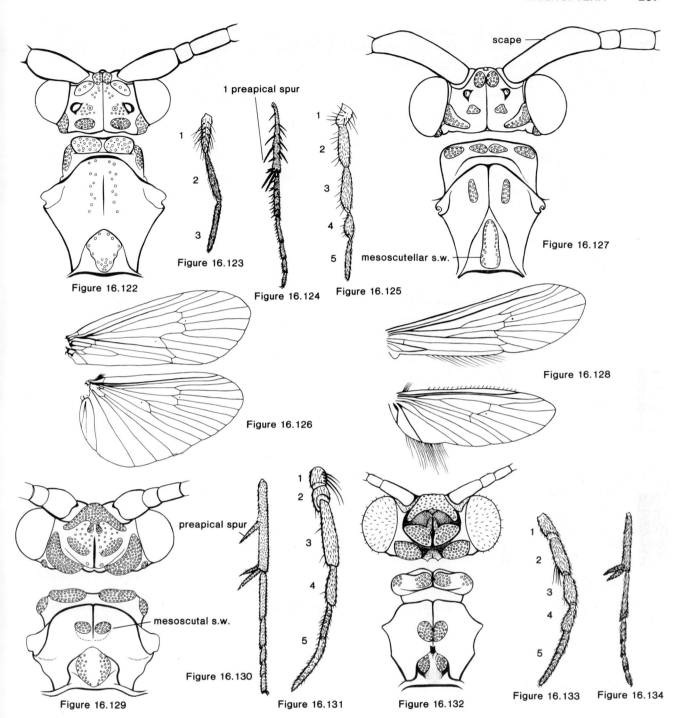

Figure 16.122. Dorsal view of head, pro-, and mesonotum of *Limnephilus* sp. (Limnephilidae) adult.

Figure 16.123. Maxillary palp of *Limnephilus* sp. (Limnephilidae) male.

Figure 16.124. Middle tibia and tarsus of *Limnephilus* sp. (Limnephilidae) adult.

Figure 16.125. Maxillary palp of *Limnephilus* sp. (Limnephilidae) female.

Figure 16.126. Wings of *Dicosmoecus* sp. (Limnephilidae).

Figure 16.127. Dorsal view of head, pro-, and mesonotum of *Neothremma* sp. (Uenoidae) adult.

Figure 16.128. Wings of *Farula* sp. (Uenoidae).

Figure 16.129. Dorsal view of head, pro-, and mesonotum of *Polycentropus* sp. (Polycentropodidae) adult.

Figure 16.130. Foretibia and tarsus of *Polycentropus* sp. (Polycentropodidae) adult.

Figure 16.131. Maxillary palp of *Polycentropus* sp. (Polycentropodidae) adult.

Figure 16.132. Dorsal view of head, pro-, and mesonotum of *Psychomyia* sp. (Psychomyiidae) adult.

Figure 16.133. Maxillary palp of *Psychomyia* sp. (Psychomyiidae) adult.

Figure 16.134. Foretibia and tarsus of *Psychomyia* sp. (Psychomyiidae) adult.

15(10′,11′) Mesoscutum lacking setal warts and setae (fig. 16.138); tarsal segments, excepting basal one, with spines only around apex (fig. 16.139) .... *BERAEIDAE*

15′. Mesoscutum with setal warts (fig. 16.148) or setal area (fig. 16.141); tarsal segments with spines usually arranged irregularly (fig. 16.124) 16

16(15′). Mesoscutal setae arising in diffuse area over almost entire length of mesoscutum (fig. 16.141) 17

16′. Mesoscutal setae largely confined to pair of small discrete warts (fig. 16.145) 19

17(16). Antennae with scape at most twice as long as pedicel, dorsum of head usually with posteromesal ridge (fig. 16.140) .... *CALAMOCERATIDAE*

17′. Antennae with scape at least 3 times longer than pedicel, dorsum of head lacking posteromesal ridge (fig. 16.141) 18

18(17′). Antennae much longer than body, middle tibia lacking preapical spurs (fig. 16.142) .... *LEPTOCERIDAE*

18′. Antennae little if any longer than body, middle tibia with 2 preapical spurs (fig. 16.144) .... *MOLANNIDAE*

19(16′). Dorsum of head with posterior setal warts very large, extending from mesal margin of eye to mid-dorsal line and anteriorly to middle of head (fig. 16.145); antennae never longer than fore wing .... *HELICOPSYCHIDAE*

19′. Dorsum of head with posterior setal warts relatively smaller than above (e.g., fig. 16.146); or antennae 1½ times longer than forewing 20

20(19′). Mesoscutellum with 1 mesal setal wart (fig. 16.146) 21

20′. Mesoscutellum with a pair of setal warts (fig. 16.148), although sometimes touching along the mid-dorsal line (fig. 16.153) 22

21(20). Mesoscutellum almost entirely covered by a single setal wart, setae arising over most of wart (fig. 16.146); maxillary palpi always 5-segmented .... *ODONTOCERIDAE*

21′. Mesoscutellum with setal wart narrower, setae largely confined to periphery (fig. 16.122); maxillary palpi 5-segmented in females, but 3-segmented in males .... *LIMNEPHILIDAE* (Goerini)

22(20′). Pronotum with 1 pair of setal warts, median fissure of mesoscutum deep (fig. 16.151) .... *SERICOSTOMATIDAE*

22′. Pronotum with 2 pairs of setal warts, median fissure of mesoscutum not as deep as above (fig. 16.148) 23

23(22′). Middle tibia with 1 or 2 preapical spurs arising at a point about one-third distant from apex of tibia (fig. 16.149) or without preapical spurs; abdomen with openings of glands on venter V in a pair of rounded sclerotized lobes (fig. 16.150) .... *BRACHYCENTRIDAE*

23′. Middle tibia with 2 preapical spurs arising from approximately midpoint of tibia (fig. 16.154); abdomen with glands on venter V not apparent .... *LEPIDOSTOMATIDAE*

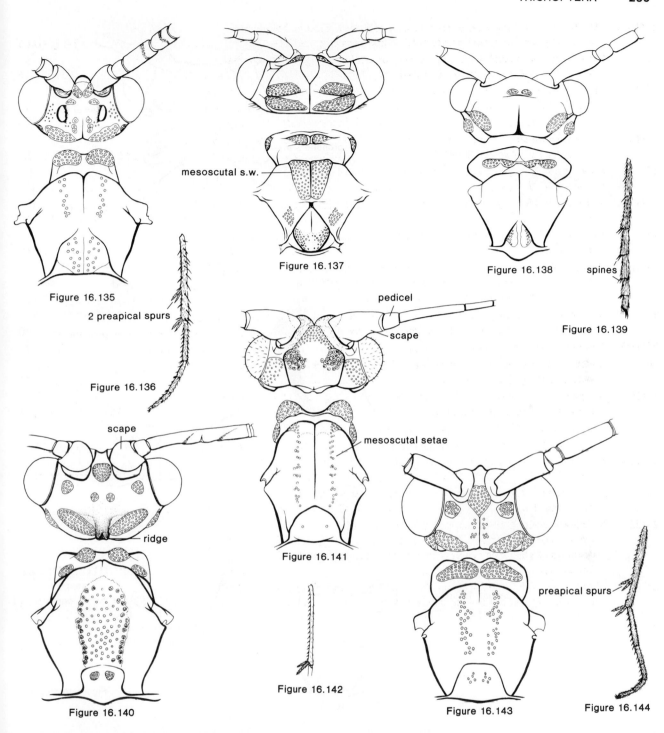

mesoscutal s.w.

Figure 16.135

Figure 16.137

Figure 16.138

spines

2 preapical spurs

Figure 16.136

Figure 16.139

pedicel

scape

scape

mesoscutal setae

ridge

Figure 16.141

Figure 16.140

Figure 16.142

preapical spurs

Figure 16.143

Figure 16.144

Figure 16.135. Dorsal view of head, pro-, and mesonotum of *Banksiola* sp. (Phryganeidae) adult.

Figure 16.136. Middle tibia and tarsus of *Banksiola* sp. (Phryganeidae) adult.

Figure 16.137. Dorsal view of head, pro-, and mesonotum of *Xiphocentron* sp. (Xiphocentronidae) adult.

Figure 16.138. Dorsal view of head, pro-, and mesonotum of *Beraea* sp. (Beraeidae) adult.

Figure 16.139. Middle tarsus of *Beraea* sp. (Beraeidae) adult.

Figure 16.140. Dorsal view of head, pro-, and mesonotum of *Heteroplectron* sp. (Calamoceratidae) adult.

Figure 16.141. Dorsal view of head, pro-, and mesonotum of *Oecetis* sp. (Leptoceridae) adult.

Figure 16.142. Middle tibia of *Oecetis* sp. (Leptoceridae) adult.

Figure 16.143. Dorsal view of head, pro-, and mesonotum of *Molanna* sp. (Molannidae) adult.

Figure 16.144. Middle tibia and tarsus of *Molanna* sp. (Molannidae) adult.

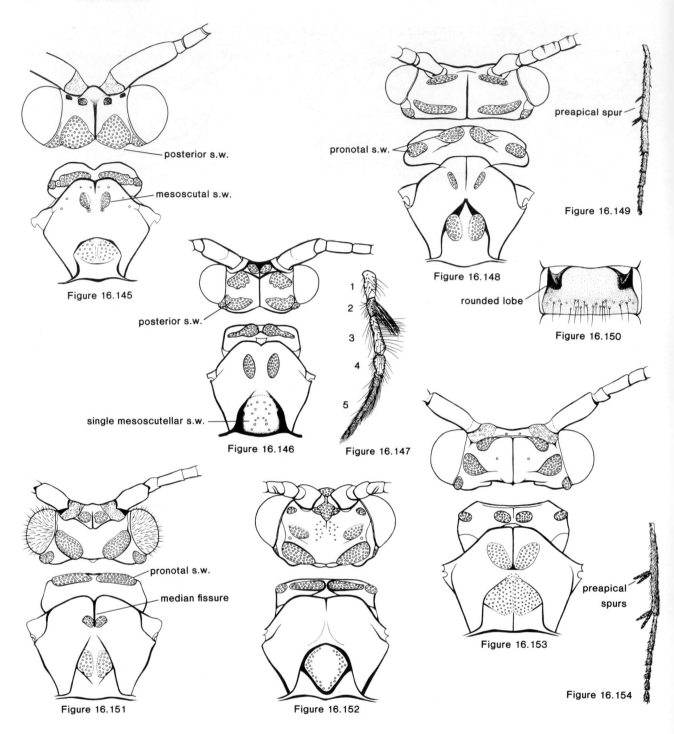

Figure 16.145. Dorsal view of head, pro-, and mesonotum of *Helicopsyche* sp. (Helicopsychidae) adult.

Figure 16.146. Dorsal view of head, pro-, and mesonotum of *Psilotreta* sp. (Odontoceridae) adult.

Figure 16.147. Maxillary palp of *Psilotreta* sp. (Odontoceridae) adult.

Figure 16.148. Dorsal view of head, pro-, and mesonotum of *Brachycentrus* sp. (Brachycentridae) adult.

Figure 16.149. Middle tibia and tarsus of *Brachycentrus* sp. (Brachycentridae) adult.

Figure 16.150. Ventral view of abdominal segment V of *Brachycentrus* sp. (Brachycentridae) adult.

Figure 16.151. Dorsal view of head, pro-, and mesonotum of *Agarodes* sp. (Sericostomatidae) adult.

Figure 16.152. Dorsal view of head, pro-, and mesonotum of *Hydropsyche* sp. (Hydropsychidae) adult.

Figure 16.153. Dorsal view of head, pro-, and mesonotum of *Lepidostoma* sp. (Lepidostomatidae) adult.

Figure 16.154. Middle tibia and tarsus of *Lepidostoma* sp. (Lepidostomatidae) adult.

ADDITIONAL TAXONOMIC REFERENCES

(L=larvae; P=pupae; A=adults)

General
Ross (1944)–L, P, A, (1959)–L; Wiggins (1977)–L; (1982 ref. #2856)–L, A; Schmid (1980)–A.

Regional faunas
Alberta: Nimmo (1971)–A, (1974)–A, (1977a,b,)–A.
California: Denning (1956)–A.
Illinois: Ross (1944)–L, P, A.
New York: Betten (1934)–A.
North and South Carolina: Unzicker *et al.* (1982)–L.
Wisconsin: Hilsenhoff (1981)–L.

Regional species lists
Arkansas: Unzicker *et al.* (1970).
British Columbia: Ross and Spencer (1952); Schmid and Guppy (1952); Nimmo and Scudder (1978).
Florida: Blickle (1962); Harris *et al.* (1982b).
Idaho: Smith (1965).
Kansas: Hamilton and Schuster (1978, 1979, 1980); Hamilton *et al.* (1983).
Kentucky: Resh (1975).
Louisiana: Harris *et al.* (1982a); Holzenthal *et al.* (1982); Lago *et al.* (1982).
Maine: Blickle (1964); Blickle and Morse (1966).
Massachusetts: Neves (1979).
Michigan: Leonard and Leonard (1949); Ellis (1962).
Minnesota: Etnier (1965); Lager *et al.* (1979).
Mississippi: Harris *et al.* (1982a); Holzenthal *et al.* (1982); Lago *et al.* (1982).
Montana: Newell and Potter (1973); Roemhild (1982).
Newfoundland: Wiggins (1961).
New Hampshire: Morse and Blickle (1953, 1957).
North Carolina: Denning (1950).
North Dakota: Harris *et al.* (1980).
Ohio: McElravy *et al.* (1977).
Oregon: Anderson (1976b).
Pennsylvania: Hyland (1948); Masteller and Flint (1979).
Quebec: Roy and Harper (1979).
South Carolina: Morse *et al.* (1980).

Tennessee: Edwards (1966); Etnier and Schuster (1979).
Texas: Edwards (1973).
Utah: Knowlton and Harmston (1938); Baumann and Unzicker (1981).
Virginia: Parker and Voshell (1981).
West Virginia: Hill and Tarter (1978).

Taxonomic treatments at the familial and generic levels
Beraeidae: Wiggins (1954)–L, P, A.
Brachycentridae: Wiggins (1965)–L.
Glossosomatidae: Ross (1956)–A.
Hydrobiosidae: Ross and King (1952)–A.
Hydropsychidae: Denning (1943)–A; Flint (1961)–L, (1974)–L, A; Schmid (1968)–A; Smith (1968a)–L, A; Gordon (1974)–A; Ross and Unzicker (1977)–A; Schuster and Etnier (1978)–L; Flint *et al.* (1979)–A; Givens and Smith (1980)–L, A; Nielsen (1981)–A.
Hydroptilidae: Flint (1970)–L, A; Denning and Blickle (1972)–A; Blickle (1979)–A; Marshall (1979)–L, A; Kelley (1982)–A; Kelley and Morse (1982)–A.
Lepidostomatidae: Ross (1946)–A; Flint and Wiggins (1961)–A; Wallace and Sherberger (1972)–A.
Leptoceridae: Yamamoto and Wiggins (1964)–L, A; Yamamoto and Ross (1966)–A; Morse (1975, 1981)–A; Resh (1976b)–L, P; Haddock (1977)–L, A; Holzenthal (1982)–A.
Limnephilidae: Ross and Merkley (1952)–A; Schmid (1955, includes references to several generic revisions)–A; Flint (1956)–L, (1960)–L; Denning (1964)–A, (1970)–A, (1975)–A; Wiggins and Anderson (1968)–L, A; Wiggins (1973b)–L, A, (1973c)–L, A; Wiggins and Richardson (1982)–L, A.
Molannidae: Sherberger and Wallace (1971)–L; Roy and Harper (1980)–A.
Philopotamidae: Ross (1956)–A.
Phryganeidae: Wiggins (1956)–A, (1960a)–L, (1962)–L, P, A.
Polycentropodidae: Flint (1964b)–L, A; Ross (1965b)–A; Morse (1972)–A; Hudson *et al.* (1981)–L.
Psychomyiidae: Ross and Merkley (1950)–A; Flint (1964b)–L, A.
Rhyacophilidae: Ross (1956)–A; Flint (1962)–L; Smith (1968b)–L; Schmid (1970, 1981)–A; Peck and Smith (1978)–L, A; Weaver and Sykora (1979)–L.
Sericostomatidae: Ross (1948)–A; Ross and Scott (1974)–A; Ross and Wallace (1974)–L, A.
Uenoidae (North American spp. previously included in Limnephilidae). Denning (1958, 1975)–A; Wiggins *et al.* 1984; ref. #2857.
Xiphocentronidae: Ross (1949)–A; Edwards (1961)–L, P.

Table 16A. Summary of ecological and distributional data for *Trichoptera (caddisflies)*. (For definition of terms see Tables 6A–6C; table prepared by K. W. Cummins, G. B. Wiggins, and J. C. Morse.)

Taxa (number of species in parentheses)*	Habitat	Habit	Trophic Relationships	North American Distribution	Ecological References*
Hydropsychoidea					81, 382, 1168, 1316, 2546, 2547, 2556, 2... 2677
Philopotamidae(38)	Generally lotic—erosional	Clingers (sac-like silk net makers)	Generally collectors—filterers		
Chimarra(17)	Lotic—erosional (warmer rivers)	Clingers (saclike silk nets)	Collectors—filterers	Widespread	81, 419, 421, 1829, 2210, 2556, 2547, 2... 2710,†
Dolophilodes(8) (=*Trentonius* =*Sortosa*)	Lotic—erosional (headwater streams and mossy seeps on rock faces)	Clingers (saclike silk nets)	Collectors—filterers	Widespread	53, 154, 1531, 1625, 2210, 2546, 2556, 2705,†
Wormaldia(13) (=*Dolophilus*)	Lotic—erosional	Clingers (saclike silk nets)	Collectors—filterers	Widespread	2158, 2547
Psychomyiidae(14)	Generally lotic—erosional	Clingers (silk-tube retreat makers)	Generally collectors—gatherers		382, 545, 1316, 188... 2099, 2106, 2675, 2...
Paduniellinae					
Paduniella(1)				Arkansas	
Psychomyiinae					
Lype(1)	Lotic—erosional		Scrapers	East, North Central	1514, 2675, 2677
Tinodes(9)	Lotic—erosional		Scrapers, collectors—gatherers	West	507, 1888, 2675
Psychomyia(3)	Lotic—erosional	Clingers (silk tube retreats)	Collectors—gatherers scrapers,	Widespread	53, 419, 421, 1888, 2210, 2675, 2677,†
Xiphocentronidae(1)					
Xiphocentron(1)	Lotic—erosional		Collectors—gatherers	Southern Texas	643, 2362, 2677
Ecnomidae(1)					
Austrotinodes(1)	Lotic—erosional	Clingers (probably silk-tube retreat makers)	Collectors—filterers?	Mexico, Texas	745, 2572
Polycentropodidae(78)	Generally lotic—erosional	Clingers (net-spinning retreat makers)	Generally collectors—filterers, some predators (engulfers)		1259, 1316, 1829, 1... 1921, 2227, 2675, 2...
Polycentropodinae					
Cernotina(7)	Lotic and lentic	Clingers (silk tube retreats)	Predators (engulfers)	Central, East	1128
Cyrnellus(1)	Lotic and lentic	Clingers (silk tube retreats)	Collectors—filterers	East, Central	2677
Neureclipsis(5)	Lotic—erosional (on vascular hydrophytes or other supports in water column)	Clingers (trumpet-shaped silk nets)	Collectors—filterers, shredders—herbivores, engulfers (predators)	East, Central	1612, 1829, 1945, 2... 2675
Nyctiophylax(8)	Lotic—erosional and depositional, lentic—littoral	Clingers (silk tube retreats)	Predators (engulfers), collectors—filterers, shredders—herbivores	Widespread, except Southwest	419, 421, 741, 1612 2675
Polycentropus(40)	Lotic—erosional, lentic—littoral	Clingers (silk tube retreats)	Predators (engulfers), collectors—filterers, shredders—herbivores	Widespread	53, 698, 1612, 1829 2210, 2391, 2392, 2... 2728
Polyplectropus(2)	Lotic—erosional	Clingers (silk tube retreats)		Southwest	
Dipseudopsinae					
Phylocentropus(5)	Lotic—depositional (sand, headwater streams)	Burrowers (branched, silk, buried tubes)	Collectors—filterers	East, Central	1508, 1514, 2558, 2...

*Emphasis on trophic relationships.
†Unpublished data, K. W. Cummins, Kellogg Biological Station and Oregon State University.

le 16A—*Continued*

a (number of species in parentheses)	Habitat	Habit	Trophic Relationships	North American Distribution	Ecological References[*]
ropsychidae(142)	Generally lotic—erosional, some lentic—erosional	Clingers (net-spinning fixed-retreat makers)	Generally collectors—filterers, some predators (engulfers)		382, 464, 545, 624, 1042, 1047, 1316, 1757, 1829, 1886, 2099, 2106, 2556, 2675, 2677
rctopsychinae					
Arctopsyche(4)	Lotic—erosional (cool streams)	Clingers (net spinners, fixed retreats)	Collectors—filterers (coarse particles, animal and plant)	Widespread	32, 154, 1008, 1625, 2266, 2544, 2547, 2556
Parapsyche(7)	Lotic—erosional	Clingers (net spinners, fixed retreats)	Collectors—filterers (coarse particles)	Widespread	32, 154, 1508, 1531, 2210, 2266, 2547, 2556, 2758
iplectroninae					
Aphropsyche(2)	Lotic—erosional (headwater streams)	Clingers (net spinners, fixed retreats)	Collectors—filterers	East	2675, 2677
Diplectrona(3)	Lotic—erosional (headwater streams)	Clingers (net spinners, fixed retreats)	Collectors—filterers (coarse particles, especially detritus)	East, West	495, 1047, 1531, 1674, 1844, 2547, 2556, 2758,†
Homoplectra(8)	Lotic—erosional (rock face springs and seeps)	Clingers (net spinners, fixed retreats)	Collectors—filters	West	53
Oropsyche(1)	Lotic—erosional	Clingers (net spinners, fixed retreats)	Collectors—filterers	North Carolina	2675
ydropsychinae					
Ceratopsyche(30)‡ (=*Symphitopsyche*)	Lotic—erosional, some lentic—erosional	Clingers (net spinners, fixed retreats)	Collectors—filterers (particles include diatoms, detritus, animals)	Widespread	32, 2189, 2556
Cheumatopsyche(40)	Lotic—erosional (especially warmer streams and rivers)	Clingers (net spinners, fixed retreats)	Collectors—filterers (particles include algae, detritus, some animals)	Widespread	32, 53, 419, 713, 799, 1671, 1843, 1844, 2026, 2545,†
Hydropsyche(43)	Lotic—erosional	Clingers (net spinners, fixed retreats)	Collectors—filterers (particles include diatoms, algae, detritus, animals)		32, 53, 81, 154, 419, 421, 464, 698, 816, 817, 818, 878, 912, 1046, 1047, 1259, 1346, 1354, 1512, 1603, 1624, 1625, 1671, 1756, 1794, 1829, 1843, 1844, 1888, 1920, 1945, 2026, 2196, 2210, 2227, 2231, 2241, 2545, 2547, 2556, 2619,†
Potamyia(1)	Lotic—erosional (larger rivers)	Clingers (net spinners, fixed retreats)	Collectors—filterers (detritus, diatoms)	East, South	799, 2210
Smicridea(4)	Lotic—erosional	Clingers (net spinners, fixed retreats)	Collectors—filterers	West, Southwest	2675, 2677
lacronematinae					
Leptonema(1)	Lotic—erosional	Clingers (net spinners, fixed retreats)	Collectors—filterers	South Texas, Mexico	740, 743, 2675
Macrostemum(3) (=*Macronema*= *Macronemum*)	Lotic—erosional (larger rivers)	Clingers (net spinners, fixed retreats)	Collectors—filterers (fine particles)	East	747, 2160, 2544, 2545, 2547, 2554, 2555, 2556
acophiloidea					
hyacophilidae(100+)	Lotic—erosional	Clingers (free ranging)	Generally predators (engulfers)		545, 1316, 1886, 2099, 2106, 2675, 2677
Himalopsyche(1)	Lotic—erosional	Clingers (free ranging) (alpine)	Predators (engulfers), scrapers	West	2675

nphasis on trophic relationships.
published data, K. W. Cummins, Kellogg Biological Station and Oregon State University.
hough some systematists follow Ross and Unzicker (1977) and Nielsen (1981) in recognizing the *morosa-bifida* group as genus *Ceratopsyche*, sound reasons
etaining *Hydropsyche sens. lat.* were given by Schmid (1979; ref. #2850).

Table 16A—*Continued*

Taxa (number of species in parentheses)	Habitat	Habit	Trophic Relationships	North American Distribution	Ecological References[*]
Rhyacophila(100+)	Lotic—erosional	Clingers (free ranging)	Predators (engulfers), a few scrapers, collectors—gatherers, shredders—herbivores (chewers)	Widespread (except Great Plains)	309, 1476, 1508, 15 1541, 1625, 1809, 1 2196, 2210, 2227, 2 2438, 2675
Hydrobiosidae(3)					
Atopsyche(3)	Lotic—erosional	Clingers (free ranging)	Predators (engulfers)	Southwest	2675, 2677
Glossosomatidae(79)	Lotic—erosional	Clingers (saddle- or turtle-shell-case makers)	Generally scrapers		545, 1042, 1316, 18 2099, 2106, 2675, 2
Glossosomatinae					
Anagapetus(6)	Lotic—erosional (including small alpine springs)	Clingers (turtle shell case, mineral)	Scrapers	Rocky Mountains	53, 56, 2677
Glossosoma(25)	Lotic—erosional (including large alpine rivers)	Clingers (turtle shell case, mineral)	Scrapers	Widespread	53, 56, 81, 382, 480 545, 912, 1259, 131 1351, 1476, 1674, 1 1886, 1888, 2099, 2 2196, 2443, 2675,†
Agapetinae					
Agapetus(30)	Lotic—erosional	Clingers (laterally compressed turtle shell case, mineral)	Scrapers, collectors—gatherers	Widespread	56, 1625, 2227
Protoptilinae					
Culoptila(4)	Lotic—erosional	Clingers (turtle shell case, mineral)	Scrapers	Widespread (primarily Southwest)	2675, 2677
Matrioptila(1)	Lotic—erosional	Clingers (depressed turtle shell case)	Scrapers	Southeast	2675, 2677
Protoptila(13)	Lotic—erosional	Clingers (laterally compressed turtle shell case, mineral)	Scrapers	Widespread	2210, 2675, †
Hydroptilidae(170) (microcaddis)	Generally lotic and lentic—erosional, lentic—littoral	Generally clingers or climbers (may fasten case down; purse- or barrel-case makers). First 4 instars free living, 5th instar case builders	Generally piercers—herbivores, scrapers, collectors—gatherers		545, 1042, 1316, 18 1886, 2099, 2106, 2 2677
Ptilocolepinae					
Palaeagapetus(3)	Lotic—erosional (cold springs and seeps)	Sprawlers (purse-type case of small leaf fragments, especially liverwort)	Shredders—detritivores	West, East	53, 2677
Hydroptilinae					
Hydroptilini					
Agraylea(3)	Lentic—vascular hydrophytes (with filamentous algae), lotic—erosional (vascular hydrophytes)	Climbers (purse-type case of silk and algal and plant stem strands)	Piercers—herbivores (filamentous algae), collectors—gatherers	Widespread	53, 104, 1671, 1794, 1810, 2210, 2227,†
Dibusa(1)	Lotic—erosional	Clingers (purse-type case of silk and *Lemanea*)	Scrapers (red alga, *Lemanea*)?	East	2675
Hydroptila(60)	Lotic—erosional and depositional (including seeps)	Clingers (purse-type case of silk and fine mineral)	Piercers—herbivores, scrapers	Widespread	53, 421, 1810, 1888, 2675,†

*Emphasis on trophic relationships.
†Unpublished data, K. W. Cummins, Kellogg Biological Station and Oregon State University.

e 16A—*Continued*

a (number of species in parentheses)	Habitat	Habit	Trophic Relationships	North American Distribution	Ecological References*
Ochrotrichia(42)	Lotic—erosional and depositional	Clingers (purse-type case of silk and fine mineral)	Collectors—gatherers, piercers—herbivores	Widespread	2675, 2758
Oxyethira(30)	Lentic—vascular hydrophytes (with filamentous algae), lotic—erosional and depositional (vascular hydrophytes)	Climbers (purse-type case, flat, flask-shaped, open at back, primarily of silk)	Piercers—herbivores collectors—gatherers, scrapers (?)	Widespread	1810, 2675,†
actobiini					
Stactobiella(3) (=Tascobia)	Lotic—erosional and depositional (small rapid streams)	Clingers? (purse-type case of silk and algal and plant stem strands)	Shredders	Widespread	53, 2675, 2677
ucotrichiini					
Leucotrichia(3)	Lotic—erosional	Clingers (purse-type case, fixed)	Scrapers, collectors—gatherers	Widespread (especially South)	53, 744, 2210, 2675,†
Zumatrichia(1)	Lotic—erosional	Clingers (purse-type case, fixed)	Scrapers, collectors—gatherers	Montana	2675
thotrichiini					
Ithytrichia(2)	Lotic—erosional (on rocks)	Clingers (purse-type case of silk)	Scrapers	Widespread	2675
Orthotrichia(6)	Lentic—vascular hydrophytes (with filamentous algae)	Clingers? (purse-type case of silk)	Piercers—herbivores	Widespread	2675
otrichiini					
Neotrichia(16)	Lotic—erosional	Clingers (case, a tube of fine mineral)	Scrapers	Widespread	2675, 2677
Mayatrichia(3)		Clingers? (case of silk, rigid)	Scrapers	Widespread	2675, 2677
rtain relationships in Hydroptilidae)					
Rioptila(1)				Arizona, Utah	209, 210
ephiloidea					
ryganeidae(27)	Generally lentic—littoral, lotic—depositional	Generally climbers (tube-case makers—cylinders open at both ends)	Generally shredders—herbivores, predators (engulfers)		545, 1316, 1886, 2099, 2106, 2675, 2677
Yphriinae					
Yphria(1)	Lotic—depositional and erosional	Clingers—sprawlers (case a curved cylinder of mineral and wood pieces)	Predators (engulfers)	West	53, 2667, 2675
Phryganeinae					
Agrypnia(9)	Lentic—littoral (ponds), lotic—depositional	Climbers (case a spirally arranged, tapered cylinder of leaf pieces)	Shredders—detritivores and herbivores (chewers), scrapers(?)	Widespread	53, 2664, 2675,†
Banksiola(5)	Lentic—vascular hydrophytes, lotic—depositional	Climbers (case similar to *Agrypnia* but with some irregular strands of vegetation)	Shredders—herbivores (chewers; early instars, filamentous green algae); last two instars predators (engulfers)	Widespread (except western Alaska)	53, 1612, 2664, 2675, 2728, 2729
Fabria(2)	Lentic—vascular hydrophytes	Climbers (case a rough, "Christmas tree shaped" tube of long vegetation strands)	Shredders—herbivores	Northeast, Central	2675

hasis on trophic relationships.
ublished data, K. W. Cummins, Kellogg Biological Station and Oregon State University.

Table 16A—*Continued*

Taxa (number of species in parentheses)	Habitat	Habit	Trophic Relationships	North American Distribution	Ecological References[*]
Hagenella(1)		Climbers (case a slightly curved cylinder of leaf pieces)		Northeast	2675
Oligostomis(2)	Lotic—erosional and depositional (detritus and vascular hydrophytes)	Climbers (case similar to *Hagenella*)	Predators (engulfers) shredders—herbivores and detritivores (chewers)	East	1337, 2249, 2675
Oligotricha(1)	Lentic—littoral	Climbers (case similar to *Agrypnia*)	Predators (engulfers)	Western Alaska	2675
Phryganea(2)	Lotic—depositional and lentic (detritus and vascular hydrophytes)	Climbers (case a spirally arranged, tapered cylinder constructed of leaf pieces)	Shredders—herbivores and detritivores (chewers), predators (engulfers)	Widespread	180, 840, 935, 1337, 1476, 2227, 2664, 2675,†
Ptilostomis(4)	Lotic—erosional and depositional (detritus and vascular hydrophytes)	Climbers (case similar to *Hagenella*)	Shredders—herbivores and detritivores (chewers), predators (engulfers)	Widespread	1476, 2664, 2675, 2
Brachycentridae(31)	Generally lotic—erosional	Generally clingers, climbers (tube-case makers, tapered, may be square in cross section)	Generally collectors—filterers and gatherers, shredders—herbivores		545, 1316, 1886, 20 2106, 2675, 2677
Adicrophleps(1)	Lotic—erosional (in moss)	Clingers, climbers (case tapered, square in cross section)	Shredders?	East	2677
Amiocentrus(1)	Lotic—erosional (rocks and vascular hydrophytes)	Clingers, climbers (case a straight, tapered tube mostly of silk)	Collectors—gatherers	West	53, 2668, 2675
Brachycentrus(9)	Lotic—erosional (on logs, branches, or vascular hydrophytes)	Clingers (case tapered, smooth, square in cross section)	Collectors—filterers (particles include algae, detritus, animals), scrapers	Widespread	828, 829, 830, 959, 1476, 1624, 1626, 1 1756, 2210, 2528
Eobrachycentrus(1)	Lotic—erosional (cold streams in moss)	Clingers (case similar to *Adicrophelps*)	Shredders—herbivores?	West (Mt. Hood area)	2668, 2675
Micrasema(18)	Lotic—erosional (on logs, branches, or vascular hydrophytes)	Clingers—sprawlers (case tapered, sometimes curved, of silk and strands of vegetation)	Shredders—herbivores (chewers), collectors—gatherers	Widespread	53, 382, 1514, 2210 2675
Oligoplectrum(1)	Lotic—erosional (on logs, branches, or vascular hydrophytes)	Clingers (case tapered, straight, smooth, of coarse mineral)	Collectors—filterers	West	2668, 2675, 2677
Lepidostomatidae(70)	Generally lotic—erosional and depositional (detritus)	Generally climbers—sprawlers—clingers (tube-case makers; tapered, often square in cross section)	Shredders—detritivores (chewers)		545, 1316, 1886, 20 2106, 2675
Lepidostoma(65)	Lotic—erosional and depositional (detritus) (headwater streams and springs)	Climbers—sprawlers—clingers (case square or "rough log cabin" type of leaf and bark fragments, or cylindrical, of sand or silk)	Shredders—detritivores (chewers) (also reported as scavengers)	Widespread	53, 58, 59, 382, 907 961, 1508, 2207, 22 2222, 2711, 2728,†
Theliopsyche(5)	Lotic—erosional (in gravel)	Climbers—sprawlers (case cylindrical, of sand)	Shredders—detritivores	East	2677

*Emphasis on trophic relationships.
†Unpublished data, K. W. Cummins, Kellogg Biological Station and Oregon State University.

e 16A— *Continued*

a (number of species in parentheses)	Habitat	Habit	Trophic Relationships	North American Distribution	Ecological References[*]
mnephilidae(300+)	All types of lotic and lentic habitats	Climbers—sprawlers—clingers (tube case makers of great variety)	Generally shredders—detritivores (chewers), collectors—gatherers, scrapers		382, 545, 737, 1042, 1316, 1886, 2099, 2106, 2675, 2677
Dicosmoecinae					
Allocosmoecus(1)	Lotic—erosional	Sprawlers (case curved, flattened, rough mineral)	Scrapers, shredders?	West	53, 2675
Amphicosmoecus(1)	Lotic—erosional and depositional, lentic—littoral	Sprawlers (case a hollowed twig with anterior bark pieces or entire case of wood pieces)	Shredders	West	1821, 2675, 2677
Cryptochia(7)	Lotic—depositional (detritus; small, cool streams, springs and seeps	Sprawlers (case flat, tapered, of wood and bark)	Scrapers, shredders	West	53, 2673, 2675, 2677
Dicosmoecus(4)	Lotic—erosional	Sprawlers (case curved, flattened, rough mineral)	Scrapers, shredders—detritivores, engulfers (predators) (also reported as scavengers)	West	53, 297, 991, 2675, 2679
Ecclisocosmoecus (1)	Lotic—depositional (sand)	Burrowers (case tapered, curved, smooth mineral)	Scrapers, shredders	Northwest	2675, 2677
Ecclisomyia(3)	Lotic—erosional (cold alpine streams)	Clingers (case a mineral tube, may have long plant pieces)	Collectors—gatherers, scrapers	West	53, 1625, 1821, 2104, 2675
Ironoquia(4) (=*Caborius*)	Lotic—depositional, lentic littoral (temporary streams and ponds)	Sprawlers (case a curved tube of leaf or bark pieces, or mineral)	Shredders	East	103, 736, 1508, 2099, 2670, 2675, 2704
Onocosmoecus(6?)	Lotic—depositional (detritus), lentic—littoral (detritus)	Sprawlers (case of wood, bark, or mineral)	Shredders	Northeast, West	1821, 2675, 2677, 2711, 2728
Apataniinae					
Apatania(15)	Lotic—erosional (especially springs), lentic—littoral (oligotrophic lakes)	Clingers—climbers—sprawlers (case tapered, strongly curved, dorsal projection, mineral)	Scrapers, collectors—gatherers	Widespread (primarily North and higher elevations)	53, 654, 737, 2675
Neophylacinae					
Neophylax(15)	Lotic—erosional	Clingers (case tapered, slightly curved, mineral with ballast stones on each side)	Scrapers	East, West	53, 419, 421, 1508, 1674, 2206, 2210, 2675
Oligophlebodes(7)	Lotic—erosional	Clingers (case strongly tapered and curved, rough mineral)	Scrapers, collectors—gatherers	West	1876, 2675
Pseudostenophylacinae					
Pseudostenophylax(3) (=*Drusinus*)	Lotic—erosional (detritus) and depositional (including seeps and temporary streams)	Sprawlers (case tapered, curved, smooth, mineral)	Shredders—detritivores (chewers), collectors—gatherers	East, West	50, 53, 58, 737, 1508, 2675, 2676

hasis on trophic relationships.

Table 16A—*Continued*

Taxa (number of species in parentheses)	Habitat	Habit	Trophic Relationships	North American Distribution	Ecological References*
Limnephilinae					
Anabolia(4)	Lentic—vascular hydrophytes, lotic—depositional (including temporary ponds)	Climbers—sprawlers (case a rough tube of leaf and wood pieces; may be three-sided)	Shredders—detritivores (chewers), collectors—gatherers	East, North	959, 1259, 2241, 26⁷
Arctopora(3) (=*Lenarchulus*)	Lentic—littoral (including temporary ponds)	Climbers—sprawlers (case a smooth tube of long leaf pieces)		Northeast, Idaho	2675
Asynarchus(10)	Lentic—littoral (including temporary ponds), lotic—depositional	Climbers (case variable tube of mineral and plant pieces)		North, Rocky Mountains	53, 737, 1821, 2675, 2711
Chilostigma(1)				Minnesota	2673, 2675
Chilostigmodes(1)				Widespread (North)	1358, 2675
Chyranda(1)	Lotic—depositional (detritus)	Sprawlers (case a flat tube of bark and leaf pieces)	Shredders—detritivores	North, Western mountains	53, 2675, 2677, 271
Clistoronia(4)	Lentic—littoral (sediments and detritus)	Sprawlers (case a rough tube of twig and bark pieces arranged longitudinally)	Collectors—gatherers, shredders—detritivores (chewers)	West	52, 53, 1984, 2675, 2728
Clostoeca(1)	Lotic—depositional (detritus, spring seepage)	Sprawlers (case a flattened tube of large leaf pieces with flanges)	Shredders—detritivores	Northwest	2675, 2677
Desmona(1)	Lotic—depositional (sand)	Sprawlers—burrowers (case a tube of mixed mineral and wood fragments)	Shredders—detritivores and herbivores (chewers)	California	680, 2675, 2677
Frenesia(2)	Lotic—erosional and depositional (detritus; including springs)	Sprawlers (case a smooth tube of mineral and wood pieces)	Shredders—detritivores (chewers)	Northeast	1476, 2106, 2675
Glyphopsyche(2)	Lentic—littoral (detritus), lotic—depositional (detritus)	Sprawlers (case a smooth tube of twig and bark pieces)		North, West, Missouri	2675
Grammotaulius(5)	Lentic—littoral and lotic—depositional (vascular hydrophytes), including temporary streams	Climbers (case a tube of long leaf pieces)		North	53, 737, 1052, 2675
Grensia(1)	Lentic—littoral(?) (tundra lakes)	Sprawlers? (case a curved tube of plant fragments and mineral)		North (tundra zone)	2675
Halesochila(1)	Lentic—littoral (sediments)	Sprawlers (case a rough tube of leaf and wood pieces)	Collectors—gatherers, shredders—detritivores (chewers)	Northwest	2675, 2728
Hesperophylax(6) (=*Platyphylax*)	Lotic—erosional and depositional (detritus), including temporary streams	Sprawlers (case a slightly curved, slightly rough, coarse mineral tube)	Shredders—detritivores and herbivores (chewers) (scrapers, collectors—gatherers)	Widespread	53, 912, 1476, 1555, 2210, 2675, 2711
Homophylax(10)	Lotic—erosional (sediments and detritus)	Clingers—sprawlers (case a smooth tube of bark pieces)	Shredders—detritivores (chewers)	West	2675
Hydatophylax(4) (=*Astenophylax*)	Lotic—depositional (detritus)	Sprawlers—climbers (case a rough cylinder of wood, bark, and some mineral, with balance sticks)	Shredders—detritivores (chewers), collectors—gatherers	East, Southeast, Northwest	53, 59, 737, 1476, 2. 2675,†

*Emphasis on trophic relationships.
†Unpublished data, K. W. Cummins, Kellogg Biological Station and Oregon State University.

e 16A—*Continued*

a (number of species in parentheses)	Habitat	Habit	Trophic Relationships	North American Distribution	Ecological References[*]
Lenarchus(9)	Lentic—littoral (including temporary ponds)	Sprawlers—climbers (case a tube of long leaf pieces or bark and leaf pieces)	Collectors—gatherers	North, West	2675, 2728, 2711
Leptophylax(1)				Northeast	2675
Limnephilus (95–100)	All types of lotic and lentic habitats (including temporary ponds and streams)	Climbers, sprawlers, clingers (case of stick, leaf and/or sand construction, variable)	Shredders—detritivores and herbivores (chewers), collectors—gatherers (and probably others)	Widespread (especially North and mountains of West)	53, 103, 737, 959, 960, 1346, 1476, 1612, 1652, 2159, 2210, 2241, 2528, 2670, 2675, 2711[†]
Nemotaulius(1) (=*Glyphotaelius*)	Lentic—littoral (detritus), lotic—depositional (detritus)	Sprawlers (case a flat "log cabin" type, of leaf pieces)	Shredders—detritivores (chewers)	Widespread in North	737, 1476, 2099, 2210, 2241, 2675
Phanocelia(1)				North	2675
Philarctus(1)	Lentic—littoral, lotic—depositional	Sprawlers (case a tube with small shells, seeds, and leaf pieces)		West, Northwest	2675
Philocasca(6)	Lotic—erosional (sediments and detritus) and depositional (detritus-semi-terrestrial)	Clingers—sprawlers (case rough, curved, coarse mineral)	Probably shredders—detritivores (chewers)	West mountains	49, 53, 2675, 2676
Platycentropus(3)	Lentic—littoral, lotic depositional (vascular hydrophytes, detritus)	Climbers (case a rough "log cabin" type of plant stems and other fine pieces)	Shredders—detritivores (and herbivores) (chewers)	East	737, 2675, 2711
Psychoglypha(15)	Lotic—erosional (detritus) and depositional	Sprawlers—clingers (case a type of mixed mineral and bark and wood pieces)	Collectors—gatherers, shredders—detritivores (chewers) (including scavengers)	North, West	53, 297, 737, 2675, 2728
Psychoronia(2)	Lotic	Sprawlers? (case a rough mineral tube)		Rocky Mountains	2675
Pycnopsyche(16)	Lotic—erosional and depositional, lentic—littoral (detritus)	Sprawlers—climbers—clingers (case smooth of mineral, or like *Hydatophylax*)	Shredders—detritivores (chewers), scrapers (last instar in some spiecies)	East, North to Rocky Mountains	419, 421, 478, 710, 911, 1122, 1476, 1509, 1510, 1513, 1671, 2675, 2706, 2711,
erinae					
Goera(6)	Lotic—erosional	Clingers (case mineral with two lateral ballast stones on each side)	Scrapers	East, West	419, 421, 2675[†]
Goeracea(2)	Lotic—erosional (including seeps)	Clingers (case like *Goera* with more than two ballast stones)	Scrapers	West	53, 2671, 2675
Goereilla(1)	Lotic—depositional (springs)	Clingers (case tapered, curved, mineral)	Collectors—gatherers	West (Montana, Idaho)	2674, 2675
Goerita(2)	Lotic—erosional	Clingers (case tapered, curved, mineral)	Scrapers	Southeast	2671, 2675
Lepania(1)	Lotic—depositional (springs and seeps)	Sprawlers (case tapered, curved, mineral)	Collectors—gatherers	Oregon, Washington	2671, 2674, 2675
ncertain relationips (within mnephilidae)					
Allomyia(11) (=*Imania*)	Lotic—erosional	Clingers (case tapered, curved, mineral, may have ballast stones)	Shredders—herbivores (chewers, mosses?), scrapers	West	2181, 2672, 2675
Manophylax(1)	Lotic—erosional (torrential)	Clingers (case tapered, curved, mineral and plant materials)	Scrapers	Idaho Mountains	2672, 2675, 2677
Moselyana(1)	Lotic—depositional (springs and seeps)	Sprawlers (case tapered, curved, fine mineral)	Collectors—gatherers?	Oregon and Washington	2672, 2675
Pedomoecus(1)	Lotic—erosional	Clingers (case tapered, curved, rough mineral)	Scrapers	West	2675, 2677

hasis on trophic relationships.
ublished data, K. W. Cummins, Kellogg Biological Station and Oregon State University.

Table 16A—*Continued*

Taxa (number of species in parentheses)	Habitat	Habit	Trophic Relationships	North American Distribution	Ecological References[*]
Rossiana(1)	Lotic—erosional and depositional (especially in moss)	Clingers (case tapered, curved, rough minerals)	Probably scrapers and shredders—herbivores (chewers)	Northwest	2675
Uenoidae(13)	Lotic—erosional	Clingers (case tapered, slender, curved, mineral)	Scrapers, collectors—gatherers	West	53, 2675, 2857
Farula(7)	Lotic—erosional (on rocks, including seeps)	Clingers (case tapered, curved, long, very slender, mineral)	Scrapers, collectors—gatherers	West	53, 2675
Neothremma(6)	Lotic—erosional (on rocks)	Clingers (case tapered, slightly curved, long, slender mineral)	Scrapers, collectors—gatherers	West	53, 737, 1625, 2675
Beraeidae(3)					
Beraea(3)	Lotic—depositional (detritus, springs)	Sprawlers (case curved, smooth, fine mineral)	Probably collectors—gatherers	Northeast, Georgia	2661, 2675
Sericostomatidae(12)	Generally lotic	Generally sprawlers	Generally shredders		545, 1193, 1194, 12 1316, 1794, 2099, 2 2436, 2675
Agarodes(9)	Lotic—erosional (detritus) and depositional (detritus)	Sprawlers (case tapered, curved, short, smooth, coarse mineral and wood fragments)	Shredders—detritivores (chewers), collectors—gatherers	East	2210, 2675
Fattigia(1)	Lotic	Sprawlers? (case curved, short, smooth, coarse mineral)	Shredders?	Southeast mountains	2675
Gumaga(2)	Lotic	Sprawlers? (case tapered, curved, long, smooth, fine mineral)	Shredders	West	2106, 2675
Odontoceridae(14)	Generally lotic—erosional and depositional (detritus)	Generally sprawlers?	Generally shredders (and scavengers)		2675
Marilia(2)	Lotic	Sprawlers? (case curved, smooth, coarse mineral)	Shredders	Southwest, Ontario	1514
Namamyia(1)	Lotic—erosional and depositional	Sprawlers? (case curved, smooth, coarse mineral)	Collectors—gatherers?	Oregon, California	2675
Nerophilus(1)	Lotic—depositional	Sprawlers? (case curved, slightly rough, coarse mineral)	Shredders—detritivores	West	2675
Parthina(2)	Lotic—erosional and depositional (small streams, springs, and seeps)	Sprawlers? (case curved, tapered, smooth, fine mineral and wood fragments)	Shredders—detritivores (chewers)?	Western mountains	53, 1514, 2675
Psilotreta(7)	Lotic—erosional (gravel, detritus) and depositional (detritus), (lentic—erosional)	Sprawlers (case curved, smooth, coarse mineral)	Scrapers, collectors—gatherers	East	419, 421, 1508, 151 2675[†]
Pseudogoera(1)	Lotic	Sprawlers? (case curved, tapered, rough, coarse mineral)	Predators (engulfers)	Southeastern mountains	2551, 2675
Molannidae(6)	Generally lentic—erosional, lotic—depositional (especially springs)	Generally sprawlers—clingers (case flat with dorsal projection and flanges)	Generally scrapers, collectors—gatherers, predators (engulfers)		545, 906, 1316, 188 2099, 2106, 2241, 2
Molanna(5)	Lentic—erosional, lotic—depositional (headwater streams and springs)	Sprawlers—clingers (case flat with dorsal projection and lateral ballast flanges, coarse to fine mineral)	Scrapers, collectors—gatherers, predators (engulfers)	Widespread	2241, 2675[†]

[*]Emphasis on trophic relationships.
[†]Unpublished data, K. W. Cummins, Kellogg Biological Station and Oregon State University.

le 16A—*Continued*

a (number of species in parentheses)	Habitat	Habit	Trophic Relationships	North American Distribution	Ecological References*
Molannodes(1)	Lotic—depositional (headwater streams and springs)	Sprawlers (case flat with dorsal projection and lateral flanges of wood fragments)	Collectors—gatherers?	Alaska, Yukon	2675
copsychidae(5)					545, 1316, 1886, 2099, 2106, 2675
Helicopsyche(5)	Lotic and lentic—erosional (including thermal springs)	Clingers (case snail shell shaped, fine mineral)	Scrapers	Widespread	419, 421, 1624, 1625, 2210, 2675
moceratidae(5)	Lotic	Sprawlers	Generally shredders—detritivores and scrapers		545, 1316, 1886, 2099, 2106, 2675
Anisocentropus(1)	Lotic—depositional (detritus)	Sprawlers? (case flat of large leaf pieces with dorsal projection)	Generally shredders—detritivores	Southeast	2552, 2675
Heteroplectron(2)	Lotic—erosional (detritus) and depositional (detritus)	Sprawlers (case a hollowed out stick or piece of bark)	Shredders—detritivores (chewers, of leaf litter and gougers of wood), scrapers?	East, West	53, 59, 1476, 1868, 2675, 2728
Phylloicus(2)	Lotic	Sprawlers? (case a flat tube with large leaf and bark pieces and dorsal projection)	Shredders—detritivores	Southwest	2675
oceridae(103)	All types of lotic and lentic habitats (including limnetic)	Climbers, sprawlers, clingers, swimmers (tube case makers of wide variety)	Collectors—gatherers and filterers, shredders—herbivores (chewers), scrapers, predators (engulfers)		545, 1316, 1886, 2099, 2106, 2675
Ceraclea(34) (=*Athripsodes*)	Lotic and lentic (some in sponges)	Sprawlers, climbers (case a fine mineral or silk tube, may have dorsal projection and flanges)	Collectors—gatherers, shredders—herbivores (chewers), predators (engulfers of sponge)	Widespread	1612, 2014, 2016, 2017, 2018, 2019, 2023, 2099, 2210, 2675
Leptocerus(1)	Lentic—vascular hydrophytes	Swimmers—climbers (case long and slender, primarily of silk)	Shredders—herbivores (chewers)	Northcentral, Northeast to South Carolina	1514, 2675
Mystacides(3)	Lotic—depositional, lentic—vascular hydrophytes	Sprawlers—climbers (case a rough tube of mineral and vegetation pieces may have balance sticks)	Collectors—gatherers, shredders—herbivores (chewers)	Widespread	53, 1052, 1476, 1612, 2675, 2783†
Nectopsyche(12) (=*Leptocella*)	Lentic—vascular hydrophytes, lotic—erosional and depositional (vascular hydrophytes)	Climbers—swimmers (case long, slender of mineral and vegetation pieces, may have long balance sticks)	Shredders—herbivores (chewers), collectors—gatherers (predators [engulfers])	Widespread	158, 1042, 1612, 1624, 1625, 1794, 2099, 2210, 2675
Oecetis(20)	Lotic—erosional and depositional, lentic—littoral	Clingers—sprawlers, climbers (case a curved tube, often tapered, of coarse mineral or plant fragments)	Predators (engulfers), shredders—herbivores (chewers)?	Widespread	180, 1612, 2099, 2210,
Setodes(8)	Lotic—erosional and depositional, lentic—littoral	Sprawlers—clingers, burrowers (case curved, stout or slender, mineral)	Collectors—gatherers (particles include algae and animals), predators (engulfers)	East	1514, 1635, 2675
Triaenodes(25)	Lentic—littoral, lotic—depositional (vascular hydrophytes)	Swimmers—climbers (case long, tapered of spirally arranged leaf and stem fragments)	Shredders—herbivores (chewers)	Widespread	158, 1514, 1612, 2442, 2675†

phasis on trophic relationships.
published data, K. W. Cummins, Kellogg Biological Station and Oregon State University.

Trichoptera Genera

17

John C. Morse and Ralph W. Holzenthal
Clemson University, South Carolina

INTRODUCTION

Through the efforts of various recent workers, especially H. H. Ross, O. S. Flint, and G. B. Wiggins, larvae of most North American caddisfly genera have been associated and described. Exceptions noted below are rare and not likely to be encountered by the general collector. Pupae for the more common genera have been described by Ross (1944). Most pupae may be identified, however, by reference to last instar larval sclerites retained in the pupal case (except Leptoceridae, which rid their pupal cases of these sclerites) and/or to structures of the pharate adult within the pupal cuticle. Adults of North American caddisfly genera may be identified through use of the keys and references provided by Betten (1934), Ross (1944), and Schmid (1980).

For the most part, the following larval keys are modified from the work by Wiggins (1977). Indeed, use of the keys and corresponding figures in this section should be viewed only as a preliminary step toward assuring accurate larval determinations. The excellent illustrations and biological discussions in the more comprehensive treatise by Wiggins (1977)

should be considered companion material for reliable identification of larval Trichoptera specimens to the generic level.

As the sequel to the preceding chapter, this section assumes the user's familiarity with the information given by Wiggins concerning ecology and life history of caddisflies and especially general trichopteran morphology. Structural features mentioned for the first time in this section are labelled in the figures. Even more so than in the chapter on family-level identification, accurate generic larval determinations are most likely obtained when last instar specimens are examined.

Of the 144 North American genera recognized in this chapter, the larvae of six have not yet been described, including four genera of Limnephilidae *(Chilostigma, Chilostigmodes, Leptophylax,* and *Phanocelia),* one of Psychomyiidae *(Paduniella)* and one of Hydroptilidae *(Rioptila).* Five families—Beraeidae, Ecnomidae, Helicopsychidae, Hydrobiosidae, and Xiphocentronidae—each contain only one North American genus *(Beraea, Austrotinodes, Helicopsyche, Atopsyche,* and *Xiphocentron,* respectively) and thus are not treated further.

KEYS TO THE GENERA OF TRICHOPTERA LARVAE

Brachycentridae

(modified from Chapin 1978)

1. Meso- and metathoracic legs long, their femora about as long as head capsule, their tibiae each produced distally into prominent process from which stout spur arises (fig. 17.1) 2

1'. Meso- and metathoracic legs shorter, their femora much shorter than head capsule (fig. 16.60), each tibia not produced distally into prominent process, although spur arises from about same point on unmodified tibia (fig. 17.2) 3

2(1). Mesonotum with mesial sclerites diverging posteriorly (fig. 17.3); head seta no. 17 not longer and stouter than other head setae; case circular in cross section, tapered, and composed of small rock fragments (fig. 17.20) .... *Oligoplectrum*

2'. Mesonotum with mesial sclerites diverging little if any posteriorly (figs. 16.58, 17.4); head seta no. 17 longer and stouter than other head setae (figs. 16.58, 17.5); case usually square in cross section, composed of small pieces of plant materials fastened transversely (figs. 16.13, 17.16), although case sometimes cylindrical and largely of silken secretion, or occasionally of small rock fragments .... *Brachycentrus*

3(1'). Ventral apotome of head longer than wide, narrowed somewhat posteriorly, rudimentary prosternal horn present on anterior part of prosternum (fig. 17.6); case 4-sided and tapered, composed of short pieces of plant material placed crosswise with loose ends often protruding (fig. 17.17) 4

3'.   Ventral apotome of head usually wider than long (fig. 17.7), sometimes squarish
        (fig. 17.8); prosternal horn absent; case cylindrical, tapered, straight or curved,
        composed of lengths of plant material wound around the circumference (figs.
        16.12, 17.18) or of silk or silk and rock material (fig. 17.19) 5

4(3).   Each half of mesonotum largely entire, lateral quarter partially delineated by
        variable suture, posterior margin raised and colored dark brown (fig. 17.9) .... *Eobrachycentrus*

4'.   Each half of mesonotum divided into 3 separate sclerites, posterior margin not
        conspicuously raised or colored (fig. 17.10) .... *Adicrophleps*

5(3'). Transverse pronotal groove curving anteriorly and usually meeting anterior margin
        (fig. 17.11), sometimes forming a rounded lateral lobe; brown, sclerotized band
        on either side of anus (fig. 17.13); mesonotal sa1 with multiple setae (fig. 17.14)
        or solitary seta .... *Micrasema*

5'.   Pronotal groove not curving anteriorly and never reaching anterior margin (fig.
        17.12); no brown, sclerotized bands near anus; mesonotal sa1 with solitary seta
        (fig. 17.15) .... *Amiocentrus*

Calamoceratidae

1.   Anterolateral corners of pronotum produced into prominent lobes (figs. 16.65,
        17.21–17.22); gills with 2 or 3 branches (fig. 17.24) 2

1'.   Anterolateral corners of pronotum somewhat extended (fig. 17.23), but much less
        than above; gill filaments single (fig. 17.25); case a hollowed-out twig (fig.
        17.26) .... *Heteroplectron*

2(1).   Metathoracic legs about as long as mesothoracic legs; anterolateral corners of
        pronotum pointed (fig. 17.22); case of pieces of bark and leaves (fig. 17.27) .... *Phylloicus*

2'.   Metathoracic legs about twice as long as mesothoracic legs; anterolateral corners
        of pronotum rounded (fig. 17.21); case of 2 leaf pieces, dorsal piece overlapping
        ventral one (fig. 16.17) .... *Anisocentropus*

Glossosomatidae

1.   Mesonotum with 2 or 3 sclerites (figs. 17.28, 17.29); head with ventromesial
        margins of genae not thickened, posterior median ventral ecdysial line about 1.5
        times as long as each anterior divergent branch (figs. 17.31, 17.32); anal opening
        without dark, sclerotized line on each side 2

1'.   Mesonotum without sclerites; head with ventromesial margins of genae thickened,
        posterior median ventral ecdysial line about as long as each anterior divergent
        branch (fig. 17.30); anal opening with dark, sclerotized line on each side (fig.
        17.33) .... (subfamily Glossosomatinae) 5

2(1).   Mesonotum with 3 sclerites (fig. 17.29); ventral apotome of head a slender, V-
        shaped sclerite (fig. 17.32) .... (subfamily Protoptilinae) 3

2'.   Mesonotum with 2 sclerites (fig. 17.28); ventral apotome of head not as slender
        (fig. 17.31) ....(subfamily Agapetinae) .... *Agapetus*

3(2).   Each tarsal claw apparently trifid, the three points subequal in length (fig. 17.34) .... *Matrioptila*

3'.   Each tarsal claw with normal single point, basal seta and basal process much
        smaller (figs. 17.35–17.36) 4

4(3'). Basal seta of each tarsal claw long, thin, and arising from side of stout basal
        process (fig. 17.36); case constructed of relatively large stones (fig. 17.39) .... *Protoptila*

4'.   Basal seta of each tarsal claw short and stout, larger than basal process (fig.
        17.35); case constructed of uniformly small stones (fig. 17.40) .... *Culoptila*

5(1'). Pronotum excised one-third anterolaterally to accommodate coxae (fig. 17.37) .... *Glossosoma*

5'.   Pronotum excised two-thirds anterolaterally to accommodate coxae (fig. 17.38) .... *Anagapetus*

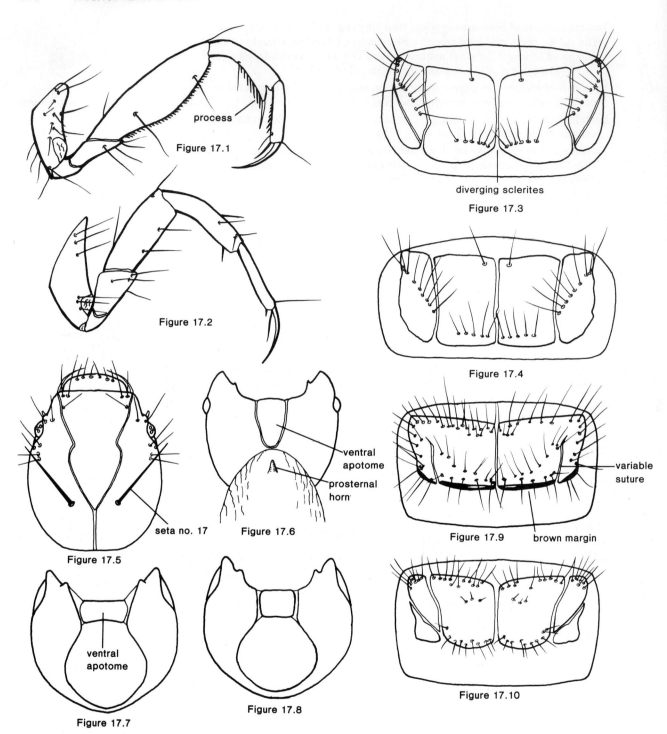

Figure 17.1

process

Figure 17.2

seta no. 17

Figure 17.5

ventral apotome

Figure 17.7

Figure 17.8

ventral apotome

prosternal horn

Figure 17.6

diverging sclerites

Figure 17.3

Figure 17.4

variable suture

Figure 17.9 · brown margin

Figure 17.10

Figure 17.1. *Brachycentrus* sp. (Brachycentridae); lateral view of right metathoracic leg.

Figure 17.2. *Micrasema wataga* Ross (Brachycentridae); lateral view of right metathoracic leg.

Figure 17.3. *Oligoplectrum echo* Ross (Brachycentridae); dorsal view of mesonotum.

Figure 17.4. *Brachycentrus* sp. (Brachycentridae); dorsal view of mesonotum.

Figure 17.5. *Brachycentrus* sp. (Brachycentridae); dorsal view of head.

Figure 17.6. *Adicrophleps hitchcocki* Flint (Brachycentridae); ventral view of head and prosternum.

Figure 17.7. *Amiocentrus aspilus* (Ross) (Brachycentridae); ventral view of head.

Figure 17.8. *Micrasema wataga* Ross (Brachycentridae); ventral view of head.

Figure 17.9. *Eobrachycentrus gelidae* Wiggins (Brachycentridae); dorsal view of mesonotum.

Figure 17.10. *Adicrophleps hitchcocki* Flint (Brachycentridae); dorsal view of mesonotum.

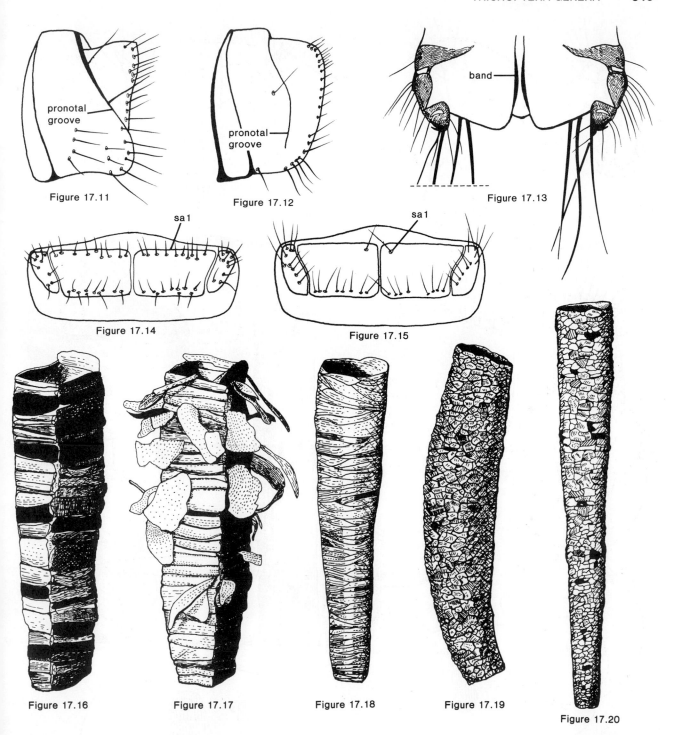

Figure 17.11

Figure 17.12

Figure 17.13

Figure 17.14

Figure 17.15

Figure 17.16

Figure 17.17

Figure 17.18

Figure 17.19

Figure 17.20

Figure 17.11. *Micrasema wataga* Ross (Brachycentridae); right lateral view of pronotum.

Figure 17.12. *Amiocentrus aspilus* (Ross) (Brachycentridae); right lateral view of pronotum.

Figure 17.13. *Micrasema wataga* Ross (Brachycentridae); posterior view of anus.

Figure 17.14. *Micrasema wataga* Ross (Brachycentridae); dorsal view of mesonotum.

Figure 17.15. *Amiocentrus aspilus* (Ross) (Brachycentridae); dorsal view of mesonotum.

Figure 17.16. *Brachycentrus* sp. (Brachycentridae); larval case.

Figure 17.17. *Adicrophleps hitchcocki* Flint (Brachycentridae); larval case.

Figure 17.18. *Micrasema wataga* Ross (Brachycentridae); larval case.

Figure 17.19. *Micrasema rusticum* (Hagen) (Brachycentridae); larval case.

Figure 17.20. *Oligoplectrum echo* Ross (Brachycentridae); larval case.

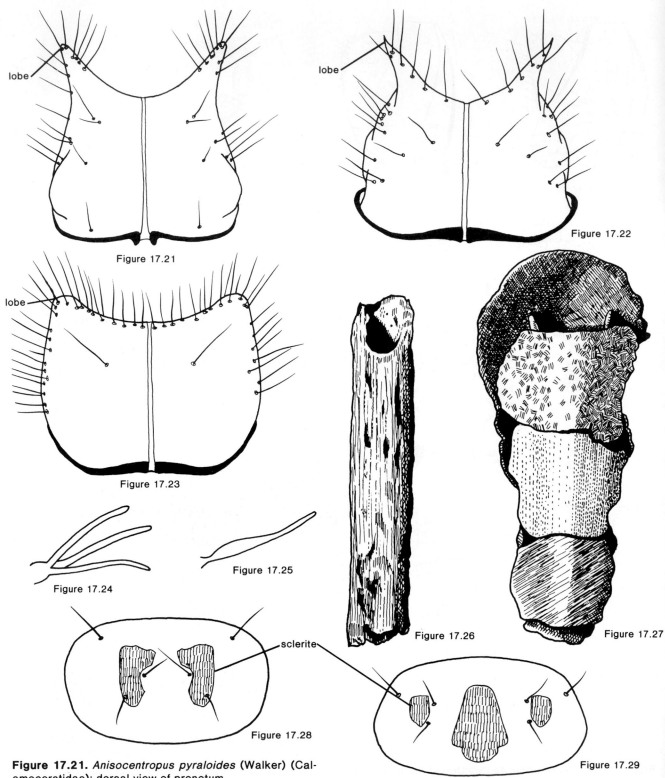

Figure 17.21

Figure 17.22

Figure 17.23

Figure 17.24

Figure 17.25

Figure 17.26

Figure 17.27

Figure 17.28

Figure 17.29

Figure 17.21. *Anisocentropus pyraloides* (Walker) (Calamoceratidae); dorsal view of pronotum.

Figure 17.22. *Phylloicus aeneus* (Banks) (Calamoceratidae); dorsal view of pronotum.

Figure 17.23. *Heteroplectron americanum* (Walker) (Calamoceratidae); dorsal view of pronotum.

Figure 17.24. *Anisocentropus pyraloides* (Walker) (Calamoceratidae); larval gill.

Figure 17.25. *Heteroplectron americanum* (Walker) (Calamoceratidae); larval gill.

Figure 17.26. *Heteroplectron americanum* (Walker) (Calamoceratidae); larval case.

Figure 17.27. *Phylloicus aeneus* (Banks) (Calamoceratidae); larval case.

Figure 17.28. *Agapetus* sp. (Glossosomatidae); dorsal view of mesonotum.

Figure 17.29. *Matrioptila jeanae* (Ross) (Glossosomatidae); dorsal view of mesonotum.

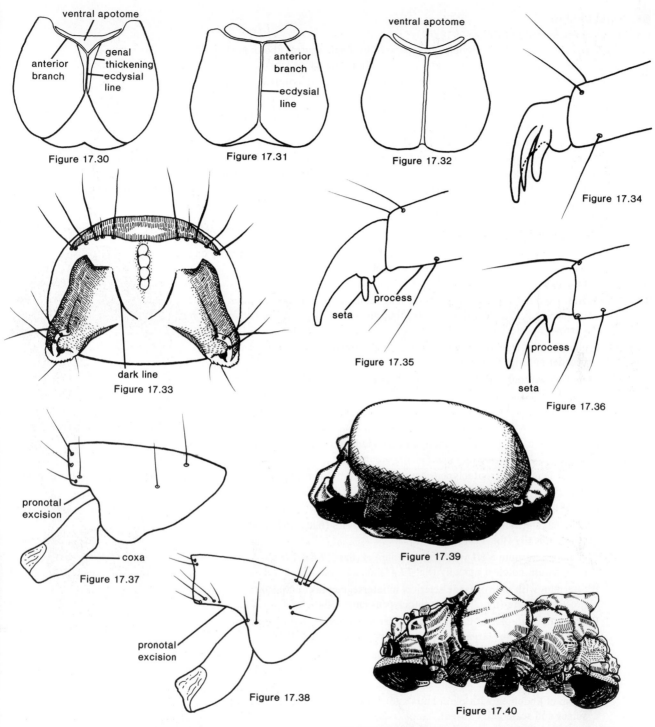

Figure 17.30. *Glossosoma nigrior* Banks (Glossosomatidae); ventral view of head.

Figure 17.31. *Agapetus* sp. (Glossosomatidae); ventral view of head.

Figure 17.32. *Matrioptila jeanae* (Ross) (Glossosomatidae); ventral view of head.

Figure 17.33. *Glossosoma nigrior* Banks (Glossosomatidae); posterior view of anus.

Figure 17.34. *Matrioptila jeanae* (Ross) (Glossosomatidae); lateral view of left mesothoracic tarsus.

Figure 17.35. *Culoptila moselyi* Denning (Glossosomatidae); lateral view of left mesothoracic tarsus.

Figure 17.36. *Protoptila* sp. (Glossosomatidae); lateral view of left mesothoracic tarsus.

Figure 17.37. *Glossosoma nigrior* Banks (Glossosomatidae); left lateral view of pronotum.

Figure 17.38. *Anagapetus* sp. (Glossosomatidae); left lateral view of pronotum.

Figure 17.39. *Protoptila* sp. (Glossosomatidae); larval case.

Figure 17.40. *Culoptila moselyi* Denning (Glossosomatidae); larval case.

Hydropsychidae

(modified from Schuster and Etnier 1978)

1. Genae of head capsule completely separated by single ventral apotome (figs. 17.41, 17.42) .... (subfamily Arctopsychinae) 4

1'. Genae touching ventrally, separating ventral apotome into anterior and posterior parts (figs. 17.43, 17.44, 17.46) or posterior part inconspicuous (fig. 17.45) 2

2(1'). Posterior ventral apotome at least one-half as long as median ecdysial line where genae touch (fig. 17.43) .... (subfamily Diplectroninae) 5

2'. Posterior ventral apotome much less than one-half as long as median ecdysial line (figs. 17.44, 17.46) or inconspicuous (fig. 17.45) 3

3(2'). Abdominal gills with up to 40 filaments arising fairly uniformly along central stalk (fig. 17.47); fore trochantin never forked (figs. 17.70–17.71) .... (subfamily Macronematinae) 12

3'. Abdominal gills with up to 10 filaments arising mostly near the apex of the central stalk (figs. 16.39, 17.48); fore trochantin usually forked (figs. 16.39, 17.50), sometimes not (fig. 17.49) .... (subfamily Hydropsychinae) 8

4(1). Most abdominal segments dorsally with tuft of long setae and/or scale hairs on sa2 and sa3 positions (fig. 17.53); ventral apotome of head usually nearly rectangular (fig. 17.42) .... *Parapsyche*

4'. Most abdominal segments with single long setae in sa2 and sa3 positions, frequently with 1 or 2 shorter setae, but not a tuft (fig. 17.54); ventral apotome narrowed posteriorly (fig. 17.41) .... *Arctopsyche*

5(2). Pronotum with transverse furrow separating narrower posterior one-third from broader anterior two-thirds (fig. 17.56) 6

5'. Pronotum without transverse furrow; constricted only slightly at posterior border (fig. 17.55) .... *Diplectrona*

6(5). Mesal surface of each meso- and metathoracic femur with palmately subdivided, stout, flattened setae (fig. 17.57) .... *Homoplectra*

6'. Mesal surface of each meso- and metathoracic femur without such subdivided setae 7

7(6'). Anterior margin of frontoclypeus convex and symmetrical (fig. 17.59) .... probably *Oropsyche*

7'. Anterior margin of frontoclypeus asymmetrical, broadly notched on left (fig. 17.58) .... *Aphropsyche*

8(3'). Abdominal sternum VIII with single median sclerite (fig. 17.62); submentum entire apically (fig. 17.45) .... *Smicridea*

8'. Abdominal sternum VIII with pair of sclerites (figs. 17.61, 17.72–17.73); submentum notched apically (fig. 17.44) 9

9(8'). Prosternum with pair of large sclerites in intersegmental fold posterior to prosternal plate (fig. 17.66); frontoclypeus entire (fig. 17.63) 10

9'. Prosternum with pair of usually small sclerites posterior to prosternal plate (fig. 17.67); if sclerites large, frontoclypeus with shallow mesal excision (fig. 17.65) 11

10(9). Dorsum of abdomen with numerous plain hairs in addition to minute spines on at least 1st 3 segments, scale hairs present on at least last 3 segments (fig. 17.68); club hairs absent .... *Hydropsyche*

10'. Dorsum of abdomen with plain hairs and club hairs only (fig. 17.69); minute spines and scale hairs absent. .... *Ceratopsyche*[1]

11(9'). Anterior ventral apotome of head with prominent anteromedian projection (fig. 17.46); posterior margin of each sclerite on abdominal sternum IX entire (fig. 17.73); lateral border of each mandible flanged (fig. 17.51); fore trochantin forked or not (fig. 17.49) .... *Potamyia*

---

1. This group of species is recognized in recent publications by different systematists as the *Hydropsyche morosa* Species Group (Ross 1944, as *H. bifida* Group, see Schefter and Unzicker 1984; ref. #2849), or as the subgenus *Ceratopsyche* of the genus *Symphitopsyche* (Ross and Unzicker 1977; Schuster and Etnier 1978), or as a separate genus *Ceratopsyche* (Nielsen 1981; Schuster 1984; ref. #2851). Schuster (1984) presented evidence for the monophyly of each of the three species groups, *Hydropsyche S.S., Symphitopsyche,* and *Ceratospyche,* as well as for their distinctive ecological roles (Mackay and Wiggins 1979). We think the last mentioned position, recognizing these as distinct genera, ultimately will prove to be in the best interest of science.

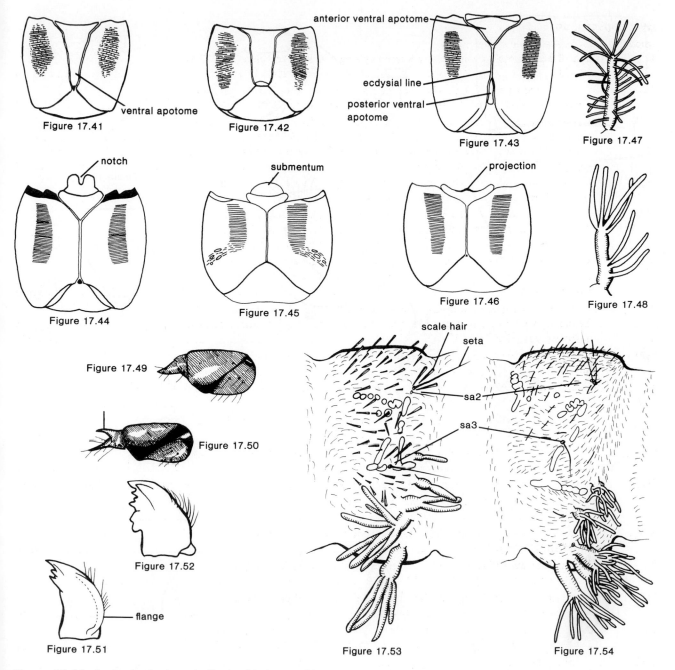

Figure 17.41
ventral apotome

Figure 17.42

anterior ventral apotome
ecdysial line
posterior ventral apotome
Figure 17.43

Figure 17.47

notch
Figure 17.44

submentum
Figure 17.45

projection
Figure 17.46

Figure 17.48

Figure 17.49

Figure 17.50

Figure 17.52

Figure 17.51
flange

scale hair
seta
sa2
sa3
Figure 17.53

Figure 17.54

Figure 17.41. *Arctopsyche irrorata* Banks (Hydropsychidae); ventral view of head.

Figure 17.42. *Parapsyche cardis* Ross (Hydropsychidae); ventral view of head.

Figure 17.43. *Diplectrona modesta* Banks (Hydropsychidae); ventral view of head.

Figure 17.44. *Hydropsyche betteni* Ross (Hydropsychidae); ventral view of head (including submentum).

Figure 17.45. *Smicridea fasciatella* Mac Lachlan (Hydropsychidae); ventral view of head (including submentum).

Figure 17.46. *Potamyia flava* (Hagen) (Hydropsychidae); ventral view of head.

Figure 17.47. *Macrostemum carolina* (Banks) (Hydropsychidae); left lateral view of gill of larval abdominal segment IV.

Figure 17.48. *Hydropsyche betteni* Ross (Hydropsychidae); left lateral view of gill of larval abdominal segment IV.

Figure 17.49. *Potamyia flava* (Hagen) (Hydropsychidae); lateral view of left foretrochantin.

Figure 17.50. *Cheumatopsyche* sp. (Hydropsychidae); lateral view of left foretrochantin.

Figure 17.51. *Potamyia flava* (Hagen) (Hydropsychidae); dorsal view of right mandible.

Figure 17.52. *Cheumatopsyche* sp. (Hydropsychidae); dorsal view of right mandible.

Figure 17.53. *Parapsyche cardis* Ross (Hydropsychidae); left lateral view of abdominal segment IV.

Figure 17.54. *Arctopsyche irrorata* Banks (Hydropsychidae); left lateral view of abdominal segment IV.

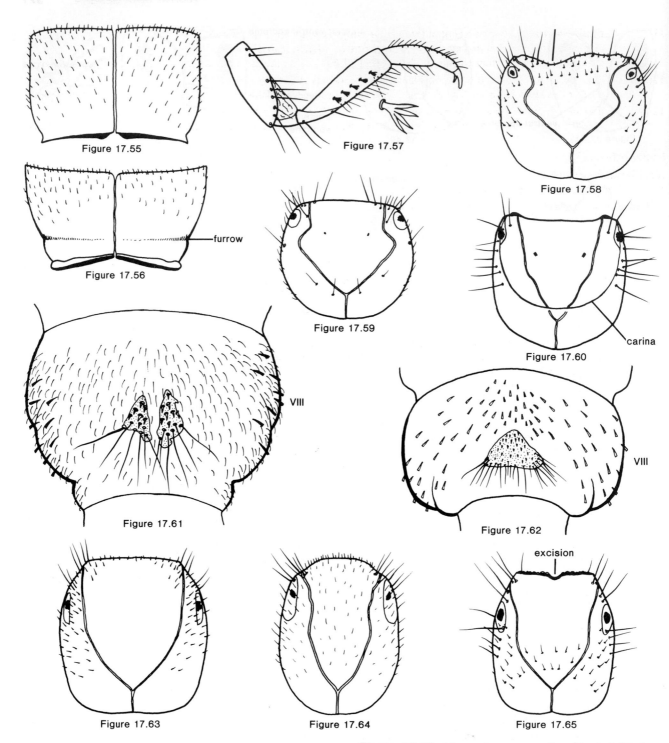

Figure 17.55

Figure 17.56

furrow

Figure 17.57

Figure 17.58

Figure 17.59

Figure 17.60

carina

VIII

Figure 17.61

VIII

Figure 17.62

excision

Figure 17.63

Figure 17.64

Figure 17.65

Figure 17.55. *Diplectrona modesta* Banks (Hydropsychidae); dorsal view of pronotum.

Figure 17.56. *Aphropsyche monticola* Flint (Hydropsychidae); dorsal view of pronotum.

Figure 17.57. *Homoplectra* sp. (Hydropsychidae); mesal view of mesothoracic leg.

Figure 17.58. *Aphropsyche monticola* Flint (Hydropsychidae); dorsal view of head.

Figure 17.59. Prob. *Oropsyche howellae* Ross (Hydropsychidae); dorsal view of head.

Figure 17.60. *Macrostemum carolina* (Banks) (Hydropsychidae); dorsal view of head.

Figure 17.61. *Hydropsyche betteni* Ross (Hydropsychidae); ventral view of abdominal sternum VIII.

Figure 17.62. *Smicridea fasciatella* Mac Lachlan (Hydropsychidae); ventral view of abdominal sternum VIII.

Figure 17.63. *Hydropsyche betteni* Ross (Hydropsychidae); dorsal view of head.

Figure 17.64. *Leptonema* sp. (Hydropsychidae); dorsal view of head.

Figure 17.65. *Cheumatopsyche* sp. (Hydropsychidae); dorsal view of head.

11'.   Anterior ventral apotome without anteromedian projection; posterior margin of each sclerite on abdominal sternum IX notched (fig. 17.72); mandibles not flanged (fig. 17.52); fore trochantin forked (fig. 17.50) .... *Cheumatopsyche*

12(3).   Tibia and tarsus of each prothoracic leg with dense, dorsal setal fringe (fig. 17.71); dorsum of head flattened and margined with sharp carina (fig. 17.60). .... *Macrostemum*

12'.   Tibia and tarsus of each prothoracic leg lacking dense, dorsal setal fringe (fig. 17.70); dorsum of head convex and without carina (fig. 17.64). .... *Leptonema*

Hydroptilidae[2]

(final larval instar only)

1.   Middorsal ecdysial line present on pronotum but usually lacking on meso- and metanota (figs. 17.76–17.77); tarsal claws short and stout, tarsi about twice as long as claws (fig. 17.74); abdominal segments V and VI usually abruptly broader than others in dorsal aspect (figs. 17.76–17.77); flat, oval, silken case, with small circular opening near each end, fastened to rock (fig. 17.97) ....
    ....(subfamily Leucotrichiinae).. 2

1'.   Middorsal ecdysial line present on all 3 thoracic nota (fig. 16.37); tarsal claws variable, but, if short and stout, tarsi much less than twice as long as claws (fig. 17.75); abdominal segments V and VI never abruptly broader than others in dorsal aspect 3

2(1).   Sclerite on abdominal tergum IX with scattered short, stout setae (fig. 17.76 inset); abdominal tergites II–VII with a pair of small circular punctures near the midline (fig. 17.76 inset). .... *Zumatrichia*

2'.   Sclerite on abdominal tergum IX usually without short, stout setae, but, if present, in transverse bands (fig. 17.77 inset); abdominal tergites II–VII solid, without punctures (fig. 17.77 inset) .... *Leucotrichia*

3(1').   Metathoracic tarsi usually short and thick, each about as long as its claw (fig. 17.79) or shorter; if metathoracic tarsi slender and slightly longer than claws (fig. 17.78), prothoracic tibiae each with prominent posteroventral lobe (fig. 17.81) 4

3'.   Metathoracic tarsi slender, each twice as long as its claw (fig. 17.80) or longer; if metathoracic tarsi only slightly longer than claws, prothoracic tibiae each without prominent lobe 10

4(3).   Larva and its case dorsoventrally depressed; each abdominal segment I–VIII with truncate, fleshy tubercle on each side (fig. 17.82); case flat, elliptical valves covered with pieces of liverwort (fig. 17.93) .... (subfamily Ptilocolepinae) .... *Palaeagapetus*

4'.   Larva and its case laterally compressed; abdominal segments without lateral tubercles (figs. 17.83–17.84) .... (subfamily Hydroptilinae) 5

5(4').   Tarsal claws stout and abruptly curved, each with thick, blunt basal spur (fig. 17.75) 6

5'.   Tarsal claws slender, gradually curved, each with thin, pointed basal spur (figs. 17.78–17.79, 17.81) 7

6(5).   Dorsal abdominal setae stout, each arising from small sclerite, dorsal rings distinct (fig. 17.83); 2 long, parallel-sided valves of case incorporate red algae on which species live (fig. 17.94) .... *Dibusa*

6'.   Dorsal abdominal setae thin and without basal sclerites, dorsal rings indistinct (fig. 17.84); 2 elliptical valves of silk case with few or no inclusions (fig. 17.95) .... *Stactobiella*

7(5').   Meso- and metathoracic legs about 2.5 times as long as prothoracic legs or longer; case entirely of silk, shaped like a flask, open posteriorly (fig. 17.96) .... *Oxyethira*

7'.   Meso- and metathoracic legs not more than 1.5 times as long as prothoracic legs (fig. 16.42) 8

2. The larva of *Rioptila* (Arizona and Utah) is unknown.

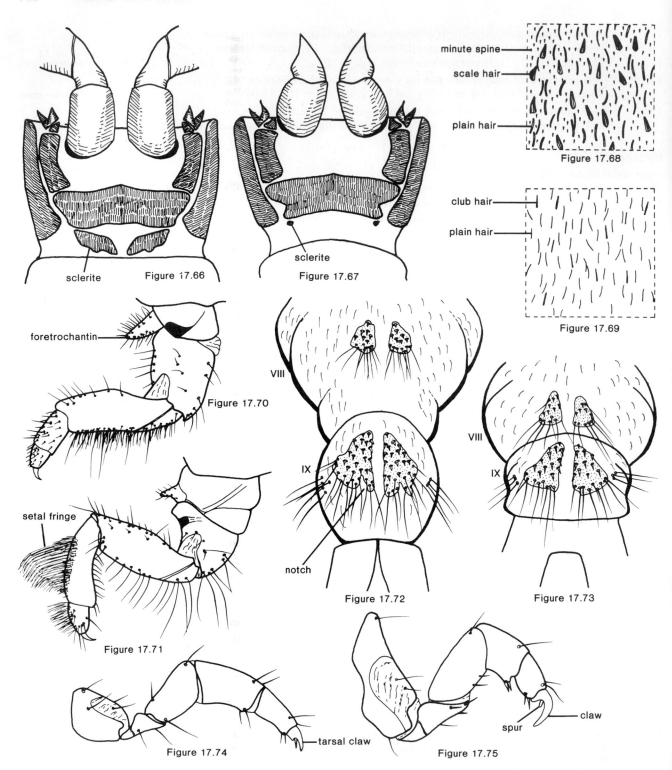

minute spine
scale hair
plain hair

Figure 17.68

club hair
plain hair

Figure 17.69

sclerite
Figure 17.66

sclerite
Figure 17.67

foretrochantin
Figure 17.70

setal fringe

Figure 17.71

VIII
IX
notch
Figure 17.72

VIII
IX
Figure 17.73

tarsal claw
Figure 17.74

claw
spur
Figure 17.75

Figure 17.66. *Hydropsyche betteni* Ross (Hydropsychidae); ventral view of prosternum.

Figure 17.67. *Cheumatopsyche* sp. (Hydropsychidae); ventral view of prosternum.

Figure 17.68. *Hydropsyche betteni* Ross (Hydropsychidae); detail of setation on abdominal tergum VIII.

Figure 17.69. *Ceratopsyche ventura* (Ross) (Hydropsychidae); detail of setation on abdominal tergum VIII.

Figure 17.70 *Leptonema* sp. (Hydropsychidae); lateral view of left prothoracic leg.

Figure 17.71. *Macrostemum carolina* (Banks) (Hydropsychidae); lateral view of left prothoracic leg.

Figure 17.72. *Cheumatopsyche* sp. (Hydropsychidae); ventral view of abdominal sternum IX.

Figure 17.73. *Potamyia flava* (Hagen) (Hydropsychidae); ventral view of abdominal sternum IX.

Figure 17.74. *Leucotrichia* sp. (Hydropsychidae); lateral view of right metathoracic leg.

Figure 17.75. *Dibusa angata* Ross (Hydroptilidae); lateral view of right metathoracic leg.

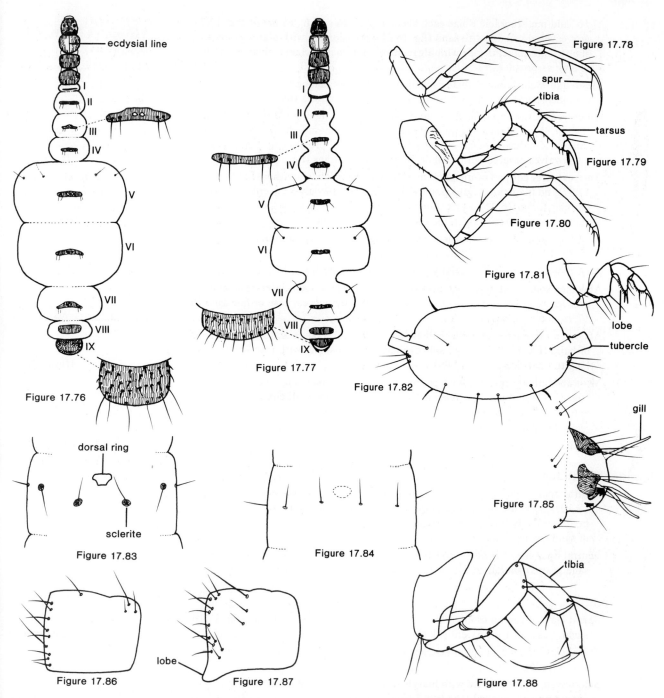

Figure 17.76

Figure 17.77

Figure 17.78

Figure 17.79

Figure 17.80

Figure 17.81

Figure 17.82

Figure 17.83

Figure 17.84

Figure 17.85

Figure 17.86

Figure 17.87

Figure 17.88

Figure 17.76. *Zumatrichia notosa* (Ross) (Hydroptilidae); dorsal view of larva: *insets,* sclerites of abdominal terga III and IX.

Figure 17.77. *Leucotrichia* sp. (Hydroptilidae); dorsal view of larva: *insets,* sclerites of abdominal terga III and IX.

Figure 17.78. *Oxyethira* sp. (Hydroptilidae); lateral view of right metathoracic leg.

Figure 17.79. *Hydroptila* sp. (Hydroptilidae); lateral view of right metathoracic leg.

Figure 17.80. *Ithytrichia* sp. (Hydroptilidae); lateral view of right metathoracic leg.

Figure 17.81. *Oxyethira* sp. (Hydroptilidae); lateral view of right prothoracic leg.

Figure 17.82. *Palaeagapetus celsus* (Ross) (Hydroptilidae); dorsal view of abdominal segment III.

Figure 17.83. *Dibusa angata* Ross (Hydroptilidae); dorsal view of abdominal segment III.

Figure 17.84. *Stactobiella delira* (Ross) (Hydroptilidae); dorsal view of abdominal segment III.

Figure 17.85. *Hydroptila* sp. (Hydroptilidae); left lateral view of posterior end of larval abdomen.

Figure 17.86. *Hydroptila* sp. (Hydroptilidae); left lateral view of metanotum.

Figure 17.87. *Ochrotrichia* sp. (Hydroptilidae); left lateral view of metanotum.

Figure 17.88. *Agraylea* sp. (Hydroptilidae); lateral view of right metathoracic leg.

8(7').   Meso- and metathoracic tibiae each about 1–2 times as long as broad (fig. 17.79); case covered usually with sand (fig. 16.22), occasionally with diatoms or filamentous algae; if case with algae, meso- and metathoracic tibiae each about as long as broad 9

8'.   Meso- and metathoracic tibiae each about 2–3 times as long as broad (fig. 17.88); case incorporating filamentous algae in concentric circles (fig. 17.102) .... *Agraylea*

9(8).   Anteroventral corners of metanotum each nearly 90° angle, with 1 or more setae (fig. 17.86); 3 filamentous gills posteriorly: 1 dorsomesally behind abdominal tergite IX, other 2 mesad of lateral sclerites of anal prolegs (fig. 17.85); case of 2 silk valves covered with sand or occasionally diatoms (fig. 16.22) .... *Hydroptila*

9'.   Anteroventral corners of metanotum each somewhat lobate, without setae (fig. 17.87); no filamentous gills posteriorly; case of 2 silk valves covered with sand (similar to fig. 16.22) or occasionally filamentous algae; sometimes one valve carried like a tortoise shell, the other a flat ventral sheet of silk .... *Ochrotrichia*

10(3').   Anal prolegs long and cylindrical, conspicuously projecting from body (figs. 17.89–17.90) 11

10'.   Anal prolegs short, not especially projecting from body (fig. 17.91) 12

11(10).   Abdomen somewhat depressed dorsoventrally, with prominent intersegmental grooves and lateral fringes of hairs (fig. 17.89); cylindrical case of fine sand (fig. 17.98) .... *Neotrichia*

11'.   Abdomen more inflated, with shallow intersegmental grooves and no lateral fringes of hairs (fig. 17.90); case of silk, cylindrical, but usually with transverse or longitudinal ridges (fig. 17.99) .... *Mayatrichia*

12(10').   Most abdominal segments with prominent, pointed, dorsal and ventral projections (fig. 17.92); flat silk case open posteriorly, reduced to small circular opening anteriorly (fig. 17.100) .... *Ithytrichia*

12'.   Abdominal segments without dorsal and ventral projections (fig. 17.91); silk case with longitudinal ridges (fig. 17.101) .... *Orthotrichia*

Lepidostomatidae

1.   Ventral apotome of head as long as, or longer than, median ecdysial line (fig. 17.103); case usually 4-sided, of quadrate pieces of leaves or bark (fig. 16.19), but pieces may be arranged irregularly, transversely, or spirally, or case may be of sand grains .... *Lepidostoma*

1'.   Ventral apotome of head shorter than median ecdysial line (fig. 17.104); case of sand grains (similar to fig. 17.132) .... *Theliopsyche*

Leptoceridae

1.   Tarsal claw of each mesothoracic leg hooked and stout; tarsus curved (fig. 17.105); slender case of transparent silk (fig. 17.119) .... *Leptocerus*

1'.   Tarsal claw of each mesothoracic leg slightly curved and slender; tarsus straight (fig. 17.106) 2

2.   Sclerotized, concave plate with marginal spines on each side of anal opening and extending onto ventral lobe (fig. 17.107); cylindrical case of stones (fig. 17.120) .... *Setodes*

2'.   Sclerotized, spiny plates absent, although patches of spines or setae may be present (fig. 17.108) 3

3.   Maxillary palpi extending far beyond labrum; mandibles long and bladelike, with sharp apical tooth separated from remainder of teeth (fig. 17.110 and inset); cases of various types and materials .... *Oecetis*

3'.   Maxillary palpi extending little, if any, beyond labrum; mandibles short, wide, with teeth grouped close to apex around central concavity (fig. 17.111 and inset) 4

4.   Mesonotum with pair of dark, curved bars on weakly sclerotized plates (fig. 16.44); abdomen broad basally, tapering posteriorly, with gills usually in clusters of 2 or more (fig. 17.112); cases of various shapes and materials, sometimes including spicules and pieces of freshwater sponges .... *Ceraclea*

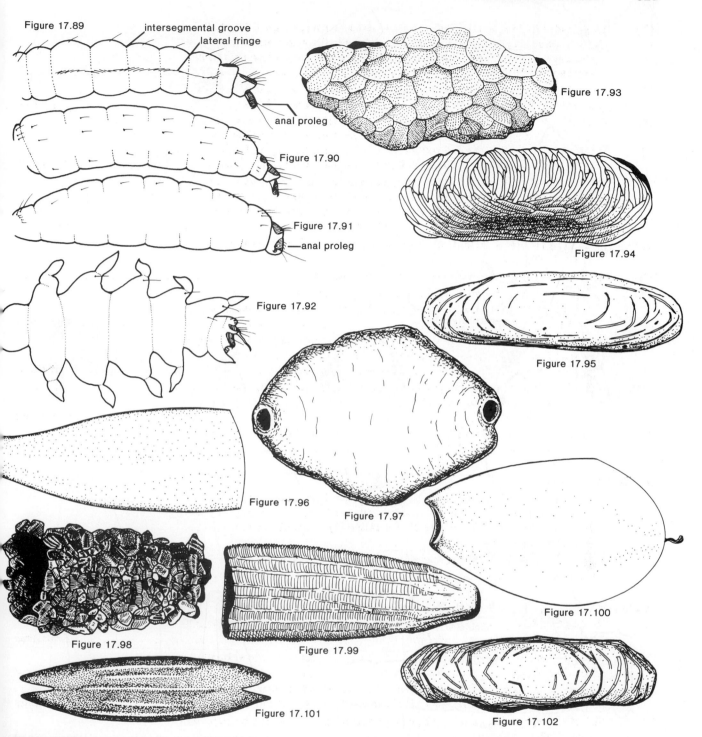

Figure 17.89

intersegmental groove
lateral fringe

anal proleg

Figure 17.90

Figure 17.91

anal proleg

Figure 17.92

Figure 17.93

Figure 17.94

Figure 17.95

Figure 17.96

Figure 17.97

Figure 17.98

Figure 17.99

Figure 17.100

Figure 17.101

Figure 17.102

Figure 17.89. *Neotrichia* sp. (Hydroptilidae); left lateral view of abdomen.

Figure 17.90. *Mayatrichia ayama* Mosely (Hydroptilidae); left lateral view of abdomen.

Figure 17.91. *Orthotrichia* sp. (Hydroptilidae); left lateral view of abdomen.

Figure 17.92. *Ithytrichia* sp. (Hydroptilidae); left lateral view of abdomen.

Figure 17.93. *Palaeagapetus celsus* (Ross) (Hydroptilidae); larval case.

Figure 17.94. *Dibusa angata* Ross (Hydroptilidae); larval case.

Figure 17.95. *Stactobiella delira* (Ross) (Hydroptilidae); larval case.

Figure 17.96. *Oxyethira* sp. (Hydroptilidae); larval case.

Figure 17.97. *Leucotrichia* sp. (Hydroptilidae); larval case.

Figure 17.98. *Neotrichia* sp. (Hydroptilidae); larval case.

Figure 17.99. *Mayatrichia ayama* Mosely (Hydroptilidae); larval case.

Figure 17.100. *Ithytrichia* sp. (Hydroptilidae); larval case.

Figure 17.101. *Orthotrichia* sp. (Hydroptilidae); larval case.

Figure 17.102. *Agraylea* sp. (Hydroptilidae); larval case.

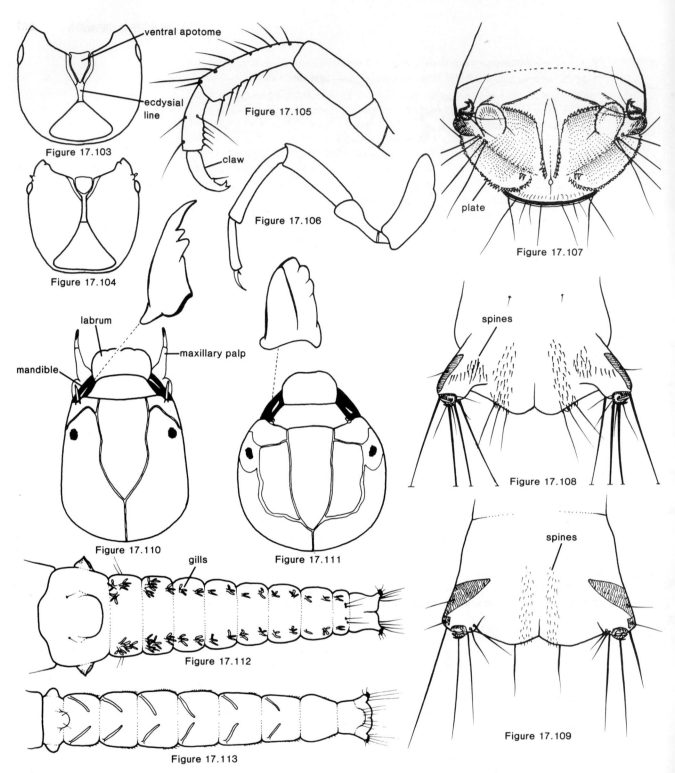

Figure 17.103. *Lepidostoma* sp. (Lepidostomatidae); ventral view of head.

Figure 17.104. *Theliopsyche* sp. (Lepidostomatidae); ventral view of head.

Figure 17.105. *Leptocerus americanus* (Banks) (Leptoceridae); lateral view of left mesothoracic leg.

Figure 17.106. *Oecetis* sp. (Leptoceridae); lateral view of left mesothoracic leg.

Figure 17.107. *Setodes incertus* (Walker) (Leptoceridae); ventral view of posterior end.

Figure 17.108. *Triaenodes tardus* Milne (Leptoceridae); ventral view of posterior end.

Figure 17.109. *Nectopsyche* sp. (Leptoceridae); ventral view of posterior end.

Figure 17.110. *Oecetis* sp. (Leptoceridae); dorsal view of head: *inset,* left mandible.

Figure 17.111. *Ceraclea maculata* (Banks) (Leptoceridae); dorsal view of head: *inset,* left mandible.

Figure 17.112. *Ceraclea* sp. (Leptoceridae); dorsal view of abdomen.

Figure 17.113. *Triaenodes tardus* Milne (Leptoceridae); dorsal view of abdomen.

4'.   Mesonotum without pair of dark bars (fig. 16.43); abdominal segments I–VII more
         slender, nearly parallel-sided, with gills single (fig. 17.113) or absent 5

5.   Ventral apotome of head triangular (fig. 17.114); tibia of each leg usually without
         apparent constriction (fig. 17.116); pair of ventral bands of uniformly small
         spines beside anal opening (fig. 17.109) or spines absent in this position, but no
         lateral patches of longer spines; slender case of plant fragments, fine sand, and/
         or diatoms with usually 1 twig or conifer needle extending length of case and
         beyond 1 or both ends (fig. 17.121) .... *Nectopsyche*

5'.   Ventral apotome of head rectangular (fig. 17.115), if triangular, case a spiral of
         plant pieces; tibia of each leg with translucent constriction, apparently dividing
         it into 2 subequal parts (figs. 17.117–17.118); patch of longer spines laterad of
         each band of short anal spines (fig. 17.108) 6

6.   Metathoracic legs each with close-set fringe of long hairs (fig. 17.117); slender
         case a spiral of plant pieces (fig. 17.122) .... *Triaenodes*

6'.   Metathoracic legs with only few, scattered, long hairs (fig. 17.118); irregular case
         of plant and mineral materials, with twigs or conifer needles extending beyond
         ends (fig. 17.123) .... *Mystacides*

Limnephilidae[3]

1.   Mesonotum with setal areas on 2 or 3 pairs of sclerites (figs. 16.79,
         17.124–17.126) 2

1'.   Mesonotum with 1 pair of sclerites closely contiguous on mid-dorsal line (figs.
         16.28, 16.41, 16.59) 8

2(1).   Mesepisternum enlarged anteriorly, either as sharp projection (figs. 16.79,
         17.124–17.125) or as short, rounded, spiny prominence (fig. 17.126) .... (subfamily Goerinae) 3

2'.   Mesepisternum not enlarged anteriorly 7

3(2).   Gills mostly 3-branched, usually on abdominal segments II–VII; case of small
         rocks, usually with 2 pairs of larger pebbles on sides (fig. 17.127) .... *Goera*

3'.   Gills single, sometimes restricted to abdominal segments III–IV or III, or gills
         absent 4

4(3'). Gills absent; smooth, tapered, slightly curved case of small rocks (fig. 17.128) .... *Goerita*

4'.   Gills present 5

5(4'). Gills on abdominal segments II–VIII; mesepisternum short, rounded, spiny
         prominence (fig. 17.126) .... *Goereilla*

5'.   Gills on abdominal segments III or III–V; mesepisternum sharp projection (figs.
         17.124–17.125) 6

6(5'). Pronotum flat or with pair of concavities, mesepisternum laterally compressed,
         each metanotal sa1 with few (1–6) setae on very small, oval sclerite (fig.
         17.124) or without sclerite; case of rocks with several larger pebbles along each
         side (fig. 17.129) .... *Goeracea*

6'.   Pronotum convex, mesepisternum dorsoventrally depressed, each metanotal sa1
         with several setae on distinct triangular sclerite (fig. 17.125); tapered, slightly
         curved case of small rocks without larger lateral pebbles (fig. 17.130) .... *Lepania*

7(2'). Dorsum of head with many unusually stout and prominent primary setae, head
         without posterolateral flanges (fig. 17.134); pronotum convex; smooth, tapered,
         slightly curved case of rocks (fig. 17.131) .... *Pedomoecus*

7'.   Dorsum of head with most primary setae unmodified, with posterolateral flanges
         (fig. 17.133); pronotum with pair of concavities (fig. 17.136); case as above
         except with rough outline and not as tapered (fig. 17.132) .... *Rossiana*

8(1'). Basal seta of each tarsal claw extending to, or nearly to, tip of claw (fig. 17.138);
         mandibles each with apical edge entire, without teeth (fig. 16.27) 9

---

3. Larvae are unknown for 4 genera: *Chilostigma* (Minnesota), *Chilostigmodes* (Alaska to Labrador), *Leptophylax* (northcentral states),
and *Phanocelia* (Manitoba and Northwest Territories).

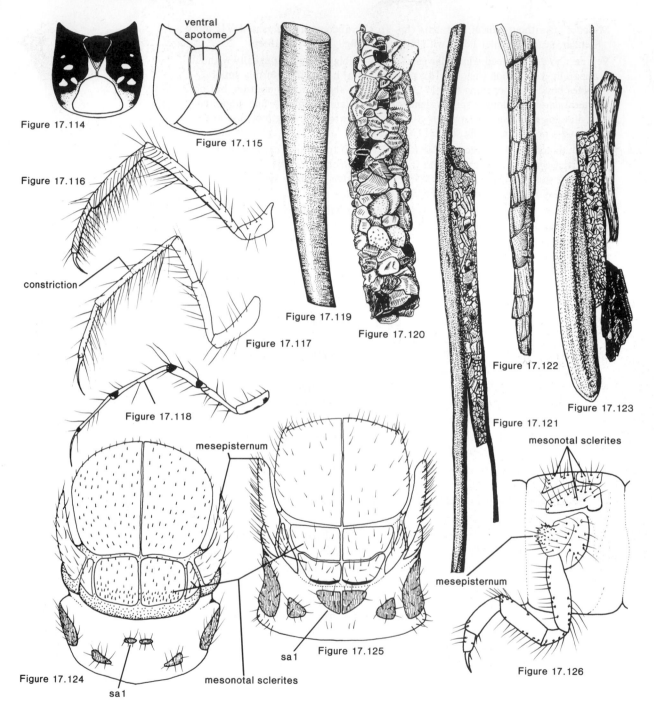

Figure 17.114

ventral apotome

Figure 17.115

Figure 17.116

constriction

Figure 17.117

Figure 17.118

Figure 17.119

Figure 17.120

Figure 17.122

Figure 17.123

Figure 17.121

mesepisternum

mesonotal sclerites

mesepisternum

Figure 17.126

sa1

Figure 17.125

Figure 17.124

sa1

mesonotal sclerites

Figure 17.120. *Setodes incertus* (Walker) (Leptoceridae); larval case.

Figure 17.114. *Nectopsyche* sp. (Leptoceridae); ventral view of head.

Figure 17.115. *Triaenodes tardus* Milne (Leptoceridae); ventral view of head.

Figure 17.116. *Nectopsyche* sp. (Leptoceridae); lateral view of left metathoracic leg.

Figure 17.117. *Triaenodes tardus* Milne (Leptoceridae); lateral view of left metathoracic leg.

Figure 17.118. *Mystacides* sp. (Leptoceridae); lateral view of left metathoracic leg.

Figure 17.119. *Leptocerus americanus* (Banks) (Leptoceridae); larval case.

Figure 17.121. *Nectopsyche* sp. (Leptoceridae); larval case.

Figure 17.122. *Triaenodes tardus* Milne (Leptoceridae); larval case.

Figure 17.123. *Mystacides* sp. (Leptoceridae); larval case.

Figure 17.124. *Goeracea* poss. *oregona* Denning (Limnephilidae); dorsal view of thorax.

Figure 17.125. *Lepania cascada* Ross (Limnephilidae); dorsal view of thorax.

Figure 17.126. *Goereilla baumanni* Denning (Limnephilidae); left lateral view of mesothorax.

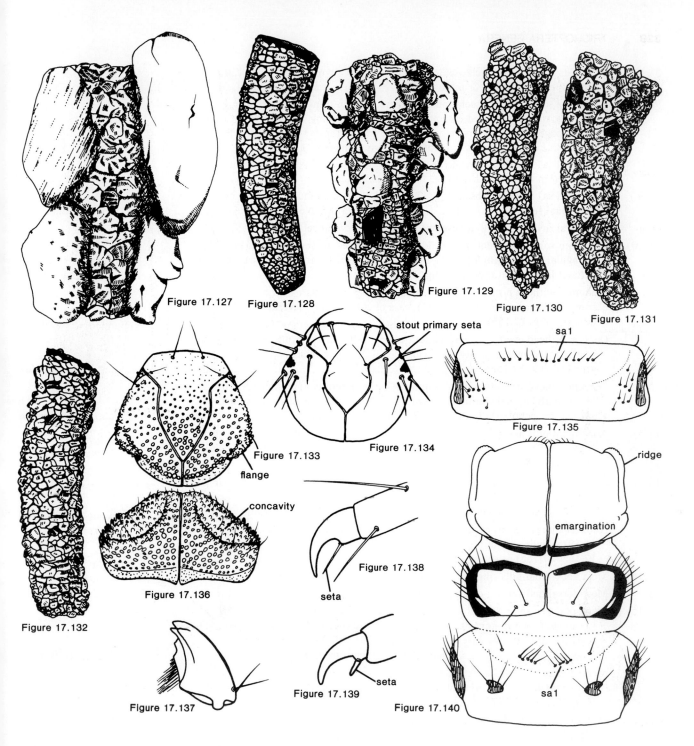

Figure 17.127. *Goera fuscula* Banks (Limnephilidae); larval case.

Figure 17.128. *Goerita semata* Ross (Limnephilidae); larval case.

Figure 17.129. *Goeracea* poss. *oregona* Denning (Limnephilidae); larval case.

Figure 17.130. *Lepania cascada* Ross (Limnephilidae); larval case.

Figure 17.131. *Pedomoecus sierra* Ross (Limnephilidae); larval case.

Figure 17.132. *Rossiana montana* Denning (Limnephilidae); larval case.

Figure 17.133. *Rossiana montana* Denning (Limnephilidae); dorsal view of head.

Figure 17.134. *Pedomoecus sierra* Ross (Limnephilidae); dorsal view of head.

Figure 17.135. *Apatania arizona* Wiggins (Limnephilidae); dorsal view of metanotum (after Wiggins 1977).

Figure 17.136. *Rossiana montana* Denning (Limnephilidae); dorsal view of pronotum.

Figure 17.137. *Limnephilus* sp. (Limnephilidae); ventral view of left mandible.

Figure 17.138. *Neophylax* sp. (Limnephilidae); lateral view of left metathoracic claw.

Figure 17.139. *Dicosmoecus* sp. (Limnephilidae); lateral view of left metathoracic claw.

Figure 17.140. *Oligophlebodes* sp. (Limnephilidae); dorsal view of thorax.

8'. Basal seta of each tarsal claw extending far short of tip of claw (fig. 17.139); mandibles each with 2 or more teeth (fig. 17.137) 13

9(8). Metanotal sa1 sclerites absent, numerous sa1 setae in transverse band (fig. 17.135); strongly tapered case of rocks, anterior opening usually oblique with dorsal edge extending beyond ventral edge for final instar (fig. 17.153) .... (subfamily Apataniinae) .... ***Apatania***

9'. Metanotal sa1 sclerites present (fig. 16.59) or, if absent, setae not numerous and arranged in transverse band (fig. 17.140) 10

10(9'). Metanotal sa1 sclerites absent (fig. 17.140) or very small and restricted to bases of individual setae (fig. 17.141) .... (subfamily Neophylacinae) 11

10'. Metanotal sa1 sclerites well developed, each with several setae (fig. 16.59) 12

11(10). Pronotum with prominent, lateral, longitudinal ridges, mesonotum with only slight triangular emargination (fig. 17.140); strongly tapered and curved case of rocks without larger lateral pebbles (fig. 17.154) .... ***Oligophlebodes***

11'. Pronotum without prominent longitudinal ridges, mesonotum with conspicuous truncate emargination (fig. 17.141); case of coarse rocks, several larger pebbles laterally (fig. 17.155) .... ***Neophylax***

12(10'). Dorsum of head evenly convex, without carina; abdominal sternite I present with small central membranous space (fig. 17.142); case of rocks with plant material attached (fig. 17.156) .... ***Manophylax***

12'. Dorsum of head flat, often with prominent carina laterally and anteriorly (fig. 17.143); abdominal sternite I absent; tapered, curved case of rocks, sometimes *Imania* with larger pebbles laterally (fig. 17.157) .... ***Allomyia***

13(8). Abdominal gills absent; tapered, curved case of fine rocks with shiny silk covering (fig. 17.158). .... ***Moselyana***

13'. Abdominal gills present 14

14(13'). Anterior margin of pronotum densely fringed with long hairs; dorsum of head flat and with 2 bands of dense scale hairs (fig. 17.144); tapered, depressed case of transverse bits of wood and bark (fig. 17.159) .... (subfamily Dicosmoecinae, in part) .... ***Cryptochia***

14'. Anterior margin of pronotum and dorsum of head without dense hairs (figs. 16.41, 16.59) or hairs not of type or arrangement described above (figs. 17.165–17.166) 15

15(14'). Most abdominal gills single 16

15'. Most dorsal and ventral gills multiple, lateral gills sometimes single 27

16(15). Metanotal sa1 and sa2 sclerites large, distance between sa2 sclerites no more than twice maximum dimension of single sa2 sclerite (fig. 17.145); slender, straight, scarcely tapered tube case of coarse rocks often with long plant material attached (fig. 17.160) .... (subfamily Dicosmoecinae, in part) .... ***Ecclisomyia***

16'. Metanotal sa1 and sa2 sclerites small, distance between sa2 sclerites more than twice maximum dimension of single sa2 sclerite, sa1 sclerites sometimes fused (figs. 17.146–17.147) 17

17(16'). One or 2 sclerites adjacent to base of each lateral hump of abdominal segment I (figs. 17.148–17.151; sclerites often only lightly pigmented but distinguishable by relatively shinier surfaces) 18

17'. No sclerites adjacent to lateral humps of abdominal segment I 23

18(17). Large single sclerite at base of each lateral hump of abdominal segment I enclosing posterior half of hump and extending posterodorsad as irregular lobe (fig. 17.149); case of leaves or bark formed into flattened tube with seams along narrow lateral flanges (fig. 17.161) .... (subfamily Limnephilinae, tribe Stenophylacini, in part) .... ***Chyranda***

18'. One or 2 small sclerites at base of each lateral hump of abdominal segment I (figs. 16.63, 17.150–17.151) 19

19(18'). Two sclerites at base of each lateral hump of abdominal segment I (figs. 16.63, 17.150) 20

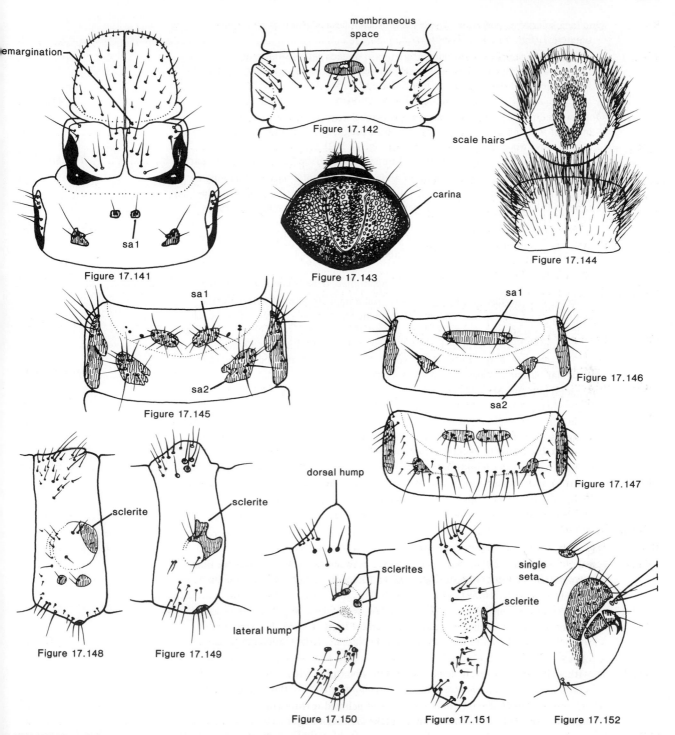

Figure 17.141. *Neophylax* sp. (Limnephilidae); dorsal view of thorax.

Figure 17.142. *Manophylax annulatus* Wiggins (Limnephilidae); ventral view of abdominal sternum I.

Figure 17.143. *Allomyia scotti* (Wiggins) (Limnephilidae); dorsal view of larval head.

Figure 17.144. *Cryptochia* sp. (Limnephilidae); dorsal view of head and pronotum.

Figure 17.145. *Ecclisomyia* sp. (Limnephilidae); dorsal view of metanotum.

Figure 17.146. *Hydatophylax* sp. (Limnephilidae); dorsal view of metanotum.

Figure 17.147. *Pycnopsyche* sp. (Limnephilidae); dorsal view of metanotum.

Figure 17.148. *Pycnopsyche* sp. (Limnephilidae); left lateral view of abdominal segment I.

Figure 17.149. *Chyranda centralis* (Banks) (Limnephilidae); left lateral view of abdominal segment I.

Figure 17.150. *Psychoglypha* sp. (Limnephilidae); left lateral view of abdominal segment I.

Figure 17.151. *Homophylax* sp. (Limnephilidae); left lateral view of abdominal segment I.

Figure 17.152. *Hydatophylax argus* (Harris) (Limnephilidae); left lateral view of abdominal segment IX.

19′.   One long sclerite at posterior edge of base of each lateral hump of abdominal
            segment I (figs. 17.148, 17.151) 21

20(19).   Two small ring sclerites posterodorsally at base of each lateral hump of abdominal
            segment I (fig. 16.63); tubular, slightly curved and tapered case largely of rocks
            with some small pieces of wood incorporated (similar to fig. 17.132) ....
            ....(subfamily Limnephilinae, tribe Stenophylacini, in part) .... ***Desmona***

20′.   One rounded posterior sclerite, one long dorsal sclerite at base of each lateral
            hump of abdominal segment I (fig. 17.150); rough, straight, untapered tube case
            of rocks and wood fragments (similar to Fig. 17.162) ....
            .... (subfamily Limnephilinae, tribe Chilostigmini, in part) .... ***Psychoglypha***

21(19′). Sclerite at base of each lateral hump of abdominal segment I only half as long as
            basal width of hump (fig. 17.151); smooth, thin-walled, nearly straight, little-
            tapered tube case of irregularly arranged bark pieces or occasional flat rocks
            (fig. 17.162), sometimes 3-sided ....
            .... (subfamily Limnephilinae, tribe Chilostigmini, in part) .... ***Homophylax***

21′.   Sclerite at base of each lateral hump of abdominal segment I nearly as long as
            basal width of hump (fig. 17.148) ....
            .... (subfamily Limnephilinae, tribe Stenophylacini, in part) 22

22(21′). Metanotal sa1 sclerites fused (fig. 17.146); abdominal sternum II with chloride
            epithelium (in which case abdominal segment IX with only single seta on each
            side of dorsal sclerite, fig. 17.152, *Hydatophylax argus,* eastern North America)
            or without chloride epithelium (in which case abdominal segment IX with tuft
            of 3–6 setae, *H. hesperus,* western North America); case of wood or leaves in
            irregular outline or case of leaves flattened (fig. 17.163) .... ***Hydatophylax***

22′.   Metanotal sa1 sclerites not fused although often contiguous (fig. 17.147),
            abdominal sternum II without chloride epithelium and abdominal segment IX
            with only single seta on each side of dorsal sclerite (similar to fig. 17.152); case
            of twigs, gravel, or leaves, variously shaped (similar to figs. 17.132, 17.163, or
            17.199), occasionally 3-sided .... ***Pycnopsyche***

23(17′). Anterior margin of pronotum with flat scale hairs, dorsum of head flat (fig.
            17.165); coarse mineral case slightly curved (similar to fig. 17.132) .... ***Philocasca***

23′.   Anterior margin of pronotum without flat scale hairs, setae normal; dorsum of
            head usually convex (flat only in western *Pseudostenophylax edwardsi,* fig.
            17.167) 24

24(23′). Mesonotal sa1 and sa2 distinct, separated by gap free of setae (figs.
            17.168–17.169) 25

24′.   Mesonotal sa1 and sa2 connected by continuous longitudinal band of setae on each
            side of meson (fig. 16.59) 26

25(24).   Pronotum covered with fine spines (fig. 17.168, inset); case of plant and rock
            fragments and apparent snail opercula (similar to fig. 17.162, but smaller
            diameter) .... (subfamily Limnephilinae, tribe Chilostigmini, in part) .... ***Grensia***

25′.   Pronotum smooth and shiny, without fine spines (fig. 17.169); case of leaf pieces
            with wide flanges at each side of depressed tube (fig. 16.10) ....
            ....(subfamily Limnephilinae, tribe Stenophylacini, in part) .... ***Clostoeca***

26(24′). Head and pronotum strongly inflated and with pebbled texture (fig. 17.166);
            smooth, tapered, curved case of small rocks (similar to figure 16.9) ....
            .... (subfamily Dicosmoecinae, in part) .... ***Ecclisocosmoecus***

26′.   Head and pronotum not unusually inflated (figs. 16.59, 16.77), although dorsum of
            head flat in Western species (fig. 17.167), sclerotized areas not pebbled; smooth,
            tapered, curved case of rocks (fig. 16.9) ....(subfamily Pseudostenophylacinae) .... ***Pseudostenophylax***

27(15′). Most gills with 3 branches, none with more than 4 28

27′.   At least some gills with more than 4 branches 43

28(27).   Dorsum of head with 2 bands of contrasting color extending from coronal suture to
            bases of mandibles (fig. 17.170) and/or narrowed posterior portion of
            frontoclypeal apotome with 3 light areas: 1 along each side and 1 at posterior
            extremity (fig. 17.173) ... (subfamily Limnephilinae, tribe Limnephilini, in part) 29

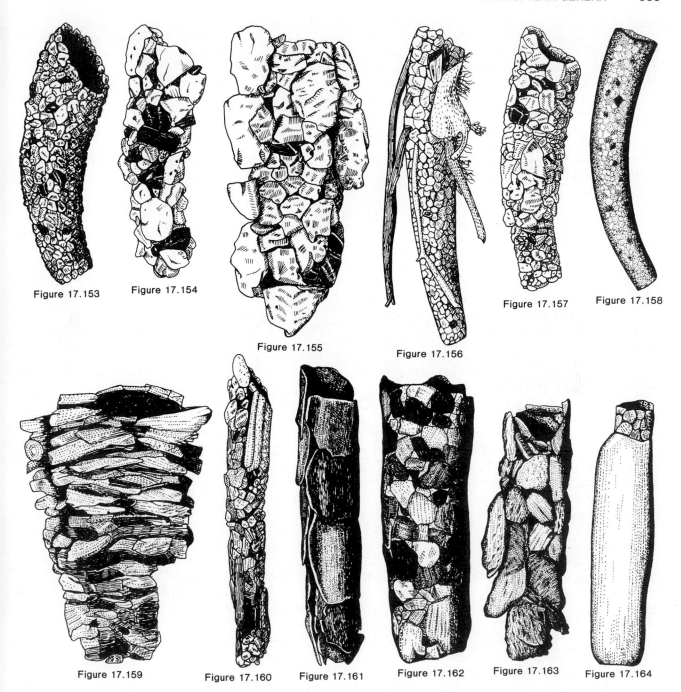

Figure 17.153   Figure 17.154

Figure 17.155

Figure 17.156

Figure 17.157   Figure 17.158

Figure 17.159   Figure 17.160   Figure 17.161   Figure 17.162   Figure 17.163   Figure 17.164

Figure 17.153. *Apatania* sp. (Limnephilidae); larval case.

Figure 17.154. *Oligophlebodes* sp. (Limnephilidae); larval case.

Figure 17.155. *Neophylax* sp. (Limnephilidae); larval case.

Figure 17.156. *Manophylax annulatus* Wiggins (Limnephilidae); larval case.

Figure 17.157. *Allomyia scotti* (Wiggins) (Limnephilidae); larval case.

Figure 17.158. *Moselyana comosa* Denning (Limnephilidae); larval case.

Figure 17.159. *Cryptochia* sp. (Limnephilidae); larval case.

Figure 17.160. *Ecclisomyia* sp. (Limnephilidae); larval case.

Figure 17.161. *Chyranda centralis* (Banks) (Limnephilidae); larval case.

Figure 17.162. *Homophylax* sp. (Limnephilidae); larval case.

Figure 17.163. *Hydatophylax argus* (Harris) (Limnephilidae); larval case.

Figure 17.164. *Amphicosmoecus canax* (Ross) (Limnephilidae); larval case (after Wiggins 1977).

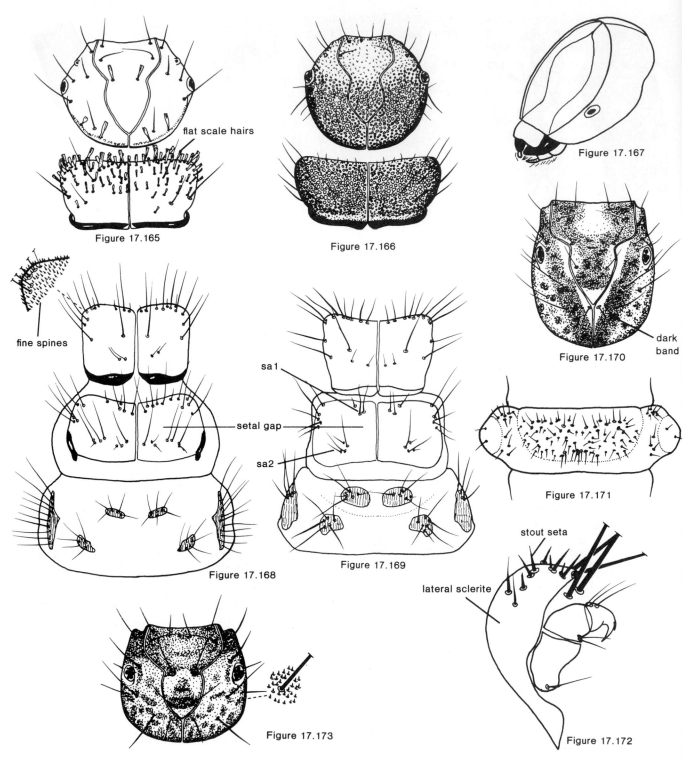

Figure 17.165

flat scale hairs

Figure 17.166

Figure 17.167

Figure 17.170

dark band

fine spines

sa1

setal gap

sa2

Figure 17.168

Figure 17.169

Figure 17.171

stout seta

lateral sclerite

Figure 17.172

Figure 17.173

Figure 17.165. *Philocasca rivularis* Wiggins (Limnephilidae); dorsal view of head and pronotum.

Figure 17.166. *Ecclisocosmoecus scylla* (Milne) (Limnephilidae); dorsal view of head and pronotum.

Figure 17.167. *Pseudostenophylax edwardsi* (Banks) (Limnephilidae); left dorsolateral oblique view of head (after Wiggins, 1977).

Figure 17.168. *Grensia praeterita* (Walker) (Limnephilidae); dorsal view of thorax: *inset*, microspines enlarged.

Figure 17.169. *Clostoeca disjuncta* (Banks) (Limnephilidae); dorsal view of thorax.

Figure 17.170. *Halesochila taylori* (Banks) (Limnephilidae); dorsal view of head.

Figure 17.171. *Clistoronia magnifica* (Banks) (Limnephilidae); ventral view of abdominal sternum I.

Figure 17.172. *Clistoronia magnifica* (Banks) (Limnephilidae); lateral view of left anal proleg.

Figure 17.173. *Clistoronia magnifica* (Banks) (Limnephilidae); dorsal view of head: *inset*, microspines enlarged.

28'.   Dorsum of head lacking bands or other well-defined, contrasting areas, usually
        uniform in color or with prominent light or dark spots only at points of muscle
        attachment (fig. 17.193) 32

29(28).   Abdominal sternum I usually with more than 100 setae overall (fig. 17.171); small
          spines on head and pronotum (fig. 17.173); short, stout setae on lateral sclerite
          of each anal proleg (fig. 17.172); cylindrical case usually of irregular pieces of
          twigs and bark, sometimes small rocks (similar to fig. 17.163) .... *Clistoronia*

29'.   Abdominal sternum I with fewer than 100 setae overall; usually without spines on
        head and pronotum; usually without short, stout setae on lateral sclerite of anal
        proleg 30

30(29').   Mesonotal sa1 consisting of single seta (fig. 17.174) 31
30'.   Mesonotal sa1 consisting of more than 1 seta (fig. 17.175) 42

31(30).   Chloride epithelia dorsally and ventrally on several abdominal segments (fig.
          17.176); rough, tubular case of wood or leaf fragments (similar to fig. 17.163),
          sometimes 3-sided, changed to fine gravel before pupation .... *Halesochila*

31'.   Chloride epithelia absent dorsally; case of leaf pieces arranged transversely or
        longitudinally (similar to fig. 17.27) .... *Nemotaulius*

32(28').   Femur of metathoracic leg with more than 2 major setae on ventral edge (fig.
          17.181) .... (subfamily Dicosmoecinae, in part) 33
32'.   Femur of metathoracic leg with 2 major setae on ventral edge (fig. 17.180) 36

33(32).   Metanotal sa1 sclerites fused (fig. 17.178); case a hollow twig with ring of bark
          pieces anteriorly (fig. 17.164) or case entirely of wood fragments .... *Amphicosmoecus*
33'.   Metanotal sa1 sclerites clearly separate (fig. 17.179) 34

34(33').   Abdominal tergum I with transverse row of setae posterior to median dorsal hump
          (fig. 17.179); scale hairs on dorsum of head (fig. 17.177); abdominal sternum II
          with 2 chloride epithelia (fig. 17.183); irregularly outlined case of small pebbles
          arranged into slightly curved and flattened cylinder (fig. 17.196) .... *Allocosmoecus*

34'.   Abdominal tergum I usually lacking setae posterior to median hump; dorsum of
        head without scale hairs; abdominal sternum II with single chloride epithelium
        (fig. 17.184), 3 epithelia (smaller epithelia laterally), or without epithelia 35

35(34').   Tibiae each with several pairs of stout spurs (fig. 17.181); case of rocks (fig.
          17.197), case of younger larva with plant materials. .... *Dicosmoecus*

35'.   Tibiae each with no more than 1 pair of stout spurs (fig. 17.182); case of pieces of
        wood and bark (similar to fig. 17.200), sometimes gravel (1 of the western
        species) .... *Onocosmoecus*

36(32').   Abdominal tergum VIII with median gap in transverse band of setae (fig. 17.186);
          cylindrical case of longitudinally arranged sedge or similar leaves (fig.
          17.198) .... (subfamily Limnephilinae, tribe Limnephilini, in part) ....*Grammotaulius*

36'.   Abdominal tergum VIII with continuous transverse band of setae (fig. 17.187) 37

37(36').   Pronotum, especially anterior margin (fig. 17.185), and lateral sclerite of anal
          proleg (fig. 17.172) both with short, stout setae ....
          .... (subfamily Limnephilinae, tribe Chilostigmini, in part) 38

37'.   Pronotum usually, lateral sclerite of anal proleg always without short, stout setae ...
        .... (subfamily Limnephilinae, tribe Limnephilini, in part) 39

38(37).   Tibiae and tarsi of all legs each with dark, contrasting band (fig. 17.180);
          cylindrical case of sand, twigs, and bark (similar to fig. 17.160) .... *Glyphopsyche*

38'.   Tibiae and tarsi each lacking dark band; smooth, cylindrical case mostly of small
        stones with wood fragments (similar to fig. 17.132) .... *Frenesia*

39(37').   Metanotal sa2 with few setae, usually 2, and no sclerite (fig. 17.188); smooth,
          cylindrical case of long leaf pieces (fig. 16.8) .... *Arctopora*
39'.   Metanotal sa2 with more than 2 setae and with sclerite (fig. 17.193) 40

40(39').   Dorsum of head with numerous large spots coalescing into diffuse blotches in some
          places, especially on frontoclypeal apotome (fig. 17.193); anterolateral corner of
          pronotum with small patch of spines (fig. 17.193); cylindrical case of plant
          materials (fig. 17.199), sometimes 3-sided .... *Anabolia*

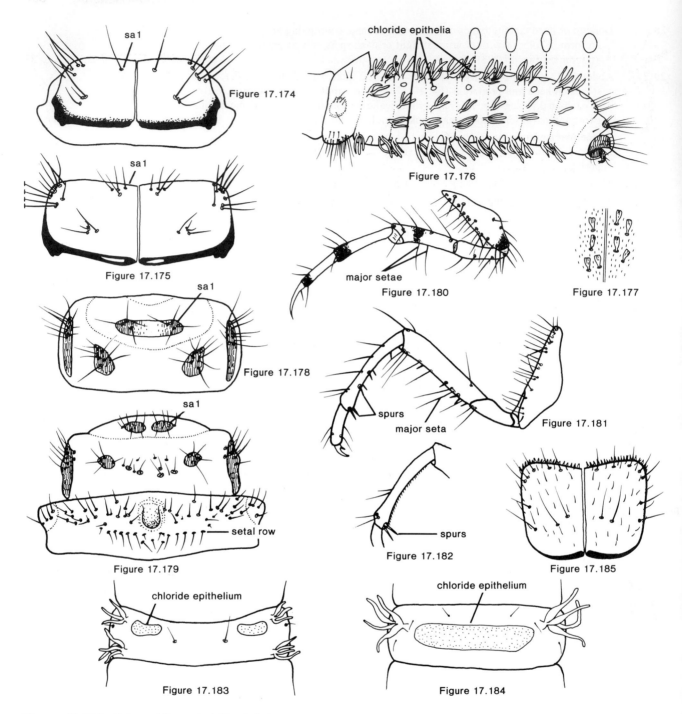

Figure 17.174. *Halesochila taylori* (Banks) (Limnephilidae); dorsal view of mesonotum.

Figure 17.175. *Asynarchus* sp. (Limnephilidae); dorsal view of mesonotum.

Figure 17.176. *Halesochila taylori* (Banks) (Limnephilidae); left lateral view of abdomen: *insets,* dorsal chloride epithelia.

Figure 17.177. *Allocosmoecus partitus* Banks (Limnephilidae); dorsal view of scale hairs on larval head.

Figure 17.178. *Amphicosmoecus canax* (Ross) (Limnephilidae); dorsal view of metanotum. (after Wiggins 1977)

Figure 17.179. *Allocosmoecus partitus* Banks (Limnephilidae); dorsal view of metanotum and abdominal tergum I.

Figure 17.180. *Glyphopsyche irrorata* (Fabricius) (Limnephilidae); lateral view of left metathoracic leg.

Figure 17.181. *Dicosmoecus* sp. (Limnephilidae); lateral view of left metathoracic leg.

Figure 17.182. *Onocosmoecus* sp. (Limnephilidae); lateral view of left metathoracic tibia.

Figure 17.183. *Allocosmoecus partitus* Banks (Limnephilidae); ventral view of abdominal sternum II.

Figure 17.184. *Dicosmoecus* sp. (Limnephilidae); ventral view of abdominal sternum II.

Figure 17.185. *Frenesia missa* (Milne) (Limnephilidae); dorsal view of pronotum.

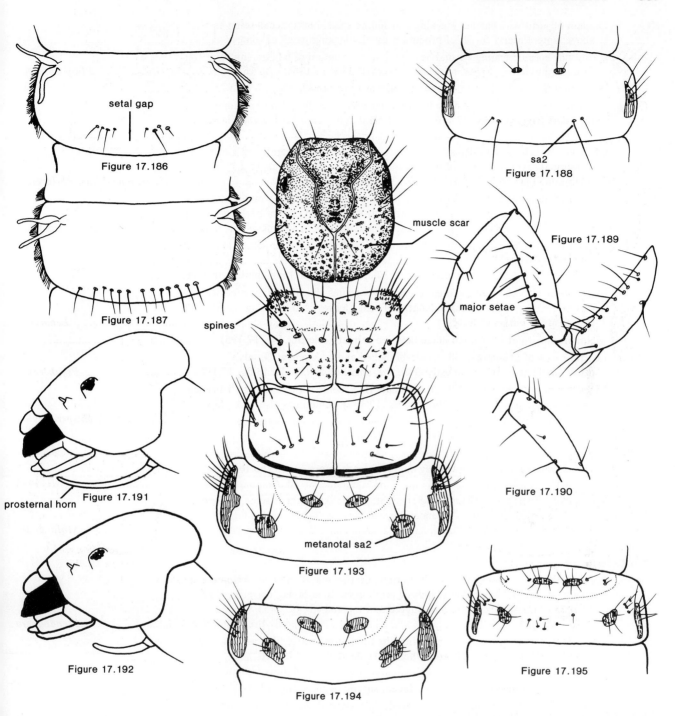

Figure 17.186. *Grammotaulius* sp. (Limnephilidae); dorsal view of abdominal tergum VIII.

Figure 17.187. *Glyphopsyche irrorata* (Fabricius) (Limnephilidae); dorsal view of abdominal tergum VIII.

Figure 17.188. *Arctopora* sp. (Limnephilidae); dorsal view of metanotum.

Figure 17.189. *Ironoquia* sp. (Limnephilidae); lateral view of left metathoracic leg.

Figure 17.190. *Hesperophylax* sp. (Limnephilidae); lateral view of left metathoracic femur.

Figure 17.191. *Platycentropus radiatus* (Say) (Limnephilidae); left lateral view of head and prosternal horn.

Figure 17.192. *Limnephilus* sp. (Limnephilidae); left lateral view of head and prosternal horn.

Figure 17.193. *Anabolia bimaculata* (Walker) (Limnephilidae); dorsal view of head and thorax.

Figure 17.194. *Lenarchus* sp. (Limnephilidae); dorsal view of metanotum.

Figure 17.195. *Hesperophylax* sp. (Limnephilidae); dorsal view of metanotum.

40'.   Dorsum of head with various markings, including spots, but not coalescing as above; anterolateral corner of pronotum usually lacking patch of spines 41

41(40'). Prosternal horn extending beyond head capsule to mentum of labium (fig. 17.191); case of transverse, narrow, projecting pieces of plant material (fig. 16.11) .... *Platycentropus*

41'.   Prosternal horn extending only to distal edge of head capsule (fig. 17.192) 42

42(30',41') Chloride epithelia present dorsally, laterally, and ventrally on most abdominal segments (similar to fig. 17.176); case of plant and rock materials (similar to fig. 17.154) .... *Asynarchus*

42'.   Chloride epithelia absent dorsally, but present ventrally and laterally on most abdominal segments; cases of wide range of shapes and materials (e.g., resembling figs. 16.7–16.8, 16.11, 17.132, and 17.200) .... *Limnephilus, Philarctus*[4]

43(27'). Femora of meso- and metathoracic legs each with approximately 5 major setae along ventral edge (fig. 17.189); curved, scarcely tapered case of bark and leaves (fig. 17.200) or of sand .... (subfamily Dicosmoecinae, in part) .... *Ironoquia*

43'.   Femora of meso- and usually metathoracic legs each with 2 major setae along ventral edge (fig. 17.190) ....
.... (subfamily Limnephilinae, tribe Limnephilini, in part) 44

44(43'). Metanotum with all setae confined to primary sclerites (fig. 17.194); cylindrical case of longitudinally arranged lengths of sedge leaves (similar to fig. 16.8) or of fragments of bark and leaves .... *Lenarchus*

44'.   Metanotum with at least a few setae between primary sclerites (fig. 17.195) 45

45(44'). Lateral series of abdominal gills single-branched and on segment II only, occasionally also III; case mostly of coarse, small rocks (similar to fig. 17.196) .... *Psychoronia*

45'.   Lateral series of abdominal gills on segments II–V, some with more than 1 branch; case mostly of small rocks (similar to fig. 17.132), sometimes also with plant pieces .... *Hesperophylax*

Molannidae

1.   Tarsal claw of each metathoracic leg curved, broad, setose, much shorter than tarsus (fig. 17.201) .... *Molanna*

1'.   Tarsal claw of each metathoracic leg straight, needlelike, without setae, as long as main body of tarsus, tarsus extended beyond claw as slender, setose filament (fig. 17.202). .... *Molannodes*

Odontoceridae

1.   Prothoracic femur about as broad as its tibia, prothoracic tibia about 4 times as long as its tarsus, single apical spur of prothoracic tibia broad, clasplike (fig. 17.203). Case of rock fragments, curved and tapered (fig. 17.215). ....
.... (subfamily Pseudogoerinae) .... *Pseudogoera*

1'.   Prothoracic femur distinctly broader than its tibia, prothoracic tibia as long as its tarsus, both apical spurs of prothoracic tibia slender (fig. 17.204) ....
.... (subfamily Odontocerinae) 2

2(1').   Anterolateral corner of pronotum produced, sharply pointed (fig. 17.205) 3

2'.   Anterolateral corner of pronotum not produced, rounded (fig. 17.206); sand case (similar to fig. 16.9) 4

3(2).   Ventral apotome of head long, completely separating genae (fig. 17.207); claw of anal proleg stout, both claw and lateral sclerite with straight spines as well as setae (fig. 17.209); case of fine sand grains with silken exterior (similar to fig. 17.158). .... *Parthina*

---

4. "Because of the close morphological similarity between larvae in *Philarctus* and *Limnephilus* and of the large number of *Limnephilus* spp. for which larvae are not known [about 65% unassociated], separation between the two genera is illusory at this stage in our knowledge" (Wiggins 1977).

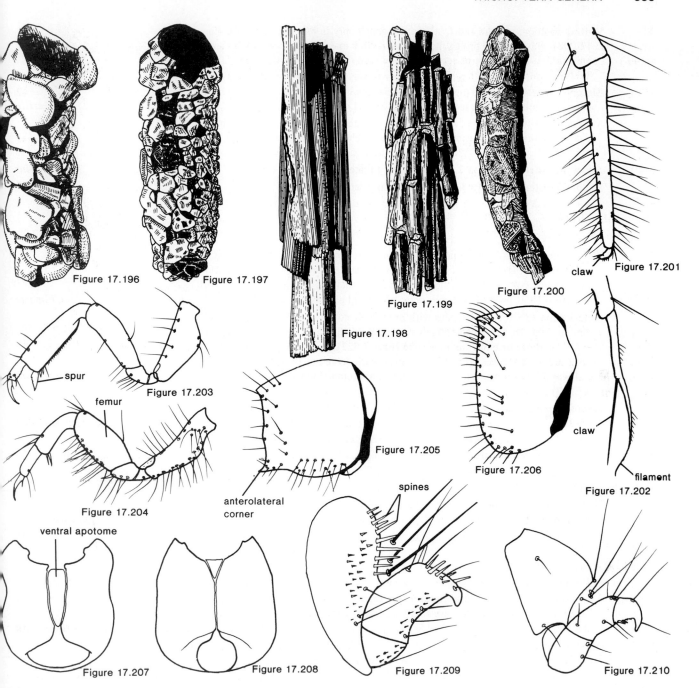

Figure 17.196. *Allocosmoecus partitus* Banks (Limnephilidae); larval case.

Figure 17.197. *Dicosmoecus* sp. (Limnephilidae); larval case.

Figure 17.198. *Grammotaulius* sp. (Limnephilidae); larval case.

Figure 17.199. *Anabolia bimaculata* (Walker) (Limnephilidae); larval case.

Figure 17.200. *Ironoquia* sp. (Limnephilidae); larval case.

Figure 17.201. *Molanna tryphena* Betten (Molannidae); lateral view of left metathoracic leg.

Figure 17.202. *Molannodes tinctus* (Zetterstedt) (Molannidae); lateral view of left metathoracic leg.

Figure 17.203. *Pseudogoera singularis* Carpenter (Odontoceridae); lateral view of left prothoracic leg.

Figure 17.204. *Psilotreta* sp. (Odontoceridae); lateral view of left prothoracic leg.

Figure 17.205. *Psilotreta* sp. (Odontoceridae); left lateral view of pronotum.

Figure 17.206. *Namamyia* sp. (Odontoceridae); left lateral view of pronotum.

Figure 17.207. *Parthina* prob. *vierra* Denning (Odontoceridae); ventral view of head.

Figure 17.208. *Psilotreta* sp. (Odontoceridae); ventral view of head.

Figure 17.209. *Parthina* prob. *vierra* Denning (Odontoceridae); lateral view of left anal claw.

Figure 17.210. *Psilotreta* sp. (Odontoceridae); lateral view of left anal claw.

3'.   Ventral apotome of head short, separating genae only in anterior one-third (fig.
        17.208); claw of anal proleg more slender, claw and lateral sclerite with setae
        only (fig. 17.210); case of coarse and fine rock fragments, very sturdy (fig.
        17.216). .... *Psilotreta*

4(2'). Mesonotal plates each subdivided into 3 sclerites, metanotal sa1 sclerites large,
        subrectangular, contiguous mesally (fig. 17.211) .... *Marilia*

4'.   Mesonotal plates undivided, metanotal sa1 sclerites small, oval, separated by a
        distance equal to, or greater than, the greatest width of one of them (fig.
        17.212) 5

5(4'). Abdominal sternum I with 2 clusters of gill filaments, 2 pairs of setae (fig. 17.213) .... *Nerophilus*

5'.   Abdominal sternum I without gills, with many setae (fig. 17.214) .... *Namamyia*

Philopotamidae

(modified from Weaver et al. 1981)

1.   Anterior margin of frontoclypeus with prominent notch asymmetrically right of
        midline (fig. 17.219); fore trochantin small, scarcely projecting (fig. 17.221) and
        prothoracic coxa with long, slender, subapical seta-bearing process; head with
        setae no. 18 at level of posterior point of ventral apotome (fig. 17.218) .... *Chimarra*

1'.   Anterior margin of frontoclypeus with prominent notch as above, or only slightly
        sinuous (fig. 16.52), or completely symmetrical (fig. 17.220); fore trochantin
        small as above or elongate, fingerlike (fig. 17.222); prothoracic coxa without
        long subapical process (fig. 17.222); head with setae no. 18 approximately
        halfway between posterior edge of ventral apotome and occipital foramen (fig.
        17.217) 2

2(1'). Anterior margin of frontoclypeus slightly (fig. 16.52) to markedly (as in fig.
        17.219) asymmetrical; fore trochantin projecting, fingerlike (fig. 17.222) .... *Dolophilodes*

2'.   Anterior margin of frontoclypeus evenly convex, symmetrical (fig. 17.220); fore
        trochantin small, scarcely projecting (as in fig. 17.221) .... *Wormaldia*

Phryganeidae

1.   Genae of head almost completely separated by ventral apotome (fig. 17.223); case
        entirely of plant fragments .... (subfamily Phryganeinae) .. 2

1'.   Genae of head mostly contiguous ventrally, separated anteriorly by tiny ventral
        apotome (fig. 17.224); case of plant and mineral fragments, mineral fragments
        mostly anterior and ventral (fig. 17.231), pupal case entirely of micalike
        fragments .... (subfamily Yphriinae) .... *Yphria*

2(1).   Mesonotal sa1 sclerite several times larger than sa3 sclerite, sa1 seta near its
        anterior edge (fig. 16.46); case slightly curved, with plant materials arranged in
        discrete rings or bands (fig. 16.15) .... *Oligostomis*

2'.   Mesonotal sa1 sclerite absent (fig. 16.45) or much smaller than sa3 sclerite (fig.
        17.230) and with its sa1 seta centrally located; case generally of ring or spiral
        (fig. 16.16) construction, slightly curved or straight, respectively 3

3(2'). Head and pronotom uniformly light brown except for darker muscle scars on head
        (fig. 17.230); case of ring construction (similar to fig. 16.15) .... probably *Hagenella*

3'.   Head and pronotum with distinct, dark bands (fig. 16.45) 4

4(3'). Ventral combs of prothoracic coxae conspicuous, their teeth evident at a
        magnification of 50 (fig. 17.225) 5

4'.   Ventral combs of prothoracic coxae small, each comb appearing as a tiny raised
        point at 50 magnification (fig. 17.226) 6

5(4).   Prothoracic sternellum usually present (fig. 17.223); ventral combs of mesothoracic
        coxae with basal axes both transverse and parallel to long axis of coxa (fig.
        17.227); case usually of spiral construction (fig. 16.16) .... *Agrypnia*

5'.   Prothoracic sternellum absent; ventral combs of mesothoracic coxae with basal
        axes only transverse to long axis of coxa (fig. 17.228); case of spiral construction
        (fig. 17.232) .... *Phryganea*

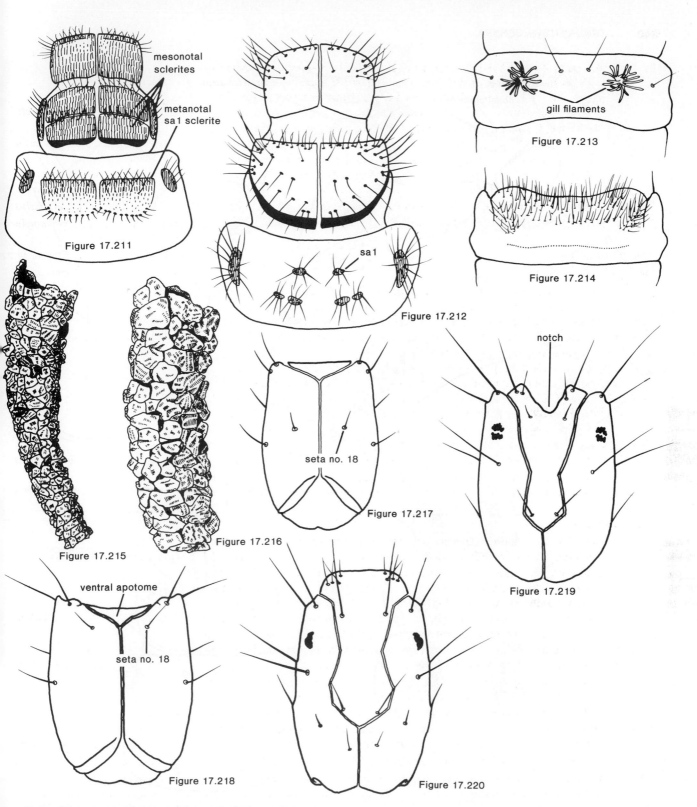

Figure 17.211. *Marilia* sp. (Odontoceridae); dorsal view of thorax.

Figure 17.212. *Nerophilus californicus* (Hagen) (Odontoceridae); dorsal view of thorax.

Figure 17.213. *Nerophilus californicus* (Hagen) (Odontoceridae); ventral view of abdominal sternum I.

Figure 17.214. *Namamyia* sp. (Odontoceridae); ventral view of abdominal sternum I.

Figure 17.215. *Pseudogoera singularis* Carpenter (Odontoceridae); larval case.

Figure 17.216. *Psilotreta* sp. (Odontoceridae); larval case.

Figure 17.217. *Dolophilodes* sp. (Philopotamidae); ventral view of head.

Figure 17.218. *Chimarra* sp. (Philopotamidae); ventral view of head.

Figure 17.219. *Chimarra* sp. (Philopotamidae); dorsal view of head.

Figure 17.220. *Wormaldia* sp. (Philopotamidae); dorsal view of head.

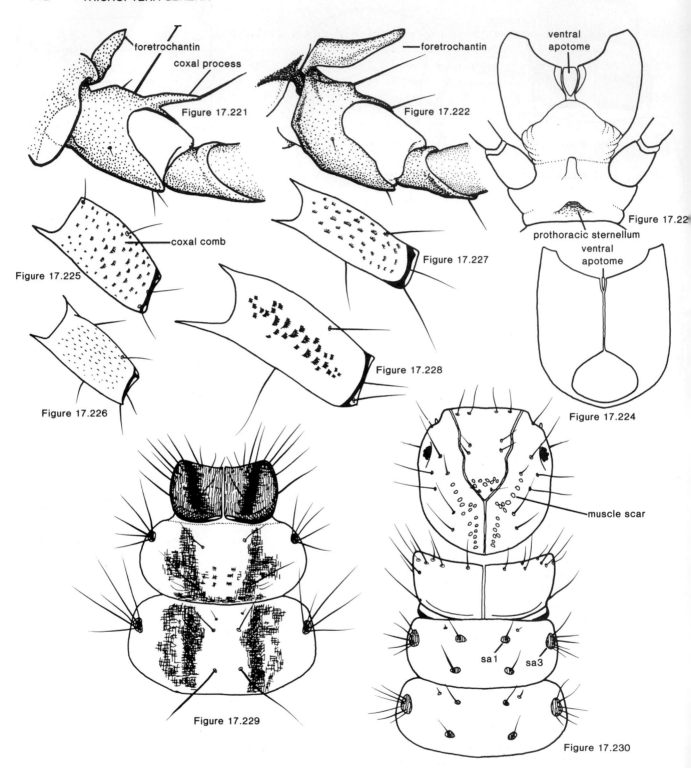

foretrochantin

coxal process

Figure 17.221

foretrochantin

Figure 17.222

ventral apotome

Figure 17.22

coxal comb

Figure 17.225

Figure 17.227

prothoracic sternellum

ventral apotome

Figure 17.226

Figure 17.228

Figure 17.224

muscle scar

Figure 17.229

sa1　sa3

Figure 17.230

Figure 17.221. *Chimmara* sp. (Philopotamidae); lateral view of right foretrochantin and prothoracic coxa.

Figure 17.222. *Dolophilodes* sp. (Philopotamidae); lateral view of right foretrochantin and prothoracic coxa.

Figure 17.223. *Agrypnia vestita* (Walker) (Phryganeidae); ventral view of head and prosternum.

Figure 17.224. *Yphria californica* (Banks) (Phryganeidae); ventral view of head.

Figure 17.225. *Phryganea* sp. (Phryganeidae); ventral view of left prothoracic coxa.

Figure 17.226. *Banksiola dossuaria* (Say) (Phryganeidae); ventral view of left prothoracic coxa.

Figure 17.227. *Agrypnia vestita* (Walker) (Phryganeidae); ventral view of left mesothoracic coxa.

Figure 17.228. *Phryganea* sp. (Phryganeidae); ventral view of left mesothoracic coxa.

Figure 17.229. *Banksiola dossuaria* (Say) (Phryganeidae); dorsal view of thorax.

Figure 17.230. Prob. *Hagenella canadensis* (Banks) (Phryganeidae); dorsal view of head and thorax.

6(4'). Meso- and metanota with pair of longitudinal, irregular, dark bands (fig. 17.229); case of spiral construction 7

6'. Meso- and metanota nearly uniform in color (fig. 16.45); case variously constructed 8

7(6). Abdominal segments VI and VII with anterodorsal gills, segment VII without posteroventral gills (fig. 17.237); case often with pieces of plant material trailing posteriorly (fig. 17.233). .... ***Banksiola***

7'. Abdominal segments VI and VII without anterodorsal gills, segment VII with posteroventral gills (fig. 17.238); case as in figure 17.232, without trailing ends. .... ***Oligotricha***

8(6'). Pronotum with dark line along anterior margin, without dark, central, transverse markings (fig. 17.236); case of spiral construction but with trailing ends of plant fragments giving a bushy appearance (fig. 17.234) .... ***Fabria***

8'. Pronotum without dark line along anterior margin, with dark transverse markings near center of each sclerite (fig. 16.45); case of ring construction without trailing ends (fig. 17.235) .... ***Ptilostomis***

Polycentropodidae
(modified from Hudson et al. 1981)

1. Tarsi all broader than their tibiae and flat (fig. 17.239); larva in branching, sand-covered silken tube in stream sand deposits (fig. 16.3) ....
.... (subfamily Dipseudopsinae) .... ***Phylocentropus***

1'. Tarsi all narrower than their tibiae and more nearly cylindrical (figs. 17.240–17.241); larva in unbranched silken tube on substrate surfaces (figs. 16.1–16.2) .... (subfamily Polycentropodinae) 2

2(1'). Anal claw with 6 or fewer conspicuous teeth along ventral, concave margin (figs. 17.242–17.243) 3

2'. Anal claw without ventral teeth (figs. 17.246–17.249) or with 10 or more tiny spines (fig. 17.244) along ventral, concave margin 4

3(2). Teeth on anal claw much shorter than apical hook, dorsal accessory spine present (fig. 17.243); pronotum with short, stout bristle near each lateral margin (fig. 17.245). .... ***Nyctiophylax***

3'. Teeth on anal claw almost as long as apical hook, dorsal accessory spine absent (fig. 17.242); pronotum without short, lateral bristles. .... ***Polyplectropus***

4(2'). Basal segment of anal proleg about as long as distal segment and with only 2 or 3 apicoventral setae (fig. 17.244); anal claw with many tiny spines along ventral, concave margin (fig. 17.244) .... ***Neureclipsis***

4'. Basal segment of anal proleg obviously longer than distal segment in mature specimens and with many setae scattered over most of its surface (figs. 17.246–17.247); anal claw without tiny ventral spines (figs. 17.246–17.249) 5

5(4'). Dorsal region between anal claw and sclerite of distal segment of anal proleg with 2 dark bands contiguous mesally (fig. 17.246, inset); meso- and metanotal sa1 setae short, not more than one-third as long as longest sa2 setae (fig. 17.250) 6

5'. Dorsal region between anal claw and sclerite of distal segment of anal proleg with 2 dark bands completely separated mesally (fig. 17.247, inset); meso- and metanotal sa1 setae about as long as longest sa2 setae (fig. 17.253) .... ***Cyrnellus***

6(5). Prothoracic tarsi broad and only one-half as long as prothoracic tibiae (fig. 17.240), *or* anal claw obtusely curved (fig. 17.248), *or* anal claw with 2 or 3 dorsal accessory spines (fig. 17.249) .... ***Polycentropus sensu lato***[5]

6'. Prothoracic tarsi narrow and at least two-thirds as long as prothoracic tibiae (fig. 17.241), *and* anal claw curved approximately 90° (fig. 17.246), *and* anal claw with only 1 dorsal accessory spine (fig. 17.246) .... ***Cernotina***

---

5. Trichoptera workers are divided as to the number of genera that should be recognized in the *Polycentropus sensu lato* complex. The issue is being studied by S. W. Hamilton (pers. comm.).

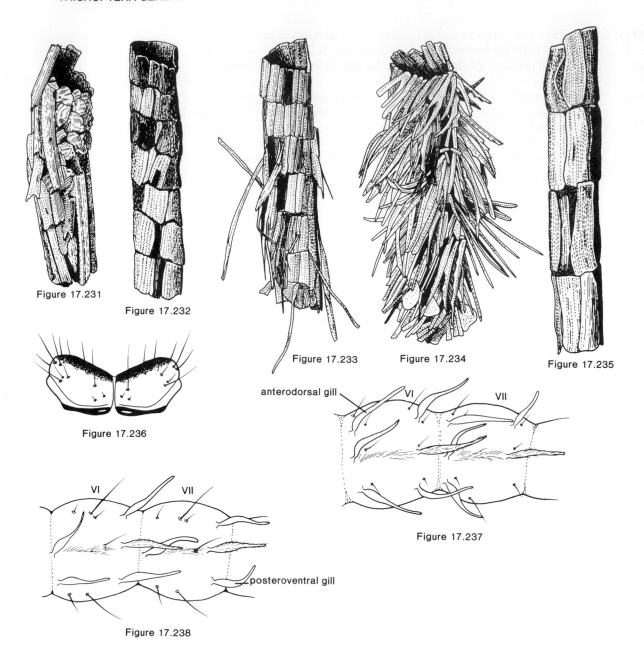

Figure 17.231

Figure 17.232

Figure 17.233   Figure 17.234

Figure 17.235

Figure 17.236

anterodorsal gill   VI   VII

Figure 17.237

VI   VII

posteroventral gill

Figure 17.238

Figure 17.231. *Yphria californica* (Banks) (Phryganeidae); larval case.

Figure 17.232. *Phryganea* sp. (Phryganeidae); larval case.

Figure 17.233. *Banksiola dossuaria* (Say) (Phryganeidae); larval case.

Figure 17.234. *Fabria inornata* (Banks) (Phryganeidae); larval case.

Figure 17.235. *Ptilostomis* sp. (Phryganeidae); larval case.

Figure 17.236. *Fabria inornata* (Banks) (Phryganeidae); dorsal view of pronotum.

Figure 17.237. *Banksiola dossuaria* (Say) (Phryganeidae); left lateral view of abdominal segments VI and VII.

Figure 17.238. *Oligotricha lapponica* (Hagen) (Phryganeidae); left lateral view of larval abdominal segments VI and VII.

Psychomyiidae[6]

1.   Anal claw with 3 or 4 conspicuous teeth along ventral, concave margin (fig.
         17.256); paired submental sclerites on ventral surface of labium longer than
         broad (fig. 17.252) .... *Psychomyia*

1'.   Anal claw without teeth on ventral, concave margin; paired submental sclerites on
         ventral surface of labium broader than long (fig. 17.251) 2

2(1').   Dorsolateral edge of each mandible without protuberance, lateral setae about one-
         third of distance from base (fig. 17.254). .... *Lype*

2'.   Dorsolateral edge of each mandible with rounded protuberance, lateral setae about
         middle (fig. 17.255). .... *Tinodes*

Rhyacophilidae

1.   Dense tuft of stout gills on sides of meso- and metathorax and abdominal segments
         I–VII (fig. 17.257); final instar larva up to 32 mm long .... *Himalopsyche*

1'.   Tufts of gills absent or not as dense or not on as many abdominal segments as
         above; final instar larva less than 30 mm long .... *Rhyacophila*

Sericostomatidae

1.   Anterolateral corners of pronotum each acute, projecting (fig. 17.258); each
         metanotal sa2 with many setae on transverse sclerite (fig. 17.260); sand case
         similar to figure 16.9 2

1'.   Anterolateral corners of pronotum each rounded, not projecting (fig. 17.259); each
         metanotal sa2 with single seta and no sclerite (fig. 17.261); case of small sand
         grains, frequently long, slender (fig. 17.262) .... *Gumaga*

2(1).   Dorsum of abdominal segment IX with about 40 setae; head flat dorsally with
         lateral carinae prominent (fig. 17.263). Higher elevations in southern
         Appalachian Mountains .... *Fattigia*

2'.   Dorsum of abdominal segment IX with about 15 setae; head rounded dorsally with
         lateral carinae not as prominent (fig. 17.264). Eastern North America, middle
         and lower elevations in Southeast .... *Agarodes*

Uenoidae

1.   Abdominal segment II with lateral setal fringe extending its full length (fig.
         17.265); anterior margin of pronotum weakly serrate (fig. 17.267); case of sand
         grains with thin, silken lining over interior and exterior surfaces (fig. 16.14) .... *Neothremma*

1'.   Abdominal segment II with lateral setae confined to anterior patch of stout setae
         and fringe of thin hairs on posterior half of either side of abdomen (fig. 17.266);
         anterior margin of pronotum smooth; case as above, but more slender .... *Farula*

6. The larva of *Paduniella* (Arkansas) is unknown.

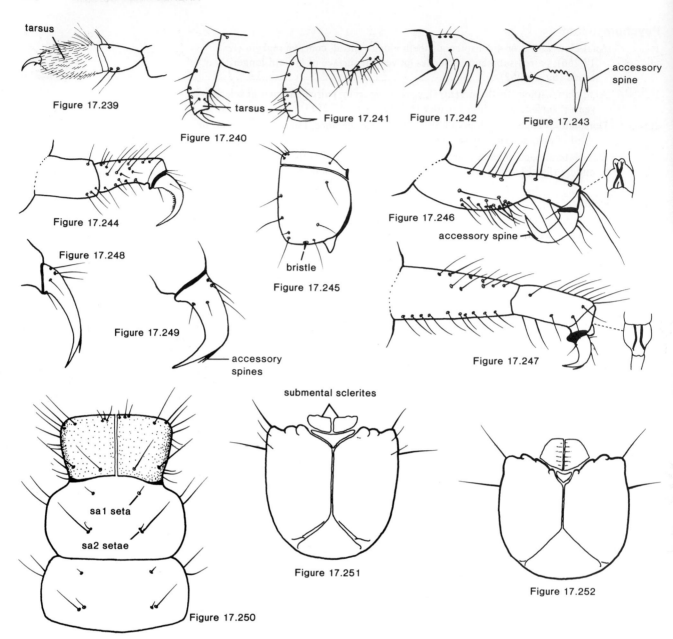

Figure 17.239

Figure 17.240

Figure 17.241

Figure 17.242

Figure 17.243

Figure 17.244

Figure 17.245

Figure 17.246

Figure 17.247

Figure 17.248

Figure 17.249

Figure 17.250

Figure 17.251

Figure 17.252

Figure 17.239. *Phylocentropus* sp. (Polycentropodidae); lateral view of left prothoracic tibia, tarsus, and claw.

Figure 17.240. *Polycentropus (P.)* sp. (Polycentropodidae); lateral view of left prothoracic tibia, tarsus, and claw.

Figure 17.241. *Cernotina spicata* Ross (Polycentropodidae); lateral view of left prothoracic leg beyond coxa.

Figure 17.242. *Polyplectropus* sp. (Polycentropodidae); lateral view of left anal claw.

Figure 17.243. *Nyctiophylax* sp. (Polycentropodidae); lateral view of left anal claw.

Figure 17.244. *Neureclipsis* sp. (Polycentropodidae); lateral view of left anal proleg and claw.

Figure 17.245. *Nyctiophylax* sp. (Polycentropodidae); left dorsolateral oblique view of pronotum.

Figure 17.246. *Cernotina spicata* Ross (Polycentropodidae); lateral view of anal proleg and claw: *inset,* dorsal region at base of anal claw.

Figure 17.247. *Cyrnellus* sp. (Polycentropodidae); lateral view of left anal proleg and claw: *inset,* dorsal region at base of anal claw.

Figure 17.248. *Polycentropus (Plectrocnemia)* sp. (Polycentropodidae); lateral view of left anal claw.

Figure 17.249. *Polycentropus (Holocentropus)* sp. (Polycentropodidae); lateral view of left anal claw.

Figure 17.250. *Polycentropus* sp. (Polycentropodidae); dorsal view of larval thorax.

Figure 17.251. *Tinodes* sp. (Psychmyiidae); ventral view of head.

Figure 17.252. *Psychomyia flavida* Hagen (Psychomyiidae); ventral view of head.

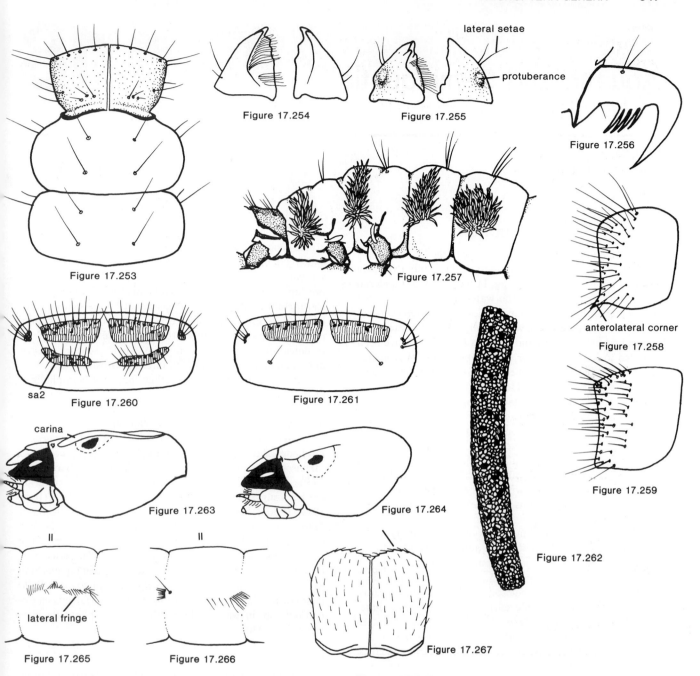

Figure 17.253.

Figure 17.254.

Figure 17.255.

Figure 17.256.

Figure 17.257.

Figure 17.258.

Figure 17.259.

Figure 17.260.

Figure 17.261.

Figure 17.262.

Figure 17.263.

Figure 17.264.

Figure 17.265.

Figure 17.266.

Figure 17.267.

Figure 17.253. *Cyrnellus fraternus* (Banks) (Polycentropodidae); dorsal view of thorax.

Figure 17.254. *Lype diversa* (Banks) (Psychomyiidae); dorsal view of mandibles.

Figure 17.255. *Tinodes* sp. (Psychomyiidae); dorsal view of mandibles.

Figure 17.256. *Psychomyia flavida* Hagen (Psychomyiidae); lateral view of left anal claw.

Figure 17.257. *Himalopsyche phryganea* (Ross) (Phyacophilidae); left lateral view of larval thorax and abdominal segments I and II (distal portions of thoracic legs omitted).

Figure 17.258. *Agarodes libalis* Ross and Scott (Sericostomatidae); left lateral view of pronotum.

Figure 17.259. *Gumaga* sp. (Sericostomatidae); left lateral view of pronotum.

Figure 17.260. *Agarodes libalis* Ross and Scott (Sericostomatidae); dorsal view of metathorax.

Figure 17.261. *Gumaga* sp. (Sericostomatidae); dorsal view of metathorax.

Figure 17.262. *Gumaga* sp. (Sericostomatidae); larval case.

Figure 17.263. *Fattigia pele* (Ross) (Sericostomatidae); left lateral view of head.

Figure 17.264. *Agarodes libalis* Ross and Scott (Sericostomatidae); left lateral view of head.

Figure 17.265. *Neothremma* sp. (Uenoidae); left lateral view of abdominal segment II.

Figure 17.266. *Farula* sp. (Uenoidae); left lateral view of abdominal segment II.

Figure 17.267. *Neothremma* sp. (Uenoidae); dorsal view of pronotum.

18

Aquatic and Semiaquatic Lepidoptera

W. H. Lange
University of California, Davis

INTRODUCTION

Adaptation to an aquatic existence in the Lepidoptera is best exemplified by certain members of the family Pyralidae where the immature stages (egg, larva, and pupa) undergo their entire development in the water. In one instance, the brachypterous form of the female of *Acentria nivea* (Olivier) spends her adult life in the water (Berg 1942). Larvae of the tropical genera *Palustra* and *Maenas* (Arctiidae) have been reported to feed underwater on aquatic plants (Wesenberg-Lund 1943), and some members of the families Nepticulidae, Cosmopterigidae, Gelechiidae, Tortricidae, Olethreutidae, Noctuidae, Arctiidae, Cossidae, and Sphingidae are also associated with aquatic or semiaquatic plants. Larval habits include leaf mining, stem or root boring, foliage feeding, and feeding on flower or seed structures. Larvae of some species of the Hawaiian genus *Hyposmocoma* (Cosmopterigidae) construct Trichoptera-like cases (fig. 18.2) and feed on lichens, algae, or mosses growing on the emergent portions of rocks in fast-flowing streams. The larvae are able to survive periodic submergence.

Among the pyralids, members of the subfamily Nymphulinae are the best suited for an aquatic existence. In the tribe Argyractini, the larvae and pupae occur in a variety of aquatic habitats, including lakes (*Eoparargyractis* sp.), deep and fast-flowing streams, hot springs, intermittent streams, and those receiving organic enrichment (*Petrophila jaliscalis* [Schaus]) (Lange 1956a; Tuskes 1981). In a western species (*Petrophila confusalis* [Walker] [= *truckeealis* Dyar]), found in well-oxygenated water of streams and lakes, the adult female usually crawls down a rock into the water and deposits groups of eggs on the underside (fig. 18.1). After hatching, the gilled larva constructs a silken tent on the rock, under which it feeds on diatoms and other algae. The pupal cocoon is made of tightly woven silk with holes along the periphery that allow for water circulation (fig. 18.1F). The pupa is located in an inner cocoon, and prior to pupation the larva cuts an "escape slit" to assist in adult emergence. The emerging adult swims (using the mid and hind legs, and wings) or floats to the surface from the underwater cocoon.

In northern California two to three generations of *Petrophila confusalis* occur a year. Tuskes (1981) reports that the larvae are most abundant in lakes and streams where the water velocity is between 0.4 and 1.4 m/sec. Other factors influencing numbers and distribution include water temperature, concentration of dissolved oxygen, substrate texture, and algal growth. Although *P. jaliscalis* (Schaus) occurs sympatrically in northern California with *P. confusalis,* the overlap in distribution is limited to streams possessing physical factors conducive to the survival of both species. *Petrophila jaliscalis* can tolerate low oxygen concentration, relatively high temperatures, reduced water velocity, and eutrophication; this allows it to have a more southern distribution and an association with intermittent streams.

In addition to the rock-dwelling species of Nymphulinae (Argyractini), the Nymphulini are associated with vascular hydrophytes and also adapted to freshwater (fig. 18.3). Many first larval instars are nongilled. Following a molt to the second instar, members of the genus *Parapoynx* (= *Paraponyx*) possess tracheal gills, whereas all instars of other genera *(Munroessa, Synclita, Neocataclysta)* lack gills (Berg 1949, 1950a). In the absence of gills, a plastron type of respiration has been suggested for *Munroessa icciusalis* (Walker) (Berg 1949, 1950a; Thorpe 1950). The first two larval instars of *Parapoynx maculalis* (Clemens) occur on the bottom and feed on submerged leaves of *Nymphaea,* whereas older larvae generally become surface feeders (Welch 1924). Periodic vibratory movements of *P. maculalis* larvae aid in replenishing oxygen (Welch and Sehon 1928). One species *Nymphuliella daeckealis* (Haimbach) (= *broweri* Heinrich), feeds on *Cephalozia* sp. in water holes in the mat of sphagnum bogs (Heinrich 1940).

Studies of the aquatic adaptations of *Pyrausta penitalis* Grote (Pyralidae) have revealed that young larvae avoid displacement by feeding under webs on the surface of *Nelumbo lutea* leaves. The older larvae tunnel into the upper end of the petioles and, if dislodged, can swim to other plants. The pupa in a *N. lutea* stem burrow is protected by a woven silk cap, or plug, made by the larva (Welch 1919; Ainslie and Cartwright 1922).

Most of the other lepidopterous larvae associated with aquatic or semiaquatic ecosystems feed on cattail (*Typha* spp.), bulrush (*Scirpus* spp.), or other vascular hydrophytes. These include genera of several pyralids (*Crambus* and *Chilo*), a nepticulid (*Nepticula*), several cosmopterigids (*Cosmopteryx* and *Lymnaecia*), noctuid borers (*Bellura, Archanara,* and *Simyra*), and a tortricid *(Archips)* (Claassen 1921). A few records are available for the aquatic habits of

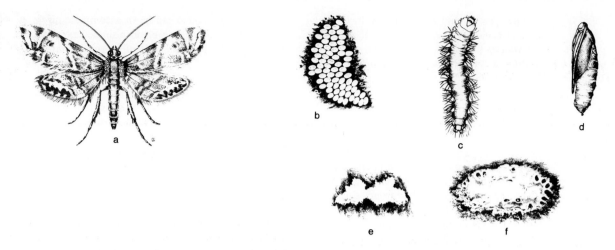

Figure 18.1

Figure 18.2

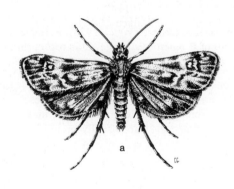

Figure 18.3

Figure 18.1. Life stages of *Petrophila (Parargyractis) confusalis* (Walker) (Pyralidae) (after Lange 1956a). *a*, adult male; *b*, eggs; *c*, mature larva; *d*, pupa; *e*, larval web; *f*, cocoon.

Figure 18.2. Case and larva of *Hyposmocoma* sp. (Cosmopterigidae) (Oahu, Hawaii).

Figure 18.3. Life stages of *Synclita occidentalis* Lange (Pyralidae) (after Lange 1956a). *a*, adult male; *b*, eggs; *c*, mature larva; *d*, pupa.

sphingid larvae (Hagen 1880), and recent papers have discussed the biology and ecology of several genera of noctuid borers *(Bellura, Apamea)* (MacKay and Rockburne 1958; Vogel and Oliver 1969; Levine 1974; Levine and Chandler 1976).

EXTERNAL MORPHOLOGY

Eggs

The eggs of Lepidoptera are laid singly or in clusters or groups. In many pyralids, the eggs are often greatly flattened and deposited in overlapping layers; in other groups eggs are of the upright type. In some Noctuidae, eggs are characteristically ribbed with a depressed micropyle (minute opening) and are laid singly. In the genus *Spodoptera* (Noctuidae), eggs are deposited in groups that the female covers with hairs from the abdomen, and in some families eggs are inserted into leaves or flower structures.

Larvae

Although many modifications occur, lepidopterous larvae are characterized by: (1) the presence of a distinct head with a ring of ocelli *(stemmata or simple eyes)*; (2) a thorax composed of pro-, meso-, and metathoracic segments, each with a pair of segmented legs; (3) 10 abdominal segments with prolegs on segments 3, 4, 5, 6, and 10 (anal prolegs); and (4) spiracles on the prothoracic segment and abdominal segments 1–8 (fig. 18.4).

Head: The head capsule can be vertical *(hypognathous)* with the mouthparts directed downward (ventrally) (fig. 18.4) or horizontal *(prognathous)* with the mouthparts directed forward (fig. 18.5). The head of leaf-mining or wood-boring species is often prognathous. An inverted *epicranial suture* and narrow *adfrontal sclerites* are distinct larval features (fig. 18.11). The *clypeus* and *labrum* are ventrad or anterad to the frons. The antennae are usually short and bear several sensillae. A distinct *spinneret* (silk-producing structure) is present and mouthparts are the chewing type with opposable mandibles. The *ocelli* are usually six in number but can be reduced, modified, or lost (fig. 18.4).

Thorax: The thorax usually bears a distinct, often sclerotized, *cervical (prothoracic) shield* (fig. 18.4). The true legs, one pair on each thoracic segment, are five-segmented with terminal claws but can be aborted or missing. Gills occur on some aquatic species.

Abdomen: In most Lepidoptera the abdomen consists of 10 segments, with pairs of fleshy prolegs on segments 3, 4, 5, 6, and 10 (fig. 18.4); however, some variations occur. In Nepticulidae prolegs occur on segments 2–7, and in the semiloopers (Noctuidae) on segments 5, 6, and 10. The truncate end of each proleg, the *planta,* bears curved hooks or *crochets* (fig. 18.4), the pattern and arrangement of which are used extensively in larval classification. If crochets are all the same length, they are termed *uniordinal;* if two or three lengths, bi- or triordinal. If they arise from a given line, they are referred to as *uniserial;* if arising from three or more lines,

multiserial. Crochets can be in a complete circle, in an interrupted circle *(penellipse),* or in single bands extending longitudinally on the mesal side of a proleg *(mesoseries),* or in a combination of *lateroseries* and mesoseries. In aquatic forms, *blood gills* or *tracheal gills* may be present or absent.

Chaetotaxy: Larvae of Lepidoptera bear setae or punctures commonly used in their classification. *Primary setae* on the head, thorax, and abdomen have a definite distribution and have a system of nomenclature utilizing Greek letters, Roman numerals, or other identifying symbols (Fracker 1915; Heinrich 1916; Hinton 1946; Common 1970). Some *subprimary setae* do not occur in the first instar but appear in the second. *Secondary setae* occur randomly and are not specifically named. A few microscopic primary setae, which occur at the anterior margin of each segment or on the prothorax, are believed to be proprioceptors (sense organs; Hinton 1946). Setae often arise from a flattened, pigmented area, a *pinaculum,* which if elevated is called a *chalaza.* In hairy caterpillars, such as the Arctiidae, a wartlike elevation bearing several to many setae pointing in different directions is called a *verruca.* The Sphingidae have a characteristic *caudal horn* or scar on the dorsum of the eighth abdominal segment, and *anal combs,* or *forks,* located ventrad of the suranal plate (fig. 18.4), are found in some Tortricidae and Olethreutidae. The cuticle of many larvae have ornamentations of granules, spicules, microspines, or pigmented areas that are sometimes useful in classification.

Pupae

The typical lepidopteran pupa is of the *obtect* type (appendages and body compactly united) and may or may not be enclosed in a cocoon (fig. 18.7). In many of the truly aquatic forms, the external spiracular openings on abdominal segments 3 and 4 are greatly enlarged and the *cremaster* (apex of the last segment of the abdomen) is hooklike and adapted to firmly anchor the pupa to its silken case (fig. 18.7).

Adults

Lepidoptera are characterized by the presence of overlapping scales on the two pairs of wings, body, and legs. Aquatic Lepidoptera usually possess a sucking proboscis or haustellum formed from the modified galeae of the maxillae.

Head: The *compound eyes* are usually prominent and one ocellus may be present over each eye. A pair of sensory organs, *chaetosemata* (Jordan's organs), is found in some of the aquatic Nymphulinae (fig. 18.28). A pair of *antennae* are located anterior to the ocelli, and the *scape* (basal segment) sometimes has a tuft of scales *(eye-cap)* over the compound eye. The antennae can be lamellate (leaflike), ciliate, clubbed, moniliform (beadlike), or serrate (sawlike). *Labial palpi* are usually present but *maxillary palpi* may be well developed or absent.

Thorax: The small *prothorax* possesses a pair of overlapping plates, the *patagia,* and the well-developed *mesothorax* has a pair of laterally placed *tegulae* (articular sclerites of insect wing). The *metathorax* is usually inconspicuous, and the *legs* are usually well developed with five-segmented tarsi.

In some of the aquatic Nymphulinae, the hind legs possess an oarlike fringe of hairs used in swimming.

Wings: Both surfaces of the wings are usually clothed with overlapping, broad scales. Wing colors and patterns are helpful in determining species, and wing venation is also used. The generalized venation is similar to primitive Trichoptera, with a tendency toward vein reduction in the higher groups. Some families may have *brachypterous* forms in one or both sexes, and in a few species (e.g., *Acentria nivea*) both winged and brachypterous females occur.

Abdomen: The 10-segmented abdomen has the terminal segments modified into the genitalia. *Tympanal organs* (hearing) occur at the base of the abdomen in some groups. The *genital* structures are helpful in characterizing taxa at the generic and specific levels, particularly in males in which modifications of the *valvae* (claspers), aedeagus, juxta, tegumen, and uncus are commonly used. Females have an egg canal and a copulatory opening, the *ductus bursae* (ostium bursae). The sclerotized portions of the ductus bursae and associated structures are particularly diagnostic in certain aquatic forms.

KEYS TO THE FAMILIES OF AQUATIC AND SEMIAQUATIC LEPIDOPTERA

Larvae

1.	Thoracic legs reduced to fleshy swellings; prolegs usually on abdominal segments 2–7 (fig. 18.8); crochets (curved hooks) lacking; small, leaf-mining species	*NEPTICULIDAE*
1′.	Thoracic legs present, segmented; crochets present (fig. 18.4)	2
2(1′).	Thorax and abdomen with filamentous gills (figs. 18.5, 18.9)	3
2′.	Thorax and abdomen without filamentous gills	5
3(2).	Head flattened dorsoventrally (fig. 18.11); prognathous (head horizontal and mouthparts directed forward); thorax and abdomen with numerous blood gills (figs. 18.1C, 18.5); mandibles prominent, adapted to scrape algae and diatoms from rocks in streams, lakes, and springs	*PYRALIDAE—Petrophila*
3′.	Head round, typical type; hypognathous (head vertical and mouthparts directed ventrally), or sometimes prognathous; feed on higher aquatic plants	4
4(3′).	Thorax and abdomen with branched or unbranched subspiracular and supraspiracular gills (fig. 18.10); living in cases cut from leaves of aquatic plants	*PYRALIDAE—Parapoynx*
5(2′).	Larvae living in cases (fig. 18.13)	6
5′.	Larvae not living in cases; stem borers, leaf miners, foliage feeders; some use plant materials to build retreats (fig. 18.14)	7
6(5).	Cases made of silk and sand particles, sometimes with operculum (lid) present; semiaquatic trichopteroid type living in conical, thornlike or saclike cases on emergent rocks in swiftly running streams; prolegs absent; crochets present with thoracic legs enlarged (figs. 18.2, 18.15); endemic to Hawaii .... *COSMOPTERIGIDAE* (Cosmopteriginae)—**Hyposmocoma**	
6′.	Case made of leaves or plant material, usually associated with lakes, ponds, or quiet water (fig. 18.3) .... *PYRALIDAE—Munroessa, Synclita, Neocataclysta*	
7(5′).	Terminal segment of abdomen with anal fork (fig. 18.16); feeds on leaves and heads of aquatic plants	*TORTRICIDAE—Archips*
7′.	Terminal segment of abdomen without anal fork	8
8(7′).	Body with prominent verrucae (elevated portions of cuticle bearing tufts of long setae) (fig. 18.17)	9
8′.	Body without prominent verrucae	10
9(8).	Crochets heteroideus (middle crochets abruptly longer on each proleg); head of *Estigmene* largely black; setae dark, long, and setal tufts dense (fig. 18.18)	*ARCTIIDAE—Estigmene*
9′.	Crochets homoideus (no abrupt change in crochet length); head of *Simyra* black and white mottled; setae light colored, bristlelike, sparsely distributed (fig. 18.19)	*NOCTUIDAE—Simyra*
10(8′).	Anal horn on 8th abdominal segment present (fig. 18.20), or reduced to prominent dark spot	*SPHINGIDAE**
10′.	Anal horn on 8th abdominal segment absent	11
11(10′).	Large larvae, 50–75 mm long at maturity	12

*Included in the key since some species are associated with aquatic habitats.

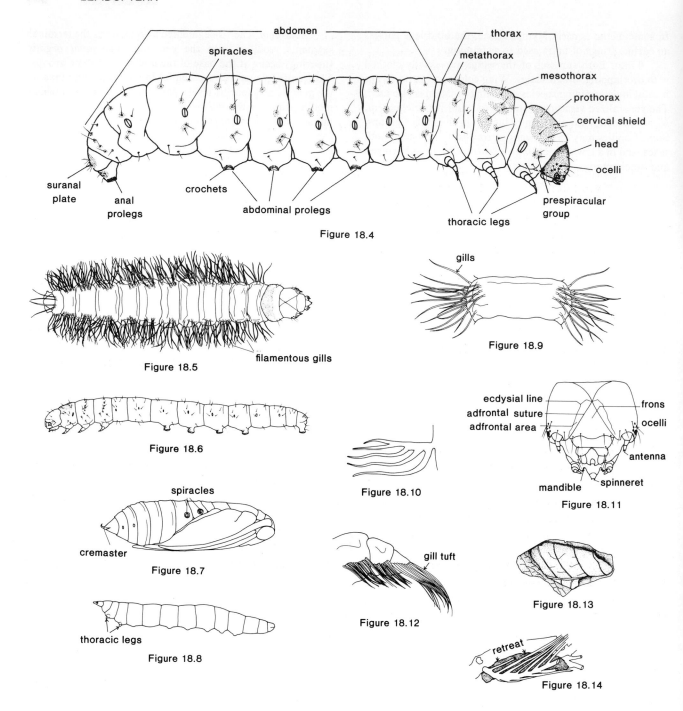

Figure 18.4

Figure 18.5

Figure 18.9

Figure 18.6

Figure 18.10

Figure 18.11

Figure 18.7

Figure 18.12

Figure 18.13

Figure 18.8

Figure 18.14

Figure 18.4. Lateral view of larva of wood-boring type, *Prionoxystus robiniae* (Peck) (Cossidae).

Figure 18.5. Dorsal view of gilled larva of rock-dwelling type, *Petrophila confusalis* (Walker) (Pyralidae).

Figure 18.6. Lateral view of stem-boring larva of *Archanara oblonga* (Grote) (Noctuidae).

Figure 18.7. Lateral view of pupa of *Petrophila confusalis* (Walker) (Pyralidae) showing enlarged spiracular openings on specific abdominal segments.

Figure 18.8. Lateral view of larva of *Nepticula* sp. (Nepticulidae).

Figure 18.9. Gills of *Petrophila confusalis* (Walker) (Pyralidae).

Figure 18.10. Branched gill of *Parapoynx* sp. (Pyralidae).

Figure 18.11. Dorsal view of head of *Petrophila confusalis* (Walker) (Pyralidae).

Figure 18.12. Gill tufts on posterior segments of a pyralid (Nymphulinae).

Figure 18.13. Larval case of *Synclita occidentalis* Lange (Pyralidae).

Figure 18.14. Larval retreat of *Acentria* sp. (Pyralidae) on *Ceratophyllum* sp.

11′. Small larvae, less than 20 mm long at maturity 13

12(11). Crochets uniordinal and arranged in a transverse band *(Archanara)* (fig. 18.21), or arranged as in fig. 18.22 *(Bellura);* spiracles narrow, height at least 3 times width (fig. 18.23); burrowers in *Typha, Nuphar, Pontederia,* and *Nymphaea* stems .... *NOCTUIDAE*

12′. Crochets triordinal to multiordinal (3 or more different lengths) (fig. 18.24); prothoracic spiracle enlarged; cervical shield smooth (fig. 18.4); body white with brown pinacula (seta-bearing papillae) (fig. 18.25); borer in *Populus* and *Salix* (fig. 18.4) .... *COSSIDAE—Prionoxystus**

13(11′). Crochets biordinal, in an incomplete ellipse with almost parallel sides and open on mesal side (fig. 18.26); body surface covered with small granules; pinacula (seta-bearing papillae) inconspicuous; in retreats made by fastening together *Ceratophyllum* or other aquatic plants .... *PYRALIDAE—Acentria*

13′. Crochets uniordinal or biordinal, in circles; body with or without granules or spicules; pinacula variable 14

14(13′). Pinacula conspicuous (fig. 18.25); body covered with granulations; crochets biordinal and arranged in a circle .... *PYRALIDAE—Crambus*

14′. Pinacula inconspicuous; body smooth; crochets uniordinal and arranged in a circle 15

15(14′). Body covered with minute spicules (fig. 18.27); primary setae short; on nut-grass .... *TORTRICIDAE* (Oleuthreutinae)—*Bactra*

15′. Body smooth, spicules lacking; pinacula not distinct; setae long; on *Helianthus* heads .... *COSMOPTERIGIDAE—Pyroderces*

Adults

1. Haustellum (proboscis) short, rudimentary, or missing 2

1′. Haustellum well developed (fig. 18.28) 5

2(1). Wings usually fully developed in males and females 3

2′. Species with brachypterous wings in some females; male with normal wings .... *PYRALIDAE—Acentria*

3(2). Small species with slender, aculeate, or lanceolate wings (fig. 18.29); body slender 4

3′. Larger species (greater than 20 mm); wings of normal width; body stout .... *COSSIDAE**

4(3). Head with ascending (recurved) labial palpi (fig. 18.30); species over 3 mm in length; eye-cap (greatly enlarged basal segment of antenna with tuft of scales over the eye) absent .... *GELECHOIDEA, (GELECHIIDAE)—(COSMOPTERIGIDAE)*

4′. Head with drooping labial palpi; very small species (3 mm); eye-cap present .... *NEPTICULIDAE*

5(1′). Small species, wing expanse under 30 mm 6

5′. Larger species, wing expanse 35–115 mm 8

6(5). Fore wings somewhat square-tipped (figs. 18.31–18.32) 7

6′. Fore wings not usually square-tipped, outer margin with projecting apex and often sloping inwardly toward body (figs. 18.33, 18.38–18.41) .... *PYRALIDAE*

7(6). Costal margin of fore wings arched (fig. 18.31) .... *TORTRICIDAE*

7′. Costal margin of fore wings not arched (fig. 18.32) .... *OLETHREUTIDAE*

8(5′). Hind wing small relative to fore wing (about one-half length of fore wing); body stout, fusiform (spindle-shaped); antennae hooked at tip (fig. 18.34) .... *SPHINGIDAE**

8′. Hind wing approaching length of fore wing; body not usually fusiform; antennae not hooked at tip (fig. 18.35) 9

9(8′). Mostly somber or dark-colored species (fig. 18.42); abdomen usually lacking dark lateral median markings; veins Sc and R in hind wing fused for only a short distance at base of discal cell (fig. 18.36) .... *NOCTUIDAE*

9′. Light-colored species or with combinations of brightly colored or banded patterns (fig. 18.43); abdomen usually with dorsal and/or lateral dark markings; Sc and R in hind wing fused to middle of discal cell (fig. 18.37) .... *ARCTIIDAE*

*Included in the key since some species are associated with aquatic habitats.

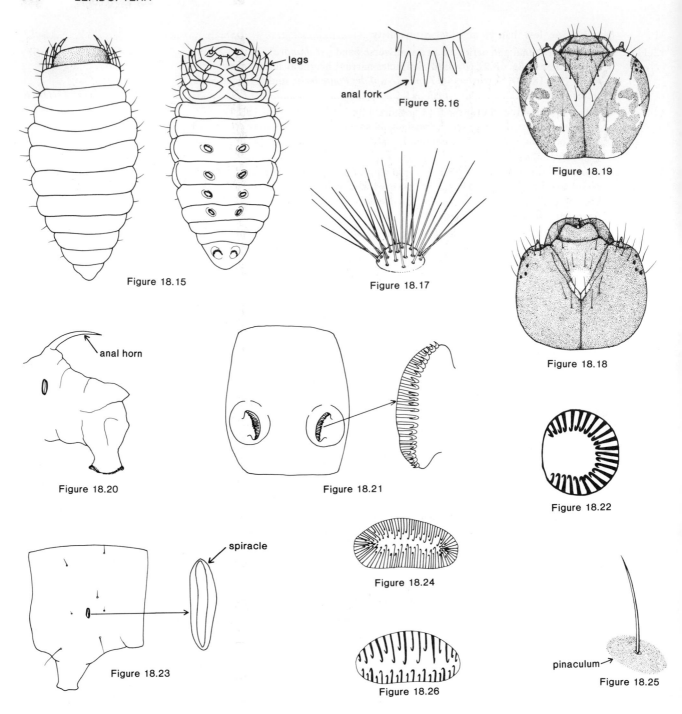

Figure 18.15.

anal fork
Figure 18.16

Figure 18.17

Figure 18.19

Figure 18.18

legs

anal horn

Figure 18.20

Figure 18.21

Figure 18.22

spiracle

Figure 18.23

Figure 18.24

Figure 18.26

pinaculum

Figure 18.25

Figure 18.15. Dorsal and ventral view of *Hyposmocoma* sp. (Cosmopterigidae).

Figure 18.16. Anal fork in *Archips* sp. (Tortricidae).

Figure 18.17. Verruca with tuft of setae.

Figure 18.18. Dorsal view of larval head of *Estigmene* sp. (Arctiidae).

Figure 18.19. Dorsal view of larval head of *Simyra* sp. (Noctuidae).

Figure 18.20. Lateral view of abdomen showing anal horn of Sphingidae.

Figure 18.21. Crochets of *Archanara oblonga* (Grote) (Noctuidae) (on abdominal segments 3-6).

Figure 18.22. Crochets of *Bellura* sp. (Noctuidae) (on abdominal segments 3-6).

Figure 18.23. Lateral view of larval abdominal segment of *Archanara* sp. (Noctuidae) showing spiracle.

Figure 18.24. Crochets of *Prionoxystus* sp. (Cossidae).

Figure 18.25. Pinaculum of *Crambus* sp. (Pyralidae).

Figure 18.26. Crochets of *Acentria* sp. (Pyralidae).

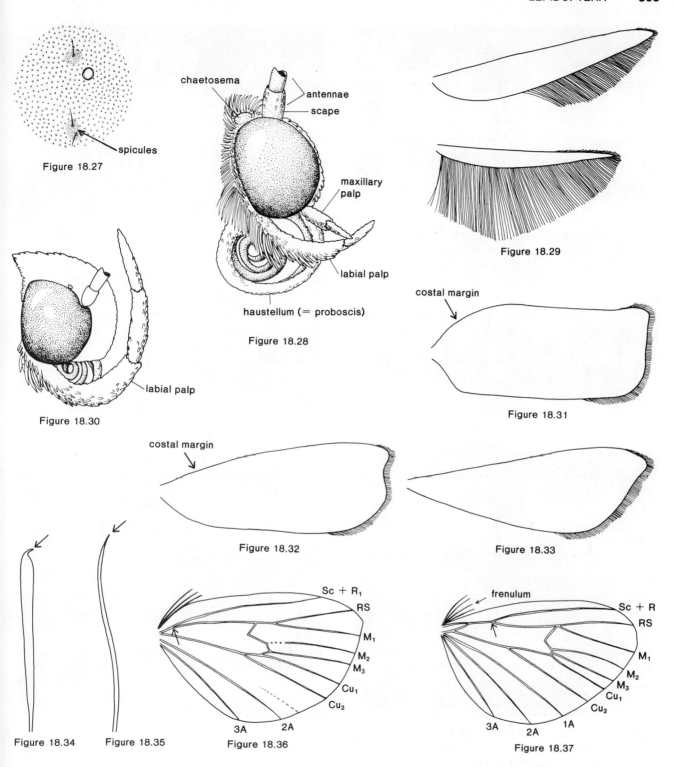

Figure 18.27

spicules

chaetosema

antennae

scape

maxillary
palp

labial palp

haustellum (= proboscis)

Figure 18.28

Figure 18.29

costal margin

Figure 18.31

labial palp

Figure 18.30

costal margin

Figure 18.32

Figure 18.33

Sc + R₁

RS

M₁

M₂

M₃

Cu₁

Cu₂

3A   2A

Figure 18.36

frenulum

Sc + R

RS

M₁

M₂

M₃

Cu₁

Cu₂

3A   2A   1A

Figure 18.37

Figure 18.34   Figure 18.35

Figure 18.27. Spicules of Olethreutidae.

Figure 18.28 Lateral view of adult Lepidoptera head showing diagnostic characters.

Figure 18.29. Front and hind wing of Cosmopterigidae.

Figure 18.30. Lateral view of adult Lepidoptera head showing recurved labial palpi (Cosmopterigidae).

Figure 18.31. Fore wing of Tortricidae.

Figure 18.32. Fore wing of Olethreutidae.

Figure 18.33. Fore wing of Pyralidae.

Figure 18.34. Antenna of Sphingidae.

Figure 18.35. Antenna of Noctuidae.

Figure 18.36. Hind wing of Noctuidae.

Figure 18.37. Hind wing of *Estigmene acrea* Dru. (Arctiidae).

Figure 18.38

Figure 18.40

Figure 18.39

Figure 18.41

Figure 18.42

Figure 18.43

Figure 18.38. Adult male of *Parapoynx maculalis* (Clemens) (Pyralidae).

Figure 18.39. Adult male of *Neocataclysta magnificalis* (Hubner) (Pyralidae).

Figure 18.40. Adult male of *Petrophila (Parargyractis) jaliscalis* (Schaus) (Pyralidae).

Figure 18.41. Adult male of *Eoparargyractis plevie* (Dyar) (Pyralidae).

Figure 18.42. Adults of Noctuidae. *a. Simyra henrici* (Grt.); *b. Archanara oblonga* (Grt.); *c. Arzama obliqua* Wlk.

Figure 18.43. Adults of Arctiidae. *a, Apantesis proxima* Guer.; *b, A. ornata* Pack.; *c, Estigmene acrea* Dru.; *d, Isia isabella* A. and S.

ADDITIONAL TAXONOMIC REFERENCES

General
Muller (1892); Quail (1904); Portier (1911, 1949); Tsou (1914); Fracker (1915); Heinrich (1916); Mosher (1916); Gerasimov (1937); Frohne (1939); Wesenberg-Lund (1943); Hinton (1946, 1948, 1956); Peterson (1948); Chu (1949, 1956); Patocka (1955); Capps (1956); Lange (1956a, b); Haggett (1955–1961); Speyer (1958); Welch (1959); Okumura (1961); MacKay (1963a, 1964, 1972); Klots (1966); Common (1970); Pennak (1978).

Regional faunas
California: Lange (1956a); Okumura (1961); Powell (1964).
Indiana and adjacent areas: McCafferty and Minno (1979).
New York: Forbes (1923, 1954, 1960).

Taxonomic treatments at the family and generic levels
(L=larvae; A=adults)
Cosmopterigidae: Hodges (1962)–A.
Cosmopterigidae (Cosmopteriginae): Hodges (1962)–A, Walsingham (1907)–A; Zimmerman (1978)–A.
Nepticulidae: Braun (1917)–L, A.
Noctuidae: Crumb (1929, 1956)–L; Forbes (1954)–L, A; MacKay and Rockburne (1958)–L; Beck (1960)–L.
Olethreutidae: MacKay and Rockburne (1958)–L; MacKay (1959, 1962a)–L; Beck (1960)–L.
Pyralidae: Forbes (1910)–L, A; Heinrich (1940)–A; Lange (1956a, b)–L, A; Hasenfuss (1960)–L; Munroe (1972–1973)–A.
Tortricidae: McDunnough (1933)–L; Swatchek (1958)–L; MacKay (1962b, 1963b)–L; Powell (1964)–L, A.

Table 18A. Summary of ecological and distributional data for *Lepidoptera*. (For definition of terms see Tables 6A–6C; table prepared by K. W. Cummins and W. H. Lange.)

Taxa (number of species in parentheses)	Habitat	Habit	Trophic Relationships	North American Distribution	Ecological References[*]
Pyralidae(148) (=Pyraustidae)	Generally lentic—vascular hydrophytes	Generally climbers, climbers—swimmers, burrowers (miners)	Generally shredders—herbivores (leaf eaters and miners, stem borers)		3, 1280, 1316, 1391, 1886, 1947, 1948, 24 2479, 2614, 2620
Nymphulinae(47) (=Hydrocampinae)	Generally lentic—vascular hydrophytes	Generally climbers, climbers—swimmers	Shredders—herbivores		1031, 1280, 1286, 13 1391, 1419, 1420, 17 2479, 2614
Ambiini(3) *Undulambia*(3)	Lentic—margins (on ferns)	Climbers	Shredders—herbivores	Southern Florida	1031, 1741
Nymphulini(23) *Chrysendeton*(3)				Southeastern United States	1391, 1741
Contiger(1)				Southeastern United States	1391, 1741
Langessa(1)	Lentic—vascular hydrophytes *(Nymphaea, Nymphoides)*	Climbers	Shredders—herbivores	Widespread (common in Florida)	1031, 1391, 1741
Munroessa(4)	Lentic and lotic—vascular hydrophytes *(Potamogeton, Vallisneria, Nymphaea, Ludwigia, Lemna, Brasenia, etc.)*	Climbers	Shredders—herbivores	Widespread	1031, 1391, 1598, 16 1741
Neocataclysta(1)	Lentic and lotic—vascular hydrophytes (floating zone: *Lemna*)	Climbers—swimmers (case constructed of *Lemna*)	Shredders—herbivores (on *Lemna*)	Nova Scotia and southern Quebec to Florida	775, 1391, 1741, 247 1598
Nymphula(1) (=*Hydrocampa* of some authors)	Lentic—vascular hydrophytes	Climbers—swimmers (case constructed of sedges, Cyperaceae)	Shredders—herbivores (chewers and miners)	Northeastern United States and southeastern Canada	101, 158, 159, 776, 8 1003, 1231, 1391, 16 1613, 1738, 1741, 21 2239, 2620, 2692‡
Nymphuliella(1)	Lentic—bog pools	Climbers (case constructed of *Cephalozia fruitans*)	Shredders	Northeastern United States	1020, 1391, 1741
Oligostigmoides(1)				Texas	1391, 1741
Parapoynx(6) (=*Paraponyx* of some authors)	Lentic—vascular hydrophytes *(Nuphar, Nymphaea, Brasenia, Potamogeton, Bacopa, Myriophyllum, Vallisneria, Nymphoides, Orortium, etc.)*	Climbers—swimmers (cases of a wide variety of aquatic plants)	Shredders—herbivores	Widespread	91, 159, 774, 989, 10 1598, 1612, 1613, 21 2608, 2611, 2612, 26
Synclita(4)	Lentic—vascular hydrophytes *(Nymphaea, Potamogeton, Lemna, Brasenia, etc.)*	Climbers—swimmers (cases constructed of pieces of leaves or *Lemna*)	Shredders—herbivores (chewers)	Widespread (introduced into Hawaii)	776, 989, 1031, 1280 1391, 1598, 1741, 27
Argyactini(21) *Eoparargyractis*(3)	Lentic—littoral?			East (Canada to Florida)	715, 1391, 1741
Neargyractis(1)				Florida	1391, 1741
Petrophila(14) (=*parargyractis*)†	Lotic—erosional, lentic—erosional (algae, diatoms)	Clingers (silk-retreat makers)	Scrapers	Widespread	153, 1391, 1419, 142 1421, 1474, 1598, 17 2479, 2481, 2482 §	
Oxyelophila(1)				Texas	1391, 1741
Usingeriessa(2)	Lotic—erosional?			California, Arizona, Texas	1391, 1741

[*]Emphasis on trophic relationships.
†See "Checklist of the Lepidoptera north of Mexico," London, 1983.
‡*Nymphula ekthlipsis* (Grote) is the only species known in the genus from North America; some of the references refer to species now placed in related genera.
§Unpublished data, K. W. Cummins, Oregon State University.
‖Unpublished data, W. H. Lange, Department of Entomology, University of California.

ble 18A—*Continued*

Taxa (number of species in parentheses)	Habitat	Habit	Trophic Relationships	North American Distribution	Ecological References[*]
ioenobiinae(13)	Generally lentic—vascular hydrophytes (emergent zone)	Generally burrowers (miners—stem borers)	Generally shredders—herbivores		1741
Acentria(1) (=*Acentropus*)	Lentic—vascular hydrophytes (*Cerato-phyllum, Potamogeton, Elodea, Hydrilla, Myriophyl-lum, Elatine,* etc.)	Climbers—swimmers, (early instars, stem borers; later instars, in retreats made of plant material)	Shredders—herbivores	Canada and eastern United States	110, 168, 299, 777, 1262, 1391, 1598, 1737, 1741, 1820, 2469, 2470
Schoenobius(12)	Lentic—vascular hydrophytes (emergent zone; *Eleocharis, Carex, Scirpus;* semiaquatic)	Burrowers (miners—stem borers below water)	Shredders—herbivores (miners)	Widespread	808, 811, 1598, 2607
Crambinae(8)	Lentic—vascular hydrophytes (emergent zone)	Burrowers (miners—stem borers below water)	Shredders—herbivores (miners)		811, 1598, 1741
Chilo(7)	Lentic—vascular hydrophytes (emergent zone; *Scirpus, Juncus, Eleocharis, Oryza*)	Burrowers (miners—stem borers)	Shredders—herbivores (miners)	Widespread	808, 810, 1598
Occidentalia(1)	Lentic—vascular hydrophytes (emergent zone; *Scirpus*)	Burrowers (miners—stem borers)	Shredders—herbivores (miners)	Eastern United States	811, 1598
Pyraustinae(80) *Ostrinia* (=*Pyrausta*)	Lentic—vascular hydrophytes *(Potamoge-ton penitalis)* (emergent and floating zone; *Eupatorium, Po-lygonum,* and Nym-phaceae)	Burrowers (in leaves—stem borers) (adapted to aquatic locomotion)	Shredders—herbivores	Widespread	3, 1598, 2610
pticulidae(70) (=Stigmellidae)					808, 811
Nepticula(70)	Lentic—vascular hydrophytes (emergent zone; *Scirpus, Eleocharis*)	Burrowers (miners—stem borers)	Shredders—herbivores (miners)	Widespread	
smopterigidae(371+) (=Lavernidae)	Generally lentic—vascular hydrophytes	Generally burrowers (miners)	Shredders—herbivores		402, 808
Cosmopteryx(20)	Lentic—vascular hydrophytes (emergent zone)	Burrowers (miners—stem borers)	Shredders—herbivores (miners)	Widespread	402
Lymnaecia(1)	Lentic—vascular hydrophytes (emergent and floating zones; *Typha*)	Burrowers (in heads, seeds, or stems)	Shredders—herbivores	Widespread	402
Cosmopteriginae(350+?) *Hyposmocoma* (350+)	Lentic—margins (on lichens, algae, and mosses) (unknown number of species semiaquatic)	Climbers (in cases of sand particles, silk, and debris on emergent portion of basalt rocks)	Shredders—herbivores (chewers and scrapers)	Endemic to Hawaii	2568, 2815‖

nphasis on trophic relationships.
npublished data, W. H. Lange, Department of Entomology, University of California.

Table 18A—*Continued*

Taxa (number of species in parentheses)	Habitat	Habit	Trophic Relationships	North American Distribution	Ecological References[*]
Noctuidae(11) (=Phalaenidae)	Generally lentic—vascular hydrophytes	Generally burrowers and climbers	Shredders—herbivores		1507
Archanara(4)	Lentic—vascular hydrophytes (emergent and floating zones; *Typha, Scirpus, Juncus, Sparganium*)	Burrowers (miners—stem borers)	Shredders—herbivores	Widespread	473, 808, 1391, 1598
Bellura(4) (=*Arzama*)	Lentic—vascular hydrophytes (emergent and floating zones; *Typha, Nuphar, Pontederia, Eichornia, Nelumbo, Symplocarpus, Sagittaria, Spanganium*)	Burrowers—leaf miners (early instars); petiole and stem borers (later instars)	Shredders—herbivores (miners)	Central, East, South	159, 402, 473, 1459, 1598, 1612, 1613, 252 2605, 2764
Neoerastria(1?)	Lentic—vascular hydrophytes (emergent zone)	Burrowers	Shredders—herbivores	Midwest	1598
Oligia(1?)	Lentic—vascular hydrophytes (emergent zone; *Scirpus*)	Burrowers—leaf miners (early instars), stem borers (later instars)	Shredders—herbivores	Midwest	1598
Simyra(1)	Lentic—vascular hydrophytes (emergent and floating zones; *Typha, Polygonum, Salix, Graminaceae*)	Climbers	Shredders—herbivores (chewers)	Widespread	473 ‖
Tortricidae(35) *Archips*(35) (=*Choristoneura*)	Lentic—vascular hydrophytes (emergent and floating zones; *Typha* and other plants)	Burrowers—climbers	Shredders—herbivores	Widespread	402

*Emphasis on trophic relationships.

‖Unpublished data, W. H. Lange, Department of Entomology, University of California.

Aquatic Coleoptera

19

David S. White
*University of Michigan,
Ann Arbor*

Warren U. Brigham
*Illinois Natural History
Survey, Champaign*

John T. Doyen
*University of California,
Berkeley*

INTRODUCTION

Coleoptera comprise the largest order of insects and, with approximately 5,000 aquatic members, ranks as one of the major groups of freshwater arthropods. Moreover, beetles occupy a broad spectrum of aquatic habitats, including such systems as cold, rapid mountain streams, brackish, stagnant waters of estuaries and salt marshes, and the intertidal zone of rocky seashores. Beetles are important in aquatic food chains—large numbers are consumed by fish and waterfowl—but few species reach the high population densities or biomass levels exhibited by some Ephemeroptera, Trichoptera, or Diptera, and beetles are not dominant organisms in most aquatic habitats. Leech and Chandler (1956) and Leach and Sanderson (1959) provide excellent discussions of the families of Coleoptera, with keys to adults and larvae of North American genera. Brigham (1982) gives keys to genera and species of the eastern fauna along with extensive summaries of ecology. The best general identification manuals for adult North American Coleoptera are Blatchley (1910) and Arnett (1960). Intertidal species are treated by Doyen (1975, 1976), and the worldwide work by Bertrand (1972) is the most comprehensive available on immatures. General treatments of aquatic Coleoptera, as well as references to more detailed taxonomic works, are given below and in table 19A.

Most aquatic beetles are substrate dwellers. Some notable exceptions, including adult Dytiscidae and Hydrophilidae, are efficient swimmers and must return to the surface periodically to renew their air supply (see chap. 4). Numerous species, including virtually all marine forms, inhabit cracks, crevices, or self-constructed burrows, and seldom if ever venture into open water.

Aquatic Coleoptera in both adult and larval stages usually are aquatic, but in Psephenidae, Helodidae, and Ptilodactylidae adults are terrestrial, sometimes occurring some distance from water. The dryopid *Helichus* is one of the few insects in which the adult is aquatic and the larva terrestrial. Adults of most species leave the water temporarily on dispersal flights, which may occur once (Elmidae) or repeatedly (many Dytiscidae, Hydrophilidae).

Feeding habits of aquatic Coleoptera are extremely variable (table 19A) and include all the categories described in chapter 6. Predators either engulf their prey or inject digestive enzymes through piercing mouthparts (especially larvae of Dytiscidae and Hydrophilidae). Some large dytiscids attack small fish or tadpoles. The hydroscaphids (*Hydroscapha*) are scrapers and unusual in that their diet consists largely of blue-green algae.

Respiration in aquatic beetles conforms to four major modes (chap. 4): (1) reliance on self-contained air reserves (e.g., Dytiscidae, Hydrophilidae, Hydraenidae); (2) transcuticular respiration, with or without tracheal gills (larvae of most families); (3) plastron respiration (adult Dryopidae, Elmidae, etc.); and (4) piercing plant tissues (e.g., larval Chrysomelidae). In most species having an air reservoir, it occupies the space beneath the elytra, and these beetles must regularly return to the surface to renew depleted air supplies. Beetles using plastron respiration mostly occupy fast-moving, well-oxygenated water and are quite sensitive to pollutants that act as wetting agents. Representatives of types 2, 3, and 4 may remain submerged indefinitely.

Adults of most aquatic beetles probably survive a single season or part of a season, but some dytiscids, hydrophilids, and elmids have been maintained for years in aquariums. Species with terrestrial adults (Psephenidae, Helodidae, Ptilodactylidae) frequently reproduce and die after a short time, sometimes without feeding.

Although *Gyrinus* species form schools of thousands of individuals, aquatic beetles do not form mating aggregations. However, species with short-lived adults often emerge synchronously and may be locally very abundant. Copulation most often occurs with the male mounted dorsally on the female and may be preceded by stroking, stridulation, or other courtship behaviors. The eggs, varying from one (Hydroscaphidae) to hundreds (Psephenidae), are deposited singly or in masses in diverse situations. Most species with truly aquatic larvae oviposit underwater, but helodids apparently oviposit in the damp marginal zone, which is also used by georyssids, heterocerids, and other families with subaquatic larvae. Some dytiscids insert the eggs into plant tissue, and a few hydrophilid females carry the egg mass about beneath the abdomen. Eggs are generally simple ovoids without a thickened or sculptured chorion. Most are laid naked, but those of hydrophilids and some hydraenids are enclosed in silken cases.

Eggs usually hatch in about one to two weeks, but eclosion may be delayed for many months in exceptional cases.

Most aquatic Coleoptera pass through from three to eight larval instars, and require an average of six to eight months to develop, with a single generation per year in temperate regions. In almost all species pupation is terrestrial, usually in cells excavated by the larvae under stones, logs, or other objects or occasionally in mud cells on aquatic vegetation (some Gyrinidae). Noteridae, Curculionidae, Chrysomelidae, and possibly some Hydrophilidae spin silk cocoons enclosing a bubble of air, within which they pupate while submerged. Psephenidae pupae are pharate, forming beneath the cuticle of the last larval instar, usually under stones at the water's edge. Just prior to pupation, the last larval instar becomes a quiescent prepupa, when diapause may occur. Few Coleoptera diapause as pupae and generally transform to adults in about two to three weeks.

EXTERNAL MORPHOLOGY

Adults

Most adult beetles, including nearly all aquatic members, are characterized by a heavily sclerotized, usually compact body. The combination of elytra (see below) and antennae with 11 or fewer segments will separate nearly all beetles from other insects with only cursory examination.

Head and Mouthparts: Coleoptera are mandibulate insects, and the mouthparts are usually visible without dissection. Mandibular structure is broadly indicative of feeding habits. In herbivore scrapers (Dryopidae, Elmidae), the mandible bears a basal flattened molar or grinding lobe as well as a sharp, anterior incisor lobe. In predaceous forms the molar lobe is usually absent.

Posterad of the labium the head capsule consists of a gula, delimited by paired gular sutures, except in Curculionidae, where the sutures are coalesced (fig. 19.309). Configuration of the antennae is used extensively in identification at all levels; important types are illustrated.

Thorax and Legs: In most beetles the pronotum has encroached ventrally to the region of the procoxae where notum and sternum are separated by a suture (fig. 19.150). In Dytiscidae and related families the lateral prothoracic region is occupied by the pleuron so that both notopleural and sternopleural sutures are present (fig. 19.99).

Dorsally, much of the thorax and abdomen are concealed by the elytra in most beetles. Morphologically the elytra represent heavily sclerotized fore wings without crossveins. Flying wings (hind wings), present in most aquatic beetles at rest, are folded beneath the elytra.

The number of tarsal segments on each leg is critical in identification to family. By convention, these numbers are designated by a three-digit tarsal formula (e.g., 5–5–5), indicating the number of tarsal segments (tarsomeres) on the anterior, middle, and posterior legs, respectively. The claws are not counted as separate segments. The tibiae and/or tarsi may bear fringes of long, slender swimming hairs (figs. 19.101, 19.150), which adhere to the leg in dried specimens and may not be visible without wetting.

Abdomen: Normally, only the abdominal sternites are visible. In Dytiscidae and related families the posterior coxae are greatly enlarged, dividing the basal sternite into two separate sclerites (fig. 19.99). In counting the number of abdominal sternites, those segments associated with the genitalia and normally drawn into the abdomen should not be tallied. They almost always differ markedly in sculpturing, color, and degree of sclerotization from the external sternites.

Larvae

Larval Coleoptera are exceedingly diverse. Among aquatic forms, the presence of a distinct, sclerotized head capsule with mandibles, maxillae, labium, and two- or three-segmented antennae (except in Helodidae, which have long, multisegmented antennae) are reliable distinguishing features. All but curculionids and a few hydrophilids have three pairs of thoracic legs bearing one or two apical claws. Beetle pupae are exarate (appendages not fused to body) and bear a general similarity to adults.

Cranial Structures: Mouthparts are extremely important in larval classification and identification, and careful dissection may be necessary to view critical structures. As in adults, the mandibles may possess or lack a molar lobe. In some larvae a fleshy cushionlike or digitate prostheca is inserted on the mandible just anterior to the molar lobe (fig. 19.168). The maxilla may bear a separate galea and lacinea or these may be united as a single lobe, the mala. The maxillary palp is inserted on the palpiger, a projection of the stipes, which is greatly enlarged in Hydrophilidae, appearing as a separate segment of the palp (fig. 19.122).

Abdominal Structures: A variety of gill-like appendages may be present laterally or ventrally on any segment (figs. 19.46, 19.131, 19.213). "Gills" may be simple or branched, dispersed or clustered, unsegmented or articulated. In some families the gills are concealed in a pocket beneath the terminal abdominal sternite (fig. 19.262), which forms a lid or operculum, and dissection is frequently necessary for examination.

Diverse unsegmented, immovable dorsal, or dorsolateral appendages occur on the apical or preapical abdominal segment (figs. 19.19, 19.21). These terminal appendages are usually relatively short and strongly sclerotized. They are termed *urogomphi* (singular, urogomphus) regardless of position or origin. Movable appendages, sometimes segmented and often elongate and filamentous (figs. 19.71, 19.167), may be present also and presumably are homologous to the cerci of many other insects.

LITTORAL COLEOPTERA

Of all the orders, except perhaps Diptera and Hemiptera, Coleoptera is unique in that it includes many semiaquatic species that inhabit littoral zone environments. Fresh, brackish, and saline waters all support littoral zone faunas, similar in family representation but differing in species composition. Aquatic marine Coleoptera are almost entirely members of families that commonly frequent the littoral zone and are discussed separately below. In freshwaters, however, families well represented in the littoral zone are almost entirely absent from truly aquatic habitats. For example, the large families Staphylinidae and Carabidae contain hundreds of species that occur regularly, if not exclusively, around water. Yet only a few Carabidae could be called aquatic, even in the loosest sense. For example, species of *Nebria* may temporarily submerge to escape predators but require terrestrial situations to survive and reproduce. In general, littoral zone existence has not been an evolutionary pathway to aquatic habits.

The littoral zone comprises several distinct habitats. The interstices in gravel or coarse sand substrates alongside bodies of water support a fauna of minute beetles such as Sphaeriidae, Hydraenidae, and Hydrophilidae. Many of these species are actually aquatic, living in the water held in interstitial spaces in the substrate. A much larger number of species frequents the surfaces of damp sand or mud adjacent to standing or running water. Adult and larval Carabidae and Staphylinidae are the most obvious and diverse element in this situation, often very dense on mud or sandbars, especially about drying ponds or intermittent streams. Limnichidae and Georyssidae also frequent this zone and may be locally abundant. Adult and larval Heteroceridae inhabit burrows they excavate beside streams. Recently emergent sandbars and banks are favorite locations, but some species dig in mud, and a few live on intertidal mud flats. Larval *Helichus* (Dryopidae) burrow through moist sand adjacent to streams and are most likely submerged during spring floods. Early instars of *Acneus* (Psephenidae) are apparently aquatic, like the other members of the family. Later instars cling to moist stones just above the waterline and drown if submerged (G. Ulrich, pers. comm.). Undersides of stones and logs, including those partially submerged, provide shelter for many inhabitants of the littoral zone, which may emerge nocturnally to forage. Accumulations of water-borne organic debris also shelter many littoral zone species. Sampling with Berlaise funnels is effective, especially in obtaining minute forms such as Ptiliidae.

In their peripheral areas, littoral zone habitats merge with purely terrestrial ones. Along steep-banked streams the transition may be abrupt, but along swampy streams and ponds it is almost imperceptible. In addition to the littoral zone inhabitants, many terrestrial taxa are often regular members of such intermediate communities. In particular, members of the terrestrial soil fauna (Pselaphidae, Ptiliidae, Leiodidae, Scydmaenidae, etc.) are likely to occur along with Lampyridae, Cantharidae, and others.

MARINE COLEOPTERA

Although numerous species representing most families of Coleoptera inhabit maritime environments, very few are marine in the sense of regularly occupying aquatic situations. Moreover, the marine representatives are almost exclusively from families found in littoral zone habitats rather than those that are truly aquatic. Thus, Staphylinidae and Carabidae are the dominant marine Coleoptera in numbers of individuals and species. Other primarily terrestrial families with marine representatives include Melyridae, Limnichidae, Salpingidae, and Curculionidae. In contrast, marine representatives of freshwater families include only a few Hydrophilidae and Hydraenidae. Nearly all marine forms in North America occur on the Pacific coast with a small number of Staphylinidae recorded from the Atlantic.

With the exception of a few Hydrophilidae genera (*Berosus, Enochrus,* etc.) that swim in brackish estuarine waters, marine Coleoptera are substrate dwellers. Some forms inhabit air-filled crevices in rocks. This group includes most Carabidae, many Staphylinidae, and *Aegialites* (Salpingidae). Many Staphylinidae (and a few exotic Carabidae) inhabit self-constructed burrows in sandy beaches. In most cases these burrows probably entrap air. Thus, most marine Coleoptera are not in direct contact with the water and have no special respiratory mechanisms. Exceptions include *Ochthebius* (Hydraenidae), which breathe with a "gill" of air held by the hydrofuge ventral cuticle.

Life histories of North American species are largely unknown, but studies of European relatives suggest that adults and larvae have similar habits and requirements. Various instars typically occur together in colonies. Dispersal is apparently by ocean currents, since most submarine forms lack wings and have fused elytra. In contrast, beetles inhabiting the supratidal zones of beaches are commonly active, powerful fliers.

KEYS TO THE FAMILIES
OF AQUATIC COLEOPTERA

Aquatic Coleoptera include members of three suborders (see chap. 8) and many subfamilies. The following keys are designed primarily for aquatic beetles, including marine forms. Families that regularly inhabit the littoral zone, though not strictly aquatic, are included since they frequently appear in aquatic samples. Many members of families that are not aquatic may occasionally appear about water, and those that have merely fallen into the water or have been caught in floods cannot be identified with the keys.

Taxonomic usage generally follows that in Arnett (1960). We are conservative by combining closely related taxa into families. For example, the Psephenoididae, Eubriidae, and Psephenidae of Bertrand (1972) are considered here as subfamilies of Psephenidae. Likewise, Hydrochinae, Sperchiinae, Epimetopinae, and Helophorinae, elevated to families in some works, are treated as subfamilies of Hydrophilidae.

The relationships of the genera included here in Ptilodactylidae are poorly understood. The genus *Stenocolus* is morphologically divergent from other Ptilodactylidae and is to be placed in a separate family, Eulachadidae. The genus *Araeopidius* is also divergent and probably will be removed from Ptilodactylidae.

The genus *Lutrochus,* included here in Limnichidae, differs from other members of that family in abdominal structure and is to be placed in the family Lutrochidae.

Helodidae (commonly accepted in North America) and Cyphonidae long have been used synonymously with Scirtidae. Since Scirtidae is the oldest name, it is nomenclaturally correct (Pope 1975) and is used here.

1. Mesothoracic wings (elytra) present, usually covering entire abdomen (fig. 19.30), sometimes only its base (figs. 19.32–19.33); antennae with at least 4 segments, usually 6 or more (figs. 19.28, 19.35); tarsi with at least 3 segments (figs. 19.30, 19.33)[a] .... ***ADULTS***

1′. Mesothoracic wings absent (figs. 19.1–19.2); antennae with 3 or fewer segments;[b] tarsi with a single segment (figs. 19.4, 19.12) .... ***LARVAE***

Larvae

1. Legs absent (fig. 19.15) 10

1′. Legs sometimes small, but always with 3–6 clearly defined segments (figs. 19.12, 19.53, 19.55, 19.74, 19.134) 2

2(1′). Legs (excluding claws) with 5 segments; tarsi with 2 claws (figs. 19.4, 19.74) (exception: HALIPLIDAE with single claw) 3

2′. Legs with 3–4 segments (figs. 19.12, 19.134); tarsi with single claw (fig. 19.134) 10

3(2). Abdomen with 2 pairs of stout, terminal hooks on segment 10 (fig. 19.47); abdominal segments 1–9 bearing lateral gills (fig. 19.46) .... ***GYRINIDAE*** (p. 373)

3′. Abdomen without hooks on terminal segment; abdominal segments usually without lateral gills, occasionally with ventral gills (fig. 19.213) 4

4(3′). Abdomen with 8 segments 6

4′. Abdomen with 9 or 10 segments 5

5(4′). Tarsi with single claw (figs. 19.53, 19.55); mandibles grooved internally (fig. 19.57); at least last larval instar with erect, dorsal projections from thoracic and abdominal tergites (figs. 19.52, 19.54) .... ***HALIPLIDAE*** (p. 374)

5′. Tarsi with 2 claws (as in fig. 19.4); mandibles not grooved; tergites without projections (fig. 19.1) .... ***CARABIDAE***[1,2,3,6]

6(4). Abdominal segment 8 with a pair of large terminal spiracles 7

6′. Abdominal segment 8 without spiracles .... ***HYGROBIIDAE***[4,6]

7(6). Cerci slender, longer (usually much longer) than 1st abdominal segment (fig. 19.71) .... ***DYTISCIDAE*** (in part) (p. 377)

7′. Cerci stout, shorter than 1st abdominal segment (fig. 19.2) or rudimentary or absent 8

8(7′). Thorax and abdomen strongly flattened; tergites expanded laterally as thin, flat projections (fig. 19.2); gular sutures single (fig. 19.3) .... ***AMPHIZOIDAE—Amphizoa*** (p. 373)

8′. Thorax and abdomen round or subcylindrical in cross section; tergites not expanded as flat, platelike projections; gular sutures double 9

9(8′). Legs short, stout, adapted for digging (fig. 19.104); mandibles with enlarged molar portion (fig. 19.105) .... ***NOTERIDAE*** (p. 388)

9′. Legs long, slender, adapted for swimming (fig. 19.74); mandibles falcate (sickleshaped), without enlarged molar portion (figs. 19.72–19.73) .... ***DYTISCIDAE*** (in part) (p. 377)

10(1,2′). Labrum separated from clypeus by distinct suture 14

10′. Labrum not represented as separate sclerite (fig. 19.130) (the labium may be visible dorsally) 11

11(10′). Body round or subcylindrical in cross section; head projecting anteriorly from prothorax and visible from above (fig. 19.131); movable cerci often visible (fig. 19.167) 12

[a]Lepiceridae, not occurring in United States, have a single tarsomere.

[b]Larvae of Helodidae have numerous, filamentous antennal segments.

[1]Subaquatic or inhabiting littoral region.

[2]Includes intertidal species in North America.

[3]Larvae of *Brachinus* spp. (Carabidae), which are ectoparasitic on pupae of Hydrophilidae, have 3 leg segments, and a single claw.

[4]Family does not occur in United States.

[6]Keys to genera not given.

11'. Body dorsoventrally flattened, with large, transverse thoracic and abdominal tergites; pronotum expanded anteriorly, usually concealing head from above (figs. 19.5–19.6) .... *LAMPYRIDAE*[1,6]

12(11). Maxilla with palpiger appearing as a segment of palp (figs. 19.122, 19.133); spiracles biforous (having 2 openings) (fig. 19.111) 13

12'. Maxilla with palpiger appearing as part of stipes (fig. 19.7); spiracles annular (ring-shaped) .... *STAPHYLINIDAE*[1,2,6] (in part) (p. 400)

13(12). Abdomen with 10 segments (fig. 19.10); cerci very short, palpilliform (fig. 19.11); legs short, 3-segmented (fig. 19.12) .... *GEORYSSIDAE*[1]—*Georyssus*

13'. Abdomen with 8 segments, or rarely , if with 10 segments, then cerci long, 2–3-segmented, and legs long, 5-segmented (figs. 19.112, 19.120, 19.131) .... *HYDROPHILIDAE* (p. 392)

14(10). Thorax and abdomen short, obese, without distinct sclerites (figs. 19.13–19.15); legs reduced (fig. 19.13) or absent (fig. 19.15) 15

14'. Thorax and abdomen cylindrical, flattened, or fusiform (spindle-shaped), but not markedly obese; thoracic and abdominal tergites clearly defined; legs adapted for walking 16

15(14). Legs very small but complete and visible (fig. 19.13); spiracles on 8th abdominal segment forming large, sclerotized dorsal hooks (fig. 19.14) .... *CHRYSOMELIDAE*[6] (p. 419)

15'. Legs entirely absent (fig. 19.15); spiracles sometimes set on tubercles, but 8th segment never with sclerotized dorsal hooks .... *CURCULIONIDAE*[2,6] (p. 422)

16(14'). At least 8th abdominal tergite bearing pairs of fleshy, articulated, fingerlike lobes (fig. 19.16); antennae very short, 2-segmented (fig. 19.17); minute larvae, less than 2 mm long 17

16'. Abdominal tergites without dorsal lobes; antennae 3-segmented or more 19

17(16). Fingerlike articulated lobes present on abdominal segments 1–8 18

17'. Fingerlike lobes present only on abdominal segments 1 and 8 (fig. 19.16) .... *HYDROSCAPHIDAE*—*Hydroscapha* (p. 390)

18(17). Fingerlike lobes on abdominal segments 1–8 approximately 1.5 times as long as wide; antenna with 2nd segment about 2–3 times as long as broad and bearing minute, lateral appendage (fig. 19.17) .... *SPHAERIIDAE*[1]—*Sphaerius*

18'. Fingerlike lobes on abdominal segments 1–8 more than 10 times as long as wide; antenna with 2nd segment about 4–5 times as long as broad, lacking appendage .... *TORRIDINICOLIDAE*[4,6]

19(16'). Abdomen with 10 segments; 9th segment bearing articulated, 1- or 2-jointed cerci (fig. 19.167) 20

19'. Abdomen with 9 segments; 8th or 9th segment sometimes bearing immovable urogomphi (figs. 19.19, 19.21), but articulated cerci never present 22

20(19). Mandibles with large, asperate (roughened) molar lobe (fig. 19.168) 21

20'. Mandibles falcate (sickle-shaped), without molar lobe (fig. 19.8) .... *STAPHYLINIDAE*[1,2,6] (in part) (p. 400)

21(20). Tenth abdominal segment with pair of recurved ventral hooks (fig. 19.169); cerci with 2 segments (fig. 19.167) .... *HYDRAENIDAE*[1,6] (p. 398)

21'. Tenth abdominal segment without hooks; cerci with single segment (as in fig. 19.9) .... *PTILIIDAE*[1,2,6]

22(19'). Antennae much longer than head (fig. 19.183), multiarticulate (many jointed) .... *SCIRTIDAE* (p. 402)

22'. Antennae short, with 2–3 segments 23

23(22'). Body cylindrical, subcylindrical, or fusiform; head and legs visible in dorsal aspect 24

23'. Body extremely flattened, with thoracic and abdominal tergites expanded laterally as thin laminae concealing head and legs from above (figs. 19.195–19.196) .... *PSEPHENIDAE* (p. 404)

24(23). Ninth abdominal segment with a lidlike operculum covering the anal region ventrally (figs. 19.221, 19.262); abdominal sternites 1–8 never bearing gills 25

---

[1]Subaquatic or inhabiting littoral region.
[2]Includes intertidal species in North America.
[4]Family does not occur in United States.
[6]Keys to genera not given.

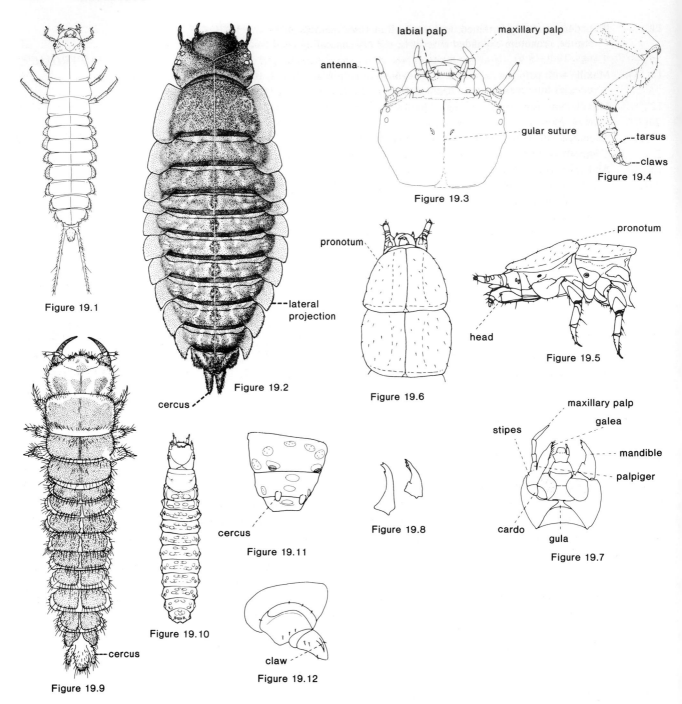

Figure 19.1

Figure 19.2

lateral projection

cercus

labial palp   maxillary palp

antenna

gular suture

tarsus

claws

Figure 19.4

Figure 19.3

pronotum

pronotum

head

Figure 19.5

Figure 19.6

cercus

Figure 19.9

Figure 19.10

cercus

Figure 19.11

Figure 19.8

maxillary palp

galea

stipes

mandible

palpiger

cardo

gula

Figure 19.7

claw

Figure 19.12

Figure 19.1. *Chlaenius* sp. (Carabidae) larva, dorsal aspect.

Figure 19.2. *Amphizoa* sp. (Amphizoidae) larva, dorsal aspect.

Figure 19.3. *Amphizoa* sp. (Amphizoidae) larva, ventral aspect of head.

Figure 19.4. *Amphizoa* sp. (Amphizoidae) larva, metathoracic leg.

Figure 19.5. Lampyridae larva, lateral aspect of head and thorax.

Figure 19.6. Lampyridae larva, dorsal aspect of head and thorax.

Figure 19.7. *Piestus* sp. (Staphylinidae) larva, ventral aspect of head.

Figure 19.8. *Oxytelus* sp. (left) and *Piestus* sp. (right) larvae (Staphylinidae), mandibles.

Figure 19.9. *Thinopinus* sp. (Staphylinidae) larva, dorsal aspect.

Figure 19.10. *Georyssus* sp. (Georyssidae) larva, dorsal aspect (after Van Emden 1956).

Figure 19.11. *Georyssus* sp. (Georyssidae) larva, abdominal apex.

Figure 19.12. *Georyssus* sp. (Georyssidae) larva, leg (after Van Emden 1956).

24′.   Ninth abdominal segment without operculum; abdominal sternites 1–8 sometimes bearing fasciculate (clustered) gills; fig. 19.213 27

25(24).   Terminal abdominal segment rounded posteriorly (fig. 19.221); head capsule with groups of 6 ocelli, 5 lateral and 1 ventral, or eyes absent 26

25′.   Terminal abdominal segment bifid or slightly emarginate (notched) posteriorly and with lateral ridges (fig. 19.231); head capsule with groups of 5 lateral ocelli .... *ELMIDAE* (p. 410)

26(25).   Opercular chamber containing 2 retractile hooks and 3 tufts of retractile gills (fig. 19.262); mandibles with prostheca (fig. 19.234) .... *LIMNICHIDAE* (p. 408)

26′.   Opercular chamber without hooks or gills; mandibles without prostheca (fig. 19.222) .... *DRYOPIDAE*[1] (p. 410)

27(24′).   Abdomen with distinct tufts of gills, either restricted to anal region (as in fig. 19.262) or present on segments 1–7 (fig. 19.213) .... *PTILODACTYLIDAE* (p. 406)

27′.   Abdomen without gills 28

28(27′).   Abdomen bearing prominent, spinelike urogomphi on terminal segment (figs. 19.19, 19.21) 29

28′.   Urogomphi absent; 9th abdominal segment rounded 31

29(28).   Urogomphi bifid (fig. 19.19); spiracles raised on tubercles; figure 19.18 .... *SALPINGIDAE*[2,6]

29′.   Urogomphi with single points (fig. 19.21); spiracles not elevated 30

30(29′).   Epicranial sutures lyre-shaped (fig. 19.20) .... *ANTHICIDAE*[1,6]

30′.   Epicranial sutures Y-shaped (fig. 19.22) .... *MELYRIDAE*[1,2,6]

31(28′).   Mouthparts prognathous; median epicranial suture absent (fig. 19.23) .... *HETEROCERIDAE*[1,6]

31′.   Mouthparts hypognathous; median epicranial suture present (fig. 19.24) .... *TENEBRIONIDAE*[1,2,6]

Adults

1.   Hind coxae expanded as broad, flattened plates covering all or part of abdominal sternites 1–3 (figs. 19.27, 19.63) 2

1′.   Hind coxae sometimes extending posteriorly along midline (figs. 19.34, 19.99), but never as broad plates 4

2(1).   Hind coxal plates meeting along midline (fig. 19.63) 3

2′.   Hind coxal plates widely separated; figure 19.27; minute, flattened beetles less than 2 mm long; figure 19.26 .... *HYDROSCAPHIDAE* (in part)—*Hydroscapha* (p. 300)

3(2).   Hind coxal plates completely covering 2 or 3 basal abdominal segments (fig. 19.63) and concealing all but apices of hind femora; beetles more than 3 mm long; figure 19.64 .... *HALIPLIDAE* (p. 374)

3′.   Hind coxal plates exposing abdominal segments laterally; bases of hind femora exposed; highly convex beetles less than 1.5 mm long; figure 19.29 .... *SPHAERIIDAE*[1]—*Sphaerius*

4(1′).   Hind coxae with medial portion extending posteriorly to divide 1st abdominal sternite into lateral sclerites (figs. 19.34, 19.99); prothorax with distinct notopleural sutures (fig. 19.99) 5

4′.   Hind coxae not extending posteriorly to divide 1st abdominal sternite (figs. 19.38, 19.150); notopleural sutures almost always absent 11

5(4).   Compound eyes divided into separate dorsal and ventral segments (figs. 19.48–19.50); antennae short, clavate (clubbed) (fig. 19.51) .... *GYRINIDAE* (p. 373)

5′.   Compound eyes undivided (fig. 19.98); antennae long, filiform or moniliform (fig. 19.193) 6

6(5′).   Hind tarsi and usually tibiae flattened, streamlined, and bearing long, stiff swimming bristles (fig. 19.101) 8

6′.   Hind tibiae and tarsi cylindrical or subcylindrical in cross section, without long, stiff swimming bristles 7

---

[1]Subaquatic or inhabiting littoral region.
[2]Includes intertidal species in North America.
[6]Keys to genera not given.

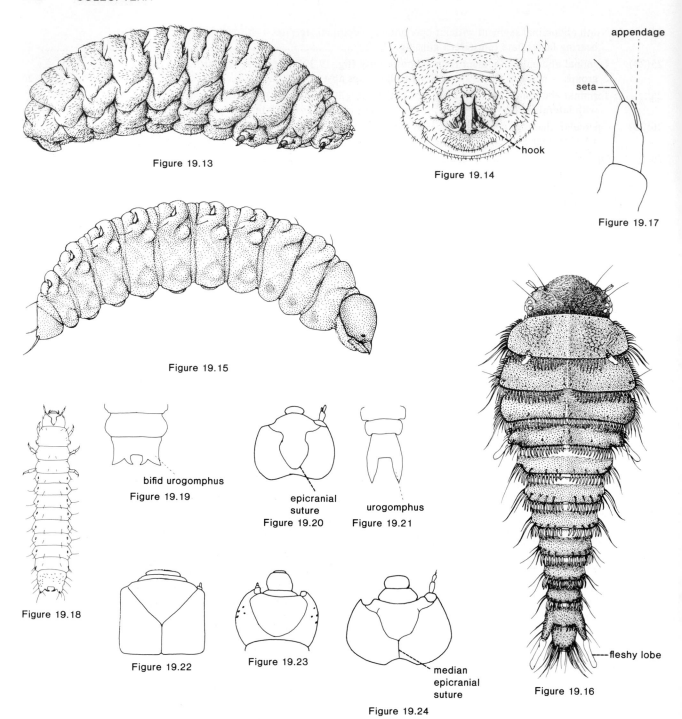

Figure 19.13

Figure 19.14

hook

appendage

seta

Figure 19.17

Figure 19.15

Figure 19.18

bifid urogomphus
Figure 19.19

epicranial suture
Figure 19.20

urogomphus
Figure 19.21

Figure 19.22

Figure 19.23

median epicranial suture
Figure 19.24

fleshy lobe
Figure 19.16

Figure 19.13. *Donacia* sp. (Chrysomelidae) larva, lateral aspect.

Figure 19.14. *Donacia* sp. (Chrysomelidae) larva, ventral aspect of terminal abdominal segment.

Figure 19.15. Curculionidae larva, lateral aspect.

Figure 19.16. *Hydroscapha* sp. (Hydroscaphidae) larva, dorsal aspect.

Figure 19.17. *Sphaerius* sp. (Sphaeriidae) larva, antenna.

Figure 19.18. *Aegialites* sp. (Salpingidae) larva, dorsal aspect.

Figure 19.19. *Aegialites* sp. (Salpingidae) larva, abdominal apex.

Figure 19.20. *Anthicus* sp. (Anthicidae) larva, dorsal aspect of cranium.

Figure 19.21. *Endeodes* sp. (Melyridae) larva, abdominal apex.

Figure 19.22. *Collops* sp. (Melyridae) larva, dorsal aspect of cranium.

Figure 19.23. Heteroceridae larva, dorsal aspect of cranium.

Figure 19.24. Tenebrionidae larva, dorsal aspect of cranium.

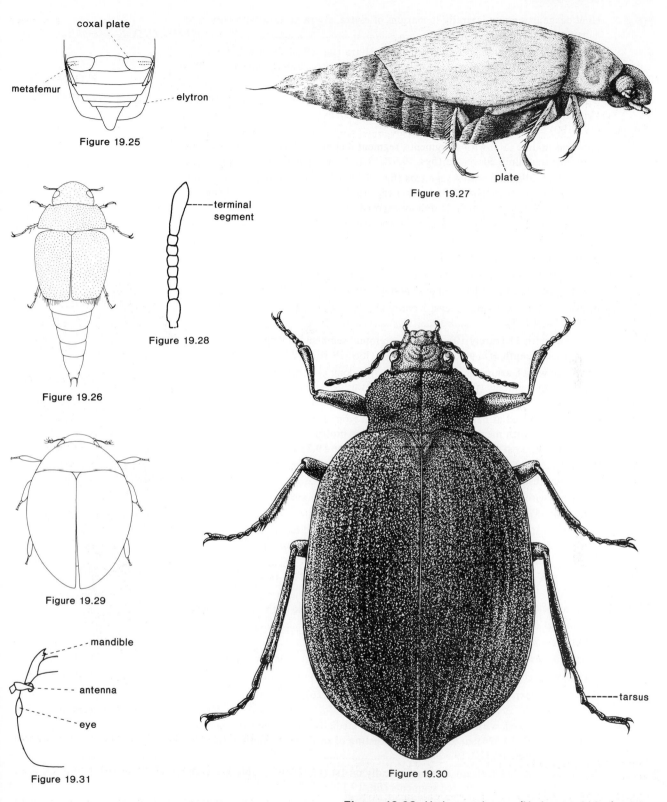

Figure 19.25

Figure 19.27

Figure 19.26

Figure 19.28

Figure 19.29

Figure 19.30

Figure 19.31

Figure 19.25. *Hydroscapha* sp. (Hydroscaphidae) adult, ventral aspect of abdomen and metathorax.

Figure 19.26. *Hydroscapha* sp. (Hydroscaphidae) adult, dorsal aspect.

Figure 19.27. *Hydroscapha* sp. (Hydroscaphidae) adult, lateral aspect.

Figure 19.28. *Hydroscapha* sp. (Hydroscaphidae) adult, antenna.

Figure 19.29. *Sphaerius* sp. (Sphaeriidae) adult, dorsal aspect.

Figure 19.30. *Amphizoa* sp. (Amphizoidae) adult, dorsal aspect.

Figure 19.31. *Endeodes* sp. (Melyridae) adult, dorsal aspect of head (after Chamberlin and Ferris 1929).

7(6'). Hind coxae extending laterally to margins of elytra; elytra at most with very short
        hairs; figure 19.30 .... *AMPHIZOIDAE—Amphizoa* (p. 373)

7'.   Hind coxae not extending laterally as far as elytra (fig. 19.34); elytra bearing
        several long, slender, erect sensory hairs; representative genera shown in figures
        19.34a–d .... *CARABIDAE*[1,2,6]

8(6).   Metasternum with transverse suture (as in fig. 19.34); eyes strongly protruberant .... *HYGROBIIDAE*[4,6]

8'.   Metasternum without transverse suture (fig. 19.99); eyes streamlined (figs. 19.97,
        19.100) 9

9(8'). Fore and middle tarsi with 5 segments, segment 4 similar in size to segment 3 (fig.
        19.75); scutellum concealed (figs. 19.97, 19.100) or exposed (fig. 19.78) 10

9'.   Fore and middle tarsi with 4 segments (fig. 19.100) or with segment 4 very small,
        concealed between lobes of segment 3 (fig. 19.76); scutellum concealed (figs.
        19.97, 19.100) (exception: scutellum exposed in *Celina*) .... *DYTISCIDAE* (in part) (p. 377)

10(9). Hind tarsi with 2 similar claws (figs. 19.106–19.107); scutellum concealed (as in
        figs. 19.97, 19.100) .... *NOTERIDAE* (p. 388)

10'.   Hind tarsi with a single claw (fig. 19.101); if 2 claws are present, scutellum is
        large, exposed .... *DYTISCIDAE* (in part) (p. 377)

11(4'). Elytra covering entire abdomen or exposing only part of 1 abdominal tergite 14

11'.   Elytra truncate, exposing at least 2 entire abdominal tergites (figs. 19.26, 19.32,
        19.172–19.175) 12

12(11'). Antennae with 11 (rarely 10) segments, terminal segment no longer than
        combined length of 2 preceding segments (figs. 19.193, 19.211, 19.216, 19.298) 13

12'.   Antennae with 8 segments, terminal segment as long as combined length of 4
        preceding segments (fig. 19.28); minute beetles, less than 1.5 mm long; figure
        19.26 .... *HYDROSCAPHIDAE* (in part)—*Hydroscapha* (p. 390)

13(12). Antennae inserted at base of mandibles distant from eyes (fig. 19.31); abdomen
        and thorax with membranous yellow or orange protrusible (extendible) vesicles
        (fig. 19.32; most apparent in living beetles); figure 19.33 .... *MELYRIDAE*[1,2,6]

13'.   Antennae inserted laterally on frons close to eyes or between eyes; protrusible
        vesicles absent .... *STAPHYLINIDAE*[1,2] (p. 400)

14(11). Antennae with terminal segment as long as combined length of 3–4 preceding
        segments (fig. 19.28) 16

14'.   Antennae with terminal segment no longer than combined length of 2 preceding
        segments (fig. 19.298); terminal segments may be fused into a globular or
        elongate club 15

15(14'). Antennae terminating in abrupt, globular (figs. 19.35, 19.311) or elongate (fig.
        19.170) club 18

15'.   Antennae slender, elongate (fig. 19.216) or very short, thick, with basal segment
        enlarged (fig. 19.227) 23

16(15'). Antennae with 9 segments; minute flattened beetles 17

16'.   Antennae with 4 segments; minute, coarsely sculptured, globular beetles .... *LEPICERIDAE*[4,6]

17(16). Elytra completely covering abdomen; tarsal formula 4-4-4 .... *TORRIDINICOLIDAE*[4,6]

17'.   Elytra short, exposing 2–5 abdominal tergites (fig. 19.26); tarsal formula
        3–3–3 .... *HYDROSCAPHIDAE* (in part)—*Hydroscapha* (p. 390)

18(15). Antennae elbowed, with 2nd segment attached medially on elongate 1st segment
        (figs. 19.320, 19.324); antennal club consisting of several compactly fused
        segments (figs. 19.320, 19.324) 19

18'.   Antennae with 2nd segment attached apically on 1st (fig. 19.227); antennal club
        consisting of 2–5 articulated segments (fig. 19.170) 20

---

[1]Subaquatic or inhabiting littoral region.
[2]Includes intertidal species in North America.
[4]Family does not occur in United States.
[6]Keys to genera not given.

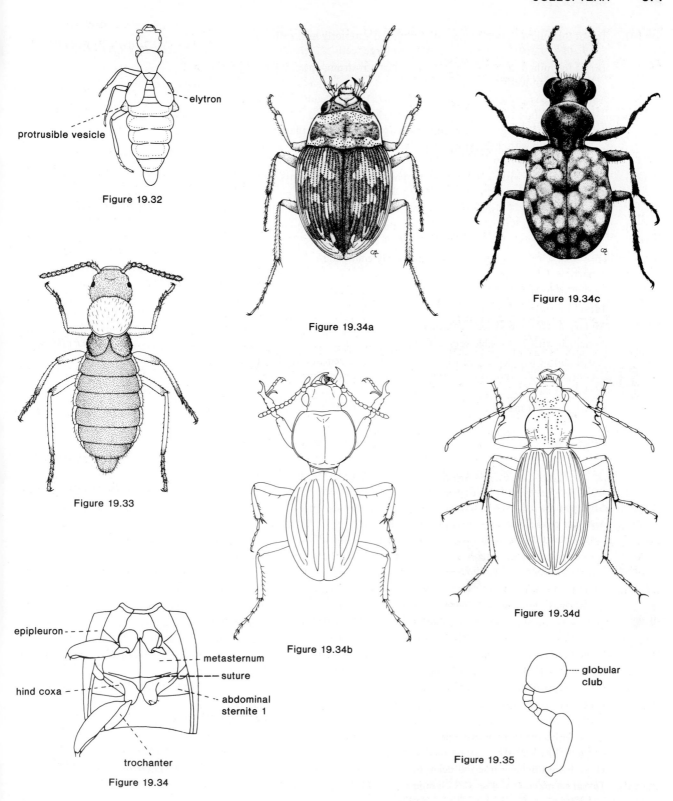

Figure 19.32

protrusible vesicle

elytron

Figure 19.34a

Figure 19.34c

Figure 19.33

Figure 19.34b

Figure 19.34d

epipleuron

metasternum

suture

hind coxa

abdominal
sternite 1

trochanter

Figure 19.34

globular
club

Figure 19.35

Figure 19.32. Melyridae adult, dorsal aspect.

Figure 19.33. *Endeodes* sp. (Melyridae) adult, dorsal aspect.

Figure 19.34. *Harpalus* sp. (Carabidae) adult, ventral aspect of thoracic region (after Larson 1975). (Figs. 19.34a–d give the dorsal aspect of several representative Carabidae often found around water: 19.34a, Omophroninae, *Omophron* sp.; 19.34b, Scaratinae, *Dyschirius* sp.; 19.34c, Elaphrinae, *Elaphrus* sp.; 19.34d, Chlaeninae, *Chlaenius* sp.).

Figure 19.35. *Neopachylopus* sp. (Histeridae) adult, antenna.

19(18).   Tarsal formula 4–4–4; head usually produced anteriorly as a rostrum (figs.
          19.309–19.310); anterior tibiae without large teeth .... *CURCULIONIDAE* (p. 422)

19'.   Tarsal formula 5–5–5; head not produced as a rostrum; anterior tibiae with several
          large lateral teeth .... *HISTERIDAE*[1,6]

20(18'). Antennae about as long as head (figs. 19.147, 19.150); club with 3–5 segments
          (fig. 19.170); tarsal formula 4–4–4, 5–5–5, or 5–4–4 21

20'.   Antennae much longer than head, length approaching half that of body (fig.
          19.36); club with 2–3 loosely articulated segments (fig. 19.37); tarsal formula
          3–3–3; figure 19.36 .... *PTILIIDAE*[1,2,6] (in part)

21(20).   Abdomen with 5 visible sternites; antennal club with 3 segments (not including
          segment 6) 22

21'.   Abdomen with 6–7 visible sternites; antennal club with 5 segments (fig. 19.170) .... *HYDRAENIDAE* (p. 398)

22(21).   Fore tarsi with 4 segments; metacoxae widely separated, intercoxal process broadly
          truncate (fig. 19.38); figures 19.39–19.40 .... *GEORYSSIDAE—Georyssus*

22'.   Fore tarsi with 5 segments; metacoxae nearly contiguous, intercoxal process
          narrow (fig. 19.150) .... *HYDROPHILIDAE*[5] (p. 392)

23(15'). Tarsal formula 5–5–5 24

23'.   Tarsal formula 5–5–4 or less 33

24(23).   Abdomen with 5–6 visible segments 25

24'.   Abdomen with 7–8 visible segments .... *LAMPYRIDAE*[1,6]

25(24).   Prosternum expanded anteriorly as prominent lobe beneath head, usually
          contracted into thorax concealing antennae and eyes (figs. 19.228–19.229,
          19.297) 26

25'.   Prosternum not markedly expanded anteriorly beneath head, antennae clearly
          visible 29

26(25).   Antennae usually thick, with enlarged basal segment (figs. 19.227, 19.229), about
          as long as head 27

26'.   Antennae filiform or serrate (figs. 19.193, 19.216, 19.298), much longer than head 28

27(26).   Antennae with 10 or fewer segments; hind coxae contiguous .... *LIMNICHIDAE*[1] (p. 408)

27'.   Antennae with 11 segments; hind coxae separated .... *DRYOPIDAE* (in part) (p. 410)

28(26'). Anterior coxae transverse with trochantin visible (fig. 19.229); antennae (if visible)
          very short, thick, with enlarged basal segment (fig. 19.227) .... *DRYOPIDAE* (in part) (p. 410)

28'.   Anterior coxae round, trochantin concealed (figs. 19.269, 19.274), antennae
          slender, filiform (fig. 19.298) .... *ELMIDAE* (in part) (p. 410)

29(25).   Tarsi with 4th segment deeply bilobed .... *SCIRTIDAE*[1] (p. 402)

29'.   Tarsi usually filiform, 4th segment not bilobed 30

30(29'). Antennae serrate or pectinate (figs. 19.202, 19.211, 19.216), never concealed 31

30'.   Antennae filiform or clavate (figs. 19.193, 19.298), or partly concealed within
          prosternum .... *ELMIDAE* (in part) (p. 410)

31(30).   Abdomen with 6 or 7 segments; maxillary palp with 2nd segment longer than next
          2 combined .... *PSEPHENIDAE* (in part) (p. 404)

31'.   Abdomen with 5 segments; maxillary palp with 2nd segment much shorter than
          next 2 combined 32

32(31'). Head with antennae inserted close together between eyes constricting clypeus from
          frons (fig. 19.210) .... *PSEPHENIDAE* (in part) (p. 404)

32'.   Head with antennae inserted below eyes, not constricting clypeus (fig. 19.217) ..... *PTILODACTYLIDAE*[1] (p. 406)

33(23'). Tarsal formula 4–4–4 or 3–3–3; hind coxae contiguous or nearly so (as in fig.
          19.34) 36

33'.   Tarsal formula 5–5–4; hind coxae usually separated 34

---

[1]Subaquatic or inhabiting littoral region.
[2]Includes intertidal species in North America.
[5]The genus *Phanocerus* (Elmidae), with 1 species in southern Texas, has distinctly clubbed antennae, and will key to Hydrophilidae.
[6]Keys to genera not given.

34(33′).   Hind coxae separated by less than coxal width; basal 2 abdominal sternites
separated by suture 35

34′.   Hind coxae separated by much more than coxal width; basal 2 abdominal
segments fused; figure 19.41 .... *SALPINGIDAE*[2,6]

35(34).   Eyes emarginate (notched) anteriorly; procoxal cavities enclosed behind by
prothorax .... *TENEBRIONIDAE*[1,6]

35′.   Eyes oval or round; procoxal cavities enclosed behind by mesothorax (as in fig.
19.229) .... *ANTHICIDAE*[1,6]

36(33).   Tarsal formula 4–4–4; beetles larger than 2 mm 37

36′.   Tarsal formula 3–3–3; minute beetles less than 2 mm long; figure 19.36 .... *PTILIIDAE*[1,2,6] (in part)

37(36).   Antennae thickened apically, shorter than head and thorax; mandibles long,
projecting horizontally before head; figure 19.42 .... *HETEROCERIDAE*[1,6]

37′.   Antennae thickened apically, longer than head and thorax; mandibles small,
directed ventrally .... *CHRYSOMELIDAE* (p. 419)

KEYS TO THE GENERA OF AQUATIC COLEOPTERA

Amphizoidae (Trout-Stream Beetles)

The family Amphizoidae contains a single genus: *Amphizoa* LeConte. Presently, four species are recognized, all from northwestern North America where the larvae and adults live in mountain streams. They are especially abundant on driftwood and trash floating in frothy eddies, along undercut banks among roots, or among accumulations of submerged pine needles. Although often rare in collections, large numbers can be collected once their habitat is recognized.

Eggs of amphizoids have been found in cracks on the undersurface of driftwood, though oviposition sites may more typically occur in high-humidity or splash zones in partly submerged brush piles. Hatching takes place during mid to late August, and the larvae usually reach the second instar by winter. Larvae (fig. 19.2) are predaceous and seem to restrict their diet to Plecoptera nymphs. They usually are found crawling on twigs or other wood; mature larvae are almost invariably entirely out of, but near, the water. Such larvae readily enter the water to seize prey, but quickly return to a twig or other support to eat the victim.

When dislodged into relatively quiet water, amphizoid larvae assume a characteristic posture with the abdomen at and horizontal to the water's surface (spiracles of the eighth abdominal tergite at the surface), and the thorax and head folded under the abdomen so that the mandibles lie beneath its apex. This posture permits the larva to respire while afloat and enables it to quickly capture any prey that comes into reach or to grasp any solid object it touches.

Mature larvae have been observed crawling from the water in late July and early August, and two have been found in protective cases lodged in debris-filled crevices between logs; however, pupation has not been observed. Newly emerged adults frequently are mud-covered; this suggests that pupation may occur in muddy creek banks.

Adult amphizoids (fig. 19.30) are poor swimmers usually found crawling on twigs or other submerged plant material. They are predaceous and, like the larvae, show a preference for Plecoptera nymphs. Earlier reports that these beetles were scavengers are incorrect.

Adult amphizoids have been observed surfacing briefly, then carrying a bubble of air beneath and surrounding the elytral apices while submerged. The highly oxygenated habitat may enable the air bubble to serve as a physical gill, precluding the need for surfacing or greatly extending the time submerged.

Gyrinidae (Whirligig Beetles)

The Gyrinidae is a small family of aquatic insects with approximately 700 species. Nearly 60 species and subspecies are recorded for the United States and Canada. Whirligig beetles often are a familiar sight on freshwater ponds, lake margins, open flowing streams, quiet stream margins, bog pools, swamps, and roadside ditches where they may form large aggregations or schools in late summer and autumn. These aggregations may contain a single species or as many as 13. In autumn, Wisconsin pond-inhabiting species fly to overwinter along large streams and lakes.

Copulation occurs on the water surface and the female lays her eggs on stems of emergent vegetation a few centimeters below the surface of the water. After hatching in 1–2 weeks, larvae (fig. 19.46) pass through three instars. They crawl about over submerged objects, using their characteristic apical abdominal hooks (fig. 19.47), and feed on small aquatic organisms. They can swim in an undulating fashion by using the abdominal gills, possibly as an escape mechanism. Pupation takes place on shore above water level. Adults are unique in having eyes divided into two portions (figs. 19.48–19.49). The lower portion remains completely submerged surveying the aquatic habitat; the upper portion views the above water habitat. Divided vision and quick swimming movements allow them to avoid predators from above or below. They are predominantly scavengers, feeding upon live or dead insects trapped or floating on the water surface.

---

[1] Subaquatic or inhabiting littoral region.

[2] Includes intertidal species in North America.

[6] Keys to genera not given.

Gyrinidae

Larvae[1]

1.   Head suborbicular with collum (neck) narrow and distinct (fig. 19.43); mandible without retinaculum (tooth) on inner margin; nasale with median produced lobe, which may or may not be emarginate, and with a lower tooth on each side (fig. 19.43); figure 19.46 .... *Dineutus*

1'.   Head elongate, with collum not distinct, nearly as wide as remainder of head (figs. 19.44–19.45); mandible with retinaculum or without 2

2(1').   Nasale with 2–4 teeth in a transverse row (fig. 19.44) .... *Gyrinus*

2'.   Nasale without teeth (fig. 19.45) (based upon early instar larvae from Missouri) .... *Gyretes*

Adults

1.   Dorsal and ventral compound eyes in contact on lateral margin of head, separated only by a narrow ridge (fig. 19.48); meso- and metatarsal segments as long as or longer than broad; length less than 3 mm .... *Spanglerogyrus*

1'.   Dorsal and ventral compound eyes divided, upper eyes inset from lateral margin of head for a distance of at least half the width of an eye (fig. 19.49); meso- and metatarsal segments 2, 3, and 4 much broader than long; length 3–15 mm 2

2(1').   Lateral margins of pronotum and elytron pubescent (fig. 19.50); elytron without striae; apical abdominal sternites with median longitudinal row of long hairs; scutellum concealed; length 3–5 mm .... *Gyretes*

2'.   Pronotum and elytron entirely glabrous; apical abdominal sternites without longitudinal row of hairs 3

3(2').   Larger species, 9–15 mm in length; elytron smooth or with indistinct striae; scutellum concealed .... *Dineutus*

3'.   Smaller species, 4–7 mm in length; elytron with 11 distinct striae; scutellum exposed .... *Gyrinus*

Haliplidae (Crawling Water Beetles)

The Haliplidae is a relatively small family of slightly more than 200 species with 69 species representing four genera from the United States and Canada. Females of the genus *Haliplus* have been observed to cut a hole with their mandibles in the side of a filament of *Ceratophyllum* or *Nitella* and deposit several eggs within the plant cell. Eggs of the genus *Peltodytes* are deposited on the leaves and stems of aquatic plants where hatching occurs within 8–14 days.

Haliplid larvae pass through three instars and are herbivorous. Pupation occurs from 20–25 days after hatching in a spherical pupal chamber constructed by the larva in rather dry mud. The mature larva remains in the pupal chamber from 4–6 days before transformation.

Numerous investigators have discussed the feeding habits of adult haliplids. Early studies reported that the adults were carnivorous but later studies have shown them to be herbivorous.

The greatly expanded hind coxal plates of Haliplidae are unique among aquatic Coleoptera. The air store retained by these plates is taken in by way of the tip of the abdomen, retained under the elytra, and acts as both a supplemental air store and in hydrostatic functions.

Haliplidae

Larvae

1.   Body segments each with 2 or more erect, segmented, hollow, spine-tipped filaments, each filament half as long as body (fig. 19.52); fore legs chelate, 4th segment produced apically and edged with a solid row of small teeth so that 5th segment and claw can be closed on it (fig. 19.53) .... *Peltodytes*

1'.   Body spines, except in 1st instar, never stalked or much longer than length of 1st body segment (fig. 19.54); apical abdominal segment produced posteriorly in a forked or unforked horn; fore legs, if chelate, with 4th segment less produced and without solid row of small teeth (fig. 19.55) 2

---

[1]The larva of *Spanglerogyrus* is unknown.

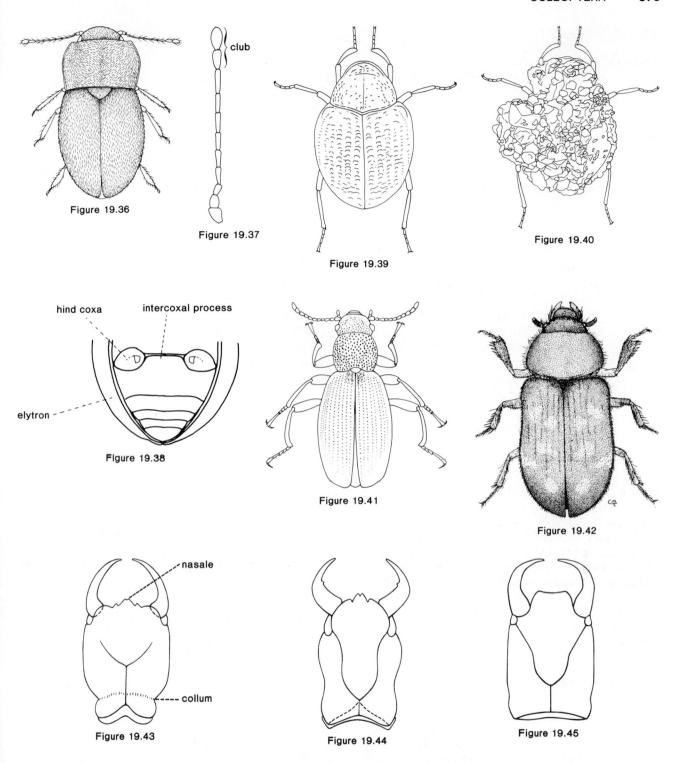

Figure 19.36.

Figure 19.37.

club

hind coxa   intercoxal process

elytron

Figure 19.38.

Figure 19.39

Figure 19.40

Figure 19.41

Figure 19.42

nasale

collum

Figure 19.43

Figure 19.44

Figure 19.45

Figure 19.36. *Actidium* sp. (Ptiliidae) adult, dorsal aspect.

Figure 19.37. *Actidium* sp. (Ptiliidae) adult, antenna.

Figure 19.38. *Georyssus* sp. (Georyssidae) adult, ventral aspect of abdomen and metathorax.

Figure 19.39. *Georyssus* sp. (Georyssidae) adult, dorsal aspect with camouflage of sand grains removed.

Figure 19.40. *Georyssus* sp. (Georyssidae) adult, dorsal aspect with camouflage of sand grains.

Figure 19.41. *Aegilites* sp. (Salpingidae) adult, dorsal aspect.

Figure 19.42. Heteroceridae adult, dorsal aspect.

Figure 19.43. *Dineutus* sp. (Gyrinidae) larva, dorsal aspect of head (after Sanderson 1982).

Figure 19.44. *Gyrinus* sp. (Gyrinidae) larva, dorsal aspect of head (after Sanderson 1982).

Figure 19.45. *Gyretes* sp. (Gyrinidae) larva, dorsal aspect of head (after Sanderson 1982).

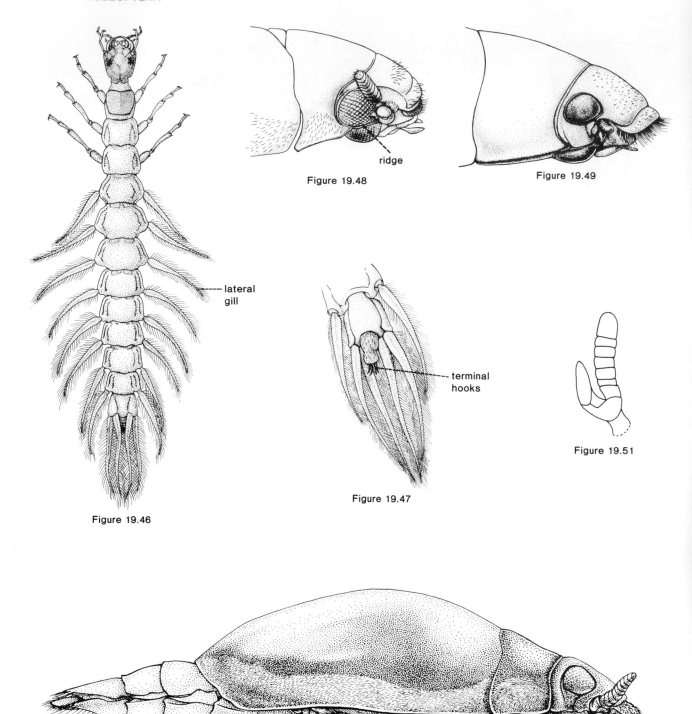

ridge

Figure 19.48

Figure 19.49

lateral
gill

terminal
hooks

Figure 19.51

Figure 19.47

Figure 19.46

Figure 19.50

Figure 19.46. *Dineutus* sp. (Gyrinidae) larva, dorsal aspect.

Figure 19.47. *Dineutus* sp. (Gyrinidae) larva, ventral aspect of last abdominal segments.

Figure 19.48. *Spanglerogyrus* sp. (Gyrinidae) adult, lateral aspect of head and pronotum.

Figure 19.49. *Dineutus* sp. (Gyrinidae) adult, lateral aspect of head and pronotum.

Figure 19.50. *Gyretes* sp. (Gyrinidae) adult, lateral aspect.

Figure 19.51. *Gyrinus* sp. (Gyrinidae) adult, antenna.

2(1′).   Third antennal segment shorter than 2nd; fore legs moderately chelate, but 3rd instead of 4th segment produced, edged with 2 blunt teeth; apical abdominal segment unforked, strongly curved ventrally (fig. 19.56); body without conspicuous spines .... ***Brychius***

2′.   Third antennal segment 2–3 times as long as 2nd; body with or without conspicuous spines 3

3(2′).   Fore leg with 3rd segment produced and edged by 2 blunt teeth; apical abdominal segment unforked (except in 1st instar); body with conspicuous spines only on lateral margins .... ***Apteraliplus***

3′.   Fore leg weakly to moderately chelate, 4th segment more or less produced, usually bearing 2–3 spines (fig. 19.55); body with or without conspicuous spines .... ***Haliplus***

Adults

1.   Pronotum with black blotch on each side of middle near posterior margin (fig. 19.58); last segment of both labial and maxillary palpi cone-shaped, as long as or longer than next to last; hind coxal plates large, only last abdominal sternite completely exposed; elytron with fine sutural stria in at least apical half .... ***Peltodytes***

1′.   Pronotum immaculate or with median blotch anteriorly (fig. 19.60), posteriorly, or both; last segment of both labial and maxillary palpi sublate, shorter than next to last; hind coxal plates smaller, leaving last 3 abdominal sternites exposed; elytron without fine sutural stria 2

2(1′).   Pronotum with sides of basal two-thirds nearly parallel (fig. 19.59); epipleuron broad, extending almost to tip of elytron, which is never truncate; metasternum reaching epipleuron .... ***Brychius***

2′.   Pronotum with sides widest at base, convergent anteriorly (fig. 19.60); epipleuron evenly narrowed, usually ending near base of last abdominal sternite, never reaching elytral apex; episternum completely separating metasternum from epipleuron 3

3(2′).   Median part of prosternum and base of prosternal process forming a plateaulike elevation, at least in part angularly separated from sides of prosternum (fig. 19.62) .... ***Haliplus***

3′.   Prosternum evenly rounded from side to side, process raised above base (fig. 19.61); tiny, length 1.5–2.5 mm; California .... ***Apteraliplus***

Dytiscidae (Predaceous Diving Beetles)

The Dytiscidae is perhaps the best adapted for aquatic existence and the most diverse of the water beetles with 2,500 described species, more than 500 of which occur in North America.

Despite the size and importance of the group among water beetles, surprisingly little is known of the life history of North American dytiscids. Mating occurs from early spring through autumn. Oviposition sites of dytiscids appear to correlate well with structural modifications of the ovipositor. Species having a long, flexible ovipositor (some *Acilius*) place their eggs loosely, usually 30–50 in a mass, above water in moist soil among grass roots or under organic debris. Most species possessing a cutting ovipositor (some *Agabus, Coptotomus, Cybister, Dytiscus, Hydaticus, Ilybius, Laccophilus,* and *Thermonectus*) insert their eggs into parts of living plants. A third group places its eggs on plant surfaces or, at most, inserts them halfway into the plant tissues (some *Agabus, Colymbetes, Deronectes,* some *Hydroporus,* and some *Rhantus*).

The larval stage of the Dytiscidae consists of three instars and requires from several weeks to several months, depending mainly upon season and the availability of food. Most dytiscid larvae rise to the surface and take in air through the large terminal spiracles. Cuticular respiration, however, appears to be common among first-instar larvae of many species. *Agabus,* some *Hydroporus,* and *Ilybius* have an extensive network of tracheae near the ventral cuticle and are believed to exchange gases through this structure. Larvae of the genus *Coptotomus* possess lateral gills and can remain beneath the surface continuously. All mature dytiscid larvae leave the water to prepare a pupal cell on land near the water's edge.

As the common name for the group implies, larval dytiscids are predaceous. Their selection of food appears to be governed by their ability to catch and overcome their prey. Although most adult dytiscids are active predators, many are also scavengers.

Adult dytiscids readily leave the water and fly. They are unable to take off directly from the water and first crawl onto an object above the water level. This behavior appears to be linked to the shift of the respiratory function: the large thoracic air-sacs connected with the first pair of spiracles that are used in flight remain collapsed while the insect is in the water.

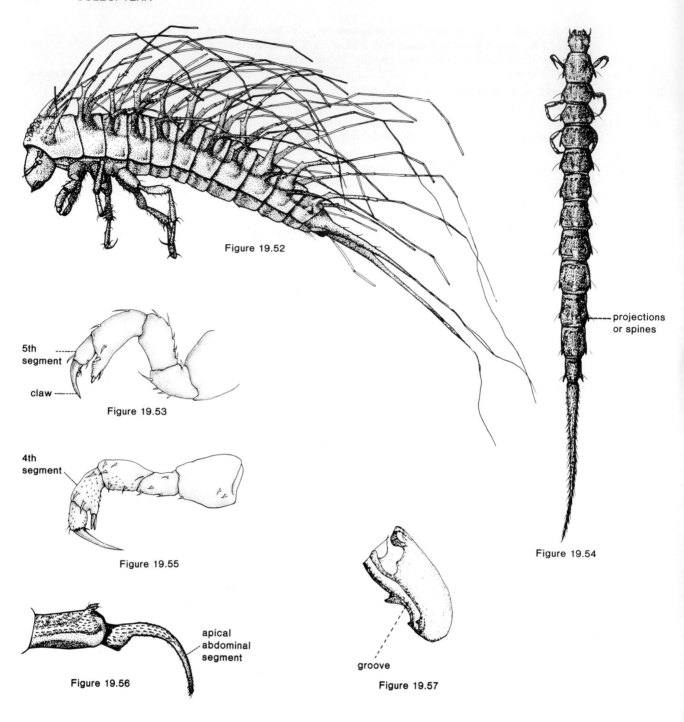

Figure 19.52

5th
segment

claw

Figure 19.53

4th
segment

Figure 19.55

apical
abdominal
segment

Figure 19.56

groove

Figure 19.57

projections
or spines

Figure 19.54

Figure 19.52. *Peltodytes* sp. (Haliplidae) larva, lateral aspect.

Figure 19.53. *Peltodytes* sp. (Haliplidae) larva, fore leg.

Figure 19.54. *Haliplus* sp. (Haliplidae) larva, dorsal aspect.

Figure 19.55. *Haliplus* sp. (Haliplidae) larva, fore leg.

Figure 19.56. *Brychius* sp. (Haliplidae) larva, lateral aspect of apex of abdomen.

Figure 19.57. *Peltodytes* sp. (Haliplidae) larva, mandible.

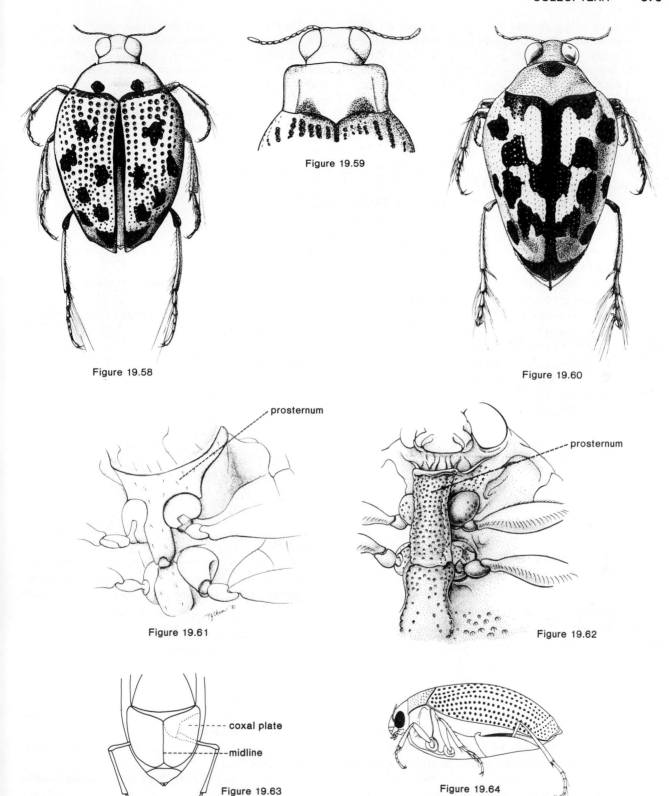

Figure 19.58

Figure 19.59

Figure 19.60

prosternum

Figure 19.61

prosternum

Figure 19.62

coxal plate

midline

Figure 19.63

Figure 19.64

Figure 19.58. *Peltodytes* sp. (Haliplidae) adult, dorsal aspect.

Figure 19.59. *Brychius* sp. (Haliplidae) adult, dorsal aspect of head and pronotum.

Figure 19.60. *Haliplus* sp. (Haliplidae) adult, dorsal aspect.

Figure 19.61. *Apteraliplus* sp. (Haliplidae) adult, prosternum.

Figure 19.62. *Haliplus* sp. (Haliplidae) adult, prosternum.

Figure 19.63. Haliplidae adult, ventral aspect of metathorax and abdomen.

Figure 19.64. *Peltodytes* sp. (Haliplidae) adult, lateral aspect.

Dytiscids splash directly into the water since the extreme modification of the legs for swimming makes them useless for alighting on surfaces. Impact usually carries them through the surface film, but frequently they return to the surface after a few seconds to fill the subelytral air chamber. Presumably, the tracheal system undergoes a reversal of the process of preparation for flight.

The taxonomy of the Hydroporinae remains as unsettled as it was 25 years ago (Leech and Chandler 1956). We have taken a conservative approach regarding most Hydroporini and followed previous works on Dytiscidae of the United States. Thus, the genera *Deuteronectes* Guignot and *Nectoporus* Guignot are considered *Oreodytes,* and the genus *Neonectes* Zimmermann is considered *Deronectes. Deronectes* is retained for those hydroporines normally placed in it.

Dytiscidae

Mature Larvae[1]

1. Head with a frontal projection (figs. 19.65–19.67); maxillary palp usually 3-segmented (4-segmented in *Celina*) 2

1'. Head without a frontal projection (fig. 19.68); maxillary palp with 4 or more segments 13

2(1). Last abdominal segment with recurved extension of lateral tracheal trunks reaching beyond apex of abdomen (fig. 19.69) .... Methlinae   Celinini .... ***Celina***

2'. Lateral tracheal trunks not extending beyond apex of last abdominal segment, terminating on apex .... Hydroporinae 3

3(2'). Frontal projection of head elongate, constricted near base and broadly spatulate at apex, a lateral branch arising from each side near base (figs. 19.65–19.66) 4

3'. Frontal projection usually broadly triangular, not constricted near base and without a lateral branch on each side, although a notch may be present on each side (fig. 19.67) 6

4(3). Lateral branch of frontal projection long and curved medially, extending well beyond midpoint of frontal projection anterior to base of lateral branch (fig. 19.65) .... Vatellini .... ***Derovatellus***

4'. Lateral branch of frontal projection short, not reaching midpoint of frontal projection anterior to base of lateral branch (fig. 19.66) .... Hyphydrini 5

5(4'). Apical segment of antenna bifurcate .... ***Desmopachria***

5'. Apical segment of antenna simple .... ***Pachydrus***

6(3'). Cercus with more than 7 setae .... Hydroporini (in part) 7

6'. Cercus with only 7 setae 8

7(6). Cercus short .... ***Deronectes***

7'. Cercus long or very long .... ***Oreodytes***

8(6'). Cercus very short, about one-half length of last abdominal segment .... Hydroporini (in part) .... ***Laccornis***

8'. Cercus distinctly longer than last abdominal segment 9

9(8'). Frontal projection with a notch at each side (fig. 19.67) .... Hydroporini (in part) 10

9'. Frontal projection without notches 12

10(9). Ocelli absent; cavernicolous, known only from artesian wells in Texas .... ***Haideoporus***

10'. Ocelli present; surface dwelling, not normally confined to artesian waters 11

11(10'). Head narrow, maximum width nearly equal to length from base to antenna; frontal projection with a deep notch and a denticle behind it .... ***Hygrotus***

11'. Head broad, maximum width greater than length from base to antenna; notch on frontal projection weak, denticle weak or absent .... ***Hydroporus***

12(9'). Larva greatly widened in middle, greatest width approximately 0.25 of total length .... Hydrovatini .... ***Hydrovatus***

12'. Larva not greatly widened in middle, greatest width 0.20 or less of total length .... Bidessini

13(1'). Maxillary stipes broad, suboval, usually with 1–2 strong inner marginal spines or hooks 14

[1]The larvae of *Anodocheilus, Bidessonotus, Brachyvatus, Carrhydrus, Laccodytes, Liodessus, Lioporius, Megadytes, Neobidessus, Neoclypeodytes,* and *Uvarus* are unknown or undescribed.

13'.   Maxillary stipes long and slender, usually without inner marginal hooks 29

14(13).   Abdominal segments 7 and/or 8 without lateral fringe of long swimming hairs 15

14'.   Abdominal segments 7 and 8 with swimming hairs 25

15(14).   Last (4th) segment of antenna less than two-thirds the length of the 3rd segment 18

15'.   Last segment of antenna more than two-thirds the length of the 3rd segment ....

          ....Colymbetinae (in part)   Colymbetini 16

16(15'). Tarsal claw with small spines on lower margin in basal half 17

16'.   Tarsal claw without small spines on lower margin in basal half .... *Hoperius*

17(16).   Mandible almost 3 times as long as broad (fig. 19.71) .... *Rhantus*

17'.   Mandible short, slightly more than twice as long as broad .... *Colymbetes*

18(15).   Last antennal segment double, although the lesser lobe may be represented only as
          a stout seta arising from the apex of the 3rd segment beside the greater lobe ... Colymbetinae (in part) 19

18'.   Last antennal segment simple; mandible not toothed 20

19(18).   Last antennal segment consisting of 2 unequal lobes; mandible toothed along inner
          edge .... Copelatini .... *Copelatus*

19'.   Last antennal segment consisting of a short lobe about one-sixth as long as 3rd
          segment and a stout seta, each arising from the apex of the 3rd segment;
          mandible falciform, stout at base, slender and tapering to sharp apex, deeply
          grooved along inner surface, bearing a cluster of short setae ventrobasally .... Agabetini .... *Agabetes*

20(18'). Fore and middle legs chelate (fig. 19.70) .... Colymbetinae (in part) .... Matini .... *Matus*

20'.   Fore and middle legs simple 21

21(20'). Cercus with numerous secondary hairs .... Laccophilinae .... Laccophilini ....*Laccophilus*

21'.   Cercus usually with 7 primary hairs in 2 whorls, 3 near middle, 4 apically ....
          .... Colymbetinae (in part) .... Agabini 22

22(21'). Thorax as wide as long, about equal in length to abdomen; sides of head nearly
          round, neck area not set off by shallow groove .... *Hydrotrupes*

22'.   Thorax longer than wide, never as long as abdomen; sides of head round or
          squarish, but with neck area set off by occipital suture or shallow groove 23

23(22'). Tibia and tarsus with conspicuous spines confined to apical half, mostly terminal;
          dorsal margin of middle and hind femora without row of spines; tergites, from
          2nd thoracic segment to 8th abdominal segment, each bearing 3 or more pairs of
          long, conspicuous setae; sternites of abdominal segments 4 through 6 each with
          a similar pair of setae .... *Agabinus*

23'.   Tibia and tarsus with spines not confined to apical half; dorsal margin of middle
          and hind femora each with row of spines; tergites and sternites (see above)
          usually without conspicuous setae, or, if present, they are much smaller than
          those of 8th and 9th tergites 24

24(23'). Lateral margin of head more or less compressed or keeled, temporal spines on a
          line that would intersect ocelli or just pass below them .... *Ilybius*

24'.   Lateral margin of head not keeled, temporal spines on a line that would run well
          below ocelli .... *Agabus*

25(14'). Anterior 6 abdominal segments each with a pair of long lateral gills .... Coptotomini .... *Coptotomus*

25'.   Abdominal segments without gills .... Dytiscinae (in part) 26

26(25'). Ligula very short, armed with 4 spines .... Eretini .... *Eretes*

26'.   Ligula long, simple or bifid, but without 4 spines .... Thermonectini 27

27(26'). Ligula bifid apically .... *Acilius*

27'.   Ligula simple 28

28(27')   Ligula not as long as 1st segment of labial palp .... *Thermonectus*

28'.   Ligula nearly equal to or exceeding length of 1st segment of labial palp .... *Graphoderus*

29(13'). Head dentate anteriorly; ligula long; cerci absent .... Cybistrinae .... *Cybister*

29'.   Head lacking dentation anteriorly; ligula absent, or low and bilobed; cerci present
    (fig. 19.68) .... Dytiscinae (in part) 30

30(29').   Cercus with lateral fringe; labium without projecting lobes .... Dytiscini .... ***Dytiscus***

30'.   Cercus without fringe; labium with 2 projecting lobes .... Hydaticini .... ***Hydaticus***

Adults

1.   Fore and middle tarsi distinctly 5-segmented, 4th segment approximately as long
    as 3rd (fig. 19.75) 2

1'.   Fore and middle tarsi each 4-segmented or with 4th segment small and concealed
    between lobes of 3rd so that 5th segment appears to be 4th (fig. 19.76) (except
    in *Bidessonotus,* which has 4th segment small, but not concealed by lobes of 3rd
    [fig. 19.77]) 5

2(1).   Scutellum entirely visible (fig. 19.78) 3

2'.   Scutellum covered by pronotum, or rarely a small tip visible; hind tarsus with a
    single straight claw .... Laccophilinae .... Laccophilini 6

3(2).   Eye emarginate above base of antenna (fig. 19.79); basal 3 segments of fore tarsus
    of male widened and with adhesion disks, but never together forming an oval or
    nearly round plate .... Colymbetinae 26

3'.   Eye not emarginate above base of antenna; 1st 3 segments of fore tarsus of male
    greatly broadened, forming a nearly round or oval plate with adhesion disks 4

4(3').   Inferior spur at apex of hind tibia dilated, much broader than the other large spur
    (fig. 19.80); basal 3 segments of male fore tarsus forming an oval plate; large
    beetles, 20–32 mm long .... Cybistrinae 38

4'.   Inferior spur not as broad as or but little broader than, other spur (fig. 19.81);
    basal 3 segments of male fore tarsus forming a nearly round plate; medium to
    large beetles, 8–38 mm long .... Dytiscinae 39

5(1').   Scutellum fully visible .... Methlinae .... Celinini .... ***Celina***

5'.   Scutellum covered by pronotum .... Hydroporinae 7

6(2').   Spines of hind tibia notched or bifid apically; apical third of prosternal process
    lanceolate, only moderately broad; larger species, 2.5–6.5 mm in length .... ***Laccophilus***

6'.   Spines of hind tibia simple, acute apically; apical third of prosternal process
    somewhat diamond-shaped .... ***Laccodytes***

7(5').   Metepisternum not reaching mesocoxal cavity, excluded by mesepimeron;
    prosternal process short, broad, not reaching metasternum, its tip ending at
    front of the contiguous middle coxae .... Vatellini .... ***Derovatellus***

7'.   Metepisternum reaching mesocoxal cavity; apex of prosternal process reaching
    metasternum 8

8(7').   Apices of hind coxal processes broad, conjointly divided into 3 parts: 2 widely
    separated narrow lateral lobes and a broad, depressed middle region (fig. 19.82);
    small, broadly ovate beetles about 2.5 mm long .... Hydrovatini .... ***Hydrovatus***

8'.   Hind coxal processes not conjointly divided into 3 parts as described above, either
    without lateral lobes (fig. 19.83) or with these lobes covering bases of hind
    trochanters (fig. 19.84) 9

9(8').   Hind coxal process without lateral lobe, base of hind trochanter entirely free (fig.
    19.83) 10

9'.   Sides of hind coxal processes diverging posteriorly, more or less produced into lobes
    that cover bases of hind trochanters (fig. 19.84) .... Hydroporini 18

10(9).   Hind tibia straight, of almost uniform width from near base to apex; hind tarsal
    claws unequal; epipleuron with diagonal carina crossing near base; shining,
    ventrally convex beetles .... Hyphydrini 11

10'.   Hind tibia slightly arcuate, narrow at base, gradually widening to apex; hind tarsal
    claws equal; epipleuron without diagonal carina crossing near base (except in
    Brachyvatus, which has a carina) .... Bidessini 12

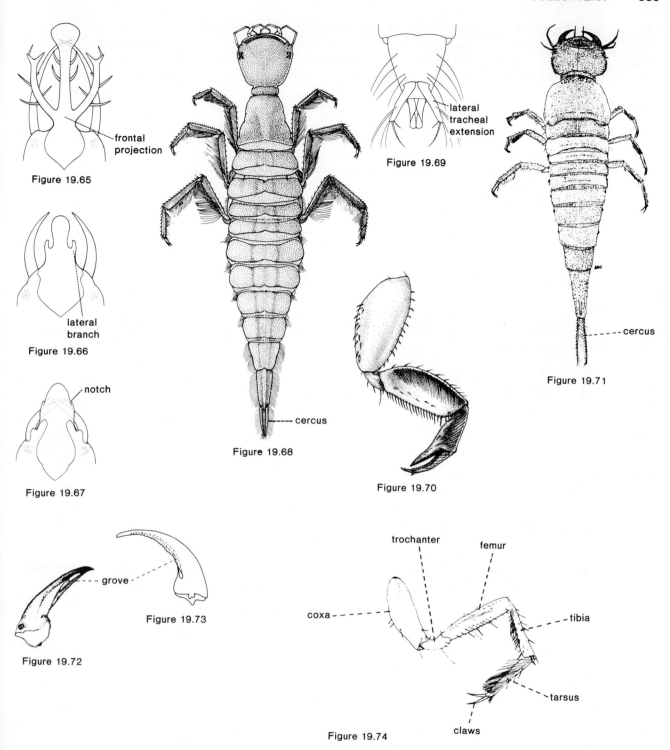

Figure 19.65

Figure 19.66

Figure 19.67

Figure 19.68

Figure 19.69

Figure 19.70

Figure 19.71

Figure 19.72

Figure 19.73

Figure 19.74

Figure 19.65. *Derovatellus* sp. (Dytiscidae) larva, dorsal aspect of frontal projection of head (after Spangler and Folkerts 1973).

Figure 19.66. *Pachydrus* sp. (Dytiscidae) larva, dorsal aspect of frontal projection of head (after Spangler and Folkerts 1973).

Figure 19.67. *Hydroporus* sp. (Dytiscidae) larva, dorsal aspect of frontal projection of head.

Figure 19.68. *Cybister* sp. (Dytiscidae) larva, dorsal aspect.

Figure 19.69. *Celina* sp. (Dytiscidae) larva, apex of abdomen (after Spangler 1973).

Figure 19.70. *Matus* sp. (Dytiscidae) larva, mesothoracic leg.

Figure 19.71. *Rhantus* sp. (Dytiscidae) larva, dorsal aspect.

Figure 19.72. *Rhantus* sp. (Dytiscidae) larva, mandible.

Figure 19.73. *Copelatus* sp. (Dytiscidae) larva, mandible.

Figure 19.74. *Rhantus* sp. (Dytiscidae) larva, metathoracic leg.

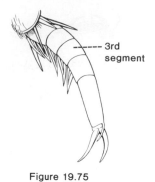

3rd segment

Figure 19.75

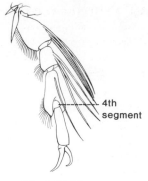

4th segment

Figure 19.76

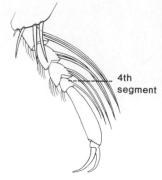

4th segment

Figure 19.77

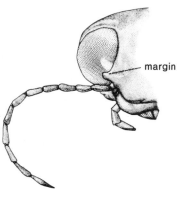

margin

Figure 19.79

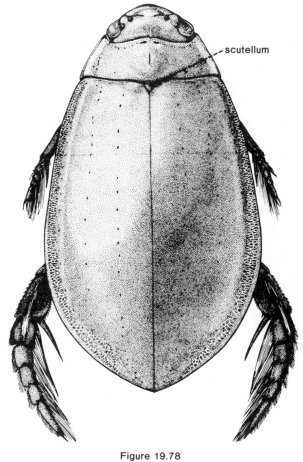

scutellum

Figure 19.78

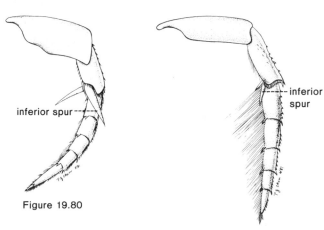

inferior spur

Figure 19.80

inferior spur

Figure 19.81

Figure 19.75. *Coptotomus* sp. (Dytiscidae) adult, tarsus of fore leg.

Figure 19.76. *Hydroporus* sp. (Dytiscidae) adult, tarsus of fore leg.

Figure 19.77. *Bidessonotus* sp. (Dytiscidae) adult, tarsus of fore leg.

Figure 19.78. *Cybister* sp. (Dytiscidae) adult, dorsal aspect.

Figure 19.79. *Coptotomus* sp. (Dytiscidae) adult, anterior aspect of head.

Figure 19.80. *Cybister* sp. (Dytiscidae) adult, hind leg.

Figure 19.81. *Acilius* sp. (Dytiscidae) adult, hind leg.

11(10). Middle coxae separated by about width of a middle coxa; prosternal process short and broad, apex obtuse .... *Pachydrus*

11'. Middle coxae separated by only one-half width of a middle coxa; prosternal process rhomboid, apex acute .... *Desmopachria*

12(10'). Head with a transverse cervical stria or suture behind eyes (fig. 19.85) 13

12'. Head without a cervical stria .... *Uvarus*

13(12). Pronotum and elytron plicate or with impressed strioles (figs. 19.86–19.88) 14

13'. Basal pronotal striole distinct, elytron without basal striole or sutural or accessory striae; figure 19.85 .... *Brachyvatus*

14(13). Clypeal margin thickened anteriorly, upturned, tuberculate, or distinctly rimmed 15

14'. Clypeal margin not thickened or only feebly so, not margined, upturned, tuberculate, or rimmed 16

15(14). Basal pronotal plicae connected by transverse depression; elytron with suture not thickened and without sutural stria (fig. 19.86) .... *Anodocheilus*

15'. Basal pronotal plicae distinct, but area between them essentially flat; elytron with suture thickened, sutural stria more or less distinct .... *Neoclypeodytes*

16(14'). Tarsi clearly 5-segmented, the 4th small, but not concealed by lobes of 3rd (fig. 19.77) .... *Bidessonotus*

16'. Tarsi each with 4th segment small and concealed between lobes of 3rd so that 5th segment appears to be 4th (as in fig. 19.76) 17

17(16'). Elytron without sutural stria, but with accessory discal stria of impressed punctures between suture and basal striole (fig. 19.87); apical sternite broad, without lateral impressions .... *Neobidessus*

17'. Elytron with sutural stria, but without accessory discal striae of impressed punctures (fig. 19.88); apical sternite narrow, impressed on either side of middle .... *Liodessus*

18(9'). Cavernicolous, known only from artesian wells in Texas; eyes minute and apparently nonfunctional; body pigmentation reduced; fore and middle coxae enlarged; prosternal process short, not reaching metasternum between middle coxae .... *Haideoporus*

18'. Surface-dwelling, not normally confined to artesian waters; eyes normal; body pigmentation normal; fore and middle coxae not enlarged; prosternal process reaching metasternum between middle coxae 19

19(18'). Base of hind femur contacting hind coxal lobe .... *Laccornis*

19'. Hind femur separated from hind coxal lobe by basal part of trochanter 20

20(19'). Epipleuron with diagonal carina crossing near base (fig. 19.89); fore and middle tarsi 4-segmented .... *Hygrotus*

20'. Epipleuron without diagonal carina crossing near base; fore and middle tarsi 5-segmented, with 4th segment small and concealed between lobes of 3rd so that 5th segment appears to be 4th (fig. 19.76) 21

21(20'). Hind margin of conjoined hind coxal processes slightly to deeply, and more or less triangularly, incised medially, lateral lobes more produced posteriorly 22

21'. Hind margin of conjoined hind coxal processes not in the least abbreviated behind, the apex either truncate or more or less angularly prominent at the middle (fig. 19.84) 23

22(21). Pronotum with a longitudinally impressed line or crease on each side, and usually with a shallow transverse impression near base or an impression on each side near base; hind femur with median row of setigerous punctures, otherwise sparsely punctate or nearly smooth; venter densely and finely punctate, with scattered or numerous coarser punctures .... *Oreodytes*

22'. Pronotum without sublateral impressed lines, usually without basal impression; hind femur usually densely punctate over entire surface; venter densely and finely punctate or somewhat granulate, usually lacking scattered large punctures .... *Deronectes* (in part)

23(21'). Hind margin of conjoined hind coxal processes either truncate or obtusely angulate medially (fig. 19.84) .... *Hydroporus* (in part)

23'.   Hind margin of conjoined hind coxal processes sinuate and somewhat angularly prominent medially (fig. 19.90) 24

24(23'). Prosternal process not protuberant; male with 4th or 4th and 5th antennal segments enlarged; basal segment of male protarsus with a ventral cupule; length greater than 3.3 mm .... *Lioporius*

24'.   Prosternal process usually protuberant (if not protuberant, then length less than 3.3 mm); male with 4th and 5th antennal segments not enlarged; male with protarsal cupule absent 25

25(24'). Hind angle of pronotum rectangular or obtuse .... *Hydroporus* (in part)

25'.   Hind angle of pronotum acute .... *Deronectes* (in part)

26(3).   Inner side of hind femur with a more or less thick group of cilia arising from a linear depression on the inner half of the inner apical angle (fig. 19.91) .... Agabini 27

26'.   Hind femur without such cilia 31

27(26). Hind coxal processes parallel-sided, lateral margins straight to apex .... *Agabinus*

27'.   Hind coxal processes not parallel-sided, lateral margins each forming a rounded lobe laterally 28

28(27'). Hind tarsal claws of equal length, if slightly unequal, then both very small, only one-third length of 5th tarsal segment 29

28'.   Hind tarsal claws obviously unequal, outer one of each pair two-thirds or less length of inner claw 30

29(28). Labial palp very short, apical segment quadrate .... *Hydrotrupes*

29'.   Labial palp approximately as long as maxillary palp, apical segment cylindrical .... *Agabus*

30(28'). Labial palp with penultimate segment triangular in cross section, the faces concave and unequal (fig. 19.92); genital valves of female dorsoventrally compressed, not armed with teeth .... *Carrhydrus*

30'.   Labial palp with penultimate segment cylindrical, not enlarged and triangular; genital valves of female laterally compressed, sawlike, with series of sharp teeth along dorsal edge .... *Ilybius*

31(26'). Prosternum with median longitudinal furrow; basal 4 hind tarsal segments lobate, each distinctly produced at upper (inner) posterior corner .... Matini .... *Matus*

31'.   Prosternum convex or keeled, without such a furrow; basal 4 hind tarsal segments not lobate at upper posterior corners 32

32(31'). Hind coxal lines divergent anteriorly, coming so close together posteriorly as to almost touch median line, then turning outward almost at right angles onto hind coxal processes (fig. 19.93); hind tarsal claws equal; pronotum narrowly, but clearly margined laterally .... Copelatini .... *Copelatus*

32'.   Hind coxal lines never almost touching median line; hind tarsal claws equal or not; pronotum margined or not 33

33(32'). Hind tarsal claws of equal length or virtually so; smaller species, 6–9 mm in length 34

33'.   Hind tarsal claws obviously unequal, outer claw only from one-third to two-thirds length of inner claw; larger species, 9–20 mm in length .... Colymbetini 35

34(33). Apical segment of palpi notched or emarginate at tip; pronotum clearly though narrowly margined laterally .... Coptotomini .... *Coptotomus*

34'.   Apical segment of palpi entire, not notched or emarginate at tip; pronotum with an exceedingly fine line along lateral edge, but not margined .... Agabetini .... *Agabetes*

35(33'). Anterior tip of metasternum (between middle coxae) clearly triangularly split to receive apex of prosternal process, the triangular channel usually deep with its apex about in line with posterior margins of middle coxae; pronotum usually margined laterally 36

35'.   Anterior tip of metasternum depressed, with shallow pit or broad notch to receive apex of prosternal process, never with sharply outlined triangular excavation; pronotum not margined 37

36(35). Prosternal process flat; dorsum unusually flat; pronotum widely margined laterally; elytron lightly reticulate throughout, the meshes rather coarse, unequal, and irregular in shape .... *Hoperius*

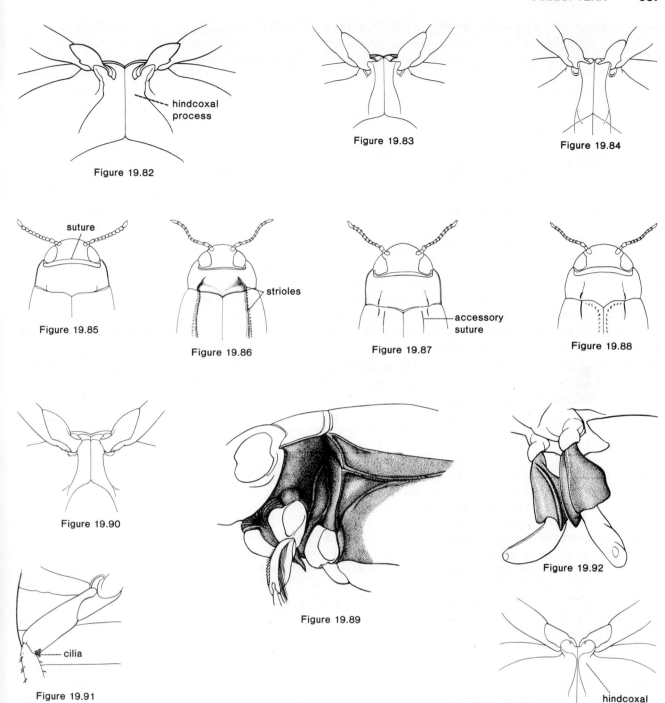

Figure 19.82. *Hydrovatus* sp. (Dytiscidae) adult, region of hind coxal processes.

Figure 19.83. *Desmopachria* sp. (Dytiscidae) adult, region of hind coxal processes.

Figure 19.84. *Hydroporus* sp. (Dytiscidae) adult, region of hind coxal processes.

Figure 19.85. *Brachyvatus* sp. (Dytiscidae) adult, head, pronotum, and bases of elytra.

Figure 19.86. *Anodocheilus* sp. (Dytiscidae) adult, head, pronotum, and bases of elytra.

Figure 19.87. *Neobidessus* sp. (Dytiscidae) adult, head, pronotum, and bases of elytra.

Figure 19.88. *Liodessus* sp. (Dytiscidae) adult, head, pronotum, and bases of elytra.

Figure 19.89. *Hygrotus* sp. (Dytiscidae) adult, ventrolateral aspect of epipleuron.

Figure 19.90. *Lioporius* sp. (Dytiscidae) adult, region of hind coxal processes (after Wolfe and Matta 1981).

Figure 19.91. *Agabus* sp. (Dytiscidae) adult, hind femur.

Figure 19.92. *Carrhydrus* sp. (Dytiscidae) adult, labial palp.

Figure 19.93. *Copelatus* sp. (Dytiscidae) adult, region of hind coxal processes.

36'.   Prosternal process convex or carinate; elytron with reticulation lightly impressed, meshes of unequal sizes and shapes, but very small (a superimposed secondary reticulation of deeply impressed lines occurs over parts of the elytron of some females) .... ***Rhantus***

37(35').   Elytral sculpture consisting of numerous parallel transverse grooves .... ***Colymbetes***

37'.   Elytron coarsely reticulate, without transverse grooves .... ***Neoscutopterus***

38(4).   Hind tarsus of male with 2 claws, of female with longer outer claw and rudimentary inner claw .... ***Megadytes***

38'.   Hind tarsus of male always, of female usually, with only 1 claw (fig. 19.80) .... ***Cybister***

39(4').   Large beetles, 20–38 mm long; posterior margins of 1st 4 hind tarsal segments bare .... Dytiscini .... ***Dytiscus***

39'.   Smaller beetles, 8–15 mm long; posterior margins of 1st 4 hind tarsal segments with a dense fringe of flat, golden cilia 40

40(39').   Posterolateral margin of elytron edged with row of small spines (figs. 19.94–19.95); apex of prosternal process sharply pointed; pronotum margined laterally; dorsal surface of hind tarsus punctate, bearing fine appressed hairs ... Eretini .... ***Eretes***

40'.   Elytron without spines on posterolateral margin; apex of prosternal process rounded; pronotum not margined laterally; dorsal surface of hind tarsus bare, except for marginal cilia 41

41(40').   Outer (shorter) spur at apex of hind tibia acute .... Hydaticini .... ***Hydaticus***

41'.   Outer spur at apex of hind tibia blunt, more or less emarginate .... Thermonectini 42

42(41').   Elytron densely punctate, also usually fluted and hairy in female .... ***Acilius***

42'.   Elytron with extremely fine punctation or none; some females with superimposed sculpture of elongate grooves, or granulate 43

43(42').   Elytron basically yellowish, uniformly speckled or vermiculate with black; hind margin of middle femur with series of stiff setae which are only about one-half as long as femur is wide .... ***Graphoderus***

43'.   Elytron black with yellow maculae or transverse bands, or yellow with black spots, or irrorate; hind margin of middle femur with series of stiff setae which are as long or longer than the femur is wide (fig. 19.96) (caution: these setae are brittle and may be broken in old or roughly handled specimens) .... ***Thermonectus***

Noteridae (Burrowing Water Beetles)

The family Noteridae is distributed widely throughout the tropical regions of both hemispheres with only a few genera and species reaching the temperate zone. The family is represented in North America north of Mexico by five genera and about 15 species.

The Palaearctic species *Noterus capricornis* Herbst has been investigated thoroughly, and its burrowing habits are the source of the family common name. Observations of noterid larvae in eastern North America indicate that most, if not all, of these species do not share the strict burrowing habits of their European relatives. In fact, they lack the chitinous point at the apex of the abdomen with which *N. capricornis* is presumed to pierce plant roots for the purpose of obtaining intercellular air.

Food habits of the larvae are unknown. Larval *N. capricornis* have been observed working their mandibles upon the surface of plant roots without, however, appearing to remove any tissue. Noterid larvae also readily attack dead chironomid larvae. The morphology of the mandible suggests an omnivorous diet; adults are predaceous.

In shallow water, larvae of *N. capricornis* renew their air supplies by bringing the apex of the abdomen to the surface. However, in the typical method of obtaining air, the apical spine of the abdomen is used to pierce plant tissue in order to tap intercellular air in the manner of chrysomelid beetles of the genus *Donacia* (chap. 4).

Pupation of *N. capricornis* also is similar to that of *Donacia*. The larva constructs a cocoon from small pieces of vegetable material mixed with mud particles on the roots of various species of aquatic plants. Larvae chew or pierce the plant root at the point of attachment of the cocoon. Air escaping from the lacerated tissue is caught in the cocoon as it is being constructed and sealed within when the larva closes the distal end. Whether North American larvae of Noteridae behave in a similar manner to *N. capricornus* is unknown. The length of the pupal period is unknown, but presumably lasts no more than a few weeks.

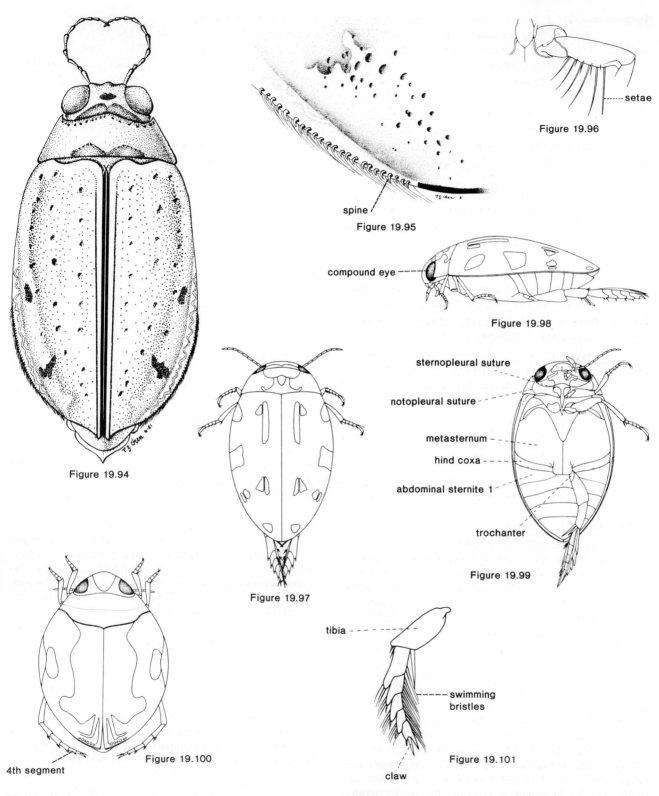

setae

Figure 19.96

spine

Figure 19.95

Figure 19.94

compound eye

Figure 19.98

sternopleural suture

notopleural suture

metasternum

hind coxa

abdominal sternite 1

trochanter

Figure 19.99

Figure 19.97

tibia

swimming bristles

Figure 19.101

claw

4th segment

Figure 19.100

Figure 19.94. *Eretes* sp. (Dytiscidae) adult, dorsal aspect.

Figure 19.95. *Eretes* sp. (Dytiscidae) adult, margin of elytron.

Figure 19.96. *Thermonectus* sp. (Dytiscidae) adult, middle femur.

Figure 19.97. *Laccophilus* sp. (Dytiscidae) adult, dorsal aspect.

Figure 19.98. *Laccophilus* sp. (Dytiscidae) adult, lateral aspect.

Figure 19.99. *Laccophilus* sp. (Dytiscidae) adult, ventral aspect.

Figure 19.100. *Desmopachria* sp. (Dytiscidae) adult, dorsal aspect.

Figure 19.101. *Laccophilus* sp. (Dytiscidae) adult, hind tibia and tarsus.

Noteridae

Larvae[1]

1.   Third antennal segment not longer than 4th; mandible with stout preapical tooth .... *Suphisellus*

1'.   Third antennal segment more than twice as long as 4th; mandible not strongly
        toothed 2

2(1').   Body globular (fig. 19.102); 3rd antennal segment about 12 times as long as 4th;
        mandible serrulate .... *Suphis*

2'.   Body cylindriform, not globular (fig. 19.103); 3rd antennal segment about 3 times
        longer than 4th; mandible simple .... *Hydrocanthus*

Adults

1.   Apex of foretibia with curved hook or spur (fig. 19.106); length usually over 2.0
        mm 2

1'.   Apex of foretibia without curved hook or spur (fig. 19.107); length usually less
        than 1.5 mm .... *Notomicrus*

2(1).   Fore tibial spurs strong, curved, and conspicuous (fig. 19.106); hind femur with
        angular cilia; prosternal process truncate posteriorly, or if rounded in the male,
        form is very broad, almost hemispherical 3

2'.   Fore tibial spurs weak and inconspicuous; hind femur usually without angular cilia;
        prosternal process rounded posteriorly in both sexes .... *Pronoterus*

3(2).   Body form very broad, almost hemispherical (fig. 19.108); color opaque black with
        irregular reddish marks on each elytron .... *Suphis*

3'.   Body form elongate, not hemispherical (fig. 19.109); elytron uniformly black,
        reddish brown, or yellowish brown, without markings or with an oblique
        yellowish crossbar just behind the middle, never with reddish marks 4

4(3').   Length usually less than 3 mm; apical segment of maxillary palpus emarginate at
        apex; prosternal process not broader than long, apex at least twice its breadth
        between the anterior coxae .... *Suphisellus*

4'.   Length usually over 4 mm; apical segment of maxillary palpus truncate at apex;
        prosternal process broader than long, apex very broad, at least 2.5–3 times its
        breadth between the anterior coxae; figure 19.109 .... *Hydrocanthus*

Hydroscaphidae (Skiff Beetles)

The Hydroscaphidae is a small family of worldwide distribution, though mainly tropical. Three genera and fewer than a dozen species are recognized. Only *Hydroscapha* LeConte is known from the United States, represented by *H. natans* LeConte, which extends northward from Mexico through the western states to Idaho.

Hydroscaphids are rare in collections probably because most collecting is done with nets having too coarse a mesh to retain them. Once located, hydroscaphids frequently are very abundant and hundreds may be collected in a rather short time. Although adults may be found under stones as much as a meter below the surface of fast-flowing streams, larvae and adults occur most commonly on algae over which a thin film of water is flowing. Often the water is so shallow that the adults are only partially submerged. *Hydroscapha natans* occurs over a wide range of temperatures, from hot springs (46°C) to mountain streams that freeze nightly throughout summer.

A single, remarkably large egg develops at a time, occupying a fourth of the female's abdomen. Larvae (fig. 19.16) and adults (fig. 19.26) remain in and feed upon algae. Pupation occurs at the edge of the water film or even among algae over which the water film is flowing. Pupae lie partially within the last larval exuviae.

In larval *H. natans,* only the first pair of thoracic spiracles and those of the first and eighth abdominal segments are functional. All three pairs are balloonlike, more than twice as long as wide. Presumably gas exchange takes place across the walls of these "balloons" providing a water-air interface available for respiration that is about an order of magnitude greater per milligram wet body weight than that across the spiracles of terrestrial insects.

Adult *Hydroscapha* apparently breathe by means of an air bubble carried under the elytra (physical gills, see chap. 4). A fringe of cilia on the hind wings and setae on the dorsum covered by the elytra serve to retain this bubble.

[1]The larvae of *Notomicrus* and *Pronoterus* are unknown.

Figure 19.102

Figure 19.103

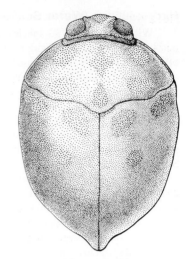

Figure 19.108

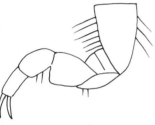

Figure 19.104

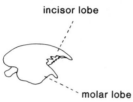

incisor lobe

molar lobe

Figure 19.105

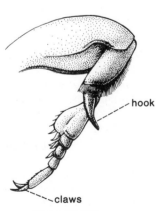

hook

claws

Figure 19.106

Figure 19.107

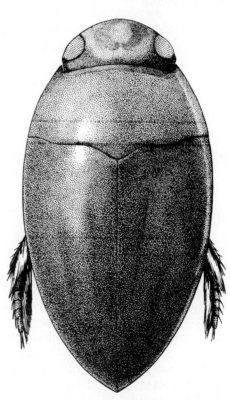

Figure 19.109

Figure 19.102. *Suphis* sp. (Noteridae) larva, dorsal aspect (after Spangler and Folkerts 1973).

Figure 19.103. *Hydrocanthus* sp. (Noteridae) larva, dorsal aspect.

Figure 19.104. *Noterus* sp. (Noteridae) larva, fore leg (not in key) (after Bertrand 1972).

Figure 19.105. *Noterus* sp. (Noteridae) larva, mandible (not in key) (after Bertrand 1972).

Figure 19.106. *Hydrocanthus* sp. (Noteridae) adult, fore leg.

Figure 19.107. *Notomicrus* sp. (Noteridae) adult, fore leg.

Figure 19.108. *Suphis* sp. (Noteridae) adult, dorsal aspect.

Figure 19.109. *Hydrocanthus* sp. (Noteridae) adult, dorsal aspect.

Hydrophilidae (Water Scavenger Beetles)

With more than 230 species, Hydrophilidae ranks second in abundance to Dytiscidae, and these two families most often come to mind when one considers aquatic Coleoptera. Although dytiscids often are distasteful to predators, hydrophilids usually are not, which seems to have led to mimicry, particularly common in lentic species.

The common name is not accurate since most hydrophilid larvae are predators, most adults are omnivores, consuming both living and dead materials, and the subfamily Sphaeridiinae is not aquatic.

Eggs are deposited underwater in silk cases that may contain more than 100 eggs. Larvae go through three instars rapidly in one to several months. Even though a few species possess lateral gills allowing them to occupy deeper habitats, most must obtain oxygen at the waterline through terminal abdominal spiracles. The larvae are poor swimmers and tend to lie in wait for prey. The genera *Hydrophilus, Tropisternus* and *Hydrobius* often consume their prey out of water. When mature, larvae leave the water to construct pupal chambers in moist soil, under rocks, and in organic debris. Some species may pupate in emergent vegetation and floating algal mats some distance from shore.

Adults generally are good swimmers but not as active as many of the Dytiscidae. They must return to the surface to renew their air supply. Typically they break the surface film with the antennae and side of the head; this allows gas exchange along the plastron and air passage on the ventral surface of the thorax. Some gas exchange, providing an auxiliary oxygen source, may occur via the plastron while submerged. Adults are active flyers and have been shown capable of leaving the water many times. Mass emergence and flight periods are not uncommon, and large numbers may be attracted to lights.

Hydrophilidae are most common in small pools and ponds with emergent vegetation and few predators. Adults can be collected throughout most of the year. With the exception of a few of the more common genera, larvae are rarely collected, perhaps because of the relatively short larval cycle, compared with most other families of aquatic Coleoptera.

Hydrophilidae

Larvae[1]

1.	Nine complete abdominal segments, 10th reduced but distinct (fig. 19.110); integument noticeably chitinized	***Helophorus***
1'.	Eight complete abdominal segments, segments 9 and 10 reduced and forming a stigmatic atrium (atrium absent in *Berosus*)	2
2(1').	Antennae with points of insertion nearer anterolateral angles of head than are insertion points of mandibles; labium and maxillae inserted in furrow beneath head	***Hydrochus***
2'.	Antennae with points of insertion further from anterolateral angles than those of mandibles; labium and maxillae inserted at anterior margin of ventral side of head	3
3(2').	Abdominal segments with broad (fig. 19.129) or long (fig. 19.112) lateral projections	4
3'.	Lateral projections usually absent; if projections present (fig. 19.128), not nearly so prominent	5
4(3).	First 7 abdominal segments with long, lateral tracheal gills (fig. 19.112); mandibles as in figure 19.113, clypeus as in figure 19.114	***Berosus***
4'.	Abdominal segments and posterior thoracic segments with broad, lateral projections (fig. 19.129)	***Crenitis***
5(3').	Antennae biramal, terminal articles accompanied by a fingerlike antennal appendage	6
5'.	Antennae not biramal, fingerlike antennal appendages absent	16
6(5).	Legs completely invisible from above and very reduced, without claws; ligula present	***Chaetarthria***
6'.	Legs sometimes very small and not visible from above, but always complete, with claws (fig. 19.134); ligula present or absent	7
7(6').	Frontal sutures parallel and not uniting to form an epicranial suture (fig. 19.115); ligula absent	***Laccobius***
7'.	Frontal sutures not parallel (as in fig. 19.142); epicranial suture present or not; ligula present	8

[1]The larvae of *Crenitulus, Dibolocelus,* and *Epimetopus* either are not well known or are not yet described for North America.

8(7').   Ligula shorter than segment 1 of labial palp .... *Helobata*

8'.   Ligula longer than segment 1 of labial palp 9

9(8').   Antenna short; epicranial suture absent; legs reduced 10

9'.   Antenna longer; epicranial suture present, but usually short; legs fairly long, not
reduced 11

10(9).   Frons truncate behind; clypeus as in figure 19.117; mandible with 2 inner teeth
(fig. 19.116); ligula about as long as palp, apparently 2-segmented; anterior
margin of pronotum without a fringe of stout setae; legs not visible from above .... *Paracymus*

10'.   Frons rounded behind; clypeus with 4 teeth (fig. 19.119); mandible with 3 inner
teeth (fig. 19.118); ligula not as long as palp, 1-segmented; anterior margin of
pronotum with a fringe of stout setae; legs barely visible from above .... *Anacaena*

11(9').   Mandibles asymmetrical, the left with 2 inner teeth, the right with only 1 (fig.
19.121); abdomen with prolegs on segments 3 through 7; figure 19.120 .... *Enochrus*

11'.   Mandibles symmetrical, each with 2–3 teeth (fig. 19.122); abdomen without
prolegs 12

12(11').   Clypeus with 4 distinct teeth (fig. 19.123) .... *Ametor*

12'.   Clypeus with 5 or more distinct teeth 13

13(12').   Clypeus with 5 distinct teeth though middle tooth may be small (fig. 19.140) 20

13'.   Clypeus with 6 or more distinct teeth; mandible with 2 inner teeth 14

14(13').   Clypeus with 6 distinct teeth, placed in 2 groups, 2 on the left and 4 on the right
(fig. 19.125); figure 19.124 .... *Helochares*

14'.   Clypeus with more than 6 teeth, those toward right not as clearly defined and with
several smaller teeth (fig. 19.126) 15

15(14').   Clypeus with tooth on left side smaller than tooth on right side (fig. 19.126) .... *Cymbiodyta*

15'.   Clypeus with left and right side teeth equal in size .... *Helocombus*

16(5').   Mesothorax, metathorax, and 1st abdominal segment each with 3 setiferous,
lateral gills (fig. 19.127); abdominal segments 2 through 6 each with 4
moderately long, setiferous, lateral gills (fig. 19.128); femur without fringe of
long swimming hairs .... *Derallus*

16'.   Gills absent or, if present, with only a single lateral gill on each side of abdominal
segments; femur with fringe of long swimming hairs 17

17(16').   Head subspherical; mandibles not symmetrical, left mandible very robust, right
mandible much more slender (fig. 19.130); pronotum not entirely sclerotized .... *Hydrophilus*

17'.   Head subquadrangular or subrectangular, mandibles symmetrical or not (figs.
19.132, 19.139), pronotum entirely sclerotized 18

18(17').   Mentum convex toward basal half, anterolateral angles less prominent (figs.
19.132–19.133); lateral abdominal gills well developed and pubescent (fig.
19.131) .... *Hydrochara*

18'.   Mentum with sides almost straight, anterolateral angles very prominent; lateral
abdominal gills rudimentary, but indicated by tubercular projections, each with
several terminal setae (fig. 19.135) 19

19(18').   Mesonotal and metanotal sclerites much reduced, triangular, hind margins very
narrow, almost pedunculate (fig. 19.135); apex of ligula not bifid; lateral
abdominal gills of 9th segment short (fig. 19.136) .... *Tropisternus*

19'.   Mesonotal and metanotal sclerites not much reduced, trapezoidal hind margins
almost as wide as anterior margin; apex of ligula shallowly bifid; lateral
abdominal gills of 9th segment very long, conspicuous; clypeus with numerous
irregular teeth (fig. 19.137) .... *Hydrobiomorpha*

20(13).   Middle tooth on clypeus smaller than the others (figs. 19.139–19.140); prosternum
entire; figure 19.138 .... *Sperchopsis*

20'.   All teeth on clypeus subequal, outer left tooth usually a little distant from the rest
(fig. 19.142); prosternum with a mesal fracture; figure 19.141 .... *Hydrobius*

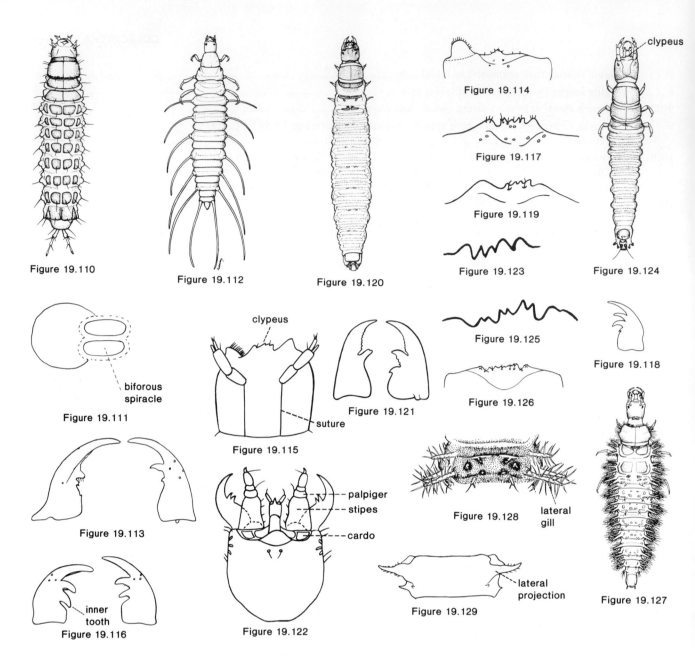

Figure 19.110

Figure 19.112

Figure 19.120

Figure 19.114

Figure 19.117

Figure 19.119

Figure 19.123

clypeus

Figure 19.124

biforous spiracle

Figure 19.111

clypeus

suture

Figure 19.115

Figure 19.121

Figure 19.125

Figure 19.126

Figure 19.118

Figure 19.113

palpiger
stipes
cardo

Figure 19.122

lateral gill

Figure 19.128

Figure 19.127

inner tooth
Figure 19.116

lateral projection

Figure 19.129

Figure 19.110. *Helophorus* sp. (Hydrophilidae) larva, dorsal aspect.

Figure 19.111. Hydrophilidae larva, spiracle.

Figure 19.112. *Berosus* sp. (Hydrophilidae) larva, dorsal aspect.

Figure 19.113. *Berosus* sp. (Hydrophilidae) larva, dorsal aspect of mandibles.

Figure 19.114. *Berosus* sp. (Hydrophilidae) larva, clypeus.

Figure 19.115. *Laccobius* sp. (Hydrophilidae) larva, dorsal aspect of head.

Figure 19.116. *Paracymus* sp. (Hydrophilidae) larva, dorsal aspect of mandibles (after Richmond 1920).

Figure 19.117. *Paracymus* sp. (Hydrophilidae) larva, clypeus (after Richmond 1920).

Figure 19.118. *Anacaena* sp. (Hydrophilidae) larva, dorsal aspect of right mandible (after Bertrand 1972).

Figure 19.119. *Anacaena* sp. (Hydrophilidae) larva, clypeus (after Brigham 1982).

Figure 19.120. *Enochrus* sp. (Hydrophilidae) larva, dorsal aspect.

Figure 19.121. *Enochrus* sp. (Hydrophilidae) larva, dorsal aspect of mandibles.

Figure 19.122. *Ametor* sp. (Hydrophilidae) larva, ventral aspect of head (after Bertrand 1972).

Figure 19.123. *Ametor* sp. (Hydrophilidae) larva, clypeus (after Bertrand 1972).

Figure 19.124. *Helochares* sp. (Hydrophilidae) larva, dorsal aspect.

Figure 19.125. *Helochares* sp. (Hydrophilidae) larva, clypeus.

Figure 19.126. *Cymbiodyta* sp. (Hydrophilidae) larva, clypeus (after Richmond 1920).

Figure 19.127. *Derallus* sp. (Hydrophilidae) larva, dorsal aspect.

Figure 19.128. *Derallus* sp. (Hydrophilidae) larva, dorsal aspect of 2nd abdominal segment.

Figure 19.129. *Crenitus* sp. (Hydrophilidae) larva, dorsal aspect of 2nd abdominal segment (after Bertrand 1972).

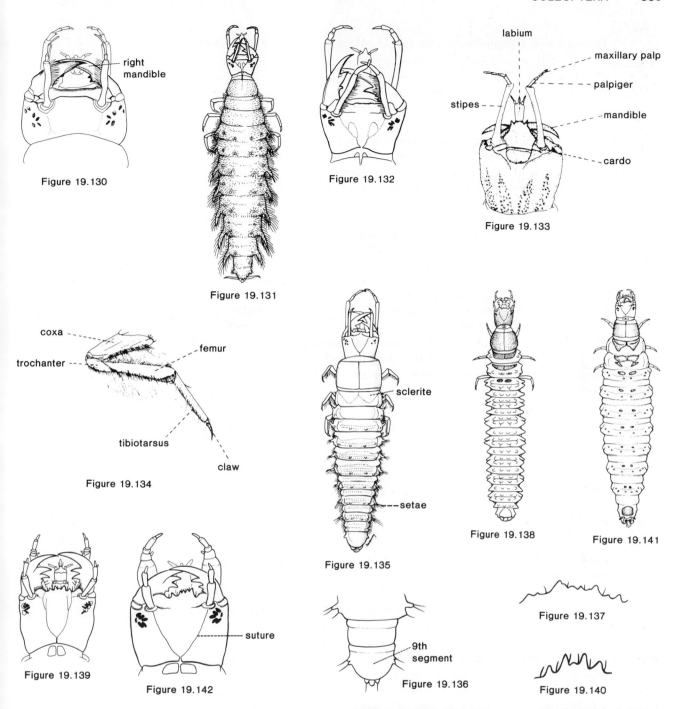

Figure 19.130

Figure 19.131

Figure 19.132

Figure 19.133

Figure 19.134

Figure 19.135

Figure 19.136

Figure 19.137

Figure 19.138

Figure 19.139

Figure 19.140

Figure 19.141

Figure 19.142

Figure 19.130. *Hydrophilus* sp. (Hydrophilidae) larva, dorsal aspect of head.

Figure 19.131. *Hydrochara* sp. (Hydrophilidae) larva, dorsal aspect.

Figure 19.132. *Hydrochara* sp. (Hydrophilidae) larva, dorsal aspect of head.

Figure 19.133. *Hydrochara* sp. (Hydrophilidae) larva, ventral aspect of head.

Figure 19.134. *Hydrochara* sp. (Hydrophilidae) larva, leg.

Figure 19.135. *Tropisternus* sp. (Hydrophilidae) larva, dorsal aspect.

Figure 19.136. *Tropisternus* sp. (Hydrophilidae) larva, dorsal aspect of last abdominal segments.

Figure 19.137. *Hydrobiomorpha* sp. (Hydrophilidae) larva, clypeus (after Bertrand 1972).

Figure 19.138. *Sperchopsis* sp. (Hydrophilidae) larva, dorsal aspect.

Figure 19.139. *Sperchopsis* sp. (Hydrophilidae) larva, dorsal aspect of head.

Figure 19.140. *Sperchopsis* sp. (Hydrophilidae) larva, clypeus.

Figure 19.141. *Hydrobius* sp. (Hydrophilidae) larva, dorsal aspect.

Figure 19.142. *Hydrobius* sp. (Hydrophilidae) larva, dorsal aspect of head.

Adults

1.   Pronotum with 5 longitudinal grooves (fig. 19.143) or expanded anteriorly (as in
        fig. 19.144) 2

1'.   Pronotum not as above 3

2(1).   Pronotum with 5 longitudinal grooves (fig. 19.143) .... Helophorinae .... *Helophorus*

2'.   Pronotum lacking grooves, expanded anteriorly at middle to cover much of head
        (fig. 19.144) .... Epimetopinae .... *Epimetopus*

3(1'). Eyes protruding, pronotum distinctly narrower than elytra bases (fig. 19.145);
        scutellum small; antenna with 3 or fewer segments before cupule .... Hydrochinae .... *Hydrochus*

3'.   Eyes prominent or not; pronotum not distinctly narrower than elytra (some
        Berosini may have narrow pronotum but scutellum is long and triangular);
        antenna often having 5 segments before cupule 4

4(3'). First segment of hind tarsi shorter than 2nd; antenna shorter or only about same
        length as maxillary palp; last glabrous segment of antenna asymmetrical and
        often cuplike, embracing 1st segment of pubescent, triarticulate club; 2nd
        segment of maxillary palpi similar in thickness to 3rd or 4th 5

4'.   First segment of hind tarsi longer than 2nd; antennae usually longer than
        maxillary palpi, last glabrous segment of antennae obconic (form of a reversed
        cone) and fitted tightly against pubescent club; 2nd segment of maxillary palpi
        noticeably thicker than 3rd or 4th .... terrestrial subfamily Sphaeridiinae not considered here

5(4).   Mesosternum and metasternum with a continuous median longitudinal keel which
        is prolonged posteriorly into a spine between the hind coxae (fig. 19.146) .... Hydrophilinae 6

5'.   Mesosternum and metasternum without a continuous spine 10

6(5).   Size smaller, length usually less than 16 mm 7

6'.   Size larger, length usually more than 25 mm 9

7(6).   Length rarely exceeding 12 mm; prosternum sulcate; metasternal spine long (fig.
        19.146) .... *Tropisternus*

7'.   Length usually greater than 13 mm; prosternum carinate; metasternal spine short
        (fig. 19.150) 8

8(7'). Clypeus broadly emarginate on its anterior border (fig. 19.148), exposing
        articulation of the labrum; figure 19.147 .... *Hydrobiomorpha*

8'.   Clypeus truncate; figures 19.149–19.151 .... *Hydrochara*

9(6'). Prosternal process closed in front, hood-shaped (fig. 19.153) .... *Hydrophilus*

9'.   Prosternal process not closed in front, bifurcate (fig. 19.156) .... *Dibolocelus*

10(5'). Basal 2 abdominal sternites with a common excavation on each side that is covered
        with a bilobed ciliated plate .... Chaetarthriinae .... *Chaetarthria*

10'.   Basal abdominal sternites without such an excavation on each side and without a
        bilobed plate 11

11(10'). Middle and hind tibiae fringed on the inner side with long swimming hairs;
        pronotum not continuous in outline with elytra (fig. 19.155) .... Berosinae 12

11'.   Middle and hind tibiae without swimming hairs; pronotum and elytra continuous
        in outline .... Hydrobiinae 13

12(11). Smaller species, 1.5–2 mm long; black, very convex beetles (fig. 19.154) .... *Derallus*

12'.   Larger species, 2–6 mm long, usually greater than 3 mm long; brown to yellowish
        beetles, usually with a highly patterned elytra and dark pronotal markings (fig.
        19.155) .... *Berosus*

13(11'). Elytron without striae, including the sutural stria (fig. 19.157) .... *Laccobius*

13'.   Elytron with at least a sutural stria (fig. 19.158) 14

14(13'). Maxillary palp short and stout, about the same length as antenna, last segment as
        long or longer than penultimate segment 15

14'.   Maxillary palp slender, much longer than antenna; last segment usually shorter
        than penultimate segment 21

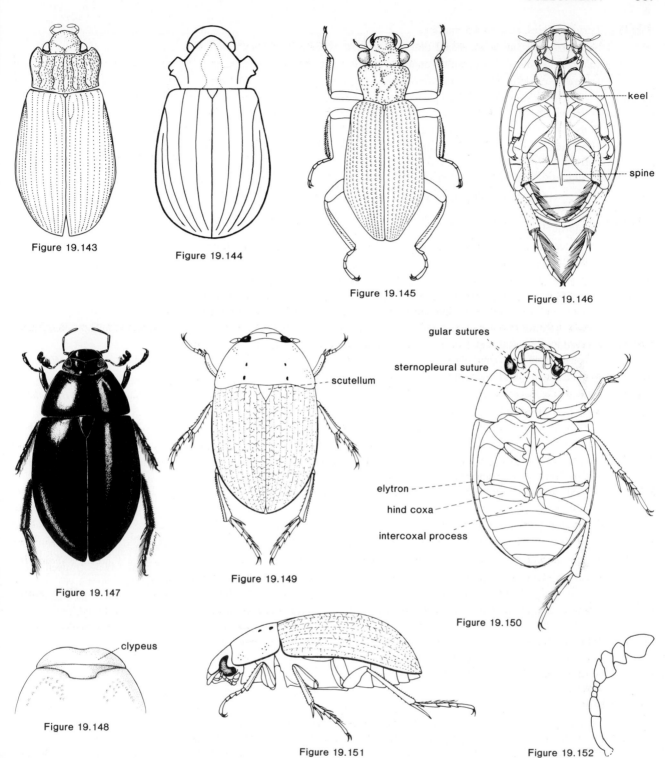

Figure 19.143

Figure 19.144

Figure 19.145

Figure 19.146

keel

spine

Figure 19.147

scutellum

Figure 19.149

gular sutures

sternopleural suture

elytron

hind coxa

intercoxal process

Figure 19.150

clypeus

Figure 19.148

Figure 19.151

Figure 19.152

Figure 19.143. *Helophorus* sp. (Hydrophilidae) adult, dorsal aspect.

Figure 19.144. *Epimetopus* sp. (Hydrophilidae) adult, dorsal aspect.

Figure 19.145. *Hydrochus* sp. (Hydrophilidae) adult, dorsal aspect.

Figure 19.146. *Tropisternus* sp. (Hydrophilidae) adult, ventral aspect.

Figure 19.147. *Hydrobiomorpha* sp. (Hydrophilidae) adult, dorsal aspect.

Figure 19.148. *Hydrobiomorpha* sp. (Hydrophilidae) adult, clypeus.

Figure 19.149. *Hydrochara* sp. (Hydrophilidae) adult, dorsal aspect.

Figure 19.150. *Hydrochara* sp. (Hydrophilidae) adult, ventral aspect.

Figure 19.151. *Hydrochara* sp. (Hydrophilidae) adult, lateral aspect.

Figure 19.152. *Hydrochara* sp. (Hydrophilidae) adult, antenna.

15(14).   Larger species, at least 4.5 mm long 16

15'.   Smaller species, not more than 3 mm long 18

16(15).   Lateral margins of elytron and pronotum smooth .... *Hydrobius*

16'.   Lateral margins of elytron and pronotum serrate or emarginate (fig. 19.158) 17

17(16').   Body shape strongly convex, clypeus deeply emarginate; eastern North America;
             figures 19.158–19.159 .... *Sperchopsis*

17'.   Body oval; clypeus shallowly emarginate; western North America .... *Ametor*

18(15').   Hind tarsal segments united longer than tibia; elytra narrowed posteriorly almost
             from the humerus .... *Crenitulus*

18'.   Hind tarsus at most no longer than tibia; body shape short and convex 19

19(18').   Prosternum longitudinally carinate (fig. 19.161); hind femur at most sparsely
             pubescent (fig. 19.160) .... *Paracymus*

19'.   Prosternum not carinate; hind femur densely pubescent 20

20(19').   Mesosternum simple, not carinate or with a small transverse protuberance before
             middle coxae .... *Crenitis*

20'.   Mesosternum with a prominent angularly elevated or dentiform protuberance
             before middle coxae (fig. 19.162) .... *Anacaena*

21(14').   All tarsi 5-segmented, basal segment may be very small and difficult to see 22

21'.   Middle and hind tarsi 4-segmented 24

22(21).   Curved pseudobasal segment (actual basal segment very small) of maxillary palp
             convex anteriorly (fig. 19.163) .... *Enochrus*

22'.   Curved pseudobasal segment of maxillary palp convex posteriorly 23

23(22').   Labrum visible .... *Helochares*

23'.   Labrum concealed beneath clypeus that projects laterally in front of eyes (fig.
             19.164) .... *Helobata*

24(21').   Mesosternum with a compressed conical process (fig. 19.165); maxillary palp long
             and slender .... *Helocombus*

24'.   Mesosternal carina transverse or elevated at the middle forming a pyramidal or
             dentiform protuberance (fig. 19.166); maxillary palp shorter and stouter .... *Cymbiodyta*

Hydraenidae (Minute Moss Beetles)

As both adults and larvae, the Hydraenidae are small (1–2 mm), inconspicuous, and semiaquatic. More than 80 species presently are recognized for the United States and Canada, most of which have been described in the past few years. Most adults and larvae occur along a narrow band from the waterline to less than 8 cm above it. They may be found also as much as 2–3 cm deep in the littoral zone substrate. Hydraenids may occur very commonly in lotic systems but, because of their habitat, are not often collected by usual stream sampling methods.

Eggs are deposited singly on wood and stones just beneath the waterline. Newly hatched larvae leave the water once the cuticle has hardened and begin feeding on protozoans and periphyton from leaves and twigs trapped above the water's edge. After larvae mature, in one year or less, pupal chambers are constructed in sand along the littoral zone. Little is known of adult life histories, although they appear to be long lived, feeding on bacteria and fungus from decaying leaves.

Hydraenidae

Larvae

1.   Setae on clypeus not placed at anterior margin and 2 median ones distant from
             each other; lacinia mobilis narrower; inner lobe of maxillae not distinctly divided
             apically; cerci nearly contiguous proximally and divergent (fig. 19.167) .... *Ochthebius*

1'.   Setae on clypeus placed at anterior margin and equidistant; lacinia mobilis
             broader; inner maxillary lobe distinctly divided apically; cerci widely separated
             proximally and nearly parallel 2

2(1').   Third antennal segment without inner swellings, segment 2 with a single antennal
             appendage; a pair of pectinate setae at anterior margin of labrum .... *Hydraena*

2'.   Third antennal segment with an inner swelling; segment 2 with 2 slender antennal
             appendages; no pectinate setae at anterior labral margin; inner maxillary lobe
             strongly divided .... *Limnebius*

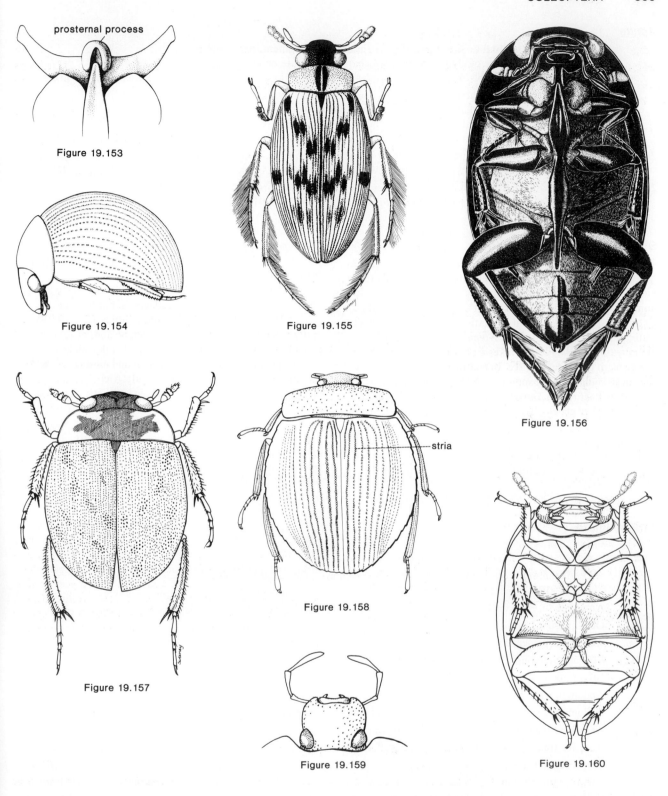

prosternal process

Figure 19.153

Figure 19.154

Figure 19.155

Figure 19.156

Figure 19.157

stria

Figure 19.158

Figure 19.159

Figure 19.160

Figure 19.153. *Hydrophilus* sp. (Hydrophilidae) adult, prosternal process.

Figure 19.154. *Derallus* sp. (Hydrophilidae) adult, lateral aspect.

Figure 19.155. *Berosus* sp. (Hydrophilidae) adult, dorsal aspect.

Figure 19.156. *Dibolocelus* sp. (Hydrophilidae) adult, ventral aspect.

Figure 19.157. *Laccobius* sp. (Hydrophilidae) adult, dorsal aspect.

Figure 19.158. *Sperchopsis* sp. (Hydrophilidae) adult, dorsal aspect.

Figure 19.159. *Sperchopsis* sp. (Hydrophilidae) adult, dorsal aspect of head.

Figure 19.160. *Paracymus* sp. (Hydrophilidae) adult, ventral aspect.

Adults

1.   Second segment of hind tarsi elongate; longer than the 3rd segment; pronotum as broad basally as base of elytra, smooth, not coarsely punctate or sculptured, sides evenly arcuate; black or rufescent beetles, about 1 mm long .... Limnebiinae .... *Limnebius*

1'.   Second segment of hind tarsi short, about as long as 3rd; pronotum at base slightly or decidedly narrower than base of elytra, surface uneven, coarsely punctate or with a transparent lateral boarder, sides sinuate or irregular; black, reddish, or aenescent beetles, 1–2 mm long .... Hydraeninae 2

2(1').   Maxillary palpi very long, much longer than antennae (antenna as in fig. 19.170); pronotum coarsely, closely punctate, sides without a transparent border .... *Hydraena*

2'.   Maxillary palpi shorter than antennae; pronotum variously sculptured, often with deep fossae and grooves, almost always with a transparent border in at least basal half; figure 19.171 .... *Ochthebius*

Staphylinidae (Rove Beetles)

The abbreviated elytra (figs. 19.172–19.175) of most of these beetles (and the Melyridae) differentiate them from all other aquatic Coleoptera. Staphylinidae are extremely common in damp habitats, including the littoral zone of fresh and saline waters; however, few are truly aquatic. For example, in fresh water, genera such as *Bledius, Stenus,* and *Carpelimus* are abundant in streamside and lakeside environments, but none live beneath the water surface. In contrast, Staphylinidae are the most common Coleoptera in North American marine habitats with at least 12 genera occupying intertidal habitats. A host of other genera frequent decaying wrack (or marine vegetation) on supertidal beaches but are only rarely submerged by excessively high tides and cannot be considered aquatic. Many of the intertidal species inhabit air spaces in crevices in rocks. This group includes the genera *Diaulota, Diglotta, Bryothinusa, Amblopusa,* and *Liparocephalus.* Other species occupy burrows they excavate in sandy beaches

(*Thinopinus, Bledius, Micralymma, Diglotta, Pontamalota, Thinusa*), and a few are found in *Salicornia* (glasswort) flats (*Bledius, Carpelimus, Thinobius*).

Biology of most aquatic Staphylinidae is poorly known. Most species are likely to be predaceous, but little precise information is available. Larval staphylinids (fig. 19.9) generally resemble the adults in body shape and, at least in the case of known marine species, occupy similar niches.

Staphylinidae is one of the largest and most poorly known families of Coleoptera. The subfamily Aleocharinae, which includes most of the marine forms, is in drastic need of comprehensive study. The following key includes only adults of taxa believed to have aquatic members. Larvae, which are very incompletely studied, are not included here. The large number of semiaquatic and littoral genera are best identified with general taxonomic works (Arnett 1960; Moore and Legner 1974). Maritime species are treated by Moore and Legner (1976).

Staphylinidae

Adults

1.   Antennae inserted on side margins of head, between eyes and mandibles (figs. 19.172–19.173) 2

1'.   Antennae inserted on vertex between inner margins of eyes; figures 19.174, 19.175 8

2(1).   Ocelli absent 4

2'.   Two ocelli present between eyes .... Omaliinae 3

3(2').   Elytra much longer than wide, covering all but 3–4 terminal abdominal segments .... *Psephidonus*

3'.   Elytra about as long as wide, exposing 5–6 abdominal segments .... *Micralymma*

4(2).   Abdomen with 7 visible sternites 5

4'.   Abdomen with 6 visible sternites (1st and 2nd sternites coalesced); figure 19.173 .... *Thinopinus*

5(4).   Anterior tibiae bearing 2 rows of stiff, projecting spines (fig. 19.176) 6

5'.   Anterior tibiae pubescent, lacking large, stiff spines 7

6(5).   Tarsal segmentation 4–4–4 .... *Bledius*

6'.   Tarsal segmentation 3–3–3 .... *Psamathobledius, Microbledius*

7(5').   Scutellum concealed; tarsi with 3 segments .... *Carpelimus*

7'.   Scutellum visible; tarsi with 2 segments .... *Thinobius*

8(1').   Hind coxae expanded laterally (fig. 19.177) .... Aleocharinae 9

8'.   Hind coxae conical, not extending laterally (fig. 19.178) .... Steninae .... *Stenus*

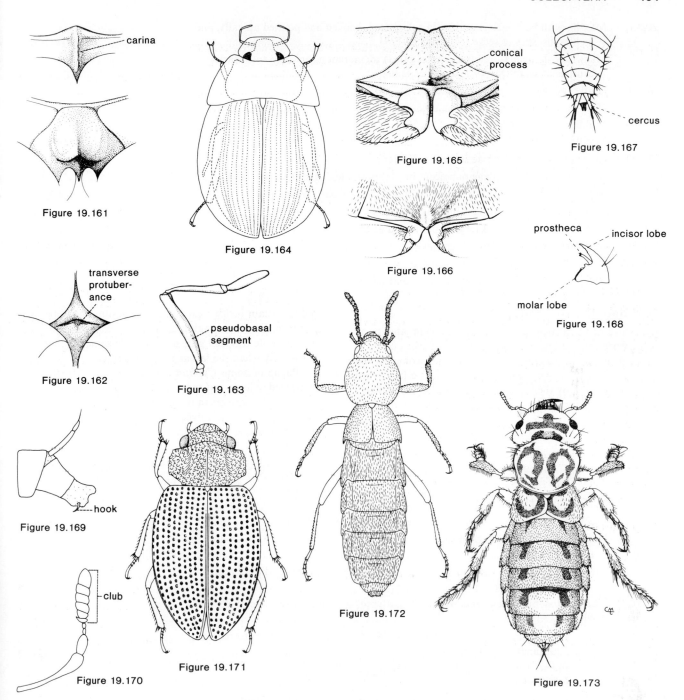

carina

Figure 19.161

conical process

Figure 19.165

cercus

Figure 19.167

Figure 19.164

Figure 19.166

prostheca

incisor lobe

molar lobe

Figure 19.168

transverse protuberance

Figure 19.162

pseudobasal segment

Figure 19.163

hook

Figure 19.169

club

Figure 19.170

Figure 19.171

Figure 19.172

Figure 19.173

Figure 19.161. *Paracymus* sp. (Hydrophilidae) adult, pro- and mesosternum.

Figure 19.162. *Anacaena* sp. (Hydrophilidae) adult, mesosternum.

Figure 19.163. *Enochrus* sp. (Hydrophilidae) adult, maxillary palp.

Figure 19.164. *Helobata* sp. (Hydrophilidae) adult, dorsal aspect.

Figure 19.165. *Helocombus* sp. (Hydrophilidae) adult, mesosternum.

Figure 19.166. *Cymbiodyta* sp. (Hydrophilidae) adult, mesosternum.

Figure 19.167. *Ochthebius* sp. (Hydraenidae) larva, dorsal aspect of last abdominal segments.

Figure 19.168. *Ochthebius* sp. (Hydraenidae) larva, mandible.

Figure 19.169. *Limnebius* sp. (Hydraenidae) larva, lateral view of last abdominal segments.

Figure 19.170. *Hydraena* sp. (Hydraenidae) adult, antenna.

Figure 19.171. *Ochthebius* sp. (Hydraenidae) adult, dorsal aspect.

Figure 19.172. *Pontamalota* sp. (Staphylinidae) adult, dorsal aspect.

Figure 19.173. *Thinopinus* sp. (Staphylinidae) adult, dorsal aspect.

9(8). Maxilla with both lacinia and galea sclerotized, hooked and pointed apically, and
lacking brushes of setae (as in fig. 19.179) .... *Bryothinusa*

9'. Maxilla with lacinia (and usually the galea) membranous apically and bearing
brushes of setae (fig. 19.180) 10

10(9'). Hind tarsi with 5 segments 11

10'. Hind tarsi with 4 segments .... *Diglotta*

11(10). Middle tarsi with 4 segments .... Bolitocharini 12

11'. Middle tarsi with 5 segments .... *Pontamalota*

12(11). Anterior and middle tibiae set with stiff spines 13

12'. Anterior and middle tibiae pubescent or glabrous, lacking stiff spines 14

13(12). Abdominal tergite 5 with transverse impression near base; figure 19.172 .... *Phytosus*

13'. Abdominal tergite 5 without impression near base; figure 19.174 .... *Thinusa*

14(12'). Abdomen with at least 3 tergites impressed at base 15

14'. Abdomen without impressed tergites (fig. 19.174) .... *Liparocephalus*

15(14). Abdomen with 5th tergite impressed at base .... *Amblopusa*

15'. Abdomen with 5th tergite not impressed at base .... *Diaulota*

Scirtidae (Marsh Beetles)

The Scirtidae (=Helodidae) are more common in other parts
of the world, but at least 30 species in seven genera occur in
North America. In general, the taxonomy and ecology of the
group are poorly known even though the aquatic larvae are
easily recognized by their many segmented, long antennae.

Larvae go through 4–8 instars and mature within one
year, grazing on rotting leaves and decaying vegetation. They
tend to remain just beneath the surface film and obtain oxygen from the air through a modified spiracle on segment 8.
The retractile trachael gills may provide some auxiliary oxygen supply when the larvae are submerged.

Pupae of some *Cyphon* and *Scirtes* hang freely from
submerged objects, but most species leave the water to construct pupal chambers in wood, mud, moss, or sand. The terrestrial adults are short lived, and it is not known if they feed.
Little is known of mating or egg deposition.

Scirtidae

Larvae[1]

1. Head with 3 ocelli on each side; anterior margin of hypopharynx with a central
cone bearing 1 pair of flat, usually serrate spines (fig. 19.181) .... *Elodes*

1'. Head with 1–2 ocelli on each side; cone of hypopharynx with 2 pairs of spines (fig.
19.182) 2

2(1'). Abdominal segments 3–6 with a regular series of short, flattened, differentiated
setae along lateral margin 4

2'. Sides of abdominal segments with only scattered, thin setae, like those of dorsum
(fig. 19.183) 3

3(2'). Last segment of maxillary palpi short (fig. 19.184); head with only scattered, long
setae, no spines along margins .... *Cyphon*

3'. Last segment of maxillary palpi very large (fig. 19.185); setae reduced on head but
with marginal spines .... *Microcara*

4(2). Anterior angle of labrum bent under, inner margin projecting from under
transverse front margin (fig. 19.186); figure 19.187 .... *Prionocyphon*

4'. Anterior angle of labrum on same plane as rest, labrum thus simply emarginate
(fig. 19.188) .... *Scirtes*

Adults

1. Hind femur similar to front and middle femora, not greatly enlarged for jumping 2

1'. Hind femur greatly enlarged, broadened, modified for jumping (fig. 19.189) 6

2(1'). Meso- and metasternal processes in contact between middle coxae, separating
them 3

---

[1]The Larvae of *Ora* and *Sarabandus* are unknown.

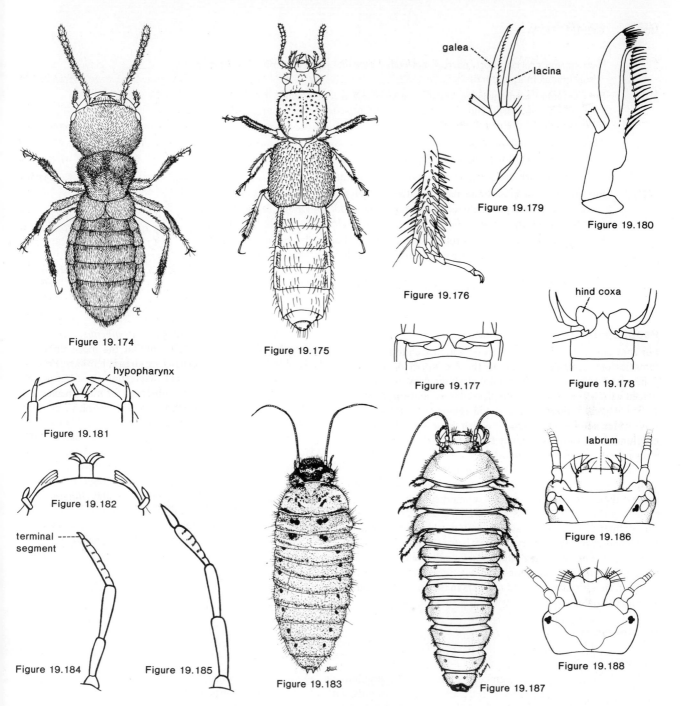

galea
lacina

Figure 19.179

Figure 19.180

Figure 19.176

hind coxa

Figure 19.174

Figure 19.175

Figure 19.177

Figure 19.178

hypopharynx

Figure 19.181

labrum

Figure 19.186

Figure 19.182

terminal segment

Figure 19.184

Figure 19.185

Figure 19.183

Figure 19.188

Figure 19.187

Figure 19.174. *Liparocephalus* sp. (Staphylinidae) adult, dorsal aspect.

Figure 19.175. *Bledius* sp. (Staphylinidae) adult, dorsal aspect.

Figure 19.176. *Bledius* sp. (Staphylinidae) adult, anterior tibia.

Figure 19.177. *Aleochara* sp. (Staphylinidae) adult (not in key), hind coxae and legs.

Figure 19.178. *Stenus* sp. (Staphylinidae) adult, hind coxae and legs.

Figure 19.179. *Myllaena* sp. (Staphylinidae) adult (not in key), maxilla.

Figure 19.180. *Liparocephalus* sp. (Staphylinidae) adult, maxilla.

Figure 19.181. *Elodes* sp. (Scirtidae) larva, dorsal aspect of anterior portion of head (after Hilsenhoff 1981).

Figure 19.182. *Microcara* sp. (Scirtidae) larva, dorsal aspect of anterior portion of head (after Bertrand 1972).

Figure 19.183. *Elodes* sp. (Scirtidae) larva, dorsal aspect.

Figure 19.184. *Cyphon* sp. (Scirtidae) larva, maxillary palp.

Figure 19.185. *Microcara* sp. (Scirtidae) larva, maxillary palp.

Figure 19.186. *Prionocyphon* sp. (Scirtidae) larva, dorsal aspect of head.

Figure 19.187. *Prionocyphon* sp. (Scirtidae) larva, dorsal aspect.

Figure 19.188. *Scirtes* sp. (Scirtidae) larva, dorsal aspect of head.

2'. Mesosternal process short, narrow, not contacting metasternum; middle coxae contiguous in apical half 5

3(2). First antennal segment large, fully twice as broad as any of those following, expanded anteriorly; 2nd segment arising from posterior apical angle of 1st and from under a slight margin (fig. 19.190). .... *Prionocyphon*

3'. Antennae not as above (fig. 19.193) 4

4(3'). Labial palpi with 3rd segment arising from side of 2nd (as in fig. 19.191) .... *Microcara*

4'. Labial palpi with 3rd segment arising from tip of 2nd .... *Cyphon*

5(2'). First segment of hind tarsus flattened above, finely margined laterally, 2nd with part of hind margin prolonged, concealing basal portion of 3rd; labial palp with 3rd segment arising from side of 2nd near the midpoint (as in fig. 19.191) .... *Elodes*

5'. First segment of hind tarsus rounded, not margined laterally, 2nd not produced posteriorly, not concealing base of 3rd; labial palp with 3rd segment arising from apex of 2nd .... *Sarabandus*

6(1'). Hind coxae meeting along full length of midline (fig. 19.189) .... *Scirtes*

6'. Hind coxae touching each other only anteriorly (fig. 19.192) .... *Ora*

Psephenidae (Water Pennies)

For convenience, we take a conservative approach to the systematics of Psephenidae, placing the six North American genera and 15 species in one family although they have been placed variously in Psephenidae, Dascillidae, and Eubriidae. Morphologically there may be good reason to separate the false water pennies (Eubriinae), which possess a ventral operculum, from those without it (the genera *Eubrianax* and *Psephenus*—true water pennies).

The life history of only *Psephenus herricki* has been studied in detail. The bright yellow eggs laid in masses of several thousand can be found on submerged and emergent objects in the swifter parts of riffles. Larval growth occurs in the warmer months and maturity may not be reached until the second year. Mature larvae either leave the water in early summer to construct pupal chambers in soft, moist soils, or they pupate underwater in air-filled chambers (some western species). In both cases, pupation occurs in the last larval skin. The adult stage is very short with little to no feeding.

With the exception of the genus *Psephenus,* information on psephenids is scant. Adults inhabit the moist undersurfaces of logs and rocks overhanging stream habitats. Presumably, these individuals are near oviposition sites, but neither oviposition nor eggs have been observed for most species. Eubriinae apparently do not exhibit the active "play" behavior associated with *Psephenus* mating.

Larvae exhibit positive rheotaxis and thigmokinesis, and a negative phototaxis. Presumably, all genera are scrapers utilizing similar food sources, primarily periphyton. As with *Psephenus,* larval *Ectopria* appear to be gregarious. Larvae of the genera *Acneus, Dicranopselaphus,* and *Alabameubria* are extremely rare and usually have been taken singly. Mature larvae undoubtedly leave the water or are stranded by receding water prior to pupation as in *Psephenus.*

Psephenidae

Larvae

1. Ninth abdominal segment with a ventral operculum closing a caudal chamber containing 3 tufts of retractile filamentous gills; without gills on other parts of abdomen; expanded lateral portions of abdominal segments separated (figs. 19.195, 19.197, 19.199) .... Eubriinae 2

1'. Ninth abdominal segment without ventral operculum; with pairs of ventral tufts of filamentous gills on 4–5 abdominal segments; expanded lateral portions of abdominal segments fitting tightly together at margin (fig. 19.201) 5

2(1). Apex of 9th abdominal segment with a distinct median notch (figs. 19.194–19.197) 3

2'. Apex of 9th abdominal segment truncate or arcuate, without a median notch (figs. 19.198–19.199) 4

3(2). Notch on apex of 9th abdominal segment very shallow, apices broad and flat; lateral (pleural) extensions of thoracic and 1st 7 abdominal segments broad and flattened (figs. 19.194–19.196) .... *Acneus*

3'. Notch on apex of 9th abdominal segment very deep, about half length of segment, apices acute; pleural extensions of thoracic and abdominal segments very slender and curved posteriorly (fig. 19.197) .... *Alabameubria*

4(2').   Ninth abdominal segment almost rectangular; pleural extensions of 8th abdominal
          segment forming part of body outline (fig. 19.198) .... *Ectopria*

4'.   Ninth abdominal segment not rectangular, the sides expanding from base toward
          broadly arcuate apex; lateral extensions of 8th abdominal segment short, not
          forming part of lateral margin of body (fig. 19.199) .... *Dicranopselaphus*

5(1').   Eighth abdominal segment with lateral expansions; abdomen with 4 pairs of gills
          (fig. 19.200) .... *Eubrianax*

5'.   Eighth abdominal segment without lateral expansions; abdomen with 5 pairs of
          gills (fig. 19.201) .... *Psephenus*

Adults[1]

1.   Posterior margin of pronotum crenulate or finely beaded; males with at least the
          anterior claw on each tarsus forked at apex (fig. 19.205); adults not aquatic .... Eubriinae 2

1'.   Posterior margin of pronotum smooth (fig. 19.209) 4

2(1).   Prosternum narrow, depressed between coxae; antenna with 3rd segment at least as
          long as either 1st 2 segments or next 3 segments combined; male with flabellate
          antenna (fig. 19.202) and tarsal claws toothed at base; female larger than male,
          with serrate antenna and tarsal claws not toothed at base .... *Acneus*

2'.   Prosternum of moderate width, not depressed between coxae; tarsal claws of both
          sexes each with basal tooth (fig. 19.203); antenna of male not flabellate (fig.
          19.206) 3

3(2').   Tibia sinuate, length approximately equal to length of tarsus, femur slender,
          narrowing gradually toward apices (fig. 19.207); tarsus slender, 5th segment 3.8
          times as long as its maximum width, 4th segment smaller than 3rd and not
          prolonged beneath 5th (figs. 19.207–19.208) .... *Ectopria*

3'.   Tibia straight, length approximately 1.25 times length of tarsus, femur stout,
          narrow toward apex, but much less than in *Ectopria* (fig. 19.204); tarsus slightly
          dilated, 2nd, 3rd, and 4th segments feebly emarginate (fig. 19.205), the 4th
          slightly prolonged beneath 5th (fig. 19.204) .... *Dicranopselaphus*

4(1').   Head usually hidden beneath broadly expanded pronotum (fig. 19.209); base of
          claws with a membranous appendage nearly reaching to tip of claw; antenna of
          male pectinate (fig. 19.211); that of female serrate (fig. 19.209) .... *Eubrianax*

4'.   Head visible from above (fig. 19.212); base of claws without membranous
          appendage; antenna of female moniliform, that of male subserrate to serrate .... *Psephenus*

Ptilodactylidae[2] (Toed-Winged Beetles)

At present we are considering only three North American genera, each with a single species, to be aquatic. The one species of the western *Areopidius* and one of the central *Odontonyx* most likely are aquatic as well, but descriptions of the larvae have not been published. Adults of these genera can be identified using Arnett (1960) under the family Dascillidae. It is likely that *Stenocolus* will be moved to its own family. Ptilodactylids are widespread, but only locally common.

Larvae of *Anchytarsus* occur in small, cool, clear streams, often along with Elmidae and Dryopidae. The number of instars is unknown but may be as many as 10, and the life cycle may take up to three years. Mature larvae leave the water to construct puparia in leaf litter where, on rare occasions, adults have been found along streams. Little is known of adult ecology, mating, or egg deposition.

Ptilodactylidae

Larvae

1.   Abdominal segments 1–7 each with 2 ventral tufts of filamentous gills (fig.
          19.213); submentum not divided; 9th abdominal segment without prehensile
          appendages bearing hooks .... *Stenocolus*

1'.   Abdominal segments 1–7 without gill tufts; submentum divided longitudinally into
          3 parts; anal region of 9th abdominal segment with 2 curved prehensile
          appendages covered with short spines (fig. 19.214) 2

[1]The adult of *Alabameubria* is unknown.
[2]*Araeopidius* and *Odontonyx*, not included here, most likely are aquatic but habits have not been described.

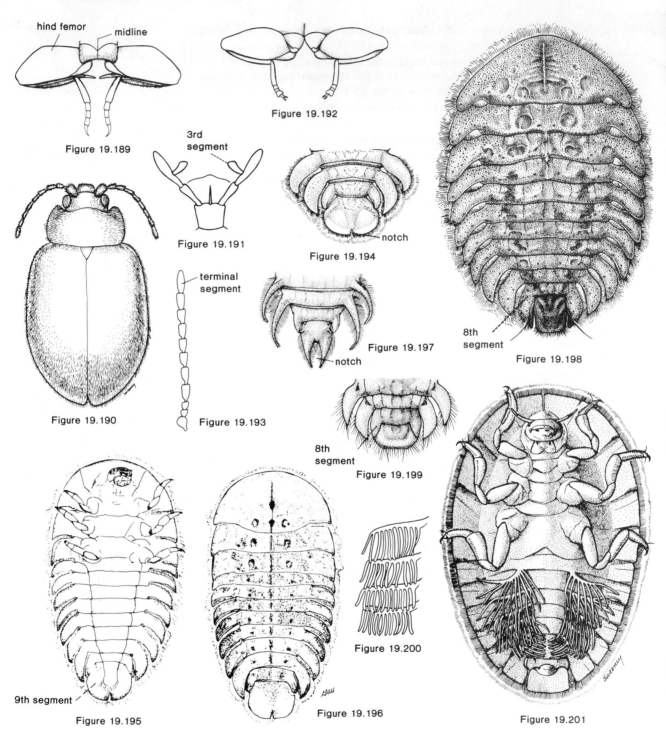

Figure 19.189. *Scirtes* sp. (Scirtidae) adult, hind legs.

Figure 19.190. *Prionocyphon* sp. (Scirtidae) adult, dorsal aspect.

Figure 19.191. *Elodes* sp. (Scirtidae) adult, labial palpi.

Figure 19.192. *Ora* sp. (Scirtidae) adult, hind legs.

Figure 19.193. *Cyphon* sp. (Scirtidae) adult, antenna.

Figure 19.194. *Acneus* sp. (Psephenidae) larva, dorsal aspect of last abdominal segment.

Figure 19.195. *Acneus* sp. (Psephenidae) larva, ventral aspect.

Figure 19.196. *Acneus* sp. (Psephenidae) larva, dorsal aspect.

Figure 19.197. *Alabameubria* sp. (Psephenidae) larva, dorsal aspect of last abdominal segment.

Figure 19.198. *Ectopria* sp. (Psephenidae) larva, dorsal aspect.

Figure 19.199. *Dicranopselaphus* sp. (Psephenidae) larva, dorsal aspect of last abdominal segment.

Figure 19.200. *Eubrianix* sp. (Psephenidae) larva, abdominal gills.

Figure 19.201. *Psephenus* sp. (Psephenidae) larva, ventral aspect.

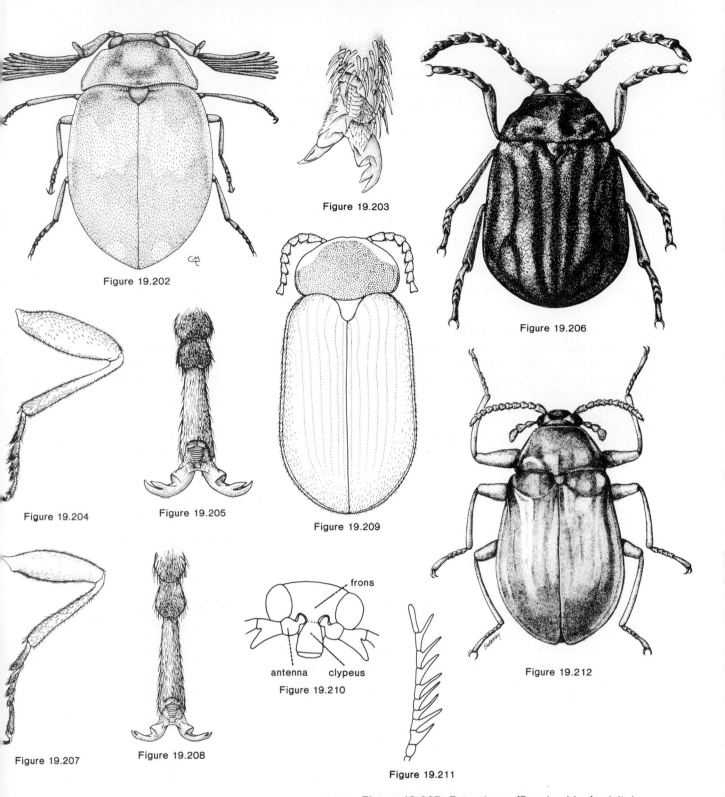

Figure 19.202

Figure 19.203

Figure 19.206

Figure 19.204

Figure 19.205

Figure 19.209

Figure 19.212

Figure 19.207

Figure 19.208

frons

antenna   clypeus

Figure 19.210

Figure 19.211

Figure 19.202. *Acneus* sp. (Psephenidae) adult, dorsal aspect.

Figure 19.203. *Dicranopselaphus* sp. (Psephenidae) adult, apex of tarsus.

Figure 19.204. *Dicranopselaphus* sp. (Psephenidae) adult, leg.

Figure 19.205. *Dicranopselaphus* sp. (Psephenidae) adult, 4th and 5th tarsal segments.

Figure 19.206. *Ectopria* sp. (Psephenidae) adult, dorsal aspect.

Figure 19.207. *Ectopria* sp. (Psephenidae) adult, leg.

Figure 19.208. *Ectopria* sp. (Psephenidae) adult, 4th and 5th tarsal segments.

Figure 19.209. *Eubrianix* sp. (Psephenidae) adult, dorsal aspect.

Figure 19.210. *Eubrianix* sp. (Psephenidae) adult, frontal aspect of head.

Figure 19.211. *Eubrianix* sp. (Psephenidae) adult, antenna.

Figure 19.212. *Psephenus* sp. (Psephenidae) adult, dorsal aspect.

2(1′). Ninth abdominal segment with numerous fingerlike anal gills (fig. 19.214), apex without projection .... *Anchytarsus*

2′. Ninth abdominal segment with 3 median anal gills and 1 gill lateral to each prehensile appendage; dorsal, flattened apex of 9th segment with small raised projection .... *Anchycteis*

Adults

1. Mandibles prominent, acutely margined above, rectangularly flexed at tip; head not retracted, moderately deflexed; 14–22 mm long .... *Stenocolus*

1′. Mandibles not prominent, arcuate at tip, not acutely margined above; head strongly deflexed; less than 12 mm long 2

2(1′). Antennae serrate in female, pectinate in male (fig. 19.216); middle coxae twice as widely separated as anterior coxae; margin of pronotum obtusely rounded laterally (fig. 19.215); 10 mm long .... *Anchycteis*

2′. Antennae slender; middle coxae no more widely separated than anterior coxae; pronotum obtusely margined laterally; 5–6 mm long .... *Anchytarsus*

Limnichidae (Marsh-Loving Beetles)

Relationships among the limnichid genera are not well understood. Although we have included only *Lutrochus* and *Throscinus* here, adults of *Limnichus* also may be found around streams. It is likely that *Lutrochus* will be moved to its own family, Lutrochidae, and that *Throscinus* may be separated from *Limnichus* and its related genera.

Throscinus is marine, occurring along west coast beaches. The larvae are undescribed but probably occur with the adults as in most littoral zone taxa. The two eastern species of *Lutrochus* are widely distributed in small streams though they are only locally common. Larvae of *Lutrochus* are morphologically similar to elmids and often share the same habitat among rocks and larger organic debris of small, cool, fast-flowing streams. Adults cling to emergent objects at the same locations one finds the larvae. If disturbed, they either fly or enter the water carrying a film of air trapped in the hairs covering the body. It is assumed that adults are short lived and it is unknown if they feed. Little has been published on any portion of the life cycle of larvae and adults, mating, oviposition, or eggs.

Limnichidae

Larvae

1. Larvae of *Limnichus* and *Throscinus* have not been described. *Limnichus* may be terrestrial, and *Throscinus* most likely will be found with the adults on mudflats and beaches. It is not expected that either will be similar to *Lutrochus,* which later may be placed in a separate family Lutrochidae. The following description should separate *Lutrochus,* which is truly aquatic.

1′. Abdomen with pleurites on 1st 4 abdominal segments; each undivided thoracic pleurite with erect hairs along medial margin; thoracic sternites membranous or absent; apex of 9th abdominal segment evenly rounded; each eyespot with 5 ocelli and with 1 ventral ocellus below base of antenna; head often retracted within body; figure 19.218 .... *Lutrochus*

Adults

1. Pronotal hypomeron with a transverse or oblique ridge; body plump and convex; figure 19.219; near streams .... Limnichinae 2

1′. Hypomeron without a ridge; body more elongate; on ocean mudflats or beaches .. Cephalobyrrhinae .. *Throscinus*

2(1). Small, less than 2 mm long; antenna slender, with 10 segments; 1st abdominal sternite with grooves for reception of folded hind legs (generally terrestrial) .... *Limnichus*

2′. Larger, at least 2.5 mm long; antenna with 11 segments, the 1st two enlarged and the remaining 9 subpectinate; 1st abdominal sternite without grooves for the reception of folded legs; figure 19.219 .... *Lutrochus*

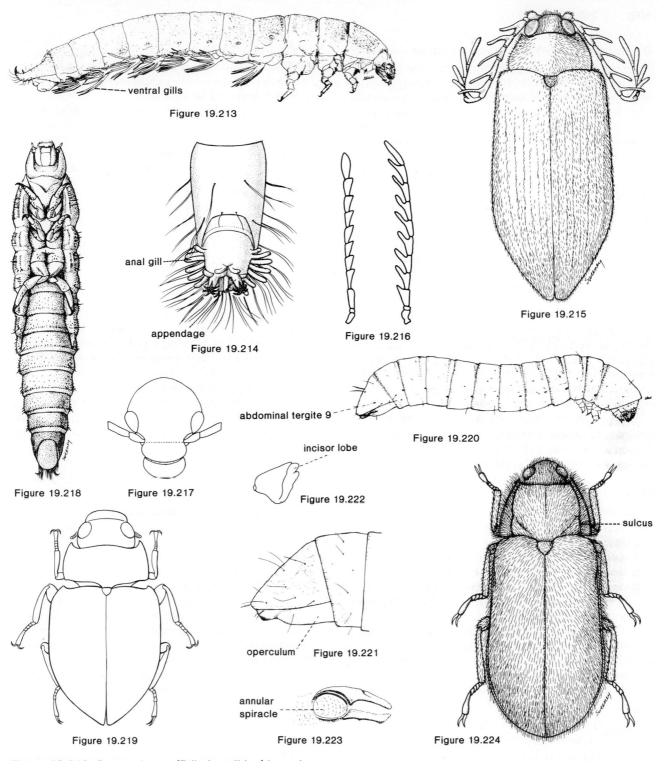

Figure 19.213. *Stenocolus* sp. (Ptilodactylidae) larva, lateral aspect.

Figure 19.214. *Anchydarsus* sp. (Ptilodactylidae) larva, 9th abdominal segment.

Figure 19.215. *Anchyctesis* sp. (Ptilodactylidae) adult, dorsal aspect.

Figure 19.216. *Anchycteis* sp. (Ptilodactylidae) adult, male and female antennae.

Figure 19.217. *Anchycteis* sp. (Ptilodactylidae) adult, frontal aspect of head.

Figure 19.218. *Lutrochus* sp. (Limnichidae) larva, ventral aspect.

Figure 19.219. *Lutrochus* sp. (Limnichidae) adult, dorsal aspect.

Figure 19.220. *Helichus* sp. (Dryopidae) larva, lateral aspect.

Figure 19.221. *Helichus* sp. (Dryopidae) larva, lateral aspect of abdominal apex.

Figure 19.222. *Helichus* sp. (Dryopidae) larva, mandible.

Figure 19.223. *Helichus* sp. (Dryopidae) larva, spiracle and closing apparatus.

Figure 19.224. *Dryops* sp. (Dryopidae) adult, dorsal aspect.

Dryopidae (Long-Toed Water Beetles)

Fourteen species of this primarily tropical family occur in America north of Mexico and represent a variety of associations with the aquatic environment. Only the genus *Helichus* is common and widespread. The adults are found in flowing waters along with the Elmidae, but the larvae appear to be terrestrial, a condition unique among the aquatic insects. *Pelonomus* may be semiaquatic to aquatic, most often occurring in small woodland pools with accumulated leaf litter. *Dryops* is rare, but both adults and larvae are aquatic. Beyond the above, virtually nothing is known of life cycles of the North American Dryopidae.

Helichus larvae have been discovered, but no description published, thus limiting the generic key. The key given here is modified from Brown (1972b), and we have included some previously published drawings of *Helichus* that seem also to be almost identical to known specimens of *Pelonomus*.

Dryopidae

Larvae[1]

1.	Tergites with anterior margins smooth; gular sutures present	*Dryops*
1′.	Tergites (except pronotum) with numerous longitudinal carinae arising near each anterior margin; gular sutures obliterated, with 2 pairs of setae near where sutures would be	*Pelonomus*

Adults

1.	Pronotum on each side with a conspicuous, complete sublateral longitudinal sulcus; pubescent (fig. 19.224)	*Dryops*
1′.	Pronotum without such a sublateral sulcus (fig. 19.230)	2
2(1′).	Second segment of antenna not enlarged; antennae pubescent (fig. 19.225); bases of antennae very close together; both 3rd and 4th segments of maxillary palp very elongate; without tomentum but extremely hairy; figure 19.226	*Pelonomus*
2′.	First, and, even more, 2nd segment of antenna enlarged and heavily sclerotized, forming a shield beneath which remaining segments may be retracted and protected (fig. 19.227); bases of antennae widely separated; parts of body and legs with tomentum; figures 19.228–19.230	*Helichus*

Elmidae (Riffle Beetles)

The nearly 100 species and 26 genera present in North America are typical inhabitants of the swifter portions of streams and rivers. Only the genera *Stenelmis, Optioservus,* and *Dubiraphia,* with a combined total of 51 species, are common and widespread. The remaining 23 genera occur primarily in localized populations in eastern, western and southwestern mountain ranges.

The terminal gills of the larvae and the highly efficient plastron of the adults make the elmids among the most truly aquatic insects. The gills of the larvae, which are retractile and protected by an operculum, can be rhythmically expanded and contracted to increase ventilation when oxygen levels are low. The adult plastron is an extremely fine hydrofuge pile with hairs as dense as several million per mm². Although efficient, this adaptation limits adult distribution to habitats rich in oxygen, such as riffles.

Eggs are deposited singly or in small groups on submerged rocks, organic debris, and vegetation. Larvae undergo 6–8 instars, which may take three years or more. Terrestrial pupal chambers are constructed in moist soils, under rocks, or in rotting wood. Newly emerged adults undergo a short flight period but, after entering the water, most are incapable of further aerial activity. Adult life spans are unknown, though many species may not reach maturity until the second year. Adults occupy habitats similar to the larvae with which they often are collected.

Elmidae

Larvae[2]

1.	Abdomen with pleura on first 8 segments (fig. 19.232)	2
1′.	Abdomen with pleura on first 6–7 segments (fig. 19.256)	7
2(1).	Body rather broad, lateral margins expanded (fig. 19.233)	3
2′.	Body slender, elongate, cylindrical or hemicylindrical (as in fig. 19.243)	4

---

[1]*Helichus* has not been described adequately to be included here but most likely will key near *Pelonomus*. Figures 19.220–19.223 provide some description of the terrestrial larvae. The adult is aquatic.

[2]The larvae of *Atractelmis* is unknown.

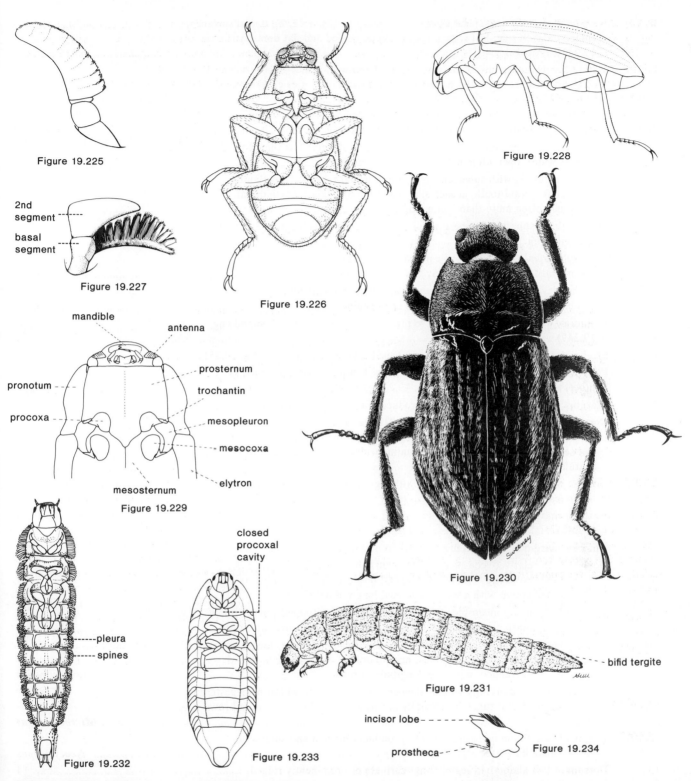

Figure 19.225

2nd segment

basal segment

Figure 19.227

Figure 19.226

Figure 19.228

mandible

antenna

prosternum

pronotum

trochantin

procoxa

mesopleuron

mesocoxa

mesosternum

elytron

Figure 19.229

Figure 19.230

pleura

spines

closed procoxal cavity

bifid tergite

Figure 19.231

Figure 19.232

Figure 19.233

incisor lobe

prostheca

Figure 19.234

Figure 19.225. *Pelonomus* sp. (Dryopidae) adult, antenna.

Figure 19.226. *Pelonomus* sp. (Dryopidae) adult, ventral aspect.

Figure 19.227. *Helichus* sp. (Dryopidae) adult, antenna.

Figure 19.228. *Helichus* sp. (Dryopidae) adult, lateral aspect.

Figure 19.229. *Helichus* sp. (Dryopidae) adult, ventral aspect of head.

Figure 19.230. *Helichus* sp. (Dryopidae) adult, dorsal aspect.

Figure 19.231. *Lara* sp. (Elmidae) larva, lateral aspect.

Figure 19.232. *Lara* sp. (Elmidae) larva, ventral aspect.

Figure 19.233. *Phanocerus* sp. (Elmidae) larva, ventral aspect.

Figure 19.234. Elmidae larva, mandible.

3(2).   With coarse, prominent spines along lateral margins (fig. 19.232); dorsal surface ridged on each side; last segment rather square-sided and flat dorsally (fig. 19.231); procoxal cavities open behind .... ***Lara***

3'.   Without marginal spines; body quite flattened and with rather smooth surface; testaceous to brown, somewhat translucent; procoxal cavities closed behind; figure 19.233 .... ***Phanocerus***

4(2').   Last abdominal segment very long and slender (at least 4 times as long as wide), operculum confined to posterior third of segment (fig. 19.235) .... ***Dubiraphia***

4'.   Last abdominal segment not conspicuously long or slender (less than 4 times as long as wide), operculum not confined to apical third 5

5(4').   Head tuberculate, with suberect spines; anterior margin of head without a prominent frontal tooth on each side (fig. 19.246); body subcylindrical, yellowish; often more than 8 mm long .... ***Narpus***

5'.   Head without suberect spines, anterior margin with a prominent frontal tooth on each side (fig. 19.248) 6

6(5').   Body cylindrical (fig. 19.237); pleural sutures extend to basal half of 9th abdominal segment; procoxal cavities closed behind .... ***Cylloepus***

6'.   Body hemicylindrical (fig. 19.238); pleural sutures not extending onto 9th abdominal segment; procoxal cavities open behind .... ***Rhizelmis***

7(1').   Prothorax with a posterior sternum so procoxal cavities are closed behind (fig. 19.249) 8

7'.   Prothorax without posterior sternum; procoxal cavities open behind (fig. 19.251) 17

8(7).   Posterolateral margins of abdominal segments 1–8 produced into spinelike processses; body rather robust (figs. 19.239–19.240) .... ***Ancyronyx***

8'.   Margins of abdominal segments not produced into spines; body elongate 9

9(8').   Dorsum of all but last segment bearing spatulate tubercles or short spines arranged in about 10 conspicuous longitudinal or diagonal rows (fig. 19.241); last segment with a middorsal longitudinal ridge and lateral margins bearing spatulate tubercles .... ***Heterelmis***

9'.   Dorsum without such spiny tubercles, although there may be rows of small, flat tubercles 10

10(9').   Anterior margin of head on each side with a distinct frontal tooth (figs. 19.246, 19.248) 13

10'.   Anterior margin of head without distinct frontal tooth (fig. 19.244) 11

11(10').   Dorsum with relatively conspicuous, flattened tubercles often arranged in longitudinal rows (fig. 19.243); abdominal tergites often with middorsal pale spots; last segment with a weak middorsal longitudinal ridge 12

11'.   Tubercles of dorsum inconspicuous, not arranged in longitudinal rows; without middorsal pale spots; last segment convex dorsally, without median ridge .... ***Neoelmis***

12(11).   Last abdominal segment conspicuously long and slender (3 times longer than wide, fig. 19.242); middorsal spots widest near middle of each segment; dorsal tubercles not arranged in parallel longitudinal rows .... ***Hexacylloepus***

12'.   Last segment not unusually long or slender; middorsal spots widest near posterior of segments; dorsal tubercles partially arranged in parallel longitudinal rows (fig. 19.243) .... ***Microcylloepus***

13(10).   Tergite of last abdominal segment with prominent median and sublateral, longitudinal, carinate ridges (fig. 19.245) .... ***Neocylloepus***

13'.   Dorsum of last abdominal segment not carinate or prominently ridged 14

14(13').   Second segment of antenna more than twice as long as 1st (fig. 19.246); prosternum with anterior suture obliterated; no suture extending from procoxal cavity to lateral margin of prontum .... ***Ordobrevia***

14'.   Second segment of antenna less than twice as long as 1st; prosternum with anterior median suture; suture from procoxal cavity to lateral margin may or may not be visible 15

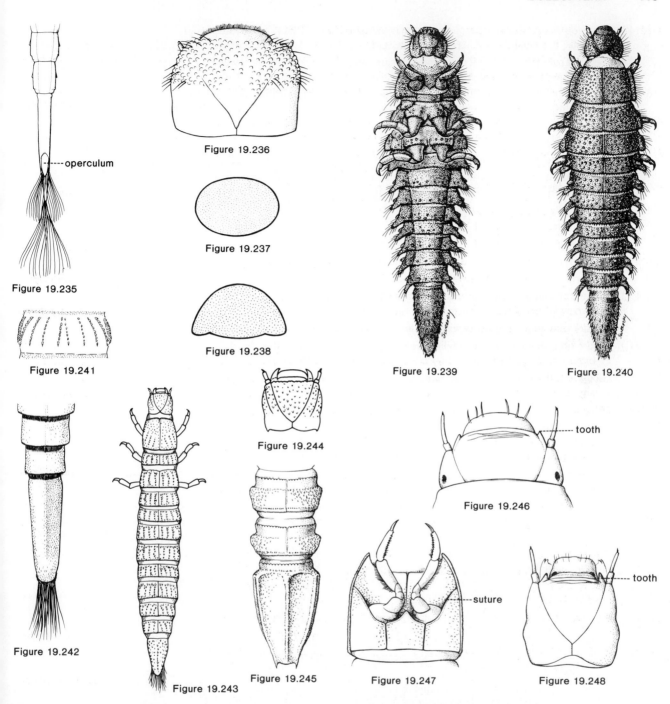

Figure 19.235

operculum

Figure 19.236

Figure 19.237

Figure 19.238

Figure 19.241

Figure 19.239

Figure 19.240

Figure 19.242

Figure 19.243

Figure 19.244

Figure 19.245

tooth

Figure 19.246

suture

tooth

Figure 19.247

Figure 19.248

Figure 19.235. *Dubiraphia* sp. (Elmidae) larva, ventral aspect of last abdominal segments.

Figure 19.236. *Narpus* sp. (Elmidae) larva, dorsal aspect of head.

Figure 19.237. *Cylloepus* sp. (Elmidae) larva, shape of abdominal cross section.

Figure 19.238. *Rhizelmis* (Elmidae) larva, shape of abdominal cross section.

Figure 19.239. *Ancyronyx* sp. (Elmidae) larva, ventral aspect.

Figure 19.240. *Ancyronyx* sp. (Elmidae) larva, dorsal aspect.

Figure 19.241. *Heterelmis* sp. (Elmidae) larva, dorsal aspect of an abdominal segment.

Figure 19.242. *Hexacylloepus* sp. (Elmidae) larva, dorsal aspect of last abdominal segments.

Figure 19.243. *Microcylloepus* sp. (Elmidae) larva, dorsal aspect.

Figure 19.244. *Microcylloepus* sp. (Elmidae) larva, dorsal aspect of head.

Figure 19.245. *Neocylloepus* sp. (Elmidae) larva, dorsal aspect of last abdominal segments.

Figure 19.246. *Ordobrevia* sp. (Elmidae) larva, dorsal aspect of head.

Figure 19.247. *Elsianus* sp. (Elmidae) larva, ventral aspect of prothorax segment.

Figure 19.248. *Stenelmis* sp. (Elmidae) larva, dorsal aspect of head.

15(14'). Suture from procoxal cavity to lateral margin distinct (fig. 19.247); body large and
rather flattened .... *Elsianus*

15'. Suture from procoxal cavity to lateral margin indistinct or absent (fig. 19.249);
body more convex and elongate, smaller 16

16(15'). Pleuron on each side of prothorax divided into pre- and postpleurites, division may
be faint; Arizona and Southwest .... *Huleechius*

16'. Pleuron not divided (fig. 19.249); from Texas and Oregon eastward .... *Stenelmis*

17(7'). Postpleurite composed of 1 part (fig. 19.251) 18

17'. Postpleurite composed of 2 parts (fig. 19.254) 19

18(17). Body robust, broad, subtriangular in cross section; with spatulate spines along
lateral margins (fig. 19.251) and middorsal line (fig. 19.250) .... *Ampumixis*

18'. Body long and slender, hemicylindrical; without prominent clusters of spines .... *Cleptelmis*

19(17'). Mesopleuron composed of 1 part (fig. 19.255) 20

19'. Mesopleuron composed of 2 parts (fig. 19.257) 21

20(19). Dorsum of each segment with median and sublateral humps (fig. 19.252) .... *Promoresia*

20'. Dorsum without such humps (also see figs. 19.253–19.255) .... *Optioservus*

21(19'). First 5 or 6 abdominal segments with pleura; last segment with 2 long, acute,
narrowly separated apical processes (fig. 19.256) .... *Macronychus*

21'. First 7 abdominal segments with pleura 22

22(21'). Body long, slender, and hemicylindrical; apex of last segment rather deeply
emarginate, the lateral angles produced and acute (fig. 19.258) .... *Zaitzevia*

22'. Body usually less elongate, subtriangular in cross section; apex of last segment
shallowly emarginate, lateral angles less acute (fig. 19.261) 23

23(22'). Abdominal segments with middorsal humps that are especially prominent toward
the rear (fig. 19.259), each hump bearing conspicuous scalelike hairs; dorsum of
each thoracic segment with 2 longitudinal dark spots on each side .... *Gonielmis*

23'. Abdominal segments without middorsal humps; thorax usually without dark
markings 24

24(23'). Western; tubercles of dorsum relatively dense, separated by less than their own
widths, crowded along posterior margins of segments; mesothorax with anterior
portion of pleuron much smaller than posterior portion; mature larva 4–5 mm
long; figure 19.260 .... *Heterlimnius*

24'. Eastern; tubercles of dorsum sparse, separated by more than their own widths
except along middorsal line, marginal tubercles separated by their own widths;
mesothorax with anterior portion of pleuron subequal to posterior portion;
mature larva not over 3 mm long; figure 19.261 .... *Oulimnius*

Adults

1. Riparian, usually not underwater; agile fliers; rather soft-bodied; pubescent, but
without tomentum; procoxae transverse and with trochantin exposed (fig.
19.265) 2

1'. Aquatic; typically slow moving, clinging to submerged objects; rarely flying except
at night; hard-bodied; with tomentum on various ventral parts; procoxae
rounded and trochantin concealed 3

2(1). Less than 4 mm long; antennae clubbed (fig. 19.263); pronotum with sublateral
sulci (fig. 19.264) .... *Phanocerus*

2'. More than 5 mm long; black, antennae not clubbed; pronotum without sublateral
sulci (fig. 19.266) .... *Lara*

3(1'). Hind coxae globular and about same size as other coxae (fig. 19.269); posterior
margin of prosternal process almost as wide as head 4

3'. Hind coxae transverse and larger than other coxae (figs. 19.274, 19.275); posterior
margin of prosternal process much narrower than width of head 5

4(3). Black; elytra with sublateral carinae (fig. 19.268); antennae with 7 segments,
enlarged at apex (fig. 19.267); pronotum without transverse impressions .... *Macronychus*

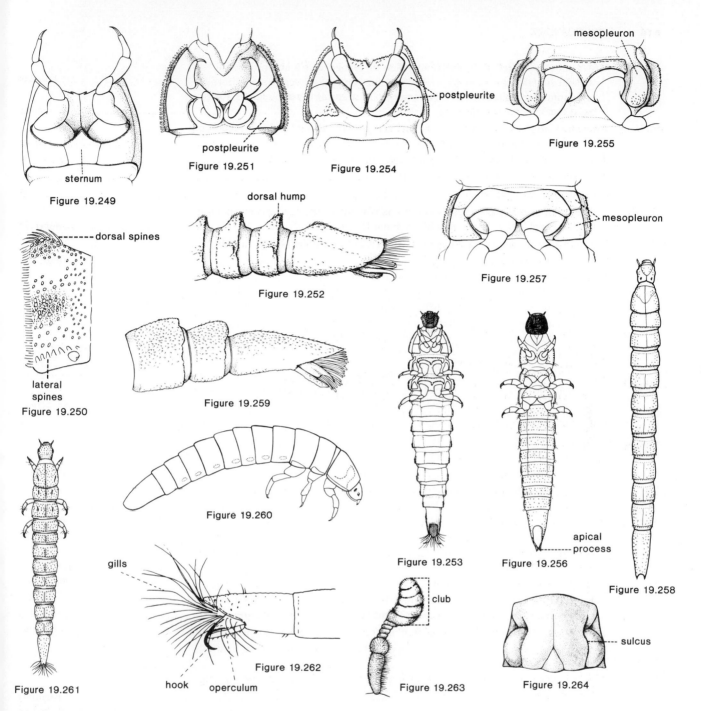

Figure 19.249. *Stenelmis* sp. (Elmidae) larva, vental aspect of prothorax segment.

Figure 19.250. *Ampumixis* sp. (Elmidae) larva, lateral aspect of an abdominal segment.

Figure 19.251. *Ampumixis* sp. (Elmidae) larva, ventral aspect of prothorax segment.

Figure 19.252. *Promoresia* sp. (Elmidae) larva, lateral aspect of last abdominal segment.

Figure 19.253. *Optioservus* sp. (Elmidae) larva, ventral aspect.

Figure 19.254. *Optioservus* sp. (Elmidae) larva, ventral aspect of prothorax.

Figure 19.255. *Optioservus* sp. (Elmidae) larva, ventral aspect of mesothorax.

Figure 19.256. *Macronychus* sp. (Elmidae) larva, ventral aspect.

Figure 19.257. *Macronychus* sp. (Elmidae) larva, ventral aspect of mesothorax.

Figure 19.258. *Zaitzevia* sp. (Elmidae) larva, dorsal aspect.

Figure 19.259. *Gonielmis* sp. (Elmidae) larva, lateral aspect of last abdominal segments.

Figure 19.260. *Heterlimnius* sp. (Elmidae) larva, lateral aspect.

Figure 19.261. *Oulimnius* sp. (Elmidae) larva, dorsal aspect.

Figure 19.262. *Cleptelmis* sp. (Elmidae) larva, lateral aspect of last abdominal segments.

Figure 19.263. *Phanocerus* sp. (Elmidae) adult, antenna.

Figure 19.264. *Phanocerus* sp. (Elmidae) adult, pronotum.

4'.   Conspicuously colored with black and yellow or orange; elytra and pronotum without sublateral carinae (fig. 19.270); antennae with 11 segments, filiform; pronotum with oblique transverse impressions at apical third; tarsal claw with a basal tooth .... ***Ancyronyx***

5(3').   Antennae with 8 segments, the apical one being enlarged (fig. 19.271); pronotum with median longitudinal groove; elytra with 3 sublateral carinae .... ***Zaitzevia***

5'.   Antennae with 10–11 segments (fig. 19.298), usually filiform 6

6(5').   Anterior tibia with fringe of tomentum (fig. 19.299) 8

6'.   Anterior tibia without fringe of tomentum 7

7(6').   Elytron with an accessory stria (sutural stria confluent with 2nd stria at about 5th puncture, fig. 19.272); granules of head and legs elongate .... ***Ordobrevia***

7'.   Elytron without such an accessory stria (fig. 19.273); granules of head and legs round .... ***Stenelmis***

8(6).   Lateral margin of 4th or 5th abdominal sternite produced as a prominent lobe or tooth, which is bent upward to clasp the epipleuron (fig. 19.300); epipleuron widened to receive tooth, then usually narrowing abruptly toward apex 14

8'.   Lateral margin of abdominal sternites not produced into a prominent upturned tooth; epipleuron usually tapering uniformly toward apex (fig. 19.278) 9

9(8').   Pronotum with sublateral carinae (fig. 19.279) 10

9'.   Pronotum smooth, without sublateral carinae (fig. 19.284) 13

10(9).   Prosternum projecting beneath head (fig. 19.276); epipleuron extending to middle of 5th abdominal segment; black; 2.5–2.6 mm long .... ***Rhizelmis***

10'.   Prosternum not projecting beneath head (fig. 19.278); epipleuron ending at base of 5th abdominal segment; less than 2.3 mm long 11

11(10').   Pronotal carinae forked at base (fig. 19.279) .... ***Cleptelmis***

11'.   Pronotal carinae not forked 12

12(11').   Sides of pronotum converging anteriorly from base (fig. 19.280); body rather spindle-shaped; black, each elytron with a broad humeral and an oblique, narrow, subapical spot; tarsi and claws prominent .... ***Atractelmis***

12'.   Sides of pronotum parallel or divergent anteriorly at base (fig. 19.281), strongly convergent apically; hump-backed; black, elytra black to red, uniformly colored or with basal half red, with or without broad apical red spots; tarsi and claws not unusually prominent .... ***Ampumixis***

13(9').   Maxillary palpi 3-segmented (fig. 19.282); markings, if present, transverse .... ***Narpus***

13'.   Maxillary palpi 4-segmented (fig. 19.283); markings, if present, longitudinal ...... ***Dubiraphia***

14(8).   Tooth that clasps epipleuron arising from lateral margin of 5th abdominal sternite 15

14'.   Tooth that clasps epipleuron arising from apical (posterior) lateral margin of 4th abdominal sternite (fig. 19.300) 22

15(14).   Elytron at base with a short accessory stria between sutural and 2nd major stria (fig. 19.285) .... ***Elsianus***

15'.   Elytron without such an accessory stria (fig. 19.286); testis usually bilobate 16

16(15').   Elytron with 1 sublateral carina; pronotum without oblique sculpturing (fig. 19.286) 17

16'.   Elytron with 2 sublateral carinae (rarely only 1 in *Microcylloepus,* which has oblique sculpturing on posterior half of pronotum) 18

17(16).   Posterior half of pronotum divided by a conspicuous median longitudinal impression, with a transverse impression slightly anterior to middle; figure 19.286; brown to black .... ***Neocylloepus***

17'.   Pronotum undivided except by transverse impression at anterior two-fifths (fig. 19.287); testaceous .... ***Neoelmis***

18(16').   Hypomeron of pronotum with a belt of tomentum extending from coxa to lateral margin; pronotum with a shallow, median, longitudinal impression, but with no transverse impressions; testaceous to black .... ***Hexacylloepus***

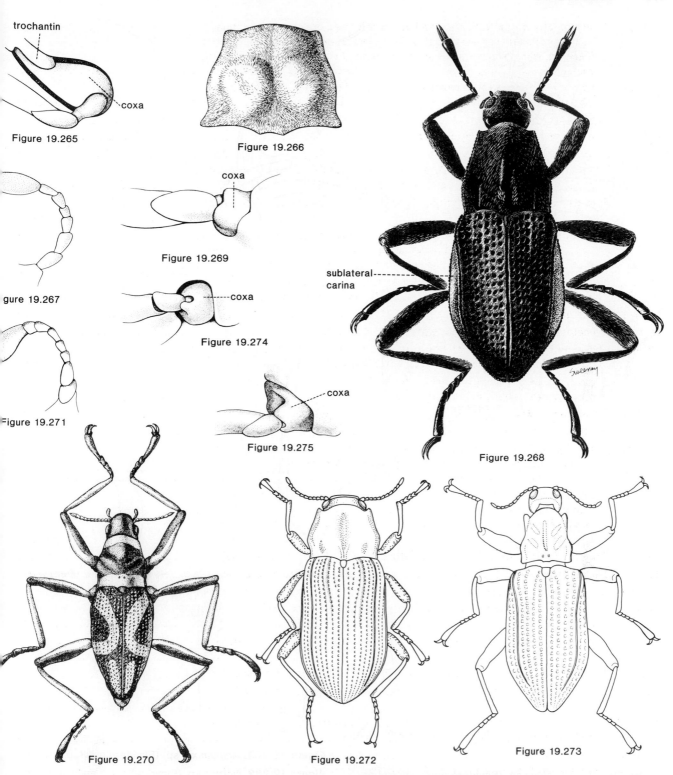

trochantin

coxa

Figure 19.265

Figure 19.266

coxa

Figure 19.269

gure 19.267

coxa

Figure 19.274

Figure 19.271

coxa

Figure 19.275

sublateral carina

Figure 19.268

Figure 19.270

Figure 19.272

Figure 19.273

Figure 19.270. *Ancyronyx* sp. (Elmidae) adult, dorsal aspect.

Figure 19.265. *Lara* sp. (Elmidae) adult, procoxa.

Figure 19.271. *Zaitzevia* sp. (Elmidae) adult, antenna.

Figure 19.266. *Lara* sp. (Elmidae) adult, pronotum.

Figure 19.267. *Macronychus* sp. (Elmidae) adult, antenna.

Figure 19.272. *Ordobrevia* sp. (Elmidae) adult, dorsal aspect.

Figure 19.268. *Macronychus* sp. (Elmidae) adult, dorsal aspect.

Figure 19.273. *Stenelmis* sp. (Elmidae) adult, dorsal aspect.

Figure 19.269. *Ancyronyx* sp. (Elmidae) adult, hind coxa.

Figure 19.274. *Stenelmis* sp. (Elmidae) adult, procoxa.

Figure 19.275. *Stenelmis* sp. (Elmidae) adult, hind coxa.

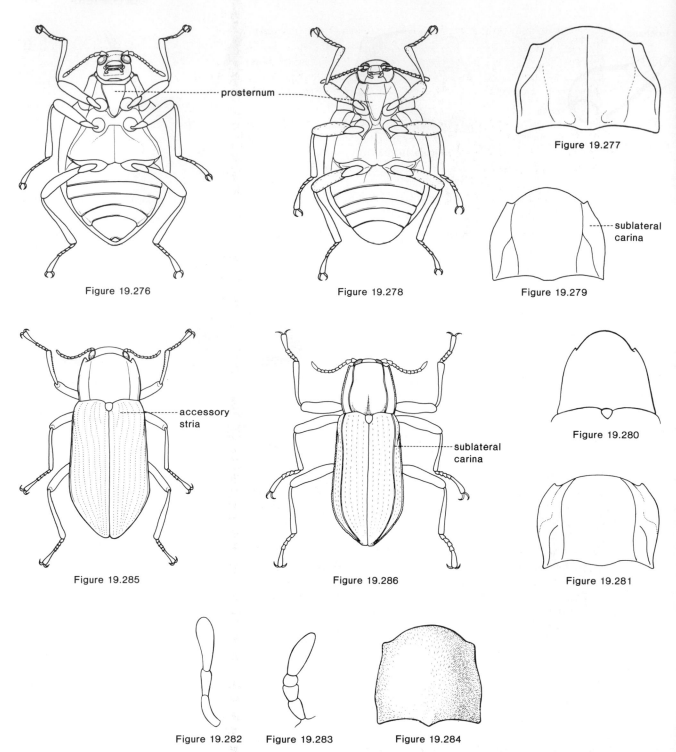

Figure 19.276

Figure 19.278

prosternum

Figure 19.277

sublateral carina

Figure 19.279

accessory stria

Figure 19.285

sublateral carina

Figure 19.286

Figure 19.280

Figure 19.281

Figure 19.282   Figure 19.283

Figure 19.284

Figure 19.276. *Rhizelmis* sp. (Elmidae) adult, ventral aspect.

Figure 19.277. *Rhizelmis* sp. (Elmidae) adult, pronotum.

Figure 19.278. *Cleptelmis* sp. (Elmidae) adult, ventral aspect.

Figure 19.279. *Cleptelmis* sp. (Elmidae) adult, pronotum.

Figure 19.280. *Actractelmis* sp. (Elmidae) adult, pronotum (after Brown 1972b).

Figure 19.281. *Ampumixis* sp. (Elmidae) adult, pronotum.

Figure 19.282. *Narpus* sp. (Elmidae) adult, maxillary palp.

Figure 19.283. *Dubiraphia* sp. (Elmidae) adult, maxillary palp.

Figure 19.284. *Dubiraphia* sp. (Elmidae) adult, pronotum.

Figure 19.285. *Elsianus* sp. (Elmidae) adult, dorsal aspect.

Figure 19.286. *Neocylloepus* sp. (Elmidae) adult, dorsal aspect.

18′.   Hypomeron with or without tomentum, but if present it does not reach lateral margin 19

19(18′).   Prosternal process broad and truncate; pronotum without median longitudinal impression, usually with transverse impression at middle (fig. 19.288); pronotal hypomeron with tomentum near coxa; body usually plump; mandible with a lateral lobe .... *Heterelmis*

19′.   Prosternal process relatively narrow, elongate with apex tapering or rounded; pronotum with median longitudinal impression (figs. 19.289, 19.291); hypomeron without tomentum; body not plump 20

20(19′).   Pronotum with a transverse impression at anterior two-fifths (fig. 19.289); mandible with a lateral lobe; epipleuron without tomentum; small, less than 2.3 mm long .... *Microcylloepus*

20′.   Pronotum without such a transverse impression; epipleuron with tomentum 21

21(20′).   Gula distinctly narrower than submentum or mentum (fig. 19.290) .... *Huleechius*

21′.   Gula not distinctly narrower than submentum or mentum; figure 19.291 .... *Cylloepus*

22(14′).   Pronotum with sublateral carinae extending from base to anterior margin; elytron with 3 sublateral carinae; figure 19.292; brown to black; 1.25–1.6 mm long .... *Oulimnius*

22′.   Pronotum with sublateral carinae absent or not extending beyond about middle; elytron without sublateral carinae; larger species, longer than 1.6 mm 23

23(22′).   Pronotum smooth, without or with only a trace of carinae; body elongate and spindle-shaped; black, elytron with 2 oblique yellowish spots (fig. 19.293); legs long, claws prominent and recurved; 2–2.6 mm long .... *Gonielmis*

23′.   Pronotum with short, sublateral carinae (fig. 19.294) 24

24(23′).   Body rather elongate; tarsi and claws long and prominent; lateral and posterior margins of pronotum smooth; eastern; figure 19.294 .... *Promoresia*

24′.   Body plump; tarsi and claws not conspicuously enlarged; lateral margin of pronotum usually slightly serrate, posterior margin usually with many small, closely placed teeth 25

25(24′).   Convex, giving a rather hump-backed appearance, with sutural intervals slightly raised; with 3rd or 4th elytral stria converging and merging with 2nd or 3rd stria at about apical third; major striae entire, extending to apex of elytron; antennae with 10–11 segments, last 3 somewhat enlarged; apex of 5th abdominal sternite usually somewhat truncate or emarginate; tarsal claws relatively slender; in Western mountains; figure 19.295 .... *Heterlimnius*

25′.   Less convex; sutural interval usually not raised; elytral striae not ordinarily merging as described above, either being entire or becoming obsolete in posterior portion of elytron; antennae with 11 segments, the last 3 less enlarged; apex of 5th abdominal sternite usually evenly rounded; claws somewhat larger and more curved; figure 19.296 .... *Optioservus*

Chrysomelidae (Leaf Beetles)

The Chrysomelidae is a large family of more than 14,000 species, but only a few genera have aquatic species. The genus *Donacia* Fabricius is the largest aquatic or semiaquatic chrysomelid genus, with 50 North American species. Some authors give generic status to *Plateumaris* Thomson, but it is treated here as a subgenus of *Donacia. Neohaemonia* Szekessy contains three species. Most existing works include *Galerucella* Crotch (Galerucellinae); however, *Pyrrhalta* Joannis has priority. At least two genera and five species of Chrysomelinae are known to contain aquatic or semiaquatic species in North America: *Prasocuris* Latreille, with a single species, and *Hydrothassa* Thomson with four species. A number of flea beetles (Alticinae) in the large genus *Disonycha* Chevrolat are known to feed upon aquatic plants, and this number is growing, principally from work on the biological control of alligatorweed *(Alternanthera philoxeroides).*

Mating of aquatic chrysomelids occurs above water, with the flowers of water lilies *(Nuphar, Nymphaea)* being preferred mating sites. North American Donaciinae usually deposit their eggs in masses, with the structure and location of the egg mass distinct for each known species. Upon hatching, larval aquatic chrysomelids must locate the correct host plant. Field studies indicate that most Donaciinae have at least a two-year life cycle.

Larvae of most species form their cocoons in the same positions on the plants in which the larvae occurred. Cocoons, spun of silk from glands opening in the mouth, are both water- and airtight and are filled with intercellular air obtained from the host plant. *Agasicles* pupates within the stem cavities of the host plant.

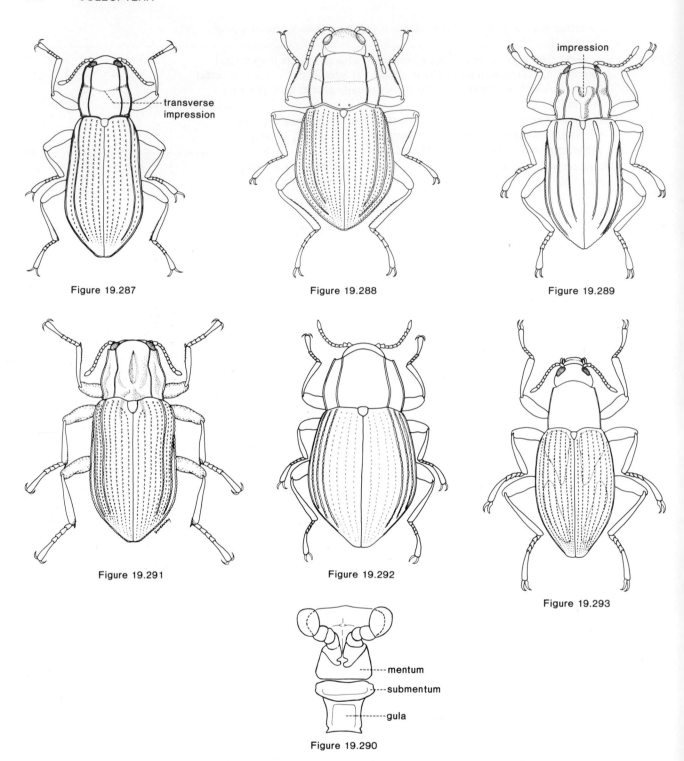

Figure 19.287

Figure 19.288

Figure 19.289

Figure 19.291

Figure 19.292

Figure 19.293

Figure 19.290

Figure 19.287. *Neoelmis* sp. (Elmidae) adult, dorsal aspect.

Figure 19.288. *Heterelmis* sp. (Elmidae) adult, dorsal aspect.

Figure 19.289. *Microcylloepus* sp. (Elmidae) adult, dorsal aspect.

Figure 19.290. *Huleechius* sp. (Elmidae) adult, ventral aspect of gula, mentum, and submentum (after Brown 1981).

Figure 19.291. *Cylloepus* sp. (Elmidae) adult, dorsal aspect.

Figure 19.292. *Oulimnius* sp. (Elmidae) adult, dorsal aspect.

Figure 19.293. *Gonielmis* sp. (Elmidae) adult, dorsal aspect.

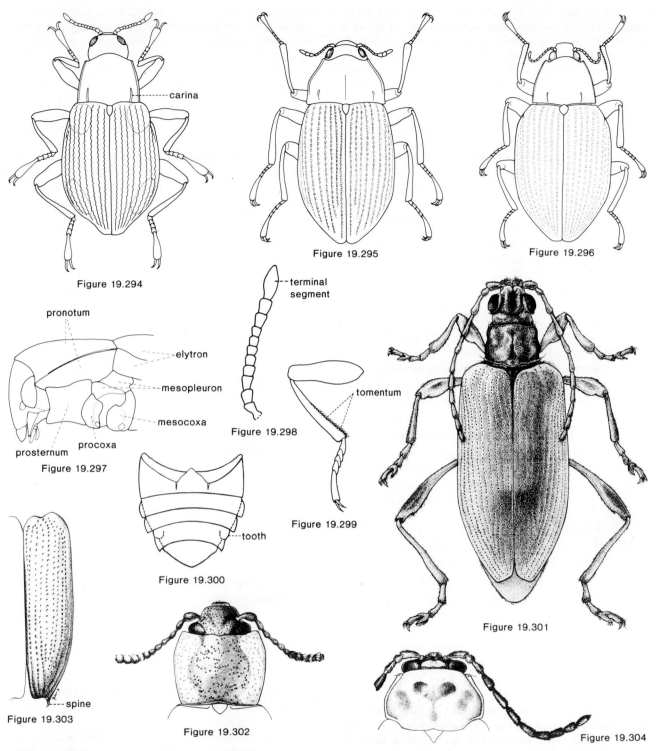

Figure 19.294

Figure 19.295

Figure 19.296

carina

pronotum

elytron

mesopleuron

mesocoxa

prosternum

procoxa

Figure 19.297

terminal segment

tomentum

Figure 19.298

Figure 19.299

tooth

Figure 19.300

spine

Figure 19.303

Figure 19.302

Figure 19.301

Figure 19.304

Figure 19.294. *Promoresia* sp. (Elmidae) adult, dorsal aspect.

Figure 19.295. *Heterlimnius* sp. (Elmidae) adult, dorsal aspect.

Figure 19.296. *Optioservus* sp. (Elmidae) adult, dorsal aspect.

Figure 19.297. *Optioservus* sp. (Elmidae) adult, lateral aspect of head.

Figure 19.298. *Optioservus* sp. (Elmidae) adult, antenna.

Figure 19.299. *Optioservus* sp. (Elmidae) adult, foreleg.

Figure 19.300. *Optioservus* sp. (Elmidae) adult, ventral aspect of abdomen.

Figure 19.301. *Donacia* sp. (Chrysomelidae) adult, dorsal aspect.

Figure 19.302. *Prasocuris* sp. (Chrysomelidae) adult, dorsal aspect of head and pronotum.

Figure 19.303. *Neohaemonia* sp. (Chrysomelidae) adult, elytron.

Figure 19.304. *Disonycha* sp. (Chrysomelidae) adult, dorsal aspect of head and pronotum.

Larvae and adults of aquatic and semiaquatic Chrysomelidae are live vascular plant shredders and, as far as is known, have a definite preference for a single-host plant taxon or, at most, several species of plants that occupy the same habitat. Although the larvae of Donaciinae feed almost exclusively upon the submerged roots, leaves, and petioles of aquatic plants, the adults may feed upon pollen. *Pyrrhalta nymphaeae* is unique among the Galerucinae in that both larvae and adults feed on the upper surface of floating leaves. Rather than mining, they chew away the epidermis of the leaf, producing an irregular trench that gives the leaf a characteristic brownish, etched appearance.

The larvae of *Donacia* pass their lives underwater even though they do not possess any of the usual morphological adaptations for an aquatic existence. They are equipped with a pair of caudal spines that, at least in some instances, may be used to penetrate the tissues of aquatic plants. It has long been suspected that the caudal spines permit the larva to use oxygen contained in air spaces within the plants. Some larvae, however, can live submerged for as long as 21 days without penetrating plants, so it is likely that they obtain oxygen by other means.

Except for some groups that contain important economic pests, the immature stages of the Chrysomelidae (fig. 19.13) are poorly known. As a result, it is impossible to provide a key for the separation of aquatic and semiaquatic genera. In fact, although the key to families of larvae provided here will separate chrysomelids from the larvae of other aquatic and semiaquatic families, the key is not adequate for separating aquatic and semiaquatic chrysomelids from the great number of other grublike larvae that may fall into the water. The inexperienced coleopterist would do well to look for the caudal spines diagnostic for the Donaciinae (fig. 19.14) and to consider all other identifications as tentative unless supported by reared and associated adult material.

Chrysomelidae

Adults

1. Antennal insertions nearly contiguous (fig. 19.301); 1st visible abdominal sternite as long as all others combined .... Donaciinae 2

1'. Antennal insertions separated by entire width of frons (fig. 19.302); if nearly contiguous, 1st visible abdominal sternite no longer than 2nd and 3rd combined 3

2(1). Elytron with outer apical angle produced into a strong spine (fig. 19.303) .... *Neohaemonia*

2'. Elytron without spine at outer apical angle (fig. 19.301) .... *Donacia*

3(1'). Antennal insertions separated by entire width of frons (fig. 19.302) ....
.... Chrysomelinae .... Prasocurini 4

3'. Antennae inserted closely on front of head (fig. 19.304) 5

4(3). Basal margin of pronotum with a fine elevated bead (fig. 19.302); form very elongate, at least 2.5 times width; sutural dark stripe not much wider around scutellum (fig. 19.305) .... *Prasocuris*

4'. Basal margin of pronotum without such a bead; form broader, length less than 2.5 times width; sutural dark stripe abruptly widened around scutellum (fig. 19.306) .... *Hydrothassa*

5(3'). Posterior femur greatly enlarged, adapted for jumping (fig. 19.307) .... Alticinae 6

5'. Posterior femur not greatly enlarged, slender, adapted for walking (fig. 19.308) .. Galerucinae .... *Pyrrhalta*

6(5). Pronotum narrow, its width approximately two-thirds that of bases of elytra; pronotum unicolorous, black .... *Agasicles*

6'. Pronotum wide, its width approximately three-fourths that of bases of elytra; pronotum unicolorous, yellow, or yellow with 2 or 3 medial black spots (fig. 19.304) .... *Disonycha*

Curculionidae (Weevils)

The Curculionidae is one of the largest families of animals. The total world fauna through 1971 approached 45,000 described species. About one-tenth of this number is known to occur within North America. For such a large and diverse group, it is surprising that only a few species have invaded the aquatic environment. Approximately 55 species are known from genera in which at least one species is aquatic.

Lissorhoptrus simplex Say is a serious pest of cultivated rice. Eggs of this species are deposited in roots of rice plants, and other species are known to deposit in and on leaves of aquatic plants. Early instar *L. simplex* larvae feed within the roots, but later instars move to the mud around the roots and continue to feed upon them. Pupation occurs within an air-filled, watertight mud cocoon located on the roots.

The respiratory mechanism of *L. simplex* is unique. Abdominal segments 2 through 7 each bears a pair of dorsal hooks that connect by large tracheae to the main longitudinal tracheal trunks. The hooks appear to be modified spiracles. The larvae pierce air cells within the rice roots and obtain air from them. Denied access to living roots, submerged larvae, as a rule, die within 24 hours.

Larval *Bagous americanus* mine the floating leaves of *Nymphaea* spp. for approximately three larval instars. These mines remain air-filled. *Bagous* larvae have the abdomen truncate behind, with a pair of enlarged spiracles on the truncated surface and the other abdominal spiracles reduced or absent. Thus, larvae can utilize the air-filled mines behind them for respiration. Larvae of *B. longirostris* have been found as deep as 2 m below the water in air-filled mines in petioles of *Nymphaea*.

Pupation of aquatic weevils occurs on or within leaf petioles. The pupal chamber remains dry. *L. simplex* in the laboratory required 32–77 days from deposition of egg to transformation to the adult.

Larvae of Curculionidae (fig. 19.15) may be separated readily from larvae of other families of aquatic Coleoptera because they do not possess legs. However, as the larvae of many genera and most species of aquatic Curculionidae are unknown or have not been described, it is impossible to provide larval keys at this time. Association of adults (which can be keyed) and larvae on host plants is a method of tentative identification of immature weevils.

Curculionidae

Adults

1.   Rostrum free, not received in prosternum 2

1'.   Rostrum received in prosternum in repose; upper surface of body very often
        uneven 6

2(1).   Lateral angle of 1st sternite covered by elytron 3

2'.   Lateral angle of 1st sternite exposed .... Cleonini .... ***Lixus***

3(2).   Tibiae fossorial (fig. 19.312); mandible biemarginate, tridentate at apex; procoxae
        contiguous .... Emphyastini .... ***Emphyastes***

3'.   Tibiae not fossorial; mandible emarginate or biemarginate; procoxae contiguous or
        separated 4

4(3'). Mandible usually emarginate and bidentate at apex .... Hyperini 12

4'.   Mandible biemarginate, tridentate at apex 5

5(4'). Tibiae each with inner apical angle drawn into a strong, curved apical claw (fig.
        19.313); size large, middorsal length (excluding head) usually greater than 7
        mm .... Hylobiini .... ***Steremnius***

5'.   Tibiae without strong apical claw, truncate at apex, if claw present *(Bagous* and
        Pnigodes), then size small, middorsal length (excluding head) usually less than 5
        mm .... Hydronomini (in part) 13

6(1'). Procoxae contiguous .... Hydronomini (in part) 13

6'.   Procoxae separated (except in *Listronotus*) .... Ceutorhynchini 7

7(6'). Second abdominal segment prolonged at sides, cutting off 3rd, which fails to reach
        margins (fig. 19.314); pectoral groove extending behind procoxae into
        mesosternum .... ***Auleutes***

7'.   Second abdominal segment not prolonged at sides; pectoral groove not extending
        behind procoxae, sometimes absent 8

8(7'). Third tarsal segment narrow, not or scarcely bilobed; 4th tarsal segment as long as
        preceding segments united 9

8'.   Third tarsal segment bilobed, 4th tarsal segment shorter than the 2 preceding
        segments united 10

9(8).   Base of thorax prolonged posteriorly as an acute triangular process .... ***Phytobius*** (in part)

9'.   Base of thorax not prolonged posteriorly .... ***Perenthis***

10(8'). Prosternum deeply sulcate before coxae, sulcus more or less evidently marked by
        carinae or bounded by very strongly formed carinae 11

10'.   Prosternum not or feebly sulcate before coxae, lateral margin of sulcus not defined
        by carinae .... ***Phytobius*** (in part)

11(10). Eye with distinct supraorbital ridge (fig. 19.315); funicle of antenna 6-segmented;
        front coxae separated by one-third the distance of middle coxae .... ***Mecopeltus***

11'.   Eye without supraorbital ridge; funicle of antenna 7-segmented; front coxae
        separated by one-half the distance of middle coxae .... ***Rhinoncus***

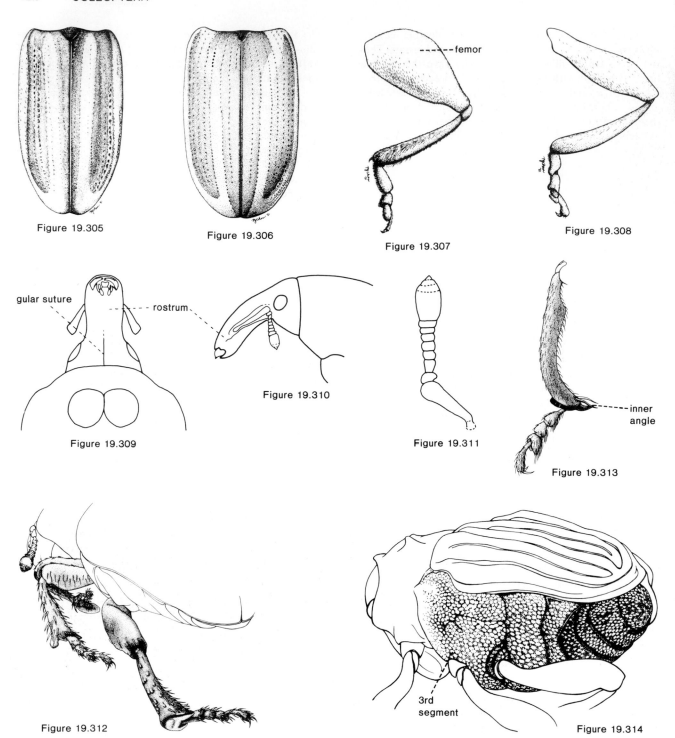

Figure 19.305

Figure 19.306

femor

Figure 19.307

Figure 19.308

gular suture

rostrum

Figure 19.309

Figure 19.310

Figure 19.311

inner angle

Figure 19.313

Figure 19.312

3rd segment

Figure 19.314

Figure 19.305. *Prasocuris* sp. (Chrysomelidae) adult, scutellum and elytra.

Figure 19.306. *Hydrothassa* sp. (Chrysomelidae) adult, scutellum and elytra.

Figure 19.307. *Disonycha* sp. (Chrysomelidae) adult, hind leg.

Figure 19.308. *Pyrrhalta* sp. (Chrysomelidae) adult, hind leg.

Figure 19.309. *Emphyastes* sp. (Curculionidae) adult, ventral aspect of head and prothorax.

Figure 19.310. *Emphyastes* sp. (Curculionidae) adult, lateral aspect of head and prothorax.

Figure 19.311. *Emphyastes* sp. (Curculionidae) adult, antenna.

Figure 19.312. *Emphyastes* sp. (Curculionidae) adult, lateral oblique aspect.

Figure 19.313. *Steremnius* sp. (Curculionidae) adult, dorsolateral aspect of hind leg.

Figure 19.314. *Auleutes* sp. (Curculionidae) adult, lateral oblique aspect.

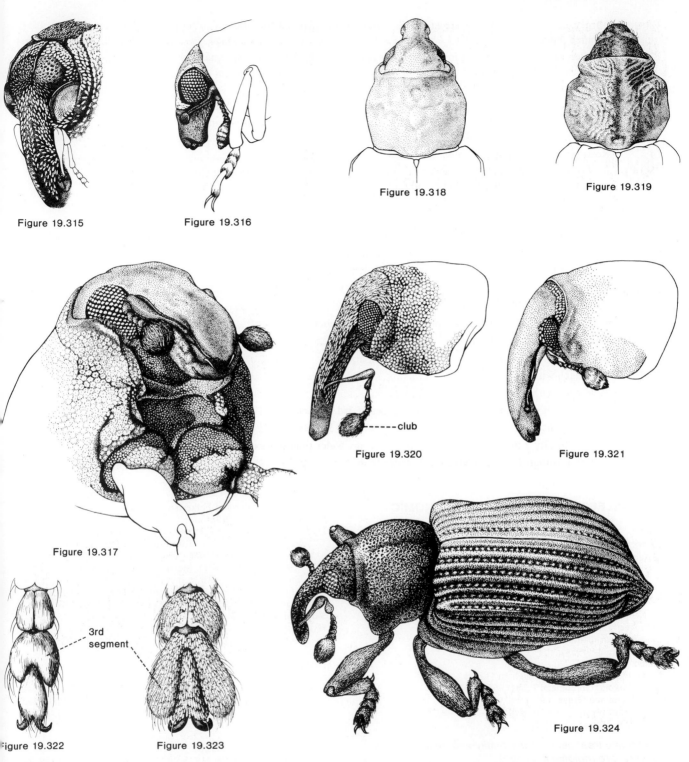

Figure 19.315

Figure 19.316

Figure 19.318

Figure 19.319

Figure 19.317

Figure 19.320

- - - - - club

Figure 19.321

3rd
segment

Figure 19.322

Figure 19.323

Figure 19.324

Figure 19.315. *Mecopeltus* sp. (Curculionidae) adult, anterior oblique aspect of head.

Figure 19.316. *Stenopelmus* sp. (Curculionidae) adult, lateral aspect of head.

Figure 19.317. *Bagous* sp. (Curculionidae) adult, ventrolateral aspect of head and prothorax.

Figure 19.318. *Bagous* sp. (Curculionidae) adult, dorsal aspect of head and pronotum.

Figure 19.319. *Pnigodes* sp. (Curculionidae) adult, dorsal aspect of head and pronotum.

Figure 19.320. *Anchodemus* sp. (Curculionidae) adult, lateral aspect of head and pronotum.

Figure 19.321. *Brachybamus* sp. (Curculionidae) adult, lateral aspect of head and pronotum.

Figure 19.322. *Onychylis* sp. (Curculionidae) adult, lateral aspect of apical segments of tarsus.

Figure 19.323. *Endalus* sp. (Curculionidae) adult, lateral aspect of apical segments of tarsus.

Figure 19.324. *Tanysphyrus* sp. (Curculionidae) adult, dorsolateral aspect.

12(4).	Larger, usually more than 5 mm in length; 2nd segment of funicle of antenna much longer than 1st	.... *Listronotus*
12′.	Smaller, seldom over 4.5 mm in length; 2nd segment of funicle of antenna equal to or just slightly longer than 1st	.... *Hyperodes*
13(5′,6).	Metasternum one-third length of 1st sternite	.... *Phycocoetes*
13′.	Metasternum as long as 1st sternite	 14
14(13′).	Rostrum very short and broad, not longer than head (fig. 19.316); 3rd segment of hind tarsus deeply emarginate, bilobed	.... *Stenopelmus*
14′.	Rostrum cylindrical, much longer than head	 15
15(14′).	Prosternum broadly and deeply excavated in front of coxae to receive rostrum (fig. 19.317); club of antenna entirely pubescent; tibia slender, curved, armed with a distal hooked spine	 16
15′.	Not fitting above description exactly	 18
16(15).	Funicle of antenna 6-segmented	.... *Neochetina*
16′.	Funicle of antenna 7-segmented	 17
17(16′).	Pronotum feebly constricted anteriorly (fig. 19.318)	.... *Bagous*
17′.	Pronotum very strongly constricted anteriorly (fig. 19.319)	.... *Pnigodes*
18(15′).	Third segment of hind tarsus emarginate or bilobed	 19
18′.	Third segment of hind tarsus simple; legs long and slender	.... *Lissorhoptrus*
19(18).	Rostrum straight or only slightly curved (fig. 19.320)	.... *Anchodemus*
19′.	Rostrum more curved (fig. 19.321)	 20
20(19′).	Tarsi each with a single claw	.... *Brachybamus*
20′.	Tarsi each with 2 claws	 21
21(20′).	Last segment of tarsus projecting beyond lobes of 3rd segment (fig. 19.322)	.... *Onychylis*
21′.	Last segment of tarsus not projecting beyond lobes of 3rd segment (fig. 19.323)	 22
22(21′).	Length usually 2 mm or more; elytra slightly if any wider than thorax	.... *Endalus*
22′.	Length less than 1.5 mm; elytra much wider than thorax (fig. 19.324)	.... *Tanysphyrus*

SELECTED ADDITIONAL TAXONOMIC REFERENCES

General

Blatchley (1910); Boving and Craighead (1930); Leech and Chandler (1956); Leech and Sanderson (1959); Arnett (1960); Klots (1966); Bertrand (1972); Doyen (1976); Pennak (1978); Lehmkuhl (1979); McCafferty (1981).

Regional faunas

California: Leech and Chandler (1956).
Canada (Southhampton Island): Young (1960).
Florida: Young (1954).
Maine: Malcolm (1971).
North and South Carolina: Brigham (1982).
North Dakota: Gordon and Post (1965)
Ohio: Melin and Graves (1971).
Pacific Northwest: Hatch (1962, 1965).
Wisconsin: Hilsenhoff (1981).

Taxonomic treatments at the family and generic levels (several are regional in scope)

Amphizoidae: Edwards (1951).
Gyrinidae: Roberts (1895); Fall (1922a); Hatch (1930); Wood (1962).
Haliplidae: Matheson (1912); Roberts (1913); Wallis (1933); Matta (1976); Hilsenhoff and Brigham (1978).
Dytiscidae: Fall (1919, 1922a, 1923); Wallis (1939a, b); Leech (1938, 1940, 1942a); Young (1953, 1956, 1963, 1967, 1974, 1979b); Anderson, R. D. (1962, 1971, 1976); McWilliams (1969); Zimmerman (1970, 1980, 1981); Hilsenhoff (1975, 1980); Zimmerman and Smith (1975a, b); Larson (1975); Michael and Matta (1977); Matta (1979); Gordon (1981); Matta and Wolf (1981); Wolf and Matta (1981).

Noteridae: Spangler and Folkerts (1973); Young (1979a).
Sphaeriidae: Britton (1966).
Hydrophilidae: Horn (1873); Richmond (1920); LaRivers (1954); Spangler (1960); Van Tassell (1966); Miller (1964, 1974); Wooldridge (1965, 1966, 1967); McCorkle (1967); Wilson, (1967); Cheary (1971); Matta (1974); Smetana (1974, 1980); Gundersen (1978); Malcolm (1979).
Staphylinidae: Herman (1972); Moore and Legner (1974, 1976).
Melyridae: Moore and Legner (1975).
Salpingidae: Spilman (1967).
Hydraenidae: Perkins (1975, 1980).
Psephenidae: Brown (1972b); Brown and Murvosh (1974); Brigham (1981).
Dryopidae: Musgrave (1935); Brown (1972b).
Scirtidae: Tetrault (1967).
Elmidae: Sanderson (1938, 1953, 1954); LaRivers (1950a); Brown and Shoemake (1964); Brown (1970a, 1972a, b, 1981); Collier (1970); Hilsenhoff (1973); Finni and Skinner (1975); Brown and White (1978); White (1978b, 1982).
Ptilodactylidae: Brown (1972b).
Limnichidae: Brown (1972b).
Chrysomelidae: Schaeffer (1925, 1928); Mead (1938); Marx (1957); Wilcox, (1965); Balsbaugh and Hays (1972); Bayer and Brochmann (1975).
Curculionidae: Tanner (1943); Kissinger (1964); Bayer and Brochmann (1975).

ABLE 19A. Summary of ecological and distributional data for *aquatic Coleoptera (beetles)*. (For definition of terms see Tables 6A–6C; table epared by D. S. White, W. U. Brigham, J. T. Doyen, K. W. Cummins and R. W. Merritt.)

Taxa (number of species in parentheses)	Habitat*	Habit*	Trophic Relationships*	North American Distribution	Ecological References†
lephaga					641
Amphizoidae(4) (trout-stream beetles)					
Amphizoa(4) Larvae and adults	Lotic—erosional (especially logs)	Clingers	Predators (engulfers; especially on stoneflies)	West, Northwest	642, 1316, 1436, 1437, 1886
Gyrinidae(59)					754, 755, 1005, 1018, 1316, 1436, 1437, 1886, 2156
(whirligig beetles)					
Larvae	Lentic and lotic—vascular hydrophytes	Generally climbers and swimmers	Generally predators (engulfers)		
Adults	Lentic and lotic—depositional	Generally surface swimmers, divers	Generally predators (engulfers) and surface film (neuston) scavengers		
Dineutus(14)		Surface swimmers, divers		Widespread	144, 525, 1188
Gyretes(4)		Surface swimmers, divers		West, South	1436, 2792
Gyrinus(40)		Surface swimmers, divers	Predators (engulfers) and neuston scavengers	Widespread	312, 1188
Spanglerogyrus(1)	Lotic—depositional	Surface swimmers, divers, climbers		Alabama	753, 2329
Carabidae(2) (Predaceous ground beetles)					
Thalassotrechus(2) Larvae and adults	Marine—rocky coasts	Clingers (rock crevice dwellers)	Predators (engulfers)	Pacific Coast	586, 588, 2506
Haliplidae(69)					1044, 1316, 1436, 1437, 1886, 2069
(crawling water beetles)					
Larvae	Generally lentic—littoral, vascular hydrophytes and some lotic—depositional	Generally climbers	Generally shredders—herbivores (chewers), piercers—hervibores, some predators (engulfers)		
Adults	Generally same as larvae	Swimmers, climbers	Generally same as larvae		
Apteraliplus(1)				California	1436
Larvae	Lentic	Clingers	Shredders—herbivores (chewers), piercers—herbivores, predators (engulfers)		
Adults	Same as larvae	Swimmers, climbers	Shredders and piercers—herbivores		
Brychius(4) Larvae and adults	Lotic and lentic—erosional	Clingers	Scrapers, piercers—herbivores	West, north central	1436
Haliplus(46)				Widespread	1043, 1045, 1437
Larvae	Lentic—vascular hydrophytes	Climbers	Piercers and shredders—herbivores		
Adults	Same	Swimmers, climbers	Same		

ata listed are for adults unless noted.
mphasis on trophic relationships.

Table 19A— *Continued*

Taxa (number of species in parentheses)	Habitat*	Habit*	Trophic Relationships*	North American Distribution	Ecological References†
Peltodytes(18)				Widespread	1043, 1045, 1437, 279●
Larvae	Lentic—vascular hydrophytes, some lotic—erosional	Climbers, clingers	Piercers and shredders—herbivores, predators (engulfers)		
Adults	Same	Swimmers, climbers, clingers	Same		
Dytiscidae(532) (predaceous diving beetles)					73, 92, 755, 1093, 131● 1408, 1436, 1437, 164● 1886, 2792, 2796, 281●
Larvae	Generally lentic—vascular hydrophytes, some lotic—depositional	Generally climbers, swimmers	Generally predators (engulfers)		
Adults	Same as larvae	Generally divers, swimmers	Same as larvae		
Acilius(4)	Lentic—vascular hydrophytes	Swimmers, divers	Predators (piercers)	Widespread	1058, 1436, 1648
Agabetes(1)	Lentic—littoral	Swimmers, divers	Predators (piercers)	East	2217, 2792
Agabinus(2)	Lotic-erosional and depositional, lentic—littoral	Swimmers, divers	Predators (piercers)	West	1436
Agabus(93)	Lotic—erosional and depositional, lentic—vascular hydrophytes	Swimmers, divers	Predators (piercers)	Widespread	1057, 1198, 1201, 121● 1435, 1648, 2792
Anodocheilus(1)	Lentic—littoral, lotic—depositional (vascular hydrophytes)	Swimmers, climbers	Predators (piercers)	Southeast	2792
Bidessonotus(3)	Lentic—littoral, lotic-depositional	Swimmers, climbers	Predators (piercers)	East, especially Southeast	2792
Brachyvatus(1)	Lentic—littoral, lotic—depositional	Swimmers, climbers	Predators (piercers)	Widespread	2792
Carrhydrus(1)	Lentic—vascular hydrophytes	Swimmers, divers	Predators (piercers)	Far North	1407
Celina(9)	Lentic—vascular hydrophytes	Swimmers, climbers	Predators (piercers)	Widespread	1436, 2792
Colymbetes(7)	Lotic—depositional	Swimmers, divers	Predators (piercers)	Northern	92, 1436
Copelatus(7)	Lotic—depositional, lentic-vascular hydrophytes	Swimmers, divers	Piercers—carnivores	Widespread	1436
Coptotomus(8)	Lentic—vascular hydrophytes, lotic—depositional	Swimmers, divers, climbers	Predators (piercers)	Widespread	92, 1407, 1436, 1437, 2722, 2792
Cybister(5)	Lentic—vascular hydrophytes	Swimmers, divers	Predators (piercers)	Widespread	92, 752, 1251, 1252, 1436
Deronectes(18)	Lotic—erosional and depositional, lentic—vascular hydrophytes	Swimmers, climbers	Predators (piercers)	Widespread	1436
Derovatellus(1)	Lentic—littoral	Swimmer, climbers	Predators (piercers)	Florida	2792
Desmopachria(9)	Lotic—depositional, lentic—vascular hydrophytes	Swimmers, climbers	Predators (piercers)	Widespread	1407, 1437, 2722, 279●
Dytiscus(14)	Lentic—vascular hydrophytes, lotic—depositional	Swimmers, divers	Predators (piercers)	Widespread	92, 1436, 2175, 2788, 781
Eretes(1)	Lentic—vascular hydrophytes	Swimmers, divers		West, Southwest	1436

*Data listed are for adults unless noted.
†Emphasis on trophic relationships.

le 19A—*Continued*

Taxa (number of species in parentheses)	Habitat*	Habit*	Trophic Relationships*	North American Distribution	Ecological References†
Graphoderus(6)	Lentic—vascular hydrophytes	Swimmers, divers	Predators (piercers)	Widespread	1436
Haideoporus(1)	Subterranean			Texas	2804, 1979
Hoperius(1)		Swimmers, divers, climbers	Predators (piercers)	Arkansas	2287
Hydaticus(4)	Lentic—vascular hydrophytes, lotic—depositional	Swimmers, divers, climbers	Predators (piercers)	Widespread	1436, 1437, 2722
Hydroporus(176)	Lotic—depositional, lentic—vascular hydrophytes	Swimmers, climbers	Predators (piercers)	Widespread	92, 1407, 1436, 1571, 2792
Hydrotrupes(1)	Lotic—erosional and depositional	Clingers, climbers	Predators (piercers)	West Coast	1436
Hydrovatus(8)	Lotic—depositional		Predators (piercers)	Widespread	1436, 2792
Hygrotus(52)	Lotic—depositional, lentic—vascular hydrophytes	Swimmers, climbers	Predators (piercers)	Widespread	1407, 1436
Illybius(15)	Lotic—depositional, lentic—vascular hydrophytes	Swimmers, divers	Predators (piercers)	East of Rocky Mountains	1407, 1436, 2792
Laccodytes(1)	Lentic—littoral		Predators (piercers)	Florida	2792
Laccophilus(10)	Lotic—depositional, lentic—vascular hydrophytes	Swimmers, divers, climbers		Widespread	1213, 1214, 1436, 2070, 2792, 2816
Laccornis(5)	Lentic—vascular hydrophytes	Swimmers, climbers	Predators (piercers)	East	1407, 1433
Liodessus(5)	Lotic—erosional and depositional, lentic—vascular hydrophytes	Swimmers, climbers	Predators (piercers)	Widespread	1436, 2792
Lioporius(2)	Lotic—erosional and depositional, lentic—vascular hydrophytes	Swimmers, climbers	Predators (piercers)	East	1436, 2792
Matus(4)	Lotic—depositional, lentic—vascular hydrophytes	Swimmers, divers	Predators (piercers)	East, South	1436, 2792
Megadytes(2)			Predators (piercers)	Florida	2792
Neobidessus(1)	Lotic—erosional and depositional, lentic—vascular hydrophytes	Swimmers, climbers	Predators (piercers)	Florida, Louisiana	1436, 2792
Neoclypeodytes(8)	Lotic—erosional and depositional, lentic—littoral	Swimmers, climbers	Predators (piercers)	West, Southwest	1436
Neoscutopterus(2)	Lentic—vascular hydrophytes			Extreme North	1436
Oreodytes(16)	Lotic—erosional and depositional, lentic—littoral	Swimmers, climbers	Predators (piercers)	Widespread (primarily West)	1436
Pachydrus(1)	Lentic—littoral, lotic—depositional	Swimmers, climbers		Florida	2792
Rhantus(11)	Lentic—vascular hydrophytes, lotic—depositional	Swimmers, divers	Predators (piercers)	Widespread	1407, 1436, 1437, 2261, 2722

a listed are for adults unless noted.
phasis on trophic relationships.

Table 19A—*Continued*

Taxa (number of species in parentheses)	Habitat*	Habit*	Trophic Relationships*	North American Distribution	Ecological References†
Thermonectes(6)	Lentic—vascular hydrophytes	Swimmers, divers, climbers	Predators (piercers)	Southwest	1436
Uvarus(9)	Lotic—erosional and depositional, lentic—vascular hydrophytes	Swimmers, climbers	Predators (piercers)	Widespread	1436, 2792
Noteridae(18) (burrowing water beetles)					95, 96, 1316, 1436, 1437, 1886, 2792
Larvae	Generally lentic—vascular hydrophytes	Generally burrowers, climbers	Predators (engulfers), collectors—gatherers		
Adults	Same as larvae	Generally swimmers, climbers, burrowers	Predators (engulfers)		
Hydrocanthus(6)	Lentic—vascular hydrophytes	Climbers		East, South	2792
Notomicrus(2)	Lotic—depositional, lentic—littoral	Burrowers		South	2217, 2792
Pronoterus(2)	Lentic—vascular hydrophytes	Climbers		East, South	2792
Suphis(1)	Lentic—vascular hydrophytes	Climbers		East, South	2792
Suphisellus(7)	Lotic—depositional, lentic—vascular hydrophytes	Climbers		Widespread	2792
Myxophaga Hydroscaphidae(1) (skiff beetles) *Hydroscapha*(1)					1075, 1077, 1316, 14 1436, 1437, 1886, 21
Larvae and adults	Lotic—erosional and margins (including thermal springs)	Clingers	Scrapers (blue-green algae)	West (especially Southwest)	
Sphaeriidae(3) (minute bog beetles) *Sphaerius*(3)					260, 1436
Larvae and adults	Lentic and lotic—margins (semiaquatic)	Burrowers, climbers	Scrapers?	Texas, Southern California, Washington	
Polyphaga Hydrophilidae(203) (water scavenger beetles)					121, 1126, 1316, 143 1437, 1886
Larvae	Lentic—vascular hydrophytes, lotic—depositional	Generally climbers	Generally predators (engulfers)		
Adults	Same as larvae	Generally divers, swimmers	Generally collectors—gatherers		
Ametor(2)	Lentic—littoral, lotic—depositional	Clingers		West	2286
Anacaena(3)	Lentic—littoral, lotic—depositional (detritus, fine sediments)	Burrowers (silt)		East and West Coasts, Illinois	1386, 1387, 1436
Berosus(26)	Lentic—littoral, lotic—depositional	Swimmers, divers, climbers	Piercers—herbivores, collectors—gatherers	Widespread	92, 2032, 2792
Chaetarthria(5)	Lentic—littoral, lotic—depositional	Climbers?		Widespread	1892

*Data listed are for adults unless noted.
†Emphasis on trophic relationships.

le 19A—*Continued*

Taxa (number of species in parentheses)	Habitat*	Habit*	Trophic Relationships*	North American Distribution	Ecological References†
Crenitis(11)	Lentic—littoral, lotic—depositional	Burrowers (sand and gravel)		East	1436
Crenitulus(1)	Lentic—littoral, lotic—depositional			East	1436
Cymbiodyta(29)	Lentic—littoral, lotic—depositional	Burrowers (sand and gravel)		Widespread	1436
Derallus(1)	Lentic—littoral, lotic—depositional	Swimmers, divers, climbers		East and Gulf Coasts	1436
Dibolocelus(2)	Lentic—littoral, lotic—depositional	Swimmers, divers		East	2792
Enochrus(25)				Widespread	92, 1386, 1387, 2032
Larvae	Lentic—littoral	Burrowers—sprawlers	Collectors—gatherers		
Adults	Same	Same	Piercers—herbivores		
Epimetopus(2)				Southwest	2792
Helobata(1)				Florida, Louisiana	2288
Helochares(3)				East, Southwest	1436
Helocombus(1)				East	1436
Helophorus(18)	Lentic and lotic—erosional, especially margins	Climbers	Shredders—herbivores	Widespread	1386, 1387, 2080, 674
Hydrobiomorpha(1)	Lentic—littoral, lotic—depositional	Swimmers, divers, climbers		South	2792
Hydrobius(3)	Lentic—littoral	Climbers, clingers, sprawlers		East	94, 1386, 1387
Hydrochara(8)	Lentic—littoral, lotic—depositional	Swimmers, divers, climbers		East, South, California	2792
Hydrochus(19)	Lentic and lotic—erosional, especially margins	Climbers	Shredders—herbivores	Widespread	1436
Hydrophilus(3)	Lentic—littoral, lotic—depositional	Swimmers, divers, climbers		Widespread	92, 1648, 2516, 2721, 2813
Larvae			Predators (engulfers)		
Adults			Collectors—gatherers, piercers—herbivores		
Lacobius(9)				Widespread	92, 1892
Larvae					
Adults			Piercers—herbivores		
Paracymus(14)	Lentic—littoral, lotic—depositional	Burrowers (sand and gravel)		Widespread (primarily South)	1436
Sperchopsis(1)	Lentic—littoral, lotic—depositional (wood)	Clingers		East, South	2285
Tropisternus(15)	Lentic—littoral, lotic—depositional			Widespread	92, 1118, 2032, 2794
Larvae		Climbers	Predators (engulfers)		2136, 2137, 2138, 2139, 2813
Adults		Swimmers, divers, climbers	Collectors—gatherers, piercers—herbivores		

a listed are for adults unless noted.
phasis on trophic relationships.

Table 19A—*Continued*

Taxa (number of species in parentheses)	Habitat*	Habit*	Trophic Relationships*	North American Distribution	Ecological References†
Staphylinidae (rove beetles)	Generally shorelines and beaches—freshwater lotic and lentic—littoral, marine—intertidal and rocky coasts	Generally clingers and climbers, burrowers	Predators (engulfers)		356, 1436, 1697, 216:
Amblopusa(2)	Marine coasts (rock crevices)	Clingers		West Coast (Alaska to California)	
Bledius(100)‡	Lotic and lentic—littoral	Clingers		Widespread	
Bryothinusa(1)	Marine coasts (rock crevices)	Clingers		California coast	
Carpelimus(78)	Lotic and lentic—littoral (leaf litter)	Clingers		Widespread	
Diaulota(4)	Marine coasts (rock crevices)	Clingers		West Coast (Alaska to Baja California)	
Diglotta(1)	Beaches—marine (sand)	Burrowers		California coast	
Liparocephalus(2)	Marine coasts (rock crevices)	Clingers		West Coast (Alaska to California)	
Micralymma(1)	Marine coasts (rock crevices)	Clingers		Maine	
Microbledius(3)	Lotic and lentic—littoral	Clingers		Widespread	
Phytosus(1)				New Jersey	
Pontomalota(5)	Beaches—marine (sand)	Burrowers		West Coast (British Columbia to California)	
Psamathobledius(2)	Lotic and lentic—littoral	Clingers		Widespread	
Psephidonus(1)	Lotic—erosional	Climbers (runners)	Predators (engulfers of Simuliidae)	East	
Thinobius(2)	Lotic and lentic—littoral	Climbers		Widespread	
Thinopinus(1)	Beaches—marine (sand)	Burrowers	Predators (engulfers of amphipods)	California coast	456
Thinusa(2)	Beaches—marine (sand)	Burrowers?	Predators (engulfers)	West Coast (Alaska to California)	
Stenus(159)‡	Lotic and lentic—littoral surface	Skaters (eject oils)		Widespread	
Melyridae(5) (soft-winged flower beetles)					202, 1436
Endeodes(5)				Pacific Coast	
Larvae and adults	Beaches—marine intertidal, marine—rocky coasts (semiaquatic)	Clingers (rock crevice dwellers), beaches (supratidal)	Predators (engulfers)		
Salpingidae(3) (=Eurystethidae) (narrow-waisted bark beetles)					1436, 2299, 2373, 25(
Aegialites(3)	Marine—rocky coasts	Clingers (rock crevice dwellers)	Predators (engulfers, especially mites), shredders—herbivores	Pacific Coast	

*Data listed are for adults unless noted.
†Emphasis on trophic relationships.
‡Not all species in the genus are aquatic.

ble 19A—*Continued*

Taxa (number of species in parentheses)	Habitat*	Habit*	Trophic Relationships*	North American Distribution	Ecological References†
Hydraenidae(82) (minute moss beetles)					1002, 1316, 1436, 1437, 1886, 1891, 1892, 1893
Larvae	Lotic—erosional (or stream margins), lentic—vascular hydrophytes (emergent zone)	Generally clingers, swimmers (runners) (primary semiaquatic)	Predators (engulfers)		
Adults	Lotic—erosional (especially margins)	Generally clingers (logs, cobbles, rock crevices)	Scrapers, collectors—gatherers		
Hydraena(25)	Lotic—erosional, lentic—littoral (especially margins)	Clingers, climbers		Widespread	1891, 1892, 1893
Limnebius(14)	Lotic—erosional, lentic—littoral (especially margins)	Clingers, climbers		Widespread	1891, 1892, 1893
Ochthebius(43)	Lotic—erosional and margins (1 intertidal species)	Clingers		Widespread	1002, 1891, 1892, 1893
Psephenidae(15) (water pennies)	Generally lotic and lentic—erosional	Clingers	Scrapers		286, 1068, 1074, 1316, 1436, 1437, 1749, 1886
Larvae	Lotic and lentic—erosional	Clingers	Scrapers		2255
Adults	(Females enter water to oviposit)	Ovipositing females are clingers	Nonfeeding		
Eubrianix(1)	Lotic—erosional	Clingers	Scrapers	West	405
Psephenus(7)	Lotic—erosional	Clingers	Scrapers	*East(1 sp.), West	276, 421, 528, 1748, 1750, 2169, 2621
Eubriinae (false water pennies)					
Acneus(2)	Lotic—erosional	Clingers	Scrapers	West Coast (south to San Francisco Bay)	
Alabameubria(1)				Alabama, Tennessee	
Dicranopselaphus(1)	Lotic—erosional	Clingers	Scrapers	Widespread	280
Ectopria(3)	Lotic and lentic—erosional	Clingers	Scrapers	East	244, 245, 421, 2169, 2792
Dryopidae(14) (long-toed water beetles)					1316, 1436, 1437, 1886
Larvae	Terrestrial	Burrowers	Generally shredders—herbivores?		
Adults (all entries)	Generally lentic—littoral, lotic—erosional	Clingers, climbers	Generally scrapers, collectors—gatherers?		
Dryops(2)	Lentic—vascular hydrophytes (emergent zone)	Climbers		Southwest, Northeast	1065
Helichus(11)	Lotic—erosional	Clingers		Widespread	981
Pelonomus(1)	Lentic—vascular hydrophytes (emergent zone)	Climbers		Texas to Florida; Illinois	280, 2792

ata listed are for adults unless noted.
nphasis on trophic relationships.

Table 19A—*Continued*

Taxa (number of species in parentheses)	Habitat*	Habit*	Trophic Relationships*	North American Distribution	Ecological References†
Scirtidae(34) (=Helodidae) (marsh beetles)					1316, 1436, 1437, 188 2471
Larvae (all entries)	Generally lentic—vascular hydrophytes (emergent zone)	Generally climbers, sprawlers	Generally scrapers, collectors—gatherers, shredders—herbivores, piercers—herbivores		
Adults	Terrestrial (possibly a few semiaquatic)				
Cyphon(13)	Lentic—littoral (sediments, leaf litter; including marshes and bogs), tree holes			Widespread	
Elodes(7)	Tree holes, seeps (including mineral springs)			Widespread	1436
Microcara(1)				Michigan	
Ora(1)				Florida, Texas	
Prionocyphon(2)	Tree holes			East	897, 1436
Sarabandus(3)				Northeast	
Scirtes(7)	Lentic—vascular hydrophytes (floating zone)	Climbers	Shredders—herbivores, piercers—herbivores	Widespread	138, 1353
Elmidae(97) (riffle beetles)					281, 282, 287, 288, 30 1316, 1436, 1437, 167 1886, 5153, 2641
Larvae and adults	Generally lotic and lentic—erosional, few lentic—vascular hydrophytes	Clingers, few climbers	Generally collectors—gatherers, scrapers		
Ampumixis(1)	Lotic—erosional	Clingers, burrowers		West	
Ancyronyx(1)	Lotic—erosional and depositional (detritus)	Clingers, sprawlers		East, Southeast	
Atractelmis(1)	Lotic—erosional	Clingers		California	
Cleptelmis(2)	Lotic—erosional (cobbles and submerged roots)	Clingers		West	296
Cylloepus(2)	Lotic—erosional	Clingers		Southwest	
Dubiraphia(10)	Lentic and lotic—erosional (submerged macrophytes)	Clingers, climbers		Widespread	421
Elsianus(3)	Lotic—erosional (cobbles and gravel)	Clingers		Southwest	
Gonielmis(1)	Lotic—erosional and depositional (wood debris and submerged roots)	Clingers, climbers		East, Southeast	
Heterelmis(3)	Lotic—erosional (cobbles and wood)	Clingers		Southwest	279, 296
Huleechius(1)	Lotic—erosional	Clingers		Arizona	283
Heterlimnius(2)	Lotic—erosional (cobbles and gravel)	Clingers		West	
Hexacylloepus(1)	Lotic—erosional (cobbles, gravel, and wood)	Clingers		Southwest	

*Data listed are for adults unless noted.
†Emphasis on trophic relationships.

le 19A—*Continued*

Taxa (number of species in parentheses)	Habitat*	Habit*	Trophic Relationships*	North American Distribution	Ecological References†
ara(2)	Lotic—erosional (wood debris, including semiaquatic)	Clingers, burrowers (in wood)	Shredders—detritivores (wood)	West (montane)	59, 296
acronychus(1)	Lotic—erosional and depositional (wood debris)	Clingers		East	533
icrocylloepus(11)	Lotic—erosional and depositional	Clingers, climbers, burrowers		Widespread	
arpus(4)	Lotic—erosional (cobbles and gravel)	Clingers		West	296
eocylloepus(1)	Lotic—erosional (cobbles and gravel)	Clingers		Texas, Arizona	280
eoelmis(1)	Lotic—erosional (cobbles and gravel)	Clingers		Southwest	
ptioservus(13)	Lotic—erosional and depositional (sediments and detritus)	Clingers	Scrapers, collectors—gatherers	Widespread	97, 296, 382, 421, 1346, 2640
rdobrevia(1)	Lotic—erosional (cobbles and gravel)	Clingers		West	
ulimnius(1)	Lotic—erosional (cobbles and gravel)	Clingers		East, Southeast	280
hanocerus(1)				Texas	
Larvae	Lotic—erosional	Clingers, climbers			
Adults	Lotic—margins (semiaquatic)	Climbers			
romoresia(2)	Lotic—erosional (cobbles and gravel)	Clingers		East, Southeast	288
hizelmis(1)	Lotic—erosional	Clingers		California	
tenelmis(28)	Lotic—erosional (coarse sediments and detritus)	Clingers	Scrapers, collectors—gatherers	Widespread	280, 421
aitzevia(2)	Lotic—erosional (cobbles and gravel)	Clingers		West	
dactylidae(3) (oed-winged beetles)					1436, 1437, 2298
Larvae (all entries)	Generally lotic—erosional and depositional	Generally clingers, burrowers	Generally shredders—detritivores and herbivores		
Adults	Terrestrial (near lotic margins in leaf litter)				
nchycteis(1)	Lotic—erosional and depositional	Burrowers	Shredders—herbivores (chewers)	California	1436, 1456, 2792
nchytarsus(1)	Lotic—erosional and depositional	Clingers	Shredders—detritivores (rotting wood)	East	
enocolus(1)	Lotic—erosional and depositional	Burrowers	Shredders—herbivores (chewers)	California	
nichidae(6) (marsh-loving beetles)		Generally clingers or burrowers	Generally collectors—gatherers?		700, 1436, 1437, 2215
Larvae	Mostly terrestrial or semiaquatic				
Adults	Mostly terrestrial, some aquatic				

a listed are for adults unless noted.
phasis on trophic relationships.

Table 19A—*Continued*

Taxa (number of species in parentheses)	Habitat*	Habit*	Trophic Relationships*	North American Distribution	Ecological References†
Lutrochus(3)	Lotic—erosional (especially mineral springs)	Clingers		East, Southwest	280, 285
Throscinus(3)	Beach zone—marine intertidal	Burrowers	Collectors—gatherers?	Texas, southern California	1436
Chrysomelidae (leaf beetles)	Generally lentic—vascular hydrophytes	Generally clingers, sprawlers	Shredders—herbivores		1316, 1436, 1437
Larvae	Lentic—vascular hydrophytes (below surface in floating and submerged zones)	Clingers (obtain air directly from vascular hydrophyte tissues)	Shredders—herbivores (chewers)		
Adults	Lentic—vascular hydrophytes (generally surface of floating leaves)	Sprawlers (on floating leaf surfaces)	Shredders—herbivores (chewers)		
Agasicles(1)	On *Alternanthera*			South	
Disonycha(33)‡	On Amaranthaceae			Widespread	
Donacia(50)	On a wide variety of vascular hydrophytes			Widespread	234, 1100, 1101, 1612
Hydrothassa(4)	On *Ranunculus*			North, East	
Neohaemonia(3)	On a wide variety of vascular hydrophytes			East of Rocky Mountains	234, 1100
Prasocuris(1)	On a wide variety of vascular hydrophytes			Northeast	
Pyrrhalta(5)‡ (=*Galerucella*)	On Nymphaeaceae			East	
Curculionidae (weevils)					1436, 1437, 1612, 2393
Larvae	Generally lentic—vascular hydrophytes (most semiaquatic)	Generally clingers, climbers, sprawlers (on leaf surfaces), burrowers (in stems)	Shredders—herbivores (chewers and miners)		
Adults	Same as larvae	Generally clingers and sprawlers	Shredders—herbivores (chewers)		
Anchodemus(3)	Lentic—vascular hydrophytes (emergent zone: *Sagittaria*)			East	1612
Auleutes(12)‡	Lentic—vascular hydrophytes (emergent and floating zones)			Widespread	
Bagous(30)	Lentic—vascular hydrophytes (floating zone)	Sprawlers, clingers		Widespread	1612
Brachybamus(1)	Lentic—vascular hydrophytes (emergent zone: probably *Sagittaria*)			East	2393
Emphyastes(1)	Beach zone—marine (sand, under macroalgae)		Shredders—detritivores (decaying *Fucus*)	Pacific Coast	
Endalus(8)	Lentic—vascular hydrophytes (emergent zone: *Scirpus* and probably others)	Climbers, clingers		Widespread	

*Data listed are for adults unless noted.
†Emphasis on trophic relationships.
‡Not all species in the genus are aquatic.

ble 19A—*Continued*

Taxa (number of species in parentheses)	Habitat*	Habit*	Trophic Relationships*	North American Distribution	Ecological References†
Hyperodes(44)‡	Lentic—vascular hydrophytes (emergent and floating zones)			Widespread	
Lissorhoptrus(1)	Lentic—vascular hydrophytes (submerged zone: rice)	Climbers, clingers	Shredders—herbivores (roots and submerged foliage of rice)	East	1319, 2480
Listronotus(27)‡	Lentic—vascular hydrophytes (emergent and floating zones)			Widespread	
Lixus(69)‡	Lentic—vascular hydrophytes (emergent and floating zones)			Widespread	
Mecopeltus(6)‡	Lentic—vascular hydrophytes (emergent and floating zones)			East, west	
Neochetina(1)	Lentic—vascular hydrophytes (emergent zone: *Eichhornia*)			South	
Onychylis(3)	Lentic—vascular hydrophytes (floating zone: *Sagittaria, Nymphaea*)			East	
Perenthis(1)				East	
Phycocoetes(1)	Beach zone—marine (sand and rock crevices)			Southern California	
Phytobius(8)‡	Lentic—vascular hydrophytes (emergent and floating zones)			Widespread	
Pnigodes(3)	Lentic—vascular hydrophytes (on *Lepidium, Ptilimnium*)			South, West	2393
Rhinoncus(4)				Widespread	
Stenopelmus(1)				Widespread	2393
Steremnius(4)				East, West	
Tanysphyrus(2)	Lentic—vascular hydrophytes (floating zone: duckweeds)		Shredders—herbivores (*Lemna*)	East	

Aquatic Hymenoptera

20

Kenneth S. Hagen
University of California, Berkeley

INTRODUCTION

Although the Hymenoptera considered aquatic in this review are all parasites (parasitoids), the group is difficult to define. In the narrowest sense they are wasps that enter the water as adults to contact their aquatic hosts, and in the broadest sense (e.g., Hedqvist's [1967] European list) they are parasites of aquatic invertebrates that do not necessarily parasitize the aquatic stage of the host species.

In an earlier review of North American aquatic Hymenoptera (Hagen 1956) only species known or suspected to either dive or crawl beneath the water surface to parasitize or to obtain their hosts were included. The present coverage follows Burghele's (1959) definition of aquatic Hymenoptera as all species parasitizing aquatic stages of insects. Therefore, all known North American hymenopterous families and genera that conform to this definition, plus some selected families and genera that attack semiaquatic species and/or life stages, have been included. Thus, caution is advised if the reader attempts to identify hymenopterans reared from terrestrial (or marginally semiaquatic) stages.

Aquatic Hymenoptera are members of the suborder Apocrita, all families falling under the Section Parasitica. The one known exception is the pompilid *Anoplius depressipes* Banks, which is a member of the section Aculeata. This wasp attacks pisaurid spiders (genus *Dolomedes*) that run over and dive under the surface of the water and may stay submerged for some time. Since *A. depressipes* can crawl into the water and run on the bottom, it may sting the spiders under water before transporting them to nests made in the bank (Evans 1949; Evans and Yoshimoto 1962).

The superfamilies of Parasitica—Ichneumonoidea, Proctotrupoidea, Cynipoidea, and Chalcidoidea—contain a few species that can be considered aquatic. Most are internal parasites of aquatic immatures that are usually found in plant tissues. The few external parasite species oviposit on larvae, prepupae, and pupae that are either in terrestrial cocoons, puparia, or pupal cases, or in plant mines.

Among the Ichneumonoidea, most aquatic braconids are internal parasites of leaf miners and enter the water as adults to oviposit. *Chaenusa* oviposits into ephydrid eggs, whereas other genera *(Ademon, Chorebus, Chorebidea, Chorebidella, Dacnusa,* and *Opius)* oviposit into larvae, but all emerge from ephydrid puparia. Species of these genera have been reported to parasitize 60–90% of *Hydrellia* sp. populations in some instances (Grigarick 1959b; Deonier 1971). Aquatic ichneumonids (*Apsilops* sp. and perhaps *Cremastus* sp.) are solitary internal parasites of stem-mining Lepidoptera.

The Proctotrupoidea associated with aquatic insects belong to one of three families, the Scelionidae, Diapriidae, or Agriotypidae. All scelionids are internal parasites of insect eggs; the diapriid genus *Trichopria* oviposits in dipterous puparia; and the Agriotypidae are ectoparasitic as larvae upon the prepupae and pupae of caddisflies (Clausen 1950). Among the Cynipoidea, only the family Eucoilidae is aquatic, attacking Diptera larvae and emerging from pupae; *Hexacola* is the only genus reported from North America thus far that attacks aquatic insects.

In the Chalcidoidea, the tiny mymarid wasps or fairyflies are all internal parasites of insect eggs. The biology of *Caraphractus cinctus* Walker, which is probably the most completely known of any aquatic hymenopteran, is summarized in figures 20.1–20.10. After mating underwater, on the surface film, or on emergent plants, this hymenopteran oviposits underwater on dytiscid beetle eggs either exposed or in plant tissues (fig. 20.1). The number of eggs deposited depends upon the size of the host egg, but up to 55 progeny have been obtained from a single dytiscid egg. In such cases the adults are often micropterous (reduced wings). After the egg (fig. 20.2) is deposited, it enlarges (figs. 20.4–20.5) and the transparent first larval instar (fig. 20.6) hatches. The larva feeds by sucking in yolk spheres from the host egg, which can be seen in the gut of the second instar (fig. 20.7). As the yolk cells are digested, the gut of the third instar becomes paler (fig. 20.8). The gregarious larvae do not attack each other and face in different directions if they are in the same host egg (figs. 20.8–20.9). Opaque white areas, which probably represent excretory products, can be seen in the terminal larval instar (fig. 20.9). Wastes are stored as a single mass in the pupal stage (fig. 20.10). The adults emerge under water, respire cutaneously, and swim with their wings (Jackson 1958c, 1961b). The female of *C. cinctus* probes each egg of *Agabus* sp. with her ovipositor and usually rejects eggs already parasitized. Arrhenotokous parthenogenesis occurs as in most parasitic Hymenoptera where an unmated female will produce only male progeny and a mated female can deposit both fertilized and unfertilized eggs. When *C. cinctus* oviposits in small host eggs like *Agabus bipustulatus,* the proportion of fertilized eggs usually increases when hosts are offered in quick succession; the number of eggs deposited in each host is then reduced to two or one with a resulting sex ratio of about 17% males. In host eggs offered to a female at long intervals, three eggs are deposited, and the resulting sex ratio is usually one male and two females. Under high competition between female parasites for a few number of host

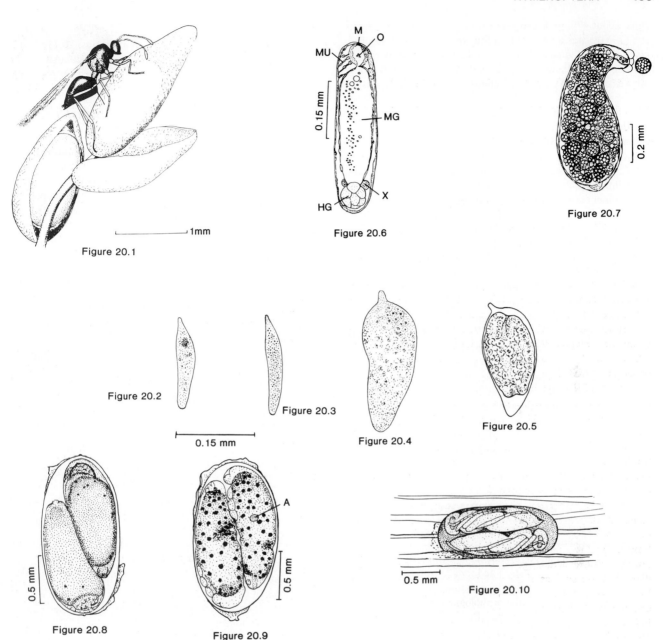

Figure 20.1

M O
MU

0.15 mm

MG

HG   X

Figure 20.6

0.2 mm

Figure 20.7

Figure 20.2

Figure 20.3

0.15 mm

Figure 20.4

Figure 20.5

A

0.5 mm

0.5 mm

Figure 20.8

Figure 20.9

0.5 mm

Figure 20.10

Figure 20.1 Female *Caraphractus cinctus* Walker (Mymaridae) ovipositing underwater in an egg of *Agabus bipustulatus* L. (Dytiscidae) laid in a sphagnum leaf. One other host egg is shown attached to the leaf with gelatinous cement (from Jackson 1958b).

Figure 20.2. *Caraphractus cinctus* ovarian eggs (from Jackson 1961b).

Figure 20.3. *Caraphractus cinctus* egg dissected from host 20 minutes after laying (from Jackson 1961b).

Figure 20.4. *Caraphractus cinctus* egg (laid by same female as egg in fig. 20.3) dissected from another host about 72 hours after laying (from Jackson 1961b).

Figure 20.5. *Caraphractus cinctus* egg of another female about 72 hours after laying; more advanced, showing reduced size and developing embryo.

Figure 20.6. *Caraphractus cinctus* first larval instar dissected from host about 70 hours after laying (from Jackson 1961b): *HG*, hindgut; *M*, mouth; *MG*, midgut; *MU*, muscle cells extending from body wall to esophagus; *O*, esophagus; *X*, probably sex cells.

Figure 20.7. *Caraphractus cinctus* second larval instar (from Jackson 1961b).

Figure 20.8. Egg of *Agabus bipustulatus* L. with two-third stage larvae of *Caraphractus cinctus*, about 9 days after laying (from Jackson 1961b).

Figure 20.9. Two full-grown parasitic larvae of *Caraphractus cinctus* in host egg. *A*, discolored spot around the oviposition puncture in shell of *Agabus bipustulatus* (from Jackson 1961b).

Figure 20.10. Eggs of *Agabus bipustulatus*, on leaf of *Juncus* sp., containing two newly formed pupae of *Caraphractus cinctus*; the one *above* is a male, the one *below*, a female (from Jackson 1961b).

eggs, about 47% male progeny results (Jackson 1966). Jackson (1961a) was able to obtain four or five generations of *C. cinctus* from *A. bipustulatus* reared in an unheated room near a window in Scotland, but by the end of October all full-grown larvae (prepupae) entered a diapause state. These diapausing prepupae pupated in the spring and emerged as adults from March to May. Interestingly, dytiscid eggs do not diapause but develop at all times of the year when the temperature is suitable. Jackson experimentally varied the photoperiod and found that 9 hours of complete darkness induced diapause in the *C. cinctus* larvae, which were sensitive to extremely low light intensity, and Jackson concluded that in ponds direct development of the parasitoid would occur with long daylight hours combined with faint light at night (twilight) or with a few hours of darkness. Temperature was not the deciding factor in the induction of diapause.

Aquatic Trichogrammatidae are all internal parasites of insect eggs. Although some species can swim with their legs, remain underwater up to five days, and have been reported to mate within the submerged host egg, most species of the large genus *Trichogramma* will undoubtedly be reared from terrestrial eggs of aquatic insect species. Thus far, no *Trichogramma* species have been reported as parasites of submerged host eggs. *Trichogramma* sp. enters a diapause state if the host eggs undergo diapause.

Species of Eulophidae and Pteromalidae have diverse habits, including hyperparasitism, a condition in which one parasitoid is in turn parasitized by another. None has been reported to invade water to find their host; however, several species are associated with the semiaquatic or terrestrial stages of aquatic insects.

EXTERNAL MORPHOLOGY

In most instances, Hymenoptera that parasitize aquatic insects do not show any external morphological adaptations in either the adult or larval stages, as compared with those parasitizing terrestrial hosts. The larvae of internal parasites are already modified to live in a liquid environment (host hemolymph), and no special morphological modifications seem to have evolved in the wasps that dive beneath the water surface to reach their host insects. Larvae of Agriotypidae are the only external parasites of hosts that live under water; they have a special morphological adaptation: the last larval instar forms a ribbonlike respiratory filament that remains functional through the pupal stage.

Suborder Apocrita

Section Parasitica

Larvae

Larvae of internal parasites are usually hypermetamorphic, that is, the first instars are distinct from later instars, which are legless and grublike. Maxillary palpi rarely project from the head surface, and the labial palpi are disklike and nonprojecting. There are rarely more than nine spiracles in mature larvae, and they are lacking in early instars of internal parasites.

Adults

Hind wings are without an anal lobe (figs. 20.11, 20.13, 20.16A) and species are rarely wingless. Hind tibiae have one or two spurs (fig. 20.20), but none are modified for preening.

KEY TO THE FAMILIES OF "AQUATIC" HYMENOPTERA

All known hymenopterous families that contain species that enter the water as adults are included in the key, as well as most families having species that parasitize terrestrial stages of aquatic insects. Since many of the hymenopterous larvae that parasitize aquatic insects cannot be separated satisfactorily on a morphological basis (particularly the Chalcidoidea and Proctotrupoidea), a key to the larvae is not presented. Rather, some general descriptive information for each family is given below.

Suborder Apocrita

Section Parasitica

Larvae

1. **Ichneumonoidea:** First instars of solitary internal parasites with large mandibles, no open spiracles and body usually ending in a long tail. First instar of external parasites segmented and with 9 spiracles; mandibles not conspicuous. Mature larvae segmented, with spiracles; head parts usually outlined by sclerotic rods.

a. *Braconidae:* First instars with large mandibles and usually without long, pointed tails *(Opius, Chorebus)*. Mature larvae usually with spiracles on pro- and metathorax and on first 7 abdominal segments.

b. *Ichneumonidae:* First instars of solitary internal parasites often have large mandibles and a long, pointed tail. Mature larvae similar to Braconidae.

2. **Chalcidoidea:** First instar of internal parasites variable, usually greatly different than mature larvae. Mature larvae either saclike with no spiracles or one pair in most egg parasites. In other hosts, segmented grublike larvae with 9, rarely 10, open spiracles; one pair on meso- and metathorax and first 7 abdominal segments.

a. *Eulophidae:* First instar is usually 13-segmented, with mandibles. Mature larva similar, with no functional spiracles in *Mestocharis* and maxillae with 2-segmented palpi. In most mature chalcidoid larvae, maxilliary palpi are disklike and not projecting.

b. *Mymaridae:* First instar *(Caraphractus)* elongate, cylindrical with no mandibles or outgrowths and no visible segmentation (fig. 20.6); first instar *(Anagrus)* saclike, head lobate, separated from body by a constriction. Mature larvae saclike, without mouth hooklets in *Caraphractus* and with hooklets in *Anagrus*.

c. *Pteromalidae:* First instar 13-segmented; mandibles present. External parasites with 4 pairs of spiracles situated in mesothorax and first 3 abdominal segments; internal parasites lack functional spiracles. Mature larvae similar to first instar but with 9 pairs of spiracles; a pair on meso- and metathorax and first 7 abdominal segments; in *Sisridivora,* 10 spiracles with the additional pair on the 8th abdominal segment. Mandibles sclerotized and supported laterally and above by sclerotic rods.

d. *Trichogrammatidae:* First instar larvae saclike, with minute mandibles. Mature larvae robust and segmented, without spines and setae; mandibles are elongated, extruded, and lie parallel to each other.

3. **Proctotrupoidea:** First instar variable. Mature larvae segmented, with mandibles and with less than 9 pairs of spiracles.

a. *Diapriidae:* First instar clearly segmented, solitary parasites with large mandibles and often with short, forked tail and no spiracles. In gregarious types (many larval parasites in one host) *(Trichopria);* first instar with mouthparts small and indistinct, but with a pair of distinct projecting papillae arising above mouth opening. Two tubercles are present on the last abdominal segment and each bear several teeth. Mature larvae *(Trichopria)* 13-segmented; papillae above mouthparts absent; mandibles sclerotized with or without teeth; spiracles on body segments 3, 4, and 5; posterior abdominal tubercles present or absent.

b. *Scelionidae:* First instar with complete lack of segmentation, but body divided by a sharp constriction into somewhat equal portions; mandibles large, external, sharply pointed, widely separated, and usually curving ventrally; abdomen terminates in a horn or tail. A transverse row of spines usually around abdomen; no spiracles present. Mature larvae elongate-ovate, mandibles (oral hooks) slender and threadlike with broad base; abdomen without spines and tail.

4. **Cynipoidea parasitic species:** First instar segmented, no spiracles, variable from an unusually elongate body with nearly every segment bearing a ventral appendage and last abdominal segment prolonged into a dorsally curved tail equal in length to the 4 preceding segments, to a body bearing no ventral appendages and a tail nearly as long as the body. Mature larvae segmented, ovoid to spindle-shaped with 6–10 spiracles; mandibles bi- or tridentate.

Eucoilidae: First instar elongate, bearing long, paired, fleshy ventral processes on the thoracic segments and a long, spined, tapering tail with a ventral projecting appendage near the base. Mature larva with 9 pairs of spiracles on the last 2 thoracic and first 7 abdominal segments; mandibles bidentate.

Section Aculeata
5. **Vespoidea**

Pompilidae: Body with head and 13 segments, legless and grublike. Head with conspicuous lobes, mandibles large and toothed, maxillary and labial palpi project as conical tubercles; maxillary palpi and galeae about equal in length. Body with 10 spiracles, but second pair on thorax vestigial.

Adults

1.	Wing venation reduced; front wings usually with no enclosed cells, but, if present, with less than 5 enclosed cells; wings usually with long marginal fringe; hind wings veinless or with one vein and vein-enclosed cells absent; rarely wingless (figs. 20.11–20.13, 20.16)	2
1'.	Wing venation well developed; front wings with more than 5 enclosed cells and without long marginal fringe, at least on anterior margins; hind wings with more than 2 veins and with at least one enclosed cell (figs. 20.19–20.22)	8
2(1).	Tarsi 4- or 5-segmented	3
2'.	Tarsi 3-segmented (fig. 20.11); parasites of insect eggs .... *TRICHOGRAMMATIDAE*
3(2).	Tarsi 4-segmented (fig. 20.13)	4
3'.	Tarsi 5-segmented (figs. 20.16, 20.20)	5
4(3).	Marginal vein short, terminating within the first third of wing's length; stigmal vein absent (fig. 20.12); body not metallic; parasites of insect eggs .... *MYMARIDAE*
4'.	Marginal vein long, extending beyond one-half of wing's length; stigmal vein present (fig. 20.13); body with metallic reflections or highly colored; parasites of dytiscid eggs, psephenid prepupae and pupae, leaf-miners, and mymarids .... *EULOPHIDAE*
5(3').	Antennae inserted on shelf at middle of face (fig. 20.14); parasites of dipterous puparia and psephenid pupae .... *DIAPRIIDAE*
5'.	Antennae not arising from shelf at middle of face (fig. 20.16B)	6
6(5').	Antennae with 2 distinctly smaller segments (anelli) between pedicel and first funicle segment; together the anelli thinner and usually shorter than first funicle segment (fig. 20.15); parasites of gyrinid and sisyrid larvae and pupae in pupal cases or cocoons, or emerging from dipterous puparia .... *PTEROMALIDAE*
6'.	Antennae without 2 distinctly smaller segments (anelli) between pedicel and first funicle segment (fig. 20.17)	7
7(6')	Scutellum with 2 pits at base and an elevated pit ("cup") on disk; fore wing without stigmal vein; abdomen compressed; parasites of Diptera larvae and pupae .... *EUCOILIDAE*

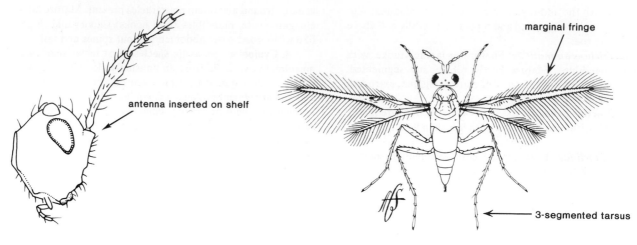

Figure 20.14

Figure 20.11

Figure 20.12

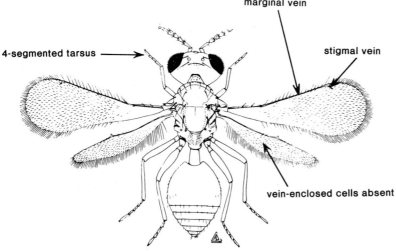

Figure 20.13

Figure 20.11. Female of *Hydrophylita aquivolans* Matheson and Crosby (Trichogrammatidae) (from Matheson and Crosby 1912).

Figure 20.12. Front wing of *Patasson gerrisophaga* (Doutt) (Mymaridae) (from Doutt 1949).

Figure 20.13. Female *Psephenivorus mexicanus* Burks (Eulophidae) (from Burks 1968).

Figure 20.14. Lateral view of a *Trichopria* sp. head (Diapriidae) (drawn by N. Vandenberg).

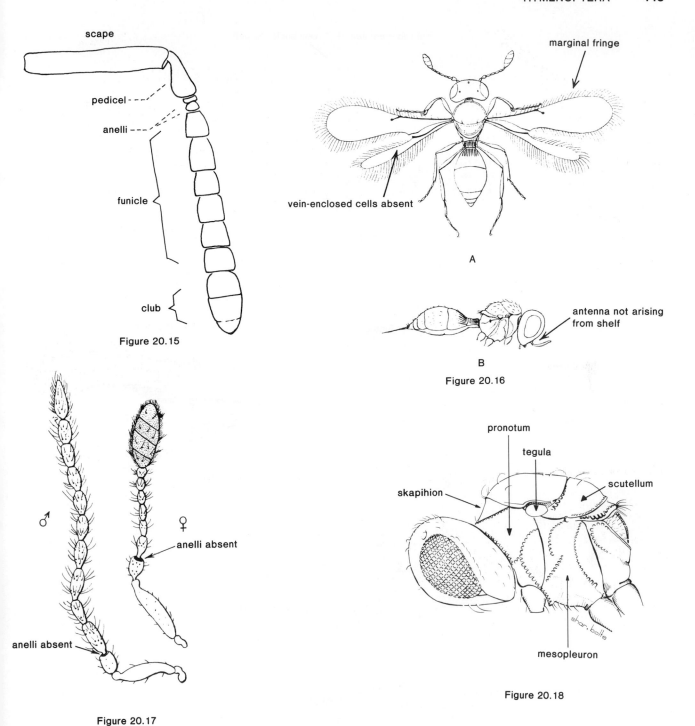

Figure 20.15

A

B

Figure 20.16

Figure 20.17

Figure 20.18

Figure 20.15. Pteromalid (*Eupteromalus* sp.) antenna (drawn by N. Vandenberg).

Figure 20.16. Female of *Tiphodytes gerriphagus* (Marchal) (Scelionidae). *A*, dorsal view; *B*, lateral view (from Marchal 1900).

Figure 20.17. Male and female antennae of *Tiphyodytes gerriphagus* (Marchal) (Scelionidae) (from Marchal 1900).

Figure 20.18. Lateral view of head and thorax of *Tiphodytes gerriphagus* (Marchal) (Scelionidae) (from Masner 1972).

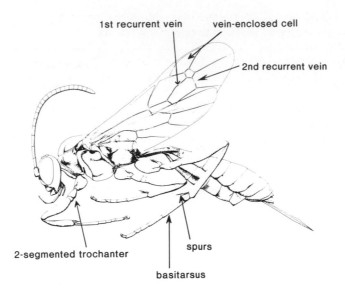

1st recurrent vein

vein-enclosed cell

2nd recurrent vein

2-segmented trochanter

spurs

basitarsus

Figure 20.20

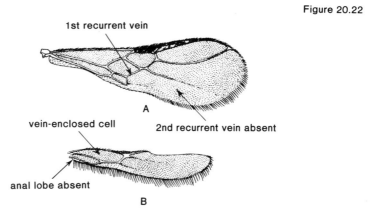

enclosed cells

anal lobe

Figure 20.19

pterostigma

1st recurrent vein

2nd recurrent vein absent

Figure 20.22

1st recurrent vein

A

2nd recurrent vein absent

vein-enclosed cell

anal lobe absent

B

Figure 20.21

Figure 20.19. Hind wing of pompilid wasp (drawn by N. Vandenberg).

Figure 20.20. Lateral view of *Apsilops hirtifrons* (Ashmead) (Ichneumonidae) (from Townes 1970).

Figure 20.21. Front *(A)* and hind *(B)* wing of *Chorebus aquaticus* Muesebeck (Braconidae) (from Muesebeck 1950).

Figure 20.22. Front wing of an *Opius* sp. (Braconidae) (drawn by N. Vandenberg).

7'.   Scutellum without an elevated cup (fig. 20.18) fore wing with stigmal vein (figs. 20.13, 20.16A); abdomen depressed; parasites of eggs of Hemiptera, Lepidoptera, and Tabanidae .... *SCELIONIDAE*

8(1').   Hind wings without an anal lobe (figs. 20.20, 20.22); hind trochanters 2-segmented (fig. 20.20); antennae with more than 15 segments; parasites of Diptera and Lepidoptera larvae and pupae 9

8'.   Hind wings with an anal lobe (fig. 20.19); hind trochanters 1-segmented; antennae with less than 15 segments and curled apically; parasites of spiders .... *POMPILIDAE*

9(8).   Fore wing with 2 recurrent veins (second recurrent vein is a crossvein in apical lower half of wing disk) (fig. 20.20); parasites of Lepidoptera larvae and pupae and Coleoptera pupae .... *ICHNEUMONIDAE*

9'.   Fore wing with one recurrent vein (no crossvein in apical lower half of wing) (figs. 20.21–20.22); parasites of Diptera larvae and puparia and Lepidoptera larvae .... *BRACONIDAE*

ADDITIONAL TAXONOMIC (AND MORPHOLOGICAL) REFERENCES

General

Matheson and Crosby (1912); Clausen (1940); Muesebeck *et al.* (1951); Short (1952); Michener (1953); Hagen (1956, 1964); Richards (1956); Hedqvist (1967); Krombein and Burks (1967); Finlayson and Hagen (1979); Krombein *et al.* (1979).

Taxonomic treatments at the family and generic levels

(L = larvae; A = adults)

Agriotypidae: Clausen (1950)–L; Mason (1971)–L, A.

Braconidae: Muesebeck (1950)–A; Burghele (1959)–A; Fischer (1964, 1971)–A; Capek (1970)–L.

Diapriidae: Kieffer (1916)–A; Muesebeck (1949, 1972)–A; Sundholm (1960)–A; O'Neill (1973)–L.

Eucoilidae: Weld (1952)–A; Quinlan (1967)–A.

Eulophidae: Parker (1924)–L; Graham (1959)–A; Boucek *et al.* (1963)–A; Jackson (1964)–L; Burks (1968)–A.

Ichneumonidae: Short (1959)–L; Townes (1969, 1970, 1971)–A.

Mymaridae: Doutt (1949)–A; Annecke and Doutt (1961)–A; Jackson (1961a)–L.

Pompilidae: Evans (1950, 1951)–A; Townes (1957)–A; Evans (1959)–L; Krombein *et al.* (1979)–A.

Pteromalidae: Parker (1924)–L; Brown (1951)–L; Graham (1969)–A.

Scelionidae: Marchal (1900)–L, A; Martin (1927)–L; Masner (1972, 1976, 1980)–A.

Trichogrammatidae: Parker (1924)–L; Martin (1927)–L; Doutt and Viggiani (1968)–A; Nagaraja and Nagarkatti (1973)–A.

Table 20A. Ecological (host-parasite) relationships and distribution (of host) of aquatic *Hymenoptera (wasps).* (Table prepared by K. Hagen, K. Cummins, and R. W. Merritt.)

Parasite Taxa	Host Order	Host Family	Host Genus	Aquatic Life Stages of Host That Are Parasitized‡	North American Distribution	
Vespoidea Pompilidae(1) *Anoplius*(1) (=*Priocnemus*)	Araenea	Pisauridae	*Dolomedes*	Adults	Northeast, Northcentral	177, 370, 690, 693, 9
Proctotrupoidea Scelionidae(4) *Pseudanteris*(1)	Hemiptera	Gerridae?		Eggs	East	1558
Telenomus(3)	Lepidoptera	Pyralidae	*Chilo, Occidentalia*	Eggs	East	812
	Diptera	Tabanidae	*Tabanus, Chrysops*	Eggs	Widespread	1364
Thoron(1) (=*Teleas, Anteris*)	Hemiptera	Nepidae	*Nepa?, Ranatra?*	Eggs	Northeast	1558
Tiphodytes(1) (=*Limnodytes, Hungaroscelio*)	Hemiptera	Gerridae	*Gerris, Trepobates*	Eggs	Widespread	939, 1547, 1558, 156 1572
Diapriidae(3) *Trichopria*(3) (=*Phaenopria*)	Diptera	Ephydridae	*Hydrellia*	Pupae	Widespread	158, 553, 923, 939
	Sciomyzidae		*Atrichomelina, Dictya, Elgiva, Sepedon*	Pupae	East	1841
	Coleoptera	Psephenidae	*Psephenus*	Prepupae, pupae	Texas	276
Ichneumonoidea Ichneumonidae(14) *Apsilops*(3) (=*Neostricklandia, Trichocryptus, Trichestema*)	Lepidoptera	Pyralidae	*Occidentalia, Chilo, Schoenobius, Nymphula*	Larvae	Widespread	158, 373, 812, 939
Bathythrix(2) (=*Hemiteles*)	Coleoptera	Gyrinidae	*Gyrinus*	Larvae in pupal cases	Iowa, Michigan	313, 1364
Cremastus(2?)	Lepidoptera	Pyralidae	*Nymphula, Occidentalia, Chilo*	Larvae, pupae	East	158, 812, 939
Oecotelma(1) (=*Hemiteles*)	Coleoptera	Gyrinidae	*Gyrinus*	Larvae in pupal cases	Michigan	313, 1364
Pleurogyrus(2) (=*Hemiteles*)	Coleoptera	Gyrinidae	*Gyrinus*	Larvae in pupal cases	Michigan	313, 1364
Mesoleptus(2)	Diptera	Sciomyzidae	*Antichaeta*	Pupae	East	1332
Near Pseuderipternis(1)	Lepidoptera	Pyralidae	*Paragyractis*	Pupae	West	939
Phygadeuon(1)	Diptera	Sciomyzidae	*Antichaeta*	Pupae	East	1332
Sulcarius	Trichoptera	Limnephilidae	*Limnephilus*	Larvae in cases	Minnesota	1652
Therascopus(1) (=*Eriplanus*)	Coleoptera	Gyrinidae	*Gyrinus*	Larvae in pupal cases	Michigan	313
Braconidae(11) *Ademon*(2)	Diptera	Ephydridae	*Hydrellia*	Larvae-pupae	Widespread	158, 303, 553, 939
Aphanta(1)	Diptera	Ephydridae	*Hydrellia*	Pupae	East	553
Asobara(1)	Diptera	Ephydridae	*Parydra*	Larvae—pupae	East	559
Bracon(1) (=*Microbracon*)	Lepidoptera	Noctuidae	*Archanara*	Larvae	East	812

‡Emphasis on trophic relationships.

—Continued

asite Taxa	Host			Aquatic Life Stages of Host That Are Parasitized‡	North American Distribution	
	Order	Family	Genus			
usa(1?)	Diptera	Ephydridae	*Hydrellia*	Eggs—pupae	Widespread	303, 553, 923
bidea(1)	Diptera	Ephydridae	*Hydrellia*	Pupae	Michigan	158, 303, 559, 939
bidella(1)	Diptera	Ephydridae	*Hydrellia*	Pupae	East, Alaska	158, 553, 939
bus(1)	Diptera	Ephydridae	*Hydrellia*	Pupae	Widespread	158, 303, 559, 923, 939
sa(1?)	Diptera	Ephydridae	*Hydrellia*	Pupae	East	158, 559, 939
(1?)	Diptera	Ephydridae	*Hydrellia*	Larvae—pupae	Widespread	303, 559, 923
ocarpa(1)	Diptera	Sciomyzidae	*Antichaeta*	Pupae	East	1332
ea						
dae(3)						
rus(1)	Hemiptera	Gyrinidae	*Gyrinus*	Eggs	Kansas	408, 939, 1097
hractus(1)	Hemiptera	Notonectidae	*Notonecta*	Eggs	East	939, 1572
	Hemiptera	Gerridae	*Gerris*	Eggs	East	1140
	Odonata	Calopterygidae	*Calopteryx*	Eggs	East	939, 1572
	Coleoptera	Dytiscidae	*Dytiscus, Agabus*	Eggs	East	939, 1199, 1200, 1572, 2054
son(1)	Hemiptera	Gerridae	*Gerris*	Eggs	California	582, 939
ema(1)	Odonata	Lestidae	*Lestes*	Eggs	Illinois	866
ammatidae(9)						
ophylita(1)	Odonata	Coenagrionidae	*Ischnura*	Eggs	East	526, 939, 1572
omeroidea(1) (Centrobiopsis)	Odonata	Lestidae	*Lestes*	Eggs	East	583, 1723
entrobia(1)	Odonata	Lestidae	*Lestes*	Eggs	Widespread	1364
wichia(1)	Hemiptera	Nepidae	*Ranatra, Nepa*	Eggs	East?	408, 812, 1028, 2134
	Coleoptera	Dytiscidae	*Dytiscus*	Eggs		408, 939, 1199
ogramma(4)	Hydracarina			Eggs	West?	939, 1097
	Megaloptera	Sialidae	*Sialis*	Eggs	West	78, 1547, 1959
	Megaloptera	Corydalidae	*Chauliodes*	Eggs	East	867
	Diptera	Sciomyzidae	*Sepedon*	Eggs	East	1264
	Diptera	Sciomyzidae	*Elgiva*	Eggs	East	1264
	Diptera	Sciomyzidae	*Tetanocera*	Eggs	East	1264
e(3)						
tocetus(1)	Odonata	Lestidae	*Lestes*	Eggs (hyperparasite)	East	306
ocharis(2)	Coleoptera	Dytiscidae	*Dytiscus?*	Eggs	East	1199, 1200, 1205
enivorus(1)	Coleoptera	Psephenidae	*Psephenus*	Prepupae, pupae	Texas	276, 307
stichus(1)	Odonata	Lestidae	*Lestes*	Eggs and hyperparasite	East	1364
lidae(5)						
romalus(2)	Diptera	Ephydridae	*Hydrellia*	Pupae	California	923
ophagus(1)	Coleoptera	Gyrinidae	*Gyrinus, Dineutes*	Larvae in pupal cases	East, Midwest	313, 2659
coptera(1)	Diptera	Ephydridae	*Hydrellia*	Larvae	California	923
ivora(1)	Neuroptera	Sisyridae	*Climacia*	Larvae, pupae in cocoons	Widespread	274, 924, 1968
a						
ae						
cola(2)	Diptera	Ephydridae	*Parydra*	Larvae—pupae	East	559
	Diptera	Chloropidae	*Hippelates*	Larvae—pupae	California	682

on trophic relationships.

Aquatic Diptera
Part One. Larvae of Aquatic Diptera

21

H. J. Teskey
Biosystematics Research Institute, Agriculture Canada, Ottawa

INTRODUCTION

Although the adults of a few Diptera are briefly aquatic (e.g., while ovipositing or emerging from submerged pupae), only the immature stages of certain species spend extended periods of time partially or fully submerged. Larvae of most species can be considered aquatic in the broadest sense since for survival they must be surrounded by a moist to wet environment, i.e., within tissues of living plants, amid decaying organic materials, as parasites of other animals, or in association with bodies of water. Only the latter habitat is normally considered to encompass aquatic species.

In some families, such as the Muscidae and Scathophagidae, only a few species are aquatic; larvae of most or all known species of the families Blephariceridae, Deuterophlebiidae, Culicidae, Chironomidae, Simuliidae, Dixidae, and others are strictly confined to lotic or lentic environments. Aquatic habits are best developed among the nematocerous Diptera.

Diptera larvae occur in almost every type of aquatic habitat, including coastal marine, saline, and brackish waters; shallow and deep waters of lakes; ponds; geyser-fed thermal pools reaching 49°C; natural seeps of crude petroleum; stagnant pools, including those associated with various types of plant and artificial receptacles; and slow to rapidly flowing streams and rivers. They are found freely suspended or swimming, attached to or among aquatic vegetation, or buried in mud, sand, gravel, or under stones. Indeed, the only watered areas of the earth where aquatic flies do not breed are the large, open seas.

Among the inhabitants of flowing water, only the larvae of the Blephariceridae, Deuterophlebiidae, Nymphomyiidae, Thaumaleidae, Simuliidae, and the genus *Maruina* of the Psychodidae remain continually exposed to the current. Larvae of the remaining families live among the silt, sand, and gravel of the streambed, where they are well protected from the dislodging influence of the current. The most notable of the former group, if only for their abundance and economic importance, are the Simuliidae, whose larvae are often found in the swift current adhering to submerged rocks or vegetation by means of their modified posterior prolegs anchored to a silk secretion deposited by the larva. Their labral fans spread to strain microscopic food particles from the water (chap. 24).

The Blephariceridae are distinctive for extreme morphological modifications, resulting from the fusion and flattening of the body segments, and for suction disks located ventrally on the body segments by means of which they adhere to smooth rocks in torrential mountain streams. Larvae of *Maruina* sp., although possessing a full complement of body segments, are similarly flattened as Blephariceridae for living in swiftly flowing water, and they also adhere to smooth rocks by a series of partially connected suction disks. The Deuterophlebiidae, or "true" mountain midges, are frequently present in the same streams as the Blephariceridae on smooth rocks very close to the water surface near the splash line. Even closer to the water surface are larvae of Thaumaleidae, which preferentially inhabit shaded, exposed, vertical rock surfaces covered by a film of water in cold streams. The larvae are partially exposed, which allows for respiration through spiracles, retained in this family but lost in most other lotic-water inhabitants. The Nymphomyiidae are also found on rocks in cold streams, but they live among aquatic mosses growing on the rocks; this probably provides these very small, delicate larvae nearly as much protection from the current as would the streambed. The adults of this rather primitive and rarely collected family of flies shed their slender, feathery wings shortly after emergence.

Larvae attached to rocks and macrophytes in flowing water are generally filterers, scrapers, or browsers of aquatic organisms, whereas some larvae burrowing in the streambed (Pelecorhynchidae, Athericidae, Empididae, and some Tabanidae and Tipulidae) are predominantly predatory on other aquatic larvae.

In standing-water habitats, some dipteran larvae lead predominantly exposed lives, whereas others burrow in the bottom or margins of the water body or in wet-to-saturated soil. The former include the Culicidae, Chaoboridae, Dixidae, and some Chironomidae and Ceratopogonidae. Larval Culicidae, Dixidae, and certain Chaoboridae live in relatively small, shallow water bodies whose surface is not subject to much wave disturbance. This allows them to respire through caudal spiracles while suspended at the water surface. The free-swimming larvae of Chironomidae, Ceratopogonidae, and *Chaoborus* sp. (Chaoboridae), being apneustic, can inhabit larger bodies of water. Their cutaneous or gill respiration is probably favored by the oxygenating effect of wave action.

The apneustic condition of the aquatic burrowing members of these two families allows some species to inhabit bottom sediments in deep lakes and rivers. Burrowing by other families, including Tipulidae, Tabanidae, Stratiomyidae, and Dolichopodidae, that respire through spiracles must stay in easy migratory distance of the air water interface. The upper two inches of damp-to-saturated soils are among the favored habitats of most representatives of these families. This respiratory problem has been alleviated for the larvae of Ptychopteridae and some Syrphidae by the presence of a slender terminal respiratory siphon extensile up to two or three times the body length. Even the pupae of Ptychopteridae have an elongate respiratory horn that allows them to remain submerged in saturated muck soils, which are the favored habitat.

Parasitoid habits are rare among aquatic dipteran larvae, but examples include the Sciomyzidae, whose hosts are freshwater snails and fingernail clams, and *Oedoparena* sp. (Dryomyzidae), which feed on barnacles. A few species of aquatic Ephydridae are predatory; however, others have very diverse habits. Some are leaf, stem, and root miners of aquatic plants, but the majority feed by filtering microorganisms in a variety of aquatic habitats, including those having high salt concentrations as in maritime marshes, tidal salt pools, or salt and alkaline lakes of arid regions.

All Diptera undergo a complete metamorphosis. Eggs of aquatic species are laid either singly or in loose or compact masses in or near water, often attached to rocks or aquatic vegetation. Hatching usually occurs after a short developmental period but may be delayed, as in some Culicidae, for prolonged periods until the eggs are again submerged. Larvae of various species, representing all functional groups (chap. 6), take an extremely wide range of plant, animal, and detrital food. Larvae usually grow through three or four (occasionally more) instars before pupation beneath the water surface. Mature larvae of some species migrate to or above the water surface before pupating. Overwintering or periods of aestivation are usually passed in the egg or larval stage but sometimes as pupae and occasionally as adults. Although some species normally complete one generation a year, many others may complete two or more under favorable conditions. In a few groups, such as certain species of Tabanidae in colder northern regions, two or more years may be required per generation.

EXTERNAL MORPHOLOGY

Aquatic dipteran larvae vary so greatly in form that the only common distinguishing feature is the absence of jointed legs on all thoracic segments. Larval head structures are extensively modified from a completely exposed, heavily sclerotized head capsule with well-developed mouthparts, including opposed mandibles (most Nematocera), through various degrees of reduction to forms with several slender rods that are partially retracted within the thorax (e.g., Tipulidae) and an accompanying rotation of the mandibles to the vertical plane (orthorrhaphous Brachycera). Cyclorrhaphous Brachycera are characterized by the loss of all external sclerotized evidence of the head capsule and modification of the portions retracted within the thorax to form a rather characteristically shaped cephalopharyngeal skeleton. The body of most larvae is usually slender, consisting of 11 or 12 segments. The segments may be secondarily subdivided or combined and some portions greatly expanded and/or flattened. The body integument is usually soft and pliable (rarely sclerotized) and in some species is covered with dense pubescence (short, fine hairs) or with scattered hairs, placed singly or in tufts or fringes. Tubercles (small, elevated, fleshy processes) may be present on one or more body segments, but most often are on the terminal segment surrounding the caudal spiracles. Tuberclelike projections in the form of prolegs on the prothorax and/or one or more abdominal segments are found in many species. Apical spines or crochets (small, curved hooks) on the prolegs assist in locomotion and attachment. Many aquatic larvae lack spiracles (*apneustic;* figs. 21.42–21.46), while others have spiracles on the prothorax and terminal segment (*amphipneustic;* fig. 21.38), or the terminal segment alone (*metapneustic;* figs. 21.3, 21.74). Some larvae are further adapted to aquatic life in the placement of the terminal pair of spiracles at the end of a respiratory siphon which may be several times the length of the body. A more detailed description of external morphological characters of Diptera larvae is given by Teskey (1981a).

The following key has been substantially expanded over the one given in the first edition to include the genera, where sufficiently well known, of smaller families that are not treated in separate chapters. These additions have been taken, with at most only minor changes, from chapters in *The Manual of Nearctic Diptera*, Vol. 1 (1981) (Coords. McAlpine *et al.*), by C. L. Hogue (Blephariceridae), C. P. Alexander (Ptychopteridae), E. F. Cook (Chaoboridae), T. M. Peters (Dixidae), M. T. James (Stratiomyidae), and G. C. Steyskal and L. V. Knutson (Empididae).

KEY TO THE FAMILIES AND SELECTED GENERA OF AQUATIC DIPTERA

Larvae

1.   Mandibles moving against one another in a horizontal or oblique plane (figs. 21.8–21.9); head capsule usually complete and fully exposed, except retracted and reduced in Tipulidae .... NEMATOCERA 2

1′.   Mandibles or mouth hooks moving parallel to one another in a vertical plane (figs. 21.59, 21.64, 21.71, 21.81). Head capsule variously reduced posteriorly; partially or almost completely retracted within thorax even if such retracted portions comprise only a few slender rods .... BRACHYCERA 29

2(1). Head capsule partially to fully retracted within thorax (figs. 21.1–21.3); usually with longitudinal incisions of varying depths dorsolaterally (figs. 21.7–21.9); in extreme cases head consisting only of several slender rods (fig. 21.8). Respiratory system metapneustic or apneustic; posterior spiracles usually bordered by 1–3 pairs of short lobes that are often fringed with short to very long hairs (figs. 21.1–21.6) .... *TIPULIDAE* (chap. 22)

2'. Head capsule complete, usually without longitudinal incisions dorsolaterally, completely exserted (figs. 21.16–21.19, 21.20–21.21, 21.29). Respiratory system amphipneustic, metapneustic, or apneustic; posterior spiracles usually without bordering fringed lobes 3

3(2'). Head not distinctly separated from thorax. Body divided into 6 major divisions, the 1st comprising the fused head, thorax, and 1st abdominal segment (fig. 21.10). Each of these divisions with a median suctorial disk ventrally (fig. 21.11) .... *BLEPHARICERIDAE* 4

3'. Head showing a distinct constrictive separation from the thorax (figs. 21.21, 21.23, 21.29–21.37). Suctorial disks absent (except in *Maruina*, Psychodidae) 8

4(3'). Dorsal proleg absent, at least from anal division of abdomen (fig. 21.15) .... *Blepharicera* Macquart

4'. Dorsal proleg present (fig. 21.10) 5

5(4'). Ventral gill tufts composed of 6 filaments, arranged in a semirosette pattern in the same plane (fig. 21.12) .... *Bibiocephala* Osten Sacken

5'. Ventral gill tufts composed of 3–5 or 7 filaments, spreading and all directed generally anterolaterally (fig. 21.11) 6

6(5'). Dorsal sclerotized plates or tubercles usually present on abdominal segments (figs. 21.10, 21.13–21.14); if absent, at least a small dorsolateral tubercle present above dorsal proleg on abdominal segment 1 7

6'. Dorsal sclerotized processes absent. If conical processes present, 2 transverse series of minute plates also present across thoracic region of anterior body division .... *Dioptopsis* Enderlein

7(6). Dorsal proleg double, with a subequal, elongate dorsal branch (fig. 21.13); or ventral gill tufts with 3 filaments (fig. 21.11) .... *Philorus* Kellogg

7'. Dorsal proleg single, with only a small proximodorsal mamillate (nipplelike) process or setal swelling (fig. 21.14); ventral gill tufts with 5–7 filaments .... *Agathon* Röder

8(3'). A pair of elongate prolegs present on each of 7 or 8 abdominal segments (fig. 21.16) 9

8'. Prolegs usually absent, but, if present, on no more than 3 abdominal segments 10

9(8). Body with 8 pairs of slender, ventrally projecting, abdominal prolegs, each terminating in a comb of clawlike spines. Antennae simple, shorter than head length (fig. 21.16) .... *NYMPHOMYIIDAE*

9'. Seven pairs of rather broad abdominal prolegs projecting ventrolaterally; their apices encircled by several transverse rows of hooked spinules. Antennae forked, longer than length of head (figs. 21.18–21.19) .... *DEUTEROPHLEBIIDAE*

10(8'). Abdomen terminating in a long, slender, telescopic respiratory siphon (fig. 21.23). Body segments with multiple transverse ridges or rows of small setae or setiferous (setae-bearing) papillae (soft projections); first 3 abdominal segments with a pair of ventral prolegs, sometimes very small, bearing a single, slender, curved claw (figs. 21.23–21.24) .... *PTYCHOPTERIDAE* 11

10'. Not having above characters 13

11(10). Hypostoma apparently fused with hypostomal bridge that closes head capsule ventrally, its anterior margin bilobed (fig. 21.25); mandible with a single outer tooth. Prolegs prominent ventrally on first 3 abdominal segments, each with a conspicuous curved claw (fig. 21.24). Coloration rusty red or black 12

11'. Hypostoma separated from hypostomal bridge, its anterior margin multitoothed (fig. 21.26); mandible with 3 large outer teeth. Prolegs and apical curved claws small and inconspicuous (fig. 21.23). Coloration pale yellow or brown .... *Ptychoptera* Meigen

12(11). Predominantly blackish in color. Respiratory siphon light yellow, entirely retractile. Very long projections encased in a black horny substance, covering entire body. Mandible with an inner comb of teeth .... *Bittacomorphella* Alexander

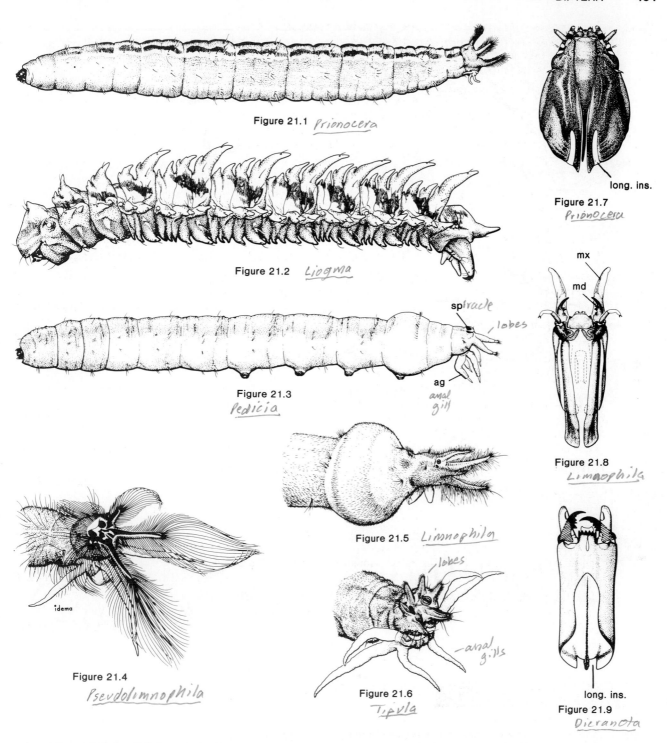

Figure 21.1. *Prionocera*

Figure 21.2. *Liogma*

Figure 21.3. *Pedicia*
sp spiracle
lobes
ag anal gill

Figure 21.4. *Pseudolimnophila*
idema

Figure 21.5. *Limnophila*

Figure 21.6. *Tipula*
lobes
anal gills

Figure 21.7. *Prionocera*
long. ins.

Figure 21.8. *Limnophila*
mx
md

Figure 21.9. *Dicranota*
long. ins.

Figure 21.1. Lateral view of *Prionocera* sp. (Tipulidae).

Figure 21.2. Lateral view of *Liogma nodicornis* (O.S.) (Tipulidae).

Figure 21.3. Lateral view of *Pedicia* sp. (Tipulidae); *ag*, anal gill; *sp*, spiracle.

Figure 21.4. Caudal segments of *Pseudolimnophila inornata* (O.S.) (Tipulidae).

Figure 21.5. Caudal segments of *Limnophila* sp. (Tipulidae).

Figure 21.6. Caudal segments of *Tipula strepens* Loew (Tipulidae).

Figure 21.7. Dorsal view of head capsule of *Prionocera* sp. (Tipulidae); *long. ins.*, longitudinal incision.

Figure 21.8. Dorsal view of head capsule of *Limnophila* sp. (Tipulidae); *md*, mandible; *mx*, maxilla.

Figure 21.9. Ventral view of head capsule of *Dicranota* sp. (Tipulidae); *long. ins.*, longitudinal incision.

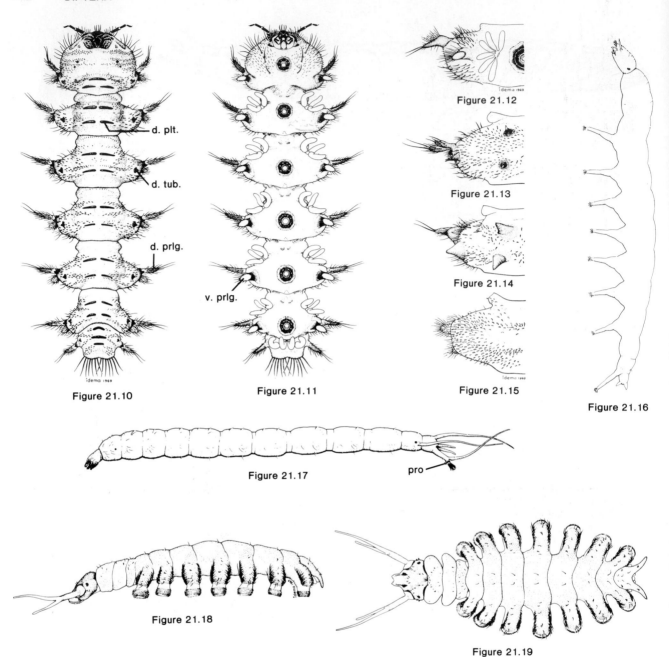

Figure 21.10

Figure 21.11

Figure 21.12

Figure 21.13

Figure 21.14

Figure 21.15

Figure 21.16

Figure 21.17

pro

Figure 21.18

Figure 21.19

Figure 21.10. Dorsal view of *Philorus californicus* Hogue (Blephariceridae); *d. pit.*, dorsal plate; *d. tub.*, dorsal tubercle; *d. prlg.*, dorsal proleg.

Figure 21.11. Ventral view of *Philorus californicus* Hogue (Blephariceridae); *v. prlg.*, ventral proleg.

Figure 21.12. Ventral view of first abdominal division of *Bibiocephala grandis* Osten Sacken (Blephariceridae).

Figure 21.13. Dorsal view of first abdominal division of *Philorus yosemite* (Osten Sacken) (Blephariceridae).

Figure 21.14. Dorsal view of first abdominal division of *Agathon elegantulus* Röder (Blephariceridae).

Figure 21.15. Dorsal view of first abdominal division of *Blepharicera tenuipes* (Walker) (Blephariceridae).

Figure 21.16. Lateral view of *Palaeodipteron walkeri* Ide (Nymphomyiidae).

Figure 21.17. Lateral view of *Protoplasa fitchii* O.S. (Tanyderidae); *pro*, proleg.

Figure 21.18. Lateral view of *Deuterophlebia neilsoni* Kennedy (Deuterophlebiidae).

Figure 21.19. Dorsal view of *Deuterophlebia nielsoni* Kennedy (Deuterophlebiidae).

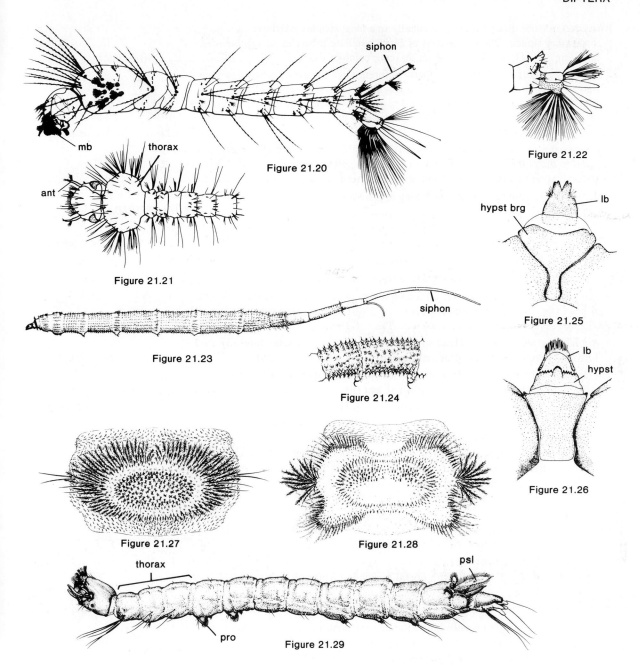

Figure 21.20

Figure 21.22

Figure 21.21

Figure 21.25

Figure 21.23

siphon

Figure 21.24

Figure 21.26

Figure 21.27

Figure 21.28

Figure 21.29

Figure 21.20. Lateral view of *Aedes fitchii* Felt and Young (Culicidae); *mb,* mouth brush.

Figure 21.21. Dorsal view of head, thorax, and seven abdominal segments of *Aedes* sp. (Culicidae); *ant,* antenna.

Figure 21.22. Lateral view of caudal segment of *Anopheles* sp. (Culicidae) showing short respiratory siphon.

Figure 21.23. Lateral view of *Ptychoptera* sp. (Ptychopteridae).

Figure 21.24. Lateral view of first two abdominal segments of *Bittacomorpha clavipes* (Fabricius) (Ptychopteridae).

Figure 21.25. Ventral view of central portion of head capsule of *Bittacomorpha clavipes* (Fabricius) (Ptchopteridae) showing absence of a separate hypostoma; *hypst brg,* hypostomal bridge; *lb,* labium.

Figure 21.26. Ventral view of central portion of head capsule of *Ptychoptera* sp. (Ptychopteridae) showing a separate hypostoma; *hypst,* hypostoma; *lb,* labium.

Figure 21.27,. Dorsal view of an abdominal segment of *Dixa* sp. (Dixidae) showing dorsal corona.

Figure 21.28. Dorsal view of an abdominal segment of *Meringodixa chalonensis* Nowell (Dixidae) showing dorsal corona and lateral tufts of long hairs.

Figure 21.29. Dorsolateral view of *Dixella* sp. (Dixidae); *pro,* proleg; *psl,* postspiracular lobe.

12′.   Rusty red in color. Body tapering gradually to a long, slender, partly retractile respiratory siphon. Transverse rows of shorter stellate tubercles covering entire body (fig. 21.24). Mandible without an inner comb of teeth. .... ***Bittacomorpha*** Westwood

13(10′). Thoracic segments fused and indistinctly differentiated, forming a single segment that is wider than any of abdominal segments (figs. 21.21, 21.30–21.31, 21.33–21.34). Thoracic and abdominal segments with prominent, lateral fanlike tufts of long setae, and/or terminal segment with an anal setal fan (figs. 21.20–21.22, 21.30–21.31, 21.33–21.34) 14

13′.   Thoracic segments usually individually distinguishable; thorax and abdomen about equal in diameter or abdomen wider (fig. 21.35). Setae on thoracic and abdominal segments not tufted and anal fan of terminal segment absent 18

14(13).   Antennae prehensile (grasping), with long apical setae; mouth brushes lacking (figs. 21.30–21.34) .... ***CHAOBORIDAE*** 15

14′.   Antennae not prehensile and with only short apical setae; prominent mouth brushes present on either side of labrum (figs. 21.20–21.21) .... ***CULICIDAE*** (chap. 23)

15(14).   Eighth abdominal segment with an elongate dorsal respiratory siphon (fig. 21.34) 16

15′.   Eighth abdominal segment without a long respiratory siphon (figs. 21.30–21.31) 17

16(15).   Antennae inserted close together; a transverse row of spiniform setae on each side of head (fig. 21.32). Terminal segment with a tuft of long setae ventrally instead of a fan .... ***Corethrella*** Coquillett

16′.   Antennae inserted far apart. Head without a transverse row of setae laterally. Terminal segment with longitudinal fanlike row of setae (fig. 21.34) .... ***Mochlonyx*** Loew

17(15′). Thorax rounded laterally. Hydrostatic air-sacs present in thorax and in 7th abdominal segment. Respiratory siphon absent (fig. 21.30) .... ***Chaoborus*** Lichtenstein

17′.   Thorax diamond-shaped in dorsal view (fig. 21.33). Hydrostatic air-sacs absent. Respiratory siphon on abdominal segment 8 short, stout, terminating in conspicuous flat spiracular apparatus (fig. 21.31) .... ***Eucorethra*** Underwood

18(13′). Paired crochet-bearing prolegs ventrally on 1st and usually 2nd abdominal segments (fig. 21.29). Abdomen posteriorly with 2 flattened dorsolateral postspiracular lobes having setose (hair-covered) margins projecting above a conical, dorsally sclerotized segment bearing the terminal anus and anal papillae (fig. 21.29) .... ***DIXIDAE*** 19

18′.   Abdominal segments without prolegs, except on anal segment. Posterior body segment without flattened, fringed postspiracular lobes and a conical, dorsally sclerotized anal segment 21

19(18).   Abdominal segments 2–7 each with dorsal coronalike fringe of plumose hairs (figs. 21.27–21.28) 20

19′.   Abdominal segments 2–7 without dorsal coronae (fig. 21.29) .... ***Dixella*** Dyar and Shannon

20(19).   Pair of prolegs ventrally on only 1st abdominal segment; tuft of longer hairs on each side of abdominal segments 2–6 below coronae (fig. 21.28) .... ***Meringodixa*** Nowell

20′.   Pair of prolegs on each of first 2 abdominal segments; lateral tufts of hairs on abdominal segments absent (fig. 21.27) .... ***Dixa*** Meigen

21(18′). Prothorax with 1 proleg or a pair of prolegs ventrally (figs. 21.35, 21.38, 21.40–21.43) 22

21′.   Prothorax lacking prolegs 25

22(21).   Head capsule usually with a pair of conspicuous, folding labral fans dorsolaterally (fig. 21.35). Abdominal segments 5–8 swollen, posterior segment terminating in a ring or circlet of numerous radiating rows of minute hooks (fig. 21.35) .... ***SIMULIIDAE*** (chap. 24)

22′.   Head capsule lacking labral fans. Posterior abdominal segments not conspicuously swollen nor with radiating rows of hooks terminally, although anal proleg(s) bearing crochets may be present 23

23(22′). Respiratory system amphipneustic (fig. 21.38); anterior spiracles on short stalks, and posterior spiracles opening into a transverse cleft between fingerlike processes on 8th abdominal segment (fig. 21.39). Prothoracic and anal prolegs unpaired .... ***THAUMALEIDAE***

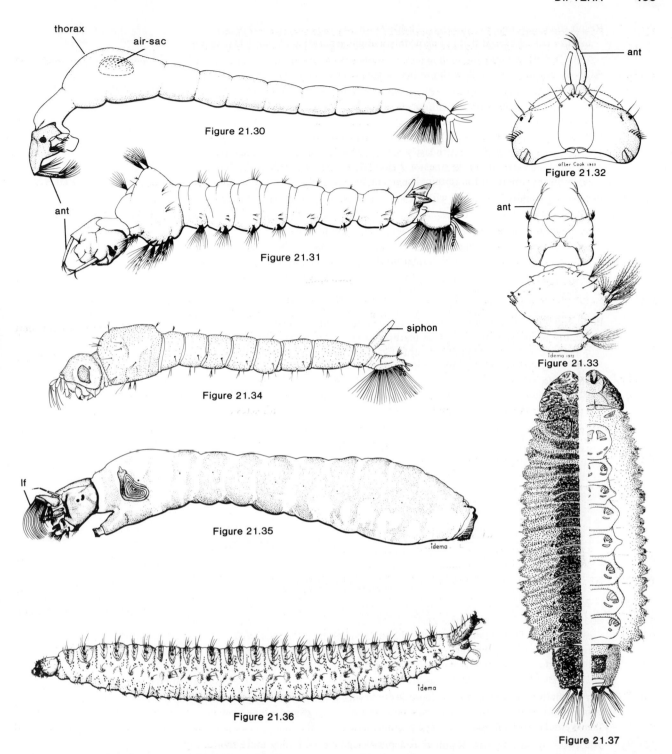

Figure 21.30

Figure 21.31

Figure 21.32

Figure 21.33

Figure 21.34

Figure 21.35

Figure 21.36

Figure 21.37

Figure 21.30. Lateral view of *Chaoborus americanus* (Johannsen) (Chaoboridae); *ant,* antenna.

Figure 21.31. Dorsolateral view of *Eucorethra underwoodi* Underwood (Chaoboridae); *ant,* antenna.

Figure 21.32. Dorsal view of head capsule of *Corethrella brakeleyi* (Coquillett) (Chaoboridae); *ant,* antenna.

Figure 21.33. Dorsal view of head, thorax, and first abdominal segment of *Eucorethra underwoodi* Underwood (Chaoboridae); *ant,* antenna.

Figure 21.34. Lateral view of *Mochlonyx* sp. (Chaoboridae).

Figure 21.35. Lateral view of *Simulium venustum* Say (Simuliidae); *lf,* labral fans.

Figure 21.36. Lateral view of *Pericoma* sp. (Psychodidae).

Figure 21.37. Half dorsal, half ventral views of *Maruina* sp. (Psychodidae).

23'.   Respiratory system apneustic (figs. 21.40–21.46). Prothoracic or anal prolegs
         usually paired even if distinction is only a slight separation of the apical spines
         (fig. 21.43) 24

24(23'). All body segments dorsally with prominent tubercles (elevated fleshy processes)
          and/or setae (fig. 21.42) .... Forcipomyiinae—*CERATOPOGONIDAE*

24'.   Body segments lacking prominent dorsal tubercles and setae (figs. 21.40–21.41,
         21.43) .... *CHIRONOMIDAE* (chap. 25)

25(21'). Last 2 abdominal segments with long filamentous processes, pairs of such processes
          arising laterally on the next to last segment, dorsolaterally on the terminal
          segment, and from near the apex of 2 elongate cylindrical prolegs that project
          posteroventrally from the terminal segment (fig. 21.17) .... *TANYDERIDAE*

25'.   Posterior abdominal segments without long filamentous processes. At most, only a
         single anal proleg present 26

26(25'). All body segments secondarily divided into 2 or 3 subdivisions with some or all of
          these subdivisions bearing dorsal sclerotized plates (figs. 21.36–21.37);
          remainder of integument with numerous dark spots that together with the dorsal
          plates impart a greyish brown coloration to larva. Respiratory system
          amphipneustic; posterior spiracles usually at apex of a relatively short, conical
          respiratory tube (fig. 21.36) .... *PSYCHODIDAE* 27

26'.   Body segments usually not secondarily divided; integument smooth, shiny, and
         creamy white, lacking all surface features except a few setae that may be
         noticeable at tip of terminal segment (figs. 21.45–21.46), and sometimes a
         retractile anal proleg bearing a few crochets (curved hooks) (fig. 21.44). Larvae
         apneustic .... Dashyheleinae, Ceratopogoninae—*CERATOPOGONIDAE*

27(26). Larva distinctly flattened, with a median row of 8 suction disks ventrally (fig.
         21.37) .... *Maruina* Müller

27'.   Larva more or less cylindrical and lacking ventral suction disks 28

28(27'). Preanal plate present and tergal plates on body segments rather uniformly sized, 2
          such plates on each of thoracic and 1st abdominal segment and 3 plates on each
          of the following 6 abdominal segments, 26 plates in all (fig. 21.36) .... *Pericoma* Walker, *Telmatoscopus* Eaton

28'.   Preanal plate absent or tergal body plates generally reduced in size or only on
         some segments, or fewer than 26 plates present .... *Psychoda* Latreille

29(1').   Sclerotized portions of head capsule exposed externally although sometimes greatly
          reduced, in which case slender tentorial and metacephalic rods prominent
          internally (figs. 21.54, 21.59, 21.64, 21.71) .... ORTHORRHAPHA 30

29'.   External sclerotized portions of head capsule absent; head reduced to an internal
         cephalopharyngeal skeleton of rather characteristic form (figs. 21.77,
         21.81–21.82, 21.89) .... CYCLORRHAPHA 63

30(29). Body somewhat depressed (figs. 21.47–21.48, 21.50–21.51); integument toughened
         and leathery from calcium deposits that are evident as numerous small
         reticulately arranged facets (fig. 21.47). Head capsule capable of only slight
         independent movement; usually with distinctive lateral eye prominences (figs.
         21.54–21.55) .... *STRATIOMYIDAE* 31

30'.   Larva usually not conspicuously depressed nor with a toughened integument
         bearing a network of facets. Head capsule capable of extensive independent
         movement; without distinctive eye prominences 40

31(29). Spiracular cleft at apex of terminal abdominal segment with long marginal
         hydrofuge (water-repelling) setae (figs. 21.47–21.48, 21.50, 21.52) 33

31'.   Spiracular cleft situated dorsally near apex of terminal abdominal segment and, if
         with bordering hydrofuge setae, very short and inconspicuous (figs. 21.49, 21.51) 32

32(31'). Abdominal segments with lateral margins thinly compressed and bilobate; anterior
          lobe small and sharply pointed. Posterior margin of terminal segment rounded
          (fig. 21.51) .... *Allognosta* Osten Sacken

32'.   Abdominal segments with lateral margins not strongly compressed or appearing
         bilobate, anterior lobe blunt and not sharply pointed. Posterior margin of
         terminal segment concave (fig. 21.49) .... *Nemotelus* Geoffroy

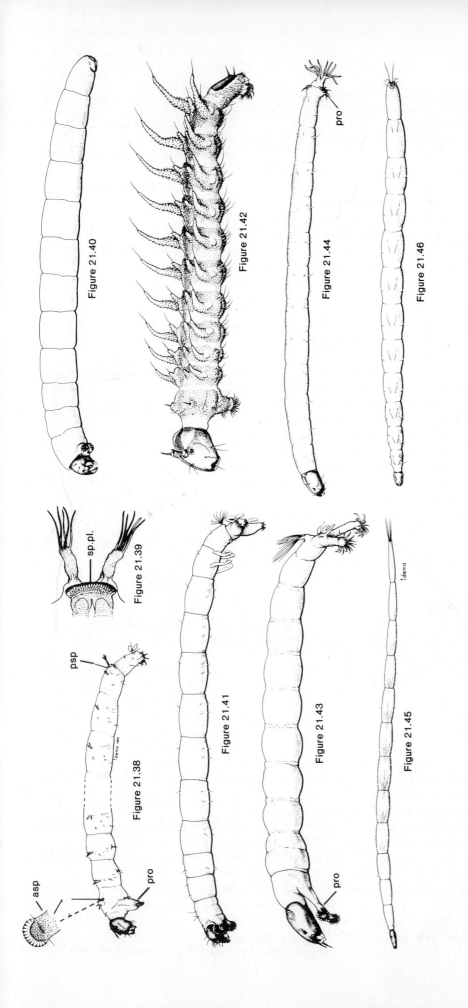

Figure 21.38. Lateral view of *Thaumalea* sp. (Thaumaleidae); *asp*, anterior spiracle; *pro*, proleg; *psp*, posterior spiracle.

Figure 21.39. Dorsal view of posterior spiracle and associated lobes of *Thaumalea* sp. (Thaumaleidae); *sp. pl.*, spiracular plate.

Figure 21.40. Lateral view of *Pseudosmittia* sp. (Chironomidae).

Figure 21.41. Lateral view of *Chironomus* sp. (Chironomidae)

Figure 21.42. Dorsolateral view of *Atrichopogon* sp. (Ceratopogonidae).

Figure 21.43. Lateral view of *Ablabesmyia* sp. (Chironomidae); *pro*, proleg.

Figure 21.44. Lateral view of *Dasyhelea* sp. (Ceratopogonidae); *pro*, proleg.

Figure 21.45. Lateral view of *Bezzia* sp. (Ceratopogonidae).

Figure 21.46. Lateral view of *Culicoides* sp. (Ceratopogonidae).

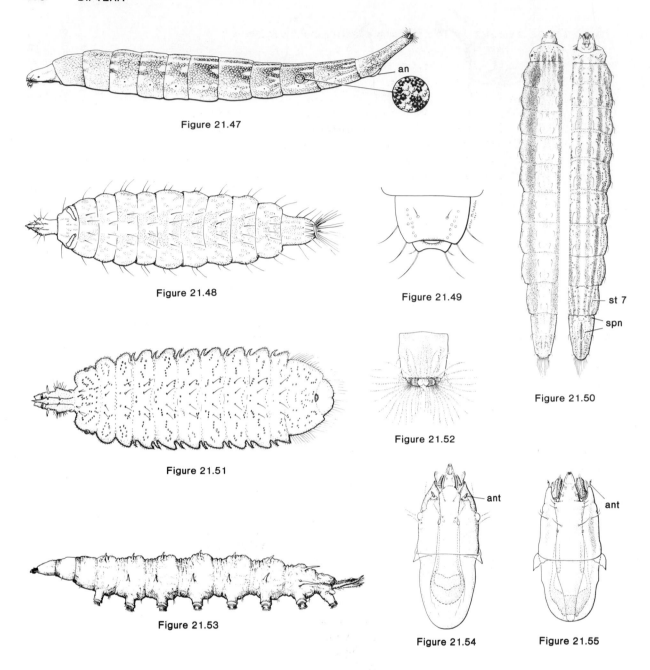

Figure 21.47

Figure 21.48

Figure 21.49

Figure 21.50

Figure 21.51

Figure 21.52

Figure 21.53

Figure 21.54

Figure 21.55

Figure 21.47. Lateral view of *Stratiomys* sp. (Stratiomyidae); *an*, anus.

Figure 21.48. Dorsal view of *Euparyphus* sp. (Stratiomyidae).

Figure 21.49. Dorsal view of terminal segment of *Nemotelus kansensis* Adams (Stratiomyidae).

Figure 21.50. Part dorsal and part ventral view of *Odontomyia cincta* Olivier (Stratiomyidae); *spn*, spine; *st 7*, sternite 7.

Figure 21.51. Dorsal view of *Allognosta* sp. (Stratiomyidae).

Figure 21.52. Dorsal view of terminal segment of *Myxosargus nigricornis* Greene (Stratiomyidae).

Figure 21.53. Lateral view of *Atherix* sp. (Athericidae).

Figure 21.54. Dorsal view of head capsule of *Caloparyphus major* (Hine) (Stratiomyidae); *ant*, antenna.

Figure 21.55. Dorsal view of head capsule of *Odontomyia cincta* Olivier (Stratiomyidae); *ant*, antenna.

33(31). Antenna situated anterolaterally on head capsule and directed anteriorly or
somewhat ventrally (fig. 21.55) 34

33'. Antenna situated dorsolaterally on head capsule and directed dorsally (fig. 21.54) 37

34(33). Terminal abdominal segment long and slender; apical portion with lateral margins
nearly parallel (fig. 21.47). Anus located anteriorly on segment and swollen .... *Stratiomys* Geoffroy

34'. Terminal abdominal segment rarely over twice as long as broad, uniformly tapered
posteriorly (fig. 21.50). Anus not conspicuously swollen 35

35(34'). Abdominal sternite 7 lacking sclerotized hooklike spines on posterior margin.
Integument covered with minute peltate scaleslike pubescence .... *Odontomyia* (*Catatasina Enderlein*)

35'. Abdominal sternite 7 with hooklike spines on posterior margin. (fig. 21.50).
Integumental pubescence variable 36

36(35'). Only abdominal sternite 7 with hooked spines. .... *Odontomyia* (*Odontomyiina Enderlein*)

36'. Abdominal sternites 6 and 7 with hooked spines (fig. 21.50). ....
.... *Odontomyia* (*Odontomyia Meigen*), *Hedriodiscus* Enderlein

37(33'). Hydrofuge setae arising from 2 lobate structures on lower lip of spiracular cleft
(fig. 21.52); anterior spiracles located at anterior corner of prothorax .... *Myxosargus* Brauer

37'. Hydrofuge setae arising from straight edge of lower lip; spiracular cleft lacking
strong lobate structures; anterior spiracles located laterally near middle of
prothorax (fig. 21.48) 38

38(37'). Terminal abdominal segment almost rectangular in outline; posterior margin more
or less indented or notched sublaterally .... *Oxycera* Meigen

38'. Terminal segment subconical with lateral and posterior margins rounded 39

39(38'). Anterior spiracle on short stalk or nearly sessile .... *Caloparyphus* James

39'. Anterior spiracle on long stalk (fig. 21.48) .... *Euparyphus* Gerstäcker

40(30'). Head capsule well developed dorsally, closed ventrally by a submental plate (figs.
21.59, 21.64); tentorial rods solidly fused with head capsule internally; a brush
of backwardly curved bristles usually present on each side of clypeus above and
near base of each mandible (figs. 21.59–21.60, 21.64) 41

40'. Head capsule reduced to a pair of slender metacephalic rods; they and tentorial
rods flexibly articulate with anterior cephalic sclerites (figs. 21.67, 21.71);
submental plate and brushes of bristles above mandibles absent 54

41(40). Posterior spiracles present, opening within slits on either side of a vertically linear
stigmatal bar (fig. 21.58) or a retractile, laterally compressed spine (figs. 21.61,
21.63). Body integument with longitudinal striations, except in some species
where integument totally covered by short, velvety pubescence. First 7
abdominal segments girdled by 3 or 4 pairs of fleshy pseudopodia (setae-bearing
swellings) or prolegs, these being the only projections from the segments (figs.
21.56–21.57) .... TABANIDAE 43

41'. Posterior spiracles absent or situated within a small terminal cavity (fig. 21.65).
Integument without striations or extensive covering of pubescence. Prolegs, if
present, limited to 1 ventral pair on each abdominal segment 42

42(41'). Larva slightly flattened dorsoventrally. Slender tubercles of progressively
increasing size situated laterally and dorsolaterally on abdominal segments 1–7;
2 longer caudal tubercles fringed with hairs on terminal segment. All abdominal
segments with a ventral pair of prolegs bearing crochets (fig. 21.53) .... ATHERICIDAE—*Atherix* Meigen

42'. Larva cylindrical, with smooth shiny integument and with segmentation beadlike;
lacking tubercles and prolegs (fig. 21.65) .... PELECORHYNCHIDAE—*Glutops* Burgess

43(41). Prolegs present only on 1st 5 abdominal segments. Body widest in region of
mesothoracic and metathoracic segments. Integument of intersegmental regions
and posterior borders of prolegs with a reticulate, fishscalelike pattern. Terminal
segment hemispherical; posterior spiracle sessile, or nearly sessile, on surface of
terminal segment. Mandible straight and bladelike .... *Apatolestes* Williston

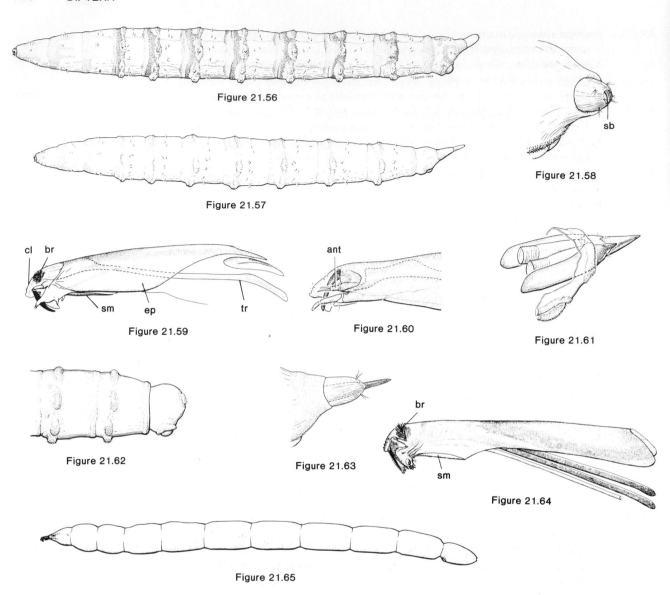

Figure 21.56

Figure 21.57

Figure 21.58

Figure 21.59

Figure 21.60

Figure 21.61

Figure 21.62

Figure 21.63

Figure 21.64

Figure 21.65

Figure 21.56. Lateral view of *Tabanus reinwardtii* Wiedemann (Tabanidae).

Figure 21.57. Lateral view of *Chrysops furcatus* Walker (Tabanidae).

Figure 21.58. Respiratory siphon of *Tabanus* sp. (Tabanidae); *sb,* stigmatal bar.

Figure 21.59. Lateral view of head capsule of *Tabanus reinwardtii* Wiedemann (Tabanidae); *br,* mandibular bristles; *cl,* clypeus; *ep,* epicranium; *sm,* submentum; *tr,* tentorial rod.

Figure 21.60. Lateral view of head capsule of *Chrysops excitans* Walker (Tabanidae); *ant,* antenna.

Figure 21.61. Respiratory siphon and spine of *Merycomyia whitneyi* (Johnson) (Tabanidae).

Figure 21.62. Terminal segments of *Leucotabanus annulatus* (Say) (Tabanidae).

Figure 21.63. Respiratory siphon and spine of *Chrysops cincticornis* Walker (Tabanidae).

Figure 21.64. Lateral view of head capsule of *Glutops rossi* Pechuman (Pelecorhynchidae); abbreviations as in Figure 21.59.

Figure 21.65. Lateral view of *Glutops rossi* Pechuman (Pelecorhynchidae).

43'.   Prolegs present on each of 1st 7 abdominal segments (figs. 21.56–21.57). Body normally widest near middle. Integument lacking reticulate, fishscalelike-patterned areas, instead often with microtrichial pubescence intersegmentally and bordering prolegs. Posterior spiracle at least slightly elevated. Mandible curved 44

44(43'). Three pairs of prolegs situated dorsally, laterally, and ventrally on each of 1st 7 abdominal segments (fig. 21.57) 45

44'.   Four pairs of prolegs, including an additional ventrolateral pair, on 1st 7 abdominal segments (fig. 21.56) 48

45(44).   Body surface, except respiratory siphon, completely clothed with a dense covering of short pubescence 46

45'.   Pubescence restricted to anterior or posterior margin or posterior border of prolegs of 1 or more segments 47

46(45).   Pubescent integumental covering conspicuously mottled with dark and paler areas; 3rd antennal segment shorter than 2nd. Respiratory siphon equal to or only slightly longer than its basal diameter .... *Chlorotabanus* Lutz

46'.   Pubescence not conspicuously mottled; 3rd antennal segment longer than 2nd segment (as in fig. 21.60). Respiratory siphon length about twice its basal diameter .... *Diachlorus* Osten Sacken

47(45).   Third antennal segment about half the length of 2nd segment. Respiratory siphon shorter than its basal diameter, lacking a respiratory spine. Prolegs with prominent hooklike crochets .... *Silvius* (*Zeuximyia* Philip)

47'.   Third antennal segment longer than 2nd segment (fig. 21.60). Respiratory siphon either longer than its basal diameter (fig. 21.57) or with a respiratory spine (fig. 21.63) .... *Chrysops* Meigen

48(44'). Respiratory siphon comprising distal ends of 2 opposed sclerotized plates between which tracheal trunks terminate in an exsertile spiracular spine (fig. 21.61). Inconspicuous and incomplete striations present only laterally on segments .... *Merycomyia* Hine

48'.   Although tracheal trunks sometimes terminating in a spiracular spine, respiratory siphon always membranous and lacking sclerotized plates. Striations on abdominal segments present or absent 49

49(48'). Respiratory siphon shorter than its basal diameter (as in fig. 21.62). Integumental striations extremely fine on all aspects of body, and usually visible only under high magnification; striations spaced at approximately 5 μm .... *Haematopota* Meigen

49'.   If respiratory siphon shorter than its basal diameter, striations more coarsely spaced at usually more than 20 μm 50

50(49'). Respiratory siphon very short, projecting no more than half its diameter. Terminal abdominal segment usually shorter than greatest diameter, hemispherical (fig. 21.62). Striations uniformly spaced on all aspects of body 51

50'.   Respiratory siphon length ranging from slightly shorter to about 4 times longer than its basal diameter. Terminal abdominal segment usually somewhat tapering posteriorly toward respiratory siphon (fig. 21.56). Striations normally absent from dorsal and ventral surfaces of at least the prothorax, and more widely spaced dorsally and ventrally than laterally on other segments 53

51(50).   Pubescence encircling anterior three-fourths of prothorax and broadly encircling posterior half of terminal abdominal segment so that anal lobes and base of respiratory siphon are covered by enlarged pubescent area .... *Silvius* (*Griseosilvius* Philip)

51'.   Pubescence encircling little more than anterior one-fourth of prothorax, and on terminal abdominal segment restricted to narrow annulus around base of respiratory siphon and on anal lobes so that pubescence on anal lobes is separated from that encircling base of respiratory siphon 52

52(51'). Terminal abdominal segment two-thirds length of penultimate segment (fig. 21.62). Larva inhabiting decaying wood and tree holes .... *Leucotabanus* Lutz

52'.   Terminal abdominal segment less than half the length of penultimate segment. Larva inhabiting damp sand on coastal beaches .... *Stenotabanus* (*Aegialomyia* Philip)

53(50').   Median lateral surfaces of terminal segment usually lacking pubescent markings. Striations present on dorsal and ventral surfaces of all abdominal segments or, if absent, pubescence restricted, at most, to a prothoracic annulus (ring) and anal ridges .... *Hybomitra* Enderlein

53'.   Either median lateral surfaces of anal segment with pubescent markings (fig. 21.56), or striations absent or poorly developed on dorsal or ventral surface or both surfaces of abdominal segments .... *Tabanus* Linnaeus, *Whitneyomyia* Bequaert, *Atylotus* Osten Sacken

54(40').   Larva metapneustic; posterior spiracles situated at the base of upper 2 of 4, smooth primary lobes of last abdominal segment (fig. 21.66). Transverse ventral creeping welts present on abdominal segments. Metacephalic rods expanded posteriorly (fig. 21.67) .... *DOLICHOPODIDAE*

54'.   Larva usually apneustic, terminal abdominal segment with 1–4 rounded lobes bearing apical setae, and abdominal segments bearing paired prolegs with apical crochets (figs. 21.68–21.70, 21.72). If metapneustic, then posterior segment with only a single lobe below spiracles, and abdominal segments with ventral creeping welts (figs. 21.73–21.74). Metacephalic rods slender posteriorly (fig. 21.71) .... *EMPIDIDAE* 55

55(54').   Respiratory system usually apneustic (posterior spiracles present in *Roederiodes* and *Oreogeton*). Seven or 8 pairs of abdominal prolegs bearing apical hooked spines or crochets. Terminal segment with elongate lobes or short tubercles ending in long setae (figs. 21.68–21.70, 21.72), rarely ending in only a tuft of apical setae. Aquatic or semiaquatic 56

55'.   Respiratory system amphipneustic. Abdominal prolegs lacking. Terminal segment rounded, with a single, bare, mid-ventral lobe (figs. 21.73–21.74). Usually terrestrial, found in soil, leaf litter, and rotting wood, but some in wet soil .... Several genera (for the most part inseparable)

56(55).   Terminal segment rounded posteriorly, at most with small dorsal and apical tubercles; each tubercle with 1–3 pairs of long setae (fig. 21.72). Seven pairs of abdominal prolegs .... *Chelifera* Macquart

56'.   Terminal segment with prominent caudal lobes (figs. 21.68–21.70). Seven or 8 pairs of abdominal prolegs 57

57(56').   Terminal segment with a single, more or less medially divided, setose caudal lobe (fig. 21.68). Seven pairs of abdominal prolegs .... *Hemerodromia* Meigen

57'.   Terminal segment with dorsal and apical caudal lobes. Eight pairs of abdominal prolegs 58

58(57').   Terminal segment with 2 dorsolateral lobes and with one more or less divided apical lobe (fig. 21.69) .... *Clinocera* (Hydrodromia)

58'.   Terminal segment with 2 pairs of lobes (fig. 21.70) 59

59(58').   Prolegs and caudal lobes rounded, very short .... *Dolichocephala* Macquart

59'.   Prolegs and caudal lobes elongate, longer 60

60(59').   Terminal segment with apical lobe short and with dorsolateral lobes long 61

60'.   Terminal segment with lobes of equal length (fig. 21.70) 62

61(60).   Posterior spiracles present .... *Roederiodes* Coquillett

61'.   Posterior spiracles absent .... *Clinocera* (*Clinocera* Meigen)

62(60').   Posterior spiracles present on dorsolateral lobes. Abdominal segments 1–7 each with a group of 6 setae on either side. Last thoracic segment with row of brushy protuberances dorsally (fig. 21.70) .... *Oreogeton* Schiner

62'.   Posterior spiracles absent. Abdominal segments without setae laterally. Last thoracic segment without brushy protuberances .... *Wiedemannia* Zetterstedt

63(29').   Posterior spiracular plates fused or very closely approximated (fig. 21.80), usually on apex of a telescopic respiratory tube (figs. 21.76, 21.78–21.79) 64

63'.   Posterior spiracular plates always distinctly separated whether mounted on a telescopic respiratory tube or not 65

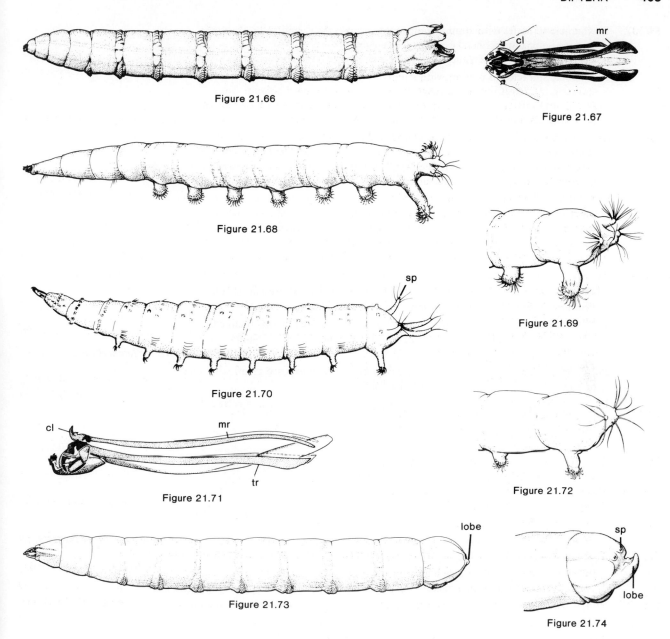

Figure 21.66

Figure 21.67

Figure 21.68

Figure 21.69

Figure 21.70

Figure 21.71

Figure 21.72

Figure 21.73

Figure 21.74

Figure 21.66. Dorsolateral view of *Rhaphium campestre* Curran (Dolichopodidae).

Figure 21.67. Dorsal view of head skeleton of *Rhaphium* sp. (Dolichopodidae); *cl,* clypeus; *mr,* metacephalic rod.

Figure 21.68. Dorsolateral view of *Hemerodromia* sp. (Empididae).

Figure 21.69. Dorsolateral view of terminal segments of *Clinocera* sp. (Empididae).

Figure 21.70. Dorsolateral view of *Oreogeton* sp. (Empididae); *sp,* spiracle.

Figure 21.71. Lateral view of head skeleton of *Hemerodromia* sp. (Empididae); *cl,* clypeus; *mr,* metacephalic rod; *tr,* tentorial rod.

Figure 21.72. Dorsolateral view of terminal segments of *Chelifera* sp. (Empididae).

Figure 21.73. Lateral view of *Rhamphomyia* sp. (Empididae).

Figure 21.74. Dorsolateral view of terminal segment of *Phyllodromia* sp. (Empididae); *sp,* spiracle.

64(63). Prothoracic spiracles with stigmatal openings on branching papillae or, if sessile, arranged along apical half of a long spiracular stalk (fig. 21.79). Cephalopharyngeal skeleton with well-developed mouth hooks (fig. 21.81) .... *CANACEIDAE*

64′.   Prothoracic spiracles, if present, with stigmatal openings near apex of a simple stalk (fig. 21.75). Cephalopharyngeal skeleton lacking mouth hooks in aquatic larvae of family, a ribbed filter chamber in area normally occupied by mouth hooks (fig. 21.77) .... *SYRPHIDAE*

65(63′). Cephalopharyngeal skeleton with a sclerotized ventral arch below base of mouth hooks, its anterior margin usually toothed (fig. 21.82). Body segments often extensively covered with short, fine hairs; posterior segment often somewhat tapered, its apex with tubercles surrounding posterior spiracles that are only slightly elevated (fig. 21.83) .... *SCIOMYZIDAE*

65′.   Cephalopharyngeal skeleton lacking a ventral arch. If body extensively covered with short, fine hairs then a respiratory siphon present, or each spiracle situated on a short tubular projection on posterior segment (figs. 21.84–21.87) 66

66(65′). Abdominal segments with short, stout, conical projections laterally. Prothoracic spiracles absent. Parasite of barnacles .... *DRYOMYZIDAE—Oedoparena* Curran

66′.   Abdominal segments usually without lateral projections, but, if present, slender. Prothoracic spiracles usually present 67

67(66′). Posterior spiracles located in a deep spiracular cavity; spiracular slits inclined more-or-less vertically (figs. 21.84–21.85). Inhabitants of pitcher plants .... *SARCOPHAGIDAE—Fletcherimyia* Townsend

67′.   Posterior spiracles not located in a deep cavity but are well exposed terminally; one or more of the spiracular slits nearly horizontal 68

68(67′). Posterior abdominal segment somewhat tapered, sometimes ending in a retractile respiratory tube (figs. 21.86–21.87). Integument of posterior abdominal segments covered with setae (fig. 21.86) or spinules, or with setaceous (setae-bearing) tubercles on some segments .... *EPHYDRIDAE*

68′.   Posterior abdominal segment rather truncate (cut off squarely) and/or integument with setae only on intersegmental areas (fig. 21.88); tubercles, if present, restricted to posterior abdominal segment 69

69(68′). Posterior abdominal segment lacking tubercles other than those bearing spiracles (fig. 21.88). Prothoracic spiracles, if present, fan-shaped and usually with fewer than 10 papillae. Accessory oral sclerite present below mouth hooks (fig. 21.89) .... *MUSCIDAE*

69′.   Posterior abdominal segment often with several pairs of tubercles surrounding spiracles. Prothoracic spiracle a cribriform (sievelike) plate, or with many papillae arranged in a bicornuate (two-horned) fan (fig. 21.90). Accessory oral sclerite absent .... *SCATHOPHAGIDAE*

ADDITIONAL TAXONOMIC REFERENCES
(Larvae)*

General
Johannsen (1934, 1935); Hennig (1948, 1950, 1952); Chu (1949); Peterson (1951); Bertrand (1954); Wirth and Stone (1956); Pennak (1978); McAlpine *et al.* (1981); McCafferty (1981).

Regional faunas
Carolinas': Webb and Brigham (1982).
Wisconsin: Hilsenhoff (1981).

Taxonomic treatments at the family level
Athericidae: Webb (1981).
Blephariceridae: Hogue (1973b, 1981).
Ceratopogonidae: Thomsen (1937); Downes and Wirth (1981).
Chaoboridae: Cook (1956, 1981).
Deuterophlebiidae: Kennedy (1981).
Dixidae: Nowell (1953); Peters (1981).
Empididae: Steyskal and Knutson (1981).
Nymphomyiidae: Kevan and Cutten (1981).
Pelecorhynchidae: Teskey (1981b).
Psychodidae: Quate (1955); Hogue (1973a).
Ptychopteridae: Alexander (1981a).
Stratiomyiidae: McFadden (1967); James (1981).
Syrphidae: Hartley (1961).
Tabanidae: Teskey (1969); Pechuman and Teskey (1981).
Tanyderidae: Alexander (1981b).
Thaumaleidae: Stone and Peterson (1981).

*Exclusive of Chironomidae, Culicidae, Simuliidae, and Tipulidae.

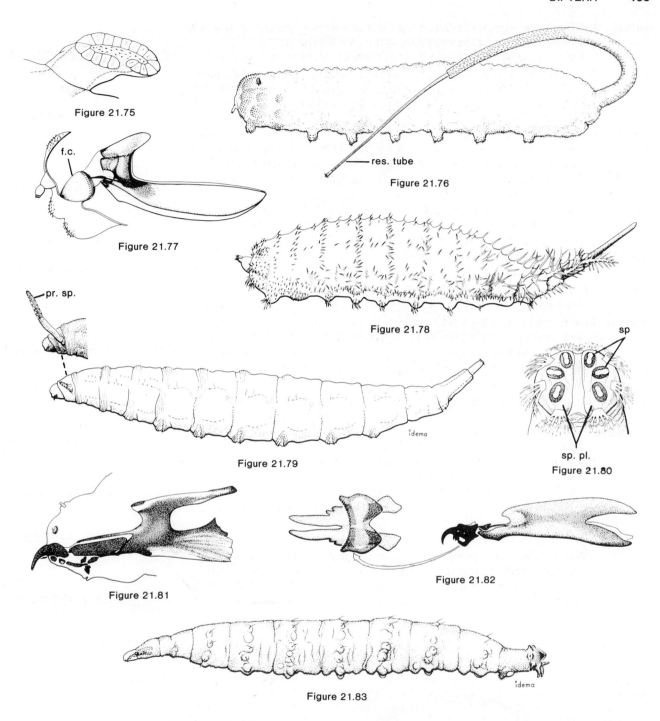

res. tube

Figure 21.76

Figure 21.75

f.c.

Figure 21.77

Figure 21.78

pr. sp.

idema

Figure 21.79

sp

sp. pl.

Figure 21.80

Figure 21.81

Figure 21.82

idema

Figure 21.83

Figure 21.75. Anterior spiracle of *Eristalis tenax* (L.) (Syrphidae).

Figure 21.76. Lateral view of *Eristalis tenax* (L.) (Syrphidae); *res.*, respiratory.

Figure 21.77. Lateral view of a cephalopharyngeal skeleton of *Eristalis tenax* (Syrphidae); *f.c.*, filter chamber.

Figure 21.78. Lateral view of *Chrysogaster* sp. (Syrphidae).

Figure 21.79. Lateral view of *Canace macateei* Malloch (Canaceidae) showing enlargement of prothoracic spiracle; *pr. sp.*, prothoracic spiracle.

Figure 21.80. Posterior spiracles of *Canace macateei* Malloch (Canaceidae); *sp*, spiracular openings; *sp. pl.*, spiracular plate.

Figure 21.81. Lateral view of cephalopharyngeal skeleton of *Canace macateei* (Canaceidae).

Figure 21.82. Lateral view of cephalopharyngeal skeleton of *Sepedon* sp. (Sciomyzidae) with enlarged ventral view of mouth hooks and serrated ventral arch.

Figure 21.83. Lateral view of *Sepedon* sp. (Sciomyzidae).

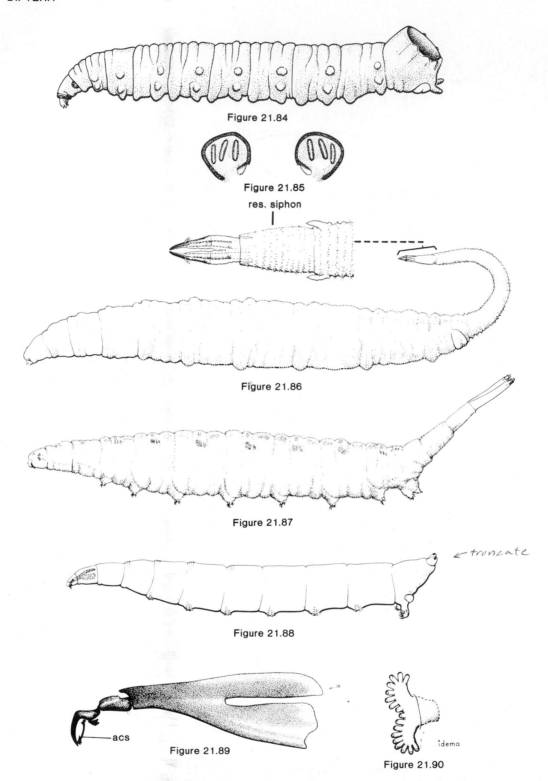

Figure 21.84

Figure 21.85

res. siphon

Figure 21.86

Figure 21.87

←truncate

Figure 21.88

acs

Figure 21.89

idema

Figure 21.90

Figure 21.84. Lateral view of *Blaesoxipha fletcheri* (Aldrich) (Sarcophagidae).

Figure 21.85. Posterior spiracles of *Blaesoxipha fletcheri* (Aldrich) (Sarcophagidae).

Figure 21.86. Lateral view of *Notiphila* sp. (Ephydridae) with enlargement of apex of respiratory siphon; *res.,* respiratory.

Figure 21.87. Lateral view of *Ephydra* sp. (Ephydridae).

Figure 21.88. Lateral view of *Limnophora* sp. (Muscidae).

Figure 21.89. Lateral view of cephalopharyngeal skeleton of *Limnophora* sp. (Muscidae); *acs,* accessory oral sclerite.

Figure 21.90. Typical bicornuate anterior spiracle of Scathophagidae.

Aquatic Diptera
Part Two. Adults of Aquatic Diptera

Richard W. Merritt
Michigan State University, East Lansing

Evert I. Schlinger
University of California, Berkeley

INTRODUCTION

Adult Diptera or true flies, which have immature stages living in a variety of aquatic and semiaquatic habitats, are found throughout the world. Adults of most aquatic and semiaquatic flies are found around or very near water, but those families whose species require a blood meal for ovarian development can often occur miles away from the nearest water source (e.g., Culicidae, Simuliidae, Tabanidae, Ceratopogonidae).

Some adult Diptera spend most of their lives "walking" on or skimming over water (e.g., some Chironomidae, Empididae, Dolichopodidae, Tipulidae); however, most groups spend little time directly associated with water. Species that oviposit directly in or on water may do so without much water contact, whereas others touch the water gently during oviposition. Collection of some of the smaller aquatic families may prove difficult; for example, one of the best places to find adult deuterophlebiids is in spider webs along streams (G. W. Courtney, pers. comm.). A summary of some common habits and habitats of adult aquatic Diptera is presented in table 21A.

The ability of adults of some families to emerge from pupae submerged in swiftly flowing water has often been cited as an extreme adaptation to an aquatic habitat. For example, in the Blephariceridae the wings expand to full size during growth within the pupal case. Thus, at emergence the adult needs only to unfold them to render them functional (Hogue 1973b). In the Nymphomyiidae, dealated adults of some species occur under water and cling to substrates with specially adapted, enlarged tarsal claws (Kevan and Cutten 1981).

Some aquatic Diptera pass through one (univoltine) or two (bivoltine) generations a year, and adults are usually present during the spring or summer (e.g., some Tipulidae, Tanyderidae, Blephariceridae, and Stratiomyidae). Other groups may undergo several generations a year (multivoltine) and adults may be found during all seasons (e.g., some Culicidae, Ceratopogonidae, and Ephydridae). The latter often occur in warmer, more southern areas of the United States.

The general classification of Diptera varies depending on the regional history of Dipterology; however, North American Dipterists usually follow that given by Stone *et al.* (1965).

The order Diptera contains three suborders: Nematocera, Brachycera, and Cyclorrhapha. The Nematocera contain six superfamilies and 23 families; the Brachycera, three superfamilies and 18 families; and the Cyclorrhapha, 14 superfamilies and 63 families. The aquatic Diptera belong mainly to the suborder Nematocera, where 20 of 23 families contain aquatic species. The Brachycera have fewer, with 6 of 18 families represented by aquatic species, and the Cyclorrhapha are the least represented with only 6 of 63 families. Although only 32 of 106 families have aquatic species, nearly 50% of the all dipterous species are aquatic (Peterson 1951).

EXTERNAL MORPHOLOGY

The morphology of adult Diptera is complex and a given structure in one family may not be the same (homologous) as in another family. For this reason, only structures thought to be homologous have been used in construction of the key. The structures discussed below should be carefully understood before attempting to use the key.

Head and Mouthparts: The *antennae* are usually inserted between the eyes and consist of three to numerous (20–30) segments.[1] When there are only three segments, the terminal segment may have an additional structure, a *style* (fig. 21.91) or an *arista* (fig. 21.93), or this segment may be annulated consisting of incomplete, segmentlike rings (fig. 21.92). In some families with three-segmented antennae, the second segment may have a dorsal, seamlike line, termed the *longitudinal seam* (fig. 21.93A). When counting the number of antennal segments, *do not* count the nonarticulating or nonmovable antennal tubercle as the first segment. The *ptilinal (frontal) suture* is a crescent-shaped groove, situated on the lower part of the frons between the bases of the antennae and the eyes (fig. 21.94A), and usually extends ventrally into the facial area. The *proboscis* is a sucking, tubelike mouthpart that is often capable of being extended and may appear rigid, as well as varying in length (figs. 21.107–21.108).

Thorax: The *mesonotum* of Diptera is strongly developed and composed of a very narrow *prescutum* and the larger *scutum, scutellum,* and *postnotum* (fig. 21.95). Several characters of the mesonotum are important in separating families

---

1. There are actually only three true segments to the antenna; the third may be divided into many flagellomeres. However, for the purpose of this key, we will use the word "segment" instead of flagellomere.

Table 21A. Some common habits and habitats of adult aquatic Diptera.[1]

	On Rocks in Splash Zone or Under Waterfalls	Flying in Mating Swarms Above Vegetation or Aggregated on Rocks	Predatory on Other Invertebrates	Feeding on Nectar or Pollen at Flowers, or on Insect Secretions on Leaves	Resting on Vegetation or Ground Near Water Source	On Host (females of blood-sucking species)
Tipulidae	(some marine spp.)	x			x	
Tanyderidae		x				
Nymphomyiidae		x				
Psychodidae	x	(aggregated)			x	
Blephariceridae	x	(aggregated)	(females of some spp. feed on insects)	x?	x	
Deuterophlebiidae		x			x	
Thaumaleidae					x	
Dixidae		(aggregated)			x	
Culicidae		x		x		x
Ceratopogonidae	x	x	(some spp. feed on insects)	x	x	x
Chironomidae	x	x		x	x	x
Simuliidae				x	x	x
Tabanidae		x		x	x	
Stratiomyidae	(some stream spp.)			x	x	
Empididae	x	x	(insects)	x	x	
Dolichopodidae	(some marine spp.)		(insects)	x	x	
Syrphidae				x	x	
Dryomyzidae	(some marine spp.)		(barnacles)			
Sciomyzidae			(snails, slugs)		x	
Canaceidae	(some marine spp.)				x	
Ephydridae	x				x	
Scathophagidae			(some spp. feed on insects)	x	x	
Muscidae	x		(some spp. feed on insects	x	x	

1. This table includes habits and habitats of exemplar species only and does not intent to show all habitats of species wihtin each family.

of Diptera. For example, the posteriorly directed V-shaped suture signifies the family Tipulidae (fig. 21.98). Also, the absence or presence of a transverse suture, complete or incomplete, separates several families (fig. 21.95). The postnotum is usually round, swollen, and smooth, but in the Chironomidae a longitudinal groove divides this structure (fig. 21.110).

Wings: These organs are probably the most important structures used to separate families of Diptera. A drawing of a generalized wing (fig. 21.97) shows the terminology of wing veins and wing cells used in the key below. When examining the wing of a fly under the microscope, the viewer must move the specimen *slowly* to obtain the proper lighting for viewing the insertion or ending of any particular vein. This is especially true when examining the subcostal vein, since this vein is often hidden by the radial vein (R_1), and is even more critical when looking for fractures in the costal vein (figs. 21.120–21.121). Because venation varies considerably from family to family, several text figures are given with the veins and cells labeled. Also, the venation within a family may be quite different from that shown in a text figure; therefore, learn the location of the veins, rather than the shape of cells enclosed by the veins.

Halteres: These small, knoblike structures are remnants of the second pair of wings, and serve as a significant character to identify the order Diptera. In one family, the Ptychopteridae, an additional structure termed the *prehalter* (fig. 21.99) is present.

Calypteres: These scalelike structures may appear to be absent, or when fully developed may cover the halteres. The calypter is often called a *squama*. There may be one or two calypteres on each side of the thorax below the wing base. The lower calypter is attached to the thorax, and the upper calypter is attached to the wing base. One calypter may be longer than the other (figs. 21.122–21.123).

Legs: The apex of the leg often contains several characters useful for separating families of Diptera. Between the tarsal claws are two padlike structures termed *pulvilli* (fig. 21.96). A hairlike or padlike structure may occur between the pulvilli, and is termed the *empodium* (fig. 21.96A, C).

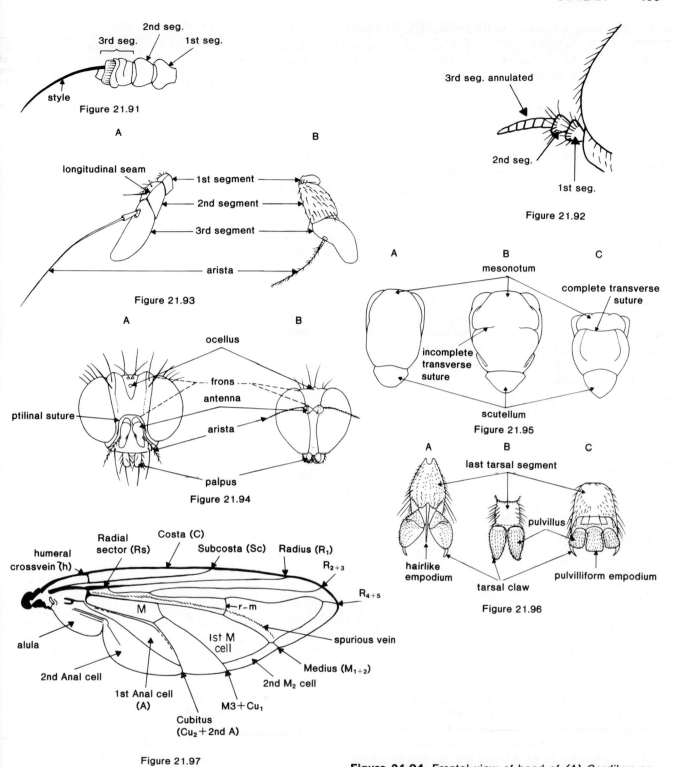

Figure 21.91

Figure 21.92

Figure 21.93

Figure 21.94

Figure 21.95

Figure 21.96

Figure 21.97

Figure 21.94. Frontal view of head of (A) Cordilura sp. (Scathophagidae), and (B) Dolichopus sp. (Dolichopodidae).

Figure 21.95. Dorsal view of thorax of (A) Dictya sp. (Sciomyzidae), (B) Cordilura sp. (Scathophagidae), and (C) Limnophora sp. (Muscidae).

Figure 21.96. Ventral view of last tarsal segment of (A) Tubifera sp. (Syrphidae), (B) Limnophora sp. (Muscidae), and (C) Tabanus sp. (Tabanidae).

Figure 21.91. Lateral view of antenna of Microchrysa sp. (Stratiomyidae).

Figure 21.92. Lateral view of antenna of Odontomyia sp. (Stratiomyidae).

Figure 21.93. Antenna of (A) Limnophora sp. (Muscidae), and (B) Dictya sp. (Sciomyzidae).

Figure 21.97. Generalized wing of Diptera showing veins and cells (Syrphidae).

KEY TO THE FAMILIES OF AQUATIC DIPTERA[2]

Adults

1. Antennae generally longer than thorax, composed of 6 or more freely articulated segments (Nematocera) (figs. 21.98–21.111) 2

1'. Antennae composed of 5 or fewer (usually 3) freely articulated segments, the last segment often annulated (fig. 21.92) or bearing a style or arista (figs. 21.91, 21.93) (Brachycera) 15

2(1). Mesonotum with an entire V-shaped suture or impression (fig. 21.98) 3

2'. Mesonotal suture transverse, not V-shaped, or wanting 5

3(2). Wings with 2 anal veins reaching the margin (fig. 21.98); legs long and slender (crane flies) .... *TIPULIDAE* (chap. 22)

3'. Wings with a single anal vein reaching the margin (figs. 21.99–21.100) 4

4(3'). Halteres with a conspicuous process ("prehalter") anterior to their base (fig. 21.99); wings with 4 branches of radius reaching the margin (fig. 21.99) (phantom crane flies) .... *PTYCHOPTERIDAE*

4'. Halteres without a conspicuous process anterior to their base; wings with 5 branches of radius reaching the margin (fig. 21.100) (primitive crane flies) .... *TANYDERIDAE*

5(2'). Wings, if present, with a marginal fringe of long hairs (fig. 21.101), very narrow and elongate with only rudiments of wing veins present anteriorly (fig. 21.101); small flies, less than 3 mm (nymphomyiid flies) .... *NYMPHOMYIIDAE*

5'. Wings without marginal fringe of long hairs, broader, not narrow and elongated 6

6(5'). M_3 vein of wing completely detached (fig. 21.102); eyes divided by an unfacetted stripe; wing venation sometimes accompanied by a fine network of folds and creases (fig. 21.102) (net-winged midges) .... *BLEPHARICERIDAE*

6'. M_3 vein of wing not detached (figs. 21.104–21.107); eyes not divided by unfacetted stripe 7

7(6'). Wings large, broadest in basal fourth and densely covered with microtrichia (fine hairs) on anterior one-half, less dense on posterior one-half; wings generally lacking most of true venation (fig. 21.103); mouthparts absent; terminal antennal segment in male may be 3–4 times body length (fig. 21.103); body size small, less than 3.0 mm (mountain midges) .... *DEUTEROPHLEBIIDAE*

7'. Wings not broadest in basal fourth and not densely covered with microtrichia; wing veins well developed, at least anteriorly; mouthparts present 8

8(7'). Costa extending around margin of wing, though weaker beyond apex (figs. 21.104–21.108) 9

8'. Costa ending at or near the apex of the wing (figs. 21.109–21.113) 13

9(8). Wings with 7 longitudinal veins reaching margin (fig. 21.104); antennae subequal to head length and shorter than palpi, with basal segments of flagellum thickened and clavate, the remaining segments filiform (fig. 21.104); small flies (3–4 mm) (solitary midges) .... *THAUMALEIDAE*

9'. Wings with at least 9 longitudinal veins reaching margin (figs. 21.105–21.108); flagellum of antennae uniformly filiform or beadlike 10

10(9'). Wings short and broad, pointed apically, usually densely hairy (mothlike) and held rooflike over the body when at rest; crossveins absent except near base of wing (fig. 21.105) (moth flies) .... *PSYCHODIDAE*

10'. Wings long, or, if broad, the apex very broadly rounded (figs. 21.106–21.108); wings held flat over the abdomen when at rest and not densely hairy (although scales may be present along wing veins or wing margins); crossveins present 11

11(10'). Apical wing veins (R_1–R_3) strongly arched (fig. 21.106); wings without scales; basal segments of antennae swollen and cylindrical, remaining segments threadlike and indistinct (fig. 21.106) .... *DIXIDAE*

2. Key modified from Wirth and Stone (1956) and Cole (1969). This key is for only those members of the included families whose larvae or pupae are aquatic or whose adults are found near, in, or on water.

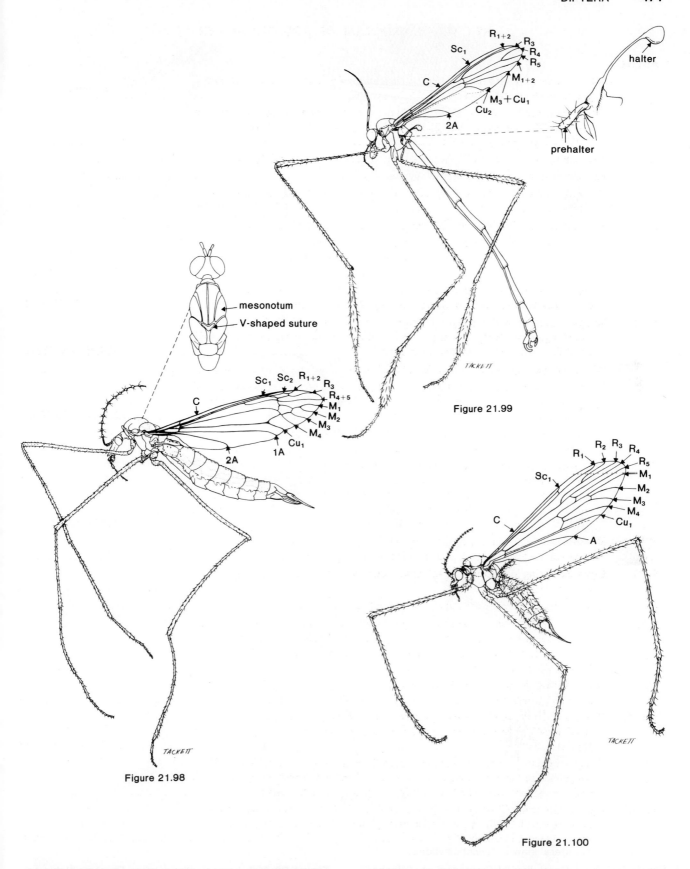

Figure 21.98. Lateral view of Tipulidae showing V-shaped mesonotal suture.

Figure 21.99. Lateral view of *Bittacomorpha* sp. (Ptych-opteridae) showing prehalter.

Figure 21.100. Lateral view of *Protoplasa* sp. (Tanyderi-dae).

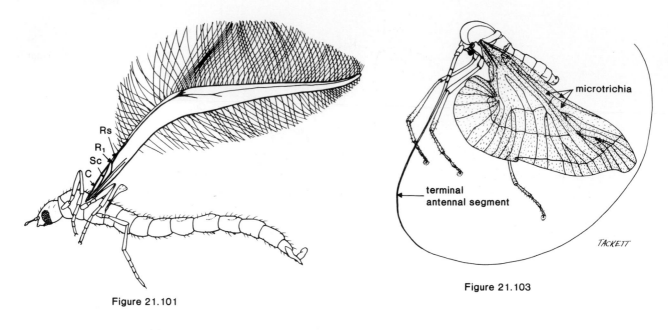

Figure 21.101

Figure 21.103

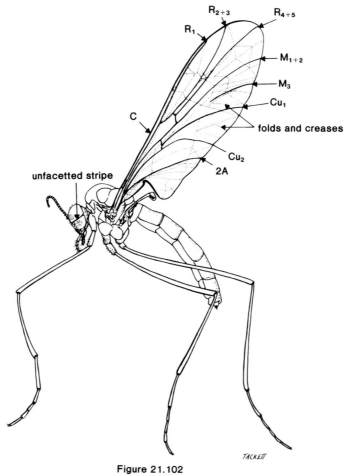

Figure 21.102

Figure 21.101. Lateral view of Nymphomyiidae.

Figure 21.102. Lateral view of *Dioptopsis* sp. (Blephariceridae).

Figure 21.103. Lateral view of male *Deuterophlebia* sp. (Deuterophlebiidae).

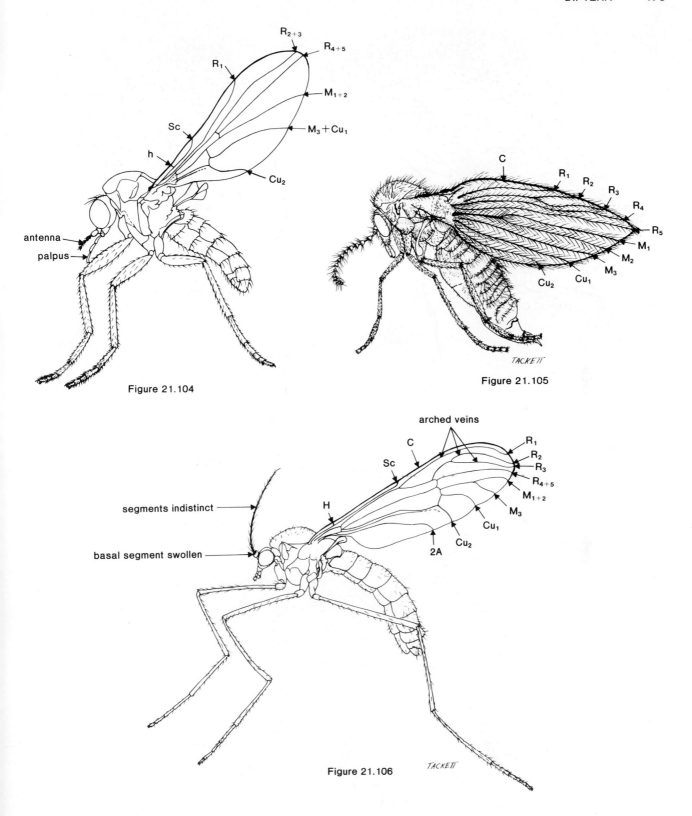

Figure 21.104

Figure 21.105

Figure 21.106

Figure 21.104. Lateral view of *Thaumalea* sp. (Thaumaleidae).

Figure 21.105. Lateral view of *Psychoda* sp. (Psychodidae).

Figure 21.106. Lateral view of *Dixa* sp. (Dixidae).

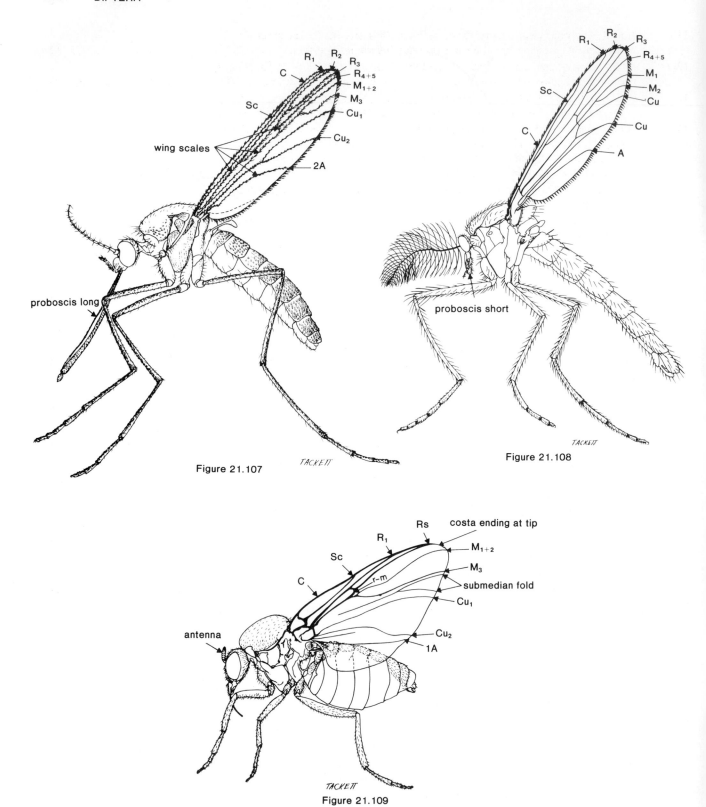

Figure 21.107

Figure 21.108

Figure 21.109

Figure 21.107. Lateral view of female *Aedes* sp. (Culicidae).

Figure 21.108. Lateral view of male *Chaoborus* sp. (Chaoboridae).

Figure 21.109. Lateral view of *Cnephia* sp. (Simuliidae).

11'.   Apical wing veins (R₁–R₃) straight or nearly so (figs. 21.107–21.108); basal
        segments of antennae not swollen and remaining segments distinct 12

12(11'). Proboscis elongated, extending far beyond the clypeus (fig. 21.107); scales present
        on wing margins and veins and usually on the body (fig. 21.107) (mosquitoes) .... *CULICIDAE* (chap. 23)

12'.   Proboscis short, extending little beyond the clypeus (fig. 21.108); scales, when
        present, confined primarily to wing margins (fig. 21.108) (phantom midges) .... *CHAOBORIDAE*

13(8'). Wings broad, anterior veins strong with posterior veins weak and poorly developed
        (fig. 21.109); antennae shorter than thorax, never plumose; dark or variously
        colored flies with humpbacked appearance, rarely over 6 mm in length (fig.
        21.109) (black flies) .... *SIMULIIDAE* (chap. 24)

13'.   Wings narrower and long, the posterior veins usually strong; antennae generally
        longer than thorax, often plumose (fig. 21.110) 14

14(13'). Postnotum elongate with a median longitudinal groove or furrow (fig. 21.110); M
        vein of wing not forked; femora not swollen; antennae of male plumose (fig.
        21.110); mouthparts not adapted for piercing (midges) .... *CHIRONOMIDAE* (chap. 25)

14'.   Postnotum rounded without a median longitudinal groove or furrow; M vein of
        wing nearly always forked (fig. 21.111); femora often swollen; mouthparts
        sclerotized and adapted for piercing (fig. 21.111) (biting midges) .... *CERATOPOGONIDAE*

15(1'). Tarsi with 3 nearly equal pads under tarsal claws (empodium pulvilliform) (fig.
        21.96C) 16

15'.   Tarsi with 2 nearly equal pads under tarsal claws (empodium hairlike or absent)
        (fig. 21.96A, B) 18

16(15). Third antennal segment annulated with 3–8 apparent segments (figs. 21.92,
        21.113–21.114); or, when base of third antennal segment annulated and
        compacted, then bearing a style (fig. 21.91) 17

16'.   Third antennal segment compact, not annulated (fig. 21.112) .... *ATHERICIDAE*[3]

17(16). Costa ending at or near wing tip (fig. 21.113); tibiae without spurs (fig. 21.113) .... *STRATIOMYIDAE*

17'.   Costa continuing well past wing tip, often around entire posterior margin of wing
        (fig. 21.114); at least middle tibiae with spurs (fig. 21.114) .... *TABANIDAE*[4]

18(15'). Anal cell long, closed just before margin of wing, therefore petiolate; a spurious
        (false) vein present running obliquely between veins R₄₊₅ and M₁₊₂ (figs. 21.97,
        21.115) .... *SYRPHIDAE*

18'.   Anal cell short, transverse, oblique, or convex apically, or rarely absent (figs.
        21.116–21.117); no spurious vein 19

19(18'). Ptilinal (frontal) suture entirely absent (fig. 21.94B); frons uniformly sclerotized;
        alula weak (fig. 21.116) 20

19'.   Ptilinal (frontal) suture present (fig. 21.94A); frons divided into distinct regions by
        ptilinal suture; alula well developed (fig. 21.123) 21

20(19). Anterior crossvein (r–m) situated at or before the basal fourth of wing (fig.
        21.116); 1st M₂ and 2nd M₂ cells united to form one long cell; vein R₄₊₅ not
        branched (fig. 21.116) .... *DOLICHOPODIDAE*

20'.   Anterior crossvein (r–m) situated far beyond basal fourth of wing (fig. 21.117); 1st
        M₂ and 2nd M₂ cells separated; vein R₄₊₅ usually branched (fig. 21.117) .... *EMPIDIDAE*

21(19'). Second antennal segment without a longitudinal seam on its upper outer edge (fig.
        21.93B); mesonotum without a complete transverse suture (fig. 21.95A, B);
        calypter (squama) small (fig. 21.118) (Acalypterate flies) 22

21'.   Second antennal segment with a longitudinal seam on its upper outer edge (fig.
        21.93A); mesonotum usually with complete transverse suture (fig. 21.95C);
        calypter (squama) large (fig. 21.122) (Calypterate flies) 25

22(21). Costa entire (not fractured); subcosta complete, ends in costa (fig. 21.118) 23

---

3. Some Rhagionidae may key out here, but they often have an elongated style.
4. Pelecorhynchidae will also key out here, but the lower calypter in this family is poorly developed.

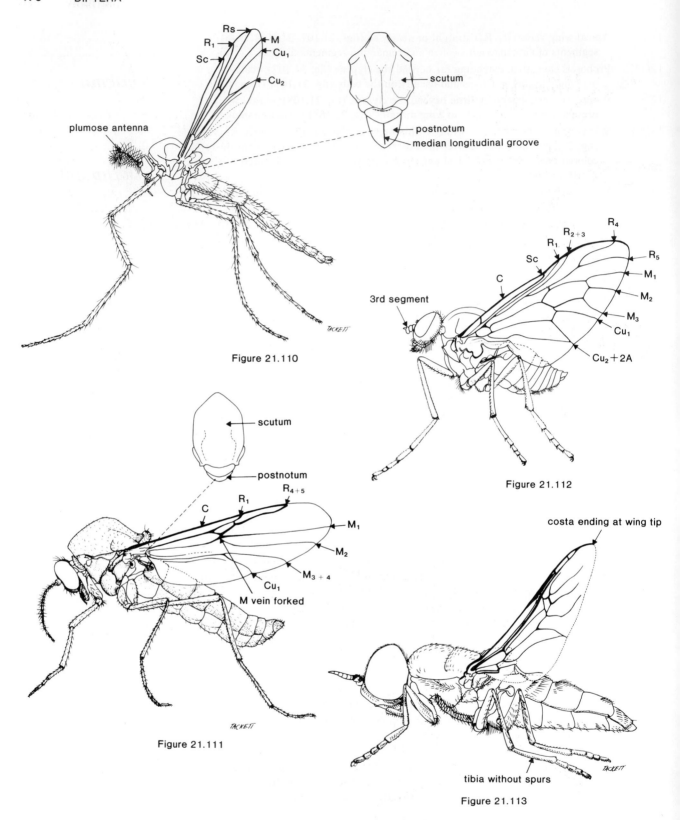

Figure 21.110

Figure 21.112

Figure 21.111

Figure 21.113

Figure 21.110. Lateral view of male Chironomini (Chironomidae) showing postnotal longitudinal groove.

Figure 21.111. Lateral view of male *Johannsenomyia* sp. (Ceratopogonidae).

Figure 21.112. Lateral view of *Atherix* sp. (Athericeridae).

Figure 21.113. Lateral view of *Odontomyia* sp. (Stratiomyidae).

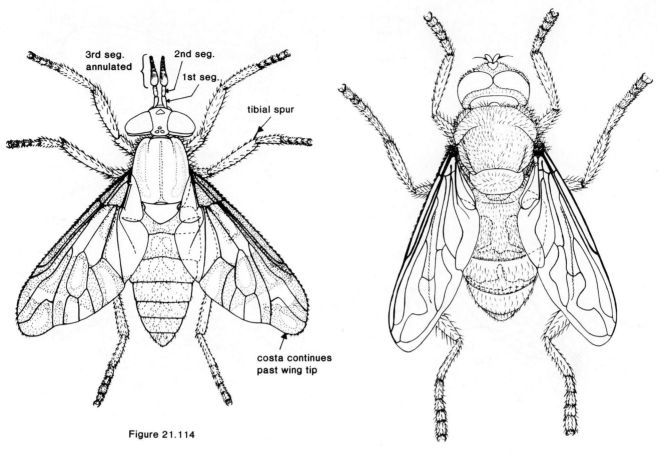

Figure 21.114

3rd seg.
annulated
2nd seg.
1st seg.
tibial spur
costa continues
past wing tip

Figure 21.115

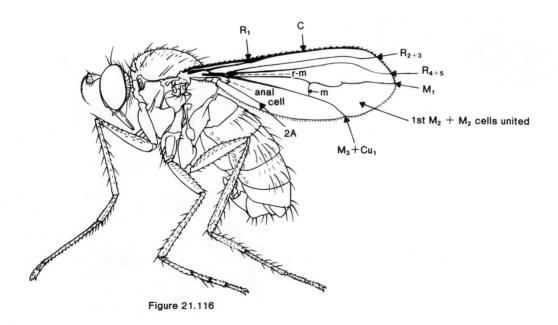

R₁
C
R₂₊₃
R₄₊₅
r-m
m
M₁
anal
cell
1st M₂ + M₂ cells united
2A
M₃+Cu₁

Figure 21.116

Figure 21.114. Dorsal view of *Chrysops* sp. (Tabanidae).

Figure 21.115. Dorsal view of *Eristalis* sp. (Syrphidae).

Figure 21.116. Lateral view of *Dolichopus* sp. (Dolicho-podidae).

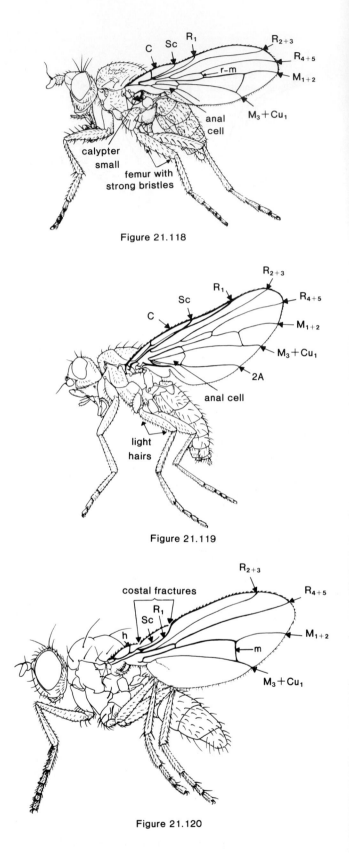

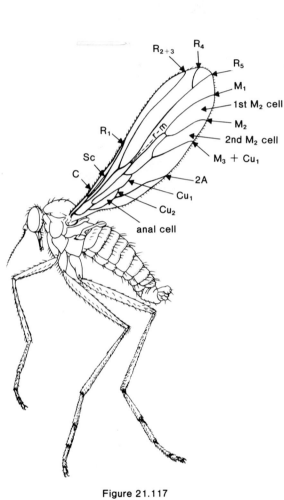

Figure 21.117

Figure 21.118

Figure 21.119

Figure 21.120

Figure 21.117. Lateral view of Empididae.

Figure 21.118. Lateral view of *Dictya* sp. (Sciomyzidae).

Figure 21.119. Lateral view of *Oedoparena* sp. (Dryomyzidae).

Figure 21.120. Lateral view of *Notiphila* sp. (Ephydridae).

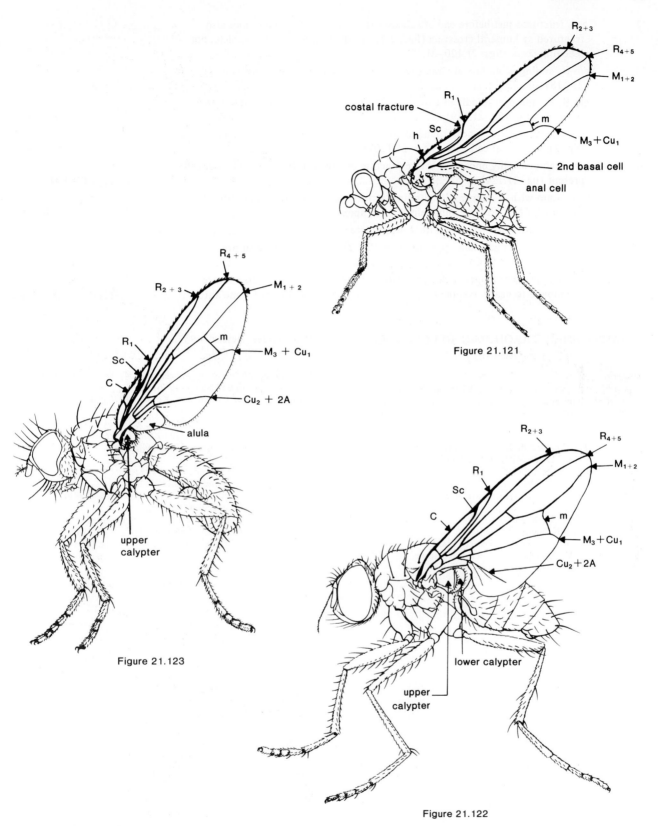

Figure 21.121

Figure 21.123

Figure 21.122

Figure 21.121. Lateral view of *Canaceoides* sp. (Canaceidae).

Figure 21.122. Lateral view of *Limnophora* sp. (Muscidae).

Figure 21.123. Lateral view of *Cordilura* sp. (Scathophagidae).

22'.   Costa fractured just before end of subcosta (fig. 21.121), and sometimes also fractured at humeral crossvein (fig. 21.120); subcosta usually incomplete, not reaching costa (figs. 21.120–21.121) **24**

23(22).   Vein R_1 ending at middle of costa (fig. 21.118); femora with strong bristles (fig. 21.118) .... *SCIOMYZIDAE*

23'.   Vein R_1 ending past middle of costa (fig. 21.119); femora with hairs but without strong bristles (fig. 21.119) .... *DRYOMYZIDAE*

24(22').   Costa fractured twice, once at junction of subcosta and once at humeral crossvein (fig. 21.120); anal cell absent (fig. 21.120) .... *EPHYDRIDAE*

24'.   Costa fractured only once, just before junction of subcosta (fig. 21.121); anal cell present (fig. 21.121) .... *CANACEIDAE*

25(21').   Mesonotum with 3 complete longitudinal stripes; venation similar to figure 21.123 except vein M_{1+2} nearly joins vein R_{4+5} at apex (*Blaesoxipha* only) .... *SARCOPHAGIDAE*

25'.   Mesonotum without stripes or with 4 incomplete stripes **26**

26(25').   Lower calypter longer than upper calypter (fig. 21.122); transverse suture complete (fig. 21.95C) .... *MUSCIDAE*

Lower calypter not longer than upper calypter (fig. 21.123); transverse suture incomplete to nearly complete (fig. 21.95A, B) (Anthomyiidae of some authors) .... *SCATHOPHAGIDAE*

ADDITIONAL TAXONOMIC REFERENCES
(Adults)[*]

General
Crampton (1942); Brues *et al.* (1954); Wirth and Stone (1956); Cole (1969); Griffiths (1972); Hennig (1973); Rohdendorf (1974); Borror *et al.* (1981); McAlpine *et al.* (1981); McCafferty (1981).

Taxonomic treatments at the family level
Athericeridae: Stuckenberg (1973); Webb (1977, 1981).
Blephariceridae: Alexander (1958); Hogue (1973b, 1981).
Canaceidae: Wirth (1951b).
Ceratopogonidae: Wirth (1952a); Wirth *et al.* (1977); Downes and Wirth (1981).
Chaoboridae: Cook (1956, 1981).
Deuterophlebiidae: Kennedy (1958, 1981).
Dixidae: Peters and Cook (1966); Peters (1981).
Dolichopodidae: Wirth and Stone (1956); Robinson and Vockeroth (1981).

Dryomyzidae: Steyskal (1957).
Empididae: Wirth and Stone (1956); Steyskal and Knutson (1981); Wilder (1981a, b, c).
Ephydridae: Sturtevent and Wheeler (1954); Wirth and Stone (1956).
Muscidae: Wirth and Stone (1956).
Nymphomyiidae: Cutten and Kevan (1970); Kevan and Cutten (1981).
Pelecorhynchidae: Krivosheina (1971); Teskey (1981b).
Psychodidae: Quate (1955); Quate and Vockeroth (1981).
Ptychopteridae: Alexander (1942, 1981a).
Sarcophagidae: Aldrich (1916).
Scathophagidae: Wirth and Stone (1956).
Sciomyzidae: Wirth and Stone (1956).
Stratiomyidae: Wirth and Stone (1956); James (1981).
Syrphidae: Wirth and Stone (1956).
Tabanidae: Wirth and Stone (1956); Pechuman and Teskey (1981).
Tanyderidae: Alexander (1942); Alexander (1981b).
Thaumaleidae: Wirth and Stone (1956); Stone (1964b); Stone and Peterson (1981).

[*]Exclusive of Chironomidae, Culicidae, Simuliidae, and Tipulidae.

le 21B. Summary of ecological and distributional data for *larval aquatic Diptera (exclusive of Tipulidae, Simuliidae, Chironomidae, and icidae).* (For definition of terms see Tables 6A.-6C; table prepared by K. W. Cummins, R. W. Merritt, E. I. Schlinger, H. J. Teskey, and B. V. erson.)

Taxa (number of species in parentheses)	Habitat	Habit	Trophic Relationships	North American Distribution	Ecological References'
uterophlebiidae(5) untain midges)					20, 1217, 1291, 1292, 1316, 1886, 2736, 2747
Deuterophlebia(5)	Lotic—erosional	Clingers (rings of hooks on abdominal segments)	Scrapers	West mountains	
phariceridae(22) net-winged nidges)	Lotic—erosional	Clingers (ventral suckers)	Generally scrapers		1106, 1217, 1240, 1316, 1886, 2747
gathon(3)	Lotic—erosional	Clingers		West mountains	
ibiocephala(3)	Lotic—erosional	Clingers		West mountains	
lepharicera(10)	Lotic—erosional	Clingers		Widespread	
ioptopsis(5)	Lotic—erosional	Clingers		West mountains	
hilorus(1)	Lotic—erosional	Clingers		West mountains	
nphomyiidae(1)					
Palaeodipteron(1)	Lotic—erosional (aquatic mosses)	Clingers (attached by elongate abdominal prolegs)	Scrapers, collectors—gatherers	Eastern Canada	79, 496, 1180, 1301
ulidae	See Table 22A.				
icidae	See Table 23A.				
oboridae(15) phantom midges)	Generally lentic—littoral, profundal, and limnetic; lotic—depositional (pools)	Generally sprawlers (day), planktonic (night)	Predators (piercers) and engulfers		434, 568, 1217, 1316, 1648, 1886, 2141, 2747, 2765
haoborus(8) (= *Corethra*)	Lentic—limnetic, profundal, and littoral (including temporary ponds and bogs)	Sprawlers (day), planktonic (night)	Predators (piercers), predators (engulfers, primarily microcrustacea)	Widespread	167, 224, 236, 1089, 1271, 1755, 1786, 2122, 2141, 2186, 2757
orethrella(3)	Lotic—depositional (pools of cold springs)			Southeast	
ucorethra(1)	Lotic—depositional (pools of cold springs)	Planktonic—swimmers	Predators (piercers, feed at surface)	North and West	1089, 1966
ochlonyx(3)	Lentic—limnetic, profundal and littoral (especially bogs and small ponds)		Predators (engulfers)	Widespread	1089, 1210, 1966
chodidae(63) noth flies)	Generally lotic—depositional, lentic—littoral (detritus)	Generally burrowers	Generally collectors—gatherers		1217, 1240, 1316, 1648, 1886, 1971, 2747
aruina(1)	Lotic—erosional	Clingers	Scrapers, collectors—gatherers	West	1105, 1973, 2747
ericoma(24)	Lotic—depositional (margins), lentic—littoral (detritus)	Burrowers	Collectors—gatherers	Widespread	419, 2747, †
sychoda(21)	Lentic—littoral (detritus), lotic—depositional, beaches—marine	Burrowers	Collectors—gatherers	Widespread	419, 1315, 1636, 2157, 2747
elmatoscopus(17)	Lentic—littoral, lotic—depositional	Burrowers	Collectors—gatherers		1240, 2747

phasis on trophic relationships.
oublished data, K. W. Cummins, Kellogg Biological Station.

Table 21B— *Continued*

Taxa (number of species in parentheses)	Habitat	Habit	Trophic Relationships	North American Distribution	Ecological References[*]
Ceratopogonidae(388) (=Heleidae; biting midges, "no-see-ums")	Generally lentic—littoral (including tree holes and small temporary ponds and pools), lotic—depositional (margins and detritus)	Generally sprawlers, burrowers, or planktonic	Generally predators (engulfers), collectors—gatherers		1217, 1316, 1472, 188 2429, 2738, 2746, 274
Dasyheleinae(29) *Dasyhelea*(2)	Lentic—tree holes, rock pools, littoral (in algal mats), lotic—depositional (margins)	Sprawlers—climbers (semiaquatic)	Collectors—gatherers, scrapers	Widespread	2429, 2747
Forcipomyiinae(103)	Generally lotic—erosional	Generally sprawlers and clingers	Collectors—gatherers and scrapers(?)		
Atrichopogon(27)	Lotic—erosional (margins, debris jams), lentic—littoral (algal mats)	Sprawlers—clingers		Widespread	218, 1812, 2429, 274
Forcipomyia(76)	Lotic—erosional (margins, including warm springs); lentic—littoral and margins (semiaquatic)	Sprawlers	Scrapers(?)	Widespread	321, 2161, 2738, 274
Ceratopogoninae(245)	Wide variety of lentic and lotic habitats	Generally burrowers, occasionally planktonic	Generally predators—(engulfers), a few collectors—gatherers		2429, 2747
Alluaudomyia(8)	Lentic—littoral (detritus and algal mats), occasionally limnetic	Burrowers, occasionally planktonic	Predators (engulfers)	Widespread	2429, 2747
Bezzia(30)	Lentic—littoral, profundal, and occasionally limnetic; lotic—hot springs (algal mats)	Burrowers, occasionally planktonic	Predators (engulfers)	Widespread	2429, 2738, 2747
Culicoides(137)	Lentic—littoral (margins), tree holes and temporary pools, brackish marshes; lotic—margins	Burrowers, occasionally planktonic	Predators (engulfers), collectors—gatherers	Widespread	111, 133, 203, 796, 1297, 1428, 1429, 27 2747
Johannsenomyia(2)	Lentic—littoral, limnetic	Burrowers, occasionally planktonic	Predators (engulfers)	East	2747
Mallochohelea(11)	Lentic—littoral (margins)	Burrowers	Predators (engulfers)	Widespread	2429
Palpomyia(23)	Lotic—erosional and depositional (detritus), lentic—littoral, profundal, and occasionally limnetic	Burrowers, occasionally planktonic	Predators (engulfers), collectors—gatherers	Widespread	419, 421, 925, 926, 2429, 2747
Probezzia(12)	Lentic—littoral and limnetic	Burrowers, occasionally planktonic	Predators (engulfers)	Widespread	2747
Serromyia(3)	Lentic—littoral (margins)	Burrowers	Probably predators (engulfers)	Widespread	2429, 2747
Sphaeromias(1)	Lentic—littoral (algal mats), occasionally limnetic	Burrowers, occasionally planktonic	Predators (engulfers)	Widespread	2429, 2747
Stilobezzia(18)	Lentic—littoral (margins)	Burrowers	Predators (engulfers)	Widespread	2429, 2747
Leptoconopinae(11) *Leptoconops*(11)	Lentic—littoral (margins), beaches—marine	Burrowers		Widespread (primarily Western)	406, 1470, 1471, 225 2745, 2747

[*]Emphasis on trophic relationships.

ble 21B—*Continued*

Taxa (number of species in parentheses)	Habitat	Habit	Trophic Relationships	North American Distribution	Ecological References[*]
nuliidae	See Table 24A.				
ronomidae	See Table 25A.				
yderidae(4) (primitive crane ies)	Lotic—erosional	Sprawlers—burrowers			
Protanyderus(3)	Lotic—erosional (sediments)	Sprawlers—burrowers		Western	694, 1320, 2091
Protoplasa(1)	Lotic—erosional (sediments)	Sprawlers—burrowers		Eastern	13
aumaleidae(5) (solitary midges)	Lotic—erosional	Clingers	Scrapers		2747
Thaumalea(4)	Lotic—erosional	Clingers	Scrapers	Widespread	1240, 2349, 2747
Trichothaumalea(1)	Lotic—erosional	Clingers	Scrapers	Western	2747
chopteridae(16) (=Liriopeidae) phantom crane ies)	Generally lotic—depositional (including springs), lentic—littoral (sediments and detritus)	Generally burrowers	Generally collectors—gatherers		1217, 1240, 1316, 1886, 2747
Bittacomorpha(2)	Lotic—depositional, lentic—vascular hydrophytes (emergent zone)	Burrowers	Collectors—gatherers	Widespread	11, 984, 2085
Bittacomorphella(4)	Lotic—depositional	Burrowers	Collectors—gatherers	Widespread	11
tychoptera(10) (=*Liriope*)	Lotic—depositional, lentic—vascular hydrophytes (bogs)	Burrowers	Collectors—gatherers, shredders (chewers—*Sphagnum*)		11, 984, 1094, 2085
idae(41) iixid midges)					
ixa(41)	Lotic—erosional (protected areas) and depositional (detritus)	Swimmers—climbers over damp surfaces	Collectors—gatherers (possibly also filterers)	Widespread	382, 1827, 2747
chycera-Orthor-ha					1217, 1239, 1240, 1316, 1610, 1611, 1886, 2747
tratiomyidae(137) (soldier flies)	Generally lentic—littoral	Generally sprawlers—swimmers	Generally collectors—gatherers		
Beris(3)	Lentic—littoral			Widespread	177
Caloparyphus(11)	Lentic—vascular hydrophytes (emergent zone)			Widespread	1610
Euparyphus(14)	Lotic—erosional and depositional margins	Sprawlers	Collectors—gatherers, scrapers	Widespread	1610, 2005
Hedriodiscus(7)	Lotic—depositional (vascular hydrophytes)	Climbers	Scrapers	Widespread	1610, 2344
Nemotelus(32)	Lentic—littoral, lotic—margins	Swimmers, sprawlers	Collectors—gatherers	Widespread	177, 1240, 1610, 2747
Odontomyia(31) (=*Eulalia*)	Lentic—vascular hydrophytes (emergent zone)	Sprawlers	Collectors—gatherers, scrapers?	Widespread	177, 1239, 1610
Oxycera(7) (=*Hermione*)	Lotic—erosional and depositional margins			East	1610, 2747
Sargus(6)	Lentic—vascular hydrophytes (emergent zone)	Climbers	Collectors—gatherers, scrapers	Widespread	1611
Stratiomys(26) (=*Stratiomyia*)	Lotic—erosional and depositional margins	Sprawlers—burrowers	Collectors—gatherers (and filterers)	Widespread	707, 1239, 1350, 1362, 1610, 2458, 2747

phasis on trophic relationships.

Table 21B— *Continued*

Taxa (number of species in parentheses)	Habitat	Habit	Trophic Relationships	North American Distribution	Ecological References[*]
Tabanidae(293) (horse and deer flies)	Generally lotic—depositional (occasionally erosional), lentic—littoral (margin, sediments, and detritus)	Generally sprawlers—burrowers	Generally predators (piercers)		76, 331, 1217, 1240, 1316, 1886, 2074, 241 2601, 2747
Apatolestes(11)	Beach zone—marine (at edge of high tide zone)	Sprawlers—burrowers	Predators (piercers)	California coast	1431
Atylotus(8)	Lentic—littoral (sediments)	Sprawlers—burrowers	Predators (piercers)	Widespread	331, 2414, 2601
Brennania(1)	Lentic—in costal sand dunes	Sprawlers—burrowers	Predators (piercers)	California coast	1653
Chlorotabanus(1)	Lentic—littoral (sediments)	Sprawlers—burrowers	Predators (piercers)	South, East Coast	899
Chrysops(80)	Lentic—littoral, beaches—marine and estuaries, lotic—depositional	Sprawlers—burrowers	Collectors—gatherers	Widespread	177, 302, 1916, 2414
Haematopota(5)	Lentic—littoral (sediments)	Sprawlers—burrowers		Widespread	331
Hybomitra(60)	Lentic—littoral, lotic	Sprawlers—burrowers	Predators (piercers)	North	2414
Leucotabanus(2)	Lentic—tree holes	Sprawlers?	Predators (piercers)	South	899
Merycomyia(2)	Lentic—littoral, lotic—depositional	Sprawlers—burrowers		East	900, 2414
Silvius(8)	Lentic—littoral, lotic—margins	Sprawlers—burrowers		Central, West	1388
Stenotabanus(8)	Beach zone—marine	Sprawlers—burrowers	Predators (piercers)	South	901
Tabanus(107)	Lentic—littoral, lotic—depositional	Sprawlers—burrowers	Predators (piercers)	Widespread	177, 419, 421
Athericidae(2) (=Rhagionidae, in part)					
Atherix(2)	Lotic—erosional and depositional	Sprawlers—burrowers	Predators (piercers)	Widespread	1217, 1240, 1316, 180 1802, 1886, 2423, 259 2599, 2747, †
Pelecorhynchidae(7)					1359
Glutops(7)	Lotic—depositional	Sprawlers—burrowers	Predators (piercers), Shredders—herbivores?	Widespread	2415, 2417
Dolichopodidae(555)	Generally lentic and lotic margins (semiaquatic)	Generally sprawlers—burrowers	Generally predators (engulfers)		450, 1081, 1240, 1648 2708, 2747
Aphrosylus(6)	Beach zone—marine (intertidal, on rocks)	Clingers (in algae on rocks)	Predators (engulfers)	West Coast	1081, 2176, 2501, 274
Argyra(45)	Lentic—littoral (margins and beach zone)	Sprawlers—burrowers,	Predators (engulfers)	Widespread	177, 1081, 2501, 274?
Asyndetus(18)	Beach zone—lakes	Sprawlers—burrowers	Predators (engulfers)	Widespread	1081, 2258
Campsicnemus(16)	Lentic—littoral (margins)	Sprawlers—burrowers	Probably collectors—gatherers	Widespread	2501, 2747
Dolichopus(294)	Lentic—littoral (margins), lotic—margins	Sprawlers—burrowers	Predators (engulfers)	Widespread	1081, 2501, 2747
Hercostomus(26)	Lotic—depositional	Sprawlers (in damp moss)	Predators (engulfers)	Widespread	2258, 2501
Hydrophorus(54)	Lentic—littoral (margins), estuaries	Sprawlers—burrowers (in fine detritus)	Predators (engulfers) (especially midges)	Widespread	2258, 2501, 2747
Hypocharassus(2)	Beach zone—marine	Sprawlers—burrowers	Predators (engulfers)	East Coast	1081, 2258, 2747
Liancalus(5)	Lotic—seeps	Sprawlers—burrowers	Predators (engulfers)	Widespread	177, 2501

*Emphasis on trophic relationships.
†Unpublished data, K. W. Cummins, Kellogg Biological Station.

ble 21B—*Continued*

Taxa (number of species in parentheses)	Habitat	Habit	Trophic Relationships	North American Distribution	Ecological References[*]
Melanderia(2)	Beach zone—marine (rocky shore line)	Clingers	Predators (engulfers)	West Coast	2176, 2747
Pelastoneurus(1)	Lotic—seeps	Burrowers (in mud)	Predators (engulfers)	West	451
Sympycnus(32)				Widespread	2501
Systenus(4)	Lentic—tree holes	Sprawlers—burrowers	Predators (engulfers) (especially *Dasyhelea*)	East and South	2739, 2747
Tachytrechus(24)	Beach zone—lakes, lotic margins	Sprawlers—burrowers	Predators (engulfers)	Widespread	2501, 2747
Telmaturgus(1)	Lotic—depositional			East	2501
Teuchophorus(4)				Widespread	2501
Thinophilus(21)	Beach zone—lakes	Sprawlers—burrowers	Predators (engulfers)	Widespread	2258
pididae(244) (dance flies)	Generally lotic—erosional and depositional (detritus), lentic—littoral	Generally sprawlers—burrowers	Generally predators (engulfers), some collectors—gatherers		1217, 1240, 1316, 1334, 1335, 1886, 2340, 2747
Boreodromia(1)	?			West	
Ceratempis(1)	?			West	
Chelifera(12)	Lotic—depositional	Sprawlers—burrowers		Widespread	250, 2747
Chelipoda(6)	?			Widespread	
Clinocera(19)	Lotic—erosional	Clingers		Widespread	250, 1818, 2500, 2747
Dolichocephala(2)	Lotic—erosional	Clingers		Widespread	2499
Heleodromia(1)				New Mexico	
Hemerodromia(15)	Lotic—erosional and depositional (detritus)	Sprawlers—burrowers	Predators (engulfers) collectors—gatherers	Widespread	177, 419, 421, 973, 1240, 1334, 2500, 2747†
Metachela(2)				Widespread	
Neoplasta(2)				Widespread	
Niphogenia(2)				West	
Oreothalia(5)				Widespread	
Phyllodromia(1)				East	
Proclinopyga(5)				Widespread	
Rhamphomyia(146)	Lentic—littoral			Widespread	2501
Roederiodes(5)	Lotic—erosional	Clingers		Widespread	177, 394, 1774, 2747
Stilpon(6)	Lotic—erosional	Clingers	Predators (engulfers)	East	2501
Thanategia(3)				Widespread	
Wiedemannia(9)	Lotic—erosional	Clingers	Predators (engulfers)	East	2501
achycera-Cyclorrhapha					
Syrphidae(125) (flower flies, rattail maggots)					998, 1217, 1240, 1316, 1886, 2071, 2747
Chrysogaster(15)	Lentic—littoral (pond margins and vascular hydrophytes)	Burrowers	Collectors—gatherers	Widespread	998, 1240, 1417, 2747
Eristalis(38)	Lentic—littoral (sediments and detritus), lotic—depositional	Burrowers (especially low O_2 organic substrates)	Collectors—gatherers	Widespread	914, 1240, 1648, 2708, 2747
Helophilus(33)	Lentic—littoral (detritus and organic sediments)	Burrowers	Collectors—gatherers	Widespread	177, 998, 1240, 2747
Mallota(10)	Lentic—tree holes		Collectors—gatherers	Widespread	177, 998, 1240, 2747
Myolepta(7)	Lentic—tree holes		Collectors—gatherers	Widespread	177, 914, 998, 2747

nphasis on trophic relationships.
npublished data, K. W. Cummins, Kellogg Biological Station.

Table 21B—*Continued*

Taxa (number of species in parentheses)	Habitat	Habit	Trophic Relationships	North American Distribution	Ecological References[*]
Neoascia(10)	Lentic—littoral (margins, marshes)		Predators—engulfers	Widespread	177, 1482
Sericomyia(12)	Lentic—littoral (bog mat pools)		Collectors—gatherers	Widespread	177, 914, 998, 2747
Phoridae(5)					
Dohrniphora(5)		Burrowers	Predators (engulfers) on Psychodidae (1 sp.)	Widespread	1315
Ephydridae(404) (shore and brine flies)	Generally lentic—littoral (margins and vascular hydrophytes)	Generally burrowers, sprawlers	Generally collectors—gatherers, shredders—herbivores (miners), scrapers, predators (engulfers)		158, 552, 1023, 1217, 1240, 1316, 1886, 217▮ 2173, 2235, 2707, 274▮ 767, 556, 2422
Psilopinae(94)	Generally lentic—littoral; marine shores, lotic—margins	Generally burrowers (some climbers, planktonic)	Generally collectors—gatherers, some shredders— herbivores, predators (piercers)		1217, 1240, 1316, 188▮ 2173, 2235, 2747, 213▮
Allotrichoma(7)	Lentic—temporary puddles (near dung), lotic—margins	Burrowers (in dung, temporary puddles and decaying snails)	Collectors—gatherers (dung and decaying snails)	Widespread	219, 552, 2173, 2747, 2130
Athyroglossa(7)	Lentic—littoral			Widespread	2176
Atissa(2)	Beach zone—marine, lentic—littoral (saline lakes and pools)			Widespread	2173, 2235
Ceropsilopa(7)	Beach zone—marine			West and South Coasts	
Clanoneurum(1)	Marine—vascular hydrophytes, emergent zone (mangrove)	Burrowers—miners	Shredders—herbivores (miners)	West and East Coasts	2235, 2747
Cressonomyia(4)	Marine—shores			East and South Coasts	
Diclasiopa(1)	Lentic—littoral, lotic—depositional			Widespread	2173
Diphuia(1)	Marine—shores			East Coast	2235
Discocerina(7)	Lentic and lotic (margins—primarily terrestrial)	Burrowers (in moss and algae)	Collectors—gatherers	Widespread	554, 771, 2173, 2747
Discomyza(2)	Lentic—littoral and margins	Burrowers	Parasites of Molluska and scavengers of carrion	West and South Coasts	177, 2235, 2747
Ditrichophora(15)	Lentic—littoral			Widespread	2173
Glenanthe(2)	Marine—salt marshes			East and West Coasts	2235
Hecamede(1)	Beach zone—marine (semiaquatic)	Burrowers	Probably collectors—gatherers (scavengers)	East Coast	2235, 2747
Hecamedoides(1)				Widespread	
Helaeomyia(2) (petroleum flies)	Lentic—pools of crude petroleum and waste oil	Sprawlers—burrowers, or large "planktonic" masses of larvae	Collectors—gatherers (organics associated with petroleum)	California, Gulf area of United States	2747
Hydrochasma(4)	Lentic—litoral, lotic—margins, marine—shores			Widespread	2235
Leptopsilopa(4)	Lentic—littoral	Burrowers—in decaying vegetation	Collectors—gatherers	Widespread	2173, 2330
Mosillus(3)	Marine—shores, lentic—littoral (alkaline lakes and ponds)			Widespread	2172, 2235
Paratissa(1)	Marine—shores			East and West Coasts	2173
Pelignellus(1)	Marine—shores			California	2235
Platygymnopa(1)	Lotic and lentic—margins	Burrowers (in decomposing snails)	Collectors—gatherers (decomposing snails)	Northern United States	2743

[*]Emphasis on trophic relationships.

Table 21B—Continued

Taxa (number of species in parentheses)	Habitat	Habit	Trophic Relationships	North American Distribution	Ecological References[*]
Polytrichophora(4)	Lentic—littoral, marine—salt marshes			Widespread	2235
Pseudohecamede(3)	Marine—shores, lentic—littoral	Burrowers	Collectors—gatherers (some in dung)	East and West Coasts (occasionally inland)	552, 2130, 2173, 2235
Psilopa(6)	Lentic—pools of crude petroleum, lentic—littoral	"Planktonic", burrowers	Collectors—gatherers, shredders—herbivores (miners)	Widespread	177, 1240, 2747
Ptilomyia(6)	Marine—shores, lentic—littoral			Widespread	2173, 2235
Rhysophora(1)				Eastern and southern United States	134, 2176
Trimerina(1)	Lentic—vascular hydrophytes (emergent zone)	Climbers	Predators (piercers) (spider egg masses)	North, West	
Trimerinoides(1)				West	
Notiphilinae(117)	Generally lentic—littoral (vascular hydrophytes), lotic—depositional, marine—shores	Generally burrowers, sprawlers	Generally collectors—gatherers		1240, 2235, 2747
Dichaeta(2)	Lentic—littoral (detritus at margins)	Burrowers	Collectors—filterers	West, Midwest	177, 617, 2173
Hydrellia(57)	Lentic—vascular hydrophytes, lotic—erosional and depositional (vascular hydrophytes—watercress), marine—shores	Burrowers—miners (especially *Potamogeton*)	Shredders—herbivores (miners)	Widespread	161, 553, 923, 1240, 1612, 1886, 2235, 2707, 2747
Ilythea(3)	Lotic—depositional (sediments)	Sprawlers	Collectors—gatherers	West, South	2173
Lemnaphila(1)	Lentic—vascular hydrophytes (floating zone—dickweeds)	Burrowers—miners (of duckweeds)	Shredders—herbivores (miners of duckweeds)	East	1886, 2195, 2747
Nostima(8)				Widespread	
Notiphila(29)	Lentic—vascular hydrophytes (including bogs), lotic—depositional (vascular hydrophytes)	Burrowers (attached to roots by respiratory spine)	Collectors—gatherers	Widespread	161, 177, 311, 558, 1023, 1119, 1575, 1612, 2235, 2513, 2747
Oedenops(1)	Marine—shores			West and South Coasts	2235
Paralimna(5)	Lentic—littoral (margins in sediments near dung)	Sprawlers	Collectors—gatherers	Widespread	2173, 2747
Philygria(4)	Lentic—vascular hydrophytes	Sprawlers	Shredders—detritivores (decay areas of vascular plants)	Widespread	2173, 2637
Typopsilopa(2)	Lentic—littoral (detritus at margins in emergent vascular hydrophyte beds)	Sprawlers	Collectors—gatherers	Widespread	2173
Zeros(5)	Lotic—depositional (sediments)	Sprawlers	Collectors—gatherers	East, South	2173
Parydrinae(73)	Generally lentic—littoral, lotic—margins, marine—shores	Generally burrowers, sprawlers	Generally collectors—gatherers, predators (engulfers)		1240, 2235, 2747
Asmeringa(1)	Marine—shores			California	2235
Axysta(3)	Lentic—littoral	Sprawlers	Scrapers (graze blue-green algae)	North, East	766, 2173

[*]Emphasis on trophic relationships.

Table 21B— *Continued*

Taxa (number of species in parentheses)	Habitat	Habit	Trophic Relationships	North American Distribution	Ecological References[*]
Brachydeutera(3)	Lentic—littoral	Sprawlers—burrowers (swimmers?)	Collectors—gatherers	Widespread	1240, 2235, 2707, 2742 2747
Gastrops(2)	Lentic—vascular hydrophytes	Burrowers	Predators (engulfers) (frog eggs)	East, South	221
Hyadina(9)	Lotic and lentic—margins	Sprawlers	Scrapers (graze blue-green algae)	Widespread	766, 2173
Lipochaeta(1)	Beaches—marine; beaches—lakes (saline)			East and West Coasts	2172, 2235
Lytogaster(7)	Lotic and lentic—margins	Sprawlers	Scrapers (graze blue-green algae)	Widespread	766, 768, 2173
Ochthera(8)	Lentic—littoral, lotic—depositional and margins	Burrowers	Predators (engulfers) (midge larvae)	Widespread	554, 2234, 2235, 2747
Parydra(34)	Lentic—littoral, lotic	Burrowers	Scrapers	Widespread	554, 559, 2173, 2235
Pelina(5)	Lotic and lentic—margins		Scrapers (graze blue-green algae)	West, Midwest	766, 769, 2173
Ephydrinae(83)	Generally lentic—littoral, lotic—depositional (thermal springs), marine—shores and salt marshes	Generally sprawlers—burrowers or climbers	Generally shredders—herbivores, collectors—gatherers, scrapers		1240, 2173, 2235, 2747
Cirrula(2)	Marine—salt marshes	Burrowers (in floating algal mats)	Shredders—herbivores (macroalgae)	Northeast coast	1578, 2235
Coenia(1)	Marine—salt marshes	Sprawlers, burrowers	Collectors—gatherers	East and West Coasts	1573, 2173, 2235
Dimecoenia(2)	Marine—salt marshes	Burrowers (in floating algal mats)	Shredders—herbivores (macroalgae)	East and West Coasts	1578, 2235
Hydropyrus(16) (=*Ephydra*)	Lentic—littoral (in algal mats, including highly alkaline lakes), lotic—depositional (in algal mats, including thermal springs)	Sprawlers—burrowers	Shredders—herbivores (macroalgae), collectors—gatherers	Widespread	7, 182, 263, 264, 430, 1240, 1924, 2173, 2235, 2744, 2747
Lamproscatella(11)	Marine—shores and salt marshes, lentic—alkaline ponds			Widespread	1576, 2173, 2235
Limnellia(10)				Widespread	1574
Neoscatella(3)	Marine—shores and salt marshes; lentic—alkaline ponds	Sprawlers—climbers	Collectors—gatherers	Widespread	2235, 2707, 2742
Paracoenia(5)	Lotic—alkaline thermal springs (in algal mats)	Sprawlers	Scrapers (graze blue-green algae), collectors—gatherers of fecal material	Widespread	263, 1903
Philotelma(1)	Lotic—depositional			West	
Setacera(6)	Lentic—littoral	Sprawlers		Widespread	766, 770, 1240, 2173, 2747
Scatella(12)	Lentic—vascular hydrophytes and algal mats (including thermal springs)	Sprawlers—climbers	Collectors—gatherers, scrapers (graze algae)	Widespread	432, 554, 766, 1578, 2235, 2483, 2742, 2807
Scatophila(22)	Lentic—littoral, marine—salt marshes	Sprawlers	Scrapers	Widespread	555, 2235, 2747
Thiomyia(1)	Lotic—sulfur spring seeps			West	2740

[*]Emphasis on trophic relationships.

Table 21B—*Continued*

Taxa (number of species in parentheses)	Habitat	Habit	Trophic Relationships	North American Distribution	Ecological References*
anaceidae(5) (beach flies)	Generally beaches— marine intertidal	Generally burrowers	Generally scrapers		1081, 2707, 2737, 2747
Canace(2)	Beach zone—marine intertidal	Burrowers		East and West Coasts of United States	1081, 2418
Canaceoides(1)	Beach zone—marine intertidal	Burrowers		California coast	1081, 2707
Nocticanace(2)	Beach zone—marine intertidal	Burrowers	Scrapers (graze algae)	West and South Coasts	1081, 2076, 2077
ryomyzidae(1)					
Oedoparena(1)	Beach zone—marine intertidal	Burrowers—inside barnacles	Predators (engulfers) (barnacles)	West Coast	301, 1329, 2176
ciomyzidae(162) (marsh flies) (=Tetanoceridae =Tetanoceratidae)	Generally lentic—littoral, lotic—depositional in snails	Generally burrowers, inside snails	Generally predators (engulfers) or "parasites" of snails		
Antichaeta(8)	Lentic—littoral (marshes and temporary ponds) in snail eggs and snails	Burrowers—in snail egg masses	Predators (engulfers) or "parasites" of snail eggs and snails	North, West	162, 163, 164, 165, 166, 730, 1217, 1240, 1316
Atrichomelina(1)	Lentic—littoral, in snails	Burrowers, inside snails	Predators (engulfers) or "parasites" of snails, some scavengers on decaying snails	Widespread	772, 1330, 1332
Colobaea(1)	Lentic—littoral			Eastern United States	
Dictya(24)	Lentic—vascular hydrophytes (emergent zone), in snails	Burrowers—inside snails	Predators (engulfers) or "parasites" of snails	Widespread	166, 2502
Elgiva(2)	Lentic—vascular hydrophytes (emergent zone), lotic—margins, in snails	Burrowers—inside snails	Predators (engulfers) or "parasites" of snails	North	162, 1333, 2747
Hedria(1)	Lentic—vascular hydrophytes (emergent zone), lotic—margins, in snails	Burrowers—inside snails	Predators (engulfers) or "parasites" of snails	North	162, 163, 764
Hoplodictya(5)	Lentic—littoral, marine—salt marshes, in snails	Burrowers—inside snails	Predators (engulfers) or "parasites" of snails; 1 sp. in *Littorina*	Widespread	1787
Limnia(17)	Lentic—vascular hydrophytes (emergent zone)			Widespread	2339
Pherbecta(1)	Lentic—littoral (bogs)			North	1331
Pherbellia(30)	Lentic—littoral (margins), marine—mud flats in snails	Burrowers—inside snails	Predators (engulfers) or "parasites" of snails	Widespread	239, 763
Poecilographa(1)	Lentic—littoral (bogs)—semiaquatic			Midwest, East	1240, 2747
Pteromicra(13)		Burrowers—inside snails	Predators (engulfers) or "parasites" of snails	Widespread	1240, 2128, 2747
Renocera(7)	Lentic—littoral (marshes and temporary ponds) in fingernail clams	Burrowers—inside fingernail clams	Predators (engulfers) or "parasites" in fingernail clams (Sphaeriidae)	North	162, 765
Sepedomerus(1)	Lentic—vascular hydrophytes (emergent zone) in snails	Burrowers—inside snails	Predators (engulfers) or "parasites" of snails	Southwest	163

Emphasis on trophic relationships.

Table 21B— *Continued*

Taxa (number of species in parentheses)	Habitat	Habit	Trophic Relationships	North American Distribution	Ecological References[*]
Sepedon(18)	Lentic—littoral (including temporary ponds)	Burrowers—inside snails	Predators (engulfers) or "parasites" of snails	Widespread	162, 1788
Tetanocera(29)	Lentic—vascular hydrophytes (emergent zone) in snails	Burrowers—inside snails	Predators (engulfers) or "parasites" of snails (and slugs)	Widespread	162, 163, 1240, 2127, 2472, 2747
Scathophagidae(80) (dung flies) (=Scatophagidae =Scopeumatidae =Cordiluridae =Anthomyiidae, in part)	Generally lentic—vascular hydrophytes	Generally burrowers—miners (in plant stems), sprawlers	Generally shredders—herbivores (miners); predators (engulfers)		1217, 1240, 1316, 188 2522, 2747
Scathophaginae	Generally lentic—vascular hydrophytes, lotic—depositional	Generally burrowers—plant miners	Shredders—herbivores (plant miners), scrapers		1240, 2747
Acanthocnema(3)	Lotic—depositional			East	
Cordilura(42)	Lentic—vascular hydrophytes (emergent zone)	Burrowers—miners (plant stems)	Shredders—herbivores (miners in stems of *Scirpus, Juncus* and *Carex*), predators (engulfers) (ceratopogonidae)		808, 809, 1240, 178 2522, 2549, 2747, 282
Hydromyza(1)	Lentic—vascular hydrophytes (submerged and floating zones)	Burrowers—miners (plant stems and roots)	Shredders—herbivores (miners in petioles of *Nuphar*, roots of *Potamogeton*)	Northeast	161, 1612, 1769, 18 2606, 2609
Orthacheta(4)	Lentic—vascular hydrophytes (emergent zone)	Burrowers—miners (plant stems)	Predators (engulfers)	Widespread	1790
Spaziphora(1)	Lentic—littoral (sewage beds in oxidation ponds)	Sprawlers	Scrapers, collectors—gatherers	Widespread	1263
Muscidae(196) (=Anthomyiidae in part, by some authors)	Generally lentic—littoral, lotic—depositional, erosional	General sprawlers	Generally predators (piercers)		1217, 1240, 1316, 188 2747
Graphomyia(1)	Lentic—depositional (small enriched ponds)	Sprawlers	Predators (piercers)	Widespread	
Limnophora(6)	Lotic—erosional	Burrowers	Predators (piercers) on Oligochaeta, Simuliidae, Tipulidae	Widespread	912, 1026, 1240, 1544 2072, 2747
Lispe(23)	Lentic—littoral, lotic—depositional (margins)	Sprawlers	Predators (piercers)	Widespread	1014, 1026, 1240, 270 2747
Lispocephala(7)	Lotic—erosional(?)			Widespread	2707, 2747
Lispoides(1)	Lotic—erosional	Sprawlers?		Widespread	1014
Mydaeina(1)	Lentic—littoral			Northern Canada	2747
Phaonia(71)	Lentic—tree holes		Predators (piercers) on mosquito larvae	Widespread	1026, 2408, 2747
Spilogona(86)	Lotic—depositional			Widespread	1026
Sarcophagidae(4)	Semiaquatic	Burrowers—miners	Collectors—gatherers		
Fletcherimyia(4) (=*Blaesoxipha*, in part)		Burrowers—miners (bases of pitcher plants)	Collectors—gatherers (scavengers on trapped invertebrates)	South, Northeast	727, 728, 782

[*]Emphasis on trophic relationships.

Tipulidae

22

George W. Byers
University of Kansas, Lawrence

INTRODUCTION

The Tipulidae or crane flies, as far as is known, comprise the largest family of Diptera. A total of 1,458 species were recorded by Stone *et al.* (1965) in America north of Mexico, and about 14,000 species are already known in the world fauna. The diversity of form among the North American tipulids is indicated by their taxonomic distribution among 3 subfamilies (Tipulinae, Cylindrotominae, Limoniinae), 5 tribes (Tipulini, Limoniini, Pediciini, Hexatomini, Eriopterini), and 64 genera.

Most crane flies are associated with moist environments, the adults usually being found in low, leafy vegetation along streams or around ponds in wooded areas. Larval tipulid abundance and distribution in woodland floodplains appear to be influenced by high soil moisture and organic content (Merritt and Lawson 1981). There are, however, several species inhabiting open fields, relatively dry rangelands, and even desert environments. The chief economic importance of the Tipulidae involves feeding by the larvae on roots of forage crops or seedling field crops. More significant, however, is the ecological importance of larvae in aquatic and semiaquatic habitats as detrital feeders and of both larval and adult tipulids as food for other invertebrates, birds, mammals, fishes, amphibians, and reptiles.

Tipulidae have successfully exploited nearly every kind of aquatic environment except the open oceans and large, deep freshwater lakes. Larvae of only a few genera, e.g., *Antocha* and *Hesperoconopa,* are truly aquatic in the sense of being apneustic (without spiracles) and able to extract oxygen from the water. Lotic waters ranging from slow, silt-laden rivers to clear, torrential mountain streams are habitats for a great number of species. Slowly flowing water, from seepages on rock cliffs, the splash zone around waterfalls, etc., commonly supports a growth of algae in which larvae of several crane fly species live. Lentic habitats include margins of ponds and lakes, freshwater and brackish marshes, and standing waters in tree-holes or axils of large leaves. A few littoral species inhabit the marine intertidal zone. To these may be added the vast numbers of species that are semiaquatic, spending their larval life in saturated plant debris, mud, or sand near the water's edge, or in wet to saturated bryophytes or sodden, partially submerged, decayed wood (table 22A).

The life cycle characteristically consists of a brief egg stage (a few days to two weeks), four larval stadia (of which the first three are relatively short as compared with the fourth), a pupal stage of 5–12 days, and an adult stage of a few days. The entire cycle may be as short as six weeks or as long as five years, depending on the species and environmental conditions, particularly temperature and moisture. The cycle of many species having aquatic larvae requires about a year; however, some species have two generations a year at temperate latitudes, with the first in May to early June and the second in August to early September. In the Arctic, some aquatic species may require four or five years to mature because of the rigorous climate (MacLean 1973). Pritchard and Hall (1971) and Pritchard (1976, 1980a) have conducted the most comprehensive study on the life cycle of a North American aquatic crane fly, *Tipula sacra* Alexander.

Only the larva can be described as aquatic, and many "aquatic" crane fly larvae depend on atmospheric oxygen and thus cannot venture far from the water surface. The extent of cutaneous respiration in aquatic tipulids has not been investigated in detail. Metapneustic larvae of several species are capable of remaining submerged for prolonged periods of time. Moreover, the large posterior spiracles of certain species are known to be closed (Pritchard and Stewart 1982; chap. 4). Elongate, membranous anal gills in some aquatic larvae, such as those of *Pseudolimnophila* sp. (fig. 22.28) or subgenus *Yamatotipula* of *Tipula* (fig. 22.4), are probably functional, but these structures are only weakly developed in some other aquatic tipulids. The pupae are also air-breathers (again with rare exceptions, such as *Antocha* spp.), and aquatic larvae leave the water to pupate in nearby soil, moss, or litter. Mating and oviposition are the primary activities of the adult flies, and when not engaged in this activity they usually rest by standing upon or suspending themselves from vegetation, rocks, or other objects in their habitat.

As indicated in table 22A, many aquatic tipulid larvae feed on organic detritus, such as decaying leaves, plant fragments, and associated microorganisms, that accumulates on pond bottoms or in backwaters of streams. Among the Limoniinae, larvae of *Hexatoma* sp., *Pedicia* sp., *Dicranota* sp., and *Limnophila* sp. are active predators. Larval diet has not been extensively studied, but Martin *et al.* (1980) recently examined the digestive mechanisms of *Tipula (Nippotipula) abdominalis* Say, a stream shredder.

Only about 10% of the North American tipulid species have been reared to the extent that larvae and pupae can definitely be associated with adults. Crane fly biology is a vast and only slightly explored field, much in need of interested students.

EXTERNAL MORPHOLOGY

Larvae

In most tipulid larvae, the body is elongate, generally subcylindrical, somewhat tapered toward the head, and less so posteriorly. The head is strongly sclerotized anteriorly, with well-developed mouthparts, and has rather sclerotized plates or rods extending backward into the thorax and separated by deep incisions (fig. 22.21). The skin is attached far forward, only a little behind the mouthparts and antennae, and the entire head can readily be withdrawn into the central thoracic region. There are three thoracic segments and eight evident abdominal segments. The spiracular disk is interpreted as the main part of the ninth abdominal segment, and the anal lobes or *anal gills* (figs. 22.4, 22.8) as the tenth segment. In the unmodified abdominal segments, a basal anterior ring and a wider (i.e., longer) posterior ring can usually be differentiated (fig. 22.2).

Larvae of Tipulidae have been given the common name "leather jackets," which applies most aptly to the larger, tough-skinned tipulines. Many of the limoniine larvae have thin, nearly transparent skin. Some aspects of the integument have been applied to the problem of identification in some species, notably the transverse, somewhat swollen zones on the basal rings of certain abdominal segments, termed *creeping welts* (fig. 22.2). These usually bear dense hairs or small spicules, or denticles, often arranged in rows or ridges.

Behind the eighth abdominal segment is a smooth posterodorsal surface bearing the two large spiracles of the dorsal tracheal trunks. This is the *spiracular disk,* which is surrounded by a variable number of *lobes* and is sclerotized to varying degrees according to the genus (figs. 22.4–22.5). This structure is a great aid in the recognition of larvae. In the Tipulinae, there are usually four subconical lobes above the spiracular disk and two blunt lobes below the disk (figs. 22.4, 22.8). Larval Limoniinae usually have only three lobes above the disk and two below (fig. 22.5), but these may be reduced in prominence, less often in number (figs. 22.16, 22.31).

Although mouthparts have been used extensively by other authors in differentiating tipulid larvae, this has been avoided where possible, because of the inconvenience of dissecting out these small parts. A mid-ventral structure, termed the *mentum,* fused *mental plates,* or *maxillary plates* by earlier authors, is usually densely sclerotized and visible without dissection. It appears to be derived from ventral extensions of the most posterior sclerotized part of the head bordering the occipital foramen (postocciput) and accordingly is called the *hypostomal bridge* (figs. 22.21–22.24). In the Hexatomini and Pediciini, the maxillae are conspicuously prolonged anteriorly (fig. 22.20).

Adults

Typically, adult crane flies possess an elongate, slender body, long and rather narrow wings, and very long, thin legs and tarsi. Tipulidae can be differentiated from other similar nematocerous flies by their V-shaped transverse mesonotal suture (fig. 21.7) and by the absence of ocelli.

Since classification at the generic level is based almost wholly on wing venation, an understanding of the nomenclature of veins and cells is necessary in order to use the accompanying key to adults. The venational nomenclature adopted here conforms to that in the *Manual of Nearctic Diptera* (McAlpine *et al.* 1981), which differs in the interpretation of the branching of the media (M) and cubitus (Cu) from virtually all earlier references on Tipulidae (e.g., the works of C. P. Alexander). In Diptera, M is thought to have only three branches; the apparent fourth is regarded as the first branch of the anterior cubitus (CuA_1). The apparent m–cu crossvein becomes the transverse basal section of the CuA_1 (labelled *bscu*). Vein M_3, the posterior branch of M, joins CuA_1 for a short distance, in most species forming the posterior border of the discal cell (cell 1st M_2, labelled *d*). Veins and cells according to this system are shown in figures 22.36 and 22.37.

Detailed structure of the male hypopygium (generally the ninth abdominal segment) is employed extensively in the differentiation of tipulid species and occasionally genera. Shapes of the ninth tergum and sternum, and also the eighth sternum, are of great taxonomic utility. The paired *basistyles* of the ninth segment, apparently of pleural origin, bear at their apices the genital claspers, or *dististyles,* which vary greatly in shape according to genus and species. There may be a single dististyle on each basistyle, or two of quite different structure (figs. 22.64—22.65).

KEY TO THE GENERA OF TIPULIDAE

In offering the keys that follow, I acknowledge a great debt to Prof. Charles P. Alexander. His extensive studies of the world's Tipulidae, spanning nearly 70 years, provide much of the basis for the present keys. I have tried to make the keys conform to his concepts of genera.

Larvae

1.   Both dorsal and lateral longitudinal rows of conspicuous, usually elongate, fleshy projections on thoracic and abdominal segments (figs. 22.3, 21.2) 2

1'.   Thoracic and abdominal segments without dorsal longitudinal rows of conspicuous projections (figs. 22.1–22.2); lateral abdominal projections, if present, blunt, shorter than their basal diameter 3

2(1).   Dorsal projections mostly long, slender; those of thoracic segments simple, posterior ones on most abdominal segments either deeply bifurcate (forked) or, if simple, approximately 10 times as long as basal diameter (fig. 22.3); in aquatic or semiaquatic mosses .... *Phalacrocera* see also p. 451

2'.   Dorsal projections shorter, length 1–3 times basal diameter (fig. 21.2); posterior pair of dorsal projections on abdominal segments 1–7 with 3 or 4 serrations, not deeply divided; body color brownish; in semiaquatic mosses .... ***Triogma***

3(1'). Spiracular disk bordered by 6 (rarely 8) usually subconical lobes, ordinarily 2 dorsal, 2 dorsolateral, 2 below spiracles; lobes sometimes short and blunt (figs. 22.4, 21.6) .... (subfamily Tipulinae) 4

3'.   Spiracular disk bordered by 5 (rarely 7) or fewer lobes, often 1 dorsomedial, 2 lateral, 2 below spiracles; lobes of variable shape (fig. 22.5); or spiracles absent .... (subfamily Limoniinae) 9

4(3).   Anal gills pinnately branched (similar branches on each side of axis) (fig. 22.6); dorsal lobes of spiracular disk short, bluntly rounded, lower lobes more than twice as long as their basal diameter; aquatic or semiaquatic in small streams, eastern North America .... ***Leptotarsus*** (=***Longurio***)

4'.   Anal gills not pinnately branched; lobes of spiracular disk variable 5

5(4'). All lobes of spiracular disk elongate; lateral and ventral lobes 3–4 times as long as their basal width; lobes bordered by numerous long hairs, outer hairs 2–3 times as long as width of lobe at point of attachment of hair (figs. 22.7, 22.10) 6

5'.   Lobes of spiracular disk not all elongate, longest ones rarely more than twice their basal width; bordering hairs usually sparse, if numerous not long (figs. 22.8–22.9, 21.6) 7

6(5).   Two pairs of elongate, retractile anal gills; lobes of spiracular disk darkened along margins, pale medially (fig. 22.7); larvae in open-ended tubes of floating vegetation .... ***Megistocera***

6'.   Three pairs of elongate anal gills (as in figs. 22.4, 21.1); lobes of spiracular disk darkened along margins but each with a thin, submedian dark line (fig. 22.10); larvae not in tubes of vegetation (included here are larvae of species of subgenus *Angarotipula* of *Tipula,* formerly assigned on basis of adult structures to *Prionocera*) .... ***Prionocera***

7(5'). Abdominal segments and posterior ring of metathorax covered with dense pilosity (fine, long hairs) giving larva a woolly appearance; thoracic segments otherwise with only short pubescence (microsetae), nearly bare by contrast; spiracular disk relatively small, only about half as wide as 8th segment; dorsal lobes of spiracular disk low, inconspicuous, with darkened posterior faces continued ventrad as wedge-shaped spots with apices between spiracles (fig. 22.11); lateral lobes only about as long as diameter of spiracle, with bluntly rounded apex; ventral lobes darkened on discal face, narrowed near mid length, expanded apically (fig. 22.11); larvae in dark, thin organic mud along small streams, in seepage areas, etc. .... ***Brachypremna***

7'.   Pilosity not dense on abdomen and contrastingly absent on thorax; spiracular disk not relatively small; ventral lobes of disk not constricted near midlength (figs. 22.8–22.9, 21.6) 8

8(7'). Spiracles large, separated by less than diameter of a spiracle; lobes of disk less than twice as long as basal width, fringed with long, dark hairs; a thin, black median line on discal face of each lobe (fig. 22.8); larvae attaining more than 50 mm length in 4th instar; in organic debris and mud at edges of ponds or small streams .... ***Holorusia***

8'.   Spiracles generally separated by more than diameter of a spiracle (figs. 22.9, 21.6); lobes of disk highly variable, from short and rounded to elongate and subconical, ventral pair rarely divided (figs. 22.1, 22.9, 21.6); large genus with larvae in a variety of aquatic and terrestrial habitats .... ***Tipula***

9(3'). Spiracles absent, tracheal system closed; dorsal and lateral lobes of 9th abdominal segment absent or extremely reduced (fig. 22.2) 10

9'.   Spiracles present, usually conspicuous (may be concealed if lobes of disk are infolded); dorsal and lateral lobes usually present, but absent in some species (fig. 22.12) 11

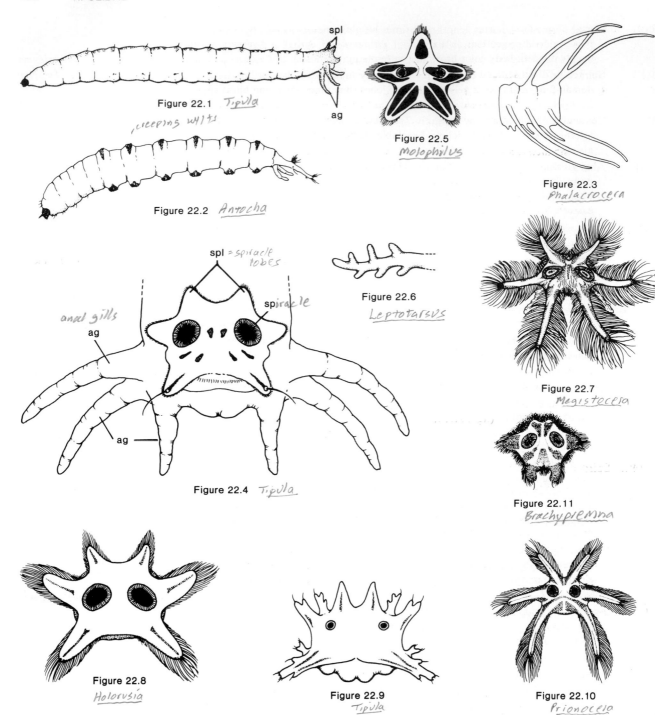

Figure 22.1 *Tipula*

(creeping welts)

Figure 22.2 *Antocha*

Figure 22.5 *Molophilus*

Figure 22.3 *Phalacrocera*

spl = spiracle lobes

anal gills

ag

spiracle

ag

Figure 22.4 *Tipula*

Figure 22.6 *Leptotarsus*

Figure 22.7 *Megistocera*

Figure 22.11 *Brachypremna*

Figure 22.8 *Holorusia*

Figure 22.9 *Tipula*

Figure 22.10 *Prionocera*

Figure 22.1. Lateral view of larva of *Tipula (Yamatotipula) furca* Walker. *ag*, anal gills; *spl*, spiracular lobes.

Figure 22.2. Lateral view of larva of *Antocha* sp.

Figure 22.3. A typical abdominal segment of *Phalacrocera* sp. (anterior at left).

Figure 22.4. Posterior end of larva of *Tipula (Yamatotipula) furca* Walker. *ag*, anal gill; *sp*, spiracle; *spl*, spiracular lobes.

Figure 22.5. Spiracular disk of *Molophilus hirtipennis* (O.S.).

Figure 22.6. Anal gill of larva of *Leptotarsus* sp.

Figure 22.7. Spiracular disk of *Megistocera longipennis* (Macquart) (after Rogers 1949).

Figure 22.8. Spiracular disk of *Holorusia rubiginosa* Loew.

Figure 22.9. Spiracular disk of *Tipula (Nippotipula) abdominalis* (Say).

Figure 22.10. Spiracular disk of *Prionocera* sp.

Figure 22.11. Spiracular disk of *Brachypremna dispellens* (Walker).

10(9).   Ventral lobes of 9th abdominal segment elongate, deeply separated, slightly divergent, with a few tufts of hairs; anal gills elongate; dorsal and ventral creeping welts conspicuous on abdominal segments 2–7 (fig. 22.2); larvae in silken tubes on stones in swift, well-oxygenated water .... ***Antocha***

10′.   Eighth and 9th abdominal segments covered with dense, long pilosity; 9th segment elongate, tapering, shallowly bifurcate (divided) at apex; anal gills short, not extending beneath 9th segment; no conspicuous creeping welts; larvae in sandy bottoms of cold, clear, rapid streams chiefly of Pacific drainage .... ***Hesperoconopa***

11(9′).   Dorsal and lateral lobes of spiracular disk absent or extremely reduced, ventral lobes elongate (fig. 22.12) (larvae of *Ornithodes* and *Nasiternella,* at present unknown, may key out here) 12

11′.   Median dorsal and/or lateral lobes of disk well developed if ventral lobes are elongate; ventral lobes usually short, less often absent (fig. 22.13) 14

12(11).   Paired prolegs (pseudopods) with sclerotized apical crochets (curved hooks) on venter of abdominal segments 3–7 (fig. 22.14); larvae in wet to saturated soil along streams .... most ***Dicranota***

12′.   Abdomen without prolegs; roughened creeping welts or broad tubercles on basal annulus of segments 4–7 (figs. 22.15, 21.3) 13

13(12′).   Creeping welts on both dorsum and venter, bearing microscopic spicules .... (subgenus *Raphidolabina*) .... ***Dicranota***

13′.   Creeping welts or broad tubercles on venter only, without spicules but with microscopic roughened surface (figs. 22.15, 21.3); larvae in wet soil of swampy woods, springs, and seepage areas .... ***Pedicia***

14(11′).   Spiracular disk surrounded by 7 lobes, 1 dorsomedian and 1 each dorsolateral, lateral, and ventral on each side; spiracles small, widely separated, at bases of lateral lobes of disk (fig. 22.13); larvae in organic silt in small streams of Pacific drainage .... ***Gonomyodes***

14′.   Spiracular disk with 5 or fewer peripheral lobes, or without distinct lobes 15

15(14′).   Spiracular disk with 4 or 5 peripheral lobes (figs. 22.16–22.17) 16

15′.   Spiracular disk with only 3 lobes, or without distinct lobes (fig. 22.18) 43

16(15).   Internal portion of head extensively sclerotized dorsally and laterally, with shallow posterior incisions (can be determined by cutting prothoracic skin at one side, or often can be seen through skin) (fig. 22.19) 17

16′.   Internal portion of head divided by deep posterior incisions into elongate, slender, rodlike to spatulate sclerites, or if sclerites are platelike, they are darkly sclerotized only along margins, giving appearance of separate rods (figs. 22.20–22.21) 37

17(16).   Hypostomal bridge (mentum or maxillary plates according to some authors) interrupted medially by membranous area (figs. 22.21–22.22) (hypostomal plates in contact though not fused in *Pseudolimnophila* (fig. 22.23)); abdominal segments without creeping welts 18

17′.   Hypostomal bridge complete, although may be deeply incised posteriorly (fig. 22.24); creeping welts present on basal ring of abdominal segments, or abdominal segments with transverse bands or patches of dense pilosity on both basal and apical rings 31

18(17).   Spiracular disk surrounded by 5 lobes in form of blackened, spatulate plates with finely toothed margins; larvae in marshy soil .... (subgenus *Scleroprocta*) .... ***Ormosia***

18′.   Spiracular disk surrounded by 4 or 5 lobes of rounded or subconical form (figs. 22.25–22.26) 19

19(18′).   Plane of spiracular disk roughly perpendicular to long axis of body (fig. 22.25); disk surrounded by 5 lobes (fig. 22.26) 20

19′.   Plane of spiracular disk diagonal to long axis of body (fig. 22.27); disk surrounded by 4 peripheral lobes (figs. 22.34, 21.4) 29

20(19).   Hypostomal prolongations expanded into sclerotized plates with anterior margins toothed (fig. 22.22) 21

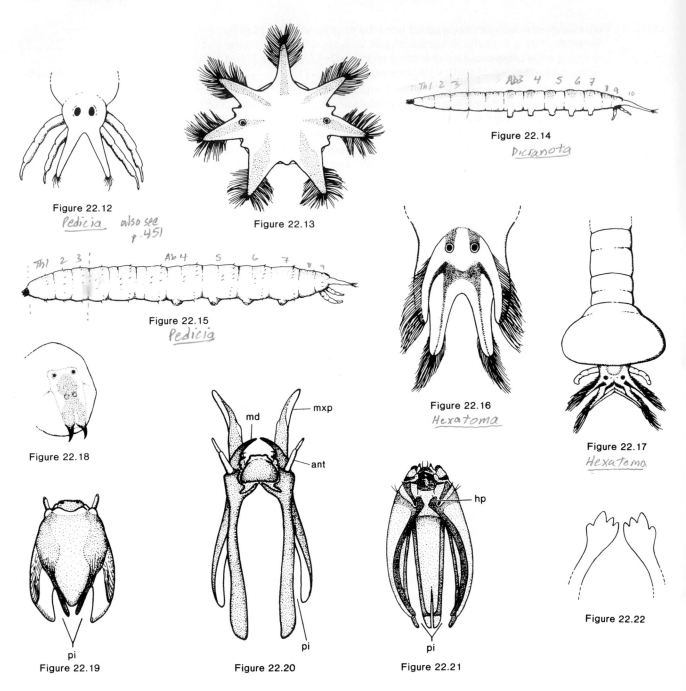

Figure 22.12

Pedicia also see p. 451

Figure 22.13

Figure 22.14
Dicranota

Figure 22.15
Pedicia

Figure 22.16
Hexatoma

Figure 22.17
Hexatoma

Figure 22.18

md mxp
ant
pi

Figure 22.19

pi

Figure 22.20

pi

hp
pi

Figure 22.21

Figure 22.22

Figure 22.12. Dorsal view of posterior end of larval abdomen of *Pedicia (Tricyphona) inconstans* (O.S.).

Figure 22.13. Spiracular disk of *Gonomyodes tacoma* (Alex.) (after Hynes 1969).

Figure 22.14. Lateral view of larva of *Dicranota* sp.

Figure 22.15. Lateral view of larva of *Pedicia albivitta* Walker.

Figure 22.16. Spiracular disk of *Hexatoma (Hexatoma) megacera* (O.S.).

Figure 22.17. Posterior end of larval abdomen of *Hexatoma (Eriocera) spinosa* (O.S.), showing expanded seventh segment.

Figure 22.18. Posterolateral view of spiracular disk of *Rhabdomastix setigera* (Alex.) (after Hynes 1969).

Figure 22.19. Dorsal view of larval head capsule of *Limonia (Geranomyia) rostrata* (Say). *pi,* posterior incisions.

Figure 22.20. Dorsal view of larval head capsule of *Limnophila* sp. *ant,* antenna; *md,* mandible; *mxp,* maxillary palp; *pi,* posterior incision.

Figure 22.21. Ventral view of larval head capsule of *Ormosia* sp. *hp,* hypostomal plate (half of incomplete hypostomal bridge); *pi,* posterior incisions.

Figure 22.22. Ventral view of incomplete hypostomal bridge of *Molophilus* sp.

20′.   Hypostomal prolongations, if expanded, not sclerotized or not toothed anteriorly
        (fig. 22.21) 22

21(20). Hypostomal plates with 4 teeth (fig. 22.22); spiracular disk extensively blackened;
        black spots on dorsolateral and ventral lobes divided medially by pale line; spot
        on dorsal lobe nearly always undivided; larvae in wet, humic soil (larvae of
        Tasiocera, at present unknown, may key out here) .... *Molophilus*

21′.   Hypostomal plates with 5–8 teeth; spiracular disk small, without extensive
        blackened areas; larvae in organic mud .... some *Erioptera*

22(20′). Posterior faces of all 5 lobes of spiracular disk bearing solidly blackened spot (fig.
        22.29) 23

22′.   Spots on some or all lobes of spiracular disk divided medially by pale line or wider
        pale zone (fig. 22.26) 24

23(22). Blackened areas of dorsolateral lobes continued between spiracles; larvae in
        organic mud near water .... some *Ormosia*

23′.   No blackened areas between spiracles (fig. 22.29); larvae in muddy stream
        banks .... (subgenus *Trimicra*) .... *Erioptera*

24(22′). Median dorsal lobe of disk bearing densely sclerotized, hornlike projection with
        apex bent downward over disk (fig. 22.26); black, wedge-shaped spots at
        periphery of disk between ventral lobes, between ventral and lateral lobes, and
        between lateral lobes and median dorsal lobe (fig. 22.26); larve in fine sand, silt,
        and organic debris at margins of clear streams, Pacific and Arctic drainage .... *Arctoconopa*

24′.   Median dorsal lobe of disk without sclerotized, hornlike projection; no wedges of
        black pigmentation between lobes of disk 25

25(24′). Dorsolateral lobes with solidly blackened spots continuous around spiracles and
        extending to midline or nearly so; spots on ventral lobes divided; larvae in moist
        earth or sand, usually near water .... some *Gonomyia*

25′.   Dorsolateral lobes and ventral lobes with spots divided (fig. 22.30); if spots of
        dorsolateral lobes are more completely darkened, 4–6 small, dark spots on
        central disk 26

26(25′). Peripheral lobes of disk short, blunt; blackened areas of dorsolateral lobes
        continuous around spiracles, fading toward midline .... some *Gonomyia*

26′.   Peripheral lobes of disk nearly as long as their width at base, or longer; blackened
        areas of dorsolateral lobes not continuous around spiracles (fig. 22.30) 27

27(26′). Blackened area of median dorsal lobe not divided (fig. 22.30); larvae in organic
        mud .... some *Ormosia*

27′.   Blackened area of median dorsal lobe (and all others) divided medially by pale line 28

28(27′). Area between spiracles generally unpigmented, not blackened; larvae in organic
        mud .... some *Ormosia*

28′.   Two rounded spots between spiracles; spiracular disk small in proportion to body
        size; larvae in organic mud .... some *Erioptera*

29(19′). Ventral lobes of disk not darkly pigmented on upper surface, not fringed with long
        hairs; spiracles pale (fig. 22.27); hypostome reduced to small, longitudinal rod
        below maxilla on each side; larvae in sandy bottoms of clear, cold streams .... *Cryptolabis*

29′.   Ventral lobes of disk darkly pigmented on upper surface, fringed with long hairs
        (longer than the lobes) (figs. 22.28, 21.4); spiracles dark; hypostome in form of
        a toothed plate at each side (fig. 22.23) 30

30(29′). Hypostomal plates (mental plates or maxillary plates of other authors) each
        bearing 4 anterior teeth; larvae in organic mud in wet woodlands .... *Paradelphomyia*

30′.   Hypostomal plates each bearing 7 or 8 anterior teeth (fig. 22.23); larvae in thin
        organic mud in swampy woods, pond margins, marshy areas .... *Pseudolimnophila*

31(17′). Spiracular disk with 5 peripheral lobes 32

31′.   Spiracular disk with 4 peripheral lobes (if vestigial median dorsal lobe is present, it
        is unpigmented) (fig. 22.28) 33

32(31).   Abdominal segments 2–7 with both dorsal and ventral creeping welts on basal
          ring; lobes of spiracular disk wider than long, broadly rounded, unpigmented or
          with only limited darkened spots; large genus with larvae in numerous aquatic
          and terrestrial habitats .... some *Limonia*

32′.   Abdominal segments 2–7 with ventral creeping welts only; ventral lobes of
          spiracular disk longer than their width at base, darkened at margins with broad
          median pale zone on each; hypostomal bridge with 5 teeth; larvae brownish with
          long, appressed (closely applied to body) pubescence, occurring in marsh borders
          in decomposing aquatic vegetation, or in marshy areas in woods .... *Helius*

33(31′). Abdominal segments 2–7 without distinct creeping welts; all segments with
          transverse bands or patches of dense pilosity; lateral lobes of disk broadly
          pigmented from spiracles outward, broadly pigmented faces of ventral lobes
          narrowly connected across lower part of disk; larvae in thin mosses and algal
          mats on wet, rocky cliffs, rarely in soil .... *Dactylolabis*

33′.   Abdominal segments 2–7 with distinct creeping welts, without transverse bands of
          dense pilosity 34

34(33′). Ventral lobes of spiracular disk longer than their width at base, tapering to
          subacute apex, fringed with long hairs (figs. 22.28, 21.4) 35

34′.   Ventral lobes of disk shorter than their width at base, broadly rounded and without
          long marginal hairs (fig. 22.31) 36

35(34).   Body wide, flattened; ventral creeping welts without minute spines; spiracles
          dorsoventrally elongated; larvae semiaquatic in indistinct tunnels beneath algal
          mats on wet cliffs, beside waterfalls, etc. .... *Elliptera*

35′.   Body nearly terete (cylindrical), only slightly flattened; ventral creeping welts with
          numerous rows of minute spines; spiracles transversely elliptical; lobes of
          spiracular disk narrowly darkened at margins; larvae in sodden, decayed wood,
          at or just below water level .... *Lipsothrix*

36(34′). Nearly entire spiracular disk except spiracles and outer margins of lobes dark
          reddish brown; spiracles horizontally elongated; larvae in wet, extremely
          decayed, pulpy wood (subgenus *Diotrepha*) .... *Orimarga*

36′.   Spiracular disk with only isolated spots of dark pigmentation, generally pale;
          spiracles oval, inclined together dorsally (fig. 22.31); large genus in a variety of
          habitats .... some *Limonia*

37(16′). Maxillae not prolonged forward, inconspicuous in dorsal aspect; plane of spiracular
          disk roughly perpendicular to long axis of body (fig. 22.25) ....
          .... (tribe Eriopterini, in part) .... return to 20

37′.   Maxillae prolonged forward, each as a dorsoventrally flattened, tapering (less often
          subconical) blade, together appearing as divergently curved tusks with apices
          visible even when head is withdrawn into thoracic segments (fig. 22.20) 38

38(37′). Mandibles complex, jointed near midlength (fig. 22.32); maxillae and labrum-
          epipharynx densely fringed with long yellowish to golden hairs; dorsal plates of
          head fused into spatulate plate widest posteriorly; spiracular disk small, its
          upper lobes often infolded, concealing spiracles, marginal hairs protruding from
          cavity formed by infolding (fig. 22.33) 39

38′.   Mandibles not jointed near midlength; maxillae and labrum-epipharynx with
          mostly short pilosity; dorsal plates of head not fused, although each may be
          widest posteriorly 40

39(38).   Pigmentation of ventral lobes of spiracular disk discontinuous, either as transverse
          striations near base of lobe, more continuous coloration toward apex, or reduced
          to short darkened median line; all (4, lateral pair sometimes reduced) lobes
          fringed with long golden hairs (fig. 22.33); basal tooth or teeth of apical portion
          of mandible much less than half as long as main outer tooth (fig. 22.32); larvae
          in moist to wet humic soil or decomposing vegetation in swampy woodlands .... *Pilaria*

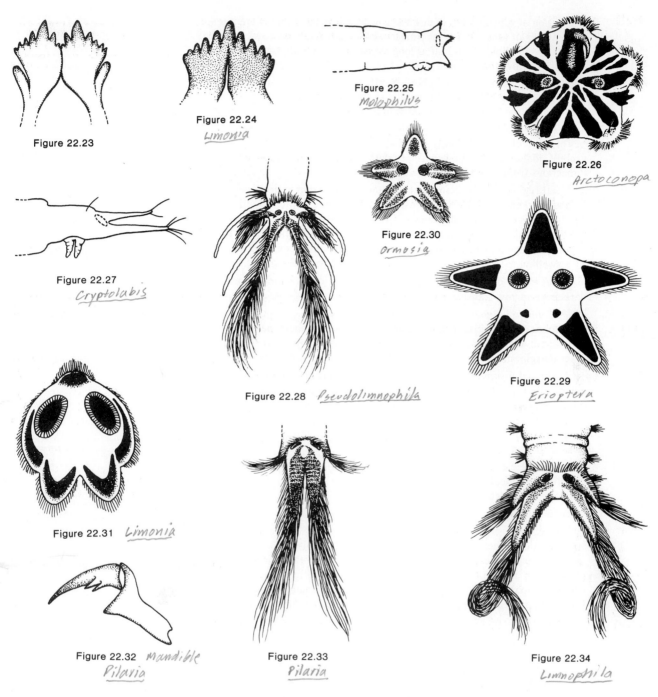

Figure 22.23

Figure 22.24
Limonia

Figure 22.25
Molophilus

Figure 22.26
Arctoconopa

Figure 22.27
Cryptolabis

Figure 22.30
Ormosia

Figure 22.28   *Pseudolimnophila*

Figure 22.29
Erioptera

Figure 22.31   *Limonia*

Figure 22.32   *Mandible*
Pilaria

Figure 22.33
Pilaria

Figure 22.34
Limnophila

Figure 22.23. Ventral view of hypostomal bridge of *Pseudolimnophila inornata* (O.S.).

Figure 22.24. Ventral view of hypostomal bridge of *Limonia* sp.

Figure 22.25. Lateral view of caudal end of larva of *Molophilus* sp. (position of spiracle indicated by dashed circle).

Figure 22.26. Spiracular disk of *Arctoconopa carbonipes* (Alex.).

Figure 22.27. Lateral view of caudal end of larva of *Cryptolabis* sp. (position of spiracle indicated by dashed circle).

Figure 22.28. Posterior end of larval abdomen of *Pseudolimnophila inornata* (O.S.).

Figure 22.29. Spiracular disk of *Erioptera (Trimicra) pilipes* (O.S.).

Figure 22.30. Spiracular disk of *Ormosia meigenii* (O.S.).

Figure 22.31. Spiracular disk of *Limonia (Dicranomyia) humidicola* (O.S.).

Figure 22.32. Mandible of *Pilaria* sp.

Figure 22.33. Spiracular disk of *Pilaria* sp.

Figure 22.34. Spiracular disk of *Limnophila macrocera* (Say) (after Alexander 1920).

39'.   Pigmentation of ventral lobes of disk more evenly distributed but more intense
             toward apex of lobe; all 4 lobes fringed with long hairs; basal tooth of apical
             portion of mandible about half as long as main outer tooth; larvae in organic
             mud in swampy woodlands .... *Ulomorpha*

40(38').   Spiracular disk surrounded by 5 short, bluntly rounded lobes; ventral lobes not
             fringed with long hairs; in some species a densely sclerotized, hornlike projection
             near apex of median dorsal lobe and lateral lobes; larvae in sandy bottoms and
             margins of clear streams .... some *Rhabdomastix*

40'.   Lobes of spiracular disk (usually 4) not all short and bluntly rounded, ventral ones
             usually elongate; ventral lobes fringed with long hairs; no sclerotized, hornlike
             projections from upper lobes (fig. 22.17) 41

41(40').   Midventral region of head before line of attachment of skin entirely membranous,
             without darkened transverse bar just beneath surface; larvae in sand or gravel
             near margins of clear, cool brooks and streams. (Note: In this genus especially,
             but also in some others in similar habitats, larvae may be found with the 7th
             abdominal segment much swollen, possibly as an aid in locomotion or anchorage.
             This swelling may persist in preserved specimens.) (fig. 22.17) .... *Hexatoma*

41'.   Midventral region of head before line of attachment of skin membranous, with
             darkened, narrow transverse bar (part of hypopharynx) visible just beneath
             surface 42

42(41').   Lateral lobes of spiracular disk unpigmented on posterior face; mandible with long
             outer tooth and two smaller teeth of similar size and shape near midlength of
             inner margin; maxillary projections subconical; larvae in wet organic debris .... *Polymera*

42'.   Lateral lobes of disk pigmented at least along one margin, usually much more
             extensively (figs. 22.34, 21.5); mandible without 2 small, similar teeth near
             midlength of inner margin (more or fewer dissimilar teeth); maxillary
             projections flattened; large genus with carnivorous, aquatic larvae found usually
             in organic mud in swampy woods, pond margins, etc., less often in bottom mud
             or sand of small streams .... *Limnophila*

43(15').   Spiracular disk broadly emarginate (indented) dorsally; larvae in a hardened,
             flattened, elliptical case, in marshy soil near small streams or springs, Pacific
             drainage (based on a European species) .... *Thaumastoptera*

43'.   Spiracular disk not broadly emarginate dorsally (figs. 22.18, 22.31); larvae not in a
             hardened case 44

44(43').   Internal portion of head divided by deep posterior incisions into elongate, slender,
             or spatulate sclerites (can be determined by cutting prothoracic skin at one side,
             or often can be seen through skin); spiracular disk lightly pigmented, vertically
             subrectangular, with 2 clawlike projections at ventral margin (fig. 22.18);
             spiracles minute, pale, separated by about 3 times the diameter of a spiracle
             (fig. 22.18); larvae yellowish, aquatic, in sandy bottoms and margins of clear
             streams .... some *Rhabdomastix*

44'.   Internal portion of head extensively sclerotized dorsally and laterally; sclerites
             platelike, with shallow posterior incisions (fig. 22.19); abdominal segments 2–7
             with both dorsal and ventral creeping welts (of differing structure in some
             species) on basal ring; spiracular disk roughly circular or broadly oval to
             transversely subrectangular; spiracles often large, oval, inclined together dorsally
             (fig. 22.31); large genus with larvae in a variety of aquatic and terrestrial
             habitats .... some *Limonia*

Adults*

1.   Terminal segment of maxillary palp elongate, longer than previous 2 segments
             combined (fig. 22.35); antennae usually 13-segmented (11 flagellomeres); rostral
             nasus usually present (fig. 22.35); vein CuA with slight deflection at bscu (fig.
             22.36) .... (subfamily Tipulinae) 2

*Adults of almost all genera of Tipulidae are likely to be found near standing or flowing water. Accordingly, the adult key identifies all
North American genera, and those whose larvae are aquatic are indicated (*).

1'.   Terminal segment of maxillary palp short, its length less than that of previous 2 segments combined; antennae usually of 14 or 16 segments (12 or 14 flagellomeres); rostral nasus absent; vein CuA not deflected at bscu (fig. 22.37) 10

2(1).   Tarsi filiform (threadlike), each tarsus longer than corresponding femur and tibia combined; legs long and slender 3

2'.   Length of tarsus not exceeding combined length of corresponding femur and tibia 5

3(2).   Antennae with only 8 segments, unusually short in both sexes (in Florida only) .... *Megistocera**

3'.   Antennae with 12 or 13 segments 4

4(3').   Wing vein R_{1+2} absent; Rs short, subequal to bscu, only slightly curved (fig. 22.38) .... *Dolichopeza*

4'.   Vein R_{1+2} present; Rs much longer than bscu, strongly curved near base (fig. 22.39) (in eastern United States) .... *Brachypremna**

5(2').   Flagellomeres 2–9 each bearing 3 or 4 pectinations (making antenna comblike) in male; antennae of female serrate (sawlike), 11-segmented (fig. 22.40) .... *Ctenophora*

5'.   Flagellomeres 2–9 not branched in male; antennae of female 13-segmented 6

6(5').   Vein R_3 deflected toward R_{4+5} near midlength, then forward toward costa, resulting in constriction of cell R_3 near its midlength (fig. 22.41) (in western states and British Columbia) .... *Holorusia**

6'.   Cell R_3 not strongly constricted by deflection of vein R_3 7

7(6').   Antennal flagellomeres without verticils (strong hairs near base), expanded subapically to give serrate appearance to antenna (fig. 22.42) .... *Prionocera**

7'.   Flagellomeres usually verticillate (fig. 22.35), if verticils absent, flagellomeres wider near their bases than apically 8

8(7').   Abdomen in both sexes greatly elongated, more than 12 times average diameter; verticils of outer flagellomeres conspicuously elongated (in eastern United States) .... *Leptotarsus (=Longurio)**

8'.   Abdomen not greatly elongated, or if so (females of a few species), flagellar verticils not conspicuously elongated 9

9(8').   Rs shorter than bscu; cell M_1 either joining cell 1st M_2 (discal cell) or separated from it by only short petiole (fig. 22.43) .... *Nephrotoma*

9'.   Rs longer than bscu; cell M_1 separated from cell 1st M_2 (discal cell) by distinct petiole (fig. 22.36) .... *Tipula**

10(').   Short terminal segment of Sc_2 present between R_1 and C; R_{1+2} absent, R_2 curving back to join R_{2+3} at a sharp angle (fig. 22.44) .... (most Cylindrotominae) 11

10'.   Terminal segment of Sc_2 usually absent (fig. 22.48) (present in some Limoniini; see couplet 15); R_{1+2} present or absent, if absent R_1 curved back to join R_{2+3} at a blunt angle 14

11(10).   Dorsum of head and prescutum (fig. 22.35) deeply pitted; prescutum with median longitudinal groove .... *Triogma**

11'.   Dorsum of head and prescutum without deep pits; no median longitudinal groove in prescutum 12

12(11').   Vein M with 3 branches (fig. 22.44) .... *Cylindrotoma*

12'.   Vein M with only 2 branches (fig. 22.45) 13

13(12').   Distal end of cell 1st M_2 closed by single crossvein; short r–m crossvein usually present (fig. 22.45) (see also couplet 16) .... *Phalacrocera* (in part)*

13'.   Distal end of cell 1st M_2 closed by two short crossveins (m and base of M_3) (fig. 22.46); antennae nodose (swelling on each segment) to bluntly serrate (sawlike) .... *Liogma*

14(10').   Eyes bare, no short hairs interspersed among ommatidia (units composing compound eye); vein Sc_1 usually short (not extending far beyond Sc_2), if long, Sc_2 is beyond level of origin of Rs (fig. 22.48) 15

14'.   Eyes with short hairs interspersed among ommatidia (fig. 22.47); vein Sc_1 long, Sc_2 before level of origin of Rs .... (Pediciini) 25

*Adults of almost all genera of Tipulidae are likely to be found near standing or flowing water. Accordingly, the adult key identifies all North American genera, and those whose larvae are aquatic are indicated (*).

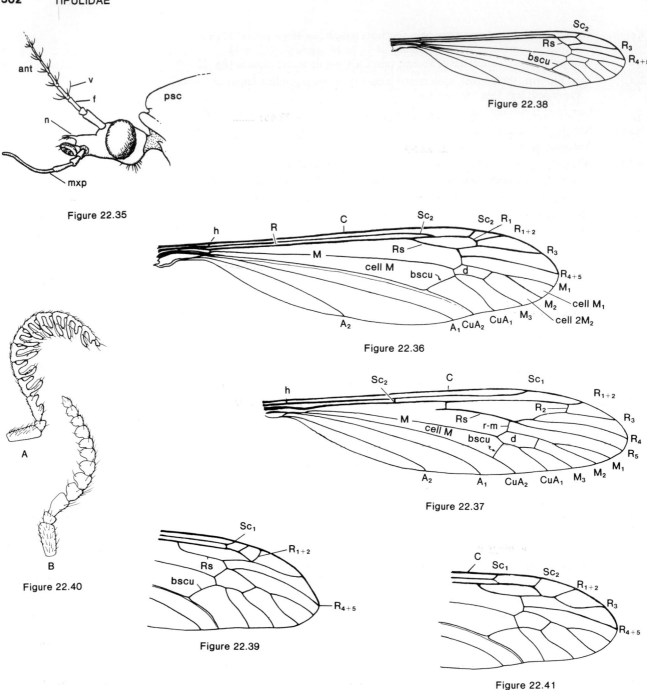

Figure 22.35.

Figure 22.36.

Figure 22.38

Figure 22.37.

Figure 22.40

Figure 22.39.

Figure 22.41.

Figure 22.35. Lateral view of head and anterior thorax of *Tipula (Yamatotipula) caloptera* Loew. *ant*, antenna; *mxp*, maxillary palp; *n*, nasus; *psc*, prescutum of mesonotum; *v*, verticil; *f*, flagellomere.

Figure 22.36. Wing of *Tipula (Yamatotipula) caloptera* Loew., showing nomenclature of veins and cells. *A*, anal veins; *bscu*, basal section of anterior cubitus; *C*, costa; *Cu*, cubitus; *d*, discal cell; *h*, humeral crossvein; *M*, media; *R*, radius; *Rs*, radial sector; *Sc*, subcosta. Cells are named from the vein (or posteriormost component of composite veins) forming their anterior border; thus, the discal cell (d) is cell first M_2 as there is a second cell $2M_2$ beyond it.

Figure 22.37. Wing of *Pedicia (Tricyphona) inconstans* (O.S.). Abbreviations as in Figure 22.36.

Figure 22.38. Wing of *Dolichopeza (Oropeza) subalbipes* (Johnson).

Figure 22.39. Wing apex of *Brachypremna dispellens* (Walker).

Figure 22.40. Antenna of *(A)* male, and *(B)* female *Ctenophora (Tanyptera) dorsalis* (Walker).

Figure 22.41. Wing apex of *Holorusia rubiginosa* Loew.

15(14).   Both short terminal segment of Sc$_2$ and R$_{1+2}$ present between R$_1$ and C (fig. 22.36) 16

15'.   Terminal segment of Sc$_2$ or R$_{1+2}$ present, but not both (fig. 22.48) 17

16(15).   Vein bscu beyond first fort of M; discal cell (1st M$_2$) present (see also couplet 13) (fig. 22.45) .... *Phalacrocera* (in part)*

16'.   Vein bscu before first fork of M; no closed discal cell (fig. 22.48) .... *Orimarga* (in part)*

17(15').   Terminal segment of Sc$_2$ often present; veins R$_4$ and R$_5$ entirely fused; only 2 branches of Rs present (fig. 22.50) .... (Limoniini) 18

17'.   Terminal segment of Sc$_2$ absent; veins R$_4$ and R$_5$ separate but R$_4$ usually merged with R$_{2+3}$; usually 3 branches of Rs present (fig. 22.55) 29

18(17).   Short section of R$_2$ present between R$_1$ and anterior branch of Rs (fig. 22.48) 19

18'.   Short section of R$_2$ absent from between R$_1$ and anterior branch of Rs (fig. 22.51) 24

19(18).   Vein bscu twice its length or more before level of 1st fork of M (fig. 22.48) 20

19'.   Vein bscu near or beyond level of 1st fork of M (fig. 22.49) 21

20(19).   Vein bscu near base of wing, far before level of origin of Rs (fig. 22.48) .... *Orimarga* (in part)*

20'.   Vein bscu 2 or 3 times its length before 1st fork of M (in California only) .... *Thaumastoptera*

21(19').   Vein R$_2$ far distad (toward wing apex) of level of discal cell (cell 1st M$_2$); bscu beyond 1st fork of M (fig. 22.37); pale longitudinal line in outer part of cell Cu .... *Dicranoptycha*

21'.   Vein R$_2$ in nearly transverse alignment with crossvein r–m (near proximal end of discal cell), or rarely beyond; no pale line in cell Cu (fig. 22.49) 22

22(21').   Antennae with 14 segments; Rs curved .... *Limonia*

22'.   Antennae with 16 segments; Rs elongate, straight, or nearly so (fig. 22.49) 23

23(22').   Anal margin of wing protruding, almost angular; Sc closely paralleling R$_1$; Sc$_2$ absent (fig. 22.49) .... *Antocha*

23'.   Anal margin of wing not protruding, smoothly curved; Sc distinctly separated from R$_1$; Sc$_2$ present but far from end of Sc$_1$ (fig. 22.50) .... *Elliptera* (in part)*

24(18').   Rostrum (snout) much shorter than rest of head; Sc$_2$ far from end of Sc$_1$ (fig. 22.50) .... *Elliptera* (in part)*

24'.   Rostrum approximately as long as rest of head, or longer; Sc$_2$ near tip of Sc$_1$ (in eastern North America) (fig. 22.51) .... *Helius**

25(14').   Membrane of wings covered with macrotrichia (large microscopic hairs) .... *Ula*

25'.   Membrane of wings without macrotrichia 26

26(25').   Antennae with 13 or 15 segments (11 or 13 flagellomeres); wings of male usually 7 mm long or less; usually no closed discal cell (fig. 22.52) .... *Dicranota**

26'.   Antennae with 14 or 16 segments; wing of male more than 7 mm long; closed discal cell usually present 27

27(26').   Rostrum (snout) prolonged to about half length of rest of head (in western North America) .... *Ornithodes**

27'.   Rostrum not prolonged, less than half length of rest of head 28

28(27').   A crossvein in cell M .... *Nasiternella**

28'.   No crossvein in cell M (fig. 22.37) .... *Pedicia**

29(17').   Tibial spurs (enlarged spines) present on distal end of tibiae (fig. 22.53) .... (Hexatomini) 30

29'.   Tibial spurs absent .... (Eriopterini) 44

30(29).   Antennae with no more than 12 segments (10 flagellomeres), although they may be very long, particularly in males .... *Hexatoma**

30'.   Antennae with more than 13 segments (11 or more flagellomeres) 31

31(30').   Rostrum (snout) greatly elongated, more than half length of entire body .... *Elephantomyia*

31'.   Rostrum short, less than length of rest of head 32

32(31').   Only two branches of Rs entending to margin of wing (fig. 22.54) .... *Atarba*

32'.   Three branches of Rs extending to margin of wing 33

*Adults of almost all genera of Tipulidae are likely to be found near standing or flowing water. Accordingly, the adult key identifies all North American genera, and those whose larvae are aquatic are indicated (*).

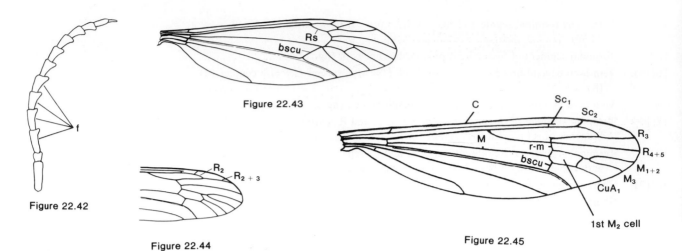

Figure 22.42

Figure 22.43

Figure 22.44

Figure 22.45

1st M₂ cell

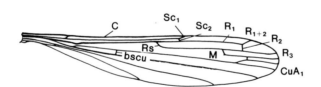

Figure 22.46

Figure 22.47

Figure 22.48

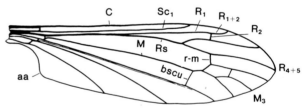

Figure 22.49

Figure 22.42. Antenna of *Prionocera* sp. *f*, flagellomere.

Figure 22.43. Wing of *Nephrotoma ferruginea* (Fabr.). *d*, discal cell.

Figure 22.44. Wing apex of *Cylindrotoma* sp.

Figure 22.45. Wing of *Phalacrocera tipulina* O.S.

Figure 22.46. Wing of *Liogma nodicornis* (O.S.).

Figure 22.47. Portion of compound eye of *Pedicia* sp., in profile, to show short hairs among ommatidia.

Figure 22.48. Wing of *Orimarga (Diotrepha) mirabilis* (O.S.).

Figure 22.49. Wing of *Antocha opalizans* O.S. *aa*, anal angle of wing.

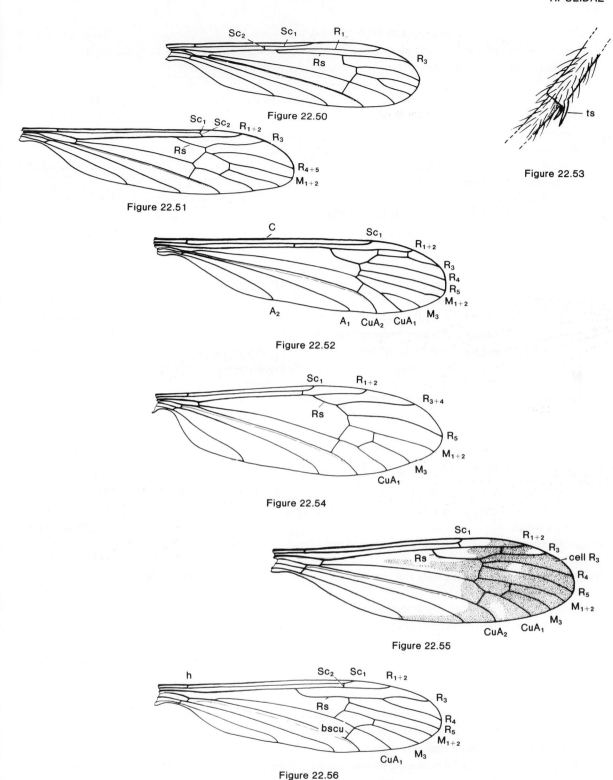

Figure 22.50

Figure 22.51

Figure 22.52

Figure 22.53

Figure 22.54

Figure 22.55

Figure 22.56

Figure 22.53. End of tibia and part of basitarsus, tribe Hexatomini; ts, tibial spur.

Figure 22.50. Wing of *Elliptera illini* Alex.

Figure 22.51. Wing of *Helius flavipes* (Macq.).

Figure 22.52. Wing of *Dicranota (Paradicranota) iowa* Alex.

Figure 22.54. Wing of *Atarba (Atarba) picticornis* O.S.

Figure 22.55. Wing of *Ulomorpha pilosella* (O.S.). Stippling = macrotrichia.

Figure 22.56. Wing of *Phyllolabis encausta* O.S.

33(32'). Macrotrichia (large microscopic hairs) present in apical cells of wings (fig. 22.55) 34

33'. No macrotrichia in apical cells, confined to stigmal area of costal margin if present 35

34(33). Macrotrichia in all cells, on all parts of membrane except near wing base; petiole
of cell R_3 very short or absent (fig. 22.55) .... *Ulomorpha**

34'. Macrotrichia in apical cells only; cell R_3 distinctly petiolate on vein R_{2+3+4} .... *Paradelphomyia*

35(33'). Crossvein in cell C between humeral crossvein and Sc_1 .... *Epiphragma*

35'. No crossvein in cell C beyond humeral crossvein (fig. 22.56) 36

36(35'). Vein R_2 absent (as crossvein between R_1 and anterior branch of Rs); vein bscu
near branching of vein M_3 and CuA_1 (fig. 22.56) .... *Phyllolabis*

36'. Vein R_2 present as crossvein between R_1 and anterior branch of Rs; bscu at or
before midlength of vein $M_3 + CuA_1$ (fig. 22.59) 37

37(36'). Anterior arculus present between R and base of M (fig. 22.57) 38

37'. Anterior arculus absent (fig. 22.58) 41

38(37). Sc short, Sc_1 joining C before level of fork of Rs (fig. 22.59) 39

38'. Sc longer, Sc_1 joining C at or beyond level of fork of Rs 40

39(38). Antennal verticils (whorls of hair) (fig. 22.35) conspicuously long; Rs longer than
vein R_3 (fig. 22.59) .... *Pilaria**

39'. Antennal verticils short; Rs short and abruptly curved or angulate near origin .... *Shannonomyia*

40(38'). Head prolonged and narrowed backward between eyes and neck (fig. 22.60) .... *Pseudolimnophila**

40'. Head not prolonged and narrowed backward behind eyes .... *Limnophila**

41(37'). No closed discal cell in wing; antennae of male elongate, most flagellomeres
constricted near midlength, binodose (2 swellings), producing appearance of 2
segments each (coastal plain of southeastern United States) .... *Polymera**

41'. Closed discal cell (cell 1st M_2) present (fig. 22.61); antennae of male without
binodose flagellomeres 42

42(41'). Vein bscu at or only slightly beyond fork of M (fig. 22.61) .... *Dactylolabis**

42'. Vein bscu distinctly beyond fork of M, usually from one-third to one-half length of
discal cell (fig. 22.62) 43

43(42'). Discal cell (cell 1st M_2) elongate, its proximal end (nearest wing base), acutely
angulate and extending much farther toward wing base than level of r–m
crossvein (fig. 22.62) .... *Prolimnophila*

43'. Discal cell not conspicuously elongate, its proximal end obtuse and at about level
of r–m .... *Austrolimnophila*

44(29'). Wings reduced to tiny vestiges; body and legs stout, giving fly a spiderlike
appearance (winter species) .... *Chionea*

44'. Wings well developed; general appearance not spiderlike 45

45(44'). Vein M_{1+2} forked, cell M_1 present (fig. 22.63) 46

45'. Vein M_{1+2} not forked, cell M_1 absent 48

46(45). Cell R_3 shorter than its petiole (R_{2+3+4}) (fig. 22.63) .... *Neolimnophila*

46'. Cell R_3 3–4 times as long as its petiole 47

47(46'). Two dististyles on each basistyle in male (fig. 22.64) .... *Neocladura*

47'. Only 1 stout dististyle on each basistyle in male (fig. 22.65) .... *Cladura*

48(45'). Rostrum elongate, about as long as rest of head and thorax combined .... *Toxorhina*

48'. Rostrum not elongate, shorter than rest of head 49

49(48'). Vein R_{3+4} unbranched, only 2 branches of Rs reaching wing margin (fig. 22.66) 50

49'. Vein R_{3+4} branched, 3 branches of Rs reaching wing margin 51

50(49). Vein R_2 absent between R_1 and anterior branch of Rs; Sc short, Sc_1 ending before
origin of short Rs; no closed discal cell (fig. 22.66) .... *Gonomyia* (in part)

50'. Vein R_2 present, near fork of Rs; Sc_1 beyond origin of Rs; R_{2+3+4} very short, Rs
long; discal cell closed .... *Teucholabis*

*Adults of almost all genera of Tipulidae are likely to be found near standing or flowing water. Accordingly, the adult key identifies all North American genera, and those whose larvae are aquatic are indicated (*).

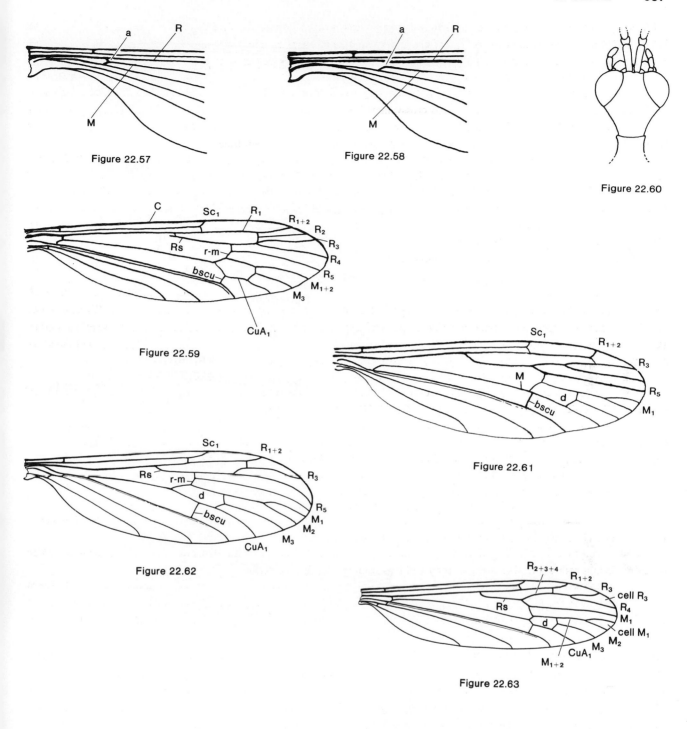

Figure 22.57

Figure 22.58

Figure 22.60

Figure 22.59

Figure 22.61

Figure 22.62

Figure 22.63

Figure 22.57. Wing base, showing anterior arculus *(a)* present between R and base of M (also see fig. 22.36).

Figure 22.58. Wing base, showing absence of anterior arculus. *a*, position of anterior arculus when present; *M*, medial vein; *R*, radial vein.

Figure 22.59. Wing of *Pilaria quadrata* (O.S.).

Figure 22.60. Dorsal view of head of *Pseudolimnophila luteipennis* (O.S.), showing narrowing behind eyes.

Figure 22.61. Wing of *Dactylolabis montana* (O.S.). *d*, discal cell.

Figure 22.62. Wing of *Prolimnophila areolata* (O.S.). *d*, discal cell.

Figure 22.63. Wing of *Neolimnophila ultima* (O.S.). *d*, discal cell.

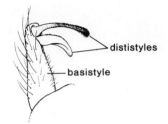

Figure 22.64

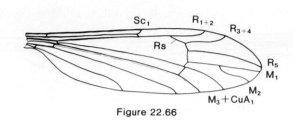

Figure 22.66

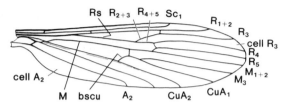

Figure 22.67

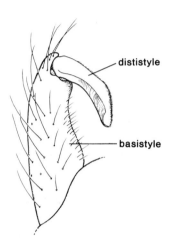

Figure 22.65

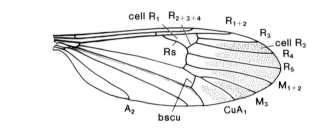

Figure 22.68

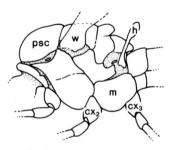

Figure 22.69

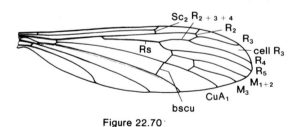

Figure 22.70

Figure 22.64. Dorsal view of right basistyle and dististyles of male *Neocladura delicatula* Alex.

Figure 22.65. Dorsal view of right basistyle and dististyle of male *Cladura flavoferruginea* O.S.

Figure 22.66. Wing of *Gonomyia (Neolipophleps) cinerea* (Doane).

Figure 22.67. Wing of *Molophilus (Molophilus) nitidus* Coq.

Figure 22.68. Wing of *Cryptolabis (Cryptolabis) paradoxa* (O.S.).

Figure 22.69. Lateral view of thorax of *Erioptera (Erioptera) chlorophylla* O.S. *cx*, coxa; *h*, halter; *m*, meron; *psc*, prescutum; *w*, base of wing.

Figure 22.70. Wing of *Lipsothrix sylvia* (Alex.).

51(49′). Rs branching into R_{2+3} and R_{4+5}; cell R_3 sessile on Rs (fig. 22.67) 52

51′. Rs branching into R_{2+3+4} and R_5; cell R_3 petiolate (fig. 22.68) 53

52(51). Cell A_2 elongate and wide; vein bscu beyond fork of M (fig. 22.67) .... *Molophilus**

52′. Cell A_2 short and narrow (i.e., vein A_2 short, close to hind margin of wing); bscu before fork of M .... *Tasiocera*

53(51′). Rs short and straight, cell R_1 (between R_1 and Rs) nearly an equilateral triangle (fig. 22.68) .... *Cryptolabis**

53′. Rs long, cell R_1 either long-triangular or not triangular 54

54(53′). Cell R_3 elongate, 3 or more times the length of its petiole (R_{2+3+4}) (figs. 22.70–22.71) 55

54′. Cell R_3 short, vein R_3 not more than twice the length of petiole of cell R_3 (fig. 22.75) 62

55(54). Coxae of middle and hind legs close together, separated by narrow meron (lateral aspect) 56

55′. Coxae of middle and hind legs separated by enlarged mesothoracic meron (lateral aspect) (fig. 22.69) 59

56(55). Veins Sc_1 and Sc_2 both short, approximately of equal length (fig. 22.70) 57

56′. Vein Sc_1 much longer than Sc_2 (fig. 22.71) 58

57(56). Vein R_{2+3+4} longer than vein bscu; veins R_2 and R_{1+2} approximately of equal length (fig. 22.70) .... *Lipsothrix**

57′. Vein R_{2+3+4} about the same length as bscu, or shorter; vein R_2 much shorter than R_{1+2} (southwestern United States) .... *Eugnophomyia*

58(56′). Body black; wings darkly tinged with brownish black; legs black, without scales .... *Gnophomyia*

58′. Body brown; wings yellowish; legs with numerous elongate scales in addition to setae (southwestern United States) .... *Idiognophomyia*

59(55′). Abundant macrotrichia in all cells of wings (fig. 22.71) .... *Ormosia**

59′. No macrotrichia in wing cells, or only a few scattered ones in outermost cells 60

60(59′). Vein Sc_1 shorter than bscu or of equal length (as in fig. 22.70) (western North America) .... *Hesperoconopa**

60′. Vein Sc_1 long, 2 or 3 times length of bscu (fig. 22.72) *61*

61. Cell 1st M_2 (discal cell) open by absence of crossvein m; vein A_2 nearly straight, not curved toward A_1 in apical portion (fig. 22.73); vein R_3 much longer than petiole of cell R_3; aedeagus simple, not divided .... *Arctoconopa**

61′. Cell 1st M_2 usually closed by crossvein m between M_{1+2} and M_3; if discal cell open by absence of m, vein A_2 curves toward A_1 apically (fig. 22.72); aedeagus bifid (forked) (fig. 22.74) .... *Erioptera**

62(54′). Vein R_2 present between R_1 and anterior branch of Rs (fig. 22.75) 63

62′. Vein R_2 absent 68

63(62). Vein R_2 immediately before point at which R_3 and R_4 diverge (fig. 22.75) .... *Gonomyia* (in part)

63′. Vein R_2 well before divergence of R_3 and R_4; R_{3+4} longer than R_2 (fig. 22.76) 64

64(63′). Vein R_4 short, subequal in length to R_{3+4}, curved caudad (backward) (fig. 22.76) .... *Rhabdomastix* (in part)*

64′. Vein R_4 longer than R_{3+4}, straight or nearly so (fig. 22.77) 65

65(64′). Vein Sc short, Sc_1 joining C before level of midlength of Rs (fig. 22.77) .... *Cheilotrichia*

65′. Vein Sc_1 joining C at level of outer one-quarter of Rs or beyond fork of Rs (fig. 22.71) 66

66(65′). Vein Sc_1 joining C at level of R_2, well beyond fork of Rs (as in fig. 22.71) .... *Gonempeda*

66′. Vein Sc_1 joining C opposite or before level of fork of Rs 67

67(66′). Abundant macrotrichia in area surrounding stigma (outer costal margin) in male .... *Empedomorpha*

67′. No macrotrichia in area surrounding stigma .... *Gonomyodes**

68(62′). Vein Sc ending before to only slightly beyond origin of Rs (fig. 22.66) .... *Gonomyia* (in part)

*Adults of almost all genera of Tipulidae are likely to be found near standing or flowing water. Accordingly, the adult key identifies all North American genera, and those whose larvae are aquatic are indicated (*).

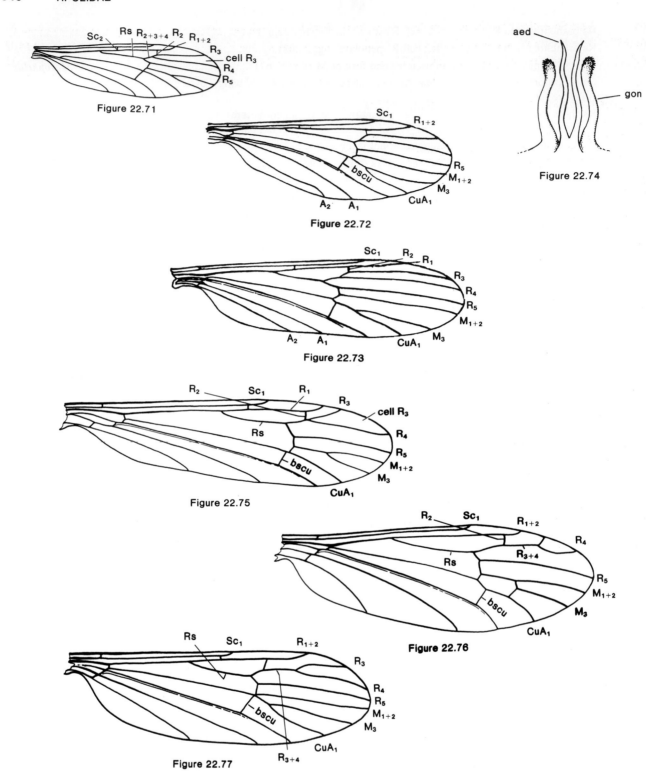

Figure 22.71. Wing of *Ormosia monticola* Alex.

Figure 22.72. Wing of *Erioptera (Erioptera) chrysocoma* O.S.

Figure 22.73. Wing of *Arctoconopa kluane* Alex.

Figure 22.74. Male aedeagus *(aed)* and gonapophyses *(gon)* of *Erioptera (Erioptera) subchlorophylla* Alex.

Figure 22.75. Wing of *Gonomyia (Progonomyia) hesperia* Alex.

Figure 22.76. Wing of *Rhabdomastix (Sacandaga) monticola* Alex.

Figure 22.77. Wing of *Cheilotrichia (Empeda) stigmatica* (O.S.).

68'.   Vein Sc ending opposite midlength of Rs, or more distally 69

69(68').   Vein bscu well before fork of M .... *Gonomyia* (in part)

69'.   Vein bscu beyond fork of M (fig. 22.76) .... *Rhabdomastix* (in part)*

ADDITIONAL TAXONOMIC REFERENCES

General
Alexander (1919, 1920, 1927, 1931, 1934, 1942, 1965); Johannsen (1934); Rees and Ferris (1939); Crampton (1942); Wirth and Stone (1956); Frommer (1963); Alexander and Byers (1981).

Regional faunas
California: Alexander (1967).
Florida (northern): Rogers (1933).
Kansas: Young (1978).
Michigan: Rogers (1942).
Northeastern United States: Alexander (1942).
Northwestern United States: Alexander (1949, 1954).
Tennessee: Rogers (1930).

Taxonomic treatments at the generic level
(L = larvae; P = pupae; A = adults)
Phalacrocera, Triogma: Brodo (1967)–L, P, A.

---

*Adults of almost all genera of Tipulidae are likely to be found near standing or flowing water. Accordingly, the adult key identifies all North American genera, and those whose larvae are aquatic are indicated (*).

Table 22A. Summary of ecological and distributional data for *Tipulidae (Diptera)*. (For definition of terms see Tables 6A–6C; table prepared by K. W. Cummins, G. W. Byers, and R. W. Merritt.)

Taxa (number of species in parentheses)	Habitat	Habit	Trophic Relationships	North American Distribution	Ecological References[§]
Tipulidae (573+) Crane flies)	Generally lentic—littoral, lotic—erosional and depositional (detritus)	Generally burrowers (and sprawlers)	Generally shredders—detritivores, collectors—gatherers	Widespread	11, 1217, 1240, 1842, 1886, 2747
Tipulinae(53+)	Generally lotic—depositional and lentic—littoral	Generally burrowers	Generally shedders?	Widespread	11, 798, 1217, 1240, 1886, 2747
Brachypremna(1)	Lotic—depositional margins (in fine sediments of springs and small streams)	Burrowers		Eastern United States	
Holorusia(1)	Lotic—depositional and lentic—margins (in detritus, moss, and fine sediments)	Burrowers	Shredders—detritivores	West	
Leptotarsus (=*Longurio*)(4)	Lotic—depositional (springs and small streams)	Burrowers?		Eastern United States	
Megistocera(1)	Lentic—littoral (vascular hydrophytes—floating zone)	Form (part of the neuston living in surface film in open-ended tubes of floating vegetation)	Shredders—herbivores?	Florida to eastern Texas	2088
Prionocera(16)	Lentic—littoral	Burrowers (in detritus)		Widespread	
Tipula(30+)	Lotic—erosional and depositional (detritus), lentic—littoral (detritus)	Burrowers (in detritus)	Shredders—detritivores and herbivores, collectors—gatherers, possibly some scrapers, predators (engulfers) with animals taken in the process of shredding?	Widespread	105, 364, 419, 421, 452, 649, 912, 945, 1022, 1317, 1415, 1416, 1671, 1842, 1953, 1957, 1958, 2012, 2085, 2646, 2747, †, *
Cylindrotominae(5)	Generally lentic and lotic—margins (in moss)	Generally burrowers—sprawlers	Generally shredders—herbivores	North	11, 17, 750, 1217, 1240, 1886, 2747
Phalacrocera(4)	Lentic—vascular hydrophytes (moss in marsh areas)	Burrowers—sprawlers	Shredders—herbivores (chewers)	Northern United States and southern Canada	1649
Triogma(1)	Lotic and lentic—margins (in moss)	Burrowers—sprawlers (semiaquatic)		Northern United States	
Limoniinae(515+)	Generally lotic—depositional, erosional, and margins, lentic—littoral and margins	Generally burrowers	Shredders, collectors, and predators (engulfers)	Widespread	11, 17, 1217
Antocha(7)	Lotic—erosional (in fast water on rocks and logs)	Clingers (in silk tube)	Collectors—gatherers	Widespread	419, 421, ‡
Arctoconopa(9)	Lotic—erosional and depositional, margins (clear streams)	Burrowers		Widespread	
Cryptolabis(12)	Lotic—depositional (sand in clear, cold streams)	Burrowers		Widespread	
Dactylolabis(18)	Lotic—erosional and depositional (in moss and algal mats, especially rocky seeps)	Burrowers—clingers		Widespread	

*Includes some important references on related terrestrial species.
†Unpublished data, K. W. Cummins and M. J. Klug, Kellogg Biological Station.
‡Unpublished data, K. W. Cummins, Kellogg Biological Station.
§Emphasis on trophic relationships.

ble 22A—*Continued*

Taxa (number of species in parentheses)	Habitat	Habit	Trophic Relationships	North American Distribution	Ecological References[§]
Dicranota(55)	Lotic—erosional and depositional (detritus), lentic—littoral (detritus); lotic and lentic margins (in damp soil)	Sprawlers—burrowers	Predators (engulfers)	Widespread	419, 1647, 1648, ‡
Elliptera(5)	Lotic—erosional (in moss and algal mats on wet rock faces)	Burrowers—clingers		Widespread	
Erioptera(35+) (includes *Trimicra* as a subgenus)	Lotic—erosional and depositional (sand, detritus, and margins), lentic margins	Burrowers (semiaquatic)	Collectors—gatherers	Widespread	2085
Gonomyia(15+)	Lotic and lentic—margins	Burrowers (semiaquatic)		Widespread	2082
Gonomyodes(4)	Lotic—depositional	Burrowers		West	
Helius(2)	Lentic and lotic—margins (in detritus in wet woodlands or marshes)	Sprawlers—burrowers		Widespread	2085
Hesperoconopa(5)	Lotic—depositional (sand in cold, clear streams)	Burrowers		West	
Hexatoma(34) (includes *Eriocera* as a subgenus)	Lotic—erosional and depositional (detritus and moss), lentic—littoral (detritus)	Burrowers—sprawlers, clingers	Predators (engulfers, Oligochaeta, Diptera)	Widespread	419, 2085, 2747
Limnophila(40+)	Lotic and lentic—margins, lotic—depositional (in fine sediments and detritus)	Burrowers	Predators (engulfers, Oligochaeta, Diptera)	Widespread	2085
Limonia(95+) (includes *Geranomyia* as a subgenus)	Lotic and lentic—margins (on exposed objects—rocks and logs; in fine organic sediments and detritus)	Burrowers—sprawlers (semiaquatic)	Shredders—herbivores (chewers—macroalgae)	Widespread	2077, 2083, 2085
Lipsothrix(4)	Lotic—depositional (soft, saturated wood)	Burrowers	Shredders (decaying wood)	Widespread	605
Molophilus(15+)	Lotic and lentic—margins	Burrowers (semiaquatic)		Widespread	937, 2085
Orimarga(5)	Lotic and lentic—margins (wet, soft, decaying wood)	Burrowers	Shredders?	Southern United States	
Ormosia(40+)	Lotic and lentic—margins (in detritus and fine organic sediments)	Burrowers (semiaquatic)	Collectors—gatherers?	Widespread	
Paradelphomyia(8)	Lentic and lotic—margins (in organic sediments—wet woodlands)	Burrowers		Widespread	
Pedicia(57)	Lotic and lentic—margins (detritus in springs, seeps, and swampy woods)	Burrowers (semiaquatic)	Predators (engulfers)	Widespread	1520
Pilaria(12)	Lentic—littoral (wet detritus and fine sediments at margin)	Burrowers	Predators (engulfers)?	Widespread	

published data, K. W. Cummins, Kellogg Biological Station.
phasis on trophic relationships.

Table 22A—*Continued*

Taxa (number of species in parentheses)	Habitat	Habit	Trophic Relationships	North American Distribution	Ecological References
Polymera(2)	Lotic—depositional (wet detritus at margin)	Burrowers		Southeastern United States	
Pseudolimnophila(5)	Lentic and lotic—margins (in organic sediments—wet woodlands and marshes)	Burrowers		Widespread	
Rhabdomastix(26)	Lotic—depositional (sand in clear streams and at margin)	Burrowers		Widespread	
Thaumastoptera(1)	Lotic—depositional (fine sediments of small streams, springs, and seeps)	Burrowers		California	
Ulomorpha(8)	Lentic and lotic—margins (in organic sediments of wet woodlands)	Burrowers	Predators (engulfers)?	Widespread	

Culicidae

23

H. D. Newson
Michigan State University, East Lansing

Introduction

Mosquitoes undergo complete metamorphosis (egg, larva, pupa, and adult). At the time of oviposition, the female instinctively selects the habitat for the aquatic immature stages. These habitats are diverse and range from large, permanent bodies of water to small seepage areas and artificial containers. Although the egg laying habits within North American genera of mosquitoes may be quite variable, some generalizations can be made. *Anopheles* sp. usually deposit eggs singly on the surface of still waters. These floating eggs often arrange themselves in star-shaped patterns due to water surface tension. *Psorophora* sp. and most North American species of *Aedes* deposit their eggs singly in moist ground depressions; their eggs may remain dormant for months or even years until flooded by rains or water from other sources. In more northern areas, *Aedes* spp. are univoltine (one generation per year) and eggs laid in the summer do not hatch until flooded the following year. Females of the genera *Culex, Mansonia, Culiseta,* and *Uranotaenia* usually glue their eggs together in raftlike masses, which they deposit directly on the surface of the water.

After mosquito eggs have been in contact with water for a sufficient time (from 24 hours to several weeks), the larvae emerge and begin to feed. Larval food consists primarily of small aquatic animals, algae, and detrital particles collected by the action of mouth brushes. Some species scrape microorganisms attached to the surface of submerged substrates. The larvae of the genus *Toxorhynchites* and some *Psorophora* are predaceous and often feed upon other species of mosquito larvae. Many species of mosquitoes complete larval development in 7–10 days if conditions are favorable, but others may require several months. All mosquito larvae, except members of the genus *Mansonia,* must come to the water surface at frequent intervals to obtain oxygen. Except when feeding or disturbed, they usually are found suspended in various positions from the water surface. Air is obtained through a pair of spiracles located dorsally on the eighth abdominal segment in *Anopheles,* and at the end of the dorsal siphon in other genera. When larvae (except *Mansonia*) are breathing, the spiracles must be in the plane of the water surface. *Mansonia* larvae and pupae attach themselves to submerged roots and stems of plants and obtain their oxygen from the plant tissues.

The fourth larval molt produces the pupa, a nonfeeding, quiescent stage that usually floats on the water surface. When disturbed by mechanical agitation or sudden changes in light intensity it dives with a tumbling, jerking motion and slowly floats to the surface again when the rapid flexions of the abdomen are stopped. The buoyancy of the pupal stage results from an air cavity between the wings of the adult developing within the pupal exoskeleton. A pair of large respiratory trumpets located dorsally on the cephalothorax enables the pupa to penetrate the water surface film and obtain air (fig. 23.2). In the genus *Mansonia,* the pupal trumpets are modified for use in penetrating and attaching to submerged vegetation. The pupal stage usually lasts only three or four days, but in some species may persist for two weeks or more. At the end of this stage, the pupa extends its abdomen nearly parallel to the surface of the water in preparation for the emergence of the adult. By ingesting the air present within the pupal skin and utilizing muscular movement, the adult is able to split the dorsum of the pupal cephalothorax and emerge. After slowly emerging, the adult uses the cast pupal skin as a float until its body and wings dry and harden.

Mosquito adults are well known for their blood feeding habits and as vectors of a great number of human and animal diseases. Females of many mosquito species take blood meals as a source of protein required for egg production *(anautogenous),* and the energy requirements of both males and females are obtained by feeding on plant juices and nectar. The mouthparts of males are not adapted for blood feeding. Some females are *autogenous,* that is, they can produce eggs without having had a previous blood meal, apparently carrying over adequate protein from the larval stage. Complete or partial autogeny is now known to exist in many species. However, the females of a great majority of mosquito species are *zoophilous,* that is, they feed in nature on vertebrate animals other than humans. Feeding preferences vary from one species to another and may include cold blooded vertebrates, birds, and a variety of mammals, including humans. Although some species are host-group specific in their blood feeding, others are much less discriminating in their choice of hosts.

Under natural conditions male mosquitoes are short-lived with a life span of about one week or less, but with optimal conditions they may survive for a considerably longer period. On the other hand, females with an adequate source of food and suitable environmental conditions commonly live much longer. Field studies have shown that females of some species survive for three or more months but the usual life span of most is from two to four weeks. For those species capable of transmitting human or animal diseases, longevity and blood-feeding preferences are critical factors in determining whether or not individuals in a given population achieve their potential as disease vectors.

There is considerable variation in the mating behavior of mosquitoes. Some species mate readily within the confines of underground animal burrows, others while swarming in a small space, and still others have larger space requirements and will mate only while swarming several meters above ground. For most species, however, mating occurs when males form a crepuscular (twilight) swarm and the females fly into it. There is evidence to indicate that the sounds formed by the swarming males is species specific and is a major factor in attracting females to the swarm. For a more complete account of the mating, host seeking, and other behavioral characteristics of mosquitoes, the reader is referred to Bates (1949), Carpenter and LaCasse (1955), Clements (1963), Carpenter (1968, 1974, 1982), and Gillett (1972).

EXTERNAL MORPHOLOGY

Larvae

Mosquito larvae have three well-differentiated body regions: the head, thorax, and abdomen. Each of these has variable structures that are used in classification (fig. 23.1). The head, which is flattened dorsoventrally, is formed of three large sclerites. The mouthparts are ventral, but some portions extend anteriorly and are visible in a dorsal view (figs. 23.6–23.7). The thorax is composed of the fused pro-, meso-, and metathorax, distinguished only by the hair group present on each segment (fig. 23.1). The first seven of the nine visible abdominal segments are somewhat similar and unmodified. The eighth segment bears the breathing apparatus posterodorsally (fig. 23.5) and the various modifications of this structure provide useful taxonomic characters. The terminal segment also has several structures of taxonomic importance (fig. 23.1).

Pupae

Mosquito pupae have only two clearly defined body regions: an enlarged anterior cephalothorax and a segmented abdomen (fig. 23.2). Two respiratory structures, the *trumpets,* are located on the dorsal portion of the cephalothorax. The abdomen is slender and terminates in a pair of flattened *paddles.* Variations in the *chaetotaxy* (arrangement of setae), the paddles, and the trumpets are important diagnostic pupal features.

Adults

The body of an adult mosquito is comprised of three distinct regions, each with important characters that can be used in classification (fig. 23.3). The large compound eyes occupy most of the lateral part of the head and the remaining portions are covered with scales of various shapes and colors. Mouthparts are elongate and highly modified for piercing and ingesting liquid foods. Long, slender, 15-segmented antennae arise between the eyes and a five-segmented maxillary palpus is located on each side of the proboscis. The thorax is composed of three fused segments, the pro-, meso-, and metathorax. The prothorax bears the front pair of legs; the mesothorax, the wings and middle pair of legs; and the metathorax, the halteres and hind pair of legs. The thoracic segments and legs are covered with various types of setae and colored scales that provide useful taxonomic characters. The wing veins and margins also are densely covered with scales of various shapes and colors. These are diagnostic features for some species, as are the configurations of certain wing veins.

KEYS TO THE GENERA OF CULICIDAE

These keys were designed to include only the species in North America that occur north of Mexico. Major taxonomic revisions of Neotropical forms are now in progress.

Characteristics given in the adult key are suitable for identifying both males and females to genus. Carpenter and LaCasse (1955) provided complete descriptions, figures, and keys for the larvae and adults of all species then known to occur in North America. Since then one additional genus, *Haemogogus,* represented by only one species, has been found to occur in the extreme southern part of Texas (Breland 1958). Darsie and Ward (1981) provide identification keys and the known distribution ranges of all species currently reported from America north of Mexico.

The key for pupae utilizes chaetotaxic characteristics to a major extent. The setal numbering system is that of Mattingly (1973) in which the individual setae on the cephalothorax and each abdominal segment are designated by sequential Arabic numbers, and abdominal segments are numbered from anterior to posterior using Roman numerals I through X. Thus, in the key, 9-C represents seta number 9 on the cephalothorax and 9-VII represents seta number 9 on the seventh abdominal segment. Segments I through VIII are distinct and clearly separated, whereas segments IX and X appear more as lobelike appendages.

Larvae (Fourth Instar)

1.	Eighth abdominal segment without an elongate dorsal siphon (fig. 23.4); abdomen with palmate hairs (fig. 23.4)	***Anopheles***
1′.	Eighth abdominal segment with an elongate dorsal siphon that is as long or longer than wide (fig. 23.5)	2
2(1′).	Mouth brushes prehensile (adapted for grasping), each composed of about 10 stout, curved rods (fig. 23.6); larvae very large (up to 15 mm long) and predaceous	***Toxorhynchites***
2′.	Mouth brushes composed of 30 or more hairs (fig. 23.7).	3

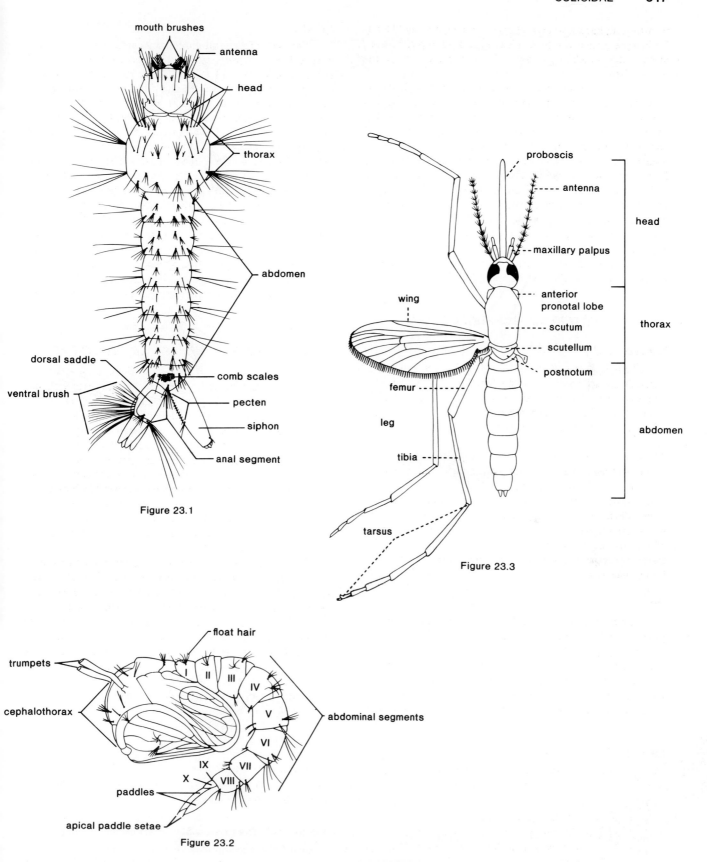

Figure 23.1

Figure 23.3

Figure 23.2

Figure 23.1. Dorsal view of mosquito larva.

Figure 23.2. Lateral view of mosquito pupa.
Figure 23.3. Dorsal view of mosquito adult.

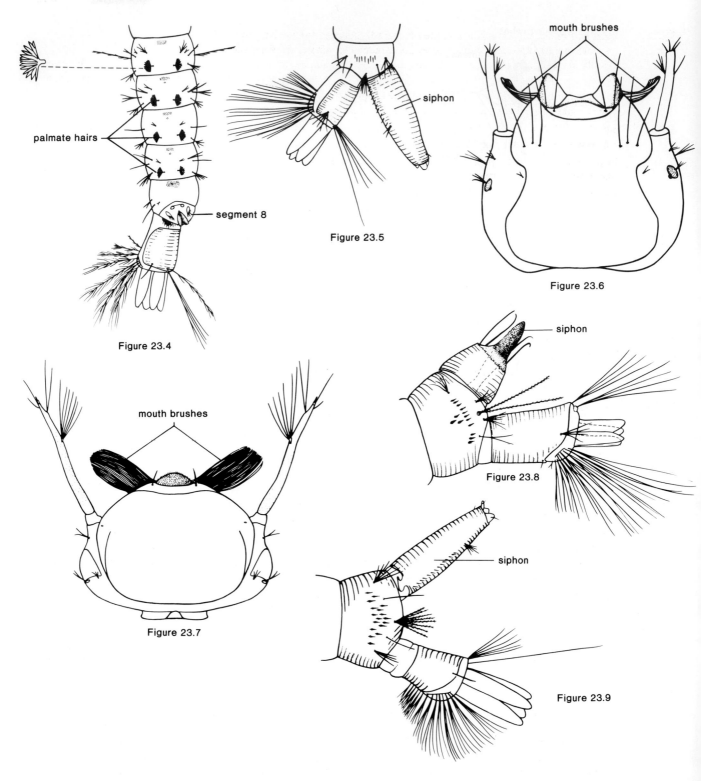

Figure 23.4. Dorsal view of *Anopheles* sp. abdomen.

Figure 23.5. Terminal abdominal segments of typical culicine larva.

Figure 23.6. Dorsal view of *Toxorhynchites* sp. mouth brushes.

Figure 23.7. Dorsal view of typical culicine mouth brushes.

Figure 23.8. Lateral view of *Mansonia* sp. siphon.

Figure 23.9. Lateral view of typically shaped culicine siphon.

3(2′). Distal half of siphon strongly attenuated (tapered), adapted for piercing roots of aquatic plants (fig. 23.8); larvae normally attached to submerged vegetation, rarely at water surface .... ***Mansonia***
(Includes *Coquillettidia* of some authors)

3′. Siphon cylindrical or fusiform (spindle-shaped) (fig. 23.9); not adapted for piercing aquatic plants 4

4(3′). Siphon with a pecten (fig. 23.10) 5

4′. Siphon without a pecten (fig. 23.11) 11

5(4). Head longer than wide (fig. 23.12); 8th abdominal segment with a sclerotized plate bearing the comb on its posterior border (fig. 23.13) .... ***Uranotaenia***

5′. Head at least as wide as long (fig. 23.14); 8th abdominal segment without a prominent sclerotized plate (fig. 23.15) (small plate present in some *Psorophora* species) 6

6(5′). Head with prominent triangular pouch on each side (fig. 23.16); anal segment with divided dorsal and ventral sclerotic plates, membranous laterally (fig. 23.17) .... ***Deinocerites***

6′. Head without a prominent triangular pouch on each side (fig. 23.18); anal segment without divided dorsal and ventral sclerotic plates (fig. 23.19) 7

7(6′). Siphon with a pair of large basal tufts (fig. 23.20); or, if tufts small, the comb scales are in a single row and have a barlike arrangement .... ***Culiseta***

7′. Siphon without a pair of basal tufts (fig. 23.21) ***8***

8(7′). Siphon with several pairs of siphonal tufts or single hairs (fig. 23.22) .... ***Culex***

8′. Siphon with one pair of median or subapical siphonal tufts (sometimes vestigial), or one pair of single hairs (fig. 23.23) 9

9(8′). Anal segment completely ringed by the dorsal saddle and pierced on the midventral line by tufts of the ventral brush (fig. 23.24) .... ***Psorophora***

9′. Anal segment not completely ringed by the dorsal saddle (fig. 23.25); or, if ringed, not pierced on the midventral line by tufts of the ventral brush (fig. 23.26) 10

10(9′). Dorsal saddle with a prominent group of long spines on posterior margin; comb scales in a single row (fig. 23.27) .... ***Haemogogus***

10′. Dorsal saddle without a prominent group of long spines on the posterior margin (fig. 23.28); or, if long spines are present on the posterior margin, comb scales are in a patch (fig. 23.29) .... ***Aedes***

11(4′). Anal segment with a prominent median ventral brush consisting of a close-set row of tufts; comb with a double row of pointed scales (fig. 23.30) .... ***Orthopodomyia***

11′. Anal segment without a median ventral brush, but with a pair of ventrolateral tufts; comb scales arranged in a single row (fig. 23.31) .... ***Wyeomyia***

Pupae

1. Segment X with a conspicuous branched hair; seta 9 on segment VIII greatly reduced; paddles without apical seta (fig. 23.32) .... ***Toxorhynchites***

1′. Segment X without branched hair; seta 9–VIII and paddles variable 2

2(1′). Paddles nearly always with an accessory seta arising anterior to, and in line with, the apical seta; if not, then seta 9 on segments IV–VII in the form of a short, stout, dark spine arising from the extreme posterior corner of the segment (fig. 23.33) and trumpets short, flared, and split nearly to base .... ***Anopheles***

2′. Paddles with accessory seta absent; or, if present, arising level with and laterad of the apical seta; seta 9 and trumpets usually different from above 3

3(2′). Trumpets modified for insertion into aquatic plant tissues (fig. 23.34); float hairs suppressed .... ***Mansonia***
(includes *Coquillettidia* of some authors)

3′. Trumpets otherwise, and/or float hair well developed (fig. 23.35) 4

4(3′). Paddles small, somewhat pointed, and without apical seta (fig. 23.36) .... ***Wyeomyia***

4′. Paddles not pointed, apical seta present (fig. 23.37) 5

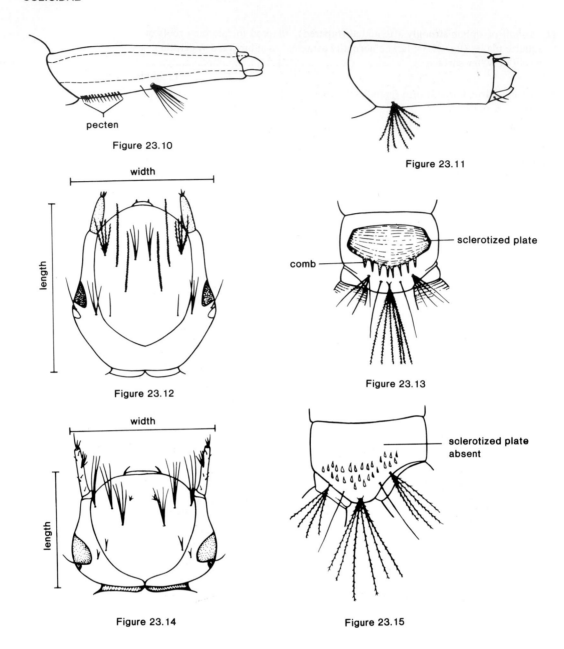

pecten

Figure 23.10

Figure 23.11

width

length

Figure 23.12

sclerotized plate

comb

Figure 23.13

width

length

Figure 23.14

sclerotized plate absent

Figure 23.15

Figure 23.13. Lateral view of eighth abdominal segment of *Uranotaenia* sp.

Figure 23.14. Dorsal view of typical culicine larval head.

Figure 23.15. Lateral view of culicine eighth abdominal segment.

Figure 23.10. Lateral view of culicine siphon.

Figure 23.11. Lateral view of culicine siphon.

Figure 23.12. Dorsal view of *Uranotaenia* sp. head.

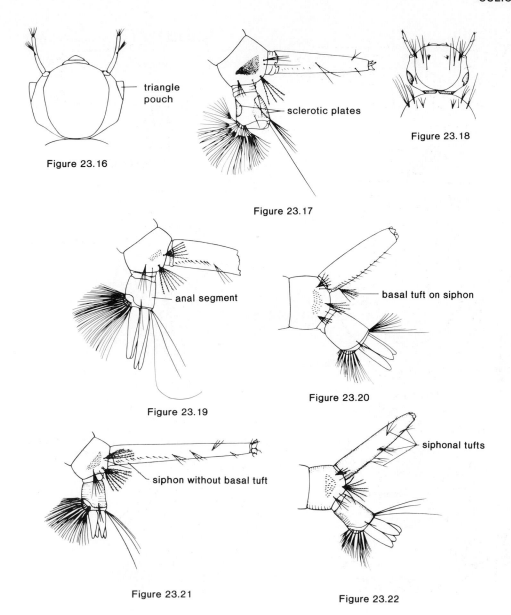

triangle
pouch

Figure 23.16

sclerotic plates

Figure 23.17

Figure 23.18

anal segment

Figure 23.19

basal tuft on siphon

Figure 23.20

siphon without basal tuft

Figure 23.21

siphonal tufts

Figure 23.22

Figure 23.16. Dorsal view of *Deinocerites* sp. head.

Figure 23.17. Lateral view of anal segment of *Deinocerites* sp.

Figure 23.18. Dorsal view of culicine head.

Figure 23.19. Lateral view of culicine anal segment.

Figure 23.20. Lateral view of *Culiseta* sp. siphon and anal segment.

Figure 23.21. Lateral view of culicine siphon and anal segment.

Figure 23.22. Lateral view of culicine siphon and anal segment.

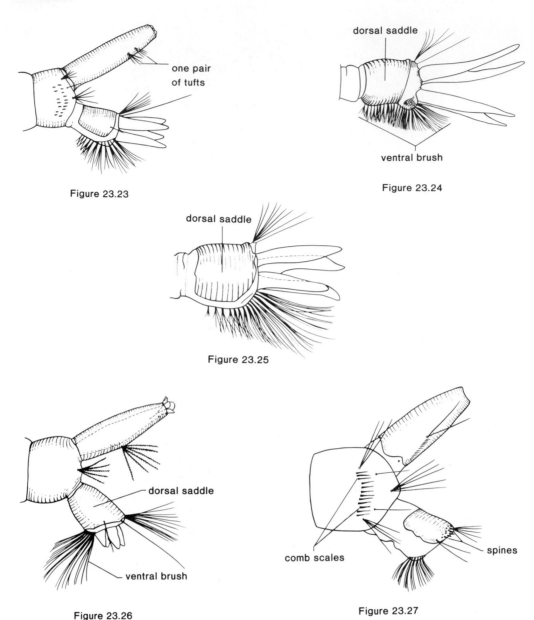

Figure 23.23

one pair of tufts

dorsal saddle

ventral brush

Figure 23.24

dorsal saddle

Figure 23.25

dorsal saddle

ventral brush

Figure 23.26

comb scales

spines

Figure 23.27

Figure 23.23. Lateral view of culicine siphon and anal segment.

Figure 23.24. Lateral view of *Psorophora* sp. anal segment.

Figure 23.25. Lateral view of culicine anal segment.

Figure 23.26. Lateral view of culicine anal segment and siphon.

Figure 23.27. Lateral view of terminal abdominal segments of *Haemogogus* sp. showing dorsal saddle and comb scales.

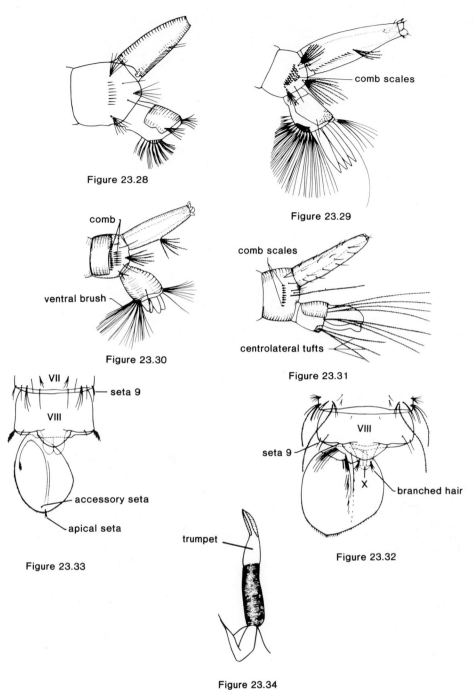

Figure 23.28

Figure 23.29

comb scales

comb

ventral brush

Figure 23.30

comb scales

centrolateral tufts

Figure 23.31

VII

seta 9

VIII

accessory seta

apical seta

Figure 23.33

VIII

seta 9

X

branched hair

Figure 23.32

trumpet

Figure 23.34

Figure 23.28. Lateral view of terminal abdominal segments of *Aedes* sp. showing dorsal saddle.

Figure 23.29. Lateral view of terminal abdominal segments of *Aedes* sp. showing comb scales.

Figure 23.30. Lateral view of terminal abdominal segments of *Orthopodomyia* sp. showing ventral brush and comb scales.

Figure 23.31. Lateral view of terminal abdominal segments of *Wyeomyia* sp. showing anal segment and comb scales.

Figure 23.32. Dorsal view of terminal abdominal segments of *Toxorhynchites* sp. showing paddle and terminal segments.

Figure 23.33. Dorsal view of paddle and terminal segments of *Anopheles* sp.

Figure 23.34. *Mansonia* sp. trumpet.

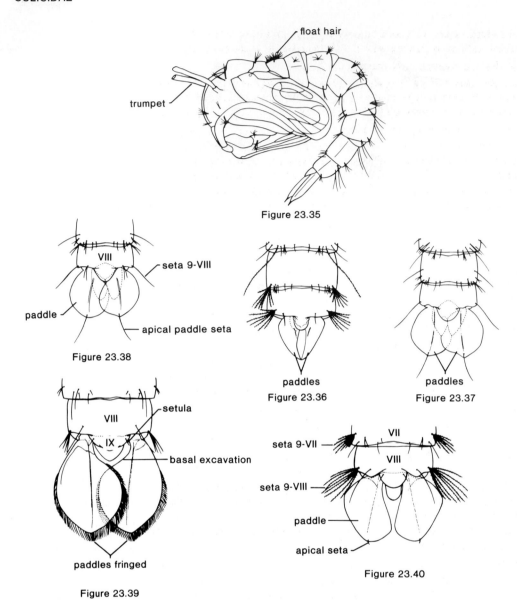

Figure 23.35

Figure 23.38

Figure 23.36

Figure 23.37

Figure 23.39

Figure 23.40

Figure 23.35. Lateral view of typical culicine pupa showing trumpets and float hairs.

Figure 23.36. Dorsal view of *Wyeomyia* sp. paddles.

Figure 23.37. Dorsal view of typical culicine paddles.

Figure 23.38. Dorsal view of *Deinocerites* sp. paddles and terminal segments.

Figure 23.39. Dorsal view of *Uranotaenia* sp. paddles and terminal segments.

Figure 23.40. Dorsal view of *Orthopodomyia* sp. paddles and terminal segments.

5(4').   Apex of paddle convex with both borders smooth; apical seta on paddle at least
          two-thirds as long as paddle; seta 9–VIII long, single, and simple (fig. 23.38) .... *Deinocerites*

5'.   Without this combination of characters 6

6(5').   Paddles with inner half deeply excavated toward base and usually much broader
          on outer half; segment IX usually with a pair of small setulae (stiff bristles);
          paddles fringed or toothed on both borders (fig. 23.39) .... *Uranotaenia*

6'.   Without this combination of characters 7

7(6').   Paddles somewhat rectangular, with the thickened basal portion of outer edge
          sometimes spiculate (having minute, pointed spines), but remaining otherwise
          smooth and hyaline (fig. 23.40); accessory paddle seta absent; apical paddle seta
          very short; seta 9 on segments VI–VIII long, stout, plumose, and on segment
          VIII about half or more the length of paddle (fig. 23.40) .... *Orthopodomyia*

7'.   Without this combination of characters 8

8(7').   Trumpets tubular for most of their length, either with or without rudimentary
          basal tracheation (fig. 23.41); seta 9–VIII arising from the posterolateral corner
          of the segment with little or no anterior displacement (fig. 23.42); and, with one
          of the following characteristics: posterior corner of abdominal segment IV
          toothed (fig. 23.43); prominent ventral lobes present on posterior border of
          segment VIII, partly covering the bases of the paddles (fig. 23.42); or, accessory
          paddle seta present (fig. 23.42) .... *Psorophora*

8'.   Without this combination of characters 9

9(8').   Seta 8–C arising laterad to, and approximately even with, the base of the trumpet,
          but very much anterior to 9–C (fig. 23.44); tracheation of trumpet absent or, at
          most, rudimentary (fig. 23.44); seta 9–VIII rarely arising cephalad of the
          posterior border of the segment (fig. 23.45) 10

9'.   Seta 8–C arising even with, or posterior to, the base of the trumpet and more
          nearly level with 9–C (fig. 23.46); trumpets frequently with extensive subbasal
          tracheation (fig. 23.46); position of seta 9–VIII variable 11

10(9).   Setae 8–C and 9–C poorly developed (fig. 23.47); setae 5–II and 5–III not
          extending to, or barely reaching, the next posterior abdominal segment; *either*
          with seta 5–VIII as long or longer than segment VI, *or* with midrib of paddle
          deeply pigmented, and seta 5 on segments IV–VI each shorter than the
          following segment; seta 9–VIII with 4 or more branches as long or longer than
          one-half the paddle length (fig. 23.48) .... *Haemogogus*

10'.   Without this combination of characters .... *Aedes*

11(9').   Trumpets with well-developed subbasal tracheation (fig. 23.49), or seta 9–VIII
          arising well cephalad of the posterior border of the segment (fig. 23.50) .... *Culex*

11'.   Trumpets with, at most, rudimentary basal tracheation (fig. 23.51); seta 9–VIII
          always arising from the posterior border of the segment (fig. 23.52) .... *Culiseta*

Adults

1.   Proboscis rigid and stout on basal half, apical half tapered toward apex and
          strongly curved downward (fig. 23.53). Large species (up to 15 mm long), with
          broad, metallic colored scales on head, thorax, abdomen, and legs .... *Toxorhynchites*

1'.   Proboscis slender, never strongly curved downward on apical half, and of nearly
          uniform thickness (fig. 23.54) 2

2(1').   Scutellum evenly rounded on posterior margin (fig. 23.55); palpi of female nearly
          as long as proboscis (fig. 23.56); abdomen bare of scales or only sparsely scaled .... *Anopheles*

2'.   Scutellum trilobed on posterior margin (fig. 23.57); palpi less than one-half as long
          as proboscis (fig. 23.58); abdomen densely scaled both dorsally and ventrally 3

3(2').   Second marginal cell of wing short, less than half as long as its petiole (fig. 23.59) .... *Uranotaenia*

3'.   Second marginal cell of wing as long or longer than its petiole (fig. 23.60) 4

4(3').   Postnotum with a tuft of setae (fig. 23.61); wing squama without fringe of hair
          (fig. 23.62) .... *Wyeomyia*

4'.   Postnotum bare (fig. 23.63); wing squama with fringe of hair (fig. 23.64) 5

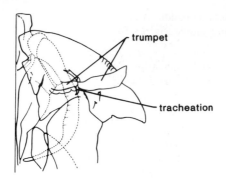

Figure 23.41

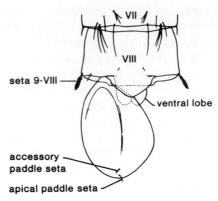

Figure 23.42

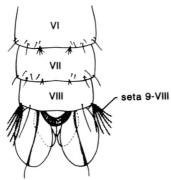

Figure 23.45

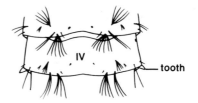

Figure 23.43

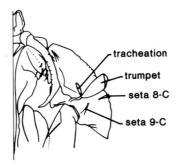

Figure 23.46

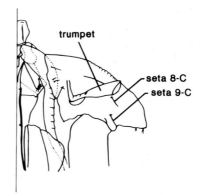

Figure 23.44

Figure 23.41. Lateral view of *Psorophora* sp. trumpets.

Figure 23.42. Dorsal view of *Psorophora* sp. paddles and terminal segments.

Figure 23.43. Dorsal view of abdominal segment IV of *Psorophora* sp.

Figure 23.44. Lateral view of culicine trumpet.

Figure 23.45. Dorsal view of culicine pupal terminal abdominal segments.

Figure 23.46. Lateral view of culicine trumpet.

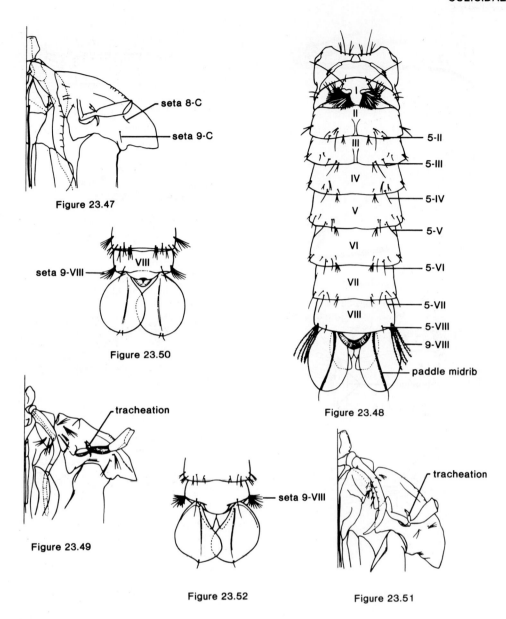

Figure 23.47

Figure 23.50

Figure 23.49

Figure 23.52

Figure 23.51

Figure 23.48

Figure 23.47. Lateral view of culicine trumpet.

Figure 23.48. Dorsal view of *Haemogogus* sp. paddles and abdominal segments.

Figure 23.49. Lateral view of *Culex* sp. trumpet.

Figure 23.50. Dorsal view of segment VIII and paddles of *Culex.*

Figure 23.51. Lateral view of *Culiseta* sp. trumpet.

Figure 23.52. Dorsal view of segment VIII and paddles of *Culiseta* sp.

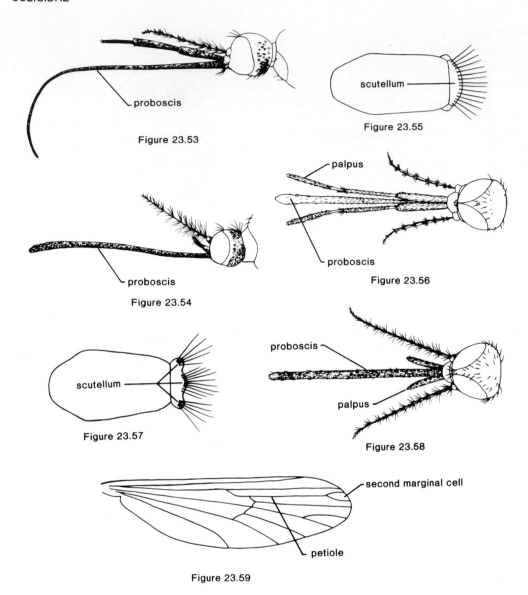

Figure 23.53

Figure 23.55

Figure 23.54

Figure 23.56

Figure 23.57

Figure 23.58

Figure 23.59

Figure 23.53. Lateral view of head showing *Toxorhynchites* sp. proboscis.

Figure 23.54. Lateral view of head showing typical culicine proboscis.

Figure 23.55. Dorsal view of thorax showing *Anopheles* sp. scutellum.

Figure 23.56. Dorsal view of head showing *Anopheles* sp. palpi.

Figure 23.57. Dorsal view of thorax showing typical culicine scutellum

Figure 3.58. Dorsal view of head showing typical culicine palpi.

Figure 23.59. *Uranotaenia* sp. wing.

5(4′).	Spiracular bristles present (fig. 23.65)	6
5′.	Spiracular bristles absent (fig. 23.66)	7
6(5).	Postspiracular bristles present (fig. 23.67); tip of abdomen pointed (fig. 23.68)	***Psorophora***
6′.	Postspiracular bristles absent (fig. 23.69); tip of abdomen blunt (fig. 23.70)	***Culiseta***
7(5′).	Anterior pronotal lobes large, collarlike, almost joining dorsally (fig. 23.71); abdominal scales bright metallic violet or silver	***Haemogogus***
7′.	Anterior pronotal lobes small, widely separated dorsally (fig. 23.72); abdomen without bright metallic scales	8
8(7′).	Postspiracular bristles present (fig. 23.67)	9
8′.	Postspiracular bristles absent (fig. 23.69)	10
9(8).	Wing scales very broad, mixed brown and white (fig. 23.73); tip of abdomen blunt (fig. 23.70)	***Mansonia*** (in part)
9′.	Wing scales narrow (rarely moderately broad) (fig. 23.74); tip of abdomen pointed (fig. 23.68)	***Aedes***
10(8′).	Antenna much longer than proboscis, 1st flagellar segment longer than the next 2 segments combined (fig. 23.75)	***Deinocerites***
10′.	Antenna not longer than proboscis, or only slightly so, 1st flagellar segment about as long as each succeeding segment (fig. 23.76)	11
11(10′).	Scutum bicolored with narrow longitudinal lines of white scales (fig. 23.77); penultimate (next to the last) segment of front tarsi very short, only about half as long as wide (fig. 23.78)	***Orthopodomyia***
11′.	Scutum without longitudinal lines of white scales (fig. 23.79); penultimate segment of front tarsi much longer than wide (fig. 23.80)	12
12(11′).	Wing scales very broad, mixed brown and white (fig. 23.73)	***Mansonia***
		(in part—includes *Coquillettidia* of some authors)
12′.	Wing scales narrow and uniformly dark (fig. 23.74)	***Culex***

ADDITIONAL TAXONOMIC REFERENCES

General
Carpenter and LaCasse (1955); Breland (1958); Darsie and Ward (1981); Stone (1981).

Regional faunas
Alaska: Gjullin et al. (1961).
Arizona: McDonald et al. (1973).
Arkansas: Carpenter (1941).
British Columbia: Curtis (1967).
California: Bohart and Washino (1978).
Canada: Wood et al. (1979).
Colorado: Harmston and Lawson (1967).
Illinois: Ross and Horsfall (1965).
Indiana: Siverly (1972).
Iowa: Knight and Wonio (1969).
Minnesota: Barr (1958).
New Jersey: Headlee (1945).
New York: Means (1979).
Northwestern United States: Gjullin and Eddy (1972).
Oklahoma: Rozeboom (1942).
Southeastern United States: King et al. (1960).
Texas: Randolph and O'Neill (1944).
Utah: Nielsen and Rees (1961).
Virginia: Gladney and Turner (1969).
Wisconsin: Dickinson (1944).

Regional species lists
Colorado: Harmston (1949).
Delaware: Darsie et al. (1951).
District of Columbia: Good (1945).
Idaho: Brothers (1971).
Kentucky: Quinby et al. (1944).
Manitoba: Trimble (1972).
Maryland: Bickley et al. (1971).
Michigan: Cassani and Newson (1980).
Mississippi: Harden et al. (1967).
Missouri: Smith and Enns (1968).
New Mexico: Sublette and Sublette (1970).
New York: Jamnback (1969).
Northeastern United States: Stojanovich (1961).
Ohio: Parsons et al. (1972).
Oklahoma: Parsons and Howell (1971).
Ontario: James et al. (1969).
Pennsylvania: Wilson et al. (1946).
Southeastern United States: Stojanovich (1961).
Texas: Sublette and Sublette (1970).
Utah: Nielsen (1968).
Virginia: Dorer et al. (1944).
West Virginia: Amrine and Butler (1978).

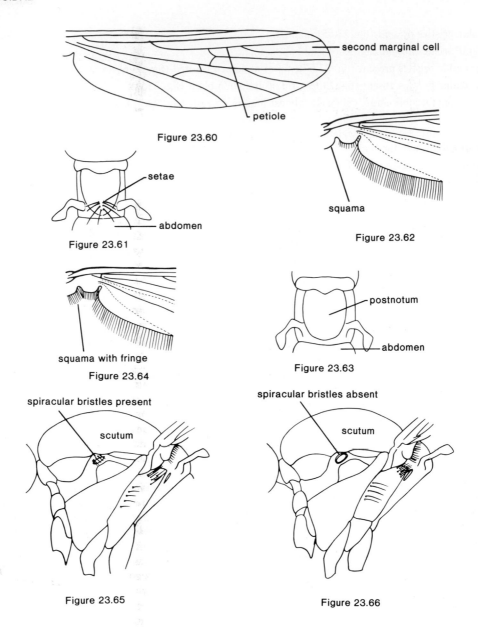

Figure 23.60

Figure 23.61

Figure 23.62

Figure 23.64

Figure 23.63

Figure 23.65

Figure 23.66

Figure 23.60. Typical culicine wing.

Figure 23.61. Dorsal view of *Wyeomyia* sp. postnotum.

Figure 23.62. *Wyeomyia* sp. squama.

Figure 23.63. Dorsal view of typical culicine postnotum.

Figure 23.64. Typical culicine squama.

Figure 23.65. Lateral view of culicine thorax.

Figure 23.66. Lateral view of culicine thorax.

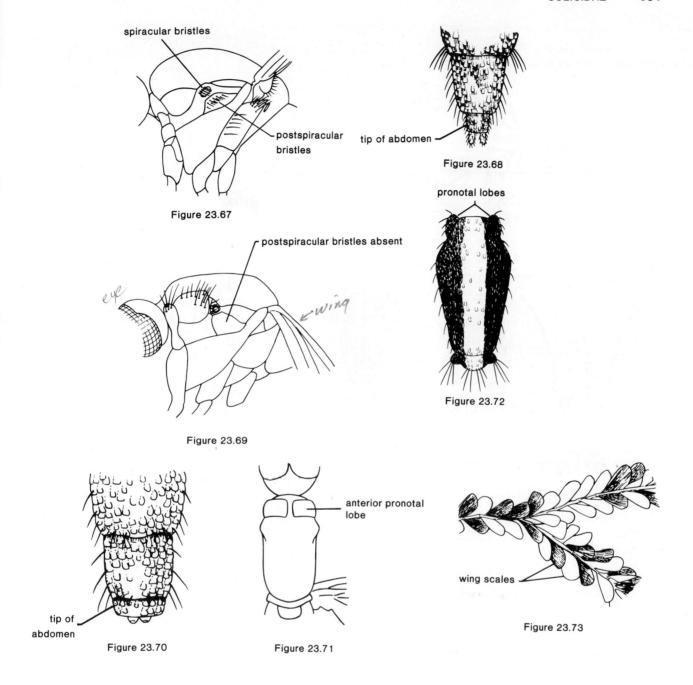

Figure 23.67

Figure 23.68

Figure 23.69

Figure 23.72

Figure 23.70

Figure 23.71

Figure 23.73

Figure 23.67. Lateral view of culicine thorax.

Figure 23.68. Dorsal view of pointed culicine abdomen.

Figure 23.69. Lateral view of culicine thorax.

Figure 23.70. Dorsal view of blunt culicine abdomen.

Figure 23.71. Dorsal view of pronotal lobes of *Haemogogus* sp.

Figure 23.72. Dorsal view of culicine thorax.

Figure 23.73. Enlarged view of *Mansonia* sp. broad wing scale, mixed brown and white.

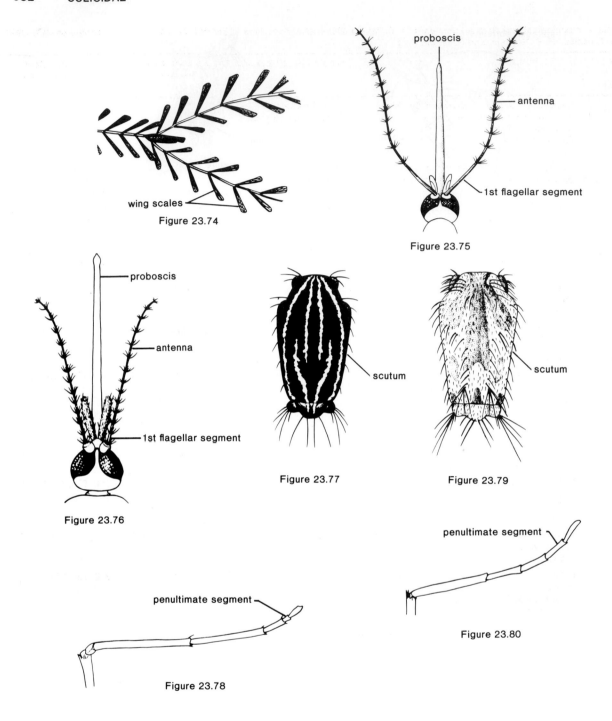

wing scales

Figure 23.74

proboscis

antenna

1st flagellar segment

Figure 23.75

proboscis

antenna

1st flagellar segment

Figure 23.76

scutum

Figure 23.77

scutum

Figure 23.79

penultimate segment

Figure 23.80

penultimate segment

Figure 23.78

Figure 23.74. Enlarged view of culicine narrow wing scales.

Figure 23.75. Dorsal view of head showing *Deinocerites* sp. antenna.

Figure 23.76. Dorsal view of culicine head showing typical mosquito antenna.

Figure 23.77. Dorsal view of *Orthopodomyia* sp. scutum.

Figure 23.78. *Orthopodomyia* sp. tarsus.

Figure 23.79. Dorsal view of culicine scutum.

Figure 23.80. Typical culicine front tarsus.

ble 23A. Summary of ecological and distributional data for *Culicidae (Diptera) (mosquitoes)*. (For definition of terms see Tables 6a–6C; table əpared by K. W. Cummins, H. D. Newson, and R. W. Merritt.)

Taxa (number of species in parentheses)	Habitat	Habit	Trophic Relationships	North American Distribution	Ecological References*
licidae(166) (mosquitoes)	Generally lentic—littoral (limnetic), lotic—depositional (pools and backwaters)	Generally planktonic—swimmers	Generally collectors—filterers and gatherers		360, 875, 964, 1217, 1316, 1886, 2377, 2548
Aedes(78)	Lentic (temporary ponds and pools)	Swimmers (divers, feeding at bottom)	Collectors—gatherers and filterers	Widespread	36, 360, 410, 565, 875, 1089, 1307, 1642, 1966, 2377
Anopheles(16)	Lentic—littoral (limnetic), lotic—depositional	Planktonic—swimmers	Collectors—filterers	Widespread	109, 139, 360, 412, 875, 1124, 1307, 1966, 2011, 2377, 2726
Culex(29)	Lentic—limnetic (lakes, ponds, ditches, and ground pools)	Planktonic—swimmers	Collectors—filterers	Widespread	360, 501, 502, 503, 504, 875, 942, 1307, 1966, 2208, 2377
Culiseta(8) (=Theobaldia)	Lentic—limnetic (ponds and ground pools)	Planktonic—swimmers, divers (feeding at bottom)	Collectors—gatherers and filterers	Widespread	360, 875, 1089, 1307, 1966
Deinocerites(3)	Beach zone—marine intertidal	Planktonic (crab holes)	Collectors—filterers	Extreme South	360, 875, 1307
Haemogogus(1)	Lentic (tree holes)	Planktonic	Collectors—filterers	Southern Texas	241
Mansonia(3)	Lentic—vascular hydrophytes	Clingers (stems and roots of plants, piercing respiratory siphon)	Collectors—gatherers and filterers	Widespread	360, 875, 1307, 2377
Orthopodomyia(3)	Lentic (tree holes and wooden artificial water containers)	Planktonic	Collectors—filterers	East, South	360, 875, 1307
Psorophora(15)	Lentic (temporary ponds and pools)	Planktonic—swimmers	Predators (piercers), collectors—filterers	Widespread	360, 875, 1307, 2377, 2747
Toxorhynchites(2) (=Megarhinus)	Lentic (in tree and rock holes, artificial water containers, and bromeliads)	Planktonic	Predators (engulfers)	East, South	360, 875, 1307, 2377, 2747
Uranotaenia(4)	Lentic—limnetic (ponds and ground pools)	Planktonic—swimmers	Collectors—filterers	Widespread (except for West and intermountain)	360, 875, 1307, 2377
Wyeomyia(4)	Lentic (bog mats in pitcher plants and small pools and water in living and dead plants)	Planktonic (in microhabitats in living and dead plants)	Collectors—filterers	East, Southeast	360, 728, 875, 1190, 1307, 2208

nphasis on trophic relationships.

Simuliidae

24

B. V. Peterson[1]
Biosystematics Research Institute
Agriculture Canada, Ottawa, Ontario

INTRODUCTION

Female black flies are among the most important insect pests of humans and animals in many parts of the world because of their role as vectors of certain parasitic disease organisms and the irritation, and toxic and allergic manifestations of their bite. Because of these factors, they have a marked impact on the economy of many regions of the world. Not all female black flies bite humans; some species feed strictly on birds or other animals, and some species do not feed on blood at all. Adults of both sexes imbibe nectar as a source of energy.

The greatest public health importance of black flies lies in their roles as vectors of the filarial nematode *Onchocerca volvulus* Leuckart, the causitive organism of human onchocerciasis ("river blindness"), in tropical Africa, Central America, northern South America, and Yemen where 20–30 million people are infected. The main vectors, as now known, include several species of the *Simulium damnosum* Theobald complex in Africa, and S. *amazonicum* Goeldi, S. *metallicum* Bellardi, S. *ochraceum* Walker, S. *sanguineum* Knab, and S. *callidum* (Dyar and Shannon) in the New World tropics. Other species serve as vectors of other filarial nematodes of humans, cattle, ducks, loons, and possibly deer and moose. In addition to filarial nematodes, some black flies are known to transmit various avian blood protozoans including the genus *Trypanosoma* and several species of *Leucocytozoon,* as well as certain viruses pathogenic to various animals. Crosskey (1973) tabulates our present knowledge of the role of black flies as vectors of pathogenic organisms.

Although the general life cycle for most black fly species is similar, much remains to be learned about individual species. The female is ready to mate and oviposit usually after egg maturation, for which a blood meal is often required. However, mating can occur shortly after emergence or just before oviposition and takes place in flight or while landed. In some species the male transfers the sperm to the female in a spermatophore (Davies 1965a).

After mating, females lay their eggs in a variety of lotic environments ranging from the smallest trickles to the largest rivers; the choice of habitat varies with the species. Most females average 200–500 eggs in a single gonotrophic cycle.

Various species oviposit in different manners, ranging from the free distribution of eggs while the female taps her abdomen on the water surface during flight, or ovipositing while landed on wet surfaces such as grass trailing in the water, to crawling underwater to deposit the eggs.

Depending on the species and water temperature, incubation time varies from four to 30 days and even longer in those species whose eggs pass through diapause. The egg burster on the larval head can be seen through the egg shell just prior to hatching. Larvae may remain at the site of hatching if the substrate and food supply are adequate, or they may drift downstream on silken threads to suitable sites. Larvae pass through a series of 4–9 molts (usually seven). Growth rates fluctuate with water temperatures and the quantity and quality of available food. The larval period varies from less than one to six or seven months in overwintering species. Some larvae are filter feeders, whereas those without labral fans are collectors of organic detritus around their attachment sites (table 24A). Last stage larvae (pharate pupae) spin variously shaped cocoons that serve to anchor and protect the developing pupae.

The duration of the pupal stage also varies according to water temperature, but usually lasts about 4–7 days. When the adult is ready to emerge, it pulls itself out of the pupal skin through a T-shaped slit originating at the back of the head and continuing along the median longitudinal line of the thorax. As the adult emerges its wings expand and the fly rises to the water surface in a bubble of air. In most instances, the adult flies immediately to a nearby support to rest and allow its cuticle to harden. After mating, and a suitable blood meal, if required, the life cycle begins again.

External Morphology

The family Simuliidae is one of the most homogeneous and easily recognized families in the order Diptera. However, generic and especially specific determinations are often difficult to make because of this homogeneity. Eleven genera and 17 subgenera are recognized in North America with about 143 described species (Peterson 1981). The family is characterized as follows.

Eggs

The eggs are small, ranging from about 0.18 to 0.46 mm in length, and ovid, but varying from triangular or kidney-shaped in one aspect to more oval in another. They are pale white when laid and gradually darken to brown with age.

1. New address: Systematic Entomology Laboratory, IIBIII,
    Agricultural Research Service, U.S.D.A.
    c/o National Museum of Natural History
    NHB 168
    Washington D.C. 20560

Larvae

The larvae are slender and somewhat cylindrical, varying from about 5.0 to 15.0 mm long, apneustic (chap. 4), and are pale whitish brown to blackish brown in color (fig. 24.1). The head is prognathus (directed forward), well developed, and heavily sclerotized (figs. 24.2–24.5), with a variable pattern of pale or dark spots especially dorsally. There is usually a pair of dorsal labral fans used for straining food particles from flowing water (fig. 24.1); these are absent in a few forms (fig. 24.6). The antennae are slender, consisting of four segments and are variously pigmented or patterned.

The head capsule has a ventral anterior wedge-shaped or subtriangular hypostoma (fig. 24.11), bearing a series of heavily sclerotized teeth along the anterior margin, and has smooth or variously serrated lateral margins. Usually the head capsule's posteroventral margin has a median incision or hypostomal cleft (fig. 24.11) that varies in size and shape. The mouthparts are well developed with the labrum forming an enlarged lobe or beaklike structure that lies anteroventral to, and is continuous medially with, the ventral surface of the stalks of the labral fans (fig. 24.4). The mandibles (figs. 24.5, 24.7–24.8) are heavily sclerotized, broadly rectangular, somewhat laterally flattened, and have 3–5 large apical teeth and two series of smaller teeth or serrations plus eight basic groups of setal brushes. The maxillae (fig. 24.5), which are situated ventral to the mandibles and dorsolateral to the labiohypopharyngeal apparatus, consist of large lobate structures with a single segmented, digitiform (finger-shaped) palpus.

The thoracic segments are stout and indistinctly delineated. The anterior segment bears a ventral two-segmented proleg having an apical ring of minute hooks arranged in rows, and a lateral sclerite of varying size and shape on each side (fig. 24.1). Developing histoblasts of legs, wings and halteres, and respiratory filaments are visible under the epidermis of later instars. The abdomen has eight poorly defined segments with the anterior ones slender and posterior ones variously enlarged. A pair of conical tubercles or a single midventral bulge is sometimes present ventrally on segment 8 (figs. 24.13–24.14). A ring of many rows of minute hooks is present posteriorly, and an anal sclerite, which is usually X-shaped (sometimes subquadrate or Y-shaped), is generally present anterodorsal to the ring of hooks (figs. 24.15–24.18). The rectum has colorless, extrusible anal papillae that are apparently osmoregulatory in function. They are composed of three simple digitiform lobes that sometimes are compound with secondary lobules. The cuticle of the abdomen is sometimes ornamented with fine setae.

Pupae

Typical pupae are shown in figures 24.27–24.28. The head is anteroventral to and flexed beneath the thorax. The frons of the female is shorter and broader than in the male. The female antennal sheaths reach the hind margin of the head, or slightly beyond, while in the male they extend about one-half to three-quarters of that distance. The thorax is enlarged, strongly arched dorsally, and usually has 2–5 dorsal and 1–2 lateral pairs of specialized setae *(trichomes)* on each half. The pupal cuticle is smooth with a faint reticulate (meshed) or densely rugose (wrinkled) pattern, and sometimes has a series or pattern of flattened to raised granules of varying sizes and shapes. A respiratory organ (gill) present at each anterolateral corner of the thorax varies in shape and size, but usually consists of one to many short or long slender filaments; it may be enlarged, clublike or antlerlike, or exhibit various combinations of these forms. The abdominal segments are beset with a varying series of setae and small hooks, and the last segment bears a pair of very short to long terminal spines. The pupae are covered by a variously shaped woven cocoon attached to the substrate.

Adults

Black fly adults are small, stout flies ranging from 1.2 to 5.5 mm in length and are usually dark brown to black but may be reddish brown, gray, orange, or yellow in color. The females have separated eyes that have facets subequal in size, whereas in males the eyes usually touch along the midline above the antennae and the facets of the upper half of each eye are usually distinctly larger than those of the lower half. There are no ocelli. The antennae are short, rather stout, and erect, with 7–9 flagellomeres (fig. 24.40). The proboscis is short and the mouthparts of the female are usually strong, with both the mandibles and the laciniae of the maxillae serrated or toothed and adapted for cutting skin and sucking blood. However, in all males and the females of some species the mouthparts are suitable only for taking nectar. The thorax is usually high and strongly arched. The legs are short and moderately stout with elongated basal tarsomeres *(basitarsi)* on all legs. On the hind leg the basal tarsomere often has an anterior process *(calcipala;* fig. 24.48) on the inner apical surface. The second hind tarsomere frequently has a variably distinct notch *(pedisulcus)* in the posterior margin (fig. 24.48). The tarsal claws are short and simple or there may be a variably sized basal or subbasal tooth (figs. 24.47–24.48, 24.50). The wings are broad, and have strong anterior and weak posterior veins (fig. 24.31). The abdomen has the first tergite modified as a collarlike basal scale. Female terminalia are generally as in figures 24.52, 24.55, and 24.56, and terminalia of the males generally as in figures 24.57 and 24.58, but both vary in size and shape in different species.

For a more detailed description of the morphology of the life history stages in the family Simuliidae, see Peterson (1981).

The following keys to genera for the larval and adult stages omit all currently recognized subgeneric categories; for the subgenera of the adult stage, consult the key by Peterson (1981). Although pupal keys to species can be constructed, a satisfactory key for separating the pupae to genus is not currently possible.

KEY TO GENERA OF SIMULIIDAE

Larvae*

1.   Lateral margins of head capsule strongly convex; labral fans absent (fig. 24.6).
      Anal sclerite Y-shaped (fig. 24.15) 2

1'.   Lateral margins of head capsule less convex; labral fans present (figs. 24.1–24.3).
      Anal sclerite X-shaped (figs. 24.17–24.18), nearly rectangular (fig. 24.16), or
      absent 3

2(1). Outer (dorsal) apical surface of mandible with a series of short fine teeth and
      about 10 rows of distinct comblike scales (fig. 24.8) .... *Gymnopais* Stone

2'.   Outer (dorsal) apical surface of mandible without a series of short fine teeth, and
      without comblike scales (fig. 24.7) .... *Twinnia* Stone and Jamnback

3(1'). Postocciput nearly complete dorsally, enclosing cervical sclerites (fig. 24.3). Basal
      2 segments of antenna pale, strongly contrasting with darkly pigmented distal
      segments (fig. 24.3). Median tooth of hypostoma distinctly trifid (fig. 24.19).
      Anal papillae consisting of 3 simple fingerlike lobes (fig. 24.17) .... *Prosimulium* Roubaud

3'.   Postocciput with a distinct and usually wide gap dorsally, not enclosing cervical
      sclerites (fig. 24.2). Basal 2 segments of antenna at least partially pigmented,
      usually yellow to brown, not strongly contrasting in color with distal segments
      (fig. 24.2). Median tooth of hypostoma single (fig. 24.20). Anal papillae
      consisting of 3 simple or compound lobes (figs. 24.17–24.18) 4

4(3'). Hypostoma with median tooth and outer lateral (corner) teeth of each side
      moderately large and subequal in height, and with 3 variably smaller but nearly
      equal sublateral (intermediate) teeth on each side (fig. 24.20). Anterodorsal
      portion of frontoclypeal apotome in lateral view not noticeably arched nor
      strongly convex (fig. 24.4). Anal papillae usually consisting of 3 compound
      lobes, but lobes simple in species of subgenus *Psilozia* and in a few species of
      subgenus *Eusimulium* .... *Simulium* Latreille

4'.   Hypostoma either with uniformly small teeth (figs. 24.23–24.24), with teeth on
      each side of median tooth confined to one large lobe (fig. 24.21), or with teeth
      clustered in 3 prominent groups (fig. 24.22). Anterodorsal portion of
      frontoclypeal apotome in lateral view often strongly convex (fig. 24.5). Anal
      papillae consisting of 3 simple lobes 5

5(4'). Hypostomal cleft reaching or extending anteriorly slightly beyond posterior margin
      of hypostoma, and of nearly uniform width throughout, with apex rather
      truncate (fig. 24.10). Hypostomal teeth all very small (fig. 24.10) .... *Metacnephia* Crosskey

5'.   Hypostomal cleft not extending much more than about half distance to posterior
      margin of hypostoma, often much less, usually shaped like an inverted U or V
      (figs. 24.11–24.12). Hypostomal teeth variable, but often large and distinct
      (figs. 24.25–24.26) 6

6(5'). Abdominal segment 8 with 2 ventral cone-shaped tubercles (fig. 24.13) 7

6'.   Abdominal segment 8 without 2 ventral cone-shaped tubercles, but sometimes with
      a single transverse midventral bulge (fig. 24.14) 10

7(6). Abdomen abruptly and greatly expanded at segment 5, with its lateral margins
      projecting ventrally beyond central portion of segment (fig. 24.13). Anal sclerite
      absent. Anterior margin of hypostoma with small indistinct teeth (fig. 24.23) .... *Ectemnia* Enderlein

7'.   Abdomen of normal shape, not abruptly nor greatly expanded at segment 5. Anal
      sclerite present. Anterior margin of hypostoma with minute lateral teeth borne
      on 2 large, nearly parallel-sided lobes that are much longer than, or subequal in
      length to, median tooth (figs. 24.21–24.22) 8

8(7'). Third antennal segment much shorter than 2nd segment, without spirallike
      microannulations .... *Greniera denaria* (Davies, Peterson, and Wood)

8'.   Third antennal segment longer than combined lengths of segments 1 and 2, and
      with spirallike microannulations (fig. 24.9) 9

*Larvae of the genus *Parasimulium* are not known

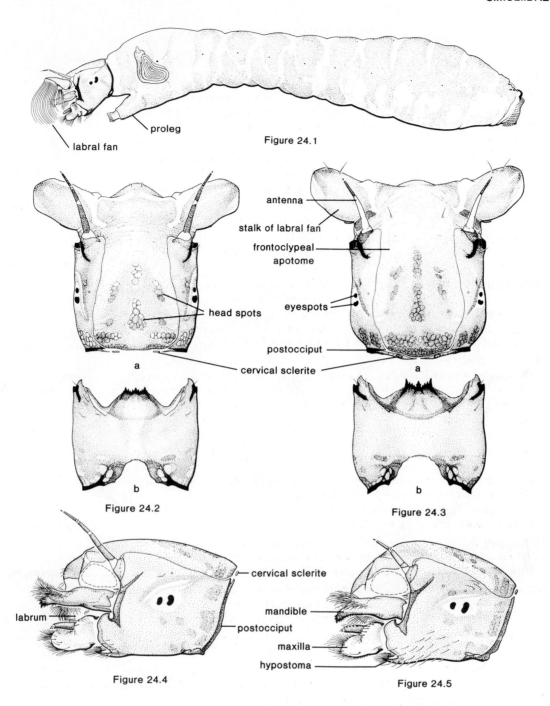

proleg

labral fan

Figure 24.1

antenna

stalk of labral fan

frontoclypeal apotome

eyespots

head spots

postocciput

cervical sclerite

a

b

a

b

Figure 24.2

Figure 24.3

cervical sclerite

labrum

mandible

postocciput

maxilla

hypostoma

Figure 24.4

Figure 24.5

Figure 24.1. Lateral view of larva of *Simulium venustum.*

Figure 24.2. Dorsal *(a)* and ventral *(b)* views of larval head capsule of *Simuliium vittatum.*

Figure 24.3. Dorsal *(a)* and ventral *(b)* views of larval head capsule of *Prosimulium ursinum.*

Figure 24.4. Lateral view of larval head capsule of *Simulium vittatum.*

Figure 24.5. Lateral view of larval head capsule of *Cnephia dacotensis.*

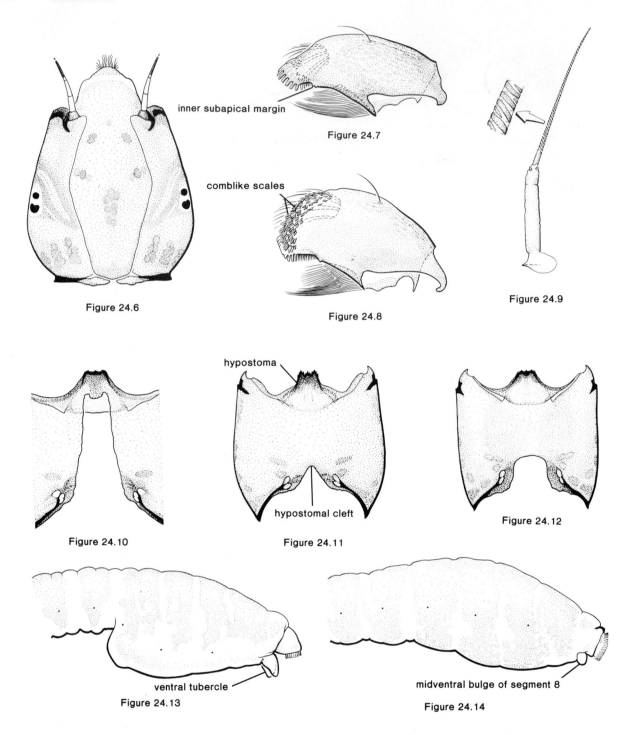

inner subapical margin

Figure 24.7

comblike scales

Figure 24.8

Figure 24.9

Figure 24.6

hypostoma

hypostomal cleft

Figure 24.10

Figure 24.11

Figure 24.12

ventral tubercle

Figure 24.13

midventral bulge of segment 8

Figure 24.14

Figure 24.6. Dorsal view of larval head capsule of *Twinnia tibblesi.*

Figure 24.7. Dorsolateral view of larval mandible of *Twinnia* sp.

Figure 24.8. Dorsolateral view of larval mandible of *Gymnopais* sp.

Figure 24.9. Larval antenna of *Greniera* sp.

Figure 24.10. Ventral view of larval head capsule of *Metacnephia saileri.*

Figure 24.11. Ventral view of larval head capsule of *Stegopterna mutata.*

Figure 24.12. Ventral view of larval head capsule of *Cnephia dacotensis.*

Figure 24.13. Lateral view of larval abdomen of *Ectemnia invenusta.*

Figure 24.14. Lateral view of larval abdomen of *Stegopterna mutata.*

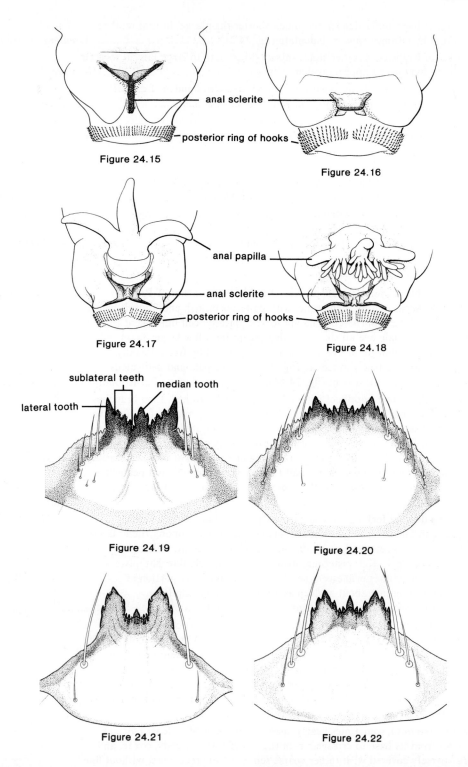

Figure 24.15

Figure 24.16

Figure 24.17

Figure 24.18

Figure 24.19

Figure 24.20

Figure 24.21

Figure 24.22

Figure 24.15. Dorsal view of posterior portion of larval abdomen of *Gymnopais* sp.

Figure 24.16. Dorsal view of posterior portion of larval abdomen of *Prosimulium decemarticulatum.*

Figure 24.17. Dorsal view of posterior portion of larval abdomen of *Simulium vittatum.*

Figure 24.18. Dorsal view of posterior portion of larval abdomen of *Simulium canadense.*

Figure 24.19. Ventral view of anterior portion of larval head capsule of *Prosimulium ursinum* showing hypostomal teeth.

Figure 24.20. Ventral view of anterior portion of larval head capsule of *Simulium vittatum* showing hypostomal teeth.

Figure 24.21. Ventral view of anterior portion of larval head capsule of *Greniera abdita* showing hypostomal teeth.

Figure 24.22. Ventral view of anterior portion of larval head capsule of *Stegopterna mutata* showing hypostomal teeth.

9(8').   Median tooth of hypostoma slender and much shorter than large, lateral toothed
         lobes so that hypostoma appears bidentate (fig. 24.21) .... ***Greniera abdita*** (Peterson) group

9'.   Median tooth of hypostoma rather stout, subequal in length to large lateral toothed
         lobes so that hypostoma appears tridentate (fig. 24.25) .... ***Greniera*** Doby and David (in part)

10(6'). Hypostomal cleft moderately deep with its anterior margin rounded (fig. 24.12).
         Hypostomal teeth uniformly small (fig. 24.24) .... ***Cnephia*** Enderlein

10'.   Hypostomal cleft narrow, shallow, and acutely pointed or narrowly rounded,
         shaped much like an inverted V (fig. 24.11). Hypostomal teeth larger and strong
         (fig. 24.22) 11

11(10'). Abdominal segment 8 with a single transverse midventral bulge (fig. 24.14).
         Hypostomal teeth as in figure 24.22; outside margin of lateral cluster of teeth
         usually sloping inwardly. Labral fan with 40–60 rays .... ***Stegopterna*** Enderlein

11'.   Abdominal segment 8 simple, without a transverse midventral bulge (fig. 24.1).
         Hypostomal teeth as in figure 24.26; outside margin of lateral cluster of teeth
         parallel or slightly sloping outwardly. Labral fan with 22–26 rays ..... ***Mayacnephia*** Wygodzinsky and Coscaron

Adults

1.   R$_1$ joining C slightly beyond middle of wing (fig. 24.29); branches of Rs
         conspicuously separated by membrane, with posterior branch ending well before
         terminus of C; false vein (m–cu fold) not forked apically; cell bm absent (fig.
         24.29). Facets of male eye all similar in size except for a few larger facets near
         middle of anterior margin of eye; eyes broadly separated by frons dorsally,
         touching or nearly so below antennae (fig. 24.38). Calcipala and pedisulcus
         absent. Mesepimeral tuft absent (fig. 24.44). .... Parasimuliinae .... ***Parasimulium*** Malloch

1'.   R$_1$ joining C well beyond middle of wing (fig. 24.30); if Rs forked, then branches
         lying closer together, with posterior branch ending near terminus of C; false vein
         (m–cu fold) distinctly forked apically; cell bm present or absent (figs.
         24.30–24.31). Facets of dorsal half of male eye usually conspicuously larger
         than those of ventral half; eyes usually touching or nearly so at middle of head
         above antennae, with frons usually small (fig. 24.39). Calcipala and pedisulcus
         present or absent (figs. 24.47–24.49). Mesepimeral tuft present (figs.
         24.45–24.46) .... Simuliinae 2

2(1').   Rs with a long distinct fork that is conspicuously longer than its petiole (fig.
         24.30); C with fine setae only, without spinules interspersed among them; basal
         section of R always setose (figs. 24.30, 24.35); cell bm present, although
         sometimes very small. Katepisternum divided by a wide, shallow katepisternal
         sulcus that is sometimes evanescent (fading) anteriorly; lower portion of
         katepisternum in profile about as deep as, or deeper than, long (figs.
         24.45–24.46). Calcipala and pedisulcus absent (fig. 24.47) 3

2'.   Rs unforked, or with a short usually obscure apical fork that is conspicuously
         shorter than its petiole (fig. 24.31); C often with spinules interspersed among its
         fine setae; basal section of R setose or bare; small cell bm present or absent
         (figs. 24.31–24.32). Katepisternum usually divided by a narrow, deep, more or
         less complete katepisternal sulcus; lower portion of katepisternum, in profile,
         often longer than deep (fig. 24.43). Calcipala and pedisulcus present or absent
         (figs. 24.48–24.49) 5

3(2).   Wing fumose (smoky), sometimes nearly opaque; petiole of M at least twice as
         long as Rs from its base to crossvein r–m (fig. 24.30). Head, body, coxae, and
         femora sparsely covered with rather coarse semierect to erect setae, without fine
         recumbent setae (fig. 24.46); clypeus bare except for a few erect setae near
         lateral margins. Postnotum rather small and strongly arched, sometimes with a
         varyingly conspicuous median longitudinal ridge or line; anepisternal membrane
         usually with some setae dorsally (apparently absent in one species). Anal lobe
         and cercus of female fused into a single, heavily sclerotized piece; spermatheca
         globular, sclerotized, with a long neck (fig. 24.55). Gonostylus of male usually
         with 2 or more minute apical spinules that cannot easily be seen under a
         dissecting microscope .... ***Gymnopais*** Stone

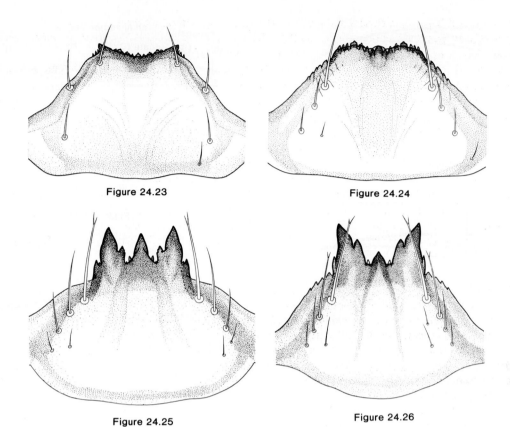

Figure 24.23

Figure 24.24

Figure 24.25

Figure 24.26

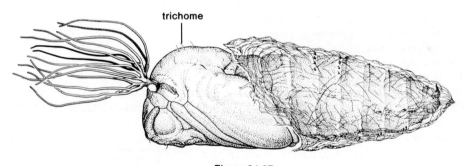

trichome

Figure 24.27

respiratory organ

Figure 24.28

Figure 24.23. Ventral view of anterior portion of larval head capsule of *Ectemnia invenusta* showing hypostomal teeth.

Figure 24.24. Ventral view of anterior portion of larval head capsule of *Cnephia dacotensis* showing hypostomal teeth.

Figure 24.25. Ventral view of anterior portion of larval head capsule of *Greniera* sp. showing hypostomal teeth.

Figure 24.26. Ventral view of anterior portion of larval head capsule of *Mayacnephia* sp. showing hypostomal teeth.

Figure 24.27. Lateral view of pupa of *Prosimulium ursinum.*

Figure 24.28. Lateral view of pupa of *Simulium vittatum.*

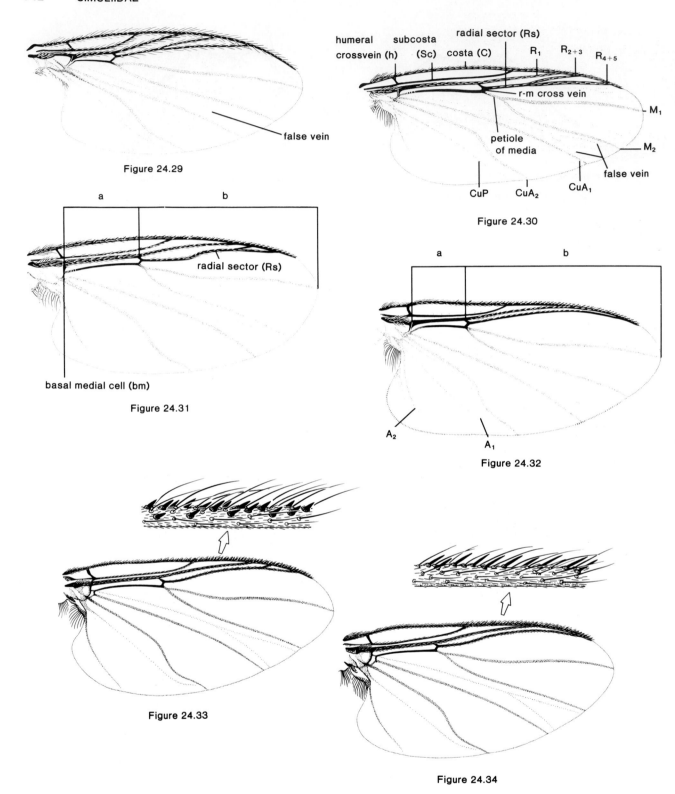

Figure 24.29

humeral
crossvein (h)   subcosta   radial sector (Rs)
                (Sc)   costa (C)   R₁   R₂₊₃   R₄₊₅
                        r-m cross vein   M₁
                petiole
                of media   M₂
                        false vein
CuP   CuA₂   CuA₁

Figure 24.30

a   b
                radial sector (Rs)
basal medial cell (bm)

Figure 24.31

a   b
A₂   A₁

Figure 24.32

Figure 24.33

Figure 24.34

Figure 24.29. Wing of *Parasimulium stonei* male.

Figure 24.30. Wing of Gymnopais holopticus female.

Figure 24.31. Wing of *Cnephia dacotensis* female.

Figure 24.32. Wing of Simulium venustum female.

Figure 24.33. Wing of *Mayacnephia* sp. female.

Figure 24.34. Wing of *Greniera* sp. female.

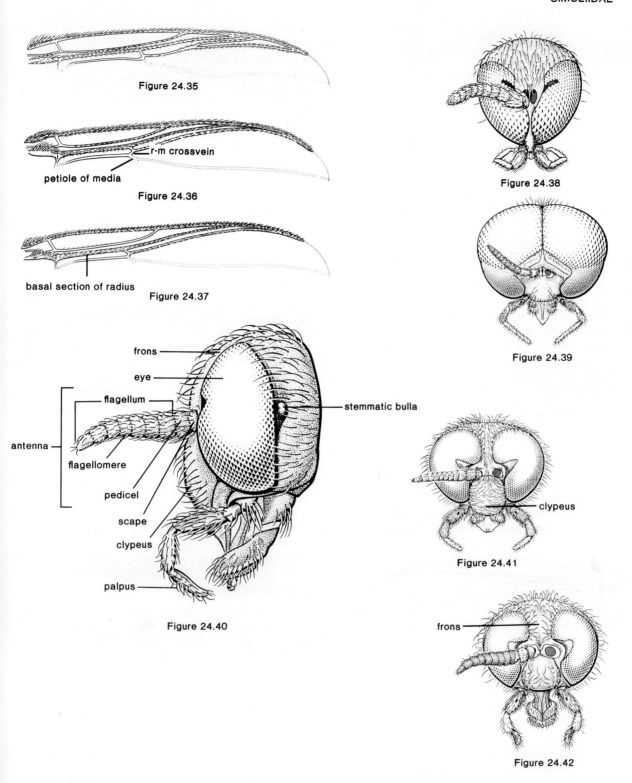

Figure 24.35

Figure 24.36

r-m crossvein

petiole of media

Figure 24.36

basal section of radius

Figure 24.37

Figure 24.38

Figure 24.39

frons

eye

flagellum

antenna

flagellomere

pedicel

scape

clypeus

palpus

stemmatic bulla

Figure 24.40

clypeus

Figure 24.41

frons

Figure 24.42

Figure 24.35. Anterior portion of wing of *Prosimulium ursinum* female.

Figure 24.36. Anterior portion of wing of *Greniera abdita* female.

Figure 24.37. Anterior portion of wing of *Metacnephia saileri* female.

Figure 24.38. Anterior view of adult head of *Parasimulium stonei* male.

Figure 24.39. Anterior view of adult head of *Simulium decorum* male.

Figure 24.40. Lateral view of adult head of *Twinnia* sp. female.

Figure 24.41. Anterior view of adult head of *Ectemnia taeniatifrons* female.

Figure 24.42. Anterior view of adult head of *Cnephia dacotensis* female.

3'.   Wing usually hyaline (clear), but, if slightly fumose or tinted, then distinctly
             transparent; petiole of M less than twice as long as Rs from its base to crossvein
             r–m (figs. 24.33–24.34). Head, body, coxae, and femora entirely covered with
             rather dense, fine, recumbent setae (fig. 24.45), with a few erect setae
             sometimes evident especially posteromedially on scutum; clypeus entirely
             covered with setae. Postnotum larger, rather evenly arched, without a median
             longitudinal ridge or line; anepisternal membrane setose or bare. Anal lobe and
             cercus of female clearly separated by membrane, usually lightly to moderately
             sclerotized; spermatheca of various shapes, but, if sclerotized, then without a
             long sclerotized neck. Gonostylus of male with a variable number of apical
             spinules that are visible under a dissecting microscope **4**

4(3').   Antenna with 7 flagellomeres (fig. 24.40), rarely with 8. Posterior margin of eye
             near middle with a slightly raised but prominent shiny stemmatic bulla (fig.
             24.40). Claws of female simple. Hypogynial valve of female rather truncate,
             short, not reaching anal lobe; spermatheca short, broader than long, with a large
             differentiated area at junction with spermathecal duct (fig. 24.52). Gonostylus
             of male with 1 (rarely 2) apical spinule; lateral margins of ventral plate of
             aedeagus strongly emarginate near junction with basal arms (fig. 24.57) .... *Twinnia* Stone and Jamnback

4'.   Antenna usually with 9 flagellomeres (figs. 24.41–24.42), but sometimes with 7 or
             8. Posterior margin of eye near middle without a prominent stemmatic bulla,
             but in some species with a weak indication of a bulla. Claws of female variable.
             Hypogynial valve of female short or elongate, but, if valve short and rather
             truncate, then claws having a variably sized but usually conspicuous basal or
             subbasal tooth; spermatheca variable. Gonostylus of male often with more than
             1 apical spinule; ventral plate of aedeagus variable, but not exactly as above .... *Prosimulium* Roubaud

5(2').   Length of basal section of R (a, fig. 24.32) equal to much less than one-third
             distance from base of Rs to apex of wing (b, fig. 24.32); R with or without setae
             dorsally; cell bm absent or greatly reduced. Calcipala usually well developed
             (figs. 24.48, 24.50), although sometimes reduced (e.g., *Psilozia* Enderlein; fig.
             24.51); pedisulcus present, usually deep and distinct (figs. 24.48, 24.50–24.51),
             rarely a shallow depression .... *Simulium* Latreille

5'.   Length of basal section of R (a, fig. 24.31) rarely less than one-third distance from
             base of Rs to apex of wing (b, fig. 24.31); R setose dorsally; cell bm present and
             distinguishable. Calcipala present, but sometimes reduced; pedisulcus absent, or,
             if present, very shallow **6**

6(5').   C with fine, uniformly colored setae, some of which are sometimes short and stiff,
             but not spiniform (spine-shaped) or darker in color (fig. 24.36) .... *Greniera* Doby and David .. **7**

6'.   C with short stout black spinules interspersed among longer and paler setae (fig.
             24.33) **8**

7(6)   Antenna with 8 flagellomeres .... *Greniera* Doby and David (in part)
                                     (1 sp., *denaria* (Davies, Peterson, and Wood); Ontario, British Columbia)

7'.   Antenna with 9 flagellomeres .... *Greniera abdita* (Peterson) group

8(6').   Rs with a short but distinct apical fork, with branches narrowly separated by
             membrane (fig. 24.33); Sc of male bare ventrally .... *Mayacnephia* Wygodzinsky and Coscaron

8'.   Rs simple, or with a short indistinct apical fork whose branches are closely
             appressed and scarcely or not separated by membrane; Sc of male bare or setose
             ventrally **9**

9(8').   Calcipala large and prominent, lamellate, rounded apically, in posterior view
             overlapping and sometimes concealing base of 2nd tarsomere (fig. 24.49); claw
             of female simple. Sc of male setose ventrally .... *Stegopterna* Enderlein

9'.   Calcipala absent, or, if present, small and bluntly pointed, in posterior view not
             concealing base of 2nd tarsomere; claw of female with a small subbasal tooth or
             a large basal thumblike projection. Sc of male bare or setose ventrally **10**

10(9').   Female **11**

10'   Male **14**

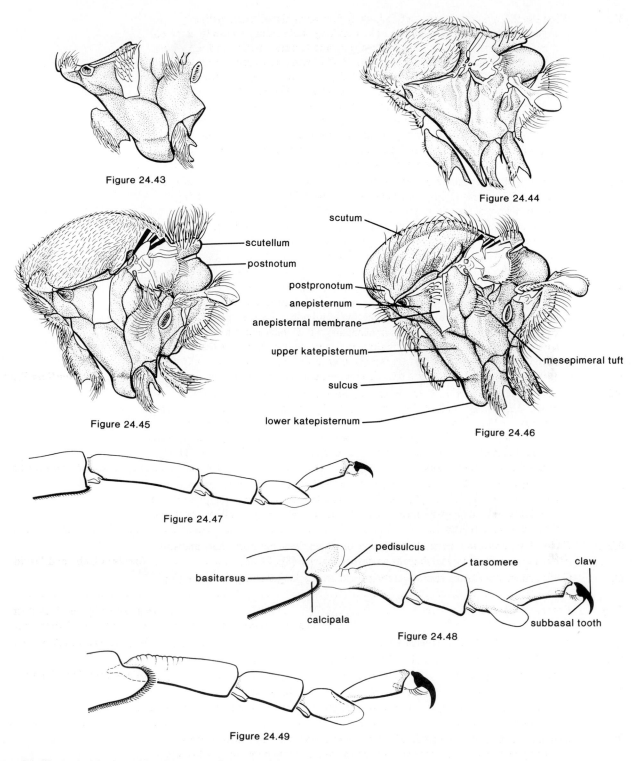

Figure 24.43

Figure 24.44

scutellum
postnotum

Figure 24.45

scutum
postpronotum
anepisternum
anepisternal membrane
upper katepisternum
mesepimeral tuft
sulcus
lower katepisternum

Figure 24.46

Figure 24.47

basitarsus
pedisulcus
tarsomere
claw
calcipala
subbasal tooth

Figure 24.48

Figure 24.49

Figure 24.43. Lateral view of anterior portion of adult thorax of *Metacnephia jeanae* female.

Figure 24.44. Lateral view of adult thorax of *Parasimulium stonei* male.

Figure 24.45. Lateral view of adult thorax of *Prosimulium mixtum* female.

Figure 24.46. Lateral view of adult thorax of *Gymnopais holopticus* female.

Figure 24.47. Hind tarsomeres of adult *Prosimulium ursinum* female.

Figure 24.48. Hind tarsomeres of adult *Simulium arcticum* female.

Figure 24.49. Hind tarsomeres of adult *Stegopterna mutata* female.

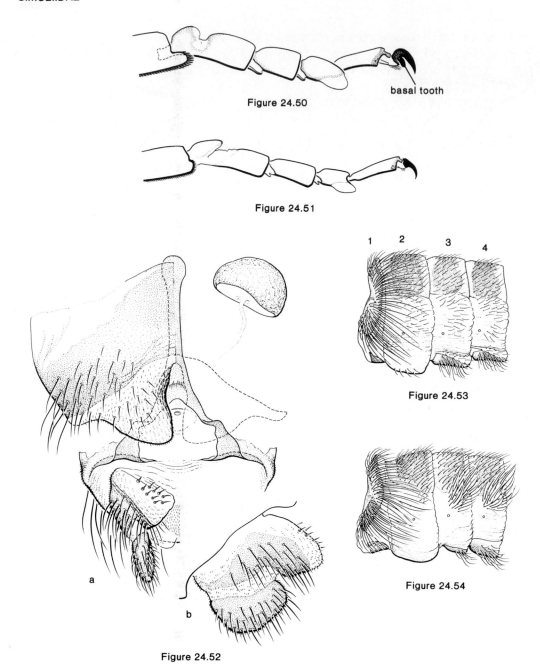

basal tooth

Figure 24.50

Figure 24.51

a

b

Figure 24.52

Figure 24.53

Figure 24.54

Figure 24.50. Hind tarsomeres of adult *Simulium meridionale* female.

Figure 24.51. Hind tarsomeres of adult *Simulium vittatum* female.

Figure 24.52. Female terminalia of adult *Twinnia tibblesi:* *a,* ventral view; *b,* lateral view.

Figure 24.53. Abdominal segments 1–4 of adult *Cnephia dacotensis* male.

Figure 24.54. Abdominal segments 1–4 of adult *Greniera* sp. male.

11(10).   R$_1$ dorsally with scattered black spinules on distal half (fig. 24.37). Anepisternal
membrane usually with tuft of pale setae dorsally (fig. 24.43) .... *Metacnephia* Crosskey (in part)

11'.   R$_1$ dorsally with setae only on distal half. If a few spinules present on R$_1$, then
anepisternal membrane bare 12

12(11').   Frons narrow, 4 times longer than wide, of nearly uniform width (fig. 24.41) .... *Ectemnia* Enderlein (in part)

12'.   Frons wider, not more than twice as long as wide, or, if narrower, then noticeably
widening above (fig. 24.42) 13

13(12').   Halter pale brown, with knob paler than stem. R$_1$ dorsally with a few spinules on
distal half .... *Cnephia* Enderlein (in part)

13'.   Halter entirely black. R$_1$ dorsally with setae only on distal half .... *Greniera* Doby and David (in part)
(1 sp; undescribed; British Columbia)

14(10').   R$_1$ dorsally with scattered black spinules on distal two-thirds or more; these more
numerous apically and as stout as spinules on C 15

14'   R$_1$ dorsally usually with setae only; if spinules present on R$_1$, these confined to
distal half or less and not as stout as spinules on C (fig. 24.34) 16

15(14).   Sc setose ventrally. Anepisternal membrane usually with tuft of pale setae dorsally
(as in fig. 24.43) .... *Metacnephia* Crosskey (in part)
(see couplet 11)

15'.   Sc bare ventrally. Anepisternal membrane bare .... *Ectemnia* Enderlein (in part)
(see couplet 12)

16(14').   Halter brown, with knob distinctly paler than stem. Fine setae on pleural
membrane of abdominal segments 3 and 4 not conspicuously long
(fig. 24.53) .... *Cnephia* Enderlein (in part)
(see couplet 13)

16'   Halter entirely black. Fine setae on pleural membrane of abdominal segments 3
and 4 long and erect (fig. 24.54) .... *Greniera* Doby and David (in part)
(see couplet 13)

ADDITIONAL TAXONOMIC REFERENCES

General
Malloch (1914); Dyar and Shannon (1927); Vargas (1945); Wirth
and Stone (1956); Davies *et al.* (1962); Wood *et al.* (1963);
Stone (1965); Crosskey (1973); Peterson (1981).

Regional faunas
Alabama: Stone and Snoddy (1969).
Alaska: Stone (1952); Sommerman (1953); Peterson (1970).
Alberta: Abdelnur (1968).
California: Wirth and Stone (1956); Hall (1974).
Canada: Peterson (1970).
Connecticut: Stone (1964a).
Eastern Canada: Twinn (1936).
Michigan: Merritt *et al.* (1978).
Minnesota: Nicholson and Mickel (1950).

New York: Stone and Jamnback (1955).
Northeastern United States: Cupp and Gordon (1983).
Ontario: Davies *et al.* (1962); Wood *et al.* (1963).
Utah: Peterson (1960).
Western United States: Stains and Knowlton (1943).
Wisconsin: Anderson (1960).

Taxonomic treatments at the generic level
(L = larvae; P = pupae; A = adults)
Gymnopais: Wood (1978)–L, P, A.
Parasimulium: Peterson (1977)–A.
Prosimulium: Peterson (1970)–L, P, A.
Simulium: Stone and Jamnback (1955)–L, P, A; Peterson (1960)–A;
Davies *et al.* (1962)–P, A; Wood *et al.* (1963)–L; Stone and
Snoddy (1969)–L, P, A.
Twinnia: Wood (1978)–L, P, A.

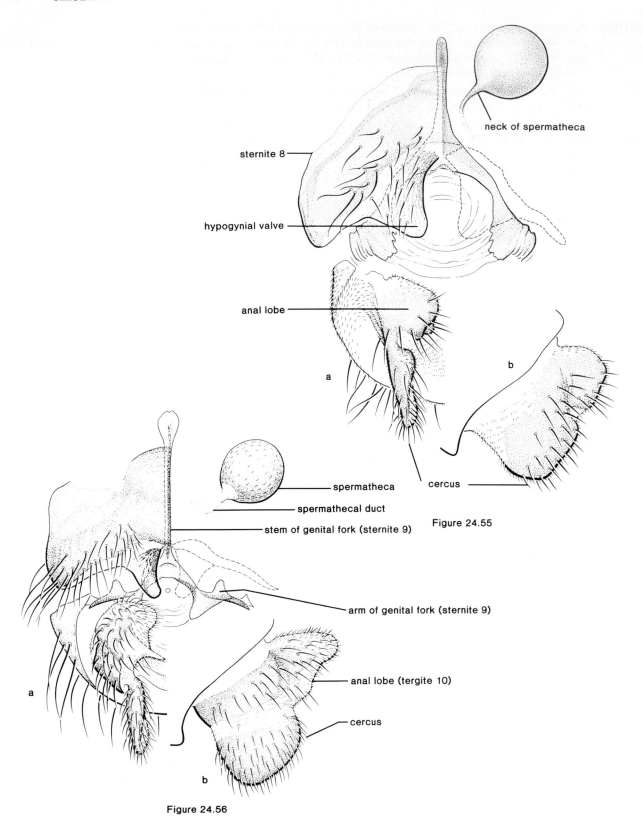

neck of spermatheca

sternite 8

hypogynial valve

anal lobe

a

b

cercus

Figure 24.55

spermatheca

spermathecal duct

stem of genital fork (sternite 9)

arm of genital fork (sternite 9)

anal lobe (tergite 10)

cercus

a

b

Figure 24.56

Figure 24.55. Female terminalia of adult *Gymnopais holopticus: a,* ventral view; *b,* lateral view.

Figure 24.56. Female terminalia of adult *Simulium vittatum: a,* ventral view; *b,* lateral view.

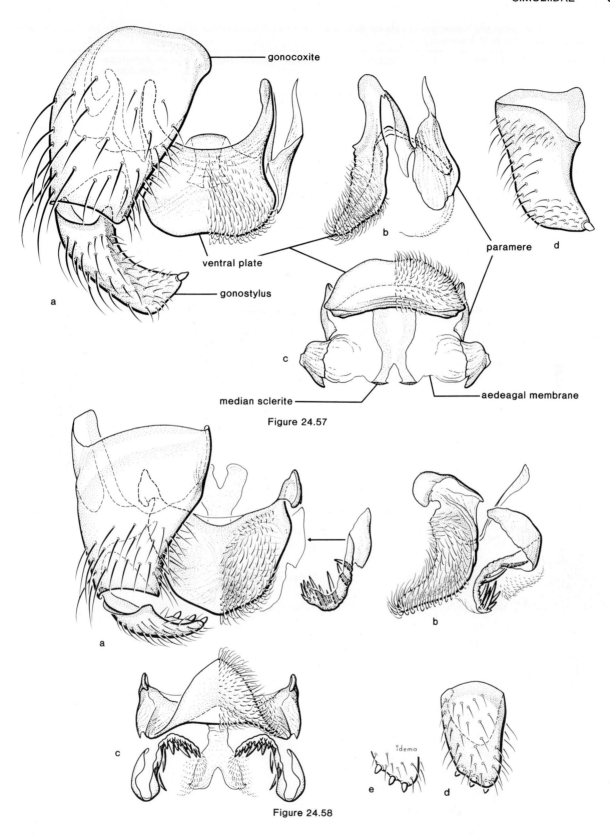

gonocoxite

ventral plate

gonostylus

paramere

median sclerite

aedeagal membrane

Figure 24.57

idema

Figure 24.58

Figure 24.57. Male terminalia of adult *Twinnia tibblesi: a,* ventral view; *b,* lateral view; *c,* terminal (end) view; *d,* inner surface of gonostylus.

Figure 24.58. Male terminalia of adult *Simulium vittatum: a,* ventral view; *b,* lateral view; *c,* terminal (end) view; *d,* outer surface of gonostylus; *e,* tip of inner surface of gonostylus.

Table 24A. Summary of ecological and distributional data for *Simuliidae (Diptera)*. (For definition of terms see Tables 6A–6C; table prepared by R. W. Merritt, K. W. Cummins, and B. V. Peterson.)

Taxa (number of species in parentheses)	Habitat	Habit	Trophic Relationships	North American Distribution	Ecological References*
Simuliidae(143) (black flies, buffalo gnats)	Generally lotic—erosional	Generally clingers (ring of minute hooks on terminal end of abdomen and proleg; silk threads)	Generally collectors—filterers		1217, 1240, 1913, 1915, 2096, 2548
Cnephia(4)	Lotic—erosional	Clingers	Collectors—filterers	Widespread	47, 376, 854, 1370, 1371, 1645, 2096, 2097, 2397, 2767
Ectemnia(2)	Lotic—erosional	Clingers	Collectors—filterers	Widespread	2218
Greniera(4)	Lotic—erosional	Clingers	Collectors—filterers	Northeastern United States and eastern Canada, British Columbia	518
Gymnopais(5)	Lotic—erosional	Clingers	Scrapers	Northwestern North America, from British Columbia to Alaska	521, 2218, 2747, 2751
Mayacnephia(4)	Lotic—erosional	Clingers	Collectors—filterers	Western North America	
Metacnephia(7)	Lotic—erosional	Clingers	Collectors—filterers	Western United States and Canada; Alaska	355, 2218, 2770, 2771
Parasimulium(4)				California, Oregon, Washington	1911, 2347
Prosimulium(42)	Lotic—erosional	Clingers	Collectors—filterers	Widespread	47, 355, 376, 522, 854, 880, 906, 1370, 1371, 1644, 1645, 1912, 2096, 2097
Simulium (66)	Lotic and lentic—erosional	Clingers	Collectors—filterers	Widespread	47, 87, 132, 308, 355, 376, 382, 421, 422, 423, 454, 679, 793, 794, 795, 963, 1295, 1346, 1370, 1371, 1373, 1374, 1375, 1376, 1377, 1528, 1603, 1642, 1645, 1698, 1727, 1756, 1798, 1799, 1800, 1909, 1913, 1969, 2004, 2096, 2097, 2214, 2218, 2397, 2713, 2714, 2766, 2767, 2768, 2769, 2771, 2772, 2781, 2808
Stegopterna(2)	Lotic—erosional	Clingers	Collectors—filterers	Widespread	1644, 1645, 2096, 2097, 2218
Twinnia(3)	Lotic—erosional	Clingers	Scrapers	Western and northeastern United States and Canada	376, 521, 906, 2751

*Emphasis on trophic relationships.

Chironomidae

25

W. P. Coffman
University of Pittsburgh, Pennsylvania

L. C. Ferrington, Jr.
State Biological Survey of Kansas, Lawrence

INTRODUCTION

The family Chironomidae is an ecologically important group of aquatic insects often occurring in high densities and diversity. The relatively short life cycles and the large total biomass of the numerous larvae confer ecological energetic significance on this taxon (as consumers and prey) and the partitioning of ecological resources by a large number of species presumably enhances the biotic stability of aquatic ecosystems.

Chironomid larvae are known to feed on a great variety of organic substrates: (1) coarse detrital particles (leaf- and wood-shredders); (2) medium detrital particles deposited in or on sediments (gatherers and scrapers); (3) fine detrital particles in suspension, transport, or deposited (filter-feeders, gatherers, and scrapers); (4) algae; benthic, planktonic, or in transport (scrapers, gatherers, and to a lesser extent filter-feeders); (5) vascular plants (miners); (6) fungal spores and hyphae (gatherers); (7) animals (as simple predators, often preying on other chironomid larvae, or as parasites on a variety of taxa, although the latter may most often be commensal relationships).

Most aquatic predators feed extensively on chironomids (larvae, pupae, and/or adults) at some point in their life cycles. As predators such as young-of-the-year fish increase in size, they tend to rely less on chironomids.

Chironomids occur in most types of aquatic ecosystems, as well as moist soils, tree holes, and dung. The range of conditions under which chironomids are found is more extensive than that of any other group of aquatic insects. Almost the complete range of gradients of temperature, pH, salinity, oxygen concentration, current velocity, depth, productivity, altitude, latitude, and others have been exploited, at least by some chironomid species. The wide ecological amplitude displayed by this family is the product of a very wide array of morphological, physiological, and behavioral adaptations. Ecologists have utilized the partitioning of gradients by various midge species to characterize the overall ecological conditions of lentic and lotic systems.

Presumably, the great species diversity in this family, with probably more than 2000 species in the Nearctic Region and from 10,000 to 15,000 species worldwide, is the product of its antiquity, relatively low vagility (instances of geographic isolation are common), and evolutionary plasticity. The overall diversity of the family is also reflected in the rich chironomid faunas of many aquatic ecosystems. The number of chironomid species present in most systems often accounts for at least 50% of the total macroinvertebrate species diversity (richness component). Natural lakes, ponds, and streams usually have at least 50 and often more than 100 species. The actual number of species present in a system is the result of the complex of physical, chemical, biological and biogeographic conditions. Obviously, the least diverse faunas are correlated with extreme conditions.

As holometabolous insects, chironomids have four distinct life stages: egg, larva, pupa, and adult (imago). Duration of the larval stage, with four instars, may last from about two weeks to several years, depending on species and environmental conditions. In general, warm water, high-quality food, and small species correlate with shorter life cycles. Average-sized chironomids (fourth instar about 5 mm long) in temperate systems usually have from one to two generations per year. First larval instars may be planktonic, are often difficult to sample, and may have a unique morphology not treated in keys that are designed for fourth instar larvae. Later instars are usually benthic. Toward the end of the fourth instar, the larval thoracic region begins to swell with the formation of the pupal integument and adult tissues. The pupal stage begins with apolysis, the separation (not shedding) of the larval from the underlying pupal integument. After ecdysis, the pupa usually remains hidden in debris until it swims to the surface where eclosion (adult emergence) takes place. Technically, the adult stage begins with the pupal-adult apolysis (pharate adult), which occurs a short time before eclosion. Chironomid adults usually live a few days, although some species survive for several weeks. The adult stage performs the functions of reproduction and dispersal. As a rule, chironomid adults do not need to feed, as reflected by the usual condition of reduced mouthparts and atrophied gut. However, many species (perhaps most) will take liquid and semiliquid carbohydrate sources such as aphid honeydew and flower nectars. The consumption of these energy rich substances presumably maximizes the potential for the completion of additional ovarian cycles.

Mating takes place in aerial swarms, on the surface in skating swarms, or on solid substrates. Females may broadcast the eggs at the water surface or, more frequently, deposit gelatinous egg masses on the open water or on emergent vegetation. Egg or larval development may be arrested under unfavorable environmental conditions. Some species are facultatively or obligatorily parthenogenetic, and larvae parasitized by nematodes or nematomorphs may produce intersexual adults. Excellent reviews of chironomid biology may be found in Oliver (1971) and Davies (1976).

In most ecological studies the larva is the life stage that is most frequently encountered. However, the quantitative collection of early instars is often difficult (chap. 3). Even when larval populations can be "adequately" sampled (chap. 3), sorting, particularly retrieval of early instars, can require prodigious amounts of time (densities of 50,000 larvae per m² are not uncommon). After sorting, the identification of the larvae also proves to be difficult because: (1) only a small percentage of the larvae of Nearctic species have been described; (2) larvae of several important groups of genera are essentially inseparable; (3) keys usually will not separate early instars; and (4) slide preparation of specimens is usually required, and even then diagnostic features are often difficult to see.

The collection of pupal exuviae has only recently become a widely used method for the investigation of chironomids (e.g., Coffman 1973; Wilson and Bright 1973), although the idea is not new (Thienemann 1910; Lenz 1955). The advantages of the technique are numerous. Most generic and species-level taxa are easily separated in the pupal stage, even if a generic or species name cannot be assigned. Large numbers of specimens can usually be collected in a short time. Collection takes advantage of the fact that pupal exuviae are not wettable for a period of time and float on the surface where they can be collected at natural or artificial blockades in streams and along the windward shore in lentic systems. Quantitative collections can be made using enclosures because all known species rise to the surface for eclosion. Since the collections are made from the surface or the water column, the substrates are not disturbed and most emerging species, regardless of larval microhabitat, are collected. Once a voucher slide series for species present in a system has been identified, most can be recognized with a dissecting microscope. Because the pupal exuviae have no tissues (except in the thoracic horns), no clearing is required. All the diagnostic features are usually discernible on every specimen because the specimen is depressed by the cover glass into two dimensions. As there is no ambiguity about the age of pupal exuviae, the size of a species is determined. On occasion, the larval and pupal exuviae as well as the adult of a specimen are collected entangled with each other providing ideal material for association. Studies for which the collection of pupal exuviae is well suited include diversity (richness and actual taxonomic composition of faunas), phenology (diel and annual), biogeography, size distribution of species, sex ratios, and production of adults.

EXTERNAL MORPHOLOGY

Larvae

Mature (fourth instar) chironomid larvae range in size from about 2 to 30 mm. There are three main body divisions: head, thorax, and abdomen, all of which have structures that are utilized for generic-level diagnosis. These divisions may appear as pale yellow or white in preserved larvae or may be variously pigmented or patterned. Common pigmentation includes dark yellow, brown, black, or yellow with a black posterior margin in the case of the head capsule and yellow, green,

blue, violet, rose, orange, or brown in the case of the thorax and abdomen. In addition the presence of hemoglobin in certain larvae produces a strong "blood red" color in living specimens, which often changes to a more diffuse red, red-orange, or brown color when preserved in ethanol.

Head: The head is in the form of a completely sclerotized capsule, and is never fully retractile. Plates that have characters of diagnostic importance associated with them are the *genae* or lateral sclerites, the *frontoclypeal apotome* or dorsal sclerite, the *labrum* or anterodorsal sclerite (figs. 25.97–25.98), and the *mentum* or medioventral sclerite (figs. 25.1–25.4).

Sensory structures situated on the dorsal aspect of the head capsule are the eyespots, antennae, and numerous setae, scales, and lamellae. Eyespots (figs. 25.1–25.4) occur on the dorsal or dorsolateral aspects of the genae. Antennae (figs. 25.1, 25.2, 25.3) also arise from the genae but occur anterior to the eyespots, except in Tanypodinae larvae which have antennae that are retractile into the head capsule (fig. 25.4). Setae originate from all head capsule sclerites, but in dorsal aspect only the S setae of the labrum are of diagnostic importance. The dorsal S setae (figs. 25.1–25.2, 25.3) are paired medial setae of the labrum and are referred to as SI through SIV setae. The anteriormost setal pair are the SI setae; setae SII through SIV originate in sequence progressing posteriorly. Various scales or lamellae (figs. 25.173, 25.175) may surround or originate in close proximity to the bases of the S setae, particularly SI.

Structures associated with feeding show extreme variation among the genera of Chironomidae. In general these structures are concentrated on the anteroventral aspect of the head capsule including the region of the mentum and the ventral surface of the labrum. Included in this category are the pecten epipharyngis, premandibles, mandibles, maxillae, prementohypopharyngeal complex, and the mentum. (See figures 25.1–25.4 for the ventral perspective and orientation of these structures.)

The pecten epipharyngis and premandibles originate from the ventral surface of the labrum. The pecten epipharyngis generally consists of three scales that may be simple or have numerous apical teeth. In some genera the scales may be fused and the pecten epipharyngis thus appears as a single plate or bar. The premandibles are movable ancillary feeding structures and may have a blunt apical cusp or, in the case of some predatory genera, may have from one to several mesally projecting teeth (fig. 25.97). Premandibles are vestigial or lacking in Tanypodinae and Podonominae larvae.

Paired mandibles and maxillae occur ventral to the premandibles. The mandibles may have strong but blunt apical and lateral teeth (figs. 25.231–25.233) or may have an elongate and sharply pointed apical tooth (fig. 25.14); the former is typical of nonpredatory species and the latter, of predatory species. The maxilla, which is usually lightly sclerotized and difficult to discern, bears a maxillary palp which is generally detectable on its anteroventral surface. In Tanypodinae larvae and in some Chironomini species (specifically "*Harnischia* Complex" genera such as *Robackia* and *Beckidia*) the maxillary palp is more elongate and often multisegmented.

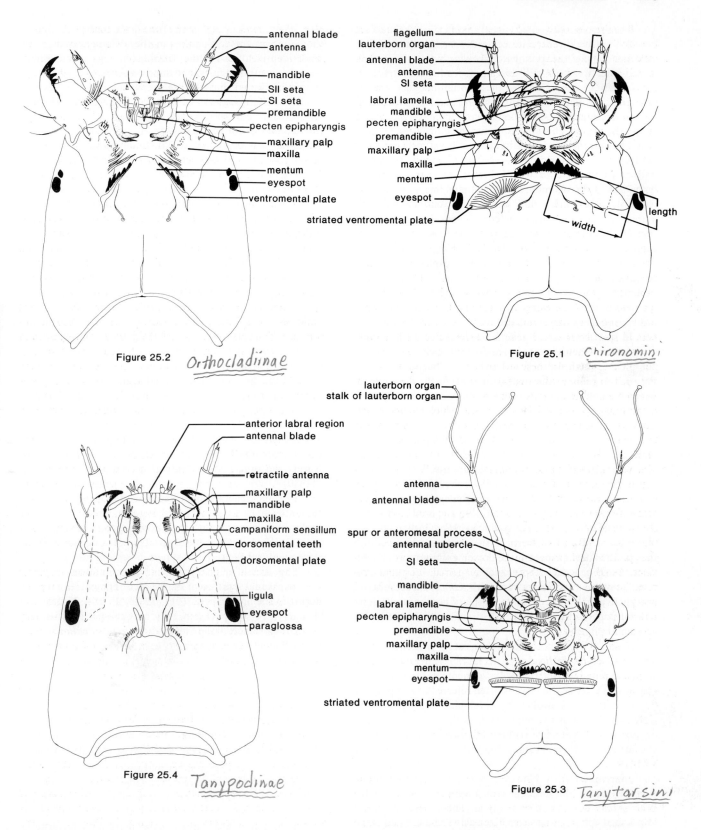

Figure 25.2   *Orthocladiinae*

Figure 25.1   *Chironomini*

Figure 25.4   *Tanypodinae*

Figure 25.3   *Tanytarsini*

Figure 25.1. Generalized Chironomini head capsule (ventral view).

Figure 25.2. Generalized Orthocladiinae head capsule (ventral view).

Figure 25.3. Generalized Tanytarsini head capsule (ventral view).

Figure 25.4. Generalized Tanypodinae head capsule (ventral view).

The prementohypopharyngeal complex and the mentum occur on the medioventral aspect of the head capsule. In Tanypodinae larvae the prementohypopharyngeal complex is armed apically with a well-developed, readily seen ligula. In most other chironomid larvae the mentum may obscure the greater part of the prementohypopharyngeal complex and, as no well-developed structure homologous to the tanypod ligula is usually present, this structure may be difficult to locate.

The current interpretation of the larval mentum holds that this structure is a double-walled, medioventral plate consisting of a dorsomentum and a ventromentum. In Chironomini, Pseudochironomini, and Tanytarsini the ventromentum is greatly expanded laterally into striated ventromental (paralabial) plates which are quite conspicuous. With the exception of the Tanypodinae, the ventromentum may be only slightly to moderately expanded laterally in the remaining chironomid genera. When only slightly expanded, the ventromental plates may appear to be absent or vestigial. In some genera the plates may be quite obvious and may even have a cardinal beard (i.e., elongate setae arising in definite rows) originating from the dorsal surface.

In most chironomid genera, again excluding Tanypodinae, the dorsomental plate is usually well sclerotized and has conspicuous teeth. In these cases the term "mentum" is simply used to refer to the toothed margin of the dorsomental plate. Notable exceptions occur within certain genera such as *Acamptocladius* and *Protanypus* in which the dorsomental plates do not meet on the ventral midline of the head capsule and the ventromental plate covers all (in the case of *Acamptocladius*) or most (in the case of *Protanypus*) of the dorsomental teeth. A more detailed discussion of the structure of the mentum is provided by Saether (1971a; ref. #2845).

In Tanypodinae larvae the ventromental plate appears to be membranous or lightly sclerotized and is difficult to see. The dorsomental plate is very reduced in Pentaneurini genera and is also difficult to discern. In the remaining Tanypodinae genera, the lateral aspect of the dorsomental plate is well developed and gives the appearance of paired, heavily sclerotized, platelike structures armed with teeth along the anterior margin. Medially the dorsomental plate has reduced sclerotization and often is not readily distinguishable from the ventromental plate.

Thorax: The larval thorax, consisting of the first three segments behind the head capsule, is only clearly demarcated from the remainder of the body segments in the late fourth instar. At this time the larva is often referred to as a prepupa since the thorax is swollen by developing pupal structures. Often structures of the pupa, such as the respiratory organ or pronounced setae, are visible, thus allowing association of the larva with the pupal stage. Ventrally, on the first thoracic segment, a pair of prolegs typically arise from a common base and bifurcate apically. However, in some genera no bifurcation may occur and a single proleg appears to exist, or the prolegs may be reduced or vestigial. The prolegs are generally armed apically with sclerotized claws, the size and structure of which may be of specific importance. Numerous setae of species-level importance may arise from the thoracic segments, most notably a distinct ring of strong setae in some case-building Tanytarsini larvae and some *Eukiefferiella* larvae.

Abdomen: The abdomen of the larva consists of all post-thoracic segments. Structures of the abdomen used for generic identification include setation, prolegs, anal tubules, procerci, ventral tubules, and supraanal setae.

In all Tanypodinae larvae except for Pentaneurini genera the lateral margins of at least the anterior five abdominal segments are equipped with a dense row of setae termed a *lateral hair fringe* (fig. 25.5). In *Natarsia* sp. the fringe is somewhat less dense but still distinguishable in most preserved specimens. A distinct lateral hair fringe is also present in the Orthocladiinae genus *Xylotopus* (fig. 25.224). Most other abdominal setae patterns appear to have only species-level significance.

As is the case with the prolegs of the thorax (anterior prolegs), those of the abdomen (posterior prolegs) show quite a bit of variation in structure. The posterior prolegs usually occur as paired structures with apical claws (figs. 25.5, 25.225, 25.227) but they may occasionally be fused or extremely reduced (figs. 25.228–25.230).

Anal tubules occur on the anal segment in most chironomid genera and may originate above, between, or occasionally along the basal margin of the posterior prolegs. Anal tubules generally occur as two paired structures, but occasionally may consist of one or three pairs, or rarely be absent.

On the dorsum of the preanal segment, a pair of fleshy tubercles, or procerci, may occur (figs. 25.258–25.259). One to several strong setae originate from the apex of the procerci and generally 0–2 weak lateral setae are present. Occasionally the procerci may have basal or lateral regions of sclerotization or pigmentation; basal spurs may also be present. Rarely the procerci are vestigial or lacking (figs. 25.227–25.230).

In some genera of Chironomini the lateral margins of the antepenultimate abdominal segment are produced into fleshy protuberances that are called *ventral tubules*. When present, these occur as one or two pairs. In the genus *Goeldichironomus* the anteriormost pair bifurcates just beyond the base (fig. 25.134).

Supraanal setae occur on the anal segment, usually just dorsal to the anal tubules (figs. 25.26, 25.258–25.259). Although these setae are generally only of species-level diagnostic importance, in the Tanypodinae genus *Pentaneura* and in the Podonominae genera *Boreochlus* and *Paraboreochlus* they appear to have generic diagnostic importance when used in concert with other body characters.

Glossary of Morphological Terms for Keys to Larvae

ACCESSORY BLADE OF MANDIBLE—bladelike structure arising on inner margin of mandible of some Tanypodinae larvae (e.g., *Hudsonimyia karelena* Roback, fig. 25.55) and oriented along the inner edge.

ANAL TUBULES—appendages of the anal segment above, between, or at the basal margin of the posterior prolegs (e.g., figs. 25.26, 25.225, 25.227, 25.229); normally two pairs, occasionally one or three pairs, rarely absent.

ANNULATIONS—areas of reduced sclerotization giving the appearance of concentric rings or annuli on certain antennal segments of most Diamesinae and Podonominae (e.g., figs. 25.246–25.247); also present on segments of one genus of Tanytarsini (fig. 25.84) and on the stalks of the lauterborn organs in another genus of Tanytarsini (fig. 25.83).

ANTENNA (plural=antennae)—paired, segmented sensory organs, one on each side of the head capsule, directed anteriorly (e.g., figs. 25.1–25.3, 25.243); retractile in Tanypodinae (e.g., figs. 25.4, 25.6–25.9); usually with conspicuous lauterborn organs in Tanytarsini (e.g., figs. 25.67–25.78) and sometimes in Chironomini (e.g., figs. 25.95–25.96), variously modified in Orthocladiinae (e.g., figs. 25.153–25.169, 25.171–25.172).

ANTENNAL BLADE—bladelike structure usually originating at the apex of the first antennal segments (e.g., figs. 25.1–25.3), occasionally originating from the margin of the second segment (e.g., figs. 25.102, 25.246) or third segment (fig. 25.103).

ANTENNAL TUBERCLE—pronounced tubercle from which the antenna originates in all Tanytarsini and in the Orthocladinae genus *Abiskomyia* (fig. 25.157); may be simple (i.e., lacking armature; e.g., figs. 25.74, 25.76–25.77), with anteromesal spur (e.g., figs. 25.78, 25.80, 25.82), elongate spine (e.g., figs. 25.67–25.68, 25.70–25.71, 25.81), or armature in the form of a palmate process (fig. 25.69).

ANTERIOR LABRAL REGION—anterior portion of the labrum (e.g., figs. 25.4, 25.97–25.98); armed with setae and peglike sensillae in most genera; occasionally with additional scales (fig. 25.245) and other armature.

ANTERIOR PROLEGS—locomotory structures originating from ventral surface of first thoracic segment (fig. 25.225) usually armed with claws; may be paired, with a common base, singular or vestigial.

APICAL DISSECTIONS—divided distally into several branches or strands; refers to structure of S setae (fig. 25.147).

BIFID—cleft or divided into two parts, forked; refers to structure of S setae (fig. 25.143).

CAMPANIFORM SENSILLUM—sense organ of the antenna or maxillary palp having the appearance of a circular structure with a central area of reduced sclerotization (e.g., figs. 25.4, 25.23–25.24, 25.29, 25.157–25.161).

CARDINAL BEARD—setae appearing to arise from underneath the ventromental plates in some Orthocladiinae (e.g., figs. 25.212–25.223) and Prodiamesinae (e.g., figs. 25.238, 25.240).

CRENULATE—with a series of indentations giving the appearance of small, blunt or evenly rounded, convex bumps on the anterior margin of the ventromental plates (e.g., figs. 25.106, 25.137–25.139); see *scalloped* for contrasting pattern of indentations.

DISTAL—near or toward the free end of any appendage; that part of a structure farthest from the body.

DORSOMENTAL PLATE—heavily sclerotized platelike structure (fig. 25.4), conspicuous in Tanypodini (fig. 25.11), Procladiini (fig. 25.12), Macropelopiini (e.g., figs. 25.18–25.20, 25.25), somewhat reduced in Natarsiini (fig. 25.17) and very reduced or vestigial in Pentaneurini.

DORSOMENTAL TEETH—teeth along the anterior margin of the dorsomental plates in Tanypodini (fig. 25.11), Procladiini (fig. 25.12), Macropelopiini (e.g., figs. 25.18–25.20, 22.25) and Natarsiini (fig. 25.17); arranged in longitudinal rows in Coelotanypodini (e.g., figs. 25.10, 25.13).

EYESPOT—dorsal or dorsolateral pigmentation patches of the head capsule used for detecting light (e.g., figs. 25.1—25.4); may consist of a single pair, two pairs, or, rarely, three pairs of pigment patches.

FLAGELLUM—the second through terminal antennal segments (fig. 25.2); used to calculate the antennal ratio, which is a ratio of the combined lengths of these segments relative to the length of the first antennal segment.

FRONTOCLYPEAL APOTOME—dorsal sclerite of the head capsule.

HEAD CAPSULE—fused sclerites of the head region, forming a hard, compact case (e.g., figs. 25.1–25.4).

HEAD RATIO—length of the head capsule divided by the maximum width of the head capsule.

LABRAL LAMELLA (plural = labral lamellae)—one or more smooth to apically pectinate, scalelike or leaflike, thin plates surrounding or anterior to the bases of the SI setae (e.g., figs. 25.173, 25.175).

LABRAL SENSILLA (plural = labral sensillae)—labral seta SIV; in some Chironomini seta SIV is greatly enlarged and two- (fig. 25.98) or three-segmented (fig. 25.97).

LATERAL HAIR FRINGE—a more or less continuous and conspicuous row of setae originating from the lateral margin of at least the five anterior abdominal segments in all Tanypodinae larvae except Pentaneurini genera (fig. 25.5), very reduced in Natarsiini larvae; also present in the Orthocladiinae genus *Xylotopus* Oliver (fig. 25.224).

LAUTERBORN ORGAN—compound sensory organ usually originating at the apex of the second antennal segment and usually having a teardrop shape; most pronounced in Tanytarsini where they may occur at the end of elongate stalks (e.g., figs. 25.3, 25.77–25.78, 25.83–25.84), arise alternately (e.g., figs. 25.67–25.68) or oppositely (e.g., figs. 25.69–25.78, 25.83–25.84), be conspicuously striated (e.g., figs. 25.67–25.70, 25.72–25.74) or simple (e.g., figs. 25.71, 25.75, 25.77–25.78, 25.83–25.84); less pronounced in most Chironomini, but occasionally well developed in certain genera (e.g., figs. 25.95–25.96); poorly developed and often inconspicuous in most Orthocladiinae; lacking (?) in Tanypodinae.

LAUTERBORN ORGAN STALK—a sclerotized structure basal to the lauterborn organ and serving as an attachment to the antenna; sometimes elongate and delicate in some Tanytarsini genera (e.g., figs. 25.3, 25.77–25.78) or short and straplike (e.g., figs. 25.67–25.70, 25.72–25.73, 25.75–25.76) or vestigial (e.g., figs. 25.71, 25.74); usually not apparent in most Chironomini and Orthocladiinae.

LIGULA—a well-sclerotized, apically toothed, internal plate of the prementohypopharyngeal complex in Tanypodinae (e.g., figs. 25.4, 25.13, 25.15–25.16, 25.41–25.53); reduced, not discernible, or absent in other subfamilies.

MANDIBLE—stout, well-sclerotized, chewing or grasping structures (e.g., figs. 25.1–25.3); usually with well-developed dentes (or "teeth") along the inner margin (e.g., figs. 25.14, 25.56–25.59, 25.99, 25.125, 25.231–25.237, 25.241–25.242), occasionally with dentes reduced or vestigial (e.g., figs. 25.4, 25.54–25.55, 25.79).

MAXILLA (plural = maxillae)—in the strictest sense the second pair of jaws or eating structures; usually poorly sclerotized and difficult to discern; located ventral and slightly posterior to the mandibles in most larvae (e.g., figs. 25.1–25.4).

MAXILLARY PALP—palp originating from the ventral margin of the maxilla and armed apically with numerous sensillae and other sensory structures; usually small in most Orthocladiinae and Tanytarsini larvae (e.g., figs. 25.1, 25.3); occasionally very elongate and/or with numerous segments in Chironomini (e.g., figs. 25.123–25.124); usually conspicuous and occasionally segmented in Tanypodinae (e.g., figs. 25.4, 25.23–25.24, 25.27–25.29); synonyms—maxillary palpus, palpus.

MENTUM—usually toothed and well-sclerotized, medioventral plate of head capsule (e.g., figs. 25.1–25.3, 25.62–25.66, 25.87–25.93, 25.100, 25.105–25.122, 25.126–25.133, 25.135–25.141, 25.176–25.223, 25.238–25.240, 25.244, 25.248–25.255, 25.257); reduced or membranous in Tanypodinae.

PALMATE—resembling the structure of a hand; with a palmlike basal portion and fingerlike apical processes; usually referring to structure of the SI seta (fig. 25.145) or armature of antennal tubercle in Tanytarsini (fig. 25.69).

PALMATE PROCESS OF ANTENNAL TUBERCLE—anteromesally projecting process of antennal tubercle in some Tanytarsini species (fig. 25.69), produced mesally to resemble a palmate structure.

PARAGLOSSA (plural = paraglossae)—curved, bifid, serrated or pectinate rod or plate originating from opposite sides at base of and running parallel to the ligula in Tanypodinae (e.g., figs. 25.4, 25.30–25.34).

PECTINATE—comblike or coarsely featherlike; usually referring to the structure of the SI seta.

PECTEN EPIPHARYNGIS—sclerotized scale or scales originating just ventral to the apex of the labral margin (e.g., figs. 25.1–25.3, 25.170, 25.174); may be smooth, spinelike, pectinate, serrate, or fused.

PLUMOSE—very finely featherlike; usually referring to the structure of the SI seta (e.g., figs. 25.173, 25.175).

POSTERIOR PROLEGS—locomotory structures originating from the ventrolateral margin of the terminal abdominal segment; usually paired and with apical claws (e.g., figs. 25.5, 25.225, 25.227), occasionally fused or extremely reduced (e.g., figs. 25.228–25.230).

PREANAL SEGMENT—the penultimate abdominal segment.

PREMANDIBLE—paired, movable, ancillary feeding appendages originating from the ventral surface of the labrum in the vicinity of the pecten epipharyngis; usually with an apical cusp or one to several mesally projecting teeth (e.g., figs. 25.1–25.3, 25.97); vestigial or lacking in Podonominae and Tanypodinae.

PREMENTOHYPOPHARYNGEAL COMPLEX—a double lobed structure ventral to the esophagus and dorsal to the mentum; usually covered by the mentum in slide mounted specimens or with only the apical portion visible; ligula arises from this structure in Tanypodinae.

PROCERCUS (plural = procerci)—fleshy tubercle originating from dorsal surface of preanal segment (e.g., figs. 25.258–25.259); usually paired and carrying several strong apical and two weak lateral setae; occasionally with lateral sclerotization, basal spurs, or pigmentation patches; rarely reduced, vestigial, or lacking (e.g., figs. 25.227–25.230).

SI SETA (plural = SI setae)—anteriormost dorsolabral seta; occurring as paired setae (e.g., figs. 25.1–25.3, 25.142–25.152, 25.170, 25.173, 25.175).

SII SETA (plural = SII setae)—dorsolabral seta immediately posterior to SI seta; occurring as paired seta (e.g., figs. 25.1, 25.150).

SCALE—small, sclerotized, flat evagination of a head capsule plate.

SCALLOPED—with a series of concave indentations giving the appearance of evenly rounded depressions on the anterior margin of the ventromental plates (e.g., figs. 25.121–25.122); see *crenulate* for contrasting pattern of indentations.

SPIRACULAR RING—lightly sclerotized or differentially pigmented margin of spiracle on the dorsum of the antepenultimate abdominal segment in some Podonominae genera (fig. 25.259).

STRIATIONS—a series of fine, longitudinal impression lines; referring to the pattern of dorsal striae on the ventromental plates of Chironomini, Tanytarsini, and Pseudochironomini (e.g., figs. 25.2–25.3, 25.62–25.66, 25.87–25.93, 25.100, 25.105–25.119, 25.121–25.122, 25.126–25.133, 25.135–25.141, 25.252–25.254).

SUPRAANAL SETA (plural = supraanal setae)—seta on anal segment just dorsal to anal tubules; occurring as paired setae (e.g., figs. 25.26, 25.258–25.259).

THORAX—first three body segments posterior to the head capsule.

VENTRAL TUBULE—fleshy protuberences originating on the ventrolateral margin of the antepenultimate abdominal segment of some genera (fig. 25.134); if present usually occurring as one or two pairs; occasionally with the anterior pair bifurcating beyond base.

VENTROMENTAL PLATE—plate occurring ventral to the mentum and extending laterally; usually occurring as well-separated, paired plates with conspicuous striations in Chironomini (e.g., figs. 25.2, 25.87–25.91, 25.93, 25.100, 25.105–25.119, 25.121–25.122, 25.126–25.131, 25.137–25.141), or without striations (fig. 25.120) or striated but closely appressed medially (e.g., figs. 25.132–25.133, 25.135–25.136); usually striated and closely appressed medially in Tanytarsini (e.g., figs. 25.3, 25.62, 25.64–25.66), less commonly widely separated (fig. 25.63); usually nonstriated, narrow, inconspicuous, or very reduced in Orthocladiinae (e.g., figs. 25.1, 25.176–25.177, 25.180–25.181, 25.185–25.817, 25.189, 25.191–25.200, 25.202–25.203, 25.205–25.206, 25.208–25.211), occasionally somewhat conspicuous, (e.g., figs. 25.178–25.179, 25.182, 25.184, 25.188, 25.190, 25.201, 25.204, 25.207) or with a cardinal beard (e.g., figs. 25.212–25.223); vestigial or large and covering the lateral mental teeth in Diamesinae (e.g., figs. 25.244, 25.248–25.251); vestigial in Podonominae (e.g., figs. 25.255, 25.257); large and with (e.g., figs. 25.238, 25.240) or without (fig. 25.239) a cardinal beard in Prodiamesinae; large, striated, and closely appressed medially in Pseudochironomini (e.g., figs. 25.252–25.254).

Pupae

Chironomid pupae range in length from about 1.5 mm to 20 mm. There are three main body divisions: head, thorax, and abdomen. The morphology of the pupa is almost competely external, since it is considered to be a modified larval integument within which the adult develops (figs. 25.260–25.262). The structures of the pupa are best seen in the cast skins (pupal exuviae), and the general description below and keys to follow are based on exuviae. (For reference to particular structures see the glossary for pupal morphology.)

Head: The head region of chironomid pupal exuviae consists primarily of eye, antenna, and mouthpart sheaths. The area of integument covering the vertex of the pharate adult head is the frontal apotome (fig. 25.260).

Thorax: The thoracic region of chironomid pupal exuviae bears the leg, wing, and halter sheaths. The thorax also has several groups of setae and the taxonomically very important thoracic horn (fig. 25.261, 25.263–25.265).

Abdomen: The abdomen of chironomid pupal exuviae consists of eight similar segments and one or more additional segments modified into anal lobes and genital sheaths (fig. 25.262). The terga (and sometimes sterna) often bear distinctive groupings of spines, recurved hooks and shagreen (fig.

25.262). The anal lobes often bear a fringe of setae and/or two or more spinelike to hairlike macrosetae (fig. 25.262).

The pigmentation of pupal exuviae is not as varied as that of larvae. However, most species have a characteristic pigmentation even if it is the absence or near absence of pigment. In others the thorax and abdomen are yellow, golden yellow, yellow brown, brown, dark brown, or gray. Many have such pigment in a distinct pattern, especially on the abdomen. Together with size and shape, the pigmentation of pupal exuviae may be an important aid in sorting and identification.

Glossary of Morphological Terms for Keys to Pupae

ANAL LOBE—usually broad "swimming fins" located at tip of abdomen; with a fringe of setae (e.g., figs. 25.262, 25.298, 25.312, 25.334, 25.336, 25.379, 25.527, 25.623, 25.628) or without (e.g., figs. 25.262, 25.266, 25.279, 25.390, 25.393, 25.420, 25.450, 25.491, 25.578); may be atypical in form (e.g., figs. 25.266, 25.323, 25.395, 25.416, 25.426, 25.501); often with one or more macrosetae.

ANAL LOBE FRINGE—a fringe of setae along outer and sometimes inner margins of anal lobes; may be sparse (e.g., figs. 25.343–25.344, 25.374) or dense (e.g., figs. 25.262, 25.312, 25.379, 25.385).

ANAL LOBE MACROSETAE—usually large lateral or terminal setae on anal lobes; two in Tanypodinae, 0–12 in other taxa (e.g., figs. 25.262, 25.266, 25.268, 25.276, 25.279, 25.296, 25.332, 25.363, 25.386–25.387, 25.416, 25.423); may be very small in some Orthocladiinae (e.g., figs. 25.400, 25.404, 25.415, 25.445, 25.447); absent in some Orthocladiinae and all Chironominae.

CAUDOLATERAL ARMATURE ON SEGMENT 8—a single spine (e.g., figs. 25.546, 25.553, 25.587, 25.606), a comb (e.g., figs. 25.560, 25.565, 25.574, 25.624) or a compound spur (figs. 25.616–25.617) on each caudolateral margin of segment 8; present in many Chironominae and a very few Orthocladiinae (however, these are probably not homologous to those in Chironominae).

CEPHALIC TUBERCLES—enlarged, sometimes ornate areas of the frontal apotome upon which the frontal setae are located (e.g., figs. 25.580, 25.582, 25.589, 25.590, 25.599); present in many Chironominae and a few Orthocladiinae (not to be confused with frontal warts [figs. 25.362, 25.514] or frontal tubercles [figs. 25.597, 25.599] that may be present in addition to simple frontal setae or cephalic tubercles).

CONJUNCTIVA—weakly chitinized connecting areas between abdominal segments (e.g., fig. 25.629).

DORSAL SETAE—a. setae located on abdominal terga; often difficult to see but they may be large, spinelike or branched (e.g., figs. 25.304, 25.312); b. one or two setae (usually lamellar) on the dorsal surface of each anal lobe (e.g., figs. 25.527, 25.539, 25.549, 25.560, 25.566).

FELT CHAMBER—the internal component of the thoracic horn which is apparent as the continuation of the connection with the tracheal system (e.g., figs. 25.267, 25.280, 25.297, 25.309, 25.317–25.318).

FRONTAL APOTOME—the chitinous region between and posterior (dorsal) to the bases of the antennae; often with frontal setae (e.g., figs. 25.260, 25.362, 25.522, 25.589, 25.598).

FRONTAL SETAE—a pair of setae usually located on the frontal apotome, often on cephalic tubercles (e.g., figs. 25.260, 25.362, 25.522, 25.589, 25.598); rarely on prefrons (fig. 25.521); often absent.

FRONTAL TUBERCLES—a pair of tubercles on frontal apotome of some Chironominae in addition to simple frontal setae or cephalic tubercles (figs. 25.597, 25.599).

FRONTAL WARTS—a pair of tubercles on the frontal apotome of some Orthocladiinae (figs. 25.362, 25.514).

GENITAL SHEATHS—usually weakly chitinized sacs that enclose the male and female genitalia; most conspicuous in male (e.g., figs. 25.266, 25.268, 25.272, 25.286, 25.447).

LAMELLAR LATERAL SETAE—large, broad setae on pluera of abdominal segments 5–8 (e.g., figs. 25.279, 25.374, 25.557, 25.607); often absent.

LATERAL ABDOMINAL FRINGE—dense rows of setae along pleura of, at least, some abdominal segments (figs. 25.276, 25.323, 25.380).

LEG SHEATHS—cuticular covering of pharate adult legs (figs. 25.263–25.265).

MULTISERIAL FRINGE—a fringe of anal lobe setae consisting of 2 or more rows (e.g., figs. 25.312, 25.385, 25.634).

"NASE"—a small to moderate "nose-shaped" tubercle near tip of wing sheath (fig. 25.575); present on most Tanytarsini.

PEARL ROWS—one or more rows of small, rounded projections along the distal margins of the wing sheaths (figs. 25.333, 25.341).

PLEURA—lateral components of each abdominal segment that connect the terga and sterna.

POSTERIOR SPINE ROW(S)—spines along the posterior margins of, at least, some terga (e.g., figs. 25.262, 25.347, 25.361, 25.372, 25.381, 25.399, 25.417, 25.459, 25.467).

PREFRONS—the cuticular region anterior (dorsal) to the frontal apotome (fig. 25.260).

PRECORNEAL SETAE—usually 3 setae close to the base of the thoracic horn (e.g., figs. 25.261, 25.339, 25.351, 25.419, 25.456, 25.469, 25.559, 25.561).

PSB II, III—lateral protuberances on segment 2 or segments 2 and 3 (e.g., figs. 25.262, 25.342, 25.355, 25.382, 25.406, 25.591).

RECURVED HOOKS (HOOKLETS)—a. one or more rows of anteriorly directed hooks on the posterior margin of segment 2 (e.g., figs. 25.262, 25.355, 25.358, 25.511, 25.515, 25.581, 25.591);

b. one row or partial row of large anteriorly directed hooks on the posterior margins (or conjunctiva) of segments 3–5; present on a few Orthocladiinae (e.g., figs. 25.473, 25.478, 25.480, 25.482, 25.484, 25.495).

SHAGREEN—complete or partial fields of small spinules on terga, pleura, or sterna (e.g., figs. 25.262, 25.370, 25.401, 25.478, 25.570, 25.573, 25.622).

SPINE GROUPS—groups of spines (long or short) on terga—usually near the center but including those along the posterior margin (e.g., figs. 25.262, 25.356, 25.359, 25.361, 25.391, 25.528, 25.534, 25.564); the spines of such groups are always, at least, slightly larger than any shagreen that may be present.

STERNA—the ventral plates of the abdominal segments.

TERGA—the dorsal plates of the abdominal segments.

THORACIC COMB—a row of spines near the base of the thoracic horn of some Tanypodinae (figs. 25.282, 25.284, 25.289).

THORACIC HORN—a structure of the anterior thorax which has been assumed to have respiratory functions; may be with a plastron (e.g., figs. 25.267, 25.278, 25.299), with a surface meshwork (e.g., figs. 25.315, 25.324), simple (e.g., figs. 25.327, 25.339, 25.346, 25.354, 25.367, 25.384, 25.398, 25.411, 25.419, 25.454, 25.474, 25.504, 25.519), with "hairs" (e.g., figs. 25.525, 25.537, 25.561), or branched (e.g., figs. 25.586, 25.615, 25.618, 25.632).

UNISERIAL FRINGE—a fringe of the anal lobes in which the setae are in a single row (e.g., figs. 25.348, 25.527, 25.546, 25.623, 25.628).

WING SHEATHS—cuticular covering of the pharate adult wings (figs. 25.261, 25.263).

Adults

Adult chironomids range in size from about 1.5 mm to 20 mm. There are three main body divisions: head, thorax, and abdomen (fig. 25.644).

Head: The most conspicuous features of the head are the eyes and antennae. The antennae of most male chironomids are plumose (figs. 25.644, 25.677). The antennae of the females are not plumose and are usually shorter than those of the males and with fewer flagellomeres. However, some male antennae are not plumose and have a reduced number of flagellomeres (fig. 25.678).

Thorax: The adult thorax bears the legs, wings, and halteres. The legs of chironomids are moderately long, especially the first pair, and consist of a femur, tibia, and five tarsomeres. The distal ends of the tibiae often carry one or two spines that are of taxonomic importance (figs. 25.649, 25.651). The fourth and fifth tarsomeres are infrequently cordiform (heart-shaped, fig. 25.650) or trilobed (fig. 25.679). The wings of chironomids have a moderately complex venation, but with few crossveins (figs. 25.645–25.648, 25.653–25.655, 25.665–25.668). The thorax may bear groups of setae and is usually patterned with brown, black, yellow, or green.

Abdomen: The abdomen of adult chironomids consists of eight segments plus several terminal segments modified as genitalia. Groups of setae are usually present on terga, sterna, and pleura and the abdomen may be patterned in brown, black, yellow, blue, or green. The genitalia (termed *hypopygium* in the male) often have a complex external and internal morphology and in the male have a large gonocoxite and a terminal (usually) gonostylus (figs. 25.644, 25.656–25.664).

NOTES ON PREPARATION OF SPECIMENS AND USE OF KEYS

General

1. The keys below include: freshwater Nearctic larvae (to subfamily and genus), freshwater Nearctic pupae (to subfamily and genus), freshwater Nearctic adults (to tribe), and marine Nearctic larvae, pupae, and adults (to tribe). The freshwater keys to genus include all known Nearctic genera for which larvae and/or pupae have been described. Additionally, these keys include taxa that cannot, at present, be assigned to any known genus. Such taxa are designated as Genera 1–20 in the keys to pupae; however, in some cases these numbered genera may simply be the undescribed pupae of named genera known only as adults, or aberrant pupae belonging to established genera. The reader must keep in mind that the number of undiscovered immature stages is, most probably, rather large. The keys do not include the extra-Nearctic taxa Aphroteniinae, Heptagyini, Lobodiamesini (all austral), Anatopyniini (Palaearctic), or Buchonomyiinae (Palaearctic-Oriental).

2. Collections from freshwater and brackish water should be keyed in the main generic keys for larvae and pupae. Marine specimens are treated (usually above the level of genus) in separate keys.

3. The Orthocladiinae, which is the most diverse of the chironomid subfamilies, has not yet been satisfactorily divided into tribes. Tentative names for a few of the orthoclad tribes are indicated by quotation marks.

4. Slides prepared for identifications may be temporary mounts with water or, preferably, permanent mounts with any suitable medium such as Euparal or Canada balsam.

Larvae

1. When possible, use the fourth larval instar. These may often be recognized by the swollen thorax of the prepupa.

2. Sever the head and mount it with the ventral side facing upward. The head must often be gently (sometimes not so gently) depressed to expose the mouthparts. Depending on the thickness of the abdomen, the head and abdomen should be placed under the same cover glass. This is usually not possible for large larvae since the abdomen prevents the depression of the head. In such cases, mount the abdomen under a separate cover glass, but on the same slide.

Pupae

1. Pupae are best determined from pupal exuviae. The identification of pupae (not exuviae) is not easy since the structures are obscured by tissues. If possible, remove pharate adults from their pupal exuviae.

2. Before dissecting pupae or pupal exuviae examine the leg sheath arrangement and type of thoracic horn. Preparation of exuviae often disrupts the leg sheath pattern, and the thoracic horn (particularly of the Chironominae) is often extremely difficult to see.

3. Pupal exuviae are best prepared as follows (these steps should be carried out with the specimen in a drop of mounting medium on a microscope slide):

   a. separate the head and thorax from the abdomen.
   b. split the thorax along the middorsal suture and open the thorax so that the two edges of the suture are on opposite sides of the specimen.
   c. turn the thorax so that the outer side of the integument is facing upwards and arrange on the slide above the abdomen.
   d. move the abdomen, dorsal side up (usually), to a position just below the thorax.
   e. place a cover glass over the specimen, depressing it just enough to cause the exuviae to flatten but not distort.

Adults

1. The keys below are designed for adult males. Males can be separated from females by their generally more slender abdomen, a rather conspicuous set of genital appendages, and, in most species, characteristic plumose antennae.

2. Most adults can be identified to subfamily and many to tribe with the use of a dissecting microscope. To be certain, however, it is best to prepare the specimen for examination with a compound microscope. This is sometimes a tedious and involved process, but has been greatly simplified here for the purposes of a key to tribes.

   a. Remove and mount:
      (1) third (hind) pair of legs
      (2) wings
   b. Remove the abdomen and heat it cautiously in 10% KOH to remove the soft obscuring tissues (alternatively, the abdomen will clear standing for 12–24 hours in 10% KOH); mount the abdomen dorsal side up, being particularly careful to orient the genitalia dorsal side up.

KEY TO TRIBES OR SUBFAMILIES OF NORTH AMERICAN FRESHWATER CHIRONOMIDAE LARVAE

1.　　　　Antennae retractile (fig. 25.4); prementohypopharyngeal complex with a 4–8 toothed ligula (figs. 25.4, 25.13, 25.15, 25.16, 25.41–25.53); mentum almost entirely membranous or with dorsomental teeth arranged in conspicuous plates (figs. 25.11–25.12, 25.17–25.20, 25.25) or longitudinal rows (figs. 25.10, 25.13) .... *Tanypodinae* (p. 560)

1′.   Antennae nonretractile (figs. 25.1–25.3); prementohypopharyngeal complex without a toothed ligula. Mentum usually entirely toothed (figs. 25.62–25.66, 25.87–25.93, 25.100, 25.105–25.122, 25.126–25.133, 25.135–25.141, 25.176–25.223, 25.238–25.239, 25.248, 25.252–25.254), or occasionally with weakly sclerotized or translucent portions (figs. 25.178–25.179, 25.240, 25.244, 25.250), but never membranous 2

2(1′).   Procerci long, at least 5 times as long as wide; premandibles absent .... *Podonominae* (p. 590)

2′.   Procerci variable, rarely more than 4 times longer than wide; premandibles present (figs. 25.1–25.3, 25.97, 25.245), usually well developed and conspicuous 3

3(2′).   Ventromental plates well developed and with conspicuous striations throughout more than one-half their width (figs. 25.62–25.66, 25.87–25.93, 25.100, 25.105–25.122, 25.126–25.133, 25.135–25.141, 25.252–25.254) .... *Chironominae** 4

3′.   Ventromental plates vestigial to well developed (figs. 25.176–25.211, 25.238–25.240, 25.244, 25.248–25.250), when well developed never with striations although occasionally with setae underneath (figs. 25.212–25.223) 6

4(3).   Antenna arising from distinct tubercle (figs. 25.67–25.71, 25.77–25.78, 25.80–25.82); first antennal segment elongate and usually at least slightly curved (figs. 25.67–25.78); lauterborn organs very large and conspicuous (figs. 25.67–25.76) or occurring at the apex of elongated stalks (figs. 25.77–25.78, 25.83–25.84) .... *Tanytarsini* (p. 567)

4′.   Antenna not arising from a distinct tubercle; if first antennal segment elongate then not curved as in figs. 25.67–25.78, and lauterborn organs not large or occurring at the apex of elongated stalks 5

5(4′).   Outermost lateral teeth of mentum rounded and directed laterally; mentum as in figs. 25.252–25.254 .... *Pseudochironomini†*

5′.   Outermost lateral teeth usually pointed and directed anteriorly (figs. 25.87–25.93, 25.100, 25.105–25.122, 25.126–25.133, 25.135–25.141); mentum never as in figures 25.252–25.254 .... *Chironomini* (p. 569)

6(3′).   Mentum as in figure 25.238, 25.239, or 25.240 .... *Prodiamesinae* (p. 590)

6′.   Mentum not as in figure 25.238, 25.239, or 25.240 7

7(6′).   Third antennal segment with areas of reduced sclerotization which give the appearance of annulations (figs. 25.246–25.247), or mentum similar to figure 25.244 and anterior labral region with large scales similar to figure 25.245 .... *Diamesinae* (p. 588)

7′.   Third antennal segment occasionally very small (figs. 25.155, 25.162, 25.165–25.167, 25.171) but never with reduced sclerotization causing an annulated appearance; mentum and anterior labral region never as in figure 25.244 or 25.245 .... *Orthocladiinae* (p. 578)

KEYS TO THE GENERA OF NORTH AMERICAN FRESHWATER CHIRONOMIDAE LARVAE

Tanypodinae

1.   Abdominal segments with a lateral hair fringe (fig. 25.5); dorsomental teeth present in well defined plates (figs. 25.11–25.12), or arranged in longitudinal rows (figs. 25.10, 25.13); head ratio 1.0 to 1.5 2

1′.   Abdominal segments lacking well defined lateral hair fringe; dorsomental teeth absent or extremely reduced; head ratio 1.5 or greater .... Pentaneurini 14

2(1).   Dorsomental teeth arranged in longitudinal rows (figs. 25.10, 25.13); ligula with 6–7 teeth (figs. 25.15, 25.16); head capsule with pronounced anterior taper (fig. 25.6) .... Coelotanypodini 3

---

*The Chironominae genus *Stenochironomus* violates the couplet in that it does not have ventromental plates with conspicuous striations. Larvae of this genus, however, can be easily recognized by the unusual structure of the mentum and the mandible (see couplet no. 24 of the key to genera of Chironomini larvae and fig. 25.120 and 25.125).

†In North America the tribe Pseudochironomini is represented by a single genus, *Pseudochironomus*. The characters used in this key to identify specimens to the tribe level thus also serve to identify to the generic level; no additional key to the genus is provided for this tribe.

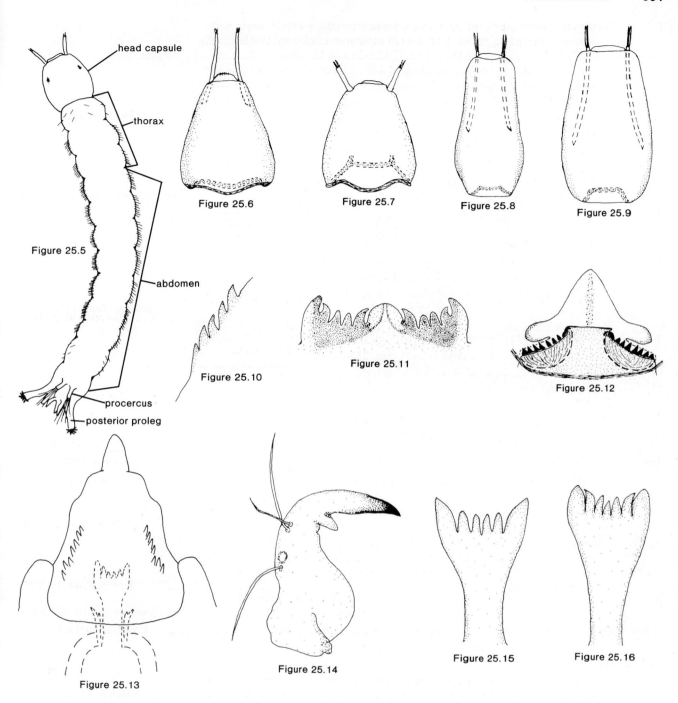

Figure 25.5. Generalized Tanypodinae larva (dorsal view) showing lateral hair fringe.

Figure 25.6. Dorsal view of *Clinotanypus* sp. head capsule.

Figure 25.7. Dorsal view of *Procladius* sp. head capsule.

Figure 25.8. Dorsal view of *Nilotanypus* sp. head capsule.

Figure 25.9. Dorsal view of *Conchapelopia* sp. head capsule.

Figure 25.10. Longitudinal arrangement of dorsomental teeth in *Coelotanypus concinnus* (Coquillett).

Figure 25.11. Dorsomental teeth of *Tanypus* sp.

Figure 25.12. Dorsomental teeth, ventromentum and prementohypopharyngeal element (in ventral view) of *Procladius* sp. (redrawn from Roback [1977]).

Figure 25.13. Longitudinal arrangement of dorsomental teeth on mental region of *Clinotanypus* sp. (ventral view).

Figure 25.14. Mandible of *Clinotanypus* sp.

Figure 25.15. Ligula of *Clinotanypus* sp.

Figure 25.16. Ligula of *Coelotanypus* sp.

2′.   Dorsomental teeth present in well defined plates (figs. 25.11–25.12); ligula with 4–5 teeth (figs. 25.43, 25.45, 25.53); head capsule more rounded anteriorly (fig. 25.7) **4**

3(2).   Ligula with 6 teeth (fig. 25.15); mandible strongly hooked (fig. 25.14); ratio of head length to antennal length approximately 1.6 .... *Clinotanypus* Kieffer

3′.   Ligula with 7 teeth (fig. 25.16); mandible not strongly hooked; ratio of head length to antennal length approximately 2.6 .... *Coelotanypus* Kieffer

4(2′).   Dorsomental plates each with 13–15 teeth .... Anatopyniini[1]

4′.   Dorsomental plates with 7 or fewer teeth **5**

5(4′).   Dorsomental plates with 2–3 teeth (fig. 25.17); antennae about one-third length of head capsule and ratio of length of first antennal segment to length of remaining segments less than 3.5 .... Natarsiini—*Natarsia* Fittkau

5′.   Dorsomental plates with more than 3 conspicuous teeth (figs. 25.18–25.20, 25.25); antennae shorter than one-third the head capsule length, or, if longer than one-third the length of head capsule, the ratio of the length of the first antennal segment to length of remaining segments always 3.5 or greater **6**

6(5′).   Mandible with bulbous base and very minute lateral teeth (fig. 25.54); ligula with 5 pale yellow to light brown teeth; teeth of ligula forming a convex arch or (less commonly) of equal lengths (fig. 25.44) .... Tanypodini—*Tanypus* Meigen

6′.   Mandible without conspicuous bulbous base; ligula with 4–5 teeth (figs. 25.41, 25.42, 25.43, 25.45, 25.53); when 5 pale yellow or light brown teeth are present on ligula the teeth form a concave arch (figs. 25.41–25.42) **7**

7(6′).   Ligula with 5 or (less commonly) 4 black teeth (figs. 25.53, 25.45); paraglossae with 1 main tooth and 1–7 accessory teeth on each side (figs. 25.30, 25.31) ..... Procladiini **8**

7′.   Ligula with 5 or 4 light yellow to brown teeth (figs. 25.41–25.43); paraglossae pectinate (figs. 25.32, 25.34); or unevenly bifid (fig. 25.33) .... Macropelopiini **9**

8(7).   Ligula with 4 teeth (fig. 25.45); antennal blade more than twice as long as the combined lengths of antennal segments 2 through 4 (fig. 25.22) .... *Djalmabatista* Fittkau

8′.   Ligula with 5 teeth (fig. 25.53); antennal blade subequal in length to the combined lengths of antennal segments 2 through 4 (fig. 25.21) .... *Procladius* Skuse

9(7′).   Ligula with 4 teeth (fig. 25.43); paraglossae pectinate (fig. 25.34); mandible with row of 4 or more inner teeth (figs. 25.58, 25.59) .... *Psectrotanypus* Kieffer **10**

9′.   Ligula with 5 teeth (figs. 25.41, 25.42); paraglossae not pectinate (figs. 25.32, 25.33); mandible not as in figure 25.58–25.59 .... **11**

10(9).   Lateral dorsomental teeth closely appressed (fig. 25.25); small claws of posterior prolegs as in figure 25.40 or simple .... *Psectrotanypus (Derotanypus)*

10′.   Lateral dorsomental teeth not closely appressed (fig. 25.19); small claws of posterior prolegs basally ovoid (fig. 25.39); or simple .... *Psectrotanypus (Psectrotanypus)*

11(9′). Inner margin of dorsomental plate produced to a point (fig. 25.18) .... *Brundiniella* Roback

11′.   Inner margins of dorsomental plate rounded (fig. 25.20) **12**

12(11′). All teeth of ligula directed anteriorly (fig. 25.42); length of palpus at least 4 times greater than width at midlength and campaniform sensillum occurring in basal one-third of palpus (fig. 25.29) .... *Macropelopia* Thienemann

12′.   First lateral teeth of ligula outcurved (fig. 25.41); length of palpus 2.9–4.1 times the width at midlength; campaniform sensillum located near middle of palpus (figs. 25.23, 25.24) **13**

13(12′). Dorsomental plate with 7 teeth; palpus about 4.1 times longer than wide at midlength (fig. 25.24); 2nd antennal segment 4.2–4.7 times longer than maximum width .... *Alotanypus* Roback

13′.   Dorsomental plate with 4–5 teeth (fig. 25.20); palpus 2.9–3.2 times longer than width at midlength (fig. 25.23); 2nd antennal segment 2.1–2.5 times longer than maximum width .... *Apsectrotanypus* Fittkau

---

1. Not recorded from North America.

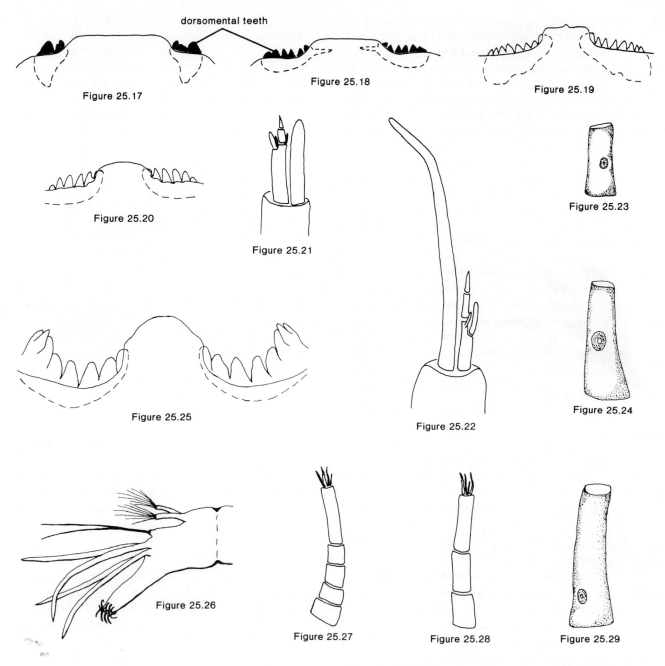

dorsomental teeth

Figure 25.17

Figure 25.18

Figure 25.19

Figure 25.20

Figure 25.21

Figure 25.23

Figure 25.25

Figure 25.22

Figure 25.24

Figure 25.26

Figure 25.27

Figure 25.28

Figure 25.29

Figure 25.17. Arrangement of dorsomental teeth in *Natarsia* sp.

Figure 25.18. Arrangement of dorsomental teeth in *Brundiniella* sp.

Figure 25.19. Arrangement of dorsometal teeth in *Psectrotanypus (Psectrotanypus) dyari* (Coquillett).

Figure 25.20. Arrangement of dorsomental teeth in *Apsectrotanypus* sp.

Figure 25.21. Apex of antenna of *Procladius* sp.

Figure 25.22. Apex of Antennna of *Djalmabatista pulcher* (Johannsen).

Figure 25.23. Basal segment of maxillary palpus of *Apsectrotanypus* sp.

Figure 25.24. Basal segment of maxillary palpus of *Alotanypus venustus* (Coquillett).

Figure 25.25. Arrangement of dorsomental teeth in *Psectrotanypus (Derotanypus) alaskensis* (Malloch).

Figure 25.26. Procerci, supraanal setae, anal tubules, and posterior prolegs of *Pentaneura* sp.

Figure 25.27. Maxillary palpus of *Ablabesmyia (Ablabesmyia) mallochi* (Walley).

Figure 25.28. Maxillary palpus of *Ablabesmyia (Ablabesmyia) parajanta* Roback.

Figure 25.29. Basal segment of maxillary palpus of *Macropelopia* sp.

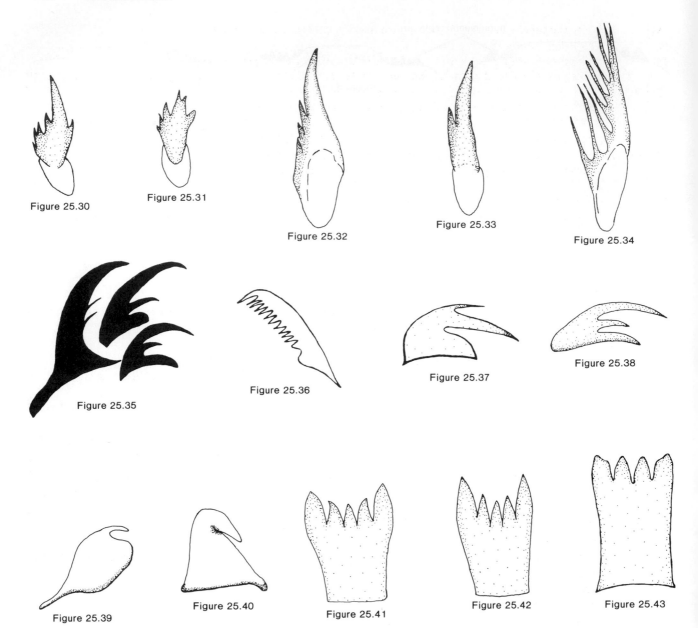

Figure 25.30. Paraglossa of *Procladius* sp.

Figure 25.31. Paraglossa of *Djalmabatista pulcher* (Johannsen).

Figure 25.32. Paraglossa of *Alotanypus venustus* (Coquillett) (redrawn from Roback [1978]).

Figure 25.33. Paraglossa of *Macropelopia decedens* (Walker) (redrawn from Roback [1978]).

Figure 25.34. Paraglossa of *Psectrotanypus (Psectrotanypus) dyari* (Coquillett).

Figure 25.35. Pigmented claws of posterior prolegs of *Paramerina smithae* (Sublette) (redrawn with modification from Roback [1972]).

Figure 25.36. Pectinate claw of posterior proleg of *Nilotanypus* sp.

Figure 25.37. Bifid claw of posterior proleg of *Labrundinia* sp.

Figure 25.38. Bifid claw of posterior proleg of *Zavrelimyia* sp.

Figure 25.39. Basally ovoid claw of posterior proleg of *Psectrotanypus (Psectrotanypus) dyari* (Coquillett).

Figure 25.40. Smallest claw of posterior proleg of *Psectrotanypus (Derotanypus) alaskensis* (Malloch) (redrawn from Roback [1978]).

Figure 25.41. Ligula of *Alotanypus venustus* (Coquillett).

Figure 25.42. Ligula of *Macropelopia* sp.

Figure 25.43. Ligula of *Psectrotanypus (Psectrotanypus) dyari* (Coquillett).

14(1'). Anterior margin of ligula straight (i.e., all teeth ending at more or less the same point) (figs. 25.50–25.51) 15

14'. Anterior margin of ligula with median tooth distinctly longer than or shorter than the 1st lateral and/or 2nd lateral teeth (figs. 25.46–25.49, 25.52) 18

15(14). Posterior prolegs with 3 smallest claws more darkly pigmented than remaining claws, the largest of the 3 more darkly pigmented claws pectinate, the remaining 2 bifid (fig. 25.35) .... ***Paramerina*** Fittkau (in part)

15'. Posterior prolegs with only 1 claw more darkly pigmented or all claws unicolorous 16

16(15'). Posterior proleg with 1 claw darkly pigmented; supraanal seta strong, and originating from distinct papillae; anal tubules longer than posterior prolegs (fig. 25.26) .... ***Pentaneura*** Philippi

16'. All claws of posterior prolegs unicolorous; supraanal seta weak, or, if conspicuous, not originating from distinct papillae; anal tubules shorter than posterior prolegs 17

17(16'). One claw of posterior proleg bifid (fig. 25.38); head capsule unicolorous; ratio of length of 1st antennal segments to combined lengths of remaining antennal segments about 3.1 .... ***Zavrelimyia*** Fittkau

17'. All claws of posterior prolegs simple; posterior ¼ of head capsule with conspicuous blackish brown pigmentation; ratio of length of 1st antennal segment to combined lengths of remaining antennal segments about 2.5 .... ***Paramerina*** Fittkau (in part)

18(14'). Median tooth of ligula longer than 1st lateral teeth (figs. 25.48–25.49) 19

18'. Median tooth of ligula shorter than (figs. 25.46–25.47) or equal in length to 1st lateral teeth; when equal in length to 1st lateral teeth, then all 3 median teeth shorter than 2nd lateral teeth (fig. 25.52) 20

19(18). Posterior prolegs with 1 bifid claw (fig. 25.37); 2nd antennal segment usually distinctly more darkly pigmented than 1st segment; ligula as in figure 25.48 .... ***Labrundinia*** Fittkau

19'. Posterior prolegs with 1 pectinate claw (fig. 25.36); all antennal segments unicolorous; ligula as in figure 25.49 .... ***Nilotanypus*** Kieffer

20(18'). Maxillary palpus with 2 or more basal segments (figs. 25.27–25.28) .... ***Ablabesmyia*** Johannsen

20'. Maxillary palpus with 1 basal segment 21

21(20'). Second antennal segment with distinct dark brown pigmentation .... ***Monopelopia*** Fittkau

21'. All antennal segments unicolorous 22

22(21'). Head capsule with granular appearance visible 100x magnification; body with undulate wrinkles; ratio of length of 1st antennal segment to combined length of remaining segments 6.0–7.5 .... ***Guttipelopia*** Fittkau

22'. Head capsule lacking granular appearance; body smooth; ratio of length of 1st antennal segment to combined lengths of remaining segments variable, but rarely greater than 5.5 23

23(22'). Mandible with at least 1 large conspicuous tooth along inner margin (figs. 25.56–25.57) 24

23'. Inner margin of mandible smooth or with only very small teeth present 25

24(23). Mandible with 1 large, pointed tooth and 1–2 smaller teeth present on inner margin (fig. 25.56) .... ***Larsia*** Fittkau

24'. Mandible with 1 large blunt tooth and 1 small tooth present on inner margin (fig. 25.57); larvae not associated for North American species .... ***Krenopelopia*** Fittkau

25(23'). Head with posterior half pigmented dark brown; mandible with 1 small tooth and well-developed accessory blade (fig. 25.55); larvae apparently restricted to mats of blue-green algae occurring on steep rock outcrops over which small volumes of water trickle .... ***Hudsonimyia*** Roback

25'. Head capsule unicolorous; mandible not as in fig. 25.55; larvae occurring in a wide variety of habitats 26

26(25'). Mandible with small but distinct teeth along inner edge; ratio of length of 1st antennal segment to combined lengths of remaining segments 3.4–3.8 .... ***Trissopelopia*** Kieffer

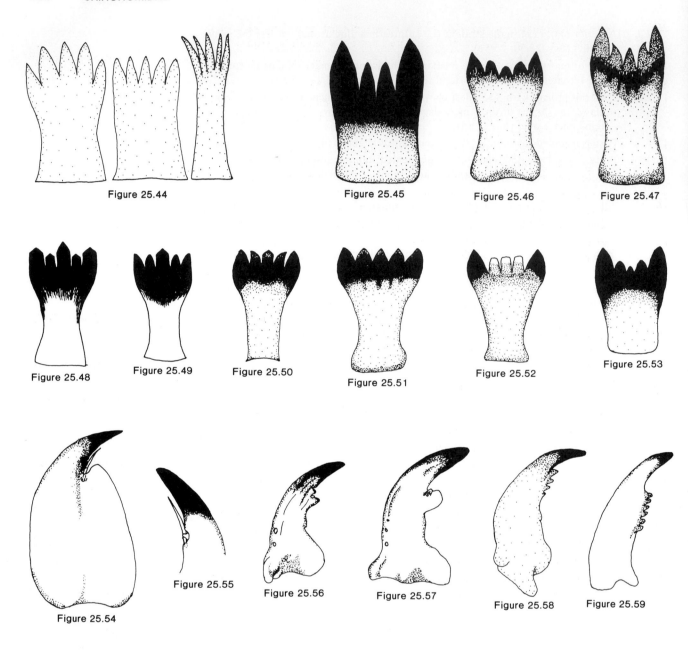

Figure 25.44.

Figure 25.45. Figure 25.46 Figure 25.47

Figure 25.48. Figure 25.49. Figure 25.50. Figure 25.51 Figure 25.52 Figure 25.53

Figure 25.54. Figure 25.55 Figure 25.56 Figure 25.57 Figure 25.58 Figure 25.59

Figure 25.44. Three types of Ligula of *Tanypus* species: *(a) Tanypus (Apelopia) neopunctipennis* Sublette; *(b) Tanypus (Tanypus) punctipennis* Meigen; *(c) Tanypus (Tanypus)* possibly *concavus* Roback. (*Tanypus (Tanypus)* possibly *concavus* Roback redrawn from Roback [1977].)

Figure 25.45. Ligula of *Djalmabatista pulcher* (Johannsen).

Figure 25.46. Ligula of *Larsia* sp.

Figure 25.47. Ligula of *Conchapelopia* sp.

Figure 25.48. Ligula of *Labrundinia* sp.

Figure 25.49. Ligula of *Nilotanypus* sp.

Figure 25.50. Ligula of *Pentaneura* sp.

Figure 25.51. Ligula of *Zavrelimyia* sp.

Figure 25.52. Ligula of *Ablabesmyia (Ablabesmyia) annulata* (Say).

Figure 25.53. Ligula of *Procladius* sp.

Figure 25.54. Mandible of *Tanypus* sp.

Figure 25.55. Apex of mandible of *Hudsonimyia karelena* Roback (redrawn with modification from Roback [1979]).

Figure 25.56. Mandible of *Larsia* sp.

Figure 25.57. Mandible of probable *Krenopelopia* sp.

Figure 25.58. Mandible of *Psectrotanypus (Derotanypus)* sp.

Figure 25.59. Mandible of *Psectrotanypus (Psectrotanypus)* sp.

26'.   Teeth of inner margin of mandible very minute, indistinct, or lacking; ratio of
         length of 1st antennal segment to combined lengths of remaining segments
         variable but usually 4.0–5.3 .... *Thienemannimyia* group[2]

Tanytarsini

1.   Ventromental plates well separated, pointed at anteromedial edge (fig. 25.63);
         larvae construct portable cases made of sand grains and/or detritus (figs.
         25.60–25.61) 2

1'.   Ventromental plates almost meeting at ventral midline of head capsule,
         anteromedial edge generally rounded or truncate (figs. 25.62, 25.64–25.66);
         larvae may construct tubes or filtering structures but never portable cases 6

2(1).   Lauterborn organs originating alternately at different heights on 2nd antennal
         segment (figs. 25.67–25.68); antennal segment 2 subequal to or longer than the
         combined lengths of segments 3–5; larval case always straight (fig. 25.60) 3

2'.   Lauterborn organs originating on opposite sides at apex of 2nd antennal segment
         (figs. 25.69–25.71); antennal segment 2 distinctly shorter than the combined
         lengths of segments 3–5; larval case straight or curved (figs. 25.60–25.61) 4

3(2).   Distal lauterborn organ arising preapically on 2nd antennal segment (fig. 25.68);
         antennal segment 2 subequal in length to the combined lengths of segments 3–5
         (fig. 25.68) .... *Zavrelia* Kieffer

3'.   Distal lauterborn organ arising from apex of 2nd antennal segment (fig. 25.67);
         antennal segment 2 distinctly longer than the combined lengths of segments 3–5
         (fig. 25.67) .... *Stempellinella* Brundin

4(2').   Antennal tubercle with a conspicuous anteromesally projecting palmate process
         (fig. 25.69); larval case curved (fig. 25.61) .... *Stempellina* Bause

4'.   Antennal tubercle lacking palmate process but with a single strong anteromesally
         directed spine (figs. 25.70–25.71); larval case curved or straight 5

5(4').   Lauterborn organs on distinct stalks, stalks subequal to or greater in length than
         antennal segment 3 (fig. 25.70); larval case curved (fig. 25.61) .... *Constempellina* Brundin

5'.   Lauterborn organs not conspicuously stalked (fig. 28.71), or if stalks are apparent
         then much shorter in length than antennal segment 3; larval case straight (fig.
         25.60) .... *Thienemanniola* Kieffer

6(1').   Mentum with only 3 distinct teeth (fig. 25.65); mandible blunt distally, lacking
         apical and lateral dentes (teeth) (fig. 25.79) .... *Corynocera* Zetterstedt

6'.   Mentum with more than 3 distinct teeth; mandible with at least 3 teeth 7

7(6').   Stalks of lauterborn organs appearing annulated along three-fourths of their length
         (fig. 25.83) .... Species near genus *Nimbocera* Reiss

7'.   Stalks of lauterborn organs never appearing annulated 8

8(7').   Second antennal segment annulated (fig. 25.84) .... Tanytarsini—*Genus "A"* (see Roback 1966)

8'.   Second antennal segment not annulated 9

9(8').   Stalks of lauterborn organs less than 1.2 times combined lengths of antennal
         segments 3–5 (figs. 25.72–25.76) 11

9'.   Stalks of lauterborn organs greater than 1.25 times (i.e., distinctly longer than) the
         combined lengths of antennal segments 3–5 (figs. 25.77–25.78) 10

10(9'). Antennal tubercle with a straight or anteromedially curved spur originating from
         medial edge (figs. 25.78, 25.80–25.82) .... *Micropsectra* Kieffer, some *Tanytarsus* van der Wulp

10'.   Antennal tubercle without a straight or anteromedially curved spur (fig. 25.77) .... *Tanytarsus* van der Wulp

11(9).   Lauterborn organs less than 0.40 times the length of their stalks (fig. 25.76) 14

11'.   Lauterborn organs about as long as or longer than the length of their stalk (figs.
         25.72–25.75) 12

12(11'). Lauterborn organs about as long as their stalk; lauterborn organs broad and
         usually with visible longitudinal striations (figs. 25.72–25.73) 13

---

2. Includes *Thienemannimyia* Fittkau, *Arctopelopia* Fittkau, *Conchapelopia* Fittkau, and possibly the larvae of the genera *Telopelopia*
Roback, *Cantopelopia* Roback, and *Xenopelopia* Fittkau. See Roback (1981; ref. #2844) for recent information on larval identification.

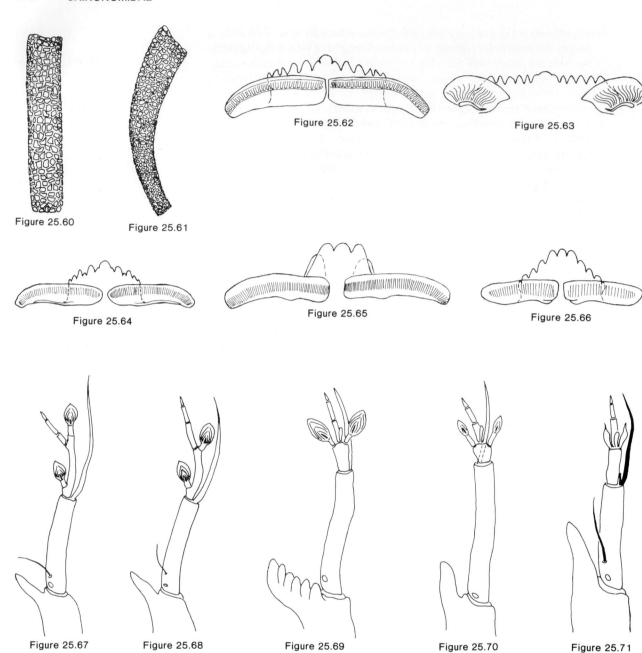

Figure 25.60

Figure 25.61

Figure 25.62

Figure 25.63

Figure 25.64

Figure 25.65

Figure 25.66

Figure 25.67

Figure 25.68

Figure 25.69

Figure 25.70

Figure 25.71

Figure 25.60. Portable sand case of *Stempellinella* sp.

Figure 25.61. Portable sand case of *Constempellina* sp.

Figure 25.62. Mentum of *Rheotanytarsus* sp.

Figure 25.63. Mentum of *Constempellina* sp.

Figure 25.64. Mentum of *Lenziella* sp.

Figure 25.65. Menum of *Corynocera* sp. (redrawn from Hirvenoja [1961]).

Figure 25.66. Mentum of *Tanytarsus (Sublettea)* sp.

Figure 25.67. Antennna of *Stempellinella* sp.

Figure 25.68. Antenna of *Zavrelia* sp. (redrawn with modification from Bause [1913]).

Figure 25.69. Antenna of *Stempellina* sp.

Figure 25.70. Antenna of *Constempellina* sp.

Figure 25.71. Antenna of *Thienemanniola* sp. (redrawn with modification from Lehmann [1973]).

12'.   Lauterborn organs at least one-third longer than their stalk (fig. 25.74); or if subequal in length then organs oval and lacking longitudinal striations (fig. 25.75) .... *Paratanytarsus* Bause

13(12).   Mentum with 2nd lateral tooth smaller than both 1st and 3rd lateral teeth (fig. 25.64); 2nd antennal segment membranous in apical half and subequal in length to 3rd antennal segment (fig. 25.72) .... *Lenziella* Kieffer

13'.   Mentum with all lateral teeth decreasing in size in an orderly manner, or if 2nd lateral teeth are reduced then 3rd antennal segment distinctly longer than 2nd segment (fig. 25.73), and 2nd segment not membranous throughout the apical one half .... *Cladotanytarsus* Kieffer

14(11).   Mentum with 5 pairs of lateral teeth 15

14'.   Mentum with 4 pairs of lateral teeth; combined length of antennal segments 2–5 subequal in length to segment 1 in 4th instar specimens .... *Neozavrelia* Goetghebuer

15(14).   Distal portion of 2nd antennal segment greatly expanded (fig. 25.86); mentum strongly arched (fig. 25.66) .... *Tanytarsus (Sublettea)* Roback

15'.   Distal portion of 2nd antennal segment only moderately expanded (fig. 25.85); mentum not strongly arched (fig. 25.62) .... *Rheotanytarsus* Bause

Chironomini

1.   Seven anterior abdominal segments subdivided, giving the appearance of a 20-segmented body; larva oligocheatelike .... *Chernovskiia* Saether

1'.   Seven anterior abdominal segments not subdivided, not giving the appearance of a 20-segmented body 2

2(1').   Antenna with 6 segments, lauterborn organs large and alternate at apices of segments 2 and 3 (figs. 25.95–25.96) 3

2'.   Antenna usually with 5, 7, or 8 segments, (figs. 25.102–25.104) or if 6 antennal segments are present then lauterborn organs not alternate at apices of 2nd and 3rd segments 8

3(2).   Mentum with a single broad light colored tooth and 6 pairs of more darkly pigmented lateral teeth (fig. 25.91) .... *Paralauterborniella* Lenz

3'.   Mentum with paired median teeth 4

4(3').   Median teeth of mentum distinctly lighter in color than outer lateral teeth (figs. 25.87, 25.89) 5

4'.   Median teeth of mentum not less darkly pigmented than outer lateral teeth (figs. 25.88, 25.90, 25.92–25.93) 6

5(4).   Two median teeth of mentum distinctly lighter in color than outer lateral teeth (fig. 25.89) .... *Microtendipes* Kieffer

5'.   Four median teeth of mentum distinctly lighter in color than outer lateral teeth (fig. 25.87) or light median teeth tiered .... *Paratendipes* Kieffer

6(4').   Antenna elongate and arising from distinct tubercle (fig. 25.96); anterior edge of ventromental plates straight; mentum as in figure 25.92; Seta posterior to ventromental plates plumose .... *Lauterborniella* Bause

6'.   Not with the above combination of characters 7

7(6').   First lateral teeth closely appressed to 2nd lateral teeth (fig. 25.90); antenna distinctly longer than mandible .... *Omisus* Townes

7'.   First lateral teeth not closely appressed to 2nd lateral teeth, much longer than median or 2nd lateral teeth (fig. 25.88); antenna subequal in length to mandible .... *Stictochironomus* Kieffer

8(2').   First antennal segment curved and with a dorsal projection originating near base (fig. 25.94); mentum as in figure 25.93 .... *Pagastiella* Brundin

8'.   Not with the above combination of characters 9

9(8').   Mentum with a dome-shaped median tooth, median tooth pale yellow in middle, lateral edges and remaining lateral teeth darkly pigmented; lateral teeth longer than the median tooth, giving the mentum an overall concave appearance (fig. 25.100) 10

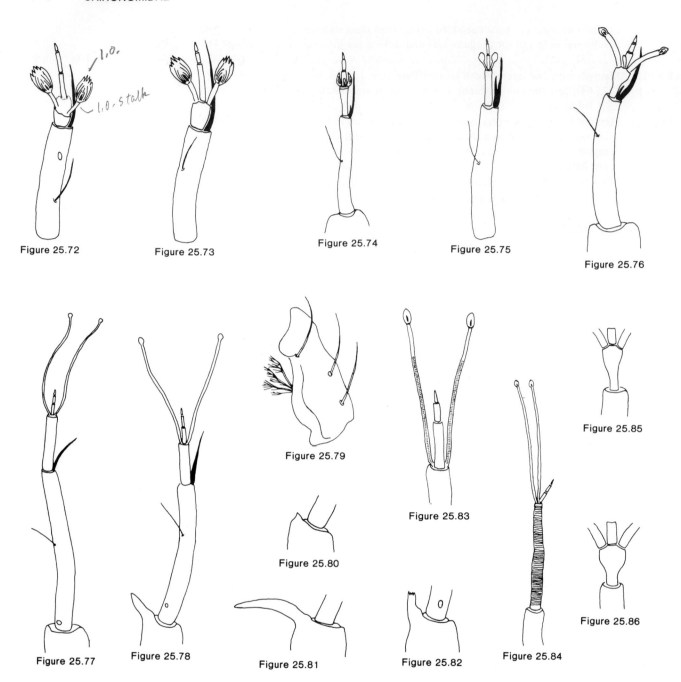

Figure 25.72

Figure 25.73

Figure 25.74

Figure 25.75

Figure 25.76

Figure 25.79

Figure 25.80

Figure 25.83

Figure 25.85

Figure 25.77

Figure 25.78

Figure 25.81

Figure 25.82

Figure 25.84

Figure 25.86

Figure 25.80. Spur on apex of antennal tubercle of *Micropsectra* sp. or *Tanytarsus* sp.

Figure 25.81. Spur on apex of antennal tubercle of *Micropsectra* sp.

Figure 25.82. Spur on apex of antennal tubercle of *Micropsectra* sp. or *Tanytarsus* sp.

Figure 25.83. Apex of antenna of genus near *Nimbocera*.

Figure 25.84. Apex of antenna of Tanytarsini Genus "A" (redrawn from Roback [1966]).

Figure 25.85. Second antennal segment of *Rheotanytarsus* sp.

Figure 25.86. Second antennal segment of *Tanytarsus* (Sublettea) sp.

Figure 25.72. Antenna of *Lenziella* sp.

Figure 25.73. Antenna of *Cladotanytarsus* sp.

Figure 25.74. Antenna of *Paratanytarsus* sp.

Figure 25.75. Antenna of *Paratanytarsus* sp.

Figure 25.76. Antenna of *Rheotanytarsus* sp.

Figure 25.77. Antenna of *Tanytarsus* sp.

Figure 25.78. Antennna of *Micropsectra* sp.

Figure 25.79. Mandible of *Corynocera* sp. (redrawn with modification from Hirvenoja [1961]).

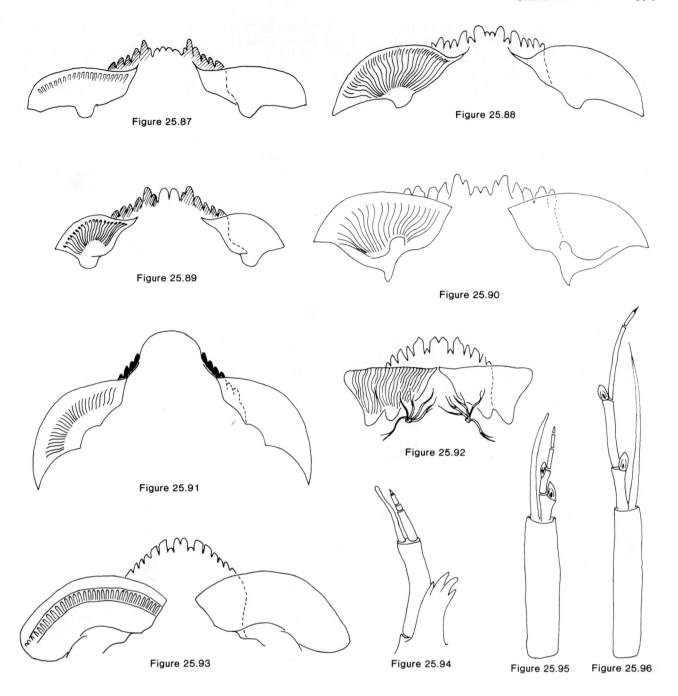

Figure 25.87

Figure 25.88

Figure 25.89

Figure 25.90

Figure 25.91

Figure 25.92

Figure 25.93

Figure 25.94

Figure 25.95

Figure 25.96

Figure 25.87. Mentum of *Paratendipes* sp.

Figure 25.88. Mentum of *Stictochironomus* sp.

Figure 25.89. Mentum of *Microtendipes* sp.

Figure 25.90. Mentum of *Omisus* sp. (redrawn with modification from Beck and Beck [1970]).

Figure 25.91. Mentum of *Paralauterborniella* sp.

Figure 25.92. Mentum of *Lauterborniella* sp.

Figure 25.93. Mentum of *Pagastiella* sp.

Figure 25.94. Antenna of *Pagastiella* sp.

Figure 25.95. Antenna of *Microtendipes* sp.

Figure 25.96. Antenna of *Lauterborniella* sp.

9'. Mentum without a dome-shaped median tooth (figs. 25.107, 25.126, 25.141), or, if median tooth is dome shaped, then lateral teeth small and not giving the impression of an overall concave mentum (figs. 25.105, 25.109, 25.114–25.115, 25.122) 13

10(9). Mentum with 5 lateral teeth (fig. 25.100) .... *Cryptochironomus* Kieffer (in part)

10'. Mentum with 7 lateral teeth 11

11(10'). Antenna with 7 segments; blade originating at apex of 3rd segment (fig. 25.103) ...... *Demicryptochironomus* Lenz

11'. Antenna with 5 segments; blade originating near apex of 2nd segment (fig. 25.102) 12

12(11'). Mentum with 7 sharp and free lateral teeth; S II bladelike, all other S setae reduced .... *Gillotia* Kieffer

12'. Mentum with 7 lateral teeth, however, 1st lateral teeth incompletely separated from the median tooth (fig. 25.101), and the outermost 2 lateral teeth fused throughout most of their base; median tooth often with 2 small spines in the center (fig. 25.101) .... *Cryptochironomus* Kieffer (in part)

13(9'). Two outermost lateral teeth of mentum distinctly enlarged as in figures 25.106–25.108, and labral sensilla 2-segmented (fig. 25.98); mentum similar to figures 25.106–25.108 14

13'. Two outermost lateral teeth of mentum usually not enlarged, if somewhat enlarged then labral sensilla 3-segmented (fig. 25.97); mentum not as in figures 25.106–25.108 16

14(13). Median tooth of mentum trifid (fig. 25.108) and antennal blade longer than the combined lengths of segments 2 through 5 .... *Microchironomus* Pagast

14'. Median tooth of mentum broadly rounded, medially notched and often giving the appearance of paired teeth (fig. 25.107), or with lateral notches (fig. 25.106); antennal blade shorter than flagellum 15

15(14'). Median tooth of mentum medially notched (fig. 25.107) .... *Cladopelma* Kieffer

15'. Median tooth of mentum broadly rounded or with lateral notches (fig. 25.106) .... *Cryptotendipes* Lenz

16(13'). Median portion of mentum lacking distinct teeth (figs. 25.112, 25.114), with a large dome-shaped tooth (figs. 25.109, 25.115), or with 1 to several notches so that the median portion forms a broad convex structure (figs. 25.110–25.111, 25.113, 25.116) 17

16'. Median portion of mentum with distinct teeth (figs. 25.117, 25.120, 25.128, 25.137) 23

17(16). Antenna more than one-third as long as head capsule; mentum and ventromental plates as in figures 25.111–25.115 .... *Paracladopelma* Harnish (in part)

17'. Antenna not more than one-third as long as head capsule; mentum and ventromental plates variable 18

18(17'). Antennal blade longer than flagellum; median tooth of mentum pointed or subtriangular (fig. 25.116); anal tubules vestigial .... *Acalcarella* Shilova

18'. Antennal blade shorter than flagellum; median tooth of mentum not pointed or subtriangular 19

19(18'). Mandible with an elongate apical tooth and 4 smaller inner teeth that originate from a common base (fig. 25.99); mentum as in figure 25.105 .... *Nilothauma* Kieffer

19'. Mandible not as in figure 25.99 and mentum not as in figure 25.105 20

20(19'). Second antennal segment about as long as 3rd segment and antenna 5-segmented; basal segment of maxillary palp about 4 times as long as wide .... *Harnischia* Kieffer

20'. Second antennal segment distinctly longer than 3rd segment or antenna 6-segmented and 2nd segment much shorter than 3rd segment; basal segment of maxillary palp at most 3 times as long as broad 21

21(20'). Antenna 6-segmented; mentum as in figure 25.109 or 25.110 .... *Saetheria* Jackson

21'. Antenna 5-segmented; mentum not as in figure 25.109 or 25.110 22

22(21'). Second antennal segment unsclerotized in basal two-thirds (fig. 25.104) .... *Cyphomella* Saether

22'. Second antennal segment fully sclerotized; mentum as in figures 25.111–25.115 .... *Paracladopelma* Harnish (in part)

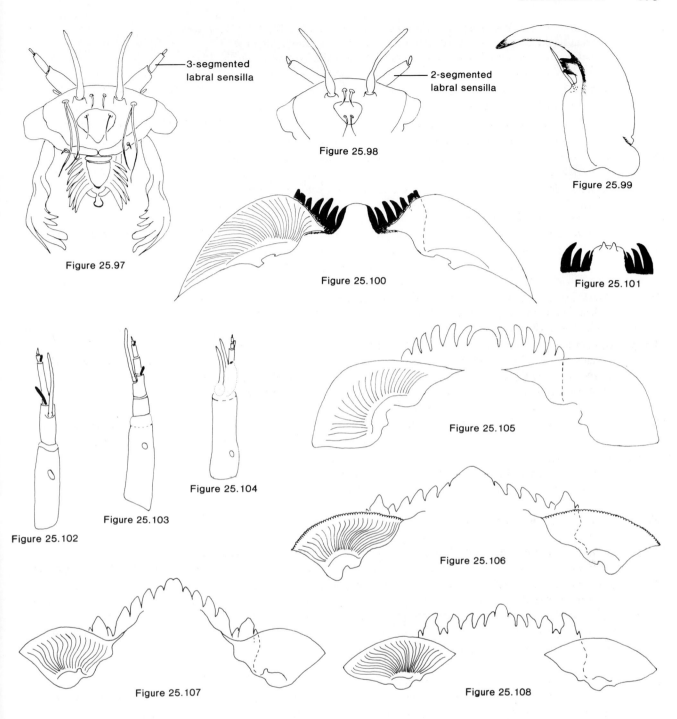

Figure 25.97. Anterior view of labral region of *Paracladopelma* sp. showing position of three-segmented labral sensillae in relation to other labral armature.

Figure 25.98. Anterior view of labral region of *Cladopelma* sp. showing two-segmented labral sensillae.

Figure 25.99. Mandible of *Nilothauma* sp.

Figure 25.100. Mentum of *Cryptochironomus* sp.

Figure 25.101. Detail of median portion of mentum of *Cryptochironomus blarina* Townes.

Figure 25.102. Antenna of *Cryptochironomus* sp.

Figure 25.103. Antenna of *Demicryptochironomus* sp.

Figure 25.104. Antenna of *Cyphomella* sp. (redrawn with modification from Saether [1977]).

Figure 25.105. Mentum of *Nilothauma* sp.

Figure 25.106. Mentum of *Cryptotendipes* sp.

Figure 25.107. Mentum of *Cladopelma* sp.

Figure 25.108. Mentum of *Microchironomus* sp. (redrawn with modification from Kugler [1971]).

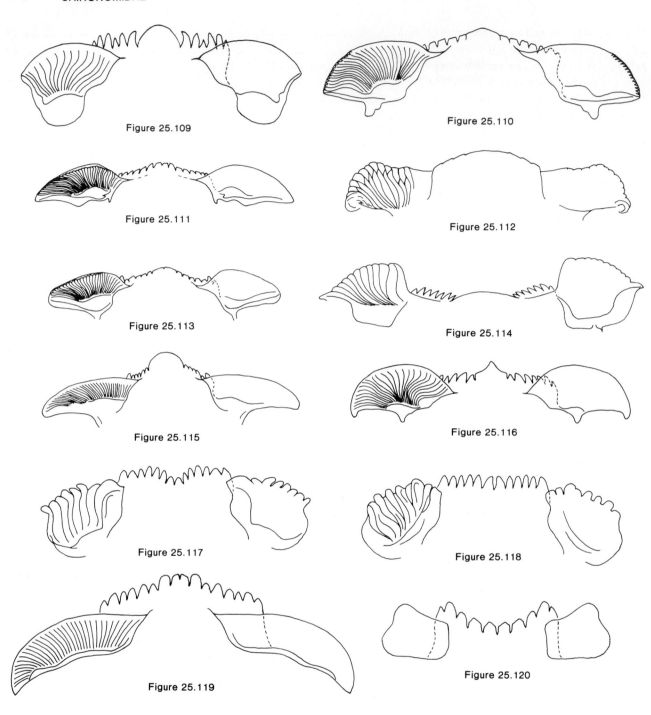

Figure 25.109

Figure 25.110

Figure 25.111

Figure 25.112

Figure 25.113

Figure 25.114

Figure 25.115

Figure 25.116

Figure 25.117

Figure 25.118

Figure 25.119

Figure 25.120

Figure 25.109. Mentum of *Saetheria tylus* (Townes).

Figure 25.110. Mentum of *Saetheria* sp. (redrawn from Jackson [1977]).

Figure 25.111. Mentum of *Paracladopelma galaptera* (Townes) (redrawn from Jackson [1977]).

Figure 25.112. Mentum of *Paracladopelma rolli* (Kirp.) (redrawn with modification from Saether [1977]).

Figure 25.113. Mentum of *Paracladopelma undine* (Townes) (redrawn from Jackson [1977]).

Figure 25.114. Mentum of *Paracladopelma doris* (Townes) (redrawn with modification from Saether [1977]).

Figure 25.115. Mentum of *Paracladopelma longanae* Beck and Beck (redrawn from Jackson [1977]).

Figure 25.116. Mentum of *Acalcarella* sp.

Figure 25.117. Mentum of *Robackia claviger* (Townes).

Figure 25.118. Mentum of *Robackia demeijerei* (Kruseman).

Figure 25.119. Mentum of *Endochironomus* sp.

Figure 25.120. Mentum of *Stenochironomus* sp.

23(16′). Mentum with an even number of teeth 24

23′. Mentum with an odd number of teeth 33

24(23). Mentum concave and consisting of 10 darkly pigmented teeth (fig. 25.120);
mandible short and robust (fig. 25.125) .... *Stenochironomus* Kieffer

24′. Mentum and mandibles not as in figures 25.120 and 25.125 25

25(24′). Pecten epipharyngis composed of 3 blunt teeth; mentum as in figure 25.128; larvae
occurring in stems and petioles of aquatic vascular plants .... *Hyporhygma* Reiss

25′. Pecten epipharyngis either a single individual plate or, more commonly, consisting
of 1–3 plates, each with 2 or more teeth; mentum not as in figure 25.128 26

26(25′). Apical segment of maxillary palp elongate and well sclerotized (fig. 25.123);
striations of ventromental plates very coarse; mentum as in figure 25.117 or
25.118 .... *Robackia* Saether

26′. Apical segment of maxillary palp not elongate, rarely well sclerotized;
ventromental plates with finer striations and mentum not as in figure 25.117 or
25.118 27

27(26′). Median pair of mental teeth partially fused and distinctly wider than each of the
remaining lateral teeth (fig. 25.121); anterior margin of ventromental plates
coarsely scalloped (fig. 25.121) .... *Parachironomus* Lenz (in part)

27′. Median pair of mental teeth not partially fused, or if partially fused then not
distinctly wider than each of the remaining lateral teeth; anterior margin of
ventromental plates not coarsely scalloped 28

28(27′). First lateral teeth of mentum much shorter than median and 2nd lateral teeth (fig.
25.126) .... *Polypedilum* Kieffer (in part)

28′. First lateral teeth of mentum subequal to or longer than the median and/or 2nd
lateral teeth 29

29(28′). Lateral teeth of mentum gradually decreasing in size and length so that anterior
margin of mentum appears to be broadly convex (figs. 25.127, 25.129) 32

29′. Second lateral teeth recessed and smaller in size than 1st lateral and 3rd lateral
teeth (fig. 25.131), or median teeth partially fused (fig. 25.119) 30

30(29′). Median teeth partially fused (fig. 25.119); ventromental plates 3–4 times wider
than their length .... *Endochironomus* Kieffer

30′. Median teeth not partially fused (fig. 25.131); ventromental plates not more than 3
times as wide as their maximum length 31

31(30′). Antennal blade distinctly longer than the combined lengths of segments 2 through
5 .... *Tribelos* Townes

31′. Antennal blade equal to or shorter than the combined lengths of segments 2
through 5 .... *Phaenopsectra* Kieffer

32(29). Ventromental plates more than 3 times wider than their maximum length and with
lateral corners rounded (fig. 25.129) .... *Pedionomus* Sublette

32′. Ventromental plates usually less than 3 times wider than their maximum length,
lateral corners never rounded (fig. 25.127) .... *Polypedilum* Kieffer (in part)

33(23′). Anterior margin of ventromental plates coarsely scalloped; median tooth of
mentum about 2 times as wide as 1st lateral teeth; all lateral teeth pointed and
gradually diminishing in size laterally (fig. 25.122) .... *Parachironomus* Lenz (in part)

33′. Anterior margin of ventromental plates smooth (figs. 25.133, 25.140) or only finely
crenulate (figs. 25.137–25.139); median tooth and lateral teeth of mentum
variable, but not as in figure 25.122 34

34(33′). Median apices of ventromental plates touching or separated from one another by a
distance less than the width of the median tooth (figs. 25.132–25.133,
25.135–25.136) 35

34′. Median apices of ventromental plates separated by a distance equal to or greater
than the width of the median tooth (figs. 25.137, 25.141) 38

35(34). Ventromental plates touching on midline; mentum as in figure 25.136 .... *Axarus* Roback

35′. Ventromental plates not touching on midline; mentum not as in figure 25.136 36

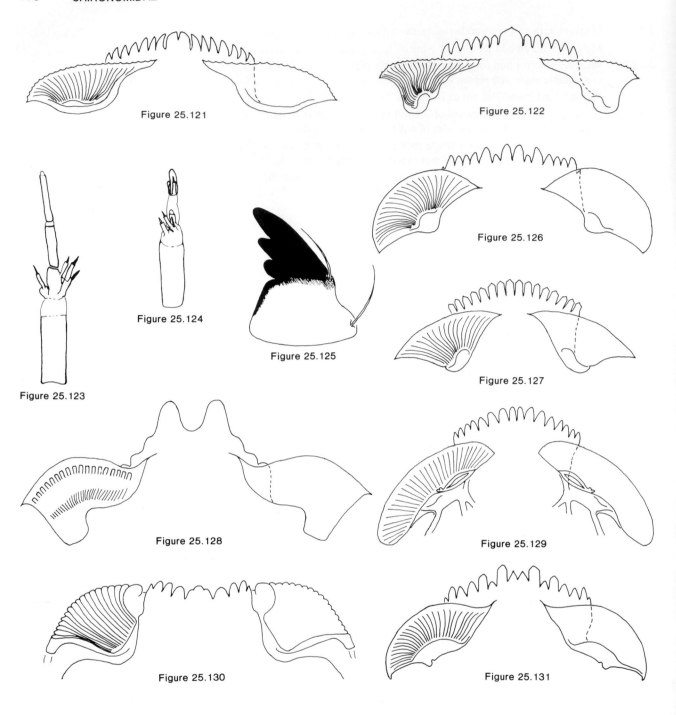

Figure 25.121

Figure 25.122

Figure 25.123

Figure 25.124

Figure 25.125

Figure 25.126

Figure 25.127

Figure 25.128

Figure 25.129

Figure 25.130

Figure 25.131

Figure 25.121. Mentum of *Parachironomus* cf. *frequens* (Johannsen).

Figure 25.122. Mentum of *Parachironomus* cf. *abortivus* (Malloch).

Figure 25.123. Maxillary palpus of *Robackia demeijerei* (Kruseman).

Figure 25.124. Maxillary palpus of *Beckidia tethys* (Townes) (redrawn with modification from Saether [1977]).

Figure 25.125. Mandible of *Stenochironomus* sp.

Figure 25.126. Mentum of *Polypedilum* sp.

Figure 25.127. Mentum of *Polypedilum* sp.

Figure 25.128. Mentum of *Hyporhygma* sp.

Figure 25.129. Mentum of *Pedionomus beckae* Sublette.

Figure 25.130. Mentum of *Beckidia tethys* (Townes) (redrawn with modification from Saether [1977]).

Figure 25.131. Mentum of *Phaenosectra* sp.

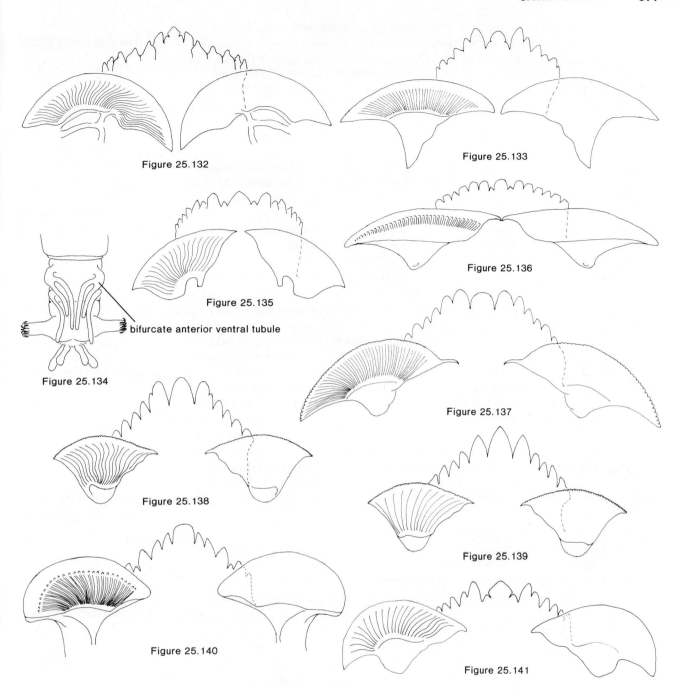

Figure 25.132

Figure 25.133

bifurcate anterior ventral tubule

Figure 25.134

Figure 25.135

Figure 25.136

Figure 25.137

Figure 25.138

Figure 25.139

Figure 25.140

Figure 25.141

Figure 25.132. Mentum of *Goeldichironomus* sp.

Figure 25.133. Mentum of *Nilodorum devineyae* (Beck) (redrawn with modification from Beck and Beck [1970]).

Figure 25.134. Posterior abdominal segments and ventral tubules of *Goeldichironomus* sp. (redrawn with modification from Fittkau [1965]).

Figure 25.135. Mentum of *Xenochironomus xenolabis* (Kieffer).

Figure 25.136. Mentum of *Axarus festivus* (Say).

Figure 25.137. Mentum of *Glyptotendipes* sp.

Figure 25.138. Mentum of *Dicrotendipes* sp.

Figure 25.139. Mentum of *Dicrotendipes* sp.

Figure 25.140. Mentum of *Einfeldia natchitocheae* (Sublette) (redrawn with modification from Sublette [1964]).

Figure 25.141. Mentum of *Chironomus* sp.

36(35'). Mentum strongly arched, and with alternating large and small teeth (fig. 25.135); larvae found in freshwater sponges .... *Xenochironomus* Kieffer

36'. Mentum not strongly arched, not as in figure 25.135; larvae found in various habitats, but apparently more common in subtropical regions of the United States 37

37(36'). Mentum with distinctly overlapping lateral teeth (fig. 25.132); abdominal segment 8 with a bifurcate anterior ventral tubule (fig. 25.134) .... *Goeldichironomus* Fittkau

37'. Lateral teeth of mentum not overlapping (fig. 25.133) abdominal segment 8 with a nonbifurcate anterior ventral tubule .... *Nilodorum* Kieffer

38(34'). Maxillary palp more than 4 times longer than wide, one apical segment elongate (fig. 25.124); lateral teeth of mentum projecting at least as far anterior as median tooth, giving the mentum an overall flat or slightly concave appearance (fig. 25.130) .... *Beckidia* Saether

38'. Maxillary palp not more than 3 times longer than wide, apical segment not as in figure 25.124; at least outermost teeth of mentum decreasing in size or length, giving the mentum an overall convex appearance (figs. 25.138, 25.140–25.141) 39

39(38'). Median tooth of mentum broadly rounded (figs. 25.137, 25.140) or pointed (figs. 25.138–25.139), but lacking lateral notches 40

39'. Median tooth with lateral notches that give it a trifid appearance (fig. 25.141) 42

40(39). Ventromental plate distinctly less than 2 times as wide as long and usually with small crenulations along anterior margin; median tooth and 1st lateral teeth enlarged and somewhat pointed; 1st laterals with (fig. 25.138) or without lateral notches (fig. 25.139) .... *Dicrotendipes* Kieffer

40'. Ventromental plates at least twice as wide as long and anterior margin with or without crenulations; median tooth rounded; 1st lateral teeth variable but never as in figures 25.138 and 25.139 41

41(40'). Median tooth extending anterior to 1st lateral teeth; 4th lateral teeth reduced (fig. 25.140) .... *Einfeldia* Kieffer (in part)

41'. Median tooth recessed within 1st lateral teeth (fig. 25.137), or very broad and extending about as far anterior as 1st lateral teeth, or if projecting farther anterior than 1st lateral teeth then 4th lateral teeth not conspicuously reduced .... *Glyptotendipes* Kieffer

42(39'). Premandible with 3 or more teeth .... *Kiefferulus* Goetghebuer

42'. Premandible at most bifid 43

43(42'). Frontal apotome with an oval depression just posterior to antennal bases and 8th abdominal segment with 1 pair of ventral tubules .... *Einfeldia* Kieffer (in part)

43'. Not with the above combination of characters 44

44(43'). Eighth abdominal segment without ventral tubules and pecten epipharyngis with 3–7 teeth .... *Einfeldia* Kieffer (in part)

44'. Not with the above combination of characters 45

45(44'). Eighth abdominal segment lacking ventral tubules, with 1 pair of ventral tubules, or with 2 pairs of ventral tubules; pecten epipharyngis with 10 or more teeth .... *Chironomus* Meigen

45'. Eighth abdominal segment with ventral tubules and pecten epipharyngis with 9 teeth; known only from California .... *Wirthiella* Sublette

Orthocladiinae

1. Antenna elongate, more than two-thirds the length of the head capsule 2

1'. Antenna not elongate, equal to or less than two-thirds the length of the head capsule 6

2(1). Second antennal segment with extensive dark brown or golden brown pigmentation (figs. 25.153–25.154) 3

2'. Second antennal segment concolorous with remaining segments, lacking distinct dark brown or golden brown pigmentation 4

3(2). Antenna longer than head capsule, 4-segmented, and usually with some darker pigmentation occurring on the 3rd segment (fig. 25.153) .... *Corynoneura* Winnertz

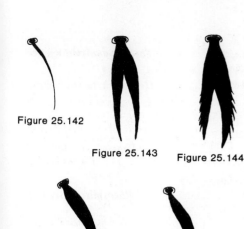

Figure 25.142

Figure 25.143

Figure 25.144

Figure 25.150

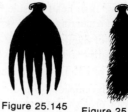

Figure 25.145

Figure 25.146

Figure 25.147

Figure 25.148

Figure 25.149

Figure 25.151

Figure 25.152

Figure 25.142. Simple SI seta of *Eukiefferiella* sp.

Figure 25.143. Bifid SI seta of *Cricotopus* sp.

Figure 25.144. Bifid SI seta with secondary feathering in *Acricotopus sp.*

Figure 25.145. Palmate SI seta of *Psectrocladius* sp.

Figure 25.146. Plumose SI seta of *Parametriocnemus* sp.

Figure 25.147. SI seta of *Hydrobaenus* sp. with strong apical dissections.

Figure 25.148. Strong and simple SI seta of *Georthocladius* sp.

Figure 25.149. SI seta with fine apical dissections.

Figure 25.150. Bifid SI and SII setal arrangement in *Pseudosmittia* sp.

Figure 25.151. SI seta with strong apical dissections in *Smittia* sp.

Figure 25.152. SI seta with weak apical dissections in *Paracricotopus* sp.

3'.	Antenna shorter than head capsule, 5-segmented, and never with dark pigmentation occurring on 3rd segment (fig. 25.154)	***Thienemanniella* Kieffer**
4(2').	Median portion of mentum concave (fig. 25.182); antenna with large lauterborn organs originating at different levels on 2nd antennal segment (fig. 25.160)	***Heterotanytarsus* Spärck**
4'.	Median portion of mentum not concave; antenna not as in figure 25.160	5
5(4').	Procercus well developed; 1 procercal seta at least twice as long as the length of the posterior prolegs; antenna with an elongate blade and whiplike apical segment (fig. 25.155); body white when preserved	***Lopescladius* Oliveira**
5'.	Procercus less well developed; all procercal setae less than twice as long as posterior prolegs; apical segment of antenna not whiplike (fig. 25.156); body often with distinctive purple or brown pigmented areas when preserved	***Rheosmittia* Brundin**
6(1').	Antenna arising from tubercle that has a large anteromedially directed spur (fig. 25.157); thoracic segments with conspicuous setae, many of which are apically dissected; larvae that build portable sand cases	***Abiskomyia* Edwards**
6'.	Not with the above combination of characters	7
7(6').	One procercal setae elongate, at least one-quarter the length of the larval body (fig. 25.225); remaining procercal setae vestigial or absent	8
7'.	All procercal setae less than one-fifth the length of the larval body	10
8(7).	Mentum consisting of a single broad, dome shaped median tooth with a central cusp and 6 pairs of narrow pointed lateral teeth (fig. 25.176); apical tooth of mandible longer than the combined widths of the lateral teeth (fig. 25.237)	***Krenosmittia* Thienemann**
8'.	Mentum consisting of paired median teeth and 5 paired lateral teeth, the outermost 2 teeth fused throughout most of their length (fig. 25.177); apical tooth of mandible shorter than combined widths of the lateral teeth (figs. 25.232–25.233)	9
9(8').	Mandible with 3 inner teeth (fig. 25.233)	***Pseudorthocladius* Goetghebuer**
9'.	Mandible with 2 inner teeth (fig. 25.232)	***Parachaetocladius* Wulker[3]**
10(7').	Ventromental plates well developed and covering all lateral teeth of mentum; 3 small median teeth visible in median concavity of mentum (fig. 25.178); larvae apparently occurring only within colonies of blue-green algae	***Acamptocladius* Brundin**
10'.	Mentum not as in figure 25.178; larvae living in a variety of habitats	11
11(10').	Cardinal beard present beneath the ventromental plates (figs. 25.212–25.223)	12
11'.	Cardinal beard not present beneath the ventromental plates (figs. 25.179–25.211)	21
12(11).	Sl seta simple (fig. 25.142), bifid (fig. 25.143) or bifid with secondary feathering (fig. 25.144)	13
12'.	Sl seta palmate (fig. 25.145), plumose (fig. 25.146), or with multiple apical dissections (fig. 25.147)	18
13(12).	Sl setae simple (fig. 25.142)	14[4]
13'.	Sl setae bifid or bifid with secondary feathering (figs. 25.143–25.144)	15
14(13).	Cardinal beard consisting of bristlelike, often branched, stellate setae; mentum with an even number of teeth (fig. 25.219); mature larvae very small, less than 4 mm total length	***Synorthocladius* Thienemann**
14'.	Cardinal beard consisting of numerous simple setae; mentum with an odd number of teeth (fig. 25.222); mature larvae 3.5–7.0 mm total length	***Parorthocladius* Thienemann**
15(13').	Sl setae bifid with secondary feathering; mentum as in figure 25.214	***Acricotopus* Kieffer**
15'.	Sl setae bifid; mentum not as in figure 25.214	16
16(15').	Mentum with paired median teeth (fig. 25.218)	***Rheocricotopus* Thienemann and Harnisch**
16'.	Mentum with an unpaired median tooth (figs. 25.212, 25.216)	17

3. The larval stages and natural history of *Parachaetocladius* specimens from western Pennsylvania are currently being described by the junior author.
4. Larvae of the recently described genus *Doncricotopus* (see Saether 1981; ref. #2848) will key to this couplet on the basis of simple SI setae. However, these larvae differ from larvae of *Synorthocladius* and *Parorthocladius* principally in the shape of the mentum, which is very similar to the mentum of *Rheocricotopus* (see fig. 25.218).

17(16'). Median tooth of mentum broad, dome-shaped, and distinctly lighter in color than remaining lateral teeth (fig. 25.216) .... *Paracladius* Hirvenoja

17'. Median tooth of mentum narrower, not dome-shaped, and usually concolorous with 1st lateral teeth (fig. 25.212) .... *Halocladius (Halocladius)* Hirvenoja

18(12'). SI seta palmate (fig. 25.145); procerci with at least 1 basal spur; apical tooth of mandible longer than the combined widths of the lateral teeth (fig. 25.234); mentum usually with a broad unpaired but peaked median tooth (fig. 25.217) or with broad paired median teeth (fig. 25.215) .... *Psectrocladius* Kieffer

18'. SI seta plumose (fig. 25.146) or with multiple apical dissections (fig. 25.147), but not with the remaining combination of characters 19

19(18'). Mentum with a broad, truncated median tooth (fig. 25.213); larvae occurring in marine littoral zones, not presently recorded from North America ...... *Halocladius (Psammocladius)* Hirvenoja

19'. Mentum with rounded or pointed median teeth (figs. 25.220–25.221, 25.223); larvae occurring in a variety of freshwater habitats 20

20(19'). Mandible with 4 inner teeth; mentum as in figure 25.220 .... *Diplocladius* Kieffer

20'. Mandible with 3 inner teeth; mentum either with 2–4 pale median teeth (fig. 25.223) or similar to figure 25.221 .... *Zalutschia* Lipina

21(11'). Procerci present 27

21'. Procerci absent 22

22(21'). Preanal segment strongly bent ventrally so that the anal segment and posterior prolegs are orientated at a right angle to the long axis of the body (figs. 25.228–25.229); anal segment and posterior prolegs retractile into preanal segment 23

22'. Preanal segment at most declivent; anal segment and posterior prolegs not oriented at right angle to main axis of body, and not retractile into preanal segment 24

23(22). Posterior prolegs each subdivided, the anterior portion bearing a semicircle of claws (fig. 25.228); no anal tubules present; antenna as in figure 25.163 .... *Gymnometriocnemus* Geotghebuer

23'. Posterior prolegs not subdivided (fig. 25.229); 4 short anal tubules present; antenna similar to figure 25.164 .... *Bryophaenocladius* Thienemann

24(22'). Larva ectoparasitic on mayflies; mouthparts reduced, mentum as in figure 25.179; body robust, especially thoracic segments, giving an overall swollen appearance (fig. 25.230) .... *Symbiocladius* Kieffer and Zavrel

24'. Larva not ectoparasitic; mouthparts, mentum, and body not as in figure 25.179 or 25.230 25

25(24'). SI seta and SII seta bifid and both well developed (fig. 25.150) .... *Pseudosmittia* Goetghebuer

25'. SII seta never bifid 26

26(25'). SI seta strong and simple (fig. 25.148) or with fine apical and lateral serrations (fig. 25.149); antenna as in figure 25.159; anal tubules elongate and with numerous constrictions throughout their length (fig. 25.227); mentum as in figure 25.180 .... *Georthocladius* Strenzke

26'. SI seta not strong and simple or with fine apical and lateral serrations, but usually with multiple apical dissections (fig. 25.151); antenna similar to figure 25.165 or 25.166; anal tubules not elongate, lacking constrictions; mentum not as in figure 25.180 .... *Smittia* Holmgren

27(21). Antenna 7-segmented, 3rd segment shorter than 4th segment and 7th segment hairlike or vestigial (fig. 25.161); mentum with 1 (*maeaeri* group, fig. 25.188) or 2 median teeth and 5 pairs of lateral teeth (fig. 25.190); labral lamella present and divided at least anteriorly (fig. 25.175); SI seta plumose .... *Heterotrissocladius* Spärck

27'. Not with the above combination of characters 28

28(27'). Larva with a dense lateral fringe of setae on at least abdominal segments 1 through 5 (fig. 25.224); mentum as in figure 25.186 .... *Xylotopus* Oliver

28'. Larva lacking a dense fringe of setae on abdominal segments; mentum not as in figure 25.186 29

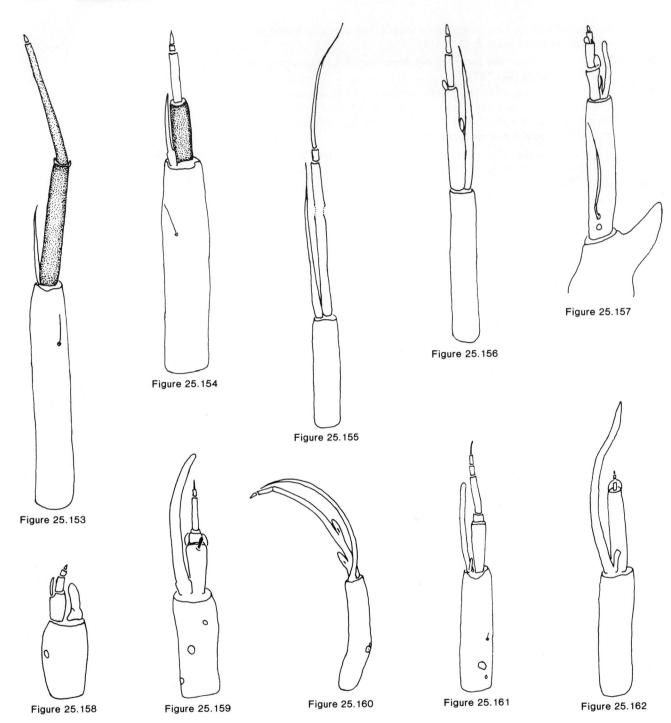

Figure 25.153. Antenna of *Corynoneura* sp.

Figure 25.154. Antenna of *Thienemanniella* sp.

Figure 25.155. Antenna of *Lopescladius* sp.

Figure 25.156. Antenna of *Rheosmittia* sp.

Figure 25.157. Antenna of *Abiskomyia* sp. (redrawn with modification from Pankratova [1970]).

Figure 25.158. Antenna of *Baeoctenus bicolor* Saether (redrawn with modification from Saether [1977]).

Figure 25.159. Antenna of *Georthocladius* sp.

Figure 25.160. Antenna of *Heterotanytarsus perennis* Saether (redrawn with modification from Saether [1975]).

Figure 25.161. Antenna of *Heterotrissocladius* sp.

Figure 25.162. Antenna of *Heleniella thienemanni* Gowin.

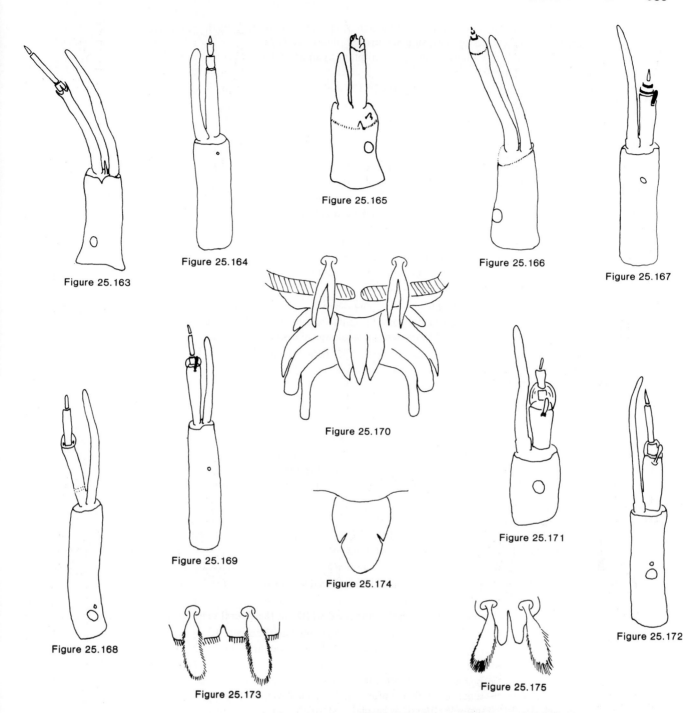

Figure 25.163

Figure 25.164

Figure 25.165

Figure 25.166

Figure 25.167

Figure 25.168

Figure 25.169

Figure 25.170

Figure 25.171

Figure 25.172

Figure 25.174

Figure 25.173

Figure 25.175

Figure 25.169. Antenna of *Parametriocnemus* sp.

Figure 25.170. Pecten epipharyngis and associated labral setae and other armature of *Cricotopus (Cricotopus)* sp.

Figure 25.163. Antenna of *Gymnometriocnemus* sp.

Figure 25.171. Antenna of *Paraphaenocladius* sp.

Figure 25.164. Antenna of *Bryophaenocladius* sp.

Figure 25.172. Antenna of *Psilometriocnemus* sp.

Figure 25.165. Antenna of *Smittia* sp.

Figure 25.173. SI and labral lamellae of *Brillia* sp.

Figure 25.166. Antenna of *Smittia aquatilis* Goetghebuer (redrawn with modification from Thienemann and Strenzke [1941]).

Figure 25.174. Pecten epipharyngis of *Cricotopus (Isocladius)* sp.

Figure 25.167. Antenna of *Epoicocladius* sp.

Figure 25.175. SI and labral lamellae of *Heterotrissocladius* sp.

Figure 25.168. Antenna of *Brillia* sp.

29(28').   Mentum strongly arched and appearing truncated at apex, only 6 anterior teeth readily discernible when head capsule not strongly depressed (figs. 25.183–25.184); larvae phoretic on Ephemeroptera nymphs or living within the gills of bivalve mollusks 30

29'.   Mentum, if strongly arched, not as in figures 25.183 and 25.184; larvae living in a variety of habitats 31

30(29).   Body with conspicuous brown setae; mentum as in figure 25.184; antenna as in figure 25.167; premandible with 2 apical teeth; larvae phoretic on Ephemeroptera .... *Epoicocladius* Zavrel

30'.   Body lacking conspicuous brown setae; mentum as in figure 25.183; antenna as in figure 25.158; premandible with 6 apical teeth; larvae living within gills of bivalve mollusks .... *Baeoctenus* Saether

31(29').   Second antennal segment elongate, more than two-thirds the length of the 1st segment; antennal segments 3–5 very reduced, their combined lengths equal to about one-fifth the length of segment 2; antennal blade curved and extending well beyond 5th antennal segment (fig. 25.162); mentum with 2 broad median teeth and 5 smaller lateral teeth; outermost lateral tooth more elongate than preceding lateral tooth (fig. 25.181) .... *Heleniella* Gowin

31'.   Antenna and mentum not as in figures 25.162 and 25.181 32

32(31').   Antenna 6-segmented; mentum broadly convex, similar to figure 25.191, 25.192, or 25.193; SI plumose or with multiple strong or weak apical dissections 33

32'.   If mentum similar to figure 25.191, 25.192, or 25.193, then antenna 4- or 5-segmented 35

33(32).   Median tooth with distinct median cusp (fig. 25.192) .... *Parakiefferiella* Brundin

33'.   Median tooth without medium cusp 34

34(33').   Median tooth truncated (fig. 25.193); SI plumose .... *Oliveridia* Saether

34'.   Mentum with paired median teeth (fig. 25.191); SI with multiple apical dissections .... *Hydrobaenus* Fries

35(32').   SI plumose, labral lamella well developed (fig. 25.173); 1st antennal segment slightly or strongly bent, 2nd antennal segment divided in the basal 3rd by an area of reduced sclerotization (fig. 25.168); mentum similar to figure 25.185 or 25.187 .... *Brillia* Kieffer

35'.   Not with the above combination of characters 36

36(35').   Mentum with strongly arcuate median tooth and 2 pairs of small lateral teeth (fig. 25.189); larvae living in submerged decomposing wood .... *Symposiocladius* Cranston

36'.   Mentum not as in figure 25.189; larvae occurring in a variety of habitats 37

37(36').   Apical tooth of mandible clearly longer than the combined widths of the lateral teeth (fig. 25.235) 38

37'.   Apical tooth of mandible not longer than the combined widths of the lateral teeth 39

38(37).   Mentum consisting of a broad median tooth with a single median cusp, and 10 pairs of sharp pointed, distinct, lateral teeth (fig. 25.205); larvae apparently restricted to high alpine or arctic regions .... *Lapposmittia* Thienemann

38.   Mentum consisting of a broad median tooth with 2 median cusps, and 6 or fewer pairs of lateral teeth, some of which are often small or indistinct; ventromental plates well developed, usually extending beyond posterolateral corner of mentum (fig. 25.204) .... *Nanocladius* Kieffer

39(37').   SI seta simple 40

39'.   SI seta bifid, plumose, palmate, or with weak (fig. 25.152) or strong apical (fig. 25.151) dissections 42

40(39).   SI seta thick and heavily sclerotized; median tooth of mentum broad, heavily sclerotized (fig. 25.194); procercus reduced; 2 procercal setae distinctly larger in diameter and longer in length than the remaining setae .... *Cardiocladius* Kieffer

40'.   If SI seta thick and heavily sclerotized then median tooth of mentum not broad and heavily sclerotized; procerus not reduced; all procercal setae similar in diameter and length 41

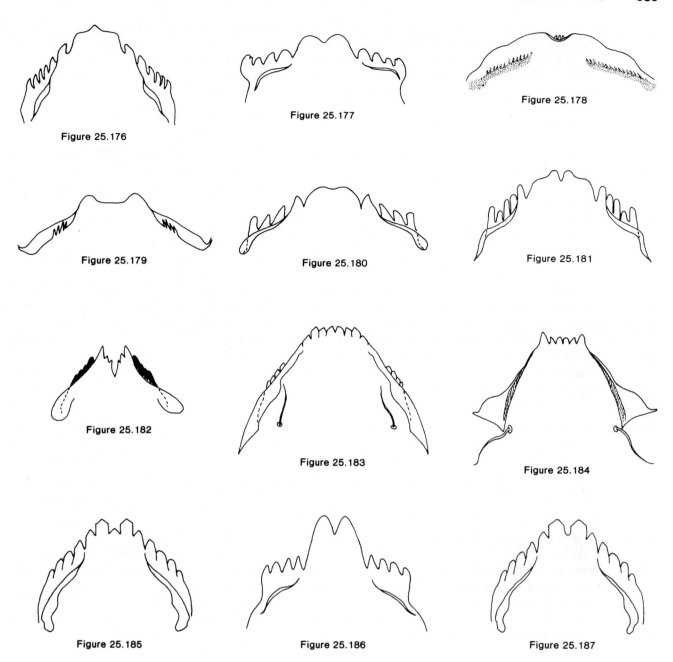

Figure 25.176. Mentum of *Krenosmittia* sp.

Figure 25.177. Mentum of *Parachaetocladius* sp.

Figure 25.178. Mentum of *Acamptocladius* sp.

Figure 25.179. Mentum of *Symbiocladius* sp.

Figure 25.180. Mentum of *Georthocladius* sp.

Figure 25.181. Mentum of *Heleniella thienemanni* Gowin.

Figure 25.182. Mentum of *Heterotanytarsus perennis* Saether (redrawn with modification from Saether [1975]).

Figure 25.183. Mentum of *Baeoctenus bicolor* Saether (redrawn with modification from Saether [1977]).

Figure 25.184. Mentum of *Epoicocladius* sp.

Figure 25.185. Mentum of *Brillia* sp.

Figure 25.186. Mentum of *Xylotopus* sp.

Figure 25.187. Mentum of *Brillia* sp.

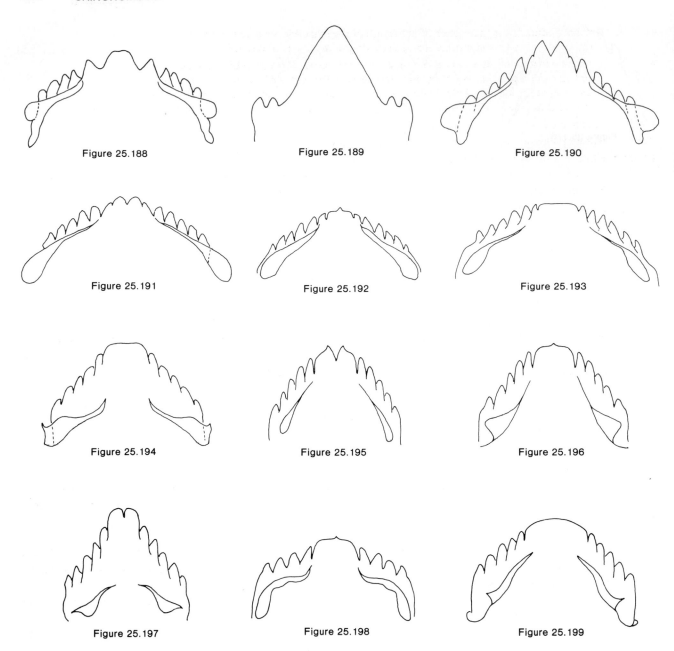

Figure 25.188

Figure 25.189

Figure 25.190

Figure 25.191

Figure 25.192

Figure 25.193

Figure 25.194

Figure 25.195

Figure 25.196

Figure 25.197

Figure 25.198

Figure 25.199

Figure 25.188. Mentum of *Heterotrissocladius maeaeri* group species.

Figure 25.189. Mentum of *Symposiocladius* sp.

Figure 25.190. Mentum of *Heterotrissocladius marcidus* group species.

Figure 25.191. Mentum of *Hydrobaenus* sp.

Figure 25.192. Mentum of *Parakiefferiella* sp.

Figure 25.193. Mentum of *Oliveridea tricornis* (Oliver) (redrawn with modification from Saether [1976]).

Figure 25.194. Mentum of *Cardiocladius* sp.

Figure 25.195. Mentum of *Tvetenia bavarica* group species.

Figure 25.196. Mentum of *Tvetenia discoloripes* group species.

Figure 25.197. Mentum of *Eukiefferiella pseudomontana* group species.

Figure 25.198. Mentum of *Eukiefferiella devonica* group species.

Figure 25.199. Mentum of *Eukiefferiella potthasti* group species.

41(40'). Antenna reduced, less than one-half the length of the mandible, or antenna about the length of the mandible and larvae occurring in the leaves of pitcher plants 51

41'. Antenna not reduced, subequal to or longer than the length of the mandible; larvae occurring in a wide variety of habitats but never in the leaves of pitcher plants; a very species rich and commonly encountered genus, mentum of some common species illustrated in figures 25.195–25.199 .... *Eukiefferiella* Thienemann (in part)[5]

42(39'). SI seta bifid 43

42'. SI seta plumose, palmate, or with weak or strong apical dissections 52

43(42). Mentum with broad median tooth and 9 pairs of lateral teeth (fig. 25.203) .... *Orthocladius (Euorthocladius)* Thienemann (in part)

43'. Mentum with fewer than 9 pairs of lateral teeth, median tooth variable 44

44(43'). Posterolateral corners of at least abdominal segments 1 through 6 with a group of setae, all of which arise from a single point (fig. 25.226) .... *Cricotopus* Van der Wulp (in part) .. 45

44'. Posterolateral corners of abdominal segments without a group of setae arising from a single point 46

45(44). Pecten epipharyngis composed of 3 nearly equal sized plates (fig. 25.170) .... *Cricotopus (Cricotopus)* Hirvenoja (in part)

45'. Pecten epipharyngis composed of 1 large conical plate, vestigial lateral plates only indicated by lateral notches in median plate (fig. 25.174) .... *Cricotopus (Isocladius)* Kieffer (in part)

46(44'). Mandible with spines along the inner margin (fig. 25.236) .... *Cricotopus (Cricotopus)* Hirvenoja (in part)

46'. Mandible smooth along inner margin 47

47(46'). Antenna 4-segmented; lauterborn organs poorly developed; eyespots dark and tripartite with 2 small anterior and 1 larger posterior pigment patch; body green ....*Orthocladius (Pogonocladius)* Brundin

47'. Antenna 5-segmented, or if 4-segmented then not with the combination of poorly developed lauterborn organs, tripartite eyespots, and green body 48

48(47'). Head capsule dark brown to black 49

48'. Head capsule yellow to light brown 50

49(48). Head capsule reddish brown to dark brown .... *Orthocladius (Eudactylocladius)* Thienemann

49'. Head capsule light brown .... *Orthocladius (Euorthocladius)* Thienemann (in part)

50(48'). Median tooth of mentum broad, 1st and 2nd lateral teeth appearing partially fused with median tooth and smaller than remaining lateral teeth (fig. 25.202) .... *Cricotopus (Cricotopus) trifascia* Edwards

50'. Mentum not as in figure 25.202 .... *Cricotopus (Cricotopus)* (in part), *Orthocladius (Orthocladius)*

51(41). SI seta short and peglike; mentum with an even number of teeth (figs. 25.206, 25.208) .... *Metriocnemus* Van der Wulp

51'. SI seta more elongate, mentum with an odd number of teeth (fig. 25.200) ....*Cricotopus (Isocladius)* Kieffer (in part)

52(42'). SI seta plumose; mentum with 2 large, rounded, median teeth and 5 lateral teeth that form a gentle arch (fig. 25.207); ventromental plates with a distinct curve such that they are anteriorly oriented parallel to the arch of the lateral mental teeth, and posteriorly to the basal margin of the mentum 53

52'. SI seta not plumose or if plumose then mentum and ventromental plates not as in figure 25.207 55

53(52). Antenna shorter than mandible (fig. 25.171) .... *Paraphaenocladius* Thienemann (in part)

53'. Antenna longer than mandible 54

54(53'). Antennal segments 2 through 5 reduced and antennal blade much longer than segments 2 through 5 .... *Paraphaenocladius* Thienemann (in part)

54'. Antennal segments 2 through 5 not abnormally reduced, antennal blade equal to or shorter than segments 2 through 5 (fig. 25.169) .... *Parametriocnemus* Thienemann

5. This genus has recently been revised by Dr. O. A. Saether and Dr. G. A. Halvorsen (1981). Larvae that key to this couplet may belong in one of the following genera: *Eukiefferiella, Tvetenia, Dratnalia,* or *Tokunagaia.* Associated pupae and/or adults may be necessary to accurately place many larvae.

55(52′).   SI seta plumose, mentum with single, broad median tooth and ventromental plates
as in figure 25.201; antenna shorter than mandible .... *Paraphaenocladius* Thienemann (in part)

55′.   Not with the above combination of characters 56

56(55′).   SI seta weak, with several fine apical dissections (fig. 25.152) 57

56′.   SI seta well developed, with several strong apical dissections 58

57(56).   Mentum with a single round median tooth and 1st lateral teeth that are set off
from the remaining lateral teeth (fig. 25.209); procercus with a preapical spine
and a basal spur; inner margin of mandible never with spines .... *Paracricotopus* Thienemann and Harnish

57′.   Mentum with a single or double median tooth; procercus lacking preapical spine
and basal spur; however, a well-developed preapical seta usually present; inner
margin of mandible with spines (fig. 25.231) which are easily worn away or are
often difficult to distinguish; a very species rich and commonly encountered
genus .... *Eukiefferiella* Thienemann (in part)[6]

58(56′).   Median pair of mental teeth extending distinctly anterior to 1st lateral teeth 59

58′.   Median pair of mental teeth shorter than 1st lateral teeth or subequal in length to
1st laterals (fig. 25.210) .... *Chaetocladius* Kieffer

59(58).   Antenna with 3rd segment much shorter than 4th segment, and blade extending
distinctly beyond apex of 5th segment; length of antennal segment 1 about equal
to the combined lengths of segments 2 through 5 (fig. 25.172); mentum as in
figure 25.211; mature larvae 5–7 mm .... *Psilometriocnemus* Saether[7]

59.   If 3rd antennal segment much shorter than 4th segment then blade not extending
beyond apex of 5th antennal segment, or 1st antennal segment distinctly larger
than the combined lengths of segments 2 through 5; mentum variable, but
occasionally with reduced or vestigial ventromental plates; length of mature
larvae variable, but many species very small, less than 4 mm .... *Limnophyes* Eaton

Diamesinae

1.   Head capsule with conspicuous dorsal tubercles (fig. 24.243); abdominal segments
with numerous small, closely set, stellate setae .... Boreoheptagyiini— *Boreoheptagyia* Brundin

1′.   Head capsule lacking dorsal tubercles; abdominal segments either lacking setae or
if present then not stellate 2

2(1′).   Labrum with large scales either forming a contiguous row across the anterior
portion (fig. 25.245), or when not contiguous then not separated by more than
the width of the largest scale; mentum as in figure 25.244 .... Protanypini—*Protanypus* Kieffer

2′.   Labrum lacking large scales, or if scales are present then not forming a contiguous
row; mentum not as in figure 25.244 3

3(2′).   Three large, sharp pointed teeth clearly visible in central area of mentum (fig.
25.249); lateral teeth covered by very darkly pigmented ventromental plates (fig.
25.248) .... *Pseudodiamesa* Goetghebuer

3′.   Central area of mentum either truncate and lacking teeth (fig. 25.251), with one
broad tooth, or with numerous small teeth; when numerous teeth are present,
ventromental plates reduced or vestigial, rarely obscuring lateral teeth 4

4(3′).   Mentum lacking teeth entirely; mandible with hook-shaped lateral tooth .... *Potthastia* Kieffer (in part)

4′.   Mentum with at least lateral teeth, though often covered by ventromental plates
(fig. 25.250); mandible without hook-shaped lateral tooth 5

5(4′).   Ventromental plates large and entirely covering at least some lateral teeth of the
mentum 7

5′.   Ventromental plates not conspicuous, or if discernible then not entirely covering
any lateral teeth of the mentum 6

---

6. This genus has recently been revised by Dr. O. A. Saether and Dr. G. A. Halvorsen (1981). Larvae that key to this couplet may belong in one of the following genera: *Eukiefferiella, Tvetenia, Dratnalia,* or *Tokunagaia.* Associated pupae and/or adults may be necessary to accurately place many larvae.
7. The larval stages and natural history of *Psilometriocnemus* specimens from western Pennsylvania are currently being described by the junior author.

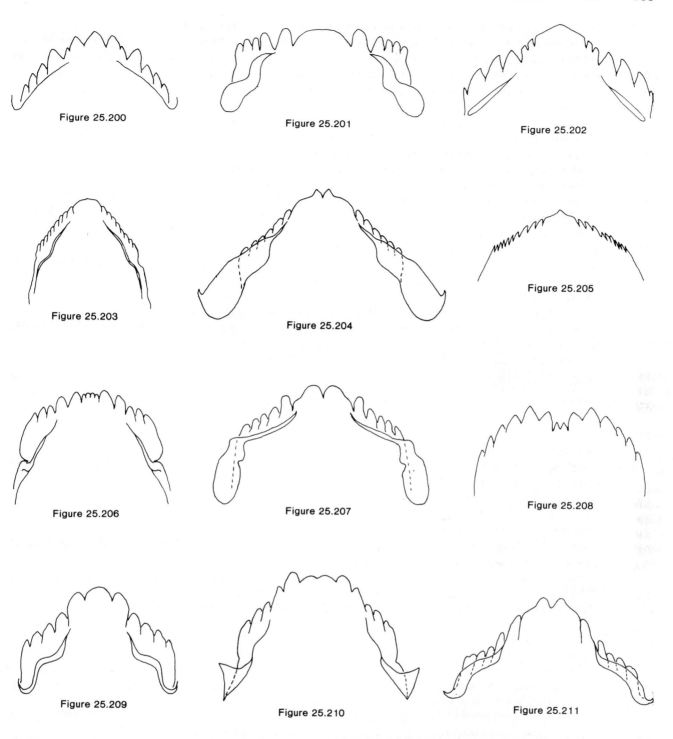

Figure 25.200. Mentum of *Cricotopus (Isocladius) elegans* Johannsen (redrawn with modification from Hirvenoja [1973]).

Figure 25.201. Mentum of *Paraphaenocladius* sp.

Figure 25.202. Mentum of *Cricotopus (Cricotopus) trifascai* Edwards.

Figure 25.203. Mentum of *Orthocladius (Euorthocladius)* sp.

Figure 25.204. Mentum of *Nanocladius* sp.

Figure 25.205. Mentum of *Lapposmittia* sp. (redrawn with modification from Thienemann [1944]).

Figure 25.206. Mentum of *Metriocnemus knabi* Coquillett.

Figure 25.207. Mentum of *Parametriocnemus* sp.

Figure 25.208. Mentum of *Metriocnemus* cf. *fuscipes* (Meigen).

Figure 25.209. Mentum of *Paracricotopus* sp.

Figure 25.210. Mentum of *Chaetocladius* sp.

Figure 25.211. Mentum of *Psilometriocnemus* sp.

6(5′).   Abdomen with numerous elongate and erect setae that are subequal to or longer in length than their corresponding abdominal segment; procercus with 1–2 basal spurs .... *Pseudokiefferiella* Zavrel

6′.   Abdominal segments either lacking elongate and erect setae, or if occasional setae are present, then distinctly shorter in length than corresponding abdominal segment .... *Diamesa* Meigen (in part)

7(5).   Median portion of mentum truncate; ventromental plates pigmented golden brown to dark brown and entirely covering all lateral teeth (figs. 25.250–25.251) .... *Pagastia* Oliver

7′.   Median portion of mentum with one broad and occasionally somewhat rounded tooth; ventromental plates not darkly pigmented, rarely entirely covering all the lateral teeth of the mentum 8

8(7′).   Second antennal segment with blade arising near middle of segment (fig. 25.246) .... *Potthastia* Kieffer (in part)

8′.   Second antennal segment with blade arising from near base (fig. 25.247), or blade absent or not conspicuous 9

9(8′).   Premandible with 1–3 teeth .... *Sympotthastia* Pagast

9′.   Premandible with more than 3 teeth .... *Diamesa* Meigen (in part)

Podonominae

1.   Median tooth of mentum subdivided into 3–4 dentes and deeply recessed from remaining lateral teeth (fig. 25.257) .... Boreochlini (in part)—*Trichotanypus* Kieffer

1′.   Median tooth of mentum not subdivided, or if appearing somewhat divided then not deeply recessed 2

2(1′).   Procercus unicolorous .... Podonomini—*Parochlus* Edwards

2′.   Procercus hyaline anteriorly and darkly pigmented posteriorly (fig. 25.256) .... Boreochlini (in part) 3

3(2′).   Eighth abdominal segment with paired spiracular rings; supraanal seta, if present, not longer than posterior prolegs (fig. 25.259) 4

3′.   Eighth abdominal segment lacking paired spiracular rings; supraanal seta conspicuous and longer than posterior prolegs (fig. 25.258) .... *Paraboreochlus* Thienemann

4(3).   Mentum with less than 9 pairs of lateral teeth (usually 7 pairs present); procercus with 5 apical setae; larvae more commonly encountered in small springs, seeps, and 1st or 2nd order streams .... *Boreochlus* Edwards

4′.   Mentum with 10 or more pairs of lateral teeth (fig. 25.255); procercus with more than 10 apical setae (usually 11, 13, or 15 setae present); larvae more commonly encountered in acid bogs or littoral regions of lakes .... *Lasiodiamesa* Kieffer

Prodiamesinae

1.   Mentum with an odd number of teeth, median tooth dome-shaped (fig. 25.240); mandible with 2 setal bunches on outer margin and inner margin greatly expanded (fig. 25.242) .... *Odontomesa* Pagast

1′.   Mentum with an even number of teeth (figs. 25.238–25.239); mandible not as in figure 25.242 2

2(1′).   Mentum strongly arched as in figure 25.239; ventromental plates with either fine setae that do not extend beyond the anterior edge of the plate or lacking easily discernible setae; mandible as in figure 25.241 .... *Monodiamesa* Kieffer

2′.   Mentum with median teeth recessed (fig. 25.238); ventromental plates with well-developed cardinal beard; mandible not as in figure 25.241 .... *Prodiamesa* Kieffer

KEY TO SUBFAMILIES OF NORTH AMERICAN FRESHWATER CHIRONOMIDAE* PUPAE

1.   Thoracic horn with a conspicuous plastron plate (e.g., figs. 25.267, 25.269, 25.278, 25.283, 25.285, 25.297, 25.307) 2

1′.   Thoracic horn, when present, without a conspicuous plastron plate (e.g., figs. 25.315, 25.326, 25.353, 25.555, 25.561, 25.632) 3

*Genera of Diamesinae, Prodiamesinae, and Orthocladiinae are keyed together since the subfamilies are not easily separated without reference to difficult characters (see couplets 6 and 7).

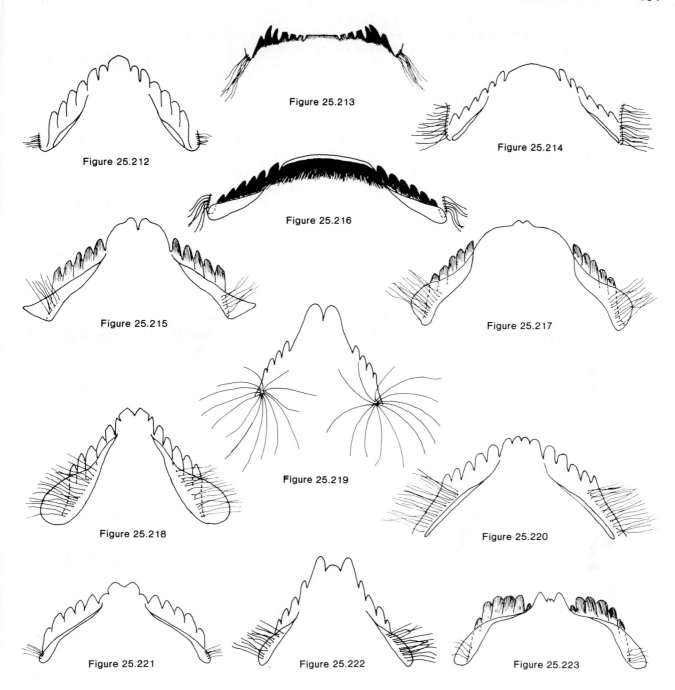

Figure 25.213

Figure 25.212

Figure 25.214

Figure 25.216

Figure 25.215

Figure 25.217

Figure 25.219

Figure 25.218

Figure 25.220

Figure 25.221

Figure 25.222

Figure 25.223

Figure 25.212. Mentum of *Halocladius (Halocladius)* sp. (redrawn with modification from Hirvenoja [1973]).

Figure 25.213. Mentum of *Halocladius (Psammocladius)* sp. (redrawn with modification from Hirvenoja [1973]).

Figure 25.214. Mentum of *Acricotopus* sp.

Figure 25.215. Mentum of *Psectrocladius* sp.

Figure 25.216. Mentum of *Paracladius* sp.

Figure 25.217. Mentum of *Psectrocladius* sp.

Figure 25.218. Mentum of *Rheocricotopus* sp.

Figure 25.219. Mentum of *Synorthocladius* sp.

Figure 25.220. Mentum of *Diplocladius* sp.

Figure 25.221. Mentum of *Zalutschia* sp.

Figure 25.222. Mentum of *Parorthocladius* sp. (redrawn with modification from Thienemann [1944]).

Figure 25.223. Mentum of *Zalutschia zalutschicola* Lipina (redrawn with modification from Saether [1976]).

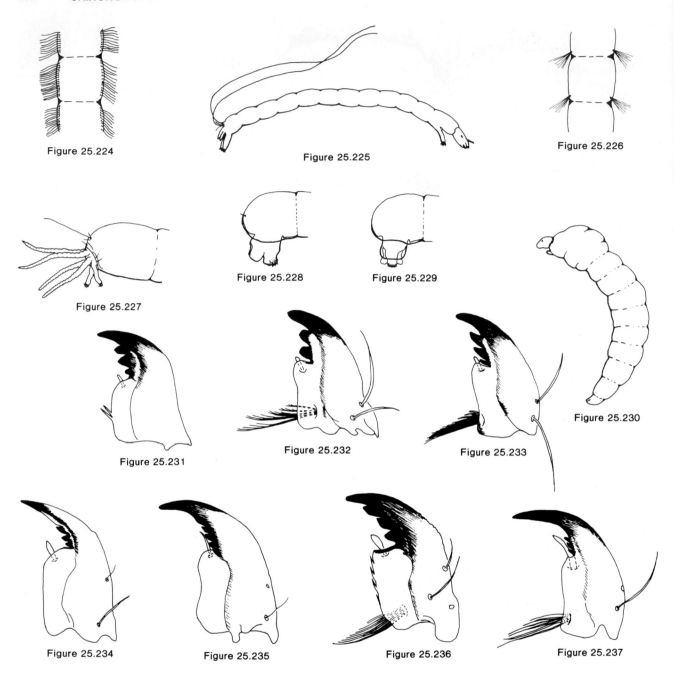

Figure 25.224. Abdominal segments of *Xylotopus* sp. showing lateral hair fringe setae.

Figure 25.225. Larva of *Krenosmittia* sp.

Figure 25.226. Abdominal segments of *Cricotopus* sp. showing setal groups arising from single points.

Figure 25.227. Posterior abdominal segment, anal tubules and posterior prolegs of *Georthocladius* sp.

Figure 25.228. Posterior abdominal segment and posterior prolegs of *Gymnometriocnemus* sp. (redrawn from Thienemann and Kruger [1941]).

Figure 25.229. Posterior abdominal segment and posterior prolegs of *Bryophaenocladius* sp.

Figure 25.230. Larva of *Symbiocladius* sp.

Figure 25.231. Mandible of *Eukiefferiella* sp.

Figure 25.232. Mandible of *Parachaetocladius* sp.

Figure 25.233. Mandible of *Pseudorthocladius* sp.

Figure 25.234. Mandible of *Psectrocladius* sp.

Figure 25.235. Mandible of *Nanocladius* sp.

Figure 25.236. Mandible of *Cricotopus (Cricotopus)* cf. *bicinctus* (Meigen).

Figure 25.237. Mandible of *Krenosmittia* sp.

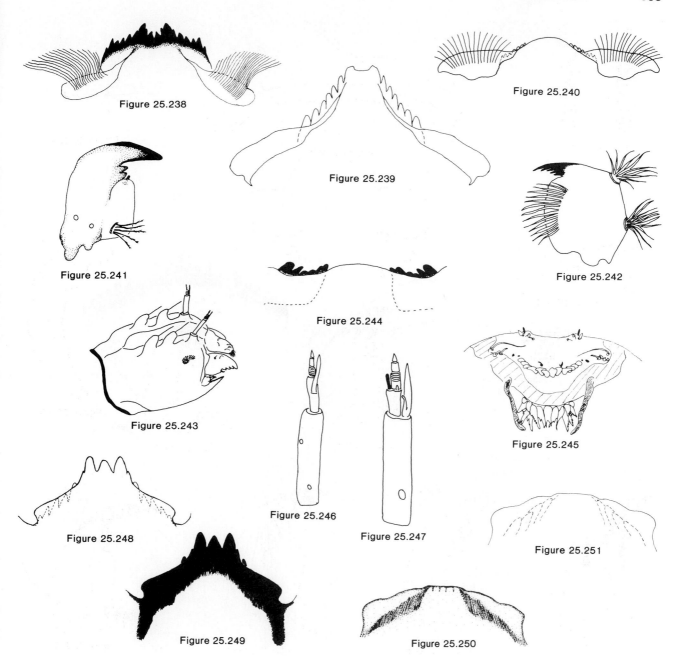

Figure 25.238
Figure 25.240
Figure 25.239
Figure 25.241
Figure 25.242
Figure 25.244
Figure 25.243
Figure 25.245
Figure 25.248
Figure 25.246
Figure 25.247
Figure 25.251
Figure 25.249
Figure 25.250

Figure 25.245. Anterior view of labral region of *Protanypus ramosus* Saether (redrawn with modification from Saether [1975]).

Figure 25.246. Antenna of *Potthastia gaedii* (Meigen).

Figure 25.247. Antenna of *Diamesa* sp.

Figure 25.248. Schematic drawing of mentum of *Pseudodiamesa* sp. showing lateral teeth covered by ventromental plates.

Figure 25.249. Mentum of *Pseudodiamesa* sp.

Figure 25.250. Mentum of *Pagastia* sp.

Figure 25.251. Schematic drawing of mentum of *Pagastia* sp. showing lateral teeth covered by ventromental plates.

Figure 25.238. Mentum of *Prodiamesa olivacea* (Meigen).

Figure 25.239. Mentum of *Monodiamesa* sp.

Figure 25.240. Mentum of *Odontomesa* sp.

Figure 25.241. Mandible of *Monodiamesa* sp.

Figure 25.242. Mandible of *Odontomesa* sp.

Figure 25.243. Head capsule of *Boreoheptagyia* sp.

Figure 25.244. Mentum of *Protanypus* sp.

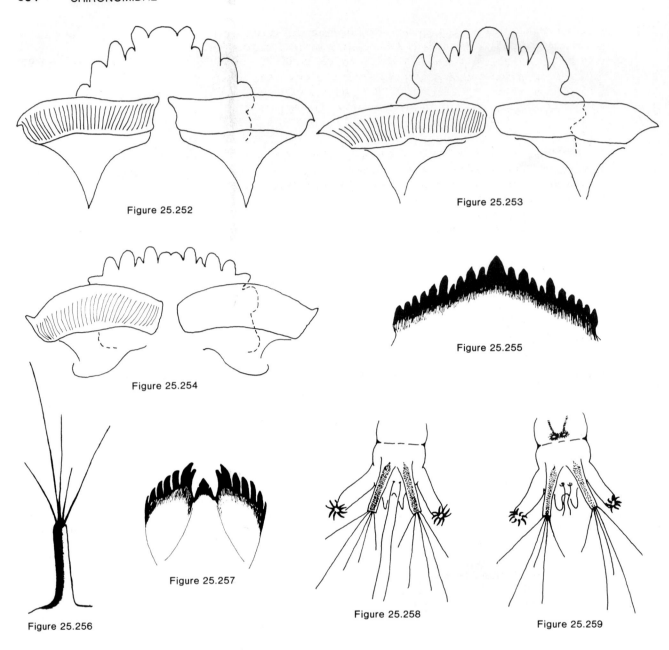

Figure 25.252

Figure 25.253

Figure 25.254

Figure 25.255

Figure 25.256

Figure 25.257

Figure 25.258

Figure 25.259

Figure 25.252. Mentum of *Pseudochironomus* cf. *articaudatus* Saether.

Figure 25.253. Mentum of *Pseudochironomus* sp.

Figure 25.254. Mentum of *Pseudochironomus fulviventris* (Johannsen).

Figure 25.255. Mentum of *Lasiodiamesa* sp.

Figure 25.256. Procercus of *Boreochlus* sp.

Figure 25.257. Mentum of *Trichotanypus* sp.

Figure 25.258. Posterior abdominal segments of *Paraboreochlus* sp.

Figure 25.259. Posterior abdominal segments of *Boreochlus* sp.

2(1).   Anal lobes with 2 large macrosetae which insert approximately in middle third of lobe margin (figs. 25.276, 25.279, 25.288) or anal lobe with a fringe of small setae or spines along the margin (figs. 25.296, 25.300, 25.302, 25.312) .... *Tanypodinae* (in part) (p. 597)

2'.   Anal lobe macrosetae often more distal, smaller or spinelike and frequently more than 2, (figs. 25.266, 25.268, 25.270, 25.272); anal lobe never with a fringe .... *Podonominae* (p. 595)

3(1').   Thoracic horn large with a surface meshwork (figs. 25.315, 25.320–25.321, 25.324) or more slender without a meshwork (figs. 25.325–25.329, 25.331); when slender and without meshwork, anal lobes with 2 large lateral macrosetae (figs. 25.288, 25.319) .... *Tanypodinae* (in part) (p. 597)

3'.   Thoracic horn not large with a meshwork, frequently absent; anal lobe often with less than or more than 2 macrosetae, when 2 are present they are not lateral **4**

4(3').   Thoracic horn, when present, unbranched, usually distinct and at least somewhat erect (figs. 25.434, 25.474, 25.504, 25.525, 25.543, 25.554) **5**

4'.   Thoracic horn with 2 or more (often many more) branches (figs. 25.586, 25.615, 25.618, 25.632), often collapsed in slide mounts .... *Chironominae* (in part) (p. 621)

5(4).   Caudolateral angles of segment 8 almost always with a spine or a group of spines (figs. 25.542, 25.549, 25.560, 25.565, 25.571, 25.574); wing sheaths almost always with a subterminal "Nase" (fig. 25.575); anal lobe fringe usually present (fig. 25.574) but may be reduced (figs. 25.549, 25.562) or absent, never with terminal macrosetae .... *Chironominae* (in part) (p. 621)

5'.   Caudolateral angles of segment 8 rarely with a spine; when present, anal lobes with macrosetae (fig. 25.490); wing sheaths without "Nase"................................... ....6 *(Orthocladiinae, Prodiamesinae, Diamesinae)* (p. 602)

6(5').   Posterior pair of leg sheaths curved under the wing sheaths, the other 2 pair distally straight (fig. 25.263) .... *Diamesinae* (p. 602)

6'.   All leg sheaths curved under wing sheaths (fig. 25.264) or, rarely, all leg sheaths distally straight (fig. 25.265) **7**

7(6').   Large species (often 8 mm or more in length) with large thoracic horns (figs. 25.383–25.384); anal lobes with more than 3 terminal (subterminal) macrosetae (figs. 25.386–25.387) or with a few weak setae on lobe surface similar to figure 25.381; when more than 3 macrosetae, terga are without spine groups as in figures 25.360–25.361; when a few weak setae on the lobe surface, posterior margins of terga without a row(s) of strong, blunt spines as in figure 25.381 .... *Prodiamesinae* (p. 602)

7'.   Often smaller species (frequently less than 5 mm in length); thoracic horns usually smaller (e.g., figs. 25.411, 25.419, 25.421, 25.427, 25.448, 25.481) often absent; anal lobes usually with 3 or fewer marginal macrosetae (e.g., figs. 25.344, 25.379, 25.407, 25.420, 25.467, 25.488); when 4 or more macrosetae, then terga with spine groups (figs. 25.360–25.361); when a few weak setae on anal lobe surface, then terga with strong posterior spines (fig. 25.381) .... *Orthocladiinae* (p. 602)

KEYS TO THE GENERA OF NORTH AMERICAN FRESHWATER CHIRONOMIDAE PUPAE

Podonominae

1.   Segment 8 with 4–5 long, filamentous or lamellar lateral setae (figs. 25.266, 25.268, 25.270) **2**

1'.   Segment 8 with 2–3 short, spinelike lateral setae (figs. 25.272, 25.275) **4**

2(1).   Anal lobes with very long slender posterior extensions (fig. 25.266); thoracic horn as in figure 25.267 .... *Lasiodiamesa*

2'.   Anal lobes with, at most, short posterior extensions (figs. 25.268, 25.270); thoracic horn as in figure 25.269 or 25.271 .... **3**

3(2').   Anal lobes with a short posterior extension (fig. 25.268); segment 8 with small caudolateral spines (fig. 25.268); thoracic horn as in figure 25.269 .... *Parochlus*

3'.   Anal lobes without posterior extension (fig. 25.270); segment 8 with large lobelike caudolateral processes (fig. 25.270); thoracic horn as in figure 25.271 .... *Trichotanypus*

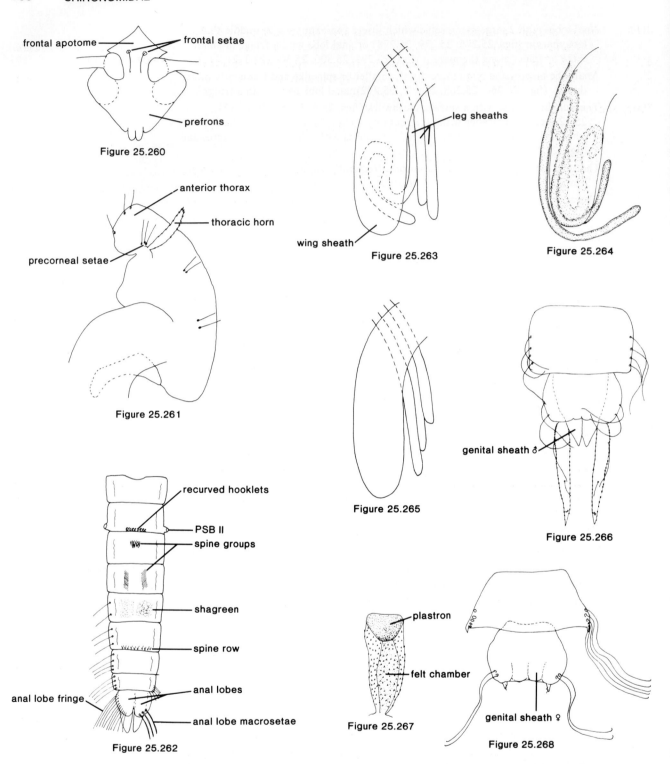

Figure 25.260

Figure 25.261

Figure 25.263

Figure 25.264

Figure 25.265

Figure 25.266

Figure 25.262

Figure 25.267

Figure 25.268

Figure 25.260. Frontal apotome and ocular field of chironomid pupa.

Figure 25.261. Thorax (left side) of chironomid pupa.

Figure 25.262. Generalized abdomen of chironomid pupa (dorsal view).

Figure 25.263. Leg sheath pattern of Diamesinae.

Figure 25.264. Leg sheath pattern of Chironomidae (except Diamesinae and a few Orthocladiinae).

Figure 25.265. Leg sheath pattern of *Lopescladius*.

Figure 25.266. Anal lobes and segment 8 of *Lasiodiamesa* sp.

Figure 25.267. Thoracic horn of *Lasiodiamesa* sp.

Figure 25.268. Anal lobes and segment 8 of *Parochlus* sp.

4(1').   Lateral margins of segment 8 with two spinelike setae (fig. 25.272); thoracic horn
        as in figure 25.273 or 25.274 .... *Boreochlus*

4'.   Lateral margins of segment 8 with three spinelike setae (fig. 25.275); thoracic
        horn as in figure 25.273 .... *Paraboreochlus*

Tanypodinae

1.   Thoracic horn with a distinct plastron plate (e.g., figs. 25.278, 25.280, 25.283,
        25.311) 2

1'.   Thoracic horn without a distinct plastron plate, either large with a reticulate
        meshwork (e.g., figs. 25.315, 25.320–25.321, 25.324) or more slender (e.g., figs.
        25.326–25.329) 26

2(1).   Anal lobes without a fringe of smaller setae or spines (figs. 25.276, 25.279, 25.286,
        25.293) 3

2'.   Anal lobes with a fringe of setae (e.g., figs. 25.296, 25.298, 25.312) in addition to
        the 2 macrosetae 17

3(2).   Anal lobes with terminal processes (fig. 25.276); abdominal segments 4–7 with a
        dense fringe of setae (fig. 25.276) .... *Djalmabatista*

3'.   Anal lobes without terminal processes, although the lobes may be long and pointed
        (e.g., figs. 25.279, 25.286, 25.293); abdominal segments with, at most, a few
        lateral setae 4

4(3'). Thoracic horn with numerous convolutions of the felt chamber (fig. 25.278) .... *Larsia*

4'.   Thoracic horn with few, if any, convolutions of the felt chamber (e.g., figs. 25.281,
        25.283, 25.290) 5

5(4'). Posterior margin of sternum 8 with a row of spines (fig. 25.279) .... *Nilotanypus*

5'.   Posterior margin of sternum 8 without a row of spines 6

6(5'). Thoracic comb present and usually well developed (figs. 25.282, 25.284) 7

6'.   Thoracic comb absent or weakly developed (fig. 25.289) 13

7(6).   Thoracic horn with felt chamber narrow with a loop at base of plastron plate (fig.
        25.281) .... *Xenopelopia*

7'.   Thoracic horn with felt chamber broader or not looped (figs. 25.282, 25.285,
        25.287, 25.290, 25.295) 8

8(7'). Plastron plate broadly joined to the felt chamber (figs. 25.282, 25.289–25.290) 9

8'.   Plastron plate narrowly joined to the felt chamber (figs. 25.283, 25.285, 25.287) 10

9(8).   Thoracic comb weakly to moderately developed (fig. 25.289) .... *Conchapelopia* (in part)

9'.   Thoracic comb well developed (fig. 25.282) .... *Trissopelopia*

10(8'). Thoracic horn with felt chamber nearly filling the internal space (figs.
        25.317–25.318) .... *Labrundinia* (in part)

10'.   Thoracic horn with felt chamber smaller (figs. 25.283, 25.285, 25.287) 11

11(10'). Plastron plate large and connected to the felt chamber by a narrow short stalk (fig.
        25.283); exuviae usually pale yellow .... *Pentaneura*

11'.   Plastron plate usually smaller with connecting stalk often longer (figs. 25.285,
        25.287); exuviae often with distinct color patterns 12

12(11'). Genital sheaths of male longer than anal lobes (fig. 25.286) .... *Paramerina*

12'.   Genital sheaths of male not longer than anal lobes .... *Zavrelimyia*

13(6'). Thoracic horn distinctly asymmetrical, i.e., the plastron plate is set at an angle to
        the long axis of the horn (figs. 25.289–25.290) .... *Conchapelopia* (in part)

13'.   Thoracic horn essentially symmetrical (figs. 25.292, 25.295), i.e., the plastron plate
        is set in line with the long axis of the horn 14

14(13'). Abdominal segment 7 with one lateral seta (fig. 25.291) .... *Natarsia*

14'.   Abdominal segment 7 with 3–4 lateral setae (fig. 25.294) 15

15(14'). Anal lobes directed posteriorly as in figure 25.288; segment 7 with 4 lateral setae
        spread along most of the margin .... *Monopelopia*

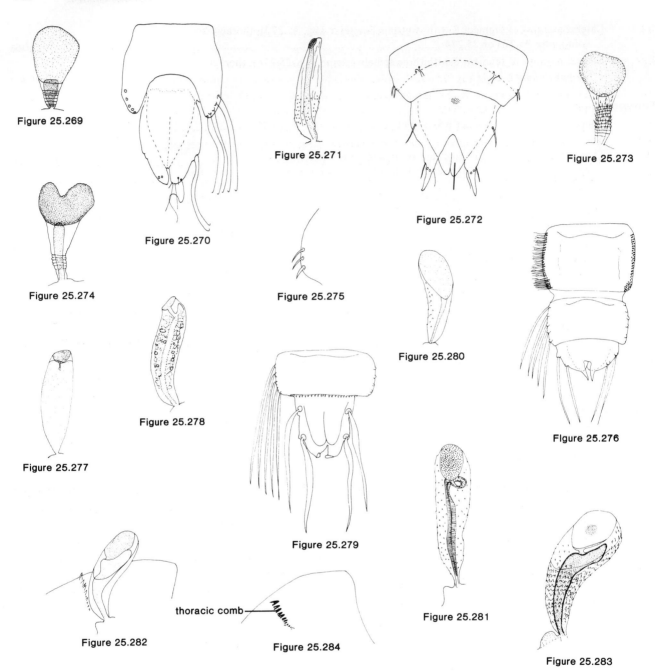

Figure 25.269. Thoracic horn of *Parochlus* sp.

Figure 25.270. Anal lobes and segment 8 of *Trichotanypus* sp.

Figure 25.271. Thoracic horn of *Trichotanypus* sp.

Figure 25.272. Anal lobes and segment 8 of *Boreochlus* sp.

Figure 25.273. Thoracic horn of *Boreochlus* sp. 1.

Figure 25.274. Thoracic horn of *Boreochlus* sp. 2.

Figure 25.275. Lateral spines on segment 8 of *Paraboreochlus* sp.

Figure 25.276. Anal lobes and segments 7 and 8 of *Djalmabatista* sp.

Figure 25.277. Thoracic horn of *Djalmabatista* sp.

Figure 25.278. Thoracic horn of *Larsia* sp.

Figure 25.279. Anal lobes and segment 8 (ventral view) of *Nilotanypus* sp.

Figure 25.280. Thoracic horn of *Nilotanypus* sp.

Figure 25.281. Thoracic horn of *Xenopelopia* sp. (after Fittkau 1962).

Figure 25.282. Thoracic horn of *Trissopelopia* sp.

Figure 25.283. Thoracic horn of *Pentaneura* sp.

Figure 25.284. Thoracic comb on anterior thorax of *Pentaneura* sp.

15'.   Anal lobes directed laterally (fig. 25.293); segment 7 with 3–4 lateral setae in a group (fig. 25.294) 16

16(15').   Anal lobes relatively short, i.e., the lateral macrosetae insert approximately midway along margin (fig. 25.293) .... ***Krenopelopia***

16'.   Anal lobes much longer, i.e., the lateral macrosetae insert at a point about one-third along margin from base .... ***Hudsonimyia***

17(2').   Segment 7 with 5 lateral setae (fig. 25.296) 18

17'.   Segment 7 with less than or more than 5 lateral setae (figs. 25.302, 25.304) 20

18(17).   Felt chamber of thoracic horn with distinct undulations (fig. 25.297) .... ***Alotanypus***

18'.   Felt chamber without undulations (figs. 25.299, 25.301) 19

19(18').   Thoracic horns with numerous dark pegs in the surface structure (fig. 25.299) .... ***Apsectrotanypus***

19'.   Thoracic horns without dark pegs (fig. 25.301) .... ***Macropelopia*** (in part)

20(17').   Segment 7 with 4 lateral setae (fig. 25.302); anal lobes with spines along margins (fig. 25.302) 21

20'.   Segment 7 with more than 5 lateral setae (fig. 25.308); anal lobes with fringe of small setae (figs. 25.304, 25.308, 25.310, 25.312) 22

21(20).   Anal lobes with small medial projections (fig. 25.302); exuviae often more than 5 mm in length .... ***Procladius (Procladius)*** (in part)

21'.   Anal lobes without small medial projections; exuviae often less than 5 mm in length .... ***Procladius (Psilotanypus)***

22(20').   Tergum 7 with at least 2 enlarged dorsal setae (lamellar or setiform), often on distinct tubercles, never branched (e.g., fig. 25.304) 23

22'.   Tergum 7 with all dorsal setae small (fig. 25.312) or, when enlarged, branched 25

23(22).   Segment 6 with a large anterior lateral seta and a smaller posterior seta (fig. 25.306); when large seta is absent, the thoracic horn is broad and flat with a plastron plate in a narrow band around the distal edge (fig. 25.307) .... ***Brundiniella***

23'.   Segment 6 without a large anterior lateral seta and thoracic horn not as in figure 25.307 24

24(23').   Inner margins of anal lobes with setae or setalike spines (fig. 25.308) .... ***Psectrotanypus***

24'.   Inner margins of anal lobes with, at most, short spines .... ***Macropelopia*** (in part)

25(22').   Anal lobes with medial setiferous projections (fig. 25.312); usually 6 lateral setae on segment 7 .... ***Clinotanypus***

25'.   Anal lobes rounded uniformly; usually 8 lateral setae on segment 7 .... ***Coelotanypus***

26(1').   Thoracic horn large, usually dark and with a conspicuous reticulate meshwork on the surface (figs. 25.315, 25.320–25.321, 25.324) 27

26'.   Thoracic horn smaller (sometimes slender) lighter and without meshwork (figs. 25.325–25.329, 25.331) 32

27(26).   Segments 7 and 8 each with no more than 5 lateral setae 28

27'.   Segments 7 or 8, or both, with more than 5 lateral setae 31

28(27).   Posterior margin of segment 8 produced laterally as lobelike projections (fig. 25.314) .... ***Guttipelopia***

28'.   Posterior margin of segment 8 not produced (figs. 25.316, 25.319) 29

29(28').   Anal lobes truncated or rounded with spines along the margin as in figure 25.302 .... ***Procladius (Procladius)*** (in part)

29'.   Anal lobes triangular (figs. 25.316, 25.319) 30

30(29').   Meshwork of thoracic horn fine (figs. 25.317–25.318); anal lobes long and narrow (fig. 25.316) .... ***Labrundinia***

30'.   Meshwork of thoracic horn coarse (fig. 25.320–25.321); anal lobes relatively short and broad (fig. 25.319) .... ***Ablabesmyia***

31(27').   Anal lobes short and rounded (figs. 25.322–25.323); dorsal setae of terga small (figs. 25.322–25.323); thoracic horn (fig. 25.324) .... ***Tanypus***

31'.   Anal lobes long and pointed as in figure 25.304; some dorsal setae large as in figure 25.304; thoracic horn (fig. 25.307) .... ***Brundiniella*** (in part)

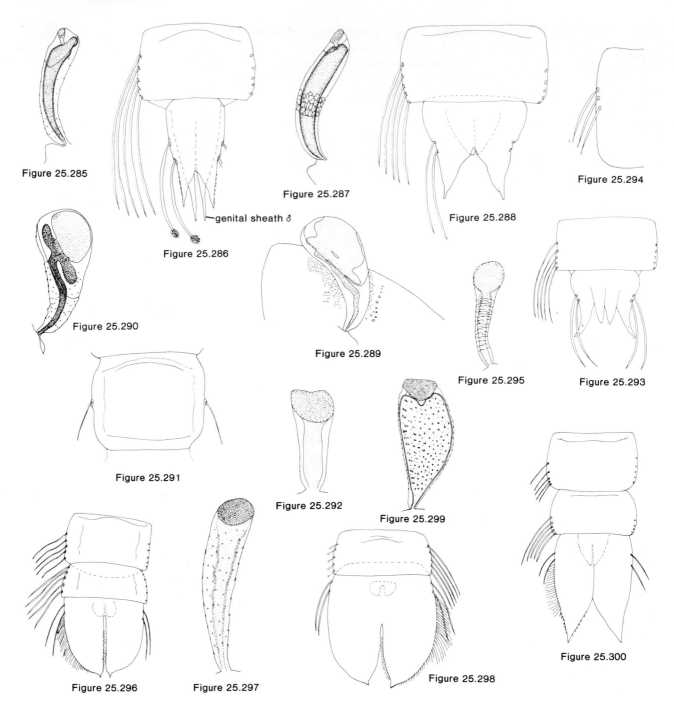

Figure 25.285

Figure 25.287

Figure 25.294

Figure 25.288

genital sheath ♂

Figure 25.286

Figure 25.290

Figure 25.289

Figure 25.295

Figure 25.293

Figure 25.291

Figure 25.292

Figure 25.299

Figure 25.300

Figure 25.296

Figure 25.297

Figure 25.298

Figure 25.285. Thoracic horn of *Paramerina* sp.

Figure 25.286. Anal lobes and segment 8 of *Paramerina* sp.

Figure 25.287. Thoracic horn of *Zavrelimyia* sp.

Figure 25.288. Anal lobes and segment 8 of *Conchapelopia* sp. 1.

Figure 25.289. Thoracic horn of *Conchapelopia* sp. 1.

Figure 25.290. Thoracic horn of *Conchapelopia* sp. 2.

Figure 25.291. Segment 7 of *Natarsia* sp.

Figure 25.292. Thoracic horn of *Natarsia* sp.

Figure 25.293. Anal lobes and segment 8 of *Krenopelopia* sp.

Figure 25.294. Lateral margin of segment 7 of *Krenopelopia* sp.

Figure 25.295. Thoracic horn of *Krenopelopia* sp.

Figure 25.296. Anal lobes and segments 7 and 8 of *Alotanypus* sp.

Figure 25.297. Thoracic horn of *Alotanypus* sp.

Figure 25.298. Anal lobes and segment 8 of *Apsectrotanypus* sp.

Figure 25.299. Thoracic horn of *Apsectrotanypus* sp.

Figure 25.300. Anal lobes and segments 7 and 8 of *Macropelopia* sp. 1.

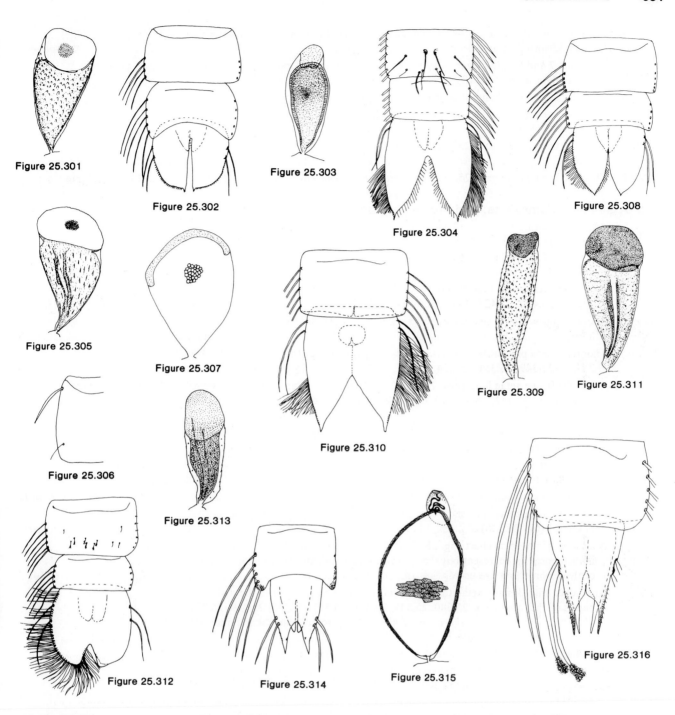

Figure 25.301. Thoracic horn of *Macropelopia* sp. 1.

Figure 25.302. Anal lobes and segments 7 and 8 of *Procladius (Procladius)* sp.

Figure 25.303. Thoracic horn of *Procladius (Procladius)* sp.

Figure 25.304. Anal lobes and segments 7 and 8 of *Brundiniella* sp. 1.

Figure 25.305. Thoracic horn of *Brundiniella* sp. 1.

Figure 25.306, Lateral margin of segment 6 of *Brundiniella* sp. 1.

Figure 25.307. Thoracic horn of *Brundiniella* sp. 2.

Figure 25.308. Anal lobes and segments 7 and 8 of *Psectrotanypus* sp.

Figure 25.309. Thoracic horn of *Psectrotanypus* sp.

Figure 25.310. Anal lobes and segment 8 of *Macropelopia* sp. 2.

Figure 25.311. Thoracic horn of *Macropelopia* sp. 2.

Figure 25.312. Anal lobes and segment 7 and 8 of *Clinotanypus* sp.

Figure 25.313. Thoracic horn of *Clinotanypus* sp.

Figure 25.314. Anal lobes and segment 8 of *Guttipelopia* sp.

Figure 25.315. Thoracic horn of *Guttipelopia* sp.

Figure 25.316. Anal lobes and segment 8 of *Labrundinia* sp.

32(26′). Segment 7 with, at most, 2 small lateral setae; segment 8 with 3–5 small setae; thoracic horn pale and slender (figs. 25.325–25.327) .... *Rheopelopia*

32′. Segments 7 and 8 with larger, lamellar setae (fig. 25.288); thoracic horn not so pale and/or more stout (figs. 25.328–25.331) 33

33(32′). Thoracic horn curved and of nearly uniform width along its length (fig. 25.328) .... *Arctopelopia*

33′. Thoracic horn not as above, particularly not of uniform width along its length (figs. 25.329–25.331) 34

34(33′). Thoracic horn as in figure 25.329–25.330; segments 2–6 with 3–6 lateral lamellar setae .... *Thienemannimyia*

34′. Thoracic horn as in figure 25.331; segments 2–6 without lateral lamellar setae .... *Conchapelopia* (in part)

Orthocladiinae, Diamesinae, and Prodiamesinae

1. Anal lobes with a fringe that consists of a dense row of long lamellar setae (e.g., figs. 25.332, 25.334–25.335, 25.348, 25.363, 25.365, 25.369, 25.371, 25.374, 25.377, 25.379, 25.381, 25.386) or short setae (figs. 25.336–25.337, 25.340, 25.343–25.345) 2

1′. Anal lobe without a fringe of setae (e.g., figs. 25.390, 25.393, 25.400, 25.404, 25.416, 25.420, 25.423, 25.426, 25.444, 25.491) 43

2(1). Thoracic horns absent (examine thorax carefully for small, hyaline, or broken horns) 3

2′. Thoracic horns present but sometimes small and/or hyaline (e.g., figs. 25.339, 25.346, 25.349, 25.351–25.354, 25.357, 25.367–25.368, 25.383–25.384) 6

3(2). Anal lobe fringe setae long (figs. 25.332, 25.334–25.335); lateral abdominal setae simple (figs. 25.332, 25.334–25.335); small species, abdomen usually 2.5 mm or less in length 4

3′. Anal lobe fringe setae short (fig. 25.337) or very short (fig. 25.336); some lateral setae of abdomen may be branched; larger species, abdomen greater than 2.5 mm in length 5

4(3). One or more pearl rows at tip of wing sheaths (fig. 25.333) .... *Corynoneura*

4′. No pearl rows on wing sheaths .... *Thienemanniella*

5(3′). Anal lobe fringe setae very short (fig. 25.336); some lateral setae of abdomen branched (fig. 25.336) .... *Sympotthastia*

5′. Anal lobe fringe setae short (fig. 25.337); all lateral setae simple; Note: thoracic horns appear to be absent but short, brown stalks indicate the attachment points of these horns that are usually lost (figs. 25.338–25.339) .... *Genus 1*

6(2′). Anal lobes with 3 macrosetae that are evenly spaced and confined to the distal halves of the lobes (figs. 25.340, 25.344, 25.348, 25.363, 25.365, 25.369, 25.371, 25.374); Note: In *Brillia* there are usually 0–1 macrosetae but "scars" indicate the lost setae (figs. 25.365, 25.369) 7

6′. Anal lobes with less than or more than 3 macrosetae (figs. 25.365, 25.377, 25.379, 25.385–25.386) or when 3 macrosetae are present they are unevenly or widely spaced (figs. 25.378); in a few forms the macrosetae are on the lobe surface (fig. 25.381) 34

7(6). Fringe setae of anal lobe short, i.e., no more than one-half the length of the lobe (figs. 25.340, 25.343–25.345); usually no more than 30 setae; Note: this must be examined carefully since long transparent setae may appear to be short and there is a tendency for the setae to break close to the lobes 8

7′. Most fringe setae of anal lobe more than one-half the length of the lobe (figs. 25.348, 25.363, 26.365, 25.369, 25.371, 25.374); often more than 30 fringe setae 14

8(7). Fringe setae of anal lobe very short, thin, weakly sclerotized, and generally concentrated in the distal half (fig. 25.340) .... *Orthocladius (Orthocladius)* (in part)

8′. Fringe setae of anal lobes longer, i.e., closer to one-half length of lobe (figs. 25.343–25.345) 9

9(8). Wing sheaths with pearl rows (fig. 25.341); PSB II elongated and pointed (fig. 25.342); anal lobes with a few fringe setae (fig. 25.343) .... *Parametriocnemus*

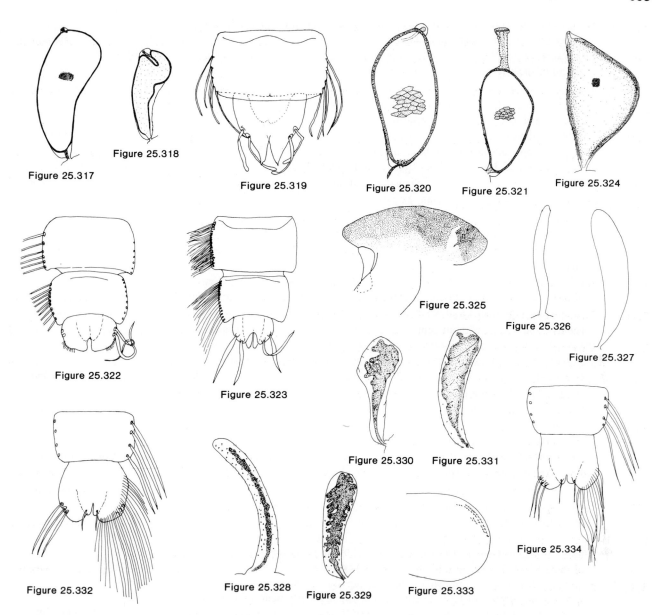

Figure 25.317. Thoracic horn of *Labrundinia* sp. 1.

Figure 25.318. Thoracic horn of *Labrundinia* sp. 2.

Figure 25.319. Anal lobes and segment 8 of *Ablabesmyia* sp. 1.

Figure 25.320. Thoracic horn of *Ablabesmyia* sp. 1.

Figure 25.321. Thoracic horn of *Ablabesymia* sp. 2.

Figure 25.322. Anal lobes and segments 7 and 8 of *Tanypus* sp. 1.

Figure 25.323. Anal lobes and segments 7 and 8 of *Tanypus* sp. 2.

Figure 25.324. Thoracic horn of *Tanypus* sp. 2.

Figure 25.325. Thorax (one-half) of *Rheopelopia* sp. 1.

Figure 25.326. Thoracic horn of *Rheopelopia* sp. 1.

Figure 25.327. Thoracic horn of *Rheopelopia* sp. 2.

Figure 25.328. Thoracic horn of *Arctopelopia* sp.

Figure 25.329. Thoracic horn of *Thienemannimyia* sp. 1.

Figure 25.330. Thoracic horn of *Thienemannimyia* sp. 2.

Figure 25.331. Thoracic horn of *Conchapelopia* sp. 3.

Figure 25.332. Anal lobes and segment 8 of *Corynoneura* sp. 1.

Figure 25.333. ''Pearl rows'' on wing sheath of *Corynoneura* sp. 1.

Figure 25.334. Anal lobes and segment 8 of *Corynoneura* sp. 2.

9'.   Wing sheaths without pearl rows; PSB if present, not elongated; anal lobes often
           with numerous setae 10

10(9'). Fringe setae of anal lobes concentrated in basal half; distal ends of lobes with
           groups of short terminal spines (fig. 25.344) in addition to the 3 macrosetae .... *Oliveridia*

10'.   Fringe setae of anal lobes variable (figs. 25.345, 25.348); anal lobes without
           terminal spines, but sometimes with terminal rugulosity 11

11(10'). Fringe setae of anal lobes mostly concentrated in basal half (fig. 25.345); thoracic
           horn well developed and serrate (fig. 25.346) .... *Hydrobaenus* (in part)

11'.   Fringe setae not concentrated in basal half (e.g., fig. 25.348); thoracic horn with
           (figs. 25.346, 25.349) or without (fig. 25.339) serrations 12

12(11'). Thoracic horn weakly sclerotized, elongated, and tapering (fig. 25.339) .... *Genus 1*

12'.   Thoracic horn serrate (figs. 25.346, 25.349) 13

13(12'). Posterior margins of terga 3–5(6) with raised areas of coarse spines (fig. 25.347);
           embedded spines often present at posterior angles of segments 6–7, 6–8, or 7–8
           (fig. 25.348) .... *Zalutschia*

13'.   Posterior margins of terga 3–5(6) without raised areas; embedded spines absent .... *Hydrobaenus* (in part)

14(7'). Tergum 5 (and usually some others) with sharply demarcated groups of spines in
           or near the center (figs. 25.350, 25.356, 25.359–25.361), rarely are there central
           spine groups on other terga when not on 5 15

14'.   Tergum 5, and others, without central groups of spines, at most, the terga may
           have shagreen of slightly larger size in the center (fig. 25.370) 20

15(14). Tergum 5, and others, with 1–2 transverse bands of spines that extend almost
           completely across the segment (fig. 25.350) .... *Paracricotopus*

15'.   Tergum 5 with 1–2 groups of central spines, but never extending across more than
           one-half the segment (figs. 25.356, 25.359, 25.361) 16

16(15'). Two precorneal setae large, 1 small, all insert on a distinct process (fig. 25.351);
           PSB II often very large (fig. 25.355); spines on tergum 5 variable (fig. 25.356);
           small species—abdomen usually less than 2.5 mm .... *Nanocladius* (in part)

16'.   All precorneal setae small (fig. 25.357); PSB II absent or weak (fig. 25.358); small
           to large species 17

17(16'). Central spine groups on terga 4–6(7) consist of weak to moderately developed
           spines that are in one group per tergum (figs. 25.356, 25.359); frontal warts
           absent 18

17'.   Central spine groups on terga 3(4)–6(7) consist of strong spines in 1–2 groups
           (figs. 25.360–25.361); frontal warts often present (fig. 25.362) 19

18(17). Posterior margin of tergum 2 with a dense group of small hooklets (fig. 25.358);
           central spine groups of terga nearly circular (fig. 25.359); moderately heavy
           shagreen often present on terga (fig. 25.359); thoracic horn as in figure 25.357 .... *Rheocricotopus* (in part)

18'.   Posterior margin of tergum 2 with a less dense group of larger hooklets (fig.
           25.355); central spine groups on terga often in short transverse rows (fig.
           25.356); shagreen on terga very weak (fig. 25.356); thoracic horn variable in
           shape (figs. 25.351–25.352, 25.354) .... *Nanocladius* (in part)

19(17'). Posterior dorsal setae of most terga almost spinelike (fig. 25.360) .... *Psectrocladius (Monopsectrocladius)*

19'.   Posterior dorsal setae not spinelike (fig. 25.361) .... *Psectrocladius (Psectrocladius)* (in part)

20(14'). Thoracic horn long and slightly bifurcate at tip (fig. 25.367) or short, dark, and
           slender (fig. 25.368); anal lobe almost always with no more than 1 macroseta,
           but "scars" indicate the presence of 3 (figs. 25.365, 25.369); posterior margin of
           sternum of male often with a strong row of spinules (fig. 25.365); sternum 8 of
           female without posterior spines (fig. 25.366) .... *Brillia*

20'.   Not with above combination of characters 21

21(20'). Male with row(s) of sharp spinules on posterior margin of sternum 8 (fig. 25.372);
           female with 2 triangular "lobes" (fig. 25.372); PSB II moderately developed
           (fig. 25.373); 8–40 setae in anal lobe fringe (fig. 25.371); wing sheaths with or
           without pearl rows; weak hooklets on posterior margin of tergum 2 (fig. 25.373) .... *Heterotrissocladius*

21'.   Not with above combination of characters 22

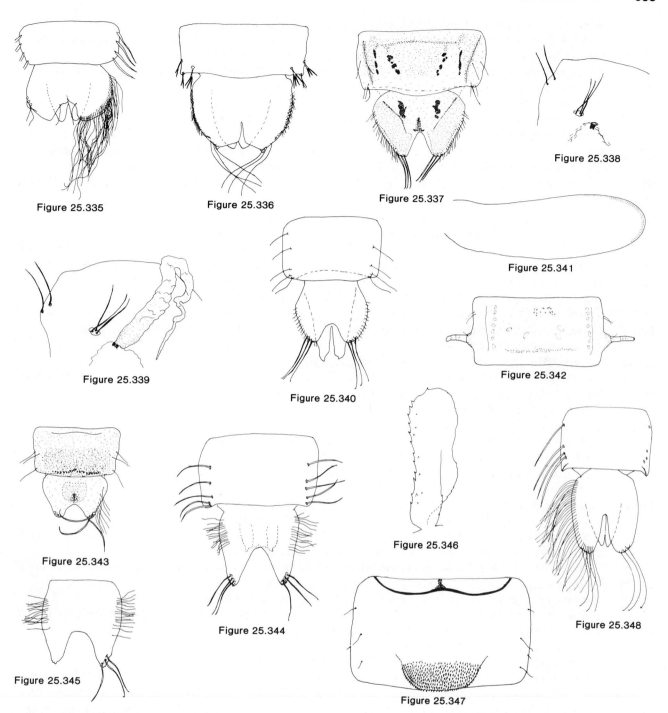

Figure 25.335

Figure 25.336

Figure 25.337

Figure 25.338

Figure 25.341

Figure 25.339

Figure 25.340

Figure 25.342

Figure 25.343

Figure 25.344

Figure 25.346

Figure 25.348

Figure 25.345

Figure 25.347

Figure 25.335. Anal lobes and segment 8 of *Thienemaniella* sp.

Figure 25.336. Anal lobes and segment 8 of *Sympotthastia* sp.

Figure 25.337. Anal lobes and segment 8 of Genus 1.

Figure 25.338. Anterior thorax with stalk of broken thoracic horn of Genus 1.

Figure 25.339. Anterior thorax with complete thoracic horn of Genus 1.

Figure 25.340. Anal lobes and segment 8 of *Orthocladius (Orthocladius)* sp. 1.

Figure 25.341. Wing sheath with "pearl rows" of *Parametriocnemus* sp.

Figure 25.342. Segment 2 of *Parametriocnemus* sp.

Figure 25.343. Anal lobes and segment 8 of *Parametriocnemus* sp.

Figure 25.344. Anal lobes and segment 8 of *Oliveridia* sp. (after Saether 1976).

Figure 25.345. Anal lobes of *Hydrobaenus* sp.

Figure 25.346. Thoracic horn of *Hydrobaenus* sp.

Figure 25.347. Segment 2 of *Zalutschia* sp.

Figure 25.348. Anal lobes and segment 8 of *Zalutschia* sp.

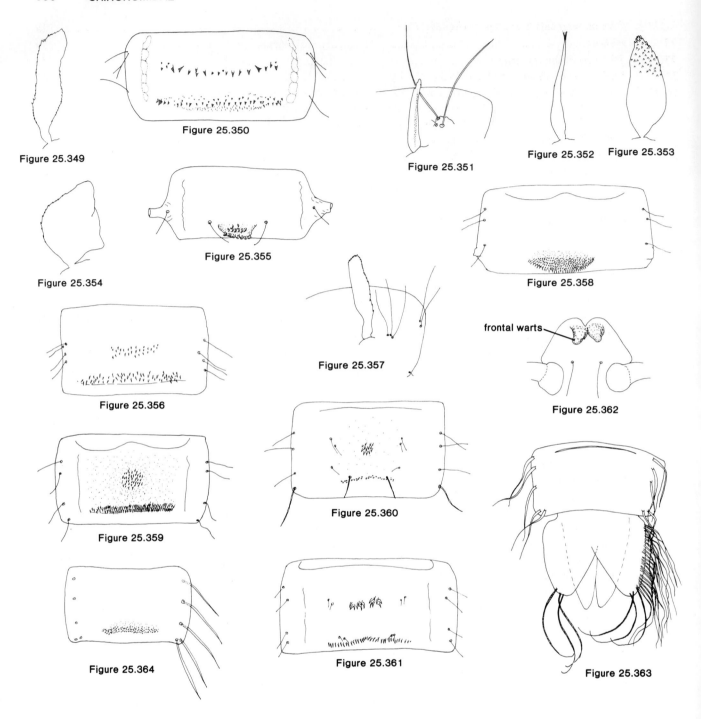

frontal warts

Figure 25.349. Thoracic horn of *Zalutschia* sp.

Figure 25.350. Tergum 5 of *Paracricotopus* sp.

Figure 25.351. Anterior thorax and thoracic horn of *Nanocladius* sp. 1.

Figure 25.352. Thoracic horn of *Nanocladius* sp. 2.

Figure 25.353. Thoracic horn of *Nanocladius* sp. 3.

Figure 25.354. Thoracic horn of *Nanocladius* sp. 4.

Figure 25.355. Segment 2 of *Nanocladius* sp. 1.

Figure 25.356. Segment 5 of *Nanocladius* sp. 1.

Figure 25.357. Anterior thorax and thoracic horn of *Rheocricotopus* sp.

Figure 25.358. Segment 2 of *Rheocricotopus* sp.

Figure 25.359. Segment 5 of *Rheocricotopus* sp.

Figure 25.360. Segment 5 of *Psectrocladius (Monopsectrocladius)* sp.

Figure 25.361. Segment 5 of *Psectrocladius (Psectrocladius)* sp. 1.

Figure 25.362. Frontal apotome with frontal setae and frontal warts of *Psectrocladius (Psectrocladius)* sp. 1.

Figure 25.363. Anal lobes and segment 8 of *Psectrocladius (Psectrocladius)* sp. 1.

Figure 25.364. Segment 8 (ventral view) of male *Brillia* sp. 1.

22(21′). PSB on segments 2 or 2 and 3 (fig. 25.375) 23

22′. PSB absent 30

23(22). PSB present on segment 2 only 24

23′. PSB present on segments 2 and 3 (fig. 25.375) 29

24(23). Anal lobes with a "fringe" consisting of a few very broad lamellar setae grading to spinelike setae; anal lobe macrosetae subterminal and inconspicuous (fig. 25.374); wing sheaths with pearl rows .... *Genus 2*

24′. Not with above combination of characters 25

25(24′). Posterior margin of tergum 2 with a distinct group of hooklets near the midline (fig. 25.355) 26

25′. Posterior margin of tergum 2 with, at most, a row(s) of spines across the margin (fig. 25.342) 28

26(25). Group of hooklets on tergum 2 weakly developed; exuviae nearly transparent .... *Genus 3*

26′. Group of hooklets on tergum 2 more developed (figs. 25.355, 25.358); exuviae almost always with pigmentation 27

27(26′). Hooklets on tergum 2 as in fig. 25.358; a trace of a spine group often present in the center of tergum 5 .... *Rheocricotopus* (in part)

27′. Hooklets on tergum 2 as in fig. 25.355; usually no trace of a central spine group on tergum 5 .... *Nanocladius* (in part)

28(25′). PSB II well developed, extended to a point (fig. 25.342); wing sheaths with pearl rows (fig. 25.341) .... *Parametriocnemus* (in part)

28′. PSB II developed, but not pointed (fig. 25.376); wing sheaths without pearl rows .... *Genus 4*

29(23′). Anal lobe macrosetae all terminal or slightly subterminal .... *Rheocricotopus* (in part)

29′. Two anal lobe macrosetae distal and close together, the 3rd much more basal, all more or less inconspicuous (fig. 25.378) .... *Mesocricotopus*

30(22′). Posterior margins of terga 3–6 without distinct rows of spines or swollen areas with spines, but may have shagreen; frontal apotome with warts as in fig. 25.362; caudolateral margins of terga 6–8 without embedded spines .... *Heterotanytarsus*

30′. Posterior margins of terga 3–6(7) with rows of spines or swollen areas with spines (fig. 25.347, 25.356, 25.359); frontal apotome with or without warts; embedded spines sometimes present on terga (fig. 25.348) 31

31(30′). Posterior margins of terga 3–6 with swollen areas that have groups of triangular spines (fig. 25.347); thoracic horn weakly serrate (fig. 25.349); terga often with embedded spines (fig. 25.348); frontal apotome with or without warts .... *Zalutschia*

31′. Posterior margins of terga 3–6(7) with distinct rows of spines (fig. 25.356, 25.359); thoracic horn with or without serrations; frontal lobe with or without warts; no embedded spines on caudolateral angles of terga 6–8 32

32(31′). Anal lobe fringe with a few, very broad setae (fig. 25.374); wing sheaths with pearl rows .... *Genus 2*

32′. Anal lobe fringe setae more numerous or not so broad; wing sheaths without pearl rows 33

33(32′). Posterior margin of tergum 2 with a dense group of hooklets (fig. 25.358); thoracic horn as in figure 25.357 .... *Rheocricotopus* (in part)

33′. Posterior margin of tergum 2 with fewer, but larger, hooklets (fig. 25.355); thoracic horn as in figures 25.351–25.353 .... *Nanocladius* (in part)

34(6′). Anal lobes with no macrosetae (figs. 25.369, 25.379) 35

34′. Anal lobes with at least one macroseta (figs. 25.365, 25.377–25.378, 25.381, 25.386) 36

35(34). Abdominal segments with a lateral fringe of setae (fig. 25.380) .... *Xylotopus*

35′. Abdominal segments without a fringe .... *Brillia* (in part)

36(34′). Anal lobes with one macroseta and 2 insertion scars (fig. 25.365) .... *Brillia* (in part)

36′. Anal lobes usually with 2 or more macrosetae (figs. 25.377–25.378, 25.385–25.387); when there is only one it is on the surface of the lobe (fig. 25.381) 37

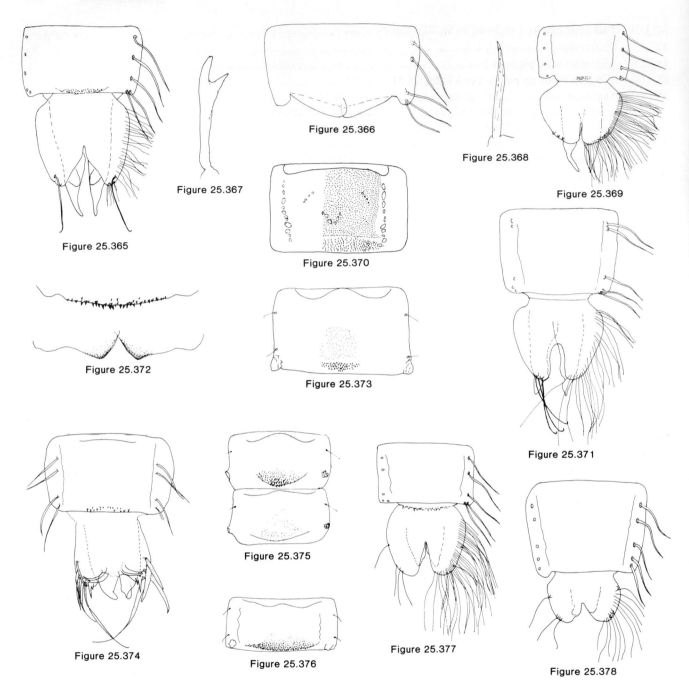

Figure 25.365. Anal lobes and segment 8 of *Brillia* sp. 1.

Figure 25.366. Segment 8 (ventral view) of female *Brillia* sp. 1.

Figure 25.367. Thoracic horn of *Brillia* sp. 1.

Figure 25.368. Thoracic horn of *Brillia* sp. 2.

Figure 25.369. Anal lobes and segment 8 of *Brillia* sp. 2.

Figure 25.370. Shagreen (partially indicated) on segment 6 of *Brillia* sp. 2.

Figure 25.371. Anal lobes and segment 8 of *Heterotrissocladius* sp.

Figure 25.372. Posterior margin of sternum 8 of male (upper) and female (lower) of *Heterotrissocladius* sp.

Figure 25.373. Segment 2 of *Heterotrissocladius* sp.

Figure 25.374. Anal lobes and segment 8 of Genus 2.

Figure 25.375. Segments 2 and 3 of *Mesocricotopus* sp.

Figure 25.376. Segment 2 of Genus 4.

Figure 25.377. Anal lobes and segment 8 of Genus 4.

Figure 25.378. Anal lobes and segment 8 of *Mesocricotopus* sp.

37(36').   Two marginal anal macrosetae located distally of the 3rd (fig. 25.378) .... *Mesocricotopus* (in part)

37'.   Anal lobe macrosetae not as above 38

38(37').   Anal lobe with 3 macrosetae located on the surface (fig. 25.381); long blunt spines
on the posterior margins of most terga (fig. 25.381) .... *Psectrocladius (Allopsectrocladius)*

38'.   Not as above 39

39(38').   Anal lobe with 1–3 macrosetae on the surface, when 3, 2 are in the distal half
similar to figure 25.381; PSB II well developed and with spinules (fig. 25.382) .... *Monodiamesa*

39'.   Anal lobe with more than 3 macrosetae (figs. 25.385–25.387); PSB II, when
present, without spinules 40

40(39').   Terga 4 and 5, at least, with central patches of spines (fig. 25.361) .... *Psectrocladius (Psectrocladius)* (in part)

40'.   Only shagreen present on terga 41

41(40').   Segment 8 extended as lobes parallel to the anal lobes (fig. 25.386) .... *Odontomesa*

41'.   Segment 8 without caudolateral lobes 42

42(41').   Anal lobes with 4 macrosetae, all of which are terminal (fig. 25.387) .... *Prodiamesa*

42'.   Anal lobes with 3 terminal and 1 more basal macroseta (fig. 25.377) .... *Genus 4*

43(1').   Anal lobes without macrosetae (figs. 25.390, 25.393, 25.395–25.396,
25.401–25.402), although short spines other than reduced macrosetae may be
present (figs. 25.390, 25.395, 25.401, 25.407); Note: taxa with very small
"macrosetae," which may be overlooked, may be keyed either way from this
couplet 44

43'.   Anal lobes with macrosetae that may be hairlike (figs. 25.400, 25.404, 25.415),
spinelike (figs. 25.435, 25.438, 25.443), or long and slender (figs. 25.420,
25.428, 25.467) 57

44(43).   Distinct, nearly circular groups of spines on the central surface of at least some
terga (figs. 25.391, 25.393–25.394) 45

44'.   Terga without such central groups of spines 46

45(44).   Spine groups on terga 4–6 (fig. 25.391); thoracic horn weakly serrate (fig. 25.389);
some thoracic setae branched (fig. 25.389) .... *Abiskomyia*

45'.   Spine groups on terga as in figures 25.393–25.394; thoracic horn long and slender
without serrations (fig. 25.392); all thoracic setae simple .... *Orthocladius (Euorthocladius)* (in part)

46(44').   Anal lobes elongate, narrow and tapering to a point (fig. 25.396) 47

46'.   Anal lobes, if pointed, not shaped as above (figs. 25.395, 25.401, 25.407) 48

47(46).   Posterior margins of terga 2–4 with a pair of broad scalelike setae (fig. 25.397);
thoracic horn absent .... *Rheosmittia (Rheosmittia)*

47'.   Posterior margins of terga with simple setae; thoracic horn a short, stout sac (fig.
25.398) .... *Genus 5*

48(46').   Posterior margins of terga 4–6, at least, with a single row of distinct spines that
may be blunt or sharp (figs. 25.399–25.401) 49

48'.   Posterior margins of terga 4–6 without a posterior row of spines or with more than
1 row (figs. 25.402, 25.404–25.405, 25.407–25.408, 25.410) 50

49(48).   Spines on posterior margins of terga forming a continuous row (fig. 25.399); the
anterior third of most terga with fine needlelike spinules (fig. 25.399); anal lobes
with or without macrosetae (fig. 25.400) .... *Metriocnemus* (in part)

49'.   Spines on posterior margins in a less continuous row (fig. 25.401); terga covered
with short broad spines (fig. 25.401); anal lobe without macrosetae (fig. 25.401) .... *Georthocladius*

50(48').   Small (2 mm), nearly transparent exuviae; terga with coarse shagreen (fig.
25.402); conjunctiva 2/3–5/6, (7/8) with groups of weak spinules in middle
third (fig. 25.402) .... *Pseudosmittia*

50'.   Not with above combination of characters 51

51(50').   Anterior abdominal segments wide, diminishing to a narrow 8th (fig. 25.403);
especially in female 52

51'.   Reduction in width of posterior segments much less 53

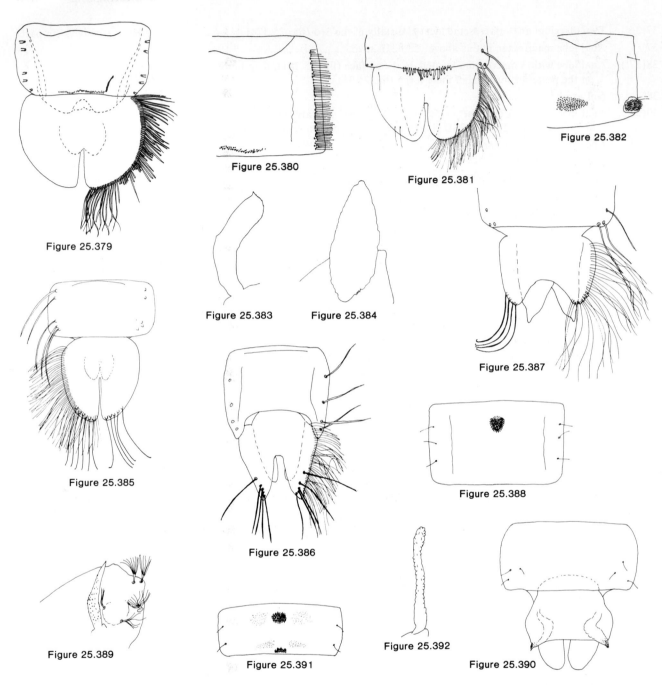

Figure 25.379. Anal lobes and segment 8 of *Xylotopus.*

Figure 25.380. Lateral margin of segment 5 of *Xylotopus.*

Figure 25.381. Anal lobes and posterior margin of segment 8 of *Psectrocladius (Allopsectrocladius)* sp.

Figure 25.382. Right half of segment 2 of *Monodiamesa* sp. 1.

Figure 25.383. Thoracic horn of *Monodiamesa* sp. 1.

Figure 25.384. Thoracic horn of *Monodiamesa* sp. 2.

Figure 25.385. Anal lobes and segment 8 of *Psectrocladius (Psectrocladius)* sp. 2.

Figure 25.386. Anal lobes and segment 8 of *Odontomesa* sp.

Figure 25.387. Anal lobes and segment 8 of *Prodiamesa* sp.

Figure 25.388. Segment 6 of *Abiskomyia* sp.

Figure 25.389. Anterior thorax and thoracic horn of *Abiskomyia* sp.

Figure 25.390. Anal lobes and segment 8 of *Abiskomyia* sp.

Figure 25.391. Segment 5 of *Orthocladius (Euorthocladius)* sp. 1.

Figure 25.392. Thoracic horn of *Orthocladius (Euorthocladius)* sp. 1.

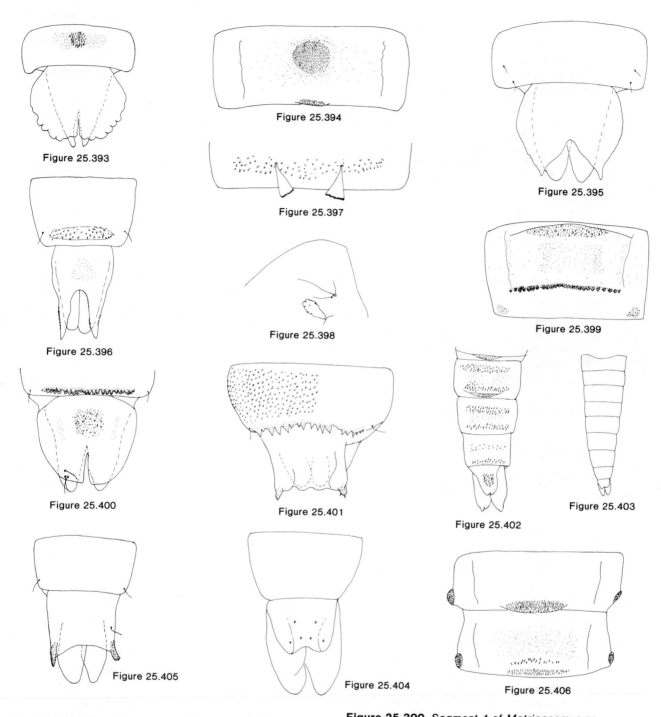

Figure 25.393.

Figure 25.394

Figure 25.397

Figure 25.395

Figure 25.396

Figure 25.398

Figure 25.399

Figure 25.400

Figure 25.401

Figure 25.402

Figure 25.403

Figure 25.405

Figure 25.404

Figure 25.406

Figure 25.393. Anal lobes and segment 8 of *Orthocladius (Euorthocladius)* sp. 1

Figure 25.394. Segment 5 of *Orthocladius (Euorthocladius)* sp. 2.

Figure 25.395. Anal lobes and segment 8 of *Orthocladius (Euorthocladius)* sp. 2.

Figure 25.396. Anal lobes and segment 8 of *Rheosmittia* sp.

Figure 25.397. Posterior margin of segment 3 of *Rheosmittia* sp.

Figure 25.398. Anterior thorax and thoracic horn of Genus

Figure 25.399. Segment 4 of *Metriocnemus* sp.

Figure 25.400. Anal lobes and segment 8 of *Metriocnemus* sp.

Figure 25.401. Anal lobes and segment 8 of *Georthocladius* sp.

Figure 25.402. Anal lobes and segments 5–8 of *Pseudosmittia* sp.

Figure 25.403. Abdomen of *Symbiocladius* sp.

Figure 25.404. Anal lobes and segment 8 of *Symbiocladius* sp.

Figure 25.405. Anal lobes and segment 8 of Genus 6.

Figure 25.406. Segments 2 and 3 of *Orthocladius (Euorthocladius)* sp. 3.

52(51).   Anal lobes terminating in spined processes (fig. 25.405); terga covered with fine
          dense shagreen; a weak anal macroseta sometimes present (fig. 25.405) .... ***Genus 6***

52'.   Anal lobes without terminal processes (fig. 25.404); terga with posterior bands of
          shagreen; tiny "macrosetae" present (fig. 25.404) .... ***Symbiocladius***

53(51'). PSB well developed on segments 2 and 3 (fig. 25.406); anal lobes with many
          terminal spines (fig. 25.407); thoracic horn as in figure 25.392 .... ***Orthocladius (Euorthocladius)*** (in part)

53'.   PSB, at most, developed on segment 2; anal lobes without spines; thoracic horn,
          when present, not as above 54

54(53'). Posterior margins (or conjunctiva) of terga 3–5 with a row of large recurved hooks
          (fig. 25.408) .... ***Eukiefferiella*** (in part)

54'.   No such large recurved hooks on conjunctiva 55

55(54'). Posterior margins of, at least, some terga with groups of several rows of weak to
          strong spines (figs. 25.410, 25.413, 25.415); thoracic horn a small yellow (fig.
          25.411) or brown sac (fig. 25.414) .... ***Orthocladius (Euorthocladius)*** (in part)

55'.   Not with above combination of characters 56

56(55'). Anal lobes as in figure 25.416; terga with fine dense shagreen that is slightly larger
          in posterior bands .... ***Bryophaenocladius*** (in part)

56'.   Anal lobes not shaped as above; terga with coarse shagreen; (Note: difficult to
          separate semiaquatic genera) .... ***Bryophaenocladius*** (in part), ***Gymnometriocnemus, Smittia, Camptocladius***

57(43'). Terga 4 and 5, at least, with central groups or rows of spines in addition to
          shagreen that may be present (figs. 25.417–25.418); thoracic horn usually
          present (figs. 25.419, 25.421–25.422), when absent, spines on tergum 4 as in
          figure 25.417; no hooklets on conjunctiva as in figures 25.451, 25.480, 25.482) 58

57'.   Terga 4 and 5 usually without central groups or rows of spines; if such spines are
          present, then the thoracic horn is either absent or present; when thoracic horn is
          present it is not as in figure 25.419, 25.421–25.422; if thoracic horn is absent,
          the tergal armature is not as in figure 25.417; hooklets may be present on some
          conjunctiva (figs. 25.451, 25.480, 25.482) 61

58(57).   Spines on terga 2–7 more or less in 4 groups (fig. 25.417); posterior margins of
          terga with very long spines (fig. 25.417); thoracic horn absent .... ***Cardiocladius***

58'.   Spines on terga in 2 groups (fig. 25.418); posterior margins of terga without long
          spines; thoracic horn present (figs. 25.419, 25.421–25.422) 59

59(58'). Thoracic horn an elongated, stalked sac without spinules (fig. 25.419) .... ***Orthocladius (Eudactylocladius)***

59'.   Thoracic horn not as above (figs. 25.421–25.422) 60

60(59'). Thoracic horn slender and tapering (fig. 25.421) .... ***Acricotopus***

60'.   Thoracic horn broad (fig. 25.422) .... ***Orthocladius (Pogonocladius)***

61(57'). Anal lobes with 8–12 spinelike macrosetae (often lost) (fig. 25.423); thoracic horn
          large (fig. 25.424) .... ***Protanypus***

61'.   Not with above characters 62

62(61'). Anal lobes long, narrow and pointed with 2–3 small macrosetae inserted
          subterminally (figs. 25.425–25.426) 63

62'.   Anal lobes not as above, when pointed, not long and tapering (figs. 25.429,
          25.444); anal macrosetae larger and usually inserted more terminally (figs.
          25.429, 25.436, 25.447, 25.465, 25.467) 64

63(62).   Thoracic horn a more or less spherical sac similar to figure 25.431 .... ***Genus 5***

63'.   Thoracic horn long and covered with scalelike ridges (fig. 25.427) .... ***Krenosmittia***

64(62'). Anal lobes terminating in sharp points (figs. 25.428–25.430, 25.432–25.433);
          thoracic horn usually a more or less spherical sac (fig. 25.431) but may be more
          elongate (fig. 25.434) 65

64'.   Anal lobes not pointed; thoracic horn very rarely as above, frequently absent 68

65(64).   Lateral margins of segments 2–8 with about 10 setae (fig. 25.428) .... ***Epoicocladius***

65'.   Lateral margins of segments 2–8 with 4–5 setae (figs. 25.429–25.430,
          25.432–25.433) 66

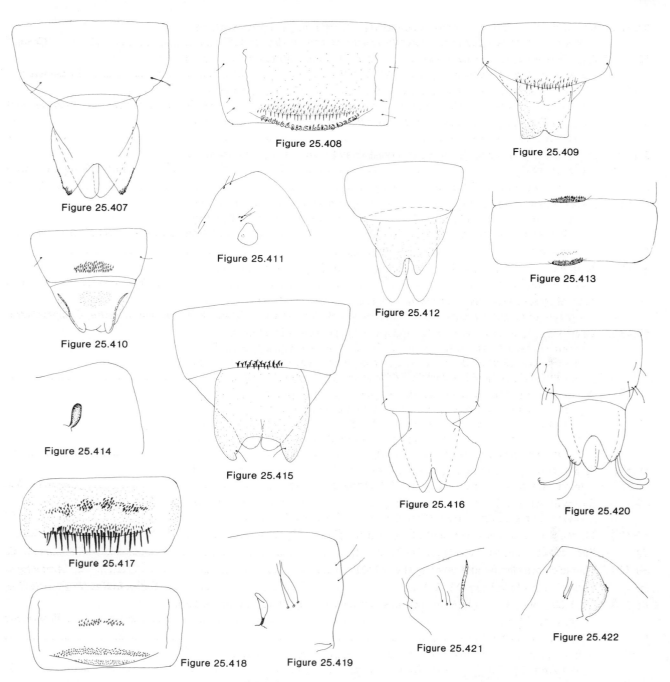

Figure 25.407. Anal lobes and segment 8 of *Orthocladius (Euorthocladius)* sp. 3.

Figure 25.408. Segment 4 of *Eukiefferiella* sp. 1.

Figure 25.409. Anal lobes and segment 8 of *Eukiefferiella* sp. 1.

Figure 25.410. Anal lobes and segment 8 of *Orthocladius (Euorthocladius)* sp. 4.

Figure 25.411. Anterior thorax and thoracic horn of *Orthocladius (Euorthocladius)* sp. 4.

Figure 25.412. Anal lobes and segment 8 of *Orthocladius (Euorthocladius)* sp. 5.

Figure 25.413. Segments 4 and 5 of *Orthocladius (Euorthocladius)* sp. 5.

Figure 25.414. Anterior thorax and thoracic horn of *Orthocladius (Euorthocladius)* sp. 5.

Figure 25.415. Anal lobes and segment 8 of *Orthocladius (Euorthocladius)* sp. 6.

Figure 25.416. Anal lobes and segment 8 of *Bryophaenocladius* sp.

Figure 25.417. Segment of *Cardiocladius* sp.

Figure 25.418. Segment 4 of *Orthocladius (Eudactylocladius)* sp.

Figure 25.419. Anterior thorax and thoracic horn of *Orthocladius (Eudactylocladius)* sp.

Figure 25.420. Anal lobes and segment 8 of *Orthocladius (Eudactylocladius)* sp.

Figure 25.421. Anterior thorax and thoracic horn of *Acricotopus* sp.

Figure 25.422. Anterior thorax and thoracic horn of *Orthocladius (Pogonocladius)* sp.

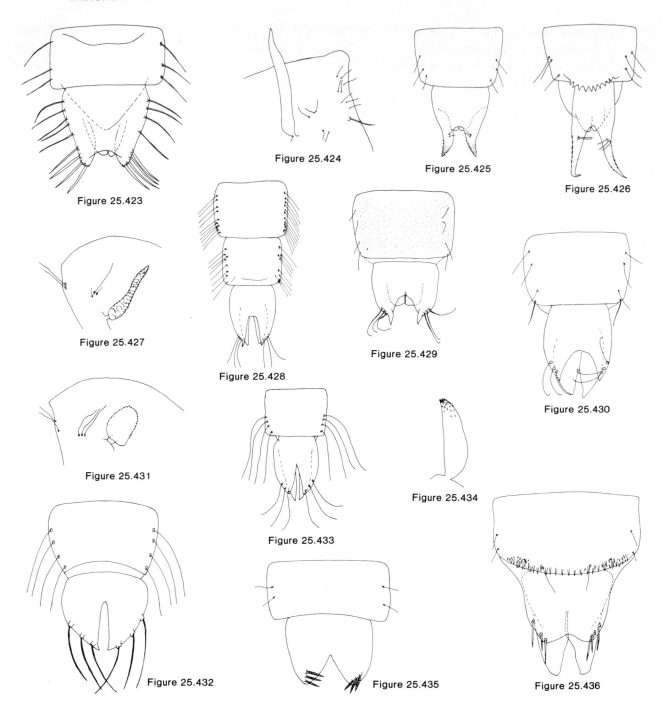

Figure 25.423

Figure 25.424

Figure 25.425

Figure 25.426

Figure 25.427

Figure 25.428

Figure 25.429

Figure 25.430

Figure 25.431

Figure 25.433

Figure 25.434

Figure 25.432

Figure 25.435

Figure 25.436

Figure 25.423. Anal lobes and segment 8 of *Protanypus* sp.

Figure 25.424. Anterior thorax and thoracic horn of *Protanypus* sp.

Figure 25.425. Anal lobes and segment 8 of Genus 5 (see Fig. 398).

Figure 25.426. Anal lobes and segment 8 of *Krenosmittia* sp.

Figure 25.427. Anterior thorax and thoracic horn of *Krenosmittia* sp.

Figure 25.428. Anal lobes and segments 7 and 8 of *Epoicocladius* sp.

Figure 25.429. Anal lobes and segment 8 of *Parakiefferiella* sp. 1.

Figure 25.430. Anal lobes and segment 8 of *Parakiefferiella* sp. 2.

Figure 25.431. Anterior thorax and thoracic horn of *Parakiefferiella* sp. 1.

Figure 25.432. Anal lobes and segment 8 of *Acamptocladius* sp. (after Saether 1971).

Figure 25.433. Anal lobes and segment 8 of *Lapposmittia* sp. (after Thienemann 1944).

Figure 25.434. Anal lobes and segment 8 of *Lapposmittia* sp. (after Thienemann 1944).

Figure 25.435. Anal lobes and segment 8 of *Baeoctenus* sp. (after Saether 1977).

Figure 25.436. Anal lobes and segment 8 of *Eukiefferiella* sp. 2.

66(65'). Thoracic horn short and globular, at most, with a few "hairs" (fig. 25.431) .... *Parakiefferiella*

66'. Thoracic horn more elongate with a few terminal spines (fig. 25.434) 67

67(66'). Anal macrosetae insert on large tubercles (fig. 25.432) .... *Acamptocladius*

67'. Not as above (fig. 25.433) .... *Lapposmittia*

68(64'). One–3 short, spinelike anal macrosetae, none hairlike (figs. 25.435–25.436, 25.438–25.440, 25.443–25.446) 69

68'. One or more long (figs. 25.455, 25.467, 25.479, 25.487, 25.501) or short (figs. 25.447, 25.449, 25.453) and hairlike anal macrosetae 75

69(68). Thoracic horn present 70

69'. Thoracic horn absent 72

70(69). Posterior margin of tergum 8 with a row(s) of spines (figs. 25.436, 25.438–25.440) 71

70'. Posterior margin of tergum 8 without a row of spines (fig. 25.435) .... *Baeoctenus*

71(70). Thoracic horn as in figure 25.437 .... *Eukiefferiella* (in part)

71'. Thoracic horn as in figures 25.441 and 25.442 .... *Chaetocladius*

72(69'). Anal lobes with 3 approximately equal macrosetae (figs. 25.444, 25.446) 73

72'. Anal lobes with 2–3 unequal macrosetae (fig. 25.443) .... *Synorthocladius*

73(72). Anal lobe macrosetae insert on a narrow, pointed, terminal process (fig. 25.444); posterior margin of tergum 8 with large spines (fig. 25.444) .... *Parachaetocladius*

73'. Anal lobe macrosetae not so inserted on a process (figs. 25.445–25.446) 74

74(73'). Anal lobe macrosetae insert terminally (fig. 25.445) .... *Halocladius*

74'. Anal lobe macrosetae insert laterally (fig. 25.446) .... *Boreoheptagyia*

75(68'). Anal lobe macrosetae all short and hairlike (figs. 25.447, 25.449, 25.453, but not fig. 25.450), sometimes inconspicuous and/or less than 3 (fig. 25.415) 76

75'. Anal lobe macrosetae longer and usually strong (figs. 25.455, 25.467, 25.479, 25.487, 25.501), but not spinelike; almost always with 3 macrosetae 82

76(75). Posterior margins of terga 3(4)–8 with distinct rows of spinules (figs. 25.413, 25.415); thoracic horn as in figure 25.414 .... *Orthocladius (Euorthocladius)* (in part)

76'. Posterior margins of terga 3(4)–8 without such spines; thoracic horn, when present, not as above 77

77(76'). Thoracic horn present 78

77'. Thoracic horn absent 79

78(77). Wing sheaths with pearl rows (fig. 25.341); PSB developed, at most, on segment 2; anal lobe with 2 weak macrosetae (fig. 25.447); thoracic horn with a few spinules (fig. 25.448) .... *Paraphaenocladius*

78'. Wing sheaths without pearl rows; PSB developed on segments 2 and 3 (fig. 25.406); anal lobe with 2–3 short macrosetae (fig. 25.407); thoracic horn without spinules (fig. 25.392) .... *Orthocladius (Euorthocladius)* (in part)

79(77'). Anal lobes without spines (figs. 25.400, 25.409, 25.450) 80

79'. Anal lobes with numerous spines (fig. 25.449) .... *Pseudorthocladius*

80(79). Some dorsal abdominal conjunctiva usually with a few large hooklets (fig. 25.408) .... *Eukiefferiella* (in part)

80'. Dorsal conjunctiva without hooklets 81

81(80'). Terga with posterior rows of spines (fig. 25.400) .... *Metriocnemus* (in part)

81'. Terga without posterior rows of spines (fig. 25.453) .... *Cricotopus* (in part)

82(75'). Posterior margins of terga and usually sterna with heavy spines that are mostly in a single row (figs. 25.455, 25.457–25.459, 25.461); thoracic horn a thin filament (fig. 25.454) or a short spur (fig. 25.456, 25.460) or absent 83

82'. Not with above combination of characters 84

83(82). Posterior margins of terga and sterna 4–7(8) with heavy spines (figs. 25.455, 25.457); thoracic horn usually a filament (fig. 25.454) but may be spurlike (fig. 25.456) .... *Diamesa*

83'. Posterior margins of terga only with heavy spines (figs. 25.458–25.459, 25.461); thoracic horn spurlike (fig. 25.460) or absent .... *Pseudokiefferiella*

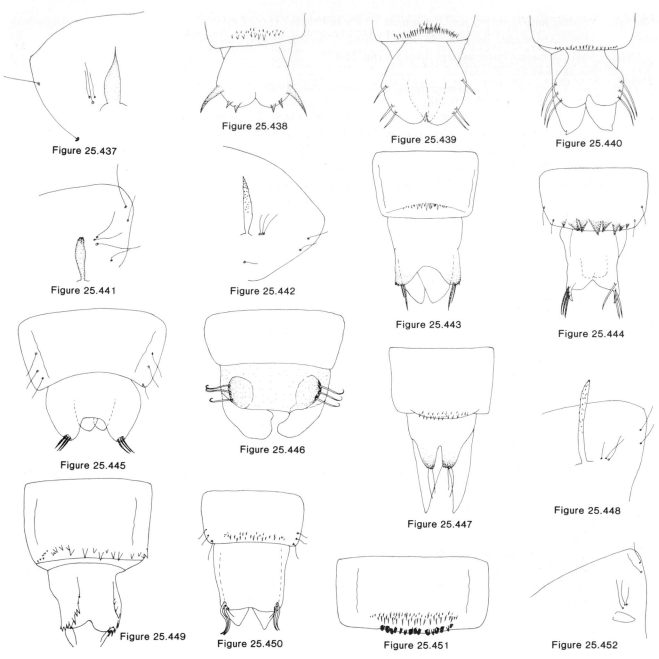

Figure 25.437. Anterior thorax and thoracic horn of *Eukiefferiella* sp. 2.

Figure 25.438. Anal lobes and segment 8 of *Chaetocladius* sp. 1.

Figure 25.439. Anal lobes and segment 8 of *Chaetocladius* sp. 2.

Figure 25.440. Anal lobes and segment 8 of *Chaetocladius* sp. 3.

Figure 25.441. Anterior thorax and thoracic horn of *Chaetocladius* sp. 2.

Figure 25.442. Anterior thorax and thoracic horn of *Chaetocladius* sp. 1.

Figure 25.443. Anal lobes and segment 8 of *Synorthocladius* sp.

Figure 25.444. Anal lobes and segment 8 of *Parachaetocladius* sp.

Figure 25.445. Anal lobes and segment 8 of *Halocladius* sp.

Figure 25.446. Anal lobes and segment 8 of *Boreoheptagyia* sp.

Figure 25.447. Anal lobes and segment 8 of *Paraphaenocladius* sp.

Figure 25.448. Anterior thorax and thoracic horn of *Paraphaenocladius* sp.

Figure 25.449. Anal lobes and segment 8 of *Pseudorthocladius* sp.

Figure 25.450. Anal lobes and segment 8 of *Eukiefferiella* sp. 3.

Figure 25.451. Segment 5 of *Eukiefferiella* sp. 3.

Figure 25.452. Anterior thorax and thoracic horn of *Eukiefferiella* sp. 3.

84(82'). Anal lobes broad, usually with short, terminal (subterminal) pointed projections (figs. 25.462–25.466); no thoracic horn; lateral abdominal setae often branched (figs. 25.462–25.465) 85
84'. Not with above combination of characters 88
85(84). Some lateral abdominal setae branched (figs. 25.462–25.465) 86
85'. No branched abdominal setae (fig. 25.466) 87
86(85). Anal lobe with a 4th seta along inner margin (figs. 25.463–25.464) .... *Pagastia*
86'. Anal lobe without a 4th seta (figs. 25.462, 25.465) .... *Potthastia*
87(85'). Terminal anal lobe projections with scalelike spines (fig. 25.465) .... *Potthastia* (in part)
87'. Terminal projections without scalelike spines (fig. 25.466) .... *Pseudodiamesa*
88(84'). Posterior margins of terga 2–8 with rows of very long, needlelike spines (fig. 25.467); thoracic horn absent .... *Limnophyes*
88'. Posterior margins of terga with or without long spines, when present then thoracic horn is present (fig. 25.474) 89
89(88'). Terga and sterna demarcated by dark lines; anal lobe as in figure 25.468; thoracic horn present (fig. 25.469) .... *Diplocladius*
89'. Not with above combination of characters 90
90(89'). Sterna 2 and 3 with anterior groups of needlelike spines (fig. 25.471); thoracic horn present (fig. 25.472) .... *Heleniella*
90'. Sterna 2 and 3 without needlelike spines, or, if present, thoracic horn absent 91
91(90'). Terga 3–4, 3–5, or 4–5 with rows of large recurved hooklets on conjunctiva (figs. 25.473, 25.478, 25.480, 24.482, 25.484); thoracic horn often "onion" shaped (figs. 25.474, 25.481, 25.483, 25.485–25.486), sometimes absent; wing sheaths without pearl rows 92
91'. Terga 3–5 without such hooklets, or, when present thoracic horn as in figures 25.492 and 25.494 and wing sheaths with pearl rows (fig. 25.341) 94
92(91). Terga 3–5 with recurved hooklets on conjunctiva (figs. 25.473, 25.478, 25.480, 25.482, 25.484); thoracic horn usually present (figs. 25.474, 25.481, 25.483, 25.485–25.486) .... *Eukiefferiella* (in part)
92'. Terga 3–4 or 4–5 with recurved hooklets on conjunctiva; thoracic horn "onion" shaped (fig. 25.489) or absent 93
93(92'). Terga 3–4 with recurved hooklets on conjunctiva; thoracic horn present (fig. 25.489); anterior areas of thorax with dark tubercles (fig. 25.489) .... *Genus 7*
93'. Terga 4–5 with recurved hooklets on conjunctiva; thoracic horn absent; anterior areas of thorax without tubercles (see fig. 25.490) .... *Tokunagaia*
94(91'). Thoracic horn "onion" shaped (figs. 25.492, 25.494); a few recurved hooklets usually present on conjunctiva 3/4–5/6 (figs. 25.493, 25.495); wing sheaths with pearl rows (fig. 25.341) .... *Tvetenia*
94'. Not with above combination of characters 95
95(94'). Anal lobes cylindrical with 3 strong macrosetae inserted at tips (figs. 25.496, 25.498, 25.501); thoracic horn present or absent 96
95'. Anal lobes broader with macrosetae inserted terminally or somewhat subterminally 100
96(95). Thoracic horn present (figs. 25.497, 25.499–25.500) 97
96'. Thoracic horn absent 99
97(96). Thoracic horn a pale, spineless sac (fig. 25.497); abdominal segments without long setae (fig. 25.496) .... "*Paratrichocladius*"
97'. Thoracic horn yellowish, long and slender with some spines (figs. 25.499–25.500); abdomen with or without long setae (fig. 25.498) 98
98(97'). Abdomen with long setae (fig. 25.498); thoracic horn very long (fig. 25.499) .... *Genus 8*
98'. Abdomen without long setae; thoracic horn shorter (fig. 25.500) .... *Psilometriocnemus*
99(96'). Posterior margins of terga 2–8 with single rows of spines which are large on 2–5 and small on 6–8 (fig. 25.502); sterna 5–7 with posterior rows of sharp spines .... *Genus 9*

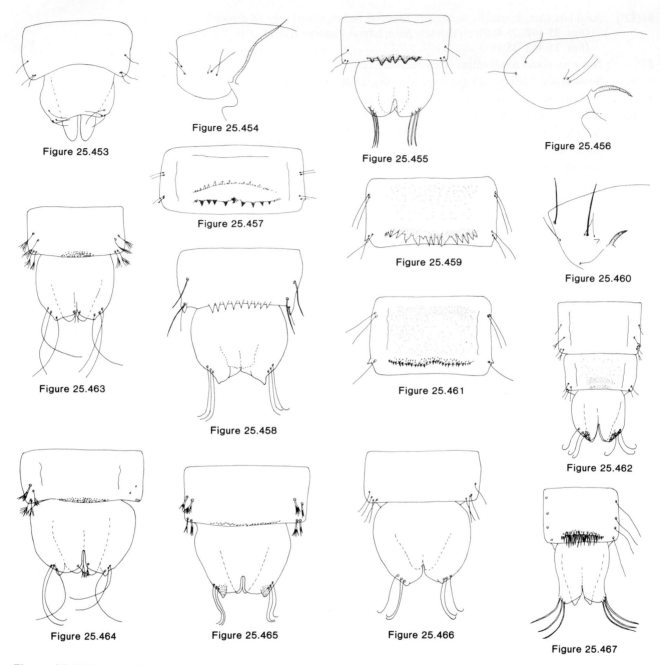

Figure 25.453. Anal lobes and segment 8 of *Cricotopus* sp. 1.

Figure 25.454. Anterior thorax and thoracic horn of *Diamesa* sp. 1.

Figure 25.455. Anal lobes and segment 8 of *Diamesa* sp. 1.

Figure 25.456. Anterior thorax and thoracic horn of *Diamesa* sp. 2.

Figure 25.457. Segment 5 of *Diamesa* sp. 2.

Figure 25.458. Anal lobes and segment 8 of *Pseudokiefferiella* sp. 1.

Figure 25.459. Segment 5 of *Pseudokiefferiella* sp. 1.

Figure 25.460. Anterior thorax and thoracic horn of *Pseudokiefferiella* sp. 1.

Figure 25.461. Segment 5 of *Pseudokiefferiella* sp. 2.

Figure 25.462. Anal lobes and segments 7 and 8 of *Potthastia* sp. 1.

Figure 25.463. Anal lobes and segment 8 of *Pagastia* sp. 1.

Figure 25.464. Anal lobes and segment 8 of *Pagastia* sp. 2.

Figure 25.465. Anal lobes and segment 8 of *Potthastia* sp. 2.

Figure 25.466. Anal lobes and segment 8 of *Pseudodiamesa* sp.

Figure 25.467. Anal lobes and segment 8 of *Limnophyes* sp.

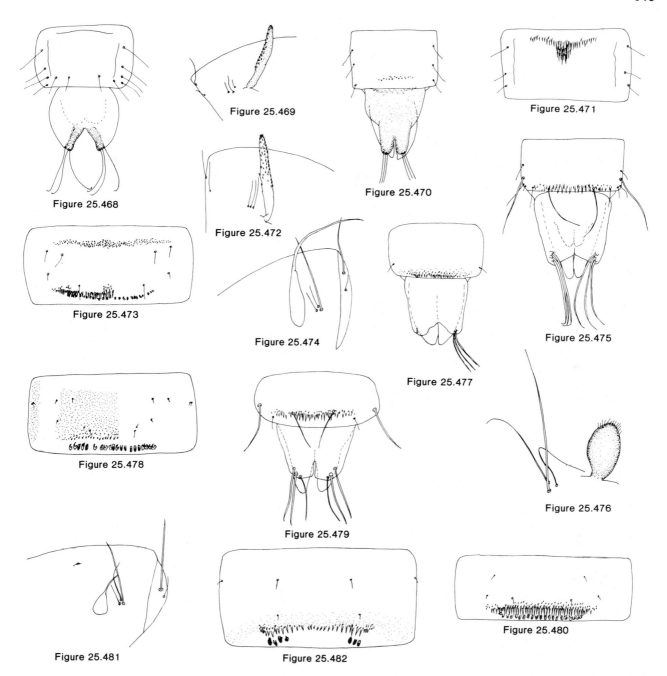

Figure 25.469

Figure 25.471

Figure 25.468

Figure 25.470

Figure 25.472

Figure 25.473

Figure 25.474

Figure 25.475

Figure 25.477

Figure 25.478

Figure 25.476

Figure 25.479

Figure 25.480

Figure 25.481

Figure 25.482

Figure 25.468. Anal lobes and segment 8 of *Diplocladius* sp.

Figure 25.469. Anterior thorax and thoracic horn of *Diplocladius* sp.

Figure 25.470. Anal lobes and segment 8 of *Heleniella* sp.

Figure 25.471. Segment 2 (ventral view) of *Heleniella* sp.

Figure 25.472. Anterior thorax and thoracic horn of *Heleniella* sp.

Figure 25.473. Segment 5 of *Eukiefferiella* sp. 4.

Figure 25.474. Anterior thorax and thoracic horn of *Eukiefferiella* sp. 4.

Figure 25.475. Anal lobes and segment 8 of *Eukiefferiella* sp. 5.

Figure 25.476. Thoracic horn and precorneal setae of *Eukiefferiella* sp. 5.

Figure 25.477. Anal lobes and segment 8 of *Eukiefferiella* sp. 6.

Figure 25.478. Segment 5 of *Eukiefferiella* sp. 6.

Figure 25.479. Anal lobes and segment 8 of *Eukiefferiella* sp. 7.

Figure 25.480. Segment 5 of *Eukiefferiella* sp. 8.

Figure 25.481. Anterior thorax and thoracic horn of *Eukiefferiella* sp. 8.

Figure 25.482. Segment 5 of *Eukiefferiella* sp. 9.

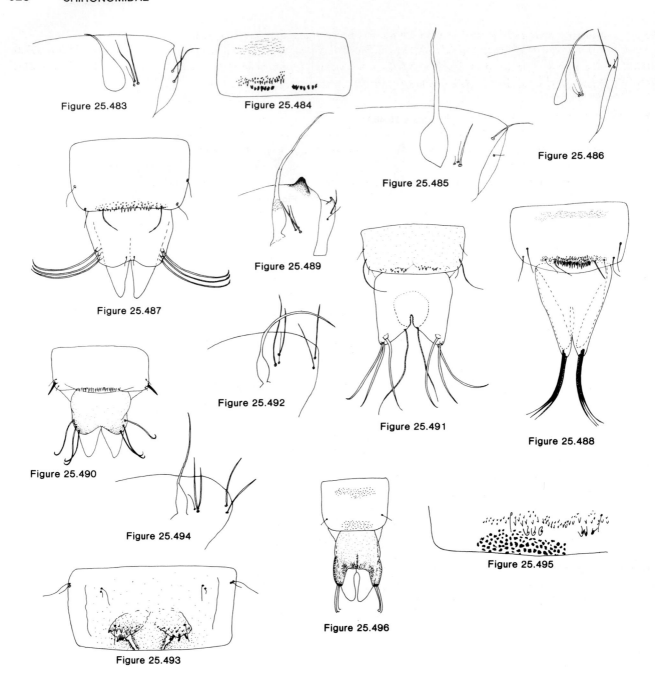

Figure 25.483

Figure 25.484

Figure 25.485

Figure 25.486

Figure 25.487

Figure 25.489

Figure 25.491

Figure 25.488

Figure 25.490

Figure 25.492

Figure 25.494

Figure 25.496

Figure 25.495

Figure 25.493

Figure 25.483. Anterior thorax and thoracic horn of *Eukiefferiella* sp. 10.

Figure 25.484. Segment 5 of *Eukiefferiella* sp. 10.

Figure 25.485. Anterior thorax and thoracic horn of *Eukiefferiella* sp. 11.

Figure 25.486. Anterior thorax and thoracic horn of *Eukiefferiella* sp. 12.

Figure 25.487. Anal lobes and segment 8 of *Eukiefferiella* sp. 13.

Figure 25.488. Anal lobes and segment 8 of Genus 7.

Figure 25.489. Anterior thorax and thoracic horn of Genus 7.

Figure 25.490. Anal lobes and segment 8 of *Tokunagaia* sp.

Figure 25.491. Anal lobes and segment 8 of *Tvetenia* sp. 1.

Figure 25.492. Anterior thorax and thoracic horn of *Tvetenia* sp. 1.

Figure 25.493. Segment 5 of *Tvetenia* sp. 1.

Figure 25.494. Anterior thorax and thoracic horn of *Tvetenia* sp. 2.

Figure 25.495. Posterior margin of segment 5 of *Tvetenia* sp. 2.

Figure 25.496. Anal lobes and segment 8 of *"Paratrichocladius"* sp.

99′.   Posterior margins of terga 1–8 with rows of spines which are approximately the same size on all terga (fig. 25.501); sterna 2–8 with posterior spines .... *Lopescladius*

100(95′). Thoracic horn brown (figs. 25.504–25.505); exuviae small (3 mm or less) .... *Stilocladius*

100′.   Thoracic horn present or absent, when present and brown, exuviae larger than 3 mm 101

101(100′) PSB II elongate and pointed (fig. 25.342) .... *Parametriocnemus*

101′.   PSB II, when present, not as above (fig. 25.511) 102

102(101′) Most terga with a posterior row of blunt spines similar to figure 25.399; thoracic horn similar to figure 25.392 .... *Thienemannia*

102′.   Terga without posterior rows of blunt spines; when present, thoracic horn not as above 103

103(102′) Posterior margins of tergum 8 with rows of sharp spines (fig. 25.440); thoracic horn as in figures 25.441 and 25.442 .... *Chaetocladius* (in part)

103′.   Only shagreen on posterior margins of tergum 8 104

104(103′) Thoracic horn short and broad (fig. 25.506); frontal setae on large tubercles .... *Paracladius*

104′.   Thoracic horn not as above (e.g., figs. 25.507, 25.512–25.513, 25.517–25.519); frontal setae not on tubercles although warts may be present (fig. 25.514) 105

105(104′) Frontal setae usually large (fig. 25.514) thoracic horn usually large and well pigmented (figs. 25.507, 25.512–25.513), never ovoid as in figure 25.518; recurved hooklets on tergum 2 almost always in more than 2 rows (fig. 25.511); anal lobes often with terminal spines (figs. 25.509–25.510); exuviae frequently yellow-golden-brown; middle abdominal segments sometimes with chitinous rings (fig. 25.508); conjunctiva sometimes with a reticulate pigmentation similar to figure 25.495; frontal setae, when present, always on frontal apotome (fig. 25.514); frontal warts sometimes present (fig. 25.514) .... *Orthocladius (Orthocladius)* (in part)

105′.   Frontal setae usually small (figs. 25.521–25.522); thoracic horn usually small and weakly pigmented (figs. 25.517–25.519), often absent; recurved hooklets on tergum 2 almost always in 2 rows (fig. 25.515); anal lobes, at most, with tiny terminal spines (fig. 25.520); exuviae often with little pigment, but may be yellow or brown; terga never with chitinous rings; conjunctiva rarely with reticulate pigmentation; frontal setae on frontal apotome (fig. 25.522) or prefrons (fig. 25.521) or absent; frontal warts absent; anal lobe macrosetae sometimes unequal (fig. 25.516) .... *Cricotopus* (in part)

Additional genera:

1. *Euryhapsis* (Orthocladiinae)—pupa will key to *Brillia* which it resembles (see Oliver 1981; ref. #2838).
2. *Doncricotopus* (Orthocladiinae)—pupa will key to *Nanocladius* or *Rheocricotopus* (see Saether 1981; ref. #2848).

Chironominae

1.   Thoracic horn always unbranched (e.g., figs. 25.525, 25.530, 25.537, 25.540, 25.543); wing sheaths almost always with a subterminal tubercle ("Nase") (fig. 25.575); if subterminal tubercle of wing sheath is absent, then at least some terga with conspicuous groups of spines (e.g., figs. 25.523, 25.534, 25.564) 2

1′.   Thoracic horn almost always with 2 or more branches (figs. 25.615, 25.618, 25.632); when unbranched, most abdominal terga have large circular areas of fine spinules (fig. 25.577) and anal lobes without fringe (fig. 25.578); wing sheaths almost never with a "Nase" 19

2(1).   Tergum 4 (and some others) with one or more distinct groups of short and/or long spines (e.g., figs. 25.523, 25.526, 25.532, 25.534, 25.541, 25.564) 3

2′.   Tergum 4 (and others) with a more or less uniform field of shagreen, although this may be loosely divided into 2–4 subfields (figs. 25.570, 25.573) 18

3(2).   Tergum 4, and sometimes 3 and 5, with conspicuous groups of long needlelike spines (e.g., figs. 25.523–25.524, 25.526, 25.528, 25.531) 4

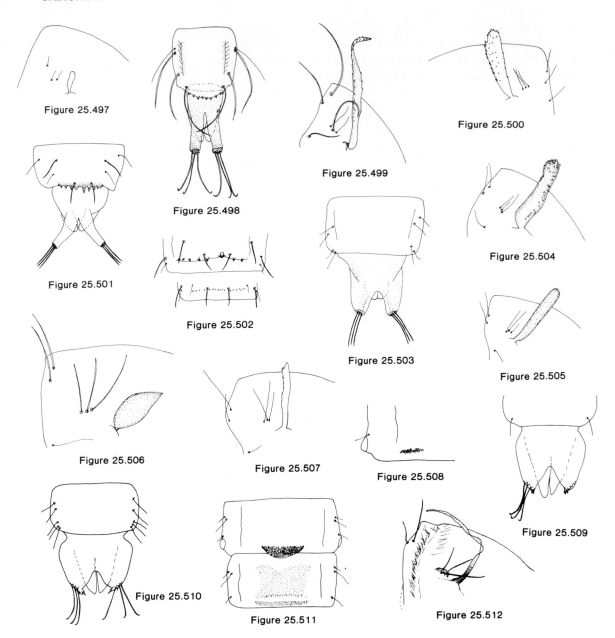

Figure 25.497. Anterior thorax and thoracic horn of "*Paratrichocladius*" sp.

Figure 25.498. Anal lobes and segment 8 of Genus 8.

Figure 25.499. Anterior thorax and thoracic horn of Genus 8.

Figure 25.500. Anterior thorax and thoracic horn of *Psilometriocnemus* sp.

Figure 25.501. Anal lobes and segment 8 of *Lopescladius*.

Figure 25.502. Posterior margins of segments 5 and 7 of Genus 9.

Figure 25.503. Anal lobes and segment 8 of *Stilocladius* sp. 1.

Figure 25.504. Anterior thorax and thoracic horn of *Stilocladius* sp. 1.

Figure 25.505. Anterior thorax and thoracic horn of *Stilocladius* sp. 2.

Figure 25.506. Anterior thorax and thoracic horn of *Paracladius* sp.

Figure 25.507. Anterior thorax and thoracic horn of *Orthocladius (Orthocladius)* sp. 2.

Figure 25.508. Lateral margin of segment 2 of *Orthocladius (Orthocladius)* sp. 2.

Figure 25.509. Anal lobes and posterior margin of segment 8 of *Orthocladius (Orthocladius)* sp. 2.

Figure 25.510. Anal lobes and segment 8 of *Orthocladius (Orthocladius)* sp. 3.

Figure 25.511. Segments 2 and 3 of *Orthocladius (Orthocladius)* sp. 3.

Figure 25.512. Anterior thorax and thoracic horn of *Orthocladius (Orthocladius)* sp. 4.

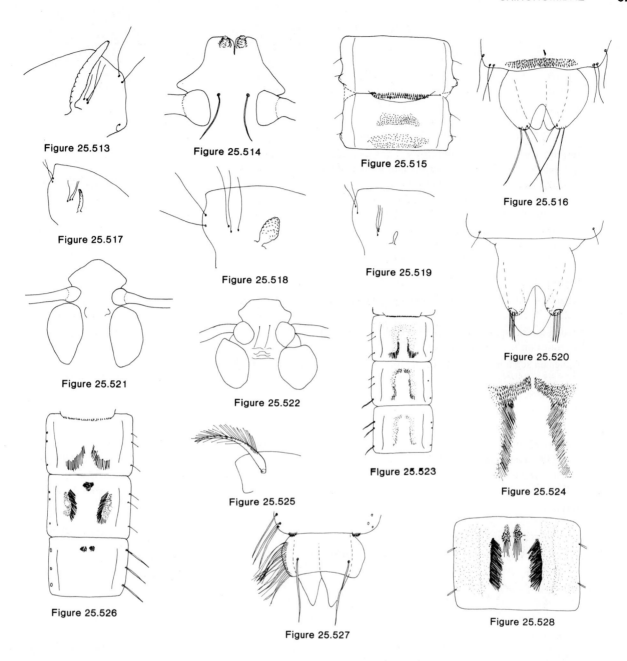

Figure 25.513. Anterior thorax and thoracic horn of *Orthocladius (Orthocladius)* sp. 5.

Figure 25.514. Frontal apotome of *Orthocladius (Orthocladius)* sp. 6.

Figure 25.515. Segments 2 and 3 of *Cricotopus* sp. 2.

Figure 25.516. Anal lobes and posterior margin of segment 8 of *Cricotopus* sp. 3.

Figure 25.517. Anterior thorax and thoracic horn of *Cricotopus* sp. 4.

Figure 25.518. Anterior thorax and thoracic horn of *Cricotopus* sp. 5.

Figure 25.519. Anterior thorax and thoracic horn of *Cricotopus* sp. 6.

Figure 25.520. Anal lobes of *Cricotopus* sp. 7.

Figure 25.521. Frontal apotome of some *Cricotopus* spp.

Figure 25.522. Frontal apotome of some *Cricotopus* spp.

Figure 25.523. Segments 3–5 of *Micropsectra* sp. 1.

Figure 25.524. Groups of spines on segment 4 of *Micropsectra* sp. 1.

Figure 25.525. Thoracic horn of *Micropsectra* sp. 1.

Figure 25.526. Segments 3–5 of *Paratanytarsus* sp. 1.

Figure 25.527. Anal lobes and posterior margin of segment 8 of *Paratanytarsus* sp. 1.

Figure 25.528. Segment 4 of *Paratanytarsus* sp. 2.

3′.   Terga 4 and 5 without groups of needlelike spines (e.g., figs. 25.538, 25.541, 25.548, 25.552, 25.564) although some long spines may be present on tergum 3 and tergum 4 and 5 may have groups of short spines 7

4(3).   Tergum 4 with 2 longitudinal rows of needlelike spines that are angled medially at their anterior ends and usually meet (figs. 25.523–25.524) .... *Micropsectra* (in part)

4′.   Tergum 4 not as above, i.e., the 2 spine rows are not joined anteriorly (e.g., figs. 25.529, 25.531, 25.533), sometimes additional spine groups are present (e.g., figs. 25.526, 25.528) or the rows are transverse (fig. 25.534) 5

5(4′).   Tergum 4 with 2 longitudinal rows of spines (although sometimes very weakly developed) and 1–2 anterior median groups of spines (figs. 25.526, 25.528); wing sheaths with or without a pearl row (fig. 25.341) .... *Paratanytarsus* (in part)

5′.   Tergum 4 with 2 longitudinal rows of spines but without median groups (figs. 25.529, 25.531–25.533) or, tergum 4 with spine rows transverse (fig. 25.534); wing sheath without pearl rows 6

6(5′).   Tergum 4 with 2 longitudinal rows of spines (figs. 25.529, 25.531–25.533) .... *Tanytarsus (Tanytarsus)*

6′.   Tergum 4 with transverse rows of spines (fig. 25.534) .... *Tanytarsus (Sublettea)*

7(3′).   Tergum 4 with a single median group of short spines (fig. 25.538) .... *Paratanytarsus* (in part)

7′.   Tergum 4 with paired groups of short spines (e.g., figs. 25.541, 25.550, 25.552, 25.557, 25.567) 8

8(7′).   Strong lateral spines on segment 8 (figs. 25.542 and 25.546); shagreen and spine groups on terga as in figures 25.541, 25.545, and 25.548 9

8′.   Spines on segment 8 usually in the form of a caudolateral comb (e.g., figs. 25.549, 25.553, 25.558, 25.560, 25.562); however, when single, tergal spine groups never as above 10

9(8).   Frontal setae usually small (fig. 25.543); when large, the spine and shagreen groups on terga 4 and 5 are as in figure 25.541 .... *Stempellina*

9′.   Frontal setae large (figs. 25.544, 25.547) and the spine and shagreen groups on tergum 5 as in figure 25.545 or 25.548 .... *Constempellina*

10(8′).   Terga 5 and 6 with large oval groups of small spines (fig. 25.550); anal lobes with fringe setae limited to distal ends (fig. 25.549) .... *Neozavrelia*

10′.   Terga 5 and 6 without such large areas of spinules but smaller groups may be present (figs. 25.552, 25.557, 25.564, 25.567); anal lobes usually with more complete fringe (figs. 25.553, 25.558, 25.560, 25.562, 25.566) 11

11(10′). Caudolateral spine on segment 8 usually a simple spur (fig. 25.553) less often with a small accessory spine .... *Rheotanytarsus*

11′.   Caudolateral spines on segment 8 in the form of a comb (figs. 25.558, 25.560, 25.562, 25.565–25.566) 12

12(11′). Each anal lobe with 1 dorsal seta (fig. 25.558) 13

12′.   Each anal lobe with 2 dorsal setae (figs. 25.560, 25.562, 25.566) 15

13(12).   Paired groups of short spines on terga 3–6 (fig. 25.556) .... *Genus 11*

13′.   Paired groups of short spines on terga 4–5 or 4–6 (fig. 25.557) 14

14(13′). Thoracic horn with "hairs" as in figure 25.525 .... *Micropsectra* (in part)

14′.   Thoracic horn without "hairs" .... *Lauterbornia*

15(12′). Combs on caudolateral corners of segment 8 wide (fig. 25.560); precorneal setae lamellar and inserting on a process (figs. 25.559, 25.561) 16

15′.   Combs on 8 usually less wide (figs. 25.562, 25.565); precorneal setae not as above 17

16(15).   Thoracic horn with short "hairs" (fig. 25.559) .... *Cladotanytarsus*

16′.   Thoracic horn with long "hairs" (fig. 25.561) .... *Lenziella*

17(15′). Fringe of anal lobes limited to distal third (fig. 25.562) .... *Corynocera*

17′.   Fringe of anal lobes usually extending along entire margin (fig. 25.566), rarely absent .... *Tanytarsus (Tanytarsus)* (in part)

18(2′).   Terga 2–6 with shagreen occupying about one-third to one-half of the surface; fields of pleura with, at most, weak shagreen (fig. 25.570) .... *Stempellinella*

18′.   Terga and pleura 2–6 with large fields of shagreen (fig. 25.573) .... *Zavrelia*

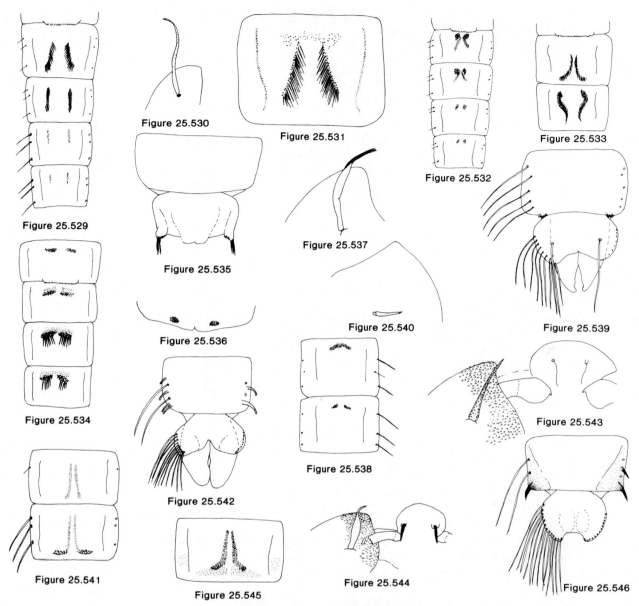

Figure 25.530

Figure 25.531

Figure 25.533

Figure 25.532

Figure 25.529

Figure 25.537

Figure 25.535

Figure 25.539

Figure 25.536

Figure 25.540

Figure 25.534

Figure 25.543

Figure 25.538

Figure 25.542

Figure 25.541

Figure 25.544

Figure 25.546

Figure 25.545

Figure 25.529. Segments 3–6 of *Tanytarsus (Tanytarsus)* sp. 1.

Figure 25.530. Thoracic horn of *Tanytarsus (Tanytarsus)* sp. 1.

Figure 25.531. Segment 3 of *Tanytarsus (Tanytarsus)* sp. 1.

Figure 25.532. Segments 3–6 of *Tanytarsus (Tanytarsus)* sp. 2.

Figure 25.533. Segments 3 and 4 of *Tanytarsus (Tanytarsus)* sp. 3.

Figure 25.534. Segments 2–5 of *Tanytarsus (Sublettea)* sp.

Figure 25.535. Anal lobes and segment 8 of *Tanytarsus (Sublettea)* sp.

Figure 25.536. Posterior margin of segment 8 (ventral view) of *Tanytarsus (Sublettea)* sp.

Figure 25.537. Thoracic horn of *Tanytarsus (Sublettea)* sp.

Figure 25.538. Segments 4 and 5 of *Paratanytarsus* sp. 3.

Figure 25.539. Anal lobes and segment 8 of *Paratanytarsus* sp. 3.

Figure 25.540. Thoracic horn of *Paratanytarsus* sp. 3.

Figure 25.541. Segments 4 and 5 of *Stempellina* sp.

Figure 25.542. Anal lobes and segment 8 of *Stempellina* sp.

Figure 25.543. Frontal apotome and anterior thorax with thoracic horn of *Stempellina* sp.

Figure 25.544. Frontal apotome and anterior thorax with thoracic horn of *Constempellina* sp. 1.

Figure 25.545. Segment 5 of *Constempellina* sp. 1.

Figure 25.546. Anal lobes and segment 8 of *Constempellina* sp. 1.

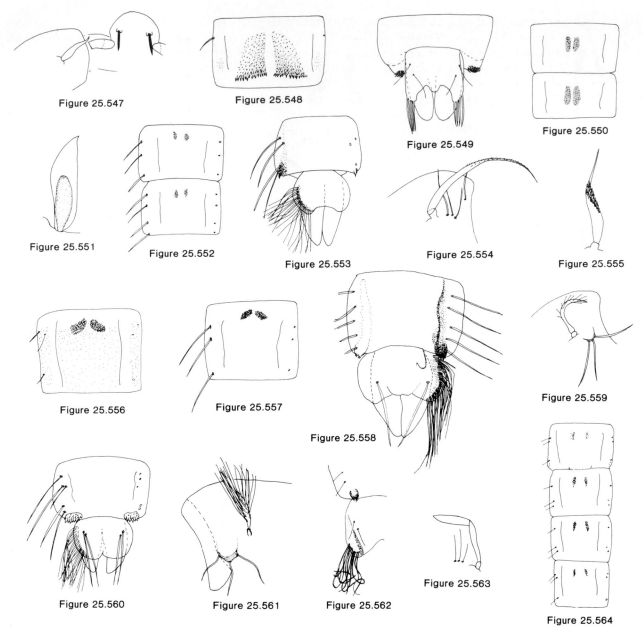

Figure 25.547

Figure 25.548

Figure 25.549

Figure 25.550

Figure 25.551

Figure 25.552

Figure 25.553

Figure 25.554

Figure 25.555

Figure 25.556

Figure 25.557

Figure 25.558

Figure 25.559

Figure 25.560

Figure 25.561

Figure 25.562

Figure 25.563

Figure 25.564

Figure 25.547. Frontal apotome and anterior thorax with thoracic horn of *Constempellina* sp. 2.

Figure 25.548. Segment 5 of *Constempellina* sp. 2.

Figure 25.549. Anal lobes and segment 8 of *Neozavrelia* sp.

Figure 25.550. Segments 5 and 6 of *Neozavrelia* sp.

Figure 25.551. Thoracic horn of *Neozavrelia* sp.

Figure 25.552. Segments 5 and 6 of *Rheotanytarsus* sp. 1.

Figure 25.553. Anal lobes and segment 8 of *Rheotany-tarsus* sp. 1.

Figure 25.554. Anterior thorax and thoracic horn of *Rheotanytarsus* sp. 1.

Figure 25.555. Thoracic horn of *Rheotanytarsus* sp. 2.

Figure 25.556. Segment 4 of Genus 11.

Figure 25.557. Segment 5 of *Micropsectra* sp. 2.

Figure 25.558. Anal lobes and segment 8 of *Micropsectra* sp. 2.

Figure 25.559. Anterior thorax and thoracic horn of *Cladotanytarsus* sp.

Figure 25.560. Anal lobes and segment 8 of *Cladotanytarsus* sp.

Figure 25.561. Anterior thorax and thoracic horn of *Lenziella* sp.

Figure 25.562. Anal lobe and segment 8 (left side) of *Corynocera* sp.

Figure 25.563. Thoracic horn and precorneal setae of *Corynocera* sp.

Figure 25.564. Segment 2–5 of *Tanytarsus* (*Tanytarsus*) sp. 4.

19(1′).   Thoracic horn unbranched (fig. 25.576); terga with large circular areas of fine spinules (fig. 25.577); anal lobes without fringe (fig. 25.578) .... ***Pseudochironomus***

19′.   Thoracic horn with 2 or more branches (e.g., figs. 25.586, 25.615, 25.618, 25.632); anal lobes with, at least, a partial fringe (e.g., figs. 25.588, 25.605, 25.623, 25.628) 20

20(19′).   Row of hooklets on posterior margin of segment 2 distinctly interrupted (figs. 25.581, 25.583, 25.591) or, rarely, absent 21

20′.   Row of hooklets on segment 2, at most, very narrowly interrupted (figs. 25.603, 25.621–25.622, 25.629, 25.640) always present 30

21(20).   Caudolateral margins of segment 8 with a spine or group of spines (e.g., figs. 25.604–25.606, 25.609, 25.616) 22

21′.   Caudolateral margins of segment 8 without spines 25

22(21).   Thoracic horn exceptionally long (fig. 25.586) .... ***Cryptotendipes*** (in part)

22′.   Thoracic horn never as long as above (figs. 25.615, 25.618, 25.632) 23

23(22′).   Tergum 6 with a posterior, median spiniferous process (fig. 25.579) .... ***Cladopelma***

23′.   Tergum 6 with, at most, rows of spines 24

24(23′).   Cephalic tubercles long (fig. 25.580); PSB II developed (fig. 25.581) .... ***Microchironomus***

24′.   Cephalic tubercles short (fig. 25.582); PSB II absent .... ***Genus 12***

25(21′).   Hooklets on posterior margin of tergum 2 absent; large tubercles on terga (fig. 25.585); thoracic horn exceptionally long (fig. 25.586) .... ***Cryptotendipes*** (in part)

25′.   Not with above characters 26

26(25′).   Caudal region with a forked posterior extension (fig. 25.588); frontal apotome often with ornate cephalic tubercles (figs. 25.589 and 25.590) .... ***Cryptochironomus***

26′.   Caudal region without a forked process; cephalic tubercles, when present, never ornate 27

27(26′).   PSB II with spinules (fig. 25.591) .... ***Beckidia***

27′.   PSB II, when present, without spinules 28

28(27′).   Cephalic tubercles absent .... ***Chernovskiia***

28′.   Cephalic tubercles present 29

29(28′).   Each caudal lobe with more than 100 fringe setae .... ***Genus 13***

29′.   Each caudal lobe with no more than about 50 setae .... ***Harnischia***

30(20′).   Caudolateral margins of segment 8 with a spine or a group of spines (e.g., figs. 25.609–25.611, 25.616, 25.624) 31

30′.   Caudolateral margins of segment 8 without spines 73

31(30).   Cephalic tubercles present (e.g., figs. 25.596–25.599) 32

31′.   Cephalic tubercles absent 65

32(31).   Thoracic horn exceptionally long (fig. 25.586) .... ***Cryptotendipes*** (in part)

32′.   Thoracic horn shorter (e.g., figs. 25.615, 25.618, 25.632) 33

33(32′).   Terga 2–6, 3–6, or 4–5 with small to large unpaired groups of spines or spiniferous processes (figs. 25.592, 25.594–25.595) 34

33′.   Terga without such groups of spines or processes 36

34(33).   Terga 2–6 with large spiniferous processes (fig. 25.592) .... ***Glyptotendipes (Phytotendipes)***

34′.   Terga 3–6 or 4–5 with small spine groups (figs. 25.594–25.595) 35

35(34′).   Terga 3–6 with small groups of spines (fig. 25.594) .... ***Glyptotendipes (Glyptotendipes)***

35′.   Terga 4–5 with very small groups of spines (fig. 25.595) .... ***Glyptotendipes (Demijerea)***

36(33′).   Cephalic tubercles truncate and with a cluster of spinules (fig. 25.596) .... ***Phaenopsectra***

36′.   Cephalic tubercles not truncate and without spinules 37

37(36′).   Cephalic tubercles extremely long and tapering (fig. 25.597) .... ***"Polypedilum"*** (in part)

37′.   Cephalic tubercles not as above (e.g., figs. 25.598–25.599) 38

38(37′).   Cephalic tubercles large, heavily sclerotized, and fused (fig. 25.598) .... ***Genus 14***

38′.   Cephalic tubercles not as above (e.g., figs. 25.580, 25.582, 25.599) 39

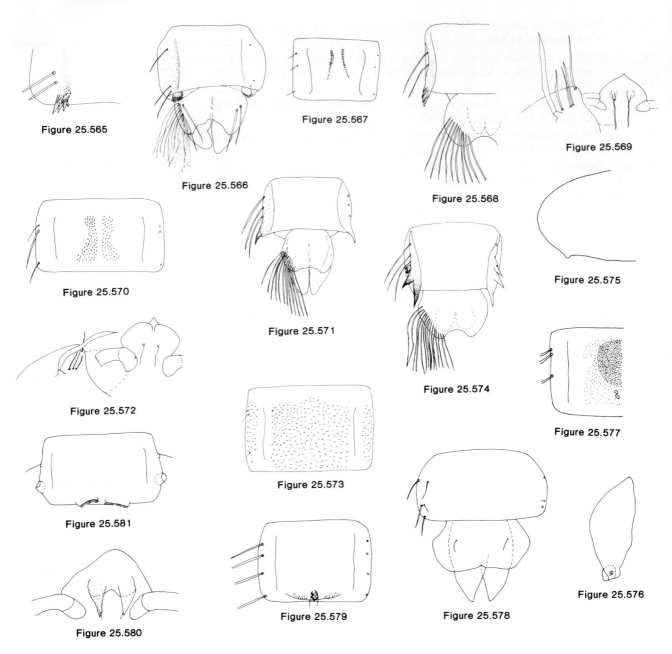

Figure 25.565

Figure 25.566

Figure 25.567

Figure 25.568

Figure 25.569

Figure 25.570

Figure 25.571

Figure 25.572

Figure 25.573

Figure 25.574

Figure 25.575

Figure 25.576

Figure 25.577

Figure 25.578

Figure 25.579

Figure 25.580

Figure 25.581

Figure 25.565. Spines on caudolateral margin of segment 8 of *Tanytarsus (Tanytarsus)* sp. 4.

Figure 25.566. Anal lobes and segment 8 of *Tanytarsus (Tanytarsus)* sp. 5.

Figure 25.567. Segment 4 of *Tanytarsus (Tanytarsus)* sp. 5.

Figure 25.568. Anal lobe and segment 8 (left half) of *Stempellinella)* sp. 1.

Figure 25.569. Frontal apotome and anterior thorax with thoracic horn of *Stempellinella* sp. 1.

Figure 25.570. Segment 4 of *Stempellinella* sp. 1.

Figure 25.571. Anal lobes and segment 8 of *Stempellinella* sp. 2.

Figure 25.572. Frontal apotome and anterior thorax with thoracic horn of *Zavrelia* sp.

Figure 25.573. Segment 4 of *Zavrelia* sp.

Figure 25.574. Anal lobes and segment 8 of *Zavrelia* sp.

Figure 25.575. Tip of wing sheath with "Nase" of *Zavrelia* sp.

Figure 25.576. Thoracic horn of *Pseudochironomus* sp. 1.

Figure 25.577. Segment 6 (left half) of *Pseudochironomus* sp. 1.

Figure 25.578. Anal lobes and segment 8 of *Pseudochironomus* sp. 1.

Figure 25.579. Segment 6 of *Cladopelma* sp.

Figure 25.580. Frontal apotome of *Microchironomus* sp.

Figure 25.581. Segment 2 of *Microchironomus* sp.

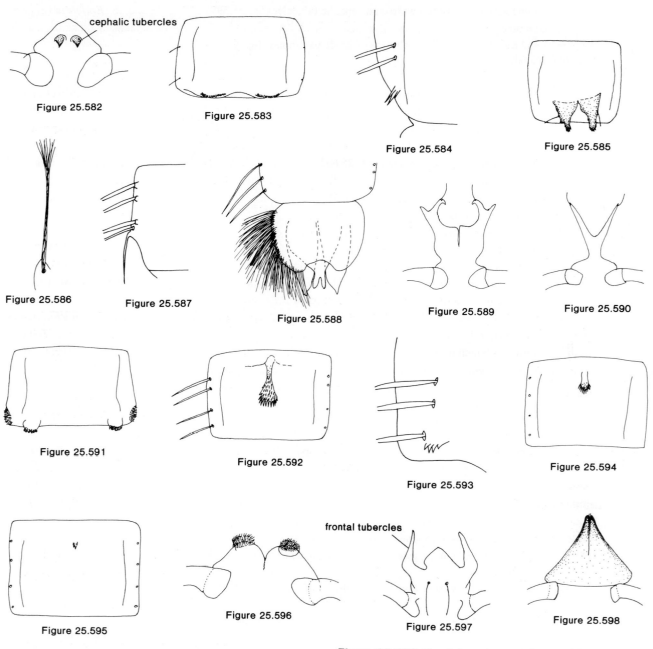

cephalic tubercles

Figure 25.582

Figure 25.583

Figure 25.584

Figure 25.585

Figure 25.586

Figure 25.587

Figure 25.588

Figure 25.589

Figure 25.590

Figure 25.591

Figure 25.592

Figure 25.593

Figure 25.594

Figure 25.595

Figure 25.596

frontal tubercles

Figure 25.597

Figure 25.598

Figure 25.582. Frontal apotome of Genus 12.

Figure 25.583. Segment 2 of Genus 12.

Figure 25.584. Caudolateral margin of segment 8 of Genus 12.

Figure 25.585. Segment 5 of *Cryptotendipes* sp.

Figure 25.586. Thoracic horn of *Cryptotendipes* sp.

Figure 25.587. Caudolateral margin of segment 8 (left half) of *Cryptotendipes* sp.

Figure 25.588. Anal lobes and segment 8 of *Cryptochironomus* sp. 1.

Figure 25.589. Frontal apotome of *Cryptochironomus* sp. 2.

Figure 25.590. Frontal apotome of *Cryptochironomus* sp. 3.

Figure 25.591. Segment 2 of *Beckidia* sp.

Figure 25.592. Segment 6 of *Glyptotendipes (Phytotendipes)* sp.

Figure 25.593. Caudolateral margin of segment 8 (left half) of *Glyptotendipes (Phytotendipes)* sp.

Figure 25.594. Segment 6 of *Glyptotendipes (Glyptotendipes)* sp.

Figure 25.595. Segment 5 of *Glyptotendipes (Demeijerea)* sp.

Figure 25.596. Frontal apotome of *Phaenopsectra* sp.

Figure 25.597. Frontal apotome of *Polypedilum* sp. 1.

Figure 25.598. Frontal apotome of Genus 14.

39(38'). Frontal apotome with large frontal warts and cephalic tubercles (fig. 25.599) .... *Einfeldia* (in part)

39'. Only cephalic tubercles present 40

40(39'). Sternum 2 and sometimes 1 and 3 with rows of needlelike spines (figs. 25.600–25.601) 41

40'. Sternum 1–3 without such spines 42

41(40). Needlelike spines on sternum 2 in transverse rows only (fig. 25.600) .... *Dicrotendipes*

41'. Needlelike spines on sternum 2 in transverse and longitudinal rows (fig. 25.601) .... *"Wirthiella"*

42(40'). Segment 5 with 1–3 lamellar lateral setae (figs. 25.602, 25.607) 43

42'. Segment 5 with 4 lamellar lateral setae (fig. 25.619) 52

43(42). Segment 5 with 1–2 lamellar lateral setae (fig. 25.602) .... *Genus 15*

43'. Segment 5 with 3 lamellar lateral setae (fig. 25.607) 44

44(43'). Segment 6 with 3 lamellar lateral setae (fig. 25.633) 45

44'. Segment 6 with 4 lamellar lateral setae (fig. 25.607) 48

45(44). Terga 2–6 with paired groups of spines (fig. 25.603); spine(s) on caudolateral margin of segment 8 as in figure 25.604 .... *Lauterborniella*

45'. Terga 2–6 without paired groups of spines; spines on segment 8 as in figure 25.605 46

46(45'). Fringe of setae on caudal lobes completely uniserial (fig. 25.605) .... *"Polypedilum"* (in part)

46'. Fringe of setae on caudal lobes at least partially multiserial 47

47(46'). Segment 8 with 3–4 lateral lamellar setae .... *Stictochironomus*

47'. Segment 8 with 5 lateral lamellar setae .... *Tribelos*

48(44'). Segment 8 with 3–4 lamellar lateral setae .... *Paratendipes*

48'. Segment 8 with 5 lamellar lateral setae 49

49(48'). Armature on caudolateral margins of segment 8 in the form of a compound spur (fig. 25.616) .... *Chironomus* (in part)

49'. Armature on margins of segment 8 consisting of a single spine (fig. 25.606) or groups of spines 50

50(49'). Armature on margins of segment 8 consisting of single spines (fig. 25.606) .... *Pagastiella*

50'. Armature on margins of segment 8 consisting of multiple spines 51

51(50'). Terga 2–5 or 3–5 with paired groups of dark spines similar to figure 25.603 .... *Omisus*

51'. Terga without such paired groups .... *Microtendipes*

52(42'). Segment 8 with 4 lamellar lateral setae 53

52'. Segment 8 with 5 lateral setae (5 lamellar or 4 lamellar and 1 hairlike) 55

53(52). Spines on caudolateral margins of segment 8 usually simple as in figures 25.608–25.609) .... *"Dicrotendipes"*

53'. Spines on caudolateral margins of segment 8 multiple as in figures 25.610 and 25.611 54

54(53'). Caudolateral margins of segment 8 with 3 or more short straight spines (fig. 25.610) .... *Paralauterborniella*

54'. Caudolateral margins of segment 8 with a series of closely set curved spines (fig. 25.611) .... *Cyphomella*

55(52'). Posterior margin of sternum 8 with 2 sclerotized spines in female and a row of spines in male (figs. 25.612–25.613) .... *Genus 16*

55'. No such spines present 56

56(55'). Sternum 1 with 2 pairs of spiniferous processes (fig. 25.614) .... *Pseudochironomus* (in part)

56'. Sternum 1 without such processes 57

57(56'). Spines on caudolateral corners of segment 8 in the form of a compound spur (figs. 25.616–25.617) .... *Chironomus* (in part)

57'. Spines on segment 8 not as above (e.g., figs. 25.620, 25.624, 25.630–25.631) 58

58(57'). Spines on caudolateral margins of segment 8 single .... *Gillotia*

58'. Spines on segment 8 multiple (e.g., figs. 25.620, 25.624, 25.630) 59

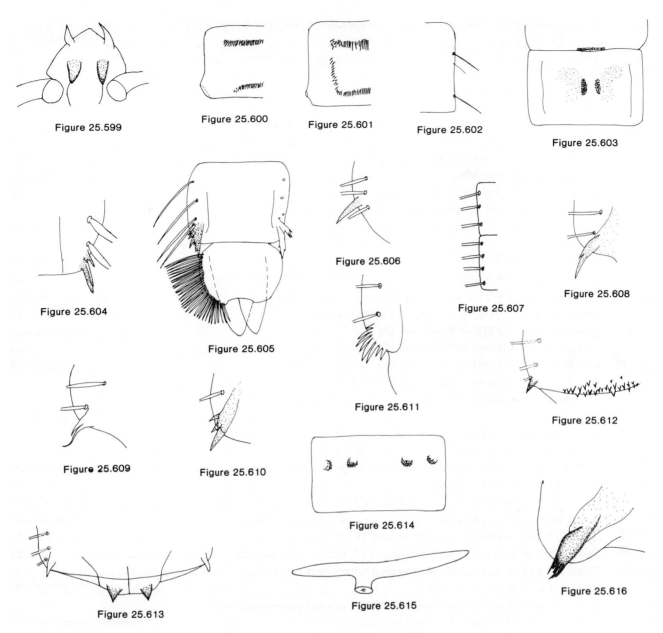

Figure 25.599.

Figure 25.600

Figure 25.601

Figure 25.602

Figure 25.603

Figure 25.604

Figure 25.605

Figure 25.606

Figure 25.607

Figure 25.608

Figure 25.609

Figure 25.610

Figure 25.611

Figure 25.612

Figure 25.614

Figure 25.613

Figure 25.615

Figure 25.616

Figure 25.599. Frontal apotome of *Einfeldia* sp. 1.

Figure 25.600. Segment 2 (ventral view, left half) of *Dicrotendipes* sp.

Figure 25.601. Segment 2 (ventral view, left half) of *"Wirthiella"* sp.

Figure 25.602. Segment 5 (right half) of Genus 15.

Figure 25.603. Posterior margin of segment 2 and segment 3 of *Lauterborniella* sp.

Figure 25.604. Caudolateral margin of segment 8 (right half) of *Lauterborniella* sp.

Figure 25.605. Anal lobes and segment 8 of *"Polypedilum"* sp.

Figure 25.606. Caudolateral margin of segment 8 (left half) of *Pagastiella* sp.

Figure 25.607. Segments 5 and 6 (left half) of *Paratendipes* sp.

Figure 25.608. Caudolateral margin of segment 8 (left half) of *"Dicrotendipes"* sp. 1.

Figure 25.609. Caudolateral margin of segment 8 (left half) of *"Dicrotendipes"* sp. 2.

Figure 25.610. Caudolateral margin of segment 8 (left half) of *Paralauterborniella* sp.

Figure 25.611. Caudolateral margin of segment 8 (left half) of *Cyphomella* sp.

Figure 25.612. Segment 8 (ventral view, left side) of male of Genus 16.

Figure 25.613. Segment 8 (ventral view of posterior margin) of female of Genus 16.

Figure 25.614. Segment 1 (ventral view) of *Pseudochironomus* sp. 2.

Figure 25.615. Thoracic horn of *Pseudochironomus* sp. 2.

Figure 25.616. Caudolateral margin of segment 8 (left half) of *Chironomus* sp. 1.

59(58′). Spines on caudolateral margins of segment 8 long, yellow, and slightly curved (fig. 25.620) .... *Einfeldia* (in part)

59′. Spines on segment 8 not as above 60

60(59′). PSB II present (fig. 25.621) 61

60′. PSB II absent 63

61(60). Shagreen on tergum 2 weak or absent .... *Parachironomus* (in part)

61′. Shagreen on tergum 2 extensive, about as on tergum 3 62

62(61′). Shagreen fields stronger posteriorly with distinct fenestra (fig. 25.622) .... *"Kiefferulus"*

62′. Shagreen fields more uniform in strength without such fenestra .... *"Goeldichironomus"*

63(60′). Fringe of setae on anal lobes uniserial (fig. 25.623) .... *Paracladopelma* (in part)

63′. Fringe of setae on anal lobes multiserial 64

64(63′). Spines on caudolateral margin of segment 8 dark and stemming from a common base (fig. 25.624) .... *Demicryptochironomus*

64′. Spines on caudolateral margin of segment 8 yellow and in a row (fig. 25.625) .... *Genus 17*

65(31′). Segment 5 with no lamellar lateral setae (fig. 25.627) 66

65′. Segment 5 with 3–4 lamellar lateral setae (figs. 25.619, 25.633) 67

66(65). Anterior regions of terga 2–5 with single rows of strong spines (fig. 25.626) .... *Pediomomus*

66′. Anterior regions of terga 2–6 with multiple rows of smaller spines (fig. 25.627) .... *Endochironomus*

67(65′). Segment 5 with 3 lateral lamellar setae (fig. 25.633) 68

67′. Segment 5 with 4 lateral lamellar setae (fig. 25.619) 72

68(67). Segment 6 with 3 lateral lamellar setae (fig. 25.633) 69

68′. Segment 6 with 4 lateral lamellar setae (fig. 25.619) 71

69(68). Fringe of setae on anal lobe extends along inner margin (fig. 25.628) .... *Genus 18*

69′. Fringe of setae does not extend along inner margin of anal lobe 70

70(69′). Fringe of setae on anal lobes almost always uniserial as in figure 25.605 .... *Polypedilum* (in part)

70′. Fringe of setae on anal lobes distally multiserial (fig. 25.634) .... *Graceus*

71(68′). Sternum 1 with 2 pairs of spiniferous processes (fig. 25.614) .... *Pseudochironomus* (in part)

71′. Sternum 1 without such processes .... *Genus 19*

72(67′). Armature on caudolateral margins of segment 8 as in figure 25.635 .... *"Nilothauma"*

72′. Armature on caudolateral margins of segment 8 as in figure 25.636 .... *Stenochironomus*

73(30′). Cephalic tubercles present (e.g., figs. 25.580, 25.582, 25.599) 74

73′. Cephalic tubercles absent 81

74(73). Terga 2–6 with median spiniferous processes (fig. 25.592) .... *Glyptotendipes (Phytotendipes)* (in part)

74′. Terga 2–6 without such processes 75

75(74′). Terga 2–5 with coarse shagreen arranged in a fenestrated pattern with many spinules located on pigmented spots of cuticle (fig. 25.637) .... *Xenochironomus* (in part)

75′. Shagreen not as above 76

76(75′). Frontal tubercles and cephalic tubercles present (fig. 25.599) .... *Einfeldia* (in part)

76′. Only cephalic tubercles present 77

77(76′). Segment 5 with 3 lateral lamellar setae (fig. 25.607) 78

77′. Segment 5 with 4 lateral lamellar setae (fig. 25.619) 79

78(77). Segment 6 with 3 lamellar lateral setae (fig. 25.633) .... *Parachironomus* (in part)

78′. Segment 6 with 4 lamellar lateral setae (fig. 25.607) .... *Pseudochironomus* (in part)

79(77′). Tergum 2 with shagreen area about the same size as that of tergum 3 (fig. 25.638) .... *Saetheria*

79′. Tergum 2 without shagreen 80

80(79′). Rows of spines on posterior margins of terga 3–6 with some spines distinctly larger than others (fig. 25.639) or with spines on tergum 6 as large or larger than those on tergum 3 (fig. 25.641) .... *Paracladopelma* (in part)

80′. Rows of spines on posterior margins of terga 3–6 all of about the same size on any one tergum (fig. 25.642) but those on tergum 6 distinctly smaller than those on tergum 3 (fig. 25.643) .... *Genus 20*

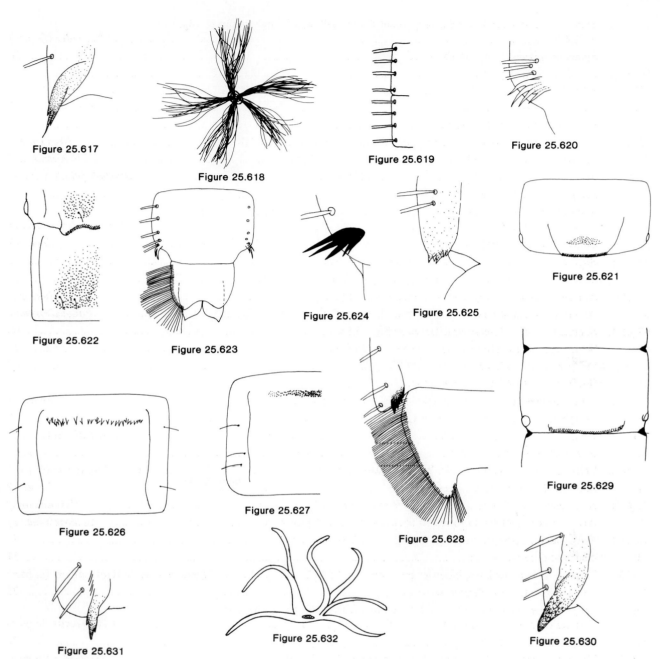

Figure 25.617

Figure 25.618

Figure 25.619

Figure 25.620

Figure 25.622

Figure 25.623

Figure 25.624

Figure 25.625

Figure 25.621

Figure 25.626

Figure 25.627

Figure 25.628

Figure 25.629

Figure 25.631

Figure 25.632

Figure 25.630

Figure 25.617. Caudolateral margin of segment 8 (left side) of *Chironomus* sp. 2.

Figure 25.618. Thoracic horn of *Chironomus* sp. 2.

Figure 25.619. Segments 5 and 6 (left side) of *Chironomus* sp. 2.

Figure 25.620. Caudolateral margin of segment 8 (left side) of *Einfeldia* sp. 2.

Figure 25.621. Segment 2 of *Parachironomus* sp.

Figure 25.622. Segments 2 and 3 (left side) of *"Kiefferulus"* sp.

Figure 25.623. Anal lobes and segment 8 of *Paracladopelma* sp. 1.

Figure 25.624. Caudolateral margin of segment 8 (left side) of *Demicryptochironomus* sp.

Figure 25.625. Caudolateral margin of segment 8 (left side) of Genus 17.

Figure 25.626. Segment 5 of *Pedionemus* sp.

Figure 25.627. Segment 5 (left side) of *Endochironomus* sp.

Figure 25.628. Caudolateral margin of segment 8 and left anal lobe of Genus 18.

Figure 25.629. Conjunctiva 1/2 and 2/3 of *Polypedilum* sp. 2.

Figure 25.630. Caudolateral margin of segment 8 (left side) of *Polypedilum* sp. 3.

Figure 25.631. Caudolateral margin of segment 8 (left side) of *Polypedilum* sp. 4.

Figure 25.632. Thoracic horn of *Polypedilum* sp. 4.

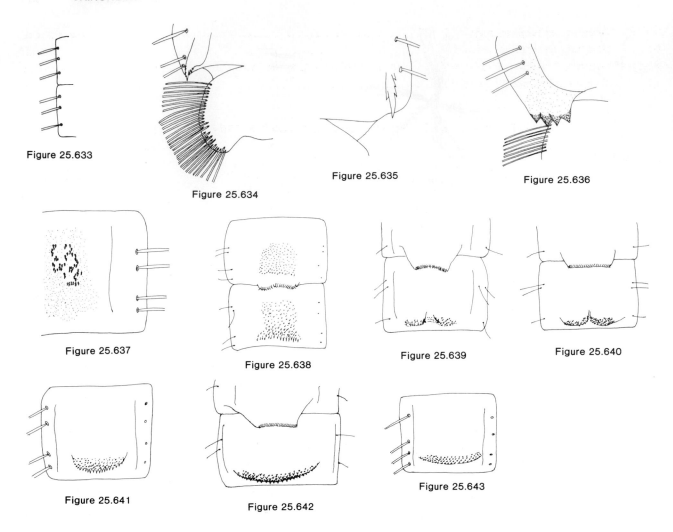

Figure 25.633

Figure 25.634

Figure 25.635

Figure 25.636

Figure 25.637

Figure 25.638

Figure 25.639

Figure 25.640

Figure 25.641

Figure 25.642

Figure 25.643

Figure 25.633. Segments 5 and 6 (left side) of *Polypedilum* sp. 4.

Figure 25.634. Anal lobe and caudolateral margin of segment 8 (left side) of *Graceus* sp.

Figure 25.635. Caudolateral margin of segment 8 (right side) of *"Nilothauma"* sp.

Figure 25.636. Caudolateral margin of segment 8 (left side) of *Stenochironomus* sp.

Figure 25.637. Segment 5 (right half) of *Xenochironomus* sp.

Figure 25.638. Segments 2 and 3 of *Saetheria* sp.

Figure 25.639. Posterior margin of segment 2 and segment 3 of *Paracladopelma* sp. 2.

Figure 25.640. Posterior margin of segment 2 and segment 3 of *Paracladopelma* sp. 3.

Figure 25.641. Segment 6 of *Paracladopelma* sp. 3.

Figure 25.642. Posterior margin of segment 2 and segment 3 of Genus 20.

Figure 25.643. Segment 6 of Genus 20.

81(73'). Shagreen on terga as in figure 25.637 .... *Xenochironomus* (in part)
81'.   Shagreen on terga not as above 82
82(81'). Sternum 2, at least, with rows of needlelike spines similar to figure 25.600 .... **Robackia**
82'.   Sterna without needlelike spines .... **Parachironomus**

KEY TO SUBFAMILIES AND TRIBES OF FRESHWATER CHIRONOMIDAE ADULTS[*]

(Males Only)

1.   Wing with crossvein M—Cu present (figs. 25.645, 25.647, 25.654–25.655) 2
1'.   Wing with crossvein M—Cu absent (figs. 25.644, 25.646, 25.665–25.668) 12
2(1).   Wing vein R_{2+3} present (figs. 25.645–25.646, 25.648, 25.654–25.655) 3
2'.   Wing vein R_{2+3} absent (fig. 25.647) .... Podonominae 11
3(2).   Vein R_{2+3} forked (figs. 25.648, 25.654–25.655) .... Tanypodinae 4
3'.   Vein R_{2+3} simple (fig. 25.645) .... Diamesinae 8
4(3).   A double comb present on distal end of tibia 3 (3rd, or hind leg) (fig. 25.649); 4th tarsal segment cordiform (heart-shaped) (fig. 25.650) .... **Coelotanypodini**
4'.   A single comb (or none) on distal end of tibia 3 (fig. 25.651); 4th tarsal segment cylindrical (fig. 25.652) 5
5(4').   Fork of Cu (fCu) sessile (figs. 25.653–25.654) 6
5'.   Fork of Cu (fCu) petiolate (stalked) (figs. 25.648, 25.655) 7
6(5).   Costa (anterior marginal wing vein) produced beyond R_{4+5} by about twice the length of R—M (fig. 25.654) .... **Macropelopiini** (in part)
6'.   Costa not or only slightly produced beyond R_{4+5} (fig. 25.648) .... **Pentaneurini**
7(5').   Petiole of cubital fork short, one-third or less the length of Cu_2 (fig. 25.648) .... **Tanypodini**
7'.   Petiole of cubital fork long, one-half or more the length of Cu_2 (fig. 25.655) .... **Macropelopiini** (in part)
8(3').   Gonostylus of genitalia narrow, simple, and attached mesally at the base of the distal third of gonocoxite (fig. 25.656) .... **Protanypini**
8'.   Gonostylus attached at the distal end of the gonocoxite (figs. 25.657–25.659) 9
9(8').   Gonostylus very short and robust (fig. 25.657) .... **Boreoheptagyini**
9'.   Gonostylus usually longer and more narrow (figs. 25.658–25.659) 10
10(9').   Gonostylus with a large dorsobasal appendage (fig. 25.658) .... **Prodiamesini** (in part)
10'.   Gonostylus simple (fig. 25.659) .... **Diamesini**
                                                                               Prodiamesini (in part)
11(2').   Gonostylus with 2 lobes (fig. 25.660) .... **Podonomini**
11'.   Gonostylus simple (figs. 25.661–25.662) .... **Boreochlini**
12(1').   Gonostylus rigidly directed backwards (somewhat flexible in one genus) (fig. 25.663) .... Chironominae 13
12'.   Gonostylus movable, often flexed inwardly toward the midline (fig. 25.664) .... Orthocladiinae 14
13(12).   Wing surface with macrotrichia (small hairs), especially near the apex; squama without a fringe of hairs; crossvein R—M almost parallel to the long axis of the wing (fig. 25.646) .... **Tanytarsini**
13'.   Wing surface with or without macrotrichia; when macrotrichia are present, squama with a fringe of hairs; crossvein R—M sharply oblique to the long axis of the wing (fig. 25.665) .... **Chironomini**
14(12'). Cu_2 straight or weakly curved; squama usually with a well-developed hair fringe (fig. 25.666) .... **"Orthocladiini"**
14'. Cu_2 usually somewhat strongly curved; hair fringe on squama usually reduced, often absent (fig. 25.667); if Cu_2 is straight, then wing as in fig. 25.668 15
15(14'). Vein R_{4+5} visible (fig. 25.667) .... **"Metriocnemini"**
15'.   Vein R_{4+5} completely fused with the thickened costa (fig. 25.668) .... **"Corynoneurini"**

[*]Couplets 4–7 modified from Roback (1971); couplets 14 and 15 modified from Brundin (1956).

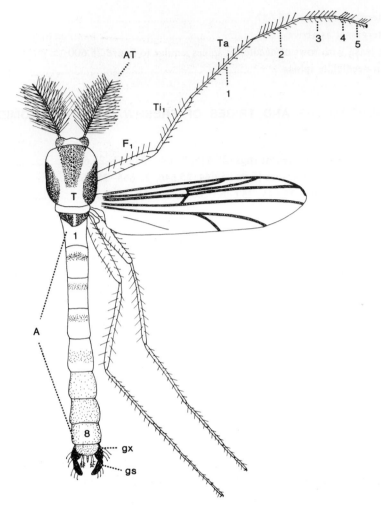

Figure 25.644

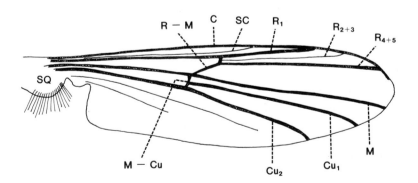

Figure 25.645

Figure 25.644. Adult chironomid male (Chironomini) in dorsal view: AT, antenna; T, thorax; A, abdominal tergites 1–8; gx, gonocoxite of male genitalia; gs, gonostylus of male genitalia; F₁, femur of foreleg; Ti₁, tibia of foreleg; Ta₁₋₅, tarsal segments of foreleg.

Figure 25.645. Diamesini wing: SQ, squama; R–M, radial-medial crossvein; C, costa; SC, subcosta: R₁, first radial; R₂₊₃, second and third radials; R₄₊₅, fourth and fifth radials; M, medius; Cu₁, first cubital; Cu₂, second cubital; M–Cu, medial-cubital crossvein.

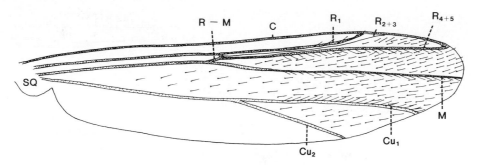

Figure 25.646

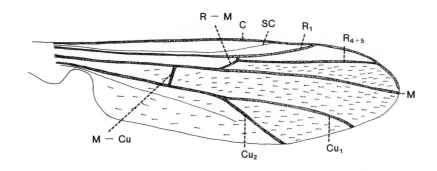

Figure 25.647

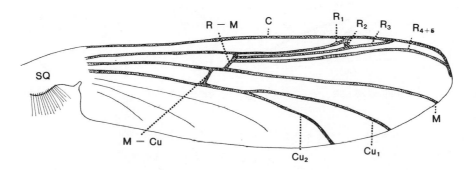

Figure 25.648

Figure 25.647. Boreochlini wing (abbreviations as in Fig. 25.645; after Goetghebuer 1939).

Figure 25.648. Tanypodini wing (abbreviations as in Fig. 25.645).

Figure 25.646. Tanytarsini wing (abbreviations as in Fig. 25.645).

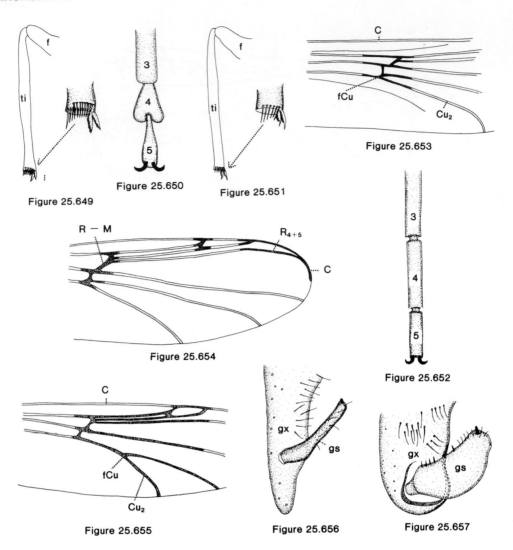

Figure 25.649

Figure 25.650

Figure 25.651

Figure 25.653

Figure 25.654

Figure 25.652

Figure 25.655

Figure 25.656

Figure 25.657

Figure 25.649. Third tibia of a Coelotanypodini adult (after Roback 1971). ti, tibia; f, femur.

Figure 25.650. Terminal tarsal segments of a Coelotanypodini adult (tarsal segments numbered).

Figure 25.651. Third tibia of a Pentaneurini adult (after Roback 1971): ti, tibia; f, femur.

Figure 25.652. Terminal tarsal segments of a Pentaneurini adult (tarsal segments numbered).

Figure 25.653. Central portion of a Pentaneurini wing: fCu, fork of cubitus; other abbreviations as in Figure 25.645.

Figure 25.654. Macropelopiini *(Natarsia)* wing (abbreviations as in Fig. 25.645).

Figure Figure 25.655. Central portion of a Macropelopiini *(Procladius)* wing (abbreviations as in Figs. 25.645, 25.653).

Figure 25.656. Dorsal view of left gonocoxite and gonostylus of a male Protanypini (after Saether 1975): gx, gonocoxite; gs, gonostylus.

Figure 25.657. Dorsal view of left gonocoxite and gonostylus of a male Boreoheptagyini (after Brundin 1966).

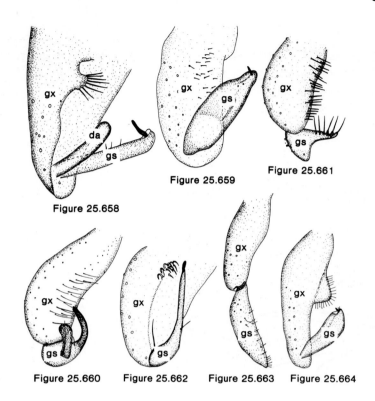

Figure 25.658

Figure 25.659

Figure 25.661

Figure 25.660 Figure 25.662 Figure 25.663 Figure 25.664

Figure 25.658. Dorsal view of left gonocoxite and gonostylus of a male Prodiamesini (*Prodiamesa* only).

Figure 25.659. Dorsal view of left gonocoxite and gonostylus of a male Diamesini.

Figure 25.660. Dorsal view of left gonocoxite and gonostylus of a male Podonomini (*Parochlus,* the only genus known from North America) (after Brundin 1966).

Figure 25.661. Dorsal view of left gonocoxite and gonostylus of a male Boreochlini.

Figure 25.662. Dorsal view of left gonocoxite and gonostylus of a male Boreochlini (after Brundin 1966).

Figure 25.663. Dorsal view of left gonocoxite and gonostylus of a male Chironomini.

Figure 25.664. Dorsal view of left gonocoxite and gonostylus of a male "Orthocladiini."

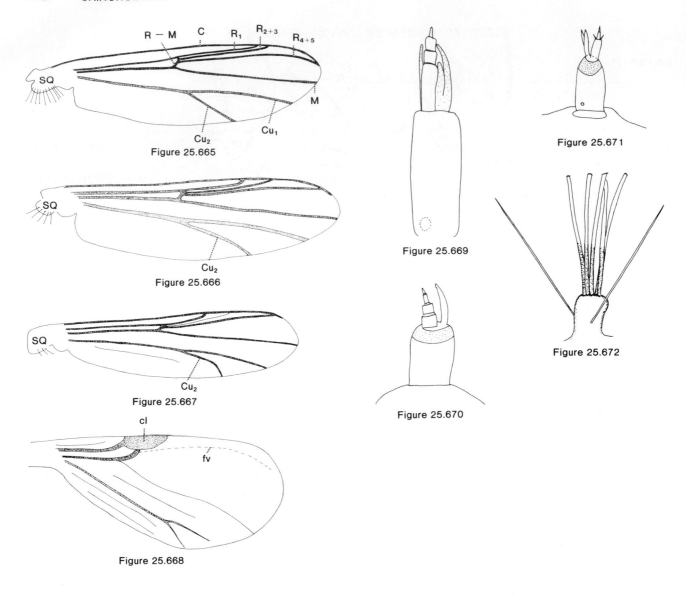

Figure 25.665

Figure 25.666

Figure 25.667

Figure 25.668

Figure 25.669

Figure 25.670

Figure 25.671

Figure 25.672

Figure 25.665. Chironomini wing (abbreviations as in Fig. 25.645).

Figure 25.666. "Orthocladiini" wing (abbreviations as in Fig. 25.645).

Figure 25.667. "Metriocnemini" wing (abbreviations as in Fig. 25.645).

Figure 25.668. "Corynoneurini" wing. Cl, clavus; fv, false vein.

Figure 25.669. Five-segmented antenna of larva of *Halocladius* sp. ("Orthocladiini") (redrawn from Hirvenoja [1973]).

Figure 25.670. Five-segmented antenna of larve of *Tethymyia* sp. (Clunionini) (redrawn from Wirth [1949]).

Figure 25.671. Four-segmented antenna of larva of *Thalassomya* sp. (Telmatogetoninae) (redrawn from Wirth [1947]).

Figure 25.672. Preanal papilla of larva of *Halocladius* sp. ("Orthocladiini") (redrawn from Hirvenoja [1973]).

KEYS TO TRIBES OF MARINE CHIRONOMIDAE*

Larvae (Marine)

1. Larval head with a ventral median mentum (labial plate), and striate ventromental plates (figs. 25.1, 25.3) .... Chironominae (go to freshwater key)

1'. Larval head with a distinct mentum, but never with striate ventromental plates 2

2(1'). Larval antenna with 5 segments (figs. 25.669–25.670) 3

2'. Larval antenna with 4 segments (fig. 25.671) .... Telmatogetoninae

3(2). Preanal papillae present, but short, with 5–6 terminal setae and 1–2 lateral setae (fig. 25.672) .... Orthocladiinae—*"Orthocladiini"* (in part) *(Halocladius)*

3'. Preanal papillae absent, replaced by 1–3 short setae or a single long seta (fig. 25.673) 4

4(3'). Preanal papillae replaced by 1–3 short setae .... Orthocladiinae (in part) .... (*Thalassosmittia,* tribe uncertain)

4'. Preanal papillae replaced by a single (may be branched) stout, long seta (fig. 25.673) .... Orthocladiinae—*Clunionini*

Pupae (Marine)

1. Anal lobes with at least a partial fringe of long hairs along edge (e.g., fig. 25.558); thoracic horn multibranched (figs. 25.618, 25.632) or simple (figs. 25.525, 25.530); a sclerotized spine or comb of spines usually present on caudolateral edges of segment 8 (figs. 25.560, 25.565, 25.616); surface of anal lobes in same plane as abdomen .... Chironominae (go to freshwater key)

1'. Anal lobes with or without a fringe of hairs, when hairs present, they are short and the surface of the anal lobe is in a plane oblique to that of the abdomen (fig. 25.674); thoracic horn, when present, always simple; no spines on caudolateral edges of segment 8 2

2(1'). Thorax with a thoracic horn; anal lobes with or without a fringe of hairs, in either case, the surface is oblique to the plane of the abdomen (fig. 25.674) .... Telmatogetoninae

2'. Thorax without a thoracic horn; anal lobes never with a fringe of hairs; surface of lobes in same plane as abdomen 3

3(2'). Anal lobes each with 3 terminal (or subterminal) setae (fig. 25.675) .... Orthocladiinae—*"Orthocladiini"* (in part) *(Halocladius)*

3'. Anal lobes without terminal setae, but there may be 1–2 spinelike projections from the margin (fig. 25.676) 4

4(3'). Dorsal surfaces of segments 2–7 (at least) heavily and somewhat uniformly shagreened (rough-surfaced) (fig. 25.676) 5

4'. Dorsal surfaces of segments 2–7 not heavily and uniformly shagreened, at most with anterior and posterior transverse rows of spines or hooks on some segments .... Orthocladiinae—*Clunionini* (in part) *(Clunio)*

5. Segment 8 with only very fine dorsal shagreen; caudolateral corners of segment 9 (anal lobe) with 2 small, closely set spines .... Orthocladiinae—*Clunionini* (in part) *(Tethymyia)*

5'. Segment 8 with heavy dorsal shagreen (as heavy as on segments 2–7) (fig. 25.676); caudolateral corners of anal lobes with an elongated spinelike projection, another located at base of distal third of the anal lobe .... Orthocladiinae (in part) (*Thalassosmittia,* tribe uncertain)

---

*The first couplet in each of the life stage keys separates the Chironominae, which has many brackish water species, from the truly marine forms. The genus *Halocladius* (Orthocladiinae: "Orthocladiini") is also known to occur in saline inland waters.

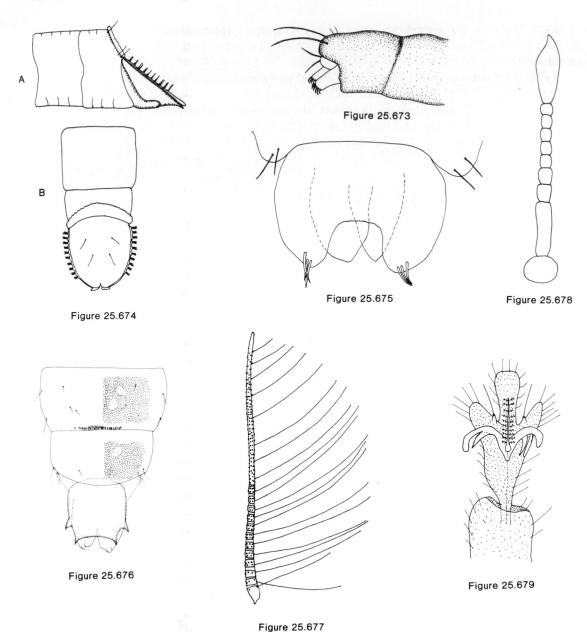

Figure 25.674

Figure 25.673

Figure 25.675

Figure 25.678

Figure 25.676

Figure 25.677

Figure 25.679

Figure 25.673. Caudal segments of larva of *Clunio* sp. (Clunionini) (redrawn from Lenz [1950]).

Figure 25.674. *A.* Lateral view of terminal abdominal segments of pupa of *Thalassomya* sp. (Telmatogetoninae). *B.* Dorsal view of same. Both redrawn from Wirth (1947).

Figure 25.675. Dorsal view of caudal lobes of pupa of *Halocladius* sp. ("Orthocladiini").

Figure 25.676. Dorsal view of segments 7 and 8 and caudal lobes of pupa of *Thalassosmittia* sp. (Orthocladiinae).

Figure 25.677. Adult male antenna of *Cricotopus* sp. (very similar to *Halocladius*); basal segment not included; only a few of the plume hairs drawn.

Figure 25.678. Adult male antenna of *Clunio* sp. (Clunionini); basal segment not included (redrawn from Goetghebuer [1950]).

Figure 25.679. Ventral view of trilobed fifth tarsal segment of *Telmatogeton* sp. (Telmatogetoninae) (redrawn from Wirth [1949]).

Adults (Marine)

1.   Antenna of male with 11–13 flagellomeres, the terminal one longer, or nearly as long, as all other segments combined (e.g., fig. 25.677); all tarsal segments cylindrical (fig. 25.652); gonostylus of male directed rigidly backward from gonocoxite (fig. 25.663; compare this to fig. 25.664) .... Chironominae (go to freshwater key)

1'.   Not with above combination of characters 2

2(1').   Antenna of male with 14 flagellomeres, the terminal one nearly as long as segments 1–13 combined (fig. 25.677); all tarsal segments cylindrical (fig. 25.652); gonostylus of male directed medially and anteriorly (fig. 25.664) ....Orthocladiinae—*"Orthocladiini"* (in part) *(Halocladius)*

2'.   Antenna of male with 6–13 flagellomeres, the terminal one never longer than combined lengths of the preceding 4 (fig. 25.678); 4th tarsal segment often cordiform (heart-shaped) (fig. 25.650); 5th tarsal segment often trilobed at apex (fig. 25.679) 3

3(2').   Antenna of male with 8, 12, or 13 flagellomeres; all tarsal segments cylindrical (fig. 25.652) .... Orthocladiinae (in part) *(Thalassosmittia,* tribe uncertain)

3'.   Antenna of male with 6, 7, or 11 flagellomeres (e.g., fig. 25.678); 4th tarsal segment often cordiform (fig. 25.650); 5th tarsal segment often trilobed at apex (fig. 25.679) 4

4(3').   Fourth and 5th tarsal segments cylindrical (fig. 25.652) .... Orthocladiinae—*Clunionini*

4'.   Either 4th tarsal segment cordiform (fig. 25.650), or 5th tarsal segment trilobed at apex (fig. 25.679) .... Telmatogetoninae

ADDITIONAL TAXONOMIC REFERENCES*

General
Johannsen (1905, 1937); Goetghebuer and Lenz (1936–1950); Townes (1945); Sublette and Sublette (1965); Frommer (1967); Hamilton *et al.* (1969); Bryce and Hobart (1972); Mason (1973); Fittkau *et al.* (1976); Hashimoto (1976); Pinder (1978); Saether (1979, 1980); Murray (1980); Hoffrichter and Reiss (1981); Oliver (1981); Simpson (1982); Wilson and Mcgill (1982).

Regional faunas
California: Sublette (1960, 1964b).
Canada: Oliver *et. al.* (1978).
Carolinas: Webb and Brigham (1982).
Connecticut: Johannsen and Townes (1952).
Eastern United States: Roback (1976, 1977; ref. #2841, 1978; ref. #2842, 1980; ref. #2843, 1981; ref #2844).
Florida: Beck and Beck (1966, 1969).

Kansas: Ferrington (1981; ref. #2829, 1982; ref. #2830, 1983a; ref. #2831, 1983b; ref. #2832)
Louisiana: Sublette (1964a).
New York: Johannsen (1905); Simpson and Bode (1980).
Pennsylvania (Philadelphia area): Roback (1957).
Southeastern United States: Beck (1968, 1975).

Taxonomic treatments at the subfamily, tribe, and generic levels (L=larvae; P=pupae; A=adults)
Clunionini: Wirth (1949)–A; Goetghebuer and Lenz (1950)–A; Lenz (1950)–L, A.
Diamesinae: Saether (1969) L, P, A; Hansen and Cook (1976)–A.
Orthocladiinae: Brundin (1956)–L, P, A; Cranston (1982)–L; Saether (1969)–L, P, A; Hirvenoja (1973)–L, P, A; Soponis (1977)–L, P, A.
Podonominae: Brundin (1966)–L, P, A; Saether (1969)–L, P, A.
Tanypodinae: Goetghebuer and Lenz (1939)–A; Fittkau (1962)–P, A; Roback (1971)–A.
Telmatogetoninae: Wirth (1947)–A.

*This is a very limited list and includes only publications of general interest and those specifically treating the Nearctic fauna.

Table 25A. Summary of ecological and distributional data for *Chironomidae (Diptera)*. (For definition of terms see Tables 6A–6C; table prepared by K. W. Cummins and W. P. Coffman.)

Taxa* (number of species in parentheses)†	Habitat	Habit	Trophic Relationships	North American Distribution	Ecological References‡
Chironomidae(~1000) (=Tendipedidae) (midges)	Essentially all types of aquatic habitats, including marine, springs, tree holes	Generally burrowers (most are tube builders)	Generally of two types: (1) collectors—gatherers and filterers. (2) Predators (engulfers and piercers)	Widespread	1241, 1242, 1538, 1837, 1886, 2060, 2617, 2747
Telmatogetoninae(4)	Generally marine (tidal pools, salt marshes, estuaries)			East and West Coasts	
Telmatogeton(1)	Beach zone—marine (rocks of intertidal)	Clingers (tube builders)	Scrapers, shredders—herbivores (chewers—macroalgae), collectors—gatherers	West Coast, Southeast Coast	391, 1795, 2162, 2747
Thalassomya(1)	Marine		Collectors—gatherers, scrapers	Florida Coast	1795, 2747
Paraclunio(2)	Beach zone—marine (rocks of intertidal)	Clingers (tube builders)	Collectors—gatherers, shredders—herbivores (chewers—macroalgae), scrapers	West Coast	1708, 1795, 2077
Tanypodinae(~140) (=Pelopiinae)	All types of lentic and lotic habitats	Generally sprawlers—swimmers (very active predators, not tube builders)	Generally predators (engulfers and piercers)	Widespread	1241, 1837, 1886, 2747
Coelotanypodini(9)	Generally lentic—littoral	Generally burrowers	Generally predators (engulfers)	Eastern United States, Canada south to California	
Clinotanypus(4)	Lentic—littoral, lotic—depositional	Burrowers	Predators (engulfers; Oligochaeta, Ostracoda, Chironomidae)	Eastern United States, Canada south to California	780, 1719, 2062
Coelotanypus(5)	Lentic—littoral	Burrowers	Predators, (engulfers; Oligochaeta, Cladocera, Chironomidae)	East	1719, 2062
Macropelopiini(~55)			Generally predators (engulfers and piercers)	Widespread	2058
Alotanypus(3)	Lotic	Burrowers—sprawlers		Widespread (especially North)	
Apsectrotanypus(2)	Lotic	Burrowers—sprawlers	Predators (engulfers; Chironomidae)	Widespread	2058
Brundiniella(2)	Lotic	Burrowers—sprawlers	Predators, (engulfers; Protozoa, Cladocera, Ostracoda, Tardigrada, Hydracarina, Chironomidae)	Widespread	2058
Djalmabatista(A)	Lotic	Sprawlers	Predators (engulfers)	Eastern United States	2058
Macropelopia(A)	Lotic—erosional, lentic—littoral	Sprawlers	Protozoa, Cladocera, Ostracoda, Crustacea, Ceratopogonidae, Chironomidae)	North	2058
Parapelopia(1)				South	

*The North American chironomid fauna includes many undescribed species and genera, especially in the subfamilies Orthocladiinae and Chironominae. New taxa are to be expected from unusual habitats and from areas of North America that have been poorly collected.
†Where available data permit, a numerical estimate of the number of described and/or known but undescribed species of a genus has been made. In other genera (most), the number of species per genus has been estimated in terms of probable range: A = 1–5 species; B = 6–19 species; C = 20 or more species. The range for any genus was derived by a subjective process based on known North American and European diversities and material in the collection of W. P. Coffman. The actual number of North American chironomid species may be more than twice the total number given here.
‡Emphasis on trophic relationships.

able 25A.—*Continued*

Taxa' (number of species in parentheses)†	Habitat	Habit	Trophic Relationships	North American Distribution	Ecological References‡
Procladius(31)	Lentic—profundal (some littoral), lotic—depositional	Sprawlers	Predators (engulfers; Protozoa, microcrustacea, Ephemeroptera, Ceratopogonidae, Gastrotricha), collectors—gatherers (winter and early instars)	Widespread (especially North)	68, 85, 120, 197, 388, 419, 421, 491, 511, 523, 711, 780, 1268, 1269, 1273, 1466, 1515, 1683, 1699, 1704, 1719, 1949, 2062, 2437, 2444, 2458, 2747
Psectrotanypus(7)	Lotic—depositional	Sprawlers	Protozoa, Cladocera, Ostracoda, Crustacea, Trichoptera, Chironomidae)	Widespread	523, 2058, 2062
Natarsiini(2)					
Natarsia(2)	Lotic—erosional	Sprawlers	Predators (engulfers; Cladocera, Ostracoda, Copepoda, Ceratopogonidae)	Widespread	419
entaneurini(70)	Generally lotic—erosional and lentic—littoral	Generally sprawlers	Generally predators (engulfers and piercers)	Widespread	
Ablabesmyia(12)	Lentic—littoral, lotic—erosional and depositional	Sprawlers	Predators (engulfers and piercers) (Rotifera, microcrustacea, Chironomidae), collectors—gatherers (early instars)	Widespread	68, 388, 511, 1515, 1683, 2062
Arctopelopia(1)	Lotic—erosional, lentic—littoral	Sprawlers	Predators (engulfers)	Rocky Mountains	
Cantopelopia(1)				North (East only?)	
Conchapelopia(14)	Lotic—erosional, lentic—littoral	Sprawlers	Predators (engulfers and piercers) (Chironomidae, Trichoptera, Ephemeroptera)	Widespread	
Guttipelopia(2)	Lentic—littoral	Sprawlers	Predators (engulfers)	Widespread	
Hudsonimyia(2)	Lotic—erosional (hygropetric)	Sprawlers		East	
Krenopelopia(1)	Lotic—erosional	Sprawlers	Predators (engulfers)	Primarily North	
Labrundinia(6)	Lotic—erosional, lentic—littoral	Sprawlers	Predators (engulfers and piercers, Oligochaeta, Cladocera, Ostracoda)	Widespread	2062
Larsia(6)	Lotic—erosional, lentic—littoral	Sprawlers	Predators (engulfers)	Widespread	
Monopelopia(2)	Lentic—littoral, lotic?	Sprawlers	Predators (engulfers)	Widespread	
Nilotanypus(2)	Lotic—erosional	Sprawlers		Widespread	
Paramerina(5)	Lotic—erosional	Sprawlers		Widespread	
Pentaneura(2)	Lentic—littoral (vascular hydrophytes and detritus), lotic—erosional and depositional	Sprawlers	Predators (engulfers and piercers, Chironomidae), collectors—gatherers (diatoms and detritus)	Eastern North America (especially Southeast)	68, 388, 419, 511, 780, 1704, 2062
Rheopelopia(3)	Lotic—erosional	Sprawlers	Predators (engulfers and piercers)	Widespread	

The North American chironomid fauna includes many undescribed species and genera, especially in the subfamilies Orthocladiinae and Chironominae. New
xa are to be expected from unusual habitats and from areas of North America that have been poorly collected.
Where available data permit, a numerical estimate of the number of described and/or known but undescribed species of a genus has been made. In other
nera (most), the number of species per genus has been estimated in terms of probable range: A = 1–5 species; B = 6–19 species; C = 20 or more species.
e range for any genus was derived by a subjective process based on known North American and European diversities and material in the collection of W. P.
offman. The actual number of North American chironomid species may be more than twice the total number given here.
mphasis on trophic relationships.

Table 25A.—*Continued*

Taxa* (number of species in parentheses)†	Habitat	Habit	Trophic Relationships	North American Distribution	Ecological References‡
Telopelopia(1)	Lotic-erosional (sandy bottom rivers)		Predators (engulfers and piercers	Midwest	
Thienemannimyia(5)	Lotic—erosional, lentic—littoral	Sprawlers	Predators (engulfers and piercers, Protozoa, Cladocera, Ostracoda, Chironomidae)	Widespread	419, 421, 1281, 2062
Trissopelopia(1)	Lotic—erosional, lentic—littoral	Sprawlers	Predators (engulfers)	Primarily North	
Xenopelopia(1)				California	
Zavrelimyia(3)	Lotic—erosional, lentic—littoral	Sprawlers	Predators (engulfers and piercers, Oligochaeta, Ostracoda, Chironomidae)	Widespread	2062
Tanypodini(11)			Generally predators (engulfers and piercers)	Widespread	
Tanypus(11) (=Pelopia)	Lentic—littoral	Sprawlers	Predators (engulfers and piercers), collectors—gatherers (diatoms, filamentous green algae, detritus)	Widespread	68, 86, 420, 523, 711, 1268, 1269, 1273, 1429, 1466, 2061, 2407, 2444
Podonominae(~14)	Generally lotic—erosional and depositional and lentic (at high altitudes and latitudes)	Generally burrowers (tube builders)		Primarily North	2747
Boreochlini(13)	Generally lotic—erosional, lentic—littoral	Generally sprawlers	Generally collectors—gatherers, scrapers		2747
Boreochlus(3)	Lotic—erosional	Sprawlers	Collectors—gatherers, scrapers	North	
Lasiodiamesa(4)	Lentic—littoral (including bogs)	Sprawlers	Collectors—gatherers, scrapers	North	
Paraboreochlus(1)	Lotic—erosional	Sprawlers	Collectors—gatherers, scrapers	Appalachians	
Trichotanypus(5)	Lotic—erosional	Sprawlers	Collectors—gatherers, scrapers	North	
Podonomini *Parochlus*(1)	Lotic—erosional	Sprawlers	Collectors—gatherers, scrapers	Primarily North	
Diamesinae(~50)	Generally lotic—erosional and depositional (cold streams), lentic—erosional (oligotrophic lakes)	Generally—clingers and some burrowers (tube builders)	Generally collectors—gatherers, scrapers	Primarily North	1241, 1837, 1886, 2747
Boreoheptagyini(1) *Boreoheptagyia*(1)	Lotic—erosional (cold, fast streams)	Sprawlers—clingers	Collectors—gatherers, scrapers?	North and mountains	
Diamesini(~45)					912, 1281, 1282, 1616, 2747
Diamesa(30)	Lotic—erosional	Sprawlers	Collectors—gatherers, scrapers?	Widespread (in uplands and mountains)	
Pagastia(3)				North	
Potthastia(A)	Lotic—erosional	Sprawlers	Collectors—gatherers, scrapers	Widespread	

*The North American chironomid fauna includes many undescribed species and genera, especially in the subfamilies Orthocladiinae and Chironominae. New taxa are to be expected from unusual habitats and from areas of North America that have been poorly collected.
†Where available data permit, a numerical estimate of the number of described and/or known but undescribed species of a genus has been made. In other genera (most), the number of species per genus has been estimated in terms of probable range: A = 1–5 species; B = 6–19 species; C = 20 or more species. The range for any genus was derived by a subjective process based on known North American and European diversities and material in the collection of W. P. Coffman. The actual number of North American chironomid species may be more than twice the total number given here.
‡Emphasis on trophic relationships.

Table 25A.—Continued

Taxa* (number of species in parentheses)†	Habitat	Habit	Trophic Relationships	North American Distribution	Ecological References‡
Pseudodiamesa(A)	Lentic—littoral (erosional)	Sprawlers	Collectors—gatherers	Probably primarily North	519, 912
Pseudokiefferiella(A)	Lotic—erosional (small mountain springs)	Sprawlers	Collectors—gatherers?	West, North	1282
Sympotthastia(A)	Lotic—erosional	Sprawlers	Collectors—gatherers, scrapers?	Widespread	128
Syndiamesa(1)	Lotic—erosional	Sprawlers		North	
"Protanypini(5)					
Protanypus(5)	Lentic—profundal	Burrowers?	Collectors—gatherers	Widespread (primarily North)	
Prodiamesinae(~8)	Generally lotic—erosional	Generally sprawlers	Generally collectors—gatherers		
Compteromesa(1)				Southeast	
Monodiamesa(A)	Lotic—erosional	Sprawlers	Collectors—gatherers?	Widespread	
Odontomesa(A)	Lotic—erosional	Sprawlers	Collectors—gatherers?	Widespread	1683
Prodiamesa(B)	Lotic—erosional and depositional (detritus)	Burrowers—sprawlers	Collectors—gatherers	Widespread	780, 1222, 1223, 1429, 1515
Orthocladiinae(~400) (=Hydrobaeninae)	Primarily lotic, but with many lentic representatives (especially oligotrophic lakes)	Generally burrowers (tube builders)	Generally collectors—gatherers, scrapers	Widespread, particularly North	382, 419, 421, 459, 1241, 1837, 1886, 2747
Clunionini(~5)					
Clunio (A)	Beach zone—marine (rocky shore)	Clingers (sand tube builders)	Collectors—gatherers, scrapers	East and West Coasts	391, 1795, 1835, 2747
Eretmoptera(1)	Beach zone—marine (rocks of intertidal)	Clingers (tube builders)	Scrapers, shredders—herbivores (chewers—macroalgae)	West Coast	2747
Tethymyia(1)	Beach zone—marine (rocks of intertidal)	Clingers (tube builders)	Scrapers, shredders—herbivores (chewers—macroalgae)	West Coast	2747
"Corynoneurini"(~20)	Generally lotic—erosional and depositional, lentic—littoral	Generally sprawlers	Generally collectors—gatherers		
Corynoneura(B)	Lotic—depositional (aquatic hydrophytes), lentic—littoral (some instar 1 planktonic)	Sprawlers	Collectors—gatherers	Widespread	419, 421, 511, 515, 1515, 2059
Thienemanniella(B)	Lotic—erosional and depositional, lentic—littoral	Sprawlers	Collectors—gatherers	Widespread	419, 421
"Orthocladiini" and "Metriocnemini"§ (~300)	Wide range of lotic and lentic habitats	Wide range of habits	Generally collectors, but other functional groups also		
Abiskomyia(1)	Lentic			Far North	
Acamptocladius(A)	Lentic—littoral	in colonial algae	Collectors—gatherers (chewers—macroalgae)	North	2846
Acricotopus(A)	Lotic—erosional, lentic—littoral	Sprawlers		North	

*The North American chironomid fauna includes many undescribed species and genera, especially in the subfamilies Orthocladiinae and Chironominae. New taxa are to be expected from unusual habitats and from areas of North America that have been poorly collected.

†Where available data permit, a numerical estimate of the number of described and/or known but undescribed species of a genus has been made. In other genera (most), the number of species per genus has been estimated in terms of probable range: A = 1–5 species; B = 6–19 species; C = 20 or more species. The range for any genus was derived by a subjective process based on known North American and European diversities and material in the collection of W. P. Coffman. The actual number of North American chironomid species may be more than twice the total number given here.

‡Emphasis on trophic relationships.

§Since the relationships among genera are poorly known in the tentative tribes "Orthocladiini" and "Metriocnemini," they have not been separated.

Table 25A.— *Continued*

Taxa* (number of species in parentheses)†	Habitat	Habit	Trophic Relationships	North American Distribution	Ecological References‡
Baeoctenus(1)	Lentic—littoral			Manitoba, New Brunswick	
Brillia(B)	Lotic—erosional and depositional (detritus)	Burrowers (miners) in rotted wood, sprawlers (in detritus)	Shredders—detritivores (chewers and miners), collectors—gatherers	Widespread	419, 421, 604, 1890, 2839 ‖
Bryophaeno-cladius(A)	Lotic—erosional	Sprawlers		Widespread	
Camptocladius(A)	Terrestrial (dung)			Widespread?	
Cardiocladius(A)	Lotic—erosional	Burrowers (loose tube construction), clingers (tube makers)	Engulfers (predators of black fly larvae)	Widespread	490, 2747
Chaetocladius(B)	Lotic—erosional	Sprawlers	Collectors—gatherers	Widespread	1282
Chasmatonotus(A)					
Cricotopus(C)	Lentic—vascular hydrophytes (and algal mats, sediments, detritus), lotic—erosional and depositional (some instar 1 planktonic)	Clingers (tube builders), burrowers (miners and tube builders)	Shredders—herbivores (miners and chewers), collectors—gatherers (detritus and algae)	Widespread	86, 160, 262, 491, 511, 515, 1241, 1281, 1515, 1616, 1732, 2282, 2741, 2747
Diplocladius(A)	Lotic—erosional	Sprawlers	Collectors—gatherers?	Widespread	
Doncricotopus(1)				Northwest Territories	
Epoicocladius(A)	Lotic—erosional and depositional		Collectors—gatherers?	Widespread	
Eukiefferiella(C)	Lotic—erosional, lentic—littoral	Sprawlers	Collectors—gatherers, scrapers, predators (engulfers of chironomid eggs and larvae)	Widespread	419, 421, 542, 912, 1281, 2437
Euryhapsis(3)	Lotic			Western	
Georthocladius(A)	Lotic—erosional			Pennsylvania, North Carolina	
Gymnometrioc-nemus(A)	Semiaquatic (lentic—margins)	Sprawlers		North	
Halocladius(A)	Beach zone—marine (in *Fucus*)	Clingers (sand tube builders)	Collectors—gatherers, scrapers	Northeast Coast	1795
Heleniella(A)	Lotic—erosional	Sprawlers		North	1281
Heterotanytarsus(A)	Lotic—erosional and lentic-littoral			North	
Heterotrissocladius(B)	Lotic—erosional, lentic—littoral and profundal	Sprawlers, burrowers	Collectors, gatherers, scrapers?	Widespread	519, 1600, 1699
Hydrobaenus(B)	Lotic—erosional, lentic—littoral	Sprawlers	Scrapers, collectors—gatherers	Widespread	382, 421
Krenosmittia(A)	Lotic—erosional (hyporheic)	Sprawlers	Collectors—gatherers	Widespread	
Lapposmittia(A)				North	
Limnophyes(B)	Lentic—littoral (macroalgae), lotic—depositional	Sprawlers	Collectors—gatherers?	Widespread	1732
Lopescladius(A)	Lotic (often hyporheic)	Sprawlers	Collectors—gatherers	Widespread	

*The North American chironomid fauna includes many undescribed species and genera, especially in the subfamilies Orthocladiinae and Chironominae. New taxa are to be expected from unusual habitats and from areas of North America that have been poorly collected.

†Where available data permit, a numerical estimate of the number of described and/or known but undescribed species of a genus has been made. In other genera (most), the number of species per genus has been estimated in terms of probable range: A = 1–5 species; B = 6–19 species; C = 20 or more species. The range for any genus was derived by a subjective process based on known North American and European diversities and material in the collection of W. P. Coffman. The actual number of North American chironomid species may be more than twice the total number given here.

‡Emphasis on trophic relationships.

‖Unpublished data, R. H. King, G. M. Ward, and K. W. Cummins, Kellogg Biological Station.

able 25A.—*Continued*

Taxa* (number of species in parentheses)†	Habitat	Habit	Trophic Relationships	North American Distribution	Ecological References‡
Mesocricotopus(A)	Lotic—erosional	Sprawlers?	Collectors—gatherers	North	
Metriocnemus(B)	Lotic—erosional and depositional (detritus), lentic—littoral (oligotrophic) (2 pitcher plant species)	Burrowers, sprawlers	Collectors—gatherers, predators (engulfers)	Widespread	419, 491, 1257, 1318, 1429, 2660
Nanocladius(B)	Lotic—erosional, lentic—littoral	Sprawlers	Collectors—gatherers	Widespread	419, 421
Oliveridia(1)	Lentic			Arctic	
Oreadomyia(1)				Alberta	
Orthocladius(C)	Lentic—littoral (erosional) and profundal, lotic—erosional	Sprawlers, burrowers	Collectors—gatherers (detritus, diatoms, filamentous algae)	Widespread	419, 519, 912, 1429, 1616, 1732, 2437
Parachaetocladius(A)	Lotic—erosional	Sprawlers	Collectors—gatherers	North	
Paracladius(A)	Lentic—littoral	Sprawlers	Collectors—gatherers	Wyoming, Montana	
Paracricotopus(A)	Lotic—erosional	Sprawlers	Collectors—gatherers	Widespread	
Parakiefferiella(B)	Lotic—erosional, lentic—littoral	Sprawlers	Collectors—gatherers	Widespread	
Parametriocnemus(B)	Lotic—erosional and depositional	Sprawlers	Collectors—gatherers	Widespread	421
Paraphaenocladius(A)	Lotic—erosional and depositional	Sprawlers?	Collectors—gatherers	Primarily North	
Paratrichocladius(A)	Lotic—erosional	Sprawlers	Collectors—gatherers	Widespread	
Parorthocladius(A)	Lotic—erosional	Sprawlers	Collectors—gatherers	Widespread	
Psectrocladius(B)	Lentic—littoral, lotic—depositional	Sprawlers, burrowers	Collectors—gatherers, shredders—herbivores (macroalgae)	Widespread	419, 511, 780, 1732
Pseudorthocladius(A)	Lotic—erosional	Sprawlers	Collectors—gatherers	East	
Pseudosmittia(A)	Lotic			Widespread	
Psilometriocnemus(A)	Lotic—erosional	Sprawlers	Collectors—gatherers	Primarily North	
Rheocricotopus(B)	Lotic—erosional	Sprawlers	Collectors—gatherers, shredders—herbivores (chewers—macroalgae), predators (engulfers)	Widespread	419, 421, 1429
Rheosmittia(A)	Lotic—Sandy substrates			Widespread	
Thalassosmittia(A) (=Saunderia)	Beach zone—marine (rocks of intertidal)	Clingers (tube builders)	Scrapers, shredders—herbivores (chewers—macroalgae), collectors—gatherers	Pacific Northwest coast	1708, 1795, 2077
Smittia(B)	Semiaquatic lentic margins	Burrowers?	Collectors—gatherers	Widespread	1732
Symbiocladius(A)	Lotic—erosional	On mayfly and stonefly nymphs	Parasites	Widespread	403, 1886, 2059, 2747
Symposiocladius(A)	Lotic	Burrowers in wood	Shredder	Widespread	2828
Synorthocladius(A)			Collectors—gatherers, scrapers?		1515
Thienemannia					
Tokunagaia(A)	Lotic—erosional	Sprawlers	Collectors—gatherers	Widespread	

*The North American chironomid fauna includes many undescribed species and genera, especially in the subfamilies Orthocladiinae and Chironominae. New axa are to be expected from unusual habitats and from areas of North America that have been poorly collected.

†Where available data permit, a numerical estimate of the number of described and/or known but undescribed species of a genus has been made. In other genera (most), the number of species per genus has been estimated in terms of probable range: A = 1–5 species; B = 6–19 species; C = 20 or more species. The range for any genus was derived by a subjective process based on known North American and European diversities and material in the collection of W. P. Coffman. The actual number of North American chironomid species may be more than twice the total number given here.

‡Emphasis on trophic relationships.

Table 25A.—*Continued*

Taxa* (number of species in parentheses)†	Habitat	Habit	Trophic Relationships	North American Distribution	Ecological References‡
Trissocladius(A)	Lotic—erosional, lentic—profundal	Commensals on mayfly nymphs, burrowers	Collectors—gatherers		519
Tvetenia(B)	Lotic	Sprawlers	Collectors—gatherers	Widespread	
Xylotopus(1)	Lotic—depositional	Burrowers in wood		East	
Zalutschia(B)	Lentic—littoral, lotic			Widespread	
Chironominae(~330)	Lentic—littoral and profundal, lotic—depositional and erosional	Generally burrowers and clingers	Generally collectors—gatherers and collectors—filterers	Widespread	169, 1242, 1837, 1886, 2747
Chironomini(~205)	Generally lentic—littoral and profundal, lotic—depositional (some instar 1 planktonic)	Generally burrowers	Generally collectors—gatherers	Widespread	1837, 1886, 2747
Acalcarella(1)	Lotic—sandy areas of rivers			North (perhaps upper Midwest)	
Axarus(4)	Lotic depositional, lentic	Sprawlers, burrowers	Collectors—gatherers	Widespread	
Beckidia(1)	Lotic			West	
Chernovskiia(2)	Lotic—sandy areas of rivers			Widespread	
Chironomus(C) (=Tendipes)	Lentic—littoral and profundal, lotic—depositional	Burrowers (tube builders)	Collectors—gatherers (a few filterers), shredders—herbivores (miners)	Widespread	160, 237, 420, 491, 509, 511, 515, 711, 780, 1053, 1095, 1242, 1255, 1274, 1341, 1429, 1465, 1466, 1612, 1615, 1732, 1949, 1964, 2008, 2031, 2079, 2437, 2563, 2567, 2747
Cladopelma(B)	Lentic—littoral	Burrowers	Collectors—gatherers	Widespread	1683, 1699, 2444
Cryptochironomus(C)	Lentic—littoral and profundal, lotic—depositional	Sprawlers, burrowers	Predators (engulfers of Protozoa, microcrustacea, Chironomidae and piercers of Oligochaeta)	Widespread	68, 491, 511, 648, 1268, 1269, 1466, 1515, 1683, 1719, 1732, 2421, 2437, 2444, 2747
Cryptotendipes(B)	Lentic—littoral, lotic—depositional	Sprawlers		Widespread	
Cyphomella(4)	Lentic and lotic (sandy rivers)	Burrowers	Collectors—gatherers	Widespread	
Demicryptochironomus(A)	Lotic—depositions	Burrowers	Collectors—gatherers	Widespread	
Dicrotendipes(B) (=Limnochironomus)	Lentic—littoral (wide range of microhabitats)	Burrowers	Collectors—gatherers and filterers, scrapers?	Widespread	68, 69, 419, 421, 1515, 1699, 1732, 1949
Einfeldia(A)	Lentic—littoral and profundal	Burrowers	Collectors—gatherers	Widespread	508
Endochironomus(B)	Lentic—littoral (algal mats) and profundal (instar 1 planktonic)	Clingers (tube builders)	Shredders—herbivores (miners and chewers—macroalgae), collectors—filterers and gatherers	Widespread	509, 515, 1196, 1683, 1732, 2567
Gillotia(1)	Lotic (sandy rivers)	Burrowers	Collectors—gatherers	Midwest	

*The North American chironomid fauna includes many undescribed species and genera, especially in the subfamilies Orthocladiinae and Chironominae. New taxa are to be expected from unusual habitats and from areas of North America that have been poorly collected.

†Where available data permit, a numerical estimate of the number of described and/or known but undescribed species of a genus has been made. In other genera (most), the number of species per genus has been estimated in terms of probable range: A = 1–5 species; B = 6–19 species; C = 20 or more species. The range for any genus was derived by a subjective process based on known North American and European diversities and material in the collection of W. P. Coffman. The actual number of North American chironomid species may be more than twice the total number given here.

‡Emphasis on trophic relationships.

Table 25A. — Continued

Taxa* (number of species in parentheses)†	Habitat	Habit	Trophic Relationships	North American Distribution	Ecological References‡
Glyptotendipes(B)	Lentic—littoral and profundal, lotic—depositional (rarely) (some instar 1 planktonic)	Burrowers (miners and tube builders), clingers (net spinners)	Shredders—herbivores (miners and chewers—filamentous algae), collectors—filterers and gatherers	Widespread	160, 310, 491, 511, 515, 711, 1274, 1305, 1515, 1683, 1699, 1732, 1949, 1964, 2437, 2567
Goeldichironomus(A)	Lentic (small stagnant ponds)	Burrowers	Collectors—gatherers	Widespread	197
Graceus(A)	Lentic—littoral, lotic	Sprawlers		Northeast	
Harnischia(A)	Lentic—vascular hydrophytes (submerged zone)	Climbers—clingers	Collectors—gatherers, scrapers?	Widespread	420, 711, 1612, 1683, 1719
Hyporhygma(A)	Lentic (vascular hydrophytes)	Burrowers	Shredders (miners in stems and petioles)		
Kiefferulus(A)	Lentic	Burrowers	Collectors—gatherers	Widespread	2567, 2747
Lauterborniella(A) (=Zavreliella)	Lentic—littoral and profundal	Climbers—sprawlers—clingers, burrowers (portable sand tube builders)	Collectors—gatherers	Widespread	519
Microchironomus(1)	Lentic (sandy littoral)	Burrowers	Collector—gatherers	Widespread?	
Microtendipes(B)	Lentic—littoral, lotic—depositional	Clingers (net spinners)	Collectors—filterers and gatherers	Widespread	160, 419, 421, 1732, 1949, 2567
Nilothauma(A)	Lotic—depositional			Widespread	
Nilodorum(A)	Lentic			South	
Omisus(A)				Widespread	
Pagastiella(A)	Lentic—littoral and profundal			West	
Parachironomus(C)	Lentic—littoral	Sprawlers (some parasites in Molluska)	Predators (engulfers), collectors—gatherers, parasites	Widespread	1257, 1450, 1515, 1683, 1732, 1949
Paracladopelma(B)	Lentic—littoral, lotic—depositional	Sprawlers		Widespread	
Paralauterborniella(A) (=Apedilum)	Lentic—vascular hydrophytes	Clingers (tube builders on plants)	Collectors—gatherers	Widespread	
Paratendipes(B)	Lotic—depositional, lentic—littoral	Burrowers (tube builders)	Collectors—gatherers	Widespread	2573, 2574
Pedionomus(A)	Lentic—littoral	Burrowers	Collectors—gatherers	South?	
Phaenopsectra(B) (=Sergentia, Lenzia)	Lentic—littoral	Clingers (tube builders)	Scrapers, collectors—gatherers (and filterers?)	Widespread	419, 421, 511, 1515
Polypedilum(C)	Lentic—vascular hydrophytes (floating zone)	Climbers, clingers	Shredders—herbivores (miners), collectors—gatherers (and filterers?), predators (engulfers)	Widespread	160, 419, 421, 491, 1272, 1274, 1612, 1699, 1700, 1719, 1732, 2437, 2444, 2567, 2747
Robackia(A)	Lentic and lotic (sandy bottom)	Burrowers	Collectors—gatherers	Widespread	
Saetheria(A)	Lentic and lotic (sandy bottom)	Burrowers	Collectors—gatherers	Widespread?	2836
Stenochironomus(A)	Lentic—vascular hydrophytes, lotic—wood	Burrowers (miners)	Collectors—gatherers shredders (wood gougers)	Widespread	604, 1890, 2747

The North American chironomid fauna includes many undescribed species and genera, especially in the subfamilies Orthocladiinae and Chironominae. New taxa are to be expected from unusual habitats and from areas of North America that have been poorly collected.
†Where available data permit, a numerical estimate of the number of described and/or known but undescribed species of a genus has been made. In other genera (most), the number of species per genus has been estimated in terms of probable range: A = 1–5 species; B = 6–19 species; C = 20 or more species. The range for any genus was derived by a subjective process based on known North American and European diversities and material in the collection of W. P. Coffman. The actual number of North American chironomid species may be more than twice the total number given here.
‡Emphasis on trophic relationships.

Table 25A. — *Continued*

Taxa* (number of species in parentheses)†	Habitat	Habit	Trophic Relationships	North American Distribution	Ecological References‡
Stictochironomus(B)	Lotic—depositional (organic sediments)	Burrowers (tube makers)	Collectors—gatherers, shredders—herbivores (miners)	Widespread	491, 1306, 1683
Tribelos(A)	Lentic and lotic (depositional)	Burrowers (wood miners)	Collectors—gatherers	Widespread	
Wirthiella(A)	Lentic (small humic ponds) (ephemeral pools)	Sprawlers	Collectors—gatherers	Widespread	2834
Xenochironomus(A)	Lotic (and lentic) in sponges	Burrowers (in sponges)	Predators (engulfers of sponges)	Widespread	
Pseudochironomini(15)	Lentic and lotic—erosional (in algae) and depositional	Burrowers	Collectors—gatherers	Widespread	491, 1732
Pseudochironomus(15)	Lentic and lotic—erosional (in algae) and depositional	Burrowers	Collectors—gatherers	Widespread	491, 1732
Tanytarsini(~110) (=Calopsectrini)	Generally lotic—erosional and depositional, lentic—littoral	Generally burrowers or clingers (tube builders)	Generally collectors—filterers and gatherers	Widespread	1837, 1886, 2533, 2747
Cladotanytarsus(B)	Lentic—vascular hydrophytes, lotic—depositional		Collectors—gatherers and filterers	Widespread	68, 511, 1732, 1949
Constempellina(A)	Lotic—erosional			Widespread	
Corynocera(1)	Lentic—littoral			Wyoming (Rocky Mountains), Northwest Canada	
Lauterbornia(A)	Lentic—littoral, lotic			Northern	2837
Lenziella(A)	Lentic, lotic—sand bottom rivers			Widespread?	
Micropsectra(C)	Lentic—littoral (including brackish), lotic—depositional	Climbers, sprawlers	Collectors—gatherers	Widespread	419, 421, 511, 1281, 1616, 1732, 2567
Nimbocera(A)	Lentic			South	
Neozavrelia(A)	Lotic—erosional			Eastern United States	
Paratanytarsus(B)	Lotic—erosional, lentic—littoral	Sprawlers		Widespread	
Rheotanytarsus(B)	Lotic—erosional	Clingers (tube and net builders)	Collectors—filterers	Widespread	419, 421, 2567
Stempellina(B)	Lotic—erosional, lentic—littoral	Climbers—sprawlers—clingers (portable, mineral tube builders)	Collectors—gatherers (detritus, algae)	Widespread	68, 419, 421, 2567
Stempellinella(A)	Lotic—erosional, lentic—littoral	Sprawlers		Widespread	
Tanytarsus(C) (=Calopsectra)	Lentic—vascular hydrophytes (floating zone) and profundal, lotic—erosional (some instar 1 planktonic)	Climbers, clingers (net spinners)	Collectors—filterers and gatherers, a few scrapers	Widespread	68, 86, 160, 371, 419, 421, 491, 511, 515, 780, 1274, 1429, 1465, 1612, 1616, 1699, 1732, 1949, 2567
Thienemanniola(A)					
Zavrelia(A)	Lotic	Climbers—sprawlers—clingers (portable, mineral tube builders)	Collectors—gatherers	Widespread	382, 419, 421, 2567

*The North American chironomid fauna includes many undescribed species and genera, especially in the subfamilies Orthocladiinae and Chironominae. New taxa are to be expected from unusual habitats and from areas of North America that have been poorly collected.

†Where available data permit, a numerical estimate of the number of described and/or known but undescribed species of a genus has been made. In other genera (most), the number of species per genus has been estimated in terms of probable range: A = 1–5 species; B = 6–19 species; C = 20 or more species. The range for any genus was derived by a subjective process based on known North American and European diversities and material in the collection of W. P. Coffman. The actual number of North American chironomid species may be more than twice the total number given here.

‡Emphasis on trophic relationships.

Bibliography

1. Abdelnur, O. M. 1968. The biology of some black flies (Diptera: Simuliidae) of Alberta. Quaest. Ent. 4:113–174.
2. Aiken, R. B. 1979. A size selective underwater light trap. Hydrobiologia 65:65–68.
3. Ainslie, G. G., and W. B. Cartwright. 1922. Biology of the lotus borer Pyrausta penitalis Grote). U.S. Dept. Agric. Tech. Bull. 1076:1–14.
4. Akov, S. 1961. A qualitative and quantitative study of the nutritional requirements of Aedes aegyptii L. larvae. J. Insect Physiol. 8:319–335.
5. Akre, B. G., and D. M. Johnson. 1979. Switching and sigmoid functional response curves by damselfly naiads with alternative prey available. J. Anim. Ecol. 48:703–720.
6. Albrecht, M. L. 1959. Die quantitative Untersuchung der Bodenfauna fliessender Gewässer, (Untersuchchungsmethoden und Arbeitsergebnisse). Z. Fisch. 8:481–550.
7. Aldrich, J. M. 1912. The biology of some western species of the dipterous genus Ephydra. J. N.Y. Ent. Soc. 20:77–99.
8. Aldrich, J. M. 1916. Sarcophaga and allies in North America. Thomas Say Found. Ent. Soc. Am. 1:1–302.
9. Alekseev, N. K. 1965. Plankton feeding of Chironomidae during larval stage. Nauch. Dok. Vysshei Shkolz. Biol. Nauk. 1:19–21.
10. Alexander, C. P. 1919. The crane flies of New York. Part I. Distribution and taxonomy of the adult flies. Mem. Cornell Univ. Agric. Exp. Sta. 25:765–993.
11. Alexander, C. P. 1920. The crane flies of New York. Part II. Biology and plylogeny. Mem. Cornell Univ. Agric. Exp. Sta. 38:691–1133.
12. Alexander, C. P. 1927. The interpretation of the radial field of the wing in the nematocerous Diptera, with special reference to the Tipulidae. Proc. Linn. Soc. N.S.W. 52:42–72.
13. Alexander, C. P. 1930. Observations on the dipterous family Tanyderidae. Proc. Linn. Soc. N.S.W. 44:221–230.
14. Alexander, C. P. 1931. Deutsche limnologische Sunda-Expedition. The crane flies (Tipulidae, Diptera). Arch. Hydrobiol. Suppl. 9, Tropische Binnengewasser 2:135–191.
15. Alexander, C. P. 1934. Family Tipulidae—the crane flies. pp. 33–58. In C. H. Curran. The families and genera of North American Diptera. Ballou, N.Y. 512 pp.
16. Alexander, C. P. 1942. Family Tipulidae. Guide to the insects of Connecticut. VI. The Diptera or true flies of Connecticut. Fasc. 1. Bull. Conn. State Geol. Nat. Hist. Surv. 64:196–485.
17. Alexander, C. P. 1949. Records and descriptions of North American craneflies (Diptera). Part VIII. The Tipuloidea of Washington, I. Am. Midl. Nat. 42:257–333.
18. Alexander, C. P. 1954. Records and descriptions of North American craneflies (Diptera). Part IX. The Tipuloidea of Oregon, I. Am. Midl. Nat. 51:1–86.
19. Alexander, C. P. 1958. Geographical distribution of the net-winged midges. Proc. 10th Int. Congr. Ent. 1:813–828.
20. Alexander, C. P. 1963. Family Deuterophlebiidae. Guide to the insects of Connecticut. VI. The Diptera or true flies of Connecticut. Fasc. 8. Bull. Conn. State Geol. Nat. Hist. Surv. 93:73–83.
21. Alexander, C. P. 1965. Family Tipulidae, pp. 16–90. In A. Stone, C. W. Sabrosky, W. W. Wirth, R. H. Foote, and J. R. Coulson (eds.). A Catalog of the Diptera of America north of Mexico. U.S. Dept. Agric. Handbk. 276.Washington, D.C. 1696 pp.
22. Alexander, C. P. 1967. The crane flies of California. Bull. Calif. Insect Surv. 8:1–269.
23. Alexander, C. P. 1981a. Chap. 22. Ptychopteridae, pp. 325–328. In J. F. McAlpine, B. V. Peterson, G. E. Shewell, H. J. Teskey, J. R. Vockeroth, and D. M. Wood (coords.). Manual of Nearctic Diptera, Vol. 1. Res. Branch, Agric. Can. Monogr. 27. Ottawa. 674 pp.
24. Alexander, C. P. 1981b. Chap. 6. Tanyderidae, pp. 149–152. In J. F. McAlpine, B. V. Peterson, G. E. Shewell, H. J. Teskey, J. R. Vockeroth, and D. M. Wood (coords.). Manual of Nearctic Diptera, Vol. 1. Res. Branch Agric. Can. Monogr. 27. Ottawa. 674 pp.
25. Alexander, C. P., and G. W. Byers. 1981. Tipulidae, pp. 153–190. In J. F. McAlpine, B. V. Peterson, G. E. Shewell, H. J. Teskey, J. R. Vockeroth, and D. M. Wood (coords.). Manual of Nearctic Diptera, Vol. 1. Res. Branch, Agric. Can. Monogr. 27. Ottawa. 674 pp.
26. Allan, I. R. H. 1951. A hand-operated quantitative grab for sampling river beds. J. Anim. Ecol. 21:159–160.
27. Allan, J. D. 1982. Feeding habits and prey consumption of three setipalpian stoneflies (Plecoptera) in a mountain stream. Ecology 63:26–34.
28. Allen, R. K. 1967. New species of new world Leptohyphinae (Ephemeroptera: Tricorythidae). Can. Ent. 99:350–375.
29. Allen, R. K. 1980. Geographic distribution and reclassification of the subfamily Ephemerellinae (Ephemeroptera: Ephemerellidae). pp. 71–91. In J. F. Flannagan and K. E. Marshall (eds.). Advances in Ephemeroptera biology. Plenum, N.Y. 552 pp.
30. Allen, R. K. and G. F. Edmunds, Jr. 1965. A revision of the genus Ephemerella (Ephemeroptera: Ephemerellidae). VIII. The subgenus Ephemerella in North America. Ent. Soc. Am. Misc. Publ. 4:243–282.
31. Allen, R. K., and G. F. Edmunds, Jr. 1976. A revision of the genus Ametropus in North America (Ephemeroptera: Ametropodidae). J. Kans. Ent. Soc. 49:625–635.
32. Alstad, D. N. 1979. Comparative biology of the common Utah Hydropsychidae (Trichoptera). Am. Midl. Nat. 103:167–174.
33. Ambühl, H. 1959. Die Bedeutung der Strömung als ökologischer Faktor. Schweiz. Z. Hydrol. 21:133–264.
34. American Public Health Association. 1971. Standard methods for the examination of water and waste-water (13th ed.). Am. Public Health Assoc., N.Y. 874 pp.
35. Amrine, J. W., and L. Butler, 1978. An annotated list of the mosquitoes of West Virginia. Mosquito News 38:101–104.
36. Andersen, N. M. 1973. Seasonal polymorphism and developmental changes in organs of flight and reproduction in bivoltine pondskaters. Ent. Scand. 4:1–20.
37. Andersen, N. M. 1975. The Limnogonus and Neogerris of the old World, with character analysis and a reclassification of the Gerrinae (Hemiptera: Gerridae). Ent. Scand. (Suppl.) 7:1–96.

38. Andersen, N. M. 1981a. Adaptations, ecological diversification, and the origin of higher taxa of semiaquatic bugs (Gerromorpha). Rostria 33 (Suppl.):3–16.

39. Andersen, N. M. 198lb. Semiaquatic bugs: phylogeny and classification of the Hebridae (Heteroptera: Gerromorpha) with revisions of *Timasius, Neotimasius* and *Hyrcanus*. Syst. Ent. 6:377–412.

40. Andersen, N. M. 1982. The semiaquatic bugs (Hemiptera, Gerromorpha). Phylogeny, adaptations, biogeography and classification. Entomonograph, Vol. 3. Scandanavian Sci. Press, Klampenborg, Denmark. 455 pp.

41. Andersen, N. M., and J. T. Polhemus. 1976. Water-striders (Hemiptera: Gerridae, Veliidae, etc.), pp. 187–224. *In* L. Cheng (ed.). Marine Insects. North Holland, Amsterdam. 581 pp.

42. Andersen, N. M. and J. T. Polhemus. 1980. Four new genera of Mesoveliidae (Hemiptera, Gerromorpha) and the phylogeny and classification of the family. Ent. Scand. 11:369–392.

43. Anderson, J. B., and W. T. Mason, Jr. 1968. A comparison of benthic macroinvertebrates collected by dredge and basket sampler. J. Wat. Poll. Contr. Fed. 40:252–259.

44. Anderson, J. F., and S. W. Hitchcock, 1968. Biology of *Chironomus atrella* in a tidal cove. Ann. Ent. Soc. Am. 61:1597–1603.

45. Anderson, J. M. E. 1976. Aquatic Hydrophilidae (Coleoptera). The biology of some Australian species with descriptions of immature stages reared in the laboratory. J. Austr. Ent. Soc. 15:219–228.

46. Anderson, J. R. 1960. The biology and taxonomy of Wisconsin black flies (Diptera: Simuliidae). Ph.D. diss., University of Wisconsin, Madison. 185 pp.

47. Anderson, J. R., and R. J. Dicke. 1960. Ecology of the immature stages of some Wisconsin black flies (Simuliidae: Diptera). Ann. Ent. Soc. Am. 53:386–404.

48. Anderson, L. D. 1932. A monograph of the genus *Metrobates*. Univ. Kans. Sci. Bull. 20:297–311.

49. Anderson, N. H. 1967. Life cycle of a terrestrial caddisfly, *Philocasca demita* (Trichoptera: Limnephilidae), in North America. Ann. Ent. Soc. Am. 60:320–323.

50. Anderson, N. H. 1974a. Observations on the biology and laboratory rearing of *Pseudostenophylax edwardsi* (Trichoptera: Limnephilidae). Can. J. Zool. 52:7–13.

51. Anderson, N. H. 1974b. The eggs and oviposition behaviour of *Agapetus fuscipes* Curtis (Trich., Glossosomatidae). Entomol. mon. Mag. 109:129–131.

52. Anderson, N. H. 1976a. Carnivory by an aquatic detritivore, *Clistoronia magnifica* (Trichoptera: Limnephilidae). Ecology 57:1081–1085.

53. Anderson, N. H. 1976b. The distribution and biology of the Oregon Trichoptera. Ore. Agric. Exp. Sta. Tech. Bull. 134:1–152.

54. Anderson, N. H. 1978. Continuous rearing of the limnephilid caddisfly, *Clistoronia magnifica* (Banks), pp. 317–329. *In* M. I. Crichton (ed.). Proc. 2nd Int. Symp. Trichoptera. Junk, The Hague, Netherlands. 359 pp.

55. Anderson, N. H., and M. J. Anderson. 1974. Making a case for the caddisfly. Insect World Digest 1:1–6.

56. Anderson, N. H. and J. R. Bourne. 1974. Bionomics of three species of glossosomatid caddisflies (Trichoptera: Glossosomatidae) in Oregon. Can. J. Zool. 52:405–411.

57. Anderson, N. H., and K. W. Cummins. 1979. The influence of diet on the life histories of aquatic insects. J. Fish. Res. Bd. Can. 36:335–342.

58. Anderson, N. H. and E. Grafius, 1975. Utilization and processing of allochthonous material by stream Trichoptera. Verh. Int. Verein. Limnol. 19:3083–3088.

59. Anderson, N. H., J. R. Sedell, L. M. Roberts, and F. J. Triska. 1978. The role of aquatic invertebrates in processing wood debris in coniferous forest streams. Am. Midl. Nat. 100:64–82.

60. Anderson, R. D. 1962. The Dytiscidae (Coleoptera) of Utah: keys, original citation, types, and Utah distribution. Great Basin Nat. 22:54–75.

61. Anderson, R. D. 1971. A revision of the Nearctic representatives of *Hygrotus* (Coleoptera: Dytiscidae). Ann. Ent. Soc. Am. 64: 503–512.

62. Anderson, R. D. 1976. A revision of the Nearctic species of *Hycrotus* groups II and III (Coleoptera: Dytiscidae). Ann. Ent. Soc. Am. 69:577–584.

63. Anderson, R. l. 1980. Chironomidae toxicity tests—biological background and procedures, pp. 70–80. *In* A. L. Buikema, Jr., and J. Cairns, Jr. (eds.). Aquatic invertebrate bioassays. Am. Soc. Test. Mater. Philadelphia. 209 pp.

64. Andre, P., P. Legerdre, and P. P. Harper. 1981. La selectivite de trois engins d'echantillonnage du benthos lacustre. Annls. Limnol. 17:25–40.

65. Annecke, D. P., and R. L. Doutt. 1961. The genera of the Mymaridae (Hym.: Chalciodoidea). Rep. S. Afr. Dept. Agric. Tech. Serv. Ent. Mem. 5:1–71.

66. Apperson, C. S., and D. G. Yows. 1976. A light trap for collecting aquatic organisms. Mosquito News 36:205–206.

67. Applegate, R. L. 1973. Corixidae (water boatmen) of the South Dakota glacial lake district. Ent. News 84:163–170.

68. Armitage, P. D. 1968. Some notes on the food of chironomid larvae of a shallow woodland lake in South Finland. Ann. Zool. Fenn. 5:6–13.

69. Armitage, P. D. 1974. Some aspects of the ecology of the Tanypodinae and other less common species of Chironomidae in Lake Kuusijarvi, South Finland. Ent. Tidskr. Suppl. 95:13–17.

70. Armitage, P. D. 1978. Catches of invertebrate drift by pump and net. Hydrobiologia 60:229–233.

71. Armitage, P. D. 1979. Folding artificial substratum sampler for use in standing water. Hydrobiologia 66:245–249.

72. Arnett, R. H. 1960. The beetles of the United States. Catholic University America Press, Washington, D.C. 1112 pp.

73. Arrow, G. J. 1924. Vocal organs in the coleopterous families Dytiscidae, Erotylidae, and Endomychidae. Trans. Ent. Soc. Lond. 72:134–143.

74. Ashley, D. L., D. C. Tarter, and W. D. Watkins. 1976. Life history and ecology of *Diploperla robusta* Stark and Gaufin (Plecoptera: Perlodidae). Psyche 83:310–318.

75. Asmus, B. S. 1973. The use of the ATP assay in terrestrial decomposition studies. Bull. Ecol. Res. Comm. 17:223–234.

76. Axtell, R. C. 1976. Coastal horseflies and deerflies (Diptera: Tabanidae), pp. 415–445. *In* L. Cheng (ed.). Marine insects. North Holland, Amsterdam. 581 pp.

77. Azam, K. M. 1969. Life history and production studies of *Sialis californica* Banks and *Sialis rotunda* Banks (Megaloptera: Sialidae), Ph.D. diss., Oregon State University, Corvallis. 111 pp.

78. Azam, K. M. and N. H. Anderson, 1969. Life history and habits of *Sialis californica* Banks and *Sialis rotunda* Banks in western Oregon. Ann. Ent. Soc. Am. 62:549–558.

79. Back, C., and D. M. Wood. 1979. *Paleodipteron walkeri* (Diptera: Nymphomyiidae) in northern Quebec. Can. Ent. 111: 1287–1291.

80. Bacon, J. A. 1956. A taxonomic study of the genus *Rhagovelia* of the Western Hemisphere. Univ. Kans. Sci. Bull. 38:695–913.

81. Badcock, R. M. 1949. Studies on stream life in tributaries of a Welsh Dee. J. Anim. Ecol. 18:193–208.

82. Badcock, R. M. 1953. Observation of oviposition under water of the aerial insect *Hydropsyche angustipennis* (Curtis) (Trichoptera). Hydrobiologia 5:222–225.

83. Baekken, T. 1981. Growth patterns and food habits of *Baetis rhodani, Capnia pygmaea* and *Diura nanseni* in a west Norwegian river. Holarct. Ecol. 4:139–144.

84. Bahr, A., and G. Schulte. 1976. Distribution of shore bugs (Heteroptera: Saldidae) in the brackish and marine littoral of the North American Pacific Coast. Mar. Biol. 36:37–46.

85. Baker, A. S., and A. J. McLachlan. 1979. Food preferences of Tanypodinae larvae (Diptera: Chironomidae). Hydrobiologia 62:283–288.

86. Baker, F. C. 1918. The productivity of invertebrate fish food on the bottom of Oneida Lake, with special reference to mollusks. Tech. Publ. N.Y. State Coll. For. 18:1–265.

87. Baker, J. H., and L. A. Bradnum. 1976. The role of bacteria in the nutrition of aquatic detritivores. Oecologia 24:95–104.

88. Baker, J. R., and H. H. Neunzig. 1968. The egg masses, eggs, and first instar larvae of eastern North American Corydalidae. Ann. Ent. Soc. Am. 61:1181–1187.

89. Baker, R. L. 1981. Behavioral interactions and use of feeding areas by nymphs of *Coenagrion resolutum* (Coenagrionidae: Odonata). Oecologia 49:353–358.

90. Baker, R. L. 1982. Effects of food abundance of growth, survival, and use of the space by nymphs of *Coenagrion resolutum* (Zygoptera). Oikos 38:47–51.

91. Balciunas, J. K., and T. D. Center. 1981. Preliminary host specificity tests of a Panamanian *Parapoynx rugosalis* as a potential biological control agent for *Hydrilla verticillata*. Environ. Ent. 10:462–467.

92. Balduf, W. V. 1935. The bionomics of entomophagous Coleoptera. John S. Swift, N.Y. 220 pp.

93. Balduf, W. V. 1939. The bionomics of entomophagous insects. Part II. John S. Swift, St. Louis. 384 pp.

94. Balfour Browne, F. 1910. On the life history of *Hydrobius fuscipes* L. Trans. R. ent. Soc. Edinb. 47:310–340.

95. Balfour Browne, F. 1947. On the false chelate leg of the water beetle. Proc. R. ent. Soc. Lond (A) 22:38–41.

96. Balfour Browne, F., and J. Balfour Browne. 1940. An outline of the habits of a water beetle: *Noterus capricornis* Herbst (Coleopt.). Proc. Zool. Soc. Lond. 15:10–12.

97. Ball, R. C., N. R. Kevern, and K. J. Linton. 1969. Red Cedar River report. II. Bioecology. Publ. Mich. State Univ. Mus. Biol. Ser. 4:105–160.

98. Balsbaugh, E. U., Jr., and K. L. Hays. 1972. The leaf beetles of Alabama (Coleoptera: Chrysomelidae). Auburn Univ. Agric. Exp. Sta. Bull. 441:1–223.

99. Bane, C. T., and O. T. Lind. 1978. The benthic invertebrate standing crop and diversity of a small desert stream in the Big Bend National Park, Texas. Southwest. Nat. 23:215–226.

100. Barber, W. E., and N. R. Kevern. 1974. Seasonal variation of sieving efficiency in a lotic habitat. Freshwat. Biol. 4:293–300.

101. Barbier, R., and G. Chauvin. 1974. The aquatic egg of *Nymphula nympheata* (Lepidoptera: Pyralidae). Cell Tiss. Res. 149:473–479.

102. Bare, C. O. 1926. Life histories of some Kansas "backswimmers." Ann. Ent. Soc. Am. 19:93–101.

103. Bärlocher, F., R. J. Mackay, and G. B. Wiggins. 1978. Detritus processing in a temporary vernal pool in southern Ontario. Arch. Hydrobiol. 81:269–295.

104. Barnard, P. C. 1971. The larva of *Agraylea sexmaculata* Curtis (Trichoptera: Hydroptilidae). Ent. Gaz. 22:253–257.

105. Barnes, H. F. 1937. Methods of investigating the bionomics of the common crane fly, *Tipula paludosa* Meigen, together with some results. Ann. Appl. Biol. 24:356–368.

106. Barr, A. R. 1958. The mosquitoes of Minnesota. Univ. Minn. Agric. Exp. Sta. Tech. Bull. 228:1–154.

107. Barton, D. R. 1980. Observations on the life histories and biology of Ephemeroptera and Plecoptera in northeastern Alberta. Aquat. Insects 2:97–111.

108. Bartsch, A. F., and W. M. Ingram. 1966. Biological analysis of water pollution in North America. Verh. Int. Verein. Limnol. 16:786–800.

109. Bates, M. 1949. The natural history of mosquitoes. Harper and Row, N.Y. 378 pp.

110. Batra, S. W. T. 1977. Bionomics of the aquatic moth *Acentropus niveus* (Olivier) a potential biological control agent for Eurasian watermilfoil and *Hydrilla*. J. N.Y. Ent. Soc. 85:143–152.

111. Battle, F. V., and E. C. Turner. 1971. The Insects of Virginia. III. A systematic review of the genus *Culicoides* (Diptera: Ceratopogonidae) in Virginia with a geographic catalog of the species occurring in the eastern United States north of Florida. Bull. Res. Div. Va. Poly. Inst. State Univ. 44:1–129.

112. Baumann, R. W. 1975. Revision of the stonefly family Nemouridae (Plecoptera): a study of the world fauna at the generic level. Smithson. Contr. Zool. 211:1–74.

113. Baumann, R. W. 1976. An annotated review of the systematics of North American stoneflies (Plecoptera). Perla 2:21–23.

114. Baumann, R. W., and A. R. Gaufin. 1970. The *Capnia projecta* complex of Western North America (Plecoptera: Capniidae). Trans. Am. Ent. Soc. 96:435–468.

115. Baumann, R. W., A. R. Gaufin, and R. F. Surdick. 1977. The stoneflies (Plecoptera) of the Rocky Mountains. Mem. Am. Ent. Soc. 31:1–208.

116. Baumann, R. W., and K. W. Stewart. 1980. The nymph of *Lednia tumana* (Ricker)(Plecoptera: Nemouridae). Proc. Ent. Soc. Wash. 82:655–659.

117. Baumann, R. W., and J. D. Unzicker, 1981. Preliminary checklist of Utah caddisflies (Trichoptera). Encyclia 58:25–29.

118. Baumgartner-Gamauf, M. 1959. Einige ufer-und wasserbewohnende Collembolen des Seewinkels. Ost. Akad. Wiss. Math. Nat. Kl. 168:363–369.

119. Bay, E. C. 1967. An inexpensive filter-aquarium for rearing and experimenting with aquatic invertebrates. Turtox News 45:146–148.

120. Bay, E. C. 1972. An observatory built in a pond provides a good view of aquatic animals and plants. Sci. Am. 227:114–118.

121. Bay, E. C. 1974. Predator-prey relationships among aquatic insects. Ann. Rev. Ent. 19:441–453.

122. Bay, E. C., and J. R. Caton. 1969. A benthos core sampler for wading depths. Calif. Vector Views 16:88–89.

123. Bayer, L. J., and H. J. Brockmann. 1975. Curculionidae and Chrysomelidae found in aquatic habitats in Wisconsin. Great Lakes Ent. 8:219–226.

124. Beak, T. W., T. C. Griffing, and A. G. Appleby. 1973. Use of artificial substrate samplers to assess water pollution, pp. 227–241. *In* Biological methods for the assessment of water quality. Am. Soc. Test. Mater. 528 pp.

125. Beatty, A. F., G. H. Beatty, and H. B. White, III. 1969. Seasonal distribution of Pennsylvania Odonata. Proc. Penn. Acad. Sci. 43:119–126.

126. Beatty, G., and A. F. Beatty. 1968. Checklist and bibliography of Pennsylvania Odonata. Penn. Acad. Sci. 42:120–129.

127. Beck, H. 1960. Die Larvalsystematik der Eulen (Noctuidae). Abhandlungen zur Larvalsystematik der Insekten. Nr. 4. Akademie, Berlin. 406 pp.

128. Beck, W. M., Jr. 1968. Chironomidae, pp. V.1–V.22. *In* F. K. Parish (ed.). Keys to water quality indicative organisms of the southeastern United States. Fed. Wat. Poll. Contr. Adm., Atlanta. 195 pp.

129. Beck, W. M., Jr. 1975. Chironomidae, pp. 159–180. *In* F. K. Parish (ed.). Keys to the water quality indicative organisms of the southeastern United States (2nd ed.). EMSL/EPA, Cincinnati. 195 pp.

130. Beck, W. M., Jr., and E. C. Beck, 1966. Chironomidae (Diptera) of Florida I. Pentaneurini (Tanypodinae). Bull. Fla. State Mus. 10:305–379.

131. Beck, W. M., Jr., and E. C. Beck. 1969. Chironomidae (Diptera) of Florida. III. The *Harnischia* complex (Chironominae). Bull. Fla. State Mus. 13:227–313.

132. Becker, C. D. 1973. Development of *Simulium (Psilozia) vittatum* Zett. (Diptera: Simuliidae) from larvae to adults at thermal increments from 17.0 to 27.0°C. Am. Midl. Nat. 89:246–251.

133. Becker, P. 1958. The behavior of larvae of *Culicoides circumscriptus* Kieff. (Dipt., Ceratopogonidae) towards light stimuli as influenced by feeding with observations on the feeding habits. Bull. Ent. Res. 49:785–802.

134. Becker, T. 1926. Ephydridae. Fam. 56, pp. 1–115. *In* E. Lindner (ed.). Die Fliegen der palaearktischen Region 6, Part I. Stuttgart. 280 pp.

135. Bednarik, A. F., and G. F. Edmunds. 1980. Descriptions of larval *Heptagenia* from the Rocky Mountain region. Pan-Pacific. Ent. 56:51–62.

136. Bednarik, A. F., and W. P. McCafferty. 1977. A checklist of the stoneflies or Plecoptera of Indiana. Great Lakes Ent. 10:223–226.

137. Bednarik, A. F., and W. P. McCafferty. 1979. Biosystematic revision of the genus *Stenonema* (Ephemeroptera: Heptageniidae). Can. Bull. Fish. Aquat. Sci. 201:1–73.

138. Beerbower, F. V. 1944. Life history of *Scirtes orbiculatus* Fabricius (Coleoptera: Helodidae). Ann. Ent. Soc. Am. 36:672–680.

139. Bekker, E. 1938. On the mechanism of feeding in larvae of *Anopheles*. Zool. Zh. 17:741–762.

140. Belle, J. 1973. A revision of the New World Genus *Progomphus* Sélys, 1854 (Anisoptera: Gomphidae). Odonatologica 2:191–348.

141. Benech, V. 1972. La fécondité de *Baetis rhodani* Pictet. Freshwat. Biol. 2:337–354.

142. Benedetta, C. 1970. Observations on the oxygen needs of some European Plecoptera. Int. Revue ges. Hydrobiol. 55:505–510.

143. Benedetto, L. A. 1970. Tagesperiodik der Flugaktivität von vier *Leuctra*-Arten am Polarkreis. Oikos Suppl. 13:87–90.

144. Benfield, E. F. 1972. A defensive secretion of *Dineutes discolor* (Coleoptera: Gyrinidae). Ann. Ent. Soc. Am. 65:1324–1327.

145. Benfield, E. F., D. S. Jones, and M. F. Patterson. 1977. Leaf pack processing in a pastureland stream. Oikos 29:99–103.

146. Bengtsson, J. 1977. Food preference experiments with nymphs of *Nemoura cinerea* (Retz.) (Plecoptera). Flora Fauna 83:36–39.

147. Benke, A. C. 1970. A method for comparing individual growth rates of aquatic insects with special reference to the Odonata. Ecology 51:328–331.

148. Benke, A. C. 1976. Dragonfly production and prey turnover. Ecology 57:915–927.

149. Benke, A. C. 1978. Interactions among coexisting predators— a field experiment with dragonfly larvae. J. Anim. Ecol. 47:335–350.

150. Benke, A. C. 1979. A modification of the Hynes method for estimating secondary production with particular significance for multivoltine populations. Limnol. Oceanogr. 24:168–171.

151. Benke, A. C., and S. S. Benke. 1975. Comparative analysis and life histories of coexisting dragonfly populations. Ecology 56:302–317.

152. Benke, A. C., D. M. Gillespie, F. K. Parrish, T. C. Van Arsdall, R. J. Hunter, and R. L. Henry. 1979. Biological basis for assessing impacts of channel modifications: Invertebrate production, drift and fish feeding in a Southeastern blackwater river. Environ. Res. Center, Ga. Inst. Tech. Atlanta Rept. No. 06–79. 187 pp.

153. Benke, A. C., T. C. Van Arsdel, Jr., D. M. Gillespie, and F. K. Parrish. 1984. Invertebrate productivity in a subtropical blackwater river: The importance of habitat and life history. Ecol. Monogr. 54:25–63.

154. Benke, A. C., and J. B. Wallace. 1980. Trophic basis of production among netspinning caddisflies in a southern Appalachian stream. Ecology 61:108–118.

155. Bennefield, B. L. 1965. A taxonomic study of the subgenus *Ladona* (Odonata: Libellulidae). Univ. Kans. Sci. Bull. 45:361–396.

156. Bennett, D. V., and E. F. Cook. 1981. The semi-aquatic Hemiptera of Minnesota (Hemiptera: Heteroptera). Minn. Agric. Exp. Sta. Tech. Bull. 332:1–59.

157. Bentinck, W. C. 1956. Structure and classification, pp. 68–73. *In* R. L. Usinger (ed.). Aquatic insects of California. Univ. Calif. Press, Berkeley. 508 pp.

158. Berg, C. O. 1949. Limnological relations of insects to plants of the genus *Potamogeton*. Trans. Am. Microsc. Soc. 68:279–291.

159. Berg, C. O. 1950a. Biology of certain aquatic caterpillars *(Pyralididae: Nymphula* spp.) which feed on *Potamogeton*. Trans. Am. Microsc. Soc. 69:254–266.

160. Berg, C. O. 1950b. Biology and certain Chironomidae reared from *Potamogeton*. Ecol. Monogr. 20:83–101.

161. Berg, C. O. 1950c. *Hydrellia* (Ephydridae) and some other acalyptrate Diptera reared from *Potamogeton*. Ann. Ent. Soc. Am. 43:374–398.

162. Berg, C. O. 1953. Sciomyzid larvae (Diptera) that feed on snails. J. Parasit. 39:630–636.

163. Berg, C. O. 1961. Biology of snail-killing Sciomyzidae (Diptera) of North America and Europe. Proc. 10th Int. Congr. Ent. 1:197–202.

164. Berg, C. O. 1964. Snail-killing sciomyzid flies: Biology of the aquatic species. Verh. Int. Verein. Limnol. 15:926–932.

165. Berg, C. O., B. A. Foote, L. V. Knutson, J. K. Barnes, S. L. Arnold, and K. Valley. 1982. Adaptive differences in phenology in sciomyzid flies. Mem. Ent. Soc. Wash. 10:15–36.

166. Berg, C. O., and L. Knutson. 1978. Biology and systematics of the Sciomyzidae. Ann. Rev. Ent. 23:239–258.

167. Berg, K. 1937. Contributions to the biology of *Corethra* Meigen *(Chaoborus* Lichtenstein). Biol. Med. 13:1–101.

168. Berg, K. 1942. Contributions to the biology of the aquatic moth *Acentropus niveus* (Oliv.). Vidensk. Medd. Dansk Naturhist. Foren. 105:59–139.

169. Berg, K. 1948. Biological studies of the River Susaa. Folia Limnol. Scand. 4:1–318.

170. Berner, L. 1950. The mayflies of Florida. Univ. Fla. Stud. Biol. Sci. Ser. 4:1–267.

171. Berner, L. 1955. The southeastern species of *Baetisca* (Ephemeroptera: Baetiscidae). Quart. J. Fla. Acad. Sci. 18:1–19.

172. Berner, L. 1956. The genus *Neoephemera* in North America (Ephemeroptera: Neoephemeridae). Ann. Ent. Soc. Am. 49:33–42.

173. Berner, L. 1959. A tabular summary of the biology of North American mayfly nymphs (Ephemeroptera). Bull. Fla. State Mus. 4:1–58.

174. Berner, L. 1975. The mayfly family Leptophlebiidae in the southeastern United States. Fla. Ent. 58:137–156.

175. Berner, L. 1978. A review of the mayfly family Metretopodidae. Trans. Am. Ent. Soc. 104:91–137.

176. Berner, L., and M. L. Pescador. 1980. The mayfly family Baetiscidae (Ephemeroptera). Part I., pp. 511–524. *In* J. F. Flannagan and K. E. Marshall (eds.). Advances in Ephemeroptera biology. Plenum, N.Y. 552 pp.

177. Bertrand, H. 1954. Les insects aquatiques d'Europe. Encyclopédie Entomologique. Ser. A. 31. 2:1–547.

178. Bertrand, H. P. I. 1972. Larves et nymphes des Coléoptères aquatiques du globe. Centre National de la Recherche Scientifique, Paris. 804 pp.

179. Betsch, J. M. 1980. Eléments pour une monographie des Collemboles Symphypléones (Hexapodes, Aptérygotes). Mem. Mus. Nat. Hist. Natur. (Paris), Ser. A. 116:1–227.

180. Betten, C. 1934. The caddis flies or Trichoptera of New York State. Bull. N.Y. State Mus. 292:1–576.

181. Betten, C. 1950. The genus *Pycnopsyche* (Trichoptera). Ann. Ent. Soc. Am. 43:508–522.

182. Beyer, A. 1939. Morphologische, ökologische und physiologische Studien an den Larven der Fliegen: *Ephydria riparia* Fallen, *E. micans* Haliday und *Cania fumosa* Stenhammar. Kieler Meeresforsch. 3:265–320.

183. Bick, G. H. 1941. Life-history of the dragonfly, *Erythemis simplicollis* (Say). Ann. Ent. Soc. Am. 34:215–230.

184. Bick, G. H. 1950. The dragonflies of Mississippi. Am. Midl. Nat. 43:66–78.

185. Bick, G. H. 1951. The early nymphal stages of *Tramea lacerata* (Odonata:Libellulidae). Ent. News 62:293–303.

186. Bick, G. H. 1957a. The dragonflies of Louisiana. Tulane Studies Zool. 5:1–135.

187. Bick, G. H. 1957b. The Odonata of Oklahoma. Southwest. Nat. 2:1–18.

188. Bick, G. H. 1959. Additional dragonflies (Odonata) from Arkansas. Southwest. Nat. 4:131–133.

189. Bick, G. H., and J. F. Aycock. 1950. The life history of *Aphylla williamsoni* Gloyd. Proc. Ent. Soc. Wash. 52:26–32.

190. Bick, G. H., and J. C. Bick. 1958. The ecology of the Odonata at a small creek in southern Oklahoma. J. Tenn. Acad. Sci. 33:240–251.

191. Bick, G. H., and J. C. Bick. 1970. Oviposition in *Archilestes grandis* (Rambur) (Odonata: Lestidae). Ent. News 81:157–163.

192. Bick, G. H., J. C. Bick, and L. E. Hornuff. 1977. An annotated list of the Odonata of the Dakotas. Fla. Ent. 60:149–165.

193. Bick, G. H., and L. E. Hornuff. 1972. Odonata collected in Wyoming, South Dakota, and Nebraska. Proc. Ent. Soc. Wash. 74:1–8.

194. Bick, G. H., and L. E. Hornuff. 1974. New records of Odonata from Montana and Colorado. Proc. Ent. Soc. Wash. 76:90–93.

195. Bickley, W. E., S. R. Joseph, J. Mallack, and R. A. Berry. 1971. An annotated checklist of the mosquitoes of Maryland. Mosquito News 31:186–190.

196. Biever, K. D. 1965. A rearing technique for the colonization of chironomid midges. Ann. Ent. Soc. Am. 58:135–136.

197. Biever, K. D. 1971. Effect on diet and competition in laboratory rearing of chironomid midges. Ann. Ent. Soc. Am. 64:1166–1169.

198. Bird, R. D. 1932. Dragonflies of Oklahoma. Publ. Univ. Okla. Biol. Surv. 4:51–57.

199. Bishop, J. E. 1973. Observations on the vertical distribution of benthos in a Malasian stream. Freshwat. Biol. 3:147–156.

200. Bishop, J. E., and H. B. N. Hynes. 1969. Downstream drift of the invertebrate fauna in a stream ecosystem. Arch. Hydrobiol. 66:56–90.

201. Bjarnov, N., and J. Thorup. 1970. A simple method for rearing running water insects, with some preliminary results. Arch. Hydrobiol. 67:201–209.

202. Blackwelder, R. E. 1932. The genus *Endeodes* LeConte (Coleoptera, Melyridae). Pan-Pacif. Ent. 8:128–136.

203. Blanton, F. S., and W. W. Wirth. 1979. The sand flies *(Culicoides)* of Florida (Diptera: Ceratopogonidae). Arthropods of Florida. Fla. Dep. Agric., Gainesville. 10:1–204.

204. Blatchley, W. S. 1910. An illustrated descriptive catalogue of the Coleoptera beetles (exclusive of the Rhyncophora) known to occur in Indiana. Bull. Ind. Dept. Geol. Nat. Res. 1:1–1386.

205. Blatchley, W. S. 1920. The Orthoptera of northeastern America. Nature, Indianapolis. 784 pp.

206. Blatchley, W. S. 1926. Heteroptera or true bugs of eastern North America. Nature, Indianapolis. 1116 pp.

207. Blickle, R. L. 1962. Hydroptilidae (Trichoptera) of Florida. Fla. Ent. 45:153–155.

208. Blickle, R. L. 1964. Hydroptilidae (Trichoptera) of Maine. Ent. News 75:159–162.

209. Blickle, R. L. 1979. Hydroptilidae (Trichoptera) of America north of Mexico. Bull. Univ. N.H. Agric. Exp. Sta. 509:1–97.

210. Blickle, R. L., and D. G. Denning. 1977. New species and a new genus of Hydroptilidae (Trichoptera). J. Kans. Ent. Soc. 50:287–300.

211. Blickle, R. L., and W. J. Morse. 1966. The caddis flies (Trichoptera) of Maine, excepting the family Hydroptilidae. Maine Agric. Exp. Sta. Tech. Bull. 24:1–12.

212. Blinn, D. W., C. Pinney, and M. W. Sanderson. 1982. Nocturnal planktonic behavior of *Ranatra montezuma* Polhemus (Nepidae: Hemiptera) in Montezuma Well, Arizona. J. Kans. Ent. Soc. 55:481–484.

213. Bloomfield, E. N. 1897. Habits of *Sericomyia borealis* Fln. Entomol. mon. Mag. 33:222–223.

214. Bobb, M. L. 1951a. Life history of *Ochterus banksi* Barber. Bull. Brooklyn Ent. Soc. 46:92–100.

215. Bobb, M. L. 1951b. The life history of *Gerris canaliculatus* Say in Virginia (Hemiptera: Gerridae). Va. J. Sci. 2:102–108.

216. Bobb, M. L. 1953. Observations on the life history of *Hesperocorixa interrupta* (Say) (Hemiptera: Corixidae). Va. J. Sci. 4:111–115.

217. Bobb, M. L. 1974. The aquatic and semiaquatic Hemiptera of Virginia. The Insects of Virginia: No. 7. Bull. Res. Div. Va. Poly. Inst. State Univ. 87:1–195.

218. Boesel, M. W., and E. G. Snyder. 1944. Observations on the early stages of the grass punky, *Atrichopogon levis* (Coquillett) (Diptera: Heleidae). Ann. Ent. Soc. Am. 37:37–46.

219. Bohart, B. E., and J. E. Gressitt. 1951. Filth-inhabiting flies of Guam. Bull. Bishop Mus. 204:1–152.

220. Bohart, R. M., and R. K. Washino. 1978. Mosquitoes of California (3rd ed.). Univ. Calif. Div. Agric. Sci. Printed Publ. No. 4084. 154 pp.

221. Bokerman, W. C. A. 1957. Frog eggs parasitized by dipterous larvae. Herpetologica 13:231–232.

222. Boling, R. H., E. D. Goodman, J. A. VanSickle, J. O. Zimmer, K. W. Cummins, R. C. Petersen, and S. R. Reice. 1975b. Toward a model of detritus processing in a woodland stream. Ecology 56:141–151.

223. Boling, R. H., Jr., R. C. Petersen, and K. W. Cummins. 1975a. Ecosystem modeling for small woodland streams, pp. 183–204. *In* B. C. Patten (ed.). Systems analysis and simulation in ecology, Vol. 3. Academic, N.Y. 601 pp.

224. Borkert, A. 1979. Systematics and bionomics of the species of the subgenus *Schadonophasma* Dyar and Shannon (*Chaoborus*, Chaoboridae, Diptera). Quaest. Ent. 15:122–255.

225. Borror, D. J. 1934. Ecological studies of *Argia moesta* Hagen (Odonata: Coenagrionidae) by means of marking. Ohio J. Sci. 34:97–108.

226. Borror, D. J. 1937. An annotated list of the dragonflies (Odonata) of Ohio. Ohio J. Sci. 37:185–196.

227. Borror, D. J. 1942. A revision of the libelluline Genus *Erythrodiplax* (Odonata). Ohio State Univ. Grad. School Stud. Contr. Zool. Ent. 4:1–286.

228. Borror, D. J. 1944. An Annotated List of the Odonata of Maine. Can. Ent. 76:134–150.

229. Borror, D. J. 1945. A key to the new world genera of Libellulidae (Odonata). Ann. Ent. Soc. Am. 38:168–194.

230. Borror, D. J., D. M. Delong, and C. A. Triplehorn. 1981. An introduction to the study of insects (5th ed.). Saunders College Publ., Philadelphia. 827 pp.

231. Borror, D. J., and R. E. White. 1970. A field guide to the insects of America north of Mexico. Houghton Mifflin, Boston. 404 pp.

232. Boucek, Z., M. W. R. de V. Graham, and G. J. Kerrich. 1963. A revision of the European species of the genus *Mestocharis* Forster (Hym.: Chalcidoidea: Eulophidae). Entomologist 96: 4–9.

233. Bournaud, M. 1963. Le courant, facteur écologique et éthologique de la vie aquatique. Hydrobiologia 22:125–165.

234. Boving, A. G. 1910. Natural history of the larvae of Donaciinae. Int. Revue ges. Hydrobiol. Biol. Suppl. 1:1–108.

235. Boving, A. G., and F. C. Craighead. 1930. An illustrated synopsis of the principal larval forms of the order Coleoptera. J. Ent. Soc. Am. 11:1–351.

236. Bradshaw, W. E. 1970. Interaction of food and photoperiod in the termination of larval diapause in *Chaeoborus americanus* (Diptera: Culicidae). Biol. Bull. 139:476–484.

237. Branch, H. E. 1923. The life history of *Chironomus cristatus* Fabr. with descriptions of the species. J. N.Y. Ent. Soc. 1:15–30.

238. Branham, J. M., and R. R. Hathaway. 1975. Sexual differences in the growth of *Pteronarcys californica* Newport and *Pteronarcella badia* (Hagen) (Plecoptera). Can. J. Zool. 53:501–506.

239. Bratt, A. D., L. V. Knutson, B. A. Foote, and C. O. Berg. 1969. Biology of *Pherbellia* (Diptera:Sciomyzidae). Mem. Cornell Univ. Exp. Sta. 404:1–247.

240. Braun, A. F. 1917.The Nepticulidae of North America. Trans. Am. Ent. Soc. 43:155–201.

241. Breland, O. P. 1958. A report on *Haemogogus* mosquitoes in the United States with notes on identification. Ann. Ent. Soc. Am. 51:217–221.

242. Brenner, R. J., and E. W. Cupp. 1980. Rearing black flies (Diptera: Simuliidae) in a closed system of water circulation. Tropenmed. Parasit. 31:247–258.

243. Brigham, A. R., W. U. Brigham, and A. Gnilka (eds.). 1982. The aquatic insects and oligochaetes of North and South Carolina. Midwest Aquatic Enterprises, Mahomet, Ill. 837 pp.

244. Brigham, W. U. 1981. *Ectopria leechi,* a new false water penny from the United States (Coleoptera: Eubriidae). Pan-Pacif. Ent. 57:313–320.

245. Brigham, W. U. 1982. Aquatic Coleoptera, pp. 10.1–10.136. *In* A. R. Brigham, W. U. Brigham, and A. Gnilka (eds.). Aquatic insects and oligochaetes of North and South Carolina. Midwest Enterprises, Mahomet, Ill. 837 pp.

246. Brimley, C. S. 1938. The Insects of North Carolina. Carolina Dep. Agric. Div. Ent. pp. 36–42.

247. Brinck, P. 1949. Studies on Swedish stoneflies. Opusc. Ent. Suppl. 11:1–250.

248. Brinck, P. 1956. Reproductive system and mating in Plecoptera. Opusc. Ent. 21:57–127.

249. Brinck, P. 1958. On a collection of stoneflies (Plecoptera) from Newfoundland and Labrador. Opusc. Ent. 23:47–58.

250. Brindle, A. 1973. Taxonomic notes on the larvae of British Diptera, 28. The larvae and pupae of *Hydrodromia stagnalis* (Holiday). Entomologist 106:249–252.

251. Brinkhurst, R. O. 1959. Alary polymorphism in the Gerroidea. J. Anim. Ecol. 28:211–230.

252. Brinkhurst, R. O. 1960. Studies on the functional morphology of *Gerris njas* DeGeer. Proc. Zool. Soc. Lond. 133:531–559.

253. Brinkhurst, R. O., K. E. Chua, and E. Batoosingh. 1969. Modifications in sampling procedures as applied to studies on bacteria and tubificid oligochaetes inhabiting aquatic sediments. J. Fish. Res. Bd. Can. 26:2581–2593.

254. Britt, N. W. 1967. Biology of two species of Lake Erie mayflies, *Ephoron album* (Say) and *Ephemera simulans* Walker. Bull. Ohio Biol. Surv. 1:1–70.

255. Brittain, J. E. 1973. The biology and life cycle of *Nemoura avicularis* Morton. Freshwat. Biol. 3:199–210.

256. Brittain, J. E. 1974. Studies on the lentic Ephemeroptera and Plecoptera in southern Norway. Nor. Ent. Tidsskr. 21:135–154.

257. Brittain, J. E. 1976. Experimental studies on nymphal growth in *Leptophlebia vespertina* (L.) (Ephemeroptera). Freshwat. Biol. 6:445–449.

258. Brittain, J. E. 1980. Mayfly strategies in a Norwegian subalpine lake, pp. 179–186. *In* J. F. Flannagan, and K. E. Marshall (eds.). Advances in Ephemeroptera biology. Plenum, N.Y. 552 pp.

259. Brittain, J. E. 1982. Biology of mayflies. Ann. Rev. Ent. 27: 119–147.

260. Britton, E. B. 1966. On the larva of *Sphaerius* and the systematic position of the Sphaeriidae (Coleoptera). Austr. J. Zool. 14:1193–1198.

261. Britton, W. E. (ed.). 1923. Guide to the insects of Connecticut. Part IV. The Hemiptera or sucking insects of Connecticut. Conn. State Geol. Nat. Hist. Surv. Bull. 34:1–807.

262. Brock, E. M. 1960. Mutualism between the midge *Cricotopus* and the alga *Nostoc*. Ecology 41:474–483.

263. Brock, M. L., R. G. Wiegert, and T. D. Brock. 1969. Feeding of *Paracoenia* and *Ephydra* (Diptera:Ephydridae) on the microorganisms of hot springs. Ecology 50:192–200.

264. Brock, T. D., and M. L. Brock. 1968. Life in a hot water basin. Nat. Hist. 77:47–53.

265. Brodo, F. 1967. A review of the subfamily Cylindrotominae in North America (Diptera: Tipulidae). Univ. Kans. Sci. Bull. 47:71–115.

266. Brodsky, K. A. 1980. Mountain torrent of the Tien Shan. A faunistic-ecology essay. (Translated from Russian by V. V. Golosov). Junk, The Hague. 311 pp.

267. Brooker, M. P. 1979. The life cycle and growth of *Sialis lutaria* L. (Megaloptera) in a drainage channel under different methods of plant management. Ecol. Ent. 4:111–117.

268. Brooks, A. R., and L. A. Kelton. 1967. Aquatic and semi-aquatic Heteroptera of Alberta, Saskatchewan and Manitoba. Mem. Ent. Soc. Can. 51:1–92.

269. Brothers, D. B. 1971. A checklist of the mosquitoes of Idaho. Tebiwa, Idaho State Univ. Mus. 14:72–73.

270. Brown, A. V., and L. C. Fitzpatrick. 1978. Life history and population energetics of the dobson fly, *Corydalus cornutus*. Ecology 59:1091–1108.

271. Brown, C. J. D. 1934. A Preliminary List of Utah Odonata. Occ. Pap. Univ. Mich. Mus. Zool. 291:1–17.

272. Brown, D. S. 1960. The ingestion and digestion of algae by *Cloeon dipterum* L. (Ephemeroptera). Hydrobiologia 16:81–96.

273. Brown, D. S. 1961. The food of the larvae of *Cloeon dipterum* L. and *Baetis rhodani* (Pictet)(Ephemeroptoera). J. Anim. Ecol. 30:55–75.

274. Brown, H. P. 1951. *Climacia areolaris* (Hagen) parasitized by a new pteromalid (Hym.: Chalcidoidea). Ann. Ent. Soc. Am. 44:103–110.

275. Brown, H. P. 1952. The life history of *Climacia areolaris* (Hagen), a neuropterous "parasite" of freshwater sponges. Am. Midl. Nat. 47:130–160.

276. Brown, H. P. 1968. *Psephenus* (Coleoptera: Psephenidae) parasitized by a new chalcidoid (Hymenoptera: Eulophidae). II. Biology of the parasite. Ann. Ent. Soc. Am. 61:452–456.

277. Brown, H. P. 1970a. A key to the dryopoid genera of the new world. Ent. News 81:171–175.

278. Brown, H. P. 1970b. *Neocyllopus*, a new genus from Texas and Central America (Coleoptera: Elmidae). Coleopt. Bull. 24:1–28.

279. Brown, H. P. 1972a. Synopsis of the genus *Heterelmis* Sharp in the United States, with description of a new species from Arizona (Coleoptera, Dryopoidea, Elmidae). Ent. News 83: 229–238.

280. Brown, H. P. 1972b. Aquatic dryopoid beetles (Coleoptera) of the United States. Biota of freshwater ecosystems identification manual no. 6. Wat. Poll. Conf. Res. Ser., E.P.A., Washington, D.C. 82 pp.

281. Brown, H. P. 1973. Survival records for elmid beetles with notes on laboratory rearing of various dryopoids. Ent. News 84: 278–284.

282. Brown, H. P. 1981a. A distribution survey of the world genera of aquatic dryopoid beetles (Coleoptera: Dryopoidea: Elmidae and Psephenidae sens. lat.). water quality indicators. Pan-Pacif. Ent. 57:133–148.

283. Brown, H. P. 1981b. *Huleechius*, a new genus of riffle beetles from Mexico and Arizona (Coleoptera: Drypoidea: Elmidae). Pan-Pacif. Ent. 57:228–244.

284. Brown, H. P. 1981c. Key to the world genera of Larinae (Coleoptera: Dryopoidea: Elmidae) with descriptions of new genera from Hispaniola, Columbia, Australia, and New Guinea. Pan-Pacif. Ent. 57:76–104.

285. Brown, H. P., and C. M. Murvosh. 1970. *Lutrochus arizonicus* new species, with notes on ecology and behavior (Coleoptera, Dryopoidea, Limnichidae). Ann. Ent. Soc. Am. 63:1030–1035.

286. Brown, H. P., and C. M. Murvosh. 1974. A revision of the genus *Psephenus* (waterpenny beetles) on the United States and Canada (Coleoptera, Dryopoidea, Psephenidae). Trans. Ent. Soc. Am. 100:289–340.

287. Brown, H. P., and C. M. Shoemake. 1964. Oklahoma riffle beetles (Coleoptera: Dryopoidea). III. Additional state and county records. Proc. Okla. Acad. Sci. 44:42–43.

288. Brown, H. P. and D. S. White. 1978. Notes on separation and identification of North American riffle beetles (Coleoptera: Dryopoidea: Elmidae). Ent. News 89:1–13.

289. Brown, J. M. 1929. Freshwater Collembola. Naturalist 2:111–113.

290. Brues, C. T. 1928. Studies on the fauna of hot springs in the Western United States and the biology of thermophilous animals. Proc. Am. Acad. Arts Sci. 63:139–228.

291. Brues, C. T., A. L. Melander, and F. M. Carpenter. 1954. Classification of insects. Bull. Harvard Mus. Comp. Zool. 108:1–917.

292. Brundin. L. 1949. Chironomiden und andere Bodentiere der südschwedischen Urgebirgsseen. Rep. Inst. Freshwat. Res. Drottningholm 30:1–94.

293. Brundin, L. 1956. Zur Systematik der Orthocladiinae (Diptera: Chironomidae). Rep. Inst. Freshwat. Res. Drottningholm 37:5–185.

294. Brundin, L. 1965. On the real nature of transantarctic relationships. Evolution 19:496–505.

295. Brundin, L. 1966. Transantarctic relationships and their significance, as evidenced by chironomid midges, with a monograph of the subfamilies Podonominae and Aphroteniinae and the Austral Heptagyinae. Kungl. Svenska Vetenskapsakad. Handl., Fjorde Sev. (4)11:1–472.

296. Brusven, M. A. 1970. Drift periodicity of some riffle beetles (Coleoptera: Elmidae). J. Kans. Ent. Soc. 43:364–371.

297. Brusven, M. A., and A. C. Scoggan. 1969. Sarcophagus habits of Trichoptera larvae on dead fish. Ent. News 80:103–105.

298. Bryce, D., and A. Hobart. 1972. The biology and identification of the larvae of the Chironomidae (Diptera). Ent. Gaz. 23:175–217.

299. Buckingham, G. R., and B. M. Ross. 1981. Notes on the biology and host specificity of *Acentria nivea*. J. Aquat. Plant Manage. 19:32–36.

300. Buikema, A. L., Jr., and J. Cairns, Jr. 1980. Aquatic invertebrate bioassays. Am. Soc. Test. Mater. Philadelphia. 209 pp.

301. Burger, J. F., J. R. Anderson, and M. F. Knudsen, 1980. The habits and life history of *Oedoparena glauca* (Diptera: Dryomyzidae), a predator of barnacles. Proc. Ent. Soc. Wash. 82:360–377.

302. Burger, J. F., D. J. Lake, and M. L. McKay. 1981. The larval habitats and rearing of some common *Chrysops* species (Diptera: Tabanidae) in New Hampshire. Proc. Ent. Soc. Wash. 83:373–389.

303. Burghele, A. 1959. New Rumanian species of Dachnusini (Hym.: Braconidae) and some ecological observations upon them. Entomol. mon. Mag. 95:121–126.

304. Burke, H. R. 1963. Notes on Texas riffle beetles (Coleoptera: Elmidae). Southwest. Nat. 8:111–114.

305. Burks, B. D. 1953. The mayflies, or Ephemeroptera, of Illinois. Bull. Ill. Nat. Hist. Surv. 26:1–216.

306. Burks, B. D. 1967. The North American species of *Aprostocetus* Westwood (Hymenoptera: Eulophidae). Ann. Ent. Soc. Am. 60:756–760.

307. Burks, B. D. 1968. *Psephenus* (Coleoptera: Psephenidae) parasitized by a new chalcidoid (Hymenoptera: Eulophidae). I. Description of the parasite. Ann. Ent. Soc. Am. 61:450–452.

308. Burton, G. J. 1973. Feeding of *Simulium hargreavesi* Gibbons larvae on *Oedogonium* algal filaments in Ghana. J. Med. Ent. 10:101–106.

309. Burton, G. J., and T. M. McRae. 1972a. Observations on trichopteran predators on aquatic stages of *Simulium damnosum* and other *Simulium* species in Ghana. J. Med. Ent. 9:289–294.

310. Burtt, E. T. 1940. A filter-feeding mechanism in a larva of the Chironomidae (Diptera:Nematocera). Proc. R. ent. Soc. Lond. (A) 15:113–121.

311. Busacca, J. D., and B. A. Foote. 1978. Biology and immature stages of two species of *Notiphila*, with notes on other shore flies occurring in cattail marshes. Ann. Ent. Soc. Am. 71:457–466.

312. Butcher, F. G. 1930. Notes on the cocooning habits of *Gyrinus*. J. Kans. Ent. Soc. 3:64–66.

313. Butcher, F. G. 1933. Hymenopterous parasites of Gyrinidae with descriptions of new species of *Hemiteles*. Ann. Ent. Soc. Am. 26:76–85.

314. Butler, E. A. 1923. A biology of the British Hemiptera-Heteroptera. H. F. Witherby, Lond. 696 pp.

315. Byers, C. F. 1927. An annotated list of the Odonata of Michigan. Occ. Pap. Univ. Mich. Mus. Zool. 183:1–16.

316. Byers, C. F. 1930. A contribution to the knowledge of Florida Odonata. Univ. Fla. Publ. 1:1–327.

317. Byers, C. F. 1937. A review of the dragonflies of the genera *Neurocordulia* and *Platycordulia*. Misc. Publ. Univ. Mich. Mus. Zool. 36:1–36.

318. Byers, C. F. 1939. A study of the dragonflies of the genus *Progomphus* (Gomphoides), with a description of a new species. Proc. Fla. Acad. Sci. 4:19–85.

319. Byers, C. F. 1941. Notes of the emergence and life history of the dragonfly *Pantala flavescens*. Proc. Fla. Acad. Sci. 6:14–25.

320. Byers, C. F. 1951. Some notes on the Odonata fauna of Mountain Lake, Virginia. Ent. News 62:164–167.

321. Bystrak, P. G., and W. W. Wirth. 1978. The North American species of *Forcipomyia*, subgenus *Euprojoannisia* (Diptera: Ceratopogonidae). U.S. Dep. Agric. Tech. Bull. 1591:1–51.

322. Caillère, L. 1972. Dynamics of the strike of *Agrion* (Syn. *Calopteryx*) *splendens* Harris 1782 larvae (Odonata: Calopterygidae). Odonatologica 1:11–19.

323. Calabrese, D. M. 1974. Keys to the adults and nymphs of the species of *Gerris* Fabricius occurring in Connecticut. Mem. Conn. Ent. Soc. 1974:228–266.

324. Calabrese, D. M. 1977. The habitats of *Gerris* F. (Hemiptera: Heteroptera: Gerridae) in Connecticut. Ann. Ent. Soc. Am. 70: 977–983.

325. Calabrese, D. M. 1978. Life history data for ten species of waterstriders (Hemiptera: Heteroptera: Gerridae) in Connecticut. Trans. Kans. Acad. Sci. 61:257–264.

326. Caldwell, B. A. 1976. The distribution of *Nigronia serricornis* and *Nigronia fasciatus* in Georgia and water quality parameters associated with the larvae (Megaloptera: Corydalidae). Bull. Ga. Acad. Sci. 34:24–31.

327. Callahan, J. R. 1974. Observations on *Gerris incognitus* and *Gerris gillettei* (Heteroptera: Gerridae). Proc. Ent. Soc. Wash. 76:15–21.

328. Calvert, P. P. 1893. Catalogue of the Odonata (dragonflies) of the vicinity of Philadelphia. Trans. Am. Ent. Soc. 20:152–272.

329. Calvert, P. P. 1934. The rates of growth, larval development, and seasonal distribution of the dragonflies of the genus *Anax* (Aeshnidae). Proc. Am. Phil. Soc. 73:1–70.

330. Calvert, P. P. 1937. Methods of rearing Odonata, pp. 270–273. *In* J. G. Needham (ed.). Culture methods for invertebrate animals. Comstock, Ithaca, N.Y. 590 pp.

331. Cameron, A. E. 1926. Bionomics of the Tabanidae (Diptera) of the Canadian prairie. Bull. Ent. Res. 17:1–42.

332. Cameron, G. N. 1976. Do tides affect coastal insect communities? Am. Midl. Nat. 95:279–287.

333. Campbell, B. C. 1979. The spatial and seasonal abundance of *Trichocorixa verticalis* (Hemiptera: Corixidae) in salt marsh intertidal pools. Can. Ent. 111:1005–1011.

334. Cannings, R. A. 1978. The distribution of *Tanypteryx hageni* (Odonata:Petaluridae) in British Columbia. J. Ent. Soc. Brit. Columbia 75:18–19.

335. Cannings, R. A. 1982a. Notes on the biology of *Aeshna sitchensis* Hagen (Anisoptera: Aeshnidae). Odonatologica 11: 219–223.

336. Cannings, R. A. 1982b. Dragonfly days. Nature, Can. 11:12–17.

337. Cannings, R. A., S. G. Cannings, and R. J. Cannings. 1980. The distribution of the genus *Lestes* in a saline lake series in central British Columbia, Canada (Zygoptera: Lestidae). Odonatologica 9:19–28.

338. Cannings, R. A., and G. P. Doerksen. 1979. Description of the larva of *Ischnura erratica* (Odonata: Coenagrionidae) with notes on the species of British Columbia. Can. Ent. 111:327–331.

339. Cannings, R. A., and K. M. Stuart, 1977. The dragonflies of British Columbia. Brit. Columbia Provin. Mus. Handbk. No. 35, 256 pp.

340. Cannings, S. G. 1981. New distributional records of Odonata from northwestern British Columbia. Syesis 13:13–15.

341. Cannings, S. G., and R. A. Cannings. 1980. The larva of *Coenagrion interrogatum* (Odonata: Coenagrionidae), with notes on the species in the Yukon. Can. Ent. 112:437–441.

342. Canterbury, L. E. 1978. Studies of the genus *Sialis* (Sialidae: Megaloptera) in eastern North America. Ph.D. diss., University of Louisville. 93 pp.

343. Canterbury, L. E., and S. E. Neff. 1980. Eggs of *Sialis* (Sialidae: Megaloptera) in eastern North America. Can. Ent. 112:409–419.

344. Capek, M. 1970. A new classification of the Braconidae (Hymenoptera) based on the cephalic structures of the final instar larva and biological evidence. Can. Ent. 102:846–875.

345. Capps, H. W. 1956. Keys for the identification of some lepidopterous larvae frequently intercepted at quarantine. U.S. Dep. Agric. E-475. 37 pp.

346. Carey, W. E., and F. W. Fisk, 1965. The effect of water temperature and dissolved oxygen content on the rate of gill movement of the hellgrammite *Corydalus cornutus*. Ohio J. Sci. 65:137–141.

347. Carle, F. L. 1979a. Two new *Gomphus* (Odonata: Gomphidae) from eastern North America with adult keys to the subgenus *Hylogomphus*. Ann. Ent. Soc. Am. 72:418–426.

348. Carle, F. L. 1979b. Environmental monitoring potential of the Odonata, with a list of rare and endangered Anisoptera of Virginia, United States. Odonatologica 8:319–323.

349. Carle, F. L. 1980. A new *Lanthus* (Odonata: Gomphidae) from eastern North America with adult and nymphal keys to American Octogomphines. Ann. Ent. Soc. Am. 73:172–179.

350. Carle, F. L. 1981. A new species of *Ophiogomphus* from eastern North America, with a key to the regional species (Anisoptera: Gomphidae). Odonatologica 10:271–278.

351. Carle, F. L. 1982. *Ophiogomphus incurvatus:* a new name for *Ophiogomphus carolinus* Hagen (Odonata: Gomphidae). Ann. Ent. Soc. Am. 75:335–339.

352. Carlson, D. 1971. A method for sampling larval and emerging insects using an aquatic black light trap. Can. Ent. 103:1365–1369.

353. Carlson, D. 1972. Comparative value of black light and cool white lamps in attracting insects to aquatic traps. J. Kans. Ent. Soc. 45:194–199.

354. Carlsson, G. 1962. Studies on Scandinavian black flies. Opusc. Ent. 21:1–280.

355. Carlsson, M., L. M. Nilsson, Bj. Svensson, and S. Ulfstrand and R. S. Wotton. 1977. Lacustrine seston and other factors influencing the blackflies (Diptera: Simuliidae) inhabiting lake outlets in Swedish Lapland. Oikos 29:229–238.

356. Carpenter, S. J. 1941. The mosquitoes of Arkansas. Ark. State Bd. Health, Little Rock. 87 pp.

357. Carpenter, S. J. 1968. Review of recent literature on mosquitoes of North America. Calif. Vector Views 15:71–98.

358. Carpenter, S. J. 1970. Review of recent literature on mosquitoes of North America. Suppl. Calif. Vector Views 17:39–65.

359. Carpenter, S. J. 1974. Review of recent literature on mosquitoes of North America. Suppl. II. Calif. Vector Views 21:73–99.

360. Carpenter, S. J., and W. J. LaCasse. 1955. Mosquitoes of North America. Univ. Calif. Press, Berkeley. 360 pp.

361. Carpenter, S. J., W. W. Middlekauff, and R. W. Chamberlain. 1946. The mosquitoes of the southern United States east of Oklahoma and Texas. Am. Midl. Nat. Monogr. 3292 pp.

362. Carpenter, S. R. 1982. Stemflow chemistry: Effects on population dynamics of detritivorous mosquitoes in tree-hole ecosystems. Oecologia 53:1–6.

363. Caspers, H. 1951. Rhythmische Erscheinungen in der Fortpflanzung von *Clunio marinus* (Dipt. Chiron.) und das Problem der lunear Periodizität bein Organismen. Arch. Hydrobiol. Suppl. 18:415–594.

364. Caspers, N. 1980. Zur Larvalentwicklung und Produktionsökologie von *Tipula maxima* Poda (Diptera, Nematocera, Tipulidae). Arch. Hydrobiol. 58:273–309.

365. Cassani, J. R., and H. D. Newson. 1980. An annotated list of mosquitoes reported from Michigan. Mosquito News 40:356–368.

366. Cather, M. R., and A. R. Gaufin. 1975. Life history of *Megarcys signata* (Plecoptera: Perlodidae), Mill Creek, Wasatch Mountains, Utah. Great Basin Nat. 35:39–48.

367. Cather, M. R., and A. R. Gaufin. 1976. Comparative ecology of three *Zapada* species of Mill Creek, Wasatch Mountains, Utah (Plecoptera: Nemouridae). Am. Midl. Nat. 95:464–471.

368. Cather, M. R., B. P. Stark, and A. R. Gaufin. 1975. Records of stoneflies (Plecoptera) from Nevada. Great Basin Nat. 35:49–50.

369. Caucci, A., and R. Nastasi. 1975. Hatches. Comparahatch, N.Y. 320 pp.

370. Caudell, A. N. 1922. A diving wasp. Proc. Ent. Soc. Wash. 24:125–126.

371. Cavenaugh, W. J. and J. E. Tilden. 1930. Algal food, feeding, and case building habits of the larva of the midge fly *Tanytarsus dissimilis* Johannsen. Ecology 5:105–115.

372. Chaffee, D. L., and D. C. Tarter. 1979. Life history and ecology of *Baetisca bajkovi* Neave, in Beech Fork of Twelvepole Creek, Wayne County, West Virginia (Ephemeroptera: Baetiscidae). Psyche 86:53–61.

373. Chagnon, G. 1922. A hymenopteran of aquatic habits. Can. Ent. 65:24.

374. Chagnon, G., and O. Fournier. 1948. Contribution à l'étude des Hemipteres aquatiques du Québec. Contr. L'Inst. Biol. Univ. Montréal, Quebec. 21:1–66.

375. Chamberlin, J. C., and G. F. Ferris. 1929. On *Liparocephalus* and allied genera (Coleoptera: Staphylinidae). Pan-Pacif. Ent. 5:137–143, 5:153–162.

376. Chance, M. M. 1970. The functional morphology of the mouthparts of black fly larvae (Diptera: Simuliidae). Quaest. Ent. 6:245–284.

377. Chandler, H. P. 1954. Four new species of dobsonflies from California. Pan Pacif. Ent. 30:105–111.

378. Chandler, H. P. 1956a. Aquatic Neuroptera, pp. 234–236. *In* R. L. Usinger (ed.). Aquatic insects of California. Univ. Calif. Press. Berkeley. 508 pp.

379. Chandler, H. P. 1956b. Megaloptera, pp. 229–233. *In* R. L. Usinger (ed.). Aquatic insects of California. Univ. Calif. Press, Berkeley. 508 pp.

380. Chang, S. L. 1966. Some physiological observations on two aquatic Collembola. Trans. Am. Microsc. Soc. 85:359–371.

381. Chapin, J. W. 1978. Systematics of Nearctic *Micrasema* (Trichoptera: Brachycentridae). Ph.D. diss., Clemson University, Clemson, S.C. 136 pp.

382. Chapman, D. W., and R. Demory. 1963. Seasonal changes in the food ingested by aquatic insect larvae and nymphs in two Oregon streams. Ecology 44:140–146.

383. Chapman, H. C. 1958. Notes on the identity, habitat and distribution of some semi-aquatic Hemiptera of Florida. Fla. Ent. 41:117–124.

384. Chapman, H. C. 1959. Distributional and ecological records for some aquatic and semi-aquatic Heteroptera of New Jersey. Bull. Brooklyn Ent. Soc. 54:8–12.

385. Chapman, H. C. 1962. The Saldidae of Nevada (Hemiptera). Pan-Pacif. Ent. 38:147–159.

386. Chapman, J. A., and J. M. Kinghorn. 1955. Window-trap for flying insects. Can. Ent. 82:46–47.

387. Chapman, R. F. 1982. The insects: structure and function (3rd ed.). Harvard Univ. Press, Cambridge. 919 pp.

388. Charles, W. N., K. East, and T. D. Murray. 1976. Production of larval Tanypodinae (Insecta: Chironomidae) in the mud at Loch Leven, Kinross. Proc. R. Soc. Edinb. 75:157–169.

389. Cheary, B. S. 1971. The biology, ecology and systematics of the genus *Laccobius (Laccobius)* of the new world. Ph.D. diss., University of California, Riverside. 178 pp.

390. Cheng, L. 1967. Studies on the biology of the Gerridae (Hem., Heteroptera). I: Observations on the feeding of *Limnogonus fossarum* (F.) Entomol. mon. ·Mag. 102:121–129.

391. Cheng, L. (ed.). 1976. Marine insects. North Holland, Amsterdam. 581 pp.

392. Cheng, L., and C. H. Fernando. 1970. The waterstriders of Ontario. Misc. Life Sci. Publ. Roy. Ont. Mus., 23 pp.

393. Cheng, L. and C. H. Fernando. 1971. Life history and biology of the riffle bug, *Rhagovelia obesa* Uhler (Heteroptera: Veliidae) in Southern Ontario. Can. J. Zool. 49:435–442.

394. Chillcott, J. G. 1961. A revision of the genus *Roederioides* Coquillett (Diptera, Empididae). Can. Ent. 93:419–428.

395. China, W. E. 1955. The evolution of the water bugs. Bull. Nat. Inst. Sci. India 7:91–103.

396. China, W. E., and N. C. E. Miller. 1959. Checklist and keys to the families and subfamilies of the Hemiptera—Heteroptera. Bull. Brit. Mus. Nat. Hist. Ent. 8:1–45.

397. Christiansen, K. 1964. Bionomics of the Collembola. Ann. Rev. Ent. 9:147–178.

398. Christiansen, K., and P. Bellinger, 1980–81. The Collembola of North America north of the Rio Grande. Grinnell College. Grinnell, Iowa 1322 pp.

399. Chu, H. F. 1949. How to know the immature insects. Wm. C. Brown, Dubuque. 234 pp.

400. Chu, H. F. 1956. The nomenclature of the chaetotaxy of lepidopterous larvae and its application. Acta Ent. Sinica 6:323–333.

401. Chutter, F. M. 1971. A reappraisal of Needham and Usinger's data on the variability of a stream fauna when sampled with a Surber sampler. Limnol. Oceanogr. 17:139–141.

402. Claassen, P. W. 1921. *Typha* insects: their ecological relationships. Mem. Cornell Univ. Agric. Exp. Sta. 57:459–531.

403. Claassen, P. W. 1922. The larva of a chironomid (*Trissolcadius equitans* n. sp.) which is parasitic upon a mayfly nymph (*Rhithrogena* sp.). Univ. Kans. Sci. Bull. 14:395–405.

404. Claassen, P. W. 1931. Plecoptera nymphs of America (north of Mexico). Thomas Say Found. Ent. Soc. Am. 3:1–199.

405. Clark, W. H., and G. L. Ralston. 1974. *Eubrianax edwardsi* in Nevada with notes on larval pupation and emergence of adults (Coleoptera: Psephenidae). Coleopt. Bull. 28:217–218.

406. Clastrier, J., and W. W. Wirth. 1978. The *Leptoconops kerteszi* complex in North America. U.S. Dep. Agric. Tech. Bull. 1573:1–58.

407. Clausen, C. P. 1931. Biological observations on *Agriotypus* (Hymenoptera). Proc. Ent. Soc. Wash. 33:29–37.

408. Clausen, C. P. 1940. Entomophagous insects. McGraw-Hill, N.Y. 688 pp.

409. Clausen, C. P. 1950. Respiratory adaptations in the immature stages of parasitic insects. Arthropoda 1:198–224.

410. Clay, M. E., and C. E. Venard. 1972. Larval diapause in the mosquito *Aedes triseriatus:* Effects of diet and temperature on photoperiod induction. J. Insect Physiol. 18:1441–1446.

411. Clemens, W. A. 1917. An ecological study of the mayfly *Chirotenetes*. Univ. Toronto Stud. Biol. Ser. 17:5–43.

412. Clements, A. N. 1963. The physiology of mosquitoes. Pergamon, N.Y. 393 pp.

413. Clifford, H. F. 1976. Observations on the life cycle of *Siphloplecton basale* (Walker)(Ephemeroptera: Metretopodidae). Pan-Pacif. Ent. 52:265–271.

414. Clifford, H. F., and D. R. Barton. 1979. Observations on the biology of *Ametropus neavei* (Ephemeroptera: Ametropidae) from a large river in northern Alberta, Canada. Can. Ent. 111:855–858.

415. Clifford, H. F., and H. Boerger. 1974. Fecundity of mayflies (Ephemeroptera), with special reference to mayflies of a brown-water stream of Alberta, Canada. Can. Ent. 106:1111–1119.

416. Clifford, H. F., H. Hamilton, and B. A. Killins. 1979. Biology of the mayfly *Leptophlebia cupida* (Say)(Ephemeroptera: Leptophlebiidae). Can. J. Zool 57:1026–1045.

417. Cobben, R. H. 1968. Evolutionary trends in Heteroptera. Part I. Eggs, architecture of the shell, gross embryology, and eclosion. Centre Agric. Publ. Documentation, Wageningen. 475 pp.

418. Cobben, R. H. 1978. Evolutionary trends in Heteroptera. Part II. Mouthpart structures and feeding strategies. Meded. Lab. Ent. 289:1–407.

419. Coffman, W. P. 1967. Community structure and trophic relations in a small woodland stream, Linesville Creek, Crawford County, Pennsylvania. Ph.D. diss., University of Pittsburgh, Pittsburgh.

420. Coffman, W. P. 1973. Energy flow in a woodland stream ecosystem: II. The taxonomic composition and phenology of the Chironomidae as determined by the collection of pupal exuviae. Arch. Hydrobiol. 71:281–322.

421. Coffman, W. P., K. W. Cummins, and J. C. Wuycheck. 1971. Energy flow in a woodland stream ecosystem. I. Tissue support trophic structure of the autumnal community. Arch. Hydrobiol. 68:232–276.

422. Colbo, M. H., and G. N. Porter. 1979. Effects of the food supply on the life history of Simuliidae (Diptera). Can. J. Zool. 57:301–306.

423. Colbo, M. H., and G. N. Porter. 1981. The interaction of rearing temperature and food supply on the life history of two species of Simuliidae (Diptera). Can. J. Zool. 59:158–163.

424. Cole, F. R. (with collaboration of E. I. Schlinger). 1969. The flies of western North America. Univ. Calif. Press, Berkeley. 693 pp.

425. Cole, G. A. 1983. Textbook of limnology (3rd ed.). C. V. Mosby Co., St. Louis. 401 pp.

426. Coleman, M. J., and H. B. N. Hynes. 1970a. The vertical distribution of the invertebrate fauna in the bed of a stream. Limnol. Oceanogr. 15:31–40.

427. Coleman, M. J. and H. B. N. Hynes. 1970b. The life-histories of some Plecoptera and Ephemeroptera in a Southern Ontario stream. Can. J. Zool. 48:1333–1339.

428. Coler, R. A., and R. C. Haynes. 1966. A practical benthos sampler. Progr. Fish Cult. 28:95.

429. Collier, J. E. 1970. A taxonomic revision of the genus *Optioservus* (Coleoptera: Elmidae) in the Nearctic region. Diss. Abstr. Int. 30(B):4648.

430. Collins, N. C. 1975. Population biology of the brine fly (Diptera: Ephydridae) in the presence of abundant algal food. Ecology 56:1139–1148.

431. Common, I. F. B. 1970. Lepidoptera, pp. 765–866. *In* The insects of Australia. CSIRO, Melbourne Univ. Press Melbourne. 1029 pp.

432. Connell, T. D., and J. F. Scheiring. 1981. The feeding ecology of the larvae of the shore fly *Scatella picea* (Walker)(Diptera: Ephydridae). Can. J. Zool. 59:1831–1835.

433. Conroy, J. C., and J. L. Kuhn. 1977. New annotated records of Odonata from the province of Manitoba with notes on their parasitism by larvae of water mites. Manitoba Ent. 11:27–40.

434. Cook, E. F. 1956. The Nearctic Chaoborinae (Diptera: Culicidae). Univ. Minn. Agric. Exp. Sta. Tech. Bull. 218: 1–102.

435. Cook, E. F. 1981. Chap. 24. Chaoboridae, pp. 335–340. *In* J. F. McAlpine, B. V. Peterson, G. E. Shewell, H. J. Teskey, J. R. Vockeroth, and D. M. Wood (coords.). Manual of Nearctic Diptera, Vol. 1. Res. Branch, Agric. Can. Monogr 27. Ottawa 674 pp.

436. Corbet, P. S. 1955. The immature stages of the emperor dragonfly, *Anax imperator* (Leach)(Odonata: Aeshnidae). Ent. Gaz. 6:189–204.

437. Corbet, P. S. 1956. The life-histories of *Lestes sponsa* (Hansemann) and *Sympetrum striolatum* (Charpentier)(Odonata). Tijdschr. Ent. 99:217–229.

438. Corbet, P. S. 1957a. The life histories of two spring species of dragonfly (Odonata: Zygoptera). Ent. Gaz. 8:79–89.

439. Corbet, P. S. 1957b. The life-history of the emperor dragonfly *Anax imperator* (Leach)(Odonata: Aeshnidae). J. Anim. Ecol. 26:1–69.

440. Corbet, P. S. 1960. Fossil history, pp. 149–163. *In* P. S. Corbet, C. Longfield, and N. W. Moore (eds.). Dragonflies. Collins, London. 260 pp.

441. Corbet, P. S. 1963. A biology of dragonflies. Quandrangle, Chicago. 247 pp.

442. Corbet, P. S. 1964. Temporal patterns of emergence in aquatic insects. Can. Ent. 96:264–279.

443. Corbet, P. S. 1965. An insect emergence trap for quantitative studies in shallow ponds. Can. Ent. 97:845–848.

444. Corbet, P. S. 1978. Concluding remarks. Symposium: Seasonality in New Zealand insects. N. Z. Ent. Soc. 6:367.

445. Corbet, P. S. 1979. Odonata. *In* H. V. Danks (ed.). Canada and its insect fauna. Mem. Ent. Soc. Can. 108:308–311.

446. Corbet, P. S. 1980. Biology of Odonata. Ann. Rev. Ent. 25: 189–217.

447. Corbet, P. S., C. Longfield, and N. W. Moore. 1960. Dragonflies. Collins, London. 260 pp.

448. Corkum, L. D. 1978. The nymphal development of *Paraleptophlebia adoptiva* (McDunnough) and *Paraleptophlebia mollis* (Eaton) (Ephemeroptera: Leptophlebiidae) and the possible influence of temperature. Can. J. Zool. 56:1842–1846.

449. Corkum, L. D., and P. J. Pointing, 1979. Nymphal development of *Baetis vagans* McDunnough (Ephemeroptera: Baetidae) and drift habits of large nymphs. Can. J. Zool. 57: 2348–2354.

450. Corpus, L. D. 1981a. A brief survey of the Dolichopodidae. Proc. Wash. State Ent. Soc. 43:617–618.

451. Corpus, L. D. 1981b. Preliminary data on the immature stages of *Pelastoneurus vagans* Loew (Diptera: Dolichopodidae). Proc. Wash. State Ent. Soc. 43:610–612.

452. Coulson, J. C. 1962. The biology of *Tipula subnodicornis* Zetterstedt with comparative observations on *Tipula paludosa* Meigen. J. Anim. Ecol. 31:1–21.

453. Craig, D. A. 1966. Techniques for rearing stream-dwelling organisms in the laboratory. Tuatara 14:65–72.

454. Craig, D. A. 1977a. Mouthparts and feeding behaviour of Tahitian larval Simuliidae (Diptera: Nematocera). Quaest. Ent. 13:195–218.

455. Craig, D. A. 1977b. A reliable chilled water stream for rheophilic insects. Mosquito News 37:773–774.

456. Craig, P. 1970. The behavior and distribution of the intertidal sand beetle, *Thinopinus pictus*. Ecology 51:1012–1017.

457. Crampton, G. C. 1930. A comparison of the more important structural details of the larva of the archaic tanyderid dipteran *Protoplasa fitchii*, with other Holometabola, from the standpoint of phylogeny. Bull. Brooklyn Ent. Soc. 35:235–258.

458. Crampton, G. C. 1942. Guide to the insects of Connecticut. Diptera or true flies of Connecticut. Part VI, Fasc. I. External Morphology. Bull. Conn. State Geol. Nat. Hist. Surv. 64:10–165.

459. Cranston, P. S. 1982. A key to the larvae of the British Orthocladiinae (Chironomidae). Sci. Publ. Freshwat. Biol. Assoc. 45:1–152.

460. Crawford, D. O. 1912. The petroleum fly of California, *Psilopa petrolei* Coq. Pomona Coll. J. Ent. 4:687–697.

461. Credland, P. F. 1973. A new method for establishing a permanent laboratory culture of *Chironomus riparius* Meigen (Diptera: Chironomidae). Freshwat. Biol. 3:45–51.

462. Crichton, M. I. 1957. The structure and function of the mouth parts of adult caddis flies (Trichoptera). Phil. Trans. Roy. Soc. Lond. (B) 241:45–91.

463. Crisp, D. T. 1962. Observations on the biology of *Corixa germani* (Fieb.) (Hemiptera: Heteroptera) in an upland reservoir. Arch. Hydrobiol. 58:261–280.

464. Crosby, T. K. 1975. Food of the New Zealand trichopterans *Hydrobiosis parumbripennis* McFarlane and *Hydropsyche colonica* McLachlan. Freshwat. Biol. 5:105–114.

465. Cross, W. H. 1955. Anisopteran Odonata of the Savannah river plant, South Carolina. J. Elisha Mitchell Sci. Soc. 71:9–17.

466. Crosskey, R. W. 1973. Simuliidae (Black-flies), pp. 109–153. *In* K. G. V. Smith (ed.). Insects and other arthropods of medical importance. Bull. Ent. Br. Mus. Nat. Hist., London 561 pp.

467. Crossman, J. S., and J. Cairns. 1974. A comparative study between two different artificial substrate samplers and regular sampling techniques. Hydrobiologia 44:517–522.

468. Crowell, R. M. 1967. The immature stages of *Albia caerulea* (Acarina: Axonopsidae), a water mite parasitizing caddisflies (Trichoptera). Can. Ent. 99:730–734.

469. Crowell, R. M. 1968. Supplementary observations of the early developmental stages of *Albia caerulea* (Acarina: Axonopsidae). Can. Ent. 100:178–180.

470. Crowley, P. H. 1979. Behavior of zygopteran nymphs in a simulated weed bed. Odonatologica 8:91–101.

471. Cruden, R. W. 1962. A preliminary survey of West Virginia dragonflies (Odonata). Ent. News 73:156–160.

472. Crumb, S. E. 1929. Tobacco cutworms. U.S. Dep. Agric. Tech. Bull. 88:1–180.

473. Crumb, S. E. 1956. The larvae of the Phalaenidae. U.S. Dep. Agric. Tech. Bull. 1135:1–356.

474. Cudney, M. D., and J. B. Wallace. 1980. Life cycles, microdistribution and production dynamics of six species of net-spinning caddisflies in a large Southeastern (U.S.A.) river. Holarct. Ecol. 3:169–182.

475. Cullen, M. J. 1969. The biology of giant water bugs (Hemiptera: Belostomatidae) in Trinidad. Proc. R. ent. Soc. Lond. (A) 44:123–136.

476. Cummings, C. 1933. The giant water bugs. Univ. Kans. Sci. Bull. 21:197–219.

477. Cummins, K. W. 1962. An evaluation of some techniques for the collection and analysis of benthic samples with special emphasis on lotic waters. Am. Midl. Nat. 67:477–504.

478. Cummins, K. W. 1964. Factors limiting the microdistribution of larvae of the caddisflies *Pycnopsyche lepida* (Hagen) and *Pycnopsyche guttifer* (Walker) in a Michigan stream. Ecol. Monogr. 34:271–295.

479. Cummins, K. W. 1972. What is a river?—zoological description, pp. 33–52. *In* R. T. Oglesby, C. A. Carlson, and J. A. McCann (eds.). River ecology and man. Academic, N.Y. 465 pp.

480. Cummins, K. W. 1973. Trophic relations of aquatic insects. Ann. Rev. Ent. 18:183–206.

481. Cummins, K. W. 1974. Structure and function of stream ecosystems. BioScience 24:631–641.

482. Cummins, K. W. 1975. Macroinvertebrates, pp. 170–198. *In* B. A. Whitton (ed.). River ecology. Blackwell, England. 725 pp.

483. Cummins, K. W. 1980a. The multiple linkages of forests to streams, pp. 191–198. *In* R. H. Waring (ed.). Forests: Fresh perspectives from ecosystem analysis. Proc. 40th Ann. Biol. Colloq., Oregon State Univ., Corvallis, 198 pp.

484. Cummins, K. W. 1980b. The natural stream ecosystem, pp. 7–24, *In* J. V. Ward and J. A. Stanford (eds.). The ecology of regulated streams. Plenum, N.Y. 398 pp.

485. Cummins, K. W., and M. J. Klug. 1979. Feeding ecology of stream invertebrates. Ann. Rev. Ecol. Syst. 10:147–172.

486. Cummins, K. W., M. J. Klug, G. M. Ward, G. L. Spengler, R. W. Speaker, R. W. Ovink, D. C. Mahan, and R. C. Petersen. 1981. Trends in particulate organic matter fluxes, community processes, and macroinvertebrate functional groups along a Great Lakes drainage basin river continuum. Verh. Int. Verein. Limnol. 21:841–849.

487. Cummins, K. W., L. D. Miller, N. A. Smith, and R. M. Fox. 1965. Experimental entomology. Reinhold, N.Y. 160 pp.

488. Cummins, K. W., R. C. Petersen, F. O. Howard, J. C. Wuycheck, and V. I. Holt. 1973. The utilization of leaf litter by stream detritivores. Ecology 54:336–345.

489. Cupp, E. W., and A. E. Gordon (eds.). 1983. Notes on the systematics, distribution, and bionomics of black flies (Diptera: Simuliidae) in the Northeastern United States. Search: Agriculture. Ithaca, N.Y.: Cornell Univ. Agric. Exp. Sta. No. 25:1–76.

490. Curry, L. L. 1954. Notes on the ecology of the midge fauna of Hunt Creek, Montmorency County, Michigan. Ecology 35:541–550.

491. Curry, L. L. 1966. Freshwater invertebrate food preferences. Unpubl. Rept. Dept. Biol., Central Michigan Univ., Mt. Pleasant.

492. Curtis, L. C. 1967. The mosquitos of British Columbia. Occ. Pap. Brit. Columbia Prov. Mus. 15:1–90.

493. Cushing, C. E. 1964. An apparatus for sampling drifting organisms in streams. J. Wildl. Manage. 28:592–594.

494. Cushing, C. E., and R. T. Rader. 1983. A note on the food of *Callibaetis* (Ephemeroptera: Baetidae). Great Basin Nat. 41:431–432.

495. Cushman, R. M., J. W. Elwood, and S. G. Hildebrand. 1975. Production dynamics of *Alloperla mediana* Banks (Plecoptera: Chloroperlidae) and *Diplectrona modesta* Banks (Trichoptera: Hydropsychidae) in Walker Branch, Tennessee. Publ. Env. Sci. Div. Oak Ridge Nat. Lab. Tenn. 785:1–66.

496. Cutten-Ali-Khan, E. A., and D. K. McE. Kevan. 1970. The Nymphomyiidae (Diptera), with special reference to *Palaeodipteron walkeri* Ide and to larva in Quebec, and a description of a new genus and species from India. Can. J. Zool. 48:1–24.

497. Cuyler, R. D. 1956. Taxonomy and ecology of larvae of sialoid Megaloptera of east-central North Carolina with a key to and description of larvae of genera known to occur in the United States. M.S. thesis. North Carolina State Univ., Raleigh. 150 pp.

498. Cuyler, R. D. 1958. The larvae of *Chauliodes* Latrielle (Megaloptera: Corydalidae). Ann. Ent. Soc. Am. 51:582–586.

499. Cuyler, R. D. 1965. The larva of *Nigronia fasciatus* Walker (Megaloptera: Corydalidae). Ent. News 76:192–194.

500. Cuyler, R. D. 1968. Range extensions of Odonata in southeastern states. Ent. News 79:29–34.

501. Dadd, R. H. 1970a. Relationship between filtering activity and ingestion of solids by larvae of the mosquito *Culex pipiens:* A method for assessing phagostimulant factors. J. Med. Ent. 7:708–712.

502. Dadd, R. H. 1970b. Comparison of rates of ingestion of particulate solids by *Culex pipiens* larvae: Phagostimulant effect of water-soluble yeast extract. Ent. Exp. Appl. 13:407–419.

503. Dadd, R. H. 1971. Effects of size and concentration of particles on rates of ingestion of latex particulates by mosquito larvae. Ann. Ent. Soc. Am. 64:687–692.

504. Dadd, R. H. 1973. Autophagostimulation by mosquito larvae. Ent. exp. appl. 16:295–300.

505. Dadd, R. H. 1975. Ingestion of colloid solutions by filter-feeding mosquito larvae: Relationship to viscosity. J. exp. Zool. 191:395–406.

506. Daly, H. V., J. T. Doyen, and P. R. Ehrlich. 1978. Introduction to insect biology and diversity. McGraw-Hill N.Y., 564 pp.

507. Danecker, E. 1961. Studien zur hygropetrischen Fauna. Biologie and Ökologie von *Stactobia* und *Tinodes* (Insect., Trichopt.). Int. Revue ges. Hydrobiol. 46:214–254.

508. Danks, H. V. 1971. Life history and biology of *Einfeldia synchrona* (Diptera: Chironomidae). Can. Ent. 103:1597–1606.

509. Danks, H. V. 1978. Some effects of photoperiod, temperature and food on emergence in three species of Chironomidae (Diptera). Can. Ent. 110:289–300.

510. Danks, H. V., and D. R. Oliver. 1972. Seasonal emergence of some high arctic Chironomidae (Diptera). Can. Ent. 104:661–686.

511. Darby, R. E. 1962. Midges associated with California rice fields, with special reference to their ecology (Diptera: Chironomidae). Hilgardia 32:1–206.

512. Darsie, R. F., D. MacCreary, and L. A. Stearns. 1951. An annotated list of the mosquitoes of Delaware. N.J. Mosquito Exterm. Assoc. Proc. 38:137–146.

513. Darsie, R. F., and R. A. Ward. 1981. Identification and geographical distribution of the mosquitoes of North America, north of Mexico. Mosquito Sys. Suppl. No. 1. Amer. Mosquito Contr. Assoc., Fresno, Calif. 313 pp.

514. Davenport, C. B. 1903. The Collembola of Cold Spring Beach, with special reference to the movements of the Poduridae. Cold Spring Harbor Monogr. 2:1–32.

515. Davies, B. R. 1976. The dispersal of Chironomidae: a review. J. Ent. Soc. S. Afr. 39:39–62.

516. Davies, D. A. L. 1981. A synopsis of the extant genera of the Odonata. Soc. Int. Odonatol. Rapid Comm. 3:1–60.

517. Davies, D. M., and B. V. Peterson. 1956. Observations on the mating, feeding, ovarian development, and oviposition of adult black flies (Simuliidae, Diptera). Can. J. Zool. 34:615–655.

518. Davies, D. M., B. V. Peterson, and D. M. Wood. 1962. The black flies (Diptera: Simuliidae) of Ontario. Part I. Adult identification and distribution with descriptions of six new species. Proc. Ent. Soc. Ont. 92:70–154.

519. Davies, I. J. 1975. Selective feeding in some arctic Chironomidae. Verh. Int. Verein. Limnol. 19:3149–3154.

520. Davies, L. 1965a. On spermatophores in Simuliidae (Diptera). Proc. R. ent. Soc. Lond., Ser. A. 40:30–34.

521. Davies, L. 1965b. The structure of certain atypical Simuliidae (Diptera) in relation to evolution within the family, and the erection of a new genus for the Crozet Island black-fly. Proc. Linn. Soc. London 176:159–180.

522. Davies, L., and C. D. Smith. 1958. The distribution and growth of *Prosimulium* larvae (Diptera: Simuliidae) in hill streams in Northern England. J. Anim. Ecol. 27:335–348.

523. Davies, R. W., and V. J. McCauley. 1970. The effects of preservatives on the regurgitation of gut contents by Chironomidae (Diptera) larvae. Can. J. Zool. 48:519–522.

524. Davis, C. C. 1961a. A study of the hatching process in aquatic invertebrates. I. The hatching process in *Amnicola limosa.* II. Hatching in *Ranatra fusca* P. Beauvois. Trans. Am. Microsc. Soc. 80:227–234.

525. Davis, C. C. 1961b. Hatching in *Dineutes assimilis* Aube (Coleoptera, Gyrinidae). Int. Revue ges. Hydrobiol. 46:429–433.

526. Davis, C. C. 1962. Ecological and morphological notes on *Hydrophylita aquivalans* (Math. and Crosby). Limnol. Oceanogr. 7:390–392.

527. Davis, C. C. 1964. A study of the hatching process in aquatic invertebrates. VII. Observations on hatching in *Notonecta melaena* Kirkaldy (Hemiptera, Notonectidae) and on *Ranatra absona* D. and DeC. (Hemiptera, Nepidae). Hydrobiologia 23:253–259.

528. Davis, C. C. 1965a. A study of the hatching process in aquatic invertebrates. XIX. Hatching in *Psephenus herricki* (DeKay) (Coleoptera, Psephenidae). Am. Midl. Nat. 74:443–450.

529. Davis, C. C. 1965b. A study of the hatching process in aquatic invertebrates. XII. The eclosion process in *Trichocorixa naias* (Kirkaldy). Trans. Am. Microsc. Soc. 84:60–65.

530. Davis, C. C. 1966. Notes on the ecology and reproduction of *Trichocorixa reticulata* in a Jamaican salt-water pool. Ecology 47:850–852.

531. Davis, K. C. 1903. Sialididae of North America. Bull. N.Y. State Mus. 18:442–486.

532. Davis, L. V., and I. E. Gray. 1966. Zonal and seasonal distribution of insects in North Carolina salt marshes. Ecol. Monogr. 36:275–295.

533. Davis, M. M., and G. R. Finni. 1974. Habitat preference of *Macronychus glabratus* Say (Coleoptera: Elmidae). Proc. Penn. Acad. Sci. 48:95–97.

534. Davis, W. T. 1933. Dragonflies of the Genus *Tetragoneuria.* Bull. Brooklyn Ent. Soc. 28:87–104.

535. Day, W. C. 1956. Ephemeroptera, pp. 79–105. *In* R. L. Usinger (ed.). Aquatic insects of California. Univ. Calif. Press, Berkeley. 508 pp.

536. Deay, H. O., and G. E. Gould. 1936. The Hemiptera of Indiana. I. Family Gerridae. Am. Midl. Nat. 17:753–769.

537. DeCoursey, R. M. 1971. Keys to the families and subfamilies of the nymphs of North American Hemiptera-Heteroptera. Proc. Ent. Soc. Wash. 73:413–428.

538. Deevy, E. S. 1941. Limnological studies in Connecticut. VI. The quantity and composition of the bottom fauna of thirty-six Connecticut and New York lakes. Ecol. Monogr. 11:413–455.

539. Delamare-Deboutteville, C. 1953. Collemboles marins de la zone souterraine humide de sables littoraux. Vie Milieu 4:290–319.

540. Delamare-Deboutteville, C. 1960. Biologie des eaux souterraines littorales et continentales. Vlg. Hermann, Paris. 740 pp.

541. De Marmels, J., and J. Racenis. 1982. An analysis of the *cophysa-* group of *Tramea* Hagen, with descriptions of two new species (Anisoptera: Libellulidae). Odonatologica 11:109–128.

542. Dendy, J. S. 1973. Predation on chironomid eggs and larvae by *Nanocladius alternantherae* Dendy and Sublette (Diptera: Chironomidae, Orthocladiinae). Ent. News 84:91–95.

543. Denning, D. G. 1943. The Hydropsychidae of Minnesota (Trichoptera). Entomologica am. 23:101–171.

544. Denning, D. G. 1950. Order Trichoptera, the caddisflies, pp. 12–23. *In* D. L. Wray (ed.). The insects of North Carolina (2nd suppl.). N. C. Dep. Agric. 59 pp.

545. Denning, D. G. 1956. Trichoptera, pp. 237–270. *In* R. L. Usinger (ed.). Aquatic insects of California. Univ. Calif. Press, Berkeley. 508 pp.

546. Denning, D. G. 1958. The genus *Farula* (Trichoptera: Limnephilidae). Ann. Ent. Soc. Am. 51:531–535.

547. Denning, D. G. 1964. The genus *Homophylax* (Trichoptera: Limnephilidae). Ann. Ent. Soc. Am. 57:253–260.

548. Denning, D. G. 1970. The genus *Psychoglypha* (Trichoptera: Limnephilidae). Can. Ent. 102:15–30.

549. Denning, D. G. 1975. New species of Trichoptera from western North America. Pan-Pacif. Ent. 51:318–326.

550. Denning, D. G., and R. L. Blickle. 1972. A review of the genus *Ochrotrichia* (Trichoptera:Hydroptilidae). Ann. Ent. Soc. Am. 65:141–151.

551. Denno, R. F. 1976. Ecological significance of wing-polymorphism in Fulgoridae which inhabit tidal salt marshes. Ecol. Ent. 1:257–266.

552. Deonier, D. L. 1964. Ecological observations on Iowa shore flies (Diptera, Ephydridae). Proc. Iowa Acad. Sci. 71:496–510.

553. Deonier, D. L. 1971. A systematic and ecological study of Nearctic *Hydrellia* (Diptera: Ephydridae). Smithson. Contr. Zool. 68:1–147.

554. Deonier, D. L. 1972. Observations on mating and food habits of certain shore flies (Diptera: Ephydridae). Ohio J. Sci. 72:22–29.

555. Deonier, D. L. 1974. Biology and descriptions of immature stages of the shore fly, *Scatophila iowana* (Diptera: Ephydridae). Iowa State J. Res. 49:17–21.

556. Deonier, D. L. (ed.). 1979. First symposium on the systematics and ecology of Ephydridae (Diptera). N. Am. Benthol. Soc. 147 pp.

557. Deonier, D. L., S. Kincaid, and J. Scheiring. 1976. Substrate and moisture preference in the common toad bug, *Gelastocoris oculatus*. Ent. News 87:257–264.

558. Deonier, D. L., W. N. Mathis, and J. T. Regensburg. 1978a. Natural history and life-cycle stages of *Notiphila carinata* (Diptera: Ephydridae). Proc. Biol. Soc. Wash. 91:798–814.

559. Deonier, D. L., and J. T. Regensburg. 1978b. Biology and immature stages of *Parydra quadrituberculata*. Ann. Ent. Soc. Am. 71:341–353.

560. de Ruiter, L., H. P. Wolvekamp, A. J. van Tooren, and A. Vlasblom. 1952. Experiments on the efficiency of the "physical gill" (*Hydrous piceus* L., *Naucoris cimicoides* L., and *Notonecta glauca* L.). Acta Physiol. Pharmacol. Neerl. 2:180–213.

561. Deshefy, G. S. 1980. Anti-predator behavior in swarms of *Rhagovelia obesa* (Hemiptera: Veliidae). Pan-Pacif. Ent. 56:111–112.

562. Deutsch, W. G. 1980. Macroinvertebrate colonization of acrylic plates in a large river. Hydrobiologia 75:65–72.

563. Dickinson, J. C., Jr. 1949. An ecological reconnaissance of the biota of some ponds and ditches in Northern Florida. Quart. J. Fla. Acad. Sci. 11:1–28.

564. Dickinson, W. E. 1944. The mosquitoes of Wisconsin. Milwaukee Pub. Mus. Bull. 8:269–385.

565. Dixon, R. D., and R. A. Burst. 1971. Mosquitoes of Manitoba, Ill. Ecology of larvae in the Winnipeg area. Can. Ent. 104:961–968.

566. Dodds, G. S., and F. L. Hisaw. 1924a. Ecological studies of aquatic insects. I. Adaptations of mayfly nymphs to swift streams. Ecology 5:137–148.

567. Dodds, G. S., and F. L. Hisaw. 1924b. Ecological studies of aquatic insects. II. Size of respiratory organs in relation to environmental conditions. Ecology 5:262–271.

568. Dodson, S. I. 1970. Complementary feeding niches sustained by size-selective predation. Limnol. Oceanogr. 15:131–137.

569. Domizi, E. A., A. L. Estevez, J. A. Schnack, and G. R. Spinelli. 1978. Ecologia y estrategia de una población de *Belostoma oxyurum* (Dufour) (Hemiptera, Belostomatidae). Ecosur 5:157–168.

570. Don, A. W. 1967. Aspects of the biology of *Microvelia macgregori* Kirkaldy (Heteroptera: Veliidae). Proc. R. ent. Soc. Lond. (A). 42:171–179.

571. Donald, D. B., and R. S. Anderson. 1977. Distribution of the stoneflies (Plecoptera) of the Waterton River drainage, Alberta, Canada. Can. Wild. Serv. Syesis 10:111–120.

572. Donnelly, T. W. 1961. The Odonata of Washington, D.C. and vicinity. Proc. Ent. Soc. Wash. 63:1–13.

573. Donnelly, T. W. 1961a. *Aeshna persephone,* a new species of dragonfly from Arizona, with notes on *Aeshna arida* Kennedy (Odonata: Aeshnidae). Proc. Ent. Soc. Wash. 63:193–202.

574. Donnelly, T. W. 1962b. *Somatochlora margarita,* a new species of dragonfly from eastern Texas. Proc. Ent. Soc. Wash. 64:235–240.

575. Donnelly, T. W. 1965. A new species of *Ischnura* from Guatemala, with revisionary notes on related North and Central American damselflies (Odonata: Coenagrionidae). Fla. Ent. 48:57–63.

576. Donnelly, T. W. 1966. A new gomphine dragonfly from eastern Texas. Proc. Ent. Soc. Wash. 68:102–105.

577. Donnelly, T. W. 1970. The Odonata of Dominican British West Indies. Smithson. Contr. Zool. 37:1–20.

578. Donnelly, T. W. 1978. Odonata of the Sam Houston National Forest and vicinity, east Texas, United States, 1960–1966. Notul. Odonatol. 1:6–7.

579. Dorer, R. E., W. E. Bickley, and H. P. Nicholson. 1944. An annotated list of the mosquitoes of Virginia. Mosquito News 4:48–50.

580. Dosdall, L., and D. M. Lehmkuhl. 1979. Stoneflies (Plecoptera) of Saskatchewan. Quaest. Ent. 15:3–116.

581. Douglas, B. 1958. The ecology of the attached diatoms and other algae in a small stony stream. Ecology 46:295–322.

582. Doutt, R. L. 1949. A synopsis of North American Anaphoidea. Pan-Pacif. Ent. 25:155–160.

583. Doutt, R. L., and G. Viggiani. 1968. The classification of the Trichogrammatidae (Hym.: Chalciodoidea). Proc. Calif. Acad. Sci. 35:477–586.

584. Downe, A. E. R., and V. G. Caspary. 1973. The swarming behavior of *Chironomus riparius* (Diptera: Chironomidae) in the laboratory. Can. Ent. 105:165–171.

585. Downes, J. A. 1974. The feeding habits of adult Chironomidae. Tijdschr. Ent. Suppl. 95:84–90.

586. Downes, J. A., and W. W. Wirth, 1981.Chap. 28. Ceratopogonidae, pp. 393–422. *In* J. P. McAlpine, B. V. Peterson, G. E. Shewell, H. J. Teskey, J. R. Vockeroth, and D. M. Wood (coords.). Manual of Nearctic Diptera, Vol. 1. Res. Branch, Agric. Can. Monogr. 27. 674 pp.

587. Doyen, J. T. 1975. Intertidal insects: order Coleoptera, pp. 446–452. *In* R. I. Smith (ed.). Intertidal invertebrates of the central California coast. Univ. Calif. Press, Berkeley. 716 pp.

588. Doyen, J. T. 1976. Marine beetles (Coleoptera excluding Staphylinidae), pp. 497–519. *In* L. Cheng (ed.). Marine insects. North Holland, Amsterdam. 581 pp.

589. Drake, C. J. 1917. A survey of the North American species of *Merragata.* Ohio J. Sci. 17:101–105.

590. Drake, C. J. 1950. Concerning North American Saldidae (Hemiptera). Bull. Brooklyn Ent. Soc. 45:1–7.

591. Drake, C. J. 1952. Alaskan Saldidae (Hemiptera). Proc. Ent. Soc. Wash. 54:145–148.

592. Drake, C. J., and H. C. Chapman. 1953. A preliminary report on the Pleidae of the Americas. Proc. Biol. Soc. Wash. 66:53–60.

593. Drake, C. J., and H. C. Chapman. 1954. New American waterstriders. Fla. Ent. 37:151–155.

594. Drake, C. J., and H. C. Chapman. 1958a. New Neotropical Hebridae, including a catalog of the American species (Hemiptera). J. Wash. Acad. Sci. 48:317–326.

595. Drake, C. J., and H. C. Chapman. 1958b. The subfamily Saldoidinae (Hemiptera: Saldidae). Ann. Ent. Soc. Am. 51:480–485.

596. Drake, C. J., and H. M. Harris. 1932. A survey of the species of *Trepobates* Uhler. Bull. Brooklyn Ent. Soc. 27:113–123.

597. Drake, C. J., and H. M. Harris. 1934. The Gerrinae of the Western Hemisphere. Ann. Carnegie Mus. 23:179–240.

598. Drake, C. J., and L. Hoberlandt. 1950. Catalog of genera and species of Saldidae. Acta Ent. Mus. Nat. Prague 26(376):1–12.

599. Drake, C. J., and F. C. Hottes. 1950. Saldidae of the Americas (Hemiptera). Great Basin Nat. 10:51–61.

600. Drake, C. J., and R. F. Hussey. 1955. Concerning the genus *Microvelia* Westwood with descriptions of two new species and checklist of the American forms (Hemiptera: Veliidae). Fla. Ent. 38:95–115.

601. Drake, C. J., and D. R. Lauck. 1959. Description, synonomy, and checklist of American Hydrometridae (Hemiptera-Heteroptera). Great Basin Nat. 19:43–52.

602. Drake, C. J., and J. Maldonado-Capriles. 1956. Some pleids and water-striders from the Dominican Republic (Hemiptera). Bull. Brooklyn Ent. Soc. 51:53–56.

603. Drees, B. M., L. Butler, and L. L. Pechuman. 1980. Horse flies and deer flies of West Virginia: An illustrated key (Diptera, Tabanidae). Bull. W.Va. Agric. For. Exp. Sta. 674:1–67.

604. Dudley, T., and N. H. Anderson. 1982. A survey of invertebrates associated with wood debris in aquatic habitats. Melanderia 39:1–21.

605. Dudley, T. L. 1982. Population and production ecology of *Lipsothrix* spp. (Diptera: Tipulidae). M.S. thesis. Oregon State University, Corvallis. 161 pp.

606. Dumont, B., and J. Verneaux. 1976. Édifice trophique partiel du cours supérieur d'un ruisseau forestier. Ann. Limnol. 12:239–252.

607. Dunkle, S. W. 1976. Larva of the dragonfly *Ophiogomphus arizonicus* (Odonata: Gomphidae). Fla. Ent. 59:317–320.

608. Dunkle, S. W. 1977a. The larva of *Somatochlora filosa* (Odonata: Corduliidae). Fla. Ent. 60:187–191.

609. Dunkle, S. W. 1977b. Larvae of the genus *Gomphaeschna* (Odonata: Aeshnidae). Fla. Ent. 60:223–225.

610. Dunkle, S. W. 1978. Notes on adult behavior and emergence of *Paltothemis lineatipes* Karsch, 1890 (Anisoptera: Libellulidae). Odonatologica 7:277–279.

611. Dunkle, S. W. 1981. The ecology and behavior of *Tachopteryx thoreyi* (Hagen) (Anisoptera: Petaluridae). Odonatologica 10: 189–199.

612. Dunkle, S. W., and M. J. Westfall, Jr. 1982. Order Odonata, pp. 32–45. *In* R. Franz (ed.). Invertebrates, Vol. 6. Rare and Endangered Biota of Florida. Univ. Presses of Florida.

613. Dunn, C. E. 1979. A revision and phylogenetic study of the genus *Hesperocorixa* Kirkaldy (Hemiptera: Corixidae). Proc. Acad. Nat. Sci. Philadelphia 131:158–190.

614. Dunson, W. A. 1980. Adaptations of nymphs of a marine dragonfly, *Erythrodiplax berenice,* to wide variations of salinity. Physiol. Zool. 53:445–452.

615. DuPorte, E. M. 1959. Manual of insect morphology. Reinhold, N.Y. 224 pp.

616. Dyar, H. G., and R. C. Shannon. 1927. The North American two-winged flies of the family Simuliidae. Proc. U.S. Nat. Mus. 69:1–54.

617. Easten, W. C., and B. A. Foote. 1971. Biology and immature stages of *Dichaeta caudata* (Diptera: Ephydridae). Ann. Ent. Soc. Am. 64:271–279.

618. Eastham, L. E. S. 1934. Metachronal rhythms and gill movements of the nymph of *Cunis horaria* (Ephemeroptera) in relation to water flow. Proc. R. Soc. Lond., Ser. B. 115:30–48.

619. Eastham, L. E. S. 1936. The rhythmical movements of the gills of nymphal *Leptophlebia marginata* (Ephemeroptera) and the currents produced by them in water. J. exp. Biol. 13:443–453.

620. Eastham, L. E. S. 1937. The gill movements of nymphal *Ecdyonurus venosus* (Ephemeroptera) and the currents produced by them in water. J. exp. Biol. 14:219–228.

621. Eastham, L. E. S. 1939. Gill movements of nymphal *Ephemera vulgata* (Ephemeroptera) and the water currents caused by them. J. exp. Biol. 16:18–33.

622. Eckblad, J. W. 1973. Experimental predation studies of malacophagous larvae of *Sepedon fuscipennis* (Diptera: Sciomyzidae). Exp. Parasitol. 33:331–342.

623. Eddington, J. M. 1968. Habitat preferences in net-spinning caddis larvae with special reference to the influence of water velocity. J. Anim. Ecol. 37:675–692.

624. Eddington, J. M., and A. H. Hildrew. 1973. Experimental observations relating to the distribution of net-spinning Trichoptera in streams. Verh. Int. Verein. Limnol. 18:1549–1558.

625. Eddy, S., and A. C. Hodson. 1961. Taxonomic keys to the common animals of the north central states (3rd ed.). Burgess, Minneapolis 162 pp.

626. Edmondson, W. T. (ed.). 1959. Freshwater Biology (2nd ed.). John Wiley & Sons, N.Y. 1248 pp.

627. Edmondson, W. T., and G. G. Winberg (eds.). 1971. A manual on methods for the assessment of secondary productivity in freshwaters. IBP Handbook 17. Blackwell, Oxford. 358 pp.

628. Edmunds, G. F., Jr. 1957. The predaceous mayfly nymphs of North America. Proc. Utah Acad. Sci. Arts Lett. 34:23–24.

629. Edmunds, G. F., Jr. 1959. Ephemeroptera, pp. 908–916. *In* W. T. Edmondson (ed.). Freshwater biology (2nd ed.). John Wiley & Sons 1248 pp.

630. Edmunds, G. F., Jr. 1960. The food habits of the nymph of the mayfly *Siphlonurus occidentalis.* Proc. Utah Acad. Sci. Arts Lett. 37:73–74.

631. Edmunds, G. F., Jr. 1961. A key to the genera of known nymphs of the Oligoneuriidae (Ephemeroptera). Proc. Ent. Soc. Wash. 63:255–256.

632. Edmunds, G. F. 1972. Biogeography and evolution of Ephemeroptera. Ann. Rev. Ent. 17:21–43.

633. Edmunds, G. F. 1975. Phylogenetic biogeography of mayflies. Ann. Mo. Bot. Gard. 62:251–263.

634. Edmunds, G. F., Jr., and R. K. Allen. 1964. The Rocky Mountain species of *Epeorus (Iron)* Eaton (Ephemeroptera: Heptageniidae). J. Kans. Ent. Soc. 37:275–288.

635. Edmunds, G. F., Jr., L. Berner, and J. R. Traver. 1958. North American mayflies of the family Oligoneuridae. Ann. Ent. Soc. Am. 51:375–382.

636. Edmunds, G. F., and S. L. Jensen. 1975. A new genus and subfamily of North American Heptageniidae (Ephemeroptera). Proc. Ent. Soc. Wash. 76:495–497.

637. Edmunds, G. F., Jr., S. L. Jensen, and L. Berner. 1976. The mayflies of North and Central America. Univ. Minnesota Press, Minneapolis. 330 pp.

638. Edmunds, G. F., and J. R. Traver. 1954. The flight mechanics and evolution of the wings of Ephemeroptera, with notes on the archetype insect wing. J. Wash. Acad. Sci. 44:390–400.

639. Edmunds, G. F., Jr., and J. R. Traver. 1959. The classification of the Ephemeroptera. I. Ephemeroidea: Behningiidae. Ann. Ent. Soc. Am. 52:43–51.

640. Edward, D. H. D. 1963. The biology of a parthenogenetic species of *Lundstroemia* (Diptera: Chironomidae), with descriptions of immature stages. Proc. R. ent. Soc. Lond.(A) 38: 165–170.

641. Edwards, J. G. 1951. Amphizoidae (Coleoptera) of the world. Wasmann J. Biol. 8:303–332.

642. Edwards, J. G. 1954. Observations on the biology of Amphizoidae. Coleopt. Bull. 8:19–24.

643. Edwards, S. W. 1961. The immature stages of *Xiphocentron mexico* (Trichoptera). Tex. J. Sci. 13:51–56.

644. Edwards, S. W. 1966. An annotated list of the Trichoptera of middle and west Tennessee. J. Tenn. Acad. Sci. 41:116–128.

645. Edwards, S. W. 1973. Texas caddis flies. Tex. J. Sci. 24:491–516.

646. Efford, I. E. 1960. A method of studying the vertical distribution of the bottom fauna in shallow waters. Hydrobiologia 16:288–292.

647. Ege, R. 1915. On the respiratory function of the air stores carried by some aquatic insects (Corixidae, Dytiscidae and Notonectidae). Z. Allg. Physiol. 17:81–124.

648. Eggleton, F. E. 1931. A limnological study of the profundal bottom fauna of certain freshwater lakes. Ecol. Monogr. 1:231–332.

649. Egglishaw, H. J., and D. W. Mackay. 1967. A survey of the bottom fauna and plant detritus in streams. J. Anim. Ecol. 33:463–476.

650. Ekman, S. 1911. Neue Apparate zur qualitativen und quantitativen Untersuchung der Bodenfauna der Binnenseen. Int. Revue ges. Hydrobiol. 3:553–561.

651. Elliott, J. M. 1965. Daily fluctuations of drift invertebrates in a Dartmoor stream. Nature 205:1127–1129.

652. Elliott, J. M. 1970a. Life history and biology of *Sericostoma personatum* Spence (Trichoptera). Oikos 20:110–118.

653. Elliott, J. M. 1970b. Methods of sampling invertebrate drift in running water. Ann. Limnol. 6:133–159.

654. Elliott, J. M. 1971. The life history and biology of *Apatania muliebris* McLachlan (Trichoptera). Ent. Gaz. 22:245–251.

655. Elliott, J. M. 1972. Effect of temperature on the time of hatching in *Baetis rhodani* (Ephemeroptera: Baetidae). Oecologia 9:47–51.

656. Elliott, J. M. 1977. Some methods for the statistical analysis of samples of benthic invertebrates (2nd ed.). Sci. Publ. Freshwat. Biol. Assoc. 25. 160 pp.

657. Elliott, J. M. 1978. Effect of temperature on the hatching time of eggs of *Ephemerella ignita* (Poda) (Ephemerellidae). Freshwat. Biol. 8:51–58.

658. Elliott, J. M., and C. M. Drake. 1981a. A comparative study of seven grabs used for sampling benthic macroinvertebrates in rivers. Freshwat. Biol. 11:99–120.

659. Elliott, J. M., and C. M. Drake. 1981b. A comparative study of four dredges used for sampling benthic macroinvertebrates in rivers. Freshwat. Biol. 11:245–261.

660. Elliott, J. M., C. M. Drake, and P. A. Tullett. 1980. The choice of a suitable sampler for benthic macroinvertebrates in deep rivers. Poll. Rep. Dep. Environ. 8:36–44.

661. Elliott, J. M., and U. H. Humpesch. 1980. Eggs of Ephemeroptera. Freshwat. Biol. Assoc. Ann. Rept. 48:41–52.

662. Elliott, J. M., and P. A. Tullett. 1978. A bibliography of samplers for benthic invertebrates. Freshwat. Biol. Assoc. Occ. Publ. 461 pp.

663. Ellis, L. L. 1952. The aquatic Hemiptera of southeastern Louisiana (exclusive of Corixidae). Am. Midl. Nat. 48:302–329.

664. Ellis, L. L. 1965. An unusual habitat for *Plea striola* (Hemiptera:Pleidae). Fla. Ent. 48:77.

665. Ellis, R. A., and J. H. Borden. 1969. Laboratory rearing of *Notonecta undulata* Say (Hemiptera, Heteroptera, Notonectidae). J. Ent. Soc. Brit. Columbia 66:51–53.

666. Ellis, R. A., and J. H. Borden. 1970. Predation by *Notonecta undulata* on larvae of the yellow fever mosquito. Ann. Ent. Soc. Am. 63:963–973.

667. Ellis, R. J. 1962. Adult caddisflies (Trichoptera) from Houghton Creek, Ogemaw County, Michigan. Occ. Pap. Univ. Mich. Mus. Zool. 624:1–15.

668. Ellis, R. J. 1970. *Alloperla* stonefly nymphs: predators or scavengers on salmon eggs and alevins. Trans. Am. Fish. Soc. 99:677–683.

669. Ellis, R. J. 1975. Seasonal abundance and distribution of adult stoneflies of Sashin Creek, Baranof Island, southern Alaska (Plecoptera). Pan-Pacif. Ent. 51:23–30.

670. Ellis, W. N., and P. F. Bellinger. 1973. An annotated list of the generic names of Collembola (insects) and their type species. Monogr. med. ent. Veren. 71:1–74.

671. Elton, C. S. 1956. Stoneflies (Plecoptera, Nemouridae), a component of the aquatic leaf-litter fauna in Wytham Woods, Berkshire. Entomol. mon. Mag. 91:231–236.

672. Elwood, J. W., and R. M. Cushman. 1975. The life history and ecology of *Peltoperla maria* (Plecoptera: Peltoperlidae) in a small spring-fed stream. Verh. Int. Verein. Limnol. 19: 3050–3056.

673. Emsley, M. G. 1969. The Schizopteridae (Hemiptera: Heteroptera) with the description of new species from Trinidad. Mem. Am. Ent. Soc. 25:1–154.

674. Engelke, M. J., Jr. 1980. Aestivation of a water scavenger beetle *Helophorus* sp. in southwestern Wyoming (Coleoptera: Hydrophilidae). Coleopt. Bull. 34:176.

675. Eriksen, C. H. 1963a. Respiratory regulation in *Ephemera simulans* (Walker) and *Hexagenia limbata* (Serville) (Ephemeroptera). J. exp. Biol. 40:455–468.

676. Eriksen, C. H. 1963b. The relation of oxygen consumption to substrate particle size in two burrowing mayflies. J. exp. Biol. 40:447–453.

677. Eriksen, C. H. 1968. Ecological significance of respiration and substrate for burrowing Ephemeroptera. Can. J. Zool. 46: 93–103.

678. Eriksen, C. H., and C. R. Feldmeth. 1967. A water-current respirometer. Hydrobiologia 29:495–504.

679. Erman, D. C., and W. C. Chouteau. 1979. Fine particulate organic carbon output from fens and its effect on benthic macroinvertebrates. Oikos 32:409–415.

680. Erman, N. A. 1981. Terrestrial feeding migration and life history of the stream-dwelling caddisfly, *Desmona bethula* (Trichoptera: Limnephilidae). Can. J. Zool. 59:1658–1665.

681. Esaki, T., and W. E. China. 1927. A new family of aquatic Hemiptera. Trans. Ent. Soc. Lond. 1927(II):279–295.

682. Eskafi, F. M., and E. F. Legner. 1974. Descriptions of immature stages of the cynipid *Hexacola* sp. near *websteri* (Eucoilinae: Hymenoptera), a larval-pupal parasite of *Hippelates* eye gnats (Diptera: Chloropidae). Can. Ent. 106:1043–1048.

683. Espinosa, L. R., and W. E. Clark. 1972. A polyprophylene light trap for aquatic invertebrates. Calif. Fish Game 58:149–152.

684. Essenberg, C. 1915. The habits and natural history of the backswimmers Notonectidae. J. Anim. Behav. 5:381–390.

685. Etnier, D. A. 1965. An annotated list of the Trichoptera of Minnesota with a description of a new species. Ent. News 76:141–152.

686. Etnier, D. A., and G. A. Schuster. 1979. An annotated list of Trichoptera (caddisflies) of Tennessee. J. Tenn. Acad. Sci. 54:15–22.

687. Ettinger, W. S. 1979. A collapsible insect emergence trap for use in shallow standing water. Ent. News 90:114–117.

688. Evans, E. D. 1972. A study of the Megaloptera of the Pacific coastal region of the United States. Ph.D. diss., Oregon State University, Corvallis. 210 pp.

689. Evans, E. D. 1984. A new genus and a new species of a dobson fly from the far western United States (Megaloptera: Corydalidae). Pan-Pacif. Ent. 60:1–3.

690. Evans, H. E. 1949. The strange habits of *Anoplius depressipes* Banks: A mystery solved. Proc. Ent. Soc. Wash. 51:206–208.

691. Evans, H. E. 1950–51. A taxonomic study of the Nearctic spider belonging to tribe Pompilini (Hym.: Pompilidae). Trans. Am. Ent. Soc. I, 75:133–270; II, 76:207–361; III, 77:203–330.

692. Evans, H. E. 1959. The larvae of Pompilidae. Ann. Ent. Soc. Am. 52:430–444.

693. Evans, H. E., and C. M. Yoshimoto. 1962. The ecology and nesting behavior of the Pompilidae (Hymenoptera) of the northeastern United States. Misc. Publ. Ent. Soc. Am. 3:67–119.

694. Exner, K., and D. A. Craig. 1976. Larvae of Alberta Tanyderidae (Diptera: Nematocera). Quaest. Ent. 12:219–237.

695. Exner, K. K., and R. W. Davies. 1979. Comments on the use of a standpipe corer in fluvial gravels. Freshwat. Biol. 9:77–78.

696. Fager, E. W., A. O. Flechsig, R. F. Ford, R. I. Clutter, and R. J. Ghelardi. 1966. Equipment for use in ecological studies using SCUBA. Limnol. Oceanog. 11:503–509.

697. Fahy, E. 1972a. An automatic separator for the removal of aquatic insects from detritus. J. Appl. Ecol. 6:655–658.

698. Fahy, E. 1972b. The feeding behavior of some common lotic insect species in two streams of differing detrital content. J. Zool. Lond. 167:337–350.

699. Falkenhan, H. H. 1932. Biologische Beobachtungen an *Sminthurides aquaticus* (Collembola). Z. Wiss. Zool. 141:525–580.

700. Fall, H. C. 1901. List of the Coleoptera of Southern California with notes on habits and distribution and descriptions of new species. Occ. Pap. Calif. Acad. Sci. 8:1–282.

701. Fall, H. C. 1919. The North American species of *Coelambus*. John D. Sherman, Jr., Mt. Vernon, N.Y. 20 pp.

702. Fall, H. C. 1922a. A revision of the North American species of *Agabus* together with a description of a new genus and species of the tribe Agabini. John D. Sherman, Jr., Mt. Vernon, N.Y. 36 pp.

703. Fall, H. C. 1922b. The North American species of *Gyrinus*. Trans. Ent. Soc. Am. 47:269–306.

704. Fall, H. C. 1923. A revision of the North American species of *Hydroporus* and *Agaporus*. Privately printed by H. C. Fall. 129 pp.

705. Farmer, R. G., and D. C. Tarter. 1976. Distribution of the superfamily Nemouroidea in West Virginia (Insecta: Plecoptera). Ent. News 87:17–24.

706. Fast, A. W. 1972. A new aquatic insect trap. Pap. Mich. Acad. Sci. Arts Lett. 5:115–124.

707. Faucheux, M. J. 1978. Contribution a l'etude de la biologie de la larvae de *Stationmyia longicornis* (Diptera, Stratiomylidae): prise de nourriture et respiration. Ann. Soc. Ent. Fr. (N.S.). 14:49–72.

708. Federley, H. 1908. Einige Libelluliden wanderungen uber die zoologische Station bei Tvärminne. Acta Soc. Fauna Flora Fenn. 31:1–38.

709. Feldmeth, C. R. 1968. The respiratory energetics of two species of stream caddisflies in relation to water flow. Ph.D. diss., University of Toronto, Canada.

710. Feldmeth, C. R. 1970. The respiratory energetics of two species of stream caddisfly larvae in relation to water flow. Comp. Biochem. Physiol. 32:193–202.

711. Felton, H. L. 1940. Control of aquatic midges with notes on the biology of certain species. J. Econ. Ent. 33:252–264.

712. Ferguson, A. 1940. A preliminary list of the Odonata of Dallas County, Texas. Field Lab. 8:1–10.

713. Ferrier, M. D., and T. E. Wissing. 1979. Larval retreat and food habits of the netspinning trichopteran *Cheumatopsyche analis* (Trichoptera: Hydropsychidae). Great Lakes Ent. 12:157–164.

714. Fiance, S. B. 1977. The genera of eastern North American Chloroperlidae (Plecoptera): Key to larval stages. Psyche 83:308–316.

715. Fiance, S. B., and R. E. Moeller. 1974. Immature stages and ecological observations on *Eoparargyractis plevie* (Pyralidae: Nymphulinae). J. Lepidopterist's Soc. 31:81–88.

716. Field, G., R. J. Duplessis, and A. P. Breton. 1967. Progress report on laboratory rearing of black flies (Diptera: Simuliidae). J. med. Ent. 4:304–305.

717. Finlayson, T., and K. S. Hagen. 1979. Final instar larvae of parasitic Hymenoptera. Pest Manage. Pap. No. 10, Simon Fraser Univ., Brit. Columbia. 111 pp.

718. Finni, G. R. 1973. Biology of winter stoneflies in a central Indiana stream (Plecoptera). Ann. Ent. Soc. Am. 66:1243–1248.

719. Finni, G. R. 1975. Feeding and longevity of the winter stonefly, *Allocapnia granulata* (Claassen) (Plecoptera: Capniidae). Ann. Ent. Soc. Am. 68:207–208.

720. Finni, G. R., and L. Chandler. 1977. Post diapause instar discrimination and life history of the capniid stonefly, *Allocapnia granulata* (Claassen) (Insecta:Plecoptera). Am. Midl. Nat. 98:243–250.

721. Finni, G. R., and L. Chandler. 1979. The micro-distribution of *Allocapnia* naiads (Plecoptera: Capniidae). J. Kans. Ent. Soc. 52:93–102.

722. Finni, G. R., and B. A. Skinner. 1975. The Elmidae and Dryopidae (Coleoptera: Dryopoidea) of Indiana. J. Kans. Ent. Soc. 48:388–395.

723. Finnish IBP/PM Group. 1969. Quantitative sampling equipment for the littoral benthos. Int. Revue ges. Hydrobiol. 54:185–193.

724. Fischer, M. 1964. Die Opiinae der Nearctic Region (Hymenoptera: Braconidae) Pol. Pismo Ent. Bull. Ent. Pol. I, 44:197–530; II, 35:1–212.

725. Fischer, M. 1971. World Opiinae (Hymenoptera), pp. 1–189. *In* V. Delucchi and G. Remaudiere (eds.). Index of entomophagous insects, 5. LeFrancois, Paris.

726. Fischer, Z. 1966. Food selection and energy transformation in larvae of *Lestes sponsa* (Odonata) in Asiatic waters. Verh. Int. Verein. Limnol. 16:600–603.

727. Fish, D. 1976. Insect-plant relationships of the insectivorous pitcher plant *Sarracenia minor*. Fla. Ent. 59:199–203.

728. Fish, D., and D. W. Hall. 1978. Succession and stratification of aquatic insects inhabiting leaves of the insectivorous pitcher plant *Saracenia purpurea*. Am. Midl. Nat. 99:172–183.

729. Fisher, E. G. 1940. A list of Maryland Odonata. Ent. News 51:37–42, 51:67–72.

730. Fisher, T. W., and R. W. Orth. 1964. Biology and immature stages of *Antichaeta testacea* Melander (Diptera: Sciomyzidae). Hilgardia 36:1–29.

731. Fittkau, E. J. 1962. Die Tanypodinae (Diptera: Chironomidae). Abh. Laralsyst. Insekt. 6:1–453.

732. Fittkau, E. J., F. Reiss, and O. Hoffrichter. 1976. A bibliography of the Chironomidae. Gunneria 26:1–177.

733. Flannagan, J. F. 1970. Efficiencies of various grabs and corers in sampling freshwater benthos. J. Fish. Res. Bd. Can. 27:1691–1700.

734. Flannagan, J. F., and D. M. Rosenberg. 1982. Types of artificial substrates used for sampling freshwater benthic macroinvertebrates, pp. 237–266. *In* J. Cairns, Jr. (ed.). Artificial substrates. Ann Arbor Sci. Publ., Mich. 279 pp.

735. Flint, O. S. 1956. The life history of the genus *Frenesia* (Trichoptera: Limnephilidae). Bull. Brooklyn Ent. Soc. 51:93–108.

736. Flint, O. S. 1958. The larva and terrestrial pupa of *Ironoquia parvula* (Trichoptera, Limnephilidae). J. N.Y. Ent. Soc. 66:59–62.

737. Flint, O. S. 1960. Taxonomy and biology of Nearctic limnephilid larvae (Trichoptera), with special reference to species in eastern United States. Entomologica Am. 40:1–117.

738. Flint, O. S. 1961. The immature stages of the Arctopsychinae occurring in eastern North America (Trichoptera: Hydropsychidae). Ann. Ent. Soc. Am. 54:5–11.

739. Flint, O. S. 1962. Larvae of the caddis fly genus *Rhyacophila* in eastern North America (Trichoptera: Rhyacophilidae). Proc. U.S. Nat. Mus. 113:465–493.

740. Flint, O. S. 1964a. The caddisflies (Trichoptera) of Puerto Rico. Univ. Puerto Rico Agric. Exp. Sta. Tech. Pap. 40.

741. Flint, O. S. 1964b. Notes on some Nearctic Psychomyiidae with special reference to their larvae (Trichoptera). Proc. U.S. Nat. Mus. 115:467–481.

742. Flint, O. S. 1965. The genus *Neohermes*. Psyche 72:255–263.

743. Flint, O. S. 1968. Bredin-Archbold-Smithsonian biological survey of Dominica.9. The Trichoptera (caddisflies) of the Lesser Antilles. Proc. U.S. Nat. Mus. 125:1–86.

744. Flint, O. S. 1970. Studies of Neotropical caddisflies, X: *Leucotrichia* and related genera from North and Central America (Trichoptera: Hydroptilidae). Smithson. Contr. Zool. 60:1–64.

745. Flint, O. S. 1973. Studies of Neotropical caddisflies, XVI.: The genus *Austrotinodes* (Trichoptera: Psychomyiidae). Proc. Biol. Soc. Wash. 86:127–142.

746. Flint, O. S. 1974. Studies of Neotropical caddisflies, XVII: The genus *Smicridea* from North and Central America (Trichoptera: Hydropsychidae). Smithson. Contr. Zool. 167:1–65.

747. Flint, O. S., Jr., and J. Bueno-Soria. 1982. Studies of Neotropical caddisflies, XXXII.: The immature stages of *Macronema variipenne* Flint and Bueno, with the division of *Macronema* by the resurrection of *Macrostemum* (Trichoptera: Hydropsychidae). Proc. Biol. Soc. Wash. 95:358–370.

748. Flint, O. S., J. R. Voshell, and C. R. Parker. 1979. The *Hydropsyche scalaris* group in Virginia, with the description of two new species (Trichoptera: Hydropsychidae). Proc. Biol. Soc. Wash. 92:837–862.

749. Flint, O. S., and G. B. Wiggins. 1961. Records and descriptions of North American species in the genus *Lepidostoma,* with a revision of the *vernalis* group (Trichoptera: Lepidostomatidae). Can. Ent. 93:279–297.

750. Flowers, R. W. 1980. Two new genera of Nearctic Heptageniidae (Ephemeroptera). Fla. Ent. 63:296–307.

751. Flowers, R. W., and W. L. Hilsenhoff. 1975. Heptageniidae (Ephemeroptera) of Wisconsin. Great Lakes Ent. 8:201–218.

752. Folkerts, G. W. 1967. Mutualistic cleaning behavior in an aquatic beetle (Coleoptera). Coleopt. Bull. 21:27–28.

753. Folkerts, G. W. 1979. *Spanglerogyrus albiventris,* a primitive new genus and species of Gyrinidae (Coleoptera) from Alabama. Coleopt. Bull. 33:1–8.

754. Folkerts, G. W., and L. A. Donavan. 1973. Resting sites of stream-dwelling gyrinids. Ent. News 84:198–201.

755. Folkerts, G. W., and L. A. Donavan. 1974. Notes on the ranges and habitats of some little-known aquatic beetles of the southeastern U.S. (Coleoptera: Gyrinidae, Dytiscidae). Coleopt. Bull. 28:203–208.

756. Folsom, J. W. 1916. North American collembolous insects of the subfamilies Achorutinae, Neanurinae, and Poduridae. Proc. U.S. Nat. Mus. 50:477–525.

757. Folsom, J. W. 1917. North American collembolous insects of the subfamily Onychiuridae. Proc. U.S. Nat. Mus. 53:637–659.

758. Folsom, J. W. 1937. Nearctic Collembola or springtails of the family Isotomidae. Bull. U.S. Nat. Mus. 168:1–138.

759. Folsom, J. W., and H. B. Mills. 1938. Contribution to the knowledge of the genus *Sminthurides* Boerner. Bull. Mus. Comp. Zool. 82:231–274.

760. Folsom, T. C., and N. C. Collins. 1982a. Food availability in nature for the larval dragonfly *Anax junius* (Odonata: Aeshnidae). Freshwat. Invert. Biol. 1:33–40.

761. Folsom, T. C., and N. C. Collins. 1982b. An index of food limitation in the field for the larval dragonfly *Anax junius* (Odonata: Aeshnidae). Freshwat. Invert. Biol. 1:25–32.

762. Foote, B. A. 1959a. Biology and life history of the snail-killing flies belonging to the genus *Sciomyza* Fallen (Diptera: Sciomyzidae). Ann. Ent. Soc. Am. 52:31–43.

763. Foote, B. A. 1959b. Biology of *Pherbellia prefixa* (Diptera: Sciomyzidae), a parasitoid-predator of the operculate snail *Valvata sincera* (Gastropoda: Valatidae). Proc. Ent. Soc. Wash. 75:141–149.

764. Foote, B. A. 1971. Biology of *Hedria mixta* (Diptera: Sciomyzidae). Ann. Ent. Soc. Am. 64:931–941.

765. Foote, B. A. 1976. Biology and larval feeding habits of three species of *Renocera* (Diptera: Sciomyzidae) that prey on fingernail clams (Mollusca:Sphaeriidae). Ann. Ent. Soc. Am. 68:121–133.

766. Foote, B. A. 1977. Utilization of blue-green algae by larvae of shore flies. Environ. Ent. 6:812–814.

767. Foote, B. A. 1979. Utilization of algae by larvae of shore flies, pp. 61–71. *In* D. L. Deonier (ed.). First symposium on the systematics and ecology of Ephydridae (Diptera). N. Am. Benthol. Soc. 147 pp.

768. Foote, B. A. 1981a. Biology and immature stages of *Lytogaster excavata*, a grazer of blue-green algae (Diptera: Ephydridae). Proc. Ent. Soc. Wash. 83:304–315.

769. Foote, B. A. 1981b. Biology and immature stages of *Pelina truncatula*, a consumer of blue-green algae (Diptera: Ephydridae). Proc. Ent. Soc. Wash. 83:607–619.

770. Foote, B. A. 1982. Biology and immature stages of *Setacera atrovirens*, a grazer of floating algal mats (Diptera: Ephydridae). Proc. Ent. Soc. Wash. 84:828–844.

771. Foote, B. A., and W. C. Eastin. 1975. Biology and immature stages of *Discocerina obscurella* (Diptera: Ephydridae). Proc. Ent. Soc. Wash. 76:401–408.

772. Foote, B. A., S. E. Neff, and C. O. Berg. 1960. Biology and immature stages of *Atrichomelina pubera* (Diptera: Sciomyzidae). Ann. Ent. Soc. Am. 53:192–199.

773. Forbes, S. A. 1887. The lake as a microcosm. Bull. Ill. Nat. Hist. Surv. 15:537–550.

774. Forbes, W. T. M. 1910. The aquatic caterpillars of Lake Quinsigamond. Psyche 17:219–227.

775. Forbes, W. T. M. 1911. Another aquatic caterpillar *(Elophila)*. Psyche 18:120–121.

776. Forbes, W. T. M. 1923. The Lepidoptera of New York and neighboring states. Mem. Cornell Univ. Agric. Exp. Sta. 68: 574–581.

777. Forbes, W. T. M. 1938. *Acentropus* in America (Lepidoptera, Pyralidae). J. N.Y. Ent. Soc. 46:338.

778. Forbes, W. T. M. 1954. Lepidoptera of New York and neighboring states. III. Noctuidae. Mem. Cornell Univ. Agric. Exp. Sta. 329:1–433.

779. Forbes, W. T. M. 1960. Lepidoptera of New York and neighboring states. IV. Agaristidae through Nymphalidae, including butterflies. Mem. Cornell Univ. Agric. Exp. Sta. 371:1–188.

780. Ford, J. B. 1962. The vertical distribution of larval Chironomidae (Dipt.) in the mud of a stream. Hydrobiologia 19: 262–272.

781. Formanowicz, D. R., Jr., and E. D. Brodie, Jr. 1981. Prepupation behavior and pupation of the predaceous diving beetle *Dytiscus verticolis* (Coleoptera: Dytiscidae). J. N.Y. Ent. Soc. 89:152–157.

782. Forsyth, A. B., and R. J. Robertson. 1975. K reproductive strategy and larval behavior of the pitcher plant sarcophagid fly, *Blaesoxipha fletcheri*. Can. J. Zool. 53:174–179.

783. Foster, W. A. 1975. The life history and population biology of an intertidal aphid, *Pemphigus trehernei* Foster. Trans. Ent. Soc. Lond. 127:193–207.

784. Foster, W. A., and J. E. Treherne. 1976. Insects of marine salt marshes: Problems and Adaptations, pp. 5–42. *In* L. Cheng (ed.). Marine Insects. Elsevier, N.Y. 581 pp.

785. Fox, H. M. 1920. Methods of studying the respiratory exchange in smaller aquatic organisms, with particular reference to the use of flagellates as an indicator for oxygen consumption. J. Gen. Physiol. 3:565–573.

786. Fox, H. M., and J. Sidney. 1953. The influence of dissolved oxygen on the respiratory movements of caddis larvae. J. exp. Biol. 30:235–237.

787. Fox, L. R. 1975a. Some demographic consequences of food shortage for the predator *Notonecta hoffmanni*. Ecology 56:868–880.

788. Fox, L. R. 1975b. Factors influencing cannibalism, a mechanism of population limitation in the predator *Notonecta hoffmanni*. Ecology 56:933–941.

789. Fracker, S. B. 1915. The classification of lepidopterous larvae. Univ. Ill. Biol. Monogr. 2:1–165.

790. Fraser, F. C. 1929. A revision of the Fissilabioidea (Cordulegasteridae, Petaliidae, and Petaluridae) (Order Odonata). Part I. Cordulegasteridae. Mem. India Mus. Zool. Surv. 9:69–167.

791. Fraser, F. C. 1933. A revision of the Fissilabioidea (Cordulegasteridae, Petaliidae, and Petaluridae) (Order Odonata). Part II. Petaliidae and Petaluridae, and Appendix to Part I. Mem. India Mus. Zool. Surv. 9:205–260.

792. Fraser, F. C. 1957. A reclassification of the order Odonata. R. Zool. Soc. New Wales 12:1–133.

793. Fredeen, F. J. H. 1959. Rearing black flies in the laboratory (Diptera: Simuliidae). Can. Ent. 91:73–83.

794. Fredeen, F. J. H. 1960. Bacteria as a source of food for black fly larvae. Nature 187:963.

795. Fredeen, F. J. H. 1964. Bacteria as food for black fly larvae in laboratory cultures and in natural streams. Can. J. Zool. 42:527–548.

796. Fredeen, F. J. H. 1969. *Culicoides (Selfia) denningi*, a unique riverbreeding species. Can. Ent. 101:539–544.

797. Fredeen, F. J. H. 1977. A review of the economic importance of black flies (Simuliidae) in Canada. Quaest. Ent. 13:219–229.

798. Freeman, B. E. 1967. Studies on the ecology of larval Tipulinae (Diptera, Tipulidae). J. Anim. Ecol. 36:123–146.

799. Fremling, C. R. 1960a. Biology and possible control of nuisance caddisflies of the upper Mississippi River. Tech. Res. Bull. Iowa State Univ. 483:856–879.

800. Fremling, C. R. 1960b. Biology of a large mayfly, *Hexagenia bilineata* (Say), of the upper Mississippi River. Res. Bull. Iowa Agric. Exp. Sta. 482:842–852.

801. Fremling, C. R. 1967. Methods for mass-rearing *Hexagenia* mayflies (Ephemeroptera: Ephemeridae). Trans. Am. Fish. Soc. 96:407–410.

802. Fremling, C. R., and W. L. Mauck. 1980. Methods for using nymphs of burrowing mayflies (Ephemeroptera, *Hexagenia*) as toxcity test organisms, pp. 81–97. *In* A. L. Buikema, Jr., and J. Cairns, Jr. (eds.). Aquatic invertebrate bioassays. Am. Soc. Test. Mater., Philadelphia, 209 pp.

803. Frick, K. E. 1949. Biology of *Microvelia capitata* Guerin, 1957, in the Panama Canal Zone and its role as a predator on anopheline larvae. Ann. Ent. Soc. Am. 42:77–100.

804. Frison, T. 1929. Fall and winter stoneflies, or Plecoptera, of Illinois. Bull. 181. Nat. Hist. Surv. 18:343–409.

805. Frison, T. H. 1935. The stoneflies, or Plecoptera, of Illinois. Bull. Ill. Nat. Hist. Surv. 20:281–471.

806. Froeschner, R. C. 1949. Contribution to a synopsis of the Hemiptera of Missouri. Part IV. Hebridae, Mesoveliidae, Cimicidae, Anthocoridae, Cryptostemmatidae, Isometopidae, Miridae. Am. Midl. Nat. 42:123–188.

807. Froeschner, R. C. 1962. Contribution to a synopsis of the Hemiptera of Missouri. Part V. Hydrometridae, Gerridae, Veliidae, Saldidae, Ochteridae, Gelastocoridae, Naucoridae, Belostomatidae, Nepidae, Notonectidae, Pleidae, Corixidae. Am. Midl. Nat. 67:208–240.

808. Frohne, W. C. 1938. Contribution to knowledge of the limnological role of the higher aquatic plants. Trans. Am. Microsc. Soc. 57:256–268.

809. Frohne, W. C. 1939a. Biology of certain subaquatic flies reared from emergent water plants. Pap. Mich. Acad. Sci. Arts Lett. 24:139–147.

810. Frohne, W. C. 1939b. Biology of *Chilo forbesellus* Fernald, an hygrophilous crambine moth. Trans. Am. Microsc. Soc. 58:304–326.

811. Frohne, W. C. 1939c. Observations on the biology of three semiaquatic lacustrine moths. Trans. Am. Microsc. Soc. 58: 327–348.

812. Frohne, W. C. 1939d. Semiaquatic Hymenoptera in north Michigan lakes. Trans. Am. Microsc. Soc. 58:228–240.

813. Frommer, S. I. 1963. Gross morphological studies of the reproductive system in representative North American crane flies (Diptera:Tipulidae). Univ. Kans. Sci. Bull. 44:535–626.

814. Frommer, S. I. 1967. Review of the anatomy of adult Chironomidae. Bull. Calif. Mosquito Cont. Assoc. Tech. Ser. 1:1–39.

815. Frost, S., A. Huni, and W. E. Kershaw. 1970. Evaluation of a kicking technique for sampling stream bottom fauna. Can. J. Zool. 49:167–173.

816. Fuller, R. L., and R. J. Mackay. 1980a. Field and laboratory studies of net-spinning activity by *Hydropsyche* larvae (Trichoptera: Hydropsychidae). Can. J. Zool. 58:2006–2014.

817. Fuller, R. L., and R. J. Mackay. 1980b. Feeding ecology of three species of *Hydropsyche* (Trichoptera:Hydropsychidae) in southern Ontario. Can. J. Zool. 58:2239–2251.

818. Fuller, R. L., and R. J. Mackay. 1981. Effects of food quality on the growth of three *Hydropsyche* species (Trichoptera: Hydropsychidae). Can. J. Zool. 59:1133–1140.

819. Fuller, R. L., and K. W. Stewart. 1977. The food habits of stoneflies (Plecoptera) in the Upper Gunnison River, Colorado. Environ. Ent. 6:293–302.

820. Fuller, R. L., and K. W. Stewart. 1979. Stonefly (Plecoptera) food habits and prey preference in the Dolores River, Colorado. Am. Midl. Nat. 101:170–181.

821. Fullington, K. E., and K. W. Stewart. 1980. Nymphs of the stonefly genus *Taeniopteryx* (Plecoptera: Taeniopterygidae) of North America. J. Kans. Ent. Soc. 53:237–259.

822. Galbraith, D. F., and C. H. Fernando. 1977. The life history of *Gerris remigis* (Heteroptera: Gerridae) in a small stream in southern Ontario. Can. Ent. 109:221–228.

823. Gale, W. F. 1971. Shallow-water core sampler. Progr. Fish Cult. 33:238–239.

824. Gale, W. F. 1981. A floatable, benthic corer for use with SCUBA. Hydrobiologia 77:273–275.

825. Gale, W. F., and D. Thompson, 1974a. Placement and retrieval of artificial substrate samplers by SCUBA. Progr. Fish Cult. 36:231–233.

826. Gale, W. F., and D. Thompson. 1974b. Aids to benthic sampling by SCUBA divers in rivers. Limnol. Oceanogr. 19: 1004–1007.

827. Gale, W. F., and D. Thompson, 1975. A suction sampler for quantitatively sampling benthos on rocky substrates in rivers. Trans. Am. Fish. Soc. 104:398–405.

828. Gallepp, G. W. 1974a. Behavioral ecology of *Brachycentrus occidentalis* Banks during the pupation period. Ecology 55:1283–1294.

829. Gallepp, G. W. 1974b. Diel periodicity in the behavior of the caddisfly *Brachycentrus americanus* (Banks). Freshwat. Biol. 4:193–204.

830. Gallepp, G. W. 1977. Responses of caddisfly larvae (*Brachycentrus* spp.) to temperature, food availability and current velocity. Am. Midl. Nat. 98:59–84.

831. Gangulyr, D. N., and B. Mitra. 1961. Observations on the fishfry destroying capacity of certain aquatic insects and the suggestion for their eradication. Indian Agric. 5:184–188.

832. Garcia, R., and E. I. Schlinger. 1972. Studies of spider predation on *Aedes dorsalis* (Meigen) in a salt marsh. Proc. Calif. Mosquito Contr. Assoc. 40:117–118.

833. Garcia-Diaz, J. 1938. An ecological survey of the fresh water insects of Puerto Rico, I. The Odonata, with new life histories. J. Agric. Univ. Puerto Rico 22:43–97.

834. Gardner, A. E. 1952. The life history of *Lestes dryas* Kirby. Ent. Gaz. 3:4–26.

835. Garman, H. 1924. Odonata from Kentucky. Ent. News 25:285–288.

836. Garman, P. 1917. The Zygoptera, or damselflies, of Illinois. Bull. Ill. State Lab. Nat. Hist. 12:411–587.

837. Garman, P. 1927. The Odonata or dragonflies of Connecticut. Bull. Conn. State Geol. Nat. Hist. Surv. 39:1–331.

838. Garrison, R. W. 1981. Description of the larva of *Ischnura gemina* with a key and new characters for the separation of sympatric *Ischnura* larvae. Ann. Ent. Soc. Am. 74:525–530.

839. Garrison, R. W., and J. E. Hafernik. 1981. The distribution of *Ischnura gemina* (Kennedy) and a description of the andromorph female (Zygoptera: Coenagrionidae). Odonatologica 10:85–91.

840. Gatjen, L. 1926. Nahrungsuntersuchung bei Phryganidenlarven (*Phryganea* and *Neuronia*). Arch. Hydrobiol. 16:649–667.

841. Gaufin, A. R. 1956. Annotated list of stoneflies of Ohio. Ohio J. Sci. 56:321–324.

842. Gaufin, A. R. 1964. The Chloroperlidae of North America. Gewasser und Abwasser 34/35:37–49.

843. Gaufin, A. R., A. V. Nebeker, and J. Sessions. 1966. The stoneflies (Plecoptera) of Utah. Univ. Utah Biol. Ser. 14:4–93.

844. Gaufin, A. R., and W. E. Ricker. 1974. Additions and corrections to a list of Montana stoneflies. Ent. News 85:285–288.

845. Gaufin, A. R., W. E. Ricker, M. Miner, P. Milam, and R. A. Hays. 1972. The stoneflies (Plecoptera) of Montana. Trans. Am. Ent. Soc. 98:1–161.

846. Gaufin, R. F., and A. R. Gaufin. 1961. The effect of low oxygen concentrations on stoneflies. Proc. Utah Acad. Sci. Arts Lett. 38:57–64.

847. Geigy, R., and G. Sarasin. 1958. Die ökologische Abhanggigkeit des Metamorphose Geschehens bei *Sialis lutaria* L. Rev. Suisse Zool. 65:323–329.

848. Geijskes, D. C. 1943. Notes on Odonata of Surinam, IV. Nine new or little known zygopterous nymphs from the inland waters. Ann. Ent. Soc. Am. 36:165–184.

849. Georgian, T. J., and J. B. Wallace. 1981. A model of seston capture by net-spinning caddisflies. Oikos 36:147–157.

850. Georgian, T. J., and J. B. Wallace. 1983. Seasonal production dynamics in a guild of periphyton-grazing insects in a southern Appalachian stream. Ecology. 64:1236–1248.

851. Gerasimov, A. 1937. Bestimmungstabelle der Familien von Schmetterlingsrapuen (Lep.) Stett. Ent. Zeitung. 98:281–300.

852. Gerber, E. J. 1970. Manual for mosquito rearing and experimental techniques. Bull. Am. Mosquito Contr. Assoc. 5:1–109.

853. Gerking, S. D. 1957. A method of sampling the littoral macrofauna and its application. Ecology 38:219–226.

854. Gersabeck, E. F., and R. W. Merritt. 1979. The effect of physical factors on the colonization and relocation behavior of immature black flies. Environ. Ent. 8:34–39.

855. Giani, N., and H. Laville. 1973. Cycle biologique et production de *Sialis lutaria* L. (Megaloptera) dans le lac de Port-Bielh (Pyrénées Centrales). Ann. Limnol. 9:45–61.

856. Gibbs, K. E. 1980. The occurrence and biology of *Siphlonisca aerodromia* Needham (Ephemeroptera: Siphloneuridae) in Maine, USA. pp. 167–168. *In* J. F. Flannigan and K. E. Marshall (eds.). Advances in Ephemeroptera biology. Plenum, N.Y. 552 pp.

857. Gibbs, R. H., Jr., and S. P. Gibbs. 1954. The Odonata of Cape Cod, Massachusetts. J. N.Y. Ent. Soc. 62:167–184.

858. Giller, P. S., and S. McNeill. 1981. Predation strategies, resource partitioning and habitat selection in *Notonecta* (Hemiptera/Heteroptera). J. Anim. Ecol. 50:789–808.

859. Gillespie, D. M., and C. J. D. Brown. 1966. A quantitative sampler for macroinvertebrates associated with aquatic macrophytes. Limnol. Oceanogr. 11:404–406.

860. Gillespie, J. 1941. Some unusual dragonfly records from New Jersey (Odonata). Ent. News 52:225–226.

861. Gillett, J. D. 1972. The mosquito, its life, activities, and impact on human affairs. Doubleday, N.Y. 358 pp.

862. Gillott, C. 1980. Entomology. Plenum, N.Y. 729 pp.

863. Gilpin, B. R., and M. A. Brusven. 1970. Food habits and ecology of mayflies of the St. Mary's River in Idaho. Melanderia 4:19–40.

864. Gilpin, B. R., and M. A. Brusven. 1976. Subsurface sampler for determining vertical distribution of stream-bed benthos. Progr. Fish Cult. 38:192–194.

865. Gilson, W. E. 1963. Differential respirometer of simplified and improved design. Science 141:531–532.

866. Girault, A. A. 1911a. Descriptions of North American Mymaridae with synonymic and other notes on described genera and species. Trans. Am. Ent. Soc. 37:253–324.

867. Girault, A. A. 1911b. Synonymic and descriptive notes on the chalcidoid family Trichogrammatidae with descriptions of new species. Trans. Am. Ent. Soc. 37:43–83.

868. Gisin, H. 1960. Collembolenfauna Europas. Geneve Educ. Mus. Nat. Hist. 312 pp.

869. Gittelman, S. H. 1974a. Locomotion and predatory strategy in backswimmers. Am. Midl. Nat. 92:496–500.

870. Gittelman, S. H. 1974b. The habitat preference and immature stages of *Neoplea striola* (Hemiptera: Pleidae). J. Kans. Ent. Soc. 47:491–503.

871. Gittelman, S.H. 1975. Physical gill efficiency and winter dormancy in the pigmy backswimmer, *Neoplea striola* (Hemiptera: Pleidae). Ann. Ent. Soc. Am. 68:1011–1017.

872. Gittelman, S. H. 1978. Optimum diet and body size in backswimmers (Heteroptera: Notonectidae, Pleidae). Ann. Ent. Soc. Am. 71:737–747.

873. Gittelman, S. H. and P. W. Severance. 1975. The habitat preference and immature stages of *Buenoa confusa* and *B. margaritacea* (Hemiptera: Notonectidae). J. Kans. Ent. Soc. 48:507–518.

874. Givens, D. R., and S. D. Smith. 1980. A synopsis of the western Arctopsychinae (Trichoptera: Hydropsychidae). Melanderia 35:1–24.

875. Gjullin, C. M., and G. W. Eddy. 1972. The mosquitos of the northwestern United States. U.S. Dept. Agric. Tech. Bull. 1447. 111 pp.

876. Gjullin, C. M., R. I. Sailer, A. Stone, and B. V. Travis. 1961. The mosquitoes of Alaska. U.S. Dept. Agric., Agric. Res. Serv. Agric. Handbk. 182:1–98.

877. Gladney, W. J., and E. C. Turner, Jr. 1969. Insects of Virginia No. 2. The mosquitoes of Virginia. Bull. Res. Div. Va. Poly. Inst. State Univ. 49. 24 pp.

878. Glasgow, J. P. 1936. The bionomics of *Hydropsyche colonica* McLach. and *H. philopotti* Till. Proc. R. ent. Soc. Lond. (A) 11:122–128.

879. Glorioso, M. J. 1981. Systematics of the dobsonfly subfamily Corydalinae (Megaloptera: Corydalidae). Syst. Ent. 6:253–290.

880. Glotzel, V. R. 1973. Populationsdynamik und Ernahrungsbiologie von Simuliidenlarven in einem mit organischen Abwassern verunreinigten Gebirgsbach. Arch. Hydrobiol. Suppl. 42: 406–451.

881. Gloyd, L. K. 1944. A new species of *Stylurus* from Mexico (Odonata: Gomphinae). Occ. Pap. Univ. Mich. Mus. Zool. 482:1–4.

882. Gloyd, L. K. 1951. Records of some Virginia Odonata. Ent. News 62:109–114.

883. Gloyd, L. K. 1958. The dragonfly fauna of the Big Bend region of Trans-Pecos Texas. Occ. Pap. Univ. Mich. Mus. Zool. 593:1–23.

884. Gloyd, L. K. 1959. Elevation of the *Macromia* group to family status (Odonata). Ent. News 70:197–205.

885. Gloyd, L. K. 1968a. The union of *Argia fumipennis* (Burmeister 1839) with *Argia violacea* (Hagen, 1861), and the recognition of three subspecies (Odonata). Occ. Pap. Univ. Mich. Mus. Zool. 658:1–6.

886. Gloyd, L. K. 1968b. The synonymy of *Diargia* and *Hyponeura* with the genus *Argia* (Odonata: Coenagrionidae: Argiinae). Mich. Entomol. 1:271–274.

887. Gloyd, L. K. 1973. The status of the generic names *Gomphoides, Negomphoides, Progomphus,* and *Ammogomphus* (Odonata: Gomphidae). Occ. Pap. Univ. Mich. Mus. Zool. 668:1–7.

888. Gloyd, L. K., and M. Wright. 1959. Odonata, pp. 917–940. *In* W. T. Edmondson (ed.). Freshwater biology (2nd ed.). John Wiley & Sons, N.Y. 1248 pp.

889. Goetghebuer, M., and F. Lenz. 1936–1950. Tendipedidae. A. Die Imagines. Pelopiinae; Tendipedinae; Diamesinae; Orthocladiinae, pp. 13b, 97:1–48, 100:49–81; 13c, 1937:1–72, 1938:73–128; 1954:129–168; 13d:1–30; 13f:1–19; 13g, 1940:7–24, 1942:25–64, 1943:113–114, 1950:145–208. *In* E. Lindner (ed.). Fliegen Palaerktischen Region. 280 pp.

890. Goetghebuer, M., and F. Lenz. 1939. Tendipedidae-Podonominae. A. Die Imagines, pp. 1–29. *In* E. Lindner (ed.). Fliegen Palaerktischen Region 13e. 280 pp.

891. Goetghebuer, M., and F. Lenz. 1950. Tendipedidae-Clunioninae. A. Die Imagines, pp. 1–23. *In* Lindner (ed.). Fliegen Palaerktischen Region 13h. 280 pp.

892. Gonsoulin, G. J. 1973a. Seven families of aquatic and semiaquatic Hemiptera in Louisiana. I. Hydrometridae. Ent. News 84:9–16.

893. Gonsoulin, G. J. 1973b. Seven families of aquatic and semiaquatic Hemiptera in Louisiana. Part II. Family Naucoridae Fallen, 1814, "Creeping water bugs." Ent. News 84:83–88.

894. Gonsoulin, G. J. 1973c. Seven families of aquatic and semiaquatic Hemiptera in Louisiana. Part III. Family Belostomatidae Leach, 1815. Ent. News 84:173–189.

895. Gonsoulin, G. J. 1974. Seven families of aquatic and semiaquatic Hemiptera in Louisiana. IV. Family Gerridae. Trans. Am. Ent. Soc. 100:513–546.

896. Gonsoulin, G. J. 1975. Seven families of aquatic and semiaquatic Hemiptera in Louisiana. Part V. Family Nepidae Latreille, 1802. Ent. News 86:23–32.

897. Good, H. G. 1924. Notes on the life history of *Prionocyphon limbatus* Lec. (Helodidae, Coleoptera). J. N.Y. Ent. Soc. 32:79–84.

898. Good, N. E. 1945. A list of the mosquitoes of the District of Columbia. Proc. Ent. Soc. Wash. 47:168–179.

899. Goodwin, J. T. 1973a. Immature stages of some eastern Nearctic Tabanidae (Diptera) II. Genera of the tribe Diachlorini. J. Ga. Ent. Soc. 8:5–11.

900. Goodwin, J. T. 1973b. Immature stages of some eastern Nearctic Tabanidae (Diptera). IV. The genus *Merycomyia*. J. Tenn. Acad. Sci. 48:115–118.

901. Goodwin, J. T. 1974. Immature stages of some eastern Nearctic Tabanidae (Diptera). V. *Stenotabanus (Aegialomyia) magnicallus* (Stone). J. Tenn. Acad. Sci. 49:14–15.

902. Gordon, A. E. 1974. A synopsis and phylogenetic outline of the Nearctic members of *Cheumatopsyche*. Proc. Acad. Nat. Sci. Philadelphia 126:117–160.

903. Gordon, R. D. 1981. New species of North American *Hydroporus, niger-tenebrosus* group (Coleoptera: Dytiscidae). Pan-Pacif. Ent. 57:105–123.

904. Gordon, R. D., and R. L. Post. 1965. North Dakota water beetles. North Dakota Insects. Publ. N. D. State Univ. Agric. Exp. Sta. 5:1–53.

905. Gower, A. M. 1967. A study of *Limnephilus lunatus* Curtis (Trichoptera: Limnephilidae) with reference to its life cycle in watercress beds. Trans. R. ent. Soc. Lond. 119:283–302.

906. Grafius, E. J., and N. H. Anderson. 1973. Literature review of foods of aquatic insects. Coniferous Forest Biome Ecosyst. Anal. Stud., Oregon State Univ., Corvallis, Internal Rept. 129. 52 pp.

907. Grafius, E. J., and N. H. Anderson. 1980. Population dynamics and role of two species of *Lepidostoma* (Trichoptera: Lepidostomatidae) in an Oregon coniferous forest stream. Ecology 61:808–816.

908. Graham, M. W. R. de V. 1959. Keys to the British genera and species of Elachertinae, Eulophinae, Entedontinae and Euderinae (Hym.: Chalcidoidea). Trans. Soc. Brit. Ent. 13: 169–204.

909. Graham, M. W. R. de V. 1969. The Pteromalidae of north-western Europe (Hym.: Chalcidoidea). Bull. Brit. Mus. Nat. Hist. Ent. 16:1–908.

910. Grant, P. M., and K. W. Stewart. 1980. The life history of *Isonychia sicca* (Ephemeroptera: Oligoneuriidae) in an intermittent stream in North Central Texas. Ann. Ent. Soc. Am. 73:747–755.

911. Grant, P. R., and R. J. Mackay. 1969. Ecological segregation of systematically related stream insects. Can. J. Zool. 47: 691–694.

912. Gray, L. J., and J. V. Ward. 1979. Food habits of stream benthos at sites of differing food availability. Am. Midl. Nat. 102:157–167.

913. Green, R. H. 1979. Sampling design and statistical methods for environmental biologists. Wiley-Interscience, N.Y. 257 pp.

914. Greene, C. T. 1923. A contribution to the biology of N. A. Diptera. Proc. Ent. Soc. Wash. 25:82–89.

915. Greenstone, M. H. 1979. A sampling device for aquatic arthropods active at the water surface. Ecology 60:642–644.

916. Grenier, P. 1949. Contribution a l'etude biologique des Simuliides de France. Physiologia Comp. Oecol. 1:165–330.

917. Grenier, S. 1970. Biologie d'*Agriotypus armatus* Curtis (Hymenoptera: Agriotypidae), parasite de nymphs de Trichopteres. Ann. Limnol. 6:317–361.

918. Grieve, E. G. 1937a. Culture methods for the damselfly, *Ischnura verticalis,* pp. 268–270. *In* J. G. Needham (ed.). Culture methods for invertebrate animals. Comstock, Ithaca, N.Y. 590 pp.

919. Grieve, E. G. 1937b. Studies on the biology of the damselfly (*Ischnura verticalis* Say), with notes on certain parasites. Am. Ent. 17:121–153.

920. Griffith, M. E. 1945. The environment, life history and structure of the water boatman, *Ramphocorixa acuminata* (Uhler). Univ. Kans. Sci. Bull. 30:241–365.

921. Griffiths, G. C. D. 1972. Studies on the phylogenetic classification of Diptera Cyclorrhapha, with special reference to the structure of the male post abdomen. Series Entomologica, 8. The Hague, Netherlands. 340 pp.

922. Grigarick, A. A. 1959a. A floating pantrap for insects associated with the water surface. J. Econ. Ent. 52:348–349.

923. Grigarick, A. A. 1959b. Bionomics of the rice leaf miner, *Hydrellia griseola* (Fallen), in California (Diptera: Ephydridae). Hilgardia 29:1–80.

924. Grigarick, A. A. 1975. The occurrence of a second genus of spongilla-fly (*Sisyra vicaria,* Walker.) at Clear Lake, Lake County, California. Pan-Pacif. Ent. 51:296–297.

925. Grogan, W. L., and W. W. Wirth. 1975. A revision of the genus *Palpomyia* Meigen of northeastern North America (Diptera: Ceratopogonidae). Contr. Md. Agric. Exp. Sta. 5076:1–49.

926. Grogan, W. L., Jr., and W. W. Wirth. 1979. The North American predaceous midges of the genus *Palpomyia* Meiger (Diptera: Ceratopogonidae). Mem. Ent. Soc. Wash. 8:1–125.

927. Grunewald, J. 1973. Die hydrochemischen Lebensbeingungen der praimaginalen Stadien von *Boophthora erythrocephala* De Geer (Diptera: Simuliidae). 2. Die Entwicklung einer Zucht unter experimentellen Bedingungen. Z. Tropenmed. Parasit. 24:232–249.

928. Gulliksen, B., and K. M. Deras. 1975. A diver-operated suction sampler for fauna on rocky bottoms. Oikos 26:246–249.

929. Gundersen, R. W. 1978. Nearctic *Enochrus* biology, keys, description (Coleoptera: Hydrophilidae). Dept. Biol. Sci., St. Cloud State Univ., St. Cloud, Minn. 54 pp.

930. Gunter, G., and J. Y. Christmas. 1959. Corixid insects as part of the off-shore fauna of the sea. Ecology 40:724–725.

931. Günther, K. K. 1975. Das genus *Neotridactylus* Günther, 1972 (Tridactylidae: Saltatoria:Insecta). Mitt. Zool. Mus. Berlin 51:305–365.

932. Gurney, A. B., and S. Parfin. 1959. Neuroptera, pp. 973–980. *In* W. T. Edmondson (ed.). Freshwater biology (2nd ed.). John Wiley & Sons, N.Y. 1248 pp.

933. Guthrie, J. E. 1903. The Collembola of Minnesota. Rep. Geol. Nat. Hist. Surv., Minn. Zool. Ser. 4:1–110.

934. Guyer, G., and R. Hutson. 1955. A comparison of sampling techniques utilized in an ecological study of aquatic insects. J. Econ. Ent. 48:662–665.

935. Haage, P. 1970. On the feeding habits of two Baltic species of caddis larvae (Trichoptera). Ent. Scand. 1:282–290.

936. Haddock, J. D. 1977. The biosystematics of the caddis fly genus *Nectopsyche* in North America with emphasis on the aquatic stages. Am. Midl. Nat. 98:382–421.

937. Hadley, M. 1971. Aspects of the larval ecology and population dynamics of *Molophilus ater* Meigen (Diptera: Tipulidae) on Pennine moorland. J. Anim. Ecol. 40:445–456.

938. Hagen, H. A. 1880. On an aquatic sphinx larva on *Nymphaea.* Psyche 3:113.

939. Hagen, K. S. 1956. Aquatic Hymenoptera, pp. 289–292. *In* R. L. Usinger (ed.). Aquatic insects of California. Univ. Calif. Press, Berkeley. 508 pp.

940. Hagen, K. S. 1964. Developmental stages of parasites, pp. 168–246. *In* P. Debach (ed.). Biological control of insects pests and weeds. Chapman and Hall, London. 844 pp.

941. Haggett, G. 1955–1961. Larvae of the British Lepidoptera not figured by Buckler. Soc. Lond. Ent. Nat. Hist. Proc. Trans. Part I, 1955:152–163; Part II, 1957:94–99; Part IV, 1959:207–214; Part V, 1960:136–137.

942. Hagstrum, D. W., and E. B. Workman. 1971. Interaction of temperature and feeding rate in determining the rate of development of larval *Culex tarsalis* (Diptera: Culicidae). Ann. Ent. Soc. Am. 64:668–671.

943. Hair, J. A., and E. C. Turner, Jr. 1966. Laboratory colonization and mass-production procedures for *Culicoides guttipennis.* Mosquito News 26:429–433.

944. Hall, F. 1974. A key to the *Simulium* larvae of southern California (Diptera: Simuliidae). Calif. Vector Views 21:65–71.

945. Hall, H. A., and G. Pritchard. 1975. The food of larvae of *Tipula sacra* Alexander in a series of abandoned beaver ponds (Diptera: Tipulidae). J. Anim. Ecol. 44:55–66.

946. Hall, R. E., and J. J. Harrod. 1963. A method of rearing *Simulium ornatum* var. *nitidifrons* (Diptera: Simuliidae) in the laboratory. Hydrobiologia 22:450–453.

947. Hall, R. J. 1975. Life history, drift and production of the stream mayfly *Tricorythodes atratus* McDunnough in the headwaters of the Mississippi River. Ph.D. diss., University of Minnesota, 228 pp.

948. Hall, T. J. 1982. Colonizing macroinvertebrates in the upper Mississippi River with a comparison of basket and multiplate samplers. Freshwat. Biol. 12:211–215.

949. Hamilton, A. L. 1969. A new type of emergence trap for collecting stream insects. J. Fish. Res. Bd. Can. 26:1685–1689.

950. Hamilton, A. L., W. Burton, and J. P. Flannagan. 1970. A multiple corer for sampling profundal benthos. J. Fish. Res. Bd. Can. 27:1867–1869.

951. Hamilton, A. L., O. Saether, and D. Oliver. 1969. A classification of the Nearctic Chironomidae. Fish. Res. Bd. Can. Tech. Rept. 124:1–42.

952. Hamilton, D. A., and D. C. Tarter. 1977. Life history and ecology of *Ephemerella funeralis* McDunnough (Ephemeroptera: Ephemerellidae) in a small West Virginia stream. Am. Midl. Nat. 98:458–462.

953. Hamilton, S. W., and G. A. Schuster. 1978. Hydroptilidae from Kansas (Trichoptera). Ent. News 89:201–205.

954. Hamilton, S. W., and G. A. Schuster. 1979. Records of Trichoptera from Kansas, II: The families Glossosomatidae, Helicopsychidae, Hydropsychidae and Rhyacophilidae. State Biol. Surv. Kans. Tech. Publ. 8:15–22.

955. Hamilton, S. W., and G. A. Schuster. 1980. Records of Trichoptera from Kansas, III: The families Limnephilidae, Phryganeidae, Polycentropodidae, and Sericostomatidae. State Biol. Surv. Kans. Tech. Publ. 9:20–29.

956. Hamilton, S. W., G. A. Schuster, and M. B. DuBois. 1983. Checklist of the Trichoptera of Kansas. Trans. Kans. Acad. Sci. In press.

957. Hammer, M. 1953. Investigations on the microfauna of northern Canada. Part II. Collembola. Acta Arct. 6:1–108.

958. Hamrum, C. L., M. A. Anderson, and M. Boole. 1971. Distribution and habitat preference of Minnesota dragonfly species (Odonata, Anisoptera) II. J. Minn. Acad. Sci. 37:93–96.

959. Hanna, H. M. 1957. A study of the growth and feeding habits of the larvae of four species of caddis flies. Proc. R. ent. Soc. Lond. (A) 32:139–146.

960. Hanna, H. M. 1959. The growth of larvae and their cases and the life cycles of five species of caddis flies (Trichoptera). Proc. R. ent. Soc. Lond. (A) 34:121–129.

961. Hansell, M. H. 1972. Case building behavior of the caddis fly larva, *Lepidostoma hirtum*. J. Zool. Lond. 167:179–192.

962. Hansen, D. C., and E. F. Cook. 1976. The systematics and morphology of the Nearctic species of *Diamesa* Meigen, 1835 (Diptera: Chironomidae). Mem. Am. Ent. Soc. 30:1–203.

963. Hansford, R. G. 1978. Life-history and distribution of *Simulium austeni* (Diptera: Simuliidae) in relation to phytoplankton in some southern English rivers. Freshwat. Biol. 8:521–531.

964. Harbach, R. E. 1977. Comparative and functional morphology of the mandibles of some fourth stage mosquito larvae. Zoomorphologie 87:217–236.

965. Harden, P., and C. Mickel. 1952. The stoneflies of Minnesota (Plecoptera). Univ. Minn. Agric. Exp. Sta. Tech. Bull. 201:1–84.

966. Hardin, F. W., H. R. Hepburn, and B. J. Ethridge. 1967. A history of mosquitoes and mosquito-borne diseases in Mississippi. 1699–1965. Mosquito News 27:60–66.

967. Harmston, F. C. 1949. An annotated list of the mosquito records from Colorado. Great Basin Nat. 9:65–75.

968. Harmston, F. C., and F. A. Lawson. 1967. Mosquitoes of Colorado. U.S. Dept. Health Educ. Welfare. 140 pp.

969. Harp, G. L., and P. A. Harp. 1980. Aquatic macroinvertebrates of Wapanocca National Wildlife Refuge. Proc. Ark. Acad. Sci. 34:115–117.

970. Harp, G. L., and J. D. Rickett. 1977. The dragonflies of Arkansas. Proc. Ark. Acad. Sci. 31:50–54.

971. Harper, P. P. 1973a. Emergence, reproduction and growth of setipalpian Plecoptera in southern Ontario. Oikos 24:94–107.

972. Harper, P. P. 1973b. Life histories of Nemouridae and Leuctridae in southern Ontario (Plecoptera). Hydrobiologia 41:309–356.

973. Harper, P. P. 1980. Phenology and distribution of aquatic dance flies (Diptera: Empididae) in a Laurentian watershed. Am. Midl. Nat. 104:110–117.

974. Harper, P. P., and H. B. N. Hynes. 1970. Diapause in the nymphs of Canadian winter stoneflies. Ecology 51:925–927.

975. Harper, P. P. and H. B. N. Hynes. 1971a. The Leuctridae of eastern Canada (Insecta: Plecoptera). Can. J. Zool. 49:915–920.

976. Harper, P. P., and H. B. N. Hynes. 1971b. The Capniidae of eastern Canada (Insecta: Plecoptera). Can. J. Zool. 49:921–940.

977. Harper, P. P., and H. B. N. Hynes. 1971c. The nymphs of the Taeniopterygidae of eastern Canada (Insecta: Plecoptera). Can. J. Zool. 49:941–947.

978. Harper, P. P., and H. B. N. Hynes. 1971d. The nymphs of the Nemouridae of eastern Canada (Insecta: Plecoptera). Can. J. Zool. 49:1129–1142.

979. Harper, P. P., and H. B. N. Hynes. 1972. Life histories of Capniidae and Taeniopterygidae in southern Ontario (Plecoptera). Arch. Hydrobiol. Suppl. 40:274–314.

980. Harper, P. P., and E. Magnin. 1969. Cycles vitaux de quelques Plecopteres des Laurentides (Insecta). Can. J. Zool. 47:483–494.

981. Harpster, H. T. 1941. An investigation of the gaseous plastron as a respiratory mechanism in *Helichus striatus* LeConte (Dryopidae). Trans. Am. Ent. Soc. 60:329–358.

982. Harpster, H. T. 1944. The gaseous plastron as a respiratory mechanism in *Stenelmis quadrimaculata* Horn (Dryopidae). Trans. Am. Microsc. Soc. 63:1–26.

983. Harris, H. M., and W. E. Shull. 1944. A preliminary list of Hemiptera of Idaho. Iowa State Coll. J. Sci. 18:199–208.

984. Harris, S. C., and R. B. Carlson. 1978. Distribution of *Bittacomorpha clavipes* (Fabricius) and *Ptychoptera quadrifasciata* Say (Diptera: Ptychopteridae) in a sandhill springbrook of southeastern North Dakota. Ann. Proc. N.D. Acad. Sci. 29:59–66.

985. Harris, S. C., P. K. Lago, and R. B. Carlson. 1980. Preliminary survey of the Trichoptera of North Dakota. Proc. Ent. Soc. Wash. 82:39–43.

986. Harris, S. C., P. K. Lago, and R. W. Holzenthal. 1982a. An annotated checklist of the caddisflies (Trichoptera) of Mississippi and southeastern Louisiana. Part II: Rhyacophiloidea. Proc. Ent. Soc. Wash. 84:509–512.

987. Harris, S. C., P. K. Lago, and J. F. Scheiring. 1982b. An annotated list of Trichoptera of several streams on Eglin Air Force Base, Florida. Ent. News 93(3):79–84.

988. Harrold, J. F. 1978. Relation of sample variations to plate orientation in the Hester-Dendy plate sampler. Progr. Fish Cult. 40:24–25.

989. Hart, C. A. 1895. On the entomology of the Illinois River and adjacent waters. Bull. Ill. State Lab. Nat. Hist. 4:1–273.

990. Hart, C. W., and S. L. H. Fuller (eds.). 1974. Pollution ecology of freshwater invertebrates. Academic, N.Y. 389 pp.

991. Hart, D. D., and V. H. Resh. 1980. Movement patterns and foraging ecology of a stream caddisfly larva. Can. J. Zool. 58:1174–1185.

992. Hart, J. W. 1970. A checklist of Indiana Collembola. Proc. Ind. Acad. Sci. 79:249–252.

993. Hart, J. W. 1971. New records of Indiana Collembola. Proc. Ind. Acad. Sci. 80:246.

994. Hart, J. W. 1973. New records of Indiana Collembola. Proc. Ind. Acad. Sci. 82:231.

995. Hart, J. W. 1974. Preliminary studies of Collembola at the Brookville Ecological Research Center, including new records of Indiana Collembola. Proc. Ind. Acad. Sci. 83:334–339.

996. Hartland-Rowe, R. 1964. Factors influencing the life-histories of some stream insects (Ephemeroptera, Plecoptera) in Alberta. Verh. Int. Verein. Limnol. 15:17–925.

997. Hartley, C. F. 1955. Rearing simuliids in the laboratory from eggs to adults. Proc. Helminth. Soc. Wash. 22:93–95.

998. Hartley, J. C. 1961. A taxonomic account of the larvae of some British Syrphidae. Proc. Zool. Soc. Lond. 136:505–573.

999. Harvey, R. S., R. L. Vannote, and B. W. Sweeney. 1979. Life history, developmental processes, and energetics of the burrowing mayfly *Dolania americana*. pp. 211–229. *In* J. F. Flannagan and K. E. Marshall (eds.). Advances in Ephemeroptera biology. Plenum, N.Y. 552 pp.

1000. Harwood, P. D. 1971. Synopsis of James G. Needham's (Cornell University) unpublished manuscript. "The dragonflies of West Virginia." Proc. W. Va. Acad. Sci. 43:72–74.

1001. Harwood, R. F., and M. T. James. 1979. Entomology in human and animal health (7th ed.). Macmillan, N.Y. 548 pp.

1002. Hase, A. 1926. Zur Kenntniss der Lebensgewohneiten und der Umwelt des marinen Kafer *Ochthebius quadricollis* Mulsant. Int. Revue ges. Hydrobiol. 16:141–179.

1003. Hasenfuss, I. 1960. Die Larvalsystematik der Zunsler (Pyralidae). Abhandlungen zur Larvalsystematik der Insekten. 5:1–263.

1004. Hashimoto, H. 1976. Non-biting insects of marine habitats, pp. 377–414. *In* L. Cheng (ed.). Marine insects. North Holland, Amsterdam. 581 pp.

1005. Hatch, M. C. 1925. An outline of the ecology of Gyrinidae. Bull. Brooklyn Ent. Soc. 20:101–104.

1006. Hatch, M. H. 1930. Records and new species of Coleoptera from Oklahoma and western Arkansas, with subsidiary studies. Publ. Okla. Biol. Surv. 2:15–26.

1007. Hatch, M. H. 1962, 1965. The beetles of the Pacific Northwest. Part III: Pselaphidae and Diversicornia (in collaboration with O. Part, J. A. Wagner, K. M. Fender, W. F. Barr, G. E. Woodroffe, and C. W. Coombs). Part IV: *Marcodactyles, Palpicornes,* and *Heteromera* (in collaboration with D. V. Miller, D. V. McCorkle, F. Werner, and D. W. Boddy). Univ. Wash. Publ. Biol. 16:1–503; 19:1–268.

1008. Hauer, R. F., and J. A. Stanford. 1981. Larval specialization and phenotypic variation in *Arctopsyche grandis* (Trichoptera: Hydropsychidae). Ecology 62:645–653.

1009. Hawkins, C. P. 1982. Ecological relationships among western Ephemerellidae: Growth, life cycles, food habits and habitat relationships. Ph.D. diss., Oregon State University, Corvallis. 213 pp.

1010. Hawkins, C. P., and J. R. Sedell. 1981. Longitudinal and seasonal changes in functional organization of macroinvertebrate communities in four Oregon streams. Ecology 62:387–397.

1011. Hayden, W., and H. T. Clifford. 1974. Seasonal movements of the mayfly *Leptophlebia cupida* (Say) in a brown water stream in Alberta, Canada. Am. Midl. Nat. 91:90–102.

1012. Hazard, E. E. 1960. A revision of the genera *Chauliodes* and *Nigronia* (Megaloptera: Corydalidae). M.S. thesis, Ohio State University, Columbus. 53 pp.

1013. Headlee, T. J. 1945. The mosquitoes of New Jersey and their control. Rutgers Univ. Press, New Brunswick. 326 pp.

1014. Heath, B. L., and W. P. McCafferty. 1975. Aquatic and semiaquatic Diptera of Indiana. Purdue Univ. Res. Bull. 930:1–17.

1015. Hedqvist, K. J. 1967. Hymenoptera, pp. 242–244. *In* J. Illies (ed.). Limnofauna Europaea. Gustav Fischer Verlag, Stuttgart. 417 pp.

1016. Heiman, D. R., and A. W. Knight. 1970. Studies on growth and development of the stonefly *Paragnetina media* Walker (Plecoptera: Perlidae). Am. Midl. Nat. 84:274–278.

1017. Heiman, D. R., and A. W. Knight. 1975. The influence of temperature on the bioenergetics of the carnivorous stonefly nymph, *Acroneuria californica* Banks (Plecoptera: Perlidae). Ecology 56:105–116.

1018. Heinrich, B., and D. Vogt. 1980. Aggregation and foraging behavior of whirligig beetles (Gyrinidae). Behav. Ecol. Sociobiol. 7:179–186.

1019. Heinrich, C. 1916. On the taxonomic value of some larval characters in the Lepidoptera. Proc. Ent. Soc. Wash. 18:154–164.

1020. Heinrich, C. 1940. Some new American pyralidoid moths. Proc. Ent. Soc. Wash. 42:31–44.

1021. Hellawell, J. M. 1978. Chap. 4. Macroinvertebrate methods, pp. 35–90. *In* Biological surveillance of rivers. A biological monitoring handbook. Dorset Press, Dorchester, England. 332 pp.

1022. Hemmingsen, A. M. 1965. The lotic cranefly, *Tipula saginata* Bergroth, and the adaptive radiation of the Tipulinae, with a test of Dyar's law. Vidensk. Medd. Dansk Naturhist. Foren 128:93–150.

1023. Hennig, W. 1943. Übersicht über die bisher bekannten Metamorphosesstadien der Ephydriden. Neubeschreibungen nach dem Material der Deutschen Limnologischen Sundaexpedition (Diptera: Ephydridae). Arb. Morph. Tax. Ent. Berlin 10:105–138.

1024. Hennig, W. 1948, 1950, 1952. Die Larvenformen der Dipteren. Akademie-Verlag, Berlin. Pt. I 185 pp.; Pt. 2 458 pp.; Pt. 3 628 pp.

1025. Hennig, W. 1966. Phylogenetic systematics. Translated by D. D. Davis and R. Zangerl, Univ. Ill. Press, Urbana. 263 pp.

1026. Hennig, W. 1967. Diptera:Muscidae, pp. 423–424. *In* J. Illies (ed.). Limnofauna Europaea. Gustav Fischer Verlag, Stuttgart. 417 pp.

1027. Hennig, W. 1973. Diptera. *In* M. Beier and W. de Gruyter (eds.). Handbuch der Zool. 4. Spezielles 31:1–337.

1028. Henriksen, K. L. 1922. Notes on some aquatic Hymenoptera. Ann. Biol. Lacustre 11:19–37.

1029. Henrikson, L., and H. Oscarson. 1978. A quantitative sampler for air-breathing aquatic insects. Freshwat. Biol. 8:73–77.

1030. Hepburn, H. R., and J. P. Woodring. 1963. Checklist of the Collembola (Insects) of Louisiana. Proc. La. Acad. Sci. 26:5–9.

1031. Herlong, D. D. 1979. Aquatic Pyralidae (Lepidoptera: *Nymphulinae*) in South Carolina. Fla. Ent. 62:188–193.

1032. Herman, L. 1972. Revision of *Bledius* and related genera. Part I. The *aequatorialis, mandibularis* and semiferrigueous groups and two new genera (Coleoptera, Staphylinidae, Oxytelinae). Bull. Am. Mus. Nat. Hist. 149:111–254.

1033. Herring, J. L. 1950. The aquatic and semiaquatic Hemiptera of northern Florida. Part II: Veliidae and Mesoveliidae. Fla. Ent. 33:145–150.

1034. Herring, J. L. 1951a. The aquatic and semiaquatic Hemiptera of northern Florida. Part III. Nepidae, Belostomatidae, Notonectidae, Pleidae and Corixidae. Fla. Ent. 34:17–29.

1035. Herring, J. L. 1951b. The aquatic and semiaquatic Hemiptera of northern Florida. Part IV. Classification of habitats and keys to the species. Fla. Ent. 34:146–161.

1036. Herring, J. L. 1958. Evidence for hurricane transport and dispersal of aquatic Hemiptera. Pan-Pacif. Ent. 34:174–175.

1037. Herring, J. L. 1961. The genus *Halobates* (Hemiptera: Gerridae). Pacif. Insects 3:223–305.

1038. Herring, J. L., and P. D. Ashlock. 1971. A key to the nymphs of the families of Hemiptera of America north of Mexico. Fla. Ent. 54:207–212.

1039. Hess, A. D. 1941. New limnological sampling equipment. Limnol. Soc. Am. Spec. Publ. 6:1–5.

1040. Hester, F. E., and J. S. Dendy. 1962. A multiple-plate sampler for aquatic macroinvertebrates. Trans. Am. Fish. Soc. 91: 420–421.

1041. Heymons, R., and H. Heymons. 1909. Collembola: Die Süsswasserfauna Deutschlands 7:1–16.

1042. Hickin, N. E. 1967. Caddis larvae. Hutchinson, London 480 pp.

1043. Hickman, J. R. 1930a. Life-histories of Michigan Haliplidae (Coleoptera). Pap. Mich. Acad. Sci. Arts Lett. 11:399–424.

1044. Hickman, J. R. 1930b. Respiration of the Haliplidae (Coleoptera). Pap. Mich. Acad. Sci. Arts Lett. 13:277–289.

1045. Hickman, J. R. 1931. Contribution to the biology of the Haliplidae (Coleoptera). Ann. Ent. Soc. Am. 24:129–142.

1046. Hildrew, A. G. 1977. Ecological aspects of life history in some net-spinning Trichoptera. pp. 269–281. *In* M. I. Crichton, (ed.). Proc. 2nd Internat. Symp. Trichop., Dr. W. Junk, Publ., The Hague 359 p.

1047. Hildrew, A. G., and J. M. Edington. 1979. Factors facilitating the coexistence of hydropsychid caddis larvae (Trichoptera) in the same river system. J. Anim. Ecol. 48:557–576.

1048. Hildrew, A. G., and C. R. Townsend. 1976. The distribution of two predators and their prey in an iron-rich stream. J. Anim. Ecol. 45:41–57.

1049. Hiley, P. D. 1969. A method of rearing Trichoptera larvae for taxonomic purposes. Entomol. mon. Mag. 105:278–279.

1050. Hiley, P. D., J. F. Wright, and A. D. Berrie. 1981. A new sampler for stream benthos, epiphytic macrofauna and aquatic macrophytes. Freshwat. Biol. 11:79–85.

1051. Hill, P., and D. Tarter. 1978. A taxonomic and distributional study of adult limnephilid caddisflies of West Virginia (Trichoptera: Limnephilidae). Ent. News 89:214–216.

1052. Hill-Griffin, A. L. 1912. New Oregon Trichoptera. Ent. News 23:17–21.

1053. Hilsenhoff, W. L. 1966. The biology of *Chironomus plumosus* (Diptera: Chironomidae) in Lake Winnebago, Wisconsin. Ann. Ent. Soc. Am. 59:465–473.

1054. Hilsenhoff, W. L. 1969. An artificial substrate sampler for stream insects. Limnol. Oceanogr. 14:465–471.

1055. Hilsenhoff, W. L. 1970. Corixidae of Wisconsin. Proc. Wisc. Acad. Sci. Arts Lett. 58:203–235.

1056. Hilsenhoff, W. L. 1973. Notes on *Dubiraphia* (Coleoptera: Elmidae) with descriptions of five new species. Ann. Ent. Soc. Am. 66:55–61.

1057. Hilsenhoff, W. L. 1974. The unusual larva and habitat of *Agabus confusus* (Dytiscidae). Ann. Ent. Soc. Am. 67: 703–705.

1058. Hilsenhoff, W. L. 1975. Notes on Nearctic *Acilius* (Dytiscidae), with the description of a new species. Ann. Ent. Soc. Am. 68:271–274.

1059. Hilsenhoff, W. L. 1980. *Coptotomus* (Coleoptera: Dytiscidae) in Eastern North America with descriptions of 2 new species. Trans. Am. Ent. Soc. 105:461–472.

1060. Hilsenhoff, W. L. 1981. Aquatic insects of Wisconsin. Nat. Hist. Council Wisc., Madison. 60 pp.

1061. Hilsenhoff, W. L., and S. J. Billmyer. 1973. Perlodidae (Plecoptera) of Wisconsin. Great Lakes Ent. 6:1–14.

1062. Hilsenhoff, W. L., and W. U. Brigham. 1978. Crawling water beetles of Wisconsin (Coleoptera: Haliplidae). Great Lakes Ent. 11:11–22.

1063. Hilsenhoff, W. L., J. L. Longridge, R. P. Narf, K. T. Tennessen, and C. P. Walton. 1972. Aquatic insects of the Pine-Popple River, Wisconsin. Wisc. Dept. Nat. Res. Tech. Bull. 54:1–44.

1064. Hinman, E. H. 1934. Predators of the Culicidae. I. The predators of larvae and pupae exclusive of fish. J. Trop. Med. Hyg. 37:129–134.

1065. Hinton, H. E. 1936. Notes on the biology of *Dryops luridus* Erichs. (Coleoptera: Dryopidae). Trans. Soc. Brit. Ent. 3:76–78.

1066. Hinton, H. E. 1946. On the homology and nomenclature of the setae of lepidopterous larvae, with some notes on the phylogeny of the Lepidoptera. Trans. R. ent. Soc. Lond. 97:1–37.

1067. Hinton, H. E. 1948. The dorsal cranial areas of caterpillars. Ann. Mag. Nat. Hist. 14:843–852.

1068. Hinton, H. E. 1955. On the respiratory adaptations, biology and taxonomy of the Psephenidae with notes on some related families (Coleoptera). Proc. Zool. Soc. Lond. 130:543–568.

1069. Hinton, H. E. 1956. The larvae of the Tineidae of economic importance. Bull. Ent. Res. 47:251–346.

1070. Hinton, H. E. 1958a. The pupa of the fly *Simulium* feeds, and spins its own cocoon. Entomol. mon. Mag. 94:14–16.

1071. Hinton, H. E. 1958b. The phylogeny of the panorpoid orders. Ann. Rev. Ent. 3:181–206.

1072. Hinton, H. E. 1960. Cryptobiosis in the larva of *Polypedilum vanderplanki* Hint. (Chironomidae). J. Insect Physiol. 5:286–300.

1073. Hinton, H. E. 1963. The origin and function of the pupal stage. Proc. R. ent. Soc. Lond. (A) 38:77–85.

1074. Hinton, H. E. 1966. Respiratory adaptations of the pupae of beetles of the family Psephenidae. Phil. Trans. R. Soc. (B) 251:211–245.

1075. Hinton, H. E. 1967. On the spiracles of the larvae of the suborder Myxophaga (Coleoptera). Aust. J. Zool. 15:955–959.

1076. Hinton, H. E. 1968. Spiracular gills. Adv. Insect Physiol. 5:65–162.

1077. Hinton, H. E. 1969. Plastron respiration in adult beetles of the suborder Myxophaga. J. Zool. Lond. 159:131–137.

1078. Hinton, H. E. 1971a. Some neglected phases in metamorphosis. Proc. R. ent. Soc. Lond. (C). 35:55–64.

1079. Hinton, H. E. 1971b. A revision of the genus *Hintonelmis* Spangler (Coleoptera: Elmidae). Trans. ent. Soc. Lond. 123:189–208.

1080. Hinton, H. E. 1976a. Plastron respiration in bugs and beetles. J. Insect Physiol. 22:1529–1550.

1081. Hinton, H. E. 1976b. Respiratory adaptations of marine insects, pp. 43–78. *In* L. Cheng (ed.). Marine Insects. North Holland, Amsterdam. 581 pp.

1082. Hinton, H. E. 1977. Enabling mechanisms. Proc. XV Int. Congr. Ent. (Washington), Ent. Soc. Am. 15:71–83.

1083. Hinton, H. E. 1981. Biology of insect eggs. Vols. I–III. Pergamon, Oxford. 1125 pp.

1084. Hirvenoja, M. 1973. Revision der Gattung *Cricotopus* van der Wulp und ihrer Verwandten (Diptera: Chironomidae). Ann. Zool. Fenn. 10:1–363.

1085. Hissom, F. K., and D. C. Tarter. 1976. Taxonomy and distribution of nymphal Perlodidae of West Virginia (Insecta: Plecoptera). J. Ga. Ent. Soc. 11:317–323.

1086. Hitchcock, S. W. 1968. *Alloperla* (Chloroperlidae: Plecoptera) of the Northeast with a key to species. J. N.Y. Ent. Soc. 76:39–46.

1087. Hitchcock, S. W. 1974. Guide to the insects of Connecticut. Part VII. The Plecoptera or stoneflies of Connecticut. Bull. Conn. State Geol. Nat. Hist. Surv. 107:1–262.

1088. Hocking, B., and L. R. Pickering. 1954. Observations on the bionomics of some northern species of Simuliidae (Diptera). Can. J. Zool. 32:99–119.

1089. Hocking, B., W. R. Richards, and C. R. Twinn. 1950. Observations on the bionomics of some northern mosquito species (Culicidae: Diptera). Can. J. Res. 28:58–80.

1090. Hodgden, B. B. 1949a. A monograph of the Saldidae of North and Central America and the West Indies. Ph.D. diss., University of Kansas, Lawrence. 511 pp.

1091. Hodgden, B. B. 1949b. New Saldidae from the western hemisphere. J. Kans. Ent. Soc. 22:149–165.

1092. Hodges, R. W. 1962. A revision of the Cosmopterygidae of America north of Mexico, with a definition of the Momphidae and Walshiidae (Lepidoptera: Gelechioidea). Entomologica 42:1–171.

1093. Hodgson, C. E. 1940. Collection and laboratory maintenance of Dytiscidae (Coleoptera). Ent. News 64:36–37.

1094. Hodkinson, I. D. 1973. The immature stages of *Ptychoptera lenis lenis* (Diptera: Ptychopteridae) with notes on their biology. Can. Ent. 105:1091–1099.

1095. Hodkinson, I. D., and K. A. Williams. 1980. Tube formation and distribution of *Chironomus plumosus* L. (Diptera: Chironomidae) in a eutrophic woodland pond, pp. 331–337. *In* D. A. Murray, (ed.). Chironomidae: ecology, systematics, cytology and physiology. Pergamon, N.Y.

1096. Hoffmann, W. E. 1924. The life history of three species of gerrids (Heteroptera: Gerridae). Ann. Ent. Soc. Am. 17:419–430.

1097. Hoffman, C. H. 1932a. Hymenopterous parasites from the eggs of aquatic and semi-aquatic insects. J. Kans. Ent. Soc. 5:33–37.

1098. Hoffman, C. H. 1932b. The biology of three North American species of *Mesovelia*. Can. Ent. 64:88–94, 113–120, 126–133.

1099. Hoffman, C. H. 1937. How to rear *Mesovelia*, pp. 305–306. *In* J. G. Needham (ed.). Culture methods for invertebrate animals. Comstock, Ithaca. 590 pp.

1100. Hoffman, C. H. 1940a. Limnological relationships of some northern Michigan Donaciini (Chrysomelidae: Coleoptera). Trans. Am. Microsc. Soc. 59:259–274.

1101. Hoffman, C. H. 1940b. The relation of *Donacia* larvae (Chrysommelidae, Coleoptera) to dissolved oxygen. Ecology 20:176–183.

1102. Hoffmann, W. E. 1925. The life history of *Velia watsoni* Drake (Heteroptera, Veliidae). Can. Ent. 57:107–112.

1103. Hoffrichter, O., and F. Reiss. 1981. Supplement 1 to "A bibliography of the Chironomidae." Gunneria 37:1–68.

1104. Hofsvang, T. 1972. *Tipula excisa* Schum. (Diptera, Tipulidae), life cycle and population dynamics. Nord. Ent. Tidsskr. 19:43–48.

1105. Hogue, C. L. 1973a. A taxonomic review of the genus *Maruina* (Diptera: Psychodidae). Los Angeles Co. Nat. Hist. Mus. Sci. Bull. 17:1–69.

1106. Hogue, C. L. 1973b. The net-winged midges or Blephariceridae of California. Bull. Calif. Insect Surv. 15:1–83.

1107. Hogue, C. L. 1981. Chap. 8. Blephariceridae, pp. 191–198. *In* J. F. McAlpine, B. V. Peterson, G. E. Shewell, H. J. Teskey, J. R. Vockeroth, and D. M. Wood (coords.). Manual of Nearctic Diptera, Vol. 1. Res. Branch, Agric. Can. Monogr. 27. Ottawa. 674 pp.

1108. Holdsworth, R. 1941a. The life history and growth of *Pteronarcys proteus* Newman. Ann. Ent. Soc. Am. 34:495–502.

1109. Holdsworth, R. 1941b. Additional information and a correction concerning the growth of *Pteronarcys proteus* Newman. Ann. Ent. Soc. Am. 34:714–715.

1110. Holopainen, I. J., and J. Sarvala. 1975. Efficiencies of two corers in sampling soft-bottom invertebrates. Ann. Zool. Fenn. 12:280–284.

1111. Holzenthal, R. W. 1982. The caddisfly genus *Setodes* in North America (Trichoptera: Leptoceridae). J. Kans. Ent. Soc. 55:253–271.

1112. Holzenthal, R. W., S. C. Harris, and P. K. Lago. 1982. An annotated checklist of the caddisflies (Trichoptera) of Mississippi and southeastern Louisiana. Part III: Limnephiloidea and conclusions. Proc. Ent. Soc. Wash. 84:513–520.

1113. Hora, S. L. 1930. Ecology, bionomics and evolution of the torrential fauna, with special reference to the organs of attachment. Phil. Trans. R. Soc. (B) 218:171–282.

1114. Horn, G. H. 1873. Revision of the genera and species of the tribe Hydrobiini. Proc. Am. Phil. Soc. 13:118–137.

1115. Horsfall, W. R. 1955. Mosquitoes: Their behavior and relation to disease. Ronald, N.Y. 723 pp.

1116. Horst, T. J. 1976. Population dynamics of the burrowing mayfly *Hexagenia limbata.* Ecology 57:199–204.

1117. Horst, T. J., and G. R. Marzolf. 1975. Production ecology of burrowing mayflies in a Kansas reservoir. Verh. Int. Verein. Limnol. 19:3029–3038.

1118. Hosseinig, S. O. 1966. Studies on the biology and life histories of aquatic beetles of the genus *Tropisternus* (Coleoptera: Hydrophilidae). Diss. Abstr. 261:4903.

1119. Houlihan, D. F. 1969a. The structure and behavior of *Notiphila riparia* and *Erioptera squalida* (Dipt.). J. Zool. Lond. 159:249–267.

1120. Houlihan, D. F. 1969b. Respiratory physiology of the larva of *Donacia simplex,* a root-piercing beetle. J. Insect Physiol. 15:1517–1536.

1121. Houlihan, D. F. 1970. Respiration in low oxygen partial pressure: The adults of *Donacia simplex* that respire from the roots of aquatic plants. J. Insect Physiol. 16:1607–1622.

1122. Howard, F. O. 1974. Natural history and ecology of *Pycnopsyche lepida, P. guttifer* and *P. scabripennis* (Trichoptera: Limnephilidae) in a woodland stream. Ph.D. diss., Michigan State University, East Lansing. 115 pp.

1123. Howe, R. H. 1917–1923. Manual of the Odonata of New England. Mem. Thoreau Mus. Nat. Hist. (Parts 1–6). Vol. II:1–149.

1124. Howland, L. J. 1930. The nutrition of mosquito larvae, with special reference to their algal food. Bull. Ent. Res. 21:431–439.

1125. Howmiller, R. P. 1971. A comparison of the effectiveness of Ekman and Ponar grabs. Trans. Am. Fish. Soc. 100:560–564.

1126. Hrbacek, J. 1950. On the morphology and function of the antennae of the central European Hydrophilidae (Coleoptera). Trans. R. ent. Soc. Lond. 101:239–256.

1127. Hrbacek, J. (ed.) 1962. Hydrobiologicke Metody. Praha. 130 pp.

1128. Hudson, P. L., J. C. Morse, and J. R. Voshell. 1981. Larva and pupa of *Cernotina spicata.* Ann. Ent. Soc. Am. 74:516–519.

1129. Huggins, D. G. 1978a. Description of the nymph of *Enallagma divagans* Selys (Odonata: Coenagrionidae). J. Kans. Ent. Soc. 51:140–143.

1130. Huggins, D. G. 1978b. Redescription of the nymph of *Enallagma basidens* Calvert (Odonata: Coenagrionidae). J. Kans. Ent. Soc. 51:222–227.

1131. Huggins, D. G. 1980. The spongillaflies (Neuroptera: Sisyridae) of Kansas. Tech. Publ. State Biol. Surv. Kans. 9:67–70.

1132. Huggins, D. G., and W. U. Brigham. 1982. Chap. 4, Odonata, pp. 4.1–4.100. *In* A. R. Brigham, W. U. Brigham, and A. Gnilka (eds.). Aquatic insects and oligochaetes of North and South Carolina. Midwest Aquatic Enterprises, Mahomet, Ill. 837 pp.

1133. Huggins, D. G., P. Liechti, and D. W. Roubik. 1976. New records of the fauna and flora for 1975. Tech. Publ. Kans. State Biol. Surv. 1:13–44.

1134. Hughes, B. D. 1975. A comparison of four samplers for benthic macroinvertebrates inhabiting coarse river deposits. Wat. Res. 9:61–69.

1135. Hummel, S., and A. C. Haman. 1975. Notes on the Odonata of Black Hawk County, Iowa. Ent. News 86:63–64.

1136. Humpesch, U. H. 1979. Life cycles and growth rates of *Baetis* spp. (Ephemeroptera: Baetidae) in the laboratory and in two stony streams in Austria. Freshwat. Biol. 9:467–479.

1137. Hungerford, H. B. 1917a. Food habits of corixids. J. N.Y. Ent. Soc. 25:1–5.

1138. Hungerford, H. B. 1917b. Life history of a boatman. J. N.Y. Ent. Soc. 25:112–122.

1139. Hungerford, H. B. 1917c. The life history of *Mesovelia mulsanti* White. Psyche 24:73–84.

1140. Hungerford, H. B. 1920. The biology and ecology of aquatic and semi-aquatic Hemiptera. Univ. Kans. Sci. Bull. 21:1–341.

1141. Hungerford, H. B. 1922a. Oxyhaemoglobin present in backswimmer, *Buenoa margaritacea.* Can. Ent. 54:262–263.

1142. Hungerford, H. B. 1922b. The life history of the toad bug *Gelastocoris oculatus* Fabr. Univ. Kans. Sci. Bull. 14:145–171.

1143. Hungerford, H. B. 1922c. The Nepidae of North America north of Mexico. Univ. Kans. Sci. Bull. 14:423–469.

1144. Hungerford, H. B. 1924. A new *Mesovelia* with some biological notes regarding it, *Mesovelia douglasensis.* Can. Ent. 56:142–144.

1145. Hungerford, H. B. 1927. The life history of the creeping water bug *Pelocoris carolinensis* Bueno (Naucoridae). Univ. Kans. Sci. Bull. 22:77–82.

1146. Hungerford, H. B. 1933. The genus *Notonecta* of the world. Univ. Kans. Sci. Bull. 21:5–195.

1147. Hungerford, H. B. 1948. The Corixidae of the Western Hemisphere (Hemiptera). Univ. Kans. Sci. Bull. 32:1–827.

1148. Hungerford, H. B. 1954. The genus *Rheumatobates* Bergroth. Univ. Kans. Sci. Bull. 36:529–588.

1149. Hungerford, H. B. 1958. Some interesting aspects of the World distribution and classification of aquatic and semiaquatic Hemiptera. Proc. 10th Int. Congr. Ent. 1:337–348.

1150. Hungerford, H. B. 1959. Hemiptera, pp. 958–972. *In* W. T. Edmondson (ed.). Freshwater Biology (2nd ed.). John Wiley & Sons, N.Y. 1248 pp.

1151. Hungerford, H. B., and N. E. Evans. 1934. The Hydrometridae of the Hungarian National Museum and other studies in the family. Ann. Mus. Nat. Hungar. 28:31–112.

1152. Hungerford, H. B., and R. Matsuda. 1960. Keys to the subfamilies, tribes, genera and subgenera of the Gerridae of the world. Univ. Kans. Sci. Bull. 41:3–23.

1153. Hungerford, H. B., P. J. Spangler, and N. A. Walker. 1955. Subaquatic light traps for insects and other animal organisms. Trans. Kans. Acad. Sci. 58:387–407.

1154. Hunt, B. P. 1953. The life history and economic importance of a burrowing mayfly, *Hexagenia limbata,* in southern Michigan lakes. Bull. Inst. Fish. Res. Ann Arbor, Mich. 4:1–151.

1155. Husbands, R. C. 1967. A subsurface light trap for sampling aquatic insect populations. Calif. Vector Views 14:81–82.

1156. Hussey, R. F., and J. L. Herring. 1949. Notes on the variation of the *Metrobates* of Florida (Hemiptera, Gerridae). Fla. Ent. 32:166–170.

1157. Hussey, R. F., and J. L. Herring. 1950. A remarkable new belostomatid from Florida and Georgia. Fla. Ent. 33:84–89.

1158. Hutchinson, G. E. 1931. On the occurrence of *Trichocorixa* Kirkaldy in salt water and its zoogeographical significance. Am. Nat. 65:573–574.

1159. Hutchinson, G. E. 1945. On the species of *Notonecta* (Hemiptera-Heteroptera) inhabiting New England. Trans. Conn. Acad. Arts Sci. 36:599–605.

1160. Hutchinson, G. E. 1957. A treatise on limnology. Vol. I. John Wiley & Sons, Inc., N.Y. 1015 pp.

1161. Hutchinson, G. E. 1981. Thoughts on aquatic insects. BioScience 31:495–500.

1162. Hutchinson, R., and A. Larochelle. 1977. Catalogue des Libellules du Quebec. Cordulia (Suppl.) 3:1–45.

1163. Hyland, K., Jr. 1948. New records of Pennsylvania caddis flies (Trichoptera). Ent. News 59:38–40.

1164. Hynes, C. D. 1969a. The immature stages of *Gonomyodes tacoma* Alex. Pan-Pacif. Ent. 45:116–119.

1165. Hynes, C. D. 1969b. The immature stages of the genus *Rhabdomastix* (Diptera: Tipulidae). Pan-Pacif. Ent. 45:229–237.

1166. Hynes, H. B. N. 1941. The taxonomy and ecology of the nymphs of British Plecoptera with notes on the adults and eggs. Trans. R. ent. Soc. Lond. 91:459–557.

1167. Hynes, H. B. N. 1948. Notes on the aquatic Hemiptera-Heteroptera of Trinidad and Tobago, B. W. I., with a description of a new species of *Martarega* B. White (Notonectidae). Trans. R. ent. Soc. Lond. 99:341–360.

1168. Hynes, H. B. N. 1961. The invertebrate fauna of a Welsh mountain stream. Arch. Hydrobiol. 57:344–388.

1169. Hynes, H. B. N. 1963. Imported organic matter and secondary productivity of streams. Int. Congr. Zool. 4:324–329.

1170. Hynes, H. B. N. 1970a. The ecology of running waters. Univ. Toronto Press, Toronto. 555 pp.

1171. Hynes, H. B. N. 1970b. The ecology of stream insects. Ann. Rev. Ent. 15:25–42.

1172. Hynes, H. B. N. 1971. Benthos of flowing water, pp. 66–80. *In* W. T. Edmondson and G. G. Winberg (eds.). A manual on methods for the assessment of secondary productivity in freshwaters. IBP Handbook 17, Blackwell, Oxford. 358 pp.

1173. Hynes, H. B. N. 1974. Further studies on the distribution of animals within the substratum. Limnol. Oceanogr. 19:92–99.

1174. Hynes, H. B. N. 1976. The biology of Plecoptera. Ann. Rev. Ent. 21:135–153.

1175. Hynes, H. B. N., and M. E. Hynes. 1975. The life histories of many of the stoneflies (Plecoptera) of southeastern mainland Australia. Australian J. Mar. Freshwat. Res. 26:113–153.

1176. Hynes, H. B. N. and N. K. Kaushik. 1968. Experimental study of the role of autumn shed leaves in aquatic environments. J. Ecol. 56:229–243.

1177. Ide, F. P. 1930. Contribution to the biology of Ontario mayflies with descriptions of new species. Can. Ent. 62:204–213, 62:218–231.

1178. Ide, F. P. 1935. Life history notes on *Ephoron, Potamanthus, Lepthophlebia* and *Blasturus* with descriptions (Ephemeroptera). Can. Ent. 67:113–125.

1179. Ide, F. P. 1940. Quantitative determination of the insect fauna of rapid water. Publ. Ontario Fish. Res. Lab. 47:1–24.

1180. Ide, F. P. 1965. A fly of the archaic family Nymphomyiidae (Diptera) from North America. Can. Ent. 97:496–507.

1181. Illies, J. 1959. Retardierte Schlupfzeit von *Baetis*-Gelegen (Ins., Ephem.). Naturwissenschaften 46:119–120.

1182. Illies, J. 1965. Phylogeny and zoogeography of the Plecoptera. Ann. Rev. Ent. 10:117–141.

1183. Illies, J. 1966. Katalog der rezenten Plecoptera. Das Tierreich, 82. Walter de Gruyter, Berlin. 623 pp.

1184. Imms. A. D. 1906. *Anurida*. Marine Biol. Mem. Liverpool 13:1–99.

1185. Imms, A. D. 1948. A general textbook of entomology (7th ed.). Dutton, New York. 727 pp.

1186. Ingram, B. R. 1976. Life histories of three species of Lestidae in North Carolina, United States (Zygoptera). Odonatologica 5:231–244.

1187. Ingram, B. R., and C. E. Jenner. 1976. Life histories of *Enallagma hageni* (Walsh) and *E. aspersum* (Hagen) (Zygoptera: Coenagrionidae). Odonatologica 5:331–345.

1188. Istock, C. A. 1966. Distribution, coexistence, and competition of whirligig beetles. Evolution 20:211–239.

1189. Istock, C. A. 1972. Population characteristics of a species ensemble of waterboatmen (Corixidae). Ecology 54:535–544.

1190. Istock, C. A., S. E. Wasserman, and H. Zimmer. 1975. Ecology and evolution of the pitcher-plant mosquito: I. Population dynamics and laboratory responses to food and population density. Evolution 29:296–312.

1191. Ivanova, S. S. 1958. Nutrition of some mayfly larvae. Proc. Mikoyan Moscow Tech. Inst. Fish. Indust. 9:102–109.

1192. Iversen, T. M. 1973. Life cycle and growth of *Sericostoma personatum* Spence (Trichoptera: Sericostomatidae) in a Danish spring. Ent. Scand. 41:323–327.

1193. Iversen, T. M. 1974. Ingestion and growth in *Sericostoma personatum* (Trichoptera) in relation to the nitrogen content of ingested leaves. Oikos 25:278–282.

1194. Iversen, T. M. 1980. Densities and energetics of two stream living larval populations of *Sericostoma personatum* (Trichoptera). Holarct. Ecol. 3:65–73.

1195. Izvekova, E. I. 1971. On the feeding habits of chironomid larvae. Limnologica 8:201–202.

1196. Izvekova, E. I., and A. A. Lvova-katchanova. 1972. Sedimentation of suspended matter by *Dreissena polymorpha* Pallas and its subsequent utilization by chironomid larvae. Pol. Arch. Hydrobiol. 19:203–210.

1197. Jaag, O., and H. Ambühl. 1964. The effect of the current on the composition of biocoenoses in flowing water streams, pp. 31–44. *In* B. A. Southgate (ed.). Advances in water pollution research; proceedings of the international conference, London, 1962. Pergamon, Oxford.

1198. Jackson, D. J. 1956a. Dimorphism of the metasternal wings in *Agabus raffrayi* Sharp and *A. labiatus* Brahn. (Coleoptera, Dytiscidae) and its relation to capacity of flight. Proc. R. ent. Soc. Lond. (A) 131:1–11.

1199. Jackson, D. J. 1956b. Notes on hymenopterous parasitoids bred from eggs of Dytiscidae in Fife. J. Soc. Brit. Ent. 5:144–149.

1200. Jackson, D. J. 1958a. A further note on a *Chrysocharis* (Hym.: Eulophidae) parasitizing the eggs of *Dytiscus marginalis* L., and comparison of its larva with that of *Caraphractus cinctus* Walker (Hym.: Mymaridae). J. Soc. Brit. Ent. 6:15–22.

1201. Jackson, D. J. 1958b. Egg-laying and egg-hatching in *Agabus bipustulatus* L., with notes on oviposition in other species of *Agabus* (Coleoptera: Dytiscidae). Trans. Ent. Soc. Lond. 110:53–80.

1202. Jackson, D. J. 1958c. Observations on the biology of *Caraphractus cinctus* Walker (Hym.: Mymaridae), a parasitoid of the eggs of Dytiscidae. 1—Methods of rearing and numbers bred on different host eggs. Trans. R. ent. Soc. Lond. 110:533–554.

1203. Jackson, D. J. 1961a. Diapause in an aquatic mymarid. Nature 192:823–824.

1204. Jackson, D. J. 1961b. Observations on the biology of *Caraphractus cinctus* Walker (Hym.: Mymaridae), a parasitoid of the eggs of Dytiscidae (Coleoptera). 2. Immature stages and seasonal history with a review of mymarid larvae. Parasitology 51:269–294.

1205. Jackson, D. J. 1964. Observations on the life-history of *Mestocharis bimacularis* (Dalman) (Hym.: Eulophidae), a parasitoid of eggs of Dytiscidae. Opusc. Ent. 29:81–97.

1206. Jackson, D. J. 1966. Observations on the biology of *Caraphractus cinctus* Walker (Hym. Mymaridae), a parasitoid of the eggs of Dytiscidae. III. The adult life and sex ratio. Trans. R. ent. Soc. Lond. 118:2349.

1207. Jacobi, G. Z. 1978. An inexpensive circular sampler for collecting benthic macroinvertebrates in streams. Arch. Hydrobiol. 83:126–131.

1208. Jaczewski, T. 1930. Notes on the American species of the genus *Mesovelia* Muls. Ann. Mus. Zool. Polon. 9:1–12.

1209. Jaczewski, T., and A. S. Kostrowicki. 1969. Number of species of aquatic and semi-aquatic Heteroptera in the fauna of various parts of the Holarctic in relation to the world fauna. Mem. Soc. Ent. Ital. 48:153–156.

1210. James, H. G. 1957. *Mochlonyx velutinus* (Ruthe) (Diptera: Culicidae), an occasional predator of mosquito larvae. Can. Ent. 89:470–480.

1211. James, H. G. 1961. Some predators of *Aedes stimulans* (Walk.) and *Aedes trichurus* (Dyar) in woodland pools. Can. J. Zool. 39:533–540.

1212. James, H. G. 1933. Collembola of the Toronto region, with notes on the biology of *Isotoma palustris* Muller. Trans. Can. Inst. 19:77–116.

1213. James, H. G. 1964a. Insect and other fauna associated with the rock pool mosquito *Aedes atropalpus* (Coq.). Mosquito News 23:325–329.

1214. James, H. G. 1964b. The role of Coleoptera in the natural control of mosquitoes in Canada. Proc. 12th Int. Congr. Ent. 12:357–358.

1215. James, H. G. 1969. Immature stages of five diving beetles (Coleoptera: Dytiscidae), notes on their habits and life history, and a key to aquatic beetles of vernal woodland pools in southern Ontario. Proc. Ent. Soc. Ont. 100:52–97.

1216. James, H. G., G. Wishart, R. E. Bellamy, M. Maw, and P. Belton. 1969. An annotated list of mosquitoes of southeastern Ontario. Proc. Ent. Soc. Ont. 100:200–230.

1217. James, M. T. 1959. Diptera, pp. 1057–1079. *In* W. T. Edmondson (ed.). Freshwater biology (2nd ed.). John Wiley & Sons, N.Y. 1248 pp.

1218. James, M. T. 1981. Chap. 36. Stratiomyidae, pp. 497–512. *In* J. F. McAlpine, B. V. Peterson, G. E. Shewell, H. J. Teskey, J. R. Vockeroth, and D. M. Wood (coords.). Manual of Nearctic Diptera, Vol. 1. Res. Branch, Agric. Can. Monogr. 27. Ottawa. 674 pp.

1219. Jamieson, G. S., and G. G. E. Scudder. 1977. Food consumption in *Gerris* (Hemiptera). Oecologia 30:23–41.

1220. Jamieson, G. S., and G. G. E. Scudder. 1979. Predation in *Gerris* (Hemiptera): Reactive distances and locomotion rates. Oecologia 44:13–20.

1221. Jamnback, H. 1969. Bloodsucking flies and other outdoor nuisance arthropods of New York state. Mem. N.Y. State Mus. Sci. Serv. 19. 90 pp.

1222. Jankovic, M. 1974. Feeding and food assimilation in larvae of *Prodiamesa olivacea*. Ent. Tidskr. Suppl. 95:116–119.

1223. Jankovic, M. 1978. Role of plant debris in the feeding of *Prodiamesa olivacea* larvae. Acta Universitatis Carolinae, Biologica 1978:77–82.

1224. Jansson, A. 1976. Audiospectrographic analysis of stridulatory signals of some North American Corixidae (Hemiptera). Ann. Zool. Fenn. 13:48–62.

1225. Jansson, A. 1977. Micronectae (Heteroptera, Corixidae) as indicators of water quality in two lakes in southern Finland. Ann. Zool. Fenn. 14:118–124.

1226. Jansson, A. 1979. A new species of *Callicorixa* from Northwestern North America. Pan-Pacif. Ent. 54:261–266.

1227. Jansson, A. 1981. Generic name *Ahuautlea* De La Llave, 1832 (Insecta, Heteroptera, Corixidae): Proposed suppression under the plenary powers Z. N. (S.) 2299. Bull. Zool. Nom. 38:197–200.

1228. Jansson, A., and G. G. E. Scudder. 1972. Corixidae (Hemiptera) as predators: rearing on frozen brine shrimp. J. Ent. Soc. Brit. Columbia 69:44–45.

1229. Jansson, A., and G. G. E. Scudder. 1974. The life cycle and sexual development of *Cenocorixa* species (Hemiptera: Corixidae) in the Pacific Northwest. Freshwat. Biol. 4:73–92.

1230. Jansson, A., and T. Vuoristo. 1979. Significance of stridulation in larval Hydropsychidae (Trichoptera). Behaviour 71:167–186.

1231. Jeffrey, R. W. 1877. *Hydrocampa stagnalis* Bred. Entomol. mon. Mag. 14:116.

1232. Jenkins, D. W. 1964. Pathogens, parasites and predators of medically important arthropods, annotated list and bibliography. Bull. World Health Org. Suppl. 30:1–150.

1233. Jenkins, M. F. 1960. On the method by which *Stenus* and *Dianous* (Coleoptera: Staphylinidae) return to the banks of a pool. Trans. R. ent. Soc. Lond. 112:1–14.

1234. Jewett, S. G., Jr. 1956. Plecoptera, pp. 155–181. *In* R. L. Usinger (ed.). Aquatic insects of California. Univ. Calif. Press, Berkeley. 508 pp.

1235. Jewett, S. G., Jr. 1959. The stoneflies of the Pacific Northwest. Ore. State Monogr. Stud. Ent. 3:1–95.

1236. Jewett, S. G., Jr. 1960. The stoneflies (Plecoptera) of California. Bull. Calif. Insect Surv. 6:122–177.

1237. Jewett, S. G., Jr. 1963. A stonefly aquatic in the adult stage. Science 139:484–485.

1238. Johannsen, O. A. 1905. Aquatic nematocerous Diptera. II-Chironomidae, pp. 76–331. *In* J. Needham, K. Morton, and O. Johannsen (eds.). Mayflies and midges of New York. Bull. New York State Mus. 86:1–352.

1239. Johannsen, O. A. 1922. Stratiomyiid larvae and puparia of the northeastern states. J. N.Y. Ent. Soc. 30:141–153.

1240. Johannsen, O. A. 1934, 1935. Aquatic Diptera. Part I. Nematocera, exclusive of Chironomidae and Ceratopogonidae. Part II. Orthorrhapha-Brachycera and Cyclorrhapha. Mem. Cornell Univ. Agric. Exp. Sta. 164:1–71; 171:1–62.

1241. Johannsen, O. A. 1937. Aquatic Diptera. III. Chironomidae: subfamilies Tanypodinae, Diamesinae, and Orthocladiinae. Mem. Cornell Univ. Agric. Exp. Sta. 205:3–84.

1242. Johannsen, O. A. 1938. Aquatic Diptera. IV. Chironomidae: subfamily Chironominae. Mem. Cornell Univ. Agric. Exp. Sta. 210:3–80.

1243. Johannsen, O. A., and H. K. Townes. 1952. Tendipedidae (Chironomidae) except Tendipedini, pp. 3–147. *In* Guide to the insects of Connecticut. Part VI. The Diptera or true flies. Fasc. 5. Midges and gnats. Bull. Conn. State Geol. Nat. Hist. Surv. 80:1–254.

1244. Johnson, C. 1968. Seasonal ecology of the dragonfly *Oplonaeschna armata* Hagen (Odonata: Aeshnidae). Am. Midl. Nat. 80:449–457.

1245. Johnson, C. 1972. The damselflies (Zygoptera) of Texas. Bull. Fla. State Mus. 16:55–128.

1246. Johnson, C. 1974. Taxonomic keys and distributional patterns for Nearctic species of *Calopteryx* damselflies. Fla. Ent. 57:231–248.

1247. Johnson, C., and M. J. Westfall. 1970. Diagnostic keys and notes on the damselflies (Zygoptera) of Florida. Bull. Fla. State Mus. 15:1–89.

1248. Johnson, D. M. 1973. Predation by damselfly naiads on cladoceran populations: fluctuating intensity. Ecology 54: 251–268.

1249. Johnson, D. M., B. G. Akre, and P. H. Crowley. 1975. Modeling arthropod predation: wasteful killing by damselfly naiads. Ecology 56:1081–1093.

1250. Johnson, D. M., and P. H. Crowley. 1980. Habitat and seasonal segregation among coexisting odonate larvae. Odonatologica 9:297–308.

1251. Johnson, G. H. 1972. Flight behavior of the predaceous diving beetle, *Cybister fimbriolatus* (Say) (Coleoptera:Dytiscidae). Coleopt. Bull. 26:23–24.

1252. Johnson, G. H., and W. Jakinovich, Jr. 1970. Feeding behavior of the predaceous diving beetle, *Cybister fimbriolatus* (Say). BioScience 20:1111.

1253. Johnson, J. H. 1981. Food habits and dietary overlap of perlid stoneflies (Plecoptera) in a tributary of Lake Ontario. Can. J. Zool. 59:2030–2037.

1254. Jonasson, P. M. 1954. An improved funnel trap for capturing emerging aquatic insects, with some preliminary results. Oikos 5:179–188.

1255. Jonasson, P. M., and J. Kristiansen. 1967. Primary and secondary production in Lake Esrom. Growth of *Chironomus anthracinus* in relation to seasonal cycles of phytoplankton and dissolved oxygen. Int. Revue ges. Hydrobiol. 52:163–217.

1256. Jones, C. M., and D. W. Anthony. 1964. The Tabanidae of Florida. U.S.D.A. Tech. Bull. 1295. 85 pp.

1257. Jones, F. M. 1916. Two insect associates of the California pitcher plant, *Darlingtonia californica* (Dipt.). Ent. News 27:385–392.

1258. Jones, F. M. 1918. *Dohrniphora venusta* Coquillett (Dipt.) in *Sarracenia flava*. Ent. News 29:299–302.

1259. Jones, J. R. E. 1950. A further ecological study of the River Rheidol: the food of the common insects of the main stream. J. Anim. Ecol. 19:159–174.

1260. Joosse, E. N. G. 1966. Some observations on the biology of *Anurida maritima* (Guerin), (Collembola). S. Morph. Okol. Tiere 57:320–328.

1261. Joosse, E. N. G. 1976. Littoral Apterygotes (Collembola and Thysanura) pp. 151–186. *In:* L. Cheng (ed.) Marine Insects, North Holland Publ. Co. Amsterdam.

1262. Judd, W. W. 1950. *Acentropus niveus* (Pyralid.) on the north shore of Lake Erie with a consideration of its distribution in North America. Can. Ent. 82:250–252.

1263. Judd, W. W. 1953. A study of the population of insects emerging as adults from the Dundas Marsh, Hamilton, Ontario, during 1948. Am. Midl. Nat. 49:801–824.

1264. Juliano, S. A. 1981. *Trichogramma* spp. (Hymenoptera: Trichogrammatidae) as egg parasitoids of *Sepedon fuscipennis* (Diptera:Sciomyzidae) and other aquatic Diptera. Can. Ent. 113:271–279.

1265. Kaiser, E. W. 1961. On the biology of *Sialis fuliginosa* Pict. and *S. nigripes* Ed. Pict. Flora Fauna, Silkeborg. 67:74–96.

1266. Kajak, Z. 1963. Analysis of quantitative benthic methods. Ekol. Polska (A) 11:1–56.

1267. Kajak, Z. 1971. Benthos of standing water, pp. 25–65. *In* W. T. Edmondson and G. G. Winberg (eds.). A manual on methods for the assessment of secondary productivity in fresh waters. IBP Handbook 17. Blackwell, Oxford. 358 pp.

1268. Kajak, Z. 1980. Role of invertebrate predators (mainly *Procladius* sp.) in benthos, pp. 339–348. *In* D. Murray (ed.). Chironomidae: ecology, systematics, cytology, and physiology. Pergamon, N.Y.

1269. Kajak, Z., and R. Dusage. 1970. Production efficiency of *Procladius choreus* Mg. (Chironomidae, Diptera) and its dependence on the trophic conditions. Pol. Arch. Hydrobiol. 17:217–224.

1270. Kajak, Z., K. Kacprzak, and R. Polkowski. 1965. Chwytacz rurowy do pobierania prob mikro-i makrobentosu, orax prob o niezaburzonej strukturze mulu dia celow ekspery mentalnych. Ekol. Polska (B) 11:159–165 (English Summary).

1271. Kajak, Z., and B. Ranke-Rybica. 1970. Feeding and production efficiency of *Chaoborus flavicans* Meigen (Diptera, Culicidae) larvae in eutrophic and dystrophic lakes. Pol. Arch. Hydrobiol. 17:225–232.

1272. Kajak, Z., and J. Rybak. 1970. Food conditions for larvae of Chironomidae in various layers of bottom sediments. Bull. Pol. Acad. Sci. Biol. 18:193–196.

1273. Kajak, Z., and A. Stanczykowska. 1968. Influence of mutual relations of organisms, especially Chironomidae in natural benthic communities, on their abundance. Ann. Zool. Fenn. 5:49–56.

1274. Kajak, Z., and J. Warda. 1968. Feeding of benthic non-predatory Chironomidae in lakes. Ann. Zool. Fenn. 5:57–64.

1275. Kalmus, H. 1963. 101 simple experiments with insects. Doubleday & Co., Inc., Garden City, N.Y. 194 pp.

1276. Kaminski, R. M., and H. R. Murkin. 1981. Evaluation of two devices for sampling nektonic invertebrates. J. Wildl. Manage. 45:493–496.

1277. Kapoor, N. N. 1972a. A recording device for measuring respiratory movements of aquatic insects. Proc. Ent. Soc. Ont. 102:71–78.

1278. Kapoor, N. N. 1972b. Rearing and maintenance of Plecoptera nymphs. Hydrobiologia 40:51–53.

1279. Karlsson, M., T. Bohlin, and J. Stenson. 1976. Core sampling and flotation: two methods to reduce costs of a chironomid population study. Oikos 27:336–338.

1280. Karny, H. H. 1934. Biologie der Wasserinsekten. F. Wagner, Vienna 311 pp.

1281. Kawecka, B., and A. Kownacki. 1974. Food conditions of Chironomidae in the River Raba. Ent. Tidskr. Suppl. 95:120–128.

1282. Kawecka, B., A. Kownacki, and M. Kownacka. 1978. Food relations between algae and bottom-fauna communities in glacial streams. Verh. Int. Verein. Limnol. 20:1527–1530.

1283. Keilin, D. 1944. Respiratory systems and respiratory adaptations in larvae and pupae of Diptera. Parasitology 36:1–66.

1284. Kellen, W. R. 1954. A new bottom sampler. Limnol. Oceanogr. Soc. Am. Spec. Publ. 22:1–3.

1285. Kelley, R. 1982. The micro-caddisfly genus *Oxyethira* (Trichoptera:Hydroptilidae): Morphology, biogeography, evolution and classification. Ph.D. diss., Clemson University, Clemson, S.C. 432 pp.

1286. Kelley, R. W., and J. C. Morse. 1982. A key to the females of the genus *Oxyethira* (Trichoptera: Hydroptilidae) from the southern United States. Proc. Ent. Soc. Wash. 84:256–269.

1287. Kellicott, D. S. 1899. The Odonata of Ohio. Spec. Pap. Ohio Acad. Sci. 2:1–114.

1288. Kelts, L. J. 1979. Ecology of a tidal marsh corixid, *Trichocorixa verticalis* (Insecta, Hemiptera). Hydrobiologia 64:37–57.

1289. Kennedy, C. H. 1915. Notes on the life history and ecology of the dragonflies (Odonata) of Washington and Oregon. Proc. U.S. Nat. Mus. 49:259–345.

1290. Kennedy, C. H. 1917. Notes on the life history and ecology of the dragonflies (Odonata) of central California and Nevada. Proc. U.S. Nat. Mus. 52:483–635.

1291. Kennedy, H. D. 1958. Biology and life history of a new species of mountain midge, *Deuterophlebia nielsoni,* from eastern California (Diptera:Deuterophlebiidae). Trans. Am. Microsc. Soc. 89:201–228.

1292. Kennedy, H. D. 1960. *Deuterophlebia inyoensis,* a new species of mountain midge from the alpine zone of the Sierra Nevada Range, California (Diptera:Deuterophlebiidae). Trans. Am. Microsc. Soc. 79:191–210.

1293. Kennedy, H. D. 1981. Chap. 9. Deuterophlebiidae, pp. 199–202. *In* J. F. McAlpine, B. V. Peterson, G. E. Shewell, H. J. Teskey, J. R. Vockeroth, and D. M. Wood (coords.). Manual of Nearctic Diptera, Vol. 1. Res. Branch Agric. Can. Monogr. 27. Ottawa. 674 pp.

1294. Kennedy, J. H., and H. B. White, III. 1979. Description of the nymph of *Ophiogomphus howei* (Odonata: Gomphidae). Proc. Ent. Soc. Wash. 81:64–69.

1295. Kershaw, W. E., T. R. Williams, S. Frost, R. E. Matchett, M. L. Mills, and R. D. Johnson. 1968. The selective control of *Simulium* larvae by particulate insecticides and its significance in river management. Trans. Roy. Soc. Trop. Med. Hyg. 62:35–40.

1296. Kerst, C. D., and N. H. Anderson. 1975. The Plecoptera community of a small stream in Oregon, U.S.A. Freshwat. Biol. 5:189–203.

1297. Kettle, D. S., and J. W. H. Lawson. 1952. The early stages of the British biting midges, *Culicoides* Latreille (Diptera: Ceratopogonidae) and allied genera. Bull. Ent. Res. 43:421–467.

1298. Kettle, D. S., C. H. Wild, and M. M. Elson. 1975. A new technique for rearing individual *Culicoides* larvae (Diptera:Ceratopogonidae). J. Med. Ent. 12:263–264.

1299. Kevan, D. K. 1979. Megaloptera, pp. 351–352. *In* H. V. Danks (ed.). Canada and its insect fauna. Mem. Ent. Soc. Can. 108. 573 pp.

1300. Kevan, D. K., and F. E. A. Cutten-Ali-Khan. 1975. Canadian Nymphomyiidae (Diptera). Can. J. Zool. 53:853–866.

1301. Kevan D. K. and F. E. A. Cutten. 1981. Chap. 10. Nymphomyiidae, pp. 203–208. *In* J. F. McAlpine, B. V. Peterson, G. E. Shewell, H. J. Teskey, J. R. Vockeroth, and D. M. Wood (coords.). Manual of Nearctic Diptera, Vol. 1. Res. Branch, Agric. Can. Monogr. 27. Ottawa. 674 pp.

1302. Khoo, S. G. 1964. Studies on the biology of *Capnia bifrons* (Newman) and notes on the diapause in the nymphs of this species. Gewasser und Abwasser 34/35:23–30.

1303. Kieffer, J. J. 1916. Diapriidae. Das Tierreich, 44. Friedlander und Sonn, Berlin. 627 pp.

1304. Kimerle, R. A., and N. H. Anderson. 1967. Evaluation of aquatic insect emergence traps. J. Econ. Ent. 60:1255–1259.

1305. Kimerle, R. A., and N. H. Anderson. 1971. Production and bioenergetic role of the midge *Glyptotendipes barbipes* (Staeger) in a waste stabilization lagoon. Limnol. Oceanogr. 16:646–659.

1306. King, R. H. 1977. Natural history and ecology of *Stictochironomus annulicrus* (Townes) (Diptera: Chironomidae), Augusta Creek, Michigan. Ph.D. diss., Michigan State University, East Lansing. 160 pp.

1307. King, W. V., G. H. Bradley, C. N. Smith, and W. C. McDuffy. 1960. A handbook of the mosquitoes of the southeastern United States. U.S. Dep. Agric. Handbk. 173. 188 pp.

1308. Kirkaldy, G. W., and J. R. de la Torre-Bueno. 1909. A catalogue of American aquatic and semi-aquatic Hemiptera, Proc. Ent. Soc. Wash. 10:173–215.

1309. Kissinger. D. G. 1964. Curculionidae of America north of Mexico. A key to genera. Taxonomic Publ., South Lancaster, Mass. 143 pp.

1310. Kittle, P. D. 1977a. A revision of the genus *Trepobates* Uhler (Hemiptera: Gerridae). Ph.D. diss., University of Arkansas, Fayetteville, 255 pp.

1311. Kittle, P. D. 1977b. Notes on the distribution and morphology of the water strider *Metrobates alacris* Drake (Hemiptera: Gerridae). Ent. News 88:67–68.

1312. Kittle, P. D. 1977c. The biology of water striders (Hemiptera: Gerridae) in northwest Arkansas. Am. Midl. Nat. 97:400–410.

1313. Kittle, P. D. 1980. The water striders (Hemiptera: Gerridae) of Arkansas. Proc. Ark. Acad. Sci. 34:68–71.

1314. Kittle, P. D. 1982. Two new species of water striders of the genus *Trepobates* (Hemiptera: Gerridae). Proc. Ent. Soc. Wash. 84:157–164.

1315. Kloter, K. O., L. R. Penner, and W. J. Widmer. 1977. Interactions between the larvae of *Psychoda alternata* and *Dohrniphora cornuta* in a trickling filter sewage bed, with descriptions of the immature stages of the latter. Ann. Ent. Soc. Am. 70:775–781.

1316. Klots, E. B. 1966. The new field book of freshwater life. G. P. Putnam's Sons, N.Y. 398 pp.

1317. Klug, M. J., and S. Kotarski. 1980. Bacteria associated with the gut tract of larval stages of the aquatic cranefly *Tipula abdominalis* (Diptera; Tipulidae). Appl. Environ. Microbiol. 40:408–416.

1318. Knab, F. 1905. A chironomid inhabitant of *Sarracenia purpurea, Metriocnemus knabi* Coq. J. N.Y. Ent. Soc. 13:69–73.

1319. Knabke, J. J. 1976. Diapause in the rice water weevil, *Lissorhoptrus oryzophilus* Kuschel (Coleoptera: Curculionidae) in California. Ph.D diss., University of California, Davis.

1320. Knight, A. W. 1963. Description of the tanyderid larva *Protanyderus marginata* Alexander from Colorado. Bull. Brooklyn Ent. Soc. 58:99–102.

1321. Knight, A. W., and A. R. Gaufin. 1963. The effect of water flow, temperature, and oxygen concentration on the Plecoptera nymph, *Acroneuria pacifica* Banks. Proc. Utah Acad. Sci. Arts Lett. 40:175–184.

1322. Knight, A. W., and A. R. Gaufin. 1964. Relative importance of varying oxygen concentration, temperature and water flow on the mechanical activity and survival of the Plecoptera nymph, *Pteronarcys californica* Newport. Proc. Utah Acad. Sci. Arts Lett. 41:14–28.

1323. Knight, A. W., and M. A. Simmons. 1975a. Factors influencing the oxygen consumption of the hellgrammite, *Corydalus cornutus* (L.) (Megaloptera: Corydalidae). Comp. Biochem. Physiol. 50A:827–833.

1324. Knight, A. W., and M. A. Simmons. 1975b. Factors influencing the oxygen consumption of larval *Nigronia serricornis* (Say) (Megaloptera: Corydalidae). Comp. Biochem. Physiol. 51A:177–183.

1325. Knight, A. W., M. A. Simmons, and C. S. Simmons. 1976. A phenomenological approach to the growth of the winter stonefly, *Taeniopteryx nivalis* (Fitch) (Plecoptera: Taeniopterygidae). Growth 40:343–367.

1326. Knight, K. L., and M. Wonio. 1969. Mosquitoes of Iowa. Spec. Rept. Iowa State Univ. 79 pp.

1327. Knopf, K. W., and K. J. Tennessen. 1980. A new species of *Progomphus* Selys, 1854 from North America (Anisoptera: Gomphidae). Odonatologica 9:247–252.

1328. Knowlton, G. F., and F. C. Harmston. 1938. Notes on Utah Plecoptera and Trichoptera. Ent. News 49:284–286.

1329. Knudsen, M. 1968. The biology and life history of *Oedoparena glauca* (Diptera: Dryomyzidae), a predator of barnacles. M.S. thesis, University of California, Berkeley.

1330. Knutson, L. V. 1970. Biology and immature stages of malacophagous flies: *Antichaeta analis, A. brevipennis* and *A. obliviosa* (Diptera: Sciomyzidae). Trans. Am. Ent. Soc. 92:67–101.

1331. Knutson, L. V. 1972. Description of the female of *Pherbecta limenitis* Steyskal (Diptera: Sciomyzidae), with notes on biology, immature stages, and distribution. Ent. News 83:15–21.

1332. Knutson, L. V., and J. Abercrombie. 1977. Biology of *Antichaeta melansoma* (Diptera: Sciomyzidae), with notes on parasitoid Braconidae and Ichneumonidae (Hymenoptera). Proc. Ent. Soc. Wash. 79:111–125.

1333. Knutson, L. V., and C. O. Berg. 1964. Biology and immature stages of snail-killing flies: the genus *Elgiva* (Diptera: Sciomyzidae). Ann. Ent. Soc. Am. 57:173–192.

1334. Knutson, L. V., and O. S. Flint, Jr. 1971. Pupae of Empididae in pupal cocoons of Rhyacophilidae and Glossosomatidae. Proc. Ent. Soc. Wash. 73:314–320.

1335. Knutson, L. V., and O. S. Flint, Jr. 1979. Do dance flies feed on caddisflies?—further evidence (Diptera: Empididae; Trichoptera). Proc. Ent. Soc. Wash. 81:32–33.

1336. Koehler, O. 1924. Sinnesphysiologische Untersuchungen an Libellenlaren. Verh. Dtsch. Zool. Ges. 29:83–91.

1337. Kolenkina, L. V. 1951. Nutrition of the larvae of some caddisflies (Trichoptera). Trudy Vsesoyuznogo Gidrobiologicheskogo Obshchest-va. 3:44–57. *In* S. G. Lepneva (ed.). Fauna of the U.S.S.R. Trichoptera. (Russian, translated by Israel Program for Scientific Translation, 1970.) U.S. Dep. Comm., Springfield, Va. 638 pp.

1338. Kondratieff, B. C., and J. R. Voshell, Jr. 1979. A checklist of the stoneflies (Plecoptera) of Virginia. Ent. News 90:241–246.

1339. Kondratieff, B. C., and J. R. Voshell, Jr. 1980. Life history and ecology of *Stenonema modestum* (Banks) (Ephemeroptera: Heptageniidae) in Virginia, U.S.A. Aquat. Insects 2: 177–189.

1340. Kondratieff, B. C., and J. R. Voshell, Jr. 1981. Influence of a reservoir with surface release on life history of the mayfly *Heterocloeon curiosum* (McDunnough) (Ephemeroptera: Baetidae). Can. J. Zool. 59:305–314.

1341. Konstantinov, A. S. 1971. Feeding habits of the chironomid larvae and certain ways to increase the food content of the water basins. Fish. Res. Bd. Can. Translation Ser. 1853.

1342. Kopelke, J. P. 1981. Morphologische und biologische studien an Belostomatiden am Beispiel der mittelamerikanischen arten *Belostoma ellipticum* und *B. thomasi* (Heteroptera). Ent. Abh. 44:59–80.

1343. Kormondy, E. J. 1958. Catalogue of the Odonata of Michigan. Misc. Publ. Univ. Mich. Mus. Zool. 104:1–43.

1344. Kormondy, E. J. 1959. The systematics of *Tetragoneuria*, based on ecological, life history, and morphological evidence (Odonata: Corduliidae). Misc. Publ. Univ. Mich. Mus. Zool. 107: 1–79.

1345. Kormondy, E. J., and J. L. Gower. 1965. Life history variations in an association of Odonata. Ecology 46:882–886.

1346. Koslucher, D. G., and G. W. Minshall. 1973. Food habits of some benthic invertebrates in a northern cool-desert stream (Deep Creek, Curlew Valley, Idaho-Utah). Trans. Am. Microsc. Soc. 92:441–452.

1347. Koss, R. W. 1968. Morphology and taxonomic use of Ephemeroptera eggs. Ann. Ent. Soc. Am. 61:696–721.

1348. Koss, R. W. 1970. The significance of the egg stage to taxonomic and phylogenetic studies of the Ephemeroptera. Proc. 1st. Int. Conf. Ephem. 1:73–78.

1349. Koss, R. W., and G. F. Edmunds, Jr. 1974. Ephemeroptera eggs and their contribution to phylogenetic studies of the order. J. Zool. Linn. Soc. Lond. 58:61–120.

1350. Koster, K. C. 1934. A study of the general biology, morphology of the respiratory system and respiration of certain aquatic *Stratiomyia* and *Odontomyia* larvae (Diptera). Pap. Mich. Acad. Sci. Arts Lett. 19:605–658.

1351. Kovalak, W. P. 1976. Seasonal and diel changes in the positioning of *Glossosoma nigrior* Banks (Trichoptera: Glossosomatidae) on artificial substrates. Can. J. Zool. 54:1585–1594.

1352. Kovalak, W. P. 1978. On the feeding habits of *Phasganophora capitata* (Plecoptera: Perlidae). Great Lakes Ent. 11:45–50.

1353. Kraatz, W. C. 1918. *Scirtes tibialis* Guer. (Coleoptera, Dascyllidae), with observations on its life history. Ann. Ent. Soc. Am. 11:393–400.

1354. Krawany, H. 1930. Trichopterenstudien im Gebiete der Lunzer Seen. Int. Revue ges. Hydrobiol. 23:417–427.

1355. Krecker, F. H. 1919. The fauna of rock bottom ponds. Ohio J. Sci. 19:427–474.

1356. Kristensen, N. P. 1975. The phylogeny of hexapod "orders." A critical review of recent accounts. Z. Zool. Syst. Evolutions Forsh 13:1–44.

1357. Kristensen, N. P. 1981. Phylogeny of insect orders. Ann. Rev. Ent. 26:135–157.

1358. Krivda, W. V. 1961. Notes on the distribution and habitat of *Chilostigma areolatum* (Walker) in Manitoba (Trichoptera: Limnephilidae). J. N.Y. Ent. Soc. 69:68–70.

1359. Krivosheina, N. P. 1971. The family Glutopidae, fam. n. and its position in the system of Diptera Brachycera Orthorrhapha (in Russian). Ent. Obozr. 50:681–694. (transl. in Ent. Rev., Wash. 50:387–395).

1360. Krogh, A. 1920. Studien über Tracheenrespiration. II. Über Gasdiffusion in den Tracheen. Pflügers Arch. ges. Physiol. 179:95–112.

1361. Krogh, A. 1943. Some experiments on the osmoregulation and respiration of *Eristalis* larvae. Entomol. Medd. 23:49–65.

1362. Krogstad, B. O. 1974. Aquatic stages of *Stratiomys normula unilimbata* Loew (Diptera: Stratiomyiidae). J. Minn. Acad. Sci. 38:86–88.

1363. Krombein, K. V., and B. D. Burks. 1967. Hymenoptera of America north of Mexico synoptic catalog. U.S. Dep. Agric. Monogr. 2. 305 pp.

1364. Krombein, K. V., P. D. Hurd, Jr., D. R. Smith, and B. D. Burks. 1979. Catalog of Hymenoptera in America north of Mexico (3 volumes). Smithson. Instit. Press, Washington, D.C. 2735 pp.

1365. Krueger, C. C., and F. B. Martin. 1980. Computation of confidence intervals for the size-frequency (Hynes) method of estimating secondary production. Limnol. Oceanogr. 25:773–777.

1366. Krull, W. H. 1929. The rearing of dragonflies from eggs. Ann. Ent. Soc. Am. 22:651–658.

1367. Kuehne, R. A. 1962. A classification of streams, illustrated by fish distribution in an eastern Kentucky creek. Ecology 43:608–614.

1368. Kuhlhorn, F. 1961. Investigations on the importance of various representatives of the hydrofauna and flora as natural limiting factors for *Anopheles* larvae. Z. Angew. Zool. 48:129–161.

1369. Kuitert, L. C. 1942. Gerrinae in the University of Kansas collections. Univ. Kans. Sci. Bull. 28:113–143.

1370. Kurtak, D. C. 1978. Efficiency of filter feeding of blackfly larvae. Can. J. Zool. 56:1608–1623.

1371. Kurtak, D. C. 1979. Food of black fly larvae (Diptera: Simuliidae): Seasonal changes in gut contents and suspended material at several sites in a single watershed. Quaest. Ent. 15:357–374.

1372. Kuusela, K., and H. Pulkkinen. 1978. A simple trap for collecting newly emerged stoneflies (Plecoptera). Oikos 31:323–325.

1373. Lacey, L. A., and M. S. Mulla. 1979. Factors affecting feeding rates of black fly larvae. Mosquito News 39:315–319.

1374. Ladle, M. 1972. Larval Simuliidae as detritus feeders in chalk streams. Mem. Inst. Ital. Idrobiol. Suppl. 29:429–439.

1375. Ladle, M. 1982. Organic detritus and its role as a food source in chalk streams. Ann. Rept. Freshwat. Biol. Assoc. 50:30–37.

1376. Ladle, M., J. A. Bass, and W. R. Jenkins. 1972. Studies on production and food consumption by the larval Simuliidae (Diptera) of a chalk stream. Hydrobiologia 39:429–448.

1377. Ladle, M., and A. Esmat. 1973. Records of Simuliidae (Diptera) from the Bere Stream, Dorset with details of the life-history and larval growth of *Simulium (Eusimulium) latipes* Meigen. Entomol. mon. Mag. 108:167–172.

1378. Lager, T. M., M. D. Johnson, S. N. Williams, and J. L. McCulloch. 1979. A preliminary report on the Plecoptera and Trichoptera of northeastern Minnesota. Great Lakes Ent. 12:109–114.

1379. Lago, P. K., R. W. Holzenthal, and S. C. Harris. 1982. An annotated checklist of the caddisflies (Trichoptera) of Mississippi and southeastern Louisiana. Part I: Introduction and Hydropsychoidea. Proc. Ent. Soc. Wash. 84:495–508.

1380. Lago, P. K., D. F. Stanford, and P. D. Hartfield. 1979. A preliminary list of Mississippi damselflies (Insects: Odonata: Zygoptera). J. Miss. Acad. Sci. 24:72–76.

1381. Laird, M. 1956. Studies of mosquitoes and freshwater ecology in the South Pacific. Bull. R. Soc. N. Z. 6:1–213.

1382. Lake, R. W. 1980. Distribution of the stoneflies (Plecoptera) of Delaware. Ent. News 9:43–48.

1383. Lamberti, G. A., and V. H. Resh. 1978. Substrate relationships, spatial distribution patterns, and sampling variability in a stream caddisfly population. Environ. Ent. 8:561–567.

1384. Lammers, R. 1977. Sampling insects with a wetland emergence trap: Design and evaluation of the trap and preliminary results. Am. Midl. Nat. 97:381–389.

1385. Lamp, W. O., and N. W. Britt. 1981. Resource partitioning by two species of stream mayflies (Ephemeroptera: Heptageniidae). Great Lakes Ent. 14:151–157.

1386. Landin, J. 1976a. Methods of sampling aquatic beetles in the transitional habitats at water margins. Freshwat. Biol. 6:81–87.

1387. Landin. J. 1976b. Seasonal patterns in abundance of water beetles belonging to the Hydrophiloidea (Coleoptera). Freshwat. Biol. 6:89–108.

1388. Lane, R. S. 1975. Immatures of some Tabanidae (Diptera) from Mendocino County, Calif. Ann. Ent. Soc. Am. 68:803–819.

1389. Lane, R. S., and J. R. Anderson. 1976. Extracting larvae of *Chrysops hirsuticallus* (Diptera: Tabanidae) from soil: efficiency of two methods. Ann. Ent. Soc. Am. 69:854–856.

1390. Lange, W. H. 1956a. Aquatic Lepidoptera, pp. 271–288. *In* R. L. Usinger (ed.). Aquatic insects of California. Univ. Calif. Press, Berkeley. 508 pp.

1391. Lange, W. H. 1956b. A generic revision of the aquatic moths of North America: (Lepidoptera: Pyralidae, Nymphulinae). Wasmann J. Biol. 14:59–144.

1392. Langford, T. E., and J. R. Daffern. 1975. The emergence of insects from a British river warmed by power station cooling-water. Part I. The use and performance of insect emergence traps in a large, spate-river and the effects of various factors on total catches, upstream and downstream of the cooling-water outfalls. Hydrobiologia 46:71–114.

1393. Lansbury, I. 1954. Some notes on the ecology of *Corixa (Halicorixa) stagnalis* Leach with some information on the measurement of salinity of brackish habitats. Entomol. mon. Mag. 90:139–140.

1394. Lansbury, I. 1956. Further observations on the ecology of *Cymatia coleoptrata* (Fabr.), (Hemiptera-Heteroptera, Corixidae) in southern England. Entomologist 89:188–195.

1395. Lansbury, I. 1957. Observations on the ecology of water-bugs (Hemiptera-Heteroptera) and their associated fauna and flora in southeast Kent. Entomologist 90:167–177.

1396. Lansbury, I. 1960. The Corixidae (Hemiptera-Heteroptera) of British Columbia. Proc. Ent. Soc. Brit. Col. 57:34–43.

1397. LaRivers, I. 1940. A preliminary synopsis of the dragonflies of Nevada. Pan-Pacif. Ent. 16:111–123.

1398. LaRivers, I. 1948. A new species of *Pelocoris* from Nevada, with notes on the genus in the United States. Ann. Ent. Soc. Am. 41:371–376.

1399. LaRivers, I. 1950a. The Dryopoidea known or expected to occur in the Nevada area (Coleoptera). Wasmann J. Biol. 8:97–111.

1400. LaRivers, I. 1950b. The staphylinoid and dascilloid aquatic coleoptera of the Nevada area. Great Basin Nat. 10:66–70.

1401. LaRivers, I. 1951. A revision of the genus *Ambrysus* in the United States. Univ. Calif. Publ. Ent. 8:277–338.

1402. LaRivers, I. 1954. Nevada Hydrophilidae (Coleoptera). Am. Midl. Nat. 52:164–175.

1403. LaRivers, I. 1971. Catalogue of taxa described in the family Naucoridae (Hemiptera). Mem. Biol. Soc. Nev. 2:65–120.

1404. LaRivers, I. 1974. Catalogue of taxa described in the family Naucoridae (Hemiptera). Supplement No. 1: Corrections, emendations and additions, with descriptions of new species. Occ. Pap. Nev. Biol. Soc. 38:1–17.

1405. LaRivers, I. 1976. Supplement No. 2 to the catalogue of taxa described in the family Naucoridae (Hemiptera), with descriptions of new species. Occ. Pap. Nev. Biol. Soc. 41:1–17.

1406. LaRow, E. J. 1970. The effect of oxygen tension on the vertical migration of *Chaoborus* larvae. Limnol. Oceanogr. 15:375–362.

1407. Larson, D. J. 1975. The predaceous water beetles (Coleoptera: Dytiscidae) of Alberta: systematics, natural history and distribution. Quaest. Ent. 11:245–498.

1408. Larson, D. J., and G. Pritchard. 1974. Organs of possible stridulatory function in waterbeetles (Coleoptera: Dytiscidae). Coleopt. Bull. 28:53–63.

1409. Lattin, J. D. 1956. Equipment and techniques, pp. 50–67. *In* R. L. Usinger (ed.). Aquatic insects of California. Univ. Calif. Press, Berkeley. 508 pp.

1410. Lauck, D. R. 1959. The taxonomy and bionomics of the aquatic Hemiptera of Illinois. M.S. thesis, University of Illinois, Urbana. 353 pp.

1411. Lauck, D. R. 1962. A monograph of the genus *Belostoma* (Hemiptera). Part I. Introduction and *B. dentatum* and *subspinosum* groups. Bull. Chi. Acad. Sci. B. 11:34–81.

1412. Lauck, D. R. 1964. A monograph of the genus *Belostoma* (Hemiptera). Part III. *B. triangulum, bergi, minor, bifoveolatum* and *flumineum* groups. Bull. Chi. Acad. Sci. B. 11: 102–154.

1413. Lauck, D. R., and A. S. Menke. 1961. The higher classification of the Belostomatidae (Hemiptera). Ann. Ent. Soc. Am. 54:644–657.

1414. Lauff, G. H., and K. W. Cummins. 1964. A model stream for studies in lotic ecology. Ecology 45:188–190.

1415. Laughlin, R. 1960. Biology of *Tipula oleracea* L.: growth of the larva. Ent. exp. Appl. 3:185–197.

1416. Laughlin, R. 1967. Biology of *Tipula paludosa;* growth of the larva in the field. Ent. exp. Appl. 10:52–68.

1417. Lavallee, A. G., and J. B. Wallace. 1974. Immature stages of Milesiinae (Syrphidae) II. *Sphegina keeniana* and *Chrysogaster nitida.* J. Ga. Ent. Soc. 9:8–15.

1418. Lavandier, P. 1979. Cycle biologique, regime alimentaire et production *d'Arcynopteryx compacta* (Plecoptera, Perlodidae) dans un torrent de haute altitude. Bull. Soc. Hist. Nat. Toulouse. 115:140–150.

1419. Lavery, M. A., and R. R. Costa. 1972. Reliability of the Surber sampler in estimating *Parargyractic fulicalis* (Clemens) (Lepidoptera: Pyralidae) populations. Can. J. Zool. 50: 1335–1336.

1420. Lavery, M. A., and R. R. Costa. 1973. Geographic distribution of the genus *Parargyractis* Lange (Lepidoptera: Pyralidae) throughout the Lake Erie and Lake Ontario watersheds (U.S.A.). J. N.Y. Ent. Soc. 81:42–49.

1421. Lavery, M. A., and R. R. Costa. 1976. Life history of *Parargyractis canadensis* Munroe (Lepidoptera: Pyralidae). Am. Midl. Nat. 96: 407–417.

1422. Lawrence, S. G. (ed.). 1981. Manual for the culture of selected freshwater invertebrates. Can. Spec. Publ. Fish. Aquat. Sci. 54:1–169.

1423. Lawson, D. L., and R. W. Merritt. 1979. A modified Ladell apparatus for the extraction of wetland macroinvertebrates. Can. Ent. 111:1389–1393.

1424. Lawson, F. A. 1959. Identification of the nymphs of common families of Hemiptera. J. Kans. Ent. Soc. 32:88–92.

1425. Lawton, J. H. 1970. Feeding and food energy assimilation in larvae of the damselfly *Pyrrhosoma nymphula* (Sulz.) (Odonata: Zygoptera). J. Anim. Ecol. 39:669–689.

1426. Lawton, J. H. 1971. Maximum and actual field feeding-rates in larvae of the damselfly *Pyrrhosoma nymphula* (Sulzer) (Odonata: Zygoptera). Freshwat. Biol. 1:99–111.

1427. Leader, J. P. 1971. Effect of temperature, salinity, and dissolved oxygen concentration upon respiratory activity of the larva of *Philanisus plebeius* (Trichoptera). J. Insect Physiol. 17:1917–1924.

1428. Leathers, A. L. 1922a. Ecological study of aquatic midges and some related insects with special reference to feeding habits. U.S. Bur. Fish. 38:1–61.

1429. Leathers, A. L. 1922b. Ecological study of aquatic midges and some related insects with special reference to feeding habits. Bull. U.S. Bur. Fish. 38:1–61.

1430. Lee, F. C. 1967. Laboratory observations on certain mosquito predators. Mosquito News 27:332–338.

1431. Lee, V. F., R. S. Lane, and C. B. Philip. 1976. Confirmation of the beach habitation of *Apatolestes actites* Philip and Steffan (Diptera: Tabanidae) on the California coast. Pan-Pacif. Ent. 52:212.

1432. Leech, H. B. 1938. A study of the Pacific Coast species of *Agabus* Leach, with a key to the nearctic species (Coleoptera: Dytiscidae). M.S. thesis, University of California, Berkeley. 106 pp.

1433. Leech, H. B. 1940. Description of a new species of *Laccornis,* with a key to the Nearctic species. Can. Ent. 72:122–128.

1434. Leech, H. B. 1942a. Key to the Nearctic genera of water beetles of the tribe Agabini, with some generic synonymy. Ann. Ent. Soc. Am. 35:76–80.

1435. Leech, H. B. 1942b. Dimorphism in the flying wings of a species of water beetle, *Agabus bifarius* (Kirby) (Coleoptera: Dytiscidae). Ann. Ent. Soc. Am. 35:355–362.

1436. Leech, H. B., and H. P. Chandler. 1956. Aquatic Coleoptera, pp. 293–371. *In* R. L. Usinger (ed.). Aquatic insects of California. Univ. Calif. Press, Berkeley. 508 pp.

1437. Leech, H. B., and M. W. Sanderson. 1959. Coleoptera, pp. 981–1023. *In* W. T. Edmondson (ed.). Freshwater biology (2nd ed.). John Wiley & Sons, N.Y. 1248 pp.

1438. Legner, E. F., R. A. Medved, and R. D. Sjogren. 1975. Quantitative water column sampler for insects in shallow aquatic habitats. Proc. Calif. Mosquito Contr. Assoc. 43:110–115.

1439. Lehmann, J. 1971. Die Chironomiden der Fulda. Arch. Hydrobiol. Suppl. 37:466–555.

1440. Lehmkuhl, D. M. 1970. A North American trichopteran larva which feeds on freshwater sponges (Trichoptera: Leptoceridae, Porifera: Spongillidae). Am. Midl. Nat. 84:278–280.

1441. Lehmkuhl, D. M. 1971. Stoneflies (Plecoptera: Nemouridae) from temporary lentic habitats in Oregon. Am. Midl. Nat. 85:514–515.

1442. Lehmkuhl, D. M. 1972a. Changes in thermal regime as a cause of reduction of benthic fauna downstream of a reservoir. J. Fish. Res. Bd. Can. 29:1329–1332.

1443. Lehmkuhl, D. M. 1972b. *Baetisca* (Ephemeroptera: Baetiscidae) from the western interior of Canada with notes on the life cycle. Can. J. Zool. 50:1017–1019.

1444. Lehmkuhl, D. M. 1976a. Mayflies. Blue Jay 34:70–81.

1445. Lehmkuhl, D. M. 1976b. Additions to the taxonomy, zoogeography, and biology of *Analetris eximia* (Acanthametropodinae: Siphlonuridae: Ephemeroptera). Can. Ent. 108:199–207.

1446. Lehmkuhl, D. M. 1979a. How to know the aquatic insects. Wm. C. Brown, Dubuque, Iowa. 168 pp.

1447. Lehmkuhl, D. M. 1979b. A new genus and species of Heptageniidae (Ephemeroptera) from western Canada. Can. Ent. 111:859–862.

1448. Leischner, T. G., and G. Pritchard. 1973. The immature stages of the alderfly, *Sialis cornuta* (Megaloptera: Sialidae). Can. Ent. 105:411–418.

1449. Lenz, F. 1950. Tendipedidae (Chironomidae). H. Clunioninae. B. Die Metamorphose den Clunioninae, pp. 8–25. *In* E. Lindner (ed.). Die Fliegen der Palaearktischen Region. 280 pp.

1450. Lenz, F. 1951. Neuue Beobachtungen zur Biologie der Jungendstadien der Tendipedidengattung *Parachironomus* Lenz. Zool. Anz. 147:95–111.

1451. Lenz, F. 1955. Der Wert der Exuviensammlung fur die Beurteilung der Tendipedidenbesielung eines Sees. Arch. Hydrobiol. Suppl. 22:415–421.

1452. Leonard, J. W., and F. A. Leonard. 1949. Noteworthy records of caddisflies from Michigan with descriptions of new species. Occ. Pap. Univ. Mich. Mus. Zool. 520:1–8.

1453. Leonard, J. W., and F. A. Leonard. 1962. Mayflies of Michigan trout streams. Cranbrook Inst. Sci., Bloomfield Hills, Mich. 139 pp.

1454. Lepneva, S. G. 1964. Larvae and pupae of Annulipalpia, Trichoptera. Fauna of the U.S.S.R. Zool. Inst. Akad. Nauk. S.S.S.R., New Ser. 88:1–638. (Transl. Israel Program Sci. Transl. 1971.)

1455. Lepneva, S. G. 1966. Larvae and pupae of Integripalpia, Trichoptera. Fauna of the U.S.S.R. Zool. Inst. Akad. Nauk. S.S.S.R., New Ser. 95:1–560. (Transl. Israel Program Sci. Transl. 1971.

1456. Lesage, L., and P. P. Harper. 1976. Notes on the life history of the toe-winged beetle *Anchytarsus bicolor* (Melsheimer) (Coleoptera: Ptilodactylidae). Coleopt. Bull. 30:233–238.

1457. LeSage, L., and A. D. Harrison. 1979. Improved traps and techniques for the study of emerging aquatic insects. Ent. News 90:65–78.

1458. Leston, D., and J. W. Pringle. 1963. Acoustic behaviour of Hemiptera, pp. 391–411. *In* R. G. Busnel (ed.). Acoustic behavior of animals. Elsevier, Amsterdam.

1459. Levine, E. 1974. Biology of *Bellura gortynoides* Walker (= *vulnifera* Grote), the yellow water lily borer (Lepidoptera: Noctuidae). Ind. Acad. Sci. 83:214–215.

1460. Levine, E., and L. Chandler. 1976. Biology of *Bellura gortynoides* (Lepidoptera: Noctuidae), a yellow water lily borer, in Indiana. Ann. Ent. Soc. Am. 69:405–414.

1461. Lewis, P. A. 1974. Taxonomy and ecology of *Stenonema* mayflies (Heptageniidae: Ephemeroptera). U.S. EPA, Environmental Monitoring Ser. Rept. EPA-670/4–74–006. 81 pp.

1462. Lewis, P. A., W. T. Mason, and C. I. Weber. 1982. Evaluation of 3 bottom grab samplers for collecting river benthos. Ohio J. Sci. 82:107–113.

1463. Lilly, C. K., D. L. Ashley, and D. C. Tarter. 1978. Observations on a population of *Sialis itasca* Ross in West Virginia (Megaloptera: Sialidae). Psyche 85:209–217.

1464. Lindeberg, B. 1958. A new trap for collecting emerging insects from small rock pools, with some examples of results obtained. Ann. Ent. Fenn. 24:186–191.

1465. Lindegaard, C., and P. Jonasson. 1975. Life cycles of *Chironomus hyperboreus* Staeger and *Tanytarsus gracilentus* (Holmgren) (Chironomidae, Diptera) in Lake Myvatn, Northern Iceland. Verh. Int. Verein. Limnol. 19:3155–3163.

1466. Lindeman, R. L. 1941. Seasonal food cycle dynamics in a senescent lake. Am. Midl. Nat. 27:428–444.

1467. Lindeman, R. L. 1942. The trophic-dynamic aspect of ecology. Ecology 23:399–418.

1468. Lindskog, P. 1968. The relations between transpiration, humidity reaction, thirst and water content in the shorebug *Saldula saltatoria* L. (Heteroptera: Saldidae). Arkiv. Zool. Ser. 2, 20:465–493.

1469. Linduska, J. P. 1942. Bottom type as a factor influencing the local distribution of mayfly nymphs. Can. Ent. 74:26–30.

1470. Linley, J. R. 1968. Studies on the larval biology of *Leptoconops becquaerti* (Kieff). (Diptera: Ceratopogonidae). Bull. Ent. Res. 58:1–24.

1471. Linley, J. R. 1969. Seasonal changes in larval populations of *Leptoconops beaquaerti* (Kieff) (Diptera: Ceratopogonidae) in Jamaica, with observations on the ecology. Bull. Ent. Res. 59:47–64.

1472. Linley, J. R. 1976. Biting midges of mangrove swamps and salt marshes (Diptera: Ceratopogonidae), pp. 335–376. *In* L. Cheng (ed.). Marine insects. North Holland, Amsterdam. 581 pp.

1473. Lippert, G., and L. Butler. 1976. Taxonomic study of Collembola of West Virginia. Bull. W. Va. Univ. Agric. Exp. Sta. 643:1–27.

1474. Lloyd, J. T. 1914. Lepidopterous larvae from rapid streams. J. N.Y. Ent. Soc. 22:145–152.

1475. Lloyd, J. T. 1915. Note on *Ithytrichia confusa* Morton. Can. Ent. 47:117–121.

1476. Lloyd, J. T. 1921. The biology of North America caddis fly larvae. Bull. Lloyd Lib. 21:1–124.

1477. Logan, E. R., and S. D. Smith. 1966. New distributional records of Intermountain stoneflies (Plecoptera). Occ. Pap. Biol. Soc. Nevada 9:1–3.

1478. Longfield, C. 1948. A vast immigration of dragonflies into the South Coast of Co. Cork. Irish. Nat. J. 9:133–141.

1479. Longley, G., and P. J. Spangler. 1977. The larva of a new subterranean water beetle: *Haideoporus texanus* (Coleoptera: Dytiscidae: Hydroporinae). Proc. Biol. Soc. Wash. 90:532–535.

1480. Louton, J. A. 1982. Lotic dragonfly (Anisoptera: Odonata) nymphs of the southeastern United States: identification, distribution and historical biogeography. Ph.D. diss., University of Tennessee, Knoxville. 357 pp.

1481. Lubbock, J. 1863. On 2 aquatic Hymenoptera, 1 of which uses its wings in swimming. Trans. Linn. Soc. Lond. 24:135–141.

1482. Lundbock, W. 1916. Diptera Danica. Genera and species of flies hitherto found in Denmark. Vol. 5. Lonchopteridae-Syrphidae. Copenhagen. 603 pp.

1483. Lutz, P. E. 1964. Life-history and photoperiodic responses of nymphs of *Tetragoneuria cynosura* (Say). Biol. Bull. 127:304–316.

1484. Lutz, P. E. 1968. Effects of temperature and photoperiod on larval development in *Lestes eurinus* (Odonata: Lestidae). Ecology 49:637–644.

1485. Lutz, P. E. 1974. Effects of temperature and photoperiod on larval development in *Tetragoneuria cynosura* (Odonata: Libellulidae). Ecology 55:370–377.

1486. Lyman, F. E. 1956. Environmental factors affecting distribution of mayfly nymphs in Douglas Lake, Michigan. Ecology 37:568–576.

1487. Macan, T. T. 1938. Evolution of aquatic habitats with special reference to the distribution of Corixidae. J. Anim. Ecol. 7:1–19.

1488. Macan, T. T. 1949. Survey of a moorland fishpond. J. Anim. Ecol. 18:160–186.

1489. Macan, T. T. 1950. Descriptions of some nymphs of the British species of *Baetis* (Ephem.). Trans. Soc. Brit. Ent. 10:143–166.

1490. Macan, T. T. 1958. Methods of sampling the bottom fauna in stony streams. Mitt. Int. Verh. Limnol. 8:1–21.

1491. Macan, T. T. 1962. The ecology of aquatic insects. Ann. Rev. Ent. 7:261–288.

1492. Macan, T. T. 1964. Emergence traps and the investigation of stream faunas. Rev. Idrobiol. 3:75–92.

1493. Macan, T. T. 1965. Predation as a factor in the ecology of water bugs. J. Anim. Ecol. 34:691–698.

1494. Macan, T. T. 1973. Ponds and lakes. Allen & Unwin, London. 148 pp.

1495. Macan, T. T. 1974. Freshwater ecology (2nd ed.). John Wiley & Sons, N.Y. 343 pp.

1496. Macan, T. T. 1976. A twenty-one-year study of the water-bugs in a moorland fishpond. J. Anim. Ecol. 45:913–922.

1497. Macan, T. T. 1977. The influence of predation on the composition of freshwater animal communities. Biol. Rev. Cambridge Philos. Soc. 52:45–70.

1498. Macan, T. T., and A. Kitching. 1976. The colonization of squares of plastic suspended in midwater. Freshwat. Biol. 6:33–40.

1499. Macan, T. T., and E. B. Worthington. 1968. Life in lakes and rivers. Collins, Lond. 272 pp.

1500. MacKay, M. R. 1959. Larvae of North American Olethreutinae (Lepidoptera). Can. Ent. 91:3–338.

1501. MacKay, M. R. 1962a. Additional larvae of the North American Olethreutinae (Lepidoptera: Tortricidae). Can. Ent. 94:626–643.

1502. MacKay, M. R. 1962b. Larvae of North American Tortricinae (Lepidoptera: Tortricidae). Can. Ent. Suppl. 28:1–182.

1503. MacKay, M. R. 1963a. Problems in naming the setae of lepidopterous larvae. Can. Ent. 95:996–999.

1504. MacKay, M. R. 1963b. Evolutional adaptation of larval characters in the Tortricidae. Can. Ent. 95:1321–1344.

1505. MacKay, M. R. 1964. The relationship of form and function of minute characters of lepidopterous larvae, and its importance in life history studies. Can. Ent. 96:991–1004.

1506. MacKay, M. R. 1972. Larval sketches of some Microlepidoptera, chiefly North American. Mem. Ent. Soc. Can. 88:1–83.

1507. MacKay, M. R., and E. W. Rockburne. 1958. Notes on life-history and larval description of *Apamea apamiformis* (Guenee), a pest of wild rice (Lepidoptera: Noctuidae). Can. Ent. 90:579–582.

1508. Mackay, R. J. 1969. Aquatic insect communities of a small stream on Mont St. Hilaire, Quebec. J. Fish. Res. Bd. Can. 26:1157–1183.

1509. Mackay, R. J. 1972. Temporal patterns in life history and flight behavior of *Pycnopsyche gentilis, P. luculenta,* and *P. scabripennis* (Trichoptera: Limnephilidae). Can. Ent. 104: 1819–1835.

1510. Mackay, R. J. 1977. Behavior of *Pycnopsyche* on mineral substrates in laboratory streams. Ecology 58:191–195.

1511. Mackay, R. J. 1978. Larval identification and instar association in some species of *Hydropsyche* and *Cheumatopsyche* (Trichoptera: Hydropsychidae). Ann. Ent. Soc. Am. 71:499–509.

1512. Mackay, R. J. 1979. Life history patterns of some species of *Hydropsyche* (Trichoptera: Hydropsychidae) in southern Ontario. Can. J. Zool. 57:963–975.

1513. Mackay, R. J., and J. Kalff. 1973. Ecology of two related species of caddisfly larvae in the organic substrates of a woodland stream. Ecology 54:499–511.

1514. Mackay, R. J., and G. B. Wiggins. 1979. Ecological diversity in Trichoptera. Ann. Rev. Ent. 24:185–208.

1515. Mackey, A. P. 1979. Trophic dependencies of some larval Chironomidae (Diptera) and fish species in the River Thames. Hydrobiologia 62:241–247.

1516. Mackey, H. E., Jr. 1972. A life history survey of *Gelastocoris oculatus* in eastern Tennessee. J. Tenn. Acad. Sci. 47:153–155.

1517. Mackie, G. L., and R. C. Bailey. 1981. An inexpensive stream bottom sampler. J. Freshwat. Ecol. 1:61–69.

1518. Macklin, J. M. 1960. Techniques for rearing Odonata. Proc. N. Central Br. Ent. Soc. Am. 15:67–71.

1519. Macklin, J. M. 1963. Notes on the life history of *Anax junius* (Drury) (Odonata: Aeshnidae). Proc. Ind. Acad. Sci. 73: 154–163.

1520. MacLean, S. F., Jr. 1973. Life cycle and growth energetics of the Arctic crane fly *Pedicia hannai antennata.* Oikos 24:436–443.

1521. MacNeill, N. 1960. A study of the caudal gills of dragonfly larvae of the suborder Zygoptera. Proc. Roy. Irish Acad. 61:115–140.

1522. Maddux, D. E. 1954. A new species of dobsonfly from California (Megaloptera: Corydalidae). Pan-Pacif. Ent. 30:70–71.

1523. Madsen, B. L. 1972. Detritus on stones in small streams. Mem. Inst. Ital. Idrobiol. Suppl. 29:385–403.

1524. Madsen, B. L. 1974. A note on the food of *Amphinemura sulcicollis.* Hydrobiologia 45:169–175.

1525. Magdych, W. P. 1979. The microdistribution of mayflies (Ephemeroptera) in *Myriophyllum* beds in Pennington Creek, Johnston County, Oklahoma. Hydrobiologia 66:161–175.

1526. Maier, C. T. 1977. The behavior of *Hydrometra championiana* (Hemiptera: Hydrometridae) and resource partitioning with *Tenagogonus quadrilineatus* (Hemiptera: Gerridae). J. Kans. Ent. Soc. 50:263–271.

1527. Maitland, P. S. 1979. The habitats of British Ephemeroptera, pp. 123–139. *In* J. F. Flannagan and K. E. Marshall, (eds). Proc. 3rd. Internat. Conf. Ephemeroptera, Plenum Press, N.Y. 552 p.

1528. Maitland, P. S., and M. M. Penny. 1967. The ecology of the Simuliidae in a Scottish river. J. Anim. Ecol. 35:179–206.

1529. Maki, A. W., K. W. Stewart, and J. K. G. Silvey. 1973. The effects of dibrom on respiratory activity of the stonefly, *Hydroperla crosbyi,* hellgrammite, *Corydalus cornutus* and the golden shiner, *Notemigonus crysoleucas.* Trans. Am. Fish. Soc. 102:806–815.

1530. Malaise, R. 1937. A new insect trap. Ent. Tidskr. 58:148–160.

1531. Malas, D., and J. B. Wallace. 1977. Strategies for coexistence in three net-spinning caddisflies (Trichoptera) in second-order southern Appalachian streams. Can. J. Zool. 55:1829–1840.

1532. Malcolm, S. E. 1971. The water beetles of Maine: including the families Gyrinidae, Haliplidae, Dytiscidae, Noteridae, and Hydrophilidae. Univ. Maine Tech. Bull. 48:1–49.

1533. Malcolm, S. E. 1979. Two new species of *Laccobius spangleri, Laccobius reflexipenis* from Eastern North America (Coleoptera: Hydrophilidae). J. N.Y. Ent. Soc. 87:59–65.

1534. Malcolm, S. E. 1980. *Oreomicrus explanatus* new genus, and elaboration of the tribe Omicrini (Coleoptera: Hydrophilidae: Sphaeridiinae). Ann. Ent. Soc. Am. 73:185–188.

1535. Malicky, H. 1973. Trichoptera (Köcherfliegen). Handb. Zool. 4:1–114.

1536. Malicky, H. 1980. Evidence for seasonal migration of the larvae of two species of philopotamid caddisflies (Trichoptera) in a mountain stream in lower Austria. Aquat. Insects 2:153–160.

1537. Malloch, J. R. 1914. American black flies or buffalo gnats. U.S. Dept. Agr. Bur. Ent. Tech. Ser. 26:1–83.

1538. Malloch, J. R. 1915. The Chironomidae, or midges, of Illinois, with particular reference to the species occurring in the Illinois River. Bull. Ill. State Lab. Nat. Hist. 10:275–543.

1539. Manton, S. M., and D. T. Anderson. 1979. Polyphyly and the evolution of arthropods, pp. 269–321. *In* M. R. House (ed.). The origin of major invertebrate groups. Academic, London. 515 pp.

1540. Mantula, J. 1911. Untersuchungen über die Funktionen der Zentralnervensystems bei Insekten. Pflüegers Arch. Ges. Physiol. 138:388–456.

1541. Manuel, K. L., and T. C. Folsom. 1982. Instar sizes, life cycles, and food habits of five *Rhyacophila* (Trichoptera: Rhyacophilidae) species from the Appalachian Mountains of South Carolina, U.S.A. Hydrobiologia 97:281–285.

1542. Marchal, P. 1900. Sur un nouvel hymenoptere aquatique, le *Limnodytes gerriphagus* n. gen. n. sp. Ann. Soc. Ent. France 69:171–176.

1543. Marchand, W. 1917. An improved method of rearing tabanid larvae. J. Econ. Ent. 10:469–472.

1544. Marchand, W. 1923. The larval stages of *Limnophora discreta* Stein (Diptera, Anthomyiidae). Bull. Brooklyn Ent. Soc. 18:58–62.

1545. Marks, E. P. 1957. The food pump of *Pelocoris* and comparative studies on other aquatic Hemiptera. Psyche 64:123–134.

1546. Marshall, J. E. 1979. A review of the genera of the Hydroptilidae (Trichoptera). Bull. Brit. Mus. Nat. Hist. 39:135–239.

1547. Martin, C. H. 1927. Biological studies of 2 hymenopterous parasites of aquatic insect eggs. Entomologica Am. 8:105–151.

1548. Martin, C. H. 1928. An exploratory survey of characters of specific value in the genus *Gelastocoris* Kirkaldy, and some new species. Univ. Kans. Sci. Bull. 18:351–369.

1549. Martin, J. O. 1900. A study of *Hydrometra lineata.* Can. Ent. 32:70–76.

1550. Martin, M. M., J. J. Kukor, J. S. Martin, and R. W. Merritt. 1981a. Digestive enzymes of larvae of three species of caddisflies (Trichoptera). Insect Biochem. 11:501–505.

1551. Martin, M. M., J. S. Martin, J. J. Kukor, and R. W. Merritt. 1980. The digestion of protein and carbohydrate by the stream detritivore, *Tipula abdominalis* (Diptera, Tipulidae). Oecologia 46:360–364.

1552. Martin, M. M., J. S. Martin, J. J. Kukor, and R. W. Merritt. 1981b. The digestive enzymes of detritus-feeding stonefly nymphs (Plecoptera: Pteronarcyidae). Can. J. Zool. 59:1947–1951.

1553. Martin, R. 1908, 1909. Aeschines. Collections zoologiques du Baron Edm. de Selys Longchamps. Impr. Acad. Hayez, Brussels. 18–20:1–223.

1554. Martin, R. D. C. 1939. Life histories of *Agrion aequabile* and *Agrion maculatum* (Agriidae: Odonata). Ann. Ent. Soc. Am. 35:601–619.

1555. Martinson, R. J., and J. D. Ward. 1982. Life history and ecology of *Hesperophylax occidentalis* (Banks) (Trichoptera: Limnephilidae) from three springs in the Piceance Basin, Colorado. Freshwat. Invert. Biol. 1:41–47.

1556. Martynova, E. F. 1972. Springtails (Collembola) inhabiting the outlets of subterranean water in the Kirghis and Uzbek SSR. Trudy Zool. Inst., Leningrad. 51:147–150.

1557. Marx, E. J. F. 1957. A review of the subgenus *Donacia* in the Western Hemisphere (Coleoptera: Donaciidae). Bull. Am. Mus. Nat. Hist. 112:191–278.

1558. Masner, L. 1972. The classification and interrelationships of Thoronini (Hym., Proctotrupoidea, Scelionidae). Can. Ent. 104: 833–849.

1559. Masner, L. 1976. Revisionary notes and keys to world genera of Scelionidae (Hym.: Proctotrupoidea). Mem. Ent. Soc. Can. 97:1–87.

1560. Masner, L. 1980. Key to genera of Scelionidae of the Holarctic region, with descriptions of new genera and species (Hymenoptera: Proctotrupoidea). Mem. Ent. Soc. Can. 113:1–54.

1561. Masner, L., and M. A. Kozlov. 1965. Four remarkable egg parasites in Europe (Hym., Scelionidae, Telenominae). Acta Ent. Bohem. 62:287–293.

1562. Mason, J. C. 1976. Evaluating a substrate tray for sampling the invertebrate fauna of small streams, with comments on general sampling problems. Arch. Hydrobiol. 78:51–70.

1563. Mason, W. R. M. 1971. An Indian *Agriotypus* (Hym.: Agriotypidae). Can. Ent. 103:1521–1524.

1564. Mason, W. T., Jr. 1973. An introduction to the identification of chironomid larvae. MERC/EPA, Cincinnati. 90 pp.

1565. Mason, W. T., J. B. Anderson, and G. E. Morrison. 1967. A limestone-filled, artificial substrate sampler-float unit for collecting macroinvertebrates in large streams. Progr. Fish Cult. 29:1–74.

1566. Mason, W. T., Jr., and P. A. Lewis. 1970. Rearing devices for stream insect larvae. Progr. Fish Cult. 32:61–62.

1567. Mason, W. T., Jr., C. I. Weber, P. A. Lewis, and E. C. Julian. 1973. Factors affecting the performance of basket and multiplate macroinvertebrate samplers. Freshwat. Biol. 3:409–436.

1568. Masteller, E. C. 1977. An aquatic emergence trap on a shale stream of western Pennsylvania. Melsheimer Ent. Ser. 23: 10–15.

1569. Masteller, E. C. and O. S. Flint. 1979. Light trap and emergence trap records of caddisflies (Trichoptera) of the Lake Erie region of Pennsylvania and adjacent Ohio. Great Lakes Ent. 12:165–177.

1570. Matheson, R. 1912. The Haliplidae of America north of Mexico. J. N.Y. Ent. Soc. 21:91–123.

1571. Matheson, R. 1914. Life-history of a dytiscid beetle *Hydroporus septentrionalis* Gyll.). Can. Ent. 46:37–50.

1572. Matheson, R., and C. R. Crosby. 1912. Aquatic Hymenoptera in America. Ann. Ent. Soc. Am. 5:65–71.

1573. Mathis, W. N. 1975. A systematic study of *Coenia* and *Paracoenia* (Diptera: Ephydridae). Great Basin Nat. 35:65–85.

1574. Mathis, W. N. 1978. A revision of the Nearctic species of *Limnellia* Malloch (Diptera: Ephydridae). Proc. Biol. Soc. Wash. 91:250–293.

1575. Mathis, W. N. 1979a. Studies of Notiphilinae (Diptera: Ephydridae), I: revision of the Nearctic species of *Notiphila* Fallen, excluding the *caudata* group. Smithson. Contr. Zool. 287:1–111.

1576. Mathis, W. N. 1979b. Studies of Ephydrinae (Diptera: Ephydridae), II: phylogeny, classification, and zoogeography of Nearctic *Lamproscatella* Hendel. Smithson. Contr. Zool. 295:1–41.

1577. Mathis, W. N., and G. E. Shewell. 1978 Studies of Ephydrinae (Diptera: Ephydridae), I: Revisions of *Parascatella* Cresson and the *triseta* group of *Scatella* Robineau-Desvoidy. Smithson, Contr. Zool. 285:1–44.

1578. Mathis, W. N., and K. W. Simpson. 1981. Studies of Ephydrinae (Diptera: Ephydridae), V. The genera *Cirrula* Cresson and *Dimecoenia* Cresson in North America. Smithson. Contr. Zool. 329:1–51.

1579. Matsuda, R. 1960. Morphology, evolution and a classification of the Gerridae. Univ. Kans. Sci. Bull. 41:25–632.

1580. Matsuda, R. 1965. Morphology and evolution of the insect head. Mem. Am. Ent. Inst. 4:1–334.

1581. Matsuda, R. 1970. Morphology and evolution of the insect thorax. Mem. Ent. Soc. Can. 76:1–431.

1582. Matsuda, R. 1976. Morphology and evolution of the insect abdomen. Pergamon, Oxford. 534 pp.

1583. Matta, J. F. 1974. The insects of Virginia: No. 8. The aquatic Hydrophilidae of Virginia (Coleoptera: Polyphaga). Bull. Res. Div. Va. Poly. Inst. State Univ. 94:1–144.

1584. Matta, J. F. 1976. Haliplidae of Virginia (Coleoptera: Adephaga). The insects of Virginia. No. 10. Va. Poly. Inst. State Univ., Res. Div. Bull. 109:1–26.

1585. Matta, J. F. 1978. An annotated list of the Odonata of southeastern Virginia. Va. J. Sci. 29:180–182.

1586. Matta, J. F. 1979. New species of Nearctic *Hydroporus* (Coleoptera: Dytiscidae) *Hydroporus sulphurius, Hydroporus ouachitus, Hydroporus allegenianus*. Proc. Biol. Soc. Wash. 92:287–293.

1587. Matta, J. F. and G. W. Wolf. 1981. A revision of the subgenus *Heterosternuta* Strand of *Hydroporus clairville* (Coleoptera: Dytiscidae). Pan-Pacif. Ent. 57:176–219.

1588. Mattingly, P. F. 1973. Culicidae (Mosquitoes), pp. 37–107. *In* K. G. V. Smith (ed.). Insects and other arthropods of medical importance. Bull. Brit. Mus. Nat. Hist. 561 pp.

1589. Mattingly, R. L., K. W. Cummins, and R. H. King. 1981. The influence of substrate organic content on the growth of a stream chironomid. Hydrobiologia 77:161–165.

1590. Maynard, E. A. 1951. A monograph of the Collembola or springtail insects of New York State. Comstock, Ithaca. 339 pp.

1591. Mayr, E. 1969. Principles of systematic zoology. McGraw-Hill, N.Y. 428 pp.

1592. McAlpine, J. F., B. V. Peterson, G. E. Shewell, H. J. Teskey, J. R. Vockeroth, and D. M. Wood (coords.). 1981. Manual of Nearctic Diptera, Vol. 1. Res. Branch, Agric. Can. Monogr. 27. 674 pp.

1593. McAtee, W. L., and J. R. Malloch. 1925. Revision of bugs of the family Cryptostemmatidae in the collection of the United States National Museum. Proc. U.S. Nat. Mus. 67:1–42.

1594. McCafferty, W. P. 1975. The burrowing mayflies (Ephemeroptera: Ephemeroidea) of the United States. Trans. Am. Ent. Soc. 101:447–504.

1595. McCafferty, W. P. 1981. Aquatic entomology. Science Books Internat., Boston. 448 pp.

1596. McCafferty, W. P., and G. F. Edmunds, Jr. 1976. Redefinition of the family Palingeniidae and its implications for the higher classification of Ephemeroptera. Ann. Ent. Soc. Am. 69:486–490.

1597. McCafferty, W. P., and G. F. Edmunds, Jr. 1979. The higher classification of the Ephemeroptera and its evolutionary basis. Ann. Ent. Soc. Am. 72:5–12.

1598. McCafferty, W. P., and M. C. Minno. 1979. The aquatic and semiaquatic Lepidoptera of Indiana and adjacent areas. Great Lakes Ent.12:179–187.

1599. McCaskill, V. H., and R. Prins. 1968. Stoneflies (Plecoptera) of northwestern South Carolina. J. Elisha Mitchell Sci. Soc. 84:448–453.

1600. McCauley, V. J. E. 1976. Efficiency of a trap for catching and retaining insects emerging from standing water. Oikos 27:339–346.

1601. McClure, R. G., and K. W. Stewart. 1976. Life cycle and production of the mayfly *Choroterpes (Neochoroterpes) mexicanus* Allen (Ephemeroptera: Leptophebiidae). Ann. Ent. Soc. Am. 69:134–148.

1602. McCorkle, D. V. 1967. A revision of the species of *Elophorus* Fabricius in America north of Mexico. Ph.D. diss., University of Washington, Seattle.

1603. McCullough, D. A., G. W. Minshall, and C. E. Cushing. 1979a. Bioenergetics of lotic filter-feeding insects *Simulium* spp. (Diptera) and *Hydropsyche occidentalis* (Trichoptera) and their function in controlling organic content in streams. Ecology 60:585–596.

1604. McCullough, D. A., G. W. Minshall, and C. E. Cushing. 1979b. Bioenergetics of a stream "collector" organism *Tricorythodes minutus* (Insecta: Ephemeroptera). Limnol. Oceanogr. 24:45–58.

1605. McDiffett, W. F. 1970. The transformation of energy by a stream detritivore *Pteronarcys scotti* (Plecoptera). Ecology 51:975–988.

1606. McDonald, J. L., T. P. Sluss, J. D. Lang, and C. C. Roan. 1973. The mosquitoes of Arizona. Univ. Arizona Agric. Exp. Sta. Tech. Bull. 205 21 pp.

1607. McDunnough, J. 1933. Notes on the biology of certain tortricid species with structural details of the larvae and pupae. Can. J. Res. 9:502–517.

1608. McElravy, E. P., T. L. Arsuffi, and B. A. Foote. 1977. New records of caddisflies (Trichoptera) for Ohio. Proc. Ent. Soc. Wash. 79:599–604.

1609. McElravy, E. P., H. Wolda, and V. H. Resh. 1982. Seasonality and annual variability of caddisfly adults (Trichoptera) in a "non-seasonal" tropical environment. Arch. Hydrobiol. 94:302–317.

1610. McFadden, M. W. 1967. Soldier fly larvae in America north of Mexico. Proc. U.S. Nat. Mus. 121:1–72.

1611. McFadden, M. W. 1972. The soldier flies of Canada and Alaska (Diptera: Stratiomyidae) I. Beridinae, Sarginae, and Clitellariinae. Can. Ent. 104:531–562.

1612. McGaha, Y. J. 1952. The limnological relations of insects to certain aquatic flowering plants. Trans. Am. Microsc. Soc. 71:355–381.

1613. McGaha, Y. J. 1954. Contribution to the biology of some Lepidoptera which feed on certain aquatic flowering plants. Trans. Am. Microsc. Soc. 73:167–177.

1614. McKinstry, A. P. 1942. A new family of Hemiptera-Heteroptera proposed for *Macrovelia hornii* Uhler. Pan-Pacif. Ent. 18:90–96.

1615. McLachlan, A. J. 1977. Some effects of tube shape on the feeding of *Chironomus plumosus* L. J. Anim. Ecol. 46:139–146.

1616. McLachlan, A. J., A. Brennan, and R. S. Wotton. 1978. Particle size and chironomid (Diptera) food in an upland river. Oikos 31:247–252.

1617. McLachlan, A. J., and M. A. Cantrell. 1980. Survival strategies in tropical rainpools. Oecologia 47:344–351.

1618. McMahon, J. A., D. J. Schimph, D. C. Anderson, K. G. Smith, and R. L. Bayr, Jr. 1981. An organism-centered approach to some community and ecosystem concepts. J. Theor. Biol. 88:287–307.

1619. McPherson, J. E. 1965. Notes on the life history of *Notonecta hoffmanni* (Hemiptera: Notonectidae). Pan-Pacif. Ent. 41:86–89.

1620. McPherson, J. E. 1966. Notes on the laboratory rearing of *Notonecta hoffmanni* (Hemiptera: Notonectidae). Pan-Pacif. Ent. 42:54–56.

1621. McWilliams, K. L. 1969. A taxonomic revision of the North American species of the genus *Thermonectus* Dejean (Coleoptera: Dytiscidae). Diss. Abstr. 29(B):3781.

1622. Mead, A. R. 1938. New subspecies and notes on *Donacia* with key to the species of the Pacific States (Coleoptera, Chrysomelidae). Pan-Pacif. Ent. 14:113–120.

1623. Means, R. G. 1979. Mosquitoes of New York, Part I. The genus *Aedes* Meigen with identification keys to genera of Culicidae. N.Y. State Mus., Albany. 221 pp.

1624. Mecom, J. O. 1970. Evidence of diurnal feeding activity in Trichoptera larvae. J. Grad. Res. Centr. S. Methodist Univ. 38:44–57.

1625. Mecom, J. O. 1972. Feeding habits of Trichoptera in a mountain stream. Oikos 23:401–407.

1626. Mecom, J. O., and K. W. Cummins. 1964. A preliminary study of the trophic relationships of the larvae of *Brachycentrus americanus* (Banks) (Trichoptera: Brachycentridae). Trans. Am. Microsc. Soc. 83:233–243.

1627. Meier, P. G., and P. G. Bartholomae. 1980. Diel periodicity in the feeding activity of *Potamanthus myops* (Ephemeroptera). Arch. Hydrobiol. 88:1–8.

1628. Meier, P. G., and H. C. Torres. 1978. A modified method for rearing midges (Diptera: Chironomidae). Great Lakes Ent. 11:89–91.

1629. Melin, B. E., and R. C. Graves. 1971. The water beetles of Miller Blue Hole, Sandusky County, Ohio (Insecta: Coleoptera). Ohio J. Sci. 71:73–77.

1630. Menke, A. S. 1958. A synopsis of the genus *Belostoma* Latreille, of America north of Mexico, with the description of a new species. Bull. S. Calif. Acad. Sci. 57:154–174.

1631. Menke, A. S. 1960. A taxonomic study of the genus *Abedus* Stål (Hemiptera: Belostomatidae). Univ. Calif. Publ. Ent. 16:393–440.

1632. Menke, A. S. 1963. A review of the genus *Lethocerus* in North and Central America, including the West Indies. Ann. Ent. Soc. Am. 56:261–267.

1633. Menke, A. E. (ed.). 1979. The semiaquatic and aquatic Hemiptera of California (Heteroptera: Hemiptera). Bull. Calif. Insect Surv. 21:1–166.

1634. Merlassino, M. B., and J. A. Schnack. 1978. Estructura comunitaria y variation estacional de la mesofauna de artropodos en el pleuston de dos afluentes de la Laguna de Chascomus. Rev. Soc. Ent. Argentina 37:1–8.

1635. Merrill, D., and G. B. Wiggins. 1971. The larva and pupa of the caddisfly genus *Setodes* in North America (Trichoptera: Leptoceridae). Occ. Pap. Life Sci. Roy. Ont. Mus. 19:1–12.

1636. Merritt, R. W. 1976. a review of the food habits of the insect fauna inhabiting cattle droppings in north central California. Pan-Pacif. Ent. 52:13–22.

1637. Merritt, R. W., and K. W. Cummins (eds.). 1978. An introduction to the aquatic insects of North America. Kendall/Hunt, Dubuque, Iowa. 441 pp.

1638. Merritt, R. W., K. W. Cummins, and J. R. Barnes. 1979. Demonstration of stream watershed community processes with some simple bioassay techniques, pp. 101–113. *In* V. H. Resh and D. M. Rosenberg (eds.). Innovative teaching in aquatic entomology. Can. Spec. Publ. Fish. Aquat. Sci. 43:1–118.

1639. Merritt, R. W., K. W. Cummins, and T. M. Burton. 1984. The role of aquatic insects in the processing and cycling of nutrients, pp. 134–163. *In* V. H. Resh and D. M. Rosenberg (eds.). The ecology of aquatic insects. Praeger Publishers, N.Y. 638 p.

1640. Merritt, R. W., and D. L. Lawson. 1979. Leaf litter processing in floodplain and stream communities, pp. 93–105. *In* R. R. Johnson and J. F. McCormick (coords.). Strategies for protection and management of floodplain wetlands and other riparian ecosystems. For. Serv./U.S.D.A. Gen. Tech. Rept. WO-12, Washington, D.C. 410 pp.

1641. Merritt, R. W., and D. L. Lawson. 1981. Adult emergence patterns and species distribution and abundance of Tipulidae in three woodland floodplains. Environ. Ent. 10:915–921.

1642. Merritt, R. W., M. M. Mortland, E. F. Gersabeck, and D. H. Ross. 1978. X-ray diffraction analysis of particles ingested by filter-feeding animals. Ent. exp. appl. 24:27–34.

1643. Merritt, R. W., and H. D. Newson. 1978. Chap. 6. Ecology and management of arthropod populations in recreational lands, pp. 125–162. *In* G. W. Frankie and C. S. Koehler (eds.). Perspectives in urban entomology. Academic Press, New York. 417 pp.

1644. Merritt, R. W., D. H. Ross, and G. J. Larson. 1982. Influence of stream temperature and seston on the growth and production of overwintering larval black flies (Diptera: Simuliidae). Ecology 63:1322–1331.

1645. Merritt, R. W., D. H. Ross, and B. V. Peterson 1978. Larval ecology of some lower Michigan black flies with keys to the immature stages. Great Lakes Ent. 11:177–208.

1646. Merritt, R. W., and J. B. Wallace. 1981. Filter-feeding insects. Sci. Am. 244:132–144.

1647. Miall, L. C. 1893. *Dicranota;* a carnivorous tipulid larva. Trans. R. ent. Soc. Lond. 1893:235–253.

1648. Miall, L. C. 1895. The natural history of aquatic insects. MacMillan, London. 395 pp.

1649. Miall, L. C., and R. Shelford. 1897. The structure and life-history of *Phalacrocera replicata.* Trans. R. ent. Soc. Lond. 1897:343–361.

1650. Michael, A. G. and J. F. Matta. 1977. The Dytiscidae of Virginia (Coleptera: Adephaga) (subfamilies: Laccophininae, Colymbetinae, Dytiscinae, Hydaticinae and Cybestrinae). The insects of Virgina. No. 12. Virginia Polytech. Inst. State Univ., Res. Div. Bull. 124:1–53.

1651. Michener, C. D. 1953. Comparative morphological and systematic studies of bee larvae with a key to the families of hymenopterous larvae. Univ. Kans. Sci. Bull. 35:987–1102.

1652. Mickel, C. E., and H. E. Milliron. 1939. Rearing the caddice fly, *Limnephilus indivisus* Walker and its hymenopterous parasite *Hemiteles biannulatus* Grav. Ann. Ent. Soc. Am. 32:575–580.

1653. Middlekauff, W. W., and R. S. Lane. 1980. Adult and immature Tabanidae (Diptera) of California. Bull. Calif. Ins. Surv. 22:1–99.

1654. Milbrink, G., and T. Wiederholm. 1973. Sampling efficiency of four types of mud bottom samplers. Oikos 24:479–482.

1655. Mill, P. J. 1973. Respiration: Aquatic insects, pp. 403–467. *In:* M. Rockstein (ed.). The physiology of Insecta, Vol. 6. 2nd ed. Academic, N.Y. 548 pp.

1656. Mill, P. J., and G. M. Hughes. 1966. The nervous control of ventilation in dragonfly larvae. J. exp. Biol. 44:297–316.

1657. Mill, P. J., and R. S. Pickard. 1972. Anal valve movement and normal ventilation in aeshnid dragonfly larvae. J. exp. Biol. 56:537–543.

1658. Miller, A. 1939. The egg and early development of the stonefly *Pteronarcys proteus* Newman. J. Morph. 64:555–609.

1659. Miller, D. C. 1964. Notes on *Enochrus* and *Cymbiodyta* from the Pacific Northwest (Coleoptera: Hydrophilidae). Coleopt. Bull. 18:69–78.

1660. Miller, D. C. 1974. Revision of the New World *Chaetarthria* (Coleoptera: Hydrophilidae). Entomologica am. 49:1–123.

1661. Miller, D. E., and W. P. Kovalak. 1979. Distribution of *Peltoperla arcuata* Needham (Ins., Plecoptera) in a small woodlawn stream. Int. Revue ges. Hydrobiol. 64:795–800.

1662. Miller, N. 1906. Some notes on the dragonflies of Waterloo, Iowa. Ent. News 17:375–361.

1663. Miller, N. C. E. 1971. The biology of the Heteroptera (2nd ed.). E. Classey, Hampton. 206 pp.

1664. Miller, P. L. 1961. Some features of the respiratory system of *Hydrocyrius columbiae* (Belostomatidae, Hemiptera). J. Insect Physiol. 6:243–271.

1665. Miller, P. L. 1964a. Respiration - aerial gas transport, pp. 557–615. *In:* M. Rockstein (ed.). The physiology of Insecta, Vol. 3. Academic, N.Y. 692 pp.

1666. Miller, P. L. 1964b. The possible role of haemoglobin in *Anisops* and *Buenoa* (Hemiptera: Notonectidae). Proc. R. ent. Soc. Lond. (A). 39:166–175.

1667. Miller, P. L. 1966. The function of haemoglobin in relation to the maintenance of neutral buoyancy in *Anisops pellucens* (Notonectidae, Hemiptera). J. exp. Biol. 44:529–543.

1668. Mills, H. B. 1934. A monograph of the Collembola of Iowa. Collegiate Press Inc., Ames. 143 pp.

1669. Milne, L. J., and M. Milne. 1978. Insects of the water surface. Sci. Am. 238(4):134–142.

1670. Milne, M. J. 1938. The "metamorphotype method" in Trichoptera. J. N.Y. Ent. Soc. 46:435–437.

1671. Minckley, W. L. 1963. The ecology of a spring stream, Doe Run, Meade County, Kentucky. Wildl. Monogr. 11:1–124.

1672. Minckley, W. L. 1964. Upstream movements of *Gammarus* (Amphipoda) in Doe Run, Meade County, Kentucky. Ecology 45:195–197.

1673. Mingo, T. M. 1979. Distribution of aquatic Dryopoidea (Coleoptera) in Maine. Ent. News 90:177–185.

1674. Minshall, G. W. 1967. Role of allochthonous detritus in the trophic structure of a woodland spring brook community. Ecology 48:139–144.

1675. Minshall, G. W., and J. N. Minshall. 1966. Notes on the life history and ecology of *Isoperla clio* (Newman) and *Isogenus decisus* Walker (Plecoptera: Perlodidae). Am. Midl. Nat. 76:340–350.

1676. Minshall, G. W., and J. N. Minshall. 1977. Microdistribution of benthic invertebrates in a Rocky Mountain (USA) stream. Hydrobiologia 55:231–249.

1677. Minshall, G. W., R. C. Petersen, K. W. Cummins, T. L. Bott, J. R. Sedell, C. E. Cushing, and R. L. Vannote. 1983. Interbiome comparison of stream ecosystem dynamics. Ecol. Monogr. 53:1–25.

1678. Minshall, J. N. 1964. An ecological life history of *Epeorus pleuralis* (Banks) in Morgan's Creek, Meade County, Kentucky. M.S. thesis, University of Louisville, Ky. 79 pp.

1679. Minshall, J. N. 1967. Life history and ecology of *Eperous pleuralis* (Banks) (Ephemeroptera: Heptageniidae). Am. Midl. Nat. 78:369–388.

1680. Mittelbach, G. G. 1981. Patterns of invertebrate size and abundance in aquatic habitats. Can. J. Fish. Aquat. Sci. 38:896–904.

1681. Moffet, J. W. 1936. A quantitative study of the bottom fauna in some Utah streams variously affected by erosion. Univ. Utah Biol. Ser. 3:1–33.

1682. Molnar, D. R., and R. J. Lavigne. 1979. The Odonata of Wyoming (dragonflies and damselflies). Sci. Monogr. Agric. Exp. Sta. Univ. Wyoming 37:1–142.

1683. Monakov, A. V. 1972. Review of studies on feeding of aquatic invertebrates conducted at the Institute of Biology of Inland Waters. Academy of Science, USSR. J. Fish. Res. Bd. Can. 29:363–383.

1684. Montgomery, B. E. 1940. The Odonata of South Carolina. J. Elisha Mitchell Sci. Soc. 56:283–301.

1685. Montgomery, B. E. 1941. Records of Indiana dragonflies, X,1937–1940. Proc. Ind. Acad. Sci. 50:229–241.

1686. Montgomery, B. E. 1947. The distribution and relative seasonal abundance of Indiana species of five families of dragonflies (Odonata, Calopterygidae, Petaluridae, Cordulegasteridae, Gomphidae and Aeshnidae). Proc. Ind. Acad. Sci. 56:163–169.

1687. Montgomery, B. E. 1948. The distribution and relative seasonal abundance of the Indiana species of Lestidae (Odonata: Zygoptera). Proc. Ind. Acad. Sci. 57:113–115.

1688. Montgomery, B. E. 1967. Geographical distribution of the Odonata of the North Central States. Proc. N. Cent. Br. Ent. Soc. Am. 22:121–129.

1689. Montgomery, B. E. 1968. The distribution of western Odonata. Proc. N. Cent. Br. Ent. Soc. Am. 23:126–136.

1690. Montgomery, B. E., and J. M. Macklin. 1962. Rates of development in the later instars of *Neotetrum pulchellum* (Drury) (Odonata, Libellulidae). Proc. N. Cent. Br. Ent. Soc. Am. 17:21–23.

1691. Moon, H. P. 1935. Methods and apparatus suitable for an investigation of the littoral region of oligotrophic lakes. Int. Revue ges. Hydrobiol. 32:319–333.

1692. Moon, H. P. 1938. The growth of *Caenis horaria, Leptophlebia marginata* and *L. vespertina.* Proc. Zool. Soc. Lond. 108:507–512.

1693. Moon, H. P. 1939. Aspects of the ecology of aquatic insects. Trans. Brit. Ent. Soc. 6:39–49.

1694. Moore, I. 1956. A revision of the Pacific coast Phytosini with a review of the foreign genera (Coleoptera: Staphylinidae). Trans. San Diego Soc. Nat. Hist. 12:103–152.

1695. Moore, I., and E. F. Legner. 1974. Keys to the genera of Staphylinidae of America north of Mexico exclusive of the Aleocharinae (Coleoptera: Staphylinidae). Hilgardia 42:548–563.

1696. Moore, I., and E. F. Legner. 1975. Revision of the genus *Endeodes* LeConte with a tabular key to the species (Coleoptera: Melyridae). J. N.Y. Ent. Soc. 85:70–81.

1697. Moore, I., and E. F. Legner. 1976. Intertidal rove beetles (Coleoptera: Staphylinidae), pp. 521–551. *In* L. Cheng (ed.). Marine insects. North Holland, Amsterdam. 581 pp.

1698. Moore, J. W. 1977. Some factors affecting algal consumption in subarctic Ephemeroptera, Plecoptera and Simuliidae. Oecologia 27:261–273.

1699. Moore, J. W. 1979a. Factors influencing algal consumption and feeding rate in *Heterotrissocladius changi* Saether and *Polypedilum nubeculosum* (Meigen). Oecologia 40:219–227.

1700. Moore, J. W. 1979b. Some factors affecting the distribution, seasonal abundance and feeding of subarctic Chironomidae (Diptera). Arch, Hydrobiol. 85:203–225.

1701. Morgan, A. H. 1911. Mayflies of Fall Creek. Ann. Ent. Soc. Am. 4:93–119.

1702. Morgan, A. H. 1913. A contribution to the biology of mayflies. Ann. Ent. Soc. Am. 6:371–413.

1703. Morgan, A. H., and H. D. O'Neil. 1931. The function of the tracheal gills in larvae of the caddisfly, *Macronema zebratum* Hagen. Physiol. Zool. 4:361–379.

1704. Morgan, J. J. 1949. The metamorphosis and ecology of some species of Tanypodinae (Dipt., Chironomidae). Entomol. mon. Mag. 85:119–126.

1705. Morgan, N. C. 1971. Factors in the design and selection of insect emergence traps, pp. 93–108. *In* W. T. Edmondson and G. G. Winberg (eds.). A manual on methods for the assessment of secondary productivity in fresh waters. IBP Handbook 17. Blackwell, Oxford. 358 pp.

1706. Morgan, N. C., A. B. Waddell, and W. B. Hall. 1963. A comparison of the catches of emerging aquatic insects in floating box and submerged funnel traps. J. Anim. Ecol. 32:203–219.

1707. Morihara, D. K., and W. P. McCafferty. 1979. The *Baetis* larvae of North America (Ephemeroptera: Baetidae). Trans. Am. Ent. Soc. 105:139–221.

1708. Morley, R. L., and R. A. Ring. 1972. The intertidal Chironomidae (Diptera) of British Columbia II. Life history and population dynamics. Can. Ent. 104:1099–1121.

1709. Morofsky, W. F. 1939. Survey of insect fauna of some Michigan trout streams in connection with improved and unimproved streams. J. Econ. Ent. 29:749–754.

1710. Morris, D. L., and M. P. Brooker. 1979. The vertical distribution of macroinvertebrates in the substratum of the upper reaches of the River Wye, Wales, Freshwat. Biol. 9:573–583.

1711. Morris, R. W. 1963. A modified Barcroft respirometer for study of aquatic animals. Turtox News 41:22–23.

1712. Morse, J. C. 1972. The genus *Nyctiophylax* in North America. J. Kans. Ent. Soc. 45:172–181.

1713. Morse, J. C. 1975. A phylogeny and revision of the caddisfly genus *Ceraclea* (Trichoptera, Leptoceridae). Contr. Am. Ent. Inst. 11:1–97.

1714. Morse, J. C. 1981. A phylogeny and classification of family-group taxa of Leptoceridae (Trichoptera), pp. 257–264. *In* G. P. Moretti (ed.). Proc. 3rd Internat. Symp. Trichoptera. Ser. Entomologica 20. Junk, The Hague, Netherlands. 472 pp.

1715. Morse, J. C., J. W. Chapin, D. D. Herlong, and R. S. Harvey. 1980. Aquatic insects of Upper Three Runs Creek, Savannah River Plant, South Carolina. Part I: Orders other than Diptera. J. Ga. Ent. Soc. 15:73–101.

1716. Morse, W. J., and R. L. Blickle. 1953. A check list of the Trichoptera (caddisflies) of New Hampshire. Ent. News 64:68–73, 97–102.

1717. Morse, W. J., and R. L. Blickle. 1957. Additions and corrections to the list of New Hampshire Trichoptera. Ent. News 68:127–131.

1718. Mosher, E. 1916. A classification of the Lepidoptera based on characters of the pupae. Bull. Ill. State Lab. Hist. 12: 14–159.

1719. Mozley, S. C. 1968. The integrative roles of the chironomid (Diptera: Chironomidae) larvae in the trophic web of a shallow, five hectare lake in the Piedmont region of Georgia. Ph.D. diss., Emory University, Atlanta. 109 pp.

1720. Muesebeck, C. F. W. 1949. A new flightless *Phaenopria* (Hym.: Diapriidae). Can. Ent. 81:234–235.

1721. Muesebeck, C. F. W. 1950. Two new genera and three new species of Braconidae. Proc. Ent. Soc. Wash. 52:77–81.

1722. Muesebeck, C. F. W. 1972. A new reared species of *Trichopria* (Proctotrupoidea: Diapriidae). Ent. News 83:141–143.

1723. Muesebeck, C. F. W., K. V.Krombein, and H. K. Townes. 1951. Hymenoptera of America north of Mexico synoptic catalog. U.S. Dep. Agric. Monogr. 21 420p.

1724. Muirhead-Thompson, R. C. 1966. Blackflies, pp. 127–144. *In* C. N. Smith (ed.). Insect colonization and mass production. Academic, N.Y. 618 pp.

1725. Muirhead-Thompson, R. C. 1969. A laboratory technique for establishing *Simulium* larvae in an experimental channel. Bull. Ent. Res. 59:533–536.

1726. Mulhern, T. D. 1942. New Jersey mechanical trap for mosquito surveys. New Jersey Agric. Exp. Sta. Circ. 421:1–8.

1727. Mulla, M. S., and L. A. Lacey. 1976. Feeding rates of *Simulium* larvae on particulates in natural streams (Diptera: Simuliidae). Environ. Ent. 5:283–287.

1728. Muller, G. W. 1892. Beobachtungen an im Wasserlebenden Schmetterlingsraupen. Zool. Jb. Syst. 6:617–630.

1729. Muller, K. 1954. Investigation on the organic drift in North Swedish streams. Rep. Inst. Freshwat. Res. Drottningholm 35:133–148.

1730. Müller, K. 1974. Stream drift as a chronobiological phenomenon in running water ecosystems. Ann. Rev. Ecol. Syst. 5:309–323.

1731. Mundie, J. H. 1956. Emergence traps for aquatic insects. Mitt. Int. Verh. Limnol. 7:1–13.

1732. Mundie, J. H. 1957. The ecology of Chironomidae in storage reservoirs. Trans. Ent. Soc. Lond. 109:149–232.

1733. Mundie, J. H. 1964. A sampler for catching emerging insects and drifting materials in streams. Limnol. Oceanogr. 9:456–459.

1734. Mundie, J. H. 1966. Sampling emerging insects and drifting materials in deep flowing water. Gewasser und Abwasser. 41/42:159–162.

1735. Mundie, J. H. 1971a. Sampling benthos and substrate materials, down to 50 microns in size, in shallow streams. J. Fish. Res. Bd. Can. 28:849–860.

1736. Mundie, J. H. 1971b. Insect emergence traps. pp. 80–93. *In* W. T. Edmondson and G. G. Winberg (eds.). A manual on methods for the assessment of secondary productivity in fresh waters. IBP Handbook 17. Blackwell, Oxford 358 pp.

1737. Munroe, E. G. 1947. Further North American records of *Acentropus niveus* (Lepidoptera, Pyralidae). Can. Ent. 79:120.

1738. Munroe, E. G. 1951a. A previously unrecognized species of *Nymphula* (Lepidoptera: Pyralidae). Can. Ent. 83:20–23.

1739. Munroe, E. G. 1951b. The identity and generic position of *Chauliodes disjunctus* Walker (Megaloptera: Corydalidae). Can. Ent. 83:33–35.

1740. Munroe, E. G. 1958. *Chauliodes disjunctus* Walker: a correction with the descriptions of a new species of a new genus (Megaloptera: Corydalidae). Can. Ent. 85:190–192.

1741. Munroe, E. G. 1972–1973. Pyraloidea. Pyralidae (in part), pp. 1–304, Fasc. 13.1, A-C. *In* R. B. Dominick (ed.). The moths of America north of Mexico. E. W Classey Ltd., London. (on-going series).

1742. Munz, P. A. 1919. A venational study of the suborder Zygoptera. Mem. Ent. Soc. Am. 3:1–307.

1743. Murphey, R. K. 1971. Sensory aspects of the control of orientation to prey by the water strider, *Gerris remigis*. Z. Vergl. Physiol 72:168–185.

1744. Murphy, H. 1919. Observations on the egg laying of the caddisfly *Brachycentrus nigrosoma* Banks, and the habits of the young larvae. J. N.Y. Ent. Soc. 27:154–158.

1745. Murphy, H. E. 1937. Rearing mayflies from egg to adult, pp. 266–267. *In* J. G. Needham (ed.). Culture methods for invertebrate animals. Comstock, Ithaca. 590 pp.

1746. Murray, D. A. (ed.). 1980. Chironomidae: ecology, systematics, cytology and physiology. Pergamon, N.Y.

1747. Murray, T. D., and W. N. Charles. 1975. A pneumatic grab for obtaining large, undisturbed mud samples: its construction and some applications for measuring the growth of larvae and emergence of adult Chironomidae. Freshwat. Biol. 5:205–210.

1748. Murvosh, C. M. 1971. Ecology of the water penny beetle *Psephenus herricki* DeKay. Ecol. Monogr. 41:79–96.

1749. Murvosh, C. M., and H. P. Brown. 1976. Mating behavior of water penny beetles (Coleoptera: Psephenidae): a hypothesis. Coleopt. Bull. 30:57–59.

1750. Murvosh, C. M., and B. W. Miller. 1974. Life history of the western water penny beetle, *Psephenus falli* (Coleoptera: Psephenidae). Coleopt. Bull. 28:85–92.

1751. Musgrave, P. N. 1935. A synopsis of the genus *Helichus* Erichson in the United States and Canada, with descriptions of new species. Proc. Ent. Soc. Wash. 37:137–145.

1752. Musser, R. J. 1962. Dragonfly nymphs of Utah. (Odonata: Anisoptera). Univ. Utah Biol. Ser. 12:1–71.

1753. Muttkowski, R. A. 1908. Review of the dragonflies of Wisconsin. Bull. Wisc. Nat. Hist. Soc. 6:57–127.

1754. Muttkowski, R. A. 1910. Catalogue of the Odonata of North America. Bull. Mus. Milwaukee 207 pp.

1755. Muttkowski, R. A. 1918. The fauna of Lake Mendota—a qualitative and quantitative survey with special reference to insects. Trans. Wisc. Acad. Sci. Arts Lett. 19:374–482.

1756. Muttkowski, R. A., and G. M. Smith. 1929. The food of trout stream insects in Yellowstone National Park. Ann. Roosevelt Wildl. 2: 241–263.

1757. Nagagawa, A. 1952. Food habits of hydropsychid larvae. Jap. J. Limnol. 16:130–138.

1758. Nagaraja, H., and S. Nagarkatti. 1973. A key to some New World species of *Trichogramma* (Hymenoptera; Trichogrammatidae), with descriptions of four new species. Proc. Ent. Soc. Wash. 75:288–297.

1759. Nagell, B. 1973. The oxygen consumption of mayfly (Ephemeroptera) and stonefly (Plecoptera) larvae at different oxygen concentration. Hydrobiologia 42:461–489.

1760. Nagell, B. 1974. The basic picture and the ecological implications of the oxygen consumption/oxygen concentration curve of some aquatic insect larvae. Ent. Tidskr. (Suppl.) 95:182–187.

1761. Neave, F. 1930. Migratory habits of the mayfly, *Blasturus cupidus* Say. Ecology 11:568–576.

1762. Nebeker, A. V. 1971. Effect of water temperature on nymphal feeding rate, emergence, and adult longevity of the stonefly, *Pteronarcys dorsata*. J. Kans. Ent. Soc. 44:21–26.

1763. Nebeker, A. V., and A. R. Gaufin. 1965. The *Capnia columbiana* complex of North America (Capniidae, Plecoptera). Trans. Am. Ent. Soc. 91:467–487.

1764. Needham, J. G. 1899. Directions for collecting and rearing dragonflies, stoneflies, and mayflies. Bull. U.S. Nat. Mus. 39:1–9.

1765. Needham, J. G. 1900. The fruiting of the Blue Flag (*Iris versicolor* L.). Am. Nat. 34:361–386.

1766. Needham, J. G. 1901a. Aquatic insects of the Adirondacks. Ephemeridae. Bull. N.Y. State Mus. 47:418–429.

1767. Needham, J. G. 1901b. Aquatic insects of the Adirondacks. Odonata. Bull. N.Y. State Mus. 47:429–540.

1768. Needham, J. G. 1903. Aquatic insects in New York state. Part 3. Life histories of Odonata suborder Zygoptera. Bull. N.Y. State Mus. 68:218–279.

1769. Needham, J. G. 1907. Notes on the aquatic insects of Walnut Lake, pp. 252–271. *In* T. C. Hankinson (ed.). A biological survey of Walnut Lake, Michigan. Rept. Mich. Geol. Surv. 1907. 288 pp.

1770. Needham, J. G. 1928. A list of the insects of New York. Mem. Cornell Univ. Agric. Exp. Sta. 101:45–56.

1771. Needham, J. G. 1941. Life history studies on *Progomphus* and its nearest allies (Odonata: Aeschnidae). Trans. Am. Ent. Soc. 67:221–245.

1772. Needham, J. G. 1951. Prodrome for a manual of the dragonflies of North America, with extended comments on wing venation systems. Trans. Am. Ent. Soc. 77:21–62.

1773. Needham, J. G., and C. Betten. 1901a. Family Sialidae. Aquatic insects of the Adirondacks. Bull. N.Y. State Mus. 47:541–544.

1774. Needham, J. G., and C. Betten. 1901b. Aquatic insects in the Adirondacks. Diptera. Bull. N.Y. State Mus. 47:545–612.

1775. Needham, J. G., and P. W. Claassen. 1925. A monograph on the Plecoptera or stoneflies of America north of Mexico. Thomas Say Found. Ent. Soc. Am. 2:1–397.

1776. Needham, J. G., and E. Fisher. 1936. The nymphs of North American libelluline dragonflies (Odonata). Trans. Am. Ent. Soc. 62:107–116.

1777. Needham, J. G., and C. A. Hart. 1901. The Dragonflies (Odonata) of Illinois Part 1. Petaluridae, Aeschnidae, and Gomphidae. Bull. Ill. State Lab. Nat. Hist. Surv. 6:1–94.

1778. Needham, J. G., and H. B. Heywood. 1929. A handbook of the dragonflies of North America. C. C. Thomas, Springfield, Ill. 378 pp.

1779. Needham, J. G., and J. T. Lloyd. 1928. The life of inland waters. The Amer. Viewpoint Soc., N.Y. 438 pp.

1780. Needham, J. G., and P. R. Needham. 1962. A guide to the study of fresh-water biology (5th ed.). Holden-Day, San Francisco 108 pp.

1781. Needham, J. G., and L. W. Smith. 1916. The stoneflies of the genus *Peltoperla*. Can. Ent. 48:80–88.

1782. Needham, J. G., J. R. Traver, and Y. C. Hsu. 1935. The biology of mayflies with a systematic account of North American species. Comstock, Ithaca. 759 pp.

1783. Needham, J. G., and M. J. Westfall, Jr. 1955. A manual of the dragonflies of North America (Anisoptera) including the Greater Antilles and the provinces of the Mexican border. Univ. Calif. Press, Berkeley. 615 pp.

1784. Needham, P. R. 1934. Quantitative studies of stream bottom foods. Trans. Am. Fish. Soc. 64:238–247.

1785. Needham, P. R., and R. L. Usinger. 1956. Variability in the macrofauna of a single riffle in Prosser Creek, California, as indicated by the Surber sampler. Hilgardia 24:383–409.

1786. Neff, S. E. 1955. Studies on a Kentucky knobs lake. II. Some aquatic Nematocera (Diptera) from Tom Wallace Lake. Trans. Ky. Acad. Sci. 16:1–13.

1787. Neff, S. E., and C. O. Berg. 1962. Biology and immature stages of *Hoplodictya spinicornis* and *H. setosa* (Diptera: Sciomyzidae). Trans. Am. Ent. Soc. 88:77–93.

1788. Neff, S. E., and C. O. Berg. 1966. Biology and immature stages of malacophagous Diptera of the genus *Sepedon* (Sciomyzidae). Bull. Va. Polytech. Inst. Agric. Exp. Sta. 566. 113 pp.

1789. Neff, S. E., and J. B. Wallace. 1969a. Observations on the immature stages of *Cordilura (Achaetella) deceptiva* and *C. (A.) varipes*. Ann. Ent. Soc. Am. 62:775–785.

1790. Neff, S. E., and J. B. Wallace. 1969b. Biology and description of immature stages of *Orthacheta hirtipes*, a predator of *Cordilura* spp. Ann. Ent. Soc. Am. 62:785–790.

1791. Nelson, C. H., and J. F. Hanson. 1971. Contribution to the anatomy and phylogeny of the family Pteronarcidae (Plecoptera). Trans. Am. Ent. Soc. 97:123–200.

1792. Nelson, C. H., and J. F. Hanson. 1973. The genus *Perlomyia*. J. Kans. Ent. Soc. 46:187–199.

1793. Nelson, C. H., D. C. Tarter, and M. L. Little. 1977. Description of the adult male of *Allonarcys comstocki* (Smith) (Plecoptera: Pteronarcidae). Ent. News 88:33–36.

1794. Nelson, D. J., and D. C. Scott. 1962. Role of detritus in the productivity of a rock-outcrop community in a Piedmont Stream. Limnol. Oceanogr. 7:396–413.

1795. Neumann, D. 1976. Adaptations of chironomids to intertidal environments. Ann. Rev. Ent. 21:387–414.

1796. Neunzig, H. H. 1966. Larvae of the genus *Nigronia* Banks. Proc. Ent. Soc. Wash. 68:11–16.

1797. Neves, R. J. 1979. A checklist of caddisflies (Trichoptera) from Massachusetts. Ent. News 90:167–175.

1798. Neveu, A. 1972. Introduction a l'étude de la faune des diptères à larves aquatiques d'un ruisseau des Pyrénées—Atlantiques, le Lissuraga. Ann. Hydrobiol. 3:173–196.

1799. Neveu, A. 1973a. Le cycle de développement des Simuliidae (Diptera, Nematocera) d'un ruisseau des Pyrénées-Atlantiques, le Lissuraga. Ann. Hydrobiol. 4:51–75.

1800. Neveu, A. 1973b. Estimation de la production de populations larvaires du genre *Simulium* (Diptera, Nematocera). Ann. Hydrobiol. 4:183–189.

1801. Neveu, A. 1976. Ecologie des larves d'Athericidae (Diptera, Brachycera) dans un ruisseau des Pyrénées-atlantiques. I. Structure et dynamique des populations. Ann. Hydrobiol. 7:73–90.

1802. Neveu, A. 1977. Ecologie des larves d'Athericidae (Diptera, Brachycera) dans un ruisseau Pyrénées-atlantiques. II. Production comparison de differentes methodes de calcul. Ann. Hydrobiol. 8:45–66.

1803. Nevin, F. R. 1929. Larval development of *Sympetrum vicinum* Trans. Am. Ent. Soc. 55:79–102.

1804. Newell, R. L., and G. W. Minshall. 1976. An annotated list of the aquatic insects of southeastern Idaho. Part I. Plecoptera. Great Basin Nat. 36:501–504.

1805. Newell, R. L., and G. W. Minshall. 1978. Life history of a multivoltine mayfly, *Tricorythodes minutus:* an example of the effect of temperature on life cycle. Ann. Ent. Soc. Am. 71:876–881.

1806. Newell, R. L., and D. S. Potter. 1973. Distribution of some Montana caddisflies (Trichoptera). Proc. Mont. Acad. Sci. 33:12–21.

1807. Nicholson, H. P., and C. E. Mickel. 1950. The black flies of Minnesota (Simuliidae). Univ. Minn. Agric. Exp. Sta. Tech. Bull. 192:1–64.

1808. Nicola, S. 1968. Scavenging by *Alloperla* (Plecoptera: Chloroperlidae) nymphs on dead pink *(Oncorhynchus gorbuscha)* and chum *(O. keta)* salmon. Can. J. Zool. 46:787–796.

1809. Nielson, A. 1942. Über die Entwicklung und Biologie der Trichopteren mit besonderer Berücksichtigung der Quelltrichopteren Himmerlands. Arch. Hydrobiol. Suppl. 17:255–631.

1810. Nielsen, A. 1948. Postembryonic development and biology of the Hydroptilidae. Biol. Skr. Dan. Vid. Selsk. 5:1–200.

1811. Nielsen, A. 1950. The torrential invertebrate fauna. Oikos 2:176–196.

1812. Nielsen, A. 1951a. Contributions to the metamorphosis and biology of the genus *Atrichopogon* Kieffer (Diptera, Ceratopogonidae), with remarks on the evolution and taxonomy of the genus. Kongr. Dan. Vidensk. Selsk. Biol. Skr. 6:1–95.

1813. Nielsen, A. 1951b. Is dorsoventral flattening of the body an adaptation to torrential life? Verh. Int. Verein. Limnol. 11:264–267.

1814. Nielsen, A. 1980. A comparative study of the genital segments and the genital chamber in female Trichoptera. Biol. Skr. (Kon. Danske Vid. Selsk.) 23:1–200.

1815. Nielsen, A. 1981. On the evolution of the phallus and other male terminalia in the Hydropsychidae with a proposal for a new generic name, pp. 273–278. *In* G. P. Moretti (ed.). Proc. 3rd Internat. Symp. on Trichoptera. Ser. Entomologica 20. Junk, The Hague, Netherlands. 472 pp.

1816. Nielsen, L. T. 1968. A current list of mosquitoes known to occur in Utah with a report of new records. Proc. Utah Mosquito Abate. Assoc. 21:34–37.

1817. Nielsen, L. T., and D. M. Rees. 1961. An identification guide to the mosquitoes of Utah. Univ. Utah Biol. Ser. 12:1–63.

1818. Nielsen, P., O. Ringdahl, and S. L. Tuxen. 1954. The zoology of Iceland. III, part 48a, Diptera. 1. Ejnar Munksgaard, Copenhagen, and Reykjavik. 189 pp.

1819. Nieser, N. 1977. A revision of the genus *Tenagobia* Bergroth (Heteroptera: Corixidae). Stud. Neotrop. Fauna Environ. 12:1–56.

1820. Nigmann, M. 1908. Anatomie und Biologie von *Acentropus niveus* Oliv. Zool. Jb. Syst. 26:489–560.

1821. Nimmo, A. P. 1971. The adult Rhyacophilidae and Limnephilidae (Trichoptera) of Alberta and eastern British Columbia and their post-glacial origin. Quaest. Ent. 7:3–234.

1822. Nimmo, A. P. 1974. The adult Trichoptera (Insecta) of Alberta and eastern British Columbia, and their post-glacial origins. II. The families Glossosomatidae and Philopotamidae. Quaest. Ent. 10:315–349.

1823. Nimmo, A. P. 1977a. The adult Trichoptera (Insecta) of Alberta and eastern British Columbia, and their post-glacial origins. I. The families Rhyacophilidae and Limnephilidae. Suppl. 1. Quaest. Ent. 13:25–67.

1824. Nimmo, A. P. 1977b. The adult Trichoptera (Insecta) of Alberta and eastern British Columbia, and their post-glacial origins. II. The families Glossosomatidae and Philopotamidae. Suppl. 1. Quaest. Ent. 13:69–71.

1825. Nimmo, A. P., and G. G. E. Scudder. 1978. An annotated checklist of the Trichoptera (Insecta) of British Columbia. Syesis 11:117–134.

1826. Novak, K., and F. Sehnal. 1963. The development cycle of some species of the genus *Limnephilus* (Trichoptera). Cas. Cs. Spol. Ent. 60:68–80.

1827. Nowell, W. R. 1951. The dipterous family Dixidae in western North America (Insecta: Diptera). Microentomology 16:187–270.

1828. Nowell, W. R. 1963. Guide to the insects of Connecticut Part VI, Fas. 3. Dixidae. Conn. Bull. State Geol. Nat. Hist. Surv. 93:85–102.

1829. Noyes, A. A. 1914. The biology of the net-spinning Trichoptera of Cascadilla Creek. Ann. Ent. Soc. Am. 7:251–272.

1830. Oakley, B., and J. M. Palka. 1967. Prey capture by dragonfly larvae. Am. Zool. 7:727–728.

1831. Oberndorfer, R. Y., and K. W. Stewart. 1977. The life cycle of *Hydroperla crosbyi* (Plecoptera: Perlodidae). Great Basin Nat. 37:260–273.

1832. O'Brien, C. W. 1975. A taxonomic revision of the new world subaquatic genus *Neochetina* (Coleoptera: Curculionidae: Bagoini). Ann. Ent. Soc. Am. 69:165–174.

1833. Okland, J. 1962. Litt om teknikk ved insamling og konservering av freshkvannsdyr. Fauna 15:69–92.

1834. Okumura, G. T. 1961. Identification of lepidopterous larvae attacking cotton-with illustrated key. Calif. Dept. Agric. Spec. Publ. 282 50 pp.

1835. Olander, R., and E. Palmen. 1968. Taxonomy, ecology and behaviour of the northern Baltic *Clunio marinus* Halid. Ann. Zool. Fenn. 5:97–110.

1836. Old, M. C. 1933. Observations on the Sisyridae (Neuroptera). Pap. Mich. Acad. Sci. Arts Lett. 17:681–684.

1837. Oliver, D. R. 1971. Life history of the Chironomidae. Ann. Rev. Ent. 16:211–230.

1838. Oliver, D. R. 1981. Chap. 29. Chironomidae, pp. 423–458. *In* J. F. McAlpine, B. V. Peterson, G. E. Shewell, H. J. Teskey, J. R. Vockeroth, and D. M. Wood (coords.). Manual of Nearctic Diptera, Vol. 1. Res. Branch Agric. Can. Monogr. 27. Ottawa, 674 pp.

1839. Oliver, D. R., D. McClymont, and M. E. Roussel. 1978. A key to some larvae of Chironomidae (Diptera) from the Mackenzie and Porcupine River watersheds. Fish. Environ. Can. Fish. Mar. Serv. Tech. Rept. No. 791:1–73.

1840. Omerod, E. A. 1889. *Ranatra linearis* attacking small fish. Entomologist 11:119–120.

1841. O'Neill, W. L. 1973. Biology of *Trichopria popei* and *T. atrichomelinae* (Hym., Diapriidae) parasitoids of the Sciomyzidae (Diptera). Ann. Ent. Soc. Am. 66:1043–1054.

1842. Osten-Sacken, C. R. 1869. The North American Tipulidae. Monogr. N. Am. Diptera IV. Smithson. Misc. Coll. 8:1–345.

1843. Oswood, M. W. 1976. Comparative life histories of the Hydropsychidae (Trichoptera) in a Montana lake outlet. Am. Midl. Nat. 96:493–497.

1844. Oswood, M. W. 1979. Abundance patterns of filter-feeding caddisflies (Trichoptera: Hydropsychidae) and seston in a Montana (U.S.A.) lake outlet. Hydrobiologia 63:177–183.

1845. Otto, C., and B. S. Svensson. 1981a. A comparison between food, feeding and growth of two mayflies, *Ephemera danica* and *Siphlonurus aestivalis* (Ephemeroptera) in a South Swedish stream. Arch. Hydrobiol. 91:341–350.

1846. Otto, C., and B. S. Svensson. 1981b. How do macrophytes growing in or close to water reduce their consumption by aquatic herbivores? Hydrobiologia 78:107–112.

1847. Paclt, J. 1956. Biologie der primar flugellosen Insekten. Gustav Fischer Verlag, Jena. 258p.

1848. Page, T. L., and D. A. Neitzel. 1979. A device to hold and identify rock-filled baskets for benthic sampling in large rivers. Limnol. Oceanogr. 24:988–990.

1849. Pajunen, V. 1970. Adaptations of *Arctocorisa carinata* (Sahlb.) and *Callocorixa producta* (Reut.) populations to a rock pool environment. Proc. Adv. Stud. Dynam. Pop. 1970:148–158.

1850. Pajunen, V. I. 1977. Population structure in rock-pool corixids (Hemiptera: Corixidae) during the reproductive season. Ann. Zool. Fenn. 14:26–47.

1851. Pajunen, V. I. 1979a. Competition between rock pool corixids. Ann. Zool. Fenn. 16:138–143.

1852. Pajunen, V.I. 1979b. Quantitative analysis of competition between *Arctocorisa carinata* (Sahlb.) and *Callicorixa producta* (Reut.) (Hemiptera, Corixidae). Ann. Zool. Fenn. 16:195–200.

1853. Parfin, S. I. 1952. The Megaloptera and Neuroptera of Minnesota. Am. Midl. Nat. 47:421–434.

1854. Parfin, S. I., and A. B. Gurney. 1956. The spongilla-flies, with special reference to those of the Western Hemisphere (Sisyridae, Neuroptera). Proc. U.S. Nat. Mus. 105:421–529.

1855. Parker, C. R., and J. R. Voshell. 1981. A preliminary checklist of the caddisflies (Trichoptera) of Virginia. J. Ga. Ent. Soc. 16:1–7.

1856. Parker, H. L. 1924. Recherches sur les formes post-embryonnaires des chalcidiens. Ann. Soc. Ent. France 93:261–379.

1857. Parr, M. J. 1970. The life histories of *Ischnura elegans* (van der Linden) and *Coenagrion puella* (L.) (Odonata) in south Lancashire. Proc. R. ent. Soc. Lond.(A) 45:172–181.

1858. Parrish, F. K. 1975. Keys to water quality indicative organisms of the southeastern United States (2nd ed.). EMSL/EPA, Cincinnati. 195 pp.

1859. Parshley, H. M. 1925. A bibliography of the North American Hemiptera-Heteroptera. Smith College, Northampton. 252 pp.

1860. Parsons, M. A., R. L. Berry, M. Jalil, and R. A. Masterson. 1972. A revised list of the mosquitoes of Ohio with some new distribution and species records. Mosquito News 32:223–226.

1861. Parsons, M. C. 1970. Respiratory significance of the thoracic and abdominal morphology of the three aquatic bugs *Ambrysus*, *Notonecta* and *Hesperocorixa* (Insecta, Heteroptera). Z. Morph. Tiere 66:242–298.

1862. Parsons, M. C. 1972. Respiratory significance of the thoracic and abdominal morphology of *Belostoma* and *Ranatra* (Insecta, Heteroptera). Z. Morph. Tiere. 73:163–194.

1863. Parsons, M. C. 1974. Anterior displacements of the metathoracic spiracle and lateral intersegmental boundary in the pterothorax of Hydrocorisae. Z. Morphol. Tiere. 79:165–198.

1864. Parsons, M. C., and R. J. Hewson. 1974. Plastral respiratory devices in adult *Cryphocricos* (Naucoridae: Heteroptera). Psyche 81:510–527.

1865. Parsons, R. E., and D. E. Howell. 1971. A list of Oklahoma mosquitoes. Mosquito News 31:168–169.

1866. Patocka, J. 1955. Die Puppen der Schmetterlinge—Schaedlinge der Eichen, die in oder an der Erde ruhen. Lesn. Sborn. 2:20–101.

1867. Patrick, R., J. Cairns, Jr., and S. S. Roback. 1967. An ecosystematic study of the fauna and flora of the Savannah River. Proc. Acad. Nat. Sci. Phila. 118:109–407.

1868. Patterson, J. W., and R. L. Vannote. 1979. Life history and population dynamics of *Heteroplectron americanum*. Environ. Ent. 8:665–669.

1869. Paulson, D. R. 1966. The dragonflies (Odonata: Anisoptera) of southern Florida. Ph.D. Diss., University of Miami, Miami, Fla. 603 pp.

1870. Paulson, D. R. 1970. A list of the Odonata of Washington with additions to and deletions from the state list. Pan-Pacif. Ent. 46:194–198.

1871. Paulson, D. R., and R. A. Cannings. 1980. Distribution, natural history and relationship of *Ischnura erratica* Calvert (Zygoptera: Coenagrionidae). Odonatologica 9:147–153.

1872. Paulson, D. R., and R. W. Garrison. 1977. A list and new distributional records of Pacific coast Odonata. Pan-Pacif. Ent. 53:147–160.

1873. Paulson, D. R., and C. E. Jenner. 1971. Population structure in overwintering larval Odonata in North Carolina in relation to adult flight season. Ecology 52:96–107.

1874. Pearlstone, P. S. M. 1973. The food of damselfly larvae in Marion Lake, British Columbia. Syesis 6:33–39.

1875. Pearse, A. S. 1932. Animals in brackish water ponds and pools at Dry Tortugas. Papers Tortugas Lab. Carnegie Inst. Washington 28:125–142.

1876. Pearson, W. D., and R. H. Kramer. 1972. Drift and production of two aquatic insects in a mountain stream. Ecol. Monogr. 42:365–385.

1877. Pechuman, L. L., and H. J. Teskey. 1981. Chap. 31. Tabanidae, pp. 463–478. *In* J. F. McAlpine, B. V. Peterson, G. E. Shewell, J. J. Teskey, J. R. Vockeroth, and D. M. Wood (coords.). Manual of Nearctic Diptera, Vol. 1. Res. Branch, Agric. Can. Monogr. 27. Ottawa. 674 pp.

1878. Peck, D. L., and S. D. Smith. 1978. A revision of the *Rhyacophila coloradensis* complex (Trichoptera: Rhyacophilidae). Melandaria 27:1–24.

1879. Peckarsky, B. L. 1979. A review of the distribution, ecology and evolution of the North American species of *Acroneuria* and six related genera (Plecoptera: Perlidae). J. Kans. Ent. Soc. 52:787–809.

1880. Peckarsky, B. L. 1980. Predator-prey interactions between stoneflies and mayflies: behavioral observations. Ecology 61:932–943.

1881. Peckarsky, B. L., and S. I. Dodson. 1980. Do stonefly predators influence benthic distributions in streams? Ecology 61:1275–1282.

1882. Pedigo, L. P. 1968. Pond shore Collembola: a redescription of *Salina banksi* MacGillivray (Entomobryidae) and new Sminthuridae. J. Kans. Ent. Soc. 41:548–556.

1883. Pedigo, L. P. 1970. Activity and local distribution of surface active Collembola II: pond-shore populations. Ann. Ent. Soc. Am. 63:753–760.

1884. Pellerin, P., and J. Pilon. 1975. Cycle biologique de *Lestes eurinus* Say (Odonata: Lestidae), methode d'elevage en milieu conditionne. Odonatologica 6:83–96.

1885. Penland, D. R. 1953. A detailed study of the life cycle and respiratory system of a new species of western dobsonfly, *Neohermes aridus*. M. S. thesis, Chico State College, Chico, Calif. 34 pp.

1886. Pennak, R. W. 1978. Freshwater invertebrates of the United States (2nd ed.). J. Wiley & Sons, N.Y. 803 pp.

1887. Percival, E., and H. Whitehead. 1928. Observations on the ova and oviposition of certain Ephemeroptera and Plecoptera. Proc. Leeds Phil. Lit. Soc. 1:271–288.

1888. Percival, E., and H. Whitehead. 1929. A quantitative study of the fauna of some types of streambed. J. Ecol. 17:282–314.

1889. Pereira, C. R. D., and N. H. Anderson. 1982. Observations on the life histories and feeding of *Cinygma integrum* Eaton and *Ironodes nitidus* (Eaton) (Ephemeroptera: Heptageniidae). Melandaria 39:35–45.

1890. Pereira, C. R. D., N. H. Anderson, and T. Dudley. 1982. Gut content analyses of aquatic insects from wood substrates. Melandaria 39:23–33.

1891. Perkins, P. D. 1975. Biosystematics of Western Hemisphere aquatic beetles (Coleoptera: Hydraenidae). Ph.D. diss., University of Maryland, College Park. 765 pp.

1892. Perkins, P. D. 1976. Psammophilous aquatic beetles in southern California: A study of microhabitat preferences with notes on response to stream alteration (Coleoptera: Hydraenidae and Hydrophilidae). Coleopt. Bull. 30:309–324.

1893. Perkins, P. D. 1980. Aquatic beetles of the family Hydraenidae in the Western Hemisphere: classification, biogeography and inferred phylogeny (Insecta: Coleoptera). Quaest. Ent. 16:3–554.

1894. Pescador, M. L., and L. Berner. 1981. The mayfly family Baetiscidae (Ephemeroptera). Part II. Biosystematics of the genus *Baetisca*. Trans. Ann. Ent. Soc. 107:163–228.

1895. Pescador, M. L., and W. L. Peters. 1974. The life history of *Baetisca rogersi* Berner (Ephemeroptera: Baetiscidae). Bull. Fla. State Mus. Biol. Sci. 17:151–209.

1896. Pescador, M. L., and W. L. Peters. 1980. A revision of the genus *Homoeoneuria* (Ephemeroptera: Oligoneuriidae). Trans. Am. Ent. Soc. 106:357–393.

1897. Peters, T. M. 1981. Chap. 23. Dixidae, pp. 329–334. *In* J. F. McAlpine, B. V. Peterson, G. E. Shewell, H. J. Teskey, J. R. Vockeroth, and D. M. Wood (coords.). Manual of Nearctic Diptera, Vol. 1. Res. Branch, Agric. Can. Monogr. 27. Ottawa. 674 pp.

1898. Peters, T. M., and E. F. Cook. 1966. The Nearctic Dixidae (Diptera). Misc. Publ. Ent. Soc. Am. 5:233–278.

1899. Peters, W. L. 1980. Phylogeny of the Leptophlebiidae (Ephemeroptera): An introduction, pp. 33–42. *In* J. F. Flannagan and K. E. Marshall (eds.). Advances in Ephemeroptera biology. Plenum, N.Y. 552 pp.

1900. Peters, W. L., and J. G. Peters, 1977. Adult life and emergence of *Dolania americana* in northwestern Florida (Ephemeroptera: Behningiidae). Int. Revue ges. Hydrobiol. 62:409–438.

1901. Peters, W., and J. Spurgeon. 1971. Biology of the waterboatmen *Kirzousacorixa femorata* (Heteroptera: Corixidae). Am. Midl. Nat. 86:197–207.

1902. Peters, W., and R. Ulbrich. 1973. The life history of the water boatman, *Trichocorisella mexicana* (Heteroptera: Corixidae) (Hem.). Can. Ent. 105:277–282.

1903. Petersen, C. E., and R. G. Wiegert. 1982. Coprophagous nutrition in a population of *Paracoenia bisetosa* (Ephydridae) from Yellowstone National Park, USA. Oikos 39:251–255.

1904. Petersen, R. C. 1974. Life history and bionomics of *Nigronia serricornis* (Say) (Megaloptera: Corydalidae). Ph.D. diss., Michigan State Univ., East Lansing. 210 pp.

1905. Petersen, R. C., and K. W. Cummins. 1974. Leaf processing in a woodland stream ecosystem. Freshwat. Biol. 4:343–368.

1906. Peterson, A. 1934. Entomological techniques. Edwards Bros., Ann Arbor. 435 pp.

1907. Peterson, A. 1948. Larvae of insects. (Lepidoptera and Plant Infesting Hymenoptera). Part I. Edwards Bros., Ann Arbor. 315 pp.

1908. Peterson, A. 1951. Larvae of insects. Part II. Coleoptera, Diptera, Neuroptera, Siphonaptera, Mecoptera, Trichoptera. Edwards Bros., Ann Arbor 416 pp.

1909. Peterson, B. V. 1956. Observations on the biology of Utah black flies (Diptera: Simuliidae). Can Ent. 88:496–507.

1910. Peterson, B. V. 1960. The Simuliidae (Diptera) of Utah, Part I. Keys, original citations, types and distribution. Great Basin Nat. 20:81–104.

1911. Peterson, B. V. 1970. The *Prosimulium* of Canada and Alaska (Diptera: Simuliidae). Mem. Ent. Soc. Can. 69:1–216.

1912. Peterson, B. V. 1977. A synopsis of the genus *Parasimulium* Malloch (Diptera: Simuliidae), with descriptions of one new subgenus and two new species. Proc. Ent. Soc. Wash. 79:96–106.

1913. Peterson, B. V. 1981. Simuliidae, pp. 355–391. *In* J. F. McAlpine, B. V. Peterson, G. E. Shewell, H. J. Teskey, J. R. Vockeroth, and D. M. Wood (coords.). Manual of Nearctic Diptera, Vol. 1. Res. Branch, Agric. Can. Monogr. 27. Ottawa. 674 pp.

1914. Peterson, C. G. J., and P. Boysen Tensen. 1911. Valuation of the sea. I. Animal life of the sea bottom: its food and quantity. Rept. Dan. Biol. Sta. 20:1–76.

1915. Peterson, D. G., and L. S. Wolfe. 1958. The biology and control of black flies (Diptera: Simuliidae) in Canada. Proc. 10th Int. Congr. Ent. 3:551–564.

1916. Philip, C. B. 1931. The Tabanidae (horseflies) of Minnesota, with special reference to their biologies and taxonomy. Univ. Minn. Agric. Exp. Sta. Tech. Bull. 80:1–128.

1917. Philipson, G. N. 1953. A method of rearing Trichoptera larvae collected from swift flowing waters. Proc. R. ent. Soc. Lond. (A) 28:15–16.

1918. Philipson, G. N. 1954. The effect of water flow and oxygen concentration on six species of caddisfly (Trichoptera) larvae. Proc. Zool. Soc. Lond. 124:547–564.

1919. Philipson, G. N. 1977. The undulatory behavior of larvae of *Hydropsyche pellucidula* Curtis and *Hydropsyche siltalai* Dohler, pp. 241–247. *In:* M. I. Crichton (ed.). Proc. 2nd Int. Symp. Trichoptera. Junk, The Hague. 359 pp.

1920. Philipson, G. N., and B. H. S. Moorhouse. 1974. Observations on ventilatory and net-spinning activities of larvae of the genus *Hydropsyche* Pictet (Trichoptera, Hydropsychidae) under experimental conditions. Freshwat. Biol. 4:525–533.

1921. Philipson, G. N., and B. H. S. Moorhouse. 1976. Respiratory behaviour of larvae of four species of the family Polycentropodidae (Trichoptera). Freshwat. Biol. 6:347–353.

1922. Phillips, R. S. 1955. Seeking the secrets of the water springtail. Nature 48:241–243.

1923. Pinder, L. C. V. 1978. A key to the adult males of the British Chironomidae (Diptera). Sci. Publ. Freshwat. Biol. Assoc. 37:1–169.

1924. Ping, C. 1921. The biology of *Ephydra subopaca* Loew. Mem. Cornell Univ. Agric. Exp. Sta. 49:557–616.

1925. Poirrier, M. A. 1969. Some freshwater sponge hosts of Louisiana and Texas spongillaflies, with new locality records. Am. Midl. Nat. 81:573–575.

1926. Poirrier, M. A., and Y. M. Arceneaux. 1972. Studies on southern Sisyridae (spongillaflies) with a key to the third-instar larvae and additional sponge-host records. Am. Midl. Nat. 88:455–458.

1927. Poirrier, M. A., and R. W. Holzenthal. 1980. Records of Spongillaflies (Neuroptera: Sisyridae) from Mississippi. J. Miss. Acad. Sci. 15:1–2.

1928. Polhemus, J. T. 1966. Some Hemiptera new to the United States (Notonectidae, Saldidae). Proc. Ent. Soc. Wash. 68:57.

1929. Polhemus, J. T. 1967. Notes on North American Saldidae (Hemiptera). Proc. Ent. Soc. Wash. 69:24–30.

1930. Polhemus, J. T. 1973. Notes on aquatic and semi-aquatic Hemiptera from the southwestern United States (Insecta: Hemiptera). Great Basin Nat. 33:113–119.

1931. Polhemus, J. T. 1974. The *austrina* group of the genus *Microvelia* (Hemiptera: Veliidae). Great Basin Nat. 34:207–217.

1932. Polhemus, J. T. 1976a. A reconsideration of the status of the genus *Paravelia* Breddin, with other notes and a checklist of species. J. Kans. Ent. Soc. 49:509–513.

1933. Polhemus, J. T. 1976b. Notes on North American Nepidae (Hemiptera: Heteroptera). Pan-Pacif. Ent. 52:204–208.

1934. Polhemus, J. T. 1976c. Shore bugs (Hemiptera: Saldidae, etc.), pp. 225–261. *In* Cheng, L. (ed.). Marine insects. North-Holland, Amsterdam. 581 pp.

1935. Polhemus, J. T. 1977. The biology and systematics of the Saldidae of Mexico and Middle America. Ph.D. diss., University of Colorado, Boulder. 606 pp.

1936. Polhemus, J. T., and H. C. Chapman. 1966. Notes on some Hebridae from the United States with the description of a new species (Hemiptera). Proc. Ent. Soc. Wash. 68:209–211.

1937. Polhemus, J. T., and C. N. McKinnon. 1983. Notes on the Hebridae of the Western Hemisphere with a description of two new species (Heteroptera: Hemiptera). Proc. Ent. Soc. Wash. 85:110–115.

1938. Polhemus, J. T., and M. S. Polhemus. 1976. Aquatic and semiaquatic Heteroptera of the Grand Canyon (Insecta: Hemiptera). Great Basin Nat. 36:221–226.

1939. Pollard, J. E. 1981. Investigator differences associated with a kicking method for sampling macroinvertebrates. J. Freshwat. Ecol. 1:215–224.

1940. Poole, W. C., and K. W. Stewart. 1976. The vertical distribution of macrobenthos within the substratum of the Brazos River, Texas. Hydrobiologia 50:151–160.

1941. Pope, R. D. 1975. Nomenclatural notes on the British Scirtidae (=Helodidae) Entomol. mon. Mag. 111:186–187.

1942. Popham, E. J. 1960. On the respiration of aquatic Hemiptera Heteroptera with special reference to the Corixidae. Proc. Zool. Soc. Lond. 135:209–242.

1943. Popham, E. J. 1962. A repetition of Ege's experiments and a note on the efficiency of the physical gill of *Notonecta* (Hemiptera-Heteroptera). Proc. R. ent. Soc. Lond. (A) 37:154–160.

1944. Popham, E. J. 1964. The migration of aquatic bugs with special reference to the Corixidae (Hemiptera, Heteroptera). Arch. Hydrobiol. 60:450–496.

1945. Popowa, A. N. 1927. Uber die Ernahrung der Trichopterenlarven (*Neureclipsis bimaculata* L. und *Hydropsyche ornatula* McLach). Arch. Wiss. Insektenbiol. 22:147–159.

1946. Porter, T. W. 1950. Taxonomy of the American Hebridae and the natural history of selected species. Ph.D. diss., University of Kansas, Lawrence. 165 pp.

1947. Portier, P. 1911. Recherches physiologiques sur les insectes aquatiques. Arch. Zool. Exp. Gen. 8:89–379.

1948. Portier, P. 1949. La biologie des Lepidopteres. Paul Lechevalier, Paris. 643 pp.

1949. Potter, D. W. B., and M. A. Learner. 1974. A study of the benthic macroinvertebrates of a shallow eutrophic reservoir in South Wales with emphasis on the Chironomidae (Diptera); their life histories and production. Arch. Hydrobiol. 74:186–226.

1950. Powell, J. A. 1964. Biological and taxonomic studies on tortricine moths, with reference to the species in California. Univ. Calif. Publ. Ent. 32:1–317.

1951. Powers, C. F., and A. Robertson. 1967. Design and evaluation of an all-purpose benthos sampler, pp. 126–131. *In* J. C. Ayers and D. C. Chandler (eds.). Studies on the environment and eutrophication of Lake Michigan. Univ. Mich. Great Lakes Res. Div. Spec. Rept. 30. 163 pp.

1952. Pritchard, G. 1964. The prey of dragonfly larvae (Odonata: Anisoptera) in ponds in northern Alberta. Can. J. Zool. 42:785–795.

1953. Pritchard, G. 1976. Growth and development of larvae and adults of *Tipula sacra* Alexander (Insecta: Diptera) in a series of abandoned beaver ponds. Can. J. Zool. 54:266–284.

1954. Pritchard, G. 1978. Study of dynamics of populations of aquatic insects: the problem of variability in life history exemplified by *Tipula sacra* Alexander (Diptera; Tipulidae). Verh. Int. Verein. Limnol. 20:2634–2640.

1955. Pritchard, G. 1980a. Life budgets for a population of *Tipula sacra* (Diptera: Tipulidae). Ecol. Ent. 5:165–173.

1956. Pritchard, G. 1980b. The life cycle of *Argia vivida* Hagen in the northern part of its range (Zygoptera: Coenagrionidae). Odonatologica 9:101–106.

1957. Pritchard, G. 1983. Biology of Tipulidae. Ann. Rev. Ent. 28:1–22.

1958. Pritchard, G., and H. A. Hall. 1971. An introduction to the biology of craneflies in a series of abandoned beaver ponds, with an account of the life cycle of *Tipula sacra* Alexander (Diptera: Tipulidae). Can. J. Zool. 49:467–482.

1959. Pritchard, G., and T. G. Leischner. 1973. The life history and feeding habits of *Sialis cornuta* Ross in a series of abandoned beaver ponds (Insecta: Megaloptera). Can. J. Zool. 51:121–131.

1960. Pritchard, G., and P. J. Scholefield. 1980. An adult emergence trap for use in small shallow ponds. Mosquito News 40:294–296.

1961. Pritchard, G., and M. Stewart. 1982. How cranefly larvae breathe. Can. J. Zool. 60:310–317.

1962. Proctor, D. L. C. 1973. The effect of temperature and photoperiod in Odonata. Can J. Zool. 51:1165–1170.

1963. Provonsha, A. V., and W. P. McCafferty. 1975. New techniques for associating the stages of aquatic insects. Great Lakes Ent. 8:105–109.

1964. Provost, M. W., and N. Branch. 1959. Food of chironomid larvae in Polk County Lakes. Fla. Ent. 42:49–62.

1965. Pruess, N. C. 1968. Checklist of Nebraska Odonata. Proc. N. Cent. Br. Ecol. Soc. Am. 22:112.

1966. Pucat, A. M. 1965. The functional morphology of the mouthparts of some mosquito larvae. Quaest. Ent. 1:41–86.

1967. Puchkova, L. V. 1969. On the trophic relationships of water crickets (Corixidae). Zool. Zh. 48:1581–1583.

1968. Pupedis, R. J. 1978. Tube feeding by *Sisyridivora cavigena* (Hymenoptera: Pteromalidae) on *Climacia areolaris* (Neuroptera: Sisyridae). Ann. Ent. Soc. Am. 71:773–775.

1969. Puri, I. M. 1925. On the life history and structure of the early stages of Simuliidae (Diptera: Nematocera). Parasitology 17:295–334.

1970. Quail, A. 1904. On the tubercles of thorax and abdomen in first larval stage of Lepidoptera. Entomologist 37:269.

1971. Quate, L. W. 1955. A revision of the Psychodidae (Diptera) in American north of Mexico. Univ. Calif. Publ. Ent. 10:103–273.

1972. Quate, L. W., and J. R. Vockeroth. 1981. Chap. 17. Psychodidae, pp. 293–300. *In* J. F. McAlpine, B. V. Peterson, G. E. Shewell, H. J. Teskey, J. R. Vockeroth, and D. M. Wood (coords.). Manual of Nearctic Diptera, Vol. 1. Res. Branch, Agric. Can. Monogr. 27. Ottawa. 674 p.

1973. Quate, L. W. and W. W. Wirth. 1951. A taxonomic revision of the genus *Maruina* (Diptera: Psychodidae). Wasmann J. Biol. 9:151–166.

1974. Quinby, G. E., R. E. Serfling, and J. K. Neel. 1944. Distribution and prevalence of the mosquitoes of Kentucky. J. Econ. Ent. 37:547–550.

1975. Quinlan, J. 1967. The brachypterous genera and species of Eucoilidae (Hymenoptera), with descriptions and figures of some type species. Proc. R. ent. Soc. Lond. (B) 36:1–10.

1976. Rabeni, C. F., and K. E. Gibbs. 1978. Comparison of two methods used by divers for sampling benthic invertebrates in deep rivers. J. Fish. Res. Bd. Can. 35:332–336.

1977. Rabeni, C. F., and G. W. Minshall. 1977. Factors affecting microdistribution of stream benthic insects. Oikos 29:33–43.

1978. Radford, D. S., and R. Hartland-Rowe. 1971. The life-cycles of some stream insects (Ephemeroptera, Plecoptera) in Alberta. Can. Ent. 103:609–617.

1979. Radinovsky, S. 1964. Cannibal of the pond. Nat. Hist. 73:16–25.

1980. Rahn, H., and C. V. Paganelli. 1968. Gas exchange in gas gills of diving insects. Resp. Physiol. 5:145–164.

1981. Randolph, N. M., and K. O'Neill. 1944. The mosquitoes of Texas. Texas State Hlth. Dept. 100 pp.

1982. Rankin, K. P. 1935. Life history of *Lethocerus americanus* Leidy (Belostomatidae, Hemiptera). Univ. Kans. Sci. Bull. 22:479–491.

1983. Rapoport, E. H., and L. Sanchez. 1963. On the epineuston or superaquatic fauna. Oikos 14:96–109.

1984. Rau, G. H., and N. H. Anderson. 1981. Use of $^{13}C/^{12}C$ to trace dissolved and particulate organic matter utilization by populations of an aquatic invertebrate. Oecologia 48:19–21.

1985. Rawat, B. L. 1939. On the habits, metamorphosis and reproductive organs of *Naucoris cimicoides* L. (Hemiptera-Heteroptera). Trans. R. ent. Soc. Lond. 88:119–138.

1986. Raybould, J. N. 1967. A method of rearing *Simulium damnosum* Theobald (Diptera: Simuliidae) under artificial conditions. Bull. World Health Org. 37:447–453.

1987. Raybould, J. N., and J. Grunewald. 1975. Present progress towards the laboratory colonization of African Simuliidae (Diptera). Tropenmed. Parasit. 26:155–168.

1988. Raybould, J. N., and H. K. Mhiddin. 1974. A simple technique for maintaining *Simulium* adults, including onchocerciasis vectors, in the laboratory. Bull. World Health Org. 51:309–310.

1989. Rees, B. E., and G. F. Ferris. 1939. The morphology of *Tipula reesi* Alexander (Diptera: Tipulidae). Microentomology 4:143–178.

1990. Rees, D. M. 1943. The mosquitoes of Utah. Bull. Univ. Utah 33:1–99.

1991. Reger, S. J., C. F. Brothersen, T. G. Osborn, and W. T. Helm. 1982. Rapid and effective processing of macroinvertebrate samples. J. Freshwat. Ecol. 1:451–465.

1992. Rehn, J. A. G., and D. C. Eades. 1961. The tribe Leptysmini (Orthoptera: Acrididae: Cyrtacanthacridinae) as found in North America and Mexico. Proc. Acad. Nat. Sci. Phila. 113:81–134.

1993. Rehn, J. A. G., and H. J. Grant. 1961. A monograph of the Orthoptera of North America (north of Mexico). Monogr. Acad. Nat. Sci. Phila. 12:1–257.

1994. Rehn, J. A. G. and M. Hebard. 1915a. Studies in American Tettigoniidae (Orthoptera). IV. A synopsis of the species of the genus *Orchelimum*. Trans. Am. Ent. Soc. 41:11–83.

1995. Rehn, J. A. G., and M. Hebard. 1915b. Studies in American Tettigoniidae (Orthoptera); V. A synopsis of the species of the genus *Conocephalus* found in North America north of Mexico. Trans. Am. Ent. Soc. 41:155–224.

1996. Reice, S. R. 1980. The role of substratum in benthic macroinvertebrate microdistribution and litter decomposition in a woodland stream. Ecology 61:580–590.

1997. Reichart, C. V. 1949. An ecological and taxonomic study of the aquatic insects of Blacklick Creek (Franklin County, Ohio). Abstr. Doct. Dissert., Ohio State Univ. 56:105–111.

1998. Reichart, C. V. 1971. A new *Buenoa* from Florida. Fla. Ent. 54:311–313.

1999. Reichart, C. V. 1976. Aquatic Hemiptera of Rhode Island. Part I. Notonectidae. Biol. Notes, Providence College 1:1–15.

2000. Reichart, C. V. 1977. Aquatic Hemiptera of Rhode Island. Part II. Naucoridae. Biol. Notes, Providence College 2:1–4.

2001. Reichart, C. V. 1978. Aquatic Hemiptera of Rhode Island. Part III. Belostomatidae. Biol. Notes, Providence College 3:1–10.

2002. Reid, G. K. 1965. Ecology of inland waters and estuaries. Reinhold Publ. Co., N.Y. 375 pp.

2003. Reisen, W. K. 1973. Invertebrate and chemical serial progression in temporary pool communities at Turner's Falls, Murray County, Oklahoma. J. Kans. Ent. Soc. 46:294–301.

2004. Reisen, W. K. 1975. Quantitative aspects of *Simulium virgatum* Coq. and *S.* species life history in a southern Oklahoma stream. Ann. Ent. Soc. Am. 68:949–954.

2005. Reisen, W. K. 1975. The ecology of Honey Creek, Oklahoma: spatial and temporal distributions of the macroinvertebrates. Proc. Okla. Acad. Sci. 55:25–31.

2006. Reiss, F. 1968. Okologische und systematische Untersuchungen und Chironomiden (Diptera) des Bodensees. Ein Beitrag zur lacustrischen Chironomidenfauna des nordlichen Alpenvorlandes. Arch. Hydrobiol. 64:176–323.

2007. Remmert, H. 1962. Der Schlupfrhythmus der Insekten. Franz Steiner, Wiesbaden. 73 pp.

2008. Rempel, J. G. 1936. The life history and morphology of *Chironomus hyperboreus*. J. Biol. Bd. Can. 2:209–220.

2009. Rempel, J. G. 1953. The mosquitoes of Saskatchewan. Can. J. Zool. 31:433–509.

2010. Rempel, J. G. 1975. The evolution of the insect head: The endless dispute. Quaest. Ent. 11:7–25.

2011. Renn, C. E. 1941. The food economy of *Anopheles quadrimaculatus* and *A. crucians* larvae. pp. 329–342. *In* A symposium on hydrobiology. Univ. Wisc. Press, Madison. 405 pp.

2012. Rennie, J. 1917. On the biology and economic significance of *Tipula paludosa*. Ann. Appl. Biol. 3:116–137.

2013. Rensing, L. 1962. Bietrage zur vergleichenden Morphologie, Physiologie und Ethologie der Wasserlaufer (Gerroidea). Zool. Beitr. 7:447–485.

2014. Resh, V. H. 1972. A technique for rearing caddisflies (Trichoptera). Can. Ent. 104:1959–1961.

2015. Resh, V. H. 1975. A distributional study of the caddisflies of Kentucky. Trans. Ky. Acad. Sci. 36:6–16.

2016. Resh, V. H. 1976a. Life cycles of invertebrate predators of freshwater sponge, pp. 299–314. *In* F. W. Harrison and R. R. Cowden (eds.). Aspects of sponge biology. Academic, N.Y. 354 pp.

2017. Resh, V. H. 1976b. The biology and immature stages of the caddisfly genus *Ceraclea* in eastern North America (Trichoptera: Leptoceridae). Ann. Ent. Soc. Am. 69:1039–1061.

2018. Resh, V. H. 1976c. Life histories of coexisting species of *Ceraclea* caddisflies (Trichoptera: Leptoceridae): The operation of independent functional units in a stream ecosystem. Can. Ent. 108:1303–1318.

2019. Resh, V. H. 1977. Habitat and substrate influences on population and production dynamics of a stream caddisfly, *Ceraclea ancylus* (Leptoceridae). Freshwat. Biol. 7:261–277.

2020. Resh, V. H. 1979a. Sampling variability and life history features: Basic considerations in the design of aquatic insect studies. J. Fish. Res. Bd. Can. 36:290–311.

2021. Resh, V. H. 1979b. Biomonitoring, species diversity indices, and taxonomy, pp. 241–253. *In* J. F. Grassle, G. P. Patil, W. K. Smith, and C. Taillie (eds.). Ecological diversity in theory and practice. Internat. Coop. Publ. House, Fairland, Md. 365 pp.

2022. Resh, V. H. and K. H. Haag. 1974. New records of parasitism of caddisflies by erythraeid mites. J. Parasit. 60:382–383.

2023. Resh, V. H., J. C. Morse, and J. D. Wallace. 1976. The evolution of the sponge feeding habit in the caddisfly genus *Ceraclea* (Trichoptera: Leptoceridae). Ann. Ent. Soc. Am. 69:937–941.

2024. Resh, V. H., and D. M. Rosenberg (eds.). 1984. The ecology of aquatic insects. Praeger Publishers, N.Y. 625 p.

2025. Resh, V. H., and J. D. Unzicker. 1975. Water quality monitoring and aquatic organisms: the importance of species identification. J. Wat. Poll. Contr. Fed. 47:9–19.

2026. Rhame, R. E., and K. W. Stewart. 1976. Life cycles and food habits of three Hydropsychidae (Trichoptera) species in the Brazos River, Texas. Trans. Am. Ent. Soc. 102:65–99.

2027. Rice, L. A. 1954. Observations on the biology of ten notonectoid species found in the Douglas Lake, Michigan region. Am. Midl. Nat. 51:105–132.

2028. Richards, O. W. 1956. Hymenoptera, introduction and keys to families. Handbooks for identification of British insects 6 (pt. 1) 94 pp.

2029. Richardson, J. W., and A. R. Gaufin. 1971. Food habits of some Western stonefly nymphs. Trans. Am. Ent. Soc. 97:91–121.

2030. Richardson, M. Y., and D. C. Tarter. 1976. Life histories of *Stenonema vicarium* (Walker) and *S. tripunctatum* (Banks) in a West Virginia stream (Ephemeroptera:Heptageniidae). Am. Midl. Nat. 95:1–9.

2031. Richardson, R. E. 1928. The bottom fauna of the middle Illinois River, 1913–1925. Bull. Ill. Nat. Hist. Surv. 8:363–522.

2032. Richmond, E. A. 1920. Studies on the biology of the aquatic Hydrophilidae. Bull. Am. Mus. Nat. Hist. 42:1–94.

2033. Ricker, W. E. 1943. Stoneflies of southwestern British Columbia. Ind. Univ. Publ. Sci. Ser. 12:1–145.

2034. Ricker, W. E. 1944. Some Plecoptera from the far North. Can. Ent. 76:174–185.

2035. Ricker, W. E. 1945. A first list of Indiana stoneflies (Plecoptera). Proc. Ind. Acad. Sci. 54:225–230.

2036. Ricker, W. E. 1946. Some prairie stoneflies (Plecoptera). Trans. Roy. Can. Inst. 26:3–8.

2037. Ricker, W. E. 1947. Stoneflies of the Maritime Provinces and Newfoundland. Trans. Roy. Can. Inst. 26:401–414.

2038. Ricker, W. E. 1949. The North American species of *Paragnetina* (Plecoptera, Perlidae). Ann. Ent. Soc. Am. 42:279–288.

2039. Ricker, W. E. 1952. Systematic studies in Plecoptera. Ind. Univ. Publ. Sci. Ser. 18:1–200.

2040. Ricker, W. E. 1959a. The species of *Isocapnia* Banks (Insecta, Plecoptera, Nemouridae). Can. J. Zool. 37:639–653.

2041. Ricker, W. E. 1959b. Plecoptera, pp. 941–957. *In* W. T. Edmondson (ed.). Freshwater biology. John Wiley & Sons, N.Y. 1248 pp.

2042. Ricker, W. E., R. Malouin, P. Harper, and H. H. Ross. 1968. Distribution of Quebec stoneflies (Plecoptera). Nat. Can. 95:1085–1123.

2043. Ricker, W. E. and H. H. Ross. 1968. North American species of *Taeniopteryx* (Plecoptera, Insecta). J. Fish. Res. Bd. Can. 25:1423–1439.

2044. Ricker, W. E., and H. H. Ross. 1969. The genus *Zealeuctra* and its position in the family Leuctridae. Can. J. Zool. 47:1113–1127.

2045. Ricker, W. E., and H. H. Ross. 1975. Synopsis of the Brachypterinae (Insecta: Plecoptera: Taeniopterygidae). Can. J. Zool. 53:132–153.

2046. Ricker, W. E., and G. G. E. Scudder. 1975. An annotated checklist of the Plecoptera (Insecta) of British Columbia. Syesis 8:333–348.

2047. Riek, E. F. 1970. Hymenoptera, pp. 867–983. *In* Insects of Australia. Melbourne Univ. Press, Melbourne. 1029 pp.

2048. Riek, E. F. 1971. The origin of insects. Proc. 13th Int. Congr. Ent. 13:292–293.

2049. Ries, M. D. 1967. Present state of knowledge of the distribution of Odonata in Wisconsin. Proc. N. Cent. Br. Ent. Soc. Am. 22:113–115.

2050. Ries, M. D. 1969. Odonata new to the Wisconsin list. Mich. Ent. 2:22–27.

2051. Riley, C. F. C. 1918. Food of aquatic Hemiptera. Science 48:545–547.

2052. Riley, C. V. 1874. Descriptions and natural history of two insects which brave the dangers of *Sarracenia variolaris*. Trans. St. Louis Acad. Sci. 3:235–240.

2053. Riley, C. V. 1879. On the larval characteristics of *Corydalus* and *Chauliodes* and on the development of *Corydalus cornutus*. Can. Ent. 11:96–98.

2054. Rimski-Korsakov, M. N. 1917. Observations biologiques sur les Hymenopteres aquatiques. Rev. Russe Ent. 16:209–225.

2055. Rimski-Korsakov, M. N. 1940. Key to the freshwater Collembola of U.S.S.R. with descriptive notes. Freshwat. Life, U.S.S.R. 1:108–110.

2056. Ris, F. 1909–1916. Libellulinen. Collections zoologiques du Baron Edm. de Selys Longchamps. Impr. Acad. Hayez, Brussels 9–13:1–1245.

2057. Ris, F. 1930. A revision of the libelluline genus *Perithemis* (Odonata). Misc. Publ. Univ. Mich. Mus. Zool. 21:1–50.

2058. Roback, S. 1978. The immature chironomids of the eastern United States III. Tanypodinae-Anatopyniini, Macropelopiini and Natarsiini. Proc. Acad. Nat. Sci. Philadelphia 129:151–202.

2059. Roback, S. S. 1953. Savannah River tendipedid larvae (Diptera: Tendipedidae-Chironomidae). Proc. Acad. Nat. Sci. Philadelphia 105:91–132.

2060. Roback, S. S. 1957. The immature tendipedids of the Philadelphia area. Monogr. Acad. Nat. Sci. Philadelphia 9:1–152.

2061. Roback, S. S. 1968. The immature stages of the genus *Tanypus* Meigen (Diptera: Chironomidae: Tanypodinae). Trans. Am. Ent. Soc. 94:407–428.

2062. Roback, S. S. 1969. Notes on the food of Tanypodinae larvae. Ent. News 80:13–18.

2063. Roback, S. S. 1971. The adults of the subfamily Tanypodinae in North America (Diptera: Chironomidae). Monogr. Acad. Nat. Sci. Philadelphia 17:1–410.

2064. Roback, S. S. 1976. The immature chironomids of the eastern United States. I. Introduction and Tanypodinae—Coelotanypodini. Proc. Acad. Nat. Sci. Philadelphia 127:147–201.

2065. Roback, S. S., and J. W. Richardson. 1969. The effects of acid mine drainage on aquatic insects. Proc. Acad. Nat. Sci. Philadelphia 21:81–107.

2066. Roback, S. S., and M. J. Westfall, Jr. 1967. New records of Odonata nymphs from the United States and Canada with water quality data. Trans. Am. Ent. Soc. 93:101–124.

2067. Robert, A. 1963. Les libellules du Quebec. Bull. Sta. Biol. Mt. Tremblant Quebec 1:1–223.

2068. Roberts, C. H. 1895. The species of *Dineutes* of America north of Mexico. Trans. Ent. Soc. Am. 22:279–288.

2069. Roberts, C. H. 1913. Critical notes on the Haliplidae. J. N. Y. Ent. Soc. 21:91–123.

2070. Roberts, D. R., L. W. Smith, and W. R. Enns. 1967. Laboratory observations on predation activities of *Laccophilus* beetles on the immature stages of some dipterous pests found in Missouri oxidation lagoons. Ann. Ent. Soc. Am. 60:908–910.

2071. Roberts, M. J. 1970. The structure of the mouthparts of syrphid larvae (Diptera) in relation to feeding habits. Acta Zool. (Stockholm) 51:43–65.

2072. Roberts, M. J. 1971. The structure and mouthparts of some calypterate dipteran larvae in relation to their feeding habits. Acta Zool. (Stockholm) 52:171–188.

2073. Roberts, R. H. 1966. A technique for rearing the immature stage of Tabanidae (Diptera). Ent. News 77:79–82.

2074. Roberts, R. H., and R. J. Dicke. 1964. The biology and taxonomy of some immature Nearctic Tabanidae (Diptera). Ann. Ent. Soc. Am. 57:31–40.

2075. Robinson, H. and J. R. Vockeroth. 1981. Chap. 48. Dolichopodidae, pp. 625–639. *In* J. F. McAlpine, B. V. Peterson, G. E. Shewell, H. J. Teskey, J. R. Vockeroth, and D. M. Wood (coords.). Manual of Nearctic Diptera, Vol. 1. Res. Branch Agric. Can. Monogr. 27. Ottawa. 647 p.

2076. Robles, C. 1982. Disturbance and predation in an assemblage of herbivorous Diptera and algae on rocky shores. Oecologia 54:23–31.

2077. Robles, C. D., and J. Cubit. 1981. Influence of biotic factors in an intertidal community: Dipteran larvae grazing on algae. Ecology 62:1536–1547.

2078. Roby, K. B., J. D. Newbold, and D. C. Erman. 1978. Effectiveness of an artificial substrate for sampling macroinvertebrates in small streams. Freshwat. Biol. 8:1–8.

2079. Rodina, A. G. 1971. The role of bacteria in the feeding of the tendipedid larvae. Trans. Ser., Fish. Res. Bd. Can. 1848.

2080. Rodionov, Z. 1928. *Helophorus micans,* un ennemi des Graminees. Def. Veget. (Leningrad) 4:951–954.

2081. Roemhild, G. 1982. Trichoptera of Montana with distributional and ecological notes. Northwest Sci. 56:8–13.

2082. Rogers, J. S. 1926. On the biology and immature stages of *Gonomyia pleuralis* Williston. Fla. Ent. 10:33–38.

2083. Rogers, J. S. 1927. On the biology and immature stages of *Geranomyia:* I, *Geranomyia rostrata* (Say). Fla. Ent. 11:17–26.

2084. Rogers, J. S. 1930. The summer crane-fly fauna of the Cumberland Plateau in Tennessee. Occ. Pap. Univ. Mich. Mus. Zool. 215:1–50.

2085. Rogers, J. S. 1933. The ecological distribution of the craneflies of northern Florida. Ecol. Monogr. 3:2–74.

2086. Rogers, J. S. 1937. Craneflies, pp. 368–376. *In* J. G. Needham (ed.). Culture methods for invertebrate animals. Comstock, Ithaca. 590 pp.

2087. Rogers, J. S. 1942. The crane-flies (Tipulidae) of the George Reserve, Michigan. Misc. Publ. Univ. Mich. Mus. Zool. 53:1–128.

2088. Rogers, J. S. 1949. The life history of *Megistocera longipennis* (Macquart) (Tipulidae, Diptera), a member of the neuston fauna. Occ. Pap. Mus. Zool. Univ. Mich. 52:1–17.

2089. Rohdendorf, B. 1974. The historical development of Diptera. Transl. from Russian by J. E. Moore, I. Thiele, B. Hocking, H. Oldroyd, and G. Ball. Univ. Alberta Press, Edmonton. 360 pp.

2090. Root, R. B. 1973. Organization of a plant-arthropod association in simple and diverse habitats: The fauna of collards *(Brassica oleracea).* Ecol. Monogr. 67:95–124.

2091. Rose, J. H. 1963. Supposed larva of *Protanyderus vipio* (Osten Sacken) discovered in California (Diptera: Tanyderidae). Pan-Pacif. Ent. 39:272–275.

2092. Rosenberg, D. M. 1978. Practical sampling of freshwater macrozoobenthos: A bibliography of useful texts, reviews, and recent papers. Can. Fish. Mar. Serv. Tech. Rept. 790:1–15.

2093. Rosenberg, D. M., and V. H. Resh. 1982. The use of artificial substrates in the study of freshwater macroinvertebrates, pp. 175–235. *In* J. Cairns, Jr. (ed.). Artificial substrates. Ann Arbor Sci. Publ., Mich. 279 pp.

2094. Rosenberg, D. M., A. P. Wiens, and B. Bilyj. 1980. Sampling emerging Chironomidae (Diptera) with submerged funnel traps in a new northern Canadian reservoir, Southern Indian Lake, Manitoba. Can. J. Fish. Aquat. Sci. 37:927–936.

2095. Rosenberg, D. M., A. P. Wiens, and O. A. Saether. 1977. Life histories of *Cricotopus (Cricotopus) bicinctus* and *C. (C.) machenziensis* (Diptera: Chironomidae) in the Fort Simpson area, Northwest Territories. J. Fish. Res. Bd. Can. 34:247–253.

2096. Ross, D. H., and D. A. Craig. 1980. Mechanisms of fine particle capture by larval black flies (Diptera: Simuliidae). Can. J. Zool. 58:1186–1192.

2097. Ross, D. H., and R. W. Merritt. 1978. The larval instars and population dynamics of five species of blackflies (Diptera: Simuliidae) and their responses to selected environmental factors. Can. J. Zool. 56:163–1642.

2098. Ross, H. H. 1937. Nearctic alder flies of the genus *Sialis* (Megaloptera, Sialidae). Bull. Ill. Nat. Hist. Surv. 21:57–78.

2099. Ross, H. H. 1944. The caddis flies, or Trichoptera, of Illinois. Bull. Ill. Nat. Hist. Surv. 23:1–326.

2100. Ross, H. H. 1946. A review of the Nearctic Lepidostomatidae (Trichoptera). Ann. Ent. Soc. Am. 39:265–291.

2102. Ross, H. H. 1947. The mosquitoes of Illinois. Bull. Ill. Nat. Hist. Surv. 24:1–96.

2102. Ross, H. H. 1948. New species of sericostomatoid Trichoptera. Proc. Ent. Soc. Wash. 50:151–157.

2103. Ross, H. H. 1949. Xiphocentronidae, a new family of Trichoptera. Ent. News 60:1–7.

2104. Ross, H. H. 1950. Synoptic notes on some Nearctic limnephilid caddisflies (Trichoptera, Limnephilidae). Am. Midl. Nat. 43:410–429.

2105. Ross, H. H. 1956. Evolution and classification of mountain caddisflies. Univ. Ill. Press, Urbana. 213 pp.

2106. Ross, H. H. 1959. Trichoptera, pp. 1024–1049. *In* W. T. Edmondson (ed.). Freshwater biology (2nd ed.). John Wiley & Sons, N.Y. 1248 pp.

2107. Ross, H. H. 1963. Stream communities and terrestrial biomes. Arch. Hydrobiol. 59:235–242.

2108. Ross, H. H. 1965a. A textbook of Entomology (3rd ed.). John Wiley & Sons, N.Y. 539 pp.

2109. Ross, H. H. 1965b. The evolutionary history of *Phylocentropus* (Trichoptera: Psychomyiidae). J. Kans. Ent. Soc. 38:398–400.

2110. Ross, H. H. 1967a. Aquatic insects and ecological problems. Bull. Ent. Soc. Am. 13:112–113.

2111. Ross, H. H. 1967b. The evolution and past dispersal of the Trichoptera. Ann. Rev. Ent. 12:169–207.

2112. Ross, H. H. 1974. Biological systematics. Addison-Wesley, Mass. 345 pp.

2113. Ross, H. H., and W. R. Horsfall. 1965. A synopsis of the mosquitoes of Illinois. Biol. Notes Nat. Hist. Surv. Div. St. Ill. 52:1–50.

2114. Ross, H. H., and E. W. King. 1952. Biogeographic and taxonomic studies in *Atopsyche* (Trichoptera, Rhyacophilidae). Ann. Ent. Soc. Am. 45:177–204.

2115. Ross, H. H., and D. R. Merkley. 1950. The genus *Tinodes* in North America. J. Kans. Ent. Soc. 23:64–67.

2116. Ross, H. H., and D. R. Merkley. 1952. An annotated key to the Nearctic males of *Limnephilus* (Trichoptera: Limnephilidae). Am. Midl. Nat. 47:435–455.

2117. Ross, H. H., and W. E. Ricker. 1971. The classification, evolution, and dispersal of the winter stonefly genus *Allocapnia*. Univ. Ill. Biol. Monogr. 45:1–166.

2118. Ross, H. H., and D. C. Scott. 1974. A review of the caddisfly genus *Agarodes,* with descriptions of new species (Trichoptera: Sericostomatidae). J. Ga. Ent. Soc. 9:147–155.

2119. Ross, H. H., and G. J. Spencer. 1952. A preliminary list of the Trichoptera of British Columbia. Proc. Ent. Soc. Brit. Columbia 48:43–51.

2120. Ross, H. H., and J. D. Unzicker. 1977. The relationships of the genera of American Hydropsychinae as indicated by phallic structures (Trichoptera, Hydropsychidae). J. Ga. Ent. Soc. 12:298–312.

2121. Ross, H. H., and J. B. Wallace. 1974. The North American genera of the family Sericostomatidae (Trichoptera). J. Ga. Ent. Soc. 9:42–48.

2122. Roth, J. C., and S. Parma. 1970. A *Chaoborus* bibliography. Bull. Ent. Soc. Am. 16:100–110.

2123. Roy, D., and P. P. Harper. 1975. Nouvelles mentions de trichoptères du Quebéc et description de *Limnephilus nimmoi* sp. nov. (Limnephilidae). Can. J. Zool. 53:1080–1088.

2124. Roy, D., and P. P. Harper. 1979. Liste préliminaire des Trichopterès (insectes) du Québec. Ann. Ent. Soc. Québec 24:148–172.

2125. Roy, D., and P. P. Harper. 1980. Females of the Nearctic *Molanna* (Trichoptera: Molannidae). Proc. Ent. Soc. Wash. 82:229–236.

2126. Rozeboom, L. E. 1942. The mosquitoes of Oklahoma. Okla. Agric. Exp. Sta. Tech. Bull. 16:1–56.

2127. Rozkosny, R. 1965. Neue Metamorphosestadien mancher *Tetanocera*—Arten (Diptera, Sciomyzidae). Zool. Listy 14:367–371.

2128. Rozkosny, R., and L. V. Knutson. 1970. Taxonomy, biology, and immature stages of Palearctic *Pteromicra*, snail-killing Diptera (Sciomyzidae). Ann. Ent. Soc. Am. 63:1434–1459.

2129. Ruhoff, E. A. 1968. Bibliography and index to scientific contributions of Carl J. Drake for the years 1914–1967. Bull. U.S. Nat. Mus. 267:1–81.

2130. Runyan, J. T., and D. L. Deonier. 1979. A comparative study of *Pseudohecamede* and *Allotrichoma* (Diptera: Ephydridae). pp. 123–137. *In* D. L. Deonier (ed.). First symposium on the systematics and Ecology of Ephydridae (Diptera). N. Am. Benthol. Soc. 147 pp.

2131. Rupprecht, R. 1967. Das Trommeln der Plecopteren. Z. Vergl. Physiol. 59:38–71.

2132. Rupprecht, R. 1972. Dialektbildung bei den Trommelsignalen von *Diura* (Plecoptera). Oikos 23:410–412.

2133. Rupprecht, R. 1977. Nachweis von Trommelsignalen bei einem europaischen Vertreter der Steinfliegen-familie Leuctridae (Plecoptera). Ent. Germ. 3:333–336.

2134. Ruschka, F., and A. Thienemann. 1913. Zur Kenntnis der Wasser-Hymenopteren. A Wiss. Insektenbiol. 9:48–52, 82–87.

2135. Ruttner, F. 1953. Fundamentals of limnology (Translated by D. G. Frey and F. E. J. Fry). Univ. of Toronto Press, Toronto, Canada. 242 pp.

2136. Ryker, L. C. 1972. Acoustic behavior of four sympatric species of water scavenger beetles (Coleoptera, Hydrophilidae, *Tropisternus*). Occ. Pap. Mus. Zool. Univ. Mich. 666:1–19.

2137. Ryker, L. C. 1975a. Calling chirps in *Tropisternus natator* (D'Orchymont) and *T. lateralis nimbatus* (Say) (Coleoptera: Hydrophilidae). Ent. News 86:179–186.

2138. Ryker, L. C. 1975b. Observations on the life cycle and flight dispersal of a water beetle, *Tropisternus ellipticus* LeConte, in western Oregon (Coleoptera: Hydrophilidae). Pan-Pacif. Ent. 51:184–194.

2139. Ryker, L. C. 1976. Acoustic behavior of *Tropisternus ellipticus, T. columbianus,* and *T. lateralis limbalis* in western Oregon (Coleoptera: Hydrophilidae). Coleopt. Bull. 30:147–156.

2140. Saether, O. A. 1969. Some Nearctic Podonominae, Diamesinae, and Orthocladiinae (Diptera: Chironomidae). Bull. Fish. Res. Bd. Can. 170:1–154.

2141. Saether, O. A. 1972. Chaoboridae, pp. 257–280. *In* H. J. Elster and W. Ohle (eds.). Das Zooplankton der Binnengewasser. Die Binnengewasser 26 Stuttgart, E. Schweizebart'sche Verlagsbuchhandlung. 294 pp.

2142. Saether, O. A. 1975. Two new species of *Protanypus* Kieffer, with keys to Nearctic and Palaearctic species of the genus (Diptera: Chironomidae). J. Fish. Res. Bd. Can. 32:367–388.

2143. Saether, O. A. 1977. Taxonomic studies on Chironomidae: *Nanocladius, Pseudochironomus* and the *Harnischia* complex. Bull. Fish. Res. Bd. Can. 196:1–143.

2144. Saether, O. A. (ed.). 1979. Recent developments in chironomid studies (Diptera: Chironomidae). Ent. Scand. 10:1–150.

2145. Saether, O. A. 1980a. Glossary of chironomid morphology terminology (Diptera: Chironomidae). Ent. Scand., Suppl. 14:1–51.

2146. Saether, O. A. 1980b. The influence of eutrophication on deep lake benthic invertebrate communities. Prog. Wat. Tech. 12:161–180.

2147. Sailer, R. I. 1948. The genus *Trichocorixa*. Univ. Kans. Sci. Bull. 32:289–407.

2148. Sailer, R. I. 1972. Biological control of aquatic weeds, recent progress. Proc. N.E. Weed Sci. Soc. 26:180–182.

2149. Sailer, R. I., and S. E. Lienk. 1954. Insect predators of mosquito larvae and pupae in Alaska. Mosquito News 14:14–16.

2150. Salmon, J. T. 1964. An index to the Collembola. Roy. Soc. New Zealand 7:1–644.

2151. Salt, G. 1937. The egg-parasite of *Sialis lutaria:* a study of the influence of the host upon a dimorphic parasite. Parasitology 29:539–558.

2152. Sanderson, M. W. 1938. A monographic revision of the North American species of *Stenelmis* (Dryopidae: Coleoptera). Univ. Kans. Sci. Bull. 25:635–717.

2153. Sanderson, M. W. 1953. A revision of the Nearctic genera of Elmidae (Coleoptera). I. J. Kans. Ent. Soc. 26:148–163.

2154. Sanderson, M. W. 1954. A revision of the Nearctic Elmidae (Coleoptera). II. J. Kans. Ent. Soc. 27:1–13.

2155. Sanderson, M. W. 1982a. Aquatic and semiaquatic Heteroptera. pp. 6.1–6.94. *In* A. R. Brigham, W. V. Brigham, and A. Gnilka (eds.). Aquatic insects and oligochaetes of North and South Carolina. Midwest Aquatic Enterprises, Mahomet, Ill. 837 pp.

2156. Sanderson, M. W. 1982b. Gyrinidae, pp. 10.29–10.38. *In* A. R. Brigham, W. U. Brigham, and A. Gnilka (eds.). Aquatic insects and oligochaetes of North and South Carolina. Midwest Aquatic Enterprises, Mahomet, Ill. 837 pp.

2157. Satchell, G. H. 1947. The ecology of the British species of *Psychoda* (Diptera: Psychodidae). Ann. Appl. Biol. 34:611–621.

2158. Satija, G. R. 1959. Food in relation to mouth parts of *Wormaldia occipitalis* Pictet. Res. Bull. Punjab Univ. N.S. 10:169–178.

2159. Satija, R. C., and G. R. Satija. 1959. Food, mouth parts and alimentary canal of *Limnophilus stigma* Curtis. Res. Bull. Punjab Univ. N.S. 11:11–24.

2160. Sattler, W. 1963. Uber den Korperbau, die Okologie und Ethologie der Larvae und Puppe von *Macronema* Pict. (Hydropsychidae). Arch. Hydrobiol. 59:26–60.

2161. Saunders, L. G. 1924. On the life history and the anatomy of the early stage of *Forcipomyia* (Diptera, Nemat., Ceratopogonidae). Parasitology 16:164–213.

2162. Saunders, L. G. 1928. Some marine insects of the Pacific coast of Canada. Ann. Ent. Soc. Am. 21:521–545.

2163. Savan, B. I., and D. L. Gibo. 1974. A mass culture technique ensuring synchronous emergence for *Leucorrhinia intacta* (Hagen) (Anisoptera: Libellulidae). Odonatologica 3:269–272.

2164. Sawchyn, W. E., and N. S. Church. 1974. The life histories of three species of *Lestes* (Odonata:Zygoptera) in Saskatchewan. Can. Ent. 106:1283–1293.

2165. Sawchyn, W. W., and C. Gillott, 1974. The life history of *Lestes congener* (Odonata: Zygoptera) on the Canadian prairies. Can. Ent. 106:367–376.

2166. Schaefer, K. F. 1966. The aquatic and semi-aquatic Hemiptera of Oklahoma. Ph.D. diss., Oklahoma State University, Stillwater. 102 pp.

2167. Schaeffer, C. 1925. Revision of the New World species of the tribe Donaciini of the coleopterous family Chrysomelidae. Bull. Brooklyn Mus. Sci. 3:45–165.

2168. Schaeffer, C. 1928. The North American species of *Hydrothassa* with notes on other Chrysomelidae and a description of new species and a variety (Col.). J. N.Y. Ent. Soc. 36:287–291.

2169. Schafer, D. A. 1950. Life history studies of *Psephenus lecontei* LeC. and *Ectopria nervosa* Melsh. (Coleoptera: Psephenidae: Dascillidae). M. S. thesis, Ohio State University, Columbus 51 pp.

2170. Schaller, F. 1970. I. Uberordnung und 1. Ordnung Collembola (Springschwanze). Handb. Zool. 4:1–72.

2171. Scheiring, J. F. 1974. Diversity of shore flies (Diptera: Ephydridae) in inland freshwater habitats. J. Kans. Ent. Soc. 47:485–491.

2172. Scheiring, J. F. 1976. Ecological notes on the brine flies of northwestern Oklahoma (Diptera: Ephydridae). J. Kans. Ent. Soc. 49:450–452.

2173. Scheiring, J. F., and B. A. Foote. 1973. Habitat distribution of the shore flies of northeastern Ohio (Diptera: Ephydridae). Ohio J. Sci. 73:152–166.

2174. Schell, D. V. 1943. The Ochteridae of the Western Hemisphere. J. Kans. Ent. Soc. 16:29–47.

2175. Schildknecht, H., R. Sieverdt, and U. Maschivitz. 1966. A vertebrate hormone (cortisone) as defensive substance of the water beetle *Dytiscus marginalis*. Agnew. Chem. Int. Engl. 5:421–422.

2176. Schlinger, E. I. 1975. Diptera, pp. 436–446. *In* R. I. Smith and J. T. Carlton (eds.). Light's manual: Intertidal invertebrates of the central California coast (3rd ed.). Univ. Calif. Press, Berkeley. 716 pp.

2177. Schliwa, W., and F. Schaller. 1963. Die Paarbildung des Springschwanzes *Podura aquatica*. Naturwissenschaften 50:698.

2178. Schmid, F. 1955. Contribution à l'étude des Limnophilidae (Trichoptera). Mitt. Schweiz. Ges. Ent. 28:1–245.

2179. Schmid, F. 1968. La famille des Arctopsychides (Trichoptera). Mem. Ent. Soc. Québec 1:1–84.

2180. Schmid, F. 1970. Le genre *Rhyacophila* et la famille des Rhyacophilidae (Trichoptera). Mem. Ent. Soc. Can. 66:1–230.

2181. Schmid, F. 1980. Genera des Trichoptères du Canada et des États adjacents. Les insectes et arachnides du Canada, Part. 7. Agric. Can. Publ. 1692. 296 pp.

2182. Schmid, F. 1981. Révision des Trichopterès Canadiens. I. La famille des Rhyacophilidae (Annulipalpia). Mem. Soc. Ent. Can. 116:1–83.

2183. Schmid, F., and R. Guppy. 1952. An annotated list of Trichoptera collected on southern Vancouver Island. Proc. Ent. Soc. Brit. Columbia 48:41–42.

2184. Schneider, R. F. 1967. An aquatic rearing apparatus for insects. Turtox News 44:90.

2185. Schoonbee, H. J., and J. H. Swanepoel. 1979. Observations on the use of the radio-isotope ^{32}P in the study of food uptake, pp. 343–352. *In* J. F. Flannagan and K. E. Marshall (eds.). Advances in Ephemeroptera biology. Plenum, N.Y. 552 pp.

2186. Schremmer, F. 1950. Zue Morphologie und funktionellen Anatomie des Larvenkopfes von *Chaoborus (Corethra* auct.) *obscuripes* v.d. Wulp (Diptera, Chaoboridae). Ost, Zool. Z. 2:471–516.

2187. Schremmer, F. 1951. Die Mundteil der Brachycerenlarven und der Kopfbau der Larve von *Stratiomys chamaeleon* L. Ost. Zool. Z. 3:326–397.

2188. Schuh, R. T. 1967. The shore bugs (Hemiptera: Saldidae) of the Great Lakes region. Contr. Am. Ent. Inst. 2:1–35.

2189. Schuster, G. A., and D. A. Etnier. 1978. A manual for the identification of the larvae of the caddisfly genera *Hydropsyche* Pictet and *Symphitopsyche* Ulmer in eastern and central North America (Trichoptera: Hydropsychidae). U.S. Environ. Prot. Agency 600/4–78–060, Cincinnati. 129 pp.

2190. Schuster, R. 1965. Die Okologie der terrestrischen Kleinfauna des Meeresstrandes. Zool. Anz. Suppl. 28:492–521.

2191. Schwardt, H. H. 1937. Methods for collecting and rearing horseflies, pp. 405–409. In J. G. Needham (ed.). Culture methods for invertebrate animals. Comstock, Ithaca. 590 pp.

2192. Schwartz, E. A. 1914. Aquatic beetles, especially *Hydroscapha,* in hot springs in Arizona. Proc. Ent. Soc. Wash. 16:163–168.

2193. Schwarz, P. 1970. Autokologische Untersuchungen zum Lebenszyklus von Setipalpia-Arten (Plecoptera). Arch. Hydrobiol. 67:103–140.

2194. Schweibert, E. 1973. Nymphs. Winchester, N.Y. 339 pp.

2195. Scotland, M. B. 1940. Review and summary of studies of insects associated with *Lemna minor.* J. N.Y. Ent. Soc. 48:319–333.

2196. Scott, D. 1958. Ecological studies on the Trichoptera of the River Dean, Cheshire. Arch. Hydrobiol. 54:340–392.

2197. Scott, D. B., Jr. 1956. Aquatic Collembola, pp. 74–78. In R. L. Usinger (ed.). Aquatic insects of California. Univ. Calif. Press, Berkeley. 508 pp.

2198. Scott, D. B., and R. Yosii. 1972. Notes on some Collembola of the Pacific coast of North America. Contr. Biol. Lab. Kyoto Univ., Kyoto 23:101–114.

2199. Scott, D. C., L. Berner, and A. Hirsch. 1959. The nymph of the mayfly genus *Tortopus* (Ephemeroptera: Polymitarcidae). Ann. Ent. Soc. Am. 52:205–213.

2200. Scott, H. M. 1924. Observations on the habits and life history of *Galerucella nymphaea* (Coleoptera). Trans. Am. Microsc. Soc. 43:11–16.

2201. Scudder, G. G. E. 1965. The Notonectidae (Hemiptera) of British Columbia. Proc. Ent. Soc. Brit. Columbia 62:38–41.

2202. Scudder, G. G. E. 1971a. Comparative morphology of insect genitalia. Ann. Rev. Ent. 16:379–406.

2203. Scudder, G. G. E. 1971b. The Gerridae (Hemiptera) of British Columbia. J. Ent. Soc. Brit. Columbia. 68:3–10.

2204. Scudder, G. G. E. 1976. Water-Boatmen of saline waters (Hemiptera: Corixidae), pp. 263–289. In L. Cheng (ed.). Marine Insects. North Holland, Amsterdam. 581 pp.

2205. Scudder, G. G. E., R. A. Cannings, and K. M. Stuart. 1976. An annotated checklist of the Odonata (Insecta) of British Columbia. Syesis 9:143–162.

2206. Sedell, J. R. 1971. Trophic ecology and natural history of *Neophylax concinnus* and *N. oligius.* Ph.D. diss., University of Pittsburgh, Pittsburgh. 154 pp.

2207. Sedell, J. R., F. J. Triska, and N. M. Triska. 1975. The processing of conifer and hardwood leaves in two coniferous forest streams. I. Weight loss and associated invertebrates. Verh. Int. Verein. Limnol. 19:1617–1627.

2208. Seifert, R. P. 1980. Mosquito fauna of *Heliconia aurea.* J. Anim. Ecol. 49:687–697.

2209. Service, M. W. 1976. Mosquito ecology: Field sampling methods. Halsted, N.Y. 583 pp.

2210. Shapas, T. J., and W. L. Hilsenhoff. 1976. Feeding habits of Wisconsin's predominant lotic Plecoptera, Ephemeroptera and Trichoptera. Great Lakes Ent. 9:175–188.

2211. Sheldon, A. L. 1969. Size relationship of *Acroneuria californica* (Perlidae: Plecoptera) and its prey. Hydrobiologia 34:85–94.

2212. Sheldon, A. L. 1972. Comparative ecology of *Arcynopteryx* and *Diura* in a California stream. Arch. Hydrobiol. 69:521–546.

2213. Sheldon, A. L. 1980. Resource division by perlid stoneflies (Plecoptera) in a lake outlet ecosystem. Hydrobiologia 71:155–161.

2214. Sheldon, A. L., and M. W. Oswood. 1977. Blackfly (Diptera: Simuliidae) abundance in a lake outlet: test of a predictive model. Hydrobiologia 56:113–120.

2215. Shepard, W. D. 1979. Co-occurrence of a marine and freshwater species of Limnichidae (Coleoptera) in Aransas County, Texas. Ent. News 90:88.

2216. Sherberger, F. F., and J. B. Wallace. 1971. Larvae of the southeastern species of *Molanna.* J. Kans. Ent. Soc. 44:217–224.

2217. Sherman, J. D. 1913. Some habits of the Dytiscidae. J. N.Y. Ent. Soc. 21:43–54.

2218. Shewell, G. E. 1958. Classification and distribution of artic and subarctic Simuliidae. Proc. 10th Int. Contr. Ent. 1:635–643.

2219. Short, J. R. T. 1952. The morphology of the head of larval Hymenoptera with special reference to the head of Ichneumonoidea, including a classification of the final instar larvae of Braconidae. Trans. Ent. Soc. Lond. 103:27–84.

2220. Short, J. R. T. 1959. A description and classification of the final instar larvae of the Ichneumonidae. (Insecta, Hymenoptera). Proc. U.S. Nat. Mus. 110:391–511.

2221. Short, J. R. T. 1970. On the classification of the final instar larvae of the Ichneumonidae (Hymenoptera). Trans. Ent. Soc. Lond. Suppl. 122:185–210.

2222. Short, R. A., S. P. Canton, and J. V. Ward. 1980. Detrital processing and associated macroinvertebrates in a Colorado mountain stream. Ecology 61:727–732.

2223. Short, R. A., and J. V. Ward. 1980. Life cycle and production of *Skwala parallela* (Frison) (Plecoptera: Perlodidae) in a Colorado montane stream. Hydrobiologia 69:273–275.

2224. Short, R. A., and J. V. Ward. 1981. Trophic ecology of three winter stoneflies (Plecoptera). Am. Midl. Nat. 105:341–347.

2225. Siegfried, C. A., and A. W. Knight. 1976. Trophic relations of *Acroneuria (Calineuria) california* (Plecoptera: Perlidae) in a Sierra foothill stream. Environ. Ent. 5:575–581.

2226. Sih, A. 1981. Stability, prey density and age/dependent interference in an aquatic insect predator, *Notonecta hoffmanni.* J. Anim. Ecol. 50:625–636.

2227. Siltala, A. J. 1907. Uber die Nahrung der Trichopteren. Acta. Soc. Flora Fauna Fenn. 29:1–34.

2228. Silvey, J. K. G. 1931. Observations on the life history of *Rheumatobates rileyi* (Berg.) (Hemiptera-Gerridae). Pap. Mich. Acad. Sci. Arts Lett. 13:433–446.

2229. Simmons, K. R., and J. D. Edman. 1981. Sustained colonization of the black fly *Simulium decorum* Walker (Diptera: Simuliidae). Can. J. Zool. 59:1–7.

2230. Simmons, K. R., and J. D. Edman. 1982. Laboratory colonization of the human onchocerciasis vector *Simulium damnosum* complex (Diptera: Simuliidae), using an enclosed, gravity-trough rearing system. J. Med. Ent. 19:117–126.

2231. Simmons, P., D. F. Barnes, C. K. Fisher, and G. F. Kaloostian. 1942. Caddisfly larvae fouling a water tunnel. J. Econ. Ent. 35:77–79.

2232. Simpson, K. 1982. A guide to basic taxonomic literature for the genera of North American Chironomidae (Diptera)-adults, pupae, and larvae. Bull. New York State Mus. 447:1–43.

2233. Simpson, K., and R. Bode. 1980. Common larvae of Chironomidae (Diptera) from New York state streams and rivers, with particular reference to the fauna of artificial substrates. Bull. New York State Mus. 439:1–105.

2234. Simpson, K. W. 1975. Biology and immature stages of three species of Nearctic *Ochthera* (Diptera: Ephydridae). Proc. Ent. Soc. Wash. 77:129–155.

2235. Simpson, K. W. 1976. Shore flies and brine flies (Diptera: Ephydridae), pp. 465–495. In L. Cheng (ed.). Marine insects. North Holland, Amsterdam. 581 pp.

2236. Simpson, K. W. 1980. Abnormalities in the tracheal gills of aquatic insects collected from streams receiving chlorinated or crude oil wastes. Freshwat. Biol. 10:581–583.

2237. Sinclair, R. N. 1964. Water quality requirements for elmid beetles with larval and adult keys for the eastern genera. Tenn. Stream Poll. Contr. 15 pp.

2238. Sioli, H. 1975. Tropical river: The Amazon, pp. 461–488. In B. A. Whitton (ed.). River Ecology. Univ. Calif. Press, Berkeley. 725 pp.

2239. Sison, P. 1938. Some observations on the life history, habits, and control of the rice caseworm, *Nymphula depunctalis* Guen. Philippine J. Agr. 9:273–299.

2240. Siverly, R. E. 1972. Mosquitoes of Indiana. Publ. Indiana State Bd. Hlth. 126 pp.

2241. Slack, H. D. 1936. The food of caddis fly (Trichoptera) larvae. J. Anim. Ecol. 5:105–115.

2242. Sladeckova, A. 1962. Limnological investigation methods for the periphyton ("aufwuchs") community. Bot. Rev. 28:286–350.

2243. Sladeckova, A., and E. Pieczynska. 1971. Periphyton, pp. 109–122. *In* W. T. Edmondson and G. G. Winberg (eds.). A manual of methods for the assessment of secondary productivity in fresh waters. IBP Handbook 17. Blackwell, Oxford 358 pp.

2244. Slater, Alex. 1981. Aquatic and semiaquatic Heteroptera in the collection of the State Biological Survey of Kansas. State Biol. Surv. Kans. Tech. Publ. 10:71–88.

2245. Slater, J. A. 1974. A preliminary analysis of the derivation of the Heteroptera fauna of the northeastern United States with special reference to the fauna of Connecticut, 25th Anniv. Mem. Conn. Ent. Soc. pp. 145–213.

2246. Slater, J. A., and R. M. Baranowski. 1978. How to know the true-bugs (Hemiptera-Heteroptera). Wm. C. Brown, Dubuque. 256 pp.

2247. Smetana, A. 1974. Revision of the genus *Cymbiodyta* Bed. (Coleoptera: Hydrophilidae). Mem. Ent. Soc. Can. 93:1–113.

2248. Smetana, A. 1980. Revision of the genus *Hydrochara* Berth. (Coleoptera: Hydrophilidae). Mem. Ent. Soc. Can. 111:1–100.

2249. Smirnov, N. N. 1962. On nutrition of caddis worms *Phryganea grandis* L. Hydrobiologia 19:252–261.

2250. Smith, C. L. 1980. A taxonomic revision of the genus *Microvelia* Westwood (Heteroptera: Veliidae) of North American including Mexico. Ph.D. diss., University of Georgia, Athens. 372 pp.

2251. Smith, C. L., and J. T. Polhemus. 1978. The Veliidae of America north of Mexico—Keys and checklist. Proc. Ent. Soc. Wash. 80:56–68.

2252. Smith, C. N. (ed.). 1966. Insect colonization and mass production. Academic, N.Y. 618 pp.

2253. Smith, E. L. 1970. Biology and structure of the dobsonfly, *Neohermes californicus* (Walker). Pan-Pacif. Ent. 46:142–150.

2254. Smith, G. E., S. G. Breeland, and E. Pickard. 1965. The Malaise trap—a survey tool in medical entomology. Mosquito News 25:398–400.

2255. Smith, J. A., and A. J. Dartnall. 1980. Boundary layer control by water pennies (Coleoptera: Psephenidae). Aquat. Insects 2:65–72.

2256. Smith, L. M., and H. Lowe. 1948. The black gnats of California. Hilgardia 18:157–183.

2257. Smith, L. W., Jr., and W. R. Enns. 1968. A list of Missouri mosquitoes. Mosquito News 28:50–51.

2258. Smith, M. E. 1952. Immature stages of the marine fly *Hypocharassus pruinosus* Wh., with a review of the biology of immature Dolichopodidae. Am. Midl. Nat. 48:421–432.

2259. Smith, R. F., and A. E. Pritchard. 1956. Odonata, pp. 106–153. *In* R. L. Usinger (ed.). Aquatic insects of California. Univ. Calif. Press, Berkeley. 508 pp.

2260. Smith, R. I., and J. T. Carlton (eds.). 1975. Light's manual: Intertidal invertebrates of the central California coast (3rd ed.). Univ. of Calif. Press, Berkeley. 716 pp.

2261. Smith, R. L. 1973. Aspects of the biology of three species of the genus *Rhantus* (Coleoptera: Dytiscidae) with special reference to the acoustical behavior of two. Can. Ent. 105:909–919.

2262. Smith, R. L. 1974. Life history of *Abedus herberti* in central Arizona (Hemiptera: Belostomatidae). Psyche 81:272–283.

2263. Smith, R. L. 1976a. Brooding behavior of a male water bug *Belostoma flumineum* (Hemiptera: Belostomatidae). J. Kans. Ent. Soc. 49:333–343.

2264. Smith, R. L. 1976b. Male brooding behavior of the water bug *Abedus herberti* (Hemiptera: Belostomatidae). Ann. Ent. Soc. Am. 69:740–747.

2265. Smith, S. D. 1965. Distributional and biological records of Idaho caddisflies (Trichoptera). Ent. News 76:242–245.

2266. Smith, S. D. 1968a. The Arctopsychinae of Idaho (Trichoptera: Hydropsychidae). Pan-Pacif. Ent. 44:102–112.

2267. Smith, S. D. 1968b. The *Rhyacophila* of the Salmon River drainage of Idaho with special reference to larvae. Ann. Ent. Soc. Am. 61:655–674.

2268. Smith, W., and A. D. McIntyre. 1954. A spring-loaded bottom sampler. J. Mar. Biol. Ass. U.K. 33:257–264.

2269. Sneath, P. H. A. and R. R. Sokal. 1973. Numerical taxonomy. W. H. Freeman, San Francisco. 573 pp.

2270. Snellen, R. K., and K. W. Stewart. 1979a. The life cycle and drumming behavior of *Zealeuctra claasseni* (Frison) and *Zealeuctra hitei* Ricker and Ross (Plecoptera: Leuctridae) in Texas, USA. Aquat. Insects 1:65–89.

2271. Snellen, R. K., and K. W. Stewart. 1979b. The life cycle of *Perlesta placida* (Plecoptera: Perlidae) in an intermittent stream in Northern Texas. Ann. Ent. Soc. Am. 72:659–666.

2272. Snider, R. J. 1967. An annotated list of the Collembola (springtails) of Michigan. Mich. Ent. 1:179–243.

2273. Snider, R. J., and S. J. Loring. 1982. *Sminthurus incognitus,* new species from Florida (Collembola: Sminthuridae). Fla. Ent. 65:216–221.

2274. Snodgrass, R. E. 1935. Principles of insect morphology. McGraw-Hill, N.Y. 667 pp.

2275. Snodgrass, R. E. 1954. The dragonfly larva. Smithson. Misc. Coll. 123:4175.

2276. Sokal, R. R., and F. J. Rohlf. 1969. Biometry. W. H. Freeman, San Francisco. 776 pp.

2277. Sokal, R. R. and F. J. Rohlf. 1981. Biometry: the principles and practice of statistics in biological research (2nd ed.). W. H. Freeman, San Francisco. 859 pp.

2278. Solem, J. O. 1973. Diel rhythmic pattern of *Leptophlebia marginata* L. and *L. vespertina* L. (Ephemeroptera). Aquilo Ser. Zool. 14:80–83.

2279. Solem, J. O., and V. H. Resh. 1981. Larval and pupal description, life cycle, and adult flight behaviour of the sponge-feeding caddisfly, *Ceraclea nigronervosa* (Retzius), in central Norway. Ent. Scand. 12:311–319.

2280. Sommerman, K. M. 1953. Identification of Alaskan black fly larvae (Diptera, Simuliidae). Proc. Ent. Soc. Wash. 55:258–273.

2281. Soponis, A. R. 1977. A revision of the Nearctic species of *Orthocladius (Orthocladius)* van der Wulp (Diptera: Chironomidae). Mem. Ent. Soc. Can. 102:1–187.

2282. Sorokin, Y. I. 1966. Use of radioactive carbon for the study of the nutrition and food relationship of aquatic animals. Inst. Biol. Vnutr. Vod. Trudy 12:83–132.

2283. Southwood, T. R. E. 1978. Ecological methods with particular reference to the study of insect populations (2nd ed.). Methuen, London. 391 pp.

2284. Spangler, P. J. 1960. A revision of the genus *Tropisternus* (Coleoptera: Hydrophilidae). Ph.D. diss., University of Missouri, Columbia. 365 pp.

2285. Spangler, P. J. 1961. Notes on the biology and distribution of *Sperchopsis tesselatus* (Ziegler), (Coleoptera, Hydrophilidae). Coleopt. Bull. 15:105–112.

2286. Spangler, P. J. 1962. A new species of the genus *Oosternum* and a key to the U.S. species (Coleoptera: Hydrophilidae). Proc. Biol. Soc. Wash. 75:97–100.

2287. Spangler, P. J. 1973. The bionomics, immature stages, and distribution of the rare predaceous water beetle, *Hoperius planatus* (Coleoptera: Dytiscidae). Proc. Biol. Soc. Wash. 86:423–434.

2288. Spangler, P. J., and J. L. Cross. 1972. A description of the egg case and larva of the water scavenger beetle, *Helobata striata* (Coleoptera, Hydrophilidae). Proc. Biol. Soc. Wash. 85:413–418.

2289. Spangler, P. J., and G. W. Folkerts. 1973. Reassignment of *Colpius inflatus* and a description of its larva (Coleoptera: Noteridae). Proc. Biol. Soc. Wash. 86:261–277.

2290. Spence, J. R. 1980. Density estimation for water-striders (Heteroptera: Gerridae). Freshwat. Biol. 10:563–570.

2291. Spence, J. R., and G. G. E. Scudder. 1980. Habitats, life cycles, and guild structure among water striders (Heteroptera: Gerridae) on the Fraser Plateau of British Columbia. Can. Ent. 112:779–792.

2292. Spence, J. R., D. H. Spence, and G. G. E. Scudder. 1980. The effects of temperature on growth and development of water strider species (Heteroptera: Gerridae) of Central British Columbia and implications for species packing. Can. J. Zool. 58:1813–1820.

2293. Spencer, G. J. 1937. Rearing of Collembola, pp. 263. *In* J. G. Needham (ed.). Culture methods for invertebrate animals. Comstock, Ithaca. 590 pp.

2294. Speyer, W. 1958. Lepidopteren-Puppen an Obstgewaechsen und in ihrer naehern Umgebung: Versuch einer Bestimmungseubersicht. Mitt. Biol. Reichsanst. Ld-U. Forstw. 93:1–40.

2295. Spieth, H. T. 1938. A method of rearing *Hexagenia* nymphs (Ephemerida). Ent. News 49:29–32.

2296. Spieth, H. T. 1941. Taxonomic studies on the Ephemeroptera. II. The genus *Hexagenia*. Am. Midl. Nat. 26:233–280.

2297. Spieth, H. T. 1947. Taxonomic studies on the Ephemeroptera: IV. The genus *Stenonema*. Ann. Ent. Soc. Am. 40:87–122.

2298. Spilman, R. L. 1961. On the immature stages of the Ptilodactylidae (Col.). Ent. News 72:105–107.

2299. Spilman, T. J. 1967. The heteromerous intertidal beetles. Pacif. Insects 9:1–21.

2300. Sprague, I. B. 1956. The biology and morphology of *Hydrometra martini* Kirkaldy. Univ. Kans. Sci. Bull. 38:579–693.

2301. Stach, J. 1947. The Apterygoten fauna of Poland in relation to the world fauna of this group of insects. Family: Isotomidae. Acta. Mon. Mus. Nat. Hist. Poland. 482 pp.

2302. Stach, J. 1949a. The Apterygoten fauna of Poland in relation to the world fauna of this group of insects. Families: Neogastruridae and Brachystomellidae. Acta. Mon. Mus. Hist. Nat. Poland. 341 pp.

2303. Stach, J. 1949b. The Apterygoten fauna of Poland in relation to the world fauna of this group of insects. Families: Anuridae and Pseudachorutidae. Acta. Mon. Mus. Nat. Hist. Poland. 122 pp.

2304. Stach, J. 1951. The Apterygoten fauna of Poland in relation to the world fauna of this group of insects. Family: Bilobidae. Acta. Mon. Mus. Nat. Hist. Poland. 97 pp.

2305. Stach, J. 1954. The Apterygoten fauna of this group of insects. Family: Onychiuridae. Acta. Mon. Mus. Nat. Hist. Poland. 219 pp.

2306. Stach, J. 1956. The Apterygoten fauna of Poland in relation to the world fauna of this group of insects. Family: Sminthuridae. Acta. Mon. Mus. Hist. Nat. Poland. 287 pp.

2307. Stach, J. 1957. The Apterygoten fauna of Poland in relation to the world fauna of this group of insects. Families: Neelidae and Dicyrtomidae. Acta. Mon. Mus. Hist. Nat. Poland. 113 pp.

2308. Stach, J. 1960. The Apterygoten fauna of Poland in relation to the world fauna of this group of insects. Tribe: Orchesellini. Acta. Mon. Mus. Hist. Nat. Poland. 151 pp.

2309. Stach, J. 1963. The Apterygoten fauna of Poland in relation to the world fauna of this group of insects. Tribe: Entomobryini. Acta. Mon. Mus. Hist. Nat. Poland. 126 pp.

2310. Stains, G. S., and G. F. Knowlton. 1943. A taxonomic and distributional study of Simuliidae of western United States. Ann. Ent. Soc. Am. 36:259–280.

2311. Stanford, J. A., and A. R. Gaufin. 1974. Hyporheic communities of two Montana rivers. Science 185:700–702.

2312. Stark, B. P. 1979. The stoneflies (Plecoptera) of Mississippi. J. Miss. Acad. Sci. 24:109–122.

2313. Stark, B. P., and R. W. Baumann. 1978. New species of Nearctic *Neoperla* (Plecoptera: Perlidae), with notes on the genus. Great Basin Nat. 38:97–114.

2314. Stark, B. P., and A. R. Gaufin. 1974a. The species of *Calineuria* and *Doroneuria* (Plecoptera: Perlidae). Great Basin Nat. 34:83–94.

2315. Stark, B. P., and A. R. Gaufin. 1974b. The genus *Diploperla* (Plecoptera: Peroldidae). J. Kans. Ent. Soc. 47:433–436.

2316. Stark, B. P., and A. R. Gaufin. 1976a. The Nearctic genera of Perlidae (Plecoptera). Misc. Publ. Ent. Soc. Am. 10:1–80.

2317. Stark, B. P., and A. R. Gaufin. 1979. The stoneflies (Plecoptera) of Florida. Trans. Am. Ent. Soc. 104:391–433.

2318. Stark, B. P., and P. K. Lago. 1980. New records of Nearctic *Sialis* (Megaloptera: Sialidae), with emphasis on Mississippi fauna. Ent. News 91:117–121.

2319. Stark, B. P., B. R. Oblad, and A. R. Gaufin. 1973. An annotated list of the stoneflies (Plecoptera) of Colorado. Ent. News 84:269–277.

2320. Stark, B. P., and K. W. Stewart. 1973. Distribution of stoneflies (Plecoptera) in Oklahoma. J. Kans. Ent. Soc. 46:563–577.

2321. Stark, B. P., and K. W. Stewart. 1981. The Nearctic genera of Peltoperlidae (Plecoptera). J. Kans. Ent. Soc. 54:285–311.

2322. Stark, B. P., and S. W. Szczytko. 1976. The genus *Beloneuria* (Plecoptera: Perlidae). Ann. Ent. Soc. Am. 69:1120–1124.

2323. Stark, B. P., T. A. Wolff, and A. R. Gaufin. 1975. New records of stoneflies (Plecoptera) from New Mexico. Great Basin Nat. 35:97–99.

2324. Statzner, B. 1981. A method to estimate the population size of benthic macroinvertebrates in streams. Oecologia 51:157–161.

2325. Statzner, B., and T. F. Holm. 1982. Morphological adaptations of benthic invertebrates to stream flow—an old question studied by means of a new technique (laser doppler anemometry). Oecologia 53:290–292.

2326. Steele, B. D., and D. C. Tarter. 1977. Distribution of the family Perlidae in West Virginia. Ent. News 88:18–22.

2327. Steelman, C. D. 1976. Effects of external and internal arthropod parasites on domestic livestock production. Ann. Rev. Ent. 21:155–178.

2328. Steelman, C. D., and A. R. Colmer. 1970. Some effects of organic wastes on aquatic insects in impounded habitats. Ann. Ent. Soc. Am. 63:397–400.

2329. Steiner, W. E., Jr., and J. J. Anderson. 1981. Notes on the natural history of *Spanglerogyrus albiventris* Folkerts, with a new distribution record (Coleoptera: Gyrinidae). Pan-Pacif. Ent. 57:124–132.

2330. Steinley, B. A., and J. T. Runyan. 1979. The life history of *Leptopsilopa atrimana* (Diptera: Ephydridae). pp. 139–147. *In* D. L. Deonier (ed.). First symposium on the systematics and ecology of Ephydridae (Diptera). N. Am. Benthol. Soc. 147 pp.

2331. Stewart, K. W., R. W. Baumann, and B. P. Stark. 1974. The distribution and past dispersal of southwestern United States Plecoptera. Trans. Am. Ent. Soc. 99:507–546.

2332. Stewart, K. W., G. P. Friday, and R. E. Rhame. 1973. Food habits of hellgrammite larvae, *Corydalus cornutus* (Megaloptera: Corydalidae), in the Brazos River, Texas. Ann. Ent. Soc. Am. 66:959–963.

2333. Stewart, K. W., and D. W. Huggins. 1977. The stoneflies of Kansas. Tech. Publ. Kans. State Biol. Surv. 4:31–40.

2334. Stewart, K. W., L. E. Milliger, and B. M. Solon. 1970. Dispersal of algae, protozoans, and fungi by aquatic Hemiptera, Trichoptera, and other aquatic insects. Ann. Ent. Soc. Am. 63:139–144.

2335. Stewart, K. W., and B. P. Stark. 1977. Reproductive system and mating of *Hydroperla crosbyi*: a newly discovered method of sperm transfer in Insecta. Oikos 28:84–89.

2336. Stewart, K. W., B. P. Stark, and T. G. Huggins. 1976. The stoneflies (Plecoptera) of Louisiana. Great Basin Nat. 36:366–384.

2337. Stewart, M., and G. Pritchard. 1982. Pharate phases in *Tipula paludosa* (Diptera: Tipulidae). Can. Ent. 114:275–278.

2338. Steyskal, G. C. 1957. A revision of the family Dryomyzidae. Pap. Mich. Acad. Sci. Arts Lett. 42:55–68.

2339. Steyskal, G. C., T. W. Fisher, L. Knutson, and R. E. Orth. 1978. Taxonomy of North American flies of the genus *Limnia* (Diptera: Sciomyzidae). Univ. Calif. Publ. Ent. 83:1–48.

2340. Steyskal, G. C., and L. V. Knutson. 1981. Chap. 47. Empididae, pp. 607–624. *In* J. F. McAlpine, B. V. Peterson, G. E. Shewell, H. J. Teskey, J. R. Vockeroth, and D. M. Wood (coords.). Manual of Nearctic Diptera, Vol. 1. Res. Branch, Agr. Can. Mon. 27. 674 pp.

2341. Stobbart, R. H., and J. Shaw, 1974. Salt and water balance; excretions pp. 361–446. *In* Rockstein (ed.). The physiology of Insecta. (2nd ed.) Vol. V. Academic Press, New York. 648 pp.

2342. Stock, M. W., and J. D. Lattin. 1976. Biology of intertidal *Saldula palustris* (Douglas) on the Oregon coast (Heteroptera: Saldidae). J. Kans. Ent. Soc. 49:313–326.

2343. Stocker, Z. S. J., and D. D. Williams. 1972. A freezing core method for describing the vertical distribution of sediments in a streambed. Limnol. Oceanogr. 17:136–139.

2344. Stockner, J. G. 1971. Ecological energetics and natural history of *Hedriodiscus truquii* (Diptera) in two thermal spring communities. J. Fish. Res. Bd. Can. 28:73–94.

2345. Stojanovich, C. J. 1961. Illustrated key to common mosquitoes of northeastern North America. C. J. Stojanovich, Campbell, Calif. 49 pp.

2346. Stone, A. 1952. The Simuliidae of Alaska (Diptera). Proc. Ent. Soc. Wash. 54:69–96.

2347. Stone, A. 1963. A new *Parasimulium* and further records for the type species (Diptera: Simuliidae). Bull. Brooklyn Ent. Soc. 58:127–129.

2348. Stone, A. 1964a. Guide to the insects of Connecticut. Part VI. The Diptera or true flies of Connecticut. Fasc. 9. Family Simuliidae. Bull. Conn. State Geol. Nat. Hist. Surv. 97:1–117.

2349. Stone, A. 1964b. Guide to the insects of Connecticut. Part VI. The Diptera or true flies of Connecticut. Fasc. 9. Family Thaumaleidae. Bull. Conn. State Geol. Nat. Hist. Surv. 97:119–122.

2350. Stone, A. 1965. Family Simuliidae, pp. 181–189. *In* A. Stone, C. W. Sabrosky, W. W. Wirth, R. H. Foote, and J. R. Coulson (eds.). A catalog of the Diptera of America north of Mexico. U.S. Dept. Agric. Handbk. 276. 1696 pp.

2351. Stone, A. 1981. Culicidae, pp. 341–350. *In* J. F. McAlpine, B. V. Peterson, G. E. Shewell, H. J. Teskey, J. R. Vockeroth, and D. M. Wood. (coords). Manual of Nearctic Diptera. Vol. I. Monogr. 27, Res. Branch, Agric. Can. Monogr 27 Ottawa, 674 pp.

2352. Stone, A., and H. A. Jamnback. 1955. The black flies of New York State (Diptera: Simuliidae). Bull. N.Y. State Mus. 349:1–144.

2353. Stone, A., and B. V. Peterson. 1981. Chap.26. Thaumaleidae, pp. 351–353. *In* J. F. McAlpine, B. V. Peterson, G. E. Shewell, H. J. Teskey, J. R. Vockeroth, and D. M. Wood (coords.). Manual of Nearctic Diptera, Vol. 1. Res. Branch, Agric. Can. Monogr 27. Ottawa, 674 pp.

2354. Stone, A., C. W. Sabrosky, W. W. Wirth, R. H. Foote, and J. R. Coulson. 1965. A catalog of the Diptera of America north of Mexico. U.S. Dep. Agric. Handbk. 276. 1696 pp.

2355. Stone, A., and E. L. Snoddy. 1969. The black flies of Alabama (Diptera: Simuliidae). Bull. Alabama Agric. Exp. Sta. Auburn Univ. 390:1–93.

2356. Stonedahl, G. M., and J. D. Lattin. 1982. The Gerridae or water striders of Oregon and Washington (Hemiptera: Heteroptera). Oregon State Univ. Agric. Exp. Sta. Tech. Bull. 144:1–36.

2357. Stout, R. J. 1981. How abiotic factors affect the distribution of two species of tropical predaceous aquatic bugs (Family: Naucoridae). Ecology 62:1170–1178.

2358. Streams, F. A. 1974. Size and competition in Connecticut *Notonecta*. 25th Anniv. Mem. Connecticut Ent. Soc. pp. 215–225.

2359. Streams, F. A., and S. Newfield. 1972. Spatial and temporal overlap among breeding populations of New England *Notonecta*. Univ. Conn. Occ. Pap. (Biol. Sci. Ser.) 2:139–157.

2360. Strenzke, K. 1955. Thalassabionte und thalassophile Collembola (Lief. 36), pp. 1–52. *In* A. Remane (ed.). Die Tierwelt der Nordund Ostee. Akad., Leipzig.

2361. Strickland, E. H. 1953. An annotated list of the Hemiptera (S.L.) of Alberta. Can. Ent. 85:193–214.

2362. Sturm, H. 1960. Die terrestrischen Puppengehäuse von *Xiphocentron sturmi* Ross (Xiphocentronidae, Trichoptera). Zool. Jb. (Syst.) 87:387–394.

2363. Stuckenberg, B. R. 1973. A new family in the lower Brachycera (Diptera). Ann. Nat. Mus. 21:646–673.

2364. Sturtevant, A. H., and M. R. Wheeler. 1954. Synopsis of Nearctic Ephydridae (Diptera). Trans. Am. Ent. Soc. 79:151–261.

2365. Stys, P. 1970. On the morphology and classification of the family Dipsocoridae s. lat., with particular reference to the genus *Hypsipteryx* Drake (Heteroptera). Acta. Ent. Bohem. 67:21–46.

2366. Sublette, J. E. 1960. Chironomid midges of California I. Chironominae exclusive of Tanytarsini. Proc. U.S. Nat. Mus. 112:197–226.

2367. Sublette, J. E. 1964a. Chironomidae (Diptera) of Louisiana. I. Systematics and immature stages of some benthic chironomids of west-central Louisiana. Tulane Stud. Zool. 11:109–150.

2368. Sublette, J. E. 1964b. Chironomid midges of California II. Tanypodinae, Podonominae and Diamesinae. Proc. U.S. Nat. Mus. 115:85–136.

2369. Sublette, J. E., and M. S. Sublette. 1965. Family Chironomidae, pp. 142–181. *In* A. Stone, C. W. Sabrosky, W. W. Wirth, R. H. Foote, and J. R. Coulson (eds.). A catalog of the Diptera of America north of Mexico. U.S. Dept. Agric. Handbk. 276. 1,696 pp.

2370. Sublette, J. E., and M. S. Sublette. 1967. The limnology of playa lakes on the Llano Estacado, New Mexico and Texas. Southwest. Nat. 12:369–406.

2371. Sublette, M. S., and J. E. Sublette. 1970. Distributional records of mosquitoes in the southern high plains with a checklist of species from New Mexico and Texas. Mosquito News 30:533–538.

2372. Sudia, W. D., and R. W. Chamberlain. 1967. Collection and processing of medically important arthropods for arbovirus isolation. Nat. Commun. Disease Centr., Atlanta. 29 pp.

2373. Sughara, Y. 1938. An observation on the intertidal rock-dwelling beetle *Aegialites stejnegeri sugiharae* Kono in the Kuriles. Ent. World 6:6–12.

2374. Sundholm, A. 1960. On *Diapria* Latreille and allied genera (Hym.: Diapriidae). Opusc. Ent. 25:215–223.

2375. Surber, E. W. 1937. Rainbow trout and bottom fauna production in one mile of stream. Trans. Am. Fish. Soc. 66:193–202.

2376. Surdick, R. F., and K. C. Kim. 1976. Stoneflies (Plecoptera) of Pennsylvania, a synopsis. Bull. Penn. State Univ. Agric. Exp. Sta. 808:1073.

2377. Surtees, G. 1959. Functional and morphological adaptations of the larval mouthparts in the subfamily Culicinae (Diptera) with a review of some related studies by Montchadsky. Proc. R. ent. Soc. Lond. (A) 34:7–16.

2378. Sutton, M. 1951. On the food, feeding mechanism and alimentary canal of Corixidae (Hemiptera, Heteroptera). Proc. Zool. Soc. Lond. 121:465–499.

2379. Svensson, B. W. 1974. Population movements of adult Trichoptera at a south Swedish stream. Oikos 25:157–175.

2380. Svihla, A. 1959. The life history of *Tanypteryx hageni* Selys (Odonata). Trans. Am. Ent. Soc.85:219–232.

2381. Swanson, G. A. 1978. A water column sampler for invertebrates in shallow wetlands. J. Wildl. Manage. 42:670–672.

2382. Swatchek, B. 1958. Die Larvalsystematik der Winkler (Tortricidae und Carposinidae). Abh. Larvalsyst. Insekt. 3. Akad., Berlin 269 pp.

2383. Sweeney, B. W. 1978. Bioenergetic and developmental response of a mayfly to thermal variation. Limnol. Oceanogr. 23:461–477.

2384. Sweeney, B. W., and J. A. Schnack. 1977. Egg development, growth and metabolism of *Sigara alternata* (Say) (Hemiptera: Corixidae) in fluctuating thermal environments. Ecology 58:265–277.

2385. Sweeney, B. W., and R. L. Vannote. 1978. Size variation and the distribution of hemimetabolous aquatic insects: two thermal equilibrium hypotheses. Science 200:444–446.

2386. Sweeney, B. W., and R. L. Vannote. 1981. *Ephemerella* mayflies of White Clay Creek: Bioenergetic and ecological relationships among six coexisting species. Ecology 62:1353–1369.

2387. Swisher, D., and C. Richards, 1971. Selective trout. Crown, N.Y. 184 pp.

2388. Syms, E.E. 1934. Biological notes on British Megaloptera. Proc. Lond. Ent. Nat. Hist. Soc. 35:121–124.

2389. Szczytko, S. W., and K. W. Stewart. 1977. The stoneflies (Plecoptera) of Texas. Trans. Am. Ent. Soc. 103:327–378.

2390. Szczytko, S. W., and K. W. Stewart, 1979. The genus *Isoperla* of western North America; holomorphology and systematics, and a new stonefly genus *Cascadoperla*. Mem. Am. Ent. Soc. 32:1–120.

2391. Tachet, H. 1965a. Recherches sur l'alimentation des larves de *Polycentropus* (Trichoptera) dans leur milieu naturel. Ann. Soc. Ent. France 1:627–633.

2392. Tachet, H. 1965b. Influence du stade larvaire et de la saison sur l'alimentation des larves de *Polycentropus* (Trichoptera) dan des conditions naturelles., Ann. Soc. Ent. France 1:635–640.

2393. Tanner, V. M. 1943. Study of subtribe Hydronomi with description of new species. Great Basin Nat. 4:1–38.

2394. Tarshis, I. B. 1968. Collecting and rearing black flies. Ann. Ent. Soc. Am. 61:1072–1083.

2395. Tarshis, I. B. 1971. Individual black fly rearing cylinders (Diptera: Simuliidae). Ann. Ent. Soc. Am. 64:1192–1193.

2396. Tarshis, I. B. 1973. Studies on the collection, rearing, and biology of the black fly *Cnephia ornithophilia*. U.S. Dep. Int., Fish Widl. Serv. Spec. Sci. Rept. 165. 16 pp.

2397. Tarshis, I. B., and W. Neil. 1970. Mass movement of black fly larvae on silken threads (Diptera: Simuliidae). Ann. Ent. Soc. Am. 63:607–610.

2398. Tarter D. C. 1976. Limnology in West Virginia: A lecture and laboratory manual. Marshall Univ. Book Store, Huntington, W. Va. 249 pp.

2399. Tarter, D. C., and R. F. Kirchner. 1980. List of the stoneflies (Plecoptera) of West Virginia. Ent. News 91:49–53.

2400. Tarter, D. C., and L. A. Krumholz. 1971. Life history and ecology of *Paragnetina media* (Walker) in Doe Run, Meade County, Kentucky. Am. Midl. Nat. 86:169–180.

2401. Tarter, D. C., and W. D. Watkins. 1974. Distribution of the fishfly genera *Chauliodes* Latreille and *Nigronia* Banks in West Virginia. Proc. W. Va. Acad. Sci. 46:146–150.

2402. Tarter, D. C., W. D. Watkins, D. L. Ashley, and J. T. Goodwin. 1978. New state records and seasonal emergence patterns of alderflies east of the Rocky Mountains (Megaloptera: Sialidae). Ent. News 89:231–239.

2403. Tarter, D. C., W. D. Watkins, and D. A. Etnier. 1979. Larval description and habitat notes of the fishfly *Neohermes concolor* (Davis) (Megaloptera: Corydalidae). Ent. News 90:29–32.

2404. Tarter, D. C., W. D. Watkins, and M. L. Little. 1975. Life history of the fishfly *Nigronia fasciatus* (Megaloptera: Corydalidae). Psyche 82:81–88.

2405. Tarter, D. C., W. D. Watkins, and M. L. Little. 1976. Distribution, including new state records, of fishflies in Kentucky (Megaloptera: Corydalidae). Trans. Ky. Acad. Sci. 37:26–28.

2406. Tarter, D. C., W. D. Watkins, M. L. Little, and D. L. Ashley. 1977. Seasonal emergence patterns of fishflies east of the Rocky Mountains (Megaloptera: Corydalidae). Ent. News 88:69–76.

2407. Tarwid, M. 1969. Analysis of the contents of the alimentary tract of predatory Pelopiinae larvae (Chironomidae). Ekol. Polska (A) 17:125–131.

2408. Tate, P. 1935. The larvae of *Phaonia mirabilis* Ringdahl, predatory on mosquito larvae (Diptera, Anthomyiidae). Parasitology 27:556–560.

2409. Taylor, O. R., Jr. 1968. Coexistence and competitive interactions in fall and winter populations of six sympatric *Notonecta* (Hemiptera: Notonectidae) in New England: Univ. Conn. Occ. Pap. Biol. Sci. Ser. 1:109–139.

2410. Tennessen, K. J. 1975. Description of the nymph of *Somatochlora provocans* Calvert (Odonata: Corduliidae). Fla. Ent. 58:105–110.

2411. Tennessen, K. J., and K. W. Knopf. 1975. Description of the nymph of *Enallagma minusculum* (Odonata: Coenagrionidae). Fla. Ent. 58:199–201.

2412. Terwilliger, R. C. 1980. Structures of invertebrate hemoglobins. Am. Zool. 20:53–67.

2413. Teskey, H. J. 1962. A method and apparatus for collecting larvae of Tabanidae (Diptera) and other invertebrate inhabitants of wetlands. Proc. Ent. Soc. Ont. 92:204–206.

2414. Teskey, H. J. 1969. Larvae and pupae of some eastern North American Tabanidae (Diptera). Mem. Ent. Soc. Can. 63:1–147.

2415. Teskey, H. J. 1970. The immature stages and phyletic position of *Glutops rossi* (Diptera: Pelecorhynchidae). Can. Ent. 102:1130–1135.

2416. Teskey, H. J. 1981a. Chap. 3. Morphology and Terminology-Larvae, pp. 65–88. *In* J. F. McAlpine, B. V, Peterson, G. E. Shewell, H. J. Teskey, J. R. Vockeroth, and D. M. Wood (coords). Manual of Nearctic Diptera, Vol. 1. Res. Branch, Agric. Can. Monogr. 27. Ottawa. 674 pp.

2417. Teskey, H. J. 1981b. Chap. 30. Pelecorhynchidae, pp. 459–462. *In* J. F. McAlpine, B. V. Peterson, G. E. Shewell, H. J. Teskey, J. R. Vockeroth, and D. M. Wood (coords). Manual of Nearctic Diptera, Vol. 1. Res. Branch, Agric. Can. Monogr. 27. Ottawa. 674 pp.

2418. Teskey, H. J., and I. Valiela. 1977. The mature larva and puparium of *Canace macateei* Malloch (Diptera: Canaceidae). Can. Ent. 109:545–547.

2419. Tetrault, R. C. 1967. A revision of the family Helodidae (Coleoptera) for America north of Mexico. Ph.D. diss., University of Wisconsin, Madison. 160 pp.

2420. Thienemann, A. 1910. Das Sammeln von Puppenhauten der Chironomiden. Arch. Hydrobiol. 6:213–214.

2421. Thienemann, A. 1954. *Chironomus*. Die Binnengewasser 20:1–834.

2422. Thier, R. W., and B. A. Foote. 1980. Biology of mud-shore Ephydridae (Diptera). Proc. Ent. Soc. Wash. 82:517–535.

2423. Thomas, A. G. B. 1974. Dipteres torrenticoles peu connus. Parts I, II. Athericidae (larves et imagos) du Sud de la France (Brachycera, Orthorrhapa). Ann. Limnol. 10:55–84; 121–130.

2424. Thomas, E. 1966. Orientierung der Imagines von *Capnia atra* Morton (Plecoptera). Oikos 17:278–280.

2425. Thomas, E. S., and R. D. Alexander. 1962. Systematic and behavioral studies on the meadow grasshoppers of the *Orchelimum concinnum* group. (Orthoptera: Tettigoniidae). Occ. Pap. Univ. Mich. Mus. Zool. 626:1–31.

2426. Thomas, L. J. 1946. Black fly incubator-aerator cabinet. Science 103:21–23.

2427. Thompson, D. J. 1978a. The natural prey of larvae of the damselfly *Ischnura elegans* (Odonata: Zygoptera). Freshwat. Biol. 8:377–384.

2428. Thompson, D. J. 1978b. Prey size selection by larvae of the damselfly *Ischnura elegans* (Odonata). J. Anim. Ecol. 47:769–785.

2429. Thomsen, L. 1937. Aquatic Diptera. Part V. Ceratopogonidae. Mem. Cornell Univ. Agric. Exp. Sta. 210:57–80.

2430. Thorpe, W. H. 1931. The biology of the petroleum fly. Science 73:101–103.

2431. Thorpe, W. H. 1950. Plastron respiration in aquatic insects. Biol. Rev. 25:344–390.

2432. Thorpe, W. H., and D. J. Crisp. 1947a. Studies on plastron respiration. I. The biology of *Aphelocheirus*, [Hemiptera, Aphelocheiridae (Naucoridae)] and the mechanism of plastron retention. J. exp. Biol. 24:227–269.

2433. Thorpe, W. H., and D. J. Crisp. 1947b. Studies on plastron respiration. II. The respiratory efficiency of the plastron of *Aphelocheirus*. J. exp. Biol. 24:270–303.

2434. Thorpe, W. H., and D. J. Crisp. 1947c. Studies on plastron respiration. III. The orientation responses of *Aphelocheirus*, [Hemiptera, Aphelocheiridae (Naucoridae)] in relation to plastron respiration; together with an account of specialized pressure receptors in aquatic insects. J. exp. Biol. 24:310–328.

2435. Thorpe, W.H., and D. J. Crisp. 1949. Studies on plastron respiration. IV. Plastron respiration in the Coleoptera. J. exp. Biol. 26:219–260.

2436. Thorup, J., and T. M. Iversen. 1974. Ingestion by *Sericostoma personatum* Spence (Trichoptera: Sericotomatidae). Arch. Hydrobiol. 74:39–47.

2437. Thut, R. N. 1969a. A study of the profundal bottom fauna of Lake Washington. Ecol. Monogr. 39:77–100.

2438. Thut, R. N. 1969b. Feeding habits of larvae of seven *Rhyacophila* species with notes on other life-history features. Ann. Ent. Soc. Am. 62:894–898.

2439. Thut, R. N. 1969c. Feeding habits of stonefly nymphs of the suborder Setipalpia. Rept. Weyerhaeuser Co., Longview, Wash. 4 pp.

2440. Tillyard, R. J. 1917. The biology of dragonflies (Odonata or Paraneuroptera). Cambridge Univ. Press. Cambridge. 396 pp.

2441. Tillyard, R. J. 1932. Kansas Permian insects 15. The order Plectoptera. Am. J. Sci. 23:97–134, 237–242.

2442. Tindall, A. R. 1960. The larval case of *Triaenodes bicolor* Curtis (Trichoptera: Leptoceridae). Proc. R. ent. Soc. Lond. (A) 35:93–96.

2443. Tindall, J. J., and W. P. Kovalak. 1979. Food particle sizes consumed by larval *Glossosoma nigrior* (Trichoptera: Glossosomatidae). Great Lakes Ent. 12:105–108.

2444. Titmus, G., and R. M. Badcock. 1981. Distribution and feeding of larval Chironomidae in a gravel-pit lake. Freshwat. Biol. 11:263–271.

2445. Tjonneland, A. 1960. The flight activity of mayflies as expressed in some East African species. Univ. Gergen Arbok Met. Naturv. Serv. 1:1–88.

2446. Tkac, M. A., and B. A. Foote. 1978. Annotated list of stoneflies (Plecoptera) from Stebbins Gulch in northeastern Ohio. Great Lakes Ent. 11:139–142.

2447. Todd, E. L. 1955. A taxonomic revision of the family Gelastocoridae. Univ. Kans. Sci. Bull. 37:277–475.

2448. Todd, E. L. 1961. A checklist of the Gelastocoridae (Hemiptera). Proc. Hawaii. Ent. Soc. 17:461–467.

2449. Torre-Bueno, J. R. de la. 1903. Brief notes toward the life history of *Pelecoris femorata* Pal. B. with a few remarks on habits. J. N.Y. Ent. Soc. 11:166–173.

2450. Torre-Bueno, J. R. de la. 1906. Life history of *Ranatra quadridentata*. Can. Ent. 38:242–252.

2451. Torre-Bueno, J. R. de la. 1910. Life histories of North American water bugs. III. *Microvelia americana* Uhler. Can. Ent. 42:176–186.

2452. Torre-Bueno, J. R. de la. 1917a. Aquatic Hemiptera. A study in the relation of structure to environment. Ann. Ent. Soc. Am. 9:353–365.

2453. Torre-Bueno, J. R. de la. 1917b. Life history of the northern *Microvelia—Microvelia borealis* Bueno. Ent. News 28:354–359.

2454. Torre-Bueno, J. R. de la. 1926. The family Hydrometridae in the western hemisphere. Entomologica Am. 7:83–128.

2455. Torre-Bueno, J. R. de la. 1937. A glossary of entomology. Science, Lancaster, Penn. 336 pp.

2456. Toth, R. S., and R. M. Chew. 1972a. Development and energetics of *Notonecta undulata* during predation on *Culex tarsalis*. Ann. Ent. Soc. Am. 65:1270–1279.

2457. Toth, R. S., and R. N. Chew. 1972b. Notes on behavior and colonization of *Buenoa scimitra*, a predator of mosquito larvae. Environ. Ent. 1:534–545.

2458. Townes, H. K. 1937. Studies on the food organisms of fish. Ann. Rept. N.Y. State Cons. Dep. 27 Suppl. 222:162–175.

2459. Townes, H. K. 1945. The Nearctic species of Tendipedini (Diptera: Tendipedidae). Am. Midl. Nat. 34:1–206.

2460. Townes, H. K. 1957. Nearactic wasps of the subfamilies Pepsinae and Ceropalinae. Bull. U.S. Nat. Mus. 209 286 pp.

2461. Townes, H. K. 1962. Design for a malaise trap. Proc. Ent. Soc. Wash. 64:253–262.

2462. Townes H. K. 1969, 1970, 1971. The genera Ichneumonidae. Parts 1, 2, 4. Mem. Am. Ent. Inst. 11:300 pp.; 12:537 pp.; 17:372 pp.

2463. Townes H. K. 1972. A light-weight malaise trap. Ent. News 83: 239–247

2464. Towns, D. R. 1981. Life histories of benthic invertebrates in a kauri forest stream in northern New Zealand. Aust. J. Mar. Freshwat. Res. 32:191–211.

2465. Townsend, L. H. 1939. A new species of *Sialis* (Megaloptera: Sialidae) from Kentucky. Proc. Ent. Soc. Wash. 4:224–226.

2466. Tozer, W. 1979. Underwater behavioral thermoregulation in the adult stonefly, *Zapada cinctipes*. Nature 281:566–567.

2467. Trama, F. B. 1972. The transformation of energy by an aquatic herbivore *Stenonema pulchellum* (Ephemeroptera). Pol. Arch. Hydrobiol. 19:113–121.

2468. Traver, J. R., and G. F. Edmunds, Jr. 1967. A revision of the genus *Thraulodes* (Ephemeroptera: Leptophlebiidae). Misc. Publ. Ent. Soc. Am. 5:349–395.

2469. Treat, A. E. 1954. *Acentropus niveus* in Massachusetts, remote from water. Lep. News 8:23–25.

2470. Treat, A. E. 1955. Flightless females of *Acentropus niveus* reared from Massachusetts progenitors. Lep. News 9:69–73.

2471. Treherne, J. R. 1951. The respiration of the larva of *Helodes minuta* (Col.). Proc. 9th Int. Congr. Ent. 1:311–314.

2472. Trelka, D. G., and B. A. Foote, 1970. Biology of slugkilling *Tetanocera* (Diptera: Sciomyzidae). Ann. Ent. Soc. Am. 63:877–895.

2473. Trimble, R. M. 1972. Occurrence of *Culiseta minnesotae* and *Aedes trivittatus* in Manitoba, including a list of mosquitoes from Manitoba. Can. Ent. 104:1535–1537.

2474. Trost, L. M. W., and L. Berner, 1963. The biology of *Callibaetis floridanus* Banks (Ephemeroptera: Baetidae). Fla. Ent. 46:285–299.

2475. Truxal, F. S. 1949. A study of the genus *Martarega* (Hemiptera: Notonectidae). J. Kans. Ent. Soc. 22:1–24.

2476. Truxal, F. S. 1953. A revision of the genus *Buenoa*. Univ. Kans. Sci. Bull. 35:1351–1523.

2477. Tsou, Y. H. 1914. The body setae of lepidopterous larvae. Trans. Am. Miscrosc. Soc. 33:223–260.

2478. Tsui, P. T. P., and M. D. Hubbard. 1979. Feeding habits of the predaceous nymphs of *Dolania americana* in northwestern Florida (Ephemeroptera: Behningiidae). Hydrobiologia 67:119–123.

2479. Tubb, R. A., and T. C. Dorris. 1965. Herbivorous insect populations in oil refinery effluent holding pond series. Limnol. Oceanogr. 10:121–134.

2480. Tucker, E. S. 1912. The rice water-weevil and methods of its control. U.S. Dept. Agric. Circ. 152 20 pp.

2481. Tuskes, P. M. 1977. Biological observations and larval competition in two species of aquatic pyralid moths of the genus *Paragyractis*. Can. Ent. 109:695–699.

2482. Tuskes, P. M. 1981. Factors influencing the abundance and distribution of two aquatic moths of the genus *Parargyractis* (Pyralidae). J. Lepid. Soc. 35:161–168.

2483. Tuxen, S. L. 1944. The hot springs, their animal communities and their zoogeographical significance. Zool. Iceland 1:1–206.

2484. Tuxen, S. L. 1970. Taxonomist's glossary of genitalia in insects. Munksgaard, Copenhagen. 359 pp.

2485. Twinn, C. R. 1936. The blackflies of eastern Canada (Simuliidae, Diptera). Can. J. Res. 14:97–150.

2486. Uchida, H. 1971. Tentative key to the Japanese genera of Collembola, in relation to the world general of this order. I. Sci. Rep. Hirosaki Univ. 18:64–76.

2487. Uchida, H. 1972a. Tentative key to the Japanese genera of Collembola, in relation to the world genera of this Order. II. Sci. Rep. Hirosaki Univ. 19:19–42.

2488. Uchida, H. 1972b. Tentative key to the Japanese genera of Collembola, in relation to the world genera of this order. III. Sci. Rep. Hirosaki Univ. 19:79–114.

2489. Ulfstrand, S. 1968. Life cycles of benthic insects in Lapland streams (Ephemeroptera, Plecoptera, Trichoptera, Diptera: Simuliidae). Oikos 19:167–190.

2490. Unzicker, J. D., L. Aggus, and L. O. Warren. 1970. A preliminary list of the Arkansas Trichoptera. J. Ga. Ent. Soc. 5:167–174.

2491. Unzicker, J. D., V. H. Resh, and J. C. Morse. 1982. Trichoptera, pp. 9.24–9.124. *In* A. R. Brigham, W. U. Brigham, and A. Gnilka (eds.). Aquatic insects and oligochaetes of North Carolina. Midwest Aquatic Enterprises, Mahomet, Ill. 837 pp.

2492. Usinger, R. L. 1941. Key to the subfamilies of Naucoridae with a generic synopsis of the new subfamily Ambrysinae. Ann. Ent. Soc. Am. 34:5–16.

2493. Usinger, R. L. 1945. Notes on the genus *Cryptostemma* with a new record for Georgia and a new species from Puerto Rico. Ent. News 56:238–241.

2494. Usinger, R. L. 1946. Notes and descriptions of *Ambrysus* Stal, with an account of the life history of *Ambrysus mormon* Montd. Univ. Kans. Sci. Bull. 31:185–210.

2495. Usinger, R. L. (ed.). 1956a. Aquatic insects of California. Univ. Calif. Press, Berkeley 508 pp.

2496. Usinger, R. L. 1956b. Aquatic Hemiptera, pp. 182–228. *In* R. L. Usinger (ed.). Aquatic insects of California. Univ. Calif. Press, Berkeley. 508 pp.

2497. Usinger, R. L., and P. R. Needham. 1956. A drag-type rifflebottom sampler. Progr. Fish Cult. 18:42–44.

2498. Vaillant, F. 1951. Un empidide destructeur de simulies. Bull. Soc. Zool. France 76:371–379.

2499. Vaillant, F. 1952. *Kowarzia barbatula* Mik et *Dolichocephala ocellata* Costa, deux empides a larves hygropétriques (Dipterès). Bull. Soc. Zool. France 77:286–291.

2500. Vaillant, F. 1953. *Hemerodromia seguyi,* nouvel empidide d'Algerie destructeur de simulies. Hydrobiologia 5:180–188.

2501. Vaillant, F. 1967. Diptera: Dolichopodidae, Empididae, pp. 401–409. *In* J. Illies (ed.). Limnofauna Europaea. Gustav Fischer Verlag, Stuttgart 474 pp.

2502. Valley, K., and C. O. Berg. 1977. Biology, immature stages, and new species of snail-killing Diptera of the genus *Dictya* (Sciomyzidae). Search Agric., Cornell Agric. Exp. Sta. 7:1–44.

2503. Van Dam, L. 1938. On the utilization of oxygen and regulation of breathing in some aquatic animals. Volharding, Groningen.

2504. Vandel, A. 1964. Biospéologie. La biologie des animaux cavernicoles. Gauthier-Villars, Paris, 619 pp.

2505. Van Duzee, E. P. 1917. Catalogue of the Hemiptera of America north of Mexico. Univ. Calif. Publ. Ent. 2:1–902.

2506. Van Dyke, E. C. 1918. New intertidal rock dwelling Coleoptera from California. Ent. News 29:303–308.

2507. Van Emden, F. 1956. The *Georyssus* larva, a hydrophilid. Proc. R. ent. Soc. Lond. (A) 31:20–24.

2508. Vannote, R. L., G. W. Minshall, K. W. Cummins, J. R. Sedell, and C. E. Cushing. 1980. The river continuum concept. Can. J. Fish. Aquat. Sci. 37:130–137.

2509. Vannote, R. L., and B. W. Sweeney. 1980. Geographic analysis of thermal equilibria: a conceptual model for evaluating the effect of natural and modified thermal regimes on aquatic insect communities. Am. Nat. 115:667–695.

2510. Van Tassel, E. R. 1963. A new *Berosus* from Arizona, with a key to the Arizona species (Coleoptera, Hydrophilidae). Coleopt. Bull. 17:1–5.

2511. Van Tassell, E. R. 1966. Taxonomy and biology of the subfamily Berosinae of North and Central America and the West Indies (Coleoptera: Hydrophilidae). Ph.D. diss., Catholic University of Amer., Washington, D.C. 329 pp.

2512. Vargas, L. 1945. Simulidos del Nuevo Mundo. Monogr. Inst. Salub. Enferm. Trop. 1:1–241.

2513. Varley, G. C. 1937. Aquatic insect larvae which obtain oxygen from the roots of plants. Proc. R. ent. Soc. Lond. (A) 12:55–60.

2514. Varvin-Aha, S. 1981. The effects of ecological differences on the amount of enzyme gene variation in Finnish water-strider *(Gerris)* species. Hereditas 94:35–39.

2515. Vaught, G. L., and K. W. Stewart. 1974. The life-history and ecology of the stonefly *Neoperla clymene* (Newman) (Plecoptera: Perlidae). Ann. Ent. Soc. Am. 67:167–178.

2516. Veneski, R., and R. K. Washino. 1970. Ecological studies of *Hydrophilus triangularis* in the laboratory and in a rice field habitat, a preliminary report. Proc. Calif. Mosquito Contr. Assoc. 38:95–97.

2517. Vepsäläinen, K. 1971a. The role of gradually changing daylength in determination of wing length, alary polymorphism and diapause in a *Gerris odontogaster* (Zett.) population in South Finland. Ann. Acad. Sci. Fenn. (A) 183:1–25.

2518. Vepsäläinen, K. 1971b. The roles of photoperiodism and genetic switch in alary polymorphism in *Gerris*. Acta Ent. Fenn. 28:101–102.

2519. Vepsäläinen, K. 1971b. The roles of photoperiodism and genetic switch in alary polymorphism in *Gerris*. Acta Ent. Fenn. 28:101–102.

2519. Vepsäläinen, K. 1974. Determination of wing length and diapause in waterstriders. Hereditas 77:163–176.

2520. Verollet, G., and H. Tachet. 1978. A suction sampler for sampling benthic macroinvertebrates in large rivers. Arch. Hydrobiol. 84:55–64.

2521. Vickery, V. R., and D. E. Johnstone. 1970. Generic status of some Nemobiinae (Orthoptera: Gryllidae) in northern North America. Ann. Ent. Soc. Am. 63:1740–1749.

2522. Vockeroth, J. R. 1967. Diptera Scatophagidae, p. 422. *In* J. Illies (ed.). Liomnofauna Europaea. Gustav Fischer Verlag, Stuttgart. 417 pp.

2523. Vogel, E. and A. D. Oliver, Jr. 1969. Life history and some factors affecting the population of *Arzama densa* in Louisiana. Ann. Ent. Soc. Am. 16:374–383.

2524. Vogel, S., and M. LaBarbera. 1978. Simple flow tanks for teaching and research. BioScience 28:638–643.

2525. Vogt, G. G., J. U. McGuire, Jr., and A. D. Cushman. 1979. Probable evolution and morphological variation in South American disonychine flea beetles (Coleoptera: Chrysomelidae) and their amaranthaceous hosts. U.S. Dept. Agric. Tech. Bull. 1593:1–148.

2526. Voigt, W. G., and R. Garcia. 1976. Keys to the *Notonecta* nymphs of the West Coast United States (Hemiptera: Notonectidae). Pan-Pacif. Ent. 52:172–176.

2527. Voigts, D. K. 1976. Aquatic invertebrate abundance in relation to changing marsh vegetation. Am. Midl. Nat. 95:313–322.

2528. Vorhies, C. 1909. Studies on the Trichoptera of Wisconsin. Trans. Wisc. Acad. Sci. Arts Lett. 16:647–738.

2529. Voshell, J. R. 1982. Life history and ecology of *Siphlonurus mirus* Eaton (Ephemeroptera: Siphlonuridae) in an intermittant pond. Freshwat. Invert. Biol. 1:17–26.

2530. Voshell, J. R., and G. M. Simmons, Jr. 1977. An evaluation of artificial substrates for sampling macrobenthos in reservoirs. Hydrobiologia 53:257–269.

2531. Voshell, J. R., Jr., and G. M. Simmons, Jr. 1978. The Odonata of a new reservoir in the southeastern United States. Odonatologica 7:67–76.

2532. Waldbauer, G. 1968. The consumption and utilization of food by insects. Adv. Insect Physiol. 5:229–288.

2533. Walentowicz, A. T., and A. J. McLachlan. 1980. Chironomids and particles: A field experiment with peat in an upland stream, pp. 179–185. *In* D. A. Murray (ed.). Chironomidae: Ecology, systematics, cytology and physiology. Pergamon Press, N.Y.

2534. Walker, C. R. 1955. A core sampler for obtaining samples of bottom muds. Progr. Fish Cult. 17:140.

2535. Walker, E. M. 1912. The North American dragonflies of the genus *Aeshna*. Toronto Stud. Biol. Ser. 11:1–213.

2536. Walker, E. M. 1925. The North American dragonflies of the genus *Somatochlora*. Univ. Toronto Stud. Biol. Ser. 26:1–202.

2537. Walker, E. M. 1928. The nymphs of the *Stylurus* group of the genus *Gomphus* with notes on the distribution of the group in Canada (Odonata). Can. Ent. 60:79–88.

2538. Walker, E. M. 1933. The nymphs of the Canadian species of *Ophiogomphus* Odonata, Gomphidae. Can. Ent. 65:217–229.

2539. Walker, E. M. 1953. The Odonata of Canada and Alaska. Part I, General, Part II. The Zygoptera-damselflies. Vol. I. Univ. Toronto Press, Toronto. 292 pp.

2540. Walker, E. M. 1958. The Odonata of Canada and Alaska. Anisoptera. Vol. 2. Univ. Toronto Press, Toronto. 318 pp.

2541. Walker, E. M., and P. S. Corbet. 1975. The Odonata of Canada and Alaska. Anisoptera, Macromiidae, Corduliidae, Libellulidae. Vol. 3. Univ. Toronto Press, Toronto. 307 pp.

2542. Walker, T. J. 1971. *Orchelimum carinatum,* a new meadow katydid from the southeastern United States (Orthoptera: Tettigoniidae). Fla. Ent. 54:277–281.

2543. Walkotten, W. J. 1976. An improved technique for freeze sampling streambed sediments. U.S. Dep. Agric. For. Serv. Res. Note PNW-281:1–9.

2544. Wallace, J. B. 1975a. The larval retreat and food of *Arctopsyche;* with phylogenetic notes on feeding adaptations in Hydropsychidae larvae (Trichoptera). Ann. Ent. Soc. Am. 68:167–173.

2545. Wallace, J. B. 1975b. Food partitioning in net-spinning Trichoptera larvae: *Hydropsyche venularis, Cheumatopsyche etrona* and *Macronema zebratum* (Hydropsychidae). Ann. Ent. Soc. Am. 68:463–472.

2546. Wallace, J. B., and D. Malas. 1976a. The fine structure of capture nets of larval Philopotamidae (Trichoptera), with special emphasis on *Dolophilodes distinctus.* Can. J. Zool. 54:1788–1802.

2547. Wallace, J. B., and D. Malas. 1976b. The significance of the elongate, rectangular mesh found in capture nets of fine particle filter feeding Trichoptera larvae. Arch. Hydrobiol. 77:205–212.

2548. Wallace, J. B., and R. W. Merritt. 1980. Filter-feeding ecology of aquatic insects. Ann. Rev. Ent. 25:103–132.

2549. Wallace, J. B., and S. E. Neff. 1971. Biology and immature stages of the genus *Cordilura* (Diptera: Scatophagidae) in the eastern United States. Ann. Ent. Soc. Am. 64:1310–1330.

2550. Wallace, J. B., and J. O'hop. 1979. Fine particle suspension-feeding capabilities of *Isonychia* spp. (Ephemeroptera: Siphlonuridae). Ann. Ent. Soc. Am. 72:353–357.

2551. Wallace, J. B., and H. H. Ross. 1971. Pseudogoerinae: a new subfamily of Odontoceridae (Trichoptera). Ann. Ent. Soc. Am. 64(4):890–894.

2552. Wallace, J. B., and F. F. Sherberger. 1970. The immature stages of *Anisocentropus pyraloides* (Trichoptera: Calamoceratidae). J. Ga. Ent. Soc. 5(4):217–224.

2553. Wallace, J. B., and F. F. Sherberger. 1972. New Nearctic species of *Lepidostoma* in the *vernalis* group from the southern Appalachians (Trichoptera: Lepidostomatidae). Ent. News 83:222–228.

2554. Wallace, J. B., and F. F. Sherberger. 1974. The larval retreat and feeding net of *Macronema carolina* Banks (Trichoptera: Hydropsychidae). Hydrobiologia 45:177–184.

2555. Wallace, J. B., and F. F. Sherberger. 1975. The larval retreat and feeding net of *Macronema transversum* Hagen (Trichoptera: Hydropsychidae). Anim. Behav. 23:592–596.

2556. Wallace, J. B., J. R. Webster, and W. R. Woodall. 1977. The role of filter feeders in flowing waters. Arch. Hydrobiol. 79:506–532.

2557. Wallace, J. B., W. R. Woodall, and F. F. Sherberger. 1970. Breakdown of leaves by feeding of *Peltoperla maria* nymphs (Plecoptera: Peltoperlidae). Ann. Ent. Soc. Am. 63:563–567.

2558. Wallace, J. B., W. R. Woodall, and A. A. Staats. 1976. The larval dwelling-tube, capture net and food of *Phylocentropus placidus* (Trichoptera: Polycentropodidae). Ann. Ent. Soc. Am. 69:149–154.

2559. Wallis, J. B. 1933. Revision of the North American species (north of Mexico) of the genus *Haliplus* Latreille. Trans. Roy. Can. Inst. 19:1–76.

2560. Wallis, J. B. 1939a. The genus *Graphoderus* Aube in North America (north of Mexico). Can. Ent. 71:128–130.

2561. Wallis, J. B. 1939b. The genus *Ilybius* Er. in North America. Can. Ent. 82:50–52.

2562. Walsh, B. D. 1963. Notes on the Neuroptera. Proc. Ent. Soc. Phila. 15:182–272.

2563. Walshe, B. M. 1947a. Feeding mechanisms of *Chironomus* larvae. Nature 160:474.

2564. Walshe, B. M. 1947b. On the function of haemoglobin in *Chironomus* after oxygen lack. J. exp. Biol. 24:329–342.

2565. Walshe, B. M. 1947c. The function of haemoglobin in *Tanytarsus* (Chironomidae). J. exp. Biol. 24:343–351.

2566. Walshe, B. M. 1950. The function of haemoglobin in *Chironomus plumosus* under natural conditions. J. exp. Biol. 27:73–95.

2567. Walshe, B. M. 1951. The feeding habits of certain chironomid larvae (subfamily Tendipedinae). Proc. Zool. Soc. Lond. 121:63–79.

2568. Walsingham, L. 1907. Microlepidoptera. Fauna Hawaiiensis 1:549–640.

2569. Walton, E., Jr. 1980. Invertebrate drift from predator-prey associations. Ecology 61:1486–1497.

2570. Walton, O. E., Jr., S. R. Reice, and R. W. Andrews. 1977. The effects of density, sediment, particle size and velocity on drift of *Acroneuria abnormis* (Plecoptera). Oikos 28:291–298.

2571. Waltz, R. D., and W. P. McCafferty. 1979. Freshwater springtails (Hexapoda: Collembola) of North America. Purdue Univ. Agric. Exp. Sta. Res. Bull. 960. Lafayette, Ind.

2572. Waltz, R. D., and W. P. McCafferty, 1983. *Austrotinodes* Schmid (Trichoptera: Psychomyiidae), a first U.S. record from Texas. Proc. Ent. Soc. Wash. 85:181–182.

2573. Ward, G. M., and K. W. Cummins. 1978, Life history and growth pattern of *Paratendipes albimanus* in a Michigan headwater stream. Ann. Ent. Soc. Am. 71:272–284.

2574. Ward, G. M., and K. W. Cummins. 1979. Effects of food quality on growth of a stream detritivore, *Paratendipes albimanus* (Meigen) (Diptera: Chironomidae). Ecology 60:57–64.

2575. Ward, H. B., and G. C. Whipple (eds.). 1918. Fresh-water biology. John Wiley & Sons, N.Y. 1111 pp.

2576. Ward, J. V. 1976. Comparative limnology of differentially regulated sections of a Colorado mountain river. Arch. Hydrobiol. 78:319–342.

2577. Ward, J. V., and J. A. Stanford (eds.). 1979. The ecology of regulated streams. Plenum, N.Y. 398 pp.

2578. Ward, J. V., and J. A. Stanford. 1982. Thermal responses in the evolutionary ecology of aquatic insects. Ann. Rev. Ent. 27:97–117.

2579. Warren, C. E. 1971. Biology and water pollution control. W. B. Saunders, Philadelphia. 434 pp.

2580. Wartinbee, D. C., and W. P. Coffman. 1976. Quantitative determination of chironomid emergence from enclosed channels in a small lotic ecosystem. Am. Midl. Nat. 95:479–484.

2581. Warwick, W. F. 1980. Chironomidae (Diptera) responses to 2800 years of cultural influence: a palaeolimnological study with special reference to sedimentation, eutrophication, and contamination processes. Can. Ent. 112:1193–1238.

2582. Washino, R. K. 1969. Progress in biological control of mosquitoes—invertebrate and vertebrate predators. Proc. Calif. Mosquito Contr. Assoc. 27:16–19.

2583. Washino, R. K., and Y. Hokama. 1968. Quantitive sampling of aquatic insects in a shallow-water habitat. Ann. Ent. Soc. Am. 61:785–786.

2584. Waters, T. F. 1965. Interpretation of invertebrate drift in streams. Ecology 46:327–334.

2585. Waters, T. F. 1969a. The turnover ratio in production ecology of freshwater invertebrates. Am. Nat. 103:173–185.

2586. Waters, T. F. 1969b. Subsampler for dividing large samples of stream invertebrate drift. Limnol. Oceanogr. 14:813–815.

2587. Waters, T. F. 1972. The drift of stream insects. Ann. Rev. Ent. 17:253–272.

2588. Waters. T. F. 1977. Secondary production in inland waters. Adv. Ecol. Res. 10:91–164.

2589. Waters, T. F. 1979a. Influence of benthos life history upon the estimation of secondary production. J. Fish. Res. Bd. Can. 36:1425–1430.

2590. Waters, T. F. 1979b. Benthic life histories: summary and future needs. J. Fish. Res. Bd. Can. 36:342–45.

2591. Waters, T. F., and G. W. Crawford. 1973. Annual production of a stream mayfly population: a comparison of methods. Limnol. Oceanogr. 18:286–296.

2592. Waters, T. F., and J. C. Hokenstrom. 1980. Annual production and drift of the stream amphipod *Gammarus pseudolimnaeus* in Valley Creek, Minnesota. Limnol. Oceanogr. 25:700–710.

2593. Waters, T. F., and R. J. Knapp. 1961. An improved stream bottom fauna sampler. Trans. Am. Fish. Soc. 90:225–226.

2594. Waters, W. E., and V. H. Resh. 1979. Ecological and statistical features of sampling insect populations in forest and aquatic environments, pp. 569–617. *In* G. P. Patil and M. Rosenzweig (eds.). Contemporary quantitative ecology and related ecometrics. Internat. Coop. Publ. House, Fairland, Md. 695 pp.

2595. Watkins, W. D., D. C. Tarter, M. L. Little, and S. D. Hopkin. 1975. New records of fishflies for West Virginia (Megaloptera: Corydalidae). Proc. W. Va Acad. Sci. 47:1–5.

2596. Weaver, J. S., III, J. A. Wojtowicz, and D. A. Etnier. 1981. Larval and pupal descriptions of *Dolophilodes (Fumonta) major* (Banks) (Trichoptera: Philopotomidae). Ent. News 92:85–90.

2597. Weaver, J. S. and J. L. Sykora. 1979. The *Rhyacophila* of Pennsylvania, with larval descriptions of *R. banksi* and *R. carpenteri* (Trichoptera: Rhyacophilidae). Ann. Carnegie Mus. 48:403–423.

2598. Webb, D. W. 1977. The Nearctic Athericidae. J. Kans. Ent. Soc. 50:473–495.

2599. Webb. D. W. 1981. Chap. 32. Athericidae, pp. 479–482. *In* J. F. McAlpine, B. V. Peterson, G. E. Shewell, H. J. Teskey, J. R. Vockeroth, and D. M. Wood (coords). Manual of Nearctic Diptera, Vol. 1. Res. Branch, Agric. Can. Monogr. 27. Ottawa. 674 pp.

2600. Webb, D. W., and W. U. Brigham. 1982. Aquatic Diptera, pp. 11.1–11.11. *In* A. R. Brigham, W. U. Brigham, and A. Gnilka. Aquatic insects and oligochaetes of the Carolina Piedmont. Duke Power Training Manual. Duke Power, Charlotte, N.C. 837 pp.

2601. Webb, J. L. and H. W. Wells. 1924. Horseflies: biologies and relation to western agriculture. Bull. U.S. Dept. Agric. 1218 35 pp.

2602. Weber, C. I. (ed.). 1973. Biological field and laboratory methods for measuring the quality of surface waters and effluents. NERC/EPA, Cincinnati, 176 pp.

2603. Wefring, D. R., and J. C. Teed. 1980. Device for collecting replicate artificial substrate samples of benthic invertebrates in large rivers. Progr. Fish-Cult. 42:26–29.

2604. Weiss, H. B., and E. West. 1920. Notes on *Galerucella nymphaea* L. the pond-lily leaf-beetle (Coleoptera). Can. Ent. 52:237–239.

2605. Welch, P. S. 1914a. Habits of the larva of *Bellura melanopyga* Grote (Lepidoptera). Biol. Bull. 27:97–114.

2606. Welch, P. S. 1914b. Observations on the life history and habits of *Hydromyza confluens* Loew (Diptera). Ann. Ent. Soc. Am. 7:135–147.

2607. Welch, P. S. 1915. The Lepidoptera of the Douglas Lake region, northern Michigan. Ent. News 26:115–119.

2608. Welch, P. S. 1916. Contributions to the biology of certain aquatic Lepidoptera. Ann. Ent. Soc. Am. 9:159–187.

2609. Welch, P. S. 1917. Further studies on *Hydromyza confluens* Loew (Diptera). Ann. Ent. Soc. Am. 10:35–45.

2610. Welch, P. S. 1919. The aquatic adaptations of *Pyrausta penitalis* Grt. Ann. Ent. Soc. Am. 12:213–226.

2611. Welch, P. S. 1922. The respiratory mechanisms in certain aquatic Lepidoptera. Trans. Am. Microsc. Soc. 41:29–50.

2612. Welch, P. S. 1924. Observations on the early larval activities of *Nymphula maculalis* Clemens (Lepidoptera). Ann. Ent. Soc. Am. 17:395–402.

2613. Welch, P. S. 1948. Limnological methods. McGraw-Hill, N.Y. 382 pp.

2614. Welch, P. S. 1959. Lepidoptera, pp. 1050–1056. *In* W. T. Edmondson (ed.). Freshwater biology (2nd ed.). John Wiley & Sons. N.Y. 1,248 pp.

2615. Welch, P. S., and G. L. Sehon. 1928. The periodic vibratory movements of the larva of *Nymphula maculalis* Clemens (Lepidoptera) and their respiratory significance. Ann. Ent. Soc. Am. 21:243–258.

2616. Weld, L. H. 1952. Cynipoidea (Hym.) 1905–1950. Privately printed, Ann Arbor, Mich. 351 pp.

2617. Wene, G. 1940, The soil as an ecological factor in the abundances of aquatic chironomid larvae. Ohio J. Sci. 40:193–199.

2618. Wentworth, C. K. 1922. A scale of grade and class terms for clastic sediments. J. Geol. 30:377–392.

2619. Wesenberg-Lund, C. 1911. Biologische Studien uber netzspinnende Trichopteren-Larven. Int. Revue ges. Hydrobiol. Suppl. 3:1–64.

2620. Wesenberg-Lund, C. 1943. Biologie der Süsswasserinsekten. Springer, Berlin. 682 pp.

2621. West, L. S. 1929. Life history notes on *Psephenus lecontei* (Coleoptera: Dryopoidea; Psephenidae). Bull. Battle Cr. Coll. 3:3–20.

2622. Westfall, M. J. 1942. A list of the dragonflies (Odonata) taken near Brevard, North Carolina. Ent. News 53:94–100, 127–132.

2623. Westfall, M. J. 1952. Additions to the list of dragonflies of Mississippi (Odonata: Anisoptera). Ent. News 63:200–203.

2624. Westfall, M. J. 1953. Notes on Florida Odonata, including additions to the state list. Fla. Ent. 36:165–173.

2625. Westfall, M. J., Jr. 1956. A new species of *Gomphus* from Alabama (Odonata). Quart. J. Fla. Acad. Sci. 19:251–258.

2626. Westfall, M. J., Jr. 1957. A new species of *Telebasis* from Florida (Odonata: Zygoptera). Fla. Ent. 40:19–27.

2627. Westfall, M. J., Jr. 1965. Confusion among species of *Gomphus*. Quart. J. Fla. Acad. Sci. 28:245–254.

2628. Westfall, M. J., Jr. 1974. A critical study of *Gomphus modestus* Needham, 1942, with notes on related species. Odonatologica 3:63–73.

2629. Westfall, M. J., Jr. 1975. A new species of *Gomphus* from Arkansas (Odonata: Gomphidae). Fla. Ent. 58:91–95.

2630. Westfall, M. J., Jr., and K. J. Tennessen. 1973. Description of the nymph of *Lestes inaequalis* (Odonata: Lestidae). Fla. Ent. 56:291–293.

2631. Westfall, M. J., and K. J. Tennessen. 1979. Taxonomic clarification within the genus *Dromogomphus* Selys (Odonata: Gomphidae). Fla. Ent. 62:266–273.

2632. Westfall, M. J., Jr., and R. P. Trogdon. 1962. The true *Gomphus consanguis* Selys (Odonata: Gomphidae). Fla. Ent. 45:29–41.

2633. Westlake, D. F. 1969. Macrophytes, pp. 32–41. *In* R. A. Vollenweider (ed.) A manual on methods for measuring primary production in aquatic environments. IBP Handbook 12. Blackwell Scientific, Oxford. 225 pp.

2634. Wetzel, R. G. 1975. Limnology. W. B. Saunders, Philadelphia. 743 pp.

2635. Whedon, A. D. 1914. Preliminary notes on the Odonata of southern Minnesota. Rept. Minn. State Ent. 77–103.

2636. Whedon, A. D. 1942. Some observations on rearing Odonata in the laboratory. Ann. Ent. Soc. Am. 35:339–342.

2637. Wheeler, A. G. 1973. Studies on the arthropod fauna of alfalfa. IV. Species associated with the crown. Can. Ent. 105:353–366.

2638. White, D. S. 1976. *Climacia areolaris* (Neuroptera: Sisyridae) in Lake Texoma, Texas and Oklahoma. Ent. News 87:287–291.

2639. White, D. S. 1978a. Life cycle of the riffle beetle, *Stenelmis sexlineata* (Elmidae). Ann. Ent. Soc. Am. 71:121–125.

2640. White, D. S. 1978b. A revision of the Nearctic *Optioservus* (Coleoptera: Elmidae) with descriptions of new species. System. Ent. 3:59–74.

2641. White, D. S. 1978c. Coleoptera (Dryopoidea), pp. 94–99. *In* J. C. Morse, J. W. Chapin, D. D. Herlong, and R. S. Harvey (eds.). Aquatic insects of Upper Three Runs Creek, Savanah River Plant, South Carolina. Part I: Orders other than Diptera. J. Ga. Ent. Soc. 15:73–101.

2642. White, D. S. 1982. Elmidae pp. 10.99–10.110. *In* A. R. Brigham, W. U. Brigham, and A. Gnilka (eds.). Aquatic insects and oligochaetes of North and South Carolina. Midwest Aquatic Enterprises, Mahomet, Ill. 837 pp.

2643. White, D. S., and D. E. Jennings. 1973. A rearing technique for various aquatic Coleoptera. Ann. Ent. Soc. Am. 66:1174–1176.

2644. White, H. B., and W. J. Morse. 1973. Odonata (Dragonflies) of New Hampshire: an annotated list. N.H. Agric. Exp. Sta. 30:1–46.

2645. White, H. B., III, and R. A. Raff. 1970. The nymph of *Williamsonia lintneri* (Hagen) (Odonata: Corduliidae). Psyche 77:252–257.

2646. White, J. H. 1951. Observations on the life history and biology of *Tipula lateralis* Meig. Ann. Appl. Biol. 38:847–858.

2647. White, T. R., P. H. Carlson, and R. C. Fox. 1979. Emergence patterns of fall and winter stoneflies (Plecoptera: Filipalpia) in northwestern South Carolina. Proc. Ent. Soc. Wash. 81:379–390.

2648. White, T. R., and R. C. Fox. 1980. Recolonization of streams by aquatic insects following channelization. Rept. Water Resour. Res. Inst. Clemson Univ. 87, pt. 1:120 pp., pt. 2:57 pp.

2649. White, T. R., K. J. Tennessen, R. C. Fox, and P. H. Carlson. 1980. The aquatic insects of South Carolina, Part I: Anisoptera (Odonata). Bull. S.C. Agric. Exp. Sta. 632:1–153.

2650. Whitehouse, F. C. 1941. British Columbia dragonflies (Odonata) with notes on distribution and habits. Am. Midl. Nat. 26:488–557.

2651. Whiteside, M. C., and C. Lindegaard. 1980. Complementary procedures for sampling small benthic invertebrates. Oikos 35:317–320.

2652. Whitlock, D. 1982. Dave Whitlock's guide to aquatic trout foods. N. Lyons Books, N.Y. 224 pp.

2653. Wichard, W. 1976. Morphologische Komponenten bei der Osmoregulation von Trichopterenlarven, pp. 171–177. *In* H. Malicky, (ed.). Proc. 1st Int. Symp. on Trichoptera, Lunz Am See (Austria), 1974. Junk, The Hague, Netherlands. 213 pp.

2654. Wichard, W. 1978. Structure and function of the tracheal gills of *Molanna angustata* Curt., pp. 293–296. *In:* M. I. Crichton (ed.), Proc. 2nd Internat. Symp. Trichoptera. Junk, The Hague. 359 pp.

2655. Wichard, W., and K. Hauss, 1975. Der Chloridzellenfehlbetrag als Okomorphologischer zeigerwert fur die salinitat von Binnengewassern. Acta Hydrochim. Hydrobiol. 3:347–356.

2656. Wichard, W., and H. Komnick. 1973. Fine structure and function of the abdominal chloride epithelia in caddisfly larvae. Z. Zellforsch. Mikrosk. Anat. 136:579–590.

2657. Wichard, W., and H. Komnick, 1974. Structure and function of the respiratory epithelium in the tracheal gills of stonefly larvae. J. Ins. Physiol. 20:2397–2406.

2658. Wichard, W., P. T. P. Tsui, and A. Dewall, 1975. Chloridzellen der larven von *Caenis diminuta* Walker (Ephemeroptera, Caenidae) bei unterschiedlicher Salinität. Int. Revue ges. Hydrobiol. 60:705–709.

2659. Wickham, H. F. 1894. On some aquatic larvae, with notice of their parasites. Can. Ent. 26:39–41.

2660. Wiens, A.P. 1972. Bionomics of the pitcher plant midge *Metriocnemus knabi* Coquillett (Diptera: Chironomidae). Ph.D. diss., University of Manitoba, Winnipeg.

2661. Wiggins, G. B. 1954. The caddisfly genus *Beraea* in North America. Life Sci. Contr. Roy. Ont. Mus. 39:1–18.

2662. Wiggins, G. B. 1956. A revision of the North American caddisfly genus *Banksiola* (Trichoptera: Phryganeidae). Life Sci. Contr. Roy. Ont. Mus. 43:1–12.

2663. Wiggins, G. B. 1959. A method of rearing caddisflies (Trichoptera). Can. Ent. 91:402–405.

2664. Wiggins, G. B. 1960a. A preliminary systematic study of the North American larvae of the caddisfly family Phryganeidae (Trichoptera). Can. J. Zool. 38:1153–1170.

2665. Wiggins, G. B. 1960b. The unusual pupal mandibles in the caddisfly family Phryganeidae (Trichoptera). Can. Ent. 92:449–457.

2666. Wiggins, G. B. 1961. The rediscovery of an unusual North American phryganeid, with some additional records of caddisflies from Newfoundland (Trichoptera). Can. Ent. 93:695–702.

2667. Wiggins, G. B. 1962. A new subfamily of phryganeid caddisflies from western North America (Trichoptera: Phryganeidae). Can. J. Zool. 40:879–891.

2668. Wiggins, G. B. 1965. Additions and revisions to the genera of North American caddisflies of the family Brachycentridae with special reference to the larval stages (Trichoptera). Can. Ent. 97:1089–1106.

2669. Wiggins, G. B. 1966. The critical problem of systematics in stream ecology, pp. 55–58. *In* K. W. Cummins, C. A. Tryon, Jr., and R. T. Hartman (eds.). Organism-substrate relationships in streams. Spec. Publ. Pymatuning Lab. Ecol. 4:1–145.

2670. Wiggins, G. B. 1973a. A contribution to the biology of caddisflies (Trichoptera) in temporary pools. Life Sci. Contr. Roy. Ont. Mus. 88:1–28.

2671. Wiggins, G. B. 1973b. New systematic data for the North American caddisfly genera *Lepania*, *Goeracea* and *Goerita* (Trichoptera: Limnephilidae). Life Sci. Contr. Roy. Ont. Mus. 91:1–33.

2672. Wiggins, G. B. 1973c. Contributions to the systematics of the caddisfly family Limnephilidae (Trichoptera). I. Life Sci. Contr. Roy. Ont. Mus. 94:1–32.

2673. Wiggins, G. B. 1975. Contributions to the systematics of the caddisfly family Limnephilidae (Trichoptera). II. Can. Ent. 107:325–336.

2674. Wiggins, G. B. 1976. Contributions to the systematics of the caddisfly family Limnephilidae (Trichoptera). III, pp. 7–19. *In* H. Malicky (ed.). Proc. 1st Int. Symp. Trichoptera, Lunz am See (Austria), 1974. Junk, The Hague, Netherlands.

2675. Wiggins, G. B. 1977. Larvae of the North American caddisfly genera. Univ. Toronto Press, Toronto. 401 pp.

2676. Wiggins, G. B., and N. H. Anderson. 1968. Contributions to the systematics of the caddisfly genera *Pseudostenophylax* and *Philocasca* with special reference to the immature stages (Trichoptera: Limnephilidae). Can. J. Zool. 46:61–75.

2677. Wiggins, G. B., and R. J. Mackay. 1978. Some relationships between systematics and trophic ecology in Nearctic aquatic insects, with special reference to Trichoptera. Ecology 59:1211–1220.

2678. Wiggins, G. B., R. J. Mackay, and I. M. Smith. 1980. Evolutionary and ecological strategies of animals in annual temporary pools. Arch. Hydrobiol./Suppl. 58:97–206.

2679. Wiggins, G. B., and J. S. Richardson. 1982. Revision and synopsis of the caddisfly genus *Dicosmoecus* (Trichoptera: Limnephilidae, Dicosmoecinae). Aquat. Ins. 4:181–217.

2680. Wigglesworth, V. B. 1938. The regulation of osmotic pressure and chloride concentration in the haemolymph of mosquito larvae. J. exp. Biol. 15:235–247.

2681. Wigglesworth, V. B. 1972. The principles of insect physiology. Chapman and Hall, London. 827 pp.

2682. Wilcox, J. A. 1965. A synopsis of the North American Galerucinae (Coleoptera: Chrysomelidae). N.Y. State Mus. Bull. 400:1–226.

2683. Wilcox, R. S. 1979. Sex discrimination in *Gerris remigis:* Role of a surface wave signal. Science 206:1325–1327.

2684. Wilder, D. D. 1981a. A revision of the genus *Niphogenia* Melander (Diptera: Empididae). Pan-Pacif. Ent. 57:422–428.

2685. Wilder, D. D. 1981b. A revision of the genus *Oreothalia* Melander (Diptera: Empididae). Proc. Ent. Soc. Wash. 83: 461–471.

2686. Wilder, D. D. 1981c. A review of the genus *Roederoides* Coquillett with the description of a new species (Diptera: Empididae). Pan-Pacif. Ent. 57:415–421.

2687. Wilding, J. L. 1940. A new square-foot aquatic sampler. Limnol. Soc. Am. Spec. Publ. 4:1–4.

2688. Wiley, G. O. 1922. Life history notes on two species of Saldidae. Univ. Kans. Sci. Bull. 14:301–311.

2689. Wiley, G. O. 1924. On the biology of *Curicta drakei* Hungerford. Ent. News 35:324–331.

2690. Wilhm, J. L., and T. C. Dorris. 1968. Biological parameters of water quality. BioScience 18:447–481.

2691. Wilkey, R. F. 1959. Preliminary list of the Collembola of California. Bull. Dep. Agric. Calif. 48:222–224.

2692. Willem, M. 1907. *Nymphula stratiotata*. Ann. Soc. Ent. Belgique 51:289–290.

2693. Willey, R. L., and H. O. Eiler. 1972. Drought resistance in subalpine nymphs of *Somatochlora semicircularis* Sélys. Am. Midl. Nat. 87:215–221.

2694. Williams, C. E. 1976. *Neurocordulia (Platycordulia) xanthosoma* (Williamson) in Texas (Odonata: Libellulidae: Corduliinae). Great Lakes Ent. 9:63–73.

2695. Williams, C. E. 1977. Courtship display in *Belonia croceipennis* (Selys), with notes on copulation and oviposition (Anisoptera: Libellulidae). Odonatologica 6:283–287.

2696. Williams, C. E. 1979. Observations on the behavior of the nymph of *Neurocordulia xanthosoma* (Williamson) under laboratory conditions (Anisoptera: Corduliidae). Notul. Odonatol. 1:44–46.

2697. Williams, C. E. 1982. The dragonflies of McLennan County, central Texas, United States. Notul. Odonatol. 1:160–161.

2698. Williams, C. E., and S. W. Dunkle. 1976. The larva of *Neurocordulia xanthosoma* (Odonata: Corduliidae). Fla. Ent. 59:429–433.

2699. Williams, D. D. 1981a. Migrations and distributions of stream benthos, pp. 155–207. *In* M. A. Lock and D. D. Williams (eds.). Perspectives in running water ecology. Plenum, N.Y. 430 pp.

2700. Williams. D. D. 1981b. Evaluation of a standpipe corer for sampling aquatic interstitial biotopes. Hydrobiologia 83:257–260.

2701. Williams, D. D. and H. B. N. Hynes. 1974. The occurrence of benthos deep in the substratum of a stream. Freshwat. Biol. 4:233–256.

2702. Williams, D. D., and H. B. N. Hynes. 1976. The recolonization mechanisms of stream benthos. Oikos 27:265–272.

2703. Williams, D. D., and H. B. N. Hynes. 1979. Reply to comments by Exner and Davies on the use of a standpipe corer. Freshwat. Biol. 9:79–80.

2704. Williams, D. D., and N. E. Williams. 1975. A contribution to the biology of *Ironoquia punctatissima* (Trichoptera: Limnephilidae). Can. Ent. 107:829–832.

2705. Williams, D. D., and N. E. Williams. 1981. Some aspects of the life history and feeding ecology of *Dolophilodes distinctus* (Walker) in two Ontario streams. Ser. Ent. 20:433–442.

2706. Williams, D. D., and N. E. Williams. 1982. Morphological and dietary variations in a riverine population of *Pycnopsyche guttifer* (Trichoptera: Limnephilidae). Aquat. Insects 4:21–27.

2707. Williams, F. X. 1938. Biological studies in Hawaiian water-loving insects. Part III. Diptera or flies. A. Ephydridae and Anthomyiidae. Proc. Hawaii Ent. Soc. 10:85–119.

2708. Williams, F. X. 1939. Biological studies in Hawaiian water-loving insects. Part III. Diptera or flies. B. Asteiidae, Syrphidae, and Dolichopodidae. Proc. Hawaii Ent. Soc. 10:281–315.

2709. Williams, F. X. 1944. Biological studies in Hawaiian water-loving insects. Part IV. Lepidoptera or moths and butterflies. Proc. Hawaii Ent. Soc. 12:180–185.

2710. Williams, N. E., and H. B. N. Hynes. 1973. Microdistribution and feeding of the net-spinning caddisflies (Trichoptera) of a Canadian stream. Oikos 24:73–84.

2711. Williams, N. E., and D. D. Williams. 1980. Distribution and feeding records of the caddisflies (Trichoptera) of the Matamek River region Quebec. Can. J. Zool. 57:2402–2412.

2712. Williams, R. W. 1951. Observations on the bionomics of *Culicoides tristratulus* Hoffman with notes on *C. alaskensis* Wirth and other species at Valdez, Alaska, summer 1949 (Diptera, Heleidae). Ann. Ent. Soc. Am. 44:173–440.

2713. Williams, T. R., R. Connolly, H. B. N. Hynes, and W. E. Kershaw. 1961a. Size of particles ingested by *Simulium* larvae. Nature 189:78.

2714. Williams, T. R., R. C. Connolly, H. B. N. Hynes, and W. E. Kershaw. 1961b. The size of particulate material ingested by *Simulium* larvae. Ann. Trop. Med. Parasit. 55:125–127.

2715. Williamson, E. B. 1900, Dragonflies of Indiana. Dept. Geol. Ann. Rept. Nat. Res. Ind. 24:229–333, 1003–1011.

2716. Williamson, E. B. 1903. The dragonflies (Odonata) of Tennessee, with a few records for Virginia and Alabama. Ent. News 14:221–229.

2717. Williamson, E. B. 1917. An annotated list of the Odonata of Indiana. Misc. Publ. Univ. Mich. Mus. Zool. 2:1–13.

2718. Williamson, E. B. 1932. Dragonflies collected in Missouri. Occ. Pap. Univ. Mich. Mus. Zool. 240:1–40.

2719. Wilson, C. A. 1958. Aquatic and semiaquatic Hemiptera of Mississippi. Tulane Stud. Zool. 6:115–170.

2720. Wilson, C. A., R. C. Barnes, and H. L. Fulton. 1946. A list of the mosquitoes of Pennsylvania with notes on their distribution and aundance. Mosquito News 6:78–84.

2721. Wilson, C. B. 1923a. Life history of the scavenger water-beetle *Hydrous (Hydrophilus) triangularis*, and its economic importance to fish breeding. Bull. U.S. Bur. Fish. 39:9–38.

2722. Wilson, C. B. 1923b. Water beetles in relation to pond-fish culture, with life histories of those found in fish ponds at Fairport, Iowa. Bull. U.S. Bur. Fish. 39:231–345.

2723. Wilson, R. B. 1967. The Hydrophilidae of Michigan with keys to species of the Great Lakes region. M.S. thesis, Michigan State University. 100 pp.

2724. Wilson, R. S., and P. L. Bright. 1973. The use of chironomid pupal exuviae for characterizing streams. Freshwat. Biol. 3:283–302.

2725. Wilson, R. S., and J. D. McGill. 1982. A practical key to the genera of pupal exuviae of the British Chironomidae. Univ. Bristol. 62 pp.

2726. Wilton, D. P., L. E. Fetzer, Jr., and R. W. Fay. 1972. Quantitative determination of feeding rates of *Anopheles albimanus* larvae. Mosquito News 32:23–27.

2727. Wingfield, C. A. 1939. The function of the gills of mayfly nymphs from different habitats. J. exp. Biol. 16:363–373.

2728. Winterbourn, M. J. 1971a. The life histories and trophic relationships of the Trichoptera of Marion Lake, British Columbia. Can. J. Zool. 49:623–635.

2729. Winterbourn, M. J. 1971b. An ecological study of *Banksiola crotchi* Banks (Trichoptera, Phryganeidae) in Marion Lake, British Columbia. Can. J. Zool. 49:636–645.

2730. Winterbourn, M. J. 1974. The life histories, trophic relations and production of *Stenoperla prasina* (Plecoptera) and *Deleatidium* sp. (Ephemeroptera) in a New Zealand river. Freshwat. Biol. 4:507–524.

2731. Winterbourn, M. J. 1978. The macroinvertebrate fauna of a New Zealand forest stream. N.Z.J. Zool. 5:157–169.

2732. Winterbourn, M. J., and N. H. Anderson, 1980. The life history of *Philanisus plebeius* Walker (Trichoptera: Chathamiidae), a caddisfly whose eggs were found in a starfish. Ecol. Ent. 5:293–303.

2733. Winters, F. E. 1927. Key to the subtribe Helocharae Orchym. (Coleoptera-Hydrophilidae) of Boreal America. Pan-Pacif. Ent. 4:19–29.

2734. Wirth, E. 1947. Notes on the genus *Thalassomya* Schiner, with descriptions of two new species (Diptera: Tendipedidae). Proc. Hawaii Ent. Soc. 13:117–139.

2735. Wirth, W. 1949. A revision of the clunionine midges with descriptions of a new genus and four new species (Diptera: Tendipedidae). Univ. Calif. Publ. Ent 8:151–182.

2736. Wirth, W. W. 1951a. A new mountain midge from California (Diptera: Deuterophlebiidae). Pan-Pacif. Ent. 27:49–57.

2737. Wirth, W. W. 1951b. A revision of the dipterous family Canaceidae. Occ. Pap. Bishop Mus. Honolulu 20:245–275.

2738. Wirth, W. W. 1952a. The Heleidae of California. Univ. Calif. Publ. Ent. 9:95–266.

2739. Wirth, W. W. 1952b. Three new species of *Systenus* (Diptera, Dolichopodidae), with a description of the immature stages from tree cavities. Proc. Ent. Soc. Wash. 54:236–244.

2740. Wirth, W. W. 1954. A new genus and species of Ephydridae (Diptera) from a California sulfur spring. Wasmann J. Biol. 12:195–202.

2741. Wirth, W. W. 1957. The species of *Cricoptopus* midges living in the blue-green alga *Nostoc* in California (Diptera: Tendipedidae). Pan-Pacif. Ent. 33:121–126.

2742. Wirth, W. W. 1964. A revision of the shore flies of the genus *Brachydeutera* Loew (Diptera: Ephydridae). Ann. Ent. Soc. Am. 57:3–12.

2743. Wirth, W. W. 1971a. *Platygymnopa*, a new genus of Ephydridae reared from decaying snails in North America (Diptera). Can. Ent. 103:266–270.

2744. Wirth, W. W. 1971b. The brine flies of the genus *Ephydra* in North America (Diptera: Ephydridae). Ann. Ent. Soc. Am. 64:357–377.

2745. Wirth, W. W., and W. R. Atchley. 1973. A review of the North American *Leptoconops* (Diptera: Ceratopogonidae). Texas Tech. Univ. Grad. Stud. 5. 57 pp.

2746. Wirth, W. W., N. C. Ratanaworabhan, and D. H. Messersmith. 1977. Natural history of Plumbers Island, Maryland. XXII. Biting midges (Diptera: Ceratopogonidae). I. Introduction and key to genera. Proc. Biol. Soc. Wash. 90:615–647.

2747. Wirth, W. W. and A. Stone. 1956. Aquatic Diptera, pp. 372–482. *In* R. L. Usinger (ed.). Aquatic insects of California. Univ. Calif. Press, Berkeley. 508 pp.

2748. Wodsedalek, J. E. 1912. Natural history and general behavior of the Ephemeridae nymphs *Heptagenia interpunctata* (Say). Ann. Ent. Soc. Am. 5:31–40.

2749. Wohlschlag, D. E. 1950. Vegetation and invertebrate life in a marl lake. Invest. Ind. Lakes 3:321–372.

2750. Wolfe, G. W., and J. F. Matta. 1981. Notes on nomenclature and classification of *Hydroporus* subgenera with the description of a new genus of Hydroporini (Coleoptera: Dytiscidae). Pan-Pacif. Ent. 57:149–175.

2751. Wood, D. M. 1978, Taxonomy of the Nearctic species of *Twinnia* and *Gymnopais* (Diptera: Simuliidae) and a discussion of the ancestry of the Simuliidae. Can. Ent. 110:1297–1337.

2752. Wood, D. M., P. T. Dang, and R. A. Ellis. 1979. The insects and arachnids of Canada. Part 6. The mosquitoes of Canada. Agric. Can. Publ. 1686:1–390.

2753. Wood, D. M., and D. M. Davies. 1964. The rearing of simuliids. Proc. 12th Int. Congr. Ent. 12:821–823.

2754. Wood, D. M., and D. M. Davies. 1966. Some methods of rearing and collecting blackflies (Diptera: Simuliidae). Proc. Ent. Soc. Ont. 96:81–90.

2755. 1963. Wood, D. M., B. V. Peterson, D. M. Davies, and H. Gyorkos. 1963. The black flies (Diptera: Simuliidae) of Ontario. Part II. Larval identification, with descriptions and illustrations. Proc. Ent. Soc. Ont. 93:99–129.

2756. Wood, F. E. 1962. A synopsis of the genus *Dineutus* (Coleoptera: Gyrinidae) in the Western Hemisphere. M.S. thesis, University of Missouri, Columbia. 99 pp.

2757. Wood, K. G. 1956. Ecology of *Chaoborus* (Diptera: Culicidae) in an Ontario lake. Ecology 37:639–643.

2758. Woodall, W. R., Jr., and J. B. Wallace. 1972. The benthic fauna in four small southern Appalachian streams. Am. Midl. Nat. 88: 393–407.

2759. Woodrum, J. E., and D. C. Tarter. 1972. The life history of the alderfly *Sialis aequalis* Banks, in an acid mine stream. Am. Midl. Nat. 89:360–368.

2760. Wooldridge, D. P. 1965. A preliminary checklist of the aquatic Hydrophilidae of Illinois. Trans. Ill. State Acad. Sci. 58:205–206.

2761. Wooldridge, D. P. 1966. Notes on nearactic *Paracymus* with descriptions of new species (Coleoptera: Hydrophilidae). J. Kans. Ent. Soc. 39:712–725.

2762. Wooldridge, D. P. 1967. The aquatic Hydrophilidae of Illinois. Trans. Ill. State Acad. Sci. 60:422–431.

2763. Wooten, R. J. 1972. The evolution of insects in freshwater ecosystems, pp. 69–82. *In* R. B. Clark and R. J. Wooten (eds.). Essays in hydrobiology. Univ. of Exeter, Exeter. 136 pp.

2764. Worthington, C. E. 1878. Miscellaneous memoranda. Can. Ent. 10:15–17.

2765. Worthington, E. B. 1931. Vertical movements of freshwater macroplankton. Int. Revue ges. Hydrobiol. 25:394–436.

2766. Wotton, R. S. 1976. Evidence that blackfly larvae can feed on particles of colloidal size. Nature 261:697.

2767. Wotton, R. S. 1977. The size of particles ingested by moorland stream blackfly larvae (Simuliidae). Oikos 29:332–335.

2768. Wotton, R. S. 1978a. Life-histories and production of blackflies (Diptera: Simuliidae) in moorland streams in Upper Teesdale, Northern England. Arch. Hydrobiol. 83:232–250.

2769. Wotton, R. S. 1978b. Growth, respiration, and assimilation of blackfly larvae (Diptera: Simuliidae) in a lake-outlet in Finland. Oecologia 33:279–290.

2770. Wotton, R. S. 1978c. The feeding-rate of *Metacnephia tredecimatum* larvae (Diptera: Simuliidae) in a Swedish lake outlet. Oikos 30:121–125.

2771. Wotton, R. S. 1979. The influence of a lake on the distribution of blackfly species (Diptera: Simuliidae) along a river. Oikos 32:368–372.

2772. Wotton, R. S. 1980. Coprophagy as an economic feeding tactic in black fly larvae. Oikos 34:282–286.

2773. Wray, D. L. 1967. Insects of North Carolina. Third Suppl. N.C. Dep. Agric. Div. Ent. 4:158–159.

2774. Wright, F. N. 1957. Rearing of *Simulium damnosum* Theobald (Diptera, Simuliidae) in the laboratory. Nature 180:1059.

2775. Wright, M. 1938. A review of the literature on the Odonata of Tennessee. Tenn. Acad. Sci. 13:26–33.

2776. Wright, M. 1946a. A description of the nymph of *Sympetrum ambiguum* (Rambur) with habitat notes. J. Tenn. Acad. Sci. 21:135–138.

2777. Wright, M. 1946b. A description of the nymph of *Agrion dimidiatum* (Burmeister). J. Tenn. Acad. Sci. 21:336–338.

2778. Wright, M., and A. Peterson. 1944. A key to the genera of anisopterous dragonfly nymphs of the United States and Canada (Odonata, suborder Anisopteral). Ohio J. Sci. 44:151–166.

2779. Wrona, F. J., J. M. Culp, and R. W. Davies. 1982. Macroinvertebrate subsampling: A simplified apparatus and approach. Can. J. Fish. Aquat. Sci. 39:1051–1054.

2780. Wu, C. 1923. Morphology, anatomy and ethology of *Nemoura*. Bull. Lloyd Lib. 3:1–81.

2781. Wu, Y. F. 1931. A contribution to the biology of *Simulium* (Diptera). Pap. Mich. Acad. Sci. Arts Lett. 13:543–599.

2782. Yamamoto, T., and H. H. Ross. 1966. A phylogenetic outline of the caddisfly genus *Mystacides* (Trichoptera: Leptoceridae). Can. Ent. 98:627–632.

2783. Yamamoto, T., and G. B. Wiggins. 1964. A comparative study of the North American species in the caddisfly genus *Mystacides* (Trichoptera: Leptoceridae). Can. J. Zool. 42:1105–1126.

2784. Yoshimoto, C. M. 1976. Synopsis of the genus *Mestocharis* Forster in America north of Mexico (Chalcidoidea: Eulophidae) Can. Ent. 108:755–758.

2785. Yoshitake, S. 1974. Studies on the contents of the digestive tract of *Chironomus* sp. on the bottom of Lake Yunoko. Jap. J. Limnol. 35:25–31.

2786. Yosii, R. 1960. Studies on the Collembola genus *Hypogastrura*. Am. Midl. Nat. 64:257–281.

2787. Young, A. M. 1966. The culturing of the diving beetle, *Dytiscus verticalis,* in the laboratory for observation of holometabolic development in aquatic insects. Turtox News 44:224–228.

2788. Young, A. M. 1967. Predation in the larvae of *Dytiscus marginalis* Linnaeus. Pan-Pacif. Ent. 43:113–117.

2789. Young. C. W. 1978. Comparison of the crane flies (Diptera: Tipulidae) of two woodlands in eastern Kansas, with a key to the adult crane flies of eastern Kansas. Univ. Kans. Sci. Bull. 51:407–440.

2790. Young, E. C. 1965. Flight muscle polymorphism in British Corixidae: Ecological observations. J. Anim. Ecol. 34:353–390.

2791. Young, F. N. 1953. Two new species of *Matus,* with a key to the known species and subspecies of the genus (Coleoptera: Dytiscidae). Ann. Ent. Soc. Am. 46:49–55.

2792. Young, F. N. 1954. The water beetles of Florida. Univ. Fla. Stud. Biol. Ser. 5:1–238.

2793. Young, F. N. 1956. A preliminary key to the species of *Hydrovatus* of the Eastern United States (Coleoptera: Dytiscidae). Coleopt. Bull. 10:53–54.

2794. Young, F. N. 1958. Notes on the care and rearing of *Tropisternus* in the laboratory (Coleoptera: Hydrophilidae). Ecology 39:166–167.

2795. Young, F. N. 1960. Notes on the water beetles of Southampton Island in the Canadian Arctic (Coleoptera: Dytiscidae and Haliplidae). Can. Ent. 92:275–278.

2796. Young, F. N. 1961a. Effects of pollution on natural associations of water beetles. Eng. Bull. Purdue Univ. 45:373–380.

2797. Young, F. N. 1961b. Geographical variation in the *Tropisternus mexicanus* (Castelnau) complex (Coleoptera, Hydrophilidae). Proc. 11th Int. Congr. Ent. 11:112–116.

2798. Young, F. N. 1961c. Pseudosibling species in the genus *Peltodytes* (Coleoptera: Haliplidae). Ann. Ent. Soc. Am. 54:214–222.

2799. Young, F. N. 1963. The Nearctic species of *Copelatus* Erickson (Coleoptera: Dytiscidae). Quart. J. Fla. Acad. Sci. 26:56–77.

2800. Young, F. N. 1967. A key to the genera of American bidessine water beetles, with descriptions of three new genera (Coleoptera: Dytiscidae, Hydroporinae). Coleopt. Bull. 21:75–84.

2801. Young, F. N. 1974. Review of the predaceous water beetles of the genus *Anodocheilus* (Coleoptera: Dytiscidae, Hydroporinae). Occ. Pap. Univ. Mich. Mus. Zool. 670:1–128.

2802. Young, F. N. 1979a. A key to Nearctic species of *Celina* with descriptions of new species (Coleoptera: Dytiscidae) *Celina imitatrix, Celina hubbelli, Celina occidentalis, Celina palustris,* new taxa, from North America. J. Kans. Ent. Soc. 52:820–830.

2803. Young, F. N. 1979b. Water beetles of the genus *Suphisellus* Crotch in the Americas north of Colombia (Coleoptera: Noteridae). Southwest. Nat. 24:409–429.

2804. Young, F. N., and G. Longley. 1976. A new subterranean aquatic beetle from Texas (Coleoptera: Dytiscidae: Hydroporinae). Ann. Ent. Soc. Am. 69:787–792.

2805. Young, W. C., and C. W. Bayer. 1979. The dragonfly nymphs (Odonata: Anisoptera) of the Guadelupe River Basin, Texas. Texas J. Sci. 31:85–98.

2806. Yount, J. 1966. A method for rearing large numbers of pond midge larvae, with estimates of productivity and standing crop. Am. Midl. Nat. 76:230–238.

2807. Zack, R. S., Jr., and B. A. Foote. 1978. Utilization of algal monocultures by larvae of *Scatella stagnalis.* Environ. Ent. 7:509–511.

2808. Zahar, A. R. 1951. The ecology and distribution of black flies in southeast Scotland. J. Anim. Ecol. 20:33–36.

2809. Zahner, R. 1959. Uber die Bindung der Mitteleuropäichen *Calopteryx*-arten (Odonata) an den Lebensraum des strömenden Wassers. I. Der Anteil der Larven an der Biotopbindung. Int. Revue ges. Hydrobiol. 44:51–130.

2810. Zalom, F. G. 1977. The Notonectidae (Hemiptera) of Arizona. Southwest Natur. 22:327–336.

2811. Zalom, F. G. 1978. A comparison of predation rates and prey handling times of adult *Notonecta* and *Buenoa* (Hemiptera: Notonectidae). Ann. Ent. Soc. Am. 71:143–148.

2812. Zalom, F. G. 1980. Diel flight periodicities of some Dytiscidae (Coleoptera) associated with California rice paddies. Ecol. Ent. 5:183–187.

2813. Zalom, F. G., and A. A. Grigarick. 1980. Predation by *Hydrophilus triangularis* and *Tropisternus lateralis* in California rice fields. Ann. Ent. Soc. Am. 73:167–171.

2814. Zeigler, D. D., and K. W. Stewart. 1977. Drumming behavior of eleven Nearctic stonefly (Plecoptera) species. Ann. Ent. Soc. Am. 70:495–505.

2815. Zimmerman, E. C. 1978. Insects of Hawaii (Microlepidoptera, Part II). Univ. Press, Hawaii, Honolulu. 9:1–1903.

2816. Zimmerman, J. R. 1960. Seasonal population changes and habitat preferences of the genus *Laccophilus* (Coleoptera: Dytiscidae). Ecology 41:141–152.

2817. Zimmerman, J. R. 1970. A taxonomic revision of the aquatic beetle genus *Laccophilus* (Dytiscidae) of North America. Mem. Ent. Soc. Am. 16:1–275.

2818. Zimmerman, J. R. 1980. Use of multivariate procedures in studies of species problems in the *sculptilis* group of North American *Colymbetes* (Coleoptera: Dytiscidae). Coleopt. Bull. 34:213–226.

2819. Zimmerman, J. R. 1981. A revision of the *Colymbetes* of North America (Dytiscidae). Coleopt. Bull 35:1–52.

2820. Zimmerman, J. R., and R. L. Smith. 1975a. The genus *Rhampus* (Coleoptera: Dytiscidae) in North America. Part I. General account of the species. Trans. Am. Ent. Soc. 101:33–123.

2821. Zimmerman, J. R., and A. H. Smith. 1975b. A survey of the *Deronectes* (Coleoptera: Dytiscidae) of Canada, United States and northern Mexico. Trans. Am. Ent. Soc. 101:651–722.

2822. Zimmerman, M. C., and T. E. Wissing. 1978. Effects of temperature on gut-loading and gut-clearing times of the burrowing mayfly *Hexagenia limbata.* Freshwat. Biol. 8:269–277.

2823. Zimmerman, M. C., and T. E. Wissing. 1979. The nutritional dynamics of the burrowing mayfly, *Hexagenia limbata.* pp. 231–257. *In* J. F. Flannagan, and K. E. Marshall (eds.). Advances in Ephemeroptera biology. Plenum, N.Y. 552 pp.

2824. Zimmerman, M. C., T. E. Wissing, and R. P. Rutter. 1975. Bioenergetics of the burrowing mayfly, *Hexagenia limbata* in a pond ecosystem. Verh. Int. Verein. Limnol. 19:3039–3049.

2825. Zimmerman, R. H., and E. C. Turner, Jr. 1982. *Cordilura varipes* (Scatophagidae), a predator of *Culicoides variipennis* (Ceratopogonidae). Mosquito News 42:279.

2826. Zismann, L. 1969. A light trap for sampling aquatic organisms. Israel J. Zool. 18:343–348.

2827. Zwick, P. 1973. Insecta: Plecoptera. Phylogenetisches System und Katalog. Das Tierreich 94. Walter de Gruyter, Berlin. 465 pp.

ADDENDUM (MARCH 1984)

2828. Cranston, P. S. 1982a. The metamorphosis of *Symposiocladius lignicola* (Kieffer) n. gen., n. comb., a wood-mining Chironomidae (Diptera). Ent. Scand. 13:419–429.

2829. Ferrington, L. C., Jr. 1981. Kansas Chironomidae, Part I, pp. 45–51. *In:* R. Brooks (ed.). New records of the fauna and flora of Kansas for 1980. St. Biol. Surv. Kansas Tech. Pub. 10.

2830. Ferrington, L. C., Jr. 1982. Kansas Chironomidae, Part II: The Tanypodinae, pp. 49–60. *In:* R. Brooks (ed.). New records of the fauna and flora of Kansas for 1981. St. Biol. Surv. Kansas Tech. Publ. 12.

2831. Ferrington, L. C., Jr. 1983a. Kansas Chironomidae, Part III: The *Harnischia* complex, pp. 48–62. *In:* R. Brooks (ed.). New records of the fauna and flora of Kansas for 1982. St. Biol. Surv. Kansas Tech. Publ. 13.

2832. Ferrington, L. C., Jr. 1983b. Interdigitating broadscale distributional patterns in some Kansas Chironomidae. Mem. Ent. Soc. Am. 34:101–113.

2833. Gaufin, A. R. 1964. Systematic list of Plecoptera of the Intermountain region. Proc. Utal Acad. Sci. 41:221–227.

2834. Grodhaus, G. G. 1980. Aestivating chironomid larvae associated with vernal pools, pp. 315–322. *In:* D. A. Murray (ed.). Chironomidae ecology, systematics, cytology and physiology. Pergammon Press, Oxford, England. 354 p.

2835. Jewett, S. G., Jr. 1971. Some Alaskan stoneflies (Plecoptera). Pan-Pacif. Ent. 47:189–192.

2836. Mozley, S. C. and L. C. Garcia. 1972. Benthic macrofauna in a coastal zone of southeastern Lake Michigan. Proc. 15th Conf. Great Lakes, pp. 102–116.

2837. Oliver, D. R. 1976. Chironomidae (Diptera) of Char Lake, Cornwallis Island, N.W.T., with descriptions of two new species. Can. Ent. 108:1053–1064.

2838. Oliver, D. R. 1981. Description of *Euryhapsis* new genus including three new species (Diptera: Chironomidae). Can. Ent. 113:711–722.

2839. Oliver, D. R. 1982. *Xylotopus,* a new genus of Orthocladiinae (Diptera: Chironomidae). Can. Ent. 114:167–168.

2840. Resh, V. H. and D. M. Rosenberg (eds.). 1979. Innovative teaching in aquatic entomology. Can. Spec. Publ. Fish. Aquat. Sci. 43:1–118.

2841. Roback, S. S. 1977. The immature chironomids of the eastern United States II. Tanypodinae-Tanypodini. Proc. Acad. Nat. Sci. Philadelphia 128:55–87.

2842. Roback, S. S. 1978. The immature chironomids of the eastern United States III. Tanypodinae-Anatopyniini, Macropelopiini and Natarsiini. Proc. Acad. Nat. Sci. Philadelphia 129:151–202.

2843. Roback, S. S. 1980. The immature chironomids of the eastern United States IV. Tanypodinae-Procladiini. Proc. Acad. Nat. Sci. Philadelphia 132:1–63.

2844. Roback, S. S. 1981. The immature chironomids of the eastern United States V. Pentaneurini-*Thienemannimyia* group. Proc. Acad. Nat. Sci. Philadelphia 133:73–129.

2845. Saether, O. A. 1971a. Notes on general morphology and terminology of the Chironomidae (Diptera). Can. Ent. 103:1237–1260.

2846. Saether, O. A. 1971b. Four new and unusual Chironomidae (Diptera). Can. Ent. 103:1799–1827.

2847. Saether, O. A. 1977. *Habrobaenus hudsoni,* n. gen., n. sp. and the immatures of *Baeoctenus bicolor* Saether (Diptera: Chironomidae). J. Fish. Res. Bd. Can. 34:2354–2361.

2848. Saether, O. A. 1981. *Doncricotopus bicaudatus* n. gen., n. sp. (Diptera: Chironomidae, Orthocladiinae) from the Northwest Territories, Canada. Ent. Scand. 12:223–229.

2849. Schefter, P. W. and J. D. Unzicker. 1984. A review of the *Hydropsyche morosa-bifida*—complex in North America (Trichoptera: Hydropsychidae). *In:* J. C. Morse (ed.). Proc. 4th Int. Symp. Trichoptera, Dr. W. Junk, Publ., The Hague (In press).

2850. Schmid, F. 1979. On some new trends in trichopterology. Bull. Ent. Soc. Can. 11:48–57.

2851. Schuster, G. A. 1984. *Hydropsyche?-Symphitopsyche?-Certopsyche?:* A taxonomic enigma. *In:* J. C. Morse (ed.). Proc. 4th Int. Symp. Trichoptera, Dr. W. Junk, Publ., The Hague (In press).

2852. Sheldon, A. L. and S. G. Jewett, Jr. 1967. Stonefy emergence in a Sierra Nevada stream. Pan-Pacif. Ent. 43:1–8.

2853. Stark, B. P. and A. R. Gaufin. 1976b. The nearctic species of *Acroneuria* (Plecoptera:Perlidae). J. Kans. Ent. Soc. 49:221–253.

2854. Surdick, R. F. 1981. Nearctic genera of Chloroperlinae (Plecoptera: Chloroperlidae). Ph.D. Thesis, Univ. of Utah. Univ. Microfilms #DA 8208937.

2855. Thienemann, A. 1944. Bestimmungstabellen fur die bis jetzt bekannten larven and puppen der Orthocladiinen (Diptera: Chironomidae). Arch. Hydrobiol. 39:551–664.

2856. Wiggins, G. B. 1982. Trichoptera, pp. 599–612. *In:* S. P. Parker (ed.). Synopsis and classification of living organisms. McGraw-Hill, N.Y.

2857. Wiggins, G. B., J. S. Weaver, and J. D. Unzicker. 1984. Revision of the caddisfly family Uenoidae (Trichoptera). Can. Ent. (In press).

Index

Z